DISTRICT OF COLUMBIA RULES OF COURT

VOLUME II – FEDERAL

2012

Mat #41130268

ISBN 978–0–314–94247–0

PREFACE

This edition of the *District of Columbia Rules of Court, Volume II – Federal, 2012*, replaces the 2011 edition and any accompanying supplements. This volume provides in convenient form court rules governing federal practice in the District of Columbia and is current with amendments received through January 1, 2012.

THE PUBLISHER

February 2012

ADDITIONAL INFORMATION OR RESEARCH ASSISTANCE

For additional information or research assistance call the West reference attorneys at 1-800-REF-ATTY (1-800-733-2889). Contact West's editorial department directly with your questions and suggestions by e-mail at west.editor@thomson.com.

Visit West's home page at west.thomson.com.

TABLE OF CONTENTS

*

FEDERAL
RULES OF CIVIL PROCEDURE
FOR THE
UNITED STATES DISTRICT COURTS

Effective September 16, 1938

Including Amendments Effective December 1, 2010

Research Note

These rules may be searched electronically on Westlaw in the US-RULES database; updates to these rules may be found on Westlaw in US-RULESPDATES. For search tips, and a detailed summary of database content, consult the Westlaw Scope Screen of each database.

TITLE VII. JUDGMENT

TITLE VIII. PROVISIONAL AND FINAL REMEDIES

TITLE IX. SPECIAL PROCEEDINGS

TITLE X. DISTRICT COURTS AND CLERKS: CONDUCTING BUSINESS; ISSUING ORDERS

TITLE XI. GENERAL PROVISIONS

APPENDIX OF FORMS

SUPPLEMENTAL RULES FOR ADMIRALTY OR MARITIME CLAIMS AND ASSET FORFEITURE ACTIONS

TITLE I. SCOPE OF RULES; FORM OF ACTION

RULE 1. SCOPE AND PURPOSE

These rules govern the procedure in all civil actions and proceedings in the United States district courts, except as stated in Rule 81. They should be construed and administered to secure the just, speedy, and inexpensive determination of every action and proceeding.

(Amended December 29, 1948, effective October 20, 1949; February 28, 1966, effective July 1, 1966; April 22, 1993, effective December 1, 1993; April 30, 2007, effective December 1, 2007.)

RULE 2. ONE FORM OF ACTION

There is one form of action—the civil action.

(Amended April 30, 2007, effective December 1, 2007.)

TITLE II. COMMENCING AN ACTION; SERVICE OF PROCESS, PLEADINGS, MOTIONS, AND ORDERS

RULE 3. COMMENCING AN ACTION

A civil action is commenced by filing a complaint with the court.

(Amended April 30, 2007, effective December 1, 2007.)

RULE 4. SUMMONS

(a) Contents; Amendments.

(1) ***Contents.*** A summons must:

(A) name the court and the parties;

(B) be directed to the defendant;

(C) state the name and address of the plaintiff's attorney or—if unrepresented—of the plaintiff;

(D) state the time within which the defendant must appear and defend;

(E) notify the defendant that a failure to appear and defend will result in a default judgment against the defendant for the relief demanded in the complaint;

(F) be signed by the clerk; and

(G) bear the court's seal.

(2) ***Amendments.*** The court may permit a summons to be amended.

(b) Issuance. On or after filing the complaint, the plaintiff may present a summons to the clerk for signature and seal. If the summons is properly completed, the clerk must sign, seal, and issue it to the plaintiff for service on the defendant. A summons—or a copy of a summons that is addressed to multiple defendants—must be issued for each defendant to be served.

(c) Service.

(1) ***In General.*** A summons must be served with a copy of the complaint. The plaintiff is responsible for having the summons and complaint served within the time allowed by Rule 4(m) and must furnish the necessary copies to the person who makes service.

(2) ***By Whom.*** Any person who is at least 18 years old and not a party may serve a summons and complaint.

(3) ***By a Marshal or Someone Specially Appointed.*** At the plaintiff's request, the court may order that service be made by a United States marshal or deputy marshal or by a person specially appointed by the court. The court must so order if the plaintiff is authorized to proceed in forma pauperis under 28 U.S.C. § 1915 or as a seaman under 28 U.S.C. § 1916.

(d) Waiving Service.

(1) ***Requesting a Waiver.*** An individual, corporation, or association that is subject to service under Rule 4(e), (f), or (h) has a duty to avoid

unnecessary expenses of serving the summons. The plaintiff may notify such a defendant that an action has been commenced and request that the defendant waive service of a summons. The notice and request must:

(A) be in writing and be addressed:

(i) to the individual defendant; or

(ii) for a defendant subject to service under Rule 4(h), to an officer, a managing or general agent, or any other agent authorized by appointment or by law to receive service of process;

(B) name the court where the complaint was filed;

(C) be accompanied by a copy of the complaint, two copies of a waiver form, and a prepaid means for returning the form;

(D) inform the defendant, using text prescribed in Form 5, of the consequences of waiving and not waiving service;

(E) state the date when the request is sent;

(F) give the defendant a reasonable time of at least 30 days after the request was sent—or at least 60 days if sent to the defendant outside any judicial district of the United States—to return the waiver; and

(G) be sent by first-class mail or other reliable means.

(2) ***Failure to Waive.*** If a defendant located within the United States fails, without good cause, to sign and return a waiver requested by a plaintiff located within the United States, the court must impose on the defendant:

(A) the expenses later incurred in making service; and

(B) the reasonable expenses, including attorney's fees, of any motion required to collect those service expenses.

(3) ***Time to Answer After a Waiver.*** A defendant who, before being served with process, timely returns a waiver need not serve an answer to the complaint until 60 days after the request was sent—or until 90 days after it was sent to the defendant outside any judicial district of the United States.

(4) ***Results of Filing a Waiver.*** When the plaintiff files a waiver, proof of service is not required and these rules apply as if a summons and complaint had been served at the time of filing the waiver.

(5) ***Jurisdiction and Venue Not Waived.*** Waiving service of a summons does not waive any objection to personal jurisdiction or to venue.

(e) Serving an Individual Within a Judicial District of the United States. Unless federal law provides otherwise, an individual—other than a minor, an incompetent person, or a person whose waiver has been filed—may be served in a judicial district of the United States by:

(1) following state law for serving a summons in an action brought in courts of general jurisdiction in the state where the district court is located or where service is made; or

(2) doing any of the following:

(A) delivering a copy of the summons and of the complaint to the individual personally;

(B) leaving a copy of each at the individual's dwelling or usual place of abode with someone of suitable age and discretion who resides there; or

(C) delivering a copy of each to an agent authorized by appointment or by law to receive service of process.

(f) Serving an Individual in a Foreign Country. Unless federal law provides otherwise, an individual—other than a minor, an incompetent person, or a person whose waiver has been filed—may be served at a place not within any judicial district of the United States:

(1) by any internationally agreed means of service that is reasonably calculated to give notice, such as those authorized by the Hague Convention on the Service Abroad of Judicial and Extrajudicial Documents;

(2) if there is no internationally agreed means, or if an international agreement allows but does not specify other means, by a method that is reasonably calculated to give notice:

(A) as prescribed by the foreign country's law for service in that country in an action in its courts of general jurisdiction;

(B) as the foreign authority directs in response to a letter rogatory or letter of request; or

(C) unless prohibited by the foreign country's law, by:

(i) delivering a copy of the summons and of the complaint to the individual personally; or

(ii) using any form of mail that the clerk addresses and sends to the individual and that requires a signed receipt; or

(3) by other means not prohibited by international agreement, as the court orders.

(g) Serving a Minor or an Incompetent Person. A minor or an incompetent person in a judicial district of the United States must be served by following state law for serving a summons or like process on such a defendant in an action brought in the courts of general jurisdiction of the state where service is made. A minor or an incompetent person who is not within any judicial district of the United States must be served in the manner prescribed by Rule 4(f)(2)(A), (f)(2)(B), or (f)(3).

(h) **Serving a Corporation, Partnership, or Association.** Unless federal law provides otherwise or the defendant's waiver has been filed, a domestic or foreign corporation, or a partnership or other unincorporated association that is subject to suit under a common name, must be served:

(1) in a judicial district of the United States:

(A) in the manner prescribed by Rule 4(e)(1) for serving an individual; or

(B) by delivering a copy of the summons and of the complaint to an officer, a managing or general agent, or any other agent authorized by appointment or by law to receive service of process and—if the agent is one authorized by statute and the statute so requires—by also mailing a copy of each to the defendant; or

(2) at a place not within any judicial district of the United States, in any manner prescribed by Rule 4(f) for serving an individual, except personal delivery under (f)(2)(C)(i).

(i) **Serving the United States and Its Agencies, Corporations, Officers, or Employees.**

(1) ***United States.*** To serve the United States, a party must:

(A)(i) deliver a copy of the summons and of the complaint to the United States attorney for the district where the action is brought—or to an assistant United States attorney or clerical employee whom the United States attorney designates in a writing filed with the court clerk—or

(ii) send a copy of each by registered or certified mail to the civil-process clerk at the United States attorney's office;

(B) send a copy of each by registered or certified mail to the Attorney General of the United States at Washington, D.C.; and

(C) if the action challenges an order of a nonparty agency or officer of the United States, send a copy of each by registered or certified mail to the agency or officer.

(2) ***Agency; Corporation; Officer or Employee Sued in an Official Capacity.*** To serve a United States agency or corporation, or a United States officer or employee sued only in an official capacity, a party must serve the United States and also send a copy of the summons and of the complaint by registered or certified mail to the agency, corporation, officer, or employee.

(3) ***Officer or Employee Sued Individually.*** To serve a United States officer or employee sued in an individual capacity for an act or omission occurring in connection with duties performed on the United States' behalf (whether or not the officer or employee is also sued in an official capacity), a party must serve the United States and also serve the officer or employee under Rule 4(e), (f), or (g).

(4) ***Extending Time.*** The court must allow a party a reasonable time to cure its failure to:

(A) serve a person required to be served under Rule 4(i)(2), if the party has served either the United States attorney or the Attorney General of the United States; or

(B) serve the United States under Rule 4(i)(3), if the party has served the United States officer or employee.

(j) **Serving a Foreign, State, or Local Government.**

(1) ***Foreign State.*** A foreign state or its political subdivision, agency, or instrumentality must be served in accordance with 28 U.S.C. § 1608.

(2) ***State or Local Government.*** A state, a municipal corporation, or any other state-created governmental organization that is subject to suit must be served by:

(A) delivering a copy of the summons and of the complaint to its chief executive officer; or

(B) serving a copy of each in the manner prescribed by that state's law for serving a summons or like process on such a defendant.

(k) **Territorial Limits of Effective Service.**

(1) ***In General.*** Serving a summons or filing a waiver of service establishes personal jurisdiction over a defendant:

(A) who is subject to the jurisdiction of a court of general jurisdiction in the state where the district court is located;

(B) who is a party joined under Rule 14 or 19 and is served within a judicial district of the United States and not more than 100 miles from where the summons was issued; or

(C) when authorized by a federal statute.

(2) ***Federal Claim Outside State-Court Jurisdiction.*** For a claim that arises under federal law, serving a summons or filing a waiver of service establishes personal jurisdiction over a defendant if:

(A) the defendant is not subject to jurisdiction in any state's courts of general jurisdiction; and

(B) exercising jurisdiction is consistent with the United States Constitution and laws.

(*l*) **Proving Service.**

(1) ***Affidavit Required.*** Unless service is waived, proof of service must be made to the court. Except for service by a United States marshal

or deputy marshal, proof must be by the server's affidavit.

(2) ***Service Outside the United States.*** Service not within any judicial district of the United States must be proved as follows:

(A) if made under Rule 4(f)(1), as provided in the applicable treaty or convention; or

(B) if made under Rule 4(f)(2) or (f)(3), by a receipt signed by the addressee, or by other evidence satisfying the court that the summons and complaint were delivered to the addressee.

(3) ***Validity of Service; Amending Proof.*** Failure to prove service does not affect the validity of service. The court may permit proof of service to be amended.

(m) **Time Limit for Service.** If a defendant is not served within 120 days after the complaint is filed, the court—on motion or on its own after notice to the plaintiff—must dismiss the action without prejudice against that defendant or order that service be made within a specified time. But if the plaintiff shows good cause for the failure, the court must extend the time for service for an appropriate period. This subdivision (m) does not apply to service in a foreign country under Rule 4(f) or 4(j)(1).

(n) **Asserting Jurisdiction over Property or Assets.**

(1) ***Federal Law.*** The court may assert jurisdiction over property if authorized by a federal statute. Notice to claimants of the property must be given as provided in the statute or by serving a summons under this rule.

(2) ***State Law.*** On a showing that personal jurisdiction over a defendant cannot be obtained in the district where the action is brought by reasonable efforts to serve a summons under this rule, the court may assert jurisdiction over the defendant's assets found in the district. Jurisdiction is acquired by seizing the assets under the circumstances and in the manner provided by state law in that district.

(Amended January 21, 1963, effective July 1, 1963; February 28, 1966, effective July 1, 1966; April 29, 1980, effective August 1, 1980; amended by Pub.L. 97-462, § 2, January 12, 1983, 96 Stat. 2527, effective 45 days after January 12, 1983; amended March 2, 1987, effective August 1, 1987; April 22, 1993, effective December 1, 1993; April 17, 2000, effective December 1, 2000; April 30, 2007, effective December 1, 2007.)

RULE 4.1. SERVING OTHER PROCESS

(a) **In General.** Process—other than a summons under Rule 4 or a subpoena under Rule 45—must be served by a United States marshal or deputy marshal or by a person specially appointed for that purpose. It may be served anywhere within the territorial limits of the state where the district court is located and, if authorized by a federal statute, beyond those limits. Proof of service must be made under Rule 4(*l*).

(b) **Enforcing Orders: Committing for Civil Contempt.** An order committing a person for civil contempt of a decree or injunction issued to enforce federal law may be served and enforced in any district. Any other order in a civil-contempt proceeding may be served only in the state where the issuing court is located or elsewhere in the United States within 100 miles from where the order was issued.

(Adopted April 22, 1993, effective December 1, 1993; amended April 30, 2007, effective December 1, 2007.)

RULE 5. SERVING AND FILING PLEADINGS AND OTHER PAPERS

(a) **Service: When Required.**

(1) ***In General.*** Unless these rules provide otherwise, each of the following papers must be served on every party:

(A) an order stating that service is required;

(B) a pleading filed after the original complaint, unless the court orders otherwise under Rule 5(c) because there are numerous defendants;

(C) a discovery paper required to be served on a party, unless the court orders otherwise;

(D) a written motion, except one that may be heard ex parte; and

(E) a written notice, appearance, demand, or offer of judgment, or any similar paper.

(2) ***If a Party Fails to Appear.*** No service is required on a party who is in default for failing to appear. But a pleading that asserts a new claim for relief against such a party must be served on that party under Rule 4.

(3) ***Seizing Property.*** If an action is begun by seizing property and no person is or need be named as a defendant, any service required before the filing of an appearance, answer, or claim must be made on the person who had custody or possession of the property when it was seized.

(b) **Service: How Made.**

(1) ***Serving an Attorney.*** If a party is represented by an attorney, service under this rule must be made on the attorney unless the court orders service on the party.

(2) ***Service in General.*** A paper is served under this rule by:

(A) handing it to the person;

(B) leaving it:

(i) at the person's office with a clerk or other person in charge or, if no one is in charge, in a conspicuous place in the office; or

(ii) if the person has no office or the office is closed, at the person's dwelling or usual place of abode with someone of suitable age and discretion who resides there;

(C) mailing it to the person's last known address—in which event service is complete upon mailing;

(D) leaving it with the court clerk if the person has no known address;

(E) sending it by electronic means if the person consented in writing—in which event service is complete upon transmission, but is not effective if the serving party learns that it did not reach the person to be served; or

(F) delivering it by any other means that the person consented to in writing—in which event service is complete when the person making service delivers it to the agency designated to make delivery.

(3) ***Using Court Facilities.*** If a local rule so authorizes, a party may use the court's transmission facilities to make service under Rule 5(b)(2)(E).

(c) Serving Numerous Defendants.

(1) ***In General.*** If an action involves an unusually large number of defendants, the court may, on motion or on its own, order that:

(A) defendants' pleadings and replies to them need not be served on other defendants;

(B) any crossclaim, counterclaim, avoidance, or affirmative defense in those pleadings and replies to them will be treated as denied or avoided by all other parties; and

(C) filing any such pleading and serving it on the plaintiff constitutes notice of the pleading to all parties.

(2) ***Notifying Parties.*** A copy of every such order must be served on the parties as the court directs.

(d) Filing.

(1) ***Required Filings; Certificate of Service.*** Any paper after the complaint that is required to be served—together with a certificate of service—must be filed within a reasonable time after service. But disclosures under Rule 26(a)(1) or (2) and the following discovery requests and responses must not be filed until they are used in the proceeding or the court orders filing: depositions, interrogatories, requests for documents or tangible things or to permit entry onto land, and requests for admission.

(2) ***How Filing Is Made—In General.*** A paper is filed by delivering it:

(A) to the clerk; or

(B) to a judge who agrees to accept it for filing, and who must then note the filing date on the paper and promptly send it to the clerk.

(3) ***Electronic Filing, Signing, or Verification.*** A court may, by local rule, allow papers to be filed, signed, or verified by electronic means that are consistent with any technical standards established by the Judicial Conference of the United States. A local rule may require electronic filing only if reasonable exceptions are allowed. A paper filed electronically in compliance with a local rule is a written paper for purposes of these rules.

(4) ***Acceptance by the Clerk.*** The clerk must not refuse to file a paper solely because it is not in the form prescribed by these rules or by a local rule or practice.

(Amended January 21, 1963, effective July 1, 1963; March 30, 1970, effective July 1, 1970; April 29, 1980, effective August 1, 1980; March 2, 1987, effective August 1, 1987; April 30, 1991, effective December 1, 1991; April 22, 1993, effective December 1, 1993; April 23, 1996, effective December 1, 1996; April 17, 2000, effective December 1, 2000; April 23, 2001, effective December 1, 2001; April 12, 2006, effective December 1, 2006; April 30, 2007, effective December 1, 2007.)

RULE 5.1. CONSTITUTIONAL CHALLENGE TO A STATUTE—NOTICE, CERTIFICATION, AND INTERVENTION

(a) Notice by a Party. A party that files a pleading, written motion, or other paper drawing into question the constitutionality of a federal or state statute must promptly:

(1) file a notice of constitutional question stating the question and identifying the paper that raises it, if:

(A) a federal statute is questioned and the parties do not include the United States, one of its agencies, or one of its officers or employees in an official capacity; or

(B) a state statute is questioned and the parties do not include the state, one of its agencies, or one of its officers or employees in an official capacity; and

(2) serve the notice and paper on the Attorney General of the United States if a federal statute is questioned—or on the state attorney general if a state statute is questioned—either by certified or registered mail or by sending it to an electronic address designated by the attorney general for this purpose.

(b) Certification by the Court. The court must, under 28 U.S.C. § 2403, certify to the appropriate attorney general that a statute has been questioned.

(c) Intervention; Final Decision on the Merits. Unless the court sets a later time, the attorney general may intervene within 60 days after the notice is filed or after the court certifies the challenge, whichever is earlier. Before the time to intervene expires, the court may reject the constitutional challenge, but may not enter a final judgment holding the statute unconstitutional.

(d) No Forfeiture. A party's failure to file and serve the notice, or the court's failure to certify, does not forfeit a constitutional claim or defense that is otherwise timely asserted.

(Adopted April 12, 2006, effective December 1, 2006; amended April 30, 2007, effective December 1, 2007.)

RULE 5.2. PRIVACY PROTECTION FOR FILINGS MADE WITH THE COURT

(a) Redacted Filings. Unless the court orders otherwise, in an electronic or paper filing with the court that contains an individual's social-security number, taxpayer-identification number, or birth date, the name of an individual known to be a minor, or a financial-account number, a party or nonparty making the filing may include only:

(1) the last four digits of the social-security number and taxpayer-identification number;

(2) the year of the individual's birth;

(3) the minor's initials; and

(4) the last four digits of the financial-account number.

(b) Exemptions from the Redaction Requirement. The redaction requirement does not apply to the following:

(1) a financial-account number that identifies the property allegedly subject to forfeiture in a forfeiture proceeding;

(2) the record of an administrative or agency proceeding;

(3) the official record of a state-court proceeding;

(4) the record of a court or tribunal, if that record was not subject to the redaction requirement when originally filed;

(5) a filing covered by Rule 5.2(c) or (d); and

(6) a pro se filing in an action brought under 28 U.S.C. §§ 2241, 2254, or 2255.

(c) Limitations on Remote Access to Electronic Files; Social–Security Appeals and Immigration Cases. Unless the court orders otherwise, in an action for benefits under the Social Security Act, and in an action or proceeding relating to an order of removal, to relief from removal, or to immigration benefits or detention, access to an electronic file is authorized as follows:

(1) the parties and their attorneys may have remote electronic access to any part of the case file, including the administrative record;

(2) any other person may have electronic access to the full record at the courthouse, but may have remote electronic access only to:

(A) the docket maintained by the court; and

(B) an opinion, order, judgment, or other disposition of the court, but not any other part of the case file or the administrative record.

(d) Filings Made Under Seal. The court may order that a filing be made under seal without redaction. The court may later unseal the filing or order the person who made the filing to file a redacted version for the public record.

(e) Protective Orders. For good cause, the court may by order in a case:

(1) require redaction of additional information; or

(2) limit or prohibit a nonparty's remote electronic access to a document filed with the court.

(f) Option for Additional Unredacted Filing Under Seal. A person making a redacted filing may also file an unredacted copy under seal. The court must retain the unredacted copy as part of the record.

(g) Option for Filing a Reference List. A filing that contains redacted information may be filed together with a reference list that identifies each item of redacted information and specifies an appropriate identifier that uniquely corresponds to each item listed. The list must be filed under seal and may be amended as of right. Any reference in the case to a listed identifier will be construed to refer to the corresponding item of information.

(h) Waiver of Protection of Identifiers. A person waives the protection of Rule 5.2(a) as to the person's own information by filing it without redaction and not under seal.

(Adopted April 30, 2007, effective December 1, 2007.)

RULE 6. COMPUTING AND EXTENDING TIME; TIME FOR MOTION PAPERS

(a) Computing Time. The following rules apply in computing any time period specified in these rules, in any local rule or court order, or in any statute that does not specify a method of computing time.

(1) ***Period Stated in Days or a Longer Unit.*** When the period is stated in days or a longer unit of time:

(A) exclude the day of the event that triggers the period;

(B) count every day, including intermediate Saturdays, Sundays, and legal holidays; and

(C) include the last day of the period, but if the last day is a Saturday, Sunday, or legal holiday, the period continues to run until the end of the next day that is not a Saturday, Sunday, or legal holiday.

(2) ***Period Stated in Hours.*** When the period is stated in hours:

(A) begin counting immediately on the occurrence of the event that triggers the period;

(B) count every hour, including hours during intermediate Saturdays, Sundays, and legal holidays; and

(C) if the period would end on a Saturday, Sunday, or legal holiday, the period continues to run until the same time on the next day that is not a Saturday, Sunday, or legal holiday.

(3) ***Inaccessibility of the Clerk's Office.*** Unless the court orders otherwise, if the clerk's office is inaccessible:

(A) on the last day for filing under Rule 6(a)(1), then the time for filing is extended to the first accessible day that is not a Saturday, Sunday, or legal holiday; or

(B) during the last hour for filing under Rule 6(a)(2), then the time for filing is extended to the same time on the first accessible day that is not a Saturday, Sunday, or legal holiday.

(4) ***"Last Day" Defined.*** Unless a different time is set by a statute, local rule, or court order, the last day ends:

(A) for electronic filing, at midnight in the court's time zone; and

(B) for filing by other means, when the clerk's office is scheduled to close.

(5) ***"Next Day" Defined.*** The "next day" is determined by continuing to count forward when the period is measured after an event and backward when measured before an event.

(6) ***"Legal Holiday" Defined.*** "Legal holiday" means:

(A) the day set aside by statute for observing New Year's Day, Martin Luther King Jr.'s Birthday, Washington's Birthday, Memorial Day, Independence Day, Labor Day, Columbus Day, Veterans' Day, Thanksgiving Day, or Christmas Day;

(B) any day declared a holiday by the President or Congress; and

(C) for periods that are measured after an event, any other day declared a holiday by the state where the district court is located.

(b) Extending Time.

(1) ***In General.*** When an act may or must be done within a specified time, the court may, for good cause, extend the time:

(A) with or without motion or notice if the court acts, or if a request is made, before the original time or its extension expires; or

(B) on motion made after the time has expired if the party failed to act because of excusable neglect.

(2) ***Exceptions.*** A court must not extend the time to act under Rules 50(b) and (d), 52(b), 59(b), (d), and (e), and 60(b).

(c) Motions, Notices of Hearing, and Affidavits.

(1) ***In General.*** A written motion and notice of the hearing must be served at least 14 days before the time specified for the hearing, with the following exceptions:

(A) when the motion may be heard ex parte;

(B) when these rules set a different time; or

(C) when a court order—which a party may, for good cause, apply for ex parte—sets a different time.

(2) ***Supporting Affidavit.*** Any affidavit supporting a motion must be served with the motion. Except as Rule 59(c) provides otherwise, any opposing affidavit must be served at least 7 days before the hearing, unless the court permits service at another time.

(d) Additional Time After Certain Kinds of Service. When a party may or must act within a specified time after service and service is made under Rule 5(b)(2)(C), (D), (E), or (F), 3 days are added after the period would otherwise expire under Rule 6(a).

(Amended December 27, 1946, effective March 19, 1948; January 21, 1963, effective July 1, 1963; February 28, 1966, effective July 1, 1966; December 4, 1967, effective July 1, 1968; March 1, 1971, effective July 1, 1971; April 28, 1983, effective August 1, 1983; April 29, 1985, effective August 1, 1985; March 2, 1987, effective August 1, 1987; April 29, 1999, effective December 1, 1999; April 23, 2001, effective December 1, 2001; April 25, 2005, effective December 1, 2005; April 30, 2007, effective December 1, 2007; March 26, 2009, effective December 1, 2009.)

TITLE III. PLEADINGS AND MOTIONS

RULE 7. PLEADINGS ALLOWED; FORM OF MOTIONS AND OTHER PAPERS

(a) **Pleadings.** Only these pleadings are allowed:

(1) a complaint;

(2) an answer to a complaint;

(3) an answer to a counterclaim designated as a counterclaim;

(4) an answer to a crossclaim;

(5) a third-party complaint;

(6) an answer to a third-party complaint; and

(7) if the court orders one, a reply to an answer.

(b) **Motions and Other Papers.**

(1) ***In General.*** A request for a court order must be made by motion. The motion must:

(A) be in writing unless made during a hearing or trial;

(B) state with particularity the grounds for seeking the order; and

(C) state the relief sought.

(2) ***Form.*** The rules governing captions and other matters of form in pleadings apply to motions and other papers.

(Amended December 27, 1946, effective March 19, 1948; January 21, 1963, effective July 1, 1963; April 28, 1983, effective August 1, 1983; April 30, 2007, effective December 1, 2007.)

RULE 7.1. DISCLOSURE STATEMENT

(a) **Who Must File; Contents.** A nongovernmental corporate party must file two copies of a disclosure statement that:

(1) identifies any parent corporation and any publicly held corporation owning 10% or more of its stock; or

(2) states that there is no such corporation.

(b) **Time to File; Supplemental Filing.** A party must:

(1) file the disclosure statement with its first appearance, pleading, petition, motion, response, or other request addressed to the court; and

(2) promptly file a supplemental statement if any required information changes.

(Adopted April 29, 2002, effective December 1, 2002; April 30, 2007, effective December 1, 2007.)

RULE 8. GENERAL RULES OF PLEADING

(a) **Claim for Relief.** A pleading that states a claim for relief must contain:

(1) a short and plain statement of the grounds for the court's jurisdiction, unless the court already has jurisdiction and the claim needs no new jurisdictional support;

(2) a short and plain statement of the claim showing that the pleader is entitled to relief; and

(3) a demand for the relief sought, which may include relief in the alternative or different types of relief.

(b) **Defenses; Admissions and Denials.**

(1) ***In General.*** In responding to a pleading, a party must:

(A) state in short and plain terms its defenses to each claim asserted against it; and

(B) admit or deny the allegations asserted against it by an opposing party.

(2) ***Denials—Responding to the Substance.*** A denial must fairly respond to the substance of the allegation.

(3) ***General and Specific Denials.*** A party that intends in good faith to deny all the allegations of a pleading—including the jurisdictional grounds—may do so by a general denial. A party that does not intend to deny all the allegations must either specifically deny designated allegations or generally deny all except those specifically admitted.

(4) ***Denying Part of an Allegation.*** A party that intends in good faith to deny only part of an allegation must admit the part that is true and deny the rest.

(5) ***Lacking Knowledge or Information.*** A party that lacks knowledge or information sufficient to form a belief about the truth of an allegation must so state, and the statement has the effect of a denial.

(6) ***Effect of Failing to Deny.*** An allegation—other than one relating to the amount of damages—is admitted if a responsive pleading is required and the allegation is not denied. If a responsive pleading is not required, an allegation is considered denied or avoided.

(c) **Affirmative Defenses.**

(1) ***In General.*** In responding to a pleading, a party must affirmatively state any avoidance or affirmative defense, including:

- accord and satisfaction;
- arbitration and award;
- assumption of risk;
- contributory negligence;
- duress;
- estoppel;

- failure of consideration;
- fraud;
- illegality;
- injury by fellow servant;
- laches;
- license;
- payment;
- release;
- res judicata;
- statute of frauds;
- statute of limitations; and
- waiver.

(2) ***Mistaken Designation.*** If a party mistakenly designates a defense as a counterclaim, or a counterclaim as a defense, the court must, if justice requires, treat the pleading as though it were correctly designated, and may impose terms for doing so.

(d) Pleading to Be Concise and Direct; Alternative Statements; Inconsistency.

(1) ***In General.*** Each allegation must be simple, concise, and direct. No technical form is required.

(2) ***Alternative Statements of a Claim or Defense.*** A party may set out 2 or more statements of a claim or defense alternatively or hypothetically, either in a single count or defense or in separate ones. If a party makes alternative statements, the pleading is sufficient if any one of them is sufficient.

(3) ***Inconsistent Claims or Defenses.*** A party may state as many separate claims or defenses as it has, regardless of consistency.

(e) Construing Pleadings. Pleadings must be construed so as to do justice.

(Amended February 28, 1966, effective July 1, 1966; March 2, 1987, effective August 1, 1987; April 30, 2007, effective December 1, 2007; April 28, 2010, effective December 1, 2010.)

RULE 9. PLEADING SPECIAL MATTERS

(a) Capacity or Authority to Sue; Legal Existence.

(1) ***In General.*** Except when required to show that the court has jurisdiction, a pleading need not allege:

(A) a party's capacity to sue or be sued;

(B) a party's authority to sue or be sued in a representative capacity; or

(C) the legal existence of an organized association of persons that is made a party.

(2) ***Raising Those Issues.*** To raise any of those issues, a party must do so by a specific denial, which must state any supporting facts that are peculiarly within the party's knowledge.

(b) Fraud or Mistake; Conditions of Mind. In alleging fraud or mistake, a party must state with particularity the circumstances constituting fraud or mistake. Malice, intent, knowledge, and other conditions of a person's mind may be alleged generally.

(c) Conditions Precedent. In pleading conditions precedent, it suffices to allege generally that all conditions precedent have occurred or been performed. But when denying that a condition precedent has occurred or been performed, a party must do so with particularity.

(d) Official Document or Act. In pleading an official document or official act, it suffices to allege that the document was legally issued or the act legally done.

(e) Judgment. In pleading a judgment or decision of a domestic or foreign court, a judicial or quasi-judicial tribunal, or a board or officer, it suffices to plead the judgment or decision without showing jurisdiction to render it.

(f) Time and Place. An allegation of time or place is material when testing the sufficiency of a pleading.

(g) Special Damages. If an item of special damage is claimed, it must be specifically stated.

(h) Admiralty or Maritime Claim.

(1) ***How Designated.*** If a claim for relief is within the admiralty or maritime jurisdiction and also within the court's subject-matter jurisdiction on some other ground, the pleading may designate the claim as an admiralty or maritime claim for purposes of Rules 14(c), 38(e), and 82 and the Supplemental Rules for Admiralty or Maritime Claims and Asset Forfeiture Actions. A claim cognizable only in the admiralty or maritime jurisdiction is an admiralty or maritime claim for those purposes, whether or not so designated.

(2) ***Designation for Appeal.*** A case that includes an admiralty or maritime claim within this subdivision (h) is an admiralty case within 28 U.S.C. § 1292(a)(3).

(Amended February 28, 1966, effective July 1, 1966; December 4, 1967, effective July 1, 1968; March 30, 1970, effective July 1, 1970; March 2, 1987, effective August 1, 1987; April 11, 1997, effective December 1, 1997; April 12, 2006, effective December 1, 2006; April 30, 2007, effective December 1, 2007.)

RULE 10. FORM OF PLEADINGS

(a) Caption; Names of Parties. Every pleading must have a caption with the court's name, a title, a file number, and a Rule 7(a) designation. The title of the complaint must name all the parties; the title of other pleadings, after naming the first party on each side, may refer generally to other parties.

(b) Paragraphs; Separate Statements. A party must state its claims or defenses in numbered paragraphs, each limited as far as practicable to a single set of circumstances. A later pleading may refer by number to a paragraph in an earlier pleading. If doing so would promote clarity, each claim founded on a separate transaction or occurrence—and each defense other than a denial—must be stated in a separate count or defense.

(c) Adoption by Reference; Exhibits. A statement in a pleading may be adopted by reference elsewhere in the same pleading or in any other pleading or motion. A copy of a written instrument that is an exhibit to a pleading is a part of the pleading for all purposes.

(Amended April 30, 2007, effective December 1, 2007.)

RULE 11. SIGNING PLEADINGS, MOTIONS, AND OTHER PAPERS; REPRESENTATIONS TO THE COURT; SANCTIONS

(a) Signature. Every pleading, written motion, and other paper must be signed by at least one attorney of record in the attorney's name—or by a party personally if the party is unrepresented. The paper must state the signer's address, e-mail address, and telephone number. Unless a rule or statute specifically states otherwise, a pleading need not be verified or accompanied by an affidavit. The court must strike an unsigned paper unless the omission is promptly corrected after being called to the attorney's or party's attention.

(b) Representations to the Court. By presenting to the court a pleading, written motion, or other paper—whether by signing, filing, submitting, or later advocating it—an attorney or unrepresented party certifies that to the best of the person's knowledge, information, and belief, formed after an inquiry reasonable under the circumstances:

(1) it is not being presented for any improper purpose, such as to harass, cause unnecessary delay, or needlessly increase the cost of litigation;

(2) the claims, defenses, and other legal contentions are warranted by existing law or by a nonfrivolous argument for extending, modifying, or reversing existing law or for establishing new law;

(3) the factual contentions have evidentiary support or, if specifically so identified, will likely have evidentiary support after a reasonable opportunity for further investigation or discovery; and

(4) the denials of factual contentions are warranted on the evidence or, if specifically so identified, are reasonably based on belief or a lack of information.

(c) Sanctions.

(1) ***In General.*** If, after notice and a reasonable opportunity to respond, the court determines that Rule 11(b) has been violated, the court may impose an appropriate sanction on any attorney, law firm, or party that violated the rule or is responsible for the violation. Absent exceptional circumstances, a law firm must be held jointly responsible for a violation committed by its partner, associate, or employee.

(2) ***Motion for Sanctions.*** A motion for sanctions must be made separately from any other motion and must describe the specific conduct that allegedly violates Rule 11(b). The motion must be served under Rule 5, but it must not be filed or be presented to the court if the challenged paper, claim, defense, contention, or denial is withdrawn or appropriately corrected within 21 days after service or within another time the court sets. If warranted, the court may award to the prevailing party the reasonable expenses, including attorney's fees, incurred for the motion.

(3) ***On the Court's Initiative.*** On its own, the court may order an attorney, law firm, or party to show cause why conduct specifically described in the order has not violated Rule 11(b).

(4) ***Nature of a Sanction.*** A sanction imposed under this rule must be limited to what suffices to deter repetition of the conduct or comparable conduct by others similarly situated. The sanction may include nonmonetary directives; an order to pay a penalty into court; or, if imposed on motion and warranted for effective deterrence, an order directing payment to the movant of part or all of the reasonable attorney's fees and other expenses directly resulting from the violation.

(5) ***Limitations on Monetary Sanctions.*** The court must not impose a monetary sanction:

(A) against a represented party for violating Rule 11(b)(2); or

(B) on its own, unless it issued the show-cause order under Rule 11(c)(3) before voluntary dismissal or settlement of the claims made by or against the party that is, or whose attorneys are, to be sanctioned.

(6) ***Requirements for an Order.*** An order imposing a sanction must describe the sanctioned conduct and explain the basis for the sanction.

(d) Inapplicability to Discovery. This rule does not apply to disclosures and discovery requests, responses, objections, and motions under Rules 26 through 37.

(Amended April 28, 1983, effective August 1, 1983; March 2, 1987, effective August 1, 1987; April 22, 1993, effective December 1, 1993; April 30, 2007, effective December 1, 2007.)

RULE 12. DEFENSES AND OBJECTIONS: WHEN AND HOW PRESENTED; MOTION FOR JUDGMENT ON THE PLEADINGS; CONSOLIDATING MOTIONS; WAIVING DEFENSES; PRETRIAL HEARING

(a) Time to Serve a Responsive Pleading.

(1) ***In General.*** Unless another time is specified by this rule or a federal statute, the time for serving a responsive pleading is as follows:

(A) A defendant must serve an answer:

(i) within 21 days after being served with the summons and complaint; or

(ii) if it has timely waived service under Rule 4(d), within 60 days after the request for a waiver was sent, or within 90 days after it was sent to the defendant outside any judicial district of the United States.

(B) A party must serve an answer to a counterclaim or crossclaim within 21 days after being served with the pleading that states the counterclaim or crossclaim.

(C) A party must serve a reply to an answer within 21 days after being served with an order to reply, unless the order specifies a different time.

(2) ***United States and Its Agencies, Officers, or Employees Sued in an Official Capacity.*** The United States, a United States agency, or a United States officer or employee sued only in an official capacity must serve an answer to a complaint, counterclaim, or crossclaim within 60 days after service on the United States attorney.

(3) ***United States Officers or Employees Sued in an Individual Capacity.*** A United States officer or employee sued in an individual capacity for an act or omission occurring in connection with duties performed on the United States' behalf must serve an answer to a complaint, counterclaim, or crossclaim within 60 days after service on the officer or employee or service on the United States attorney, whichever is later.

(4) ***Effect of a Motion.*** Unless the court sets a different time, serving a motion under this rule alters these periods as follows:

(A) if the court denies the motion or postpones its disposition until trial, the responsive pleading must be served within 14 days after notice of the court's action; or

(B) if the court grants a motion for a more definite statement, the responsive pleading must be served within 14 days after the more definite statement is served.

(b) How to Present Defenses. Every defense to a claim for relief in any pleading must be asserted in the responsive pleading if one is required. But a party may assert the following defenses by motion:

(1) lack of subject-matter jurisdiction;

(2) lack of personal jurisdiction;

(3) improper venue;

(4) insufficient process;

(5) insufficient service of process;

(6) failure to state a claim upon which relief can be granted; and

(7) failure to join a party under Rule 19.

A motion asserting any of these defenses must be made before pleading if a responsive pleading is allowed. If a pleading sets out a claim for relief that does not require a responsive pleading, an opposing party may assert at trial any defense to that claim. No defense or objection is waived by joining it with one or more other defenses or objections in a responsive pleading or in a motion.

(c) Motion for Judgment on the Pleadings. After the pleadings are closed—but early enough not to delay trial—a party may move for judgment on the pleadings.

(d) Result of Presenting Matters Outside the Pleadings. If, on a motion under Rule 12(b)(6) or 12(c), matters outside the pleadings are presented to and not excluded by the court, the motion must be treated as one for summary judgment under Rule 56. All parties must be given a reasonable opportunity to present all the material that is pertinent to the motion.

(e) Motion for a More Definite Statement. A party may move for a more definite statement of a pleading to which a responsive pleading is allowed but which is so vague or ambiguous that the party cannot reasonably prepare a response. The motion must be made before filing a responsive pleading and must point out the defects complained of and the details desired. If the court orders a more definite statement and the order is not obeyed within 14 days after notice of the order or within the time the court sets, the court may strike the pleading or issue any other appropriate order.

(f) Motion to Strike. The court may strike from a pleading an insufficient defense or any redundant, immaterial, impertinent, or scandalous matter. The court may act:

(1) on its own; or

(2) on motion made by a party either before responding to the pleading or, if a response is not allowed, within 21 days after being served with the pleading.

(g) Joining Motions.

(1) ***Right to Join.*** A motion under this rule may be joined with any other motion allowed by this rule.

(2) ***Limitation on Further Motions.*** Except as provided in Rule 12(h)(2) or (3), a party that makes a motion under this rule must not make another motion under this rule raising a defense or objection that was available to the party but omitted from its earlier motion.

(h) Waiving and Preserving Certain Defenses.

(1) ***When Some Are Waived.*** A party waives any defense listed in Rule 12(b)(2)-(5) by:

(A) omitting it from a motion in the circumstances described in Rule 12(g)(2); or

(B) failing to either:

(i) make it by motion under this rule; or

(ii) include it in a responsive pleading or in an amendment allowed by Rule 15(a)(1) as a matter of course.

(2) ***When to Raise Others.*** Failure to state a claim upon which relief can be granted, to join a person required by Rule 19(b), or to state a legal defense to a claim may be raised:

(A) in any pleading allowed or ordered under Rule 7(a);

(B) by a motion under Rule 12(c); or

(C) at trial.

(3) ***Lack of Subject-Matter Jurisdiction.*** If the court determines at any time that it lacks subject-matter jurisdiction, the court must dismiss the action.

(i) Hearing Before Trial. If a party so moves, any defense listed in Rule 12(b)(1)-(7)—whether made in a pleading or by motion—and a motion under Rule 12(c) must be heard and decided before trial unless the court orders a deferral until trial.

(Amended December 27, 1946, effective March 19, 1948; January 21, 1963, effective July 1, 1963; February 28, 1966, effective July 1, 1966; March 2, 1987, effective August 1, 1987; April 22, 1993, effective December 1, 1993; April 17, 2000, effective December 1, 2000; April 30, 2007, effective December 1, 2007; March 26, 2009, effective December 1, 2009.)

RULE 13. COUNTERCLAIM AND CROSSCLAIM

(a) Compulsory Counterclaim.

(1) ***In General.*** A pleading must state as a counterclaim any claim that—at the time of its service—the pleader has against an opposing party if the claim:

(A) arises out of the transaction or occurrence that is the subject matter of the opposing party's claim; and

(B) does not require adding another party over whom the court cannot acquire jurisdiction.

(2) ***Exceptions.*** The pleader need not state the claim if:

(A) when the action was commenced, the claim was the subject of another pending action; or

(B) the opposing party sued on its claim by attachment or other process that did not establish personal jurisdiction over the pleader on that claim, and the pleader does not assert any counterclaim under this rule.

(b) Permissive Counterclaim. A pleading may state as a counterclaim against an opposing party any claim that is not compulsory.

(c) Relief Sought in a Counterclaim. A counterclaim need not diminish or defeat the recovery sought by the opposing party. It may request relief that exceeds in amount or differs in kind from the relief sought by the opposing party.

(d) Counterclaim Against the United States. These rules do not expand the right to assert a counterclaim—or to claim a credit—against the United States or a United States officer or agency.

(e) Counterclaim Maturing or Acquired After Pleading. The court may permit a party to file a supplemental pleading asserting a counterclaim that matured or was acquired by the party after serving an earlier pleading.

(f) [Abrogated]

(g) Crossclaim Against a Coparty. A pleading may state as a crossclaim any claim by one party against a coparty if the claim arises out of the transaction or occurrence that is the subject matter of the original action or of a counterclaim, or if the claim relates to any property that is the subject matter of the original action. The crossclaim may include a claim that the coparty is or may be liable to the cross-claimant for all or part of a claim asserted in the action against the cross-claimant.

(h) Joining Additional Parties. Rules 19 and 20 govern the addition of a person as a party to a counterclaim or crossclaim.

(i) Separate Trials; Separate Judgments. If the court orders separate trials under Rule 42(b), it may enter judgment on a counterclaim or crossclaim under Rule 54(b) when it has jurisdiction to do so, even if the opposing party's claims have been dismissed or otherwise resolved.

(Amended December 27, 1946, effective March 19, 1948; January 21, 1963, effective July 1, 1963; February 28, 1966, effective July 1, 1966; March 2, 1987, effective August 1, 1987; April 30, 2007, effective December 1, 2007; March 26, 2009, effective December 1, 2009.)

RULE 14. THIRD–PARTY PRACTICE

(a) When a Defending Party May Bring in a Third Party.

(1) ***Timing of the Summons and Complaint.*** A defending party may, as third-party plaintiff, serve a summons and complaint on a nonparty who is or may be liable to it for all or part of the claim against it. But the third-party plaintiff must, by motion, obtain the court's leave if it files the third-party complaint more than 14 days after serving its original answer.

(2) ***Third–Party Defendant's Claims and Defenses.*** The person served with the summons and third-party complaint—the "third-party defendant":

(A) must assert any defense against the third-party plaintiff's claim under Rule 12;

(B) must assert any counterclaim against the third-party plaintiff under Rule 13(a), and may assert any counterclaim against the third-party plaintiff under Rule 13(b) or any crossclaim against another third-party defendant under Rule 13(g);

(C) may assert against the plaintiff any defense that the third-party plaintiff has to the plaintiff's claim; and

(D) may also assert against the plaintiff any claim arising out of the transaction or occurrence that is the subject matter of the plaintiff's claim against the third-party plaintiff.

(3) ***Plaintiff's Claims Against a Third–Party Defendant.*** The plaintiff may assert against the third-party defendant any claim arising out of the transaction or occurrence that is the subject matter of the plaintiff's claim against the third-party plaintiff. The third-party defendant must then assert any defense under Rule 12 and any counterclaim under Rule 13(a), and may assert any counterclaim under Rule 13(b) or any crossclaim under Rule 13(g).

(4) ***Motion to Strike, Sever, or Try Separately.*** Any party may move to strike the third-party claim, to sever it, or to try it separately.

(5) ***Third–Party Defendant's Claim Against a Nonparty.*** A third-party defendant may proceed under this rule against a nonparty who is or may be liable to the third-party defendant for all or part of any claim against it.

(6) ***Third–Party Complaint In Rem.*** If it is within the admiralty or maritime jurisdiction, a third-party complaint may be in rem. In that event, a reference in this rule to the "summons" includes the warrant of arrest, and a reference to the defendant or third-party plaintiff includes, when appropriate, a person who asserts a right under Supplemental Rule C(6)(a)(i) in the property arrested.

(b) When a Plaintiff May Bring in a Third Party. When a claim is asserted against a plaintiff, the plaintiff may bring in a third party if this rule would allow a defendant to do so.

(c) Admiralty or Maritime Claim.

(1) ***Scope of Impleader.*** If a plaintiff asserts an admiralty or maritime claim under Rule 9(h), the defendant or a person who asserts a right under Supplemental Rule C(6)(a)(i) may, as a third-party plaintiff, bring in a third-party defendant who may be wholly or partly liable—either to the plaintiff or to the third-party plaintiff—for remedy over, contribution, or otherwise on account of the same transaction, occurrence, or series of transactions or occurrences.

(2) ***Defending Against a Demand for Judgment for the Plaintiff.*** The third-party plaintiff may demand judgment in the plaintiff's favor against the third-party defendant. In that event, the third-party defendant must defend under Rule 12 against the plaintiff's claim as well as the third-party plaintiff's claim; and the action proceeds as if the plaintiff had sued both the third-party defendant and the third-party plaintiff.

(Amended December 27, 1946, effective March 19, 1948; January 21, 1963, effective July 1, 1963; February 28, 1966, effective July 1, 1966; March 2, 1987, effective August 1, 1987; April 17, 2000, effective December 1, 2000; April 12, 2006, effective December 1, 2006; April 30, 2007, effective December 1, 2007; March 26, 2009, effective December 1, 2009.)

RULE 15. AMENDED AND SUPPLEMENTAL PLEADINGS

(a) Amendments Before Trial.

(1) ***Amending as a Matter of Course.*** A party may amend its pleading once as a matter of course within:

(A) 21 days after serving it, or

(B) if the pleading is one to which a responsive pleading is required, 21 days after service of a responsive pleading or 21 days after service of a motion under Rule 12(b), (e), or (f), whichever is earlier.

(2) ***Other Amendments.*** In all other cases, a party may amend its pleading only with the opposing party's written consent or the court's leave. The court should freely give leave when justice so requires.

(3) ***Time to Respond.*** Unless the court orders otherwise, any required response to an amended pleading must be made within the time remaining to respond to the original pleading or within 14 days after service of the amended pleading, whichever is later.

(b) Amendments During and After Trial.

(1) ***Based on an Objection at Trial.*** If, at trial, a party objects that evidence is not within the issues raised in the pleadings, the court may permit the pleadings to be amended. The court should freely permit an amendment when doing so will aid in presenting the merits and the objecting party fails to satisfy the court that the evidence would prejudice that party's action or defense on the merits. The court may grant a continuance to enable the objecting party to meet the evidence.

(2) ***For Issues Tried by Consent.*** When an issue not raised by the pleadings is tried by the parties' express or implied consent, it must be treated in all respects as if raised in the pleadings. A party may move—at any time, even after judgment—to amend the pleadings to conform them to the evidence and to raise an unpleaded issue. But failure to amend does not affect the result of the trial of that issue.

(c) Relation Back of Amendments.

(1) ***When an Amendment Relates Back.*** An amendment to a pleading relates back to the date of the original pleading when:

(A) the law that provides the applicable statute of limitations allows relation back;

(B) the amendment asserts a claim or defense that arose out of the conduct, transaction, or occurrence set out—or attempted to be set out—in the original pleading; or

(C) the amendment changes the party or the naming of the party against whom a claim is asserted, if Rule 15(c)(1)(B) is satisfied and if, within the period provided by Rule 4(m) for serving the summons and complaint, the party to be brought in by amendment:

(i) received such notice of the action that it will not be prejudiced in defending on the merits; and

(ii) knew or should have known that the action would have been brought against it, but for a mistake concerning the proper party's identity.

(2) ***Notice to the United States.*** When the United States or a United States officer or agency is added as a defendant by amendment, the notice requirements of Rule 15(c)(1)(C)(i) and (ii) are satisfied if, during the stated period, process was delivered or mailed to the United States attorney or the United States attorney's designee, to the Attorney General of the United States, or to the officer or agency.

(d) Supplemental Pleadings. On motion and reasonable notice, the court may, on just terms, permit a party to serve a supplemental pleading setting out any transaction, occurrence, or event that happened after the date of the pleading to be supplemented. The court may permit supplementation even though the original pleading is defective in stating a claim or defense. The court may order that the opposing party plead to the supplemental pleading within a specified time.

(Amended January 21, 1963, effective July 1, 1963; February 28, 1966, effective July 1, 1966; March 2, 1987, effective August 1, 1987; April 30, 1991, effective December 1, 1991; amended by Pub.L. 102–198, § 11, December 9, 1991, 105 Stat. 1626; amended April 22, 1993, effective December 1, 1993; April 30, 2007, effective December 1, 2007; March 26, 2009, effective December 1, 2009.)

RULE 16. PRETRIAL CONFERENCES; SCHEDULING; MANAGEMENT

(a) Purposes of a Pretrial Conference. In any action, the court may order the attorneys and any unrepresented parties to appear for one or more pretrial conferences for such purposes as:

(1) expediting disposition of the action;

(2) establishing early and continuing control so that the case will not be protracted because of lack of management;

(3) discouraging wasteful pretrial activities;

(4) improving the quality of the trial through more thorough preparation; and

(5) facilitating settlement.

(b) Scheduling.

(1) ***Scheduling Order.*** Except in categories of actions exempted by local rule, the district judge—or a magistrate judge when authorized by local rule—must issue a scheduling order:

(A) after receiving the parties' report under Rule 26(f); or

(B) after consulting with the parties' attorneys and any unrepresented parties at a scheduling conference or by telephone, mail, or other means.

(2) ***Time to Issue.*** The judge must issue the scheduling order as soon as practicable, but in any event within the earlier of 120 days after any defendant has been served with the complaint or 90 days after any defendant has appeared.

(3) ***Contents of the Order.***

(A) *Required Contents.* The scheduling order must limit the time to join other parties, amend the pleadings, complete discovery, and file motions.

(B) *Permitted Contents.* The scheduling order may:

(i) modify the timing of disclosures under Rules 26(a) and 26(e)(1);

(ii) modify the extent of discovery;

(iii) provide for disclosure or discovery of electronically stored information;

(iv) include any agreements the parties reach for asserting claims of privilege or of protection as trial-preparation material after information is produced;

(v) set dates for pretrial conferences and for trial; and

(vi) include other appropriate matters.

(4) ***Modifying a Schedule.*** A schedule may be modified only for good cause and with the judge's consent.

(c) Attendance and Matters for Consideration at a Pretrial Conference.

(1) ***Attendance.*** A represented party must authorize at least one of its attorneys to make stipulations and admissions about all matters that can reasonably be anticipated for discussion at a pretrial conference. If appropriate, the court may require that a party or its representative be present or reasonably available by other means to consider possible settlement.

(2) ***Matters for Consideration.*** At any pretrial conference, the court may consider and take appropriate action on the following matters:

(A) formulating and simplifying the issues, and eliminating frivolous claims or defenses;

(B) amending the pleadings if necessary or desirable;

(C) obtaining admissions and stipulations about facts and documents to avoid unnecessary proof, and ruling in advance on the admissibility of evidence;

(D) avoiding unnecessary proof and cumulative evidence, and limiting the use of testimony under Federal Rule of Evidence 702;

(E) determining the appropriateness and timing of summary adjudication under Rule 56;

(F) controlling and scheduling discovery, including orders affecting disclosures and discovery under Rule 26 and Rules 29 through 37;

(G) identifying witnesses and documents, scheduling the filing and exchange of any pretrial briefs, and setting dates for further conferences and for trial;

(H) referring matters to a magistrate judge or a master;

(I) settling the case and using special procedures to assist in resolving the dispute when authorized by statute or local rule;

(J) determining the form and content of the pretrial order;

(K) disposing of pending motions;

(L) adopting special procedures for managing potentially difficult or protracted actions that may involve complex issues, multiple parties, difficult legal questions, or unusual proof problems;

(M) ordering a separate trial under Rule 42(b) of a claim, counterclaim, crossclaim, third-party claim, or particular issue;

(N) ordering the presentation of evidence early in the trial on a manageable issue that might, on the evidence, be the basis for a judgment as a matter of law under Rule 50(a) or a judgment on partial findings under Rule 52(c);

(O) establishing a reasonable limit on the time allowed to present evidence; and

(P) facilitating in other ways the just, speedy, and inexpensive disposition of the action.

(d) Pretrial Orders. After any conference under this rule, the court should issue an order reciting the action taken. This order controls the course of the action unless the court modifies it.

(e) Final Pretrial Conference and Orders. The court may hold a final pretrial conference to formulate a trial plan, including a plan to facilitate the admission of evidence. The conference must be held as close to the start of trial as is reasonable, and must be attended by at least one attorney who will conduct the trial for each party and by any unrepresented party. The court may modify the order issued after a final pretrial conference only to prevent manifest injustice.

(f) Sanctions.

(1) ***In General.*** On motion or on its own, the court may issue any just orders, including those authorized by Rule 37(b)(2)(A)(ii)-(vii), if a party or its attorney:

(A) fails to appear at a scheduling or other pretrial conference;

(B) is substantially unprepared to participate—or does not participate in good faith—in the conference; or

(C) fails to obey a scheduling or other pretrial order.

(2) ***Imposing Fees and Costs.*** Instead of or in addition to any other sanction, the court must order the party, its attorney, or both to pay the reasonable expenses—including attorney's fees—incurred because of any noncompliance with this rule, unless the noncompliance was substantially justified or other circumstances make an award of expenses unjust.

(Amended April 28, 1983, effective August 1, 1983; March 2, 1987, effective August 1, 1987; April 22, 1993, effective December 1, 1993; April 12, 2006, effective December 1, 2006; April 30, 2007, effective December 1, 2007.)

TITLE IV. PARTIES

RULE 17. PLAINTIFF AND DEFENDANT; CAPACITY; PUBLIC OFFICERS

(a) Real Party in Interest.

(1) ***Designation in General.*** An action must be prosecuted in the name of the real party in interest. The following may sue in their own names without joining the person for whose benefit the action is brought:

(A) an executor;

(B) an administrator;

(C) a guardian;

(D) a bailee;

(E) a trustee of an express trust;

(F) a party with whom or in whose name a contract has been made for another's benefit; and

(G) a party authorized by statute.

(2) ***Action in the Name of the United States for Another's Use or Benefit.*** When a federal statute so provides, an action for another's use or benefit must be brought in the name of the United States.

(3) ***Joinder of the Real Party in Interest.*** The court may not dismiss an action for failure to prosecute in the name of the real party in interest until, after an objection, a reasonable time has been allowed for the real party in interest to ratify, join, or be substituted into the action. After ratification, joinder, or substitution, the action proceeds as if it had been originally commenced by the real party in interest.

(b) Capacity to Sue or Be Sued. Capacity to sue or be sued is determined as follows:

(1) for an individual who is not acting in a representative capacity, by the law of the individual's domicile;

(2) for a corporation, by the law under which it was organized; and

(3) for all other parties, by the law of the state where the court is located, except that:

(A) a partnership or other unincorporated association with no such capacity under that state's law may sue or be sued in its common name to enforce a substantive right existing under the United States Constitution or laws; and

(B) 28 U.S.C. §§ 754 and 959(a) govern the capacity of a receiver appointed by a United States court to sue or be sued in a United States court.

(c) Minor or Incompetent Person.

(1) ***With a Representative.*** The following representatives may sue or defend on behalf of a minor or an incompetent person:

(A) a general guardian;

(B) a committee;

(C) a conservator; or

(D) a like fiduciary.

(2) ***Without a Representative.*** A minor or an incompetent person who does not have a duly appointed representative may sue by a next friend or by a guardian ad litem. The court must appoint a guardian ad litem—or issue another appropriate order—to protect a minor or incompetent person who is unrepresented in an action.

(d) Public Officer's Title and Name. A public officer who sues or is sued in an official capacity may be designated by official title rather than by name, but the court may order that the officer's name be added.

(Amended December 27, 1946, effective March 19, 1948; December 29, 1948, effective October 20, 1949; February 28, 1966, effective July 1, 1966; March 2, 1987, effective August 1, 1987; April 25, 1988, effective August 1, 1988; amended by Pub.L. 100–690, Title VII, § 7049, November 18, 1988, 102 Stat. 4401 (although amendment by Pub.L. 100–690 could not be executed due to prior amendment by Court order which made the same change effective August 1, 1988); April 30, 2007, effective December 1, 2007.)

RULE 18. JOINDER OF CLAIMS

(a) In General. A party asserting a claim, counterclaim, crossclaim, or third-party claim may join, as independent or alternative claims, as many claims as it has against an opposing party.

(b) Joinder of Contingent Claims. A party may join two claims even though one of them is contingent on the disposition of the other; but the court may grant relief only in accordance with the parties' relative substantive rights. In particular, a plaintiff may state a claim for money and a claim to set aside a conveyance that is fraudulent as to that plaintiff, without first obtaining a judgment for the money.

(Amended February 28, 1966, effective July 1, 1966; March 2, 1987, effective August 1, 1987; April 30, 2007, effective December 1, 2007.)

RULE 19. REQUIRED JOINDER OF PARTIES

(a) Persons Required to Be Joined if Feasible.

(1) ***Required Party.*** A person who is subject to service of process and whose joinder will not deprive the court of subject-matter jurisdiction must be joined as a party if:

(A) in that person's absence, the court cannot accord complete relief among existing parties; or

(B) that person claims an interest relating to the subject of the action and is so situated that disposing of the action in the person's absence may:

(i) as a practical matter impair or impede the person's ability to protect the interest; or

(ii) leave an existing party subject to a substantial risk of incurring double, multiple, or otherwise inconsistent obligations because of the interest.

(2) ***Joinder by Court Order.*** If a person has not been joined as required, the court must order that the person be made a party. A person who refuses to join as a plaintiff may be made either a defendant or, in a proper case, an involuntary plaintiff.

(3) ***Venue.*** If a joined party objects to venue and the joinder would make venue improper, the court must dismiss that party.

(b) When Joinder Is Not Feasible. If a person who is required to be joined if feasible cannot be joined, the court must determine whether, in equity and good conscience, the action should proceed among the existing parties or should be dismissed. The factors for the court to consider include:

(1) the extent to which a judgment rendered in the person's absence might prejudice that person or the existing parties;

(2) the extent to which any prejudice could be lessened or avoided by:

(A) protective provisions in the judgment;

(B) shaping the relief; or

(C) other measures;

(3) whether a judgment rendered in the person's absence would be adequate; and

(4) whether the plaintiff would have an adequate remedy if the action were dismissed for nonjoinder.

(c) Pleading the Reasons for Nonjoinder. When asserting a claim for relief, a party must state:

(1) the name, if known, of any person who is required to be joined if feasible but is not joined; and

(2) the reasons for not joining that person.

(d) Exception for Class Actions. This rule is subject to Rule 23.

(Amended February 28, 1966, effective July 1, 1966; March 2, 1987, effective August 1, 1987; April 30, 2007, effective December 1, 2007.)

RULE 20. PERMISSIVE JOINDER OF PARTIES

(a) Persons Who May Join or Be Joined.

(1) ***Plaintiffs.*** Persons may join in one action as plaintiffs if:

(A) they assert any right to relief jointly, severally, or in the alternative with respect to or arising out of the same transaction, occurrence, or series of transactions or occurrences; and

(B) any question of law or fact common to all plaintiffs will arise in the action.

(2) ***Defendants.*** Persons—as well as a vessel, cargo, or other property subject to admiralty process in rem—may be joined in one action as defendants if:

(A) any right to relief is asserted against them jointly, severally, or in the alternative with respect to or arising out of the same transaction, occurrence, or series of transactions or occurrences; and

(B) any question of law or fact common to all defendants will arise in the action.

(3) ***Extent of Relief.*** Neither a plaintiff nor a defendant need be interested in obtaining or defending against all the relief demanded. The court may grant judgment to one or more plaintiffs according to their rights, and against one or more defendants according to their liabilities.

(b) Protective Measures. The court may issue orders—including an order for separate trials—to protect a party against embarrassment, delay, expense, or other prejudice that arises from including a person against whom the party asserts no claim and who asserts no claim against the party.

(Amended February 28, 1966, effective July 1, 1966; March 2, 1987, effective August 1, 1987; April 30, 2007, effective December 1, 2007.)

RULE 21. MISJOINDER AND NONJOINDER OF PARTIES

Misjoinder of parties is not a ground for dismissing an action. On motion or on its own, the court may at any time, on just terms, add or drop a party. The court may also sever any claim against a party.

(Amended April 30, 2007, effective December 1, 2007.)

RULE 22. INTERPLEADER

(a) Grounds.

(1) ***By a Plaintiff.*** Persons with claims that may expose a plaintiff to double or multiple liability may be joined as defendants and required to interplead. Joinder for interpleader is proper even though:

(A) the claims of the several claimants, or the titles on which their claims depend, lack a common origin or are adverse and independent rather than identical; or

(B) the plaintiff denies liability in whole or in part to any or all of the claimants.

(2) ***By a Defendant.*** A defendant exposed to similar liability may seek interpleader through a crossclaim or counterclaim.

(b) Relation to Other Rules and Statutes. This rule supplements—and does not limit—the joinder of parties allowed by Rule 20. The remedy this rule provides is in addition to—and does not supersede or limit—the remedy provided by 28 U.S.C. §§ 1335, 1397, and 2361. An action under those statutes must be conducted under these rules.

(Amended December 29, 1948, effective October 20, 1949; March 2, 1987, effective August 1, 1987; April 30, 2007, effective December 1, 2007.)

RULE 23. CLASS ACTIONS

(a) Prerequisites. One or more members of a class may sue or be sued as representative parties on behalf of all members only if:

(1) the class is so numerous that joinder of all members is impracticable;

(2) there are questions of law or fact common to the class;

(3) the claims or defenses of the representative parties are typical of the claims or defenses of the class; and

(4) the representative parties will fairly and adequately protect the interests of the class.

(b) Types of Class Actions. A class action may be maintained if Rule 23(a) is satisfied and if:

(1) prosecuting separate actions by or against individual class members would create a risk of:

(A) inconsistent or varying adjudications with respect to individual class members that would establish incompatible standards of conduct for the party opposing the class; or

(B) adjudications with respect to individual class members that, as a practical matter, would be dispositive of the interests of the other members not parties to the individual adjudications or would substantially impair or impede their ability to protect their interests;

(2) the party opposing the class has acted or refused to act on grounds that apply generally to the class, so that final injunctive relief or corresponding declaratory relief is appropriate respecting the class as a whole; or

(3) the court finds that the questions of law or fact common to class members predominate over any questions affecting only individual members, and that a class action is superior to other available methods for fairly and efficiently adjudicating the controversy. The matters pertinent to these findings include:

(A) the class members' interests in individually controlling the prosecution or defense of separate actions;

(B) the extent and nature of any litigation concerning the controversy already begun by or against class members;

(C) the desirability or undesirability of concentrating the litigation of the claims in the particular forum; and

(D) the likely difficulties in managing a class action.

(c) Certification Order; Notice to Class Members; Judgment; Issues Classes; Subclasses.

(1) ***Certification Order.***

(A) *Time to Issue.* At an early practicable time after a person sues or is sued as a class representative, the court must determine by order whether to certify the action as a class action.

(B) *Defining the Class; Appointing Class Counsel.* An order that certifies a class action must define the class and the class claims, issues, or defenses, and must appoint class counsel under Rule 23(g).

(C) *Altering or Amending the Order.* An order that grants or denies class certification may be altered or amended before final judgment.

(2) ***Notice.***

(A) *For (b)(1) or (b)(2) Classes.* For any class certified under Rule 23(b)(1) or (b)(2), the court may direct appropriate notice to the class.

(B) *For (b)(3) Classes.* For any class certified under Rule 23(b)(3), the court must direct to class members the best notice that is practicable under the circumstances, including individual notice to all members who can be identified through reasonable effort. The notice must clearly and concisely state in plain, easily understood language:

(i) the nature of the action;

(ii) the definition of the class certified;

(iii) the class claims, issues, or defenses;

(iv) that a class member may enter an appearance through an attorney if the member so desires;

(v) that the court will exclude from the class any member who requests exclusion;

(vi) the time and manner for requesting exclusion; and

(vii) the binding effect of a class judgment on members under Rule 23(c)(3).

(3) ***Judgment.*** Whether or not favorable to the class, the judgment in a class action must:

(A) for any class certified under Rule 23(b)(1) or (b)(2), include and describe those whom the court finds to be class members; and

(B) for any class certified under Rule 23(b)(3), include and specify or describe those to whom the Rule 23(c)(2) notice was directed, who have not requested exclusion, and whom the court finds to be class members.

(4) ***Particular Issues.*** When appropriate, an action may be brought or maintained as a class action with respect to particular issues.

(5) ***Subclasses.*** When appropriate, a class may be divided into subclasses that are each treated as a class under this rule.

(d) Conducting the Action.

(1) ***In General.*** In conducting an action under this rule, the court may issue orders that:

(A) determine the course of proceedings or prescribe measures to prevent undue repetition or complication in presenting evidence or argument;

(B) require—to protect class members and fairly conduct the action—giving appropriate notice to some or all class members of:

(i) any step in the action;

(ii) the proposed extent of the judgment; or

(iii) the members' opportunity to signify whether they consider the representation fair and adequate, to intervene and present claims or defenses, or to otherwise come into the action;

(C) impose conditions on the representative parties or on intervenors;

(D) require that the pleadings be amended to eliminate allegations about representation of absent persons and that the action proceed accordingly; or

(E) deal with similar procedural matters.

(2) ***Combining and Amending Orders.*** An order under Rule 23(d)(1) may be altered or amended from time to time and may be combined with an order under Rule 16.

(e) Settlement, Voluntary Dismissal, or Compromise. The claims, issues, or defenses of a certified class may be settled, voluntarily dismissed, or compromised only with the court's approval. The following procedures apply to a proposed settlement, voluntary dismissal, or compromise:

(1) The court must direct notice in a reasonable manner to all class members who would be bound by the proposal.

(2) If the proposal would bind class members, the court may approve it only after a hearing and on finding that it is fair, reasonable, and adequate.

(3) The parties seeking approval must file a statement identifying any agreement made in connection with the proposal.

(4) If the class action was previously certified under Rule 23(b)(3), the court may refuse to approve a settlement unless it affords a new opportunity to request exclusion to individual class members who had an earlier opportunity to request exclusion but did not do so.

(5) Any class member may object to the proposal if it requires court approval under this subdivision (e); the objection may be withdrawn only with the court's approval.

(f) Appeals. A court of appeals may permit an appeal from an order granting or denying class-action certification under this rule if a petition for permission to appeal is filed with the circuit clerk within 14 days after the order is entered. An appeal does not stay proceedings in the district court unless the district judge or the court of appeals so orders.

(g) Class Counsel.

(1) ***Appointing Class Counsel.*** Unless a statute provides otherwise, a court that certifies a class must appoint class counsel. In appointing class counsel, the court:

(A) must consider:

(i) the work counsel has done in identifying or investigating potential claims in the action;

(ii) counsel's experience in handling class actions, other complex litigation, and the types of claims asserted in the action;

(iii) counsel's knowledge of the applicable law; and

(iv) the resources that counsel will commit to representing the class;

(B) may consider any other matter pertinent to counsel's ability to fairly and adequately represent the interests of the class;

(C) may order potential class counsel to provide information on any subject pertinent to the appointment and to propose terms for attorney's fees and nontaxable costs;

(D) may include in the appointing order provisions about the award of attorney's fees or nontaxable costs under Rule 23(h); and

(E) may make further orders in connection with the appointment.

(2) ***Standard for Appointing Class Counsel.*** When one applicant seeks appointment as class counsel, the court may appoint that applicant only if the applicant is adequate under Rule 23(g)(1) and (4). If more than one adequate applicant seeks appointment, the court must appoint the applicant best able to represent the interests of the class.

(3) ***Interim Counsel.*** The court may designate interim counsel to act on behalf of a putative class before determining whether to certify the action as a class action.

(4) ***Duty of Class Counsel.*** Class counsel must fairly and adequately represent the interests of the class.

(h) Attorney's Fees and Nontaxable Costs. In a certified class action, the court may award reasonable attorney's fees and nontaxable costs that are authorized by law or by the parties' agreement. The following procedures apply:

(1) A claim for an award must be made by motion under Rule 54(d)(2), subject to the provisions of this subdivision (h), at a time the court sets. Notice of the motion must be served on all parties and, for motions by class counsel, directed to class members in a reasonable manner.

(2) A class member, or a party from whom payment is sought, may object to the motion.

(3) The court may hold a hearing and must find the facts and state its legal conclusions under Rule 52(a).

(4) The court may refer issues related to the amount of the award to a special master or a magistrate judge, as provided in Rule 54(d)(2)(D).

(Amended February 28, 1966, effective July 1, 1966; March 2, 1987, effective August 1, 1987; April 24, 1998, effective December 1, 1998; March 27, 2003, effective December 1, 2003; April 30, 2007, effective December 1, 2007; March 26, 2009, effective December 1, 2009.)

RULE 23.1. DERIVATIVE ACTIONS

(a) Prerequisites. This rule applies when one or more shareholders or members of a corporation or an unincorporated association bring a derivative action to enforce a right that the corporation or association may properly assert but has failed to enforce. The derivative action may not be maintained if it appears that the plaintiff does not fairly and adequately represent the interests of shareholders or members who are similarly situated in enforcing the right of the corporation or association.

(b) Pleading Requirements. The complaint must be verified and must:

(1) allege that the plaintiff was a shareholder or member at the time of the transaction complained of, or that the plaintiff's share or membership later devolved on it by operation of law;

(2) allege that the action is not a collusive one to confer jurisdiction that the court would otherwise lack; and

(3) state with particularity:

(A) any effort by the plaintiff to obtain the desired action from the directors or comparable authority and, if necessary, from the shareholders or members; and

(B) the reasons for not obtaining the action or not making the effort.

(c) Settlement, Dismissal, and Compromise. A derivative action may be settled, voluntarily dismissed, or compromised only with the court's approval. Notice of a proposed settlement, voluntary dismissal, or compromise must be given to shareholders or members in the manner that the court orders.

(Adopted February 28, 1966, effective July 1, 1966; amended March 2, 1987, effective August 1, 1987; April 30, 2007, effective December 1, 2007.)

RULE 23.2. ACTIONS RELATING TO UNINCORPORATED ASSOCIATIONS

This rule applies to an action brought by or against the members of an unincorporated association as a class by naming certain members as representative parties. The action may be maintained only if it appears that those parties will fairly and adequately protect the interests of the association and its members. In conducting the action, the court may issue any appropriate orders corresponding with those in Rule 23(d), and the procedure for settlement, voluntary dismissal, or compromise must correspond with the procedure in Rule 23(e).

(Adopted February 28, 1966, effective July 1, 1966; amended April 30, 2007, effective December 1, 2007.)

RULE 24. INTERVENTION

(a) Intervention of Right. On timely motion, the court must permit anyone to intervene who:

- (1) is given an unconditional right to intervene by a federal statute; or
- (2) claims an interest relating to the property or transaction that is the subject of the action, and is so situated that disposing of the action may as a practical matter impair or impede the movant's ability to protect its interest, unless existing parties adequately represent that interest.

(b) Permissive Intervention.

- (1) ***In General.*** On timely motion, the court may permit anyone to intervene who:
  - (A) is given a conditional right to intervene by a federal statute; or
  - (B) has a claim or defense that shares with the main action a common question of law or fact.
- (2) ***By a Government Officer or Agency.*** On timely motion, the court may permit a federal or state governmental officer or agency to intervene if a party's claim or defense is based on:
  - (A) a statute or executive order administered by the officer or agency; or
  - (B) any regulation, order, requirement, or agreement issued or made under the statute or executive order.
- (3) ***Delay or Prejudice.*** In exercising its discretion, the court must consider whether the intervention will unduly delay or prejudice the adjudication of the original parties' rights.

(c) Notice and Pleading Required. A motion to intervene must be served on the parties as provided in Rule 5. The motion must state the grounds for intervention and be accompanied by a pleading that sets out the claim or defense for which intervention is sought.

(Amended December 27, 1946, effective March 19, 1948; December 29, 1948, effective October 20, 1949; January 21, 1963, effective July 1, 1963; February 28, 1966, effective July 1, 1966; March 2, 1987, effective August 1, 1987; April 30, 1991, effective December 1, 1991; April 12, 2006, effective December 1, 2006; April 30, 2007, effective December 1, 2007.)

RULE 25. SUBSTITUTION OF PARTIES

(a) Death.

- (1) ***Substitution if the Claim Is Not Extinguished.*** If a party dies and the claim is not extinguished, the court may order substitution of the proper party. A motion for substitution may be made by any party or by the decedent's successor or representative. If the motion is not made within 90 days after service of a statement noting the death, the action by or against the decedent must be dismissed.
- (2) ***Continuation Among the Remaining Parties.*** After a party's death, if the right sought to be enforced survives only to or against the remaining parties, the action does not abate, but proceeds in favor of or against the remaining parties. The death should be noted on the record.
- (3) ***Service.*** A motion to substitute, together with a notice of hearing, must be served on the parties as provided in Rule 5 and on nonparties as provided in Rule 4. A statement noting death must be served in the same manner. Service may be made in any judicial district.

(b) Incompetency. If a party becomes incompetent, the court may, on motion, permit the action to be continued by or against the party's representative. The motion must be served as provided in Rule 25(a)(3).

(c) Transfer of Interest. If an interest is transferred, the action may be continued by or against the original party unless the court, on motion, orders the transferee to be substituted in the action or joined with the original party. The motion must be served as provided in Rule 25(a)(3).

(d) Public Officers; Death or Separation from Office. An action does not abate when a public officer who is a party in an official capacity dies, resigns, or otherwise ceases to hold office while the action is pending. The officer's successor is automatically substituted as a party. Later proceedings should be in the substituted party's name, but any misnomer not affecting the parties' substantial rights must be disregarded. The court may order substitution at any time, but the absence of such an order does not affect the substitution.

(Amended December 29, 1948, effective October 20, 1949; April 17, 1961, effective July 19, 1961; January 21, 1963, effective July 1, 1963; March 2, 1987, effective August 1, 1987; April 30, 2007, effective December 1, 2007.)

TITLE V. DISCLOSURES AND DISCOVERY

RULE 26. DUTY TO DISCLOSE; GENERAL PROVISIONS GOVERNING DISCOVERY

(a) Required Disclosures.

(1) ***Initial Disclosure.***

(A) *In General.* Except as exempted by Rule 26(a)(1)(B) or as otherwise stipulated or ordered by the court, a party must, without awaiting a discovery request, provide to the other parties:

(i) the name and, if known, the address and telephone number of each individual likely to have discoverable information—along with the subjects of that information—that the disclosing party may use to support its claims or defenses, unless the use would be solely for impeachment;

(ii) a copy—or a description by category and location—of all documents, electronically stored information, and tangible things that the disclosing party has in its possession, custody, or control and may use to support its claims or defenses, unless the use would be solely for impeachment;

(iii) a computation of each category of damages claimed by the disclosing party—who must also make available for inspection and copying as under Rule 34 the documents or other evidentiary material, unless privileged or protected from disclosure, on which each computation is based, including materials bearing on the nature and extent of injuries suffered; and

(iv) for inspection and copying as under Rule 34, any insurance agreement under which an insurance business may be liable to satisfy all or part of a possible judgment in the action or to indemnify or reimburse for payments made to satisfy the judgment.

(B) *Proceedings Exempt from Initial Disclosure.* The following proceedings are exempt from initial disclosure:

(i) an action for review on an administrative record;

(ii) a forfeiture action in rem arising from a federal statute;

(iii) a petition for habeas corpus or any other proceeding to challenge a criminal conviction or sentence;

(iv) an action brought without an attorney by a person in the custody of the United States, a state, or a state subdivision;

(v) an action to enforce or quash an administrative summons or subpoena;

(vi) an action by the United States to recover benefit payments;

(vii) an action by the United States to collect on a student loan guaranteed by the United States;

(viii) a proceeding ancillary to a proceeding in another court; and

(ix) an action to enforce an arbitration award.

(C) *Time for Initial Disclosures—In General.* A party must make the initial disclosures at or within 14 days after the parties' Rule 26(f) conference unless a different time is set by stipulation or court order, or unless a party objects during the conference that initial disclosures are not appropriate in this action and states the objection in the proposed discovery plan. In ruling on the objection, the court must determine what disclosures, if any, are to be made and must set the time for disclosure.

(D) *Time for Initial Disclosures—For Parties Served or Joined Later.* A party that is first served or otherwise joined after the Rule 26(f) conference must make the initial disclosures within 30 days after being served or joined, unless a different time is set by stipulation or court order.

(E) *Basis for Initial Disclosure; Unacceptable Excuses.* A party must make its initial disclosures based on the information then reasonably available to it. A party is not excused from making its disclosures because it has not fully investigated the case or because it challenges the sufficiency of another party's disclosures or because another party has not made its disclosures.

(2) ***Disclosure of Expert Testimony.***

(A) *In General.* In addition to the disclosures required by Rule 26(a)(1), a party must disclose to the other parties the identity of any witness it may use at trial to present evidence under Federal Rule of Evidence 702, 703, or 705.

(B) *Witnesses Who Must Provide a Written Report.* Unless otherwise stipulated or ordered by the court, this disclosure must be accompanied by a written report—prepared and signed by the witness—if the witness is one retained or specially employed to provide expert testimony in the case or one whose duties as the party's employee regularly involve giving expert testimony. The report must contain:

(i) a complete statement of all opinions the witness will express and the basis and reasons for them;

(ii) the facts or data considered by the witness in forming them;

(iii) any exhibits that will be used to summarize or support them;

(iv) the witness's qualifications, including a list of all publications authored in the previous 10 years;

(v) a list of all other cases in which, during the previous 4 years, the witness testified as an expert at trial or by deposition; and

(vi) a statement of the compensation to be paid for the study and testimony in the case.

(C) *Witnesses Who Do Not Provide a Written Report.* Unless otherwise stipulated or ordered by the court, if the witness is not required to provide a written report, this disclosure must state:

(i) the subject matter on which the witness is expected to present evidence under Federal Rule of Evidence 702, 703, or 705; and

(ii) a summary of the facts and opinions to which the witness is expected to testify.

(D) *Time to Disclose Expert Testimony.* A party must make these disclosures at the times and in the sequence that the court orders. Absent a stipulation or a court order, the disclosures must be made:

(i) at least 90 days before the date set for trial or for the case to be ready for trial; or

(ii) if the evidence is intended solely to contradict or rebut evidence on the same subject matter identified by another party under Rule 26(a)(2)(B) or (C), within 30 days after the other party's disclosure.

(E) *Supplementing the Disclosure.* The parties must supplement these disclosures when required under Rule 26(e).

(3) ***Pretrial Disclosures.***

(A) *In General.* In addition to the disclosures required by Rule 26(a)(1) and (2), a party must provide to the other parties and promptly file the following information about the evidence that it may present at trial other than solely for impeachment:

(i) the name and, if not previously provided, the address and telephone number of each witness—separately identifying those the party expects to present and those it may call if the need arises;

(ii) the designation of those witnesses whose testimony the party expects to present by deposition and, if not taken stenographically, a transcript of the pertinent parts of the deposition; and

(iii) an identification of each document or other exhibit, including summaries of other evidence—separately identifying those items the party expects to offer and those it may offer if the need arises.

(B) *Time for Pretrial Disclosures; Objections.* Unless the court orders otherwise, these disclosures must be made at least 30 days before trial. Within 14 days after they are made, unless the court sets a different time, a party may serve and promptly file a list of the following objections: any objections to the use under Rule 32(a) of a deposition designated by another party under Rule 26(a)(3)(A)(ii); and any objection, together with the grounds for it, that may be made to the admissibility of materials identified under Rule 26(a)(3)(A)(iii). An objection not so made—except for one under Federal Rule of Evidence 402 or 403—is waived unless excused by the court for good cause.

(4) ***Form of Disclosures.*** Unless the court orders otherwise, all disclosures under Rule 26(a) must be in writing, signed, and served.

(b) Discovery Scope and Limits.

(1) ***Scope in General.*** Unless otherwise limited by court order, the scope of discovery is as follows: Parties may obtain discovery regarding any nonprivileged matter that is relevant to any party's claim or defense—including the existence, description, nature, custody, condition, and location of any documents or other tangible things and the identity and location of persons who know of any discoverable matter. For good cause, the court may order discovery of any matter relevant to the subject matter involved in the action. Relevant information need not be admissible at the trial if the discovery appears reasonably calculated to lead to the discovery of admissible evidence. All discovery is subject to the limitations imposed by Rule 26(b)(2)(C).

(2) ***Limitations on Frequency and Extent.***

(A) *When Permitted.* By order, the court may alter the limits in these rules on the number of depositions and interrogatories or on the length of depositions under Rule 30. By order or local rule, the court may also limit the number of requests under Rule 36.

(B) *Specific Limitations on Electronically Stored Information.* A party need not provide discovery of electronically stored information from sources that the party identifies as not reasonably accessible because of undue burden or cost. On motion to compel discovery or for a protective order, the party from whom discovery is sought must show that the information is not reasonably accessible because of undue burden or cost. If that showing is made, the court may nonetheless order discovery from such sources if the requesting party shows good cause, considering the limitations of Rule 26(b)(2)(C). The court may specify conditions for the discovery.

(C) *When Required.* On motion or on its own, the court must limit the frequency or extent of discovery otherwise allowed by these rules or by local rule if it determines that:

(i) the discovery sought is unreasonably cumulative or duplicative, or can be obtained from some other source that is more convenient, less burdensome, or less expensive;

(ii) the party seeking discovery has had ample opportunity to obtain the information by discovery in the action; or

(iii) the burden or expense of the proposed discovery outweighs its likely benefit, considering the needs of the case, the amount in controversy, the parties' resources, the importance of the issues at stake in the action, and the importance of the discovery in resolving the issues.

(3) ***Trial Preparation: Materials.***

(A) *Documents and Tangible Things.* Ordinarily, a party may not discover documents and tangible things that are prepared in anticipation of litigation or for trial by or for another party or its representative (including the other party's attorney, consultant, surety, indemnitor, insurer, or agent). But, subject to Rule 26(b)(4), those materials may be discovered if:

(i) they are otherwise discoverable under Rule 26(b)(1); and

(ii) the party shows that it has substantial need for the materials to prepare its case and cannot, without undue hardship, obtain their substantial equivalent by other means.

(B) *Protection Against Disclosure.* If the court orders discovery of those materials, it must protect against disclosure of the mental impressions, conclusions, opinions, or legal theories of a party's attorney or other representative concerning the litigation.

(C) *Previous Statement.* Any party or other person may, on request and without the required showing, obtain the person's own previous statement about the action or its subject matter. If the request is refused, the person may move for a court order, and Rule 37(a)(5) applies to the award of expenses. A previous statement is either:

(i) a written statement that the person has signed or otherwise adopted or approved; or

(ii) a contemporaneous stenographic, mechanical, electrical, or other recording—or a transcription of it—that recites substantially verbatim the person's oral statement.

(4) ***Trial Preparation: Experts.***

(A) *Deposition of an Expert Who May Testify.* A party may depose any person who has been identified as an expert whose opinions may be presented at trial. If Rule 26(a)(2)(B) requires a report from the expert, the deposition may be conducted only after the report is provided.

(B) *Trial-Preparation Protection for Draft Reports or Disclosures.* Rules 26(b)(3)(A) and (B) protect drafts of any report or disclosure required under Rule 26(a)(2), regardless of the form in which the draft is recorded.

(C) *Trial-Preparation Protection for Communications Between a Party's Attorney and Expert Witnesses.* Rules 26(b)(3)(A) and (B) protect communications between the party's attorney and any witness required to provide a report under Rule 26(a)(2)(B), regardless of the form of the communications, except to the extent that the communications:

(i) relate to compensation for the expert's study or testimony;

(ii) identify facts or data that the party's attorney provided and that the expert considered in forming the opinions to be expressed; or

(iii) identify assumptions that the party's attorney provided and that the expert relied on in forming the opinions to be expressed.

(D) *Expert Employed Only for Trial Preparation.* Ordinarily, a party may not, by interrogatories or deposition, discover facts known or opinions held by an expert who has been retained or specially employed by another party in anticipation of litigation or to prepare for trial and who is not expected to be called as a witness at trial. But a party may do so only:

(i) as provided in Rule 35(b); or

(ii) on showing exceptional circumstances under which it is impracticable for the party to obtain facts or opinions on the same subject by other means.

(E) *Payment.* Unless manifest injustice would result, the court must require that the party seeking discovery:

(i) pay the expert a reasonable fee for time spent in responding to discovery under Rule 26(b)(4)(A) or (D); and

(ii) for discovery under (D), also pay the other party a fair portion of the fees and expenses it reasonably incurred in obtaining the expert's facts and opinions.

(5) ***Claiming Privilege or Protecting Trial-Preparation Materials.***

(A) *Information Withheld.* When a party withholds information otherwise discoverable by claiming that the information is privileged or subject to protection as trial-preparation material, the party must:

(i) expressly make the claim; and

(ii) describe the nature of the documents, communications, or tangible things not produced or disclosed—and do so in a manner that, without revealing information itself privileged or protected, will enable other parties to assess the claim.

(B) *Information Produced.* If information produced in discovery is subject to a claim of privilege or of protection as trial-preparation material, the party making the claim may notify any party that received the information of the claim and the basis for it. After being notified, a party must promptly return, sequester, or destroy the specified information and any copies it has; must not use or disclose the information until the claim is resolved; must take reasonable steps to retrieve the information if the party disclosed it before being notified; and may promptly present the information to the court under seal for a determination of the claim. The producing party must preserve the information until the claim is resolved.

(c) Protective Orders.

(1) ***In General.*** A party or any person from whom discovery is sought may move for a protective order in the court where the action is pending—or as an alternative on matters relating to a deposition, in the court for the district where the deposition will be taken. The motion must include a certification that the movant has in good faith conferred or attempted to confer with other affected parties in an effort to resolve the dispute without court action. The court may, for good cause, issue an order to protect a party or person from annoyance, embarrassment, oppression, or undue burden or expense, including one or more of the following:

(A) forbidding the disclosure or discovery;

(B) specifying terms, including time and place, for the disclosure or discovery;

(C) prescribing a discovery method other than the one selected by the party seeking discovery;

(D) forbidding inquiry into certain matters, or limiting the scope of disclosure or discovery to certain matters;

(E) designating the persons who may be present while the discovery is conducted;

(F) requiring that a deposition be sealed and opened only on court order;

(G) requiring that a trade secret or other confidential research, development, or commercial information not be revealed or be revealed only in a specified way; and

(H) requiring that the parties simultaneously file specified documents or information in sealed envelopes, to be opened as the court directs.

(2) ***Ordering Discovery.*** If a motion for a protective order is wholly or partly denied, the court may, on just terms, order that any party or person provide or permit discovery.

(3) ***Awarding Expenses.*** Rule 37(a)(5) applies to the award of expenses.

(d) Timing and Sequence of Discovery.

(1) ***Timing.*** A party may not seek discovery from any source before the parties have conferred as required by Rule 26(f), except in a proceeding exempted from initial disclosure under Rule 26(a)(1)(B), or when authorized by these rules, by stipulation, or by court order.

(2) ***Sequence.*** Unless, on motion, the court orders otherwise for the parties' and witnesses' convenience and in the interests of justice:

(A) methods of discovery may be used in any sequence; and

(B) discovery by one party does not require any other party to delay its discovery.

(e) Supplementing Disclosures and Responses.

(1) ***In General.*** A party who has made a disclosure under Rule 26(a)—or who has responded to an interrogatory, request for production, or request for admission—must supplement or correct its disclosure or response:

(A) in a timely manner if the party learns that in some material respect the disclosure or response is incomplete or incorrect, and if the additional or corrective information has not otherwise been made known to the other parties during the discovery process or in writing; or

(B) as ordered by the court.

(2) ***Expert Witness.*** For an expert whose report must be disclosed under Rule 26(a)(2)(B), the party's duty to supplement extends both to information included in the report and to information given during the expert's deposition. Any additions or changes to this information must be disclosed by the time the party's pretrial disclosures under Rule 26(a)(3) are due.

(f) Conference of the Parties; Planning for Discovery.

(1) ***Conference Timing.*** Except in a proceeding exempted from initial disclosure under Rule 26(a)(1)(B) or when the court orders otherwise, the parties must confer as soon as practicable—and in any event at least 21 days before a scheduling conference is to be held or a scheduling order is due under Rule 16(b).

(2) ***Conference Content; Parties' Responsibilities.*** In conferring, the parties must consider the nature and basis of their claims and defenses and the possibilities for promptly settling or resolving the case; make or arrange for the disclosures required by Rule 26(a)(1); discuss any issues about preserving discoverable information; and develop a proposed discovery plan. The attorneys of record and all unrepresented parties that have appeared in the case are jointly responsible for arranging the conference, for attempting in good faith to agree on the proposed discovery plan, and for submitting to the court within 14 days after the conference a written report outlining the plan. The court may order the parties or attorneys to attend the conference in person.

(3) ***Discovery Plan.*** A discovery plan must state the parties' views and proposals on:

(A) what changes should be made in the timing, form, or requirement for disclosures under Rule 26(a), including a statement of when initial disclosures were made or will be made;

(B) the subjects on which discovery may be needed, when discovery should be completed, and whether discovery should be conducted in phases or be limited to or focused on particular issues;

(C) any issues about disclosure or discovery of electronically stored information, including the form or forms in which it should be produced;

(D) any issues about claims of privilege or of protection as trial-preparation materials, including—if the parties agree on a procedure to assert these claims after production—whether to ask the court to include their agreement in an order;

(E) what changes should be made in the limitations on discovery imposed under these rules or by local rule, and what other limitations should be imposed; and

(F) any other orders that the court should issue under Rule 26(c) or under Rule 16(b) and (c).

(4) ***Expedited Schedule.*** If necessary to comply with its expedited schedule for Rule 16(b) conferences, a court may by local rule:

(A) require the parties' conference to occur less than 21 days before the scheduling conference is held or a scheduling order is due under Rule 16(b); and

(B) require the written report outlining the discovery plan to be filed less than 14 days after the parties' conference, or excuse the parties from submitting a written report and permit them to report orally on their discovery plan at the Rule 16(b) conference.

(g) Signing Disclosures and Discovery Requests, Responses, and Objections.

(1) ***Signature Required; Effect of Signature.*** Every disclosure under Rule 26(a)(1) or (a)(3) and every discovery request, response, or objection must be signed by at least one attorney of record in the attorney's own name—or by the party personally, if unrepresented—and must state the signer's address, e-mail address, and telephone number. By signing, an attorney or party certifies that to the best of the person's knowledge, information, and belief formed after a reasonable inquiry:

(A) with respect to a disclosure, it is complete and correct as of the time it is made; and

(B) with respect to a discovery request, response, or objection, it is:

(i) consistent with these rules and warranted by existing law or by a nonfrivolous argument for extending, modifying, or reversing existing law, or for establishing new law;

(ii) not interposed for any improper purpose, such as to harass, cause unnecessary delay, or needlessly increase the cost of litigation; and

(iii) neither unreasonable nor unduly burdensome or expensive, considering the needs of the case, prior discovery in the case, the amount in controversy, and the importance of the issues at stake in the action.

(2) ***Failure to Sign.*** Other parties have no duty to act on an unsigned disclosure, request, response, or objection until it is signed, and the court must strike it unless a signature is promptly supplied after the omission is called to the attorney's or party's attention.

(3) ***Sanction for Improper Certification.*** If a certification violates this rule without substantial justification, the court, on motion or on its own, must impose an appropriate sanction on the signer, the party on whose behalf the signer was acting, or both. The sanction may include an order to pay the reasonable expenses, including attorney's fees, caused by the violation.

(Amended December 27, 1946, effective March 19, 1948; January 21, 1963, effective July 1, 1963; February 28, 1966, effective July 1, 1966; March 30, 1970, effective July 1, 1970; April 29, 1980, effective August 1, 1980; April 28, 1983, effective August 1, 1983; March 2, 1987, effective August 1, 1987; April 22, 1993, effective December 1, 1993; April 17, 2000, effective December 1, 2000; April 12, 2006, effective December 1, 2006; April 30, 2007, effective December 1, 2007; April 28, 2010, effective December 1, 2010.)

RULE 27. DEPOSITIONS TO PERPETUATE TESTIMONY

(a) Before an Action Is Filed.

(1) ***Petition.*** A person who wants to perpetuate testimony about any matter cognizable in a United States court may file a verified petition in the district court for the district where any expected adverse party resides. The petition must ask for an order authorizing the petitioner to depose the named persons in order to perpetuate their testimony. The petition must be titled in the petitioner's name and must show:

(A) that the petitioner expects to be a party to an action cognizable in a United States court but cannot presently bring it or cause it to be brought;

(B) the subject matter of the expected action and the petitioner's interest;

(C) the facts that the petitioner wants to establish by the proposed testimony and the reasons to perpetuate it;

(D) the names or a description of the persons whom the petitioner expects to be adverse parties and their addresses, so far as known; and

(E) the name, address, and expected substance of the testimony of each deponent.

(2) ***Notice and Service.*** At least 21 days before the hearing date, the petitioner must serve each expected adverse party with a copy of the petition and a notice stating the time and place of the hearing. The notice may be served either inside or outside the district or state in the manner provided in Rule 4. If that service cannot be made with reasonable diligence on an expected adverse party, the court may order service by publication or otherwise. The court must appoint an attorney to represent persons not served in the manner provided in Rule 4 and to cross-examine the deponent if an unserved person is not otherwise represented. If any expected adverse party is a minor or is incompetent, Rule 17(c) applies.

(3) ***Order and Examination.*** If satisfied that perpetuating the testimony may prevent a failure or delay of justice, the court must issue an order that designates or describes the persons whose depositions may be taken, specifies the subject matter of the examinations, and states whether the depositions will be taken orally or by written interrogatories. The depositions may then be taken under these rules, and the court may issue orders like those authorized by Rules 34 and 35. A reference in these rules to the court where an action is pending means, for purposes of this rule, the court where the petition for the deposition was filed.

(4) ***Using the Deposition.*** A deposition to perpetuate testimony may be used under Rule 32(a) in any later-filed district-court action involving the same subject matter if the deposition either was taken under these rules or, although not so taken, would be admissible in evidence in the courts of the state where it was taken.

(b) Pending Appeal.

(1) ***In General.*** The court where a judgment has been rendered may, if an appeal has been taken or may still be taken, permit a party to depose witnesses to perpetuate their testimony for use in the event of further proceedings in that court.

(2) ***Motion.*** The party who wants to perpetuate testimony may move for leave to take the depositions, on the same notice and service as if the action were pending in the district court. The motion must show:

(A) the name, address, and expected substance of the testimony of each deponent; and

(B) the reasons for perpetuating the testimony.

(3) ***Court Order.*** If the court finds that perpetuating the testimony may prevent a failure or delay of justice, the court may permit the depositions to be taken and may issue orders like those authorized by Rules 34 and 35. The depositions may be taken and used as any other deposition taken in a pending district-court action.

(c) **Perpetuation by an Action.** This rule does not limit a court's power to entertain an action to perpetuate testimony.

(Amended December 27, 1946, effective March 19, 1948; December 29, 1948, effective October 20, 1949; March 1, 1971, effective July 1, 1971; March 2, 1987, effective August 1, 1987; April 25, 2005, effective December 1, 2005; April 30, 2007, effective December 1, 2007; March 26, 2009, effective December 1, 2009.)

RULE 28. PERSONS BEFORE WHOM DEPOSITIONS MAY BE TAKEN

(a) **Within the United States.**

(1) ***In General.*** Within the United States or a territory or insular possession subject to United States jurisdiction, a deposition must be taken before:

(A) an officer authorized to administer oaths either by federal law or by the law in the place of examination; or

(B) a person appointed by the court where the action is pending to administer oaths and take testimony.

(2) ***Definition of "Officer".*** The term "officer" in Rules 30, 31, and 32 includes a person appointed by the court under this rule or designated by the parties under Rule 29(a).

(b) **In a Foreign Country.**

(1) ***In General.*** A deposition may be taken in a foreign country:

(A) under an applicable treaty or convention;

(B) under a letter of request, whether or not captioned a "letter rogatory";

(C) on notice, before a person authorized to administer oaths either by federal law or by the law in the place of examination; or

(D) before a person commissioned by the court to administer any necessary oath and take testimony.

(2) ***Issuing a Letter of Request or a Commission.*** A letter of request, a commission, or both may be issued:

(A) on appropriate terms after an application and notice of it; and

(B) without a showing that taking the deposition in another manner is impracticable or inconvenient.

(3) ***Form of a Request, Notice, or Commission.*** When a letter of request or any other device is used according to a treaty or convention, it must be captioned in the form prescribed by that treaty or convention. A letter of request may be addressed "To the Appropriate Authority in [name of country]." A deposition notice or a commission must designate by name or descriptive title the person before whom the deposition is to be taken.

(4) ***Letter of Request—Admitting Evidence.*** Evidence obtained in response to a letter of request need not be excluded merely because it is not a verbatim transcript, because the testimony was not taken under oath, or because of any similar departure from the requirements for depositions taken within the United States.

(c) **Disqualification.** A deposition must not be taken before a person who is any party's relative, employee, or attorney; who is related to or employed by any party's attorney; or who is financially interested in the action.

(Amended December 27, 1946, effective March 19, 1948; January 21, 1963, effective July 1, 1963; April 29, 1980, effective August 1, 1980; March 2, 1987, effective August 1, 1987; April 22, 1993, effective December 1, 1993; April 30, 2007, effective December 1, 2007.)

RULE 29. STIPULATIONS ABOUT DISCOVERY PROCEDURE

Unless the court orders otherwise, the parties may stipulate that:

(a) a deposition may be taken before any person, at any time or place, on any notice, and in the manner specified—in which event it may be used in the same way as any other deposition; and

(b) other procedures governing or limiting discovery be modified—but a stipulation extending the time for any form of discovery must have court approval if it would interfere with the time set for completing discovery, for hearing a motion, or for trial.

(Amended March 30, 1970, effective July 1, 1970; April 22, 1993, effective December 1, 1993; April 30, 2007, effective December 1, 2007.)

RULE 30. DEPOSITIONS BY ORAL EXAMINATION

(a) **When a Deposition May Be Taken.**

(1) ***Without Leave.*** A party may, by oral questions, depose any person, including a party, without leave of court except as provided in Rule 30(a)(2). The deponent's attendance may be compelled by subpoena under Rule 45.

(2) ***With Leave.*** A party must obtain leave of court, and the court must grant leave to the extent consistent with Rule 26(b)(2):

(A) if the parties have not stipulated to the deposition and:

(i) the deposition would result in more than 10 depositions being taken under this rule or Rule 31 by the plaintiffs, or by the defendants, or by the third-party defendants;

(ii) the deponent has already been deposed in the case; or

(iii) the party seeks to take the deposition before the time specified in Rule 26(d), unless the party certifies in the notice, with supporting facts, that the deponent is expected to leave the United States and be unavailable for examination in this country after that time; or

(B) if the deponent is confined in prison.

(b) Notice of the Deposition; Other Formal Requirements.

(1) ***Notice in General.*** A party who wants to depose a person by oral questions must give reasonable written notice to every other party. The notice must state the time and place of the deposition and, if known, the deponent's name and address. If the name is unknown, the notice must provide a general description sufficient to identify the person or the particular class or group to which the person belongs.

(2) ***Producing Documents.*** If a subpoena duces tecum is to be served on the deponent, the materials designated for production, as set out in the subpoena, must be listed in the notice or in an attachment. The notice to a party deponent may be accompanied by a request under Rule 34 to produce documents and tangible things at the deposition.

(3) ***Method of Recording.***

(A) *Method Stated in the Notice.* The party who notices the deposition must state in the notice the method for recording the testimony. Unless the court orders otherwise, testimony may be recorded by audio, audiovisual, or stenographic means. The noticing party bears the recording costs. Any party may arrange to transcribe a deposition.

(B) *Additional Method.* With prior notice to the deponent and other parties, any party may designate another method for recording the testimony in addition to that specified in the original notice. That party bears the expense of the additional record or transcript unless the court orders otherwise.

(4) ***By Remote Means.*** The parties may stipulate—or the court may on motion order—that a deposition be taken by telephone or other remote means. For the purpose of this rule and Rules 28(a), 37(a)(2), and 37(b)(1), the deposition takes place where the deponent answers the questions.

(5) ***Officer's Duties.***

(A) *Before the Deposition.* Unless the parties stipulate otherwise, a deposition must be conducted before an officer appointed or designated under Rule 28. The officer must begin the deposition with an on-the-record statement that includes:

(i) the officer's name and business address;

(ii) the date, time, and place of the deposition;

(iii) the deponent's name;

(iv) the officer's administration of the oath or affirmation to the deponent; and

(v) the identity of all persons present.

(B) *Conducting the Deposition; Avoiding Distortion.* If the deposition is recorded non-stenographically, the officer must repeat the items in Rule 30(b)(5)(A)(i)-(iii) at the beginning of each unit of the recording medium. The deponent's and attorneys' appearance or demeanor must not be distorted through recording techniques.

(C) *After the Deposition.* At the end of a deposition, the officer must state on the record that the deposition is complete and must set out any stipulations made by the attorneys about custody of the transcript or recording and of the exhibits, or about any other pertinent matters.

(6) ***Notice or Subpoena Directed to an Organization.*** In its notice or subpoena, a party may name as the deponent a public or private corporation, a partnership, an association, a governmental agency, or other entity and must describe with reasonable particularity the matters for examination. The named organization must then designate one or more officers, directors, or managing agents, or designate other persons who consent to testify on its behalf; and it may set out the matters on which each person designated will testify. A subpoena must advise a nonparty organization of its duty to make this designation. The persons designated must testify about information known or reasonably available to the organization. This paragraph (6) does not preclude a deposition by any other procedure allowed by these rules.

(c) Examination and Cross–Examination; Record of the Examination; Objections; Written Questions.

(1) ***Examination and Cross–Examination.*** The examination and cross-examination of a deponent proceed as they would at trial under the Federal Rules of Evidence, except Rules 103 and 615. After putting the deponent under oath or affirmation, the officer must record the testimony by the method designated under Rule 30(b)(3)(A). The testimony must be recorded by the officer personally or by a person acting in the presence and under the direction of the officer.

(2) ***Objections.*** An objection at the time of the examination—whether to evidence, to a party's conduct, to the officer's qualifications, to the manner of taking the deposition, or to any other aspect of the deposition—must be noted on the record, but the examination still proceeds; the testimony is taken subject to any objection. An objection must be stated concisely in a nonargumentative and nonsuggestive manner. A person may instruct a deponent not to answer only when necessary to preserve a privilege, to enforce a limitation ordered by the court, or to present a motion under Rule 30(d)(3).

(3) ***Participating Through Written Questions.*** Instead of participating in the oral examination, a party may serve written questions in a sealed envelope on the party noticing the deposition, who must deliver them to the officer. The officer must ask the deponent those questions and record the answers verbatim.

(d) Duration; Sanction; Motion to Terminate or Limit.

(1) ***Duration.*** Unless otherwise stipulated or ordered by the court, a deposition is limited to 1 day of 7 hours. The court must allow additional time consistent with Rule 26(b)(2) if needed to fairly examine the deponent or if the deponent, another person, or any other circumstance impedes or delays the examination.

(2) ***Sanction.*** The court may impose an appropriate sanction—including the reasonable expenses and attorney's fees incurred by any party—on a person who impedes, delays, or frustrates the fair examination of the deponent.

(3) ***Motion to Terminate or Limit.***

(A) *Grounds.* At any time during a deposition, the deponent or a party may move to terminate or limit it on the ground that it is being conducted in bad faith or in a manner that unreasonably annoys, embarrasses, or oppresses the deponent or party. The motion may be filed in the court where the action is pending or the deposition is being taken. If the objecting deponent or party so demands, the deposition must be suspended for the time necessary to obtain an order.

(B) *Order.* The court may order that the deposition be terminated or may limit its scope and manner as provided in Rule 26(c). If terminated, the deposition may be resumed only by order of the court where the action is pending.

(C) *Award of Expenses.* Rule 37(a)(5) applies to the award of expenses.

(e) Review by the Witness; Changes.

(1) ***Review; Statement of Changes.*** On request by the deponent or a party before the deposition is completed, the deponent must be allowed 30 days after being notified by the officer that the transcript or recording is available in which:

(A) to review the transcript or recording; and

(B) if there are changes in form or substance, to sign a statement listing the changes and the reasons for making them.

(2) ***Changes Indicated in the Officer's Certificate.*** The officer must note in the certificate prescribed by Rule 30(f)(1) whether a review was requested and, if so, must attach any changes the deponent makes during the 30–day period.

(f) Certification and Delivery; Exhibits; Copies of the Transcript or Recording; Filing.

(1) ***Certification and Delivery.*** The officer must certify in writing that the witness was duly sworn and that the deposition accurately records the witness's testimony. The certificate must accompany the record of the deposition. Unless the court orders otherwise, the officer must seal the deposition in an envelope or package bearing the title of the action and marked "Deposition of [witness's name]" and must promptly send it to the attorney who arranged for the transcript or recording. The attorney must store it under conditions that will protect it against loss, destruction, tampering, or deterioration.

(2) ***Documents and Tangible Things.***

(A) *Originals and Copies.* Documents and tangible things produced for inspection during a deposition must, on a party's request, be marked for identification and attached to the deposition. Any party may inspect and copy them. But if the person who produced them wants to keep the originals, the person may:

(i) offer copies to be marked, attached to the deposition, and then used as originals—after giving all parties a fair opportunity to verify the copies by comparing them with the originals; or

(ii) give all parties a fair opportunity to inspect and copy the originals after they are marked—in which event the originals may be used as if attached to the deposition.

(B) *Order Regarding the Originals.* Any party may move for an order that the originals be attached to the deposition pending final disposition of the case.

(3) ***Copies of the Transcript or Recording.*** Unless otherwise stipulated or ordered by the court, the officer must retain the stenographic notes of a deposition taken stenographically or a copy of the recording of a deposition taken by another method. When paid reasonable charges, the officer must furnish a copy of the transcript or recording to any party or the deponent.

(4) ***Notice of Filing.*** A party who files the deposition must promptly notify all other parties of the filing.

(g) **Failure to Attend a Deposition or Serve a Subpoena; Expenses.** A party who, expecting a deposition to be taken, attends in person or by an attorney may recover reasonable expenses for attending, including attorney's fees, if the noticing party failed to:

(1) attend and proceed with the deposition; or

(2) serve a subpoena on a nonparty deponent, who consequently did not attend.

(Amended January 21, 1963, effective July 1, 1963; March 30, 1970, effective July 1, 1970; March 1, 1971, effective July 1, 1971; November 20, 1972, effective July 1, 1975; April 29, 1980, effective August 1, 1980; March 2, 1987, effective August 1, 1987; April 22, 1993, effective December 1, 1993; April 17, 2000, effective December 1, 2000; April 30, 2007, effective December 1, 2007.)

RULE 31. DEPOSITIONS BY WRITTEN QUESTIONS

(a) **When a Deposition May Be Taken.**

(1) ***Without Leave.*** A party may, by written questions, depose any person, including a party, without leave of court except as provided in Rule 31(a)(2). The deponent's attendance may be compelled by subpoena under Rule 45.

(2) ***With Leave.*** A party must obtain leave of court, and the court must grant leave to the extent consistent with Rule 26(b)(2):

(A) if the parties have not stipulated to the deposition and:

(i) the deposition would result in more than 10 depositions being taken under this rule or Rule 30 by the plaintiffs, or by the defendants, or by the third-party defendants;

(ii) the deponent has already been deposed in the case; or

(iii) the party seeks to take a deposition before the time specified in Rule 26(d); or

(B) if the deponent is confined in prison.

(3) ***Service; Required Notice.*** A party who wants to depose a person by written questions must serve them on every other party, with a notice stating, if known, the deponent's name and address. If the name is unknown, the notice must provide a general description sufficient to identify the person or the particular class or group to which the person belongs. The notice must also state the name or descriptive title and the address of the officer before whom the deposition will be taken.

(4) ***Questions Directed to an Organization.*** A public or private corporation, a partnership, an association, or a governmental agency may be deposed by written questions in accordance with Rule 30(b)(6).

(5) ***Questions from Other Parties.*** Any questions to the deponent from other parties must be served on all parties as follows: cross-questions, within 14 days after being served with the notice and direct questions; redirect questions, within 7 days after being served with cross-questions; and recross-questions, within 7 days after being served with redirect questions. The court may, for good cause, extend or shorten these times.

(b) **Delivery to the Officer; Officer's Duties.** The party who noticed the deposition must deliver to the officer a copy of all the questions served and of the notice. The officer must promptly proceed in the manner provided in Rule 30(c), (e), and (f) to:

(1) take the deponent's testimony in response to the questions;

(2) prepare and certify the deposition; and

(3) send it to the party, attaching a copy of the questions and of the notice.

(c) **Notice of Completion or Filing.**

(1) ***Completion.*** The party who noticed the deposition must notify all other parties when it is completed.

(2) ***Filing.*** A party who files the deposition must promptly notify all other parties of the filing.

(Amended March 30, 1970, effective July 1, 1970; March 2, 1987, effective August 1, 1987; April 22, 1993, effective December 1, 1993; April 30, 2007, effective December 1, 2007.)

RULE 32. USING DEPOSITIONS IN COURT PROCEEDINGS

(a) **Using Depositions.**

(1) ***In General.*** At a hearing or trial, all or part of a deposition may be used against a party on these conditions:

(A) the party was present or represented at the taking of the deposition or had reasonable notice of it;

(B) it is used to the extent it would be admissible under the Federal Rules of Evidence if the deponent were present and testifying; and

(C) the use is allowed by Rule 32(a)(2) through (8).

(2) ***Impeachment and Other Uses.*** Any party may use a deposition to contradict or impeach the testimony given by the deponent as a witness, or for any other purpose allowed by the Federal Rules of Evidence.

(3) ***Deposition of Party, Agent, or Designee.*** An adverse party may use for any purpose the deposition of a party or anyone who, when deposed, was the party's officer, director, managing agent, or designee under Rule 30(b)(6) or 31(a)(4).

(4) ***Unavailable Witness.*** A party may use for any purpose the deposition of a witness, whether or not a party, if the court finds:

(A) that the witness is dead;

(B) that the witness is more than 100 miles from the place of hearing or trial or is outside the United States, unless it appears that the witness's absence was procured by the party offering the deposition;

(C) that the witness cannot attend or testify because of age, illness, infirmity, or imprisonment;

(D) that the party offering the deposition could not procure the witness's attendance by subpoena; or

(E) on motion and notice, that exceptional circumstances make it desirable—in the interest of justice and with due regard to the importance of live testimony in open court—to permit the deposition to be used.

(5) ***Limitations on Use.***

(A) *Deposition Taken on Short Notice.* A deposition must not be used against a party who, having received less than 14 days' notice of the deposition, promptly moved for a protective order under Rule 26(c)(1)(B) requesting that it not be taken or be taken at a different time or place—and this motion was still pending when the deposition was taken.

(B) *Unavailable Deponent; Party Could Not Obtain an Attorney.* A deposition taken without leave of court under the unavailability provision of Rule 30(a)(2)(A)(iii) must not be used against a party who shows that, when served with the notice, it could not, despite diligent efforts, obtain an attorney to represent it at the deposition.

(6) ***Using Part of a Deposition.*** If a party offers in evidence only part of a deposition, an adverse party may require the offeror to introduce other parts that in fairness should be considered with the part introduced, and any party may itself introduce any other parts.

(7) ***Substituting a Party.*** Substituting a party under Rule 25 does not affect the right to use a deposition previously taken.

(8) ***Deposition Taken in an Earlier Action.*** A deposition lawfully taken and, if required, filed in any federal- or state-court action may be used in a later action involving the same subject matter between the same parties, or their representatives or successors in interest, to the same extent as if taken in the later action. A deposition previously taken may also be used as allowed by the Federal Rules of Evidence.

(b) Objections to Admissibility. Subject to Rules 28(b) and 32(d)(3), an objection may be made at a hearing or trial to the admission of any deposition testimony that would be inadmissible if the witness were present and testifying.

(c) Form of Presentation. Unless the court orders otherwise, a party must provide a transcript of any deposition testimony the party offers, but may provide the court with the testimony in nontranscript form as well. On any party's request, deposition testimony offered in a jury trial for any purpose other than impeachment must be presented in nontranscript form, if available, unless the court for good cause orders otherwise.

(d) Waiver of Objections.

(1) ***To the Notice.*** An objection to an error or irregularity in a deposition notice is waived unless promptly served in writing on the party giving the notice.

(2) ***To the Officer's Qualification.*** An objection based on disqualification of the officer before whom a deposition is to be taken is waived if not made:

(A) before the deposition begins; or

(B) promptly after the basis for disqualification becomes known or, with reasonable diligence, could have been known.

(3) ***To the Taking of the Deposition.***

(A) *Objection to Competence, Relevance, or Materiality.* An objection to a deponent's competence—or to the competence, relevance, or materiality of testimony—is not waived by a failure to make the objection before or during the deposition, unless the ground for it might have been corrected at that time.

(B) *Objection to an Error or Irregularity.* An objection to an error or irregularity at an oral examination is waived if:

(i) it relates to the manner of taking the deposition, the form of a question or answer, the oath or affirmation, a party's conduct, or other matters that might have been corrected at that time; and

(ii) it is not timely made during the deposition.

(C) *Objection to a Written Question.* An objection to the form of a written question under Rule 31 is waived if not served in writing on the party submitting the question within the time for serving responsive questions or, if the question is a recross-question, within 7 days after being served with it.

(4) ***To Completing and Returning the Deposition.*** An objection to how the officer transcribed the testimony—or prepared, signed, certified, sealed, endorsed, sent, or otherwise dealt with the deposition—is waived unless a motion to suppress is made promptly after the error or irregularity becomes known or, with reasonable diligence, could have been known.

(Amended March 30, 1970, effective July 1, 1970; November 20, 1972, effective July 1, 1975; April 29, 1980, effective August 1, 1980; March 2, 1987, effective August 1, 1987; April 22, 1993, effective December 1, 1993; April 30, 2007, effective December 1, 2007; March 26, 2009, effective December 1, 2009.)

RULE 33. INTERROGATORIES TO PARTIES

(a) In General.

(1) ***Number.*** Unless otherwise stipulated or ordered by the court, a party may serve on any other party no more than 25 written interrogatories, including all discrete subparts. Leave to serve additional interrogatories may be granted to the extent consistent with Rule 26(b)(2).

(2) ***Scope.*** An interrogatory may relate to any matter that may be inquired into under Rule 26(b). An interrogatory is not objectionable merely because it asks for an opinion or contention that relates to fact or the application of law to fact, but the court may order that the interrogatory need not be answered until designated discovery is complete, or until a pretrial conference or some other time.

(b) Answers and Objections.

(1) ***Responding Party.*** The interrogatories must be answered:

(A) by the party to whom they are directed; or

(B) if that party is a public or private corporation, a partnership, an association, or a governmental agency, by any officer or agent, who must furnish the information available to the party.

(2) ***Time to Respond.*** The responding party must serve its answers and any objections within 30 days after being served with the interrogatories. A shorter or longer time may be stipulated to under Rule 29 or be ordered by the court.

(3) ***Answering Each Interrogatory.*** Each interrogatory must, to the extent it is not objected to, be answered separately and fully in writing under oath.

(4) ***Objections.*** The grounds for objecting to an interrogatory must be stated with specificity. Any ground not stated in a timely objection is waived unless the court, for good cause, excuses the failure.

(5) ***Signature.*** The person who makes the answers must sign them, and the attorney who objects must sign any objections.

(c) Use. An answer to an interrogatory may be used to the extent allowed by the Federal Rules of Evidence.

(d) Option to Produce Business Records. If the answer to an interrogatory may be determined by examining, auditing, compiling, abstracting, or summarizing a party's business records (including electronically stored information), and if the burden of deriving or ascertaining the answer will be substantially the same for either party, the responding party may answer by:

(1) specifying the records that must be reviewed, in sufficient detail to enable the interrogating party to locate and identify them as readily as the responding party could; and

(2) giving the interrogating party a reasonable opportunity to examine and audit the records and to make copies, compilations, abstracts, or summaries.

(Amended December 27, 1946, effective March 19, 1948; March 30, 1970, effective July 1, 1970; April 29, 1980, effective August 1, 1980; April 22, 1993, effective December 1, 1993; April 12, 2006, effective December 1, 2006; April 30, 2007, effective December 1, 2007.)

RULE 34. PRODUCING DOCUMENTS, ELECTRONICALLY STORED INFORMATION, AND TANGIBLE THINGS, OR ENTERING ONTO LAND, FOR INSPECTION AND OTHER PURPOSES

(a) In General. A party may serve on any other party a request within the scope of Rule 26(b):

(1) to produce and permit the requesting party or its representative to inspect, copy, test, or sam-

ple the following items in the responding party's possession, custody, or control:

(A) any designated documents or electronically stored information—including writings, drawings, graphs, charts, photographs, sound recordings, images, and other data or data compilations—stored in any medium from which information can be obtained either directly or, if necessary, after translation by the responding party into a reasonably usable form; or

(B) any designated tangible things; or

(2) to permit entry onto designated land or other property possessed or controlled by the responding party, so that the requesting party may inspect, measure, survey, photograph, test, or sample the property or any designated object or operation on it.

(b) Procedure.

(1) ***Contents of the Request.*** The request:

(A) must describe with reasonable particularity each item or category of items to be inspected;

(B) must specify a reasonable time, place, and manner for the inspection and for performing the related acts; and

(C) may specify the form or forms in which electronically stored information is to be produced.

(2) ***Responses and Objections.***

(A) *Time to Respond.* The party to whom the request is directed must respond in writing within 30 days after being served. A shorter or longer time may be stipulated to under Rule 29 or be ordered by the court.

(B) *Responding to Each Item.* For each item or category, the response must either state that inspection and related activities will be permitted as requested or state an objection to the request, including the reasons.

(C) *Objections.* An objection to part of a request must specify the part and permit inspection of the rest.

(D) *Responding to a Request for Production of Electronically Stored Information.* The response may state an objection to a requested form for producing electronically stored information. If the responding party objects to a requested form—or if no form was specified in the request—the party must state the form or forms it intends to use.

(E) *Producing the Documents or Electronically Stored Information.* Unless otherwise stipulated or ordered by the court, these procedures apply to producing documents or electronically stored information:

(i) A party must produce documents as they are kept in the usual course of business or must organize and label them to correspond to the categories in the request;

(ii) If a request does not specify a form for producing electronically stored information, a party must produce it in a form or forms in which it is ordinarily maintained or in a reasonably usable form or forms; and

(iii) A party need not produce the same electronically stored information in more than one form.

(c) Nonparties. As provided in Rule 45, a nonparty may be compelled to produce documents and tangible things or to permit an inspection.

(Amended December 27, 1946, effective March 19, 1948; March 30, 1970, effective July 1, 1970; April 29, 1980, effective August 1, 1980; March 2, 1987, effective August 1, 1987; April 30, 1991, effective December 1, 1991; April 22, 1993, effective December 1, 1993; April 12, 2006, effective December 1, 2006; April 30, 2007, effective December 1, 2007.)

RULE 35. PHYSICAL AND MENTAL EXAMINATIONS

(a) Order for an Examination.

(1) ***In General.*** The court where the action is pending may order a party whose mental or physical condition—including blood group—is in controversy to submit to a physical or mental examination by a suitably licensed or certified examiner. The court has the same authority to order a party to produce for examination a person who is in its custody or under its legal control.

(2) ***Motion and Notice; Contents of the Order.*** The order:

(A) may be made only on motion for good cause and on notice to all parties and the person to be examined; and

(B) must specify the time, place, manner, conditions, and scope of the examination, as well as the person or persons who will perform it.

(b) Examiner's Report.

(1) ***Request by the Party or Person Examined.*** The party who moved for the examination must, on request, deliver to the requester a copy of the examiner's report, together with like reports of all earlier examinations of the same condition. The request may be made by the party against whom the examination order was issued or by the person examined.

(2) ***Contents.*** The examiner's report must be in writing and must set out in detail the examiner's findings, including diagnoses, conclusions, and the results of any tests.

(3) ***Request by the Moving Party.*** After delivering the reports, the party who moved for the examination may request—and is entitled to receive—from the party against whom the examination order was issued like reports of all earlier or later examinations of the same condition. But those reports need not be delivered by the party with custody or control of the person examined if the party shows that it could not obtain them.

(4) ***Waiver of Privilege.*** By requesting and obtaining the examiner's report, or by deposing the examiner, the party examined waives any privilege it may have—in that action or any other action involving the same controversy—concerning testimony about all examinations of the same condition.

(5) ***Failure to Deliver a Report.*** The court on motion may order—on just terms—that a party deliver the report of an examination. If the report is not provided, the court may exclude the examiner's testimony at trial.

(6) ***Scope.*** This subdivision (b) applies also to an examination made by the parties' agreement, unless the agreement states otherwise. This subdivision does not preclude obtaining an examiner's report or deposing an examiner under other rules.

(Amended March 30, 1970, effective July 1, 1970; March 2, 1987, effective August 1, 1987; amended by Pub.L. 100–690, Title VII, § 7047(b), November 18, 1988, 102 Stat. 4401; amended April 30, 1991, effective December 1, 1991; April 30, 2007, effective December 1, 2007.)

RULE 36. REQUESTS FOR ADMISSION

(a) Scope and Procedure.

(1) ***Scope.*** A party may serve on any other party a written request to admit, for purposes of the pending action only, the truth of any matters within the scope of Rule 26(b)(1) relating to:

(A) facts, the application of law to fact, or opinions about either; and

(B) the genuineness of any described documents.

(2) ***Form; Copy of a Document.*** Each matter must be separately stated. A request to admit the genuineness of a document must be accompanied by a copy of the document unless it is, or has been, otherwise furnished or made available for inspection and copying.

(3) ***Time to Respond; Effect of Not Responding.*** A matter is admitted unless, within 30 days after being served, the party to whom the request is directed serves on the requesting party a written answer or objection addressed to the matter and signed by the party or its attorney. A shorter or longer time for responding may be stipulated to under Rule 29 or be ordered by the court.

(4) ***Answer.*** If a matter is not admitted, the answer must specifically deny it or state in detail why the answering party cannot truthfully admit or deny it. A denial must fairly respond to the substance of the matter; and when good faith requires that a party qualify an answer or deny only a part of a matter, the answer must specify the part admitted and qualify or deny the rest. The answering party may assert lack of knowledge or information as a reason for failing to admit or deny only if the party states that it has made reasonable inquiry and that the information it knows or can readily obtain is insufficient to enable it to admit or deny.

(5) ***Objections.*** The grounds for objecting to a request must be stated. A party must not object solely on the ground that the request presents a genuine issue for trial.

(6) ***Motion Regarding the Sufficiency of an Answer or Objection.*** The requesting party may move to determine the sufficiency of an answer or objection. Unless the court finds an objection justified, it must order that an answer be served. On finding that an answer does not comply with this rule, the court may order either that the matter is admitted or that an amended answer be served. The court may defer its final decision until a pretrial conference or a specified time before trial. Rule 37(a)(5) applies to an award of expenses.

(b) Effect of an Admission; Withdrawing or Amending It. A matter admitted under this rule is conclusively established unless the court, on motion, permits the admission to be withdrawn or amended. Subject to Rule 16(e), the court may permit withdrawal or amendment if it would promote the presentation of the merits of the action and if the court is not persuaded that it would prejudice the requesting party in maintaining or defending the action on the merits. An admission under this rule is not an admission for any other purpose and cannot be used against the party in any other proceeding.

(Amended December 27, 1946, effective March 19, 1948; March 30, 1970, effective July 1, 1970; March 2, 1987, effective August 1, 1987; April 22, 1993, effective December 1, 1993; April 30, 2007, effective December 1, 2007.)

RULE 37. FAILURE TO MAKE DISCLOSURES OR TO COOPERATE IN DISCOVERY; SANCTIONS

(a) Motion for an Order Compelling Disclosure or Discovery.

(1) ***In General.*** On notice to other parties and all affected persons, a party may move for an order compelling disclosure or discovery. The motion must include a certification that the movant has in good faith conferred or attempted to confer with the person or party failing to make disclosure or discovery in an effort to obtain it without court action.

(2) ***Appropriate Court.*** A motion for an order to a party must be made in the court where the action is pending. A motion for an order to a nonparty must be made in the court where the discovery is or will be taken.

(3) ***Specific Motions.***

(A) *To Compel Disclosure.* If a party fails to make a disclosure required by Rule 26(a), any other party may move to compel disclosure and for appropriate sanctions.

(B) *To Compel a Discovery Response.* A party seeking discovery may move for an order compelling an answer, designation, production, or inspection. This motion may be made if:

(i) a deponent fails to answer a question asked under Rule 30 or 31;

(ii) a corporation or other entity fails to make a designation under Rule 30(b)(6) or 31(a)(4);

(iii) a party fails to answer an interrogatory submitted under Rule 33; or

(iv) a party fails to respond that inspection will be permitted—or fails to permit inspection—as requested under Rule 34.

(C) *Related to a Deposition.* When taking an oral deposition, the party asking a question may complete or adjourn the examination before moving for an order.

(4) ***Evasive or Incomplete Disclosure, Answer, or Response.*** For purposes of this subdivision (a), an evasive or incomplete disclosure, answer, or response must be treated as a failure to disclose, answer, or respond.

(5) ***Payment of Expenses; Protective Orders.***

(A) *If the Motion Is Granted (or Disclosure or Discovery Is Provided After Filing).* If the motion is granted—or if the disclosure or requested discovery is provided after the motion was filed—the court must, after giving an opportunity to be heard, require the party or deponent whose conduct necessitated the motion, the party or attorney advising that conduct, or both to pay the movant's reasonable expenses incurred in making the motion, including attorney's fees. But the court must not order this payment if:

(i) the movant filed the motion before attempting in good faith to obtain the disclosure or discovery without court action;

(ii) the opposing party's nondisclosure, response, or objection was substantially justified; or

(iii) other circumstances make an award of expenses unjust.

(B) *If the Motion Is Denied.* If the motion is denied, the court may issue any protective order authorized under Rule 26(c) and must, after giving an opportunity to be heard, require the movant, the attorney filing the motion, or both to pay the party or deponent who opposed the motion its reasonable expenses incurred in opposing the motion, including attorney's fees. But the court must not order this payment if the motion was substantially justified or other circumstances make an award of expenses unjust.

(C) *If the Motion Is Granted in Part and Denied in Part.* If the motion is granted in part and denied in part, the court may issue any protective order authorized under Rule 26(c) and may, after giving an opportunity to be heard, apportion the reasonable expenses for the motion.

(b) Failure to Comply with a Court Order.

(1) ***Sanctions in the District Where the Deposition Is Taken.*** If the court where the discovery is taken orders a deponent to be sworn or to answer a question and the deponent fails to obey, the failure may be treated as contempt of court.

(2) ***Sanctions in the District Where the Action Is Pending.***

(A) *For Not Obeying a Discovery Order.* If a party or a party's officer, director, or managing agent—or a witness designated under Rule 30(b)(6) or 31(a)(4)—fails to obey an order to provide or permit discovery, including an order under Rule 26(f), 35, or 37(a), the court where the action is pending may issue further just orders. They may include the following:

(i) directing that the matters embraced in the order or other designated facts be taken as established for purposes of the action, as the prevailing party claims;

(ii) prohibiting the disobedient party from supporting or opposing designated claims or defenses, or from introducing designated matters in evidence;

(iii) striking pleadings in whole or in part;

(iv) staying further proceedings until the order is obeyed;

(v) dismissing the action or proceeding in whole or in part;

(vi) rendering a default judgment against the disobedient party; or

(vii) treating as contempt of court the failure to obey any order except an order to submit to a physical or mental examination.

(B) *For Not Producing a Person for Examination.* If a party fails to comply with an order under Rule 35(a) requiring it to produce another person for examination, the court may issue any of the orders listed in Rule 37(b)(2)(A)(i)-(vi), unless the disobedient party shows that it cannot produce the other person.

(C) *Payment of Expenses.* Instead of or in addition to the orders above, the court must order the disobedient party, the attorney advising that party, or both to pay the reasonable expenses, including attorney's fees, caused by the failure, unless the failure was substantially justified or other circumstances make an award of expenses unjust.

(c) Failure to Disclose, to Supplement an Earlier Response, or to Admit.

(1) ***Failure to Disclose or Supplement.*** If a party fails to provide information or identify a witness as required by Rule 26(a) or (e), the party is not allowed to use that information or witness to supply evidence on a motion, at a hearing, or at a trial, unless the failure was substantially justified or is harmless. In addition to or instead of this sanction, the court, on motion and after giving an opportunity to be heard:

(A) may order payment of the reasonable expenses, including attorney's fees, caused by the failure;

(B) may inform the jury of the party's failure; and

(C) may impose other appropriate sanctions, including any of the orders listed in Rule 37(b)(2)(A)(i)-(vi).

(2) ***Failure to Admit.*** If a party fails to admit what is requested under Rule 36 and if the requesting party later proves a document to be genuine or the matter true, the requesting party may move that the party who failed to admit pay the reasonable expenses, including attorney's fees, incurred in making that proof. The court must so order unless:

(A) the request was held objectionable under Rule 36(a);

(B) the admission sought was of no substantial importance;

(C) the party failing to admit had a reasonable ground to believe that it might prevail on the matter; or

(D) there was other good reason for the failure to admit.

(d) Party's Failure to Attend Its Own Deposition, Serve Answers to Interrogatories, or Respond to a Request for Inspection.

(1) ***In General.***

(A) *Motion; Grounds for Sanctions.* The court where the action is pending may, on motion, order sanctions if:

(i) a party or a party's officer, director, or managing agent—or a person designated under Rule 30(b)(6) or 31(a)(4)—fails, after being served with proper notice, to appear for that person's deposition; or

(ii) a party, after being properly served with interrogatories under Rule 33 or a request for inspection under Rule 34, fails to serve its answers, objections, or written response.

(B) *Certification.* A motion for sanctions for failing to answer or respond must include a certification that the movant has in good faith conferred or attempted to confer with the party failing to act in an effort to obtain the answer or response without court action.

(2) ***Unacceptable Excuse for Failing to Act.*** A failure described in Rule 37(d)(1)(A) is not excused on the ground that the discovery sought was objectionable, unless the party failing to act has a pending motion for a protective order under Rule 26(c).

(3) ***Types of Sanctions.*** Sanctions may include any of the orders listed in Rule 37(b)(2)(A)(i)-(vi). Instead of or in addition to these sanctions, the court must require the party failing to act, the attorney advising that party, or both to pay the reasonable expenses, including attorney's fees, caused by the failure, unless the failure was substantially justified or other circumstances make an award of expenses unjust.

(e) Failure to Provide Electronically Stored Information. Absent exceptional circumstances, a court may not impose sanctions under these rules on a party for failing to provide electronically stored information lost as a result of the routine, good-faith operation of an electronic information system.

(f) Failure to Participate in Framing a Discovery Plan. If a party or its attorney fails to participate in good faith in developing and submitting a proposed discovery plan as required by Rule 26(f), the court may, after giving an opportunity to be heard, require that party or attorney to pay to any other party the reasonable expenses, including attorney's fees, caused by the failure.

(Amended December 29, 1948, effective October 20, 1949; March 30, 1970, effective July 1, 1970; April 29, 1980, effective August 1, 1980; amended by Pub.L. 96–481, Title II, § 205(a), October 21, 1980, 94 Stat. 2330, effective October 1, 1981; amended March 2, 1987, effective August 1, 1987; April 22, 1993, effective December 1, 1993; April 17, 2000, effective December 1, 2000; April 12, 2006, effective December 1, 2006; April 30, 2007, effective December 1, 2007.)

TITLE VI. TRIALS

RULE 38. RIGHT TO A JURY TRIAL; DEMAND

(a) Right Preserved. The right of trial by jury as declared by the Seventh Amendment to the Constitution—or as provided by a federal statute—is preserved to the parties inviolate.

(b) Demand. On any issue triable of right by a jury, a party may demand a jury trial by:

(1) serving the other parties with a written demand—which may be included in a pleading—no later than 14 days after the last pleading directed to the issue is served; and

(2) filing the demand in accordance with Rule 5(d).

(c) Specifying Issues. In its demand, a party may specify the issues that it wishes to have tried by a jury; otherwise, it is considered to have demanded a jury trial on all the issues so triable. If the party has demanded a jury trial on only some issues, any other party may—within 14 days after being served with the demand or within a shorter time ordered by the court—serve a demand for a jury trial on any other or all factual issues triable by jury.

(d) Waiver; Withdrawal. A party waives a jury trial unless its demand is properly served and filed. A proper demand may be withdrawn only if the parties consent.

(e) Admiralty and Maritime Claims. These rules do not create a right to a jury trial on issues in a claim that is an admiralty or maritime claim under Rule 9(h).

(Amended February 28, 1966, effective July 1, 1966; March 2, 1987, effective August 1, 1987; April 22, 1993, effective December 1, 1993; April 30, 2007, effective December 1, 2007; March 26, 2009, effective December 1, 2009.)

RULE 39. TRIAL BY JURY OR BY THE COURT

(a) When a Demand Is Made. When a jury trial has been demanded under Rule 38, the action must be designated on the docket as a jury action. The trial on all issues so demanded must be by jury unless:

(1) the parties or their attorneys file a stipulation to a nonjury trial or so stipulate on the record; or

(2) the court, on motion or on its own, finds that on some or all of those issues there is no federal right to a jury trial.

(b) When No Demand Is Made. Issues on which a jury trial is not properly demanded are to be tried by the court. But the court may, on motion, order a jury trial on any issue for which a jury might have been demanded.

(c) Advisory Jury; Jury Trial by Consent. In an action not triable of right by a jury, the court, on motion or on its own:

(1) may try any issue with an advisory jury; or

(2) may, with the parties' consent, try any issue by a jury whose verdict has the same effect as if a jury trial had been a matter of right, unless the action is against the United States and a federal statute provides for a nonjury trial.

(Amended April 30, 2007, effective December 1, 2007.)

RULE 40. SCHEDULING CASES FOR TRIAL

Each court must provide by rule for scheduling trials. The court must give priority to actions entitled to priority by a federal statute.

(Amended April 30, 2007, effective December 1, 2007.)

RULE 41. DISMISSAL OF ACTIONS

(a) Voluntary Dismissal.

(1) ***By the Plaintiff.***

(A) *Without a Court Order.* Subject to Rules 23(e), 23.1(c), 23.2, and 66 and any applicable federal statute, the plaintiff may dismiss an action without a court order by filing:

(i) a notice of dismissal before the opposing party serves either an answer or a motion for summary judgment; or

(ii) a stipulation of dismissal signed by all parties who have appeared.

(B) *Effect.* Unless the notice or stipulation states otherwise, the dismissal is without prejudice. But if the plaintiff previously dismissed any federal- or state-court action based on or including the same claim, a notice of dismissal operates as an adjudication on the merits.

(2) ***By Court Order; Effect.*** Except as provided in Rule 41(a)(1), an action may be dismissed at the plaintiff's request only by court order, on terms that the court considers proper. If a defendant has pleaded a counterclaim before being served with the plaintiff's motion to dismiss, the action may be dismissed over the defendant's objection only if the counterclaim can remain pending for independent adjudication. Unless the order states otherwise, a dismissal under this paragraph (2) is without prejudice.

(b) **Involuntary Dismissal; Effect.** If the plaintiff fails to prosecute or to comply with these rules or a court order, a defendant may move to dismiss the action or any claim against it. Unless the dismissal order states otherwise, a dismissal under this subdivision (b) and any dismissal not under this rule—except one for lack of jurisdiction, improper venue, or failure to join a party under Rule 19—operates as an adjudication on the merits.

(c) **Dismissing a Counterclaim, Crossclaim, or Third-Party Claim.** This rule applies to a dismissal of any counterclaim, crossclaim, or third-party claim. A claimant's voluntary dismissal under Rule 41(a)(1)(A)(i) must be made:

(1) before a responsive pleading is served; or

(2) if there is no responsive pleading, before evidence is introduced at a hearing or trial.

(d) **Costs of a Previously Dismissed Action.** If a plaintiff who previously dismissed an action in any court files an action based on or including the same claim against the same defendant, the court:

(1) may order the plaintiff to pay all or part of the costs of that previous action; and

(2) may stay the proceedings until the plaintiff has complied.

(Amended December 27, 1946, effective March 19, 1948; January 21, 1963, effective July 1, 1963; February 28, 1966, effective July 1, 1966; December 4, 1967, effective July 1, 1968; March 2, 1987, effective August 1, 1987; April 30, 1991, effective December 1, 1991; April 30, 2007, effective December 1, 2007.)

RULE 42. CONSOLIDATION; SEPARATE TRIALS

(a) **Consolidation.** If actions before the court involve a common question of law or fact, the court may:

(1) join for hearing or trial any or all matters at issue in the actions;

(2) consolidate the actions; or

(3) issue any other orders to avoid unnecessary cost or delay.

(b) **Separate Trials.** For convenience, to avoid prejudice, or to expedite and economize, the court may order a separate trial of one or more separate issues, claims, crossclaims, counterclaims, or third-party claims. When ordering a separate trial, the court must preserve any federal right to a jury trial.

(Amended February 28, 1966, effective July 1, 1966; April 30, 2007, effective December 1, 2007.)

RULE 43. TAKING TESTIMONY

(a) **In Open Court.** At trial, the witnesses' testimony must be taken in open court unless a federal statute, the Federal Rules of Evidence, these rules, or other rules adopted by the Supreme Court provide otherwise. For good cause in compelling circumstances and with appropriate safeguards, the court may permit testimony in open court by contemporaneous transmission from a different location.

(b) **Affirmation Instead of an Oath.** When these rules require an oath, a solemn affirmation suffices.

(c) **Evidence on a Motion.** When a motion relies on facts outside the record, the court may hear the matter on affidavits or may hear it wholly or partly on oral testimony or on depositions.

(d) **Interpreter.** The court may appoint an interpreter of its choosing; fix reasonable compensation to be paid from funds provided by law or by one or more parties; and tax the compensation as costs.

(Amended February 28, 1966, effective July 1, 1966; November 20, 1972, and December 18, 1972, effective July 1, 1975; March 2, 1987, effective August 1, 1987; April 23, 1996, effective December 1, 1996; April 30, 2007, effective December 1, 2007.)

RULE 44. PROVING AN OFFICIAL RECORD

(a) **Means of Proving.**

(1) ***Domestic Record.*** Each of the following evidences an official record—or an entry in it—that is otherwise admissible and is kept within the United States, any state, district, or commonwealth, or any territory subject to the administrative or judicial jurisdiction of the United States:

(A) an official publication of the record; or

(B) a copy attested by the officer with legal custody of the record—or by the officer's deputy—and accompanied by a certificate that the officer has custody. The certificate must be made under seal:

(i) by a judge of a court of record in the district or political subdivision where the record is kept; or

(ii) by any public officer with a seal of office and with official duties in the district or political subdivision where the record is kept.

(2) ***Foreign Record.***

(A) *In General.* Each of the following evidences a foreign official record—or an entry in it—that is otherwise admissible:

(i) an official publication of the record; or

(ii) the record—or a copy—that is attested by an authorized person and is accompanied either by a final certification of genuineness or by a certification under a treaty or convention to which the United States and the country where the record is located are parties.

(B) *Final Certification of Genuineness.* A final certification must certify the genuineness of the signature and official position of the attester or of any foreign official whose certificate of genuineness relates to the attestation or is in a chain of certificates of genuineness relating to the attestation. A final certification may be made by a secretary of a United States embassy or legation; by a consul general, vice consul, or consular agent of the United States; or by a diplomatic or consular official of the foreign country assigned or accredited to the United States.

(C) *Other Means of Proof.* If all parties have had a reasonable opportunity to investigate a foreign record's authenticity and accuracy, the court may, for good cause, either:

(i) admit an attested copy without final certification; or

(ii) permit the record to be evidenced by an attested summary with or without a final certification.

(b) Lack of a Record. A written statement that a diligent search of designated records revealed no record or entry of a specified tenor is admissible as evidence that the records contain no such record or entry. For domestic records, the statement must be authenticated under Rule 44(a)(1). For foreign records, the statement must comply with (a)(2)(C)(ii).

(c) Other Proof. A party may prove an official record—or an entry or lack of an entry in it—by any other method authorized by law.

(Amended February 28, 1966, effective July 1, 1966; March 2, 1987, effective August 1, 1987; April 30, 1991, effective December 1, 1991; April 30, 2007, effective December 1, 2007.)

RULE 44.1. DETERMINING FOREIGN LAW

A party who intends to raise an issue about a foreign country's law must give notice by a pleading or other writing. In determining foreign law, the court may consider any relevant material or source, including testimony, whether or not submitted by a party or admissible under the Federal Rules of Evidence. The court's determination must be treated as a ruling on a question of law.

(Adopted February 28, 1966, effective July 1, 1966; amended November 20, 1972, effective July 1, 1975; March 2, 1987, effective August 1, 1987; April 30, 2007, effective December 1, 2007.)

RULE 45. SUBPOENA

(a) In General.

(1) ***Form and Contents.***

(A) *Requirements—In General.* Every subpoena must:

(i) state the court from which it issued;

(ii) state the title of the action, the court in which it is pending, and its civil-action number;

(iii) command each person to whom it is directed to do the following at a specified time and place: attend and testify; produce designated documents, electronically stored information, or tangible things in that person's possession, custody, or control; or permit the inspection of premises; and

(iv) set out the text of Rule 45(c) and (d).

(B) *Command to Attend a Deposition—Notice of the Recording Method.* A subpoena commanding attendance at a deposition must state the method for recording the testimony.

(C) *Combining or Separating a Command to Produce or to Permit Inspection; Specifying the Form for Electronically Stored Information.* A command to produce documents, electronically stored information, or tangible things or to permit the inspection of premises may be included in a subpoena commanding attendance at a deposition, hearing, or trial, or may be set out in a separate subpoena. A subpoena may specify the form or forms in which electronically stored information is to be produced.

(D) *Command to Produce; Included Obligations.* A command in a subpoena to produce documents, electronically stored information, or tangible things requires the responding party to permit inspection, copying, testing, or sampling of the materials.

(2) ***Issued from Which Court.*** A subpoena must issue as follows:

(A) for attendance at a hearing or trial, from the court for the district where the hearing or trial is to be held;

(B) for attendance at a deposition, from the court for the district where the deposition is to be taken; and

(C) for production or inspection, if separate from a subpoena commanding a person's attendance, from the court for the district where the production or inspection is to be made.

(3) ***Issued by Whom.*** The clerk must issue a subpoena, signed but otherwise in blank, to a party who requests it. That party must complete it before service. An attorney also may issue and sign a subpoena as an officer of:

(A) a court in which the attorney is authorized to practice; or

(B) a court for a district where a deposition is to be taken or production is to be made, if the attorney is authorized to practice in the court where the action is pending.

(b) Service.

(1) ***By Whom; Tendering Fees; Serving a Copy of Certain Subpoenas.*** Any person who is at least 18 years old and not a party may serve a subpoena. Serving a subpoena requires delivering a copy to the named person and, if the subpoena requires that person's attendance, tendering the fees for 1 day's attendance and the mileage allowed by law. Fees and mileage need not be tendered when the subpoena issues on behalf of the United States or any of its officers or agencies. If the subpoena commands the production of documents, electronically stored information, or tangible things or the inspection of premises before trial, then before it is served, a notice must be served on each party.

(2) ***Service in the United States.*** Subject to Rule 45(c)(3)(A)(ii), a subpoena may be served at any place:

(A) within the district of the issuing court;

(B) outside that district but within 100 miles of the place specified for the deposition, hearing, trial, production, or inspection;

(C) within the state of the issuing court if a state statute or court rule allows service at that place of a subpoena issued by a state court of general jurisdiction sitting in the place specified for the deposition, hearing, trial, production, or inspection; or

(D) that the court authorizes on motion and for good cause, if a federal statute so provides.

(3) ***Service in a Foreign Country.*** 28 U.S.C. § 1783 governs issuing and serving a subpoena directed to a United States national or resident who is in a foreign country.

(4) ***Proof of Service.*** Proving service, when necessary, requires filing with the issuing court a statement showing the date and manner of service and the names of the persons served. The statement must be certified by the server.

(c) Protecting a Person Subject to a Subpoena.

(1) ***Avoiding Undue Burden or Expense; Sanctions.*** A party or attorney responsible for issuing and serving a subpoena must take reasonable steps to avoid imposing undue burden or expense on a person subject to the subpoena. The issuing court must enforce this duty and impose an appropriate sanction—which may include lost earnings and reasonable attorney's fees—on a party or attorney who fails to comply.

(2) ***Command to Produce Materials or Permit Inspection.***

(A) *Appearance Not Required.* A person commanded to produce documents, electronically stored information, or tangible things, or to permit the inspection of premises, need not appear in person at the place of production or inspection unless also commanded to appear for a deposition, hearing, or trial.

(B) *Objections.* A person commanded to produce documents or tangible things or to permit inspection may serve on the party or attorney designated in the subpoena a written objection to inspecting, copying, testing or sampling any or all of the materials or to inspecting the premises—or to producing electronically stored information in the form or forms requested. The objection must be served before the earlier of the time specified for compliance or 14 days after the subpoena is served. If an objection is made, the following rules apply:

(i) At any time, on notice to the commanded person, the serving party may move the issuing court for an order compelling production or inspection.

(ii) These acts may be required only as directed in the order, and the order must protect a person who is neither a party nor a party's officer from significant expense resulting from compliance.

(3) ***Quashing or Modifying a Subpoena.***

(A) *When Required.* On timely motion, the issuing court must quash or modify a subpoena that:

(i) fails to allow a reasonable time to comply;

(ii) requires a person who is neither a party nor a party's officer to travel more than 100 miles from where that person resides, is employed, or regularly transacts business in person—except that, subject to Rule 45(c)(3)(B)(iii), the person may be commanded to attend a trial by traveling from any such place within the state where the trial is held;

(iii) requires disclosure of privileged or other protected matter, if no exception or waiver applies; or

(iv) subjects a person to undue burden.

(B) *When Permitted.* To protect a person subject to or affected by a subpoena, the issuing court may, on motion, quash or modify the subpoena if it requires:

(i) disclosing a trade secret or other confidential research, development, or commercial information;

(ii) disclosing an unretained expert's opinion or information that does not describe specific occurrences in dispute and results from the expert's study that was not requested by a party; or

(iii) a person who is neither a party nor a party's officer to incur substantial expense to travel more than 100 miles to attend trial.

(C) *Specifying Conditions as an Alternative.* In the circumstances described in Rule 45(c)(3)(B), the court may, instead of quashing or modifying a subpoena, order appearance or production under specified conditions if the serving party:

(i) shows a substantial need for the testimony or material that cannot be otherwise met without undue hardship; and

(ii) ensures that the subpoenaed person will be reasonably compensated.

(d) Duties in Responding to a Subpoena.

(1) ***Producing Documents or Electronically Stored Information.*** These procedures apply to producing documents or electronically stored information:

(A) *Documents.* A person responding to a subpoena to produce documents must produce them as they are kept in the ordinary course of business or must organize and label them to correspond to the categories in the demand.

(B) *Form for Producing Electronically Stored Information Not Specified.* If a subpoena does not specify a form for producing electronically stored information, the person responding must produce it in a form or forms in which it is ordinarily maintained or in a reasonably usable form or forms.

(C) *Electronically Stored Information Produced in Only One Form.* The person responding need not produce the same electronically stored information in more than one form.

(D) *Inaccessible Electronically Stored Information.* The person responding need not provide discovery of electronically stored information from sources that the person identifies as not reasonably accessible because of undue burden or cost. On motion to compel discovery or for a protective order, the person responding must show that the information is not reasonably accessible because of undue burden or cost. If that showing is made, the court may nonetheless order discovery from such sources if the requesting party shows good cause, considering the limitations of Rule 26(b)(2)(C). The court may specify conditions for the discovery.

(2) ***Claiming Privilege or Protection.***

(A) *Information Withheld.* A person withholding subpoenaed information under a claim that it is privileged or subject to protection as trial-preparation material must:

(i) expressly make the claim; and

(ii) describe the nature of the withheld documents, communications, or tangible things in a manner that, without revealing information itself privileged or protected, will enable the parties to assess the claim.

(B) *Information Produced.* If information produced in response to a subpoena is subject to a claim of privilege or of protection as trial-preparation material, the person making the claim may notify any party that received the information of the claim and the basis for it. After being notified, a party must promptly return, sequester, or destroy the specified information and any copies it has; must not use or disclose the information until the claim is resolved; must take reasonable steps to retrieve the information if the party disclosed it before being notified; and may promptly present the information to the court under seal for a determination of the claim. The person who produced the information must preserve the information until the claim is resolved.

(e) Contempt. The issuing court may hold in contempt a person who, having been served, fails without adequate excuse to obey the subpoena. A nonparty's failure to obey must be excused if the subpoena purports to require the nonparty to attend or produce at a place outside the limits of Rule 45(c)(3)(A)(ii).

(Amended December 27, 1946, effective March 19, 1948; December 29, 1948, effective October 20, 1949; March 30, 1970, effective July 1, 1970; April 29, 1980, effective August 1, 1980; April 29, 1985, effective August 1, 1985; March 2, 1987, effective August 1, 1987; April 30, 1991, effective December 1, 1991; April 25, 2005, effective December 1, 2005; April 12, 2006, effective December 1, 2006; April 30, 2007, effective December 1, 2007.)

RULE 46. OBJECTING TO A RULING OR ORDER

A formal exception to a ruling or order is unnecessary. When the ruling or order is requested or made, a party need only state the action that it wants the court to take or objects to, along with the grounds for the request or objection. Failing to object does not prejudice a party who had no opportunity to do so when the ruling or order was made.

(Amended March 2, 1987, effective August 1, 1987; April 30, 2007, effective December 1, 2007.)

RULE 47. SELECTING JURORS

(a) Examining Jurors. The court may permit the parties or their attorneys to examine prospective jurors or may itself do so. If the court examines the jurors, it must permit the parties or their attorneys to make any further inquiry it considers proper, or must itself ask any of their additional questions it considers proper.

(b) Peremptory Challenges. The court must allow the number of peremptory challenges provided by 28 U.S.C. § 1870.

(c) Excusing a Juror. During trial or deliberation, the court may excuse a juror for good cause.

(Amended February 28, 1966, effective July 1, 1966; April 30, 1991, effective December 1, 1991; April 30, 2007, effective December 1, 2007.)

RULE 48. NUMBER OF JURORS; VERDICT; POLLING

(a) Number of Jurors. A jury must begin with at least 6 and no more than 12 members, and each juror must participate in the verdict unless excused under Rule 47(c).

(b) Verdict. Unless the parties stipulate otherwise, the verdict must be unanimous and must be returned by a jury of at least 6 members.

(c) Polling. After a verdict is returned but before the jury is discharged, the court must on a party's request, or may on its own, poll the jurors individually. If the poll reveals a lack of unanimity or lack of assent by the number of jurors that the parties stipulated to, the court may direct the jury to deliberate further or may order a new trial.

(Amended April 30, 1991, effective December 1, 1991; April 30, 2007, effective December 1, 2007; March 26, 2009, effective December 1, 2009.)

RULE 49. SPECIAL VERDICT; GENERAL VERDICT AND QUESTIONS

(a) Special Verdict.

(1) ***In General.*** The court may require a jury to return only a special verdict in the form of a special written finding on each issue of fact. The court may do so by:

(A) submitting written questions susceptible of a categorical or other brief answer;

(B) submitting written forms of the special findings that might properly be made under the pleadings and evidence; or

(C) using any other method that the court considers appropriate.

(2) ***Instructions.*** The court must give the instructions and explanations necessary to enable the jury to make its findings on each submitted issue.

(3) ***Issues Not Submitted.*** A party waives the right to a jury trial on any issue of fact raised by the pleadings or evidence but not submitted to the jury unless, before the jury retires, the party demands its submission to the jury. If the party does not demand submission, the court may make a finding on the issue. If the court makes no finding, it is considered to have made a finding consistent with its judgment on the special verdict.

(b) General Verdict with Answers to Written Questions.

(1) ***In General.*** The court may submit to the jury forms for a general verdict, together with written questions on one or more issues of fact that the jury must decide. The court must give the

instructions and explanations necessary to enable the jury to render a general verdict and answer the questions in writing, and must direct the jury to do both.

(2) ***Verdict and Answers Consistent.*** When the general verdict and the answers are consistent, the court must approve, for entry under Rule 58, an appropriate judgment on the verdict and answers.

(3) ***Answers Inconsistent with the Verdict.*** When the answers are consistent with each other but one or more is inconsistent with the general verdict, the court may:

(A) approve, for entry under Rule 58, an appropriate judgment according to the answers, notwithstanding the general verdict;

(B) direct the jury to further consider its answers and verdict; or

(C) order a new trial.

(4) ***Answers Inconsistent with Each Other and the Verdict.*** When the answers are inconsistent with each other and one or more is also inconsistent with the general verdict, judgment must not be entered; instead, the court must direct the jury to further consider its answers and verdict, or must order a new trial.

(Amended January 21, 1963, effective July 1, 1963; March 2, 1987, effective August 1, 1987; April 30, 2007, effective December 1, 2007.)

RULE 50. JUDGMENT AS A MATTER OF LAW IN A JURY TRIAL; RELATED MOTION FOR A NEW TRIAL; CONDITIONAL RULING

(a) Judgment as a Matter of Law.

(1) ***In General.*** If a party has been fully heard on an issue during a jury trial and the court finds that a reasonable jury would not have a legally sufficient evidentiary basis to find for the party on that issue, the court may:

(A) resolve the issue against the party; and

(B) grant a motion for judgment as a matter of law against the party on a claim or defense that, under the controlling law, can be maintained or defeated only with a favorable finding on that issue.

(2) ***Motion.*** A motion for judgment as a matter of law may be made at any time before the case is submitted to the jury. The motion must specify the judgment sought and the law and facts that entitle the movant to the judgment.

(b) Renewing the Motion After Trial; Alternative Motion for a New Trial. If the court does not grant a motion for judgment as a matter of law made under Rule 50(a), the court is considered to have submitted the action to the jury subject to the court's later deciding the legal questions raised by the motion. No later than 28 days after the entry of judgment—or if the motion addresses a jury issue not decided by a verdict, no later than 28 days after the jury was discharged—the movant may file a renewed motion for judgment as a matter of law and may include an alternative or joint request for a new trial under Rule 59. In ruling on the renewed motion, the court may:

(1) allow judgment on the verdict, if the jury returned a verdict;

(2) order a new trial; or

(3) direct the entry of judgment as a matter of law.

(c) Granting the Renewed Motion; Conditional Ruling on a Motion for a New Trial.

(1) ***In General.*** If the court grants a renewed motion for judgment as a matter of law, it must also conditionally rule on any motion for a new trial by determining whether a new trial should be granted if the judgment is later vacated or reversed. The court must state the grounds for conditionally granting or denying the motion for a new trial.

(2) ***Effect of a Conditional Ruling.*** Conditionally granting the motion for a new trial does not affect the judgment's finality; if the judgment is reversed, the new trial must proceed unless the appellate court orders otherwise. If the motion for a new trial is conditionally denied, the appellee may assert error in that denial; if the judgment is reversed, the case must proceed as the appellate court orders.

(d) Time for a Losing Party's New–Trial Motion. Any motion for a new trial under Rule 59 by a party against whom judgment as a matter of law is rendered must be filed no later than 28 days after the entry of the judgment.

(e) Denying the Motion for Judgment as a Matter of Law; Reversal on Appeal. If the court denies the motion for judgment as a matter of law, the prevailing party may, as appellee, assert grounds entitling it to a new trial should the appellate court conclude that the trial court erred in denying the motion. If the appellate court reverses the judgment, it may order a new trial, direct the trial court to determine whether a new trial should be granted, or direct the entry of judgment.

(Amended January 21, 1963, effective July 1, 1963; March 2, 1987, effective August 1, 1987; April 30, 1991, effective December 1, 1991; April 22, 1993, effective December 1, 1993; April 27, 1995, effective December 1, 1995; April 12, 2006, effective December 1, 2006; April 30, 2007, effective December 1, 2007; March 26, 2009, effective December 1, 2009.)

RULE 51. INSTRUCTIONS TO THE JURY; OBJECTIONS; PRESERVING A CLAIM OF ERROR

(a) Requests.

(1) ***Before or at the Close of the Evidence.*** At the close of the evidence or at any earlier reasonable time that the court orders, a party may file and furnish to every other party written requests for the jury instructions it wants the court to give.

(2) ***After the Close of the Evidence.*** After the close of the evidence, a party may:

(A) file requests for instructions on issues that could not reasonably have been anticipated by an earlier time that the court set for requests; and

(B) with the court's permission, file untimely requests for instructions on any issue.

(b) Instructions. The court:

(1) must inform the parties of its proposed instructions and proposed action on the requests before instructing the jury and before final jury arguments;

(2) must give the parties an opportunity to object on the record and out of the jury's hearing before the instructions and arguments are delivered; and

(3) may instruct the jury at any time before the jury is discharged.

(c) Objections.

(1) ***How to Make.*** A party who objects to an instruction or the failure to give an instruction must do so on the record, stating distinctly the matter objected to and the grounds for the objection.

(2) ***When to Make.*** An objection is timely if:

(A) a party objects at the opportunity provided under Rule 51(b)(2); or

(B) a party was not informed of an instruction or action on a request before that opportunity to object, and the party objects promptly after learning that the instruction or request will be, or has been, given or refused.

(d) Assigning Error; Plain Error.

(1) ***Assigning Error.*** A party may assign as error:

(A) an error in an instruction actually given, if that party properly objected; or

(B) a failure to give an instruction, if that party properly requested it and—unless the court rejected the request in a definitive ruling on the record—also properly objected.

(2) ***Plain Error.*** A court may consider a plain error in the instructions that has not been preserved as required by Rule 51(d)(1) if the error affects substantial rights.

(Amended March 2, 1987, effective August 1, 1987; March 27, 2003, effective December 1, 2003; April 30, 2007, effective December 1, 2007.)

RULE 52. FINDINGS AND CONCLUSIONS BY THE COURT; JUDGMENT ON PARTIAL FINDINGS

(a) Findings and Conclusions.

(1) ***In General.*** In an action tried on the facts without a jury or with an advisory jury, the court must find the facts specially and state its conclusions of law separately. The findings and conclusions may be stated on the record after the close of the evidence or may appear in an opinion or a memorandum of decision filed by the court. Judgment must be entered under Rule 58.

(2) ***For an Interlocutory Injunction.*** In granting or refusing an interlocutory injunction, the court must similarly state the findings and conclusions that support its action.

(3) ***For a Motion.*** The court is not required to state findings or conclusions when ruling on a motion under Rule 12 or 56 or, unless these rules provide otherwise, on any other motion.

(4) ***Effect of a Master's Findings.*** A master's findings, to the extent adopted by the court, must be considered the court's findings.

(5) ***Questioning the Evidentiary Support.*** A party may later question the sufficiency of the evidence supporting the findings, whether or not the party requested findings, objected to them, moved to amend them, or moved for partial findings.

(6) ***Setting Aside the Findings.*** Findings of fact, whether based on oral or other evidence, must not be set aside unless clearly erroneous, and the reviewing court must give due regard to the trial court's opportunity to judge the witnesses' credibility.

(b) Amended or Additional Findings. On a party's motion filed no later than 28 days after the entry of judgment, the court may amend its findings—or make additional findings—and may amend the judgment accordingly. The motion may accompany a motion for a new trial under Rule 59.

(c) Judgment on Partial Findings. If a party has been fully heard on an issue during a nonjury trial and the court finds against the party on that issue, the court may enter judgment against the party on a claim or defense that, under the controlling law, can be maintained or defeated only with a favorable finding on that issue. The court may, however, decline to render any judgment until the close of the evidence. A judgment on partial findings must be supported by findings of fact and conclusions of law as required by Rule 52(a).

(Amended December 27, 1946, effective March 19, 1948; January 21, 1963, effective July 1, 1963; April 28, 1983, effective August 1, 1983; April 29, 1985, effective August 1, 1985; April 30, 1991, effective December 1, 1991; April 22, 1993, effective December 1, 1993; April 27, 1995, effective December 1, 1995; April 30, 2007, effective December 1, 2007; March 26, 2009, effective December 1, 2009.)

RULE 53. MASTERS

(a) Appointment.

(1) ***Scope.*** Unless a statute provides otherwise, a court may appoint a master only to:

(A) perform duties consented to by the parties;

(B) hold trial proceedings and make or recommend findings of fact on issues to be decided without a jury if appointment is warranted by:

(i) some exceptional condition; or

(ii) the need to perform an accounting or resolve a difficult computation of damages; or

(C) address pretrial and posttrial matters that cannot be effectively and timely addressed by an available district judge or magistrate judge of the district.

(2) ***Disqualification.*** A master must not have a relationship to the parties, attorneys, action, or court that would require disqualification of a judge under 28 U.S.C. § 455, unless the parties, with the court's approval, consent to the appointment after the master discloses any potential grounds for disqualification.

(3) ***Possible Expense or Delay.*** In appointing a master, the court must consider the fairness of imposing the likely expenses on the parties and must protect against unreasonable expense or delay.

(b) Order Appointing a Master.

(1) ***Notice.*** Before appointing a master, the court must give the parties notice and an opportunity to be heard. Any party may suggest candidates for appointment.

(2) ***Contents.*** The appointing order must direct the master to proceed with all reasonable diligence and must state:

(A) the master's duties, including any investigation or enforcement duties, and any limits on the master's authority under Rule 53(c);

(B) the circumstances, if any, in which the master may communicate ex parte with the court or a party;

(C) the nature of the materials to be preserved and filed as the record of the master's activities;

(D) the time limits, method of filing the record, other procedures, and standards for reviewing the master's orders, findings, and recommendations; and

(E) the basis, terms, and procedure for fixing the master's compensation under Rule 53(g).

(3) ***Issuing.*** The court may issue the order only after:

(A) the master files an affidavit disclosing whether there is any ground for disqualification under 28 U.S.C. § 455; and

(B) if a ground is disclosed, the parties, with the court's approval, waive the disqualification.

(4) ***Amending.*** The order may be amended at any time after notice to the parties and an opportunity to be heard.

(c) Master's Authority.

(1) ***In General.*** Unless the appointing order directs otherwise, a master may:

(A) regulate all proceedings;

(B) take all appropriate measures to perform the assigned duties fairly and efficiently; and

(C) if conducting an evidentiary hearing, exercise the appointing court's power to compel, take, and record evidence.

(2) ***Sanctions.*** The master may by order impose on a party any noncontempt sanction provided by Rule 37 or 45, and may recommend a contempt sanction against a party and sanctions against a nonparty.

(d) Master's Orders. A master who issues an order must file it and promptly serve a copy on each party. The clerk must enter the order on the docket.

(e) Master's Reports. A master must report to the court as required by the appointing order. The master must file the report and promptly serve a copy on each party, unless the court orders otherwise.

(f) Action on the Master's Order, Report, or Recommendations.

(1) ***Opportunity for a Hearing; Action in General.*** In acting on a master's order, report, or recommendations, the court must give the parties notice and an opportunity to be heard; may receive evidence; and may adopt or affirm, modify, wholly or partly reject or reverse, or resubmit to the master with instructions.

(2) ***Time to Object or Move to Adopt or Modify.*** A party may file objections to—or a motion to adopt or modify—the master's order, report, or

recommendations no later than 21 days after a copy is served, unless the court sets a different time.

(3) ***Reviewing Factual Findings.*** The court must decide de novo all objections to findings of fact made or recommended by a master, unless the parties, with the court's approval, stipulate that:

(A) the findings will be reviewed for clear error; or

(B) the findings of a master appointed under Rule 53(a)(1)(A) or (C) will be final.

(4) ***Reviewing Legal Conclusions.*** The court must decide de novo all objections to conclusions of law made or recommended by a master.

(5) ***Reviewing Procedural Matters.*** Unless the appointing order establishes a different standard of review, the court may set aside a master's ruling on a procedural matter only for an abuse of discretion.

(g) **Compensation.**

(1) ***Fixing Compensation.*** Before or after judgment, the court must fix the master's compensation on the basis and terms stated in the appointing order, but the court may set a new basis and terms after giving notice and an opportunity to be heard.

(2) ***Payment.*** The compensation must be paid either:

(A) by a party or parties; or

(B) from a fund or subject matter of the action within the court's control.

(3) ***Allocating Payment.*** The court must allocate payment among the parties after considering the nature and amount of the controversy, the parties' means, and the extent to which any party is more responsible than other parties for the reference to a master. An interim allocation may be amended to reflect a decision on the merits.

(h) **Appointing a Magistrate Judge.** A magistrate judge is subject to this rule only when the order referring a matter to the magistrate judge states that the reference is made under this rule.

(Amended February 28, 1966, effective July 1, 1966; April 28, 1983, effective August 1, 1983; March 2, 1987, effective August 1, 1987; April 30, 1991, effective December 1, 1991; April 22, 1993, effective December 1, 1993; March 27, 2003, effective December 1, 2003; April 30, 2007, effective December 1, 2007; March 26, 2009, effective December 1, 2009.)

TITLE VII. JUDGMENT

RULE 54. JUDGMENT; COSTS

(a) **Definition; Form.** "Judgment" as used in these rules includes a decree and any order from which an appeal lies. A judgment should not include recitals of pleadings, a master's report, or a record of prior proceedings.

(b) **Judgment on Multiple Claims or Involving Multiple Parties.** When an action presents more than one claim for relief—whether as a claim, counterclaim, crossclaim, or third-party claim—or when multiple parties are involved, the court may direct entry of a final judgment as to one or more, but fewer than all, claims or parties only if the court expressly determines that there is no just reason for delay. Otherwise, any order or other decision, however designated, that adjudicates fewer than all the claims or the rights and liabilities of fewer than all the parties does not end the action as to any of the claims or parties and may be revised at any time before the entry of a judgment adjudicating all the claims and all the parties' rights and liabilities.

(c) **Demand for Judgment; Relief to Be Granted.** A default judgment must not differ in kind from, or exceed in amount, what is demanded in the pleadings. Every other final judgment should grant the relief to which each party is entitled, even if the party has not demanded that relief in its pleadings.

(d) **Costs; Attorney's Fees.**

(1) ***Costs Other Than Attorney's Fees.*** Unless a federal statute, these rules, or a court order provides otherwise, costs—other than attorney's fees—should be allowed to the prevailing party. But costs against the United States, its officers, and its agencies may be imposed only to the extent allowed by law. The clerk may tax costs on 14 days' notice. On motion served within the next 7 days, the court may review the clerk's action.

(2) ***Attorney's Fees.***

(A) *Claim to Be by Motion.* A claim for attorney's fees and related nontaxable expenses must be made by motion unless the substantive law requires those fees to be proved at trial as an element of damages.

(B) *Timing and Contents of the Motion.* Unless a statute or a court order provides otherwise, the motion must:

(i) be filed no later than 14 days after the entry of judgment;

(ii) specify the judgment and the statute, rule, or other grounds entitling the movant to the award;

(iii) state the amount sought or provide a fair estimate of it; and

(iv) disclose, if the court so orders, the terms of any agreement about fees for the services for which the claim is made.

(C) *Proceedings.* Subject to Rule 23(h), the court must, on a party's request, give an opportunity for adversary submissions on the motion in accordance with Rule 43(c) or 78. The court may decide issues of liability for fees before receiving submissions on the value of services. The court must find the facts and state its conclusions of law as provided in Rule 52(a).

(D) *Special Procedures by Local Rule; Reference to a Master or a Magistrate Judge.* By local rule, the court may establish special procedures to resolve fee-related issues without extensive evidentiary hearings. Also, the court may refer issues concerning the value of services to a special master under Rule 53 without regard to the limitations of Rule 53(a)(1), and may refer a motion for attorney's fees to a magistrate judge under Rule 72(b) as if it were a dispositive pretrial matter.

(E) *Exceptions.* Subparagraphs (A)-(D) do not apply to claims for fees and expenses as sanctions for violating these rules or as sanctions under 28 U.S.C. § 1927.

(Amended December 27, 1946, effective March 19, 1948; April 17, 1961, effective July 19, 1961; March 2, 1987, effective August 1, 1987; April 22, 1993, effective December 1, 1993; April 29, 2002, effective December 1, 2002; March 27, 2003, effective December 1, 2003; April 30, 2007, effective December 1, 2007; March 26, 2009, effective December 1, 2009.)

RULE 55. DEFAULT; DEFAULT JUDGMENT

(a) Entering a Default. When a party against whom a judgment for affirmative relief is sought has failed to plead or otherwise defend, and that failure is shown by affidavit or otherwise, the clerk must enter the party's default.

(b) Entering a Default Judgment.

(1) ***By the Clerk.*** If the plaintiff's claim is for a sum certain or a sum that can be made certain by computation, the clerk—on the plaintiff's request, with an affidavit showing the amount due—must enter judgment for that amount and costs against a defendant who has been defaulted for not appearing and who is neither a minor nor an incompetent person.

(2) ***By the Court.*** In all other cases, the party must apply to the court for a default judgment. A default judgment may be entered against a minor or incompetent person only if represented by a general guardian, conservator, or other like fiduciary who has appeared. If the party against whom a default judgment is sought has appeared personally or by a representative, that party or its representative must be served with written notice of the application at least 7 days before the hearing. The court may conduct hearings or make referrals—preserving any federal statutory right to a jury trial—when, to enter or effectuate judgment, it needs to:

(A) conduct an accounting;

(B) determine the amount of damages;

(C) establish the truth of any allegation by evidence; or

(D) investigate any other matter.

(c) Setting Aside a Default or a Default Judgment. The court may set aside an entry of default for good cause, and it may set aside a default judgment under Rule 60(b).

(d) Judgment Against the United States. A default judgment may be entered against the United States, its officers, or its agencies only if the claimant establishes a claim or right to relief by evidence that satisfies the court.

(Amended March 2, 1987, effective August 1, 1987; April 30, 2007, effective December 1, 2007; March 26, 2009, effective December 1, 2009.)

RULE 56. SUMMARY JUDGMENT

(a) Motion for Summary Judgment or Partial Summary Judgment. A party may move for summary judgment, identifying each claim or defense—or the part of each claim or defense—on which summary judgment is sought. The court shall grant summary judgment if the movant shows that there is no genuine dispute as to any material fact and the movant is entitled to judgment as a matter of law. The court should state on the record the reasons for granting or denying the motion.

(b) Time to File a Motion. Unless a different time is set by local rule or the court orders otherwise, a party may file a motion for summary judgment at any time until 30 days after the close of all discovery.

(c) Procedures.

(1) ***Supporting Factual Positions.*** A party asserting that a fact cannot be or is genuinely disputed must support the assertion by:

(A) citing to particular parts of materials in the record, including depositions, documents, electronically stored information, affidavits or declarations, stipulations (including those made for purposes of the motion only), admissions, interrogatory answers, or other materials; or

(B) showing that the materials cited do not establish the absence or presence of a genuine dispute, or that an adverse party cannot produce admissible evidence to support the fact.

(2) ***Objection That a Fact Is Not Supported by Admissible Evidence.*** A party may object that the material cited to support or dispute a fact cannot be presented in a form that would be admissible in evidence.

(3) ***Materials Not Cited.*** The court need consider only the cited materials, but it may consider other materials in the record.

(4) ***Affidavits or Declarations.*** An affidavit or declaration used to support or oppose a motion must be made on personal knowledge, set out facts that would be admissible in evidence, and show that the affiant or declarant is competent to testify on the matters stated.

(d) When Facts Are Unavailable to the Nonmovant. If a nonmovant shows by affidavit or declaration that, for specified reasons, it cannot present facts essential to justify its opposition, the court may:

(1) defer considering the motion or deny it;

(2) allow time to obtain affidavits or declarations or to take discovery; or

(3) issue any other appropriate order.

(e) Failing to Properly Support or Address a Fact. If a party fails to properly support an assertion of fact or fails to properly address another party's assertion of fact as required by Rule 56(c), the court may:

(1) give an opportunity to properly support or address the fact;

(2) consider the fact undisputed for purposes of the motion;

(3) grant summary judgment if the motion and supporting materials—including the facts considered undisputed—show that the movant is entitled to it; or

(4) issue any other appropriate order.

(f) Judgment Independent of the Motion. After giving notice and a reasonable time to respond, the court may:

(1) grant summary judgment for a nonmovant;

(2) grant the motion on grounds not raised by a party; or

(3) consider summary judgment on its own after identifying for the parties material facts that may not be genuinely in dispute.

(g) Failing to Grant All the Requested Relief. If the court does not grant all the relief requested by the motion, it may enter an order stating any material fact—including an item of damages or other relief—that is not genuinely in dispute and treating the fact as established in the case.

(h) Affidavit or Declaration Submitted in Bad Faith. If satisfied that an affidavit or declaration under this rule is submitted in bad faith or solely for delay, the court—after notice and a reasonable time to respond—may order the submitting party to pay the other party the reasonable expenses, including attorney's fees, it incurred as a result. An offending party or attorney may also be held in contempt or subjected to other appropriate sanctions.

(Amended December 27, 1946, effective March 19, 1948; January 21, 1963, effective July 1, 1963; March 2, 1987, effective August 1, 1987; April 30, 2007, effective December 1, 2007; March 26, 2009, effective December 1, 2009; April 28, 2010, effective December 1, 2010.)

RULE 57. DECLARATORY JUDGMENT

These rules govern the procedure for obtaining a declaratory judgment under 28 U.S.C. § 2201. Rules 38 and 39 govern a demand for a jury trial. The existence of another adequate remedy does not preclude a declaratory judgment that is otherwise appropriate. The court may order a speedy hearing of a declaratory-judgment action.

(Amended December 29, 1948, effective October 20, 1949; April 30, 2007, effective December 1, 2007.)

RULE 58. ENTERING JUDGMENT

(a) Separate Document. Every judgment and amended judgment must be set out in a separate document, but a separate document is not required for an order disposing of a motion:

(1) for judgment under Rule 50(b);

(2) to amend or make additional findings under Rule 52(b);

(3) for attorney's fees under Rule 54;

(4) for a new trial, or to alter or amend the judgment, under Rule 59; or

(5) for relief under Rule 60.

(b) Entering Judgment.

(1) ***Without the Court's Direction.*** Subject to Rule 54(b) and unless the court orders otherwise, the clerk must, without awaiting the court's direction, promptly prepare, sign, and enter the judgment when:

(A) the jury returns a general verdict;

(B) the court awards only costs or a sum certain; or

(C) the court denies all relief.

(2) ***Court's Approval Required.*** Subject to Rule 54(b), the court must promptly approve the form of the judgment, which the clerk must promptly enter, when:

(A) the jury returns a special verdict or a general verdict with answers to written questions; or

(B) the court grants other relief not described in this subdivision (b).

(c) **Time of Entry.** For purposes of these rules, judgment is entered at the following times:

(1) if a separate document is not required, when the judgment is entered in the civil docket under Rule 79(a); or

(2) if a separate document is required, when the judgment is entered in the civil docket under Rule 79(a) and the earlier of these events occurs:

(A) it is set out in a separate document; or

(B) 150 days have run from the entry in the civil docket.

(d) **Request for Entry.** A party may request that judgment be set out in a separate document as required by Rule 58(a).

(e) **Cost or Fee Awards.** Ordinarily, the entry of judgment may not be delayed, nor the time for appeal extended, in order to tax costs or award fees. But if a timely motion for attorney's fees is made under Rule 54(d)(2), the court may act before a notice of appeal has been filed and become effective to order that the motion have the same effect under Federal Rule of Appellate Procedure 4(a)(4) as a timely motion under Rule 59.

(Amended December 27, 1946, effective March 19, 1948; January 21, 1963, effective July 1, 1963; April 22, 1993, effective December 1, 1993; April 29, 2002, effective December 1, 2002; April 30, 2007, effective December 1, 2007.)

RULE 59. NEW TRIAL; ALTERING OR AMENDING A JUDGMENT

(a) **In General.**

(1) ***Grounds for New Trial.*** The court may, on motion, grant a new trial on all or some of the issues—and to any party—as follows:

(A) after a jury trial, for any reason for which a new trial has heretofore been granted in an action at law in federal court; or

(B) after a nonjury trial, for any reason for which a rehearing has heretofore been granted in a suit in equity in federal court.

(2) ***Further Action After a Nonjury Trial.*** After a nonjury trial, the court may, on motion for a new trial, open the judgment if one has been entered, take additional testimony, amend findings of fact and conclusions of law or make new ones, and direct the entry of a new judgment.

(b) **Time to File a Motion for a New Trial.** A motion for a new trial must be filed no later than 28 days after the entry of judgment.

(c) **Time to Serve Affidavits.** When a motion for a new trial is based on affidavits, they must be filed with the motion. The opposing party has 14 days after being served to file opposing affidavits. The court may permit reply affidavits.

(d) **New Trial on the Court's Initiative or for Reasons Not in the Motion.** No later than 28 days after the entry of judgment, the court, on its own, may order a new trial for any reason that would justify granting one on a party's motion. After giving the parties notice and an opportunity to be heard, the court may grant a timely motion for a new trial for a reason not stated in the motion. In either event, the court must specify the reasons in its order.

(e) **Motion to Alter or Amend a Judgment.** A motion to alter or amend a judgment must be filed no later than 28 days after the entry of the judgment.

(Amended December 27, 1946, effective March 19, 1948; February 28, 1966, effective July 1, 1966; April 27, 1995, effective December 1, 1995; April 30, 2007, effective December 1, 2007; March 26, 2009, effective December 1, 2009.)

RULE 60. RELIEF FROM A JUDGMENT OR ORDER

(a) **Corrections Based on Clerical Mistakes; Oversights and Omissions.** The court may correct a clerical mistake or a mistake arising from oversight or omission whenever one is found in a judgment, order, or other part of the record. The court may do so on motion or on its own, with or without notice. But after an appeal has been docketed in the appellate court and while it is pending, such a mistake may be corrected only with the appellate court's leave.

(b) **Grounds for Relief from a Final Judgment, Order, or Proceeding.** On motion and just terms, the court may relieve a party or its legal representative from a final judgment, order, or proceeding for the following reasons:

(1) mistake, inadvertence, surprise, or excusable neglect;

(2) newly discovered evidence that, with reasonable diligence, could not have been discovered in time to move for a new trial under Rule 59(b);

(3) fraud (whether previously called intrinsic or extrinsic), misrepresentation, or misconduct by an opposing party;

(4) the judgment is void;

(5) the judgment has been satisfied, released or discharged; it is based on an earlier judgment that has been reversed or vacated; or applying it prospectively is no longer equitable; or

(6) any other reason that justifies relief.

(c) Timing and Effect of the Motion.

(1) ***Timing.*** A motion under Rule 60(b) must be made within a reasonable time—and for reasons (1), (2), and (3) no more than a year after the entry of the judgment or order or the date of the proceeding.

(2) ***Effect on Finality.*** The motion does not affect the judgment's finality or suspend its operation.

(d) Other Powers to Grant Relief. This rule does not limit a court's power to:

(1) entertain an independent action to relieve a party from a judgment, order, or proceeding;

(2) grant relief under 28 U.S.C. § 1655 to a defendant who was not personally notified of the action; or

(3) set aside a judgment for fraud on the court.

(e) Bills and Writs Abolished. The following are abolished: bills of review, bills in the nature of bills of review, and writs of coram nobis, coram vobis, and audita querela.

(Amended December 27, 1946, effective March 19, 1948; December 29, 1948, effective October 20, 1949; March 2, 1987, effective August 1, 1987; April 30, 2007, effective December 1, 2007.)

RULE 61. HARMLESS ERROR

Unless justice requires otherwise, no error in admitting or excluding evidence—or any other error by the court or a party—is ground for granting a new trial, for setting aside a verdict, or for vacating, modifying, or otherwise disturbing a judgment or order. At every stage of the proceeding, the court must disregard all errors and defects that do not affect any party's substantial rights.

(Amended April 30, 2007, effective December 1, 2007.)

RULE 62. STAY OF PROCEEDINGS TO ENFORCE A JUDGMENT

(a) Automatic Stay; Exceptions for Injunctions, Receiverships, and Patent Accountings. Except as stated in this rule, no execution may issue on a judgment, nor may proceedings be taken to enforce it, until 14 days have passed after its entry. But unless the court orders otherwise, the following are not stayed after being entered, even if an appeal is taken:

(1) an interlocutory or final judgment in an action for an injunction or a receivership; or

(2) a judgment or order that directs an accounting in an action for patent infringement.

(b) Stay Pending the Disposition of a Motion. On appropriate terms for the opposing party's security, the court may stay the execution of a judgment—or any proceedings to enforce it—pending disposition of any of the following motions:

(1) under Rule 50, for judgment as a matter of law;

(2) under Rule 52(b), to amend the findings or for additional findings;

(3) under Rule 59, for a new trial or to alter or amend a judgment; or

(4) under Rule 60, for relief from a judgment or order.

(c) Injunction Pending an Appeal. While an appeal is pending from an interlocutory order or final judgment that grants, dissolves, or denies an injunction, the court may suspend, modify, restore, or grant an injunction on terms for bond or other terms that secure the opposing party's rights. If the judgment appealed from is rendered by a statutory three-judge district court, the order must be made either:

(1) by that court sitting in open session; or

(2) by the assent of all its judges, as evidenced by their signatures.

(d) Stay with Bond on Appeal. If an appeal is taken, the appellant may obtain a stay by supersedeas bond, except in an action described in Rule 62(a)(1) or (2). The bond may be given upon or after filing the notice of appeal or after obtaining the order allowing the appeal. The stay takes effect when the court approves the bond.

(e) Stay Without Bond on an Appeal by the United States, Its Officers, or Its Agencies. The court must not require a bond, obligation, or other security from the appellant when granting a stay on an appeal by the United States, its officers, or its agencies or on an appeal directed by a department of the federal government.

(f) Stay in Favor of a Judgment Debtor Under State Law. If a judgment is a lien on the judgment debtor's property under the law of the state where the court is located, the judgment debtor is entitled to the same stay of execution the state court would give.

(g) Appellate Court's Power Not Limited. This rule does not limit the power of the appellate court or one of its judges or justices:

(1) to stay proceedings—or suspend, modify, restore, or grant an injunction—while an appeal is pending; or

(2) to issue an order to preserve the status quo or the effectiveness of the judgment to be entered.

(h) **Stay with Multiple Claims or Parties.** A court may stay the enforcement of a final judgment entered under Rule 54(b) until it enters a later judgment or judgments, and may prescribe terms necessary to secure the benefit of the stayed judgment for the party in whose favor it was entered.

(Amended December 27, 1946, effective March 19, 1948; December 29, 1948, effective October 20, 1949; April 17, 1961, effective July 19, 1961; March 2, 1987, effective August 1, 1987; April 30, 2007, effective December 1, 2007; March 26, 2009, effective December 1, 2009.)

RULE 62.1. INDICATIVE RULING ON A MOTION FOR RELIEF THAT IS BARRED BY A PENDING APPEAL

(a) **Relief Pending Appeal.** If a timely motion is made for relief that the court lacks authority to grant because of an appeal that has been docketed and is pending, the court may:

(1) defer considering the motion;

(2) deny the motion; or

(3) state either that it would grant the motion if the court of appeals remands for that purpose or that the motion raises a substantial issue.

(b) **Notice to the Court of Appeals.** The movant must promptly notify the circuit clerk under Federal Rule of Appellate Procedure 12.1 if the district court states that it would grant the motion or that the motion raises a substantial issue.

(c) **Remand.** The district court may decide the motion if the court of appeals remands for that purpose.

(Added March 26, 2009, effective December 1, 2009.)

RULE 63. JUDGE'S INABILITY TO PROCEED

If a judge conducting a hearing or trial is unable to proceed, any other judge may proceed upon certifying familiarity with the record and determining that the case may be completed without prejudice to the parties. In a hearing or a nonjury trial, the successor judge must, at a party's request, recall any witness whose testimony is material and disputed and who is available to testify again without undue burden. The successor judge may also recall any other witness.

(Amended March 2, 1987, effective August 1, 1987; April 30, 1991, effective December 1, 1991; April 30, 2007, effective December 1, 2007.)

TITLE VIII. PROVISIONAL AND FINAL REMEDIES

RULE 64. SEIZING A PERSON OR PROPERTY

(a) **Remedies Under State Law—In General.** At the commencement of and throughout an action, every remedy is available that, under the law of the state where the court is located, provides for seizing a person or property to secure satisfaction of the potential judgment. But a federal statute governs to the extent it applies.

(b) **Specific Kinds of Remedies.** The remedies available under this rule include the following—however designated and regardless of whether state procedure requires an independent action:

- arrest;
- attachment;
- garnishment;
- replevin;
- sequestration; and
- other corresponding or equivalent remedies.

(Amended April 30, 2007, effective December 1, 2007.)

RULE 65. INJUNCTIONS AND RESTRAINING ORDERS

(a) **Preliminary Injunction.**

(1) ***Notice.*** The court may issue a preliminary injunction only on notice to the adverse party.

(2) ***Consolidating the Hearing with the Trial on the Merits.*** Before or after beginning the hearing on a motion for a preliminary injunction, the court may advance the trial on the merits and consolidate it with the hearing. Even when consolidation is not ordered, evidence that is received on the motion and that would be admissible at trial becomes part of the trial record and need not be repeated at trial. But the court must preserve any party's right to a jury trial.

(b) **Temporary Restraining Order.**

(1) ***Issuing Without Notice.*** The court may issue a temporary restraining order without written or oral notice to the adverse party or its attorney only if:

(A) specific facts in an affidavit or a verified complaint clearly show that immediate and irreparable injury, loss, or damage will result to the movant before the adverse party can be heard in opposition; and

(B) the movant's attorney certifies in writing any efforts made to give notice and the reasons why it should not be required.

(2) ***Contents; Expiration.*** Every temporary restraining order issued without notice must state the date and hour it was issued; describe the injury and state why it is irreparable; state why the order was issued without notice; and be promptly filed in the clerk's office and entered in the record. The order expires at the time after entry—not to exceed 14 days—that the court sets, unless before that time the court, for good cause, extends it for a like period or the adverse party consents to a longer extension. The reasons for an extension must be entered in the record.

(3) ***Expediting the Preliminary-Injunction Hearing.*** If the order is issued without notice, the motion for a preliminary injunction must be set for hearing at the earliest possible time, taking precedence over all other matters except hearings on older matters of the same character. At the hearing, the party who obtained the order must proceed with the motion; if the party does not, the court must dissolve the order.

(4) ***Motion to Dissolve.*** On 2 days' notice to the party who obtained the order without notice—or on shorter notice set by the court—the adverse party may appear and move to dissolve or modify the order. The court must then hear and decide the motion as promptly as justice requires.

(c) **Security.** The court may issue a preliminary injunction or a temporary restraining order only if the movant gives security in an amount that the court considers proper to pay the costs and damages sustained by any party found to have been wrongfully enjoined or restrained. The United States, its officers, and its agencies are not required to give security.

(d) **Contents and Scope of Every Injunction and Restraining Order.**

(1) ***Contents.*** Every order granting an injunction and every restraining order must:

(A) state the reasons why it issued;

(B) state its terms specifically; and

(C) describe in reasonable detail—and not by referring to the complaint or other document—the act or acts restrained or required.

(2) ***Persons Bound.*** The order binds only the following who receive actual notice of it by personal service or otherwise:

(A) the parties;

(B) the parties' officers, agents, servants, employees, and attorneys; and

(C) other persons who are in active concert or participation with anyone described in Rule 65(d)(2)(A) or (B).

(e) **Other Laws Not Modified.** These rules do not modify the following:

(1) any federal statute relating to temporary restraining orders or preliminary injunctions in actions affecting employer and employee;

(2) 28 U.S.C. § 2361, which relates to preliminary injunctions in actions of interpleader or in the nature of interpleader; or

(3) 28 U.S.C. § 2284, which relates to actions that must be heard and decided by a three-judge district court.

(f) **Copyright Impoundment.** This rule applies to copyright-impoundment proceedings.

(Amended December 27, 1946, effective March 19, 1948; December 29, 1948, effective October 20, 1949; February 28, 1966, effective July 1, 1966; March 2, 1987, effective August 1, 1987; April 23, 2001, effective December 1, 2001; April 30, 2007, effective December 1, 2007; March 26, 2009, effective December 1, 2009.)

RULE 65.1. PROCEEDINGS AGAINST A SURETY

Whenever these rules (including the Supplemental Rules for Admiralty or Maritime Claims and Asset Forfeiture Actions) require or allow a party to give security, and security is given through a bond or other undertaking with one or more sureties, each surety submits to the court's jurisdiction and irrevocably appoints the court clerk as its agent for receiving service of any papers that affect its liability on the bond or undertaking. The surety's liability may be enforced on motion without an independent action. The motion and any notice that the court orders may be served on the court clerk, who must promptly mail a copy of each to every surety whose address is known.

(Adopted February 28, 1966, effective July 1, 1966; amended March 2, 1987, effective August 1, 1987; April 12, 2006, effective December 1, 2006; April 30, 2007, effective December 1, 2007.)

RULE 66. RECEIVERS

These rules govern an action in which the appointment of a receiver is sought or a receiver sues or is sued. But the practice in administering an estate by a receiver or a similar court-appointed officer must accord with the historical practice in federal courts or with a local rule. An action in which a receiver has been appointed may be dismissed only by court order.

(Amended December 27, 1946, effective March 19, 1948; December 29, 1948, effective October 20, 1949; April 30, 2007, effective December 1, 2007.)

RULE 67. DEPOSIT INTO COURT

(a) Depositing Property. If any part of the relief sought is a money judgment or the disposition of a sum of money or some other deliverable thing, a party—on notice to every other party and by leave of court—may deposit with the court all or part of the money or thing, whether or not that party claims any of it. The depositing party must deliver to the clerk a copy of the order permitting deposit.

(b) Investing and Withdrawing Funds. Money paid into court under this rule must be deposited and withdrawn in accordance with 28 U.S.C. §§ 2041 and 2042 and any like statute. The money must be deposited in an interest-bearing account or invested in a court-approved, interest-bearing instrument.

(Amended December 29, 1948, effective October 20, 1949; April 28, 1983, effective August 1, 1983; April 30, 2007, effective December 1, 2007.)

RULE 68. OFFER OF JUDGMENT

(a) Making an Offer; Judgment on an Accepted Offer. At least 14 days before the date set for trial, a party defending against a claim may serve on an opposing party an offer to allow judgment on specified terms, with the costs then accrued. If, within 14 days after being served, the opposing party serves written notice accepting the offer, either party may then file the offer and notice of acceptance, plus proof of service. The clerk must then enter judgment.

(b) Unaccepted Offer. An unaccepted offer is considered withdrawn, but it does not preclude a later offer. Evidence of an unaccepted offer is not admissible except in a proceeding to determine costs.

(c) Offer After Liability is Determined. When one party's liability to another has been determined but the extent of liability remains to be determined by further proceedings, the party held liable may make an offer of judgment. It must be served within a reasonable time—but at least 14 days—before the date set for a hearing to determine the extent of liability.

(d) Paying Costs After an Unaccepted Offer. If the judgment that the offeree finally obtains is not more favorable than the unaccepted offer, the offeree must pay the costs incurred after the offer was made.

(Amended December 27, 1946, effective March 19, 1948; February 28, 1966, effective July 1, 1966; March 2, 1987, effective August 1, 1987; April 30, 2007, effective December 1, 2007; March 26, 2009, effective December 1, 2009.)

RULE 69. EXECUTION

(a) In General.

(1) ***Money Judgment; Applicable Procedure.*** A money judgment is enforced by a writ of execution, unless the court directs otherwise. The procedure on execution—and in proceedings supplementary to and in aid of judgment or execution—must accord with the procedure of the state where the court is located, but a federal statute governs to the extent it applies.

(2) ***Obtaining Discovery.*** In aid of the judgment or execution, the judgment creditor or a successor in interest whose interest appears of record may obtain discovery from any person—including the judgment debtor—as provided in these rules or by the procedure of the state where the court is located.

(b) Against Certain Public Officers. When a judgment has been entered against a revenue officer in the circumstances stated in 28 U.S.C. § 2006, or against an officer of Congress in the circumstances stated in 2 U.S.C. § 118, the judgment must be satisfied as those statutes provide.

(Amended December 29, 1948, effective October 20, 1949; March 30, 1970, effective July 1, 1970; March 2, 1987 effective August 1, 1987; April 30, 2007, effective December 1, 2007.)

RULE 70. ENFORCING A JUDGMENT FOR A SPECIFIC ACT

(a) Party's Failure to Act; Ordering Another to Act. If a judgment requires a party to convey land, to deliver a deed or other document, or to perform any other specific act and the party fails to comply within the time specified, the court may order the act to be done—at the disobedient party's expense—by another person appointed by the court. When done, the act has the same effect as if done by the party.

(b) Vesting Title. If the real or personal property is within the district, the court—instead of ordering a conveyance—may enter a judgment divesting any party's title and vesting it in others. That judgment has the effect of a legally executed conveyance.

(c) Obtaining a Writ of Attachment or Sequestration. On application by a party entitled to performance of an act, the clerk must issue a writ of attachment or sequestration against the disobedient party's property to compel obedience.

(d) Obtaining a Writ of Execution or Assistance. On application by a party who obtains a judgment or order for possession, the clerk must issue a writ of execution or assistance.

(e) Holding in Contempt. The court may also hold the disobedient party in contempt.

(Amended April 30, 2007, effective December 1, 2007.)

RULE 71. ENFORCING RELIEF FOR OR AGAINST A NONPARTY

When an order grants relief for a nonparty or may be enforced against a nonparty, the procedure for enforcing the order is the same as for a party.

(Amended March 2, 1987, effective August 1, 1987; April 30, 2007, effective December 1, 2007.)

TITLE IX. SPECIAL PROCEEDINGS

RULE 71.1. CONDEMNING REAL OR PERSONAL PROPERTY

(a) Applicability of Other Rules. These rules govern proceedings to condemn real and personal property by eminent domain, except as this rule provides otherwise.

(b) Joinder of Properties. The plaintiff may join separate pieces of property in a single action, no matter whether they are owned by the same persons or sought for the same use.

(c) Complaint.

(1) ***Caption.*** The complaint must contain a caption as provided in Rule 10(a). The plaintiff must, however, name as defendants both the property—designated generally by kind, quantity, and location—and at least one owner of some part of or interest in the property.

(2) ***Contents.*** The complaint must contain a short and plain statement of the following:

(A) the authority for the taking;

(B) the uses for which the property is to be taken;

(C) a description sufficient to identify the property;

(D) the interests to be acquired; and

(E) for each piece of property, a designation of each defendant who has been joined as an owner or owner of an interest in it.

(3) ***Parties.*** When the action commences, the plaintiff need join as defendants only those persons who have or claim an interest in the property and whose names are then known. But before any hearing on compensation, the plaintiff must add as defendants all those persons who have or claim an interest and whose names have become known or can be found by a reasonably diligent search of the records, considering both the property's character and value and the interests to be acquired. All others may be made defendants under the designation "Unknown Owners."

(4) ***Procedure.*** Notice must be served on all defendants as provided in Rule 71.1(d), whether they were named as defendants when the action commenced or were added later. A defendant may answer as provided in Rule 71.1(e). The court, meanwhile, may order any distribution of a deposit that the facts warrant.

(5) ***Filing; Additional Copies.*** In addition to filing the complaint, the plaintiff must give the clerk at least one copy for the defendants' use and additional copies at the request of the clerk or a defendant.

(d) Process.

(1) ***Delivering Notice to the Clerk.*** On filing a complaint, the plaintiff must promptly deliver to the clerk joint or several notices directed to the named defendants. When adding defendants, the plaintiff must deliver to the clerk additional notices directed to the new defendants.

(2) ***Contents of the Notice.***

(A) *Main Contents.* Each notice must name the court, the title of the action, and the defendant to whom it is directed. It must describe the property sufficiently to identify it, but need not describe any property other than that to be taken from the named defendant. The notice must also state:

(i) that the action is to condemn property;

(ii) the interest to be taken;

(iii) the authority for the taking;

(iv) the uses for which the property is to be taken;

(v) that the defendant may serve an answer on the plaintiff's attorney within 21 days after being served with the notice;

(vi) that the failure to so serve an answer constitutes consent to the taking and to the court's authority to proceed with the action and fix the compensation; and

(vii) that a defendant who does not serve an answer may file a notice of appearance.

(B) *Conclusion.* The notice must conclude with the name, telephone number, and e-mail address of the plaintiff's attorney and an address within the district in which the action is brought where the attorney may be served.

(3) ***Serving the Notice.***

(A) *Personal Service.* When a defendant whose address is known resides within the United States or a territory subject to the administrative or judicial jurisdiction of the United States, personal service of the notice (without a copy of the complaint) must be made in accordance with Rule 4.

(B) *Service by Publication.*

(i) A defendant may be served by publication only when the plaintiff's attorney files a certificate stating that the attorney believes the defendant cannot be personally served, because after diligent inquiry within the state where the complaint is filed, the defendant's place of residence is still unknown or, if known, that it is beyond the territorial limits of personal service. Service is then made by publishing the notice—once a week for at least 3 successive weeks—in a newspaper published in the county where the property is located or, if there is no such newspaper, in a newspaper with general circulation where the property is located. Before the last publication, a copy of the notice must also be mailed to every defendant who cannot be personally served but whose place of residence is then known. Unknown owners may be served by publication in the same manner by a notice addressed to "Unknown Owners."

(ii) Service by publication is complete on the date of the last publication. The plaintiff's attorney must prove publication and mailing by a certificate, attach a printed copy of the published notice, and mark on the copy the newspaper's name and the dates of publication.

(4) ***Effect of Delivery and Service.*** Delivering the notice to the clerk and serving it have the same effect as serving a summons under Rule 4.

(5) ***Amending the Notice; Proof of Service and Amending the Proof.*** Rule 4(a)(2) governs amending the notice. Rule 4(*l*) governs proof of service and amending it.

(e) Appearance or Answer.

(1) ***Notice of Appearance.*** A defendant that has no objection or defense to the taking of its property may serve a notice of appearance designating the property in which it claims an interest. The defendant must then be given notice of all later proceedings affecting the defendant.

(2) ***Answer.*** A defendant that has an objection or defense to the taking must serve an answer within 21 days after being served with the notice. The answer must:

(A) identify the property in which the defendant claims an interest;

(B) state the nature and extent of the interest; and

(C) state all the defendant's objections and defenses to the taking.

(3) ***Waiver of Other Objections and Defenses; Evidence on Compensation.*** A defendant waives all objections and defenses not stated in its answer. No other pleading or motion asserting an additional objection or defense is allowed. But at the trial on compensation, a defendant—whether or not it has previously appeared or answered—may present evidence on the amount of compensation to be paid and may share in the award.

(f) Amending Pleadings. Without leave of court, the plaintiff may—as often as it wants—amend the complaint at any time before the trial on compensation. But no amendment may be made if it would result in a dismissal inconsistent with Rule 71.1(i)(1) or (2). The plaintiff need not serve a copy of an amendment, but must serve notice of the filing, as provided in Rule 5(b), on every affected party who has appeared and, as provided in Rule 71.1(d), on every affected party who has not appeared. In addition, the plaintiff must give the clerk at least one copy of each amendment for the defendants' use, and additional copies at the request of the clerk or a defendant. A defendant may appear or answer in the time and manner and with the same effect as provided in Rule 71.1(e).

(g) Substituting Parties. If a defendant dies, becomes incompetent, or transfers an interest after being joined, the court may, on motion and notice of hearing, order that the proper party be substituted. Service of the motion and notice on a nonparty must be made as provided in Rule 71.1(d)(3).

(h) Trial of the Issues.

(1) ***Issues Other Than Compensation; Compensation.*** In an action involving eminent domain under federal law, the court tries all issues, including compensation, except when compensation must be determined:

(A) by any tribunal specially constituted by a federal statute to determine compensation; or

(B) if there is no such tribunal, by a jury when a party demands one within the time to answer or within any additional time the court sets, unless the court appoints a commission.

(2) ***Appointing a Commission; Commission's Powers and Report.***

(A) *Reasons for Appointing.* If a party has demanded a jury, the court may instead appoint a three-person commission to determine compensation because of the character, location, or quantity of the property to be condemned or for other just reasons.

(B) *Alternate Commissioners.* The court may appoint up to two additional persons to serve as alternate commissioners to hear the case and replace commissioners who, before a decision is filed, the court finds unable or disqualified to perform their duties. Once the commission renders its final decision, the court must discharge any alternate who has not replaced a commissioner.

(C) *Examining the Prospective Commissioners.* Before making its appointments, the court must advise the parties of the identity and qualifications of each prospective commissioner and alternate, and may permit the parties to examine them. The parties may not suggest appointees, but for good cause may object to a prospective commissioner or alternate.

(D) *Commission's Powers and Report.* A commission has the powers of a master under Rule 53(c). Its action and report are determined by a majority. Rule 53(d), (e), and (f) apply to its action and report.

(i) Dismissal of the Action or a Defendant.

(1) ***Dismissing the Action.***

(A) *By the Plaintiff.* If no compensation hearing on a piece of property has begun, and if the plaintiff has not acquired title or a lesser interest or taken possession, the plaintiff may, without a court order, dismiss the action as to that property by filing a notice of dismissal briefly describing the property.

(B) *By Stipulation.* Before a judgment is entered vesting the plaintiff with title or a lesser interest in or possession of property, the plaintiff and affected defendants may, without a court order, dismiss the action in whole or in part by filing a stipulation of dismissal. And if the parties so stipulate, the court may vacate a judgment already entered.

(C) *By Court Order.* At any time before compensation has been determined and paid, the court may, after a motion and hearing, dismiss the action as to a piece of property. But if the plaintiff has already taken title, a lesser interest, or possession as to any part of it, the court must award compensation for the title, lesser interest, or possession taken.

(2) ***Dismissing a Defendant.*** The court may at any time dismiss a defendant who was unnecessarily or improperly joined.

(3) ***Effect.*** A dismissal is without prejudice unless otherwise stated in the notice, stipulation, or court order.

(j) Deposit and Its Distribution.

(1) ***Deposit.*** The plaintiff must deposit with the court any money required by law as a condition to the exercise of eminent domain and may make a deposit when allowed by statute.

(2) ***Distribution; Adjusting Distribution.*** After a deposit, the court and attorneys must expedite the proceedings so as to distribute the deposit and to determine and pay compensation. If the compensation finally awarded to a defendant exceeds the amount distributed to that defendant, the court must enter judgment against the plaintiff for the deficiency. If the compensation awarded to a defendant is less than the amount distributed to that defendant, the court must enter judgment against that defendant for the overpayment.

(k) Condemnation Under a State's Power of Eminent Domain. This rule governs an action involving eminent domain under state law. But if state law provides for trying an issue by jury—or for trying the issue of compensation by jury or commission or both—that law governs.

(*l*) Costs. Costs are not subject to Rule 54(d).

(Adopted April 30, 1951, effective August 1, 1951; amended January 21, 1963, effective July 1, 1963; April 29, 1985, effective August 1, 1985; March 2, 1987, effective August 1, 1987; April 25, 1988, effective August 1, 1988; amended by Pub.L. 100–690, Title VII, § 7050, November 18, 1988, 102 Stat. 4401 (although amendment by Pub.L. 100–690 could not be executed due to prior amendment by Court order which made the same change effective August 1, 1988); amended April 22, 1993, effective December 1, 1993; March 27, 2003, effective December 1, 2003; April 30, 2007, effective December 1, 2007; March 26, 2009, effective December 1, 2009.)

RULE 72. MAGISTRATE JUDGES: PRETRIAL ORDER

(a) Nondispositive Matters. When a pretrial matter not dispositive of a party's claim or defense is referred to a magistrate judge to hear and decide, the magistrate judge must promptly conduct the required proceedings and, when appropriate, issue a written order stating the decision. A party may serve and file objections to the order within 14 days after being served with a copy. A party may not assign as error a defect in the order not timely objected to. The district judge in the case must consider timely objections and modify or set aside any part of the order that is clearly erroneous or is contrary to law.

(b) Dispositive Motions and Prisoner Petitions.

(1) ***Findings and Recommendations.*** A magistrate judge must promptly conduct the required proceedings when assigned, without the parties' consent, to hear a pretrial matter dispositive of a claim or defense or a prisoner petition challenging the conditions of confinement. A record must be made of all evidentiary proceedings and may, at the magistrate judge's discretion, be made of any other proceedings. The magistrate judge must enter a recommended disposition, including, if appropriate, proposed findings of fact. The clerk must promptly mail a copy to each party.

(2) ***Objections.*** Within 14 days after being served with a copy of the recommended disposition, a party may serve and file specific written objections to the proposed findings and recommendations. A party may respond to another party's objections within 14 days after being served with a copy. Unless the district judge orders otherwise, the objecting party must promptly arrange for transcribing the record, or whatever portions of it the parties agree to or the magistrate judge considers sufficient.

(3) ***Resolving Objections.*** The district judge must determine de novo any part of the magistrate judge's disposition that has been properly objected to. The district judge may accept, reject, or modify the recommended disposition; receive further evidence; or return the matter to the magistrate judge with instructions.

(Former Rule 72 abrogated December 4, 1967, effective July 1, 1968; new Rule 72 adopted April 28, 1983, effective August 1, 1983; amended April 30, 1991, effective December 1, 1991; April 22, 1993, effective December 1, 1993; April 30, 2007, effective December 1, 2007; March 26, 2009, effective December 1, 2009.)

RULE 73. MAGISTRATE JUDGES: TRIAL BY CONSENT; APPEAL

(a) Trial by Consent. When authorized under 28 U.S.C. § 636(c), a magistrate judge may, if all parties consent, conduct a civil action or proceeding, including a jury or nonjury trial. A record must be made in accordance with 28 U.S.C. § 636(c)(5).

(b) Consent Procedure.

(1) ***In General.*** When a magistrate judge has been designated to conduct civil actions or proceedings, the clerk must give the parties written notice of their opportunity to consent under 28 U.S.C. § 636(c). To signify their consent, the parties must jointly or separately file a statement consenting to the referral. A district judge or magistrate judge may be informed of a party's response to the clerk's notice only if all parties have consented to the referral.

(2) ***Reminding the Parties About Consenting.*** A district judge, magistrate judge, or other court official may remind the parties of the magistrate judge's availability, but must also advise them that they are free to withhold consent without adverse substantive consequences.

(3) ***Vacating a Referral.*** On its own for good cause—or when a party shows extraordinary circumstances—the district judge may vacate a referral to a magistrate judge under this rule.

(c) Appealing a Judgment. In accordance with 28 U.S.C. § 636(c)(3), an appeal from a judgment entered at a magistrate judge's direction may be taken to the court of appeals as would any other appeal from a district court judgment.

(Former Rule 73 abrogated December 4, 1967, effective July 1, 1968; new Rule 73 adopted April 28, 1983, effective August 1, 1983; amended March 2, 1987, effective August 1, 1987; April 22, 1993, effective December 1, 1993; April 11, 1997, effective December 1, 1997; April 30, 2007, effective December 1, 2007.)

RULE 74. METHOD OF APPEAL FROM MAGISTRATE JUDGE TO DISTRICT JUDGE UNDER TITLE 28, U.S.C. § 636(c)(4) AND RULE 73(d) [ABROGATED]

(Former Rule 74 abrogated December 4, 1967, effective July 1, 1968; new Rule 74 adopted April 28, 1983, effective August 1, 1983; amended April 22, 1993, effective December 1, 1993; abrogated April 11, 1997, effective December 1, 1997; April 30, 2007, effective December 1, 2007.)

RULE 75. PROCEEDINGS ON APPEAL FROM MAGISTRATE JUDGE TO DISTRICT JUDGE UNDER RULE 73(d) [ABROGATED]

(Former Rule 75 abrogated December 4, 1967, effective July 1, 1968; new Rule 75 adopted April 28, 1983, effective August 1, 1983; amended March 2, 1987, effective August 1, 1987; April 22, 1993, effective December 1, 1993; abrogated April 11, 1997, effective December 1, 1997; April 30, 2007, effective December 1, 2007.)

RULE 76. JUDGMENT OF THE DISTRICT JUDGE ON THE APPEAL UNDER RULE 73(d) AND COSTS [ABROGATED]

(Former Rule 76 abrogated December 4, 1967, effective July 1, 1968; new Rule 76 adopted April 28, 1983, effective August 1, 1983; amended April 22, 1993, effective December 1, 1993;

abrogated April 11, 1997, effective December 1, 1997; April 30, 2007, effective December 1, 2007.)

TITLE X. DISTRICT COURTS AND CLERKS: CONDUCTING BUSINESS; ISSUING ORDERS

RULE 77. CONDUCTING BUSINESS; CLERK'S AUTHORITY; NOTICE OF AN ORDER OR JUDGMENT

(a) When Court Is Open. Every district court is considered always open for filing any paper, issuing and returning process, making a motion, or entering an order.

(b) Place for Trial and Other Proceedings. Every trial on the merits must be conducted in open court and, so far as convenient, in a regular courtroom. Any other act or proceeding may be done or conducted by a judge in chambers, without the attendance of the clerk or other court official, and anywhere inside or outside the district. But no hearing—other than one ex parte—may be conducted outside the district unless all the affected parties consent.

(c) Clerk's Office Hours; Clerk's Orders.

(1) ***Hours.*** The clerk's office—with a clerk or deputy on duty—must be open during business hours every day except Saturdays, Sundays, and legal holidays. But a court may, by local rule or order, require that the office be open for specified hours on Saturday or a particular legal holiday other than one listed in Rule 6(a)(4)(A).

(2) ***Orders.*** Subject to the court's power to suspend, alter, or rescind the clerk's action for good cause, the clerk may:

(A) issue process;

(B) enter a default;

(C) enter a default judgment under Rule 55(b)(1); and

(D) act on any other matter that does not require the court's action.

(d) Serving Notice of an Order or Judgment.

(1) ***Service.*** Immediately after entering an order or judgment, the clerk must serve notice of the entry, as provided in Rule 5(b), on each party who is not in default for failing to appear. The clerk must record the service on the docket. A party also may serve notice of the entry as provided in Rule 5(b).

(2) ***Time to Appeal Not Affected by Lack of Notice.*** Lack of notice of the entry does not affect the time for appeal or relieve—or authorize the court to relieve—a party for failing to appeal within the time allowed, except as allowed by Federal Rule of Appellate Procedure (4)(a).

(Amended December 27, 1946, effective March 19, 1948; January 21, 1963, effective July 1, 1963; December 4, 1967, effective July 1, 1968; March 1, 1971, effective July 1, 1971; March 2, 1987, effective August 1, 1987; April 30, 1991, effective December 1, 1991; April 23, 2001, effective December 1, 2001; April 30, 2007, effective December 1, 2007.)

RULE 78. HEARING MOTIONS; SUBMISSION ON BRIEFS

(a) Providing a Regular Schedule for Oral Hearings. A court may establish regular times and places for oral hearings on motions.

(b) Providing for Submission on Briefs. By rule or order, the court may provide for submitting and determining motions on briefs, without oral hearings.

(Amended March 2, 1987, effective August 1, 1987; April 30, 2007, effective December 1, 2007.)

RULE 79. RECORDS KEPT BY THE CLERK

(a) Civil Docket.

(1) ***In General.*** The clerk must keep a record known as the "civil docket" in the form and manner prescribed by the Director of the Administrative Office of the United States Courts with the approval of the Judicial Conference of the United States. The clerk must enter each civil action in the docket. Actions must be assigned consecutive file numbers, which must be noted in the docket where the first entry of the action is made.

(2) ***Items to be Entered.*** The following items must be marked with the file number and entered chronologically in the docket:

(A) papers filed with the clerk;

(B) process issued, and proofs of service or other returns showing execution; and

(C) appearances, orders, verdicts, and judgments.

(3) ***Contents of Entries; Jury Trial Demanded.*** Each entry must briefly show the nature of the paper filed or writ issued, the substance of each proof of service or other return, and the sub-

stance and date of entry of each order and judgment. When a jury trial has been properly demanded or ordered, the clerk must enter the word "jury" in the docket.

(b) Civil Judgments and Orders. The clerk must keep a copy of every final judgment and appealable order; of every order affecting title to or a lien on real or personal property; and of any other order that the court directs to be kept. The clerk must keep these in the form and manner prescribed by the Director of the Administrative Office of the United States Courts with the approval of the Judicial Conference of the United States.

(c) Indexes; Calendars. Under the court's direction, the clerk must:

(1) keep indexes of the docket and of the judgments and orders described in Rule 79(b); and

(2) prepare calendars of all actions ready for trial, distinguishing jury trials from nonjury trials.

(d) Other Records. The clerk must keep any other records required by the Director of the Administrative Office of the United States Courts with the approval of the Judicial Conference of the United States.

(Amended December 27, 1946, effective March 19, 1948; December 29, 1948, effective October 20, 1949; January 21, 1963, effective July 1, 1963; April 30, 2007, effective December 1, 2007.)

RULE 80. STENOGRAPHIC TRANSCRIPT AS EVIDENCE

If stenographically reported testimony at a hearing or trial is admissible in evidence at a later trial, the testimony may be proved by a transcript certified by the person who reported it.

(Amended December 27, 1946, effective March 19, 1948; April 30, 2007, effective December 1, 2007.)

TITLE XI. GENERAL PROVISIONS

RULE 81. APPLICABILITY OF THE RULES IN GENERAL; REMOVED ACTIONS

(a) Applicability to Particular Proceedings.

(1) ***Prize Proceedings.*** These rules do not apply to prize proceedings in admiralty governed by 10 U.S.C. §§ 7651–7681.

(2) ***Bankruptcy.*** These rules apply to bankruptcy proceedings to the extent provided by the Federal Rules of Bankruptcy Procedure.

(3) ***Citizenship.*** These rules apply to proceedings for admission to citizenship to the extent that the practice in those proceedings is not specified in federal statutes and has previously conformed to the practice in civil actions. The provisions of 8 U.S.C. § 1451 for service by publication and for answer apply in proceedings to cancel citizenship certificates.

(4) ***Special Writs.*** These rules apply to proceedings for habeas corpus and for quo warranto to the extent that the practice in those proceedings:

(A) is not specified in a federal statute, the Rules Governing Section 2254 Cases, or the Rules Governing Section 2255 Cases; and

(B) has previously conformed to the practice in civil actions.

(5) ***Proceedings Involving a Subpoena.*** These rules apply to proceedings to compel testimony or the production of documents through a subpoena issued by a United States officer or agency under a federal statute, except as otherwise provided by statute, by local rule, or by court order in the proceedings.

(6) ***Other Proceedings.*** These rules, to the extent applicable, govern proceedings under the following laws, except as these laws provide other procedures:

(A) 7 U.S.C. §§ 292, 499g(c), for reviewing an order of the Secretary of Agriculture;

(B) 9 U.S.C., relating to arbitration;

(C) 15 U.S.C. § 522, for reviewing an order of the Secretary of the Interior;

(D) 15 U.S.C. § 715d(c), for reviewing an order denying a certificate of clearance;

(E) 29 U.S.C. §§ 159, 160, for enforcing an order of the National Labor Relations Board;

(F) 33 U.S.C. §§ 918, 921, for enforcing or reviewing a compensation order under the Longshore and Harbor Workers' Compensation Act; and

(G) 45 U.S.C. § 159, for reviewing an arbitration award in a railway-labor dispute.

(b) Scire Facias and Mandamus. The writs of scire facias and mandamus are abolished. Relief previously available through them may be obtained by appropriate action or motion under these rules.

(c) Removed Actions.

(1) ***Applicability.*** These rules apply to a civil action after it is removed from a state court.

(2) ***Further Pleading.*** After removal, repleading is unnecessary unless the court orders it. A defendant who did not answer before removal must answer or present other defenses or objections

under these rules within the longest of these periods:

(A) 21 days after receiving—through service or otherwise—a copy of the initial pleading stating the claim for relief;

(B) 21 days after being served with the summons for an initial pleading on file at the time of service; or

(C) 7 days after the notice of removal is filed.

(3) ***Demand for a Jury Trial.***

(A) *As Affected by State Law.* A party who, before removal, expressly demanded a jury trial in accordance with state law need not renew the demand after removal. If the state law did not require an express demand for a jury trial, a party need not make one after removal unless the court orders the parties to do so within a specified time. The court must so order at a party's request and may so order on its own. A party who fails to make a demand when so ordered waives a jury trial.

(B) *Under Rule 38.* If all necessary pleadings have been served at the time of removal, a party entitled to a jury trial under Rule 38 must be given one if the party serves a demand within 14 days after:

(i) it files a notice of removal; or

(ii) it is served with a notice of removal filed by another party.

(d) Law Applicable.

(1) ***"State Law" Defined.*** When these rules refer to state law, the term "law" includes the state's statutes and the state's judicial decisions.

(2) ***"State" Defined.*** The term "state" includes, where appropriate, the District of Columbia and any United States commonwealth or territory.

(3) ***"Federal Statute" Defined in the District of Columbia.*** In the United States District Court for the District of Columbia, the term "federal statute" includes any Act of Congress that applies locally to the District.

(Amended December 28, 1939, effective April 3, 1941; December 27, 1946, effective March 19, 1948; December 29, 1948, effective October 20, 1949; April 30, 1951, effective August 1, 1951; January 21, 1963, effective July 1, 1963; February 28, 1966, effective July 1, 1966; December 4, 1967, effective July 1, 1968; March 1, 1971, effective July 1, 1971; March 2, 1987, effective August 1, 1987; April 23, 2001, effective December 1, 2001; April 29, 2002, effective December 1, 2002; April 30, 2007, effective December 1, 2007; March 26, 2009, effective December 1, 2009.)

RULE 82. JURISDICTION AND VENUE UNAFFECTED

These rules do not extend or limit the jurisdiction of the district courts or the venue of actions in those courts. An admiralty or maritime claim under Rule 9(h) is not a civil action for purposes of 28 U.S.C. §§ 1391–1392.

(Amended December 29, 1948, effective October 20, 1949; February 28, 1966, effective July 1, 1966; April 23, 2001, effective December 1, 2001; April 30, 2007, effective December 1, 2007.)

RULE 83. RULES BY DISTRICT COURTS; JUDGE'S DIRECTIVES

(a) Local Rules.

(1) ***In General.*** After giving public notice and an opportunity for comment, a district court, acting by a majority of its district judges, may adopt and amend rules governing its practice. A local rule must be consistent with—but not duplicate—federal statutes and rules adopted under 28 U.S.C. §§ 2072 and 2075, and must conform to any uniform numbering system prescribed by the Judicial Conference of the United States. A local rule takes effect on the date specified by the district court and remains in effect unless amended by the court or abrogated by the judicial council of the circuit. Copies of rules and amendments must, on their adoption, be furnished to the judicial council and the Administrative Office of the United States Courts and be made available to the public.

(2) ***Requirement of Form.*** A local rule imposing a requirement of form must not be enforced in a way that causes a party to lose any right because of a nonwillful failure to comply.

(b) Procedure When There Is No Controlling Law. A judge may regulate practice in any manner consistent with federal law, rules adopted under 28 U.S.C. §§ 2072 and 2075, and the district's local rules. No sanction or other disadvantage may be imposed for noncompliance with any requirement not in federal law, federal rules, or the local rules unless the alleged violator has been furnished in the particular case with actual notice of the requirement.

(Amended April 29, 1985, effective August 1, 1985; April 27, 1995, effective December 1, 1995; April 30, 2007, effective December 1, 2007.)

RULE 84. FORMS

The forms in the Appendix suffice under these rules and illustrate the simplicity and brevity that these rules contemplate.

(Amended December 27, 1946, effective March 19, 1948; April 30, 2007, effective December 1, 2007.)

RULE 85. TITLE

These rules may be cited as the Federal Rules of Civil Procedure.

(Amended April 30, 2007, effective December 1, 2007.)

RULE 86. EFFECTIVE DATES

(a) In General. These rules and any amendments take effect at the time specified by the Supreme Court, subject to 28 U.S.C. § 2074. They govern:

(1) proceedings in an action commenced after their effective date; and

(2) proceedings after that date in an action then pending unless:

(A) the Supreme Court specifies otherwise; or

(B) the court determines that applying them in a particular action would be infeasible or work an injustice.

(b) December 1, 2007 Amendments. If any provision in Rules 1–5.1, 6–73, or 77–86 conflicts with another law, priority in time for the purpose of 28 U.S.C. § 2072(b) is not affected by the amendments taking effect on December 1, 2007.

(Amended December 27, 1946, effective March 19, 1948; December 29, 1948, effective October 20, 1949; April 17, 1961, effective July 19, 1961; January 21, 1963, and March 18, 1963, effective July 1, 1963; April 30, 2007, effective December 1, 2007.)

APPENDIX OF FORMS

(See Rule 84)

FORM 1. CAPTION

(Use on every summons, complaint, answer, motion, or other document.)

United States District Court
for the
______ District of ______

A B, Plaintiff	)	
	)	
v.	)	
	)	Civil Action No. ______
C D, Defendant	)	
	)	
v.	)	
	)	
E F, Third–Party Defendant	)	
(Use if needed.)	)	

(Name of Document)

(Added Apr. 30, 2007, eff. Dec. 1, 2007.)

FORM 2. DATE, SIGNATURE, ADDRESS, E–MAIL ADDRESS, AND TELEPHONE NUMBER

(Use at the conclusion of pleadings and other papers that require a signature.)

Date ________

____
(Signature of the attorney or unrepresented party)

____
(Printed name)

____
(Address)

____
(E-mail address)

____
(Telephone number)

(Added Apr. 30, 2007, eff. Dec. 1, 2007.)

FORM 3. SUMMONS

(Caption—See Form 1.)

To *name the defendant*:

A lawsuit has been filed against you.

Within 21 days after service of this summons on you (not counting the day you received it), you must serve on the plaintiff an answer to the attached complaint or a motion under Rule 12 of the Federal Rules of Civil Procedure. The answer or motion must be served on the plaintiff's attorney, ________, whose address is ________. If you fail to do so, judgment by default will be entered against you for the relief demanded in the complaint. You also must file your answer or motion with the court.

Date ________

____
Clerk of Court

(Court Seal)

(*Use 60 days if the defendant is the United States or a United States agency, or is an officer or employee of the United States allowed 60 days by Rule 12(a)(3).*)

(Added Apr. 30, 2007, eff. Dec. 1, 2007, and amended Mar. 26, 2009, eff. Dec. 1, 2009.)

FORM 4. SUMMONS ON A THIRD-PARTY COMPLAINT

(Caption—See Form 1.)

To *name the third-party defendant*:

A lawsuit has been filed against defendant ______, who as third-party plaintiff is making this claim against you to pay part or all of what [he] may owe to the plaintiff ______.

Within 21 days after service of this summons on you (not counting the day you received it), you must serve on the plaintiff and on the defendant an answer to the attached third-party complaint or a motion under Rule 12 of the Federal Rules of Civil Procedure. The answer or motion must be served on the defendant's attorney, ____________, whose address is, ____________, and also on the plaintiff's attorney, ____________, whose address is, ____________. If you fail to do so, judgment by default will be entered against you for the relief demanded in the third-party complaint. You also must file the answer or motion with the court and serve it on any other parties.

A copy of the plaintiff's complaint is also attached. You may—but are not required to—respond to it.

Date ______

____
Clerk of Court

(Court Seal)

(Added Apr. 30, 2007, eff. Dec. 1, 2007, and amended Mar. 26, 2009, eff. Dec. 1, 2009.)

FORM 5. NOTICE OF A LAWSUIT AND REQUEST TO WAIVE SERVICE OF A SUMMONS

(Caption—See Form 1.)

To *(name the defendant—or if the defendant is a corporation, partnership, or association name an officer or agent authorized to receive service)*:

Why are you getting this?

A lawsuit has been filed against you, or the entity you represent, in this court under the number shown above. A copy of the complaint is attached.

This is not a summons, or an official notice from the court. It is a request that, to avoid expenses, you waive formal service of a summons by signing and returning the enclosed waiver. To avoid these expenses, you must return the signed waiver within (*give at least 30 days or at least 60 days if the defendant is outside any judicial district of the United States*) from the date shown below, which is the date this notice was sent. Two copies of the waiver form are enclosed, along with a stamped, self-addressed envelope or other prepaid means for returning one copy. You may keep the other copy.

What happens next?

If you return the signed waiver, I will file it with the court. The action will then proceed as if you had been served on the date the waiver is filed, but no summons will be served on you and you will have 60 days from the date this notice is sent (see the date below) to answer the complaint (or 90 days if this notice is sent to you outside any judicial district of the United States).

If you do not return the signed waiver within the time indicated, I will arrange to have the summons and complaint served on you. And I will ask the court to require you, or the entity you represent, to pay the expenses of making service.

Please read the enclosed statement about the duty to avoid unnecessary expenses.

I certify that this request is being sent to you on the date below.

(Date and sign—See Form 2.)

(Added Apr. 30, 2007, eff. Dec. 1, 2007.)

FORM 6. WAIVER OF THE SERVICE OF SUMMONS

(Caption—See Form 1.)

To *name the plaintiff's attorney or the unrepresented plaintiff*:

I have received your request to waive service of a summons in this action along with a copy of the complaint, two copies of this waiver form, and a prepaid means of returning one signed copy of the form to you.

I, or the entity I represent, agree to save the expense of serving a summons and complaint in this case.

I understand that I, or the entity I represent, will keep all defenses or objections to the lawsuit, the court's jurisdiction, and the venue of the action, but that I waive any objections to the absence of a summons or of service.

I also understand that I, or the entity I represent, must file and serve an answer or a motion under Rule 12 within 60 days from ______, the date when this request was sent (or 90 days if it was sent outside the United States). If I fail to do so, a default judgment will be entered against me or the entity I represent.

(Date and sign—See Form 2.)

(Attach the following to Form 6.)

Duty to Avoid Unnecessary Expenses of Serving a Summons

Rule 4 of the Federal Rules of Civil Procedure requires certain defendants to cooperate in saving unnecessary expenses of serving a summons and complaint. A defendant who is located in the United States and who fails to return a signed waiver of service requested by a plaintiff located in the United States will be required to pay the expenses of service, unless the defendant shows good cause for the failure.

"Good cause" does *not* include a belief that the lawsuit is groundless, or that it has been brought in an improper venue, or that the court has no jurisdiction over this matter or over the defendant or the defendant's property.

If the waiver is signed and returned, you can still make these and all other defenses and objections, but you cannot object to the absence of a summons or of service.

If you waive service, then you must, within the time specified on the waiver form, serve an answer or a motion under Rule 12 on the plaintiff and file a copy with the court. By signing and returning the waiver form, you are allowed more time to respond than if a summons had been served.

(Added Apr. 30, 2007, eff. Dec. 1, 2007.)

FORM 7. STATEMENT OF JURISDICTION

a. (*For diversity-of-citizenship jurisdiction.*) The plaintiff is [a citizen of *Michigan*] [a corporation incorporated under the laws of *Michigan* with its principal place of business in *Michigan*]. The defendant is [a citizen of *New York*] [a corporation incorporated under the laws of *New York* with its principal place of business in *New York*]. The amount in controversy, without interest and costs, exceeds the sum or value specified by 28 U.S.C. § 1332.

b. (*For federal-question jurisdiction.*) This action arises under [the United States Constitution, *specify the article or amendment and the section*] [a United States treaty *specify*] [a federal statute, ___ U.S.C. § ___].

c. (*For a claim in the admiralty or maritime jurisdiction.*) This is a case of admiralty or maritime jurisdiction. *(To invoke admiralty status under Rule 9(h) use the following:* This is an admiralty or maritime claim within the meaning of Rule 9(h).)

(Added Apr. 30, 2007, eff. Dec. 1, 2007.)

FORM 8. STATEMENT OF REASONS FOR OMITTING A PARTY

(*If a person who ought to be made a party under Rule 19(a) is not named, include this statement in accordance with Rule 19(c).*)

This complaint does not join as a party *name* who [is not subject to this court's personal jurisdiction] [cannot be made a party without depriving this court of subject-matter jurisdiction] because *state the reason.*

(Added Apr. 30, 2007, eff. Dec. 1, 2007.)

FORM 9. STATEMENT NOTING A PARTY'S DEATH

(Caption—See Form 1.)

In accordance with Rule 25(a) *name the person,* who is [a party to this action] [a representative of or successor to the deceased party] notes the death during the pendency of this action of *name,* [*describe as party* in this action].

(Date and sign—See Form 2.)

(Added Apr. 30, 2007, eff. Dec. 1, 2007.)

FORM 10. COMPLAINT TO RECOVER A SUM CERTAIN

(Caption—See Form 1.)

1. (Statement of Jurisdiction—See Form 7.)

(Use one or more of the following as appropriate and include a demand for judgment.)

(a) On a Promissory Note

2. On *date,* the defendant executed and delivered a note promising to pay the plaintiff on *date* the sum of $_______ with interest at the rate of ___ percent. A copy of the note [is attached as Exhibit A] [is summarized as follows: _______.]

3. The defendant has not paid the amount owed.

(b) On an Account

2. The defendant owes the plaintiff $_______ according to the account set out in Exhibit A.

(c) For Goods Sold and Delivered

2. The defendant owes the plaintiff $_______ for goods sold and delivered by the plaintiff to the defendant from *date* to *date.*

(d) For Money Lent

2. The defendant owes the plaintiff $_______ for money lent by the plaintiff to the defendant on *date.*

(e) For Money Paid by Mistake

2. The defendant owes the plaintiff $_______ for money paid by mistake to the defendant on *date* under these circumstances: *describe with particularity in accordance with Rule 9(b).*

(f) For Money Had and Received

2. The defendant owes the plaintiff $_______ for money that was received from *name* on *date* to be paid by the defendant to the plaintiff.

Demand for Judgment

Therefore, the plaintiff demands judgment against the defendant for $_______, plus interest and costs.

(Date and sign—See Form 2.)

(Added Apr. 30, 2007, eff. Dec. 1, 2007.)

FORM 11. COMPLAINT FOR NEGLIGENCE

(Caption—See Form 1.)

1. (Statement of Jurisdiction—See Form 7.)
2. On *date*, at *place*, the defendant negligently drove a motor vehicle against the plaintiff.
3. As a result, the plaintiff was physically injured, lost wages or income, suffered physical and mental pain, and incurred medical expenses of $_______.

Therefore, the plaintiff demands judgment against the defendant for $_______, plus costs.

(Date and sign—See Form 2).

(Added Apr. 30, 2007, eff. Dec. 1, 2007.)

FORM 12. COMPLAINT FOR NEGLIGENCE WHEN THE PLAINTIFF DOES NOT KNOW WHO IS RESPONSIBLE

(Caption—See Form 1.)

1. (Statement of Jurisdiction—See Form 7.)
2. On *date*, at *place*, defendant *name* or defendant *name* or both of them willfully or recklessly or negligently drove, or caused to be driven, a motor vehicle against the plaintiff.
3. As a result, the plaintiff was physically injured, lost wages or income, suffered mental and physical pain, and incurred medical expenses of $_______.

Therefore, the plaintiff demands judgment against one or both defendants for $_______, plus costs.

(Date and sign—See Form 2.)

(Added Apr. 30, 2007, eff. Dec. 1, 2007.)

FORM 13. COMPLAINT FOR NEGLIGENCE UNDER THE FEDERAL EMPLOYERS' LIABILITY ACT

(Caption—See Form 1.)

1. (Statement of Jurisdiction—See Form 7.)
2. At the times below, the defendant owned and operated in interstate commerce a railroad line that passed through a tunnel located at ______.
3. On date, the plaintiff was working to repair and enlarge the tunnel to make it convenient and safe for use in interstate commerce.
4. During this work, the defendant, as the employer, negligently put the plaintiff to work in a section of the tunnel that the defendant had left unprotected and unsupported.
5. The defendant's negligence caused the plaintiff to be injured by a rock that fell from an unsupported portion of the tunnel.
6. As a result, the plaintiff was physically injured, lost wages or income, suffered mental and physical pain, and incurred medical expenses of $______.

Therefore, the plaintiff demands judgment against the defendant for $______, and costs.

(Date and sign—See Form 2.)

(Added Apr. 30, 2007, eff. Dec. 1, 2007.)

FORM 14. COMPLAINT FOR DAMAGES UNDER THE MERCHANT MARINE ACT

(Caption—See Form 1.)

1. (Statement of Jurisdiction—See Form 7.)
2. At the times below, the defendant owned and operated the vessel name and used it to transport cargo for hire by water in interstate and foreign commerce.
3. On date, at place, the defendant hired the plaintiff under seamen's articles of customary form for a voyage from ________ to ________ and return at a wage of $______ a month and found, which is equal to a shore worker's wage of $______ a month.
4. On date, the vessel was at sea on the return voyage. (*Describe the weather and the condition of the vessel.*)
5. (*Describe as in Form 11 the defendant's negligent conduct.*)
6. As a result of the defendant's negligent conduct and the unseaworthiness of the vessel, the plaintiff was physically injured, has been incapable of any gainful activity, suffered mental and physical pain, and has incurred medical expenses of $______.

Therefore, the plaintiff demands judgment against the defendant for $______, plus costs.

(Date and sign—See Form 2.)

(Added Apr. 30, 2007, eff. Dec. 1, 2007.)

FORM 15. COMPLAINT FOR THE CONVERSION OF PROPERTY

(Caption—See Form 1.)

1. (Statement of Jurisdiction—See Form 7.)
2. On *date*, at *place*, the defendant converted to the defendant's own use property owned by the plaintiff. The property converted consists of *describe*.
3. The property is worth $________.

Therefore, the plaintiff demands judgment against the defendant for $________, plus costs.

(Date and sign—See Form 2.)

(Added Apr. 30, 2007, eff. Dec. 1, 2007.)

FORM 16. THIRD–PARTY COMPLAINT

(Caption—See Form 1.)

1. Plaintiff *name* has filed against defendant *name* a complaint, a copy of which is attached.
2. (*State grounds entitling defendant's name to recover from third-party defendant's name for (all or an identified share) of any judgment for plaintiff's name against defendant's name.*)

Therefore, the defendant demands judgment against *third-party defendant's name* for *all or an identified share* of sums that may be adjudged against the defendant in the plaintiff's favor.

(Date and sign—See Form 2.)

(Added Apr. 30, 2007, eff. Dec. 1, 2007.)

FORM 17. COMPLAINT FOR SPECIFIC PERFORMANCE OF A CONTRACT TO CONVEY LAND

(Caption—See Form 1.)

1. (Statement of Jurisdiction—See Form 7.)
2. On *date*, the parties agreed to the contract [attached as Exhibit A][summarize the contract].
3. As agreed, the plaintiff tendered the purchase price and requested a conveyance of the land, but the defendant refused to accept the money or make a conveyance.
4. The plaintiff now offers to pay the purchase price.

Therefore, the plaintiff demands that:

(a) the defendant be required to specifically perform the agreement and pay damages of $_______, plus interest and costs, or

(b) if specific performance is not ordered, the defendant be required to pay damages of $_______, plus interest and costs.

(Date and sign—See Form 2.)

(Added Apr. 30, 2007, eff. Dec. 1, 2007.)

FORM 18. COMPLAINT FOR PATENT INFRINGEMENT

(Caption—See Form 1.)

1. (Statement of Jurisdiction—See Form 7.)
2. On *date*, United States Letters Patent No. _______ were issued to the plaintiff for an invention in an *electric motor*. The plaintiff owned the patent throughout the period of the defendant's infringing acts and still owns the patent.
3. The defendant has infringed and is still infringing the Letters Patent by making, selling, and using *electric motors* that embody the patented invention, and the defendant will continue to do so unless enjoined by this court.
4. The plaintiff has complied with the statutory requirement of placing a notice of the Letters Patent on all *electric motors* it manufactures and sells and has given the defendant written notice of the infringement.

Therefore, the plaintiff demands:

(a) a preliminary and final injunction against the continuing infringement;

(b) an accounting for damages; and

(c) interest and costs.

(Date and sign—See Form 2.)

(Added Apr. 30, 2007, eff. Dec. 1, 2007.)

FORM 19. COMPLAINT FOR COPYRIGHT INFRINGEMENT AND UNFAIR COMPETITION

(Caption—See Form 1.)

1. (Statement of Jurisdiction—See Form 7.)
2. Before *date*, the plaintiff, a United States citizen, wrote a book entitled ________.
3. The book is an original work that may be copyrighted under United States law. A copy of the book is attached as Exhibit A.
4. Between *date* and *date*, the plaintiff applied to the copyright office and received a certificate of registration dated ________ and identified as *date, class, number*.
5. Since *date*, the plaintiff has either published or licensed for publication all copies of the book in compliance with the copyright laws and has remained the sole owner of the copyright.
6. After the copyright was issued, the defendant infringed the copyright by publishing and selling a book entitled ________, which was copied largely from the plaintiff's book. A copy of the defendant's book is attached as Exhibit B.
7. The plaintiff has notified the defendant in writing of the infringement.
8. The defendant continues to infringe the copyright by continuing to publish and sell the infringing book in violation of the copyright, and further has engaged in unfair trade practices and unfair competition in connection with its publication and sale of the infringing book, thus causing irreparable damage.

Therefore, the plaintiff demands that:

(a) until this case is decided the defendant and the defendant's agents be enjoined from disposing of any copies of the defendant's book by sale or otherwise;

(b) the defendant account for and pay as damages to the plaintiff all profits and advantages gained from unfair trade practices and unfair competition in selling the defendant's book, and all profits and advantages gained from infringing the plaintiff's copyright (but no less than the statutory minimum);

(c) the defendant deliver for impoundment all copies of the book in the defendant's possession or control and deliver for destruction all infringing copies and all plates, molds, and other materials for making infringing copies;

(d) the defendant pay the plaintiff interest, costs, and reasonable attorney's fees; and

(e) the plaintiff be awarded any other just relief.

(Date and sign—See Form 2.)

(Added Apr. 30, 2007, eff. Dec. 1, 2007.)

FORM 20. COMPLAINT FOR INTERPLEADER AND DECLARATORY RELIEF

(Caption—See Form 1.)

1. (Statement of Jurisdiction—See Form 7.)
2. On *date*, the plaintiff issued a life insurance policy on the life of *name* with *name* as the named beneficiary.
3. As a condition for keeping the policy in force, the policy required payment of a premium during the first year and then annually.
4. The premium due on *date* was never paid, and the policy lapsed after that date.
5. On *date*, after the policy had lapsed, both the insured and the named beneficiary died in an automobile collision.
6. Defendant *name* claims to be the beneficiary in place of *name* and has filed a claim to be paid the policy's full amount.
7. The other two defendants are representatives of the deceased persons' estates. Each defendant has filed a claim on behalf of each estate to receive payment of the policy's full amount.
8. If the policy was in force at the time of death, the plaintiff is in doubt about who should be paid.

Therefore, the plaintiff demands that:

(a) each defendant be restrained from commencing any action against the plaintiff on the policy;

(b) a judgment be entered that no defendant is entitled to the proceeds of the policy or any part of it, but if the court determines that the policy was in effect at the time of the insured's death, that the defendants be required to interplead and settle among themselves their rights to the proceeds, and that the plaintiff be discharged from all liability except to the defendant determined to be entitled to the proceeds; and

(c) the plaintiff recover its costs.

(Date and sign—See Form 2.)

(Added Apr. 30, 2007, eff. Dec. 1, 2007.)

FORM 21. COMPLAINT ON A CLAIM FOR A DEBT AND TO SET ASIDE A FRAUDULENT CONVEYANCE UNDER RULE 18(b)

(Caption—See Form 1.)

1. (Statement of Jurisdiction—See Form 7.)
2. On *date*, defendant *name* signed a note promising to pay to the plaintiff on *date* the sum of $______ with interest at the rate of ___ percent. [The pleader may, but need not, attach a copy or plead the note verbatim.]
3. Defendant *name* owes the plaintiff the amount of the note and interest.
4. On *date*, defendant *name* conveyed all defendant's real and personal property *if less than all, describe it fully* to defendant *name* for the purpose of defrauding the plaintiff and hindering or delaying the collection of the debt.

Therefore, the plaintiff demands that:

(a) judgment for $______, plus costs, be entered against defendant(s) *name(s)*; and

(b) the conveyance to defendant *name* be declared void and any judgment granted be made a lien on the property.

(Date and sign—See Form 2.)

(Added Apr. 30, 2007, eff. Dec. 1, 2007.)

FORM 30. ANSWER PRESENTING DEFENSES UNDER RULE 12(b)

(Caption—See Form 1.)

Responding to Allegations in the Complaint

1. Defendant admits the allegations in paragraphs ______.
2. Defendant lacks knowledge or information sufficient to form a belief about the truth of the allegations in paragraphs ______.
3. Defendant admits *identify part of the allegation* in paragraph ______ and denies or lacks knowledge or information sufficient to form a belief about the truth of the rest of the paragraph.

Failure to State a Claim

4. The complaint fails to state a claim upon which relief can be granted.

Failure to Join a Required Party

5. If there is a debt, it is owed jointly by the defendant and *name* who is a citizen of ______. This person can be made a party without depriving this court of jurisdiction over the existing parties.

Affirmative Defense—Statute of Limitations

6. The plaintiff's claim is barred by the statute of limitations because it arose more than ______ years before this action was commenced.

Counterclaim

7. (*Set forth any counterclaim in the same way a claim is pleaded in a complaint. Include a further statement of jurisdiction if needed.*)

Crossclaim

8. (*Set forth a crossclaim against a coparty in the same way a claim is pleaded in a complaint. Include a further statement of jurisdiction if needed.*)

(Date and sign—See Form 2.)

(Added Apr. 30, 2007, eff. Dec. 1, 2007.)

FORM 31. ANSWER TO A COMPLAINT FOR MONEY HAD AND RECEIVED WITH A COUNTERCLAIM FOR INTERPLEADER

(Caption—See Form 1.)

Response to the Allegations in the Complaint
(See Form 30.)

Counterclaim for Interpleader

1. The defendant received from name a deposit of $_______.
2. The plaintiff demands payment of the deposit because of a purported assignment from name, who has notified the defendant that the assignment is not valid and who continues to hold the defendant responsible for the deposit.

Therefore, the defendant demands that:

(a) name be made a party to this action;

(b) the plaintiff and name be required to interplead their respective claims;

(c) the court decide whether the plaintiff or name or either of them is entitled to the deposit and discharge the defendant of any liability except to the person entitled to the deposit; and

(d) the defendant recover costs and attorney's fees.

(Date and sign—See Form 2.)

(Added Apr. 30, 2007, eff. Dec. 1, 2007.)

FORM 40. MOTION TO DISMISS UNDER RULE 12(B) FOR LACK OF JURISDICTION, IMPROPER VENUE, INSUFFICIENT SERVICE OF PROCESS, OR FAILURE TO STATE A CLAIM

(Caption—See Form 1.)

The defendant moves to dismiss the action because:

1. the amount in controversy is less than the sum or value specified by 28 U.S.C. § 1332;
2. the defendant is not subject to the personal jurisdiction of this court;
3. venue is improper (this defendant does not reside in this district and no part of the events or omissions giving rise to the claim occurred in the district);
4. the defendant has not been properly served, as shown by the attached affidavits of _______; or
5. the complaint fails to state a claim upon which relief can be granted.

(Date and sign—See Form 2.)

(Added Apr. 30, 2007, eff. Dec. 1, 2007.)

FORM 41. MOTION TO BRING IN A THIRD-PARTY DEFENDANT

(Caption—See Form 1.)

The defendant, as third-party plaintiff, moves for leave to serve on *name* a summons and third-party complaint, copies of which are attached.

(Date and sign—See Form 2.)

(Added Apr. 30, 2007, eff. Dec. 1, 2007.)

FORM 42. MOTION TO INTERVENE AS A DEFENDANT UNDER RULE 24

(Caption—See Form 1.)

1. *name* moves for leave to intervene as a defendant in this action and to file the attached answer.

(State grounds under Rule 24(a) or (b).)

2. The plaintiff alleges patent infringement. We manufacture and sell to the defendant the articles involved, and we have a defense to the plaintiff's claim.
3. Our defense presents questions of law and fact that are common to this action.

(Date and sign—See Form 2.)

[An Intervener's Answer must be attached. See Form 30.]

(Added Apr. 30, 2007, eff. Dec. 1, 2007.)

FORM 50. REQUEST TO PRODUCE DOCUMENTS AND TANGIBLE THINGS, OR TO ENTER ONTO LAND UNDER RULE 34

(Caption—See Form 1.)

The plaintiff name requests that the defendant name respond within ____ days to the following requests:

1. To produce and permit the plaintiff to inspect and copy and to test or sample the following documents, including electronically stored information:

(Describe each document and the electronically stored information, either individually or by category.)

(State the time, place, and manner of the inspection and any related acts.)

2. To produce and permit the plaintiff to inspect and copy—and to test or sample—the following tangible things:

(Describe each thing, either individually or by category.)

(State the time, place, and manner of the inspection and any related acts.)

3. To permit the plaintiff to enter onto the following land to inspect, photograph, test, or sample the property or an object or operation on the property.

(Describe the property and each object or operation.)

(State the time and manner of the inspection and any related acts.)

(Date and sign—See Form 2.)

(Added Apr. 30, 2007, eff. Dec. 1, 2007.)

FORM 51. REQUEST FOR ADMISSIONS UNDER RULE 36

(Caption—See Form 1.)

The plaintiff name asks the defendant name to respond within 30 days to these requests by admitting, for purposes of this action only and subject to objections to admissibility at trial:

1. The genuineness of the following documents, copies of which [are attached] [are or have been furnished or made available for inspection and copying].

(List each document.)

2. The truth of each of the following statements:

(List each statement.)

(Date and sign—See Form 2.)

(Added Apr. 30, 2007, eff. Dec. 1, 2007.)

FORM 52. REPORT OF THE PARTIES' PLANNING MEETING

(Caption—See Form 1.)

1. The following persons participated in a Rule 26(f) conference on ___*date*___ by *state the method of conferring*___:
2. Initial Disclosures. The parties [have completed] [will complete by ___*date*___] the initial disclosures required by Rule 26(a)(1).
3. Discovery Plan. The parties propose this discovery plan:

(Use separate paragraphs or subparagraphs if the parties disagree.)

(a) Discovery will be needed on these subjects: (*describe*)

(b) Disclosure or discovery of electronically stored information should be handled as follows: (*briefly describe the parties' proposals, including the form or forms for production.*)

(c) The parties have agreed to an order regarding claims of privilege or of protection as trial-preparation material asserted after production, as follows: (*briefly describe the provisions of the proposed order.*)

(d) (Dates for commencing and completing discovery, including discovery to be commenced or completed before other discovery.)

(e) (Maximum number of interrogatories by each party to another party, along with dates the answers are due.)

(f) (Maximum number of requests for admission, along with the dates responses are due.)

(g) (Maximum number of depositions for each party.)

(h) (Limits on the length of depositions, in hours.)

(i) (Dates for exchanging reports of expert witnesses.)

(j) (Dates for supplementations under Rule 26(e).)

4. Other Items:

(a) (A date if the parties ask to meet with the court before a scheduling order.)

(b) (Requested dates for pretrial conferences.)

(c) (Final dates for the plaintiff to amend pleadings or to join parties.)

(d) (Final dates for the defendant to amend pleadings or to join parties.)

(e) (Final dates to file dispositive motions.)

(f) (State the prospects for settlement.)

(g) (Identify any alternative dispute resolution procedure that may enhance settlement prospects.)

(h) (Final dates for submitting Rule 26(a)(3) witness lists, designations of witnesses whose testimony will be presented by deposition, and exhibit lists.)

(i) (Final dates to file objections under Rule 26(a)(3).)

(j) (Suggested trial date and estimate of trial length.)

(k) (Other matters.)

(Date and sign—see Form 2.)

(Added Apr. 30, 2007, eff. Dec. 1, 2007. As amended Apr. 28, 2010, eff. Dec. 1, 2010.)

FORM 60. NOTICE OF CONDEMNATION

(Caption—See Form 1.)

To *name the defendant*.

1. A complaint in condemnation has been filed in the United States District Court for the ______District of ______, to take property to use for *purpose*. The interest to be taken is *describe*. The court is located in the United States courthouse at this address: ______.
2. The property to be taken is described below. You have or claim an interest in it.

(*Describe the property.*)

3. The authority for taking this property is *cite*.
4. If you want to object or present any defense to the taking you must serve an answer on the plaintiff's attorney within 21 days [after being served with this notice][from *(insert the date of the last publication of notice)*]. Send your answer to this address: ______.
5. Your answer must identify the property in which you claim an interest, state the nature and extent of that interest, and state all your objections and defenses to the taking. Objections and defenses not presented are waived.
6. If you fail to answer you consent to the taking and the court will enter a judgment that takes your described property interest.
7. Instead of answering, you may serve on the plaintiff's attorney a notice of appearance that designates the property in which you claim an interest. After you do that, you will receive a notice of any proceedings that affect you. Whether or not you have previously appeared or answered, you may present evidence at a trial to determine compensation for the property and share in the overall award.

(Date and sign—See Form 2.)

(Added Apr. 30, 2007, eff. Dec. 1, 2007, and amended Mar. 26, 2009, eff. Dec. 1, 2009.)

FORM 61. COMPLAINT FOR CONDEMNATION

(Caption—See Form 1; name as defendants the property and at least one owner.)

1. (Statement of Jurisdiction—See Form 7.)
2. This is an action to take property under the power of eminent domain and to determine just compensation to be paid to the owners and parties in interest.
3. The authority for the taking is ______.
4. The property is to be used for ____________.
5. The property to be taken is (*describe in enough detail for identification—or attach the description and state "is described in Exhibit A, attached."*)
6. The interest to be acquired is ____________.
7. The persons known to the plaintiff to have or claim an interest in the property are: ____________. (*For each person include the interest claimed.*)
8. There may be other persons who have or claim an interest in the property and whose names could not be found after a reasonably diligent search. They are made parties under the designation "Unknown Owners."

Therefore, the plaintiff demands judgment:

(a) condemning the property;

(b) determining and awarding just compensation; and

(c) granting any other lawful and proper relief.

(Date and sign—See Form 2.)

(Added Apr. 30, 2007, eff. Dec. 1, 2007.)

FORM 70. JUDGMENT ON A JURY VERDICT

(Caption—See Form 1.)

This action was tried by a jury with Judge ______ presiding, and the jury has rendered a verdict.

It is ordered that:

[the plaintiff name recover from the defendant name the amount of $______ with interest at the rate of ___%, along with costs.]

[the plaintiff recover nothing, the action be dismissed on the merits, and the defendant name recover costs from the plaintiff name.]

Date ______

____

Clerk of Court

(Added Apr. 30, 2007, eff. Dec. 1, 2007.)

FORM 71. JUDGMENT BY THE COURT WITHOUT A JURY

(Caption—See Form 1.)

This action was tried by Judge ______ without a jury and the following decision was reached:

It is ordered that [the plaintiff *name* recover from the defendant *name* the amount of $______, with prejudgment interest at the rate of __%, postjudgment interest at the rate of __%, along with costs.] [the plaintiff recover nothing, the action be dismissed on the merits, and the defendant *name* recover costs from the plaintiff *name*.]

Date____________

____

Clerk of Court

(Added Apr. 30, 2007, eff. Dec. 1, 2007.)

FORM 80. NOTICE OF A MAGISTRATE JUDGE'S AVAILABILITY

1. A magistrate judge is available under title 28 U.S.C. § 636(c) to conduct the proceedings in this case, including a jury or nonjury trial and the entry of final judgment. But a magistrate judge can be assigned only if all parties voluntarily consent.
2. You may withhold your consent without adverse substantive consequences. The identity of any party consenting or withholding consent will not be disclosed to the judge to whom the case is assigned or to any magistrate judge.
3. If a magistrate judge does hear your case, you may appeal directly to a United States court of appeals as you would if a district judge heard it.

A form called *Consent to an Assignment to a United States Magistrate Judge* is available from the court clerk's office.

(Added Apr. 30, 2007, eff. Dec. 1, 2007.)

FORM 81. CONSENT TO AN ASSIGNMENT TO A MAGISTRATE JUDGE

(Caption—See Form 1.)

I voluntarily consent to have a United States magistrate judge conduct all further proceedings in this case, including a trial, and order the entry of final judgment. (Return this form to the court clerk—not to a judge or magistrate judge.)

Date_______________

____

Signature of the Party

(Added Apr. 30, 2007, eff. Dec. 1, 2007.)

FORM 82. ORDER OF ASSIGNMENT TO A MAGISTRATE JUDGE

(Caption—See Form 1.)

With the parties' consent it is ordered that this case be assigned to United States Magistrate Judge _______ of this district to conduct all proceedings and enter final judgment in accordance with 28 U.S.C. § 636(c).

Date _______________

____

United States District Judge

(Added Apr. 30, 2007, eff. Dec. 1, 2007.)

SUPPLEMENTAL RULES FOR ADMIRALTY OR MARITIME CLAIMS AND ASSET FORFEITURE ACTIONS

RULE A. SCOPE OF RULES

(1) These Supplemental Rules apply to:

(A) the procedure in admiralty and maritime claims within the meaning of Rule 9(h) with respect to the following remedies:

(i) maritime attachment and garnishment,

(ii) actions in rem,

(iii) possessory, petitory, and partition actions, and

(iv) actions for exoneration from or limitation of liability;

(B) forfeiture actions in rem arising from a federal statute; and

(C) the procedure in statutory condemnation proceedings analogous to maritime actions in rem, whether within the admiralty and maritime jurisdiction or not. Except as otherwise provided, references in these Supplemental Rules to actions in rem include such analogous statutory condemnation proceedings.

(2) The Federal Rules of Civil Procedure also apply to the foregoing proceedings except to the extent that they are inconsistent with these Supplemental Rules.

(Added Feb. 28, 1966, eff. July 1, 1966, and amended Apr. 12, 2006, eff. Dec. 1, 2006.)

RULE B. IN PERSONAM ACTIONS: ATTACHMENT AND GARNISHMENT

(1) When Available; Complaint, Affidavit, Judicial Authorization, and Process. In an in personam action:

(a) If a defendant is not found within the district when a verified complaint praying for attachment and the affidavit required by Rule B(1)(b) are filed, a verified complaint may contain a prayer for process to attach the defendant's tangible or intangible personal property—up to the amount sued for—in the hands of garnishees named in the process.

(b) The plaintiff or the plaintiff's attorney must sign and file with the complaint an affidavit stating that, to the affiant's knowledge, or on information and belief, the defendant cannot be found within the district. The court must review the complaint and affidavit and, if the conditions of this Rule B appear to exist, enter an order so stating and authorizing process of attachment and garnishment. The clerk may issue supplemental process enforcing the court's order upon application without further court order.

(c) If the plaintiff or the plaintiff's attorney certifies that exigent circumstances make court review impracticable, the clerk must issue the summons and process of attachment and garnishment. The plaintiff has the burden in any post-attachment hearing under Rule E(4)(f) to show that exigent circumstances existed.

(d)(i) If the property is a vessel or tangible property on board a vessel, the summons, process, and any supplemental process must be delivered to the marshal for service.

(ii) If the property is other tangible or intangible property, the summons, process, and any supplemental process must be delivered to a person or organization authorized to serve it, who may be (A) a marshal; (B) someone under contract with the United States; (C) someone specially appointed by the court for that purpose; or, (D) in an action brought by the United States, any officer or employee of the United States.

(e) The plaintiff may invoke state-law remedies under Rule 64 for seizure of person or property for the purpose of securing satisfaction of the judgment.

(2) Notice to Defendant. No default judgment may be entered except upon proof—which may be by affidavit—that:

(a) the complaint, summons, and process of attachment or garnishment have been served on the defendant in a manner authorized by Rule 4;

(b) the plaintiff or the garnishee has mailed to the defendant the complaint, summons, and process of attachment or garnishment, using any form of mail requiring a return receipt; or

(c) the plaintiff or the garnishee has tried diligently to give notice of the action to the defendant but could not do so.

(3) Answer.

(a) By Garnishee. The garnishee shall serve an answer, together with answers to any interrogatories served with the complaint, within 21 days after service of process upon the garnishee. Interrogatories to the garnishee may be served with the complaint without leave of court. If the garnishee refuses or neglects to answer on oath as to the debts, credits, or effects of the defendant in the garnishee's hands, or any interrogatories concerning such debts, credits, and effects that may be propounded by the plaintiff, the court may award compulsory process against the garnishee. If the garnishee admits any debts, credits, or effects, they shall be held in the garnishee's hands or paid into the registry of the court, and shall be held in either case subject to the further order of the court.

(b) By Defendant. The defendant shall serve an answer within 30 days after process has been executed, whether by attachment of property or service on the garnishee.

(Added Feb. 28, 1966, eff. July 1, 1966, and amended Apr. 29, 1985, eff. Aug. 1, 1985; Mar. 2, 1987, eff. Aug. 1, 1987; Apr. 17, 2000, eff. Dec. 1, 2000; Apr. 25, 2005, eff. Dec. 1, 2005; Mar. 26, 2009, eff. Dec. 1, 2009.)

RULE C. IN REM ACTIONS: SPECIAL PROVISIONS

(1) When Available. An action in rem may be brought:

(a) To enforce any maritime lien;

(b) Whenever a statute of the United States provides for a maritime action in rem or a proceeding analogous thereto.

Except as otherwise provided by law a party who may proceed in rem may also, or in the alternative, proceed in personam against any person who may be liable.

Statutory provisions exempting vessels or other property owned or possessed by or operated by or for the United States from arrest or seizure are not affected by this rule. When a statute so provides, an action against the United States or an instrumentality thereof may proceed on in rem principles.

(2) Complaint. In an action in rem the complaint must:

(a) be verified;

(b) describe with reasonable particularity the property that is the subject of the action; and

(c) state that the property is within the district or will be within the district while the action is pending.

(3) Judicial Authorization and Process.

(a) Arrest Warrant.

(i) The court must review the complaint and any supporting papers. If the conditions for an in rem action appear to exist, the court must issue an order directing the clerk to issue a warrant for the arrest of the vessel or other property that is the subject of the action.

(ii) If the plaintiff or the plaintiff's attorney certifies that exigent circumstances make court review impracticable, the clerk must promptly issue a summons and a warrant for the arrest of the vessel or other property that is the subject of the action. The plaintiff has the burden in any post-arrest hearing under Rule E(4)(f) to show that exigent circumstances existed.

(b) Service.

(i) If the property that is the subject of the action is a vessel or tangible property on board a vessel, the warrant and any supplemental process must be delivered to the marshal for service.

(ii) If the property that is the subject of the action is other property, tangible or intangible, the warrant and any supplemental process must be delivered to a person or organization authorized to enforce it, who may be: (A) a marshal; (B) someone under contract with the United States; (C) someone specially appointed by the court for that purpose; or, (D) in an action brought by the United States, any officer or employee of the United States.

(c) Deposit in Court. If the property that is the subject of the action consists in whole or in part of freight, the proceeds of property sold, or other intangible property, the clerk must issue—in addition to the warrant—a summons directing any person controlling the property to show cause why it should not be deposited in court to abide the judgment.

(d) Supplemental Process. The clerk may upon application issue supplemental process to enforce the court's order without further court order.

(4) Notice. No notice other than execution of process is required when the property that is the subject of the action has been released under Rule E(5). If the property is not released within 14 days after execution, the plaintiff must promptly—or within the time that the court allows—give public notice of the action and arrest in a newspaper designated by court order and having general circulation in the district, but publication may be terminated if the property is released before publication is completed. The notice must specify the time under Rule C(6) to file a statement of interest in or right against the seized property and to answer. This rule does not affect the notice requirements in an action to foreclose a preferred ship mortgage under 46 U.S.C. §§ 31301 et seq., as amended.

(5) Ancillary Process. In any action in rem in which process has been served as provided by this rule, if any part of the property that is the subject of the action has not been brought within the control of the court because it has been removed or sold, or because it is intangible property in the hands of a person who has not been served with process, the court may, on motion, order any person having possession or control of such property or its proceeds to show cause why it should not be delivered into the custody of the marshal or other person or organization having a warrant for the arrest of the property, or paid into court to abide the judgment; and, after hearing, the court may enter such judgment as law and justice may require.

(6) Responsive Pleading; Interrogatories.

(a) Statement of Interest; Answer. In an action in rem:

(i) a person who asserts a right of possession or any ownership interest in the property that is the subject of the action must file a verified statement of right or interest:

(A) within 14 days after the execution of process, or

(B) within the time that the court allows;

(ii) the statement of right or interest must describe the interest in the property that supports the person's demand for its restitution or right to defend the action;

(iii) an agent, bailee, or attorney must state the authority to file a statement of right or interest on behalf of another; and

(iv) a person who asserts a right of possession or any ownership interest must serve an answer within 21 days after filing the statement of interest or right.

(b) Interrogatories. Interrogatories may be served with the complaint in an in rem action without leave of court. Answers to the interrogatories must be served with the answer to the complaint.

(Added Feb. 28, 1966, eff. July 1, 1966, and amended Apr. 29, 1985, eff. Aug. 1, 1985; Mar. 2, 1987, eff. Aug. 1, 1987; Apr. 30, 1991, eff. Dec. 1, 1991; Apr. 17, 2000, eff. Dec. 1, 2000; Apr. 29, 2002, eff. Dec. 1, 2002; Apr. 25, 2005, eff. Dec. 1, 2005; Apr. 12, 2006, eff. Dec. 1, 2006; Apr. 23, 2008, eff. Dec. 1, 2008; Mar. 26, 2009, eff. Dec. 1, 2009.)

RULE D. POSSESSORY, PETITORY, AND PARTITION ACTIONS

In all actions for possession, partition, and to try title maintainable according to the course of the admiralty practice with respect to a vessel, in all actions so maintainable with respect to the possession of cargo or other maritime property, and in all actions by one or more part owners against the others to obtain security for the return of the vessel from any voyage undertaken without their consent, or by one or more part owners against the others to obtain possession of the vessel for any voyage on giving security for its safe return, the process shall be by a warrant of arrest of the vessel, cargo, or other property, and by notice in the manner provided by Rule B(2) to the adverse party or parties.

(Added Feb. 28, 1966, eff. July 1, 1966.)

RULE E. ACTIONS IN REM AND QUASI IN REM: GENERAL PROVISIONS

(1) Applicability. Except as otherwise provided, this rule applies to actions in personam with process of maritime attachment and garnishment, actions in rem, and petitory, possessory, and partition actions, supplementing Rules B, C, and D.

(2) Complaint; Security.

(a) Complaint. In actions to which this rule is applicable the complaint shall state the circumstances from which the claim arises with such particularity that the defendant or claimant will be able, without moving for a more definite statement, to commence an investigation of the facts and to frame a responsive pleading.

(b) Security for Costs. Subject to the provisions of Rule 54(d) and of relevant statutes, the court may, on the filing of the complaint or on the appearance of any defendant, claimant, or any other party, or at any later time, require the plaintiff, defendant, claimant, or other party to give security, or additional security, in such sum as the court shall direct to pay all costs and expenses that shall be awarded against the party by any interlocutory order or by the final judgment, or on appeal by any appellate court.

(3) Process.

(a) In admiralty and maritime proceedings process in rem or of maritime attachment and garnishment may be served only within the district.

(b) Issuance and Delivery. Issuance and delivery of process in rem, or of maritime attachment and garnishment, shall be held in abeyance if the plaintiff so requests.

(4) Execution of Process; Marshal's Return; Custody of Property; Procedures for Release.

(a) In General. Upon issuance and delivery of the process, or, in the case of summons with process of attachment and garnishment, when it appears that the defendant cannot be found within the district, the marshal or other person or organization having a warrant shall forthwith execute the process in accordance with this subdivision (4), making due and prompt return.

(b) Tangible Property. If tangible property is to be attached or arrested, the marshal or other person or organization having the warrant shall take it into the marshal's possession for safe custody. If the character or situation of the property is such that the taking of actual possession is impracticable, the marshal or other person executing the process shall affix a copy thereof to the property in a conspicuous place and leave a copy of the complaint and process with the person having possession or the person's agent. In furtherance of the marshal's custody of any vessel the marshal is authorized to make a written request to the collector of customs not to grant clearance to such vessel until notified by the marshal or deputy marshal or by the clerk that the vessel has been released in accordance with these rules.

(c) Intangible Property. If intangible property is to be attached or arrested the marshal or other person or organization having the warrant shall execute the process by leaving with the garnishee or other obligor a copy of the complaint and process requiring the garnishee or other obligor to answer as provided in Rules B(3)(a) and C(6); or the marshal may accept for payment into the registry of the court the amount owed to the extent of the amount claimed by the plaintiff with interest and costs, in which event the garnishee or other obligor shall not be required to answer unless alias process shall be served.

(d) Directions With Respect to Property in Custody. The marshal or other person or organization having the warrant may at any time apply to the court for directions with respect to property that has been attached or arrested, and shall give notice of such application to any or all of the parties as the court may direct.

(e) Expenses of Seizing and Keeping Property; Deposit. These rules do not alter the provisions of Title 28, U.S.C., § 1921, as amended, relative to the expenses of seizing and keeping property attached or arrested and to the requirement of deposits to cover such expenses.

(f) Procedure for Release From Arrest or Attachment. Whenever property is arrested or attached, any person claiming an interest in it shall be entitled to a prompt hearing at which the plaintiff shall be required to show why the arrest or attachment should not be vacated or other relief granted consistent with these rules. This subdivision shall have no application to suits for seamen's wages when process is issued upon a certification of sufficient cause filed pursuant to Title 46, U.S.C. §§ 603 and 604 or to actions by the United States for forfeitures for violation of any statute of the United States.

(5) Release of Property.

(a) Special Bond. Whenever process of maritime attachment and garnishment or process in rem is issued the execution of such process shall be stayed, or the property released, on the giving of security, to be approved by the court or clerk, or by stipulation of the parties, conditioned to answer the judgment of the court or of any appellate court. The parties may stipulate the amount and nature of such security. In the event of the inability or refusal of the parties so to stipulate the court shall fix the principal sum of the bond or stipulation at an amount sufficient to cover the amount of the plaintiff's claim fairly stated with accrued interest and costs; but the principal sum shall in no event exceed (i) twice the amount of the plaintiff's claim or (ii) the value of the property on due appraisement, whichever is smaller. The bond or stipulation shall be conditioned for the payment of the principal sum and interest thereon at 6 per cent per annum.

(b) General Bond. The owner of any vessel may file a general bond or stipulation, with sufficient surety, to be approved by the court, conditioned to answer the judgment of such court in all or any actions that may be brought thereafter in such court in which the vessel is attached or arrested. Thereupon the execution of all such process against such vessel shall be stayed so long as the amount secured by such bond or stipulation is at least double the aggregate amount claimed by plaintiffs in all actions begun and pending in which such vessel has been attached or arrested. Judgments and remedies may be had on such bond or stipulation as if a special bond or stipulation had been filed in each of such actions. The district court may make necessary orders to carry this rule into effect, particularly as to the giving of proper notice of any action against or attachment of a vessel for which a general bond has been filed. Such bond or stipulation shall be indorsed by the clerk with a minute of the actions wherein process is so stayed. Further security may be required by the court at any time.

If a special bond or stipulation is given in a particular case, the liability on the general bond or stipulation shall cease as to that case.

(c) Release by Consent or Stipulation; Order of Court or Clerk; Costs. Any vessel, cargo, or other property in the custody of the marshal or other person or organization having the warrant may be released forthwith upon the marshal's acceptance and approval of a stipulation, bond, or other security, signed by the party on whose behalf the property is detained or the party's attorney and expressly authorizing such release, if all costs and charges of the court and its officers shall have first been paid. Otherwise no property in the custody of the marshal, other person or organization having the warrant, or other officer of the court shall be released without an order of the court; but such order may be entered as of course by the clerk, upon the giving of approved security as provided by law and these rules, or upon the dismissal or discontinuance of the action; but the marshal or other person or organization having the warrant shall not deliver any property so released until the costs and charges of the officers of the court shall first have been paid.

(d) Possessory, Petitory, and Partition Actions. The foregoing provisions of this subdivision (5) do not apply to petitory, possessory, and partition actions. In such cases the property arrested shall be released only by order of the court, on such terms and conditions and on the giving of such security as the court may require.

(6) Reduction or Impairment of Security. Whenever security is taken the court may, on motion and hearing, for good cause shown, reduce the amount of security given; and if the surety shall be or become insufficient, new or additional sureties may be required on motion and hearing.

(7) Security on Counterclaim.

(a) When a person who has given security for damages in the original action asserts a counterclaim that arises from the transaction or occurrence that is the subject of the original action, a plaintiff for whose benefit the security has been given must give security for damages demanded in the counterclaim unless the court for cause shown, directs otherwise. Proceedings on the original claim must be stayed until this security is given unless the court directs otherwise.

(b) The plaintiff is required to give security under Rule E(7)(a) when the United States or its corporate instrumentality counterclaims and would have been required to give security to respond in damages if a private party but is relieved by law from giving security.

(8) Restricted Appearance. An appearance to defend against an admiralty and maritime claim with respect to which there has issued process in rem, or process of attachment and garnishment, may be expressly restricted to the defense of such claim, and in that event is not an appearance for the purposes of any other claim with respect to which such process is not available or has not been served.

(9) Disposition of Property; Sales.

(a) Interlocutory Sales; Delivery.

(i) On application of a party, the marshal, or other person having custody of the property, the court may order all or part of the property sold—with the sales proceeds, or as much of them as will satisfy the judgment, paid into court to await further orders of the court—if:

(A) the attached or arrested property is perishable, or liable to deterioration, decay, or injury by being detained in custody pending the action;

(B) the expense of keeping the property is excessive or disproportionate; or

(C) there is an unreasonable delay in securing release of the property.

(ii) In the circumstances described in Rule E(9)(a)(i), the court, on motion by a defendant or a person filing a statement of interest or right under Rule C(6), may order that the property, rather than being sold, be delivered to the movant upon giving security under these rules.

(b) Sales; Proceeds. All sales of property shall be made by the marshal or a deputy marshal, or by other person or organization having the warrant, or by any other person assigned by the court where the marshal or other person or organization having the warrant is a party in interest; and the proceeds of sale shall be forthwith paid into the registry of the court to be disposed of according to law.

(10) Preservation of Property. When the owner or another person remains in possession of property attached or arrested under the provisions of Rule E(4)(b) that permit execution of process without taking actual possession, the court, on a party's motion or on its own, may enter any order necessary to preserve the property and to prevent its removal.

(Added Feb. 28, 1966, eff. July 1, 1966, and amended Apr. 29, 1985, eff. Aug. 1, 1985; Mar. 2, 1987, eff. Aug. 1, 1987; Apr. 30, 1991, eff. Dec. 1, 1991; Apr. 17, 2000, eff. Dec. 1, 2000; Apr. 12, 2006, eff. Dec. 1, 2006.)

RULE F. LIMITATION OF LIABILITY

(1) Time for Filing Complaint; Security. Not later than six months after receipt of a claim in writing, any vessel owner may file a complaint in the appropriate district court, as provided in subdivision (9) of this rule, for limitation of liability pursuant to statute. The owner (a) shall deposit with the court, for the benefit of claimants, a sum equal to the amount or value of the owner's interest in the vessel and pending freight, or approved security therefor, and in addition such sums, or approved security therefor, as the court may from time to time fix as necessary to carry out the provisions of the statutes as amended; or (b) at the owner's option shall transfer to a trustee to be appointed by the court, for the benefit of claimants, the owner's interest in the vessel and pending freight, together with such sums, or approved security therefor, as the court may from time to time fix as necessary to carry out the provisions of the statutes as amended. The plaintiff shall also give security for costs and, if the plaintiff elects to give security, for interest at the rate of 6 percent per annum from the date of the security.

(2) Complaint. The complaint shall set forth the facts on the basis of which the right to limit liability is asserted and all facts necessary to enable the court to determine the amount to which the owner's liability shall be limited. The complaint may demand exoneration from as well as limitation of liability. It shall state the voyage if any, on which the demands sought to be limited arose, with the date and place of its termination; the amount of all demands including all unsatisfied liens or claims of lien, in contract or in tort or otherwise, arising on that voyage, so far as known to the plaintiff, and what actions and proceedings, if any, are pending thereon; whether the vessel was damaged, lost, or abandoned, and, if so, when and where; the value of the vessel at the close of the voyage or, in case of wreck, the value of her wreckage, strippings, or proceeds, if any, and where and in whose possession they are; and the amount of any pending freight recovered or recoverable. If the plaintiff elects to transfer the plaintiff's interest in the vessel to a trustee, the complaint must further show any prior paramount liens thereon, and what voyages or trips, if any, she has made since the voyage or trip on which the claims sought to be limited arose, and any existing liens arising upon any such subsequent voyage or trip, with the amounts and causes thereof, and the names and addresses of the lienors, so far as known; and whether the vessel sustained any injury upon or by reason of such subsequent voyage or trip.

(3) Claims Against Owner; Injunction. Upon compliance by the owner with the requirements of subdivision (1) of this rule all claims and proceedings against the owner or the owner's property with respect to the matter in question shall cease. On application of the plaintiff the court shall enjoin the further prosecution of any action or proceeding against the plaintiff or the plaintiff's property with respect to any claim subject to limitation in the action.

(4) Notice to Claimants. Upon the owner's compliance with subdivision (1) of this rule the court shall issue a notice to all persons asserting claims with respect to which the complaint seeks limitation, admonishing them to file their respective claims with the clerk of the court and to serve on the attorneys for the plaintiff a copy thereof on or before a date to be named in the notice. The date so fixed shall not be less than 30 days after issuance of the notice. For cause shown, the court may enlarge the time within which claims may be filed. The notice shall be published in such newspaper or newspapers as the court may direct once a week for four successive weeks prior to the date fixed for the filing of claims. The plaintiff not later than the day of second publication shall also mail a copy of the notice to every person known to have made any claim against the vessel or the plaintiff arising out of the voyage or trip on which the claims sought to be limited arose. In cases involving death a copy of such notice shall be mailed to the decedent at the decedent's last known address, and also to any person who shall be known to have made any claim on account of such death.

(5) Claims and Answer. Claims shall be filed and served on or before the date specified in the notice provided for in subdivision (4) of this rule. Each claim shall specify the facts upon which the claimant relies in support of the claim, the items thereof, and the dates on which the same accrued. If a claimant desires to contest either the right to exoneration from or the right to limitation of liability the claimant shall file and serve an answer to the complaint unless the claim has included an answer.

(6) Information to be Given Claimants. Within 30 days after the date specified in the notice for filing claims, or within such time as the court thereafter may allow, the plaintiff shall mail to the attorney for each claimant (or if the claimant has no attorney to the claimant) a list setting forth (a) the name of each claimant, (b) the name and address of the claimant's attorney (if the claimant is known to have one), (c) the nature of the claim, i.e., whether property loss, property damage, death, personal injury etc., and (d) the amount thereof.

(7) Insufficiency of Fund or Security. Any claimant may by motion demand that the funds deposited in court or the security given by the plaintiff be increased on the ground that they are less than the value of the plaintiff's interest in the vessel and pending freight. Thereupon the court shall cause due appraisement to be made of the value of the plaintiff's interest in the vessel and pending freight; and if the court finds that the deposit or security is either insufficient or excessive it shall order its increase or reduction. In like manner any claimant may demand that the deposit or security be increased on the ground that it is insufficient to carry out the provisions of the statutes relating to claims in respect of loss of life or bodily injury; and, after notice and hearing, the court may similarly order that the deposit or security be increased or reduced.

(8) Objections to Claims: Distribution of Fund. Any interested party may question or controvert any claim without filing an objection thereto. Upon determination of liability the fund deposited or secured, or the proceeds of the vessel and pending freight, shall be divided pro rata, subject to all relevant provisions of law, among the several claimants in proportion to the amounts of their respective claims, duly proved, saving, however, to all parties any priority to which they may be legally entitled.

(9) Venue; Transfer. The complaint shall be filed in any district in which the vessel has been attached or arrested to answer for any claim with respect to which the plaintiff seeks to limit liability; or, if the vessel has not been attached or arrested, then in any district in which the owner has been sued with respect to any such claim. When the vessel has not been attached or arrested to answer the matters aforesaid, and suit has not been commenced against the owner, the proceedings may be had in the district in which the vessel may be, but if the vessel is not within any district and no suit has been commenced in any district, then the complaint may be filed in any district. For the convenience of parties and witnesses, in the interest of justice, the court may transfer the action to any district; if venue is wrongly laid the court shall dismiss or, if it be in the interest of justice, transfer the action to any district in which it could have been brought. If the vessel shall have been sold, the proceeds shall represent the vessel for the purposes of these rules.

(Added Feb. 28, 1966, eff. July 1, 1966, and amended Mar. 2, 1987, eff. Aug. 1, 1987.)

RULE G. FORFEITURE ACTIONS IN REM

(1) Scope. This rule governs a forfeiture action in rem arising from a federal statute. To the extent that this rule does not address an issue, Supplemental Rules C and E and the Federal Rules of Civil Procedure also apply.

(2) Complaint. The complaint must:

(a) be verified;

(b) state the grounds for subject-matter jurisdiction, in rem jurisdiction over the defendant property, and venue;

(c) describe the property with reasonable particularity;

(d) if the property is tangible, state its location when any seizure occurred and — if different — its location when the action is filed;

(e) identify the statute under which the forfeiture action is brought; and

(f) state sufficiently detailed facts to support a reasonable belief that the government will be able to meet its burden of proof at trial.

(3) Judicial Authorization and Process.

(a) Real Property. If the defendant is real property, the government must proceed under 18 U.S.C. § 985.

(b) Other Property; Arrest Warrant. If the defendant is not real property:

(i) the clerk must issue a warrant to arrest the property if it is in the government's possession, custody, or control;

(ii) the court—on finding probable cause—must issue a warrant to arrest the property if it is not in the government's possession, custody, or control and is not subject to a judicial restraining order; and

(iii) a warrant is not necessary if the property is subject to a judicial restraining order.

(c) Execution of Process.

(i) The warrant and any supplemental process must be delivered to a person or organization authorized to execute it, who may be: (A) a marshal or any other United States officer or employee; (B) someone under contract with the United States; or (C) someone specially appointed by the court for that purpose.

(ii) The authorized person or organization must execute the warrant and any supplemental process on property in the United States as soon as practicable unless:

(A) the property is in the government's possession, custody, or control; or

(B) the court orders a different time when the complaint is under seal, the action is stayed before the warrant and supplemental process are executed, or the court finds other good cause.

(iii) The warrant and any supplemental process may be executed within the district or, when authorized by statute, outside the district.

(iv) If executing a warrant on property outside the United States is required, the warrant may be transmitted to an appropriate authority for serving process where the property is located.

(4) Notice.

(a) Notice by Publication.

(i) When Publication Is Required. A judgment of forfeiture may be entered only if the government has published notice of the action within a reasonable time after filing the complaint or at a time the court orders. But notice need not be published if:

(A) the defendant property is worth less than $1,000 and direct notice is sent under Rule G(4)(b) to every person the government can reasonably identify as a potential claimant; or

(B) the court finds that the cost of publication exceeds the property's value and that other means of notice would satisfy due process.

(ii) Content of the Notice. Unless the court orders otherwise, the notice must:

(A) describe the property with reasonable particularity;

(B) state the times under Rule G(5) to file a claim and to answer; and

(C) name the government attorney to be served with the claim and answer.

(iii) Frequency of Publication. Published notice must appear:

(A) once a week for three consecutive weeks; or

(B) only once if, before the action was filed, notice of nonjudicial forfeiture of the same property was published on an official internet government forfeiture site for at least 30 consecutive days, or in a newspaper of general circulation for three consecutive weeks in a district where publication is authorized under Rule G(4)(a)(iv).

(iv) Means of Publication. The government should select from the following options a means of publication reasonably calculated to notify potential claimants of the action:

(A) if the property is in the United States, publication in a newspaper generally circulated in the district where the action is filed, where the property was seized, or where property that was not seized is located;

(B) if the property is outside the United States, publication in a newspaper generally circulated in a district where the action is filed, in a newspaper generally circulated in the country where the property is located, or in legal notices published and generally circulated in the country where the property is located; or

(C) instead of (A) or (B), posting a notice on an official internet government forfeiture site for at least 30 consecutive days.

(b) Notice to Known Potential Claimants.

(i) Direct Notice Required. The government must send notice of the action and a copy of the complaint to any person who reasonably appears to be a potential claimant on the facts known to the government before the end of the time for filing a claim under Rule G(5)(a)(ii)(B).

(ii) Content of the Notice. The notice must state:

(A) the date when the notice is sent;

(B) a deadline for filing a claim, at least 35 days after the notice is sent;

(C) that an answer or a motion under Rule 12 must be filed no later than 21 days after filing the claim; and

(D) the name of the government attorney to be served with the claim and answer.

(iii) Sending Notice.

(A) The notice must be sent by means reasonably calculated to reach the potential claimant.

(B) Notice may be sent to the potential claimant or to the attorney representing the potential claimant with respect to the seizure of the property or in a related investigation, administrative forfeiture proceeding, or criminal case.

(C) Notice sent to a potential claimant who is incarcerated must be sent to the place of incarceration.

(D) Notice to a person arrested in connection with an offense giving rise to the forfeiture who is not incarcerated when notice is sent may be sent to the address that person last gave to the agency that arrested or released the person.

(E) Notice to a person from whom the property was seized who is not incarcerated when notice is sent may be sent to the last address that person gave to the agency that seized the property.

(iv) When Notice Is Sent. Notice by the following means is sent on the date when it is placed in the mail, delivered to a commercial carrier, or sent by electronic mail.

(v) Actual Notice. A potential claimant who had actual notice of a forfeiture action may not oppose or seek relief from forfeiture because of the government's failure to send the required notice.

(5) Responsive Pleadings.

(a) Filing a Claim.

(i) A person who asserts an interest in the defendant property may contest the forfeiture by filing a claim in the court where the action is pending. The claim must:

(A) identify the specific property claimed;

(B) identify the claimant and state the claimant's interest in the property;

(C) be signed by the claimant under penalty of perjury; and

(D) be served on the government attorney designated under Rule G(4)(a)(ii)(C) or (b)(ii)(D).

(ii) Unless the court for good cause sets a different time, the claim must be filed:

(A) by the time stated in a direct notice sent under Rule G(4)(b);

(B) if notice was published but direct notice was not sent to the claimant or the claimant's attorney, no later than 30 days after final publication of newspaper notice or legal notice under Rule G(4)(a) or no later than 60 days after the first day of publication on an official internet government forfeiture site; or

(C) if notice was not published and direct notice was not sent to the claimant or the claimant's attorney:

(1) if the property was in the government's possession, custody, or control when the complaint was filed, no later than 60 days after the filing, not counting any time when the complaint was under seal or when the action was stayed before execution of a warrant issued under Rule G(3)(b); or

(2) if the property was not in the government's possession, custody, or control when the complaint was filed, no later than 60 days after the government complied with 18 U.S.C. § 985(c) as to real property, or 60 days after process was executed on the property under Rule G(3).

(iii) A claim filed by a person asserting an interest as a bailee must identify the bailor, and if filed on the bailor's behalf must state the authority to do so.

(b) Answer. A claimant must serve and file an answer to the complaint or a motion under Rule 12 within 21 days after filing the claim. A claimant waives an objection to in rem jurisdiction or to venue if the objection is not made by motion or stated in the answer.

(6) Special Interrogatories.

(a) Time and Scope. The government may serve special interrogatories limited to the claimant's identity and relationship to the defendant property without the court's leave at any time after the claim is filed and before discovery is closed. But if the claimant serves a motion to dismiss the action, the government must serve the interrogatories within 21 days after the motion is served.

(b) Answers or Objections. Answers or objections to these interrogatories must be served within 21 days after the interrogatories are served.

(c) Government's Response Deferred. The government need not respond to a claimant's motion to dismiss the action under Rule G(8)(b) until 21 days after the claimant has answered these interrogatories.

(7) Preserving, Preventing Criminal Use, and Disposing of Property; Sales.

(a) Preserving and Preventing Criminal Use of Property. When the government does not have actual possession of the defendant property the court, on motion or on its own, may enter any order necessary to preserve the property, to prevent its removal or encumbrance, or to prevent its use in a criminal offense.

(b) Interlocutory Sale or Delivery.

(i) Order to Sell. On motion by a party or a person having custody of the property, the court may order all or part of the property sold if:

(A) the property is perishable or at risk of deterioration, decay, or injury by being detained in custody pending the action;

(B) the expense of keeping the property is excessive or is disproportionate to its fair market value;

(C) the property is subject to a mortgage or to taxes on which the owner is in default; or

(D) the court finds other good cause.

(ii) Who Makes the Sale. A sale must be made by a United States agency that has authority to sell the property, by the agency's contractor, or by any person the court designates.

(iii) Sale Procedures. The sale is governed by 28 U.S.C. §§ 2001, 2002, and 2004, unless all parties, with the court's approval, agree to the sale, aspects of the sale, or different procedures.

(iv) Sale Proceeds. Sale proceeds are a substitute res subject to forfeiture in place of the property that was sold. The proceeds must be held in an interest-bearing account maintained by the United States pending the conclusion of the forfeiture action.

(v) Delivery on a Claimant's Motion. The court may order that the property be delivered to the claimant pending the conclusion of the action if the claimant shows circumstances that would permit sale under Rule G(7)(b)(i) and gives security under these rules.

(c) Disposing of Forfeited Property. Upon entry of a forfeiture judgment, the property or proceeds from selling the property must be disposed of as provided by law.

(8) Motions.

(a) Motion To Suppress Use of the Property as Evidence. If the defendant property was seized, a party with standing to contest the lawfulness of the seizure may move to suppress use of the property as evidence. Suppression does not affect forfeiture of the property based on independently derived evidence.

(b) Motion To Dismiss the Action.

(i) A claimant who establishes standing to contest forfeiture may move to dismiss the action under Rule 12(b).

(ii) In an action governed by 18 U.S.C. § 983(a)(3)(D) the complaint may not be dismissed on the ground that the government did not have adequate evidence at the time the complaint was filed to establish the forfeitability of the property. The sufficiency of the complaint is governed by Rule G(2).

(c) Motion To Strike a Claim or Answer.

(i) At any time before trial, the government may move to strike a claim or answer:

(A) for failing to comply with Rule G(5) or (6), or

(B) because the claimant lacks standing.

(ii) The motion:

(A) must be decided before any motion by the claimant to dismiss the action; and

(B) may be presented as a motion for judgment on the pleadings or as a motion to determine after a hearing or by summary judgment whether the claimant can carry the burden of establishing standing by a preponderance of the evidence.

(d) Petition To Release Property.

(i) If a United States agency or an agency's contractor holds property for judicial or nonjudicial forfeiture under a statute governed by 18 U.S.C. § 983(f), a person who has filed a claim to the property may petition for its release under § 983(f).

(ii) If a petition for release is filed before a judicial forfeiture action is filed against the property, the petition may be filed either in the district where the property was seized or in the district where a warrant to seize the property issued. If a judicial forfeiture action against the property is later filed in another district — or if the government shows that the action will be filed in another district — the petition may be transferred to that district under 28 U.S.C. § 1404.

(e) Excessive Fines. A claimant may seek to mitigate a forfeiture under the Excessive Fines Clause of the Eighth Amendment by motion for summary judgment or by motion made after entry of a forfeiture judgment if:

(i) the claimant has pleaded the defense under Rule 8; and

(ii) the parties have had the opportunity to conduct civil discovery on the defense.

(9) Trial. Trial is to the court unless any party demands trial by jury under Rule 38.

(Added Apr. 12, 2006, eff. Dec. 1, 2006, and amended Mar. 26, 2009, eff. Dec. 1, 2009.)

INDEX TO FEDERAL RULES OF CIVIL PROCEDURE

*

FEDERAL RULES OF EVIDENCE

Including Amendments Effective December 1, 2011

Research Note

These rules may be searched electronically on Westlaw in the US-RULES database; updates to these rules may be found on Westlaw in US-RULESPDATES. For search tips, and a detailed summary of database content, consult the Westlaw Scope Screen of each database.

ARTICLE I. GENERAL PROVISIONS

RULE 101. SCOPE; DEFINITIONS

(a) **Scope.** These rules apply to proceedings in United States courts. The specific courts and proceedings to which the rules apply, along with exceptions, are set out in Rule 1101.

(b) **Definitions.** In these rules:

- (1) "civil case" means a civil action or proceeding;
- (2) "criminal case" includes a criminal proceeding;
- (3) "public office" includes a public agency;
- (4) "record" includes a memorandum, report, or data compilation;
- (5) a "rule prescribed by the Supreme Court" means a rule adopted by the Supreme Court under statutory authority; and
- (6) a reference to any kind of written material or any other medium includes electronically stored information.

(Pub.L. 93–595, § 1, Jan. 2, 1975, 88 Stat. 1929; Mar. 2, 1987, eff. Oct. 1, 1987; Apr. 25, 1988, eff. Nov. 1, 1988; Apr. 22, 1993, eff. Dec. 1, 1993; Apr. 26, 2011, eff. Dec. 1, 2011.)

RULE 102. PURPOSE

These rules should be construed so as to administer every proceeding fairly, eliminate unjustifiable expense and delay, and promote the development of evidence law, to the end of ascertaining the truth and securing a just determination.

(Pub.L. 93–595, § 1, Jan. 2, 1975, 88 Stat.1929; Apr. 26, 2011, eff. Dec. 1, 2011.)

RULE 103. RULINGS ON EVIDENCE

(a) **Preserving a Claim of Error.** A party may claim error in a ruling to admit or exclude evidence only if the error affects a substantial right of the party and:

- (1) if the ruling admits evidence, a party, on the record:
  - (A) timely objects or moves to strike; and
  - (B) states the specific ground, unless it was apparent from the context; or
- (2) if the ruling excludes evidence, a party informs the court of its substance by an offer of proof, unless the substance was apparent from the context.

(b) **Not Needing to Renew an Objection or Offer of Proof.** Once the court rules definitively on the record—either before or at trial—a party need not renew an objection or offer of proof to preserve a claim of error for appeal.

(c) **Court's Statement About the Ruling; Directing an Offer of Proof.** The court may make any statement about the character or form of the evidence, the objection made, and the ruling. The court may direct that an offer of proof be made in question-and-answer form.

(d) **Preventing the Jury from Hearing Inadmissible Evidence.** To the extent practicable, the court must conduct a jury trial so that inadmissible evidence is not suggested to the jury by any means.

(e) **Taking Notice of Plain Error.** A court may take notice of a plain error affecting a substantial right, even if the claim of error was not properly preserved.

(Pub.L. 93–595, § 1, Jan. 2, 1975, 88 Stat. 1929; Apr. 17, 2000, eff. Dec. 1, 2000; Apr. 26, 2011, eff. Dec. 1, 2011.)

RULE 104. PRELIMINARY QUESTIONS

(a) **In General.** The court must decide any preliminary question about whether a witness is qualified, a privilege exists, or evidence is admissible. In so deciding, the court is not bound by evidence rules, except those on privilege.

(b) **Relevance That Depends on a Fact.** When the relevance of evidence depends on whether a fact exists, proof must be introduced sufficient to support a finding that the fact does exist. The court may admit the proposed evidence on the condition that the proof be introduced later.

(c) **Conducting a Hearing So That the Jury Cannot Hear It.** The court must conduct any hearing on a preliminary question so that the jury cannot hear it if:

(1) the hearing involves the admissibility of a confession;

(2) a defendant in a criminal case is a witness and so requests; or

(3) justice so requires.

(d) **Cross-Examining a Defendant in a Criminal Case.** By testifying on a preliminary question, a defendant in a criminal case does not become subject to cross-examination on other issues in the case.

(e) **Evidence Relevant to Weight and Credibility.** This rule does not limit a party's right to introduce before the jury evidence that is relevant to the weight or credibility of other evidence.

(Pub.L. 93–595, § 1, Jan. 2, 1975, 88 Stat.1930; Mar. 2, 1987, eff. Oct. 1, 1987; Apr. 26, 2011, eff. Dec. 1, 2011.)

RULE 105. LIMITING EVIDENCE THAT IS NOT ADMISSIBLE AGAINST OTHER PARTIES OR FOR OTHER PURPOSES

If the court admits evidence that is admissible against a party or for a purpose—but not against another party or for another purpose—the court, on timely request, must restrict the evidence to its proper scope and instruct the jury accordingly.

(Pub.L. 93–595, § 1, Jan. 2, 1975, 88 Stat. 1930; Apr. 26, 2011, eff. Dec. 1, 2011.)

RULE 106. REMAINDER OF OR RELATED WRITINGS OR RECORDED STATEMENTS

If a party introduces all or part of a writing or recorded statement, an adverse party may require the introduction, at that time, of any other part—or any other writing or recorded statement—that in fairness ought to be considered at the same time.

(Pub.L. 93–595, § 1, Jan. 2, 1975, 88 Stat. 1930; Mar. 2, 1987, eff. Oct. 1, 1987; Apr. 26, 2011, eff. Dec. 1, 2011.)

ARTICLE II. JUDICIAL NOTICE

RULE 201. JUDICIAL NOTICE OF ADJUDICATIVE FACTS

(a) **Scope.** This rule governs judicial notice of an adjudicative fact only, not a legislative fact.

(b) **Kinds of Facts That May Be Judicially Noticed.** The court may judicially notice a fact that is not subject to reasonable dispute because it:

(1) is generally known within the trial court's territorial jurisdiction; or

(2) can be accurately and readily determined from sources whose accuracy cannot reasonably be questioned.

(c) **Taking Notice.** The court:

(1) may take judicial notice on its own; or

(2) must take judicial notice if a party requests it and the court is supplied with the necessary information.

(d) **Timing.** The court may take judicial notice at any stage of the proceeding.

(e) **Opportunity to Be Heard.** On timely request, a party is entitled to be heard on the propriety of taking judicial notice and the nature of the fact to be noticed. If the court takes judicial notice before notifying a party, the party, on request, is still entitled to be heard.

(f) **Instructing the Jury.** In a civil case, the court must instruct the jury to accept the noticed fact as conclusive. In a criminal case, the court must instruct the jury that it may or may not accept the noticed fact as conclusive.

(Pub.L. 93–595, § 1, Jan. 2, 1975, 88 Stat. 1930; Apr. 26, 2011, eff. Dec. 1, 2011.)

ARTICLE III. PRESUMPTIONS IN CIVIL CASES

RULE 301. PRESUMPTIONS IN CIVIL CASES GENERALLY

In a civil case, unless a federal statute or these rules provide otherwise, the party against whom a presumption is directed has the burden of producing evidence to rebut the presumption. But this rule does not shift the burden of persuasion, which remains on the party who had it originally.

(Pub.L. 93–595, § 1, Jan. 2, 1975, 88 Stat. 1931; Apr. 26, 2011, eff. Dec. 1, 2011.)

RULE 302. APPLYING STATE LAW TO PRESUMPTIONS IN CIVIL CASES

In a civil case, state law governs the effect of a presumption regarding a claim or defense for which state law supplies the rule of decision.

(Pub.L. 93–595, § 1, Jan. 2, 1975, 88 Stat. 1931; Apr. 26, 2011, eff. Dec. 1, 2011.)

ARTICLE IV. RELEVANCE AND ITS LIMITS

RULE 401. TEST FOR RELEVANT EVIDENCE

Evidence is relevant if:

(a) it has any tendency to make a fact more or less probable than it would be without the evidence; and

(b) the fact is of consequence in determining the action.

(Pub.L. 93–595, § 1, Jan. 2, 1975, 88 Stat.1931; Apr. 26, 2011, eff. Dec. 1, 2011.)

RULE 402. GENERAL ADMISSIBILITY OF RELEVANT EVIDENCE

Relevant evidence is admissible unless any of the following provides otherwise:

- the United States Constitution;
- a federal statute;
- these rules; or
- other rules prescribed by the Supreme Court.

Irrelevant evidence is not admissible.

(Pub.L. 93–595, § 1, Jan. 2, 1975, 88 Stat. 1931; Apr. 26, 2011, eff. Dec. 1, 2011.)

RULE 403. EXCLUDING RELEVANT EVIDENCE FOR PREJUDICE, CONFUSION, WASTE OF TIME, OR OTHER REASONS

The court may exclude relevant evidence if its probative value is substantially outweighed by a danger of one or more of the following: unfair prejudice, confusing the issues, misleading the jury, undue delay, wasting time, or needlessly presenting cumulative evidence.

(Pub.L. 93–595, § 1, Jan. 2, 1975, 88 Stat. 1932; Apr. 26, 2011, eff. Dec. 1, 2011.)

RULE 404. CHARACTER EVIDENCE; CRIMES OR OTHER ACTS

(a) Character Evidence.

(1) ***Prohibited Uses.*** Evidence of a person's character or character trait is not admissible to prove that on a particular occasion the person acted in accordance with the character or trait.

(2) ***Exceptions for a Defendant or Victim in a Criminal Case.*** The following exceptions apply in a criminal case:

(A) a defendant may offer evidence of the defendant's pertinent trait, and if the evidence is admitted, the prosecutor may offer evidence to rebut it;

(B) subject to the limitations in Rule 412, a defendant may offer evidence of an alleged victim's pertinent trait, and if the evidence is admitted, the prosecutor may:

(i) offer evidence to rebut it; and

(ii) offer evidence of the defendant's same trait; and

(C) in a homicide case, the prosecutor may offer evidence of the alleged victim's trait of peacefulness to rebut evidence that the victim was the first aggressor.

(3) ***Exceptions for a Witness.*** Evidence of a witness's character may be admitted under Rules 607, 608, and 609.

(b) Crimes, Wrongs, or Other Acts.

(1) ***Prohibited Uses.*** Evidence of a crime, wrong, or other act is not admissible to prove a person's character in order to show that on a particular occasion the person acted in accordance with the character.

(2) ***Permitted Uses; Notice in a Criminal Case.*** This evidence may be admissible for another purpose, such as proving motive, opportunity, intent, preparation, plan, knowledge, identity, absence of mistake, or lack of accident. On request by a defendant in a criminal case, the prosecutor must:

(A) provide reasonable notice of the general nature of any such evidence that the prosecutor intends to offer at trial; and

(B) do so before trial—or during trial if the court, for good cause, excuses lack of pretrial notice.

(Pub.L. 93–595, § 1, Jan. 2, 1975, 88 Stat.1932; Mar. 2, 1987, eff. Oct. 1, 1987; Apr. 30, 1991, eff. Dec. 1, 1991; Apr. 17, 2000, eff. Dec. 1, 2000; Apr. 12, 2006, eff. Dec. 1, 2006; Apr. 26, 2011, eff. Dec. 1, 2011.)

RULE 405. METHODS OF PROVING CHARACTER

(a) **By Reputation or Opinion.** When evidence of a person's character or character trait is admissible, it may be proved by testimony about the person's reputation or by testimony in the form of an opinion. On cross-examination of the character witness, the court may allow an inquiry into relevant specific instances of the person's conduct.

(b) **By Specific Instances of Conduct.** When a person's character or character trait is an essential element of a charge, claim, or defense, the character or trait may also be proved by relevant specific instances of the person's conduct.

(Pub.L. 93–595, § 1, Jan. 2, 1975, 88 Stat. 1932; Mar. 2, 1987, eff. Oct. 1, 1987; Apr. 26, 2011, eff. Dec. 1, 2011.)

RULE 406. HABIT; ROUTINE PRACTICE

Evidence of a person's habit or an organization's routine practice may be admitted to prove that on a particular occasion the person or organization acted in accordance with the habit or routine practice. The court may admit this evidence regardless of whether it is corroborated or whether there was an eyewitness.

(Pub.L. 93–595, § 1, Jan. 2, 1975, 88 Stat. 1932; Apr. 26, 2011, eff. Dec. 1, 2011.)

RULE 407. SUBSEQUENT REMEDIAL MEASURES

When measures are taken that would have made an earlier injury or harm less likely to occur, evidence of the subsequent measures is not admissible to prove:

- negligence;
- culpable conduct;
- a defect in a product or its design; or
- a need for a warning or instruction.

But the court may admit this evidence for another purpose, such as impeachment or—if disputed—proving ownership, control, or the feasibility of precautionary measures.

(Pub.L. 93–595, § 1, Jan. 2, 1975, 88 Stat. 1932; Apr. 11, 1997, eff. Dec. 1, 1997; Apr. 26, 2011, eff. Dec. 1, 2011.)

RULE 408. COMPROMISE OFFERS AND NEGOTIATIONS

(a) **Prohibited Uses.** Evidence of the following is not admissible—on behalf of any party—either to prove or disprove the validity or amount of a disputed claim or to impeach by a prior inconsistent statement or a contradiction:

(1) furnishing, promising, or offering—or accepting, promising to accept, or offering to accept—a valuable consideration in compromising or attempting to compromise the claim; and

(2) conduct or a statement made during compromise negotiations about the claim—except when offered in a criminal case and when the negotiations related to a claim by a public office in the exercise of its regulatory, investigative, or enforcement authority.

(b) **Exceptions.** The court may admit this evidence for another purpose, such as proving a witness's bias or prejudice, negating a contention of undue delay, or proving an effort to obstruct a criminal investigation or prosecution.

(Pub.L. 93–595, § 1, Jan. 2, 1975, 88 Stat. 1933; Apr. 12, 2006, eff. Dec. 1, 2006; Apr. 26, 2011, eff. Dec. 1, 2011.)

RULE 409. OFFERS TO PAY MEDICAL AND SIMILAR EXPENSES

Evidence of furnishing, promising to pay, or offering to pay medical, hospital, or similar expenses resulting from an injury is not admissible to prove liability for the injury.

(Pub.L. 93–595, § 1, Jan. 2, 1975, 88 Stat.1933; Apr. 26, 2011, eff. Dec. 1, 2011.)

RULE 410. PLEAS, PLEA DISCUSSIONS, AND RELATED STATEMENTS

(a) **Prohibited Uses.** In a civil or criminal case, evidence of the following is not admissible against the defendant who made the plea or participated in the plea discussions:

(1) a guilty plea that was later withdrawn;

(2) a nolo contendere plea;

(3) a statement made during a proceeding on either of those pleas under Federal Rule of Criminal Procedure 11 or a comparable state procedure; or

(4) a statement made during plea discussions with an attorney for the prosecuting authority if the

discussions did not result in a guilty plea or they resulted in a later-withdrawn guilty plea.

(b) **Exceptions.** The court may admit a statement described in Rule 410(a)(3) or (4):

(1) in any proceeding in which another statement made during the same plea or plea discussions has been introduced, if in fairness the statements ought to be considered together; or

(2) in a criminal proceeding for perjury or false statement, if the defendant made the statement under oath, on the record, and with counsel present.

(Pub.L. 93–595, § 1, Jan. 2, 1975, 88 Stat. 1933; Pub.L. 94–149, § 1(9), Dec. 12, 1975, 89 Stat. 805; Apr. 30, 1979, eff. Dec. 1, 1980; Apr. 26, 2011, eff. Dec. 1, 2011.)

RULE 411. LIABILITY INSURANCE

Evidence that a person was or was not insured against liability is not admissible to prove whether the person acted negligently or otherwise wrongfully. But the court may admit this evidence for another purpose, such as proving a witness's bias or prejudice or proving agency, ownership, or control.

(Pub.L. 93–595, § 1, Jan. 2, 1975, 88 Stat.1933; Mar. 2, 1987, eff. Oct. 1, 1987; Apr. 26, 2011, eff. Dec. 1, 2011.)

RULE 412. SEX-OFFENSE CASES: THE VICTIM'S SEXUAL BEHAVIOR OR PREDISPOSITION

(a) **Prohibited Uses.** The following evidence is not admissible in a civil or criminal proceeding involving alleged sexual misconduct:

(1) evidence offered to prove that a victim engaged in other sexual behavior; or

(2) evidence offered to prove a victim's sexual predisposition.

(b) **Exceptions.**

(1) ***Criminal Cases.*** The court may admit the following evidence in a criminal case:

(A) evidence of specific instances of a victim's sexual behavior, if offered to prove that someone other than the defendant was the source of semen, injury, or other physical evidence;

(B) evidence of specific instances of a victim's sexual behavior with respect to the person accused of the sexual misconduct, if offered by the defendant to prove consent or if offered by the prosecutor; and

(C) evidence whose exclusion would violate the defendant's constitutional rights.

(2) ***Civil Cases.*** In a civil case, the court may admit evidence offered to prove a victim's sexual behavior or sexual predisposition if its probative value substantially outweighs the danger of harm to any victim and of unfair prejudice to any party. The court may admit evidence of a victim's reputation only if the victim has placed it in controversy.

(c) **Procedure to Determine Admissibility.**

(1) ***Motion.*** If a party intends to offer evidence under Rule 412(b), the party must:

(A) file a motion that specifically describes the evidence and states the purpose for which it is to be offered;

(B) do so at least 14 days before trial unless the court, for good cause, sets a different time;

(C) serve the motion on all parties; and

(D) notify the victim or, when appropriate, the victim's guardian or representative.

(2) ***Hearing.*** Before admitting evidence under this rule, the court must conduct an in camera hearing and give the victim and parties a right to attend and be heard. Unless the court orders otherwise, the motion, related materials, and the record of the hearing must be and remain sealed.

(d) **Definition of "Victim."** In this rule, "victim" includes an alleged victim.

(Added Pub.L. 95–540, § 2(a), Oct. 28, 1978, 92 Stat. 2046, and amended Pub.L. 100–690, Title VII, § 7046(a), Nov. 18, 1988, 102 Stat. 4400; Apr. 29, 1994, eff. Dec. 1, 1994; Pub.L. 103–322, Title IV, § 40141(b), Sept. 13, 1994, 108 Stat. 1919; Apr. 26, 2011, eff. Dec. 1, 2011.)

RULE 413. SIMILAR CRIMES IN SEXUAL-ASSAULT CASES

(a) **Permitted Uses.** In a criminal case in which a defendant is accused of a sexual assault, the court may admit evidence that the defendant committed any other sexual assault. The evidence may be considered on any matter to which it is relevant.

(b) **Disclosure to the Defendant.** If the prosecutor intends to offer this evidence, the prosecutor must disclose it to the defendant, including witnesses' statements or a summary of the expected testimony. The prosecutor must do so at least 15 days before trial or at a later time that the court allows for good cause.

(c) **Effect on Other Rules.** This rule does not limit the admission or consideration of evidence under any other rule.

(d) **Definition of "Sexual Assault."** In this rule and Rule 415, "sexual assault" means a crime under federal law or under state law (as "state" is defined in 18 U.S.C. § 513) involving:

(1) any conduct prohibited by 18 U.S.C. chapter 109A;

(2) contact, without consent, between any part of the defendant's body—or an object—and another person's genitals or anus;

(3) contact, without consent, between the defendant's genitals or anus and any part of another person's body;

(4) deriving sexual pleasure or gratification from inflicting death, bodily injury, or physical pain on another person; or

(5) an attempt or conspiracy to engage in conduct described in subparagraphs (1)–(4).

(Added Pub.L. 103–322, Title XXXII, § 320935(a), Sept. 13, 1994, 108 Stat. 2136; Apr. 26, 2011, eff. Dec. 1, 2011.)

RULE 414. SIMILAR CRIMES IN CHILD-MOLESTATION CASES

(a) Permitted Uses. In a criminal case in which a defendant is accused of child molestation, the court may admit evidence that the defendant committed any other child molestation. The evidence may be considered on any matter to which it is relevant.

(b) Disclosure to the Defendant. If the prosecutor intends to offer this evidence, the prosecutor must disclose it to the defendant, including witnesses' statements or a summary of the expected testimony. The prosecutor must do so at least 15 days before trial or at a later time that the court allows for good cause.

(c) Effect on Other Rules. This rule does not limit the admission or consideration of evidence under any other rule.

(d) Definition of "Child" and "Child Molestation." In this rule and Rule 415:

(1) "child" means a person below the age of 14; and

(2) "child molestation" means a crime under federal law or under state law (as "state" is defined in 18 U.S.C. § 513) involving:

(A) any conduct prohibited by 18 U.S.C. chapter 109A and committed with a child;

(B) any conduct prohibited by 18 U.S.C. chapter 110;

(C) contact between any part of the defendant's body—or an object—and a child's genitals or anus;

(D) contact between the defendant's genitals or anus and any part of a child's body;

(E) deriving sexual pleasure or gratification from inflicting death, bodily injury, or physical pain on a child; or

(F) an attempt or conspiracy to engage in conduct described in subparagraphs (A)–(E).

(Added Pub.L. 103–322, Title XXXII, § 320935(a), Sept. 13, 1994, 108 Stat. 2135; Apr. 26, 2011, eff. Dec. 1, 2011.)

RULE 415. SIMILAR ACTS IN CIVIL CASES INVOLVING SEXUAL ASSAULT OR CHILD MOLESTATION

(a) Permitted Uses. In a civil case involving a claim for relief based on a party's alleged sexual assault or child molestation, the court may admit evidence that the party committed any other sexual assault or child molestation. The evidence may be considered as provided in Rules 413 and 414.

(b) Disclosure to the Opponent. If a party intends to offer this evidence, the party must disclose it to the party against whom it will be offered, including witnesses' statements or a summary of the expected testimony. The party must do so at least 15 days before trial or at a later time that the court allows for good cause.

(c) Effect on Other Rules. This rule does not limit the admission or consideration of evidence under any other rule.

(Added Pub.L. 103–322, Title XXXII, § 320935(a), Sept. 13, 1994, 108 Stat. 2137; Apr. 26, 2011, eff. Dec. 1, 2011.)

ARTICLE V. PRIVILEGES

RULE 501. PRIVILEGE IN GENERAL

The common law—as interpreted by United States courts in the light of reason and experience—governs a claim of privilege unless any of the following provides otherwise:

- the United States Constitution;
- a federal statute; or
- rules prescribed by the Supreme Court.

But in a civil case, state law governs privilege regarding a claim or defense for which state law supplies the rule of decision.

(Pub.L. 93–595, § 1, Jan. 2, 1975, 88 Stat. 1933; Apr. 26, 2011, eff. Dec. 1, 2011.)

RULE 502. ATTORNEY–CLIENT PRIVILEGE AND WORK PRODUCT; LIMITATIONS ON WAIVER

The following provisions apply, in the circumstances set out, to disclosure of a communication or information covered by the attorney-client privilege or work-product protection.

(a) **Disclosure Made in a Federal Proceeding or to a Federal Office or Agency; Scope of a Waiver.** When the disclosure is made in a federal proceeding or to a federal office or agency and waives the attorney-client privilege or work-product protection, the waiver extends to an undisclosed communication or information in a federal or state proceeding only if:

(1) the waiver is intentional;

(2) the disclosed and undisclosed communications or information concern the same subject matter; and

(3) they ought in fairness to be considered together.

(b) **Inadvertent Disclosure.** When made in a federal proceeding or to a federal office or agency, the disclosure does not operate as a waiver in a federal or state proceeding if:

(1) the disclosure is inadvertent;

(2) the holder of the privilege or protection took reasonable steps to prevent disclosure; and

(3) the holder promptly took reasonable steps to rectify the error, including (if applicable) following Federal Rule of Civil Procedure 26(b)(5)(B).

(c) **Disclosure Made in a State Proceeding.** When the disclosure is made in a state proceeding and is not the subject of a state-court order concerning waiver, the disclosure does not operate as a waiver in a federal proceeding if the disclosure:

(1) would not be a waiver under this rule if it had been made in a federal proceeding; or

(2) is not a waiver under the law of the state where the disclosure occurred.

(d) **Controlling Effect of a Court Order.** A federal court may order that the privilege or protection is not waived by disclosure connected with the litigation pending before the court—in which event the disclosure is also not a waiver in any other federal or state proceeding.

(e) **Controlling Effect of a Party Agreement.** An agreement on the effect of disclosure in a federal proceeding is binding only on the parties to the agreement, unless it is incorporated into a court order.

(f) **Controlling Effect of This Rule.** Notwithstanding Rules 101 and 1101, this rule applies to state proceedings and to federal court-annexed and federal court-mandated arbitration proceedings, in the circumstances set out in the rule. And notwithstanding Rule 501, this rule applies even if state law provides the rule of decision.

(g) **Definitions.** In this rule:

(1) "attorney-client privilege" means the protection that applicable law provides for confidential attorney-client communications; and

(2) "work-product protection" means the protection that applicable law provides for tangible material (or its intangible equivalent) prepared in anticipation of litigation or for trial.

(Pub.L. 110–322, § 1(a), Sept. 19, 2008, 122 Stat. 3537; Apr. 26, 2011, eff. Dec. 1, 2011.)

ARTICLE VI. WITNESSES

RULE 601. COMPETENCY TO TESTIFY IN GENERAL

Every person is competent to be a witness unless these rules provide otherwise. But in a civil case, state law governs the witness's competency regarding a claim or defense for which state law supplies the rule of decision.

(Pub.L. 93–595, § 1, Jan. 2, 1975, 88 Stat.1934; Apr. 26, 2011, eff. Dec. 1, 2011.)

RULE 602. NEED FOR PERSONAL KNOWLEDGE

A witness may testify to a matter only if evidence is introduced sufficient to support a finding that the witness has personal knowledge of the matter. Evidence to prove personal knowledge may consist of the witness's own testimony. This rule does not apply to a witness's expert testimony under Rule 703.

(Pub.L. 93–595, § 1, Jan. 2, 1975, 88 Stat. 1934; Mar. 2, 1987, eff. Oct. 1, 1987; Apr. 25, 1988, eff. Nov. 1, 1988; Apr. 26, 2011, eff. Dec. 1, 2011.)

RULE 603. OATH OR AFFIRMATION TO TESTIFY TRUTHFULLY

Before testifying, a witness must give an oath or affirmation to testify truthfully. It must be in a form designed to impress that duty on the witness's conscience.

(Pub.L. 93–595, § 1, Jan. 2, 1975, 88 Stat. 1934; Mar. 2, 1987, eff. Oct. 1, 1987; Apr. 26, 2011, eff. Dec. 1, 2011.)

RULE 604. INTERPRETER

An interpreter must be qualified and must give an oath or affirmation to make a true translation.

(Pub.L. 93–595, § 1, Jan. 2, 1975, 88 Stat. 1934; Mar. 2, 1987, eff. Oct. 1, 1987; Apr. 26, 2011, eff. Dec. 1, 2011.)

RULE 605. JUDGE'S COMPETENCY AS A WITNESS

The presiding judge may not testify as a witness at the trial. A party need not object to preserve the issue.

(Pub.L. 93–595, § 1, Jan. 2, 1975, 88 Stat. 1934; Apr. 26, 2011, eff. Dec. 1, 2011.)

RULE 606. JUROR'S COMPETENCY AS A WITNESS

(a) **At the Trial.** A juror may not testify as a witness before the other jurors at the trial. If a juror is called to testify, the court must give a party an opportunity to object outside the jury's presence.

(b) **During an Inquiry Into the Validity of a Verdict or Indictment.**

(1) **Prohibited Testimony or Other Evidence.** During an inquiry into the validity of a verdict or indictment, a juror may not testify about any statement made or incident that occurred during the jury's deliberations; the effect of anything on that juror's or another juror's vote; or any juror's mental processes concerning the verdict or indictment. The court may not receive a juror's affidavit or evidence of a juror's statement on these matters.

(2) **Exceptions.** A juror may testify about whether:

(A) extraneous prejudicial information was improperly brought to the jury's attention;

(B) an outside influence was improperly brought to bear on any juror; or

(C) a mistake was made in entering the verdict on the verdict form.

(Pub.L. 93–595, § 1, Jan. 2, 1975, 88 Stat. 1934; Pub.L. 94–149, § 1(10), Dec. 12, 1975, 89 Stat. 805; Mar. 2, 1987, eff. Oct. 1, 1987; Apr. 12, 2006, eff. Dec. 1, 2006; Apr. 26, 2011, eff. Dec. 1, 2011.)

RULE 607. WHO MAY IMPEACH A WITNESS

Any party, including the party that called the witness, may attack the witness's credibility.

(Pub.L. 93–595, § 1, Jan. 2, 1975, 88 Stat.1934; Mar. 2, 1987, eff. Oct. 1, 1987; Apr. 26, 2011, eff. Dec. 1, 2011.)

RULE 608. A WITNESS'S CHARACTER FOR TRUTHFULNESS OR UNTRUTHFULNESS

(a) **Reputation or Opinion Evidence.** A witness's credibility may be attacked or supported by testimony about the witness's reputation for having a character for truthfulness or untruthfulness, or by testimony in the form of an opinion about that character. But evidence of truthful character is admissible only after the witness's character for truthfulness has been attacked.

(b) **Specific Instances of Conduct.** Except for a criminal conviction under Rule 609, extrinsic evidence is not admissible to prove specific instances of a witness's conduct in order to attack or support the witness's character for truthfulness. But the court may, on cross-examination, allow them to be inquired into if they are probative of the character for truthfulness or untruthfulness of:

(1) the witness; or

(2) another witness whose character the witness being cross-examined has testified about.

By testifying on another matter, a witness does not waive any privilege against self-incrimination for testimony that relates only to the witness's character for truthfulness.

(Pub.L. 93–595, § 1, Jan. 2, 1975, 88 Stat.1935; Mar. 2, 1987, eff. Oct. 1, 1987; Apr. 25, 1988, eff. Nov. 1, 1988; Mar. 27, 2003, eff. Dec. 1, 2003; Apr. 26, 2011, eff. Dec. 1, 2011.)

RULE 609. IMPEACHMENT BY EVIDENCE OF A CRIMINAL CONVICTION

(a) **In General.** The following rules apply to attacking a witness's character for truthfulness by evidence of a criminal conviction:

(1) for a crime that, in the convicting jurisdiction, was punishable by death or by imprisonment for more than one year, the evidence:

(A) must be admitted, subject to Rule 403, in a civil case or in a criminal case in which the witness is not a defendant; and

(B) must be admitted in a criminal case in which the witness is a defendant, if the probative value of the evidence outweighs its prejudicial effect to that defendant; and

(2) for any crime regardless of the punishment, the evidence must be admitted if the court can readily determine that establishing the elements of the crime required proving—or the witness's admitting—a dishonest act or false statement.

(b) **Limit on Using the Evidence After 10 Years.** This subdivision (b) applies if more than 10 years have passed since the witness's conviction or release from confinement for it, whichever is later. Evidence of the conviction is admissible only if:

(1) its probative value, supported by specific facts and circumstances, substantially outweighs its prejudicial effect; and

(2) the proponent gives an adverse party reasonable written notice of the intent to use it so that the party has a fair opportunity to contest its use.

(c) **Effect of a Pardon, Annulment, or Certificate of Rehabilitation.** Evidence of a conviction is not admissible if:

(1) the conviction has been the subject of a pardon, annulment, certificate of rehabilitation, or other equivalent procedure based on a finding that the person has been rehabilitated, and the person has not been convicted of a later crime punishable by death or by imprisonment for more than one year; or

(2) the conviction has been the subject of a pardon, annulment, or other equivalent procedure based on a finding of innocence.

(d) **Juvenile Adjudications.** Evidence of a juvenile adjudication is admissible under this rule only if:

(1) it is offered in a criminal case;

(2) the adjudication was of a witness other than the defendant;

(3) an adult's conviction for that offense would be admissible to attack the adult's credibility; and

(4) admitting the evidence is necessary to fairly determine guilt or innocence.

(e) **Pendency of an Appeal.** A conviction that satisfies this rule is admissible even if an appeal is pending. Evidence of the pendency is also admissible.

(Pub.L. 93–595, § 1, Jan. 2, 1975, 88 Stat.1935; Mar. 2, 1987, eff. Oct. 1, 1987; Jan. 26, 1990, eff. Dec. 1, 1990; Apr. 12, 2006, eff. Dec. 1, 2006; Apr. 26, 2011, eff. Dec. 1, 2011.)

RULE 610. RELIGIOUS BELIEFS OR OPINIONS

Evidence of a witness's religious beliefs or opinions is not admissible to attack or support the witness's credibility.

(Pub.L. 93–595, § 1, Jan. 2, 1975, 88 Stat.1936; Mar. 2, 1987, eff. Oct. 1, 1987; Apr. 26, 2011, eff. Dec. 1, 2011.)

RULE 611. MODE AND ORDER OF EXAMINING WITNESSES AND PRESENTING EVIDENCE

(a) **Control by the Court; Purposes.** The court should exercise reasonable control over the mode and order of examining witnesses and presenting evidence so as to:

(1) make those procedures effective for determining the truth;

(2) avoid wasting time; and

(3) protect witnesses from harassment or undue embarrassment.

(b) **Scope of Cross–Examination.** Cross-examination should not go beyond the subject matter of the direct examination and matters affecting the witness's credibility. The court may allow inquiry into additional matters as if on direct examination.

(c) **Leading Questions.** Leading questions should not be used on direct examination except as necessary to develop the witness's testimony. Ordinarily, the court should allow leading questions:

(1) on cross-examination; and

(2) when a party calls a hostile witness, an adverse party, or a witness identified with an adverse party.

(Pub.L. 93–595, § 1, Jan. 2, 1975, 88 Stat. 1936; Mar. 2, 1987, eff. Oct. 1, 1987; Apr. 26, 2011, eff. Dec. 1, 2011.)

RULE 612. WRITING USED TO REFRESH A WITNESS'S MEMORY

(a) **Scope.** This rule gives an adverse party certain options when a witness uses a writing to refresh memory:

(1) while testifying; or

(2) before testifying, if the court decides that justice requires the party to have those options.

(b) **Adverse Party's Options; Deleting Unrelated Matter.** Unless 18 U.S.C. § 3500 provides otherwise in a criminal case, an adverse party is entitled to have the writing produced at the hearing, to inspect it, to cross-examine the witness about it, and to introduce in evidence any portion that relates to the witness's testimony. If the producing party claims that the writing includes unrelated matter, the court must examine the writing in camera, delete any unrelated portion, and order that the rest be delivered to the adverse party. Any portion deleted over objection must be preserved for the record.

(c) **Failure to Produce or Deliver the Writing.** If a writing is not produced or is not delivered as ordered, the court may issue any appropriate order. But if the prosecution does not comply in a criminal case, the court must strike the witness's testimony or—if justice so requires—declare a mistrial.

(Pub.L. 93–595, § 1, Jan. 2, 1975, 88 Stat. 1936; Mar. 2, 1987, eff. Oct. 1, 1987; Apr. 26, 2011, eff. Dec. 1, 2011.)

RULE 613. WITNESS'S PRIOR STATEMENT

(a) Showing or Disclosing the Statement During Examination. When examining a witness about the witness's prior statement, a party need not show it or disclose its contents to the witness. But the party must, on request, show it or disclose its contents to an adverse party's attorney.

(b) Extrinsic Evidence of a Prior Inconsistent Statement. Extrinsic evidence of a witness's prior inconsistent statement is admissible only if the witness is given an opportunity to explain or deny the statement and an adverse party is given an opportunity to examine the witness about it, or if justice so requires. This subdivision (b) does not apply to an opposing party's statement under Rule 801(d)(2).

(Pub.L. 93–595, § 1, Jan. 2, 1975, 88 Stat.1936; Mar. 2, 1987, eff. Oct. 1, 1987; Apr. 25, 1988, eff. Nov. 1, 1988; Apr. 26, 2011, eff. Dec. 1, 2011.)

RULE 614. COURT'S CALLING OR EXAMINING A WITNESS

(a) Calling. The court may call a witness on its own or at a party's request. Each party is entitled to cross-examine the witness.

(b) Examining. The court may examine a witness regardless of who calls the witness.

(c) Objections. A party may object to the court's calling or examining a witness either at that time or at the next opportunity when the jury is not present.

(Pub.L. 93–595, § 1, Jan. 2, 1975, 88 Stat.1937; Apr. 26, 2011, eff. Dec. 1, 2011.)

RULE 615. EXCLUDING WITNESSES

At a party's request, the court must order witnesses excluded so that they cannot hear other witnesses' testimony. Or the court may do so on its own. But this rule does not authorize excluding:

(a) a party who is a natural person;

(b) an officer or employee of a party that is not a natural person, after being designated as the party's representative by its attorney;

(c) a person whose presence a party shows to be essential to presenting the party's claim or defense; or

(d) a person authorized by statute to be present.

(Pub.L. 93–595, § 1, Jan. 2, 1975, 88 Stat.1937; Mar. 2, 1987, eff. Oct. 1, 1987; Apr. 25, 1988, eff. Nov. 1, 1988; Pub.L. 100–690, Nov. 18, 1988, Title VII, § 7075(a), 102 Stat. 4405; Apr. 24, 1998, eff. Dec. 1, 1998; Apr. 26, 2011, eff. Dec. 1, 2011.)

ARTICLE VII. OPINIONS AND EXPERT TESTIMONY

RULE 701. OPINION TESTIMONY BY LAY WITNESSES

If a witness is not testifying as an expert, testimony in the form of an opinion is limited to one that is:

(a) rationally based on the witness's perception;

(b) helpful to clearly understanding the witness's testimony or to determining a fact in issue; and

(c) not based on scientific, technical, or other specialized knowledge within the scope of Rule 702.

(Pub.L. 93–595, § 1, Jan. 2, 1975, 88 Stat.1937; Mar. 2, 1987, eff. Oct. 1, 1987; Apr. 17, 2000, eff. Dec. 1, 2000; Apr. 26, 2011, eff. Dec. 1, 2011.)

RULE 702. TESTIMONY BY EXPERT WITNESSES

A witness who is qualified as an expert by knowledge, skill, experience, training, or education may testify in the form of an opinion or otherwise if:

(a) the expert's scientific, technical, or other specialized knowledge will help the trier of fact to understand the evidence or to determine a fact in issue;

(b) the testimony is based on sufficient facts or data;

(c) the testimony is the product of reliable principles and methods; and

(d) the expert has reliably applied the principles and methods to the facts of the case.

(Pub.L. 93–595, § 1, Jan. 2, 1975, 88 Stat. 1937; Apr. 17, 2000, eff. Dec. 1, 2000; Apr. 26, 2011, eff. Dec. 1, 2011.)

RULE 703. BASES OF AN EXPERT'S OPINION TESTIMONY

An expert may base an opinion on facts or data in the case that the expert has been made aware of or personally observed. If experts in the particular field would reasonably rely on those kinds of facts or data in forming an opinion on the subject, they need not be admissible for the opinion to be admitted. But if the facts or data would otherwise be inadmissible, the proponent of the opinion may disclose them to the jury only if their probative value in helping the jury evaluate the opinion substantially outweighs their prejudicial effect.

(Pub.L. 93–595, § 1, Jan. 2, 1975, 88 Stat.1937; Mar. 2, 1987, eff. Oct. 1, 1987; Apr. 17, 2000, eff. Dec. 1, 2000; Apr. 26, 2011, eff. Dec. 1, 2011.)

RULE 704. OPINION ON AN ULTIMATE ISSUE

(a) In General—Not Automatically Objectionable. An opinion is not objectionable just because it embraces an ultimate issue.

(b) Exception. In a criminal case, an expert witness must not state an opinion about whether the defendant did or did not have a mental state or condition that constitutes an element of the crime charged or of a defense. Those matters are for the trier of fact alone.

(Pub.L. 93–595, § 1, Jan. 2, 1975, 88 Stat. 1937; Pub.L. 98–473, Title IV, § 406, Oct. 12, 1984, 98 Stat. 2067; Apr. 26, 2011, eff. Dec. 1, 2011.)

RULE 705. DISCLOSING THE FACTS OR DATA UNDERLYING AN EXPERT'S OPINION

Unless the court orders otherwise, an expert may state an opinion—and give the reasons for it—without first testifying to the underlying facts or data. But the expert may be required to disclose those facts or data on cross-examination.

(Pub.L. 93–595, § 1, Jan. 2, 1975, 88 Stat. 1938; Mar. 2, 1987, eff. Oct. 1, 1987; Apr. 22, 1993, eff. Dec. 1, 1993; Apr. 26, 2011, eff. Dec. 1, 2011.)

RULE 706. COURT-APPOINTED EXPERT WITNESSES

(a) Appointment Process. On a party's motion or on its own, the court may order the parties to show cause why expert witnesses should not be appointed and may ask the parties to submit nominations. The court may appoint any expert that the parties agree on and any of its own choosing. But the court may only appoint someone who consents to act.

(b) Expert's Role. The court must inform the expert of the expert's duties. The court may do so in writing and have a copy filed with the clerk or may do so orally at a conference in which the parties have an opportunity to participate. The expert:

(1) must advise the parties of any findings the expert makes;

(2) may be deposed by any party;

(3) may be called to testify by the court or any party; and

(4) may be cross-examined by any party, including the party that called the expert.

(c) Compensation. The expert is entitled to a reasonable compensation, as set by the court. The compensation is payable as follows:

(1) in a criminal case or in a civil case involving just compensation under the Fifth Amendment, from any funds that are provided by law; and

(2) in any other civil case, by the parties in the proportion and at the time that the court directs—and the compensation is then charged like other costs.

(d) Disclosing the Appointment to the Jury. The court may authorize disclosure to the jury that the court appointed the expert.

(e) Parties' Choice of Their Own Experts. This rule does not limit a party in calling its own experts.

(Pub.L. 93–595, § 1, Jan. 2, 1975, 88 Stat.1938; Mar. 2, 1987, eff. Oct. 1, 1987; Apr. 26, 2011, eff. Dec. 1, 2011.)

ARTICLE VIII. HEARSAY

RULE 801. DEFINITIONS THAT APPLY TO THIS ARTICLE; EXCLUSIONS FROM HEARSAY

(a) Statement. "Statement" means a person's oral assertion, written assertion, or nonverbal conduct, if the person intended it as an assertion.

(b) Declarant. "Declarant" means the person who made the statement.

(c) Hearsay. "Hearsay" means a statement that:

(1) the declarant does not make while testifying at the current trial or hearing; and

(2) a party offers in evidence to prove the truth of the matter asserted in the statement.

(d) Statements That Are Not Hearsay. A statement that meets the following conditions is not hearsay:

(1) **A Declarant-Witness's Prior Statement.** The declarant testifies and is subject to cross-examination about a prior statement, and the statement:

(A) is inconsistent with the declarant's testimony and was given under penalty of perjury at a trial, hearing, or other proceeding or in a deposition;

(B) is consistent with the declarant's testimony and is offered to rebut an express or implied charge that the declarant recently fabricated it or acted from a recent improper influence or motive in so testifying; or

(C) identifies a person as someone the declarant perceived earlier.

(2) **An Opposing Party's Statement.** The statement is offered against an opposing party and:

(A) was made by the party in an individual or representative capacity;

(B) is one the party manifested that it adopted or believed to be true;

(C) was made by a person whom the party authorized to make a statement on the subject;

(D) was made by the party's agent or employee on a matter within the scope of that relationship and while it existed; or

(E) was made by the party's coconspirator during and in furtherance of the conspiracy.

The statement must be considered but does not by itself establish the declarant's authority under (C); the existence or scope of the relationship under (D); or the existence of the conspiracy or participation in it under (E).

(Pub.L. 93–595, § 1, Jan. 2, 1975, 88 Stat.1938; Pub.L. 94–113, § 1, Oct. 16, 1975, 89 Stat. 576; Mar. 2, 1987, eff. Oct. 1, 1987; Apr. 11, 1997, eff. Dec. 1, 1997; Apr. 26, 2011, eff. Dec. 1, 2011.)

RULE 802. THE RULE AGAINST HEARSAY

Hearsay is not admissible unless any of the following provides otherwise:

- a federal statute;
- these rules; or
- other rules prescribed by the Supreme Court.

(Pub.L. 93–595, § 1, Jan. 2, 1975, 88 Stat. 1939; Apr. 26, 2011, eff. Dec. 1, 2011.)

RULE 803. EXCEPTIONS TO THE RULE AGAINST HEARSAY—REGARDLESS OF WHETHER THE DECLARANT IS AVAILABLE AS A WITNESS

The following are not excluded by the rule against hearsay, regardless of whether the declarant is available as a witness:

(1) **Present Sense Impression.** A statement describing or explaining an event or condition, made while or immediately after the declarant perceived it.

(2) **Excited Utterance.** A statement relating to a startling event or condition, made while the declarant was under the stress of excitement that it caused.

(3) **Then–Existing Mental, Emotional, or Physical Condition.** A statement of the declarant's then-existing state of mind (such as motive, intent, or plan) or emotional, sensory, or physical condition (such as mental feeling, pain, or bodily health), but not including a statement of memory or belief to prove the fact remembered or believed unless it relates to the validity or terms of the declarant's will.

(4) **Statement Made for Medical Diagnosis or Treatment.** A statement that:

(A) is made for—and is reasonably pertinent to—medical diagnosis or treatment; and

(B) describes medical history; past or present symptoms or sensations; their inception; or their general cause.

(5) **Recorded Recollection.** A record that:

(A) is on a matter the witness once knew about but now cannot recall well enough to testify fully and accurately;

(B) was made or adopted by the witness when the matter was fresh in the witness's memory; and

(C) accurately reflects the witness's knowledge.

If admitted, the record may be read into evidence but may be received as an exhibit only if offered by an adverse party.

(6) **Records of a Regularly Conducted Activity.** A record of an act, event, condition, opinion, or diagnosis if:

(A) the record was made at or near the time by—or from information transmitted by—someone with knowledge;

(B) the record was kept in the course of a regularly conducted activity of a business, organization, occupation, or calling, whether or not for profit;

(C) making the record was a regular practice of that activity;

(D) all these conditions are shown by the testimony of the custodian or another qualified witness, or by a certification that complies with Rule 902(11) or (12) or with a statute permitting certification; and

(E) neither the source of information nor the method or circumstances of preparation indicate a lack of trustworthiness.

(7) **Absence of a Record of a Regularly Conducted Activity.** Evidence that a matter is not included in a record described in paragraph (6) if:

(A) the evidence is admitted to prove that the matter did not occur or exist;

(B) a record was regularly kept for a matter of that kind; and

(C) neither the possible source of the information nor other circumstances indicate a lack of trustworthiness.

(8) **Public Records.** A record or statement of a public office if:

(A) it sets out:

(i) the office's activities;

(ii) a matter observed while under a legal duty to report, but not including, in a criminal case, a matter observed by law-enforcement personnel; or

(iii) in a civil case or against the government in a criminal case, factual findings from a legally authorized investigation; and

(B) neither the source of information nor other circumstances indicate a lack of trustworthiness.

(9) **Public Records of Vital Statistics.** A record of a birth, death, or marriage, if reported to a public office in accordance with a legal duty.

(10) **Absence of a Public Record.** Testimony—or a certification under Rule 902—that a diligent search failed to disclose a public record or statement if the testimony or certification is admitted to prove that:

(A) the record or statement does not exist; or

(B) a matter did not occur or exist, if a public office regularly kept a record or statement for a matter of that kind.

(11) **Records of Religious Organizations Concerning Personal or Family History.** A statement of birth, legitimacy, ancestry, marriage, divorce, death, relationship by blood or marriage, or similar facts of personal or family history, contained in a regularly kept record of a religious organization.

(12) **Certificates of Marriage, Baptism, and Similar Ceremonies.** A statement of fact contained in a certificate:

(A) made by a person who is authorized by a religious organization or by law to perform the act certified;

(B) attesting that the person performed a marriage or similar ceremony or administered a sacrament; and

(C) purporting to have been issued at the time of the act or within a reasonable time after it.

(13) **Family Records.** A statement of fact about personal or family history contained in a family record, such as a Bible, genealogy, chart, engraving on a ring, inscription on a portrait, or engraving on an urn or burial marker.

(14) **Records of Documents That Affect an Interest in Property.** The record of a document that purports to establish or affect an interest in property if:

(A) the record is admitted to prove the content of the original recorded document, along with its signing and its delivery by each person who purports to have signed it;

(B) the record is kept in a public office; and

(C) a statute authorizes recording documents of that kind in that office.

(15) **Statements in Documents That Affect an Interest in Property.** A statement contained in a document that purports to establish or affect an interest in property if the matter stated was relevant to the document's purpose—unless later dealings with the property are inconsistent with the truth of the statement or the purport of the document.

(16) **Statements in Ancient Documents.** A statement in a document that is at least 20 years old and whose authenticity is established.

(17) **Market Reports and Similar Commercial Publications.** Market quotations, lists, directories, or other compilations that are generally relied on by the public or by persons in particular occupations.

(18) **Statements in Learned Treatises, Periodicals, or Pamphlets.** A statement contained in a treatise, periodical, or pamphlet if:

(A) the statement is called to the attention of an expert witness on cross-examination or relied on by the expert on direct examination; and

(B) the publication is established as a reliable authority by the expert's admission or testimony, by another expert's testimony, or by judicial notice.

If admitted, the statement may be read into evidence but not received as an exhibit.

(19) **Reputation Concerning Personal or Family History.** A reputation among a person's family by blood, adoption, or marriage—or among a person's associates or in the community—concerning the person's birth, adoption, legitimacy, ancestry, marriage, divorce, death, relationship by blood, adoption, or marriage, or similar facts of personal or family history.

(20) **Reputation Concerning Boundaries or General History.** A reputation in a community—arising before the controversy—concerning boundaries of land in the community or customs that affect the land, or concerning general historical events important to that community, state, or nation.

(21) **Reputation Concerning Character.** A reputation among a person's associates or in the community concerning the person's character.

(22) **Judgment of a Previous Conviction.** Evidence of a final judgment of conviction if:

(A) the judgment was entered after a trial or guilty plea, but not a nolo contendere plea;

(B) the conviction was for a crime punishable by death or by imprisonment for more than a year;

(C) the evidence is admitted to prove any fact essential to the judgment; and

(D) when offered by the prosecutor in a criminal case for a purpose other than impeachment, the judgment was against the defendant.

The pendency of an appeal may be shown but does not affect admissibility.

(23) **Judgments Involving Personal, Family, or General History, or a Boundary.** A judgment that is admitted to prove a matter of personal, family, or general history, or boundaries, if the matter:

(A) was essential to the judgment; and

(B) could be proved by evidence of reputation.

(24) **[Other Exceptions.]** [Transferred to Rule 807.]

(Pub.L. 93–595, § 1, Jan. 2, 1975, 88 Stat. 1939; Pub.L. 94–149, § 1(11), Dec. 12, 1975, 89 Stat. 805; Mar. 2, 1987, eff. Oct. 1, 1987; Apr. 11, 1997, eff. Dec. 1, 1997; Apr. 17, 2000, eff. Dec. 1, 2000; Apr. 26, 2011, eff. Dec. 1, 2011.)

RULE 804. EXCEPTIONS TO THE RULE AGAINST HEARSAY—WHEN THE DECLARANT IS UNAVAILABLE AS A WITNESS

(a) **Criteria for Being Unavailable.** A declarant is considered to be unavailable as a witness if the declarant:

(1) is exempted from testifying about the subject matter of the declarant's statement because the court rules that a privilege applies;

(2) refuses to testify about the subject matter despite a court order to do so;

(3) testifies to not remembering the subject matter;

(4) cannot be present or testify at the trial or hearing because of death or a then-existing infirmity, physical illness, or mental illness; or

(5) is absent from the trial or hearing and the statement's proponent has not been able, by process or other reasonable means, to procure:

(A) the declarant's attendance, in the case of a hearsay exception under Rule 804(b)(1) or (6); or

(B) the declarant's attendance or testimony, in the case of a hearsay exception under Rule 804(b)(2), (3), or (4).

But this subdivision (a) does not apply if the statement's proponent procured or wrongfully caused the declarant's unavailability as a witness in order to prevent the declarant from attending or testifying.

(b) **The Exceptions.** The following are not excluded by the rule against hearsay if the declarant is unavailable as a witness:

(1) **Former Testimony.** Testimony that:

(A) was given as a witness at a trial, hearing, or lawful deposition, whether given during the current proceeding or a different one; and

(B) is now offered against a party who had—or, in a civil case, whose predecessor in interest had—an opportunity and similar motive to develop it by direct, cross-, or redirect examination.

(2) **Statement Under the Belief of Imminent Death.** In a prosecution for homicide or in a civil case, a statement that the declarant, while believing the declarant's death to be imminent, made about its cause or circumstances.

(3) **Statement Against Interest.** A statement that:

(A) a reasonable person in the declarant's position would have made only if the person believed it to be true because, when made, it was so contrary to the declarant's proprietary or pecuniary interest or had so great a tendency to invalidate the declarant's claim against someone else or to expose the declarant to civil or criminal liability; and

(B) is supported by corroborating circumstances that clearly indicate its trustworthiness, if it is offered in a criminal case as one that tends to expose the declarant to criminal liability.

(4) **Statement of Personal or Family History.** A statement about:

(A) the declarant's own birth, adoption, legitimacy, ancestry, marriage, divorce, relationship by blood, adoption, or marriage, or similar facts of personal or family history, even though the declarant had no way of acquiring personal knowledge about that fact; or

(B) another person concerning any of these facts, as well as death, if the declarant was related to the person by blood, adoption, or marriage or was so intimately associated with the person's family that the declarant's information is likely to be accurate.

(5) **[Other Exceptions.]** [Transferred to Rule 807.]

(6) **Statement Offered Against a Party That Wrongfully Caused the Declarant's Unavailability.** A statement offered against a party that wrongfully caused—or acquiesced in wrongfully

causing—the declarant's unavailability as a witness, and did so intending that result.

(Pub.L. 93–595, § 1, Jan. 2, 1975, 88 Stat. 1942; Pub.L. 94–149, § 1(12), (13), Dec. 12, 1975, 89 Stat. 806; Mar. 2, 1987, eff. Oct. 1, 1987; Pub.L. 100–690, Title VII, § 7075(b), Nov. 18, 1988, 102 Stat. 4405; Apr. 11, 1997, eff. Dec. 1, 1997; Apr. 28, 2010, eff. Dec. 1, 2010; Apr. 26, 2011, eff. Dec. 1, 2011.)

RULE 805. HEARSAY WITHIN HEARSAY

Hearsay within hearsay is not excluded by the rule against hearsay if each part of the combined statements conforms with an exception to the rule.

(Pub.L. 93–595, § 1, Jan. 2, 1975, 88 Stat. 1943; Apr. 26, 2011, eff. Dec. 1, 2011.)

RULE 806. ATTACKING AND SUPPORTING THE DECLARANT'S CREDIBILITY

When a hearsay statement—or a statement described in Rule 801(d)(2)(C), (D), or (E)—has been admitted in evidence, the declarant's credibility may be attacked, and then supported, by any evidence that would be admissible for those purposes if the declarant had testified as a witness. The court may admit evidence of the declarant's inconsistent statement or conduct, regardless of when it occurred or whether the declarant had an opportunity to explain or deny it. If the party against whom the statement was admitted calls the declarant as a witness, the party may examine the declarant on the statement as if on cross-examination.

(Pub.L. 93–595, § 1, Jan. 2, 1975, 88 Stat. 1943; Mar. 2, 1987, eff. Oct. 1, 1987; Apr. 11, 1997, eff. Dec. 1, 1997; Apr. 26, 2011, eff. Dec. 1, 2011.)

RULE 807. RESIDUAL EXCEPTION

(a) **In General.** Under the following circumstances, a hearsay statement is not excluded by the rule against hearsay even if the statement is not specifically covered by a hearsay exception in Rule 803 or 804:

(1) the statement has equivalent circumstantial guarantees of trustworthiness;

(2) it is offered as evidence of a material fact;

(3) it is more probative on the point for which it is offered than any other evidence that the proponent can obtain through reasonable efforts; and

(4) admitting it will best serve the purposes of these rules and the interests of justice.

(b) **Notice.** The statement is admissible only if, before the trial or hearing, the proponent gives an adverse party reasonable notice of the intent to offer the statement and its particulars, including the declarant's name and address, so that the party has a fair opportunity to meet it.

(Added Apr. 11, 1997, eff. Dec. 1, 1997; Apr. 26, 2011, eff. Dec. 1, 2011.)

ARTICLE IX. AUTHENTICATION AND IDENTIFICATION

RULE 901. AUTHENTICATING OR IDENTIFYING EVIDENCE

(a) **In General.** To satisfy the requirement of authenticating or identifying an item of evidence, the proponent must produce evidence sufficient to support a finding that the item is what the proponent claims it is.

(b) **Examples.** The following are examples only—not a complete list—of evidence that satisfies the requirement:

(1) **Testimony of a Witness with Knowledge.** Testimony that an item is what it is claimed to be.

(2) **Nonexpert Opinion About Handwriting.** A nonexpert's opinion that handwriting is genuine, based on a familiarity with it that was not acquired for the current litigation.

(3) **Comparison by an Expert Witness or the Trier of Fact.** A comparison with an authenticated specimen by an expert witness or the trier of fact.

(4) **Distinctive Characteristics and the Like.** The appearance, contents, substance, internal patterns, or other distinctive characteristics of the item, taken together with all the circumstances.

(5) **Opinion About a Voice.** An opinion identifying a person's voice—whether heard firsthand or through mechanical or electronic transmission or recording—based on hearing the voice at any time under circumstances that connect it with the alleged speaker.

(6) **Evidence About a Telephone Conversation.** For a telephone conversation, evidence that a call was made to the number assigned at the time to:

(A) a particular person, if circumstances, including self-identification, show that the person answering was the one called; or

(B) a particular business, if the call was made to a business and the call related to business reasonably transacted over the telephone.

(7) **Evidence About Public Records.** Evidence that:

(A) a document was recorded or filed in a public office as authorized by law; or

(B) a purported public record or statement is from the office where items of this kind are kept.

(8) **Evidence About Ancient Documents or Data Compilations.** For a document or data compilation, evidence that it:

(A) is in a condition that creates no suspicion about its authenticity;

(B) was in a place where, if authentic, it would likely be; and

(C) is at least 20 years old when offered.

(9) **Evidence About a Process or System.** Evidence describing a process or system and showing that it produces an accurate result.

(10) **Methods Provided by a Statute or Rule.** Any method of authentication or identification allowed by a federal statute or a rule prescribed by the Supreme Court.

(Pub.L. 93–595, § 1, Jan. 2, 1975, 88 Stat.1943; Apr. 26, 2011, eff. Dec. 1, 2011.)

RULE 902. EVIDENCE THAT IS SELF-AUTHENTICATING

The following items of evidence are self-authenticating; they require no extrinsic evidence of authenticity in order to be admitted:

(1) **Domestic Public Documents That Are Sealed and Signed.** A document that bears:

(A) a seal purporting to be that of the United States; any state, district, commonwealth, territory, or insular possession of the United States; the former Panama Canal Zone; the Trust Territory of the Pacific Islands; a political subdivision of any of these entities; or a department, agency, or officer of any entity named above; and

(B) a signature purporting to be an execution or attestation.

(2) **Domestic Public Documents That Are Not Sealed but Are Signed and Certified.** A document that bears no seal if:

(A) it bears the signature of an officer or employee of an entity named in Rule 902(1)(A); and

(B) another public officer who has a seal and official duties within that same entity certifies under seal—or its equivalent—that the signer has the official capacity and that the signature is genuine.

(3) **Foreign Public Documents.** A document that purports to be signed or attested by a person who is authorized by a foreign country's law to do so. The document must be accompanied by a final certification that certifies the genuineness of the signature and official position of the signer or attester—or of any foreign official whose certificate of genuineness relates to the signature or attestation or is in a chain of certificates of genuineness relating to the signature or attestation. The certification may be made by a secretary of a United States embassy or legation; by a consul general, vice consul, or consular agent of the United States; or by a diplomatic or consular official of the foreign country assigned or accredited to the United States. If all parties have been given a reasonable opportunity to investigate the document's authenticity and accuracy, the court may, for good cause, either:

(A) order that it be treated as presumptively authentic without final certification; or

(B) allow it to be evidenced by an attested summary with or without final certification.

(4) **Certified Copies of Public Records.** A copy of an official record—or a copy of a document that was recorded or filed in a public office as authorized by law—if the copy is certified as correct by:

(A) the custodian or another person authorized to make the certification; or

(B) a certificate that complies with Rule 902(1), (2), or (3), a federal statute, or a rule prescribed by the Supreme Court.

(5) **Official Publications.** A book, pamphlet, or other publication purporting to be issued by a public authority.

(6) **Newspapers and Periodicals.** Printed material purporting to be a newspaper or periodical.

(7) **Trade Inscriptions and the Like.** An inscription, sign, tag, or label purporting to have been affixed in the course of business and indicating origin, ownership, or control.

(8) **Acknowledged Documents.** A document accompanied by a certificate of acknowledgment that is lawfully executed by a notary public or another officer who is authorized to take acknowledgments.

(9) **Commercial Paper and Related Documents.** Commercial paper, a signature on it, and related documents, to the extent allowed by general commercial law.

(10) **Presumptions Under a Federal Statute.** A signature, document, or anything else that a federal statute declares to be presumptively or prima facie genuine or authentic.

(11) **Certified Domestic Records of a Regularly Conducted Activity.** The original or a copy of a domestic record that meets the requirements

of Rule 803(6)(A)–(C), as shown by a certification of the custodian or another qualified person that complies with a federal statute or a rule prescribed by the Supreme Court. Before the trial or hearing, the proponent must give an adverse party reasonable written notice of the intent to offer the record—and must make the record and certification available for inspection—so that the party has a fair opportunity to challenge them.

(12) **Certified Foreign Records of a Regularly Conducted Activity.** In a civil case, the original or a copy of a foreign record that meets the requirements of Rule 902(11), modified as follows: the certification, rather than complying with a federal statute or Supreme Court rule, must be signed in a manner that, if falsely made, would subject the maker to a criminal penalty in the country where the certification is signed. The proponent must also meet the notice requirements of Rule 902(11).

(Pub.L. 93–595, § 1, Jan. 2, 1975, 88 Stat. 1944; Mar. 2, 1987, eff. Oct. 1, 1987; Apr. 25, 1988, eff. Nov. 1, 1988; Apr. 17, 2000, eff. Dec. 1, 2000; Apr. 26, 2011, eff. Dec. 1, 2011.)

RULE 903. SUBSCRIBING WITNESS'S TESTIMONY

A subscribing witness's testimony is necessary to authenticate a writing only if required by the law of the jurisdiction that governs its validity.

(Pub.L. 93–595, § 1, Jan. 2, 1975, 88 Stat.1945; Apr. 26, 2011, eff. Dec. 1, 2011.)

ARTICLE X. CONTENTS OF WRITINGS, RECORDINGS, AND PHOTOGRAPHS

RULE 1001. DEFINITIONS THAT APPLY TO THIS ARTICLE

In this article:

(a) A "writing" consists of letters, words, numbers, or their equivalent set down in any form.

(b) A "recording" consists of letters, words, numbers, or their equivalent recorded in any manner.

(c) A "photograph" means a photographic image or its equivalent stored in any form.

(d) An "original" of a writing or recording means the writing or recording itself or any counterpart intended to have the same effect by the person who executed or issued it. For electronically stored information, "original" means any printout—or other output readable by sight—if it accurately reflects the information. An "original" of a photograph includes the negative or a print from it.

(e) A "duplicate" means a counterpart produced by a mechanical, photographic, chemical, electronic, or other equivalent process or technique that accurately reproduces the original.

(Pub.L. 93–595, § 1, Jan. 2, 1975, 88 Stat. 1945; Apr. 26, 2011, eff. Dec. 1, 2011.)

RULE 1002. REQUIREMENT OF THE ORIGINAL

An original writing, recording, or photograph is required in order to prove its content unless these rules or a federal statute provides otherwise.

(Pub.L. 93–595, § 1, Jan. 2, 1975, 88 Stat. 1946; Apr. 26, 2011, eff. Dec. 1, 2011.)

RULE 1003. ADMISSIBILITY OF DUPLICATES

A duplicate is admissible to the same extent as the original unless a genuine question is raised about the original's authenticity or the circumstances make it unfair to admit the duplicate.

(Pub.L. 93–595, § 1, Jan. 2, 1975, 88 Stat. 1946; Apr. 26, 2011, eff. Dec. 1, 2011.)

RULE 1004. ADMISSIBILITY OF OTHER EVIDENCE OF CONTENT

An original is not required and other evidence of the content of a writing, recording, or photograph is admissible if:

(a) all the originals are lost or destroyed, and not by the proponent acting in bad faith;

(b) an original cannot be obtained by any available judicial process;

(c) the party against whom the original would be offered had control of the original; was at that time put on notice, by pleadings or otherwise, that the original would be a subject of proof at the trial or hearing; and fails to produce it at the trial or hearing; or

(d) the writing, recording, or photograph is not closely related to a controlling issue.

(Pub.L. 93–595, § 1, Jan. 2, 1975, 88 Stat. 1946; Mar. 2, 1987, eff. Oct. 1, 1987; Apr. 26, 2011, eff. Dec. 1, 2011.)

RULE 1005. COPIES OF PUBLIC RECORDS TO PROVE CONTENT

The proponent may use a copy to prove the content of an official record—or of a document that was recorded or filed in a public office as authorized by law—if these conditions are met: the record or document is otherwise admissible; and the copy is certified as correct in accordance with Rule 902(4) or is testified to be correct by a witness who has compared it with the original. If no such copy can be obtained by reasonable diligence, then the proponent may use other evidence to prove the content.

(Pub.L. 93–595, § 1, Jan. 2, 1975, 88 Stat. 1946; Apr. 26, 2011, eff. Dec. 1, 2011.)

RULE 1006. SUMMARIES TO PROVE CONTENT

The proponent may use a summary, chart, or calculation to prove the content of voluminous writings, recordings, or photographs that cannot be conveniently examined in court. The proponent must make the originals or duplicates available for examination or copying, or both, by other parties at a reasonable time and place. And the court may order the proponent to produce them in court.

(Pub.L. 93–595, § 1, Jan. 2, 1975, 88 Stat. 1946; Apr. 26, 2011, eff. Dec. 1, 2011.)

RULE 1007. TESTIMONY OR STATEMENT OF A PARTY TO PROVE CONTENT

The proponent may prove the content of a writing, recording, or photograph by the testimony, deposition, or written statement of the party against whom the evidence is offered. The proponent need not account for the original.

(Pub.L. 93–595, § 1, Jan. 2, 1975, 88 Stat. 1947; Mar. 2, 1987, eff. Oct. 1, 1987; Apr. 26, 2011, eff. Dec. 1, 2011.)

RULE 1008. FUNCTIONS OF THE COURT AND JURY

Ordinarily, the court determines whether the proponent has fulfilled the factual conditions for admitting other evidence of the content of a writing, recording, or photograph under Rule 1004 or 1005. But in a jury trial, the jury determines—in accordance with Rule 104(b)—any issue about whether:

(a) an asserted writing, recording, or photograph ever existed;

(b) another one produced at the trial or hearing is the original; or

(c) other evidence of content accurately reflects the content.

(Pub.L. 93–595, § 1, Jan. 2, 1975, 88 Stat. 1947; Apr. 26, 2011, eff. Dec. 1, 2011.)

ARTICLE XI. MISCELLANEOUS RULES

RULE 1101. APPLICABILITY OF THE RULES

(a) To Courts and Judges. These rules apply to proceedings before:

- United States district courts;
- United States bankruptcy and magistrate judges;
- United States courts of appeals;
- the United States Court of Federal Claims; and
- the district courts of Guam, the Virgin Islands, and the Northern Mariana Islands.

(b) To Cases and Proceedings. These rules apply in:

- civil cases and proceedings, including bankruptcy, admiralty, and maritime cases;
- criminal cases and proceedings; and
- contempt proceedings, except those in which the court may act summarily.

(c) Rules on Privilege. The rules on privilege apply to all stages of a case or proceeding.

(d) Exceptions. These rules—except for those on privilege—do not apply to the following:

(1) the court's determination, under Rule 104(a), on a preliminary question of fact governing admissibility;

(2) grand-jury proceedings; and

(3) miscellaneous proceedings such as:

- extradition or rendition;
- issuing an arrest warrant, criminal summons, or search warrant;
- a preliminary examination in a criminal case;
- sentencing;
- granting or revoking probation or supervised release; and
- considering whether to release on bail or otherwise.

(e) Other Statutes and Rules. A federal statute or a rule prescribed by the Supreme Court may provide for admitting or excluding evidence independently from these rules.

(Pub.L. 93–595, § 1, Jan. 2, 1975, 88 Stat. 1947; Pub.L. 94–149, § 1(14), Dec. 12, 1975, 89 Stat. 806; Pub.L. 95–598,

Title II, § 251, Nov. 6, 1978, 92 Stat. 2673; Pub.L. 97–164, Title I, § 142, Apr. 2, 1982, 96 Stat. 45; Mar. 2, 1987, eff. Oct. 1, 1987; Apr. 25, 1988, eff. Nov. 1, 1988; Pub.L. 100–690, Title VII, § 7075(c), Nov. 18, 1988, 102 Stat. 4405; Apr. 22, 1993, eff. Dec. 1, 1993; Apr. 26, 2011, eff. Dec. 1, 2011.)

RULE 1102. AMENDMENTS

These rules may be amended as provided in 28 U.S.C. § 2072.

(Pub.L. 93–595, § 1, Jan. 2, 1975, 88 Stat.1948; Apr. 30, 1991, eff. Dec. 1, 1991; Apr. 26, 2011, eff. Dec. 1, 2011.)

RULE 1103. TITLE

These rules may be cited as the Federal Rules of Evidence.

(Pub.L. 93–595, § 1, Jan. 2, 1975, 88 Stat.1948; Apr. 26, 2011, eff. Dec. 1, 2011.)

INDEX TO FEDERAL RULES OF EVIDENCE

*

FEDERAL RULES OF APPELLATE PROCEDURE

Effective July 1, 1968

Including Amendments Effective December 1, 2011

Research Note

These rules may be searched electronically on Westlaw in the US-RULES database; updates to these rules may be found on Westlaw in US-RULESPDATES. For search tips, and a detailed summary of database content, consult the Westlaw Scope Screen of each database.

TITLE I. APPLICABILITY OF RULES

RULE 1. SCOPE OF RULES; DEFINITION; TITLE

(a) Scope of Rules.

(1) These rules govern procedure in the United States courts of appeals.

(2) When these rules provide for filing a motion or other document in the district court, the procedure must comply with the practice of the district court.

(b) Definition. In these rules, "state" includes the District of Columbia and any United States commonwealth or territory.

(c) Title. These rules are to be known as the Federal Rules of Appellate Procedure.

(As amended Apr. 30, 1979, eff. Aug. 1, 1979; Apr. 25, 1989, eff. Dec. 1, 1989; Apr. 29, 1994, eff. Dec. 1, 1994; Apr. 24, 1998, eff. Dec. 1, 1998; Apr. 29, 2002, eff. Dec. 1, 2002; Apr. 28, 2010, eff. Dec. 1, 2010.)

RULE 2. SUSPENSION OF RULES

On its own or a party's motion, a court of appeals may—to expedite its decision or for other good cause—suspend any provision of these rules in a particular case and order proceedings as it directs, except as otherwise provided in Rule 26(b).

(As amended Apr. 24, 1998, eff. Dec. 1, 1998.)

TITLE II. APPEAL FROM A JUDGMENT OR ORDER OF A DISTRICT COURT

RULE 3. APPEAL AS OF RIGHT—HOW TAKEN

(a) Filing the Notice of Appeal.

(1) An appeal permitted by law as of right from a district court to a court of appeals may be taken only by filing a notice of appeal with the district clerk within the time allowed by Rule 4. At the time of filing, the appellant must furnish the clerk with enough copies of the notice to enable the clerk to comply with Rule 3(d).

(2) An appellant's failure to take any step other than the timely filing of a notice of appeal does not affect the validity of the appeal, but is ground only for the court of appeals to act as it considers appropriate, including dismissing the appeal.

(3) An appeal from a judgment by a magistrate judge in a civil case is taken in the same way as an appeal from any other district court judgment.

(4) An appeal by permission under 28 U.S.C. § 1292(b) or an appeal in a bankruptcy case may be taken only in the manner prescribed by Rules 5 and 6, respectively.

(b) Joint or Consolidated Appeals.

(1) When two or more parties are entitled to appeal from a district-court judgment or order, and their interests make joinder practicable, they may file a joint notice of appeal. They may then proceed on appeal as a single appellant.

(2) When the parties have filed separate timely notices of appeal, the appeals may be joined or consolidated by the court of appeals.

(c) Contents of the Notice of Appeal.

(1) The notice of appeal must:

(A) specify the party or parties taking the appeal by naming each one in the caption or body of the notice, but an attorney representing more than one party may describe those parties with such terms as "all plaintiffs," "the defendants," "the plaintiffs A, B, et al.," or "all defendants except X";

(B) designate the judgment, order, or part thereof being appealed; and

(C) name the court to which the appeal is taken.

(2) A pro se notice of appeal is considered filed on behalf of the signer and the signer's spouse and minor children (if they are parties), unless the notice clearly indicates otherwise.

(3) In a class action, whether or not the class has been certified, the notice of appeal is sufficient if it names one person qualified to bring the appeal as representative of the class.

(4) An appeal must not be dismissed for informality of form or title of the notice of appeal, or for failure to name a party whose intent to appeal is otherwise clear from the notice.

(5) Form 1 in the Appendix of Forms is a suggested form of a notice of appeal.

(d) Serving the Notice of Appeal.

(1) The district clerk must serve notice of the filing of a notice of appeal by mailing a copy to each party's counsel of record—excluding the appellant's—or, if a party is proceeding pro se, to the party's last known address. When a defendant in a criminal case appeals, the clerk must also serve a copy of the notice of appeal on the defendant, either by personal service or by mail addressed to the defendant. The clerk must promptly send a copy of the notice of appeal and of the docket entries—and any later docket entries—to the clerk of the court of appeals named in the notice. The district clerk must note, on each copy, the date when the notice of appeal was filed.

(2) If an inmate confined in an institution files a notice of appeal in the manner provided by Rule 4(c), the district clerk must also note the date when the clerk docketed the notice.

(3) The district clerk's failure to serve notice does not affect the validity of the appeal. The clerk must note on the docket the names of the parties to whom the clerk mails copies, with the date of mailing. Service is sufficient despite the death of a party or the party's counsel.

(e) Payment of Fees. Upon filing a notice of appeal, the appellant must pay the district clerk all required fees. The district clerk receives the appellate docket fee on behalf of the court of appeals.

(As amended Apr. 30, 1979, eff. Aug. 1, 1979; Mar. 10, 1986, eff. July 1, 1986; Apr. 25, 1989, eff. Dec. 1, 1989; Apr. 22, 1993, eff. Dec. 1, 1993; Apr. 29, 1994, eff. Dec. 1, 1994; Apr. 24, 1998, eff. Dec. 1, 1998.)

[RULE 3.1. APPEAL FROM A JUDGMENT OF A MAGISTRATE JUDGE IN A CIVIL CASE (Abrogated Apr. 24, 1998, eff. Dec. 1, 1998)]

RULE 4. APPEAL AS OF RIGHT—WHEN TAKEN

(a) Appeal in a Civil Case.

(1) **Time for Filing a Notice of Appeal.**

(A) In a civil case, except as provided in Rules 4(a)(1)(B), 4(a)(4), and 4(c), the notice of appeal required by Rule 3 must be filed with the district clerk within 30 days after entry of the judgment or order appealed from.

(B) The notice of appeal may be filed by any party within 60 days after entry of the judgment or order appealed from if one of the parties is:

(i) the United States;

(ii) a United States agency;

(iii) a United States officer or employee sued in an official capacity; or

(iv) a current or former United States officer or employee sued in an individual capacity for an act or omission occurring in connection with duties performed on the United States' behalf—including all instances in which the United States represents that person when the judgment or order is entered or files the appeal for that person.

(C) An appeal from an order granting or denying an application for a writ of error coram nobis is an appeal in a civil case for purposes of Rule 4(a).

(2) **Filing Before Entry of Judgment.** A notice of appeal filed after the court announces a decision or order—but before the entry of the judgment or order—is treated as filed on the date of and after the entry.

(3) **Multiple Appeals.** If one party timely files a notice of appeal, any other party may file a notice of appeal within 14 days after the date when the first notice was filed, or within the time otherwise prescribed by this Rule 4(a), whichever period ends later.

(4) **Effect of a Motion on a Notice of Appeal.**

(A) If a party timely files in the district court any of the following motions under the Federal Rules of Civil Procedure, the time to file an appeal runs for all parties from the entry of the order disposing of the last such remaining motion:

(i) for judgment under Rule 50(b);

(ii) to amend or make additional factual findings under Rule 52(b), whether or not granting the motion would alter the judgment;

(iii) for attorney's fees under Rule 54 if the district court extends the time to appeal under Rule 58;

(iv) to alter or amend the judgment under Rule 59;

(v) for a new trial under Rule 59; or

(vi) for relief under Rule 60 if the motion is filed no later than 28 days after the judgment is entered.

(B)(i) If a party files a notice of appeal after the court announces or enters a judgment—but before it disposes of any motion listed in Rule 4(a)(4)(A)—the notice becomes effective to appeal a judgment or order, in whole or in part, when the order disposing of the last such remaining motion is entered.

(ii) A party intending to challenge an order disposing of any motion listed in Rule 4(a)(4)(A), or a judgment's alteration or amendment upon such a motion, must file a notice of appeal, or an amended notice of appeal—in compliance with Rule 3(c)—within the time prescribed by this Rule measured from the entry of the order disposing of the last such remaining motion.

(iii) No additional fee is required to file an amended notice.

(5) Motion for Extension of Time.

(A) The district court may extend the time to file a notice of appeal if:

(i) a party so moves no later than 30 days after the time prescribed by this Rule 4(a) expires; and

(ii) regardless of whether its motion is filed before or during the 30 days after the time prescribed by this Rule 4(a) expires, that party shows excusable neglect or good cause.

(B) A motion filed before the expiration of the time prescribed in Rule 4(a)(1) or (3) may be ex parte unless the court requires otherwise. If the motion is filed after the expiration of the prescribed time, notice must be given to the other parties in accordance with local rules.

(C) No extension under this Rule 4(a)(5) may exceed 30 days after the prescribed time or 14 days after the date when the order granting the motion is entered, whichever is later.

(6) Reopening the Time to File an Appeal. The district court may reopen the time to file an appeal for a period of 14 days after the date when its order to reopen is entered, but only if all the following conditions are satisfied:

(A) the court finds that the moving party did not receive notice under Federal Rule of Civil Procedure 77(d) of the entry of the judgment or order sought to be appealed within 21 days after entry;

(B) the motion is filed within 180 days after the judgment or order is entered or within 14 days after the moving party receives notice under Federal Rule of Civil Procedure 77(d) of the entry, whichever is earlier; and

(C) the court finds that no party would be prejudiced.

(7) Entry Defined.

(A) A judgment or order is entered for purposes of this Rule 4(a):

(i) if Federal Rule of Civil Procedure 58(a) does not require a separate document, when the judgment or order is entered in the civil docket under Federal Rule of Civil Procedure 79(a); or

(ii) if Federal Rule of Civil Procedure 58(a) requires a separate document, when the judgment or order is entered in the civil docket under Federal Rule of Civil Procedure 79(a) and when the earlier of these events occurs:

- the judgment or order is set forth on a separate document, or
- 150 days have run from entry of the judgment or order in the civil docket under Federal Rule of Civil Procedure 79(a).

(B) A failure to set forth a judgment or order on a separate document when required by Federal Rule of Civil Procedure 58(a) does not affect the validity of an appeal from that judgment or order.

(b) Appeal in a Criminal Case.

(1) Time for Filing a Notice of Appeal.

(A) In a criminal case, a defendant's notice of appeal must be filed in the district court within 14 days after the later of:

(i) the entry of either the judgment or the order being appealed; or

(ii) the filing of the government's notice of appeal.

(B) When the government is entitled to appeal, its notice of appeal must be filed in the district court within 30 days after the later of:

(i) the entry of the judgment or order being appealed; or

(ii) the filing of a notice of appeal by any defendant.

(2) Filing Before Entry of Judgment. A notice of appeal filed after the court announces a decision, sentence, or order—but before the entry of the judgment or order—is treated as filed on the date of and after the entry.

(3) Effect of a Motion on a Notice of Appeal.

(A) If a defendant timely makes any of the following motions under the Federal Rules of Criminal Procedure, the notice of appeal from a judgment of conviction must be filed within 14 days after the entry of the order disposing of the last such remaining motion, or within 14 days after the entry of the judgment of conviction, whichever period ends later. This provision applies to a timely motion:

(i) for judgment of acquittal under Rule 29;

(ii) for a new trial under Rule 33, but if based on newly discovered evidence, only if the motion is made no later than 14 days after the entry of the judgment; or

(iii) for arrest of judgment under Rule 34.

(B) A notice of appeal filed after the court announces a decision, sentence, or order—but before it disposes of any of the motions referred to in Rule 4(b)(3)(A)—becomes effective upon the later of the following:

(i) the entry of the order disposing of the last such remaining motion; or

(ii) the entry of the judgment of conviction.

(C) A valid notice of appeal is effective—without amendment—to appeal from an order disposing of any of the motions referred to in Rule 4(b)(3)(A).

(4) Motion for Extension of Time. Upon a finding of excusable neglect or good cause, the district court may—before or after the time has expired, with or without motion and notice—extend the time to file a notice of appeal for a period not to exceed 30 days from the expiration of the time otherwise prescribed by this Rule 4(b).

(5) Jurisdiction. The filing of a notice of appeal under this Rule 4(b) does not divest a district court of jurisdiction to correct a sentence under Federal Rule of Criminal Procedure 35(a), nor does the filing of a motion under 35(a) affect the validity of a notice of appeal filed before entry of the order disposing of the motion. The filing of a motion under Federal Rule of Criminal Procedure 35(a) does not suspend the time for filing a notice of appeal from a judgment of conviction.

(6) Entry Defined. A judgment or order is entered for purposes of this Rule 4(b) when it is entered on the criminal docket.

(c) Appeal by an Inmate Confined in an Institution.

(1) If an inmate confined in an institution files a notice of appeal in either a civil or a criminal case, the notice is timely if it is deposited in the institution's internal mail system on or before the last day for filing. If an institution has a system designed for legal mail, the inmate must use that system to receive the benefit of this rule. Timely filing may be shown by a declaration in compliance with 28 U.S.C. § 1746 or by a notarized statement, either of which must set forth the date of deposit and state that first-class postage has been prepaid.

(2) If an inmate files the first notice of appeal in a civil case under this Rule 4(c), the 14–day period provided in Rule 4(a)(3) for another party to file a notice of appeal runs from the date when the district court dockets the first notice.

(3) When a defendant in a criminal case files a notice of appeal under this Rule 4(c), the 30–day period for the government to file its notice of appeal runs from the entry of the judgment or order appealed from or from the district court's docketing of the defendant's notice of appeal, whichever is later.

(d) Mistaken Filing in the Court of Appeals. If a notice of appeal in either a civil or a criminal case is mistakenly filed in the court of appeals, the clerk of that court must note on the notice the date when it was received and send it to the district clerk. The notice is then considered filed in the district court on the date so noted.

(As amended Apr. 30, 1979, eff. Aug. 1, 1979; Nov. 18, 1988, Pub.L. 100–690, Title VII, § 7111, 102 Stat. 4419; Apr. 30, 1991, eff. Dec. 1, 1991; Apr. 22, 1993, eff. Dec. 1, 1993; Apr. 27, 1995, eff. Dec. 1, 1995; Apr. 24, 1998, eff. Dec. 1, 1998; Apr. 29, 2002, eff. Dec. 1, 2002; Apr. 25, 2005, eff. Dec. 1, 2005; Mar. 26, 2009, eff. Dec. 1, 2009; Apr. 28, 2010, eff. Dec. 1, 2010; Apr. 26, 2011, eff. Dec. 1, 2011.)

RULE 5. APPEAL BY PERMISSION

(a) Petition for Permission to Appeal.

(1) To request permission to appeal when an appeal is within the court of appeals' discretion, a party must file a petition for permission to appeal. The petition must be filed with the circuit clerk with proof of service on all other parties to the district-court action.

(2) The petition must be filed within the time specified by the statute or rule authorizing the appeal or, if no such time is specified, within the time provided by Rule 4(a) for filing a notice of appeal.

(3) If a party cannot petition for appeal unless the district court first enters an order granting permission to do so or stating that the necessary conditions are met, the district court may amend its order, either on its own or in response to a party's motion, to include the required permission or statement. In that event, the time to petition runs from entry of the amended order.

(b) Contents of the Petition; Answer or Cross–Petition; Oral Argument.

(1) The petition must include the following:

(A) the facts necessary to understand the question presented;

(B) the question itself;

(C) the relief sought;

(D) the reasons why the appeal should be allowed and is authorized by a statute or rule; and

(E) an attached copy of:

(i) the order, decree, or judgment complained of and any related opinion or memorandum, and

(ii) any order stating the district court's permission to appeal or finding that the necessary conditions are met.

(2) A party may file an answer in opposition or a cross-petition within 10 days after the petition is served.

(3) The petition and answer will be submitted without oral argument unless the court of appeals orders otherwise.

(c) Form of Papers; Number of Copies. All papers must conform to Rule 32(c)(2). Except by the court's permission, a paper must not exceed 20 pages, exclusive of the disclosure statement, the proof of service, and the accompanying documents required by Rule 5(b)(1)(E). An original and 3 copies must be filed unless the court requires a different number by local rule or by order in a particular case.

(d) Grant of Permission; Fees; Cost Bond; Filing the Record.

(1) Within 14 days after the entry of the order granting permission to appeal, the appellant must:

(A) pay the district clerk all required fees; and

(B) file a cost bond if required under Rule 7.

(2) A notice of appeal need not be filed. The date when the order granting permission to appeal is entered serves as the date of the notice of appeal for calculating time under these rules.

(3) The district clerk must notify the circuit clerk once the petitioner has paid the fees. Upon receiving this notice, the circuit clerk must enter the appeal on the docket. The record must be forwarded and filed in accordance with Rules 11 and 12(c).

(As amended Apr. 30, 1979, eff. Aug. 1, 1979; Apr. 29, 1994, eff. Dec. 1, 1994; Apr. 24, 1998, eff. Dec. 1, 1998; Apr. 29, 2002, eff. Dec. 1, 2002; Mar. 26, 2009, eff. Dec. 1, 2009.)

[RULE 5.1. APPEAL BY LEAVE UNDER 28 U.S.C. § 636(c)(5) (Abrogated Apr. 24, 1998, eff. Dec. 1, 1998)]

RULE 6. APPEAL IN A BANKRUPTCY CASE FROM A FINAL JUDGMENT, ORDER, OR DECREE OF A DISTRICT COURT OR BANKRUPTCY APPELLATE PANEL

(a) Appeal From a Judgment, Order, or Decree of a District Court Exercising Original Jurisdiction in a Bankruptcy Case. An appeal to a court of appeals from a final judgment, order, or decree of a district court exercising jurisdiction under 28 U.S.C. § 1334 is taken as any other civil appeal under these rules.

(b) Appeal From a Judgment, Order, or Decree of a District Court or Bankruptcy Appellate Panel Exercising Appellate Jurisdiction in a Bankruptcy Case.

(1) **Applicability of Other Rules.** These rules apply to an appeal to a court of appeals under 28 U.S.C. § 158(d) from a final judgment, order, or decree of a district court or bankruptcy appellate panel exercising appellate jurisdiction under 28 U.S.C. § 158(a) or (b). But there are 3 exceptions:

(A) Rules 4(a)(4), 4(b), 9, 10, 11, 12(b), 13–20, 22–23, and 24(b) do not apply;

(B) the reference in Rule 3(c) to "Form 1 in the Appendix of Forms" must be read as a reference to Form 5; and

(C) when the appeal is from a bankruptcy appellate panel, the term "district court," as used in any applicable rule, means "appellate panel."

(2) **Additional Rules.** In addition to the rules made applicable by Rule 6(b)(1), the following rules apply:

(A) **Motion for rehearing.**

(i) If a timely motion for rehearing under Bankruptcy Rule 8015 is filed, the time to appeal for all parties runs from the entry of the order disposing of the motion. A notice of appeal filed after the district court or bankruptcy appellate panel announces or enters a judgment, order, or decree—but before disposition of the motion for rehearing—becomes effective when the order disposing of the motion for rehearing is entered.

(ii) Appellate review of the order disposing of the motion requires the party, in compliance with Rules 3(c) and 6(b)(1)(B), to amend a previously filed notice of appeal. A party intending to challenge an altered or amended judgment, order, or decree must file a notice of appeal or amended notice of appeal within the time prescribed by Rule 4—excluding Rules 4(a)(4) and 4(b)—measured from the entry of the order disposing of the motion.

(iii) No additional fee is required to file an amended notice.

(B) **The record on appeal.**

(i) Within 14 days after filing the notice of appeal, the appellant must file with the clerk possessing the record assembled in accordance with Bankruptcy Rule 8006—and serve on the appellee—a statement of the issues to be presented on appeal and a designation of the record to be certified and sent to the circuit clerk.

(ii) An appellee who believes that other parts of the record are necessary must, within 14 days after being served with the appellant's designation, file with the clerk and serve on the appellant a designation of additional parts to be included.

(iii) The record on appeal consists of:

- the redesignated record as provided above;
- the proceedings in the district court or bankruptcy appellate panel; and
- a certified copy of the docket entries prepared by the clerk under Rule 3(d).

(C) Forwarding the record.

(i) When the record is complete, the district clerk or bankruptcy appellate panel clerk must number the documents constituting the record and send them promptly to the circuit clerk together with a list of the documents correspondingly numbered and reasonably identified. Unless directed to do so by a party or the circuit clerk, the clerk will not send to the court of appeals documents of unusual bulk or weight, physical exhibits other than documents, or other parts of the record designated for omission by local rule of the court of appeals. If the exhibits are unusually bulky or heavy, a party must arrange with the clerks in advance for their transportation and receipt.

(ii) All parties must do whatever else is necessary to enable the clerk to assemble and forward the record. The court of appeals may provide by rule or order that a certified copy of the docket entries be sent in place of the redesignated record, but any party may request at any time during the pendency of the appeal that the redesignated record be sent.

(D) Filing the record. Upon receiving the record—or a certified copy of the docket entries sent in place of the redesignated record—the circuit clerk must file it and immediately notify all parties of the filing date.

(Added Apr. 25, 1989, eff. Dec. 1, 1989, and amended Apr. 30, 1991, eff. Dec. 1, 1991; Apr. 22, 1993, eff. Dec. 1, 1993; Apr. 24, 1998, eff. Dec. 1, 1998; Mar. 26, 2009, eff. Dec. 1, 2009.)

RULE 7. BOND FOR COSTS ON APPEAL IN A CIVIL CASE

In a civil case, the district court may require an appellant to file a bond or provide other security in any form and amount necessary to ensure payment of costs on appeal. Rule 8(b) applies to a surety on a bond given under this rule.

(As amended Apr. 30, 1979, eff. Aug. 1, 1979; Apr. 24, 1998, eff. Dec. 1, 1998.)

RULE 8. STAY OR INJUNCTION PENDING APPEAL

(a) Motion for Stay.

(1) Initial Motion in the District Court. A party must ordinarily move first in the district court for the following relief:

(A) a stay of the judgment or order of a district court pending appeal;

(B) approval of a supersedeas bond; or

(C) an order suspending, modifying, restoring, or granting an injunction while an appeal is pending.

(2) Motion in the Court of Appeals; Conditions on Relief. A motion for the relief mentioned in Rule 8(a)(1) may be made to the court of appeals or to one of its judges.

(A) The motion must:

(i) show that moving first in the district court would be impracticable; or

(ii) state that, a motion having been made, the district court denied the motion or failed to afford the relief requested and state any reasons given by the district court for its action.

(B) The motion must also include:

(i) the reasons for granting the relief requested and the facts relied on;

(ii) originals or copies of affidavits or other sworn statements supporting facts subject to dispute; and

(iii) relevant parts of the record.

(C) The moving party must give reasonable notice of the motion to all parties.

(D) A motion under this Rule 8(a)(2) must be filed with the circuit clerk and normally will be considered by a panel of the court. But in an exceptional case in which time requirements make that procedure impracticable, the motion may be made to and considered by a single judge.

(E) The court may condition relief on a party's filing a bond or other appropriate security in the district court.

(b) Proceeding Against a Surety. If a party gives security in the form of a bond or stipulation or other undertaking with one or more sureties, each surety submits to the jurisdiction of the district court and irrevocably appoints the district clerk as the surety's agent on whom any papers affecting the surety's liability on the bond or undertaking may be served. On motion, a surety's liability may be enforced in the district court without the necessity of an independent action. The motion and any notice that the district court prescribes may be served on the district clerk, who must promptly mail a copy to each surety whose address is known.

(c) Stay in a Criminal Case. Rule 38 of the Federal Rules of Criminal Procedure governs a stay in a criminal case.

(As amended Mar. 10, 1986, eff. July 1, 1986; Apr. 27, 1995, eff. Dec. 1, 1995; Apr. 24, 1998, eff. Dec. 1, 1998.)

RULE 9. RELEASE IN A CRIMINAL CASE

(a) Release Before Judgment of Conviction.

(1) The district court must state in writing, or orally on the record, the reasons for an order regarding the release or detention of a defendant in a criminal case. A party appealing from the order must file with the court of appeals a copy of the district court's order and the court's statement of reasons as soon as practicable after filing the notice of appeal. An appellant who questions the factual basis for the district court's order must file a transcript of the release proceedings or an explanation of why a transcript was not obtained.

(2) After reasonable notice to the appellee, the court of appeals must promptly determine the appeal on the basis of the papers, affidavits, and parts of the record that the parties present or the court requires. Unless the court so orders, briefs need not be filed.

(3) The court of appeals or one of its judges may order the defendant's release pending the disposition of the appeal.

(b) Release After Judgment of Conviction. A party entitled to do so may obtain review of a district-court order regarding release after a judgment of conviction by filing a notice of appeal from that order in the district court, or by filing a motion in the court of appeals if the party has already filed a notice of appeal from the judgment of conviction. Both the order and the review are subject to Rule 9(a). The papers filed by the party seeking review must include a copy of the judgment of conviction.

(c) Criteria for Release. The court must make its decision regarding release in accordance with the applicable provisions of 18 U.S.C. §§ 3142, 3143, and 3145(c).

(As amended Apr. 24, 1972, eff. Oct. 1, 1972; Oct. 12, 1984, Pub.L. 98–473, Title II, § 210, 98 Stat. 1987; Apr. 29, 1994, eff. Dec. 1, 1994; Apr. 24, 1998, eff. Dec. 1, 1998.)

RULE 10. THE RECORD ON APPEAL

(a) Composition of the Record on Appeal. The following items constitute the record on appeal:

(1) the original papers and exhibits filed in the district court;

(2) the transcript of proceedings, if any; and

(3) a certified copy of the docket entries prepared by the district clerk.

(b) The Transcript of Proceedings.

(1) Appellant's Duty to Order. Within 14 days after filing the notice of appeal or entry of an order disposing of the last timely remaining motion of a type specified in Rule 4(a)(4)(A), whichever is later, the appellant must do either of the following:

(A) order from the reporter a transcript of such parts of the proceedings not already on file as the appellant considers necessary, subject to a local rule of the court of appeals and with the following qualifications:

(i) the order must be in writing;

(ii) if the cost of the transcript is to be paid by the United States under the Criminal Justice Act, the order must so state; and

(iii) the appellant must, within the same period, file a copy of the order with the district clerk; or

(B) file a certificate stating that no transcript will be ordered.

(2) Unsupported Finding or Conclusion. If the appellant intends to urge on appeal that a finding or conclusion is unsupported by the evidence or is contrary to the evidence, the appellant must include in the record a transcript of all evidence relevant to that finding or conclusion.

(3) Partial Transcript. Unless the entire transcript is ordered:

(A) the appellant must—within the 14 days provided in Rule 10(b)(1)—file a statement of the issues that the appellant intends to present on the appeal and must serve on the appellee a copy of both the order or certificate and the statement;

(B) if the appellee considers it necessary to have a transcript of other parts of the proceedings, the appellee must, within 14 days after the service of the order or certificate and the statement of the issues, file and serve on the appellant a designation of additional parts to be ordered; and

(C) unless within 14 days after service of that designation the appellant has ordered all such parts, and has so notified the appellee, the appellee may within the following 14 days either order the parts or move in the district court for an order requiring the appellant to do so.

(4) Payment. At the time of ordering, a party must make satisfactory arrangements with the reporter for paying the cost of the transcript.

(c) Statement of the Evidence When the Proceedings Were Not Recorded or When a Transcript Is Unavailable. If the transcript of a hearing or trial is unavailable, the appellant may prepare a statement of the evidence or proceedings from the best available means, including the appellant's recollection. The statement must be served on the appellee, who may serve objections or proposed amendments within 14 days after being served. The statement and any objections or proposed amendments must then be submitted to the district court for settlement and approval. As settled and approved, the statement must be included by the district clerk in the record on appeal.

(d) Agreed Statement as the Record on Appeal. In place of the record on appeal as defined in Rule 10(a), the parties may prepare, sign, and submit to the district court a statement of the case showing how the issues presented by the appeal arose and were decided in the district court. The statement must set forth only those facts averred and proved or sought to be proved that are essential to the court's resolution of the issues. If the statement is truthful, it—together with any additions that the district court may consider necessary to a full presentation of the issues on appeal—must be approved by the district court and must then be certified to the court of appeals as the record on appeal. The district clerk must then send it to the circuit clerk within the time provided by Rule 11. A copy of the agreed statement may be filed in place of the appendix required by Rule 30.

(e) Correction or Modification of the Record.

(1) If any difference arises about whether the record truly discloses what occurred in the district court, the difference must be submitted to and settled by that court and the record conformed accordingly.

(2) If anything material to either party is omitted from or misstated in the record by error or accident, the omission or misstatement may be corrected and a supplemental record may be certified and forwarded:

(A) on stipulation of the parties;

(B) by the district court before or after the record has been forwarded; or

(C) by the court of appeals.

(3) All other questions as to the form and content of the record must be presented to the court of appeals.

(As amended Apr. 30, 1979, eff. Aug. 1, 1979; Mar. 10, 1986, eff. July 1, 1986; Apr. 30, 1991, eff. Dec. 1, 1991; Apr. 22, 1993, eff. Dec. 1, 1993; Apr. 27, 1995, eff. Dec. 1, 1995; Apr. 24, 1998, eff. Dec. 1, 1998; Mar. 26, 2009, eff. Dec. 1, 2009.)

RULE 11. FORWARDING THE RECORD

(a) Appellant's Duty. An appellant filing a notice of appeal must comply with Rule 10(b) and must do whatever else is necessary to enable the clerk to assemble and forward the record. If there are multiple appeals from a judgment or order, the clerk must forward a single record.

(b) Duties of Reporter and District Clerk.

(1) Reporter's Duty to Prepare and File a Transcript. The reporter must prepare and file a transcript as follows:

(A) Upon receiving an order for a transcript, the reporter must enter at the foot of the order the date of its receipt and the expected completion date and send a copy, so endorsed, to the circuit clerk.

(B) If the transcript cannot be completed within 30 days of the reporter's receipt of the order, the reporter may request the circuit clerk to grant additional time to complete it. The clerk must note on the docket the action taken and notify the parties.

(C) When a transcript is complete, the reporter must file it with the district clerk and notify the circuit clerk of the filing.

(D) If the reporter fails to file the transcript on time, the circuit clerk must notify the district judge and do whatever else the court of appeals directs.

(2) District Clerk's Duty to Forward. When the record is complete, the district clerk must number the documents constituting the record and send them promptly to the circuit clerk together with a list of the documents correspondingly numbered and reasonably identified. Unless directed to do so by a party or the circuit clerk, the district clerk will not send to the court of appeals documents of unusual bulk or weight, physical exhibits other than documents, or other parts of the record designated for omission by local rule of the court of appeals. If the exhibits are unusually bulky or heavy, a party must arrange with the clerks in advance for their transportation and receipt.

(c) Retaining the Record Temporarily in the District Court for Use in Preparing the Appeal. The parties may stipulate, or the district court on motion may order, that the district clerk retain the record temporarily for the parties to use in preparing the papers on appeal. In that event the district clerk must certify to the circuit clerk that the record on appeal is complete. Upon receipt of the appellee's brief, or earlier if the court orders or the parties agree, the appellant must request the district clerk to forward the record.

(d) [Abrogated.]

(e) Retaining the Record by Court Order.

(1) The court of appeals may, by order or local rule, provide that a certified copy of the docket entries be forwarded instead of the entire record. But a party may at any time during the appeal request that designated parts of the record be forwarded.

(2) The district court may order the record or some part of it retained if the court needs it while the appeal is pending, subject, however, to call by the court of appeals.

(3) If part or all of the record is ordered retained, the district clerk must send to the court of appeals a copy of the order and the docket entries together with the parts of the original record allowed by the district court and copies of any parts of the record designated by the parties.

(f) Retaining Parts of the Record in the District Court by Stipulation of the Parties. The parties may agree by written stipulation filed in the district court that designated parts of the record be retained in the district court subject to call by the court of appeals or request by a party. The parts of the record so designated remain a part of the record on appeal.

(g) Record for a Preliminary Motion in the Court of Appeals. If, before the record is forwarded, a party makes any of the following motions in the court of appeals:

- for dismissal;
- for release;
- for a stay pending appeal;
- for additional security on the bond on appeal or on a supersedeas bond; or
- for any other intermediate order—

the district clerk must send the court of appeals any parts of the record designated by any party.

(As amended Apr. 30, 1979, eff. Aug. 1, 1979; Mar. 10, 1986, eff. July 1, 1986; Apr. 24, 1998, eff. Dec. 1, 1998.)

RULE 12. DOCKETING THE APPEAL; FILING A REPRESENTATION STATEMENT; FILING THE RECORD

(a) Docketing the Appeal. Upon receiving the copy of the notice of appeal and the docket entries from the district clerk under Rule 3(d), the circuit clerk must docket the appeal under the title of the district-court action and must identify the appellant, adding the appellant's name if necessary.

(b) Filing a Representation Statement. Unless the court of appeals designates another time, the attorney who filed the notice of appeal must, within 14 days after filing the notice, file a statement with the circuit clerk naming the parties that the attorney represents on appeal.

(c) Filing the Record, Partial Record, or Certificate. Upon receiving the record, partial record, or district clerk's certificate as provided in Rule 11, the circuit clerk must file it and immediately notify all parties of the filing date.

(As amended Apr. 30, 1979, eff. Aug. 1, 1979; Mar. 10, 1986, eff. July 1, 1986; Apr. 22, 1993, eff. Dec. 1, 1993; Apr. 24, 1998, eff. Dec. 1, 1998; Mar. 26, 2009, eff. Dec. 1, 2009.)

RULE 12.1. REMAND AFTER AN INDICATIVE RULING BY THE DISTRICT COURT ON A MOTION FOR RELIEF THAT IS BARRED BY A PENDING APPEAL

(a) Notice to the Court of Appeals. If a timely motion is made in the district court for relief that it lacks authority to grant because of an appeal that has been docketed and is pending, the movant must promptly notify the circuit clerk if the district court states either that it would grant the motion or that the motion raises a substantial issue.

(b) Remand After an Indicative Ruling. If the district court states that it would grant the motion or that the motion raises a substantial issue, the court of appeals may remand for further proceedings but retains jurisdiction unless it expressly dismisses the appeal. If the court of appeals remands but retains jurisdiction, the parties must promptly notify the circuit clerk when the district court has decided the motion on remand.

(Added Mar. 26, 2009, eff. Dec. 1, 2009.)

TITLE III. REVIEW OF A DECISION OF THE UNITED STATES TAX COURT

RULE 13. REVIEW OF A DECISION OF THE TAX COURT

(a) How Obtained; Time for Filing Notice of Appeal.

(1) Review of a decision of the United States Tax Court is commenced by filing a notice of appeal with the Tax Court clerk within 90 days after the entry of the Tax Court's decision. At the time of filing, the appellant must furnish the clerk with enough copies of the notice to enable the clerk to comply with Rule 3(d). If one party files a timely notice of appeal, any other party may file a notice of appeal within 120 days after the Tax Court's decision is entered.

(2) If, under Tax Court rules, a party makes a timely motion to vacate or revise the Tax Court's decision, the time to file a notice of appeal runs from the entry of the order disposing of the motion or from the entry of a new decision, whichever is later.

(b) Notice of Appeal; How Filed. The notice of appeal may be filed either at the Tax Court clerk's office in the District of Columbia or by mail addressed to the clerk. If sent by mail the notice is considered filed on the postmark date, subject to § 7502 of the Internal Revenue Code, as amended, and the applicable regulations.

(c) Contents of the Notice of Appeal; Service; Effect of Filing and Service. Rule 3 prescribes the contents of a notice of appeal, the manner of service, and the effect of its filing and service. Form 2 in the Appendix of Forms is a suggested form of a notice of appeal.

(d) The Record on Appeal; Forwarding; Filing.

(1) An appeal from the Tax Court is governed by the parts of Rules 10, 11, and 12 regarding the record on appeal from a district court, the time and manner of forwarding and filing, and the docketing in the court of appeals. References in those rules and in Rule 3 to the district court and district clerk are to be read as referring to the Tax Court and its clerk.

(2) If an appeal from a Tax Court decision is taken to more than one court of appeals, the original record must be sent to the court named in the first notice of appeal filed. In an appeal to any other court of appeals, the appellant must apply to that other court to make provision for the record.

(As amended Apr. 30, 1979, eff. Aug. 1, 1979; Apr. 29, 1994, eff. Dec. 1, 1994; Apr. 24, 1998, eff. Dec. 1, 1998.)

RULE 14. APPLICABILITY OF OTHER RULES TO THE REVIEW OF A TAX COURT DECISION

All provisions of these rules, except Rules 4–9, 15–20, and 22–23, apply to the review of a Tax Court decision.

(As amended Apr. 24, 1998, eff. Dec. 1, 1998.)

TITLE IV. REVIEW OR ENFORCEMENT OF AN ORDER OF AN ADMINISTRATIVE AGENCY, BOARD, COMMISSION, OR OFFICER

RULE 15. REVIEW OR ENFORCEMENT OF AN AGENCY ORDER—HOW OBTAINED; INTERVENTION

(a) Petition for Review; Joint Petition.

(1) Review of an agency order is commenced by filing, within the time prescribed by law, a petition for review with the clerk of a court of appeals authorized to review the agency order. If their interests make joinder practicable, two or more persons may join in a petition to the same court to review the same order.

(2) The petition must:

(A) name each party seeking review either in the caption or the body of the petition—using such terms as "et al.," "petitioners," or "respondents" does not effectively name the parties;

(B) name the agency as a respondent (even though not named in the petition, the United States is a respondent if required by statute); and

(C) specify the order or part thereof to be reviewed.

(3) Form 3 in the Appendix of Forms is a suggested form of a petition for review.

(4) In this rule "agency" includes an agency, board, commission, or officer; "petition for review" includes a petition to enjoin, suspend, modify, or otherwise review, or a notice of appeal, whichever form is indicated by the applicable statute.

(b) Application or Cross–Application to Enforce an Order; Answer; Default.

(1) An application to enforce an agency order must be filed with the clerk of a court of appeals authorized to enforce the order. If a petition is filed to review an agency order that the court may enforce, a party opposing the petition may file a cross-application for enforcement.

(2) Within 21 days after the application for enforcement is filed, the respondent must serve on the applicant an answer to the application and file it with the clerk. If the respondent fails to answer in time, the court will enter judgment for the relief requested.

(3) The application must contain a concise statement of the proceedings in which the order was entered, the facts upon which venue is based, and the relief requested.

(c) Service of the Petition or Application. The circuit clerk must serve a copy of the petition for review, or an application or cross-application to enforce an agency order, on each respondent as prescribed by Rule 3(d), unless a different manner of service is prescribed by statute. At the time of filing, the petitioner must:

(1) serve, or have served, a copy on each party admitted to participate in the agency proceedings, except for the respondents;

(2) file with the clerk a list of those so served; and

(3) give the clerk enough copies of the petition or application to serve each respondent.

(d) Intervention. Unless a statute provides another method, a person who wants to intervene in a proceeding under this rule must file a motion for leave to intervene with the circuit clerk and serve a copy on all parties. The motion—or other notice of intervention authorized by statute—must be filed within 30 days after the petition for review is filed and must contain a concise statement of the interest of the moving party and the grounds for intervention.

(e) Payment of Fees. When filing any separate or joint petition for review in a court of appeals, the petitioner must pay the circuit clerk all required fees.

(As amended Apr. 22, 1993, eff. Dec. 1, 1993; Apr. 24, 1998, eff. Dec. 1, 1998; Mar. 26, 2009, eff. Dec. 1, 2009.)

RULE 15.1. BRIEFS AND ORAL ARGUMENT IN A NATIONAL LABOR RELATIONS BOARD PROCEEDING

In either an enforcement or a review proceeding, a party adverse to the National Labor Relations Board proceeds first on briefing and at oral argument, unless the court orders otherwise.

(Added Mar. 10, 1986, eff. July 1, 1986, and amended Apr. 24, 1998, eff. Dec. 1, 1998.)

RULE 16. THE RECORD ON REVIEW OR ENFORCEMENT

(a) Composition of the Record. The record on review or enforcement of an agency order consists of:

(1) the order involved;

(2) any findings or report on which it is based; and

(3) the pleadings, evidence, and other parts of the proceedings before the agency.

(b) Omissions From or Misstatements in the Record. The parties may at any time, by stipulation, supply any omission from the record or correct a misstatement, or the court may so direct. If necessary, the court may direct that a supplemental record be prepared and filed.

(As amended Apr. 24, 1998, eff. Dec. 1, 1998.)

RULE 17. FILING THE RECORD

(a) Agency to File; Time for Filing; Notice of Filing. The agency must file the record with the circuit clerk within 40 days after being served with a petition for review, unless the statute authorizing review provides otherwise, or within 40 days after it files an application for enforcement unless the respondent fails to answer or the court orders otherwise. The court may shorten or extend the time to file the record. The clerk must notify all parties of the date when the record is filed.

(b) Filing—What Constitutes.

(1) The agency must file:

(A) the original or a certified copy of the entire record or parts designated by the parties; or

(B) a certified list adequately describing all documents, transcripts of testimony, exhibits, and other material constituting the record, or describing those parts designated by the parties.

(2) The parties may stipulate in writing that no record or certified list be filed. The date when the stipulation is filed with the circuit clerk is treated as the date when the record is filed.

(3) The agency must retain any portion of the record not filed with the clerk. All parts of the record retained by the agency are a part of the record on review for all purposes and, if the court or a party so requests, must be sent to the court regardless of any prior stipulation.

(As amended Apr. 24, 1998, eff. Dec. 1, 1998.)

RULE 18. STAY PENDING REVIEW

(a) Motion for a Stay.

(1) Initial Motion Before the Agency. A petitioner must ordinarily move first before the agency for a stay pending review of its decision or order.

(2) Motion in the Court of Appeals. A motion for a stay may be made to the court of appeals or one of its judges.

(A) The motion must:

(i) show that moving first before the agency would be impracticable; or

(ii) state that, a motion having been made, the agency denied the motion or failed to afford the relief requested and state any reasons given by the agency for its action.

(B) The motion must also include:

(i) the reasons for granting the relief requested and the facts relied on;

(ii) originals or copies of affidavits or other sworn statements supporting facts subject to dispute; and

(iii) relevant parts of the record.

(C) The moving party must give reasonable notice of the motion to all parties.

(D) The motion must be filed with the circuit clerk and normally will be considered by a panel of the court. But in an exceptional case in which time requirements make that procedure impracticable, the motion may be made to and considered by a single judge.

(b) Bond. The court may condition relief on the filing of a bond or other appropriate security.

(As amended Apr. 24, 1998, eff. Dec. 1, 1998.)

RULE 19. SETTLEMENT OF A JUDGMENT ENFORCING AN AGENCY ORDER IN PART

When the court files an opinion directing entry of judgment enforcing the agency's order in part, the agency must within 14 days file with the clerk and serve on each other party a proposed judgment conforming to the opinion. A party who disagrees with the agency's proposed judgment must within 10 days file with the clerk and serve the agency with a proposed judgment that the party believes conforms to the opinion. The court will settle the judgment and direct entry without further hearing or argument.

(As amended Mar. 10, 1986, eff. July 1, 1986; Apr. 24, 1998, eff. Dec. 1, 1998; Mar. 26, 2009, eff. Dec. 1, 2009.)

RULE 20. APPLICABILITY OF RULES TO THE REVIEW OR ENFORCEMENT OF AN AGENCY ORDER

All provisions of these rules, except Rules 3–14 and 22–23, apply to the review or enforcement of an agency order. In these rules, "appellant" includes a petitioner or applicant, and "appellee" includes a respondent.

(As amended Apr. 24, 1998, eff. Dec. 1, 1998.)

TITLE V. EXTRAORDINARY WRITS

RULE 21. WRITS OF MANDAMUS AND PROHIBITION, AND OTHER EXTRAORDINARY WRITS

(a) Mandamus or Prohibition to a Court: Petition, Filing, Service, and Docketing.

(1) A party petitioning for a writ of mandamus or prohibition directed to a court must file a petition with the circuit clerk with proof of service on all parties to the proceeding in the trial court. The party must also provide a copy to the trial-court judge. All parties to the proceeding in the trial court other than the petitioner are respondents for all purposes.

(2)(A) The petition must be titled "In re [name of petitioner]."

(B) The petition must state:

(i) the relief sought;

(ii) the issues presented;

(iii) the facts necessary to understand the issue presented by the petition; and

(iv) the reasons why the writ should issue.

(C) The petition must include a copy of any order or opinion or parts of the record that may be essential to understand the matters set forth in the petition.

(3) Upon receiving the prescribed docket fee, the clerk must docket the petition and submit it to the court.

(b) Denial; Order Directing Answer; Briefs; Precedence.

(1) The court may deny the petition without an answer. Otherwise, it must order the respondent, if any, to answer within a fixed time.

(2) The clerk must serve the order to respond on all persons directed to respond.

(3) Two or more respondents may answer jointly.

(4) The court of appeals may invite or order the trial-court judge to address the petition or may invite an amicus curiae to do so. The trial-court judge may request permission to address the petition but may not do so unless invited or ordered to do so by the court of appeals.

(5) If briefing or oral argument is required, the clerk must advise the parties, and when appropriate, the trial-court judge or amicus curiae.

(6) The proceeding must be given preference over ordinary civil cases.

(7) The circuit clerk must send a copy of the final disposition to the trial-court judge.

(c) Other Extraordinary Writs. An application for an extraordinary writ other than one provided for in Rule 21(a) must be made by filing a petition with the circuit clerk with proof of service on the respondents. Proceedings on the application must conform, so far as is practicable, to the procedures prescribed in Rule 21(a) and (b).

(d) Form of Papers; Number of Copies. All papers must conform to Rule 32(c)(2). Except by the court's permission, a paper must not exceed 30 pages, exclusive of the disclosure statement, the proof of service, and the accompanying documents required by Rule 21(a)(2)(C). An original and 3 copies must be filed unless the court requires the filing of a different number by local rule or by order in a particular case.

(As amended Apr. 29, 1994, eff. Dec. 1, 1994; Apr. 23, 1996, eff. Dec. 1, 1996; Apr. 24, 1998, eff. Dec. 1, 1998; Apr. 29, 2002, eff. Dec. 1, 2002.)

TITLE VI. HABEAS CORPUS; PROCEEDINGS IN FORMA PAUPERIS

RULE 22. HABEAS CORPUS AND SECTION 2255 PROCEEDINGS

(a) Application for the Original Writ. An application for a writ of habeas corpus must be made to the appropriate district court. If made to a circuit judge, the application must be transferred to the appropriate district court. If a district court denies an application made or transferred to it, renewal of the application before a circuit judge is not permitted. The applicant may, under 28 U.S.C. § 2253, appeal to the court of appeals from the district court's order denying the application.

(b) Certificate of Appealability.

(1) In a habeas corpus proceeding in which the detention complained of arises from process issued by a state court, or in a 28 U.S.C. § 2255 proceeding, the applicant cannot take an appeal unless a circuit justice or a circuit or district judge issues a certificate of appealability under 28 U.S.C. § 2253(c). If an applicant files a notice of appeal, the district clerk must send to the court of appeals the certificate (if any) and the statement described in Rule 11(a) of the Rules Governing Proceedings Under 28 U.S.C. § 2254 or § 2255 (if any), along with the notice of appeal and the file of the district-court proceedings. If the district judge has denied the certificate, the applicant may request a circuit judge to issue it.

(2) A request addressed to the court of appeals may be considered by a circuit judge or judges, as the court prescribes. If no express request for a certificate is filed, the notice of appeal constitutes a request addressed to the judges of the court of appeals.

(3) A certificate of appealability is not required when a state or its representative or the United States or its representative appeals.

(As amended Pub.L. 104–132, Title I, § 103, Apr. 24, 1996, 110 Stat. 1218; Apr. 24, 1998, eff. Dec. 1, 1998; Mar. 26, 2009, eff. Dec. 1, 2009.)

RULE 23. CUSTODY OR RELEASE OF A PRISONER IN A HABEAS CORPUS PROCEEDING

(a) Transfer of Custody Pending Review. Pending review of a decision in a habeas corpus proceeding commenced before a court, justice, or judge of the United States for the release of a prisoner, the person having custody of the prisoner must not transfer custody to another unless a transfer is directed in accordance with this rule. When, upon application, a custodian shows the need for a transfer, the court, justice, or judge rendering the decision under review may authorize the transfer and substitute the successor custodian as a party.

(b) Detention or Release Pending Review of Decision Not to Release. While a decision not to release a prisoner is under review, the court or judge rendering the decision, or the court of appeals, or the Supreme Court, or a judge or justice of either court, may order that the prisoner be:

(1) detained in the custody from which release is sought;

(2) detained in other appropriate custody; or

(3) released on personal recognizance, with or without surety.

(c) Release Pending Review of Decision Ordering Release. While a decision ordering the release of a prisoner is under review, the prisoner must—unless the court or judge rendering the decision, or the court of appeals, or the Supreme Court, or a judge or justice of either court orders otherwise—be released on personal recognizance, with or without surety.

(d) Modification of the Initial Order on Custody. An initial order governing the prisoner's custody or release, including any recognizance or surety, continues in effect pending review unless for special reasons shown to the court of appeals or the Supreme Court, or to a judge or justice of either court, the order is modified or an independent order regarding custody, release, or surety is issued.

(As amended Mar. 10, 1986, eff. July 1, 1986; Apr. 24, 1998, eff. Dec. 1, 1998.)

RULE 24. PROCEEDING IN FORMA PAUPERIS

(a) Leave to Proceed In Forma Pauperis.

(1) Motion in the District Court. Except as stated in Rule 24(a)(3), a party to a district-court action who desires to appeal in forma pauperis must file a motion in the district court. The party must attach an affidavit that:

(A) shows in the detail prescribed by Form 4 of the Appendix of Forms the party's inability to pay or to give security for fees and costs;

(B) claims an entitlement to redress; and

(C) states the issues that the party intends to present on appeal.

(2) Action on the Motion. If the district court grants the motion, the party may proceed on appeal without prepaying or giving security for fees and costs, unless a statute provides otherwise. If the district court denies the motion, it must state its reasons in writing.

(3) Prior Approval. A party who was permitted to proceed in forma pauperis in the district-court action, or who was determined to be financially unable to obtain an adequate defense in a criminal case, may proceed on appeal in forma pauperis without further authorization, unless:

(A) the district court—before or after the notice of appeal is filed—certifies that the appeal is not taken in good faith or finds that the party is not otherwise entitled to proceed in forma pauperis and states in writing its reasons for the certification or finding; or

(B) a statute provides otherwise.

(4) Notice of District Court's Denial. The district clerk must immediately notify the parties and the court of appeals when the district court does any of the following:

(A) denies a motion to proceed on appeal in forma pauperis;

(B) certifies that the appeal is not taken in good faith; or

(C) finds that the party is not otherwise entitled to proceed in forma pauperis.

(5) Motion in the Court of Appeals. A party may file a motion to proceed on appeal in forma pauperis in the court of appeals within 30 days after service of the notice prescribed in Rule 24(a)(4). The motion must include a copy of the affidavit filed in the district court and the district court's statement of reasons for its action. If no affidavit was filed in the district court, the party must include the affidavit prescribed by Rule 24(a)(1).

(b) Leave to Proceed In Forma Pauperis on Appeal or Review of an Administrative–Agency Proceeding. When an appeal or review of a proceeding before an administrative agency, board, commission, or officer (including for the purpose of this rule the United States Tax Court) proceeds directly in a court of appeals, a party may file in the court of appeals a motion for leave to proceed on appeal in forma pauperis with an affidavit prescribed by Rule 24(a)(1).

(c) Leave to Use Original Record. A party allowed to proceed on appeal in forma pauperis may request that the appeal be heard on the original record without reproducing any part.

(As amended Apr. 30, 1979, eff. Aug. 1, 1979; Mar. 10, 1986, eff. July 1, 1986; Apr. 24, 1998, eff. Dec. 1, 1998; Apr. 29, 2002, eff. Dec. 1, 2002.)

TITLE VII. GENERAL PROVISIONS

RULE 25. FILING AND SERVICE

(a) Filing.

(1) Filing with the Clerk. A paper required or permitted to be filed in a court of appeals must be filed with the clerk.

(2) Filing: Method and Timeliness.

(A) In general. Filing may be accomplished by mail addressed to the clerk, but filing is not timely unless the clerk receives the papers within the time fixed for filing.

(B) A brief or appendix. A brief or appendix is timely filed, however, if on or before the last day for filing, it is:

(i) mailed to the clerk by First–Class Mail, or other class of mail that is at least as expeditious, postage prepaid; or

(ii) dispatched to a third-party commercial carrier for delivery to the clerk within 3 days.

(C) Inmate filing. A paper filed by an inmate confined in an institution is timely if deposited in the institution's internal mailing system on or before the last day for filing. If an institution has a system designed for legal mail, the inmate must use that system to receive the benefit of this rule. Timely filing may be shown by a declaration in compliance with 28 U.S.C. § 1746 or by a notarized statement, either of which must set forth the date of deposit and state that first-class postage has been prepaid.

(D) Electronic filing. A court of appeals may by local rule permit or require papers to be filed, signed, or verified by electronic means that are consistent with technical standards, if any, that the Judicial Conference of the United States establishes. A local rule may require filing by electronic means only if reasonable exceptions are allowed. A paper filed by electronic means in compliance with a local rule constitutes a written paper for the purpose of applying these rules.

(3) Filing a Motion with a Judge. If a motion requests relief that may be granted by a single judge, the judge may permit the motion to be filed with the judge; the judge must note the filing date on the motion and give it to the clerk.

(4) Clerk's Refusal of Documents. The clerk must not refuse to accept for filing any paper presented for that purpose solely because it is not presented in proper form as required by these rules or by any local rule or practice.

(5) Privacy Protection. An appeal in a case whose privacy protection was governed by Federal Rule of Bankruptcy Procedure 9037, Federal Rule of Civil Procedure 5.2, or Federal Rule of Criminal Procedure 49.1 is governed by the same rule on appeal. In all other proceedings, privacy protection is governed by Federal Rule of Civil Procedure 5.2, except that Federal Rule of Criminal Procedure 49.1 governs when an extraordinary writ is sought in a criminal case.

(b) Service of All Papers Required. Unless a rule requires service by the clerk, a party must, at or before the time of filing a paper, serve a copy on the other parties to the appeal or review. Service on a party represented by counsel must be made on the party's counsel.

(c) Manner of Service.

(1) Service may be any of the following:

(A) personal, including delivery to a responsible person at the office of counsel;

(B) by mail;

(C) by third-party commercial carrier for delivery within 3 days; or

(D) by electronic means, if the party being served consents in writing.

(2) If authorized by local rule, a party may use the court's transmission equipment to make electronic service under Rule 25(c)(1)(D).

(3) When reasonable considering such factors as the immediacy of the relief sought, distance, and cost, service on a party must be by a manner at least as expeditious as the manner used to file the paper with the court.

(4) Service by mail or by commercial carrier is complete on mailing or delivery to the carrier. Service by electronic means is complete on transmission, unless the party making service is notified that the paper was not received by the party served.

(d) Proof of Service.

(1) A paper presented for filing must contain either of the following:

(A) an acknowledgment of service by the person served; or

(B) proof of service consisting of a statement by the person who made service certifying:

(i) the date and manner of service;

(ii) the names of the persons served; and

(iii) their mail or electronic addresses, facsimile numbers, or the addresses of the places of delivery, as appropriate for the manner of service.

(2) When a brief or appendix is filed by mailing or dispatch in accordance with Rule 25(a)(2)(B), the proof of service must also state the date and manner by which the document was mailed or dispatched to the clerk.

(3) Proof of service may appear on or be affixed to the papers filed.

(e) Number of Copies. When these rules require the filing or furnishing of a number of copies, a court may require a different number by local rule or by order in a particular case.

(As amended Mar. 10, 1986, eff. July 1, 1986; Apr. 30, 1991, eff. Dec. 1, 1991; Apr. 22, 1993, eff. Dec. 1, 1993; Apr. 29, 1994, eff. Dec. 1, 1994; Apr. 23, 1996, eff. Dec. 1, 1996; Apr. 24, 1998, eff. Dec. 1, 1998; Apr. 29, 2002, eff. Dec. 1, 2002; Apr. 12, 2006, eff. Dec. 1, 2006; Apr. 30, 2007, eff. Dec. 1, 2007; Mar. 26, 2009, eff. Dec. 1, 2009.)

RULE 26. COMPUTING AND EXTENDING TIME

(a) Computing Time. The following rules apply in computing any time period specified in these rules, in any local rule or court order, or in any statute that does not specify a method of computing time.

(1) Period Stated in Days or a Longer Unit. When the period is stated in days or a longer unit of time:

(A) exclude the day of the event that triggers the period;

(B) count every day, including intermediate Saturdays, Sundays, and legal holidays; and

(C) include the last day of the period, but if the last day is a Saturday, Sunday, or legal holiday, the period continues to run until the end of the next day that is not a Saturday, Sunday, or legal holiday.

(2) Period Stated in Hours. When the period is stated in hours:

(A) begin counting immediately on the occurrence of the event that triggers the period;

(B) count every hour, including hours during intermediate Saturdays, Sundays, and legal holidays; and

(C) if the period would end on a Saturday, Sunday, or legal holiday, the period continues to run until the same time on the next day that is not a Saturday, Sunday, or legal holiday.

(3) Inaccessibility of the Clerk's Office. Unless the court orders otherwise, if the clerk's office is inaccessible:

(A) on the last day for filing under Rule 26(a)(1), then the time for filing is extended to the first accessible day that is not a Saturday, Sunday, or legal holiday; or

(B) during the last hour for filing under Rule 26(a)(2), then the time for filing is extended to the same time on the first accessible day that is not a Saturday, Sunday, or legal holiday.

(4) "Last Day" Defined. Unless a different time is set by a statute, local rule, or court order, the last day ends:

(A) for electronic filing in the district court, at midnight in the court's time zone;

(B) for electronic filing in the court of appeals, at midnight in the time zone of the circuit clerk's principal office;

(C) for filing under Rules 4(c)(1), 25(a)(2)(B), and 25(a)(2)(C)—and filing by mail under Rule 13(b)—at the latest time for the method chosen for delivery to the post office, third-party commercial carrier, or prison mailing system; and

(D) for filing by other means, when the clerk's office is scheduled to close.

(5) "Next Day" Defined. The "next day" is determined by continuing to count forward when the period is measured after an event and backward when measured before an event.

(6) "Legal Holiday" Defined. "Legal holiday" means:

(A) the day set aside by statute for observing New Year's Day, Martin Luther King Jr.'s Birthday, Washington's Birthday, Memorial Day, Independence Day, Labor Day, Columbus Day, Veterans' Day, Thanksgiving Day, or Christmas Day;

(B) any day declared a holiday by the President or Congress; and

(C) for periods that are measured after an event, any other day declared a holiday by the state where either of the following is located: the district court that rendered the challenged judgment or order, or the circuit clerk's principal office.

(b) Extending Time. For good cause, the court may extend the time prescribed by these rules or by its order to perform any act, or may permit an act to be done after that time expires. But the court may not extend the time to file:

(1) a notice of appeal (except as authorized in Rule 4) or a petition for permission to appeal; or

(2) a notice of appeal from or a petition to enjoin, set aside, suspend, modify, enforce, or otherwise review an order of an administrative agency, board, commission, or officer of the United States, unless specifically authorized by law.

(c) Additional Time after Service. When a party may or must act within a specified time after service, 3 days are added after the period would otherwise expire under Rule 26(a), unless the paper is delivered on the date of service stated in the proof of service. For purposes of this Rule 26(c), a paper that is served electronically is not treated as delivered on the date of service stated in the proof of service.

(As amended Mar. 1, 1971, eff. July 1, 1971; Mar. 10, 1986, eff. July 1, 1986; Apr. 25, 1989, eff. Dec. 1, 1989; Apr. 30, 1991, eff. Dec. 1, 1991; Apr. 23, 1996, eff. Dec. 1, 1996; Apr. 24, 1998, eff. Dec. 1, 1998; Apr. 29, 2002, eff. Dec. 1, 2002; Apr. 25, 2005, eff. Dec. 1, 2005; Mar. 26, 2009, eff. Dec. 1, 2009.)

RULE 26.1. CORPORATE DISCLOSURE STATEMENT

(a) Who Must File. Any nongovernmental corporate party to a proceeding in a court of appeals must file a statement that identifies any parent corporation and any publicly held corporation that owns 10% or more of its stock or states that there is no such corporation.

(b) Time for Filing; Supplemental Filing. A party must file the Rule 26.1(a) statement with the principal brief or upon filing a motion, response, petition, or answer in the court of appeals, whichever occurs first, unless a local rule requires earlier filing. Even if the statement has already been filed, the party's principal brief must include the statement before the table of contents. A party must supplement its statement whenever the information that must be disclosed under Rule 26.1(a) changes.

(c) Number of Copies. If the Rule 26.1(a) statement is filed before the principal brief, or if a supplemental statement is filed, the party must file an original and 3 copies unless the court requires a different number by local rule or by order in a particular case.

(Added Apr. 25, 1989, eff. Dec. 1, 1989, and amended Apr. 30, 1991, eff. Dec. 1, 1991; Apr. 29, 1994, eff. Dec. 1, 1994; Apr. 24, 1998, eff. Dec. 1, 1998; Apr. 29, 2002, eff. Dec. 1, 2002.)

RULE 27. MOTIONS

(a) In General.

(1) Application for Relief. An application for an order or other relief is made by motion unless these rules prescribe another form. A motion must be in writing unless the court permits otherwise.

(2) Contents of a Motion.

(A) Grounds and relief sought. A motion must state with particularity the grounds for the motion, the relief sought, and the legal argument necessary to support it.

(B) Accompanying documents.

(i) Any affidavit or other paper necessary to support a motion must be served and filed with the motion.

(ii) An affidavit must contain only factual information, not legal argument.

(iii) A motion seeking substantive relief must include a copy of the trial court's opinion or agency's decision as a separate exhibit.

(C) Documents barred or not required.

(i) A separate brief supporting or responding to a motion must not be filed.

(ii) A notice of motion is not required.

(iii) A proposed order is not required.

(3) Response.

(A) Time to file. Any party may file a response to a motion; Rule 27(a)(2) governs its contents. The response must be filed within 10 days after service of the motion unless the court shortens or extends the time. A motion authorized by Rules 8, 9, 18, or 41 may be granted before the 10-day period runs only if the court gives reasonable notice to the parties that it intends to act sooner.

(B) Request for affirmative relief. A response may include a motion for affirmative relief. The time to respond to the new motion, and to reply to that response, are governed by Rule 27(a)(3)(A) and (a)(4). The title of the response must alert the court to the request for relief.

(4) Reply to Response. Any reply to a response must be filed within 7 days after service of the response. A reply must not present matters that do not relate to the response.

(b) Disposition of a Motion for a Procedural Order. The court may act on a motion for a procedural order—including a motion under Rule 26(b)—at any time without awaiting a response, and may, by rule or by order in a particular case, authorize its clerk to act on specified types of procedural motions. A party adversely affected by the court's, or the clerk's, action may file a motion to reconsider, vacate, or modify that action. Timely opposition filed after the motion is granted in whole or in part does not constitute a request to reconsider, vacate, or modify the disposition; a motion requesting that relief must be filed.

(c) Power of a Single Judge to Entertain a Motion. A circuit judge may act alone on any motion, but may not dismiss or otherwise determine an appeal or other proceeding. A court of appeals may provide by rule or by order in a particular case that only the court may act on any motion or class of motions. The court may review the action of a single judge.

(d) Form of Papers; Page Limits; and Number of Copies.

(1) Format.

(A) Reproduction. A motion, response, or reply may be reproduced by any process that yields a clear black image on light paper. The paper must be opaque and unglazed. Only one side of the paper may be used.

(B) Cover. A cover is not required, but there must be a caption that includes the case number, the name of the court, the title of the case, and a brief descriptive title indicating the purpose of the motion and identifying the party or parties for whom it is filed. If a cover is used, it must be white.

(C) Binding. The document must be bound in any manner that is secure, does not obscure the text, and permits the document to lie reasonably flat when open.

(D) Paper size, line spacing, and margins. The document must be on 8½ by 11 inch paper. The text must be double-spaced, but quotations more than two lines long may be indented and single-spaced. Headings and footnotes may be single-spaced. Margins must be at least one inch on all four sides. Page numbers may be placed in the margins, but no text may appear there.

(E) Typeface and type styles. The document must comply with the typeface requirements of Rule 32(a)(5) and the type-style requirements of Rule 32(a)(6).

(2) Page Limits. A motion or a response to a motion must not exceed 20 pages, exclusive of the corporate disclosure statement and accompanying documents authorized by Rule 27(a)(2)(B), unless the court permits or directs otherwise. A reply to a response must not exceed 10 pages.

(3) Number of Copies. An original and 3 copies must be filed unless the court requires a different number by local rule or by order in a particular case.

(e) Oral Argument. A motion will be decided without oral argument unless the court orders otherwise.

(As amended Apr. 30, 1979, eff. Aug. 1, 1979; Apr. 25, 1989, eff. Dec. 1, 1989; Apr. 29, 1994, eff. Dec. 1, 1994; Apr. 24, 1998, eff. Dec. 1, 1998; Apr. 29, 2002, eff. Dec. 1, 2002; Apr. 25, 2005, eff. Dec. 1, 2005; Mar. 26, 2009, eff. Dec. 1, 2009.)

RULE 28. BRIEFS

(a) Appellant's Brief. The appellant's brief must contain, under appropriate headings and in the order indicated:

(1) a corporate disclosure statement if required by Rule 26.1;

(2) a table of contents, with page references;

(3) a table of authorities—cases (alphabetically arranged), statutes, and other authorities—with references to the pages of the brief where they are cited;

(4) a jurisdictional statement, including:

(A) the basis for the district court's or agency's subject-matter jurisdiction, with citations to applicable statutory provisions and stating relevant facts establishing jurisdiction;

(B) the basis for the court of appeals' jurisdiction, with citations to applicable statutory provisions and stating relevant facts establishing jurisdiction;

(C) the filing dates establishing the timeliness of the appeal or petition for review; and

(D) an assertion that the appeal is from a final order or judgment that disposes of all parties' claims, or information establishing the court of appeals' jurisdiction on some other basis;

(5) a statement of the issues presented for review;

(6) a statement of the case briefly indicating the nature of the case, the course of proceedings, and the disposition below;

(7) a statement of facts relevant to the issues submitted for review with appropriate references to the record (see Rule 28(e));

(8) a summary of the argument, which must contain a succinct, clear, and accurate statement of the arguments made in the body of the brief, and which must not merely repeat the argument headings;

(9) the argument, which must contain:

(A) appellant's contentions and the reasons for them, with citations to the authorities and parts of the record on which the appellant relies; and

(B) for each issue, a concise statement of the applicable standard of review (which may appear in the discussion of the issue or under a separate heading placed before the discussion of the issues);

(10) a short conclusion stating the precise relief sought; and

(11) the certificate of compliance, if required by Rule 32(a)(7).

(b) Appellee's Brief. The appellee's brief must conform to the requirements of Rule 28(a)(1)–(9) and (11), except that none of the following need appear unless the appellee is dissatisfied with the appellant's statement:

(1) the jurisdictional statement;

(2) the statement of the issues;

(3) the statement of the case;

(4) the statement of the facts; and

(5) the statement of the standard of review.

(c) Reply Brief. The appellant may file a brief in reply to the appellee's brief. Unless the court permits, no further briefs may be filed. A reply brief must contain a table of contents, with page references, and a table of authorities—cases (alphabetically arranged), statutes, and other authorities—with references to the pages of the reply brief where they are cited.

(d) References to Parties. In briefs and at oral argument, counsel should minimize use of the terms "appellant" and "appellee." To make briefs clear, counsel should use the parties' actual names or the designations used in the lower court or agency proceeding, or such descriptive terms as "the employee," "the injured person," "the taxpayer," "the ship," "the stevedore."

(e) References to the Record. References to the parts of the record contained in the appendix filed with the appellant's brief must be to the pages of the appendix. If the appendix is prepared after the briefs are filed, a party referring to the record must follow one of the methods detailed in Rule 30(c). If the original record is used under Rule 30(f) and is not consecutively paginated, or if the brief refers to an unreproduced part of the record, any reference must be to the page of the original document. For example:

- Answer p. 7;
- Motion for Judgment p. 2;
- Transcript p. 231.

Only clear abbreviations may be used. A party referring to evidence whose admissibility is in controversy must cite the pages of the appendix or of the transcript at which the evidence was identified, offered, and received or rejected.

(f) Reproduction of Statutes, Rules, Regulations, etc. If the court's determination of the issues presented requires the study of statutes, rules, regulations, etc., the relevant parts must be set out in the brief or in an addendum at the end, or may be supplied to the court in pamphlet form.

(g) [Reserved]

(h) [Deleted]

(i) Briefs in a Case Involving Multiple Appellants or Appellees. In a case involving more than one appellant or appellee, including consolidated cases, any number of appellants or appellees may join in a brief, and any party may adopt by reference a part of another's brief. Parties may also join in reply briefs.

(j) Citation of Supplemental Authorities. If pertinent and significant authorities come to a party's attention after the party's brief has been filed—or after oral argument but before decision—a party may promptly advise the circuit clerk by letter, with a copy to all other parties, setting forth the citations. The letter must state the reasons for the supplemental citations, referring either to the page of the brief or to a point argued orally. The body of the letter must not exceed 350 words. Any response must be made promptly and must be similarly limited.

(As amended Apr. 30, 1979, eff. Aug. 1, 1979; Mar. 10, 1986, eff. July 1, 1986; Apr. 25, 1989, eff. Dec. 1, 1989; Apr. 30, 1991, eff. Dec. 1, 1991; Apr. 22, 1993, eff. Dec. 1, 1993; Apr. 29, 1994, eff. Dec. 1, 1994; Apr. 24, 1998, eff. Dec. 1, 1998; Apr. 29, 2002, eff. Dec. 1, 2002; Apr. 25, 2005, eff. Dec. 1, 2005.)

RULE 28.1. CROSS-APPEALS

(a) Applicability. This rule applies to a case in which a cross-appeal is filed. Rules 28(a)-(c), 31(a)(1), 32(a)(2), and 32(a)(7)(A)-(B) do not apply to such a case, except as otherwise provided in this rule.

(b) Designation of Appellant. The party who files a notice of appeal first is the appellant for the purposes of this rule and Rules 30 and 34. If notices are filed on the same day, the plaintiff in the proceeding below is the appellant. These designations may be modified by the parties' agreement or by court order.

(c) Briefs. In a case involving a cross-appeal:

(1) Appellant's Principal Brief. The appellant must file a principal brief in the appeal. That brief must comply with Rule 28(a).

(2) Appellee's Principal and Response Brief. The appellee must file a principal brief in the cross-appeal and must, in the same brief, respond to the principal brief in the appeal. That appellee's brief must comply with Rule 28(a), except that the brief need not include a statement of the case or a statement of the facts unless the appellee is dissatisfied with the appellant's statement.

(3) Appellant's Response and Reply Brief. The appellant must file a brief that responds to the principal brief in the cross-appeal and may, in the same brief, reply to the response in the appeal. That brief must comply with Rule 28(a)(2)–(9) and (11), except that none of the following need appear unless the appellant is dissatisfied with the appellee's statement in the cross-appeal:

(A) the jurisdictional statement;

(B) the statement of the issues;

(C) the statement of the case;

(D) the statement of the facts; and

(E) the statement of the standard of review.

(4) Appellee's Reply Brief. The appellee may file a brief in reply to the response in the cross-appeal. That brief must comply with Rule 28(a)(2)–(3) and (11) and must be limited to the issues presented by the cross-appeal.

(5) No Further Briefs. Unless the court permits, no further briefs may be filed in a case involving a cross-appeal.

(d) Cover. Except for filings by unrepresented parties, the cover of the appellant's principal brief must be blue; the appellee's principal and response brief, red; the appellant's response and reply brief, yellow; the appellee's reply brief, gray; an intervenor's or amicus curiae's brief, green; and any supplemental brief, tan. The front cover of a brief must contain the information required by Rule 32(a)(2).

(e) Length.

(1) Page Limitation. Unless it complies with Rule 28.1(e)(2) and (3), the appellant's principal brief must not exceed 30 pages; the appellee's principal and response brief, 35 pages; the appellant's response and reply brief, 30 pages; and the appellee's reply brief, 15 pages.

(2) Type-Volume Limitation.

(A) The appellant's principal brief or the appellant's response and reply brief is acceptable if:

(i) it contains no more than 14,000 words; or

(ii) it uses a monospaced face and contains no more than 1,300 lines of text.

(B) The appellee's principal and response brief is acceptable if:

(i) it contains no more than 16,500 words; or

(ii) it uses a monospaced face and contains no more than 1,500 lines of text.

(C) The appellee's reply brief is acceptable if it contains no more than half of the type volume specified in Rule 28.1(e)(2)(A).

(3) Certificate of Compliance. A brief submitted under Rule 28.1(e)(2) must comply with Rule 32(a)(7)(C).

(f) Time to Serve and File a Brief. Briefs must be served and filed as follows:

(1) the appellant's principal brief, within 40 days after the record is filed;

(2) the appellee's principal and response brief, within 30 days after the appellant's principal brief is served;

(3) the appellant's response and reply brief, within 30 days after the appellee's principal and response brief is served; and

(4) the appellee's reply brief, within 14 days after the appellant's response and reply brief is served, but at least 7 days before argument unless the court, for good cause, allows a later filing.

(As added April 25, 2005, eff. Dec. 1, 2005, and amended Mar. 26, 2009, eff. Dec. 1, 2009.)

RULE 29. BRIEF OF AN AMICUS CURIAE

(a) When Permitted. The United States or its officer or agency or a state may file an amicus-curiae brief without the consent of the parties or leave of court. Any other amicus curiae may file a brief only by leave of court or if the brief states that all parties have consented to its filing.

(b) Motion for Leave to File. The motion must be accompanied by the proposed brief and state:

(1) the movant's interest; and

(2) the reason why an amicus brief is desirable and why the matters asserted are relevant to the disposition of the case.

(c) Contents and Form. An amicus brief must comply with Rule 32. In addition to the requirements of Rule 32, the cover must identify the party or parties supported and indicate whether the brief supports affirmance or reversal. An amicus brief need not comply with Rule 28, but must include the following:

(1) if the amicus curiae is a corporation, a disclosure statement like that required of parties by Rule 26.1;

(2) a table of contents, with page references;

(3) a table of authorities—cases (alphabetically arranged), statutes, and other authorities—with references to the pages of the brief where they are cited;

(4) a concise statement of the identity of the amicus curiae, its interest in the case, and the source of its authority to file;

(5) unless the amicus curiae is one listed in the first sentence of Rule 29(a), a statement that indicates whether:

(A) a party's counsel authored the brief in whole or in part;

(B) a party or a party's counsel contributed money that was intended to fund preparing or submitting the brief; and

(C) a person—other than the amicus curiae, its members, or its counsel—contributed money that was intended to fund preparing or submitting the brief and, if so, identifies each such person;

(6) an argument, which may be preceded by a summary and which need not include a statement of the applicable standard of review; and

(7) a certificate of compliance, if required by Rule 32(a)(7).

(d) Length. Except by the court's permission, an amicus brief may be no more than one-half the maximum length authorized by these rules for a party's principal brief. If the court grants a party permission to file a longer brief, that extension does not affect the length of an amicus brief.

(e) Time for Filing. An amicus curiae must file its brief, accompanied by a motion for filing when necessary, no later than 7 days after the principal brief of the party being supported is filed. An amicus curiae that does not support either party must file its brief no later than 7 days after the appellant's or petitioner's principal brief is filed. A court may grant leave for later filing, specifying the time within which an opposing party may answer.

(f) Reply Brief. Except by the court's permission, an amicus curiae may not file a reply brief.

(g) Oral Argument. An amicus curiae may participate in oral argument only with the court's permission.

(As amended Apr. 24, 1998, eff. Dec. 1, 1998; Apr. 28, 2010, eff. Dec. 1, 2010.)

RULE 30. APPENDIX TO THE BRIEFS

(a) Appellant's Responsibility.

(1) Contents of the Appendix. The appellant must prepare and file an appendix to the briefs containing:

(A) the relevant docket entries in the proceeding below;

(B) the relevant portions of the pleadings, charge, findings, or opinion;

(C) the judgment, order, or decision in question; and

(D) other parts of the record to which the parties wish to direct the court's attention.

(2) Excluded Material. Memoranda of law in the district court should not be included in the appendix unless they have independent relevance. Parts of the record may be relied on by the court or the parties even though not included in the appendix.

(3) Time to File; Number of Copies. Unless filing is deferred under Rule 30(c), the appellant must file 10 copies of the appendix with the brief and must serve one copy on counsel for each party separately represented. An unrepresented party proceeding in forma pauperis must file 4 legible copies with the clerk, and one copy must be served on counsel for each separately represented party. The court may by local rule or by order in a particular case require the filing or service of a different number.

(b) All Parties' Responsibilities.

(1) Determining the Contents of the Appendix. The parties are encouraged to agree on the contents of the appendix. In the absence of an agreement, the appellant must, within 14 days after the record is filed, serve on the appellee a designation of the parts of the record the appellant intends to include in the appendix and a statement of the issues the appellant intends to present for review. The appellee may, within 14 days after receiving the designation, serve on the appellant a designation of additional parts to which it wishes to direct the court's attention. The appellant must include the designated parts in the appendix. The parties must not engage in unnecessary designation of parts of the record, because the entire record is available to the court. This paragraph applies also to a cross-appellant and a cross-appellee.

(2) Costs of Appendix. Unless the parties agree otherwise, the appellant must pay the cost of the appendix. If the appellant considers parts of the record designated by the appellee to be unnecessary, the appellant may advise the appellee, who must then advance the cost of including those parts. The cost of the appendix is a taxable cost. But if any party causes unnecessary parts of the record to be included in the appendix, the court may impose the cost of those parts on that party. Each circuit must, by local rule, provide for sanctions against attorneys who unreasonably and vexatiously increase litigation costs by including unnecessary material in the appendix.

(c) Deferred Appendix.

(1) Deferral Until After Briefs Are Filed. The court may provide by rule for classes of cases or by order in a particular case that preparation of the appendix may be deferred until after the briefs have been filed and that the appendix may be filed 21 days after the appellee's brief is served. Even though the filing of the appendix may be deferred, Rule 30(b) applies; except that a party must designate the parts of the record it wants included in the appendix when it serves its brief, and need not include a statement of the issues presented.

(2) References to the Record.

(A) If the deferred appendix is used, the parties may cite in their briefs the pertinent pages of the record. When the appendix is prepared, the record pages cited in the briefs must be indicated by inserting record page numbers, in brackets, at places in the appendix where those pages of the record appear.

(B) A party who wants to refer directly to pages of the appendix may serve and file copies of the brief within the time required by Rule 31(a), containing appropriate references to pertinent pages of the record. In that event, within 14 days after the appendix is filed, the party must serve and file copies of the brief, containing references to the pages of the appendix in place of or in addition to the references to the pertinent pages of the record. Except for the correction of typographical errors, no other changes may be made to the brief.

(d) Format of the Appendix. The appendix must begin with a table of contents identifying the page at which each part begins. The relevant docket entries must follow the table of contents. Other parts of the record must follow chronologically. When pages from the transcript of proceedings are placed in the appendix, the transcript page numbers must be shown in brackets immediately before the included pages. Omissions in the text of papers or of the transcript must be indicated by asterisks. Immaterial formal matters (captions, subscriptions, acknowledgments, etc.) should be omitted.

(e) Reproduction of Exhibits. Exhibits designated for inclusion in the appendix may be reproduced in a separate volume, or volumes, suitably indexed. Four copies must be filed with the appendix, and one copy must be served on counsel for each separately represented party. If a transcript of a proceeding before an administrative agency, board, commission, or officer was used in a district-court action and has been designated for inclusion in the appendix, the transcript must be placed in the appendix as an exhibit.

(f) Appeal on the Original Record Without an Appendix. The court may, either by rule for all cases or classes of cases or by order in a particular case, dispense with the appendix and permit an appeal to proceed on the original record with any copies of the record, or relevant parts, that the court may order the parties to file.

(As amended Mar. 30, 1970, eff. July 1, 1970; Mar. 10, 1986, eff. July 1, 1986; Apr. 30, 1991, eff. Dec. 1, 1991; Apr. 29, 1994, eff. Dec. 1, 1994; Apr. 24, 1998, eff. Dec. 1, 1998; Mar. 26, 2009, eff. Dec. 1, 2009.)

RULE 31. SERVING AND FILING BRIEFS

(a) Time to Serve and File a Brief.

(1) The appellant must serve and file a brief within 40 days after the record is filed. The appellee must serve and file a brief within 30 days after the appellant's brief is served. The appellant may serve and file a reply brief within 14 days after service of the appellee's brief but a reply brief must be filed at least 7 days before argument, unless the court, for good cause, allows a later filing.

(2) A court of appeals that routinely considers cases on the merits promptly after the briefs are filed may shorten the time to serve and file briefs, either by local rule or by order in a particular case.

(b) Number of Copies. Twenty-five copies of each brief must be filed with the clerk and 2 copies must be served on each unrepresented party and on counsel for each separately represented party. An unrepresented party proceeding in forma pauperis must file 4 legible copies with the clerk, and one copy must be served on each unrepresented party and on counsel for each separately represented party. The court may by local rule or by order in a particular case require the filing or service of a different number.

(c) Consequence of Failure to File. If an appellant fails to file a brief within the time provided by this rule, or within an extended time, an appellee may move to dismiss the appeal. An appellee who fails to file a brief will not be heard at oral argument unless the court grants permission.

(As amended Mar. 30, 1970, eff. July 1, 1970; Mar. 10, 1986, eff. July 1, 1986; Apr. 29, 1994, eff. Dec. 1, 1994; Apr. 24, 1998, eff. Dec. 1, 1998; Apr. 29, 2002, eff. Dec. 1, 2002; Mar. 26, 2009, eff. Dec. 1, 2009.)

RULE 32. FORM OF BRIEFS, APPENDICES, AND OTHER PAPERS

(a) Form of a Brief.

(1) Reproduction.

(A) A brief may be reproduced by any process that yields a clear black image on light paper. The paper must be opaque and unglazed. Only one side of the paper may be used.

(B) Text must be reproduced with a clarity that equals or exceeds the output of a laser printer.

(C) Photographs, illustrations, and tables may be reproduced by any method that results in a good copy of the original; a glossy finish is acceptable if the original is glossy.

(2) Cover. Except for filings by unrepresented parties, the cover of the appellant's brief must be blue; the appellee's, red; an intervenor's or amicus curiae's, green; any reply brief, gray; and any supplemental brief, tan. The front cover of a brief must contain:

(A) the number of the case centered at the top;

(B) the name of the court;

(C) the title of the case (see Rule 12(a));

(D) the nature of the proceeding (e.g., Appeal, Petition for Review) and the name of the court, agency, or board below;

(E) the title of the brief, identifying the party or parties for whom the brief is filed; and

(F) the name, office address, and telephone number of counsel representing the party for whom the brief is filed.

(3) Binding. The brief must be bound in any manner that is secure, does not obscure the text, and permits the brief to lie reasonably flat when open.

(4) Paper Size, Line Spacing, and Margins. The brief must be on 8½ by 11 inch paper. The text must be double-spaced, but quotations more than two lines long may be indented and single-spaced. Headings and footnotes may be single-spaced. Margins must be at least one inch on all four sides. Page numbers may be placed in the margins, but no text may appear there.

(5) Typeface. Either a proportionally spaced or a monospaced face may be used.

(A) A proportionally spaced face must include serifs, but sans-serif type may be used in headings and captions. A proportionally spaced face must be 14–point or larger.

(B) A monospaced face may not contain more than 10½ characters per inch.

(6) Type Styles. A brief must be set in a plain, roman style, although italics or boldface may be used for emphasis. Case names must be italicized or underlined.

(7) Length.

(A) Page limitation. A principal brief may not exceed 30 pages, or a reply brief 15 pages, unless it complies with Rule 32(a)(7)(B) and (C).

(B) Type-volume limitation.

(i) A principal brief is acceptable if:

- it contains no more than 14,000 words; or
- it uses a monospaced face and contains no more than 1,300 lines of text.

(ii) A reply brief is acceptable if it contains no more than half of the type volume specified in Rule 32(a)(7)(B)(i).

(iii) Headings, footnotes, and quotations count toward the word and line limitations. The corporate disclosure statement, table of contents, table of citations, statement with respect to oral argument, any addendum containing statutes, rules or regulations, and any certificates of counsel do not count toward the limitation.

(C) Certificate of compliance.

(i) A brief submitted under Rules 28.1(e)(2) or 32(a)(7)(B) must include a certificate by the attorney, or an unrepresented party, that the brief complies with the type-volume limitation. The person preparing the certificate may rely on the word or line count of the word-processing system used to prepare the brief. The certificate must state either:

- the number of words in the brief; or
- the number of lines of monospaced type in the brief.

(ii) Form 6 in the Appendix of Forms is a suggested form of a certificate of compliance. Use of Form 6 must be regarded as sufficient to meet the requirements of Rules 28.1(e)(3) and 32(a)(7)(C)(i).

(b) Form of an Appendix. An appendix must comply with Rule 32(a)(1), (2), (3), and (4), with the following exceptions:

(1) The cover of a separately bound appendix must be white.

(2) An appendix may include a legible photocopy of any document found in the record or of a printed judicial or agency decision.

(3) When necessary to facilitate inclusion of odd-sized documents such as technical drawings, an appendix may be a size other than 8½ by 11 inches, and need not lie reasonably flat when opened.

(c) Form of Other Papers.

(1) Motion. The form of a motion is governed by Rule 27(d).

(2) Other Papers. Any other paper, including a petition for panel rehearing and a petition for hearing or rehearing en banc, and any response to such a petition, must be reproduced in the manner prescribed by Rule 32(a), with the following exceptions:

(A) A cover is not necessary if the caption and signature page of the paper together contain the information required by Rule 32(a)(2). If a cover is used, it must be white.

(B) Rule 32(a)(7) does not apply.

(d) Signature. Every brief, motion, or other paper filed with the court must be signed by the party filing the paper or, if the party is represented, by one of the party's attorneys.

(e) Local Variation. Every court of appeals must accept documents that comply with the form requirements of this rule. By local rule or order in a particular case a court of appeals may accept documents that do not meet all of the form requirements of this rule.

(As amended Apr. 24, 1998, eff. Dec. 1, 1998; Apr. 29, 2002, eff. Dec. 1, 2002; Apr. 25, 2005, eff. Dec. 1, 2005.)

RULE 32.1. CITING JUDICIAL DISPOSITIONS

(a) Citation Permitted. A court may not prohibit or restrict the citation of federal judicial opinions, orders, judgments, or other written dispositions that have been:

(i) designated as "unpublished," "not for publication," "non-precedential," "not precedent," or the like; and

(ii) issued on or after January 1, 2007.

(b) Copies Required. If a party cites a federal judicial opinion, order, judgment, or other written disposition that is not available in a publicly accessible electronic database, the party must file and serve a copy of that opinion, order, judgment, or disposition with the brief or other paper in which it is cited.

(Added Apr. 12, 2006, eff. Dec. 1, 2006.)

RULE 33. APPEAL CONFERENCES

The court may direct the attorneys—and, when appropriate, the parties—to participate in one or more conferences to address any matter that may aid in disposing of the proceedings, including simplifying the issues and discussing settlement. A judge or other person designated by the court may preside over the conference, which may be conducted in person or by telephone. Before a settlement conference, the attorneys must consult with their clients and obtain as much authority as feasible to settle the case. The court may, as a result of the conference, enter an order controlling the course of the proceedings or implementing any settlement agreement.

(As amended Apr. 29, 1994, eff. Dec. 1, 1994; Apr. 24, 1998, eff. Dec. 1, 1998.)

RULE 34. ORAL ARGUMENT

(a) In General.

(1) Party's Statement. Any party may file, or a court may require by local rule, a statement explaining why oral argument should, or need not, be permitted.

(2) Standards. Oral argument must be allowed in every case unless a panel of three judges who have examined the briefs and record unanimously agrees that oral argument is unnecessary for any of the following reasons:

(A) the appeal is frivolous;

(B) the dispositive issue or issues have been authoritatively decided; or

(C) the facts and legal arguments are adequately presented in the briefs and record, and the decisional process would not be significantly aided by oral argument.

(b) Notice of Argument; Postponement. The clerk must advise all parties whether oral argument will be scheduled, and, if so, the date, time, and place for it, and the time allowed for each side. A motion to postpone the argument or to allow longer argument must be filed reasonably in advance of the hearing date.

(c) Order and Contents of Argument. The appellant opens and concludes the argument. Counsel must not read at length from briefs, records, or authorities.

(d) Cross-Appeals and Separate Appeals. If there is a cross-appeal, Rule 28.1(b) determines which party is the appellant and which is the appellee for purposes of oral argument. Unless the court directs otherwise, a cross-appeal or separate appeal must be argued when the initial appeal is argued. Separate parties should avoid duplicative argument.

(e) Nonappearance of a Party. If the appellee fails to appear for argument, the court must hear appellant's argument. If the appellant fails to appear for argument, the court may hear the appellee's argument. If neither party appears, the case will be decided on the briefs, unless the court orders otherwise.

(f) Submission on Briefs. The parties may agree to submit a case for decision on the briefs, but the court may direct that the case be argued.

(g) Use of Physical Exhibits at Argument; Removal. Counsel intending to use physical exhibits other than documents at the argument must arrange to place them in the courtroom on the day of the argument before the court convenes. After the argument, counsel must remove the exhibits from the courtroom, unless the court directs otherwise. The clerk may destroy or dispose of the exhibits if counsel does not reclaim them within a reasonable time after the clerk gives notice to remove them.

(As amended Apr. 30, 1979, eff. Aug. 1, 1979; Mar. 10, 1986, eff. July 1, 1986; Apr. 30, 1991, eff. Dec. 1, 1991; Apr. 22, 1993, eff. Dec. 1, 1993; Apr. 24, 1998, eff. Dec. 1, 1998; Apr. 25, 2005, eff. Dec. 1, 2005.)

RULE 35. EN BANC DETERMINATION

(a) When Hearing or Rehearing En Banc May Be Ordered. A majority of the circuit judges who are in regular active service and who are not disqualified may order that an appeal or other proceeding be heard or reheard by the court of appeals en banc. An en banc hearing or rehearing is not favored and ordinarily will not be ordered unless:

(1) en banc consideration is necessary to secure or maintain uniformity of the court's decisions; or

(2) the proceeding involves a question of exceptional importance.

(b) Petition for Hearing or Rehearing En Banc. A party may petition for a hearing or rehearing en banc.

(1) The petition must begin with a statement that either:

(A) the panel decision conflicts with a decision of the United States Supreme Court or of the court to which the petition is addressed (with citation to the conflicting case or cases) and consideration by the full court is therefore necessary to secure and maintain uniformity of the court's decisions; or

(B) the proceeding involves one or more questions of exceptional importance, each of which must be concisely stated; for example, a petition may assert that a proceeding presents a question of exceptional importance if it involves an issue on which the panel decision conflicts with the authoritative decisions of other United States Courts of Appeals that have addressed the issue.

(2) Except by the court's permission, a petition for an en banc hearing or rehearing must not exceed 15 pages, excluding material not counted under Rule 32.

(3) For purposes of the page limit in Rule 35(b)(2), if a party files both a petition for panel rehearing and a petition for rehearing en banc, they are considered a single document even if they are filed separately, unless separate filing is required by local rule.

(c) Time for Petition for Hearing or Rehearing En Banc. A petition that an appeal be heard initially en banc must be filed by the date when the appellee's brief is due. A petition for a rehearing en banc must be filed within the time prescribed by Rule 40 for filing a petition for rehearing.

(d) Number of Copies. The number of copies to be filed must be prescribed by local rule and may be altered by order in a particular case.

(e) Response. No response may be filed to a petition for an en banc consideration unless the court orders a response.

(f) Call for a Vote. A vote need not be taken to determine whether the case will be heard or reheard en banc unless a judge calls for a vote.

(As amended Apr. 30, 1979, eff. Aug. 1, 1979; Apr. 29, 1994, eff. Dec. 1, 1994; Apr. 24, 1998, eff. Dec. 1, 1998; Apr. 25, 2005, eff. Dec. 1, 2005.)

RULE 36. ENTRY OF JUDGMENT; NOTICE

(a) Entry. A judgment is entered when it is noted on the docket. The clerk must prepare, sign, and enter the judgment:

(1) after receiving the court's opinion—but if settlement of the judgment's form is required, after final settlement; or

(2) if a judgment is rendered without an opinion, as the court instructs.

(b) Notice. On the date when judgment is entered, the clerk must serve on all parties a copy of the opinion—or the judgment, if no opinion was written—and a notice of the date when the judgment was entered.

(As amended Apr. 24, 1998, eff. Dec. 1, 1998; Apr. 29, 2002, eff. Dec. 1, 2002.)

RULE 37. INTEREST ON JUDGMENT

(a) When the Court Affirms. Unless the law provides otherwise, if a money judgment in a civil case is affirmed, whatever interest is allowed by law is payable from the date when the district court's judgment was entered.

(b) When the Court Reverses. If the court modifies or reverses a judgment with a direction that a money judgment be entered in the district court, the mandate must contain instructions about the allowance of interest.

(As amended Apr. 24, 1998, eff. Dec. 1, 1998.)

RULE 38. FRIVOLOUS APPEAL—DAMAGES AND COSTS

If a court of appeals determines that an appeal is frivolous, it may, after a separately filed motion or notice from the court and reasonable opportunity to respond, award just damages and single or double costs to the appellee.

(As amended Apr. 29, 1994, eff. Dec. 1, 1994; Apr. 24, 1998, eff. Dec. 1, 1998.)

RULE 39. COSTS

(a) Against Whom Assessed. The following rules apply unless the law provides or the court orders otherwise:

(1) if an appeal is dismissed, costs are taxed against the appellant, unless the parties agree otherwise;

(2) if a judgment is affirmed, costs are taxed against the appellant;

(3) if a judgment is reversed, costs are taxed against the appellee;

(4) if a judgment is affirmed in part, reversed in part, modified, or vacated, costs are taxed only as the court orders.

(b) Costs For and Against the United States. Costs for or against the United States, its agency, or officer will be assessed under Rule 39(a) only if authorized by law.

(c) Costs of Copies. Each court of appeals must, by local rule, fix the maximum rate for taxing the cost of producing necessary copies of a brief or appendix, or copies of records authorized by Rule 30(f). The rate must not exceed that generally charged for such work in the area where the clerk's office is located and should encourage economical methods of copying.

(d) Bill of Costs: Objections; Insertion in Mandate.

(1) A party who wants costs taxed must—within 14 days after entry of judgment—file with the circuit clerk, with proof of service, an itemized and verified bill of costs.

(2) Objections must be filed within 14 days after service of the bill of costs, unless the court extends the time.

(3) The clerk must prepare and certify an itemized statement of costs for insertion in the mandate, but issuance of the mandate must not be delayed for taxing costs. If the mandate issues before costs are finally determined, the district clerk must—upon the circuit clerk's request—add the statement of costs, or any amendment of it, to the mandate.

(e) Costs on Appeal Taxable in the District Court. The following costs on appeal are taxable in the district court for the benefit of the party entitled to costs under this rule:

(1) the preparation and transmission of the record;

(2) the reporter's transcript, if needed to determine the appeal;

(3) premiums paid for a supersedeas bond or other bond to preserve rights pending appeal; and

(4) the fee for filing the notice of appeal.

(As amended Apr. 30, 1979, eff. Aug. 1, 1979; Mar. 10, 1986, eff. July 1, 1986; Apr. 24, 1998, eff. Dec. 1, 1998; Mar. 26, 2009, eff. Dec. 1, 2009.)

RULE 40. PETITION FOR PANEL REHEARING

(a) Time to File; Contents; Answer; Action by the Court if Granted.

(1) Time. Unless the time is shortened or extended by order or local rule, a petition for panel rehearing may be filed within 14 days after entry of judgment. But in a civil case, unless an order shortens or extends the time, the petition may be filed by any party within 45 days after entry of judgment if one of the parties is:

(A) the United States;

(B) a United States agency;

(C) a United States officer or employee sued in an official capacity; or

(D) a current or former United States officer or employee sued in an individual capacity for an act or omission occurring in connection with duties performed on the United States' behalf—including all instances in which the United States represents that person when the court of appeals' judgment is entered or files the petition for that person.

(2) Contents. The petition must state with particularity each point of law or fact that the petitioner believes the court has overlooked or misapprehended and must argue in support of the petition. Oral argument is not permitted.

(3) Answer. Unless the court requests, no answer to a petition for panel rehearing is permitted. But ordinarily rehearing will not be granted in the absence of such a request.

(4) Action by the Court. If a petition for panel rehearing is granted, the court may do any of the following:

(A) make a final disposition of the case without reargument;

(B) restore the case to the calendar for reargument or resubmission; or

(C) issue any other appropriate order.

(b) Form of Petition; Length. The petition must comply in form with Rule 32. Copies must be served and filed as Rule 31 prescribes. Unless the court permits or a local rule provides otherwise, a petition for panel rehearing must not exceed 15 pages.

(As amended Apr. 30, 1979, eff. Aug. 1, 1979; Apr. 29, 1994, eff. Dec. 1, 1994; Apr. 24, 1998, eff. Dec. 1, 1998; Apr. 26, 2011, eff. Dec. 1, 2011.)

RULE 41. MANDATE: CONTENTS; ISSUANCE AND EFFECTIVE DATE; STAY

(a) Contents. Unless the court directs that a formal mandate issue, the mandate consists of a certified copy of the judgment, a copy of the court's opinion, if any, and any direction about costs.

(b) When Issued. The court's mandate must issue 7 days after the time to file a petition for rehearing expires, or 7 days after entry of an order denying a timely petition for panel rehearing, petition for rehearing en banc, or motion for stay of mandate, whichever is later. The court may shorten or extend the time.

(c) Effective Date. The mandate is effective when issued.

(d) Staying the Mandate.

(1) On Petition for Rehearing or Motion. The timely filing of a petition for panel rehearing, petition for rehearing en banc, or motion for stay of mandate, stays the mandate until disposition of the petition or motion, unless the court orders otherwise.

(2) Pending Petition for Certiorari.

(A) A party may move to stay the mandate pending the filing of a petition for a writ of certiorari in the Supreme Court. The motion must be served on all parties and must show that the certiorari petition would present a substantial question and that there is good cause for a stay.

(B) The stay must not exceed 90 days, unless the period is extended for good cause or unless the party who obtained the stay files a petition for the writ and so notifies the circuit clerk in writing within the period of the stay. In that case, the stay continues until the Supreme Court's final disposition.

(C) The court may require a bond or other security as a condition to granting or continuing a stay of the mandate.

(D) The court of appeals must issue the mandate immediately when a copy of a Supreme

Court order denying the petition for writ of certiorari is filed.

(As amended Apr. 29, 1994, eff. Dec. 1, 1994; Apr. 24, 1998, eff. Dec. 1, 1998; Apr. 29, 2002, eff. Dec. 1, 2002; Mar. 26, 2009, eff. Dec. 1, 2009.)

RULE 42. VOLUNTARY DISMISSAL

(a) Dismissal in the District Court. Before an appeal has been docketed by the circuit clerk, the district court may dismiss the appeal on the filing of a stipulation signed by all parties or on the appellant's motion with notice to all parties.

(b) Dismissal in the Court of Appeals. The circuit clerk may dismiss a docketed appeal if the parties file a signed dismissal agreement specifying how costs are to be paid and pay any fees that are due. But no mandate or other process may issue without a court order. An appeal may be dismissed on the appellant's motion on terms agreed to by the parties or fixed by the court.

(As amended Apr. 24, 1998, eff. Dec. 1, 1998.)

RULE 43. SUBSTITUTION OF PARTIES

(a) Death of a Party.

(1) After Notice of Appeal Is Filed. If a party dies after a notice of appeal has been filed or while a proceeding is pending in the court of appeals, the decedent's personal representative may be substituted as a party on motion filed with the circuit clerk by the representative or by any party. A party's motion must be served on the representative in accordance with Rule 25. If the decedent has no representative, any party may suggest the death on the record, and the court of appeals may then direct appropriate proceedings.

(2) Before Notice of Appeal Is Filed—Potential Appellant. If a party entitled to appeal dies before filing a notice of appeal, the decedent's personal representative—or, if there is no personal representative, the decedent's attorney of record—may file a notice of appeal within the time prescribed by these rules. After the notice of appeal is filed, substitution must be in accordance with Rule 43(a)(1).

(3) Before Notice of Appeal Is Filed—Potential Appellee. If a party against whom an appeal may be taken dies after entry of a judgment or order in the district court, but before a notice of appeal is filed, an appellant may proceed as if the death had not occurred. After the notice of appeal is filed, substitution must be in accordance with Rule 43(a)(1).

(b) Substitution for a Reason Other Than Death. If a party needs to be substituted for any reason other than death, the procedure prescribed in Rule 43(a) applies.

(c) Public Officer: Identification; Substitution.

(1) Identification of Party. A public officer who is a party to an appeal or other proceeding in an official capacity may be described as a party by the public officer's official title rather than by name. But the court may require the public officer's name to be added.

(2) Automatic Substitution of Officeholder. When a public officer who is a party to an appeal or other proceeding in an official capacity dies, resigns, or otherwise ceases to hold office, the action does not abate. The public officer's successor is automatically substituted as a party. Proceedings following the substitution are to be in the name of the substituted party, but any misnomer that does not affect the substantial rights of the parties may be disregarded. An order of substitution may be entered at any time, but failure to enter an order does not affect the substitution.

(As amended Mar. 10, 1986, eff. July 1, 1986; Apr. 24, 1998, eff. Dec. 1, 1998.)

RULE 44. CASE INVOLVING A CONSTITUTIONAL QUESTION WHEN THE UNITED STATES OR THE RELEVANT STATE IS NOT A PARTY

(a) Constitutional Challenge to Federal Statute. If a party questions the constitutionality of an Act of Congress in a proceeding in which the United States or its agency, officer, or employee is not a party in an official capacity, the questioning party must give written notice to the circuit clerk immediately upon the filing of the record or as soon as the question is raised in the court of appeals. The clerk must then certify that fact to the Attorney General.

(b) Constitutional Challenge to State Statute. If a party questions the constitutionality of a statute of a State in a proceeding in which that State or its agency, officer, or employee is not a party in an official capacity, the questioning party must give written notice to the circuit clerk immediately upon the filing of the record or as soon as the question is raised in the court of appeals. The clerk must then certify that fact to the attorney general of the State.

(As amended Apr. 24, 1998, eff. Dec. 1, 1998; Apr. 29, 2002, eff. Dec. 1, 2002.)

RULE 45. CLERK'S DUTIES

(a) General Provisions.

(1) Qualifications. The circuit clerk must take the oath and post any bond required by law. Neither the clerk nor any deputy clerk may practice as an attorney or counselor in any court while in office.

(2) When Court Is Open. The court of appeals is always open for filing any paper, issuing and returning process, making a motion, and entering an order. The clerk's office with the clerk or a deputy in attendance must be open during business hours on all days except Saturdays, Sundays, and legal holidays. A court may provide by local rule or by order that the clerk's office be open for specified hours on Saturdays or on legal holidays other than New Year's Day, Martin Luther King, Jr.'s Birthday, Washington's Birthday, Memorial Day, Independence Day, Labor Day, Columbus Day, Veterans' Day, Thanksgiving Day, and Christmas Day.

(b) Records.

(1) The Docket. The circuit clerk must maintain a docket and an index of all docketed cases in the manner prescribed by the Director of the Administrative Office of the United States Courts. The clerk must record all papers filed with the clerk and all process, orders, and judgments.

(2) Calendar. Under the court's direction, the clerk must prepare a calendar of cases awaiting argument. In placing cases on the calendar for argument, the clerk must give preference to appeals in criminal cases and to other proceedings and appeals entitled to preference by law.

(3) Other Records. The clerk must keep other books and records required by the Director of the Administrative Office of the United States Courts, with the approval of the Judicial Conference of the United States, or by the court.

(c) Notice of an Order or Judgment. Upon the entry of an order or judgment, the circuit clerk must immediately serve a notice of entry on each party, with a copy of any opinion, and must note the date of service on the docket. Service on a party represented by counsel must be made on counsel.

(d) Custody of Records and Papers. The circuit clerk has custody of the court's records and papers. Unless the court orders or instructs otherwise, the clerk must not permit an original record or paper to be taken from the clerk's office. Upon disposition of the case, original papers constituting the record on appeal or review must be returned to the court or agency from which they were received. The clerk must preserve a copy of any brief, appendix, or other paper that has been filed.

(As amended Mar. 1, 1971, eff. July 1, 1971; Mar. 10, 1986, eff. July 1, 1986; Apr. 24, 1998, eff. Dec. 1, 1998; Apr. 29, 2002, eff. Dec. 1, 2002; Apr. 25, 2005, eff. Dec. 1, 2005.)

RULE 46. ATTORNEYS

(a) Admission to the Bar.

(1) Eligibility. An attorney is eligible for admission to the bar of a court of appeals if that attorney is of good moral and professional character and is admitted to practice before the Supreme Court of the United States, the highest court of a state, another United States court of appeals, or a United States district court (including the district courts for Guam, the Northern Mariana Islands, and the Virgin Islands).

(2) Application. An applicant must file an application for admission, on a form approved by the court that contains the applicant's personal statement showing eligibility for membership. The applicant must subscribe to the following oath or affirmation:

"I, ________________, do solemnly swear [or affirm] that I will conduct myself as an attorney and counselor of this court, uprightly and according to law; and that I will support the Constitution of the United States."

(3) Admission Procedures. On written or oral motion of a member of the court's bar, the court will act on the application. An applicant may be admitted by oral motion in open court. But, unless the court orders otherwise, an applicant need not appear before the court to be admitted. Upon admission, an applicant must pay the clerk the fee prescribed by local rule or court order.

(b) Suspension or Disbarment.

(1) Standard. A member of the court's bar is subject to suspension or disbarment by the court if the member:

(A) has been suspended or disbarred from practice in any other court; or

(B) is guilty of conduct unbecoming a member of the court's bar.

(2) Procedure. The member must be given an opportunity to show good cause, within the time prescribed by the court, why the member should not be suspended or disbarred.

(3) Order. The court must enter an appropriate order after the member responds and a hearing is held, if requested, or after the time prescribed for a response expires, if no response is made.

(c) Discipline. A court of appeals may discipline an attorney who practices before it for conduct unbecoming a member of the bar or for failure to comply with any court rule. First, however, the court must afford the attorney reasonable notice, an opportunity to show cause to the contrary, and, if requested, a hearing.

(As amended Mar. 10, 1986, eff. July 1, 1986; Apr. 24, 1998, eff. Dec. 1, 1998.)

RULE 47. LOCAL RULES BY COURTS OF APPEALS

(a) **Local Rules.**

(1) Each court of appeals acting by a majority of its judges in regular active service may, after giving appropriate public notice and opportunity for comment, make and amend rules governing its practice. A generally applicable direction to parties or lawyers regarding practice before a court must be in a local rule rather than an internal operating procedure or standing order. A local rule must be consistent with—but not duplicative of—Acts of Congress and rules adopted under 28 U.S.C. § 2072 and must conform to any uniform numbering system prescribed by the Judicial Conference of the United States. Each circuit clerk must send the Administrative Office of the United States Courts a copy of each local rule and internal operating procedure when it is promulgated or amended.

(2) A local rule imposing a requirement of form must not be enforced in a manner that causes a party to lose rights because of a nonwillful failure to comply with the requirement.

(b) Procedure When There Is No Controlling Law. A court of appeals may regulate practice in a particular case in any manner consistent with federal law, these rules, and local rules of the circuit. No sanction or other disadvantage may be imposed for noncompliance with any requirement not in federal law, federal rules, or the local circuit rules unless the alleged violator has been furnished in the particular case with actual notice of the requirement.

(As amended Apr. 27, 1995, eff. Dec. 1, 1995; Apr. 24, 1998, eff. Dec. 1, 1998.)

RULE 48. MASTERS

(a) Appointment; Powers. A court of appeals may appoint a special master to hold hearings, if necessary, and to recommend factual findings and disposition in matters ancillary to proceedings in the court. Unless the order referring a matter to a master specifies or limits the master's powers, those powers include, but are not limited to, the following:

(1) regulating all aspects of a hearing;

(2) taking all appropriate action for the efficient performance of the master's duties under the order;

(3) requiring the production of evidence on all matters embraced in the reference; and

(4) administering oaths and examining witnesses and parties.

(b) Compensation. If the master is not a judge or court employee, the court must determine the master's compensation and whether the cost is to be charged to any party.

(As amended Apr. 29, 1994, eff. Dec. 1, 1994; Apr. 24, 1998, eff. Dec. 1, 1998.)

APPENDIX OF FORMS

FORM 1. NOTICE OF APPEAL TO A COURT OF APPEALS FROM A JUDGMENT OR ORDER OF A DISTRICT COURT

United States District Court for the ______
District of ______
File Number ______

A.B., Plaintiff	)	
	)	
v.	)	*Notice of Appeal*
	)	
C.D., Defendant	)	

Notice is hereby given that [(here name all parties taking the appeal) , (plaintiffs) (defendants) in the above named case,[1]] hereby appeal to the United States Court of Appeals for the ______ Circuit (from the final judgment) (from an order (describing it)) entered in this action on the ______ day of ______, 20__.

(s) ______________________
Attorney for [______________]
[Address:______________]

(As amended Apr. 22, 1993, eff. Dec. 1, 1993; Mar. 27, 2003, eff. Dec. 1, 2003.)

1 See Rule 3(c) for permissible ways of identifying appellants.

FORM 2. NOTICE OF APPEAL TO A COURT OF APPEALS FROM A DECISION OF THE UNITED STATES TAX COURT

UNITED STATES TAX COURT

Washington, D.C.

A.B., Petitioner	)	
	)	
v.	)	Docket No. ________
	)	
Commissioner of Internal	)	
Revenue, Respondent	)	

Notice of Appeal

Notice is hereby given that [___here name all parties taking the appeal[1]___], hereby appeals to the United States Court of Appeals for the ______ Circuit from (that part of) the decision of this court entered in the above captioned proceeding on the ______ day of ______, 20__ (relating to ______).

(s) ________________
Counsel for [________________]
[Address:________________]

(As amended Apr. 22, 1993, eff. Dec. 1, 1993; Mar. 27, 2003, eff. Dec. 1, 2003.)

1 See Rule 3(c) for permissible ways of identifying appellants.

FORM 3. PETITION FOR REVIEW OF ORDER OF AN AGENCY, BOARD, COMMISSION OR OFFICER

United States Court of Appeals for the ______ Circuit

A.B., Petitioner)
)
v.) Petition for Review
XYZ Commission, Respondent)

[(here name all parties bringing the petition[1])] hereby petitions the court for review of the Order of the XYZ Commission (describe the order) entered on ______, 20___.

[(s)] ______________________
Attorney for Petitioners
Address:__________________

(As amended Apr. 22, 1993, eff. Dec. 1, 1993; Mar. 27, 2003, eff. Dec. 1, 2003.)

[1] See Rule 15.

FORM 4. AFFIDAVIT ACCOMPANYING MOTION FOR PERMISSION TO APPEAL IN FORMA PAUPERIS

United States District Court
for the
_____ District of _____

A.B., Plaintiff
v. Case No. __________
C.D., Defendant

Affidavit in Support of Motion

I swear or affirm under penalty of perjury that, because of my poverty, I cannot prepay the docket fees of my appeal or post a bond for them. I believe I am entitled to redress. I swear or affirm under penalty of perjury under United States laws that my answers on this form are true and correct. (28 U.S.C. § 1746; 18 U.S.C. § 1621.)

Signed: ________________________

Instructions

Complete all questions in this application and then sign it. Do not leave any blanks: if the answer to a question is "0," "none," or "not applicable (N/A)," write in that response. If you need more space to answer a question or to explain your answer, attach a separate sheet of paper identified with your name, your case's docket number, and the question number.

Date: ________________________

My issues on appeal are:

1. For both you and your spouse estimate the average amount of money received from each of the following sources during the past 12 months. Adjust any amount that was received weekly, biweekly, quarterly, semiannually, or annually to show the monthly rate. Use gross amounts, that is, amounts before any deductions for taxes or otherwise.

Income source	**Average monthly amount during the past 12 months**		**Amount expected next month**	
	You	**Spouse**	**You**	**Spouse**
Employment	$_____	$_____	$_____	$_____
Self-employment	$_____	$_____	$_____	$_____
Income from real property (such as rental income)	$_____	$_____	$_____	$_____
Interest and dividends	$_____	$_____	$_____	$_____
Gifts	$_____	$_____	$_____	$_____
Alimony	$_____	$_____	$_____	$_____
Child support	$_____	$_____	$_____	$_____
Retirement (such as social security, pensions, annuities, insurance)	$_____	$_____	$_____	$_____
Disability (such as social security, insurance payments)	$_____	$_____	$_____	$_____
Unemployment payments	$_____	$_____	$_____	$_____
Public-assistance (such as welfare)	$_____	$_____	$_____	$_____
Other (specify): ________	$_____	$_____	$_____	$_____
Total monthly income:	$_____	$_____	$_____	$_____

2. List your employment history, most recent employer first. (Gross monthly pay is before taxes or other deductions.)

Employer	Address	Dates of employment	Gross monthly pay

3. List your spouse's employment history, most recent employer first. (Gross monthly pay is before taxes or other deductions.)

Employer	Address	Dates of employment	Gross monthly pay

4. How much cash do you and your spouse have? $________

Below, state any money you or your spouse have in bank accounts or in any other financial institution.

Financial institution	Type of account	Amount you have	Amount your spouse has
		$	$
		$	$
		$	$

If you are a prisoner, you must attach a statement certified by the appropriate institutional officer showing all receipts, expenditures, and balances during the last six months in your institutional accounts. If you have multiple accounts, perhaps because you have been in multiple institutions, attach one certified statement of each account.

5. List the assets, and their values, which you own or your spouse owns. Do not list clothing and ordinary household furnishings.

Home (Value)	**Other real estate** (Value)	**Motor vehicle #1** (Value)
		Make & year:
		Model:
		Registration #:

Motor vehicle #2 (Value)	**Other assets** (Value)	**Other assets** (Value)
Make & year:		
Model:		
Registration #:		

6. State every person, business, or organization owing you or your spouse money, and the amount owed.

Person owing you or your spouse money	Amount owed to you	Amount owed to your spouse

7. State the persons who rely on you or your spouse for support.

Name [or, if under 18, initials only]	Relationship	Age

8. Estimate the average monthly expenses of you and your family. Show separately the amounts paid by your spouse. Adjust any payments that are made weekly, biweekly, quarterly, semiannually, or annually to show the monthly rate.

	You	Your Spouse
Rent or home-mortgage payment (include lot rented for mobile home)	$____	$____
Are real-estate taxes included? ☐ Yes ☐ No		
Is property insurance included? ☐ Yes ☐ No		
Utilities (electricity, heating fuel, water, sewer, and Telephone)	$____	$____
Home maintenance (repairs and upkeep)	$____	$____
Food	$____	$____
Clothing	$____	$____
Laundry and dry-cleaning	$____	$____
Medical and dental expenses	$____	$____
Transportation (not including motor vehicle payments)	$____	$____
Recreation, entertainment, newspapers, magazines, etc.	$____	$____
Insurance (not deducted from wages or included in Mortgage payments)	$____	$____
Homeowner's or renter's	$____	$____
Life	$____	$____
Health	$____	$____
Motor Vehicle	$____	$____
Other: ____________	$____	$____
Taxes (not deducted from wages or included in Mortgage payments) (specify): __	$____	$____
Installment payments	$____	$____
Motor Vehicle	$____	$____
Credit card (name): ________	$____	$____
Department store (name): ______	$____	$____
Other: ____________	$____	$____
Alimony, maintenance, and support paid to others	$____	$____
Regular expenses for operation of business, profession, or farm (attach detailed statement)	$____	$____
Other (specify): ____________	$____	$____
Total monthly expenses:	$____	$____

9. Do you expect any major changes to your monthly income or expenses or in your assets or liabilities during the next 12 months?
☐ Yes ☐ No If yes, describe on an attached sheet.

10. Have you paid—or will you be paying—an attorney any money for services in connection with this case, including the completion of this form? Yes No
If yes, how much? $________
If yes, state the attorney's name, address, and telephone number:
____
____
____

11. Have you paid—or will you be paying—anyone other than an attorney (such as a paralegal or a typist) any money for services in connection with this case, including the completion of this form?
☐ Yes ☐ No
If yes, how much? $________
If yes, state the person's name, address, and telephone number:
____
____
____

12. Provide any other information that will help explain why you cannot pay the docket fees for your appeal.

13. State the city and state of your legal residence.

____

____

Your daytime phone number: (___) ____________
Your age: ______ Your years of schooling: ______
Last four digits of your social-security number: ____________

(As amended Apr. 24, 1998, eff. Dec. 1, 1998; Apr. 28, 2010, eff. Dec. 1, 2010.)

FORM 5. NOTICE OF APPEAL TO A COURT OF APPEALS FROM A JUDGMENT OR ORDER OF A DISTRICT COURT OR A BANKRUPTCY APPELLATE PANEL

United States District Court for the ....
District of ....

In re)
)
.................................,)
Debtor)
) File No...........
.................................,)
Plaintiff)
)
v.)
)
.................................,)
Defendant)

Notice of Appeal to
United States Court of Appeals
for the .... Circuit

.........................., the plaintiff [or defendant or other party] appeals to the United States Court of Appeals for the .... Circuit from the final judgment [or order or decree] of the district court for the district of ... [or bankruptcy appellate panel of the .... circuit], entered in this case on ...., 20.... [here describe the judgment, order, or decree] ....

The parties to the judgment [or order or decree] appealed from and the names and addresses of their respective attorneys are as follows:

Dated ....
Signed ....
Attorney for Appellant

Address: ....
....

(Added Apr. 25, 1989, eff. Dec. 1, 1989; Mar. 27, 2003, eff. Dec. 1, 2003.)

FORM 6. CERTIFICATE OF COMPLIANCE WITH RULE 32(a)

Certificate of Compliance With Type-Volume Limitation, Typeface Requirements, and Type Style Requirements

1. This brief complies with the type-volume limitation of Fed. R. App. P. 32(a)(7)(B) because:

☐ this brief contains [*state the number of*] words, excluding the parts of the brief exempted by Fed. R. App. P. 32(a)(7)(B)(iii), *or*

☐ this brief uses a monospaced typeface and contains [*state the number of*] lines of text, excluding the parts of the brief exempted by Fed. R. App. P. 32(a)(7)(B)(iii).

2. This brief complies with the typeface requirements of Fed. R. App. P. 32(a)(5) and the type style requirements of Fed. R. App. P. 32(a)(6) because:

☐ this brief has been prepared in a proportionally spaced typeface using [*state name and version of word processing program*] in [*state font size and name of type style*], *or*

☐ this brief has been prepared in a monospaced typeface using [*state name and version of word processing program*] with [*state number of characters per inch and name of type style*].

(s)____________________

Attorney for ____________________

Dated: ____________

(Added Apr. 29, 2002, eff. Dec. 1, 2002.)

*

INDEX TO FEDERAL RULES OF APPELLATE PROCEDURE

*

UNITED STATES COURT OF APPEALS
FOR THE
DISTRICT OF COLUMBIA CIRCUIT

Adopted February 1, 1971

Including Amendments Received Through January 1, 2012

Research Note

These rules may be searched electronically on Westlaw in the US-RULES database; updates to these rules may be found on Westlaw in US-RULESUPDATES. For search tips, and a detailed summary of database content, consult the Westlaw Scope Screen of each database.

TITLE I. APPLICABILITY OF RULES

FRAP 1. SCOPE OF RULES; DEFINITION; TITLE

[For text of rule, see Federal Rules of Appellate Procedure]

RULE 1. SCOPE OF RULES; GENERAL PROVISIONS

The Circuit Rules of the United States Court of Appeals for the District of Columbia Circuit are adopted pursuant to Rule 47, Federal Rules of Appellate Procedure ("FRAP"), to replace all General Rules heretofore adopted by this court. Circuit Rules are keyed to correspondingly numbered provisions of the FRAP. (Several rules dealing with miscellaneous subjects are included after Circuit Rule 47.)

The court's Handbook of Practice and Internal Procedures ("Handbook") should also be consulted. In the event of any conflict between the Circuit Rules and the Handbook, the Circuit Rules prevail.

***(a)* Name, Seal, and Process.**

(1) Name. *The name of this court, as fixed by Chapter 3 of Title 28 of the United States Code, is "United States Court of Appeals for the District of Columbia Circuit."*

(2) Seal. *The seal of the court will contain the words "United States" on the upper part of the outer edge, preceded and followed by a star; the words "Court of Appeals" on the lower part of the outer edge, running from left to right; and the words "for the District of Columbia Circuit" in 5 lines in the center.*

(3) Process. *Writs, process, orders, and judgments of this court must be signed by a judge or judges of the court, or by the clerk at the direction of the court.*

(b) Sessions.

(1) No Formal Terms—Court Always Open. *The court does not hold formal terms but is open the year round for such purposes as docketing appeals; filing pleadings, records, and opinions; and entering orders and judgments.*

(2) Regular Sessions. *Regular sessions of the court are held at Washington, D.C., commencing on such day in September as the court may designate, and terminating at such time as the court may designate, and are adjourned as the court may from time to time direct.*

(3) Special Sessions. *Special sessions may be held at any time by order of the court.*

(c) Court Employees Not to Practice Law. *No one employed in any capacity by the court may engage in the practice of law while continuing in such position; no former employee may practice as an attorney in any matter connected with any case pending in the court during his or her term of service. For the purposes of this rule, a case is pending in this court upon the docketing of a notice of appeal, or the filing of a petition, in this court. See also FRAP 45(a).*

[Effective January 1, 1994. Amended on an interim basis May 6, 1999, effective May 6, 1999, adopted without changes December 22, 1999, effective January 3, 2000.]

FRAP 2. SUSPENSION OF RULES

[For text of rule, see Federal Rules of Appellate Procedure]

RULE 2. SUSPENSION OF RULES

In the interest of expediting decisions or for other good cause, the court may suspend the requirements of these Circuit Rules.

[Effective January 1, 1994. Amended April 24, 1998, effective December 1, 1998.]

TITLE II. APPEAL FROM A JUDGMENT OR ORDER OF A DISTRICT COURT

FRAP 3. APPEAL AS OF RIGHT—HOW TAKEN

[For text of rule, see Federal Rules of Appellate Procedure]

RULE 3. APPEAL AS OF RIGHT—HOW TAKEN

[There is no corresponding Circuit Rule.]

FRAP 3.1 APPEAL FROM A JUDGMENT OF A MAGISTRATE JUDGE IN A CIVIL CASE [ABROGATED]

FRAP 4. APPEAL AS OF RIGHT—WHEN TAKEN

[For text of rule, see Federal Rules of Appellate Procedure]

RULE 4. APPEAL AS OF RIGHT—WHEN TAKEN

[There is no corresponding Circuit Rule.]

FRAP 5. APPEAL BY PERMISSION

[For text of rule, see Federal Rules of Appellate Procedure]

RULE 5. APPEAL BY PERMISSION

***(a) Certificate of Parties and Disclosure Statement to be Attached.** A certificate of parties and amici curiae, as described in Circuit Rule 28(a)(1)(A), and a disclosure statement, as described in Circuit Rule 26.1, must be attached as an addendum to the petition. Any required disclosure statement must also be attached to any answer to the petition.*

***(b) Reply.** A party may file a reply to an answer within 7 days after the answer is served. A reply may not exceed 10 pages.*

***(c) Number of Copies.** Unless the court directs otherwise, the original and 4 copies of every petition, cross-petition, answer, and reply must be filed with the clerk.*

***(d) Motions to Extend Time or Exceed Page Limits.** Motions to extend time for filing answers or replies and motions to exceed page limits for petitions, answers, and replies are governed by Circuit Rule 27(h).*

[Adopted without changes November 4, 2002, effective December 1, 2002. Amended effective December 1, 2005. Amended November 16, 2009, effective December 1, 2009.]

FRAP 5.1. APPEAL BY LEAVE UNDER 28 U.S.C. § 636(c)(5) [Abrogated]

FRAP 6. APPEAL IN A BANKRUPTCY CASE FROM A FINAL JUDGMENT, ORDER, OR DECREE OF A DISTRICT COURT OR BANKRUPTCY APPELLATE PANEL

[For text of rule, see Federal Rules of Appellate Procedure]

RULE 6. APPEAL IN A BANKRUPTCY CASE FROM A FINAL JUDGMENT, ORDER, OR DECREE OF A DISTRICT COURT OR BANKRUPTCY APPELLATE PANEL

[There is no corresponding Circuit Rule.]

FRAP 7. BOND FOR COSTS ON APPEAL IN A CIVIL CASE

[For text of rule, see Federal Rules of Appellate Procedure]

RULE 7. BOND FOR COSTS ON APPEAL IN A CIVIL CASE

[There is no corresponding Circuit Rule.]

FRAP 8. STAY OR INJUNCTION PENDING APPEAL

[For text of rule, see Federal Rules of Appellate Procedure]

RULE 8. STAY AND EMERGENCY RELIEF PENDING APPEAL FROM A JUDGMENT OR ORDER OF THE DISTRICT COURT

(a) Criteria; Service.

(1) A motion for a stay of a judgment or of an order of the district court or any other motion seeking emergency relief must state whether such relief was previously requested from the district court and the ruling on that request. The motion must state the reasons for granting the stay or other emergency relief sought and discuss, with specificity, each of the following factors: (i) the likelihood that the moving party will prevail on the merits; (ii) the prospect of irreparable injury to the moving party if relief is withheld; (iii) the possibility of harm to other parties if relief is granted; and (iv) the public interest.

(2) Except in extraordinary circumstances, for any motion that is not filed electronically and for any party who has not consented to electronic service, the motion must be served by hand or, in the case of a party located outside the greater Washington metropolitan area, by other form of expedited service. The movant must attempt to notify the opposing side by telephone in advance of the filing of the motion and describe in the motion the efforts made to so notify the opposing side.

(3) There must be attached to each copy of the motion a copy of the judgment or order involved, and of any pertinent decision, memorandum, opinion, or findings issued by the district court. If the district court's reasons were given orally, the pertinent extract from the reporter's transcript must be attached, if available.

(4) A certificate of parties and amici curiae, as described in Circuit Rule 28(a)(1)(A), and a disclosure statement, as described in Circuit Rule 26.1, must be attached as an addendum to the motion, and any required disclosure statement must also be attached to any response to the motion, unless such documents have been filed previously with the court.

(b) Dispositive Motion Combined with Motion for Stay or Opposition Thereto. *A party filing or opposing a motion for a stay or other emergency relief may, in addition or in the alternative, file a motion to dispose of the appeal in its entirety. When a response to a motion for a stay or other emergency relief is combined with a dispositive motion, the combined pleading may not exceed 30 pages. The response to such a combined pleading may not exceed 15 pages, and the final reply may not exceed 10 pages.*

See also *Circuit Rule 18 (Stay Pending Review of an Agency Order), Circuit Rule 25 (Filing and Service), and Circuit Rule 27 (Motions).*

[Effective January 1, 1994. Amended on an interim basis May 6, 1999, effective May 6, 1999, adopted without changes December 22, 1999, effective January 3, 2000; November 4, 2002, effective December 1, 2002; December 1, 2005; May 15, 2009, effective June 8, 2009; November 16, 2009, effective December 1, 2009.]

FRAP 9. RELEASE IN A CRIMINAL CASE

[For text of rule, see Federal Rules of Appellate Procedure]

RULE 9. RELEASE IN A CRIMINAL CASE

(a) Appeal From a Pretrial Release or Detention Order. *An appeal from a pretrial release or detention order must be expedited. Appellant must make immediate arrangements for preparation of all necessary transcripts, including the transcript of proceedings before a magistrate judge, and notify the court in writing of those arrangements. Unless otherwise ordered by the court or a judge thereof, the following schedule will apply:*

(1) Not later than 10 days after the transcript of record is filed, the appellant must serve and file an original and 4 copies of a memorandum of law and fact setting forth as many of the matters required by Circuit Rule 9(b) as are relevant. The memorandum of law and fact must be accompanied by a copy of the order under review and the statement of reasons (including related findings of fact and conclusions of law) entered by the district court.

(2) The appellee may file a responsive memorandum not later than 10 days after the filing of appellant's memorandum.

(3) The appellant may file a memorandum in reply within 7 days after the filing of appellee's memorandum.

(4) The memorandum, any response thereto, and the reply must comply with FRAP 27(d)(1)–(2).

(5) The appeal will be determined by a panel of the court on the record and pleadings filed, unless oral argument is directed by the court.

(b) Release Pending Appeal From a Judgment of Conviction. *The applicant must file an original and 4 copies of an application pertaining to release pending appeal from a judgment of conviction. The application, any response thereto, and a reply to the response must comply with FRAP 27(d)(1)–(2). The space limi-*

tations imposed by FRAP 27(d)(2) may be exceeded only if authorized by order of the court, or a judge thereof, on motion showing good cause. The application must contain, in the following order:

(1) The name of the applicant, the district court number of the case, the offense of conviction, and the date and terms of sentence.

(2) The reasons given by the district court for the denial or, in the absence of reasons stated by the district court, an account of the facts and reasons relevant to that court's failure to grant the relief sought by the applicant.

(3) Where the applicant is the defendant, a concise statement of the question or questions involved in the appeal, with a showing that the appeal raises a substantial question of law or fact likely to result in reversal or in an order for a new trial. See also *FRAP 9(c). Sufficient facts must be set forth to present the essential background and the manner in which the question or questions arose in the district court.*

(4) Where the applicant is the defendant, a certificate by counsel, or by the applicant if acting pro se, that the appeal is not taken for delay.

(5) The application will be ruled upon by a panel of the court.

[Effective January 1, 1994. Amended on an interim basis May 6, 1999, effective May 6, 1999, adopted without changes December 22, 1999, effective January 3, 2000. Amended December 1, 2005. Amended November 16, 2009, effective December 1, 2009.]

FRAP 10. THE RECORD ON APPEAL

[For text of rule, see Federal Rules of Appellate Procedure]

RULE 10. THE RECORD ON APPEAL

[There is no corresponding Circuit Rule.]

FRAP 11. FORWARDING THE RECORD

[For text of rule, see Federal Rules of Appellate Procedure]

RULE 11. FORWARDING THE RECORD ON APPEAL FROM A JUDGMENT OR ORDER OF THE DISTRICT COURT

(a) When Forwarded. *Except as provided in Circuit Rule 47.2, the record in all cases must be forwarded to this court by the clerk of the district court at a time designated by the clerk of this court.*

(b) Transcript in Criminal Case. *The court reporter must expedite the preparation and furnishing of the transcript. A copy of any order of the district court directing that transcripts be furnished to appellant must be forwarded by the clerk of the district court to this court.*

See also *Circuit Rule 47.1 (Matters Under Seal).*

[Effective January 1, 1994. Amended on an interim basis May 6, 1999, effective May 6, 1999, adopted without changes December 22, 1999, effective January 3, 2000; November 4, 2002, effective December 1, 2002.]

FRAP 12. DOCKETING THE APPEAL; FILING A REPRESENTATION STATEMENT; FILING THE RECORD

[For text of rule, see Federal Rules of Appellate Procedure]

RULE 12. DOCKETING STATEMENT IN APPEAL FROM A JUDGMENT OR ORDER OF THE DISTRICT COURT; STATEMENT BY APPELLEE, INTERVENOR, OR AMICUS CURIAE

(a) Timing. *As directed by the court, appellant must file a docketing statement and serve a copy on all parties and amici curiae appearing at that time.*

(b) Docketing Statement Form. *The docketing statement must be on a form furnished by the clerk's office and contain such information as the form prescribes. An incomplete docketing statement will be lodged, and the party submitting it will be directed to provide a conforming one.*

(c) Provisional Certificate. *Attached to the docketing statement must be a provisional certificate prepared by appellant setting forth the information required by Circuit Rule 28(a)(1).*

(d) Knowledge and Information. *The docketing statement and the provisional certificate will be prepared on the basis of the knowledge and information reasonably available to appellant at the time of filing.*

(e) Errors in Docketing Statement. *Any party or amicus curiae must bring any errors in the docketing statement or provisional certificate to the attention of the clerk by letter served on all parties and amici within 7 days of service of the docketing statement.*

(f) Statement by Appellee, Intervenor, or Amicus Curiae. *Within 7 days of service of the docketing statement, an appellee must file with the court any statement required by Circuit Rule 26.1. Any disclosure statement required by Circuit Rule 26.1 must accompany a motion to intervene, a written representation of consent to participate as amicus curiae, or a motion for leave to participate as amicus.*

See also *Circuit Rule 46 (Attorneys; Appearance by Law Student).*

[Effective January 1, 1994. Amended on an interim basis May 6, 1999, effective May 6, 1999, adopted without changes

December 22, 1999, effective January 3, 2000; as amended on an interim basis December 10, 1999, effective December 10, 1999, adopted without changes effective May 9, 2000; November 4, 2002, effective December 1, 2002; December 1, 2005; May 15, 2009, effective June 8, 2009; November 16, 2009, effective December 1, 2009.]

FRAP 12.1 REMAND AFTER AN INDICATIVE RULING BY THE DISTRICT COURT ON A MOTION FOR RELIEF THAT IS BARRED BY A PENDING APPEAL

[For text of rule, see Federal Rules of Appellate Procedure]

RULE 12.1. REMAND AFTER AN INDICATIVE RULING BY THE DISTRICT COURT ON A MOTION FOR RELIEF THAT IS BARRED BY A PENDING APPEAL

See Circuit Rule 41(b) (Issuance of Mandate; Stay of Mandate; Remand).

[Adopted November 16, 2009, effective December 1, 2009.]

TITLE III. REVIEW OF A DECISION OF THE UNITED STATES TAX COURT

FRAP 13. REVIEW OF A DECISION OF THE TAX COURT

[For text of rule, see Federal Rules of Appellate Procedure]

RULE 13. REVIEW OF A DECISION OF THE TAX COURT

[There is no corresponding Circuit Rule.]

FRAP 14. APPLICABILITY OF OTHER RULES TO THE REVIEW OF A TAX COURT DECISION

[For text of rule, see Federal Rules of Appellate Procedure]

RULE 14. APPLICABILITY OF OTHER RULES TO THE REVIEW OF A TAX COURT DECISION

[There is no corresponding Circuit Rule.]

TITLE IV. REVIEW OR ENFORCEMENT OF AN ORDER OF AN ADMINISTRATIVE AGENCY, BOARD, COMMISSION, OR OFFICER

FRAP 15. REVIEW OR ENFORCEMENT OF AN AGENCY ORDER—HOW OBTAINED; INTERVENTION

[For text of rule, see Federal Rules of Appellate Procedure]

RULE 15. PETITION FOR REVIEW OR APPEAL FROM AGENCY ACTION; DOCKETING STATEMENT

(a) Service of Petition for Review. *In carrying out the service obligations of FRAP 15(c), in cases involving informal agency rulemaking such as, for example, those conducted pursuant to 5 U.S.C. § 553, a petitioner or appellant need serve copies only on the respondent agency, and on the United States if required by statute, see, e.g., 28 U.S.C. § 2344.*

(b) Intervention. *For purposes of FRAP 15(d), a motion to intervene in a case before this court regarding review of agency action must be served on all parties to the case before the court. A motion to intervene in a case before this court concerning direct review of an agency action will be deemed a motion to intervene in all cases before this court involving the same agency action or order, including later filed cases, unless the moving party specifically states otherwise, and an order granting such motion has the effect of granting intervention in all such cases.*

*(c) **Docketing Statement.***

(1) Timing. *As directed by the court, appellant or petitioner must file a docketing statement and serve a copy on all parties (including intervenors) and amici curiae appearing before this court at that time.*

(2) Docketing Statement Form. *The docketing statement must be on a form furnished by the clerk's office and contain such information as the form prescribes. In cases involving direct review in this court of administrative actions, the docketing statement must contain a brief statement of the basis for the appellant's or petitioner's claim of standing. This statement may include reference to arguments, evidence, or the administrative record supporting the claim of standing.* See Sierra Club v. EPA, *292 F.3d 895, 900–01 (D.C. Cir. 2002). An incomplete docketing statement will be lodged, and the party submitting it will be directed to provide a conforming one.*

(3) Provisional Certificate. *Attached to the docketing statement must be a provisional certificate prepared by appellant or petitioner setting forth the information required by Circuit Rule 28(a)(1).*

(4) Knowledge and Information. *The docketing statement and the provisional certificate will be prepared on the basis of the knowledge and information reasonably available to appellant or petitioner at the time of filing.*

(5) Errors in Docketing Statement. *Any party or amicus curiae must bring any errors in the docketing statement or provisional certificate to the attention of the clerk by letter served on all parties and amici within 7 days of service of the docketing statement.*

(6) Statement by Respondent, Appellee, Intervenor, or Amicus Curiae. *Within 7 days of service of the docketing statement, a respondent or appellee must file with the court any statement required by Circuit Rule 26.1. Any disclosure statement required by Circuit Rule 26.1 must accompany a motion to intervene, a written representation of consent to participate as amicus curiae, or a motion for leave to participate as amicus.*

[Effective January 1, 1994. Amended on an interim basis May 6, 1999, effective May 6, 1999, adopted without changes December 22, 1999, effective January 3, 2000; as amended on an interim basis December 10, 1999, effective December 10, 1999, adopted without changes effective May 9, 2000; November 4, 2002, effective December 1, 2002; December 1, 2005; July 1, 2006; May 15, 2009, effective June 8, 2009; November 16, 2009, effective December 1, 2009.]

FRAP 15.1 BRIEFS AND ORAL ARGUMENT IN A NATIONAL LABOR RELATIONS BOARD PROCEEDING

[For text of rule, see Federal Rules of Appellate Procedure]

RULE 15.1 BRIEFS AND ORAL ARGUMENT IN NATIONAL LABOR RELATIONS BOARD AND FEDERAL LABOR RELATIONS AUTHORITY PROCEEDINGS

The provisions of FRAP 15.1 also apply to parties adverse to the Federal Labor Relations Authority in an enforcement or a review proceeding.

[Effective January 1, 1994. Amended on an interim basis May 6, 1999, effective may 6, 1999, adopted without changes December 22, 1999, effective January 3, 2000.]

FRAP 16. THE RECORD ON REVIEW OR ENFORCEMENT

[For text of rule, see Federal Rules of Appellate Procedure]

RULE 16. THE RECORD ON REVIEW OR ENFORCEMENT

[There is no corresponding Circuit Rule.]

FRAP 17. FILING THE RECORD

[For text of rule, see Federal Rules of Appellate Procedure]

RULE 17. FILING THE RECORD FOR REVIEW OR ENFORCEMENT OF AN AGENCY ORDER

*(a) **Immigration Case.** On petition for review in immigration matters, the Executive Office for Immigration Review must transmit the record to this court within 40 days after the filing of the petition for review.*

*(b) **Other Agency Case.** On petition for review or on direct appeal of any other agency action, the agency must transmit a certified list of the contents of the administrative record to the court within 40 days after the filing of the petition for review or direct appeal, and transmit no other portion of the record to this court unless the court so requests.*

See also *Circuit Rule 47.1 (Matters under Seal).*

[Effective January 1, 1994. Amended on an interim basis May 6, 1999, effective May 6, 1999; adopted without changes December 22, 1999, effective January 3, 2000; December 1, 2005.]

FRAP 18. STAY PENDING REVIEW

[For text of rule, see Federal Rules of Appellate Procedure]

RULE 18. STAY AND EMERGENCY RELIEF PENDING REVIEW OF AN AGENCY ORDER

(a) Criteria; Service.

(1) A motion for a stay of an order of an agency or any other motion seeking emergency relief must state whether such relief was previously requested from the agency and the ruling on that request. The motion must state the reasons for granting the stay or other emergency relief sought and discuss, with specificity, each of the following factors: (i) the likelihood that the moving party will prevail on the merits; (ii) the prospect of irreparable injury to the moving party if relief is withheld; (iii) the possibility of harm to other parties if relief is granted; and (iv) the public interest.

(2) Except in extraordinary circumstances, for any motion that is not filed electronically and for any party who has not consented to electronic service, the motion must be served by hand or, in the case of a party located outside the greater Washington metropolitan area, by other form of expedited service. The movant must attempt to notify the opposing side by telephone in advance of the filing of the motion and describe in the motion the efforts made to so notify the opposing side.

(3) There must be attached to each copy of the motion a copy of the order involved, and of any pertinent rule, decision, memorandum, opinion, or findings issued by the agency.

(4) A certificate of parties and amici curiae, as described in Circuit Rule 28(a)(1)(A), and a disclosure statement, as described in Circuit Rule 26.1, must be attached as an addendum to the motion, and any required disclosure statement must also be attached to any response to the motion, unless such documents have been filed previously with the court.

(b) Dispositive Motion Combined with Motion for Stay or Opposition Thereto. *A party filing or opposing a motion for a stay or other emergency relief may, in addition or in the alternative, file a motion to dispose of the petition for review or direct appeal in its entirety. When a response to a motion for a stay or other emergency relief is combined with a dispositive motion, the combined pleading may not exceed 30 pages. The response to such a combined pleading may not exceed 15 pages, and the final reply may not exceed 10 pages.*

See also *Circuit Rule 8 (Stay and Emergency Relief Pending Appeal from a Judgment or Order of the District Court), Circuit Rule 25 (Filing and Service), and Circuit Rule 27 (Motions).*

[Effective January 1, 1994. Amended on an interim basis May 6, 1999, effective May 6, 1999; adopted without changes December 22, 1999, effective January 3, 2000; November 4, 2002, effective December 1, 2002; December 1, 2005; May 15, 2009, effective June 8, 2009; November 16, 2009, effective December 1, 2009.]

FRAP 19. SETTLEMENT OF A JUDGMENT ENFORCING AN AGENCY ORDER IN PART

[For text of rule, see Federal Rules of Appellate Procedure]

RULE 19. SETTLEMENT OF A JUDGMENT ENFORCING AN AGENCY ORDER IN PART

[There is no corresponding Circuit Rule.]

FRAP 20. APPLICABILITY OF RULES TO THE REVIEW OR ENFORCEMENT OF AN AGENCY ORDER

[For text of rule, see Federal Rules of Appellate Procedure]

RULE 20. APPLICABILITY OF RULES TO THE REVIEW OR ENFORCEMENT OF AN AGENCY ORDER

[There is no corresponding Circuit Rule.]

TITLE V. EXTRAORDINARY WRITS

FRAP 21. WRITS OF MANDAMUS AND PROHIBITION, AND OTHER EXTRAORDINARY WRITS

[For text of rule, see Federal Rules of Appellate Procedure]

RULE 21. WRITS OF MANDAMUS AND PROHIBITION AND OTHER EXTRAORDINARY WRITS AND COMPLAINTS OF UNREASONABLE DELAY

(a) *No responsive pleading to a petition for an extraordinary writ to the district court or an administrative agency, including a petition seeking relief from unreasonable agency delay, is permitted unless* *requested by the court. No such petition will be granted in the absence of such a request.*

(b) *A petition for a writ of mandamus or a writ of prohibition to the district court must not bear the name of the district judge, but instead be titled, "In re ______, Petitioner." Unless otherwise ordered, the district judge will be represented pro forma by counsel for the party opposing the relief, who will appear in the name of such party and not that of the judge.*

(c) *Unless the court directs otherwise, the original and 4 copies of a petition for an extraordinary writ, and of any responsive pleading or reply authorized by the court, must be filed with the clerk.*

(d) *A certificate of parties and amici curiae, as described in Circuit Rule 28(a)(1)(A), and a disclosure statement, as described in Circuit Rule 26.1, must be attached as an addendum to the petition, unless such documents have been filed previously with the court. Any required disclosure statement must also be attached to any answer to the petition.*

(e) *Motions to extend time for filing and to exceed page limits for petitions, answers, and replies are governed by Circuit Rule 27(h).*

[Effective January 1, 1994. Amended May 6, 1999, effective May 6, 1999, adopted without changes December 22, 1999, effective January 3, 2000; November 4, 2002, effective December 1, 2002; November 1, 2009, effective December 1, 2009.]

TITLE VI. HABEAS CORPUS; PROCEEDINGS IN FORMA PAUPERIS

FRAP 22. HABEAS CORPUS AND SECTION 2255 PROCEEDINGS

[For text of rule, see Federal Rules of Appellate Procedure]

RULE 22. HABEAS CORPUS AND SECTION 2255 PROCEEDINGS

See *Circuit Rule 47.2 (Appeal Expedited by Statute; Habeas Corpus Proceeding).*

[Effective January 1, 1994. Amended on an interim basis May 6, 1999, effective May 6, 1999, adopted without changes December 22, 1999, effective January 3, 2000.]

FRAP 23. CUSTODY OR RELEASE OF A PRISONER IN A HABEAS CORPUS PROCEEDING

[For text of rule, see Federal Rules of Appellate Procedure]

RULE 23. CUSTODY OR RELEASE OF A PRISONER IN A HABEAS CORPUS PROCEEDING

[There is no corresponding Circuit Rule.]

FRAP 24. PROCEEDING IN FORMA PAUPERIS

[For text of rule, see Federal Rules of Appellate Procedure]

RULE 24. PROCEEDING IN FORMA PAUPERIS

(a) *A case may be considered on the record without the necessity of an appendix when the appellant or petitioner is proceeding in forma pauperis and is not represented by counsel. If an appendix is not used, unrepresented appellants and petitioners must furnish with the brief the following items:*

(1) The pages of the court reporter's transcript to be called to the attention of the court (any method of duplication may be used which produces a clear black image on light paper), and a list setting forth the page numbers of the transcripts so furnished.

(2) Other portions of the record to be presented for the court's consideration, which must in every case include the findings of fact, conclusions of law, and opinion, if any, of the district court.

The appellant or petitioner is required to submit one copy of the above-listed documents; however, the appellant or petitioner is encouraged to submit 4 copies of each if able to do so.

(b) *Appellee or respondent must furnish with the brief 4 copies of an appendix containing any pages of the transcript or other portions of the record to be called to the court's attention and which were not furnished by appellant or petitioner.*

(c) *An appellant or petitioner who is represented by counsel and an amicus curiae appointed by the court must prepare an appendix as prescribed by FRAP 30 and Circuit Rule 30.*

See also Circuit Rule 30 (Appendix to the Briefs), and Circuit Rule 31 (Serving and Filing Briefs).

[Effective January 1, 1994. Amended on an interim basis May 6, 1999, effective May 6, 1999, adopted without changes December 22, 1999, effective January 3, 2000. Amended effective May 10, 2010.]

TITLE VII. GENERAL PROVISIONS

FRAP 25. FILING AND SERVICE

[For text of rule, see Federal Rules of Appellate Procedure]

RULE 25. FILING AND SERVICE

(a) Filing by Electronic Means. *The court will accept for filing documents submitted, signed, or verified by electronic means that comply with procedures established by the court. In cases assigned to the court's Case Management/Electronic Case Files (CM/ECF) system, the clerk is authorized to permit or to require a party to file by electronic means. The clerk also may require paper copies of any document filed electronically.*

(b) Exceptions. *Upon motion and a showing of good cause, the court may exempt a party from the electronic filing requirements and authorize filing by means other than use of the CM/ECF system.*

(c) Service of Documents by Electronic Means. *Registration for the court's CM/ECF system constitutes consent to electronic service of all documents as provided in these rules and the Federal Rules of Appellate Procedure. The Notice of Docket Activity that is generated by the court's CM/ECF system constitutes service of the filed document on all parties who have consented to electronic service. For any document that is not filed electronically and for any party who has not consented to electronic service, the document must be served by an alternative method of service, in accordance with the Federal Rules of Appellate Procedure and this court's rules. The Notice of Docket Activity generated by the court's CM/ECF system does not replace the certificate of service required by FRAP 25.*

(d) Non-Electronic Filing. *When electronic filing is not utilized, a non-emergency paper may be filed at the United States court house after the regular hours of the clerk's office pursuant to procedures established by the clerk's office. In emergencies or other compelling circumstances, when electronic filing is not utilized, the clerk may authorize that papers be filed with the court through facsimile transmission. Except when specifically so permitted, such filing is not authorized.*

[Effective January 1, 1994; adopted without change November 4, 2002, effective December 1, 2002; December 1, 2005. Amended May 15, 2009, effective June 8, 2009.]

FRAP 26. COMPUTING AND EXTENDING TIME

[For text of rule, see Federal Rules of Appellate Procedure]

RULE 26. COMPUTING AND EXTENDING TIME

For the purpose of computing response and reply periods, all filed papers will be presumed to have been served by mail unless the certificate of service clearly indicates that service was made by hand or other means authorized by FRAP 25(c).

[Effective January 1, 1994. Amended on an interim basis May 6, 1999, effective May 6, 1999, adopted without changes December 22, 1999, effective January 3, 2000; November 4, 2002, effective December 1, 2002.]

FRAP 26.1 CORPORATE DISCLOSURE STATEMENT

[For text of rule, see Federal Rules of Appellate Procedure]

RULE 26.1 DISCLOSURE STATEMENT

(a) *A corporation, association, joint venture, partnership, syndicate, or other similar entity appearing as a party or amicus curiae in any proceeding must file a disclosure statement, at the time specified in FRAP 26.1; Circuit Rules 5, 8, 12, 15, 18, 21, 27, and 35(c); or as otherwise ordered by the court, identifying all parent companies and any publicly-held company that has a 10% or greater ownership interest (such as stock or partnership shares) in the entity. A revised corporate disclosure statement must be filed any time there is a change in corporate ownership interests that would affect the disclosures required by this rule. For the purposes of this rule, "parent companies" include all companies controlling the specified entity directly, or indirectly through intermediaries.*

(b) *The statement must identify the represented entity's general nature and purpose, insofar as relevant to the litigation. If the entity is an unincorporated entity whose members have no ownership interests, the statement must include the names of any members of the entity that have issued shares or debt securities to the public. No such listing need be made, however, of the names of members of a trade association or professional association. For purposes of this rule, a "trade association" is a continuing association of numerous organizations or individuals operated for the purpose of promoting the general commercial, professional, legislative, or other interests of the membership.*

See also *Circuit Rule 5 (Appeal by Permission), Circuit Rule 8 (Stay and Emergency Relief Pending Appeal from a Judgment or Order of the District Court), Circuit Rule 12(f) (Docketing Statement in Appeal from a Judgment or Order of the District*

Court; Statement by Appellee, Intervenor, or Amicus Curiae), Circuit Rule 15(c)(6) (Petition for Review or Appeal from Agency Action; Docketing Statement), Circuit Rule 18 (Stay Pending Review), Circuit Rule 21 (Extraordinary Writs), Circuit Rule 27 (Motions), and Circuit Rule 35(c) (Petition for Panel Rehearing and Petition for Hearing or Rehearing En Banc).

[Effective January 1, 1994. Amended on an interim basis May 6, 1999, effective May 6, 1999, adopted without changes December 22, 1999, effective January 3, 2000. Amended on an interim basis December 10, 1999, effective December 10, 1999, adopted without changes effective May 9, 2000; November 4, 2002, effective December 1, 2002; December 1, 2005.]

FRAP 27. MOTIONS

[For text of rule, see Federal Rules of Appellate Procedure]

RULE 27. MOTIONS

(a) Form of Pleadings.

(1) In Writing; Service. *Every motion must be in writing and signed by counsel of record or by the movant if not represented by counsel, with proof of service on all other parties to the proceeding before this court, unless the motion is made in open court in opposing counsel's or movant's presence or this court provides otherwise.*

(2) Format. *Motions, responses thereto, and replies to responses must comply with FRAP 27(d)(1)–(2).*

(3) Reference to Oral Argument and Submission Without Oral Argument. *If a case has been scheduled for oral argument, has already been argued, or is being submitted without oral argument, a motion, and any response or reply, must so state in capital letters at the top of the first page and, where applicable, include the date of argument.*

(4) Certificate of Parties and Disclosure Statement to Be Attached. *A certificate of parties and amici curiae, as described in Circuit Rule 28(a)(1)(A), and a disclosure statement, as described in Circuit Rule 26.1, must be attached as an addendum to the motion, and any required disclosure statement must also be attached to any response to the motion, unless such documents have been filed previously with the court.*

(b) Number of Copies. *Unless the court directs otherwise, the original and 4 copies of every motion, response, and reply must be filed with the clerk.*

(c) Response That Also Seeks Affirmative Relief. *When a party opposing a motion also seeks affirmative relief, that party must submit with the response a motion so stating. Such a combined motion and response may not exceed 30 pages, the response to such a combined filing may not exceed 20 pages, and the final reply for such a combined filing may not exceed 10 pages.*

(d) Reply to Response That Also Seeks Affirmative Relief; Limits on Further Pleadings. *When a response includes a motion for affirmative relief, the reply may be joined in the same pleading with a response to the motion for affirmative relief. That combined pleading must be filed within 10 days of service of the motion for affirmative relief.*

After a party files a reply, no further pleading pertaining to the motion may be filed by that party except upon leave of the court.

(e) Clerk May Dispose of Certain Motions.

(1) Procedural Motions. *The clerk may dispose of procedural motions, in accordance with the court's instructions. Instead of granting or denying a motion under the authority afforded by this subparagraph, the clerk may submit it to a panel or to an individual judge of the court.*

(2) Reconsideration of Clerk's Orders on Procedural Motions. *Any interested party adversely affected by an order of the clerk disposing of a motion may move for reconsideration thereof within 10 days after entry of the order. The clerk will submit the motion for reconsideration to a panel or an individual judge of the court.*

(f) Requests for Expeditious Consideration. *Any party may request expedited action on a motion on the ground that, to avoid irreparable harm, relief is needed in less time than would ordinarily be required for this court to receive and consider a response. The motion on which expedited action is sought must be labeled an "Emergency Motion" and the request for expedition must state the nature of the emergency and the date by which court action is necessary. The motion must be filed at least 7 days before the date by which court action is necessary or counsel must explain why it was not so filed. Counsel for the party seeking expedition must communicate the request and the reasons therefor in person or by telephone to the clerk's office and to opposing counsel.*

(g) Dispositive Motions.

(1) Timing. *Any motion which, if granted, would dispose of the appeal or petition for review in its entirety, or transfer the case to another court, must be filed within 45 days of the docketing of the case in this court, unless, for good cause shown, the court grants leave for a later filing. This requirement does not apply to a motion by an appellant to dismiss its own appeal, or by a petitioner to dismiss its own petition, either of which may be filed at any time.*

(2) Required Attachments. *There must be attached to each copy of a dispositive motion a copy of any pertinent opinion or findings issued by the district court or agency or, if the reasons were given orally,*

the pertinent extract from the reporter's transcript must be attached, if available.

(3) Deferral of Briefing Pending Resolution of Dispositive Motion. *Unless otherwise ordered by the court, briefing, if scheduled, will be deferred pending resolution of any dispositive motion filed within 45 days of the docketing of the case in this court. If such a motion is filed more than 45 days after the docketing of the case in this court, briefing will be deferred only if ordered by the court.*

(4) Response to an Untimely Motion. *When a substantive motion is filed along with a procedural motion for leave to file out of time or to exceed the length limitations, no response is required to the substantive motion until a decision is rendered on the procedural motion to file out of time or to exceed length limitations.*

(h) Motions to Extend Time for Filing and to Exceed Page Limits.

(1) Timeliness of Request. *A motion to extend the time for filing motions, responses, and replies, or to exceed the page limits for such pleadings, must be filed at least 5 days before the pleading is due. Motions filed less than 5 days before the due date will be denied absent exceptional circumstances, except that the clerk may grant unopposed late filed motions for extension of time for good cause shown.*

(2) Consultation. *Before filing a motion to extend the time for filing a pleading or for leave to exceed page limits, the moving party must attempt to obtain the consent of the opposing side. If consent is not obtained, the moving party must attempt to inquire whether an opposition or other form of response will be filed. The opening paragraph of any such motion must recite the position taken by the opposing party in response to these inquiries, or the efforts made to obtain a response.*

The following requirements pertain to service (i) on an opposing party who has not consented to electronic service or (ii) for motions to extend the time for filing or for leave to exceed page limits that are not filed electronically. If the opposing side has stated an intention to file an opposition or other response, or has not been reached after reasonable effort, the moving party must serve the motion by personal service or, if personal service is not feasible, give telephone notice of the filing and serve the motion by the most expeditious form of service. If the moving party is unable to effect personal service or telephone notice at the time of filing, the opening paragraph of the motion must recite the efforts made to do so.

(3) Pleadings in Excess of Page Limits. *The court disfavors motions to exceed page limits; such motions will be granted only for extraordinarily compelling reasons.*

(4) Automatic Extensions for Timely Filed Motions. *If a motion is filed in accordance with the requirements of subparagraphs (1) and (2) above and the court does not act on the motion by the end of the second business day before the filing deadline, the time for filing the pleading is automatically extended until the court rules on the motion. If the motion is denied by the court under these circumstances, the time for filing will be extended automatically for 7 days after the date of the order denying the motion. If a timely filed motion to exceed length limitations is not acted upon by the filing date for the document, the overlong document may be filed; if the motion is subsequently denied, the movant will be given a short period in which to file a document that conforms to the rules. This rule does not apply to the filing of briefs. See Circuit Rule 28.*

See also *Circuit Rule 25 (Filing and Service), and Circuit Rule 47.1 (Matters Under Seal).*

[Effective January 1, 1994. Amended effective December 8, 1998; as amended on an interim basis May 6, 1999, effective May 6, 1999, adopted without changes December 22, 1999, effective January 3, 2000; November 4, 2002, effective December 1, 2002; December 1, 2005; January 16, 2007; May 15, 2009, effective June 8, 2009; November 16, 2009, effective December 1, 2009.]

FRAP 28. BRIEFS

[For text of rule, see Federal Rules of Appellate Procedure]

RULE 28. BRIEFS

(a) Contents of Briefs: Additional Requirements. *Briefs for an appellant/petitioner and an appellee/respondent, and briefs for an intervenor and an amicus curiae, must contain the following in addition to the items required by FRAP 28:*

(1) Certificate. *Immediately inside the cover and preceding the table of contents, a certificate titled "Certificate as to Parties, Rulings, and Related Cases," which contains a separate paragraph or paragraphs, with the appropriate heading, corresponding to, and in the same order as, each of the subparagraphs below.*

(A) Parties and Amici. The appellant or petitioner must furnish a list of all parties, intervenors, and amici who have appeared before the district court, and all persons who are parties, intervenors, or amici in this court. An appellee or respondent, intervenor, or amicus may omit from its certificate those persons who were listed by the appellant or petitioner, but must state: "[Except for the following,] all parties, intervenors, and amici appearing [before the district court and] in this court are listed in the Brief for ______." Any party or amicus curiae that is a corporation, asso-

ciation, joint venture, partnership, syndicate, or other similar entity must make the disclosure required by Circuit Rule 26.1.

(B) Rulings Under Review. Appropriate references must be made to each ruling at issue in this court, including the date, the name of the district court judge (if any), the place in the appendix where the ruling can be found, and any official citation in the case of a district court or Tax Court opinion, the Federal Register citation and/or other citation in the case of an agency decision, or a statement that no such citation exists. Such references need not be included if they are contained in a brief previously filed by another person, but the certificate must state: "[Except for the following,] references to the rulings at issue appear in the Brief for ______."

(C) Related Cases. A statement indicating whether the case on review was previously before this court or any other court and, if so, the name and number of such prior case. The statement must also contain similar information for any other related cases currently pending in this court or in any other court of which counsel is aware. For purposes of this rule, the phrase "any other court" means any other United States court of appeals or any other court (whether federal or local) in the District of Columbia. The phrase "any other related cases" means any case involving substantially the same parties and the same or similar issues. If there are no related cases, the certificate must so state.

(2) Principal Authorities. *In the left-hand margin of the table of authorities in all briefs, an asterisk must be placed next to those authorities on which the brief principally relies, together with a notation at the bottom of the first page of the table stating: "Authorities upon which we chiefly rely are marked with asterisks." If there are no such authorities, the notation must so state. The table of authorities must identify each page of the brief on which the authority is cited;* passim *or similar terms may not be used.*

*(3)** Glossary. *All briefs containing abbreviations, including acronyms, must provide a "Glossary" defining each such abbreviation on a page immediately following the table of authorities. Abbreviations that are part of common usage need not be defined.*

(4) Statements of Jurisdiction and the Case. *The brief of the appellant or petitioner must set forth the jurisdictional statement required by FRAP 28(a)(4). Any party, intervenor, or amicus curiae may include in its brief a counter statement regarding jurisdiction. The parties need not include in their briefs a statement of the case.*

(5) Statutes and Regulations. *Pertinent statutes and regulations must be set forth either in the body of the brief following the statement of the issues presented for review or in an addendum introduced by a table of contents and bound with the brief or separately; in the latter case a statement must appear in the body of the brief referencing the addendum. If the statutes and regulations are included in an addendum bound with the brief, the addendum must be separated from the body of the brief (and from any other addendum) by a distinctly colored separation page. If the pertinent statutes and regulations are contained in a brief previously submitted by another party, they need not be repeated but, if they are not repeated, a statement must appear under this heading as follows: "[Except for the following,] all applicable statutes, etc., are contained in the Brief for ______."*

(6) Summary of Argument. *Except when a brief contains a "Standing" section as required by Circuit Rule 28(a)(7), in each brief, including a reply brief, a summary of argument must immediately precede the argument; the summary of argument must contain a succinct, clear statement of the arguments made in the body of the brief and not merely repeat the argument headings.*

(7) Standing. *In cases involving direct review in this court of administrative actions, the brief of the appellant or petitioner must set forth the basis for the claim of standing. This section, entitled "Standing," must follow the summary of argument and immediately precede the argument. When the appellant's or petitioner's standing is not apparent from the administrative record, the brief must include arguments and evidence establishing the claim of standing.* See Sierra Club v. EPA, *292 F.3d 895, 900–01 (D.C. Cir. 2002). If the evidence is lengthy, and not contained in the administrative record, it may be presented in a separate addendum to the brief.*

(8) Reference to Oral Argument and Submission Without Oral Argument. *If a case has been scheduled for oral argument, has already been argued, or is being submitted without oral argument, a brief must so state in capital letters at the top of the first page and, where applicable, include the date of the argument.*

(b) References to Authorities and Other Material. *When citing to the record, authorities, or any other material, citations must refer to specific pages of the source; passim or similar terms may not be used.*

(c) Length of Briefs. *The length of briefs is governed by FRAP 28.1, 32(a)(7), and Circuit Rule 32(a).*

(d) Briefs for Intervenors. *The rules stated below apply with respect to the brief for an intervenor in this court. For purposes of this rule, an intervenor is an interested person who has sought and obtained the court's leave to participate in an already instituted proceeding.*

(1) Except by permission or direction of the court, the brief must conform to the brief lengths set out in Circuit Rule 32(a)(2).

(2) The brief must avoid repetition of facts or legal arguments made in the principal (appellant/petitioner or appellee/respondent) brief, and focus on points not made or adequately elaborated upon in the principal brief, although relevant to the issues before this court.

(3) Except as otherwise directed by the court, the brief must be filed in accordance with the time limitations described in FRAP 29.

(4) Intervenors on the same side must join in a single brief to the extent practicable. This requirement does not apply to a governmental entity. (For this purpose, the term "governmental entity" includes the United States or an officer or agency thereof, the District of Columbia, or a State, Territory, or Commonwealth of the United States.) Any separate brief for an intervenor must contain a certificate of counsel plainly stating why the separate brief is necessary. Generally unacceptable grounds for the filing of separate briefs include representations that the issues presented require greater length than these rules allow (appropriately addressed by a motion to exceed length limits), that counsel cannot coordinate their efforts due to geographical dispersion, or that separate presentations were allowed in earlier proceedings.

(5) A reply brief may be filed for an intervenor on the side of appellant or petitioner at the time the appellant's or petitioner's reply brief is due.

(e) Request to Exceed the Limits on the Length of Briefs and for Extension of Time for Filing.

(1) The court disfavors motions to exceed limits on the length of briefs, and motions to extend the time for filing briefs; such motions will be granted only for extraordinarily compelling reasons.

(2) A motion to exceed the limits on length of briefs or to extend the filing time for a brief must be filed at least 7 days before the brief is due. Motions filed less than 7 days before the due date will be denied absent exceptional circumstances, except that the clerk may grant unopposed late filed motions for extension of time that do not affect the oral argument schedule, for good cause shown.

(3) Before filing a motion to exceed the limits on length of briefs, or to extend the time for filing, the moving party must attempt to obtain the consent of the opposing side. If consent is not obtained, the moving party must attempt to inquire whether an opposition or other form of response will be filed. The opening paragraph of any such motion must recite the position taken by the opposing party in response to these inquiries, or the efforts made to obtain a response.

The following requirements pertain to service (i) on an opposing party who has not consented to electronic service or (ii) for motions to exceed the limits on length of briefs or to extend the time for filing that are not filed electronically. If the opposing side has stated an intention to file an opposition or other response, or has not been reached after reasonable effort, the moving party must serve the motion by hand, or if such service is not feasible, by giving telephone notice of the filing and serving the motion by the most expeditious form of service. If the moving party is unable to effect service by hand or telephone notice at the time of filing, the opening paragraph of the motion must recite the efforts made to do so.

(4) Submission of a motion to exceed the limits on length of briefs or extend the filing time for a brief does not toll the time for compliance with filing requirements. Movants will be expected to meet all filing requirements in the absence of an order granting a waiver.

(f) Citation of Supplemental Authorities. *After briefing has been completed, a party may file an original and 4 copies of a letter pursuant to FRAP 28(j).*

See also *Circuit Rule 28.1 (Cross–Appeals), Circuit Rule 29 (Brief of an Amicus Curiae), Circuit Rule 32.1 (Citing Judicial Dispositions), and Circuit Rule 47.1 (Matters Under Seal).*

[Effective January 1, 1994. Amended on an interim basis May 6, 1999, effective May 6, 1999, adopted without changes December 22, 1999, effective January 3, 2000; January 1, 2002; November 4, 2002, effective December 1, 2002; December 1, 2005; July 1, 2006; December 1, 2006; January 16, 2007; May 15, 2009, effective June 8, 2009; November 16, 2009, effective December 1, 2009.]

* **Publishers Note:** On or about January 26, 2010, the Clerk of the Court provided the following notice concerning D.C. Cir. Rule 28(a)(3):

The D.C. Circuit Rules permit the use of abbreviations, including acronyms, in briefs, provided the brief contains a glossary defining the abbreviations, other than those that are part of common usage. D.C. Cir. Rule 28(a)(3). To enhance the clarity of the brief, the court strongly urges parties to limit the use of acronyms. While acronyms may be used for entities and statutes with widely recognized initials, such as FERC and FOIA, parties should avoid using acronyms that are not widely known.

FRAP 28.1 CROSS–APPEALS

[For text of rule, see Federal Rules of Appellate Procedure]

RULE 28.1 CROSS–APPEALS

(a) Designation of Appellant. *When, pursuant to FRAP 28.1, the parties agree that a party other than the first one to file a notice of appeal will be deemed the appellant for purposes of this rule, they must so notify the court. In a civil case, this notice must be* *given at the time the docketing statement is filed. In a criminal case, the parties must so notify the court at the time of the filing of the final transcript status report.*

(b) Contents of Briefs. *Briefs in cross-appeals must comply with all applicable provisions of FRAP 28, FRAP 28.1, and D.C. Cir. Rule 28.*

(c) Time to Serve and File a Brief. *Parties must serve and file their briefs in accordance with the scheduling order issued by the court.*

[Effective December 1, 2005.]

FRAP 29. BRIEF OF AN AMICUS CURIAE

[For text of rule, see Federal Rules of Appellate Procedure]

RULE29. BRIEF OF AN AMICUS CURIAE

The rules stated below apply with respect to the brief for an amicus curiae not appointed by the court. A brief for an amicus curiae appointed by the court is governed by the provisions of Circuit Rule 28.

(a) Contents of Brief. *The brief must avoid repetition of facts or legal arguments made in the principal (appellant/petitioner or appellee/respondent) brief and focus on points not made or adequately elaborated upon in the principal brief, although relevant to the issues before this court.*

(b) Leave to File. *Any individual or non-governmental entity intending to participate as amicus curiae must file either a written representation that all parties consent to such participation, or, in the absence of such consent, a motion for leave to participate as amicus curiae. (For this purpose, the term "governmental entity" includes the United States or an officer or agency thereof, the District of Columbia, or a State, Territory, or Commonwealth of the United States.) Any disclosure statement required by Circuit Rule 26.1 must accompany a written representation of consent to participate as amicus curiae or a motion for leave to participate as amicus. The time for filing is governed by FRAP 29(e); however, the court encourages individuals and non-governmental entities to file a written representation of consent or motion for leave to participate, and governmental entities to file a notice of intent to file an amicus brief, as promptly as practicable after the case is docketed in this court. Leave to participate as amicus will not be granted and an amicus brief will not be accepted if the participation of amicus would result in the recusal of a member of the panel that has been assigned to the case or a member of the en banc court when participation is sought with respect to a petition for rehearing en banc.*

(c) Timely Filing. *Generally, a brief for amicus curiae will be due as set by the briefing order in each case. In the absence of provision for such a brief in the order, the brief must be filed in accordance with the time limitations described in FRAP 29(e).*

(d) Single Brief. *Amici curiae on the same side must join in a single brief to the extent practicable. This requirement does not apply to a governmental entity. Any separate brief for an amicus curiae must contain a certificate of counsel plainly stating why the separate brief is necessary. Generally unacceptable grounds for the filing of separate briefs include representations that the issues presented require greater length than these rules allow (appropriately addressed by a motion to exceed length limits), that counsel cannot coordinate their efforts due to geographical dispersion, or that separate presentations were allowed in earlier proceedings.*

See *Circuit Rule 28(d) (Briefs for Intervenors), and Circuit Rule 34(e) (Participation in Oral Argument by Amici Curiae).*

[Effective January 1, 1994. Amended effective December 1, 1997. As amended on an interim basis May 6, 1999, effective May 6, 1999; adopted without changes December 22, 1999, effective January 3, 2000. Amended on an interim basis December 10, 1999, effective December 10, 1999, adopted without changes effective May 9, 2000. Amended November 4, 2002, effective December 1, 2002. Amended effective December 1, 2005; December 1, 2006; December 1, 2010.]

FRAP 30. APPENDIX TO THE BRIEFS

[For text of rule, see Federal Rules of Appellate Procedure]

RULE 30. APPENDIX TO THE BRIEFS

(a) Filing and Form. *Except as provided in Circuit Rules 9 or 24, an appendix must be prepared as prescribed by FRAP 30. Appellant or petitioner must file 8 copies of the appendix with the court, and serve one copy on counsel for each separately represented party, at the time the brief for appellant or petitioner is filed, unless filing is to be deferred pursuant to FRAP 30(c). When an appendix is filed electronically, 7 paper copies must be filed in addition to the electronic version. The appendix must be reproduced on light paper by any duplicating or copying process capable of producing a clear black image; such duplication may be made on both sides of each page.*

(b) Record Items to Be Included. *The appendix must contain a copy of relevant portions of all pleadings, transcripts, and exhibits that are cited in the briefs. Counsel must not, however, burden the appendix with material of excessive length or items that do not bear directly on the issues raised on appeal. Costs will not be awarded for unnecessary reproduc-*

tion of items such as discovery materials, memoranda, pretrial briefs, or interlocutory motions or rulings that lack direct relevance to the appeal; appropriate sanctions will be imposed, after notice and opportunity to respond, if the court finds counsel to have been unreasonable in including such material. Any portion of the record, whether or not included in an appendix, may be relied upon by the parties and by the court.

(c) Deferred Appendix Option. *If all parties consent, they may utilize the deferred appendix option described at FRAP 30(c).*

(d) Motion to Dispense With Appendix. *For good cause shown, appellant or petitioner may be excused from the requirement of producing an appendix or any part thereof.*

(e) Supplementing the Appendix. *If anything material to the appeal or petition is omitted from the appendix, the clerk, on the duly served and filed written request of any party, may allow the appendix to be supplemented.*

See also *Circuit Rule 47.1 (Matters Under Seal).*

[Effective January 1, 1994. Amended on an interim basis May 6, 1999, effective May 6, 1999, adopted without changes December 22, 1999, effective January 3, 2000; May 15, 2009, effective June 8, 2009.]

FRAP 31. SERVING AND FILING BRIEFS

[For text of rule, see Federal Rules of Appellate Procedure]

RULE 31. SERVING AND FILING BRIEFS

(a) Time to Serve and File a Brief. *Parties must serve and file their briefs in accordance with the scheduling order issued by the court.*

(b) Number of Copies. *Except for unrepresented persons proceeding in forma pauperis, the original and 8 copies of every brief must be filed. When the deferred appendix method is used, 6 copies of the initial briefs must be filed (when filed electronically, 5 paper copies in addition to the electronic version), followed by the original and 8 copies in final form. An unrepresented person proceeding in forma pauperis must file with the clerk one original brief, and the clerk will duplicate the necessary copies.*

See also *Circuit Rule 47.1(d)(1) (Matters Under Seal).*

[Effective January 1, 1994. Amended on an interim basis May 6, 1999, effective May 6, 1999, adopted without changes December 22, 1999, effective January 3, 2000. Amended on interim basis April 1, 2004. Amended effective December 1, 2005; May 15, 2009, effective June 8, 2009.]

FRAP 32. FORM OF BRIEFS, APPENDICES, AND OTHER PAPERS

[For text of rule, see Federal Rules of Appellate Procedure]

RULE 32. FORM OF BRIEFS, APPENDICES, AND OTHER PAPERS

(a) Form of Briefs. *Except as provided below, the form of briefs is governed by FRAP 28.1 and 32(a).*

(1) Length of Briefs. *In calculating the number of words and lines that do not count toward the word and line limitations, the certificate required by Circuit Rule 28(a)(1), the glossary, and any addendum containing evidence in support of the claim of standing required by Circuit Rule 28(a)(7), may be excluded, in addition to the items listed in FRAP 32(a)(7)(B)(iii).*

(2) Length of Briefs for Intervenors.

(A) Page limitation. ***A principal brief for an intervenor may not exceed 19 pages, and a reply brief 9 pages, unless it complies with Circuit Rule 32(a)(2)(B).***

(B) Type-volume limitation.

(i) A principal brief is acceptable if:

- *it contains no more than 8,750 words; or*
- *it uses a monospaced face and contains no more than 813 lines of text.*

(ii) A reply brief is acceptable if it contains no more than half of the type volume specified in Circuit Rule 32(a)(2)(B)(i).

(C) Certificate. If a type-volume limitation is used, the brief must contain the certificate of compliance required by FRAP 32(a)(7)(C).

(3) Length of Briefs for Amici Curiae Not Appointed by the Court. *See FRAP 29(d).*

(b) Pleading by Letter. *Except as prescribed by FRAP 28(j), parties, other than pro se litigants proceeding in forma pauperis, may not plead by letter.*

(c) Nonconforming Papers. *If the court receives any submission that does not conform substantially to the requirements of the FRAP or these rules, the clerk will promptly notify the person making the submission and direct that person to cure the defect or submit an appropriate motion. See FRAP 25(a)(4).*

See also *Circuit Rule 28 (Briefs).*

[Effective January 1, 1994. Amended on an interim basis May 6, 1999, effective May 6, 1999, adopted without changes

December 22, 1999, effective January 3, 2000. Amended effective December 1, 2005; July 1, 2006; March 2, 2009.]

FRAP 32.1 CITING JUDICIAL DISPOSITIONS

[For text of rule, see Federal Rules of Appellate Procedure]

RULE 32.1 CITING JUDICIAL DISPOSITIONS

(a) Citation to Published Opinions and to Statutes. *Citations to decisions of this court must be to the Federal Reporter. Dual or parallel citation of cases is not required. Citations of state court decisions included in the National Reporter System must be to that system in both the text and the table of authorities. Citations to all federal statutes, including those statutes applicable to the District of Columbia, must refer to the current official code or its supplement, or if there is no current official code, to a current unofficial code or its supplement. Citation to the official session laws is not required unless there is no code citation.*

(b) Citation to Unpublished Dispositions.

(1) Unpublished Dispositions of this Court.

(A) Unpublished dispositions entered before January 1, 2002. Unpublished orders or judgments of this court, including explanatory memoranda and sealed dispositions, entered before January 1, 2002, are not to be cited as precedent. Counsel may refer to an unpublished disposition, however, when the binding (i.e., the res judicata or law of the case) or preclusive effect of the disposition, rather than its quality as precedent, is relevant.

(B) Unpublished dispositions entered on or after January 1, 2002. All unpublished orders or judgments of this court, including explanatory memoranda (but not including sealed dispositions), entered on or after January 1, 2002, may be cited as precedent. Counsel should review the criteria governing published and unpublished opinions in Circuit Rule 36, in connection with reliance upon unpublished dispositions of this court.

(2) Unpublished Opinions of Other Courts. *Unpublished dispositions of other courts of appeals and district courts entered before January 1, 2007, may be cited when the binding (i.e., the res judicata or law of the case) or preclusive effect of the disposition is relevant. Otherwise, unpublished dispositions of other courts of appeals entered before January 1, 2007, may be cited only under the circumstances and for the purposes permitted by the court issuing the disposition, and unpublished dispositions of district courts entered before that date may not be cited. Unpublished dispositions of other federal courts entered on or after January 1, 2007, may be cited in accordance with FRAP 32.1.*

(3) Procedures Governing Citation to Unpublished Dispositions. *A copy of each unpublished disposition cited in a brief that is not available in a publicly accessible electronic database must be included in an appropriately labeled addendum to the brief. The addendum may be bound together with the brief, but separated from the body of the brief (and from any other addendum) by a distinctly colored separation page. If the addendum is bound separately, it must be filed and served concurrently with, and in the same number of copies as, the brief itself.*

[Effective December 1, 2006.]

FRAP 33. APPEAL CONFERENCES

[For text of rule, see Federal Rules of Appellate Procedure]

RULE 33. APPEAL CONFERENCES

[There is no corresponding Circuit Rule.]

FRAP 34. ORAL ARGUMENT

[For text of rule, see Federal Rules of Appellate Procedure]

RULE 34. ORAL ARGUMENT

(a) Substance and Style of Oral Argument. *Oral argument should undertake to emphasize and clarify the written argument appearing in the briefs. This court will not entertain any oral argument that is read from a prepared text.*

(b) Time Allowed for Argument. *Counsel will be afforded such time for oral argument as the court may provide and will be so advised by order.*

(c) Notice by Counsel. *Unless the court orders otherwise, no less than 7 days before the date of scheduled argument, the court must be notified of the names of counsel who will argue. Not more than 2 counsel may be heard for each side except by leave of the court, granted on motion for good cause shown. Such requests are not favored. In cases in which 15 minutes or less per side is allotted for argument, only one counsel may be heard for each side except by leave of the court, granted on motion for good cause shown.*

(d) Apportionment of Time Among Parties. *In the absence of an order of this court, and subject to the provision as to number of counsel stated in paragraph (c), counsel for the parties on each side of a case, including counsel for any intervenor, may agree on the apportionment of the time allotted. In the event of a failure to agree, the court will allocate the time* *upon motion duly filed and served. Unless otherwise ordered, counsel for an intervenor will be permitted to argue only to the extent that counsel for the party whose side the intervenor supports is willing to share allotted time.*

(e) Participation in Oral Argument by Amici Curiae. *An amicus curiae, other than one appointed by the court, will not be permitted to participate in the oral argument without leave of the court granted for extraordinary reasons on motion, except that counsel for the party supported by amicus curiae may consent to such participation subject to the provision as to number of counsel stated in paragraph (c) above. A motion by amicus curiae seeking leave to participate in oral argument must be filed at least 14 days prior to the date oral argument is scheduled.*

(f) Failure to File Brief. *A party who fails to file a brief will not be heard at the time of oral argument except by permission of the court.*

(g) Continuance of Oral Argument. *When a case has been set for oral argument, it may not be continued by stipulation of the parties, but only by order of the court upon a motion evidencing extraordinary cause for a continuance.*

(h) Consolidation. *Where 2 or more cases are consolidated under FRAP 3(b) or for other reason by this court, the consolidated cases will be considered as one case for the purpose of this rule unless the court directs otherwise.*

(i) Exhibits and Handouts. *If counsel intends to use exhibits during argument or to hand out prepared materials, notice of this intent must be provided to the court and all other counsel presenting argument by letter received not less than 7 days before the date of the argument. The letter must set forth justification for the use of the exhibits or handouts.*

(j) Disposition Without Oral Argument.

(1) Procedure. *Whenever the court, on its own motion, or on the motion of a party or stipulation of the parties, concludes that oral argument is not needed, the court may, after causing notice of that determination to be given to the parties by the clerk, proceed to dispose of the case without oral argument.*

(2) Reconsideration. *Motions for reconsideration of a decision to dispose of a case without oral argument may be made within 10 days of the date of the order advising counsel of this court's determination that the case is to be decided without oral argument. Such motions are disfavored.*

[Effective January 1, 1994. Amended on an interim basis May 6, 1999, effective May 6, 1999, adopted without changes December 22, 1999, effective January 3, 2000; November 4, 2002, effective December 1, 2002; November 16, 2009, effective December 1, 2009.]

FRAP 35. EN BANC DETERMINATION

[For text of rule, see Federal Rules of Appellate Procedure]

RULE 35. PETITION FOR PANEL REHEARING AND PETITION FOR HEARING OR REHEARING EN BANC

(a) Time Within Which to File. *In all cases in which a party is one of those listed in FRAP 40(a)(1)(A)–(D), the time within which any party may seek panel rehearing or rehearing en banc is 45 days after entry of judgment or other form of decision. In all other cases, any petition for panel rehearing or petition for rehearing en banc must be filed within 30 days after entry of judgment or other form of decision. The time for filing a petition for panel rehearing or rehearing en banc will not be extended except for good cause shown.*

(b) Number of Copies and Length. *An original and 4 copies of a petition for panel rehearing, and an original and 19 copies of a petition for hearing or rehearing en banc must be filed. Such petitions must conform to the page limits of FRAP 35. This court disfavors motions to exceed page limits, and such motions will be granted only for extraordinarily compelling reasons.*

(c) Panel Opinion, Certificate of Parties, and Disclosure Statement to be Attached. *A copy of the opinion of the panel from which rehearing is being sought; a certificate of parties and amici curiae, as described in Circuit Rule 28(a)(1)(A); and a disclosure statement, as described in Circuit Rule 26.1, must be attached as an addendum to the petition. Any required disclosure statement must also be attached to any response to a petition.*

(d) Disposition of Petition. *A petition for rehearing ordinarily will not be granted, nor will an opinion or judgment be modified in any significant respect in response to a petition for rehearing, in the absence of a request by the court for a response to the petition.*

A petition for panel rehearing will not be acted upon until action is ready to be taken on any timely petition for rehearing en banc. If rehearing en banc is granted, the panel's judgment, but ordinarily not its opinion, will be vacated, and the petition for panel rehearing may be acted upon without awaiting final termination of the en banc proceeding. Upon termination of the en banc proceeding, a new judgment will be issued. If the en banc court divides evenly, a new judgment affirming the decision under review will be issued.

(e) Filing Copies of Brief. *When a petition for rehearing is granted, the court will issue an appro-*

priate order if further briefing is needed or if more copies of the original briefs are required.

(f) Brief of an Amicus Curiae. *No amicus curiae brief in response to or in support of a petition for rehearing en banc will be received by the clerk except by invitation of the court.*

[Effective January 1, 1994. Amended on an interim basis May 6, 1999, effective May 6, 1999, adopted without changes December 22, 1999, effective January 3, 2000. Amended on an interim basis December 10, 1999, effective December 10, 1999, adopted effective May 9, 2000; November 4, 2002, effective December 1, 2002; November 16, 2009, effective December 1, 2009. Amended effective December 1, 2011.]

FRAP 36. ENTRY OF JUDGMENT; NOTICE

[For text of rule, see Federal Rules of Appellate Procedure]

RULE 36. ENTRY OF JUDGMENT; NOTICE; DECISIONS OF THE COURT

(a) Entry. *In cases assigned to the court's Case Management/Electronic Case Files (CM/ECF) system, all judgments will be filed electronically in accordance with Circuit Rule 25 and the procedures established by the court. That filing constitutes entry of the judgment on the docket as required by FRAP 36(a).*

(b) Notice. *Upon the entry of the judgment in a case assigned to the CM/ECF system, the clerk will electronically transmit a Notice of Docket Activity to all parties who have consented to electronic service. Electronic transmission of the Notice of Docket Activity constitutes the notice and service required by FRAP 36(b) and 45(c). For any party who has not consented to electronic service, the clerk must serve in paper form a copy of the opinion or the judgment, if no opinion was written, which notes the date the judgment was entered.*

(c) Opinions of the Court.

(1) Policy. *It is the policy of this court to publish opinions and explanatory memoranda that have general public interest.*

(2) Published Opinions. *An opinion, memorandum, or other statement explaining the basis for the court's action in issuing an order or judgment will be published if it meets one or more of the following criteria:*

(A) with regard to a substantial issue it resolves, it is a case of first impression or the first case to present the issue in this court;

(B) it alters, modifies, or significantly clarifies a rule of law previously announced by the court;

(C) it calls attention to an existing rule of law that appears to have been generally overlooked;

(D) it criticizes or questions existing law;

(E) it resolves an apparent conflict in decisions within the circuit or creates a conflict with another circuit;

(F) it reverses a published agency or district court decision, or affirms a decision of the district court upon grounds different from those set forth in the district court's published opinion;

(G) it warrants publication in light of other factors that give it general public interest.

All published opinions of the court, prior to issuance, will be circulated to all judges on the court; printed prior to release, unless otherwise ordered; and rendered by being filed with the clerk.

(d) Abbreviated Dispositions. *The court may, while according full consideration to the issues, dispense with published opinions where the issues occasion no need therefor, and confine its action to such abbreviated disposition as it may deem appropriate, e.g., affirmance by order of a decision or judgment of a court or administrative agency, a judgment of affirmance or reversal, containing a notation of precedents or accompanied by a brief memorandum. If the parties have agreed to such disposition, they may so state in their briefs or may so stipulate at any time prior to decision. In any such case the court will promptly issue a judgment unless compelling reasons dictate otherwise.*

(e) Unpublished Opinions.

(1) An opinion, memorandum, or other statement explaining the basis for this court's action in issuing an order or judgment under subsection (b) above, which does not satisfy any of the criteria for publication set out in subsection (a) above, will nonetheless be circulated to all judges on the court prior to issuance. A copy of each such unpublished opinion, memorandum, or statement will be retained as part of the case file in the clerk's office and be publicly available there on the same basis as any published opinion.

(2) While unpublished dispositions may be cited to the court in accordance with FRAP 32.1 and Circuit Rule 32.1(b)(1), a panel's decision to issue an unpublished disposition means that the panel sees no precedential value in that disposition.

(f) Motion to Publish. *Any person may, by motion made within 30 days after judgment or, if a timely petition for rehearing is made, within 30 days after action thereon, request that an unpublished opinion be published. Motions filed out of time will not be considered unless good cause is shown. Motions for publication must be based upon one or more of the criteria listed in subsection (a). Such motions are not* *favored and will be granted only for compelling reasons.*

[Effective January 1, 1994. Amended on an interim basis May 6, 1999, effective May 6, 1999, adopted without changes December 22, 1999, effective January 3, 2000; January 1, 2002; November 4, 2002, effective December 1, 2002; December 1, 2006; May 15, 2009, effective June 8, 2009.]

FRAP 37. INTEREST ON JUDGMENT

[For text of rule, see Federal Rules of Appellate Procedure]

RULE 37. INTEREST ON JUDGMENT

[There is no corresponding Circuit Rule.]

FRAP 38. FRIVOLOUS APPEAL—DAMAGES AND COSTS

[For text of rule, see Federal Rules of Appellate Procedure]

RULE 38. SANCTIONS

When any party to a proceeding before this court or any attorney practicing before the court fails to comply with the FRAP, these rules, or an order of this court, or takes an appeal or files a petition or motion that is frivolous or interposed for an improper purpose, such as to harass or to cause unnecessary delay, the court may, on its own motion, or on motion of a party, impose appropriate sanctions on the offending party, the attorney, or both. Sanctions include dismissal for failure to prosecute; imposition of costs, expenses, and attorneys' fees; and disciplinary proceedings. See *28 U.S.C. §§ 1912, 1927.*

[Effective January 1, 1994. Amended effective December 1, 2005.]

FRAP 39. COSTS

[For text of rule, see Federal Rules of Appellate Procedure]

RULE 39. COSTS

(a) Allowable Items. *Costs will be allowed for the docketing fee and for the cost of reproducing the number of copies of briefs and appendices to be filed with the court or served on parties, intervenors, and amici curiae, plus 3 copies for the prevailing party. The costs of reproducing the required copies of briefs and appendices will be taxed at actual cost or at a rate periodically set by the clerk to reflect the per page cost for the most economical means of reproduction available in the Washington metropolitan area, whichever is less. Charges incurred for covers and fasteners may also be claimed, at actual cost not to exceed a rate similarly determined by the clerk. The rates set by the clerk will be published by posting in the clerk's office and on the court's web site, and publication in The Daily Washington Law Reporter.*

(b) Procedure for Requesting Taxation of Costs. *Forms furnished by the clerk's office, or facsimiles thereof, must be used in requesting taxation of costs. Parties submitting bills of costs that are not itemized as required by the clerk or not presented on clerk's office forms or reasonable facsimiles thereof will be directed to provide a conforming request.*

(c) No Costs Taxed for Briefs for Amici or Intervenors. *No taxation of costs for briefs for intervenors or amici curiae or separate replies thereto will be assessed unless allowed by the court on motion.*

(d) Costs of Producing Separate Briefs and Appendices Where Record is Sealed. *The costs under Circuit Rule 47.1 of preparing 2 sets of briefs, and/or 2 segments of appendices, may be assessed if such costs are otherwise allowable.*

[Effective January 1, 1994. Amended on an interim basis May 6, 1999, effective May 6, 1999, adopted without changes December 22, 1999, effective January 3, 2000; November 4, 2002, effective December 1, 2002; December 1, 2005.]

FRAP 40. PETITION FOR PANEL REHEARING

[For text of rule, see Federal Rules of Appellate Procedure]

RULE 40. PETITION FOR PANEL REHEARING

See *Circuit Rule 35.*

[Effective January 1, 1994. Amended on an interim basis May 6, 1999, effective May 6, 1999, adopted without changes December 22, 1999, effective January 3, 2000.]

FRAP 41. MANDATE: CONTENTS; ISSUANCE AND EFFECTIVE DATE; STAY

[For text of rule, see Federal Rules of Appellate Procedure]

RULE 41. ISSUANCE OF MANDATE; STAY OF MANDATE; REMAND

(a) Mandate.

(1) Time for Issuance. *While retaining discretion to direct immediate issuance of its mandate in an appropriate case, the court ordinarily will include as part of its disposition an instruction that the clerk withhold issuance of the mandate until the expiration*

of the time for filing a petition for rehearing or a petition for rehearing en banc and, if such petition is timely filed, until 7 days after disposition thereof. Such an instruction is without prejudice to the right of any party at any time to move for expedited issuance of the mandate for good cause shown.

(2) Stay of Mandate. *A motion for a stay of the issuance of mandate will not be granted unless the motion sets forth facts showing good cause for the relief sought. If the motion is granted, the stay ordinarily will not extend beyond 90 days from the date that the mandate otherwise would have issued. If a timely motion to stay issuance of the mandate has been filed, the mandate will not issue while the motion is pending. If a party obtains a stay of issuance of the mandate, that party must inform the clerk of this court whether a petition for a writ of certiorari has been filed with the Supreme Court within the period of the stay.*

The clerk may grant an unopposed motion to stay issuance of the mandate for a period not longer than 90 days from the date that the mandate otherwise would have issued. No motion to stay issuance of the mandate will be granted by the clerk until after the response time has passed, unless the moving party represents in the motion that all other parties either consent to the stay or do not object thereto. The clerk may submit any motion governed by this subparagraph to the panel of the court that decided the case.

(3) Writs. *No mandate will issue in connection with an order granting or denying a writ of mandamus or other special writ, but the order or judgment granting or denying the relief sought will become effective automatically 21 days after issuance in the absence of an order or other special direction of this court to the contrary.*

(4) Mandate Recall if Rehearing En Banc Granted. *When rehearing en banc is granted, the court will recall the mandate if it has issued.*

(b) Remand. *If the record in any case is remanded to the district court or to an agency, this court retains jurisdiction over the case. If the case is remanded, this court does not retain jurisdiction, and a new notice of appeal or petition for review will be necessary if a party seeks review of the proceedings conducted on remand.*

[Effective January 1, 1994. Amended on an interim basis May 6, 1999, effective May 6, 1999, adopted without changes December 22, 1999, effective January 3, 2000; November 4, 2002, effective December 1, 2002; November 16, 2009, effective December 1, 2009.]

FRAP 42. VOLUNTARY DISMISSAL

[For text of rule, see Federal Rules of Appellate Procedure]

RULE 42. VOLUNTARY DISMISSAL

See *Circuit Rule 27(g) (Motions, Dispositive Motions).*

[Effective January 1, 1994; adopted without changes November 4, 2002, effective December 1, 2002.]

FRAP 43. SUBSTITUTION OF PARTIES

[For text of rule, see Federal Rules of Appellate Procedure]

RULE 43. SUBSTITUTION OF PARTIES

[There is no corresponding Circuit Rule.]

FRAP 44. CASE INVOLVING A CONSTITUTIONAL QUESTION WHEN THE UNITED STATES OR THE RELEVANT STATE IS NOT A PARTY

[For text of rule, see Federal Rules of Appellate Procedure]

RULE 44. CASE INVOLVING A CONSTITUTIONAL QUESTION WHEN THE UNITED STATES OR THE RELEVANT STATE IS NOT A PARTY

[There is no corresponding Circuit Rule.]

FRAP 45. CLERK'S DUTIES

[For text of rule, see Federal Rules of Appellate Procedure]

RULE 45. CLERK'S DUTIES; FEES FOR SERVICES

(a) Attendance at Sessions. *The clerk or a deputy of the clerk will attend in person the sessions of this court.*

(b) Office Hours. *The clerk's office will be open for the transaction of business from 9:00 A.M. until 4:00 P.M. daily, except Saturdays, Sundays, federal holidays, and any other day the chief judge designates. The court is always open for the receipt of emergency papers and the transaction of emergency business.*

(c) Entry of Court–Issued Documents. *Except as otherwise provided by these rules or court order, all orders, opinions, judgments, and other documents issued by the court in cases assigned to the court's Case Management/Electronic Case Files (CM/ECF) system will be filed electronically in accordance with Circuit Rule 25 and the procedures established by the* *court. Any such filing constitutes under FRAP 36 and 45(b) entry on the docket maintained by the clerk. Any order, judgment, or other court-issued document filed electronically without the original signature of a judge or authorized court personnel has the same force and effect as if the judge or clerk had signed a paper copy. Orders also may be issued as "text-only" entries on the docket, without an attached document. Such orders are official and binding.*

(d) Notice of Orders and Judgments. *Immediately upon the entry of an order or judgment in a case assigned to the CM/ECF system, the clerk will electronically transmit a Notice of Docket Activity to all parties who have consented to electronic service. Electronic transmission of the Notice of Docket Activity constitutes the notice and service required by FRAP 36(b) and 45(c). For any party who has not consented to electronic service, the clerk must immediately serve in paper form a notice of entry with a copy of any opinion.*

(e) Fees for Services. *Fees, as prescribed by the Judicial Conference of the United States, are to be charged for the following services performed by the clerk, except that no fees are to be charged for services rendered on behalf of the United States. The schedule of currently applicable fees will be posted on the court's web site and distributed periodically as an appendix to these rules.*

(1) Docketing a case or docketing any other proceeding. A separate fee must be paid by each party filing a notice of appeal in the district court, but parties filing a joint notice of appeal in the district court are required to pay only one fee. A docketing fee will not be charged for the docketing of a petition for permission to appeal under FRAP 5, unless the appeal is allowed.

(2) Search of the records of this court and certifying the results.

(3) Certifying any document or paper, whether certification is made directly on the document or by separate instrument.

(4) Reproducing any record or paper.

(5) Comparing with the original thereof any copy of any transcript of record, entry, or paper, when such copy is furnished by any person requesting certification.

(f) Printed Copies of Opinions. *For each printed copy of the decision in a case, including all separate and dissenting opinions, the clerk will charge such sum as the court may from time to time direct, and copies may be supplied without charge or at such reduced charge as the court may from time to time designate. Each party in a case will receive 2 paper copies of the decision without charge.*

(g) Other Fees Not Authorized. *No fees for services other than those authorized pursuant to law may be charged.*

See also *Circuit Rule 1 (Scope of Rules; General Provisions), and Circuit Rule 25 (Filing and Service).*

[Effective January 1, 1994. Amended on an interim basis May 6, 1999, effective May 6, 1999, adopted without changes December 22, 1999, effective January 3, 2000; November 4, 2002, effective December 1, 2002; December 1, 2005; May 15, 2009, effective June 8, 2009; April 14, 2011, effective April 14, 2011.]

FRAP 46. ATTORNEYS

[For text of rule, see Federal Rules of Appellate Procedure]

RULE 46. ATTORNEYS; APPEARANCE BY LAW STUDENT

(a) Appearances. *Except as otherwise provided by law, the docketing statement and all papers filed thereafter in this court must be signed by at least one member of the bar of this court, and only members of the bar of this court may present oral argument. However, on motion for good cause shown, the court may allow argument to be presented in a case by an attorney who is not a member of the bar of this court.*

(b) Admission. *Each applicant for admission to the bar of this court must file with the clerk an application for admission on a form approved by the court and furnished by the clerk and append an original certificate, executed not more than 60 days prior to the date of the application, from the court upon which the application is based, evidencing the applicant's admission to practice before that court and current good standing. Upon the court's grant of an application for admission, the clerk will mail to the applicant a certificate of admission. Applicants for admission to the bar of this court need not appear in person for the purpose of taking the oath or affirmation of admission. The fee for admission will be set periodically by order of the court and must be tendered with the application.*

(c) Change of Address. *Changes in the address of counsel and pro se litigants must be immediately reported to the clerk in writing.*

(d) Change of Name of Attorney After Admission. *Any member of the bar of this court may file with the clerk a certificate that he or she is engaged in practice under a new name. The clerk will note such change of name on the roll of attorneys and on the records of this court.*

(e) Disbarment and Suspension. *For provisions governing the discipline of members of the bar of this court, see the court's Rules of Disciplinary Enforcement.*

(f) Committee on Admissions and Grievances. *For provisions governing the Committee on Admissions and Grievances and the referral of matters to that committee, see the court's Rules of Disciplinary Enforcement.*

(g) Appearance by Law Student.

(1) Entry of Appearance on Written Consent of Party. *An eligible law student may enter an appearance in this court on behalf of any party including the United States or a governmental agency, provided that the party on whose behalf the student appears has consented thereto in writing, and that a supervising lawyer has also indicated in writing approval of that appearance. In each case, the written consent and approval must be filed with the clerk.*

(2) Appearance on Briefs and Participation in Oral Argument. *A law student who has entered an appearance in a case pursuant to paragraph (1) may appear on the brief, provided the supervising attorney also appears on the brief; may participate in oral argument, provided the supervising attorney is present in court; and may take part in other activities in connection with the case, subject to the direction of the supervising attorney.*

(3) Eligibility. *In order to be eligible to make an appearance pursuant to this rule, the law student must:*

(A) be duly enrolled in a law school accredited by the American Bar Association;

(B) have completed legal studies amounting to at least 4 semesters, or the equivalent if the school is on some basis other than a semester basis;

(C) be enrolled in or have passed a clinical program of an accredited law school for credit, held under the direction of a faculty member of such law school, in which a law student obtains practical experience by participating in cases and matters pending before the courts;

(D) be certified by the dean of the law school as being of good character and competent legal ability, and as being adequately trained to perform as a legal intern.

(4) Students Not to Be Compensated by Parties. *A law student appearing pursuant to this rule may neither ask for nor receive any compensation or remuneration of any kind for services from any party on whose behalf the services are rendered; this rule does not prevent a lawyer, legal aid bureau, law school, public defender agency, or the government from paying compensation to the eligible law student, nor does it prevent any agency from making such charges for its services as may otherwise be proper.*

(5) Withdrawal or Termination of Certification. *The certification of a student by the law school dean must be filed with the clerk of this court and, unless it is sooner withdrawn, will remain in effect for 18 months, or until the announcement of the results of the first bar examination following the student's graduation, whichever is earlier. For any student who passes that examination, or who is admitted to the bar without taking an examination, the certification will continue in effect until the date the student is admitted to the bar. The certification may be withdrawn by the dean at any time by mailing a notice to that effect to the student and to the clerk of this court. It is not necessary that the notice state the cause for withdrawal, unless requested by the student. The certification may be terminated by this court at any time without notice or hearing and without any showing of cause.*

(6) Supervising Attorney. *An attorney under whose supervision an eligible law student undertakes any activity permitted by this rule must:*

(A) be a member in good standing of the bar of this court;

(B) assume responsibility for the quality of the student's work;

(C) guide and assist the student in preparation to the extent necessary or appropriate under the circumstances.

[Effective January 1, 1994. Amended on an interim basis May 6, 1999, effective May 6, 1999, adopted without changes December 22, 1999, effective January 3, 2000; November 4, 2002, effective December 1, 2002.]

FRAP 47. LOCAL RULES BY COURTS OF APPEALS

[For text of rule, see Federal Rules of Appellate Procedure]

RULE 47. LOCAL RULES BY COURTS OF APPEALS

(a) Amendment—Notice and Opportunity for Comment. *These rules may be amended by the court as provided herein. The court will give notice and opportunity for comment as provided in this rule with respect to any proposed changes in these rules except where emergency or other conditions render it impractical or unnecessary.*

(b) Proposal for Change. *Any person may propose a change in these rules by submitting a written suggestion to the court or to its Advisory Committee on Procedures.*

(c) Notice of Proposed Amendment by Court. *Upon consideration of a proposal from any person or from the Advisory Committee on Procedures, or upon its own motion, the court will, whenever necessary or appropriate, give notice of a proposed change in these rules. Such notice will consist of the text of the* *proposed change, or a description of the subjects and issues involved, together with a brief explanation of the purpose of the proposal. The notice will be made public as follows:*

(1) by posting a copy on the bulletin board next to the public counter in the clerk's office and on the court's web site;

(2) by delivering a copy to The Daily Washington Law Reporter *for publication;*

(3) by sending a copy to the chair of the Advisory Committee on Procedures;

(4) by sending copies to:

(A) the president of the District of Columbia Bar;

(B) the president of the Bar Association of the District of Columbia;

(C) the president of the Washington Bar Association;

(D) the president of the Women's Bar Association;

(E) the presidents of any nationwide bar associations, local chapters of nationwide bar associations, or other voluntary groups of lawyers or citizens that notify the clerk of this court in writing that they wish to receive copies of these notices.

(d) Comments by Public and Advisory Committee on Procedures. *The notice will specify a period of not less than 45 days from the date of its publication in* The Daily Washington Law Reporter *within which any person may submit written comments on the proposed changes to the Advisory Committee on Procedures. That committee must give consideration to all written comments timely received and within 45 days from the close of the comment period transmit to this court its recommendations with respect to the proposal and the written comments it has received.*

(e) Final Action by Court. *Following receipt of the committee's recommendation, this court may determine that the proposed change should be adopted, that it should be amended and adopted, or that it should be withdrawn. The court will publish notice of its final action respecting the proposal, including the effective date of any change in these rules, in the manner provided in paragraph (c).*

(f) Publication of Amendments Made Without Opportunity for Comment. *If an amendment to these rules is made without notice or opportunity for comment, it will be made public in the manner provided in paragraph (c). Such publication will state the effective date of the amendment, which may not be earlier than the date of publication.*

[Effective January 1, 1994. Amended on an interim basis May 6, 1999, effective May 6, 1999, adopted without changes December 22, 1999, effective January 3, 2000; December 1, 2005.]

RULE 47.1 MATTERS UNDER SEAL

(a) Case with Record Under Seal. *Any portion of the record that was placed under seal in the district court or before an agency remains under seal in this court unless otherwise ordered. Parties and their counsel are responsible for assuring that materials under seal remain under seal and are not publicly disclosed.*

(b) Agreement to Unseal. *In any case in which the record in the district court or before an agency is under seal in whole or in part and a notice of appeal or petition for review has been filed, each party must promptly review the record to determine whether any portions of the record under seal need to remain under seal on appeal. If a party determines that some portion should be unsealed, that party must seek an agreement on the unsealing. Such agreement must be presented promptly to the district court or agency for its consideration and issuance of an appropriate order.*

(c) Motion to Unseal. *A party or any other interested person may move at any time to unseal any portion of the record in this court, including confidential briefs or appendices filed under this rule. On appeals from the district court, the motion will ordinarily be referred to the district court, and, if necessary, the record remanded for that purpose, but the court may, when the interests of justice require, decide that motion, and, if unsealing is ordered, remand the record for unsealing. Unless otherwise ordered, the pendency of a motion under this rule will not delay the filing of any brief under any scheduling order.*

(d) Briefs Containing Material Under Seal.

(1) Two Sets of Briefs. *If a party deems it necessary to refer in a brief to material under seal, 2 sets of briefs must be filed which are identical except for references to sealed materials. One set of briefs must bear the legend "Under Seal" on the cover, and each page containing sealed material must bear the legend "Under Seal" at the top of the page. The second set of briefs must bear the legend "Public Copy—Sealed Material Deleted" on the cover, and each page from which material under seal has been deleted must bear a legend stating "Material Under Seal Deleted" at the top of the page. The party must file the original and 6 copies of the sealed brief and the original and 14 copies of the public brief. Both sets of briefs must comply with the remainder of these rules, including Circuit Rule 32(a) on length of briefs.*

(2) Service. *Each party must be served with 2 copies of the public brief and 2 copies of the brief under seal, if the party is entitled to receive the material under seal.* See, e.g., *Fed. R. Crim. P. 6(e).*

(3) Non-availability to the Public. *Briefs filed with the court under seal are available only to authorized*

court personnel and will not be made available to the public.

(e) Appendices Containing Matters Under Seal.

(1) Sealed Supplement to the Appendix; Number of Copies. *If a party deems it necessary to include material under seal in an appendix, the appendix must be filed in 2 segments. One segment must contain all sealed material and bear the legend "Supplement—Under Seal" on the cover, and each page of that supplement containing sealed material must bear the legend "Under Seal" at the top of the page. The second appendix segment must bear the legend "Public Appendix—Sealed Material in Separate Supplement" on the cover; each page from which material under seal has been deleted must bear the legend "Material Under Seal Deleted" at the top of the page. The party must file 7 copies of the sealed supplement and 7 copies of the public appendix.*

(2) Service; Number of Copies. *Each party must be served with one copy of the public appendix and one copy of the sealed supplement, if the party is entitled to receive the material under seal.* See, e.g., *Fed. R. Crim. P. 6(e).*

(3) Non-availability to the Public. *Supplements to appendices filed with the court under seal are available only to authorized court personnel and will not be made available to the public.*

(f) Disposal of Sealed Records.

(1) In any case in which all or part of the record of this court (including briefs and appendices) has been maintained under seal, the clerk will, in conjunction with the issuance of the mandate (or the entry of the final order, in a case in which no mandate will issue), order the parties to show cause why the record (or sealed portions) should not be unsealed. If the parties agree to unsealing, the record will be unsealed by order of the court, issued by the clerk. No order to show cause will be issued in cases where the nature of the materials themselves (e.g., grand jury materials) makes it clear that unsealing would be impermissible. If the parties do not agree to unsealing, the order to show cause, and any responses thereto, will be referred to the court for disposition.

(2) Any record material not unsealed pursuant to this rule will be designated "Temporary Sealed Records," and transferred to the Federal Records Center under applicable regulations. The records will be returned to the court for reconsideration of unsealing after a period of 20 years.

(3) The court may, on its own motion, issue an order to show cause and consider the unsealing of any records in the court's custody, at any time.

(4) Counsel to an appeal involving sealed records must promptly notify the court when it is no longer necessary to maintain the record or portions of the record under seal.

[Effective January 1, 1994. Amended effective December 8, 1998; as amended on an interim basis May 6, 1999, effective May 6, 1999, adopted without changes December 22, 1999, effective January 3, 2000; December 1, 2005.]

RULE 47.2 APPEAL EXPEDITED BY STATUTE; HABEAS CORPUS PROCEEDING; SENTENCING APPEAL

(a) Appeal Expedited by Statute and Habeas Corpus Proceeding. *Upon filing a notice of appeal in a case invoking 18 U.S.C. § 3145 or § 3731, 28 U.S.C. chapter 153, or 28 U.S.C. § 1826, the appellant must so advise the clerks of this court and of the district court immediately both orally and by letter. Pursuant to 28 U.S.C. § 1657, this practice will also be followed in an action seeking temporary or preliminary injunctive relief. In such cases, the clerk of the district court must transmit a copy of the notice of appeal and a certified copy of the docket entries to the clerk of this court forthwith. The clerk of this court will thereupon enter the appeal upon the docket and prepare an expedited schedule for briefing and argument. If a hearing occurred, appellant must order the necessary portions of the transcript on an expedited basis and make arrangements with the clerk of the district court for prompt transmittal of the record to this court.*

(b) Sentencing Appeal Pursuant to 18 U.S.C. § 3742.

(1) In an appeal from a sentence the court will, where appropriate upon motion, establish an expedited briefing and argument schedule. Memoranda and replies as provided below must be filed and served in accordance therewith. An original and 14 copies must be filed in each case.

(2) The appellant must file and serve a memorandum of law and fact setting forth appellant's challenge to the sentence. Appellee must file and serve a memorandum of law and fact setting forth the response to appellant's challenge. Appellant may file and serve a reply.

(3) Except by permission or direction of this court, the memoranda of law may not exceed 20 pages, exclusive of pages containing the certificate required by Circuit Rule 28(a)(1). The reply memorandum may not exceed 10 pages. The documents must comply with the typeface requirements of FRAP 32(a)(5) and the type-style requirements of FRAP 32(a)(6).

(4) The memoranda need not contain a table of authorities, a statement of jurisdiction, or a summary of argument.

(5) The filings will be placed in the public record. Parties should avoid matters that could compromise

the confidentiality of the presentence report. Where inclusion of confidential matters is unavoidable, the party should move to have the submission placed under seal.

(6) Where the court is reviewing both sentence and conviction in the same proceeding, the rules set out above, except for Circuit Rule 47.2(b)(5), will not apply.

[Effective January 1, 1994. Amended on an interim basis May 6, 1999, effective May 6, 1999, adopted without changes December 22, 1999, effective January 3, 2000; December 1, 2005.]

RULE 47.3 JUDICIAL CONFERENCE

(a) Purpose. *In accordance with 28 U.S.C. § 333, the chief judge of this circuit may summon biennially, and may summon annually, a conference of all the circuit, district, and bankruptcy judges of the circuit in active service, for the purpose of considering the business of the courts and means to improve the administration of justice within the circuit. The conference will be called "The Judicial Conference of the District of Columbia Circuit."*

(b) Conference Arrangements and Procedures.

(1) The chief judge of the circuit will appoint a committee on arrangements for the conference to submit for approval of the circuit judicial council a conference plan including the proposed location and program for the conference. The committee on arrangements will include both district and circuit judges, and members of the bar.

(2) The chief judge of the circuit presides at the conference. The circuit executive of this circuit serves as conference secretary, and will make and preserve a record of conference proceedings. The chief judge may appoint committees to pursue or carry out conference actions or advice, and may fill vacancies in or reconstitute or, upon completion of their assignments, discharge such committees.

(c) Composition. *In addition to the circuit, district, and bankruptcy judges, persons invited to participate in the conference must include:*

(1) the senior and retired judges of this court and of the district court;

(2) the United States magistrate judges of the District of Columbia;

(3) the circuit executive of this circuit;

(4) the clerks of this court, the district court, and the bankruptcy court;

(5) the librarian of this circuit;

(6) the director of this court's legal division;

(7) the chief United States probation officer of the District of Columbia;

(8) the chief judge of the United States Tax Court, or such representative of the tax court as the chief judge of that court designates;

(9) the director of the Administrative Office of the United States Courts;

(10) the director of the Federal Judicial Center;

(11) the United States Attorney for the District of Columbia;

(12) the Federal Public Defender for the District of Columbia;

(13) the director of the District of Columbia Public Defender Service;

(14) the deans of law schools located in the District of Columbia;

(15) the Attorney General of the District of Columbia;

(16) members of the bar in such numbers as will permit and promote participation by those engaged in the various fields of federal court practice;

(17) other individuals whose background, position, or achievement will contribute to the purpose and program of the conference.

[Effective January 1, 1994. Amended on an interim basis May 6, 1999, effective May 6, 1999. Adopted without changes December 22, 1999, effective January 3, 2000; November 4, 2002, effective December 1, 2002; December 1, 2005.]

RULE 47.4 ADVISORY COMMITTEE ON PROCEDURES

(a) Establishment of Committee; Membership. *In accordance with 28 U.S.C. § 2077(b), there will be an Advisory Committee on Procedures which consists of not less than 15 members of the bar of this court selected by the judges of the court in regular active service in such a way as to represent a broad cross section of those appearing in the federal courts of the District of Columbia, including representatives from government agencies, law schools, public interest groups, and private practitioners.*

(b) Committee Functions. *The committee will, among other things:*

(1) provide a forum for study of the internal operating procedures and rules of this court;

(2) serve as a conduit from the bar and the public to the court regarding procedural matters and suggestions for changes;

(3) draft, consider, and recommend, for the court's adoption, rules and internal operating procedures, and amendments thereto;

(4) render reports from time to time, on its own initiative and on request, to the court and to the

Judicial Conference of the District of Columbia Circuit on the activities and recommendations of the committee.

(c) Terms of Members. *The members of the committee will serve 3–year terms that will be staggered in such a way as to enable the court to appoint or reappoint one-third of the committee each year. The court will appoint one of the members to chair the committee.*

[Effective January 1, 1994. Amended on an interim basis May 6, 1999, effective May 6, 1999, adopted without changes December 22, 1999, effective January 3, 2000.]

RULE 47.5 PROCESSING DIRECT CRIMINAL APPEALS

Absent extraordinary circumstances, a direct criminal appeal will not be held in abeyance pending resolution of a postconviction proceeding in district court.

[Adopted effective March 27, 1996. Amended on an interim basis May 6, 1999, effective May 6, 1999, adopted without changes December 22, 1999, effective January 3, 2000.]

RULE 47.6 APPEALS FROM THE ALIEN TERRORIST REMOVAL COURT

(a) In General.

(1) Perfection. *A party seeking to appeal from a decision of the Alien Terrorist Removal Court must do so by filing a notice of appeal in the office of the clerk of the court of appeals.*

(2) Appeals Treated as Motions. *Unless otherwise specified herein or ordered by the court, appeals will be treated and processed by the court as motions. See generally FRAP 27(d); Circuit Rule 27. The appellant must file, simultaneously with the notice of appeal, 5 copies of a memorandum in support of the appeal, not to exceed 20 pages in length. No response will be permitted unless specified by this rule. All submissions must be filed and, if served, served by hand. An alien not represented by counsel who is unable to file or serve submissions by hand must do so by the most expeditious means available to the alien that are effective to reach the Department of Justice promptly.*

(3) Submissions to Be Filed Under Seal. *Unless otherwise specified herein, all submissions filed in the court in an appeal from the Alien Terrorist Removal Court must be filed under seal. In addition, any submission containing or referring to classified information must so indicate in an appropriate legend on the face of the submission. The court and all parties to a removal proceeding must comply with all applicable statutory provisions for the protection of classified information, and with the "Security Procedures Established Pursuant to Pub. L. 96–456, 94 Stat. 2025, by the Chief Justice of the United States for the Protection of Classified Information."*

(4) Appointment of Counsel. *Counsel appointed to represent or assist an alien in the Alien Terrorist Removal Court, including any "special attorney" designated under 8 U.S.C. § 1534(e)(3), must continue to represent or assist the alien in any proceedings in this court, without additional appointment.*

(5) Expedition. *All appeals from the Alien Terrorist Removal Court must be disposed of by this court as expeditiously as practicable. Any party to an appeal seeking disposition within a definite time period may move for such relief, stating the grounds in support.*

(b) Appeal From the Denial of a Removal Application (8 U.S.C. § 1535(a)).

(1) Perfection. *The United States may appeal the denial of an application to use the alien terrorist removal procedure, by filing in the court of appeals clerk's office, within 20 days of the date of the order appealed from, a notice of appeal accompanied by a memorandum in support of the appeal.*

(2) Record. *The United States must serve a copy of the notice of appeal on the Alien Terrorist Removal Court. Upon receipt of the notice, the Removal Court must transmit, under seal, the entire record of the application proceeding to the court of appeals.*

(3) Ex Parte Appeal. *An appeal from the denial of a removal application must be conducted ex parte and under seal. No submissions, including the notice of appeal and the memorandum in support of the appeal, will be served on the alien.*

(c) Interlocutory Appeal From Discovery Orders (8 U.S.C. § 1535(b)).

(1) Perfection. *The United States may appeal a determination of the Removal Court regarding a request for approval of an unclassified summary of evidence, or refusing to make requested findings under 8 U.S.C. § 1534(e)(3), by filing in the court of appeals clerk's office a notice of appeal accompanied by a memorandum in support of the appeal.*

(2) Record. *The United States must serve a copy of the notice of appeal on the Alien Terrorist Removal Court. Upon receipt of the notice, the Removal Court must transmit the entire record of the removal proceeding to the court of appeals. Any portion of the record sealed in the Removal Court must be transmitted to and maintained by this court under seal.*

(3) Ex Parte Appeal. *An appeal from a discovery determination will be conducted ex parte and under seal. No submissions, except the notice of appeal, will be served on the alien.*

(d) Appeal From a Decision After a Removal Hearing (8 U.S.C. § 1535(c)) .

(1) Perfection. *The United States or the alien may appeal the decision of the Removal Court after a removal hearing, by filing in the court of appeals clerk's office, within 20 days of the date of the order appealed from, a notice of appeal accompanied by a memorandum in support of the appeal.*

(2) Automatic Appeal. *In the case of a permanent resident alien in which the alien was denied an unclassified summary of evidence under 8 U.S.C. § 1534(e)(3), and in which appeal is automatic unless waived, the alien must file, within 20 days of the date of the Removal Court's order, a memorandum in support of the appeal, or a notice that the appeal has been waived. Failure to file a timely memorandum in support of the appeal, or a timely notice of waiver, will result in dismissal of the automatic appeal for lack of prosecution.*

(3) Record. *The appellant (except in the case of an automatic appeal) must serve a copy of the notice of appeal on the Alien Terrorist Removal Court. Upon receipt of the notice, the Removal Court must transmit the entire record of the removal proceeding to the court of appeals. Any portion of the record sealed in the Removal Court must be transmitted to and maintained by this court under seal.*

In the case of an automatic appeal, the Removal Court must, upon the filing of the court's order after the removal hearing, transmit a certified copy of the order, together with the record of the removal proceedings, to the court of appeals.

(4) Briefing. *Within 10 days of the filing of the appellant's memorandum in support of the appeal, the appellee must file a responsive brief, not to exceed 20 pages in length. Appellant's reply, if any, is due 5 days after the date the response is filed, and may not exceed 10 pages in length. Briefs or memoranda must be filed under seal, to the extent necessary to comply with subsection (a)(3) of this rule.*

(5) Hearing and Disposition. *As soon as practicable after the filing of the appeal, the court will inform the parties whether it will hear argument on the appeal or dispose of the appeal on the written submissions. The court will dispose of the appeal as expeditiously as practicable.*

(e) Appeal From a Release or Detention Order (8 U.S.C. § 1535(e)). *Any appeal from a release or detention order of the Removal Court will be governed by Circuit Rule 9, except that the appellant's memorandum in support of the appeal must be filed simultaneously with the notice of appeal.*

[Adopted, on an interim basis, effective December 5, 1996. Amended on an interim basis May 6, 1999, effective May 6, 1999, adopted without changes December 22, 1999, effective January 3, 2000. Amended effective November 4, 2002, effective December 1, 2002; December 1, 2005.]

FRAP 48. MASTERS

[For text of rule, see Federal Rules of Appellate Procedure]

RULE 48. MASTERS

[There is no corresponding Circuit Rule.]

[Effective January 1, 1994; May 6, 1999.]

APPENDIX OF FORMS FOR THE FEDERAL RULES OF APPELLATE PROCEDURE

FORM 1. NOTICE OF APPEAL TO A COURT OF APPEALS FROM A JUDGMENT OR ORDER OF A DISTRICT COURT

[For text of form, see Federal Rules of Appellate Procedure]

FORM 2. NOTICE OF APPEAL TO A COURT OF APPEALS FROM A DECISION OF THE UNITED STATES TAX COURT

[For text of form, see Federal Rules of Appellate Procedure]

FORM 3. PETITION FOR REVIEW OF ORDER OF AN AGENCY, BOARD, COMMISSION OR OFFICER

[For text of form, see Federal Rules of Appellate Procedure]

FORM 4. AFFIDAVIT ACCOMPANYING MOTION FOR PERMISSION TO APPEAL IN FORMA PAUPERIS

[For text of form, see Federal Rules of Appellate Procedure]

FORM 5. NOTICE OF APPEAL TO A COURT OF APPEALS FROM A JUDGMENT OR ORDER OF A DISTRICT COURT OR A BANKRUPTCY APPELLATE PANEL

[For text of form, see Federal Rules of Appellate Procedure]

FORM 6. CERTIFICATE OF COMPLIANCE WITH RULE 32(a)

[For text of form, see Federal Rules of Appellate Procedure]

APPENDIX TO THE CIRCUIT RULES OF THE U.S. COURT OF APPEALS FOR THE DISTRICT OF COLUMBIA

APPENDIX I. COURT OF APPEALS FEE SCHEDULES

(Issued in accordance with 28 U.S.C. § 1913)

(Eff. 11/01/2011)

The fees included in the Court of Appeals Miscellaneous Fee Schedule are to be charged for services provided by the courts of appeals.

- The United States should not be charged fees under this schedule, except as prescribed in Items 2, 4, and 5 when the information requested is available through remote electronic access.
- Federal agencies or programs that are funded from judiciary appropriations (agencies, organizations, and individuals providing services authorized by the Criminal Justice Act, 18 U.S.C. § 3006A, and bankruptcy administrators) should not be charged any fees under this schedule.

(1) For docketing a case on appeal or review, or docketing any other proceeding, $450.

- Each party filing a notice of appeal pays a separate fee to the district court, but parties filing a joint notice of appeal pay only one fee.
- There is no docketing fee for an application for an interlocutory appeal under 28 U.S.C. § 1292(b) or other petition for permission to appeal under Fed. R. App. P. 5, unless the appeal is allowed.

• There is no docketing fee for a direct bankruptcy appeal or a direct bankruptcy cross appeal, when the fee has been collected by the bankruptcy court in accordance with item 14 of the Bankruptcy Court Miscellaneous Fee Schedule.

(2) For conducting a search of the court of appeals records, $30 per name or item searched. This fee applies to services rendered on behalf of the United States if the information requested is available through remote electronic access.

(3) For certification of any document, $11.

(4) For reproducing any document, $.50 per page. This fee applies to services rendered on behalf of the United States if the document requested is available through remote electronic access.

(5) For reproducing recordings of proceedings, regardless of the medium, $30, including the cost of materials. This fee applies to services rendered on behalf of the United States if the recording is available through remote electronic access.

(6) For reproducing the record in any appeal in which the court of appeals does not require an appendix pursuant to Fed. R. App. P.30(f), $83.

(7) For retrieving a record from a Federal Records Center, National Archives, or other storage location removed from the place of business of the court, $53.

(8) For a check paid into the court which is returned for lack of funds, $53.

(9) For copies of opinions, a fee commensurate with the cost of printing, as fixed by each court.

(10) For copies of the local rules of court, a fee commensurate with the cost of distributing the copies. The court may also distribute copies of the local rules without charge.

(11) For filing:

- Any separate or joint notice of appeal or application for appeal from the Bankruptcy Appellate Panel, $5;
- A notice of the allowance of an appeal from the Bankruptcy Appellate Panel, $5.

(12) For counsel's requested use of the court's videoconferencing equipment in connection with each oral argument, the court may charge and collect a fee of $200 per remote location.

(13) For original admission of attorney to practice, including a certificate of admission, $176. For a duplicate certificate of admission or certificate of good standing, $18.

[The D.C. Circuit collects a local attorney admission fee of $50 in addition to the national attorney admission fee of $176 imposed by this fee schedule. The payment of the combined fee of $226 should be made payable to the "Clerk, U.S. Court of Appeals."]

ELECTRONIC PUBLIC ACCESS FEE SCHEDULE

(Issued in accordance with 28 U.S.C. §§ 1913, 1914, 1926, 1930, 1932)

*(Eff. 1/1/2009)**

As directed by Congress, the Judicial Conference has determined that the following fees are necessary to reimburse expenses incurred by the judiciary in providing electronic public access to court records. These fees shall apply to the United States unless otherwise stated. No fees under this schedule shall be charged to federal agencies or programs which are funded from judiciary appropriations, including, but not limited to, agencies, organizations, and individuals providing services authorized by the Criminal Justice Act, 18 U.S.C. § 3006A, and bankruptcy administrator programs.

I. For electronic access to court data via a federal judiciary Internet site: eight cents per page, with the total for any document, docket sheet, or case-specific report not to exceed the fee for thirty pages-provided however that transcripts of federal court proceedings shall not be subject to the thirty-page fee limit. For electronic access to an audio file of a hearing in a district court, bankruptcy court, or the Court of Federal Claims via a federal judiciary Internet site: $2.40 per audio file.

Attorneys of record and parties in a case (including pro se litigants) receive one free electronic copy of all documents filed electronically, if receipt is required by law or directed by the filer. No fee is owed under this provision until an account holder accrues charges of more than $10 in a quarterly billing cycle. Consistent with Judicial Conference policy, courts may, upon a showing of cause, exempt indigents, bankruptcy case trustees, individual researchers associated with educational institutions, courts, section 501(c)(3) not-for-profit organizations, court appointed pro bono attorneys, and pro bono ADR neutrals from payment of these fees. Courts must find that parties from the classes of persons or entities listed above seeking exemption have demonstrated that an exemption is necessary in order to avoid unreasonable burdens and to promote public access to information. Any user granted an exemption agrees not to sell for profit the data obtained as a result. Any transfer of data obtained as the result of a fee exemption is prohibited unless expressly authorized by the court. Exemptions may be granted for a definite period of time and may be revoked at the discretion of the court granting the exemption.

II. For printing copies of any record or document accessed electronically at a public terminal in the courthouse: ten cents per page. This fee shall apply to services rendered on behalf of the United States if the record requested is remotely available through electronic access.

III. For every search of court records conducted by the PACER Service Center, $26 per name or item searched.

IV. For the PACER Service Center to reproduce on paper any record pertaining to a PACER account, if this information is remotely available through electronic access, 50 cents per page.

V. For a check paid to the PACER Service Center which is returned for lack of funds, $45.

JUDICIAL CONFERENCE POLICY NOTES

Courts should not exempt local, state or federal government agencies, members of the media, attorneys or others not members of one of the groups listed above. Exemptions should be granted as the exception, not the rule. A court may not use this exemption language to exempt all users. An exemption applies only to access related to the case or purpose for which it was given. The prohibition on transfer of information received without fee is not intended to bar a quote or reference to information received as a result of a fee exemption in a scholarly or other similar work.

The electronic public access fee applies to electronic court data viewed remotely from the public records of individual cases in the court, including filed documents and the docket sheet. Electronic court data may be viewed free at public terminals at the courthouse and courts may provide other local court information at no cost. Examples of information that can be provided at no cost include: local rules, court forms, news items, court calendars, opinions, and other information—such as court hours, court location, telephone listings—determined locally to benefit the public and the court.

[Effective July 1, 2001. Amended December 18, 2001, effective January 1, 2002. Amended effective September 23, 2003; November 1, 2003; January 1, 2005; April 9, 2006; July 1, 2006; September 20, 2006; January 1, 2007; March 11, 2008; January 1, 2009.]

* [**Publisher's Note:** So in original. *See also* Electronic Public Access Fee Schedule, effective September 7, 2011, published herein under the heading "Federal Courts Miscellaneous Fee Schedules", *post*.]

APPENDIX II. RULES OF DISCIPLINARY ENFORCEMENT FOR THE UNITED STATES COURT OF APPEALS FOR THE DISTRICT OF COLUMBIA CIRCUIT

INTRODUCTION

The United States Court of Appeals for the District of Columbia Circuit, in furtherance of its power and responsibility under Rule 46 of the Federal Rules of Appellate Procedure, and its inherent power and responsibility to supervise the conduct of attorneys who are admitted to practice before it, or are admitted for the purpose of a particular proceeding (pro hac vice), promulgates the following Rules of Disciplinary Enforcement.

RULE I. STANDARDS FOR PROFESSIONAL CONDUCT

(a) For misconduct as defined in paragraph (b) below, or for failure to comply with these Rules or any rule or order of this Court, and after notice and opportunity to be heard, any attorney admitted to practice before this Court may be reprimanded (publicly or privately), suspended from practice before this Court, disbarred, or subjected to such other disciplinary action as the circumstances may warrant.

(b) Acts or omissions by an attorney admitted to practice before this Court, individually or in concert with any other person or persons, which violate any Code of Professional Responsibility or other officially-adopted body of disciplinary rules applicable to the conduct of the attorney constitute misconduct. The Code of Professional Responsibility adopted by this Court is the Code of Professional Responsibility adopted by the District of Columbia Court of Appeals, as amended from time to time by that Court, except as otherwise provided by specific Rule of this Court.

RULE II. COMMITTEE ON ADMISSIONS AND GRIEVANCES

(a) The Committee. The Court shall appoint a standing committee of six members of the bar of this Court to be known as the Committee on Admissions and Grievances. Each member shall be appointed to serve for a term of three years. A member is eligible for reappointment to one additional term. Each member may serve until a successor has been appointed. If a member holds over after the expiration of the term for which that member was appointed, the period of the member's holdover shall be treated as part of the term of his or her successor. The Court may revoke any appointment at any time. In the case of any vacancy, the successor appointed shall serve the unexpired term of his or her predecessor. The Court shall designate one of the members of the Committee to serve as Chair.

(b) Confidentiality. Except to the extent reasonably necessary to carry out its responsibilities and unless otherwise ordered by the Court, the Committee shall treat in confidence the referral to it of an application for admission or a grievance, its consideration of such a matter, and its report to the Court.

(c) Admissions.

(1) The Court may refer to the Committee an application for admission to practice before the Court whenever that application or other available information raises a question as to whether the applicant is qualified for admission under the standards set forth in Rule 46(a) of the Federal Rules of Appellate Procedure.

(2) Upon referral by the Court of any such application for admission, the Committee shall take such action as is appropriate, subject to any special instruc-

tions from the Court, and shall report its findings and recommendations to the Court. The Committee shall provide the applicant with a copy of its findings and recommendations if the Committee recommends denial of the application.

(3) In considering applications for admission referred to it by the Court, the Committee may solicit relevant information from the applicant or from others. In addition, the applicant may submit to the Committee any information that he or she deems to be relevant, and shall be entitled to be represented by counsel.

(4) The applicant shall have the burden of establishing that he or she has the character and qualifications necessary for admission and shall cooperate with the Court and the Committee in their consideration of the application.

(d) Grievances.

(1) The Court may refer to the Committee any accusation or suggestion of misconduct on the part of any member of the bar, or any failure to comply with these rules or any rule or order of this Court, for such investigation, hearing and report as the Court deems advisable. Any such matter shall be referred to in these Rules as a Grievance.

(2) Upon referral by the Court of any Grievance, the Committee shall take such action as is appropriate, subject to any special instructions from the Court, and shall report its findings and recommendations to the Court. In such matters, the Committee shall be guided by Rule I of these Rules.

(3) The Committee shall consider each Grievance referred to it and, if in its opinion further action is warranted, it shall serve a statement thereof on the member of the bar of this Court to whom the Grievance relates, by certified mail, return receipt requested, addressed to the last office address filed with the Clerk. As respondent thereto, the member shall file an answer with the Chair of the Committee subscribed and sworn to under oath on or before thirty (30) days after the date of mailing. The Chair of the Committee, upon good cause shown, may extend the time to answer.

(4) If the Committee concludes after investigation and review that a hearing is unnecessary because (a) the facts are not in dispute, (b) sufficient evidence to support the Grievance is not present, (c) there is pending another proceeding against the respondent, the disposition of which in the judgment of the Committee should be awaited before further action is considered, or (d) a hearing is otherwise not warranted under the circumstances presented, the Committee shall report to the Court its recommendation for disposition of the matter.

(e) Hearings by the Committee.

(1) The Committee may sit as a fact-finding body and upon reasonable notice to the respondent may hold hearings on the Grievance.

(2) The respondent shall be entitled to be represented by counsel. The respondent may submit to the Committee all relevant information he or she deems appropriate and may request that the Committee consider the testimony of witnesses. The Committee may require that witnesses, including the respondent, testify under oath.

(3) The persons who may be present at the hearing are the members of the Committee, the respondent, the respondent's counsel, if any, and a witness providing testimony.

(4) At the respondent's request and expense, the hearing will be recorded.

(5) The Committee shall report its findings and recommendations to the Court. A copy of its findings and recommendations shall be forwarded simultaneously to the respondent.

(f) Duty of Respondent to Cooperate. It shall be the duty and responsibility of the respondent and his or her counsel to cooperate with the Committee. If a respondent fails to respond to the Committee, the Committee may recommend to the Court that discipline be imposed.

(g) Show Cause Order or Hearing by the Court.

(1) Upon receipt of the Committee's finding that misconduct occurred, the Court may issue an order requiring the respondent to show cause why discipline should not be imposed. The Court may invite the Committee or any member of the bar of this Court to reply to the respondent's answer to the show cause order or to pursue the Grievance against the respondent at a show cause hearing.

(2) If the Grievance is sustained, the Court may reprimand, suspend, disbar or otherwise discipline the respondent.

[Amended effective January 31, 2003.]

RULE III. ATTORNEYS CONVICTED OF CRIMES

(a) Upon the filing with this Court of a certified copy of a judgment of conviction demonstrating that any attorney admitted to practice before the Court has been convicted in any court of the United States, or of the District of Columbia, or of any state, territory, commonwealth or possession of the United States of a serious crime as defined in paragraph (f) below, the Clerk shall enter an order immediately suspending that attorney, regardless of the pendency of any appeal, until final disposition of a disciplinary proceeding to be commenced upon such conviction. The Clerk shall immediately serve a copy of such order upon the attorney by certified mail, return receipt requested, addressed to the last office address filed with the Clerk. Upon good cause shown, the Court may set aside such order when it appears in the interest of justice to do so.

(b) Upon the filing of a certified copy of a judgment of conviction of an attorney for a serious crime, the Court shall refer the matter to the Committee on Admissions and Grievances for a recommendation to the Court on the extent of the final discipline to be imposed as a result of the conduct resulting in the conviction, provided that the recommendation for final discipline shall not be made until all appeals from the conviction are concluded.

(c) Upon the filing of a certified copy of a judgment of conviction of an attorney for a crime not constituting a "serious crime," the Court may refer the matter to the Committee for a recommendation to the Court for appropriate action, including the institution of a disciplinary proceeding.

(d) In any disciplinary proceedings instituted against an attorney based upon a conviction, a certified copy of a judgment of conviction of an attorney for a crime shall be conclusive evidence of the commission of that crime.

(e) An attorney suspended under the provisions of this Rule shall be reinstated immediately upon the filing of a certificate demonstrating that the underlying conviction of a serious crime has been reversed, but the reinstatement shall not terminate any disciplinary proceeding then pending against the attorney. In any such proceeding, evidence relating to the conduct which resulted in the conviction may be considered despite the reversal of the conviction.

(f) The term "serious crime" includes any felony and also includes any lesser crime, a necessary element of which, as determined by the statutory or common law definition of such crime in the jurisdiction where the judgment was entered, involves interference with the administration of justice, false swearing, misrepresentation, fraud, willful failure to file income tax returns, deceit, bribery, extortion, misappropriation, theft, or an attempt or a conspiracy or solicitation of another to commit a "serious crime."

RULE IV. DISCIPLINE IMPOSED BY OTHER COURTS OR AGENCIES

(a) Upon the filing of a certified or exemplified copy of a judgment or order demonstrating that an attorney admitted to practice before this Court has been disciplined for professional misconduct as defined in Rule I.B to another court, or by an agency of the United States as defined in 5 U.S.C. § 551, this Court may refer the matter to the Committee on Admissions and Grievances for a recommendation for appropriate action, or may issue a notice directed to the attorney containing:

(1) a copy of the judgment or order from the other court or agency; and

(2) an order to show cause directing that the attorney inform this Court within the time specified of any claim by the attorney predicated upon the grounds set forth in paragraph (c) below that the imposition of the identical discipline by this Court would be unwarranted and the reasons therefor.

(b) In the event the discipline imposed in the other jurisdiction has been stayed there, any reciprocal discipline imposed in this Court may be deferred until such stay expires.

(c) After consideration of the response called for by the order issued pursuant to paragraph (a) above or after expiration of the time specified in the order, this Court shall impose the identical discipline unless the attorney demonstrates, or this Court is satisfied that:

(1) the procedure was so lacking in notice or opportunity to be heard as to constitute a deprivation of due process; or

(2) there was such an infirmity of proof establishing the misconduct as to give rise to the clear conviction that this Court could not, consistent with its duty, accept as final the conclusion on that subject; or

(3) the imposition of the same discipline by this Court would result in grave injustice; or

(4) the misconduct warrants substantially different discipline.

When this Court determines that any of these elements exists, it shall enter such other order as it deems appropriate.

(d) Except as provided in paragraph (c) above, a final adjudication in another court or in an agency of the United States that an attorney has been guilty of misconduct shall establish conclusively the misconduct for purposes of a disciplinary proceeding in this Court.

(e) This Court may at any stage ask the Committee to conduct disciplinary proceedings or to make recommendations to the Court for appropriate action in light of the imposition of professional discipline by another court or by an agency.

RULE V. DISBARMENT ON CONSENT OR RESIGNATION IN OTHER COURTS

Any attorney admitted to practice before this Court who is disbarred on consent or resigns from the bar of any other court of the United States or the District of Columbia, or from the bar of any state, territory, commonwealth or possession of the United States while an investigation into allegations of misconduct is pending, shall, upon the filing with this Court of a certified or exemplified copy of the judgment or order accepting such disbarment on consent or resignation, be disbarred.

RULE VI. DISBARMENT ON CONSENT WHILE UNDER DISCIPLINARY INVESTIGATION OR PROSECUTION

(a) Any attorney admitted to practice before this Court who is the subject of an investigation into, or a pending proceeding involving, allegations of misconduct may consent to disbarment from practicing law before this Court, but only by delivering to this Court an affidavit stating that the attorney desires to consent to disbarment and that:

(1) the attorney's consent is freely and voluntarily rendered; the attorney is not being subject to coercion or duress; the attorney is fully aware of the implications of so consenting;

(2) the attorney is aware that there is a presently pending investigation or proceeding involving allegations that there exist grounds for the attorney's discipline, the nature of which the attorney shall specifically set forth;

(3) the attorney acknowledges that the material facts so alleged are true or that he has no defense to the allegations; and

(4) the attorney so consents because the attorney knows that if a Grievance were predicated upon the matters under investigation, or if the proceeding were prosecuted, the attorney could not successfully defend himself.

(b) Upon receipt of the required affidavit, the Clerk shall enter an order disbarring the attorney.

(c) An order disbarring an attorney on consent shall be a matter of public record. However, the affidavit required under the provisions of this Rule shall not be publicly disclosed or made available for use in any other proceeding except upon order of this Court.

RULE VII. REINSTATEMENT

(a) After Disbarment or Suspension. An attorney who is suspended for a definite period shall automatically be reinstated at the end of the period of suspension upon the filing with the Clerk of an affidavit of compliance with the provisions of the order. An attorney who is suspended indefinitely or disbarred may not resume practice until reinstated by order of this Court. A suspension may be directed to run concurrently with a suspension mandated by another court, in which event the attorney shall be eligible for reinstatement in this Court when that suspension expires, and will automatically be reinstated upon filing with the Clerk an affidavit indicating that the period of suspension has run and that the attorney has been reinstated by the other court.

(b) Hearing on Application. Petitions for reinstatement by a disbarred or indefinitely suspended attorney under this Rule shall be filed with the Clerk. Upon receipt of the petition, the Clerk shall promptly refer the petition to the Committee, which shall assign the matter for prompt hearing before the Committee. At the hearing the petitioner shall have the burden of demonstrating by clear and convincing evidence that he or she possesses the moral and professional qualifications required for admission to practice law before this Court and that the petitioner's resumption of the practice of law will not be detrimental to the integrity and standing of the bar or to the administration of justice. The Committee shall make its recommendation to the Court, which may adopt its findings, schedule a hearing on the matter, or take such other action as it deems appropriate.

(c) Conditions of Reinstatement. If the petitioner is found by the Court to be unfit to resume the practice of law, the petition shall be dismissed. If the petitioner is found fit to resume the practice of law, the petitioner will be ordered reinstated. Reinstatement may be conditional upon the payment of all or part of the costs of the proceedings, and upon the making of partial or complete restitution to parties harmed by the misconduct which led to the suspension or disbarment. If the petitioner has been suspended or disbarred for five years or more, reinstatement may also be conditioned upon the furnishing of proof of competency and learning in the law, which proof may include certification by the bar examiners of a state or other jurisdiction of the attorney's successful completion of an examination for admission to practice subsequent to the date of suspension or disbarment.

(d) Successive Petitions. No petition for reinstatement under this Rule may be filed within one year following an adverse decision upon a petition for reinstatement filed by or on behalf of the same person.

RULE VIII. ATTORNEYS SPECIALLY ADMITTED

Whenever an attorney applies to be admitted or is admitted to this Court for purposes of a particular proceeding (*pro hac vice*), the attorney shall be deemed thereby to have conferred disciplinary jurisdiction upon this Court for any alleged misconduct of that attorney arising in the course of, in the preparation for, or in connection with such proceedings.

RULE IX. PROCEEDINGS WHERE AN ATTORNEY IS DECLARED TO BE MENTALLY INCOMPETENT OR IS ALLEGED TO BE INCAPACITATED

(a) Attorneys Declared Mentally Incompetent. Where an attorney who is a member of the bar of this

Court has been judicially declared incompetent or involuntarily committed to a mental hospital, the Court, upon proper proof of the fact, shall enter an order suspending such attorney from the practice of law effective immediately and for an indefinite period until further order of the Court. A copy of such order shall be served upon the attorney, his guardian and the Director of the mental health hospital in such a manner as the Court may direct.

(b) Attorneys Alleged to Be Incapacitated. Whenever it appears to the Court that a member of the bar may be incapacitated by reason of mental infirmity or illness or because of the use of drugs or intoxicants, the Court may take or direct such action as it deems necessary or proper to determine whether the attorney is so incapacitated, including the examination of the attorney by such qualified medical experts as the Court shall designate, and including reference of the matter to the Committee. Failure or refusal to submit to such examination shall be *prima facie* evidence of incapacity. If the Court concludes that the attorney is incapacitated and should not be permitted to continue to practice law before the Court, it shall enter an order suspending the attorney for an indefinite period and until further order of the Court. The Court may provide for such notice to the respondent attorney of proceedings in the matter as is deemed proper and advisable and may appoint an attorney to represent the respondent if the respondent is without representation.

(c) Claim of Disability During Disciplinary Proceedings. If during the course of a disciplinary proceeding the respondent contends that he or she is suffering from a disability by reason of a mental or physical infirmity or illness or because of the use of drugs or intoxicants, and that this disability makes it impossible for the respondent to make an adequate defense, the Court shall enter an order immediately suspending the respondent from continuing to practice law before this Court until a determination is made of the respondent's capacity to continue to practice law in a proceeding instituted in accordance with the provisions of paragraph (b) above.

(d) Application for Reinstatement. Any attorney suspended for incompetency, mental illness or because of the use of drugs or intoxicants may apply to the Court for reinstatement once a year or at such shorter intervals as the Court may direct in the order of suspension. The application shall be granted by the Court upon a showing by clear and convincing evidence that the attorney's disability has been removed and he or she is fit to resume the practice of law. The Court may take or direct such action as it deems necessary or proper to make a determination of whether the attorney's disability has been remedied, including a direction for an examination of the attorney by such qualified medical experts as the Court shall designate. The Court may direct that the expenses of such an examination shall be paid by the attorney.

Where an attorney has been suspended because of a judicial declaration of incompetence or involuntary commitment to a mental hospital and has thereafter been judicially declared to be competent, the court may dispense with further evidence and direct the reinstatement of the attorney upon such terms as are deemed proper and advisable.

(e) Waiver of Physician–Patient Privilege. The filing of an application for reinstatement by an attorney who has been suspended for disability shall constitute a waiver of any doctor-patient privilege with respect to any treatment of the attorney during the period of his disability for the condition underlying the suspension. The attorney may be required to disclose the name of every psychiatrist, psychologist, physician and hospital by whom or in which the attorney has been examined or treated since his suspension for the condition underlying the suspension, and may be required to furnish the Court with written consent for such psychiatrists, psychologists, physicians or hospitals to divulge such information or records as may be requested by the medical experts designated by the Court.

RULE X. DUTY OF ATTORNEYS TO NOTIFY THE COURT OF CONVICTIONS OR DISCIPLINE BY OTHER COURTS OR AGENCIES

If an attorney admitted to practice before this Court (a) is subjected to public discipline for professional misconduct as defined in Rule I.B; (b) is indicted or charged with a felony or serious crime as defined in Rule III.F; (c) is convicted of a felony or misdemeanor; (d) is disbarred on consent; or (e) resigns from the bar of any court while an investigation into an allegation of misconduct is pending, the attorney shall so notify the Clerk of this Court in writing within ten days of such discipline, indictment, charge, conviction, disbarment on consent or resignation.

RULE XI. DUTIES OF THE CLERK

(a) Upon being informed that an attorney admitted to practice before this Court has been convicted of any crime or has been subjected to discipline by another court, the Clerk of this Court shall determine whether the clerk of the court in which such conviction occurred or in which such discipline was imposed has forwarded a certificate of such conviction or discipline to this Court. If a certificate has not been so forwarded, the Clerk shall promptly obtain a certificate and file it with this Court.

(b) Whenever it appears that any person disbarred, suspended, publicly reprimanded, or disbarred on consent by this Court is admitted to practice law in any other jurisdiction or before any other court, the Clerk of this Court shall, within ten days of that action transmit a certified copy of the order of disbarment, suspension, reprimand, or disbarment on consent to the disciplinary authority for each other jurisdiction or court, and the administrative tribunal, if any, affected by the misconduct.

(c) The Clerk of this Court shall promptly notify the National Discipline Data Bank operated by the American Bar Association of any order of this Court imposing public discipline upon any attorney admitted to practice before this Court.

RULE XII. JURISDICTION

Nothing contained in these Rules shall be construed to deny to this Court such powers as are necessary for the Court to maintain control over proceedings conducted before it, such as proceedings for contempt under Title 18 of the United States Code or under Rule 42 of the Federal Rules of Criminal Procedure, or to deprive the Court of its inherent disciplinary powers.

RULE XIII. EFFECTIVE DATE

These Rules shall become effective on July 1, 1984, and shall apply to proceedings brought thereafter and also shall apply to pending proceedings unless their application would not be feasible or would be unjust.

APPENDIX III. APPELLATE MEDIATION PROGRAM

The Appellate Mediation Program was created in 1987. Originally conceived as a one-year experiment, it has become an integral part of the Court's case management system. Mediation was originally intended to supplement the Court's 1986 Case Management Plan, which was undertaken to accommodate a sixty percent increase in filings and pending cases over a two-year period. It was also intended to help parties by curtailing the expense involved in protracted appeals and by providing a forum to stimulate the development of creative resolution options that are not likely to be achieved through Court order or through the independent action of the parties.

The Appellate Mediation Program uses mediation to achieve settlement of cases. It also encourages the settlement of some issues in a case and the procedural streamlining of cases to simplify briefing and to reduce motions activity. Mediation efforts that are unsuccessful initially may result, weeks or even months later, in settlement.

Mediation differs considerably from arbitration and negotiation. In arbitration, an outcome is imposed upon the parties. In negotiation, discussion takes place between the parties, usually with no assistance from a neutral. In mediation, a neutral helps parties reach a resolution that is acceptable to them. Cases are settled only if the parties agree to a course of action that will terminate their case so that no further Court involvement is required.

The Appellate Mediation Program has had a significant impact on the Court's workload. Cases that are settled do not proceed to oral argument, thus saving the time of judges and law clerks who would otherwise prepare for argument. Issues and positions are clarified in the mediation process so that, even if settlement is not achieved, the Court benefits from more efficient briefing. Finally, mediation frequently saves time and money for the litigants themselves. It can also produce agreements that meet their needs more effectively than the relief that could be provided through judicial disposition. Mediation is offered at no cost to the parties.

CASE SELECTION

Cases filed with the Court of Appeals are selected for mediation by attorneys in the Legal Division of the Clerk's Office. Screening occurs after dispositive motions have been decided and, in any event, no sooner than 45 days after a case has been docketed in the Court of Appeals.

No criminal cases enter the program. Civil cases are reviewed on an individual basis, with a number of factors considered in making the eligibility determination. These factors include the nature of the underlying dispute, the relationship of the issues on appeal to the underlying dispute, the availability of incentives to reach settlement or limit the issues on appeal, the susceptibility of these issues to mediation, the possibility of effectuating a resolution, the number of parties, and the number of related pending cases. Uncounseled cases, while not categorically excluded, are rarely referred to mediation.

Parties are encouraged to request mediation by completing a "Request to Enter Appellate Mediation Program" form and sending it to the Clerk *in duplicate.* The Court treats such requests as confidential. Although requests to enter mediation are not automatically granted, the Legal Division staff give them special consideration.

PROGRAM MEDIATORS

The Court has selected distinguished senior members of the bar, academicians from local law schools, and attorneys with broad experience mediating complex civil cases to serve as mediators. The mediators are experienced attorneys who enjoy the Court's full confidence.

The mediators protect the confidentiality of all proceedings and do not communicate with the Court about what transpires during mediation sessions. Mediators are required to recuse themselves from handling any cases in which they perceive a conflict of interest.

Mediators are not paid for their services, but are reimbursed by the Court for minor out-of-pocket expenses such as trips to the Courthouse. The Court also provides parking, administrative support and limited secretarial services if needed.

The primary role of program mediators is to make every effort to help parties reach a settlement or, at a minimum, to help parties resolve some issues in the case. If settlement is not possible, the mediators will help parties clarify or eliminate issues to expedite the litigation process.

CONFIDENTIALITY

Confidentiality is ensured throughout the mediation process. Attorneys in the Legal Division do not confer with judges in selecting cases for mediation. Mediators protect the confidentiality of all proceedings and are prohibited from complying with subpoenas or other requests for information about mediated cases. Papers generated by the mediation process are not included in Court files, and information about what transpires in the mediation process is not at any time made known to the Court. The Circuit Executive's Office, which is responsible for program administration and evaluation and liaison between the mediators and Court personnel, maintains strict confidentiality about the content of the mediation in particular cases. The Court expects participating counsel to refrain from commenting publicly about the fact that a case is in mediation or from disclosing any information about the parties' discussions or the status of the talks to anyone who is not, directly or indirectly, a party to the negotiations.

The above is not intended to guarantee absolute secrecy about the identity of the cases that are chosen for mediation. Nor is it meant to preclude dissemination of information about the types of cases going through the mediation process and about overall program results. Generic information about the program and cases entering it is available, and reports are generated for analysis and evaluation. Individual cases that have been resolved through mediation may be publicly identified or brought to the Court's attention as program successes if the litigants consent to such a disclosure.

MEDIATION PROCEDURES

The Director of the Legal Division of the Clerk's Office identifies cases for mediation no earlier than 45 days after they have been docketed in the Court of Appeals. Lead counsel and intervenors involved in cases selected for mediation receive a letter from the Court describing the program and assigning a mediator. A copy of the Court's en banc Order defining the procedures to be followed is included in the mailing. At the same time, the Court sends to the assigned mediator a copy of the judgment or order on appeal, any opinion issued by the District Court or agency, the appellant's or petitioner's statement of issues on appeal, D.C. Cir. Rule 28(a)(1) statements, and all relevant motions.

Within fifteen days of the selection of a case for mediation, counsel are required to submit a position paper, not to exceed ten pages, to the mediator. The position paper will outline the key facts and legal issues in the case and will include a statement of motions filed and their status. Position papers **are not briefs, are not filed with the Court, and need not be served on the other party unless the mediator so directs.**

The mediator sets the date for the initial mediation session, which must be held within 45 days of the selection of the case for mediation, and schedules follow-up sessions as needed. The initial session is normally held at the Court. However, a mediator may decide to hold this or subsequent meetings in his/her office or at another location. All cases in mediation are subject to normal scheduling for briefing and oral argument. If it appears that the briefing schedule will interfere with the mediator's ability to convene necessary sessions or otherwise proceed with the mediation, the attorneys shall file a motion to defer or postpone the briefing and/or oral argument date(s), representing that the mediator, whom they shall not identify by name, concurs in the request. **The motion must indicate, in both the caption and the first paragraph, that the change is needed to accommodate a pending mediation.** Attorneys may not file any other motions that would notify the Court that the case is in mediation.

The Court requires that counsel for parties attend all mediation sessions. All parties are also strongly urged by the Court to attend each mediation session. Each party represented must have counsel or another person present with actual authority to enter into a settlement agreement during the session. In cases involving the United States government or the District of Columbia government, senior attorneys on either side of the case may attend mediation sessions so long as someone with settlement authority can be reached by telephone during conference sessions. It is the responsibility of the United States Department of Justice and the District of Columbia Corporation Counsel attorneys during these sessions to furnish the mediator with the names and titles of the government officials who are authorized under applicable laws and regulations to effectuate settlement, including the Justice Department officials who possess settlement authority under 28 CFR, Part O, Subpart Y. The attorneys who participate in the mediation sessions shall also identify the officials whose participation in the discussions would be helpful, even though such officials may lack ultimate settlement authority. When settlement authority for the United States rests with an official at the rank of Assistant Attorney General, its equivalent or higher, or with members of an independent agency, or when settlement authority for the District of Columbia rests with officials above the rank of Corporation Counsel, the requirement that the official or members be reachable during the mediation session is waived unless the mediator for good reason specifically provides otherwise in writing after reviewing the mediation papers.

If settlement is reached, the agreement, which shall be binding upon all parties, will be put into writing, and counsel will file a stipulation of dismissal. If the case is not settled, it will remain on the docket and proceed as though mediation had not been initiated. Regardless of the outcome of a case, mediators will complete a case evaluation form for each case mediated. Each attorney participating in the mediation will be asked to complete an evaluation form.

THE MEDIATION PROCESS

Mediation begins at a joint meeting attended by the mediator, counsel for the parties and, whenever possible, the parties themselves. The mediator explains how the mediation is to be conducted. After this introduction, each party is asked to explain to the other party or parties and to the mediator its views on the matter in dispute. The party who filed the appeal typically speaks first. The mediator is likely to refrain from asking questions or allowing the parties to ask questions of each other until all parties have had an opportunity to speak.

Once the views of all parties have been stated in the joint session, the mediator usually caucuses individually with each of the parties. The purpose of these caucuses is to allow the mediator and the parties to explore more fully the needs and interests underlying their stated positions. It is also to help the parties begin thinking about settlement options that perhaps go beyond what could be accomplished in the court proceeding alone. The mediator encourages the parties to think broadly about the problem and helps them explore options for settlement.

After the initial series of meetings, the mediator may convene follow-up sessions to help the parties continue to explore settlement possibilities. These discussions may take place in person or over the telephone, whichever the mediator thinks likely to be most beneficial under the circumstances of the particular case.

ORDER ESTABLISHING APPELLATE MEDIATION PROGRAM

REVISED ORDER

BEFORE: EDWARDS, Chief Judge; WALD, SILBERMAN, WILLIAMS, GINSBURG, SENTELLE, HENDERSON, RANDOLPH, ROGERS, TATEL, AND GARLAND, Circuit Judges

ORDERED, by the Court, *en banc*, that civil appeals from the United States District Court, petitions for review of agency action, and original actions may be referred to a mediator designated by the Court to meet with counsel and parties to facilitate settlement of the case, to simplify issues or otherwise to assist in the expeditious handling of an appeal. It is

FURTHER ORDERED that mediation sessions must be attended by counsel for each party or another person with actual authority to settle the case. Additionally, the parties themselves are strongly encouraged to attend the sessions. In cases involving the United States government or the District of Columbia government, senior attorneys on either side of the case may attend mediation sessions so long as someone with settlement authority can be reached by telephone during conference sessions. When settlement authority for the United States rests with officials of the rank of Assistant Attorney General (or its equivalent) or higher, or with the members of an independent agency, or in cases in which settlement authority for the District of Columbia rests with officials above the rank of Corporation Counsel, the requirement that the officials or members be reachable during the mediation session is waived unless the mediator for good reason specifically provides otherwise in writing after reviewing the mediation papers. Failure of counsel to attend sessions may result in the imposition of sanctions.

The Circuit Executive for the D.C. Circuit shall serve as the program administrator of the Appellate Mediation Program. A party may request mediation, but the Director of the Legal Division of the Clerk's Office will ultimately determine which cases are appropriate for mediation. Case selection will take place no sooner than 45 days after a case has been docketed in the Court of Appeals. Lead counsel will receive notice of case selection and of the mediator assigned.

An initial mediation session will be held by the mediator within 45 days of a case's selection for mediation. The mediator will schedule additional sessions as needed. Mediation sessions will normally be held at the E. Barrett Prettyman United States Courthouse, 333 Constitution Avenue, N.W., Washington, D.C. The mediator has discretion, however, to hold sessions at any other location he/she thinks appropriate.

The Court will send the mediator a copy of the judgment or order on appeal, any opinion issued by the District Court or agency, the appellant's or petitioner's statement of issues on appeal, D.C.Cir.Rule 28(a)(1) statements, and all relevant motions. Within fifteen days of the case's selection for mediation, counsel shall prepare and submit to the mediator a position paper of no more than ten pages, stating their views on the key facts and legal issues in the case. The position paper will include a statement of motions filed and their disposition. Mediation statements *shall not* be filed with the Court and need not be served on opposing counsel unless the mediator so directs.

All motions filed or decided while mediation is underway are to be identified for the mediator and submitted to him/her upon request. Like mediation statements, documents submitted to the mediator or prepared for mediation sessions need not be served on opposing counsel unless the mediator so directs and *shall not* be filed with the Clerk's Office.

All cases in mediation remain subject to normal scheduling for briefing and oral argument by the Clerk's Office. If the mediator, in consultation with the parties, believes that additional mediation sessions or discussions are required and that the briefing schedule in the case would interfere with such efforts, the attorneys shall request an extension by filing a joint motion to defer or postpone the briefing and/or oral argument date(s). The motion must indicate, in both the caption and the first paragraph, that the change is needed to accommodate a pending mediation. The attorneys shall represent that the mediator, whom they shall not identify by name, concurs in the request. Attorneys may not file any other motions that would notify the Court that the case is in mediation, nor may they use information obtained through the mediation as a basis for any other motion.

The content of mediation discussions and proceedings, including any statement made or document prepared by any party, attorney or other participant, is privileged and shall not be disclosed to the Court or construed for any purpose, in any proceeding in any forum, as an admission against interest. Mediators shall not comply with requests for information about mediated cases and, if subpoenaed, are hereby instructed not to testify. Participating counsel and their clients will refrain from commenting publicly about the fact that a case is in mediation or from disclosing any information about the parties' discussions or the status of the talks to anyone who is not, directly or indirectly, a party to the negotiations. No party shall be bound by anything said or done at a mediation session unless a settlement is reached. If a settlement is reached, the agreement shall be reduced to writing and shall be binding upon all parties to the agreement.

Mediators who have been selected by the Court to serve in the Appellate Mediation Program are highly experienced members of the bar who have been involved in the types of litigation that come before the Court. Mediators, who will serve without compensation, have received special training to help parties reach agreement and avoid the time, expense and uncertainty of further litigation. Mediation is offered to parties at no cost.

Mediators may, in their discretion, call or write to private clients or to representatives of government agencies to request their attendance at mediation sessions. Any communication by the mediator with such persons must, however, be fully disclosed to the counsel of record. Mediators may communicate, in the presence of counsel, settlement offers or other appropriate information to private clients or to representatives of government agencies. If a mediator makes any oral or written suggestion as to the advisability of a change in any party's position with respect to settlement, counsel for that party shall promptly transmit the suggestion to his or her client if that client is not present at the mediation session. Counsel shall explain to clients, whether present at mediation or not, the suggestions put forward by mediators and their import. It is

FURTHER ORDERED that if a case is settled, counsel shall file a stipulation of dismissal. Such stipulation must be filed within 30 days after the settlement is reached unless a short extension is requested by the attorneys by motion. If a case cannot be resolved through mediation, it will remain on the docket and proceed as if mediation had not been initiated; therefore, no notification to the Court is necessary.

A copy of this Order will be posted in the Office of the Clerk of the United States District Court for the District of Columbia and the Office of the Clerk of the United States Court of Appeals for the District of Columbia Circuit.

Per Curiam

[Effective November 28, 1988. Amended April 19, 1989; May 1, 1992; and March 20, 1993; April 14, 1998; December 1, 2005.]

APPENDIX IV. ADMINISTRATIVE ORDER REGARDING ELECTRONIC CASE FILING

BEFORE: Sentelle, Chief Judge; Ginsburg, Henderson, Rogers, Tatel, Garland, Brown, Griffith, and Kavanaugh, Circuit Judges

ADMINISTRATIVE ORDER REGARDING ELECTRONIC CASE FILING

Pursuant to Federal Rule of Appellate Procedure 25(a)(2)(D) and 25(c), the United States Court of Appeals for the District of Columbia Circuit has authorized the filing and service of documents by electronic means. See D.C. Cir. Rule 25 (as amended, effective June 8, 2009). To implement the Case Management/Electronic Case Files (CM/ECF) system, the court hereby adopts the following provisions that will govern in cases before the court, effective June 8, 2009. These provisions may be amended from time to time as necessary, with or without prior notice, by further order of the court. The court may deviate from these provisions in specific cases if deemed appropriate in the exercise of its discretion.

ECF–1. Scope of Electronic Filing System

Except as otherwise prescribed by Circuit rule or order of the court, all cases filed on and after September 1, 2009, will be assigned to the court's CM/ECF system. Case-initiating documents, including petitions for permission to appeal, petitions for review or notices of appeal from agency action, and petitions for writ of mandamus and other original proceedings in this court, must be filed in paper form. Except as otherwise prescribed by Circuit rule or court order, all briefs, motions, petitions for rehearing, and other documents subsequently filed in any case by a filer registered in accordance with ECF–2 must be filed electronically using the CM/ECF system. Upon the court's request, an ECF filer must promptly provide the clerk, in a format designated by the court, an identical electronic version of any paper document previously filed in the same case by that filer.

ECF–2. Registration as an ECF Filer; Passwords; Consent to Service

(A) Attorneys who appear before this court must register for the court's CM/ECF system. An attorney must enter an appearance in each case in which the attorney wishes to participate as an ECF filer. Registration requirements will be posted on the court's web site and may include training as a prerequisite to registration as an ECF filer.

(B) At the discretion of the court, a party to a pending civil case who is not represented by an attorney may be permitted to register as an ECF filer solely for purposes of that case. A pro se party who desires to register as an ECF filer must file a motion in this court, describing the party's access to the internet and confirming the capacity to file and receive documents electronically on a regular basis. If permission is granted, the pro se party may be required to complete CM/ECF training provided by the clerk as a prerequisite to registration as an ECF filer. If a pro se party retains an attorney, the attorney must enter an appearance.

(C) ECF filers agree to protect the security of their passwords and to notify the PACER Service Center and the clerk immediately if they learn that their password has been compromised. ECF filers may be sanctioned for failure to comply with this provision.

(D) Registration as an ECF filer constitutes consent to electronic service of all documents as provided in the Federal Rules of Appellate Procedure and the rules of this court. See D.C. Cir. Rule 25(c).

ECF–3. Electronic Signatures

(A) The ECF Filer. The filer log-in and password required to submit documents to the CM/ECF system serve as the filer's signature for all purposes under the Federal Rules of Appellate Procedure and the rules of this court. The name of the filer under whose log-in and password a document is submitted must be preceded by an "/s/" and typed in the space where the signature would otherwise appear, followed by the firm name, if any, and the attorney's or party's street address, telephone number, and e-mail address. No ECF filer or other person may knowingly permit or cause to permit a filer's log-in and password to be used by anyone other than an authorized agent of the ECF filer.

(B) Other Signatures. Documents requiring signatures of more than one party must be electronically filed either by: (1) submitting a scanned document containing all necessary signatures; (2) representing the consent of the other parties on the document; or (3) in any other manner approved by the court. Electronically represented signatures of all parties and ECF filers as described above are presumed to be valid signatures. If any party, counsel of record, or ECF filer objects to the representation of his or her signature on an electronic document as described above, he or she must, within 14 days of the filing, file a notice setting forth the basis of the objection.

ECF–4. CM/ECF Retention Requirements

Documents that are electronically filed and require original signatures other than that of the filer must be maintained in paper form by the filer until issuance of the mandate (or entry of the final order, in a case in which no mandate will issue) or until such later date as the court prescribes. On request of the court, the filer must provide original documents for review.

ECF–5. Consequences of Electronic Filing

(A) The Docket. Electronic transmission of a document to the CM/ECF system consistent with this order, together with the transmission of a Notice of Docket Activity from the court, constitute filing of the document under the Federal Rules of Appellate Procedure and the rules of this court, and constitute under FRAP 36 and 45(b) entry of the document on the docket maintained by the clerk. If the court requires a party to file a motion for leave to file, both the motion and document at issue should be submitted electronically. If leave is granted, the underlying document will remain on the docket; if leave is denied, the docket will so reflect.

(B) Format. Before filing a document with the court, an ECF filer must verify its legibility and completeness. Documents created by the filer and filed electronically must be in Portable Document Format (PDF), which is generated from an original word-processing file and is text searchable. PDF images created by scanning paper documents do not comply with this requirement. Appendix items and attachments to an electronically-filed document may be scanned if a word-processing version is not available. When a document has been filed electronically, the official record is the electronic document stored by the court, and the filing party is bound by the document as filed.

(C) Time of Filing. Except in the case of documents first filed in paper form and subsequently submitted electronically under ECF–1, a document filed electronically is deemed filed on the date and at the time stated on the Notice of Docket Activity from the court. Unless a time for filing is specified by court order, filing must be completed before midnight Eastern Time to be considered timely filed that day.

(D) Technical Failures. An ECF filer whose filing is made untimely as the result of a technical failure may seek appropriate relief from the court.

ECF–6. Paper Copies of Electronic Filings

(A) In General. Except for documents listed below or unless the court directs otherwise, documents filed by an ECF filer in accordance with this order are not to be submitted to the court in paper form.

(B) Motions. In addition to filing electronically, paper copies must be filed with the court of the following motions, including any accompanying documents, and any responses thereto, and replies: dispositive motions (e.g., motions for summary disposition, motions to transfer or remand, and motions to dismiss except those seeking voluntary dismissal in civil cases and in criminal cases where the government is the appellant), procedural motions unless the motion states it is unopposed, motions for stay and emergency relief pursuant to Circuit Rules 8 and 18, motions to expedite, motions or applications under Circuit Rule 9, motions for leave to proceed in forma pauperis, motions for appointment of counsel, and motions to exceed the length limits. The number of paper copies is governed by Circuit Rule 27(b); the "original" is the electronic filing.

(C) Other Documents. Except as provided in ECF–8(C), electronic filing is required for any portion of an appendix that is available in electronic format and fully text searchable. In addition to filing electronically, paper copies of the following documents must be filed with the court: briefs, appendices, memoranda of law and fact, responsive pleadings to petitions and replies thereto, letters pursuant to FRAP 28(j), proposed judgments in a National Labor Relations Board proceeding, petitions for panel rehearing and hearing or rehearing en banc, and responses to orders to show cause. The number of paper copies is governed by the rules pertaining to that document or by order in a particular case; the "original" is the electronic filing.

(D) Time of Filing Paper Copies. Unless the court has ordered filing by hand or other means, filing of paper copies of non-emergency documents may be accomplished by First–Class Mail addressed to the clerk, or other class of mail that is at least as expeditious, postage prepaid, within two business days of the electronic filing.

ECF–7. Service of Documents by Electronic Means

The Notice of Docket Activity that is generated by the court's CM/ECF system constitutes service of the filed document on all parties who have registered for the CM/ECF system but does not replace the certificate of service required by FRAP 25. Any party who has not consented to electronic service must be served by an alternative method of service, in accordance with the Federal Rules of Appellate Procedure and this court's rules. See D.C. Cir. Rule 25(c).

ECF–8. Exceptions to Requirement of Electronic Filing And Service

(A) A party proceeding pro se must file documents in paper form with the clerk and must be served with documents in paper form, unless the pro se party has been permitted to register as an ECF filer for that case.

(B) A motion to file documents under seal, including any exhibits and attachments, and all documents containing material under seal may not be filed or served electronically unless the court orders otherwise. Matters under seal are governed by Circuit Rule 47.1.

(C) Exhibits, attachments, or appendix items that (1) exceed 500 pages or 1500 kilobytes; (2) are not in a format that readily permits electronic filing, such as odd-sized documents; or (3) are illegible when scanned into electronic format may be filed in paper form. Documents filed pursuant to this subsection must be served by an alternative method of service authorized by FRAP 25, and the filer must file electronically a notice of paper filing.

(D) Upon motion and a showing of good cause, the court may exempt a party from the electronic filing requirements and authorize filing by means other than use of the CM/ECF system. See D.C. Cir. Rule 25(b).

ECF–9. Privacy Protection

Unless the court orders otherwise, parties must refrain from including or must redact the following personal data identifiers from documents filed with the court to the extent required by FRAP 25(a)(5):

- Social Security numbers. If an individual's Social Security number must be included, use the last four digits only.
- Financial account numbers. If financial account numbers are relevant, use the last four digits only.
- Names of minors. If the involvement of an individual known to be a minor must be mentioned, use the minor's initials only.
- Dates of birth. If an individual's date of birth must be included, use the year only.
- Home addresses. In criminal cases, if a home address must be included, use the city and state only.

The filer bears sole responsibility for ensuring a document complies with these requirements. Guidance on redacting personal data identifiers is posted on the court's web site and must be followed.

ECF–10. Hyperlinks

(A) Electronically filed documents may contain the following types of hyperlinks:

- Hyperlinks to other portions of the same document or to other documents filed in the case;
- Hyperlinks to documents that are part of the record on appeal or the record on review or enforcement of an agency order;
- Hyperlinks to authorities cited in the document.

(B) Hyperlinks do not replace standard citations to authority and parts of the record; standard citations must be provided in addition to any hyperlink. Hyperlinks are simply mechanisms for accessing material cited in a filed document and are not considered part of this court's record. The court accepts no responsibility for the availability or functionality of any hyperlink and does not endorse any product, organization, or content at any hyperlinked site.

[Dated May 15, 2009, effective June 8, 2009.]

UNITED STATES COURT OF APPEALS FOR THE DISTRICT OF COLUMBIA CIRCUIT PLAN TO IMPLEMENT THE CRIMINAL JUSTICE ACT OF 1964

Pursuant to approval of the Judicial Council for the District of Columbia Circuit (Judicial Council), the United States Court of Appeals for the District of Columbia Circuit hereby adopts the following revised plan for furnishing representation for persons financially unable to obtain adequate representation in the cases and situations defined in 18 U.S.C. § 3006A, as amended (hereinafter, "the Act"). This plan supplements the plan of the United States District Court for the District of Columbia Circuit, unless otherwise specified herein.

I. PROVISION FOR FURNISHING COUNSEL

a) This plan provides for the furnishing of legal services on appeal by the Federal Defender organization for the District of Columbia, established in accordance with the November 8, 1988, amendment to the CJA Plan for the United States District Court for the District of Columbia, which was approved by the Judicial Council on December 15, 1988. In addition, this plan provides for the appointment and compensation of appellate counsel from the list of attorneys established and maintained in accordance with part (b) of this section.

Insofar as practicable, attorney appointments from the list will be made in at least 25 percent of the cases.

b) The Court shall establish a list of attorneys who are members of the Bar of the Court and who have demonstrated experience in appellate litigation. No attorney with less than one year's active membership in the District of Columbia or a state bar shall be included on the list. Completion of an appellate litigation training course may substitute for demonstrated experience.The Chief Judge shall appoint an Attorney Selection Committee to evaluate attorneys' eligibility for the list. This Committee shall consist of two active Circuit Judges, the Federal Public Defender, one experienced criminal law practitioner who is on the list and one who is not on the list. The attorney members shall serve staggered three-year terms and shall be eligible for reappointment to an additional term. The Committee shall re-examine the list annually to assure that it is current, and that its members are qualified. The Committee shall also review the operation and administration of the CJA list over the preceding year and recommend to the Court any changes deemed necessary or appropriate by the Committee regarding the appointment process and panel management.

c) Attorneys who wish to be included on the list may petition the Court in writing, stating their eligibility as defined in section (b) above. The Court may direct the Clerk to add any attorney when satisfied of his or her eligibility.

d) Attorneys may petition the Court in writing to be removed from the list and the Court may so direct the Clerk. A panel, on its own motion, may also recommend to the CJA Committee that an attorney be removed from the list and the CJA Committee may remove an attorney on such a motion or on its own motion.

e) In accordance with Circuit Rule 46(g), law school students may provide assistance to appointed counsel. Counsel may claim costs of compensating students for services rendered, but not for expenses incurred by such students.

II. DETERMINATION OF NEED FOR APPOINTMENT OR CONTINUANCE OF COUNSEL

a) In cases where appointment of counsel was first made by the District Court, the Court will accept the District Court's determination that the party is financially unable to obtain counsel and will make appointment of counsel without further inquiry.

b) In cases where a party for the first time seeks appointment of counsel under the Act on appeal, as further defined in section III(e), the District Court will make appropriate inquiry to determine whether the party is financially unable to obtain counsel. This Court will accept the District Court's determination that the party is financially unable to obtain counsel and make appointment of counsel without further inquiry.

c) If at any stage of an appeal the party claims and the Court, on appropriate inquiry, finds that the party is financially unable to pay counsel whom the party has retained, the Court may make such appointment of counsel or the Federal Public Defender as the interests of justice dictate.

d) The Court may at any time examine or re-examine the financial status of a party for whom counsel has been appointed, and if it is found that any funds are available for payment from or on behalf of the party, it may authorize or direct that such funds be paid to the appointed attorney in lieu of compensation under the Act or to the Court for deposit in the Treasury.

e) It shall be the duty of counsel appointed under the Act to notify the Court of any information coming to counsel's attention indicating that funds may be available for payment from or on behalf of the party, unless the source of the attorney's information is protected as a privileged communication. Counsel may not request or accept from anyone a promise or a payment of any nature in relation to representation of the party, except as authorized or directed by the Court.

f) A copy of the Court's Plan shall be provided to all counsel appointed under the Plan.

III. APPOINTMENT OF COUNSEL

a) In all cases on appeal, where a party was represented in the District Court by court-appointed counsel, such counsel shall continue to represent the party on appeal, except as otherwise noted in subsections (c) and (d).

b) The party may file a written notice with the United States District Court that he or she does not desire to appeal. In such event there shall be no further obligation on counsel to proceed.

c) Application by District Court counsel to be relieved of further obligation to represent the party, or by a party that he or she no longer be represented by District Court counsel, shall be in writing and shall state the reason for the request. Counsel shall state in the application that his or her client has been advised of counsel's desire to be relieved. Counsel shall continue to represent the defendant until relieved by this Court.

d) In situations where counsel is appointed by the District Court under the discretionary power conferred by the Act in petty offenses or other instances, counsel shall advise his or her client of the right to appeal, and if requested to do so, shall file a notice of appeal. Thereafter, application shall be made to this Court for appointment of counsel, and this Court shall determine whether an appointment is required.

e) Where appointed District Court counsel is relieved from further representation, a party who is eligible under the Act is entitled to be represented by appointed counsel on appeal.

Where a party who is eligible under the Act seeks appointment of counsel for the first time on appeal, the Clerk of the District Court shall advise the party that if he or she desires the appointment of counsel, the party must complete the appropriate CJA form and file it with the District Court. The District Court will rule on the application in the first instance; if the District Court determines that the party is not financially eligible for representation, the request for representation may be renewed before the Court of Appeals without filing a new notice of appeal. The Chief Judge, delegate Judge, or panel will review the statement of financial need.

If the party does not desire the appointment of counsel, the party may so advise the Clerk of the

Court of Appeals, by filing with the Clerk a signed statement to that effect.

f) Appointments by the Court of Appeals will be made to the Federal Defender Organization, if the Federal Public Defender so requests, or by selection from the list of attorneys defined in section I(b). In order to ensure the effective supervision and management of the Federal Defender Organization, the Federal Public Defender will be responsible for the assignment of cases among the staff attorneys in that office.

g) Upon the determination of a need for counsel, the Clerk shall notify the Federal Public Defender of that need and the nature of the case. The Federal Defender Organization shall either provide the representation or select as counsel the next attorney on the list who has handled or assisted in a case of equal or greater complexity and who is available to accept the appointment. In making the decision whether to provide the representation or to select an attorney from the list, the Federal Defender Organization must take into account the requirement of section I(a) that insofar as practicable, panel attorney appointments be made in at least 25 percent of the cases.

The Federal Public Defender shall maintain a current list of all attorneys included on the CJA list, with current office addresses and telephone numbers. The Federal Public Defender shall also maintain a record of qualifications and experience of each attorney on the list. The Federal Public Defender shall maintain a public record of assignments to private counsel, as well as statistical data reflecting the proration of appointments between the Federal Defender Organization and private attorneys, according to the formula described in section I(a). Every effort shall be made to ensure that counsel is selected as expeditiously as possible, that selections are equitably distributed and that information on availability of counsel is maintained.

Selections from the list should be made on a rotational basis, subject to the Court's or the Federal Public Defender's discretion to make exceptions in unusual cases due to the nature and complexity of the case and attorney availability. This procedure should result in a balanced distribution of appointments and compensation among the members of the list of attorneys, and quality representation for each person for whom counsel is appointed.

A party is not entitled to have a particular attorney appointed. Counsel appointed shall serve until further order of the Court. Applications to withdraw shall be governed by section III(c).

h) In cases of multiple parties who have been tried together, appointment of counsel on appeal may be one or more attorneys to represent all parties, except that separate counsel shall be appointed for parties who have such conflicting interests that they cannot properly be represented by the same attorney, or when other good cause is shown.

i) The court may, in the interests of justice, substitute one appointed counsel for another at any stage of the appeal proceedings.

j) Subsection (b) of the Act provides, in part, that:

Counsel furnishing representation under the plan shall be selected from a panel of attorneys designated or approved by the court, or from a bar association, legal aid agency, or defender organization furnishing representation pursuant to the plan.

However, when the chief judge, or a circuit judge designated by the chief judge to act on his or her behalf, determines that the appointment of an attorney, who is not a member of the CJA panel, is in the interest of justice, judicial economy or continuity of representation, or there is some other compelling circumstance warranting his or her appointment, the attorney may be admitted to the CJA panel pro hac vice and appointed to represent the CJA defendant. Consideration for preserving the integrity of the panel selection process suggests that such appointments should be made only in exceptional circumstances. Further, the attorney, who may or may not maintain an office in this district, should possess such qualities as would qualify him or her for admission to this district's CJA panel in the ordinary course of panel selection.

IV. DUTY OF COUNSEL AS TO CERTIORARI

The duties of representation by counsel on appeal, where the appeal has been unsuccessful, shall extend to advising the party of the right to file a petition for a writ of certiorari in the Supreme Court of the United States and counsel's opinion on the merits and likelihood of success in obtaining the writ. If the party asks counsel to file a petition for a writ of certiorari and there are non-frivolous grounds for doing so, counsel shall prepare and file a petition. If counsel determines that there are no non-frivolous grounds for seeking a writ of certiorari, counsel shall, within twenty days of judgment, notify the client in writing that counsel will not file a petition, briefly explaining why. Counsel shall also inform the client about the procedures both for filing a petition for certiorari pro se and for asking the Court of Appeals to appoint new counsel to prepare a petition for certiorari. Counsel should caution the party that it is unlikely the Court will appoint new counsel and that the party should be prepared to file a petition for certiorari pro se within the prescribed time. Once counsel has provided this notice to the party, counsel shall notify the Court that counsel's representation has ceased. The Clerk shall notify the party in writing of the effective date of the termination of counsel's appointment. Failure to comply with these procedures may result in the Court's refusal to approve counsel's voucher.

V. PAYMENT OF CLAIMS FOR COMPENSATION AND EXPENSES

a) A person for whom counsel is appointed under the Act is not required to pay filing fees and costs.

b) An attorney appointed by the Court pursuant to Part I(b) of the Plan shall be compensated for services and reimbursed for expenses reasonably incurred within the limitations and subject to the conditions of the Act.

c) The hourly rates of compensation established in accordance with the Act are intended to be maximum rates only and shall be treated as such.

d) For services rendered in this Court on the main appeal from the judgment in a felony or misdemeanor case or a case under subsection (a)(2) of the Act, the total compensation, exclusive of expenses, shall not exceed that authorized by law. However, payments in excess of these limitations may be made to provide fair compensation in a case involving extended or complex representation when so certified by a United States Circuit Judge and approved by the Chief Judge of the Court, or an active Circuit Judge to whom the Chief Judge has delegated review authority.

e) No counsel appointed under the Plan shall accept payment from or on behalf of a party without prior authorization by a United States Circuit Judge on the form provided for such purpose.

f) Each counsel appointed under Part I(b) of the Plan shall be entitled to reimbursement for expenses reasonably incurred in accordance with standards established by the United States Judicial Conference.

g) All claims for compensation and reimbursement for expenses reasonably incurred shall be submitted on the appropriate CJA form, to the Office of the Clerk of the Court of Appeals. Counsel shall identify with specificity the activities for which compensation is claimed. Time claimed for legal research shall be identified by reasonable reference to each issue, whether included or not in the briefs; time claimed for drafting and editing shall be identified by reference to each pleading or section of the brief prepared. Failure to provide sufficient detail to permit meaningful review of a claim may result in delay or denial of approval of the claim. In evaluating the reasonableness of the detail provided for claims relating to legal research and writing done before September 30, 1997, the court will bear in mind that such work was done without notice of the requirement of specificity. The Clerk of the Court of Appeals shall promulgate, with the approval of the Chief Judge, guidelines to assist counsel in meeting this specificity requirement.

The Clerk shall review the claim form for mathematical and technical accuracy and for conformity with the Guidelines for the Administration of the Criminal Justice Act (Volume VII, *Guide to Judiciary Policies and Procedures*). If the form is correct, the Clerk shall forward it to the appropriate judge for consideration. All such claims should be submitted promptly and in any event not more than 45 days after the conclusion of the attorney's representation.

h) Any active member of the Court, if designated by the panel of judges hearing the appeal, shall fix the compensation and allow the reimbursement for expenses to be paid to the appropriate counsel as provided in the Act. If the Court proposes to reduce counsel's compensation, the amount remaining after the proposed reduction shall be paid on an interim basis, and counsel shall be given an opportunity to resubmit a final voucher again claiming the questioned amount, together with any additional information supporting payment of that amount.

i) Counsel's time and expenses involved in the preparation of a petition for a writ of certiorari shall be treated as part of his or her representation before this Court.

j) If an attorney is substituted for one previously appointed in the same case, the total compensation which may be paid both attorneys shall not exceed the statutory maximum for one party, unless the case involves extended or complicated representation. Vouchers for attorney's services shall not be approved until the conclusion of the appeal, unless the Chief Judge directs that interim payment be made in cases where representation is extended or complex.

k) Compensation for services furnished by a partner or associate may be claimed within the maximum compensation allowed by the Act, except that in-court services and travel expenses incurred in connection therewith cannot be allowed unless such partner or associate has been appointed under the Criminal Justice Act.

VI. OPERATION OF THE PLAN

a) This plan incorporates the Guidelines for the Administration of the Criminal Justice Act (18 U.S.C. § 3006A) by reference.

b) The Court will comply with all directives of the Judicial Conference of the United States or the Administrative Office of the U.S. Courts regarding operation of the plan, including allowable reimbursements and the use, preparation, and submission of required forms and reports.

c) This Plan shall be effective on July 1, 1991.

[Effective July 1, 1991. Amended April 8, 1996; October 23, 1996; March 19, 1998; January 3, 2005; June 26, 2007.]

RULES FOR JUDICIAL–CONDUCT AND JUDICIAL–DISABILITY PROCEEDINGS

PREFACE

These Rules were promulgated by the Judicial Conference of the United States, after public comment, pursuant to 28 U.S.C. §§ 331 and 358, to establish standards and procedures for addressing complaints filed by complainants or identified by chief judges, under the Judicial Conduct and Disability Act, 28 U.S.C. §§ 351–364.

ARTICLE I. GENERAL PROVISIONS

RULE 1. SCOPE

These Rules govern proceedings under the Judicial Conduct and Disability Act, 28 U.S.C. §§ 351–364 (the Act), to determine whether a covered judge has engaged in conduct prejudicial to the effective and expeditious administration of the business of the courts or is unable to discharge the duties of office because of mental or physical disability.

[Adopted March 11, 2008, effective April 10, 2008.]

Commentary on Rule 1

In September 2006, the Judicial Conduct and Disability Act Study Committee, appointed in 2004 by Chief Justice Rehnquist and known as the "Breyer Committee," presented a report, known as the "Breyer Committee Report," 239 F.R.D. 116 (Sept. 2006), to Chief Justice Roberts that evaluated implementation of the Judicial Conduct and Disability Act of 1980, 28 U.S.C. §§ 351–364. The Breyer Committee had been formed in response to criticism from the public and the Congress regarding the effectiveness of the Act's implementation. The Executive Committee of the Judicial Conference directed the Judicial Conference Committee on Judicial Conduct and Disability to consider the recommendations made by the Breyer Committee and to report on their implementation to the Conference.

The Breyer Committee found that it could not evaluate implementation of the Act without establishing interpretive standards, Breyer Committee Report, 239 F.R.D. at 132, and that a major problem faced by chief judges in implementing the Act was the lack of authoritative interpretive standards. Id. at 212–15. The Breyer Committee then established standards to guide its evaluation, some of which were new formulations and some of which were taken from the "Illustrative Rules Governing Complaints of Judicial Misconduct and Disability," discussed below. The principal standards used by the Breyer Committee are in Appendix E of its Report. Id. at 238.

Based on the findings of the Breyer Committee, the Judicial Conference Committee on Judicial Conduct and Disability concluded that there was a need for the Judicial Conference to exercise its power under Section 358 of the Act to fashion standards guiding the various officers and bodies who must exercise responsibility under the Act. To that end, the Judicial Conference Committee proposed rules that were based largely on Appendix E of the Breyer Committee Report and the Illustrative Rules.

The Illustrative Rules were originally prepared in 1986 by the Special Committee of the Conference of Chief Judges of the United States Courts of Appeals, and were subsequently revised and amended, most recently in 2000, by the predecessor to the Committee on Judicial Conduct and Disability. The Illustrative Rules were adopted, with minor variations, by circuit judicial councils, to govern complaints under the Judicial Conduct and Disability Act.

After being submitted for public comment pursuant to 28 U.S.C. § 358(c), the present Rules were promulgated by the Judicial Conference on March 11, 2008.

RULE 2. EFFECT AND CONSTRUCTION

(a) Generally. These Rules are mandatory; they supersede any conflicting judicial-council rules. Judicial councils may promulgate additional rules to implement the Act as long as those rules do not conflict with these Rules.

(b) Exception. A Rule will not apply if, when performing duties authorized by the Act, a chief judge, a special committee, a judicial council, the Judicial Conference Committee on Judicial Conduct and Disability, or the Judicial Conference of the United States expressly finds that exceptional circumstances render application of that Rule in a particular proceeding manifestly unjust or contrary to the purposes of the Act or these Rules.

[Adopted March 11, 2008, effective April 10, 2008.]

Commentary on Rule 2

Unlike the Illustrative Rules, these Rules provide mandatory and nationally uniform provisions governing the substantive and procedural aspects of misconduct and disability proceedings under the Act. The mandatory nature of these Rules is authorized by 28 U.S.C. § 358(a) and (c). Judicial councils retain the power to promulgate rules consistent with these Rules. For example, a local rule may authorize the electronic distribution of materials pursuant to Rule 8(b).

Rule 2(b) recognizes that unforeseen and exceptional circumstances may call for a different approach in particular cases.

RULE 3. DEFINITIONS

(a) Chief Judge. "Chief judge" means the chief judge of a United States Court of Appeals, of the United States Court of International Trade, or of the United States Court of Federal Claims.

(b) Circuit Clerk. "Circuit clerk" means a clerk of a United States court of appeals, the clerk of the United States Court of International Trade, the clerk of the United States Court of Federal Claims, or the circuit executive of the United States Court of Appeals for the Federal Circuit.

(c) Complaint. A complaint is:

(1) a document that, in accordance with Rule 6, is filed by any person in his or her individual capacity or on behalf of a professional organization; or

(2) information from any source, other than a document described in (c) (1), that gives a chief judge probable cause to believe that a covered judge, as defined in Rule 4, has engaged in misconduct or may have a disability, whether or not the information is framed as or is intended to be an allegation of misconduct or disability.

(d) Court of Appeals, District Court, and District Judge. "Courts of appeals," "district court," and "district judge," where appropriate, include the United States Court of Federal Claims, the United States Court of International Trade, and the judges thereof.

(e) Disability. "Disability" is a temporary or permanent condition rendering a judge unable to discharge the duties of the particular judicial office. Examples of disability include substance abuse, the inability to stay awake during court proceedings, or a severe impairment of cognitive abilities.

(f) Judicial Council and Circuit. "Judicial council" and "circuit," where appropriate, include any courts designated in 28 U.S.C. § 363.

(g) Magistrate Judge. "Magistrate judge," where appropriate, includes a special master appointed by the Court of Federal Claims under 42 U.S.C. § 300aa–12(c).

(h) Misconduct. Cognizable misconduct:

(1) is conduct prejudicial to the effective and expeditious administration of the business of the courts. Misconduct includes, but is not limited to:

(A) using the judge's office to obtain special treatment for friends or relatives;

(B) accepting bribes, gifts, or other personal favors related to the judicial office;

(C) having improper discussions with parties or counsel for one side in a case;

(D) treating litigants or attorneys in a demonstrably egregious and hostile manner;

(E) engaging in partisan political activity or making inappropriately partisan statements;

(F) soliciting funds for organizations; or

(G) violating other specific, mandatory standards of judicial conduct, such as those pertaining to restrictions on outside income and requirements for financial disclosure.

(2) is conduct occurring outside the performance of official duties if the conduct might have a prejudicial effect on the administration of the business of the courts, including a substantial and widespread lowering of public confidence in the courts among reasonable people.

(3) does not include:

(A) an allegation that is directly related to the merits of a decision or procedural ruling. An allegation that calls into question the correctness of a judge's ruling, including a failure to recuse, without more, is merits-related. If the decision or ruling is alleged to be the result of an improper motive, e.g., a bribe, ex parte contact, racial or ethnic bias, or improper conduct in rendering a decision or ruling, such as personally derogatory remarks irrelevant to the issues, the complaint is not cognizable to the extent that it attacks the merits.

(B) an allegation about delay in rendering a decision or ruling, unless the allegation concerns an improper motive in delaying a particular decision or habitual delay in a significant number of unrelated cases.

(i) Subject Judge. "Subject judge" means any judge described in Rule 4 who is the subject of a complaint.

[Adopted March 11, 2008, effective April 10, 2008.]

Commentary on Rule 3

Rule 3 is derived and adapted from the Breyer Committee Report and the Illustrative Rules.

Unless otherwise specified or the context otherwise indicates, the term "complaint" is used in these Rules to refer both to complaints identified by a chief judge under Rule 5 and to complaints filed by complainants under Rule 6.

Under the Act, a "complaint" may be filed by "any person" or "identified" by a chief judge. See 28 U.S.C. § 351(a) and (b). Under Rule 3(c)(1), complaints may be submitted by a person, in his or her individual capacity, or by a professional organization. Generally, the word "complaint" brings to mind the commencement of an adversary proceeding in which the contending parties are left to present the evidence and legal arguments, and judges play the role of an essentially passive arbiter. The Act, however, establishes an administrative, inquisitorial process. For example, even absent a complaint under Rule 6, chief judges are expected in some circumstances to trigger the process—"identify a complaint," see 28 U.S.C. § 351(b) and Rule 5—and conduct an investigation without becoming a party. See 28 U.S.C. § 352(a); Breyer Committee Report, 239 F.R.D. at 214; Illustrative Rule 2(j). Even when a complaint is filed by someone other than the chief judge, the complainant lacks many rights that a litigant would have, and the chief judge, instead of being limited to the "four corners of the complaint," must, under Rule 11, proceed as though misconduct or disability has been alleged where the complainant reveals information of misconduct or disability but does not claim it as such. See Breyer Committee Report, 239 F.R.D. at 183–84.

An allegation of misconduct or disability filed under Rule 6 is a "complaint," and the Rule so provides in subsection (c)(1). However, both the nature of the process and the use of the term "identify" suggest that the word "complaint" covers more than a document formally triggering the process. The process relies on chief judges considering known information and triggering the process when appropriate. "Identifying" a "complaint," therefore, is best understood as the chief judge's concluding that information known to the judge constitutes probable cause to believe that misconduct occurred or a disability exists, whether or not the information is framed as, or intended to be an accusation. This definition is codified in (c)(2).

Rule 3(e) relates to disability and provides only the most general definition, recognizing that a fact-specific approach is the only one available.

The phrase "prejudicial to the effective and expeditious administration of the business of the courts" is not subject to precise definition, and subsection (h)(1) therefore provides some specific examples. Although the Code of Conduct for United States Judges may be informative, its main precepts are highly general; the Code is in many potential applications aspirational rather than a set of disciplinary rules. Ultimately, the responsibility for determining what constitutes misconduct under the statute is the province of the judicial council of the circuit subject to such review and limitations as are ordained by the statute and by these Rules.

Even where specific, mandatory rules exist—for example, governing the receipt of gifts by judges, outside earned income, and financial disclosure obligations—the distinction between the misconduct statute and the specific, mandatory rules must be borne in mind. For example, an inadvertent, minor violation of any one of these Rules, promptly remedied when called to the attention of the judge, might still be a violation but might not rise to the level of misconduct under the statute. By contrast, a pattern of such violations of the Code might well rise to the level of misconduct.

An allegation can meet the statutory standard even though the judge's alleged conduct did not occur in the course of the performance of official duties. The Code of Conduct for United States Judges expressly covers a wide range of extra-official activities, and some of these activities may constitute misconduct. For example, allegations that a judge solicited funds for a charity or participated in a partisan political event are cognizable under the Act.

On the other hand, judges are entitled to some leeway in extra-official activities. For example, misconduct may not include a judge being repeatedly and publicly discourteous to a spouse (not including physical abuse) even though this might cause some reasonable people to have diminished confidence in the courts. Rule 3(h)(2) states that conduct of this sort is covered, for example, when it might lead to a "substantial and widespread" lowering of such confidence.

Rule 3(h)(3)(A) tracks the Act, 28 U.S.C. § 352(b)(1)(A)(ii), in excluding from the definition of misconduct allegations "[d]irectly related to the merits of a decision or procedural ruling." This exclusion preserves the independence of judges in the exercise of judicial power by ensuring that the complaint procedure is not used to collaterally attack the substance of a judge's ruling. Any allegation that calls into question the correctness of an official action of a judge—without more—is merits-related. The phrase "decision or procedural ruling" is not limited to rulings issued in deciding Article III cases or controversies. Thus, a complaint challenging the correctness of a chief judge's determination to dismiss a prior misconduct complaint would be properly dismissed as merits-related—in other words, as challenging the substance of the judge's administrative determination to dismiss the complaint—even though it does not concern the judge's rulings in Article III litigation. Similarly, an allegation that a judge had incorrectly declined to approve a Criminal Justice Act voucher is merits-related under this standard.

Conversely, an allegation—however unsupported—that a judge conspired with a prosecutor to make a particular ruling is not merits-related, even though it "relates" to a ruling in a colloquial sense. Such an allegation attacks the propriety of conspiring with the prosecutor and goes beyond a challenge to the correctness—"the merits"—of the ruling itself. An allegation that a judge ruled against the complainant because the complainant is a member of a particular racial or ethnic group, or because the judge dislikes the complainant personally, is also not merits-related. Such an allegation attacks the propriety of arriving at rulings with an illicit or improper motive. Similarly, an allegation that a judge used an inappropriate term to refer to a class of people is not merits-related even if the judge used it on the bench or in an opinion; the correctness of the judge's rulings is not at stake. An allegation that a judge treated litigants or attorneys in a demonstrably egregious and hostile manner while on the bench is also not merits-related.

The existence of an appellate remedy is usually irrelevant to whether an allegation is merits-related. The merits-related ground for dismissal exists to protect judges' independence in making rulings, not to protect or promote the appellate process. A complaint alleging an incorrect ruling is merits-related even though the complainant has no recourse from that ruling. By the same token, an allegation that is otherwise cognizable under the Act should not be dismissed merely because an appellate remedy appears to exist (for example, vacating a ruling that resulted from an improper ex parte communication). However, there may be occasions when appellate and misconduct proceedings overlap, and consideration and disposition of a complaint under these Rules may be properly deferred by a chief judge until the appellate proceedings are concluded in order to avoid, inter alia, inconsistent decisions.

Because of the special need to protect judges' independence in deciding what to say in an opinion or ruling, a somewhat different standard applies to determine the merits-relatedness of a non-frivolous allegation that a judge's language in a ruling reflected an improper motive. If the judge's language was relevant to the case at hand—for example a statement that a claim is legally or factually "frivolous"—then the judge's choice of language is presumptively merits-related and excluded, absent evidence apart from the ruling itself suggesting an improper motive. If, on the other hand, the challenged language does not seem relevant on its face, then an additional inquiry under Rule 11 is necessary.

With regard to Rule 3(h)(3)(B), a complaint of delay in a single case is excluded as merits-related. Such an allegation may be said to challenge the correctness of an official action of the judge—in other words, assigning a low priority to deciding the particular case. But, by the same token, an allegation of a habitual pattern of delay in a significant number of unrelated cases, or an allegation of deliberate delay in a single case arising out of an illicit motive, is not merits-related.

The remaining subsections of Rule 3 provide technical definitions clarifying the application of the Rules to the various kinds of courts covered.

RULE 4. COVERED JUDGES

A complaint under these Rules may concern the actions or capacity only of judges of United States courts of appeals, judges of United States district courts, judges of United States bankruptcy courts, United States magistrate judges, and judges of the courts specified in 28 U.S.C. § 363.

[Adopted March 11, 2008, effective April 10, 2008.]

Commentary on Rule 4

This Rule tracks the Act. Rule 8(c) and (d) contain provisions as to the handling of complaints against persons not covered by the Act, such as other court personnel, or against both covered judges and noncovered persons.

ARTICLE II. INITIATION OF A COMPLAINT

RULE 5. IDENTIFICATION OF A COMPLAINT

(a) Identification. When a chief judge has information constituting reasonable grounds for inquiry into whether a covered judge has engaged in misconduct or has a disability, the chief judge may conduct an inquiry, as he or she deems appropriate, into the accuracy of the information even if no related complaint has been filed. A chief judge who finds probable cause to believe that misconduct has occurred or that a disability exists may seek an informal resolution that he or she finds satisfactory. If no informal resolution is achieved or is feasible, the chief judge may identify a complaint and, by written order stating the reasons, begin the review provided in Rule 11. If the evidence of misconduct is clear and convincing and no informal resolution is achieved or is feasible, the chief judge must identify a complaint. A chief judge must not decline to identify a complaint merely because the person making the allegation has not filed a complaint under Rule 6. This Rule is subject to Rule 7.

(b) Noncompliance with Rule 6(d). Rule 6 complaints that do not comply with the requirements of Rule 6(d) must be considered under this Rule.

[Adopted March 11, 2008, effective April 10, 2008.]

Commentary on Rule 5

This Rule is adapted from the Breyer Committee Report, 239 F.R.D. at 245–46.

The Act authorizes the chief judge, by written order stating reasons, to identify a complaint and thereby dispense with the filing of a written complaint. See 28 U.S.C. § 351(b). Under Rule 5, when a chief judge becomes aware of information constituting reasonable grounds to inquire into possible misconduct or disability on the part of a covered judge, and no formal complaint has been filed, the chief judge has the power in his or her discretion to begin an appropriate inquiry. A chief judge's decision whether to informally seek a resolution and/or to identify a complaint is guided by the results of that inquiry. If the chief judge concludes that there is probable cause to believe that misconduct has occurred or a disability exists, the chief judge may seek an informal resolution, if feasible, and if failing in that, may identify a complaint. Discretion is accorded largely for the reasons police officers and prosecutors have discretion in making arrests or bringing charges. The matter may be trivial and isolated, based on marginal evidence, or otherwise highly unlikely to lead to a misconduct or disability finding. On the other hand, if the inquiry leads the chief judge to conclude that there is clear and convincing evidence of misconduct or a disability, and no satisfactory informal resolution has been achieved or is feasible, the chief judge is required to identify a complaint.

An informal resolution is one agreed to by the subject judge and found satisfactory by the chief judge. Because an informal resolution under Rule 5 reached before a complaint is filed under Rule 6 will generally cause a subsequent Rule 6 complaint alleging the identical matter to be concluded, see Rule 11(d), the chief judge must be sure that the resolution is fully appropriate before endorsing it. In doing so, the chief judge must balance the seriousness of the matter against the particular judge's alacrity in addressing the issue. The availability of this procedure should encourage attempts at swift remedial action before a formal complaint is filed.

When a complaint is identified, a written order stating the reasons for the identification must be provided; this begins the process articulated in Rule 11. Rule 11 provides that once the chief judge has identified a complaint, the chief judge, subject to the disqualification provisions of Rule 25, will perform, with respect to that complaint, all functions assigned to the chief judge for the determination of complaints filed by a complainant.

In high-visibility situations, it may be desirable for the chief judge to identify a complaint without first seeking an informal resolution (and then, if the circumstances warrant, dismiss or conclude the identified complaint without appointment of a special committee) in order to assure the public that the allegations have not been ignored.

A chief judge's decision not to identify a complaint under Rule 5 is not appealable and is subject to Rule 3(h)(3)(A), which excludes merits-related complaints from the definition of misconduct.

A chief judge may not decline to identify a complaint solely on the basis that the unfiled allegations could be raised by one or more persons in a filed complaint, but none of these persons has opted to do so.

Subsection (a) concludes by stating that this Rule is "subject to Rule 7." This is intended to establish that only: (i) the chief judge of the home circuit of a potential subject judge, or (ii) the chief judge of a circuit in which misconduct is alleged to have occurred in the course of official business while the potential subject judge was sitting by designation, shall have the power or a duty under this Rule to identify a complaint.

Subsection (b) provides that complaints filed under Rule 6 that do not comply with the requirements of Rule 6(d), must be considered under this Rule. For instance, if a complaint has been filed but the form submitted is unsigned, or the truth of the statements therein are not verified in writing under penalty of perjury, then a chief judge must nevertheless consider the allegations as known information, and proceed to follow the process described in Rule 5(a).

RULE 6. FILING A COMPLAINT

(a) Form. A complainant may use the form reproduced in the appendix to these Rules or a form designated by the rules of the judicial council in the circuit in which the complaint is filed. A complaint form is also available on each court of appeals' website or may be obtained from the circuit clerk or any district court or bankruptcy court within the circuit. A form is not necessary to file a complaint, but the complaint must be written and must include the information described in (b).

(b) Brief Statement of Facts. A complaint must contain a concise statement that details the specific facts on which the claim of misconduct or disability is based. The statement of facts should include a description of:

(1) what happened;

(2) when and where the relevant events happened;

(3) any information that would help an investigator check the facts; and

(4) for an allegation of disability, any additional facts that form the basis of that allegation.

(c) Legibility. A complaint should be typewritten if possible. If not typewritten, it must be legible. An illegible complaint will be returned to the complainant with a request to resubmit it in legible form. If a resubmitted complaint is still illegible, it will not be accepted for filing.

(d) Complainant's Address and Signature; Verification. The complainant must provide a contact address and sign the complaint. The truth of the statements made in the complaint must be verified in writing under penalty of perjury. If any of these requirements are not met, the complaint will be accepted for filing, but it will be reviewed under only Rule 5(b).

(e) Number of Copies; Envelope Marking. The complainant shall provide the number of copies of the complaint required by local rule. Each copy should be in an envelope marked "Complaint of Misconduct" or "Complaint of Disability." The envelope must not show the name of any subject judge.

[Adopted March 11, 2008, effective April 10, 2008.]

Commentary on Rule 6

The Rule is adapted from the Illustrative Rules and is self-explanatory.

RULE 7. WHERE TO INITIATE COMPLAINTS

(a) Where to File. Except as provided in (b),

(1) a complaint against a judge of a United States court of appeals, a United States district court, a United States bankruptcy court, or a United States magistrate judge must be filed with the circuit clerk in the jurisdiction in which the subject judge holds office.

(2) a complaint against a judge of the United States Court of International Trade or the United States Court of Federal Claims must be filed with the respective clerk of that court.

(3) a complaint against a judge of the United States Court of Appeals for the Federal Circuit must be filed with the circuit executive of that court.

(b) Misconduct in Another Circuit; Transfer. If a complaint alleges misconduct in the course of official business while the subject judge was sitting on a court by designation under 28 U.S.C. §§ 291–293 and 294(d), the complaint may be filed or identified with the circuit clerk of that circuit or of the subject judge's home circuit. The proceeding will continue in the circuit of the first-filed or first-identified complaint. The judicial council of the circuit where the complaint was first filed or first identified may transfer the complaint to the subject judge's home circuit or to the circuit where the alleged misconduct occurred, as the case may be.

[Adopted March 11, 2008, effective April 10, 2008.]

Commentary on Rule 7

Title 28 U.S.C. § 351 states that complaints are to be filed with "the clerk of the court of appeals for the circuit." However, in many circuits, this role is filled by circuit executives. Accordingly, the term "circuit clerk," as defined in Rule 3(b) and used throughout these Rules, applies to circuit executives.

Section 351 uses the term "the circuit" in a way that suggests that either the home circuit of the subject judge or the circuit in which misconduct is alleged to have occurred is the proper venue for complaints. With an exception for judges sitting by designation, the Rule requires the identifying or filing of a misconduct or disability complaint in the circuit in which the judge holds office, largely based on the administrative perspective of the Act. Given the Act's emphasis on the future conduct of the business of the courts, the circuit in which the judge holds office is the appropriate forum because that circuit is likely best able to influence a judge's future behavior in constructive ways.

However, when judges sit by designation, the non-home circuit has a strong interest in redressing misconduct in the course of official business, and where allegations also involve a member of the bar—ex parte contact between an attorney and a judge, for example—it may often be desirable to have the judicial and bar misconduct proceedings take place in the same venue. Rule 7(b), therefore, allows transfer to, or filing or identification of a complaint in, the non-home circuit. The proceeding may be transferred by the judicial council of the filing or identified circuit to the other circuit.

RULE 8. ACTION BY CLERK

(a) Receipt of Complaint. Upon receiving a complaint against a judge filed under Rule 5 or 6, the circuit clerk must open a file, assign a docket number according to a uniform numbering scheme promulgated by the Judicial Conference Committee on Judicial Conduct and Disability, and acknowledge the complaint's receipt.

(b) Distribution of Copies. The clerk must promptly send copies of a complaint filed under Rule 6 to the chief judge or the judge authorized to act as chief judge under Rule 25(f), and copies of complaints filed under Rule 5 or 6 to each subject judge. The clerk must retain the original complaint. Any further distribution should be as provided by local rule.

(c) Complaints Against Noncovered Persons. If the clerk receives a complaint about a person not holding an office described in Rule 4, the clerk must not accept the complaint for filing under these Rules.

(d) Receipt of Complaint About a Judge and Another Noncovered Person. If a complaint is received about a judge described in Rule 4 and a person not holding an office described in Rule 4, the clerk must accept the complaint for filing under these Rules only with regard to the judge and must inform the complainant of the limitation.

[Adopted March 11, 2008, effective April 10, 2008.]

Commentary on Rule 8

This Rule is adapted from the Illustrative Rules and is largely self-explanatory.

The uniform docketing scheme described in subsection (a) should take into account potential problems associated with a complaint that names multiple judges. One solution may be to provide separate docket numbers for each subject judge. Separate docket numbers would help avoid difficulties in tracking cases, particularly if a complaint is dismissed with respect to some, but not all of the named judges.

Complaints against noncovered persons are not to be accepted for processing under these Rules but may, of course, be accepted under other circuit rules or procedures for grievances.

RULE 9. TIME FOR FILING OR IDENTIFYING A COMPLAINT

A complaint may be filed or identified at any time. If the passage of time has made an accurate and fair investigation of a complaint impractical, the complaint must be dismissed under Rule 11(c)(1)(E).

[Adopted March 11, 2008, effective April 10, 2008.]

Commentary on Rule 9

This Rule is adapted from the Act, 28 U.S.C. §§ 351, 352(b)(1)(A)(iii), and the Illustrative Rules.

RULE 10. ABUSE OF THE COMPLAINT PROCEDURE

(a) Abusive Complaints. A complainant who has filed repetitive, harassing, or frivolous complaints, or has otherwise abused the complaint procedure, may be restricted from filing further complaints. After giving the complainant an opportunity to show cause in writing why his or her right to file further complaints should not be limited, a judicial council may prohibit, restrict, or impose conditions on the complainant's use of the complaint procedure. Upon written request of the complainant, the judicial council may revise or withdraw any prohibition, restriction, or condition previously imposed.

(b) Orchestrated Complaints. When many essentially identical complaints from different complainants are received and appear to be part of an orchestrated campaign, the chief judge may recommend that the judicial council issue a written order instructing the circuit clerk to accept only a certain number of such complaints for filing and to refuse to accept further ones. The clerk must send a copy of any such order to anyone whose complaint was not accepted.

[Adopted March 11, 2008, effective April 10, 2008.]

Commentary on Rule 10

This Rule is adapted from the Illustrative Rules.

Rule 10(a) provides a mechanism for a judicial council to restrict the filing of further complaints by a single complainant who has abused the complaint procedure. In some instances, however, the complaint procedure may be abused in a manner for which the remedy provided in Rule 10(a) may not be appropriate. For example, some circuits have been inundated with submissions of dozens or hundreds of essentially identical complaints against the same judge or judges, all submitted by different complainants. In many of these instances, persons with grievances against a particular judge or judges used the Internet or other technology to orchestrate mass complaint-filing campaigns against them. If each complaint submitted as part of such a campaign were accepted for filing and processed according to these Rules, there would be a serious drain on court resources without any benefit to the adjudication of the underlying merits.

A judicial council may, therefore, respond to such mass filings under Rule 10(b) by declining to accept repetitive complaints for filing, regardless of the fact that the complaints are nominally submitted by different complainants. When the first complaint or complaints have been dismissed on the merits, and when further, essentially identical submissions follow, the judicial council may issue a second order noting that these are identical or repetitive complaints, directing the circuit clerk not to accept these complaints or any further such complaints for filing, and directing the clerk to send each putative complainant copies of both orders.

ARTICLE III. REVIEW OF A COMPLAINT BY THE CHIEF JUDGE

RULE 11. REVIEW BY THE CHIEF JUDGE

(a) Purpose of Chief Judge's Review. When a complaint is identified by the chief judge or is filed, the chief judge must review it unless the chief judge is disqualified under Rule 25. If the complaint contains information constituting evidence of misconduct or disability, but the complainant does not claim it as such, the chief judge must treat the complaint as if it did allege misconduct or disability and give notice to the subject judge. After reviewing the complaint, the chief judge must determine whether it should be:

(1) dismissed;

(2) concluded on the ground that voluntary corrective action has been taken;

(3) concluded because intervening events have made action on the complaint no longer necessary; or

(4) referred to a special committee.

(b) Inquiry by Chief Judge. In determining what action to take under Rule 11(a), the chief judge may conduct a limited inquiry. The chief judge, or a designee, may communicate orally or in writing with the complainant, the subject judge, and any others who may have knowledge of the matter, and may review transcripts or other relevant documents. In conducting the inquiry, the chief judge must not determine any reasonably disputed issue.

(c) Dismissal.

(1) *Allowable Grounds.* A complaint must be dismissed in whole or in part to the extent that the chief judge concludes that the complaint:

(A) alleges conduct that, even if true, is not prejudicial to the effective and expeditious administration of the business of the courts and does not indicate a mental or physical disability resulting in inability to discharge the duties of judicial office;

(B) is directly related to the merits of a decision or procedural ruling;

(C) is frivolous;

(D) is based on allegations lacking sufficient evidence to raise an inference that misconduct has occurred or that a disability exists;

(E) is based on allegations which are incapable of being established through investigation;

(F) has been filed in the wrong circuit under Rule 7; or

(G) is otherwise not appropriate for consideration under the Act.

(2) *Disallowed Grounds.* A complaint must not be dismissed solely because it repeats allegations of a previously dismissed complaint if it also contains material information not previously considered and does not constitute harassment of the subject judge.

(d) Corrective Action. The chief judge may conclude the complaint proceeding in whole or in part if:

(1) an informal resolution under Rule 5 satisfactory to the chief judge was reached before the complaint was filed under Rule 6, or

(2) the chief judge determines that the subject judge has taken appropriate voluntary corrective action that acknowledges and remedies the problems raised by the complaint.

(e) Intervening Events. The chief judge may conclude the complaint proceeding in whole or in part upon determining that intervening events render some or all of the allegations moot or make remedial action impossible.

(f) Appointment of Special Committee. If some or all of the complaint is not dismissed or concluded, the chief judge must promptly appoint a special committee to investigate the complaint or any relevant portion of it and to make recommendations to the judicial council. Before appointing a special committee, the chief judge must invite the subject judge to respond to the complaint either orally or in writing if the judge was not given an opportunity during the limited inquiry. In the chief judge's discretion, separate complaints may be joined and assigned to a single special committee. Similarly, a single complaint about more than one judge may be severed and more than one special committee appointed.

(g) Notice of Chief Judge's Action; Petitions for Review.

(1) *When Special Committee Is Appointed.* If a special committee is appointed, the chief judge must notify the complainant and the subject judge that the matter has been referred to a special committee and identify the members of the committee. A copy of the order appointing the special committee must be sent to the Judicial Conference Committee on Judicial Conduct and Disability.

(2) *When Chief Judge Disposes of Complaint Without Appointing Special Committee.* If the chief judge disposes of the complaint under Rule 11(c), (d), or (e), the chief judge must prepare a supporting memorandum that sets forth the reasons for the disposition. Except as authorized by 28 U.S.C. § 360, the memorandum must not include the name of the complainant or of the subject judge. The order and the supporting memorandum, which may be one document, must be provided to the complainant, the subject judge, and the Judicial Conference Committee on Judicial Conduct and Disability.

(3) *Right of Petition for Review.* If the chief judge disposes of a complaint under Rule 11(c), (d), or (e), the complainant and subject judge must be notified of the right to petition the judicial council for review of the disposition, as provided in Rule 18. If a petition for review is filed, the chief judge must promptly transmit all materials obtained in connection with the inquiry under Rule 11(b) to the circuit clerk for transmittal to the judicial council.

(h) Public Availability of Chief Judge's Decision. The chief judge's decision must be made public to the extent, at the time, and in the manner provided in Rule 24.

[Adopted March 11, 2008, effective April 10, 2008.]

Commentary on Rule 11

Subsection (a) lists the actions available to a chief judge in reviewing a complaint. This subsection provides that where a complaint has been filed under Rule 6, the ordinary doctrines of waiver do not apply. A chief judge must identify as a complaint any misconduct or disability issues raised by the factual allegations of the complaint even if the complainant makes no such claim with regard to those issues. For example, an allegation limited to misconduct in fact-finding that mentions periods during a trial when the judge was asleep must be treated as a complaint regarding disability. Some formal order giving notice of the expanded scope of the proceeding must be given to the subject judge.

Subsection (b) describes the nature of the chief judge's inquiry. It is based largely on the Breyer Committee Report, 239 F.R.D. at 243–45. The Act states that dismissal is appropriate "when a limited inquiry . . . demonstrates that the allegations in the complaint lack any factual foundation or are conclusively refuted by objective evidence." 28 U.S.C. § 352(b)(1)(B). At the same time, however, Section 352(a) states that "[t]he chief judge shall not undertake to make findings of fact about any matter that is reasonably in dispute." These two statutory standards should be read together, so that a matter is not "reasonably" in dispute if a limited inquiry shows that the allegations do not constitute misconduct or disability, that they lack any reliable factual foundation, or that they are conclusively refuted by objective evidence.

In conducting a limited inquiry under subsection (b), the chief judge must avoid determinations of reasonably disputed issues, including reasonably disputed issues as to whether the facts alleged constitute misconduct or disability, which are ordinarily left to a special committee and the judicial council. An allegation of fact is ordinarily not "refuted" simply because the subject judge denies it. The limited inquiry must reveal something more in the way of refutation before it is appropriate to dismiss a complaint that is otherwise cognizable. If it is the complainant's word against the subject judge's—in other words, there is simply no other significant evidence of what happened or of the complainant's unreliability—then there must be a special-committee investigation. Such a credibility issue is a matter "reasonably in dispute" within the meaning of the Act.

However, dismissal following a limited inquiry may occur when the complaint refers to transcripts or to witnesses and the chief judge determines that the transcripts and witnesses all support the subject judge. Breyer Committee Report, 239 F.R.D. at 243. For example, consider a complaint alleging that the subject judge said X, and the complaint mentions, or it is independently clear, that five people may have heard what the judge said. Id. The chief judge is told by the subject judge and one witness that the judge did not say X, and the chief judge dismisses the complaint without questioning the other four possible witnesses. Id. In this example, the matter remains reasonably in dispute. If all five witnesses say the judge did not say X, dismissal is appropriate, but if potential witnesses who are reasonably accessible have not been questioned, then the matter remains reasonably in dispute. Id.

Similarly, under (c)(1)(A), if it is clear that the conduct or disability alleged, even if true, is not cognizable under these Rules, the complaint should be dismissed. If that issue is reasonably in dispute, however, dismissal under (c)(1)(A) is inappropriate.

Essentially, the standard articulated in subsection (b) is that used to decide motions for summary judgment pursuant to Fed. R. Civ. P. 56. Genuine issues of material fact are not resolved at the summary judgment stage. A material fact is one that "might affect the outcome of the suit under the governing law," and a dispute is "genuine" if "the evidence is such that a reasonable jury could return a verdict for the nonmoving party." *Anderson v. Liberty Lobby*, 477 U.S. 242, 248 (1986). Similarly, the chief judge may not resolve a genuine issue concerning a material fact or the existence of misconduct or a disability when conducting a limited inquiry pursuant to subsection (b).

Subsection (c) describes the grounds on which a complaint may be dismissed. These are adapted from the Act, 28 U.S.C. § 352(b), and the Breyer Committee Report, 239 F.R.D. at 239–45. Subsection (c)(1)(A) permits dismissal of an allegation that, even if true, does not constitute misconduct or disability under the statutory standard. The proper standards are set out in Rule 3 and discussed in the Commentary on that Rule. Subsection (c)(1)(B) permits dismissal of complaints related to the merits of a decision by a subject judge; this standard is also governed by Rule 3 and its accompanying Commentary.

Subsections (c)(1)(C)–(E) implement the statute by allowing dismissal of complaints that are "frivolous, lacking sufficient evidence to raise an inference that misconduct has occurred, or containing allegations which are incapable of being established through investigation." 28 U.S.C. § 352(b)(1)(A)(iii).

Dismissal of a complaint as "frivolous," under Rule 11(c)(1)(C), will generally occur without any inquiry beyond the face of the complaint. For instance, when the allegations are facially incredible or so lacking in indicia of reliability that no further inquiry is warranted, dismissal under this subsection is appropriate.

A complaint warranting dismissal under Rule 11(c)(1)(D) is illustrated by the following example. Consider a complainant who alleges an impropriety and asserts that he knows of it because it was observed and reported to him by a person who is identified. The judge denies that the event occurred. When contacted, the source also denies it. In such a case, the chief judge's proper course of action may turn on whether the source had any role in the allegedly improper conduct. If the complaint was based on a lawyer's statement that he or she had an improper ex parte contact with a judge, the lawyer's denial of the impropriety might not be taken as wholly persuasive, and it would be appropriate to conclude that a real factual issue is raised. On the other hand, if the complaint quoted a disinterested third party and that disinterested party denied that the statement had been made, there would be no value in opening a formal investigation. In such a case, it would be appropriate to dismiss the complaint under Rule 11(c)(1)(D).

Rule 11(c)(1)(E) is intended, among other things, to cover situations when no evidence is offered or identified, or when the only identified source is unavailable. Breyer Committee Report, 239 F.R.D. at 243. For example, a complaint alleges that an unnamed attorney told the complainant that the judge did X. Id. The subject judge denies it. The chief judge requests that the complainant (who does not purport to have observed the judge do X) identify the unnamed witness, or that the unnamed witness come forward so that the chief judge can learn the unnamed witness's account. Id. The complainant responds that he has spoken with the unnamed witness, that the unnamed witness is an attorney who practices in federal court, and that the unnamed witness is unwilling to be identified or to come forward. Id. at 243–44. The allegation is then properly dismissed as containing allegations that are incapable of being established through investigation. Id.

If, however, the situation involves a reasonable dispute over credibility, the matter should proceed. For example, the complainant alleges an impropriety and alleges that he or she observed it and that there were no other witnesses; the subject judge denies that the event occurred. Unless the complainant's allegations are facially incredible or so lacking indicia of reliability warranting dismissal under Rule 11(c)(1)(C), a special committee must be appointed because there is a material factual question that is reasonably in dispute.

Dismissal is also appropriate when a complaint is filed so long after an alleged event that memory loss, death, or changes to unknown residences prevent a proper investigation.

Subsection (c)(2) indicates that the investigative nature of the process prevents the application of claim preclusion principles where new and material evidence becomes available. However, it also recognizes that at some point a renewed investigation may constitute harassment of the subject judge and should be foregone, depending of course on the seriousness of the issues and the weight of the new evidence.

Rule 11(d) implements the Act's provision for dismissal if voluntary appropriate corrective action has been taken. It is largely adapted from the Breyer Committee Report, 239 F.R.D. 244–45. The Act authorizes the chief judge to conclude the proceedings if "appropriate corrective action has been taken." 28 U.S.C. § 352(b)(2). Under the Rule, action taken after the complaint is filed is "appropriate" when it acknowledges and remedies the problem raised by the complaint. Breyer Committee Report, 239 F.R.D. at 244. Because the Act deals with the conduct of judges, the emphasis is on correction of the judicial conduct that was the subject of the complaint. Id. Terminating a complaint based on corrective action is premised on the implicit understanding that voluntary self-correction or redress of misconduct or a disability is preferable to sanctions. Id. The chief judge may facilitate this process by giving the subject judge an objective view of the appearance of the judicial conduct in question and by suggesting appropriate corrective measures. Id. Moreover, when corrective action is taken under Rule 5 satisfactory to the chief judge before a complaint is filed, that informal resolution will be sufficient to conclude a subsequent complaint based on the identical conduct.

"Corrective action" must be voluntary action taken by the subject judge. Breyer Committee Report, 239 F.R.D. at 244. A remedial action directed by the chief judge or by an appellate court without the participation of the subject judge in formulating the directive or without the subject judge's subsequent agreement to such action does not constitute the requisite voluntary corrective action. Id. Neither the chief judge nor an appellate court has authority under the Act to impose a formal remedy or sanction; only the judicial council can impose a formal remedy or sanction under 28 U.S.C. § 354(a)(2). Id. Compliance with a previous council order may serve as corrective action allowing conclusion of a later complaint about the same behavior. Id.

Where a judge's conduct has resulted in identifiable, particularized harm to the complainant or another individual, appropriate corrective action should include steps taken by that judge to acknowledge and redress the harm, if possible, such as by an apology, recusal from a case, or a pledge to refrain from similar conduct in the future. Id. While the Act is generally forward-looking, any corrective action should, to the extent possible, serve to correct a specific harm to an individual, if such harm can reasonably be remedied. Id. In some cases, corrective action may not be "appropriate" to justify conclusion of a complaint unless the complainant or other individual harmed is meaningfully apprised of the nature of the corrective action in the chief judge's order, in a direct communication from the subject judge, or otherwise. Id.

Voluntary corrective action should be proportionate to any plausible allegations of misconduct in the complaint. The form of corrective action should also be proportionate to any sanctions that a judicial council might impose under Rule 20(b), such as a private or public reprimand or a change in case assignments. Breyer Committee Report, 239 F.R.D at 244–45. In other words, minor corrective action will not suffice to dispose of a serious matter. Id.

Rule 11(e) implements Section 352(b)(2) of the Act, which permits the chief judge to "conclude the proceeding," if "action on the complaint is no longer necessary because of intervening events," such as a resignation from judicial office. Ordinarily, however, stepping down from an administrative post such as chief judge, judicial-council member, or court-committee chair does not constitute an event rendering unnecessary any further action on a complaint alleging judicial misconduct. Breyer Committee Report, 239 F.R.D. at 245. As long as the subject of the complaint performs judicial duties, a complaint alleging judicial misconduct must be addressed. Id.

If a complaint is not disposed of pursuant to Rule 11(c), (d), or (e), a special committee must be appointed. Rule 11(f) states that a subject judge must be invited to respond to the complaint before a special committee is appointed, if no earlier response was invited.

Subject judges, of course, receive copies of complaints at the same time that they are referred to the chief judge, and they are free to volunteer responses to them. Under Rule 11(b), the chief judge may request a response if it is thought necessary. However, many complaints are clear candidates for dismissal even if their allegations are accepted as true, and there is no need for the subject judge to devote time to a defense.

The Act requires that the order dismissing a complaint or concluding the proceeding contain a statement of reasons and that a copy of the order be sent to the complainant. 28 U.S.C. § 352(b). Rule 24, dealing with availability of information to the public, contemplates that the order will be made public, usually without disclosing the names of the complainant or the subject judge. If desired for administrative purposes, more identifying information can be included in a non-public version of the order.

When complaints are disposed of by chief judges, the statutory purposes are best served by providing the complainant with a full, particularized, but concise explanation, giving reasons for the conclusions reached. See also Commentary on Rule 24, dealing with public availability.

Rule 11(g) provides that the complainant and subject judge must be notified, in the case of a disposition by the chief judge, of the right to petition the judicial council for review. A copy of a chief judge's order and memorandum, which may be one document, disposing of a complaint must be sent by the circuit clerk to the Judicial Conference Committee on Judicial Conduct and Disability.

ARTICLE IV. INVESTIGATION AND REPORT BY SPECIAL COMMITTEE

RULE 12. COMPOSITION OF SPECIAL COMMITTEE

(a) Membership. Except as provided in (e), a special committee appointed under Rule 11(f) must consist of the chief judge and equal numbers of circuit and district judges. If the complaint is about a district judge, bankruptcy judge, or magistrate judge, then, when possible, the district-judge members of the committee must be from districts other than the district of the subject judge. For the courts named in 28 U.S.C. § 363, the committee must be selected from the judges serving on the subject judge's court.

(b) Presiding Officer. When appointing the committee, the chief judge may serve as the presiding officer or else must designate a committee member as the presiding officer.

(c) Bankruptcy Judge or Magistrate Judge as Adviser. If the subject judge is a bankruptcy judge or magistrate judge, he or she may, within 14 days after being notified of the committee's appointment, ask the chief judge to designate as a committee adviser another bankruptcy judge or magistrate judge, as the case may be. The chief judge must grant such a request but may otherwise use discretion in naming the adviser. Unless the adviser is a Court of Federal Claims special master appointed under 42 U.S.C. § 300aa–12(c), the adviser must be from a district other than the district of the subject bankruptcy judge or subject magistrate judge. The adviser cannot vote but has the other privileges of a committee member.

(d) Provision of Documents. The chief judge must certify to each other member of the committee and to any adviser copies of the complaint and statement of facts in whole or relevant part, and any other relevant documents on file.

(e) Continuing Qualification of Committee Members. A member of a special committee who was qualified to serve when appointed may continue to serve on the committee even though the member relinquishes the position of chief judge, active circuit judge, or active district judge, as the case may be, but only if the member continues to hold office under Article III, Section 1, of the Constitution of the United States, or under 28 U.S.C. § 171.

(f) Inability of Committee Member to Complete Service. If a member of a special committee can no longer serve because of death, disability, disqualification, resignation, retirement from office, or other reason, the chief judge must decide whether to appoint a replacement member, either a circuit or district judge as needed under (a). No special committee appointed under these Rules may function with only a single member, and the votes of a two-member committee must be unanimous.

(g) Voting. All actions by a committee must be by vote of a majority of all members of the committee.

[Adopted March 11, 2008, effective April 10, 2008.]

Commentary on Rule 12

This Rule is adapted from the Act and the Illustrative Rules.

Rule 12 leaves the size of a special committee flexible, to be determined on a case-by-case basis. The question of committee size is one that should be weighed with care in view of the potential for consuming the members' time; a large committee should be appointed only if there is a special reason to do so.

Although the Act requires that the chief judge be a member of each special committee, 28 U.S.C. § 353(a)(1), it does not require that the chief judge preside. Accordingly, Rule 12(b) provides that if the chief judge does not preside, he or she must designate another committee member as the presiding officer.

Rule 12(c) provides that the chief judge must appoint a bankruptcy judge or magistrate judge as an adviser to a special committee at the request of a bankruptcy or magistrate subject judge.

Subsection (c) also provides that the adviser will have all the privileges of a committee member except a vote. The adviser, therefore, may participate in all deliberations of the committee, question witnesses at hearings, and write a separate statement to accompany the special committee's report to the judicial council.

Rule 12(e) provides that a member of a special committee who remains an Article III judge may continue to serve on the committee even though the member's status otherwise changes. Thus, a committee that originally consisted of the chief judge and an equal number of circuit and district judges, as required by the law, may continue to function even though changes of status alter that composition. This provision reflects the belief that stability of membership will contribute to the quality of the work of such committees.

Stability of membership is also the principal concern animating Rule 12(f), which deals with the case in which a special committee loses a member before its work is complete. The Rule permits the chief judge to determine whether a replacement member should be appointed. Generally, appointment of a replacement member is desirable in these situations unless the committee has conducted evidentiary hearings before the vacancy occurs. However, cases may arise in which a committee is in the late stages of its work, and in which it would be difficult for a new member to play a meaningful role. The Rule also preserves the collegial character of the committee process by prohibiting a single surviving member from serving as a committee and by providing that a committee of two surviving members will, in essence, operate under a unanimity rule.

Rule 12(g) provides that actions of a special committee must be by vote of a majority of all the members. All the members of a committee should participate in committee decisions. In that circumstance, it seems reasonable to require that committee decisions be made by a majority of the membership, rather than a majority of some smaller quorum.

RULE 13. CONDUCT OF AN INVESTIGATION

(a) Extent and Methods of Special–Committee Investigation. Each special committee must determine the appropriate extent and methods of the investigation in light of the allegations of the complaint. If, in the course of the investigation, the committee has cause to believe that the subject judge may have engaged in misconduct or has a disability that is beyond the scope of the complaint, the committee must refer the new matter to the chief judge for action under Rule 5 or Rule 11.

(b) Criminal Conduct. If the committee's investigation concerns conduct that may be a crime, the committee must consult with the appropriate prosecutorial authorities to the extent permitted by the Act to avoid compromising any criminal investigation. The committee has final authority over the timing and extent of its investigation and the formulation of its recommendations.

(c) Staff. The committee may arrange for staff assistance to conduct the investigation. It may use existing staff of the judicial branch or may hire special staff through the Director of the Administrative Office of the United States Courts.

(d) Delegation of Subpoena Power; Contempt. The chief judge may delegate the authority to exercise the committee's subpoena powers. The judicial council or special committee may institute a contempt proceeding under 28 U.S.C. § 332(d) against anyone who fails to comply with a subpoena.

[Adopted March 11, 2008, effective April 10, 2008.]

Commentary on Rule 13

This Rule is adapted from the Illustrative Rules.

Rule 13, as well as Rules 14, 15, and 16, are concerned with the way in which a special committee carries out its mission. They reflect the view that a special committee has two roles that are separated in ordinary litigation. First, the committee has an investigative role of the kind that is characteristically left to executive branch agencies or discovery by civil litigants. 28 U.S.C. § 353(c). Second, it has a formalized fact-finding and recommendation-of-disposition role that is characteristically left to juries, judges, or arbitrators. Id. Rule 13 generally governs the investigative stage. Even though the same body has responsibility for both roles under the Act, it is important to distinguish between them in order to ensure that appropriate rights are afforded at appropriate times to the subject judge.

One of the difficult questions that can arise is the relationship between proceedings under the Act and criminal investigations. Rule 13(b) assigns responsibility for coordination to the special committee in cases in which criminal conduct is suspected, but gives the committee the authority to determine the appropriate pace of its activity in light of any criminal investigation.

Title 28 U.S.C. § 356(a) provides that a special committee will have full subpoena powers as provided in 28 U.S.C. § 332(d). Section 332(d)(1) provides that subpoenas will be issued on behalf of judicial councils by the circuit clerk "at the direction of the chief judge of the circuit or his designee." Rule 13(d) contemplates that, where the chief judge designates someone else as presiding officer of a special committee, the presiding officer also be delegated the authority to direct the circuit clerk to issue subpoenas related to committee proceedings. That is not intended to imply, however, that the decision to use the subpoena power is exercisable by the presiding officer alone. See Rule 12(g).

RULE 14. CONDUCT OF HEARINGS BY SPECIAL COMMITTEE

(a) Purpose of Hearings. The committee may hold hearings to take testimony and receive other evidence, to hear argument, or both. If the committee is investigating allegations against more than one judge, it may hold joint or separate hearings.

(b) Committee Evidence. Subject to Rule 15, the committee must obtain material, nonredundant evidence in the form it considers appropriate. In the committee's discretion, evidence may be obtained by committee members, staff, or both. Witnesses offering testimonial evidence may include the complainant and the subject judge.

(c) Counsel for Witnesses. The subject judge has the right to counsel. The special committee has discretion to decide whether other witnesses may have counsel present when they testify.

(d) Witness Fees. Witness fees must be paid as provided in 28 U.S.C. § 1821.

(e) Oath. All testimony taken at a hearing must be given under oath or affirmation.

(f) Rules of Evidence. The Federal Rules of Evidence do not apply to special-committee hearings.

(g) Record and Transcript. A record and transcript must be made of all hearings.

[Adopted March 11, 2008, effective April 10, 2008.]

Commentary on Rule 14

This Rule is adapted from Section 353 of the Act and the Illustrative Rules.

Rule 14 is concerned with the conduct of fact-finding hearings. Special-committee hearings will normally be held only after the investigative work has been completed and the committee has concluded that there is sufficient evidence to warrant a formal fact-finding proceeding. Special-committee proceedings are primarily inquisitorial rather than adversarial. Accordingly, the Federal Rules of Evidence do not apply to such hearings. Inevitably, a hearing will have something of an adversary character. Nevertheless, that tendency should be moderated to the extent possible. Even though a proceeding will commonly have investigative and hearing stages, committee members should not regard themselves as prosecutors one day and judges the next. Their duty—and that of their staff—is at all times to be impartial seekers of the truth.

Rule 14(b) contemplates that material evidence will be obtained by the committee and presented in the form of affidavits, live testimony, etc. Staff or others who are organizing the hearings should regard it as their role to present evidence representing the entire picture. With respect to testimonial evidence, the subject judge should normally be called as a committee witness. Cases may arise in which the judge will not testify voluntarily. In such cases, subpoena powers are available, subject to the normal testimonial privileges. Although Rule 15(c) recognizes the subject judge's statutory right to call witnesses on his or her own behalf, exercise of this right should not usually be necessary.

RULE 15. RIGHTS OF SUBJECT JUDGE

(a) Notice.

(1) *Generally.* The subject judge must receive written notice of:

(A) the appointment of a special committee under Rule 11(f);

(B) the expansion of the scope of an investigation under Rule 13(a);

(C) any hearing under Rule 14, including its purposes, the names of any witnesses the committee intends to call, and the text of any statements that have been taken from those witnesses.

(2) *Suggestion of Additional Witnesses.* The subject judge may suggest additional witnesses to the committee.

(b) Report of the Special Committee. The subject judge must be sent a copy of the special committee's report when it is filed with the judicial council.

(c) Presentation of Evidence. At any hearing held under Rule 14, the subject judge has the right to present evidence, to compel the attendance of witnesses, and to compel the production of documents. At the request of the subject judge, the chief judge or the judge's designee must direct the circuit clerk to issue a subpoena to a witness under 28 U.S.C. § 332(d)(1). The subject judge must be given the opportunity to cross-examine committee witnesses, in person or by counsel.

(d) Presentation of Argument. The subject judge may submit written argument to the special committee and must be given a reasonable opportunity to present oral argument at an appropriate stage of the investigation.

(e) Attendance at Hearings. The subject judge has the right to attend any hearing held under Rule 14 and to receive copies of the transcript, of any documents introduced, and of any written arguments submitted by the complainant to the committee.

(f) Representation by Counsel. The subject judge may choose to be represented by counsel in the exercise of any right enumerated in this Rule. As provided in Rule 20(e), the United States may bear the costs of the representation.

[Adopted March 11, 2008, effective April 10, 2008.]

Commentary on Rule 15

This Rule is adapted from the Act and the Illustrative Rules.

The Act states that these Rules must contain provisions requiring that "the judge whose conduct is the subject of a complaint ... be afforded an opportunity to appear (in person or by counsel) at proceedings conducted by the investigating panel, to present oral and documentary evidence, to compel the attendance of witnesses or the production of documents, to cross-examine witnesses, and to present argument orally or in writing." 28 U.S.C. § 358(b)(2). To implement this provision, Rule 15(e) gives the judge the right to attend any hearing held for the purpose of receiving evidence of record or hearing argument under Rule 14.

The Act does not require that the subject judge be permitted to attend all proceedings of the special committee. Accordingly, the Rules do not give a right to attend other proceedings—for example, meetings at which the committee is engaged in investigative activity, such as interviewing persons to learn whether they ought to be called as witnesses or examining for relevance purposes documents delivered pursuant to a subpoena duces tecum, or meetings in which the committee is deliberating on the evidence or its recommendations.

RULE 16. RIGHTS OF COMPLAINANT IN INVESTIGATION

(a) Notice. The complainant must receive written notice of the investigation as provided in Rule 11(g)(1). When the special committee's report to the judicial council is filed, the complainant must be notified of the filing. The judicial council may, in its discretion, provide a copy of the report of a special committee to the complainant.

(b) Opportunity to Provide Evidence. If the committee determines that the complainant may have evidence that does not already exist in writing, a representative of the committee must interview the complainant.

(c) Presentation of Argument. The complainant may submit written argument to the special committee. In its discretion, the special committee may permit the complainant to offer oral argument.

(d) Representation by Counsel. A complainant may submit written argument through counsel and, if permitted to offer oral argument, may do so through counsel.

(e) Cooperation. In exercising its discretion under this Rule, a special committee may take into account the degree of the complainant's cooperation in preserving the confidentiality of the proceedings, including the identity of the subject judge.

[Adopted March 11, 2008, effective April 10, 2008.]

Commentary on Rule 16

This Rule is adapted from the Act and the Illustrative Rules.

In accordance with the view of the process as fundamentally administrative and inquisitorial, these Rules do not give the complainant the rights of a party to litigation, and leave the complainant's role largely to the discretion of the special committee. However, Rule 16(b) provides that, where a special committee has been appointed and it determines that the complainant may have additional evidence, the complainant must be interviewed by a representative of the committee. Such an interview may be in person or by telephone, and the representative of the committee may be either a member or staff.

Rule 16 does not contemplate that the complainant will ordinarily be permitted to attend proceedings of the special committee except when testifying or presenting oral argument. A special committee may exercise its discretion to permit the complainant to be present at its proceedings, or to permit the complainant, individually or through counsel, to participate in the examination or cross-examination of witnesses.

The Act authorizes an exception to the normal confidentiality provisions where the judicial council in its discretion provides a copy of the report of the special committee to the complainant and to the subject judge. 28 U.S.C. § 360(a)(1). However, the Rules do not entitle the complainant to a copy of the special committee's report.

In exercising their discretion regarding the role of the complainant, the special committee and the judicial council should protect the confidentiality of the complaint process. As a consequence, subsection (e) provides that a special committee may consider the degree to which a complainant has cooperated in preserving the confidentiality of the proceedings in determining what role beyond the minimum required by these Rules should be given to that complainant.

RULE 17. SPECIAL–COMMITTEE REPORT

The committee must file with the judicial council a comprehensive report of its investigation, including findings and recommendations for council action. The report must be accompanied by a statement of the vote by which it was adopted, any separate or dissenting statements of committee members, and the record of any hearings held under Rule 14. A copy of the report and accompanying statement must be sent to the Judicial Conference Committee on Judicial Conduct and Disability.

[Adopted March 11, 2008, effective April 10, 2008.]

Commentary on Rule 17

This Rule is adapted from the Illustrative Rules and is self-explanatory. The provision for sending a copy of the special-committee report and accompanying statement to the Judicial Conference Committee is new.

ARTICLE V. JUDICIAL–COUNCIL REVIEW

RULE 18. PETITIONS FOR REVIEW OF CHIEF JUDGE DISPOSITIONS UNDER RULE 11(c), (d), OR (e)

(a) Petitions for Review. After the chief judge issues an order under Rule 11(c), (d), or (e), a complainant or subject judge may petition the judicial council of the circuit to review the order. By rules promulgated under 28 U.S.C. § 358, the judicial council may refer a petition for review filed under this Rule to a panel of no fewer than five members of the council, at least two of whom must be district judges.

(b) When to File; Form; Where to File. A petition for review must be filed in the office of the circuit clerk within 35 days of the date on the clerk's letter informing the parties of the chief judge's order. The petition should be in letter form, addressed to the circuit clerk, and in an envelope marked "Misconduct Petition" or "Disability Petition." The name of the subject judge must not be shown on the envelope. The letter should be typewritten or otherwise legible. It should begin with "I hereby petition the judicial council for review of . . ." and state the reasons why the petition should be granted. It must be signed.

(c) Receipt and Distribution of Petition. A circuit clerk who receives a petition for review filed within the time allowed and in proper form must:

(1) acknowledge its receipt and send a copy to the complainant or subject judge, as the case may be;

(2) promptly distribute to each member of the judicial council, or its relevant panel, except for any member disqualified under Rule 25, or make available in the manner provided by local rule, the following materials:

(A) copies of the complaint;

(B) all materials obtained by the chief judge in connection with the inquiry;

(C) the chief judge's order disposing of the complaint;

(D) any memorandum in support of the chief judge's order;

(E) the petition for review; and

(F) an appropriate ballot;

(3) send the petition for review to the Judicial Conference Committee on Judicial Conduct and Disability. Unless the Judicial Conference Committee requests them, the clerk will not send copies of the materials obtained by the chief judge.

(d) Untimely Petition. The clerk must refuse to accept a petition that is received after the deadline in (b).

(e) Timely Petition Not in Proper Form. When the clerk receives a petition filed within the time allowed but in a form that is improper to a degree that would substantially impair its consideration by the judicial council—such as a document that is ambiguous about whether it is intended to be a petition for review—the clerk must acknowledge its receipt, call the filer's attention to the deficiencies, and give the filer the opportunity to correct the deficiencies within 21 days of the date of the clerk's letter about the deficiencies or within the original deadline for filing the petition, whichever is later. If the deficiencies are corrected within the time allowed, the clerk will proceed according to paragraphs (a) and (c) of this

Rule. If the deficiencies are not corrected, the clerk must reject the petition.

[Adopted March 11, 2008, effective April 10, 2008.]

Commentary on Rule 18

Rule 18 is adapted largely from the Illustrative Rules.

Subsection (a) permits a subject judge, as well as the complainant, to petition for review of a chief judge's order dismissing a complaint under Rule 11(c), or concluding that appropriate corrective action or intervening events have remedied or mooted the problems raised by the complaint pursuant to Rule 11(d) or (e). Although the subject judge may ostensibly be vindicated by the dismissal or conclusion of a complaint, a chief judge's order may include language disagreeable to the subject judge. For example, an order may dismiss a complaint, but state that the subject judge did in fact engage in misconduct. Accordingly, a subject judge may wish to object to the content of the order and is given the opportunity to petition the judicial council of the circuit for review.

Subsection (b) contains a time limit of thirty-five days to file a petition for review. It is important to establish a time limit on petitions for review of chief judges' dispositions in order to provide finality to the process. If the complaint requires an investigation, the investigation should proceed; if it does not, the subject judge should know that the matter is closed.

The standards for timely filing under the Federal Rules of Appellate Procedure should be applied to petitions for review. See Fed. R. App. P. 25(a)(2)(A) and (C).

Rule 18(e) provides for an automatic extension of the time limit imposed under subsection (b) if a person files a petition that is rejected for failure to comply with formal requirements.

RULE 19. JUDICIAL–COUNCIL DISPOSITION OF PETITIONS FOR REVIEW

(a) Rights of Subject Judge. At any time after a complainant files a petition for review, the subject judge may file a written response with the circuit clerk. The clerk must promptly distribute copies of the response to each member of the judicial council or of the relevant panel, unless that member is disqualified under Rule 25. Copies must also be distributed to the chief judge, to the complainant, and to the Judicial Conference Committee on Judicial Conduct and Disability. The subject judge must not otherwise communicate with individual council members about the matter. The subject judge must be given copies of any communications to the judicial council from the complainant.

(b) Judicial–Council Action. After considering a petition for review and the materials before it, a judicial council may:

(1) affirm the chief judge's disposition by denying the petition;

(2) return the matter to the chief judge with directions to conduct a further inquiry under Rule 11(b) or to identify a complaint under Rule 5;

(3) return the matter to the chief judge with directions to appoint a special committee under Rule 11(f); or

(4) in exceptional circumstances, take other appropriate action.

(c) Notice of Council Decision. Copies of the judicial council's order, together with any accompanying memorandum in support of the order or separate concurring or dissenting statements, must be given to the complainant, the subject judge, and the Judicial Conference Committee on Judicial Conduct and Disability.

(d) Memorandum of Council Decision. If the council's order affirms the chief judge's disposition, a supporting memorandum must be prepared only if the judicial council concludes that there is a need to supplement the chief judge's explanation. A memorandum supporting a council order must not include the name of the complainant or the subject judge.

(e) Review of Judicial–Council Decision. If the judicial council's decision is adverse to the petitioner, and if no member of the council dissented on the ground that a special committee should be appointed under Rule 11(f), the complainant must be notified that he or she has no right to seek review of the decision. If there was a dissent, the petitioner must be informed that he or she can file a petition for review under Rule 21(b) solely on the issue of whether a special committee should be appointed.

(f) Public Availability of Judicial–Council Decision. Materials related to the council's decision must be made public to the extent, at the time, and in the manner set forth in Rule 24.

[Adopted March 11, 2008, effective April 10, 2008.]

Commentary on Rule 19

This Rule is largely adapted from the Act and is self-explanatory.

The council should ordinarily review the decision of the chief judge on the merits, treating the petition for review for all practical purposes as an appeal. The judicial council may respond to a petition by affirming the chief judge's order, remanding the matter, or, in exceptional cases, taking other appropriate action.

RULE 20. JUDICIAL–COUNCIL CONSIDERATION OF REPORTS AND RECOMMENDATIONS OF SPECIAL COMMITTEES

(a) Rights of Subject Judge. Within 21 days after the filing of the report of a special committee, the subject judge may send a written response to the members of the judicial council. The judge must also be given an opportunity to present argument through counsel, written or oral, as determined by the council. The judge must not otherwise communicate with council members about the matter.

(b) Judicial–Council Action.

(1) *Discretionary Actions.* Subject to the judge's rights set forth in subsection (a), the judicial council may:

(A) dismiss the complaint because:

(i) even if the claim is true, the claimed conduct is not conduct prejudicial to the effective and expeditious administration of the business of the courts and does not indicate a mental or physical disability resulting in inability to discharge the duties of office;

(ii) the complaint is directly related to the merits of a decision or procedural ruling;

(iii) the facts on which the complaint is based have not been established; or

(iv) the complaint is otherwise not appropriate for consideration under 28 U.S.C. §§ 351–364.

(B) conclude the proceeding because appropriate corrective action has been taken or intervening events have made the proceeding unnecessary.

(C) refer the complaint to the Judicial Conference of the United States with the council's recommendations for action.

(D) take remedial action to ensure the effective and expeditious administration of the business of the courts, including:

(i) censuring or reprimanding the subject judge, either by private communication or by public announcement;

(ii) ordering that no new cases be assigned to the subject judge for a limited, fixed period;

(iii) in the case of a magistrate judge, ordering the chief judge of the district court to take action specified by the council, including the initiation of removal proceedings under 28 U.S.C. § 631(i) or 42 U.S.C. § 300aa–12(c)(2);

(iv) in the case of a bankruptcy judge, removing the judge from office under 28 U.S.C. § 152(e);

(v) in the case of a circuit or district judge, requesting the judge to retire voluntarily with the provision (if necessary) that ordinary length-of-service requirements will be waived; and

(vi) in the case of a circuit or district judge who is eligible to retire but does not do so, certifying the disability of the judge under 28 U. S.C. § 372(b) so that an additional judge may be appointed.

(E) take any combination of actions described in (b)(1)(A)–(D) of this Rule that is within its power.

(2) *Mandatory Actions.* A judicial council must refer a complaint to the Judicial Conference if the council determines that a circuit judge or district judge may have engaged in conduct that:

(A) might constitute ground for impeachment; or

(B) in the interest of justice, is not amenable to resolution by the judicial council.

(c) Inadequate Basis for Decision. If the judicial council finds that a special committee's report, recommendations, and record provide an inadequate basis for decision, it may return the matter to the committee for further investigation and a new report, or it may conduct further investigation. If the judicial council decides to conduct further investigation, the subject judge must be given adequate prior notice in writing of that decision and of the general scope and purpose of the additional investigation. The judicial council's conduct of the additional investigation must generally accord with the procedures and powers set forth in Rules 13 through 16 for the conduct of an investigation by a special committee.

(d) Council Vote. Council action must be taken by a majority of those members of the council who are not disqualified. A decision to remove a bankruptcy judge from office requires a majority vote of all the members of the council.

(e) Recommendation for Fee Reimbursement. If the complaint has been finally dismissed or concluded under (b)(1)(A) or (B) of this Rule, and if the subject judge so requests, the judicial council may recommend that the Director of the Administrative Office of the United States Courts use funds appropriated to the Judiciary to reimburse the judge for reasonable expenses incurred during the investigation, when those expenses would not have been incurred but for the requirements of the Act and these Rules. Reasonable expenses include attorneys' fees and expenses related to a successful defense or prosecution of a proceeding under Rule 21(a) or (b).

(f) Council Action. Council action must be by written order. Unless the council finds that extraordinary reasons would make it contrary to the interests of justice, the order must be accompanied by a memorandum setting forth the factual determinations on which it is based and the reasons for the council action. The order and the supporting memorandum must be provided to the complainant, the subject judge, and the Judicial Conference Committee on Judicial Conduct and Disability. The complainant and the subject judge must be notified of any right to review of the judicial council's decision as provided in Rule 21(b).

[Adopted March 11, 2008, effective April 10, 2008.]

Commentary on Rule 20

This Rule is largely adapted from the Illustrative Rules.

Rule 20(a) provides that within twenty-one days after the filing of the report of a special committee, the subject judge may address a written response to all of the members of the judicial council. The subject judge must also be given an opportunity to present oral argument to the council, personally or through counsel. The subject judge may not otherwise communicate with council members about the matter.

Rule 20(c) provides that if the judicial council decides to conduct an additional investigation, the subject judge must be given adequate prior notice in writing of that decision and of the general scope and purpose of the additional investigation. The conduct of the investigation will be generally in accordance with the procedures set forth in Rules 13 through 16 for the conduct of an investigation by a special committee. However, if hearings are held, the council may limit testimony or the presentation of evidence to avoid unnecessary repetition of testimony and evidence before the special committee.

Rule 20(d) provides that council action must be taken by a majority of those members of the council who are not disqualified, except that a decision to remove a bankruptcy judge from office requires a majority of all the members of the council as required by 28 U.S.C. § 152(e). However, it is inappropriate to apply a similar rule to the less severe actions that a judicial council may take under the Act. If some members of the council are disqualified in the matter, their disqualification should not be given the effect of a vote against council action.

With regard to Rule 20(e), the judicial council, on the request of the subject judge, may recommend to the Director of the Administrative Office of the United States Courts that the subject judge be reimbursed for reasonable expenses, including attorneys' fees, incurred. The judicial council has the authority to recommend such reimbursement where, after investigation by a special committee, the complaint has been finally dismissed or concluded under subsection (b)(1)(A) or (B) of this Rule. It is contemplated that such reimbursement may be provided for the successful prosecution or defense of a proceeding under Rule 21(a) or (b), in other words, one that results in a Rule 20(b)(1)(A) or (B) dismissal or conclusion.

Rule 20(f) requires that council action normally be supported with a memorandum of factual determinations and reasons and that notice of the action be given to the complainant and the subject judge. Rule 20(f) also requires that the notification to the complainant and the subject judge include notice of any right to petition for review of the council's decision under Rule 21(b).

ARTICLE VI. REVIEW BY JUDICIAL CONFERENCE COMMITTEE ON CONDUCT AND DISABILITY

RULE 21. COMMITTEE ON JUDICIAL CONDUCT AND DISABILITY

(a) Review by Committee. The Committee on Judicial Conduct and Disability, consisting of seven members, considers and disposes of all petitions for review under (b) of this Rule, in conformity with the Committee's jurisdictional statement. Its disposition of petitions for review is ordinarily final. The Judicial Conference of the United States may, in its sole discretion, review any such Committee decision, but a complainant or subject judge does not have a right to this review.

(b) Reviewable Matters.

(1) *Upon Petition.* A complainant or subject judge may petition the Committee for review of a judicial-council order entered in accordance with:

(A) Rule 20(b)(1)(A), (B), (D), or (E); or

(B) Rule 19(b)(1) or (4) if one or more members of the judicial council dissented from the order on the ground that a special committee should be appointed under Rule 11(f); in that event, the Committee's review will be limited to the issue of whether a special committee should be appointed.

(2) *Upon Committee's Initiative.* At its initiative and in its sole discretion, the Committee may review any judicial-council order entered under Rule 19(b)(1) or (4), but only to determine whether a special committee should be appointed. Before undertaking the review, the Committee must invite that judicial council to explain why it believes the appointment of a special committee is unnecessary, unless the reasons are clearly stated in the judicial council's order denying the petition for review. If the Committee believes that it would benefit from a submission by the subject judge, it may issue an appropriate request. If the Committee determines that a special committee should be appointed, the Committee must issue a written decision giving its reasons.

(c) Committee Vote. Any member of the Committee from the same circuit as the subject judge is disqualified from considering or voting on a petition for review. Committee decisions under (b) of this Rule must be by majority vote of the qualified Committee members. If only six members are qualified to vote on a petition for review, the decision must be made by a majority of a panel of five members drawn from a randomly selected list that rotates after each decision by a panel drawn from the list. The members who will determine the petition must be selected based on committee membership as of the date on which the petition is received. Those members selected to hear the petition should serve in that capacity until final disposition of the petition, whether or not their term of committee membership has ended. If only four members are qualified to vote, the Chief Justice must appoint, if available, an ex-member of the Committee or, if not, another United States judge to consider the petition.

(d) Additional Investigation. Except in extraordinary circumstances, the Committee will not conduct an additional investigation. The Committee may return the matter to the judicial council with directions to undertake an additional investigation. If the Committee conducts an additional investigation, it will exercise the powers of the Judicial Conference under 28 U.S.C. § 331.

(e) Oral Argument; Personal Appearance. There is ordinarily no oral argument or personal appearance before the Committee. In its discretion, the Committee may permit written submissions from the complainant or subject judge.

(f) Committee Decisions. Committee decisions under this Rule must be transmitted promptly to the Judicial Conference of the United States. Other distribution will be by the Administrative Office at the direction of the Committee chair.

(g) Finality. All orders of the Judicial Conference or of the Committee (when the Conference does not exercise its power of review) are final.

[Adopted March 11, 2008, effective April 10, 2008.]

Commentary on Rule 21

This Rule is largely self-explanatory.

Rule 21(a) is intended to clarify that the delegation of power to the Judicial Conference Committee on Judicial Conduct and Disability to dispose of petitions does not preclude review of such dispositions by the Conference. However, there is no right to such review in any party.

Rules 21(b)(1)(B) and (b)(2) are intended to fill a jurisdictional gap as to review of dismissals or conclusions of complaints under Rule 19(b)(1) or (4). Where one or more members of a judicial council reviewing a petition have dissented on the ground that a special committee should have been appointed, the complainant or subject judge has the right to petition for review by the Committee but only as to that issue. Under Rule 21(b)(2), the Judicial Conference Committee on Judicial Conduct and Disability may review such a dismissal or conclusion in its sole discretion, whether or not such a dissent occurred, and only as to the appointment of a special committee. No party has a right to such review, and such review will be rare.

Rule 21(c) provides for review only by Committee members from circuits other than that of the subject judge. To avoid tie votes, the Committee will decide petitions for review by rotating panels of five when only six members are qualified. If only four members are qualified, the Chief Justice must appoint an additional judge to consider that petition for review.

Under this Rule, all Committee decisions are final in that they are unreviewable unless the Judicial Conference, in its discretion, decides to review a decision. Committee decisions, however, do not necessarily constitute final action on a complaint for purposes of Rule 24.

RULE 22. PROCEDURES FOR REVIEW

(a) Filing a Petition for Review. A petition for review of a judicial-council decision may be filed by sending a brief written statement to the Judicial Conference Committee on Judicial Conduct and Disability, addressed to:

Judicial Conference Committee on
Judicial Conduct and Disability
Attn: Office of General Counsel
Administrative Office of the United States Courts
One Columbus Circle, NE
Washington, D.C. 20544

The Administrative Office will send a copy of the petition to the complainant or subject judge, as the case may be.

(b) Form and Contents of Petition for Review. No particular form is required. The petition must contain a short statement of the basic facts underlying the complaint, the history of its consideration before the appropriate judicial council, a copy of the judicial council's decision, and the grounds on which the petitioner seeks review. The petition for review must specify the date and docket number of the judicial-council order for which review is sought. The petitioner may attach any documents or correspondence arising in the course of the proceeding before the judicial council or its special committee. A petition should not normally exceed 20 pages plus necessary attachments.

(c) Time. A petition must be submitted within 63 days of the date of the order for which review is sought.

(d) Copies. Seven copies of the petition for review must be submitted, at least one of which must be signed by the petitioner or his or her attorney. If the petitioner submits a signed declaration of inability to pay the expense of duplicating the petition, the Administrative Office must accept the original petition and must reproduce copies at its expense.

(e) Action on Receipt of Petition for Review. The Administrative Office must acknowledge receipt of a petition for review submitted under this Rule, notify the chair of the Judicial Conference Committee on Judicial Conduct and Disability, and distribute the petition to the members of the Committee for their deliberation.

[Adopted March 11, 2008, effective April 10, 2008.]

Commentary on Rule 22

Rule 22 is self-explanatory.

ARTICLE VII. MISCELLANEOUS RULES

RULE 23. CONFIDENTIALITY

(a) General Rule. The consideration of a complaint by the chief judge, a special committee, the judicial council, or the Judicial Conference Committee on Judicial Conduct and Disability is confidential. Information about this consideration must not be disclosed by any judge or employee of the judicial branch or by any person who records or transcribes testimony except as allowed by these Rules. In extraordinary circumstances, a chief judge may disclose the existence of a proceeding under these Rules when necessary to maintain public confidence in the federal judiciary's ability to redress misconduct or disability.

(b) Files. All files related to complaints must be separately maintained with appropriate security precautions to ensure confidentiality.

(c) Disclosure in Decisions. Except as otherwise provided in Rule 24, written decisions of the chief judge, the judicial council, or the Judicial Conference Committee on Judicial Conduct and Disability, and dissenting opinions or separate statements of members of the council or Committee may contain information and exhibits that the authors consider appropriate for inclusion, and the information and exhibits may be made public.

(d) Availability to Judicial Conference. On request of the Judicial Conference or its Committee on Judicial Conduct and Disability, the circuit clerk must furnish any requested records related to a complaint. For auditing purposes, the circuit clerk must provide access to the Committee to records of proceedings under the Act at the site where the records are kept.

(e) Availability to District Court. If the judicial council directs the initiation of proceedings for removal of a magistrate judge under Rule 20(b)(1)(D)(iii), the circuit clerk must provide to the chief judge of the district court copies of the report of the special committee and any other documents and records that were before the judicial council at the time of its decision. On request of the chief judge of the district court, the judicial council may authorize release to that chief judge of any other records relating to the investigation.

(f) Impeachment Proceedings. If the Judicial Conference determines that consideration of impeachment may be warranted, it must transmit the record of all relevant proceedings to the Speaker of the House of Representatives.

(g) Subject Judge's Consent. If both the subject judge and the chief judge consent in writing, any materials from the files may be disclosed to any person. In any such disclosure, the chief judge may require that the identity of the complainant, or of witnesses in an investigation conducted by a chief judge, a special committee, or the judicial council, not be revealed.

(h) Disclosure in Special Circumstances. The Judicial Conference, its Committee on Judicial Conduct and Disability, or a judicial council may authorize disclosure of information about the consideration of a complaint, including the papers, documents, and transcripts relating to the investigation, to the extent that disclosure is justified by special circumstances and is not prohibited by the Act. Disclosure may be made to judicial researchers engaged in the study or evaluation of experience under the Act and related modes of judicial discipline, but only where the study or evaluation has been specifically approved by the Judicial Conference or by the Judicial Conference Committee on Judicial Conduct and Disability. Appropriate steps must be taken to protect the identities of the subject judge, the complainant, and witnesses from public disclosure. Other appropriate safeguards to protect against the dissemination of confidential information may be imposed.

(i) Disclosure of Identity by Subject Judge. Nothing in this Rule precludes the subject judge from acknowledging that he or she is the judge referred to in documents made public under Rule 24.

(j) Assistance and Consultation. Nothing in this Rule precludes the chief judge or judicial council acting on a complaint filed under the Act from seeking the help of qualified staff or from consulting other judges who may be helpful in the disposition of the complaint.

[Adopted March 11, 2008, effective April 10, 2008.]

Commentary on Rule 23

Rule 23 was adapted from the Illustrative Rules.

The Act applies a rule of confidentiality to "papers, documents, and records of proceedings related to investigations conducted under this chapter" and states that they may not be disclosed "by any person in any proceeding," with enumerated exceptions. 28 U.S.C. § 360(a). Three questions arise: Who is bound by the confidentiality rule, what proceedings are subject to the rule, and who is within the circle of people who may have access to information without breaching the rule?

With regard to the first question, Rule 23(a) provides that judges, employees of the judicial branch, and those persons involved in recording proceedings and preparing transcripts are obliged to respect the confidentiality requirement. This of course includes subject judges who do not consent to identification under Rule 23(i).

With regard to the second question, Rule 23(a) applies the rule of confidentiality broadly to consideration of a complaint at any stage.

With regard to the third question, there is no barrier of confidentiality among a chief judge, judicial council, the

Judicial Conference, and the Judicial Conference Committee on Judicial Conduct and Disability. Each may have access to any of the confidential records for use in their consideration of a referred matter, a petition for review, or monitoring the administration of the Act. A district court may have similar access if the judicial council orders the district court to initiate proceedings to remove a magistrate judge from office, and Rule 23(e) so provides.

In extraordinary circumstances, a chief judge may disclose the existence of a proceeding under these Rules. The disclosure of such information in high-visibility or controversial cases is to reassure the public that the federal judiciary is capable of redressing judicial misconduct or disability. Moreover, the confidentiality requirement does not prevent the chief judge from "communicat[ing] orally or in writing with ... [persons] who may have knowledge of the matter," as part of a limited inquiry conducted by the chief judge under Rule 11(b).

Rule 23 recognizes that there must be some exceptions to the Act's confidentiality requirement. For example, the Act requires that certain orders and the reasons for them must be made public. 28 U.S.C. § 360(b). Rule 23(c) makes it explicit that memoranda supporting chief judge and council orders, as well as dissenting opinions and separate statements, may contain references to information that would otherwise be confidential and that such information may be made public. However, subsection (c) is subject to Rule 24(a) which provides the general rule regarding the public availability of decisions. For example, the name of a subject judge cannot be made public in a decision if disclosure of the name is prohibited by that Rule.

The Act makes clear that there is a barrier of confidentiality between the judicial branch and the legislative. It provides that material may be disclosed to Congress only if it is believed necessary to an impeachment investigation or trial of a judge. 28 U.S.C. § 360(a)(2). Accordingly, Section 355(b) of the Act requires the Judicial Conference to transmit the record of the proceeding to the House of Representatives if the Conference believes that impeachment of a subject judge may be appropriate. Rule 23(f) implements this requirement.

The Act provides that confidential materials may be disclosed if authorized in writing by the subject judge and by the chief judge. 28 U.S.C. § 360(a)(3). Rule 23(g) implements this requirement. Once the subject judge has consented to the disclosure of confidential materials related to a complaint, the chief judge ordinarily will refuse consent only to the extent necessary to protect the confidentiality interests of the complainant or of witnesses who have testified in investigatory proceedings or who have provided information in response to a limited inquiry undertaken pursuant to Rule 11. It will generally be necessary, therefore, for the chief judge to require that the identities of the complainant or of such witnesses, as well as any identifying information, be shielded in any materials disclosed, except insofar as the chief judge has secured the consent of the complainant or of a particular witness to disclosure, or there is a demonstrated need for disclosure of the information that, in the judgment of the chief judge, outweighs the confidentiality interest of the complainant or of a particular witness (as may be the case where the complainant is delusional or where the complainant or a particular witness has already demonstrated a lack of concern about maintaining the confidentiality of the proceedings).

Rule 23(h) permits disclosure of additional information in circumstances not enumerated. For example, disclosure may be appropriate to permit a prosecution for perjury based on testimony given before a special committee. Another example might involve evidence of criminal conduct by a judge discovered by a special committee.

Subsection (h) also permits the authorization of disclosure of information about the consideration of a complaint, including the papers, documents, and transcripts relating to the investigation, to judicial researchers engaged in the study or evaluation of experience under the Act and related modes of judicial discipline. The Rule envisions disclosure of information from the official record of complaint proceedings to a limited category of persons for appropriately authorized research purposes only, and with appropriate safeguards to protect individual identities in any published research results that ensue. In authorizing disclosure, the judicial council may refuse to release particular materials when such release would be contrary to the interests of justice, or that constitute purely internal communications. The Rule does not envision disclosure of purely internal communications between judges and their colleagues and staff.

Under Rule 23(j), chief judges and judicial councils may seek staff assistance or consult with other judges who may be helpful in the process of complaint disposition; the confidentiality requirement does not preclude this. The chief judge, for example, may properly seek the advice and assistance of another judge who the chief judge deems to be in the best position to communicate with the subject judge in an attempt to bring about corrective action. As another example, a new chief judge may wish to confer with a predecessor to learn how similar complaints have been handled. In consulting with other judges, of course, the chief judge should disclose information regarding the complaint only to the extent the chief judge deems necessary under the circumstances.

RULE 24. PUBLIC AVAILABILITY OF DECISIONS

(a) General Rule; Specific Cases. When final action has been taken on a complaint and it is no longer subject to review, all orders entered by the chief judge and judicial council, including any supporting memoranda and any dissenting opinions or separate statements by members of the judicial council, must be made public, with the following exceptions:

(1) if the complaint is finally dismissed under Rule 11(c) without the appointment of a special committee, or if it is concluded under Rule 11(d) because of voluntary corrective action, the publicly available materials must not disclose the name of the subject judge without his or her consent.

(2) if the complaint is concluded because of intervening events, or dismissed at any time after a special committee is appointed, the judicial council must determine whether the name of the subject judge should be disclosed.

(3) if the complaint is finally disposed of by a privately communicated censure or reprimand, the publicly available materials must not disclose either

the name of the subject judge or the text of the reprimand.

(4) if the complaint is finally disposed of under Rule 20(b)(1)(D) by any action other than private censure or reprimand, the text of the dispositive order must be included in the materials made public, and the name of the subject judge must be disclosed.

(5) the name of the complainant must not be disclosed in materials made public under this Rule unless the chief judge orders disclosure.

(b) Manner of Making Public. The orders described in (a) must be made public by placing them in a publicly accessible file in the office of the circuit clerk or by placing the orders on the court's public website. If the orders appear to have precedential value, the chief judge may cause them to be published. In addition, the Judicial Conference Committee on Judicial Conduct and Disability will make available on the Federal Judiciary's website, www.uscourts.gov, selected illustrative orders described in paragraph (a), appropriately redacted, to provide additional information to the public on how complaints are addressed under the Act.

(c) Orders of Judicial Conference Committee. Orders of this Committee constituting final action in a complaint proceeding arising from a particular circuit will be made available to the public in the office of the clerk of the relevant court of appeals. The Committee will also make such orders available on the Federal Judiciary's website, www.uscourts.gov. When authorized by the Committee, other orders related to complaint proceedings will similarly be made available.

(d) Complaints Referred to the Judicial Conference of the United States. If a complaint is referred to the Judicial Conference under Rule 20(b)(1)(C) or 20(b)(2), materials relating to the complaint will be made public only if ordered by the Judicial Conference.

[Adopted March 11, 2008, effective April 10, 2008.]

Commentary on Rule 24

Rule 24 is adapted from the Illustrative Rules and the recommendations of the Breyer Committee.

The Act requires the circuits to make available only written orders of a judicial council or the Judicial Conference imposing some form of sanction. 28 U.S.C. § 360(b). The Judicial Conference, however, has long recognized the desirability of public availability of a broader range of orders and other materials. In 1994, the Judicial Conference "urge[d] all circuits and courts covered by the Act to submit to the West Publishing Company, for publication in Federal Reporter 3d, and to Lexis all orders issued pursuant to [the Act] that are deemed by the issuing circuit or court to have significant precedential value to other circuits and courts covered by the Act." Report of the Proceedings of the Judicial Conference of the United States, Mar. 1994, at 28. Following this recommendation, the 2000 revision of the Illustrative Rules contained a public availability provision very similar to Rule 24. In 2002, the Judicial Conference again voted to encourage the circuits "to submit non-routine public orders disposing of complaints of judicial misconduct or disability for publication by on-line and print services." Report of the Proceedings of the Judicial Conference of the United States, Sept. 2002, at 58. The Breyer Committee Report further emphasized that "[p]osting such orders on the judicial branch's public website would not only benefit judges directly, it would also encourage scholarly commentary and analysis of the orders." Breyer Committee Report, 239 F.R.D. at 216. With these considerations in mind, Rule 24 provides for public availability of a wide range of materials.

Rule 24 provides for public availability of orders of the chief judge, the judicial council, and the Judicial Conference Committee on Judicial Conduct and Disability and the texts of any memoranda supporting their orders, together with any dissenting opinions or separate statements by members of the judicial council. However, these orders and memoranda are to be made public only when final action on the complaint has been taken and any right of review has been exhausted. The provision that decisions will be made public only after final action has been taken is designed in part to avoid public disclosure of the existence of pending proceedings. Whether the name of the subject judge is disclosed will then depend on the nature of the final action. If the final action is an order predicated on a finding of misconduct or disability (other than a privately communicated censure or reprimand) the name of the judge must be made public. If the final action is dismissal of the complaint, the name of the subject judge must not be disclosed. Rule 24(a)(1) provides that where a proceeding is concluded under Rule 11(d) by the chief judge on the basis of voluntary corrective action, the name of the subject judge must not be disclosed. Shielding the name of the subject judge in this circumstance should encourage informal disposition.

If a complaint is dismissed as moot, or because intervening events have made action on the complaint unnecessary, after appointment of a special committee, Rule 24(a)(2) allows the judicial council to determine whether the subject judge will be identified. In such a case, no final decision has been rendered on the merits, but it may be in the public interest—particularly if a judicial officer resigns in the course of an investigation—to make the identity of the judge known.

Once a special committee has been appointed, and a proceeding is concluded by the full council on the basis of a remedial order of the council, Rule 24(a)(4) provides for disclosure of the name of the subject judge.

Finally, Rule 24(a)(5) provides that the identity of the complainant will be disclosed only if the chief judge so orders. Identifying the complainant when the subject judge is not identified would increase the likelihood that the identity of the subject judge would become publicly known, thus circumventing the policy of nondisclosure. It may not always be practicable to shield the complainant's identity while making public disclosure of the judicial council's order and supporting memoranda; in some circumstances, moreover, the complainant may consent to public identification.

RULE 25. DISQUALIFICATION

(a) General Rule. Any judge is disqualified from participating in any proceeding under these Rules if the judge, in his or her discretion, concludes that circumstances warrant disqualification. If the complaint is filed by a judge, that judge is disqualified from participating in any consideration of the complaint except to the extent that these Rules provide for a complainant's participation. A chief judge who has identified a complaint under Rule 5 is not automatically disqualified from considering the complaint.

(b) Subject Judge. A subject judge is disqualified from considering the complaint except to the extent that these Rules provide for participation by a subject judge.

(c) Chief Judge Not Disqualified from Considering a Petition for Review of a Chief Judge's Order. If a petition for review of a chief judge's order entered under Rule 11(c), (d), or (e) is filed with the judicial council in accordance with Rule 18, the chief judge is not disqualified from participating in the council's consideration of the petition.

(d) Member of Special Committee Not Disqualified. A member of the judicial council who serves on a special committee, including the chief judge, is not disqualified from participating in council consideration of the committee's report.

(e) Subject Judge's Disqualification After Appointment of a Special Committee. Upon appointment of a special committee, the subject judge is automatically disqualified from participating in any proceeding arising under the Act or these Rules as a member of any special committee, the judicial council of the circuit, the Judicial Conference of the United States, and the Judicial Conference Committee on Judicial Conduct and Disability. The disqualification continues until all proceedings on the complaint against the subject judge are finally terminated with no further right of review.

(f) Substitute for Disqualified Chief Judge. If the chief judge is disqualified from participating in consideration of the complaint, the duties and responsibilities of the chief judge under these Rules must be assigned to the most-senior active circuit judge not disqualified. If all circuit judges in regular active service are disqualified, the judicial council may determine whether to request a transfer under Rule 26, or, in the interest of sound judicial administration, to permit the chief judge to dispose of the complaint on the merits. Members of the judicial council who are named in the complaint may participate in this determination if necessary to obtain a quorum of the judicial council.

(g) Judicial–Council Action When Multiple Judges Are Disqualified. Notwithstanding any other provision in these Rules to the contrary,

(1) a member of the judicial council who is a subject judge may participate in its disposition if:

(A) participation by one or more subject judges is necessary to obtain a quorum of the judicial council;

(B) the judicial council finds that the lack of a quorum is due to the naming of one or more judges in the complaint for the purpose of disqualifying that judge or judges, or to the naming of one or more judges based on their participation in a decision excluded from the definition of misconduct under Rule 3(h)(3); and

(C) the judicial council votes that it is necessary, appropriate, and in the interest of sound judicial administration that one or more subject judges be eligible to act.

(2) otherwise disqualified members may participate in votes taken under (g)(1)(B) and (g)(1)(C).

(h) Disqualification of Members of the Judicial Conference Committee. No member of the Judicial Conference Committee on Judicial Conduct and Disability is disqualified from participating in any proceeding under the Act or these Rules because of consultations with a chief judge, a member of a special committee, or a member of a judicial council about the interpretation or application of the Act or these Rules, unless the member believes that the consultation would prevent fair-minded participation.

[Adopted March 11, 2008, effective April 10, 2008.]

Commentary on Rule 25

Rule 25 is adapted from the Illustrative Rules.

Subsection (a) provides the general rule for disqualification. Of course, a judge is not disqualified simply because the subject judge is on the same court. However, this subsection recognizes that there may be cases in which an appearance of bias or prejudice is created by circumstances other than an association with the subject judge as a colleague. For example, a judge may have a familial relationship with a complainant or subject judge. When such circumstances exist, a judge may, in his or her discretion, conclude that disqualification is warranted.

Subsection (e) makes it clear that the disqualification of the subject judge relates only to the subject judge's participation in any proceeding arising under the Act or these Rules as a member of a special committee, judicial council, Judicial Conference, or the Judicial Conference Committee. The Illustrative Rule, based on Section 359(a) of the Act, is ambiguous and could be read to disqualify a subject judge from service of any kind on each of the bodies mentioned. This is undoubtedly not the intent of the Act; such a disqualification would be anomalous in light of the Act's allowing a subject judge to continue to decide cases and to continue to exercise the powers of chief circuit or district judge. It would also create a substantial deterrence to the appointment of special committees, particularly where a special committee is needed solely because the chief judge may not decide matters of credibility in his or her review under Rule 11.

While a subject judge is barred by Rule 25(b) from participating in the disposition of the complaint in which he or she is named, Rule 25(e) recognizes that participation in proceedings arising under the Act or these Rules by a judge who is the subject of a special committee investigation may lead to an appearance of self-interest in creating substantive and procedural precedents governing such proceedings; Rule 25(e) bars such participation.

Under the Act, a complaint against the chief judge is to be handled by "that circuit judge in regular active service next senior in date of commission." 28 U.S.C. § 351(c). Rule 25(f) provides that seniority among judges other than the chief judge is to be determined by date of commission, with the result that complaints against the chief judge may be routed to a former chief judge or other judge who was appointed earlier than the chief judge. The Rules do not purport to prescribe who is to preside over meetings of the judicial council. Consequently, where the presiding member of the judicial council is disqualified from participating under these Rules, the order of precedence prescribed by Rule 25(f) for performing "the duties and responsibilities of the chief circuit judge under these Rules" does not apply to determine the acting presiding member of the judicial council. That is a matter left to the internal rules or operating practices of each judicial council. In most cases the most senior active circuit judge who is a member of the judicial council and who is not disqualified will preside.

Sometimes a single complaint is filed against a large group of judges. If the normal disqualification rules are observed in such a case, no court of appeals judge can serve as acting chief judge of the circuit, and the judicial council will be without appellate members. Where the complaint is against all circuit and district judges, under normal rules no member of the judicial council can perform the duties assigned to the council under the statute.

A similar problem is created by successive complaints arising out of the same underlying grievance. For example, a complainant files a complaint against a district judge based on alleged misconduct, and the complaint is dismissed by the chief judge under the statute. The complainant may then file a complaint against the chief judge for dismissing the first complaint, and when that complaint is dismissed by the next senior judge, still a third complaint may be filed. The threat is that the complainant will bump down the seniority ladder until, once again, there is no member of the court of appeals who can serve as acting chief judge for the purpose of the next complaint. Similarly, complaints involving the merits of litigation may involve a series of decisions in which many judges participated or in which a rehearing en banc was denied by the court of appeals, and the complaint may name a majority of the judicial council as subject judges.

In recognition that these multiple-judge complaints are virtually always meritless, the judicial council is given discretion to determine: (1) whether it is necessary, appropriate, and in the interest of sound judicial administration to permit the chief judge to dispose of a complaint where it would otherwise be impossible for any active circuit judge in the circuit to act, and (2) whether it is necessary, appropriate, and in the interest of sound judicial administration, after appropriate findings as to need and justification are made, to permit subject judges of the judicial council to participate in the disposition of a petition for review where it would otherwise be impossible to obtain a quorum.

Applying a rule of necessity in these situations is consistent with the appearance of justice. See, e.g., In re Complaint of Doe, 2 F.3d 308 (8th Cir. Jud. Council 1993) (invoking the rule of necessity); In re Complaint of Judicial Misconduct, No. 91-80464 (9th Cir. Jud. Council 1992) (same). There is no unfairness in permitting the chief judge to dispose of a patently insubstantial complaint that names all active circuit judges in the circuit.

Similarly, there is no unfairness in permitting subject judges, in these circumstances, to participate in the review of a chief judge's dismissal of an insubstantial complaint. The remaining option is to assign the matter to another body. Among other alternatives, the council may request a transfer of the petition under Rule 26. Given the administrative inconvenience and delay involved in these alternatives, it is desirable to request a transfer only if the judicial council determines that the petition is substantial enough to warrant such action.

In the unlikely event that a quorum of the judicial council cannot be obtained to consider the report of a special committee, it would normally be necessary to request a transfer under Rule 26.

Rule 25(h) recognizes that the jurisdictional statement of the Judicial Conference Committee contemplates consultation between members of the Committee and judicial participants in proceedings under the Act and these Rules. Such consultation should not automatically preclude participation by a member in that proceeding.

RULE 26. TRANSFER TO ANOTHER JUDICIAL COUNCIL

In exceptional circumstances, a chief judge or a judicial council may ask the Chief Justice to transfer a proceeding based on a complaint identified under Rule 5 or filed under Rule 6 to the judicial council of another circuit. The request for a transfer may be made at any stage of the proceeding before a reference to the Judicial Conference under Rule 20(b)(1)(C) or 20(b)(2) or a petition for review is filed under Rule 22. Upon receiving such a request, the Chief Justice may refuse the request or select the transferee judicial council, which may then exercise the powers of a judicial council under these Rules.

[Adopted March 11, 2008, effective April 10, 2008.]

Commentary on Rule 26

Rule 26 is new; it implements the Breyer Committee's recommended use of transfers. Breyer Committee Report, 239 F.R.D. at 214–15.

Rule 26 authorizes the transfer of a complaint proceeding to another judicial council selected by the Chief Justice. Such transfers may be appropriate, for example, in the case of a serious complaint where there are multiple disqualifications among the original council, where the issues are highly visible and a local disposition may weaken public confidence in the process, where internal tensions arising in the council as a result of the complaint render disposition by a less involved council appropriate, or where a complaint calls into question policies or governance of the home court of appeals. The power to effect a transfer is lodged in the Chief Justice to avoid disputes in a council over where to transfer a sensitive matter and to ensure that the transferee council accepts the matter.

Upon receipt of a transferred proceeding, the transferee council shall determine the proper stage at which to begin consideration of the complaint—for example, reference to the transferee chief judge, appointment of a special committee, etc.

RULE 27. WITHDRAWAL OF COMPLAINTS AND PETITIONS FOR REVIEW

(a) Complaint Pending Before Chief Judge. With the chief judge's consent, a complainant may withdraw a complaint that is before the chief judge for a decision under Rule 11. The withdrawal of a complaint will not prevent a chief judge from identifying or having to identify a complaint under Rule 5 based on the withdrawn complaint.

(b) Complaint Pending Before Special Committee or Judicial Council. After a complaint has been referred to a special committee for investigation and before the committee files its report, the complainant may withdraw the complaint only with the consent of both the subject judge and either the special committee or the judicial council.

(c) Petition for Review. A petition for review addressed to a judicial council under Rule 18, or the Judicial Conference Committee on Judicial Conduct and Disability under Rule 22 may be withdrawn if no action on the petition has been taken.

[Adopted March 11, 2008, effective April 10, 2008.]

Commentary on Rule 27

Rule 27 is adapted from the Illustrative Rules and treats the complaint proceeding, once begun, as a matter of public business rather than as the property of the complainant. Accordingly, the chief judge or the judicial council remains responsible for addressing any complaint under the Act, even a complaint that has been formally withdrawn by the complainant.

Under subsection 27(a), a complaint pending before the chief judge may be withdrawn if the chief judge consents. Where the complaint clearly lacked merit, the chief judge may accordingly be saved the burden of preparing a formal order and supporting memorandum. However, the chief judge may, or be obligated under Rule 5, to identify a complaint based on allegations in a withdrawn complaint.

If the chief judge appoints a special committee, Rule 27(b) provides that the complaint may be withdrawn only with the consent of both the body before which it is pending (the special committee or the judicial council) and the subject judge. Once a complaint has reached the stage of appointment of a special committee, a resolution of the issues may be necessary to preserve public confidence. Moreover, the subject judge is given the right to insist that the matter be resolved on the merits, thereby eliminating any ambiguity that might remain if the proceeding were terminated by withdrawal of the complaint.

With regard to all petitions for review, Rule 27(c) grants the petitioner unrestricted authority to withdraw the petition. It is thought that the public's interest in the proceeding is adequately protected, because there will necessarily have been a decision by the chief judge and often by the judicial council as well in such a case.

RULE 28. AVAILABILITY OF RULES AND FORMS

These Rules and copies of the complaint form as provided in Rule 6(a) must be available without charge in the office of the clerk of each court of appeals, district court, bankruptcy court, or other federal court whose judges are subject to the Act. Each court must also make these Rules and the complaint form available on the court's website, or provide an Internet link to the Rules and complaint form that are available on the appropriate court of appeals' website.

[Adopted March 11, 2008, effective April 10, 2008.]

RULE 29. EFFECTIVE DATE

These Rules will become effective 30 days after promulgation by the Judicial Conference of the United States.

[Adopted March 11, 2008, effective April 10, 2008.]

APPENDIX—COMPLAINT FORM

JUDICIAL COUNCIL OF THE DISTRICT OF COLUMBIA CIRCUIT
COMPLAINT OF JUDICIAL MISCONDUCT OR DISABILITY

E. Barrett Prettyman U.S. Courthouse
333 Constitution Avenue, N.W.
Washington, D.C. 20001-2866
202-216-7340

This form should be completed and mailed to the above address to the attention of the "Circuit Executive". The envelope should be marked "JUDICIAL MISCONDUCT COMPLAINT" or "JUDICIAL DISABILITY COMPLAINT". Do not put the name of the judge or magistrate judge on the envelope.

The "Rules for Judicial-Conduct and Judicial-Disability Proceedings", adopted by the Judicial Conference of the United States, contain information on what to include in a complaint (Rule 6), where to file a complaint (Rule 7), and other important matters. Your complaint (this form and the statement of facts) should be typewritten and must be legible.

Number of copies. If the complaint is about a single judge of the court of appeals, submit three copies of this form, the statement of facts, and any documents. If it is about a single district court judge, magistrate judge, or bankruptcy judge, four copies must be filed. If the complaint is about more than one judge, enough copies must be filed to provide one for the clerk of the court, one for the chief judge of the circuit, one for each judge complained about, and one for the Chief Judge of the District Court if the subject judge is a district judge.

1. Complainant's Name: ______________________
   Address: ______________________
   ____
   Telephone: (____) ______________________

2. Judge or Magistrate Judge complained about: ______________________
   Name: ______________________
   Court: ______________________

3. Does this complaint concern the behavior of the judge(s) or magistrate judge(s) in a particular lawsuit or lawsuits?
   [ ] Yes [ ] No
   If "yes," give the following information about each lawsuit (use reverse side if more than one):
   Court: ______________________
   Case Number: ______________________
   Are (were) you a party or lawyer in the lawsuit?
   [ ] Party [ ] Lawyer [ ] Neither

   If a party, give the following information:
   Lawyer's Name: ______________________
   Address: ______________________
   Telephone: (____) ______________________
   Docket number(s) of any appeals of above case(s) to the Court of Appeals, D.C. Circuit: ______________________
   ____

4. Have you filed any lawsuits against the judge or magistrate judge?
[ ] Yes [ ] No
If "yes," give the following information about each lawsuit (use the reverse side if more than one):
Court: ____________
Case Number: ____________
Present status of lawsuit: ____________
Your lawyer's name: ____________
Telephone: (____)____________
Court to which any appeal has been taken in the lawsuit against the judge: ____
Docket number of the appeal: ____________
Present status of the appeal: ____________

5. **Brief Statement of Facts.** Using the next page of this form and up to four additional double-sided pages (8.5 x 11″) as necessary, submit a brief statement of the specific facts on which the claim of judicial misconduct or disability is based. Include what happened, when and where it happened, and any information that would help an investigator check the facts. If the complaint alleges judicial disability, also include any additional facts that form the basis of that allegation. See Rule 6(a) for further information on what to include in your statement of facts.

Declaration and Signature:

I declare under penalty of perjury that the statements made in this complaint are true and correct to the best of my knowledge.

(Signature)____________ (Date)____________

[Adopted March 11, 2008, effective April 10, 2008. Revised January 2011.]

SELECTED ORDERS AND NOTICES

POLICY GUIDELINES FOR THE USE OF CAMERAS AND RECORDING AND VIDEOTAPING DEVICES IN THE E. BARRETT PRETTYMAN UNITED STATES COURTHOUSE AND THE WILLIAM B. BRYANT ANNEX

The following guidelines regarding the use of cameras and recording and videotaping devices in the courthouse and annex have been approved by the Circuit Judicial Council and are effective as of March 19, 1987 (as amended by the Circuit Judicial Council on October 12, 2000, and March 3, 2008).

1. The use of any device that has the capability to photograph, record, or videotape is prohibited except in connection with ceremonial and educational functions of the courts (naturalization proceedings, investitures of new judges, memorial services, portrait presentation ceremonies, etc.). The use of such equipment is permissible within a judge's chambers and courtroom at the discretion of the judge. Videotaping, recording, or photographing court events, ceremonies, and educational programs may be permitted with prior approval of the chief judge or court unit executive[1] of the sponsoring court and under such conditions as he or she may prescribe. Acting at the direction of the chief judge of the sponsoring court, the special assistants to the chief judges are also authorized to approve these requests. The chief judge, court unit executive, or special assistant to the chief judge will notify the U.S. Marshal in writing[2] in advance of the event that use of these devices is authorized.

2. Notwithstanding the above, the Court of Appeals may decide whether to permit the taking of photographs and radio and television coverage of Court of Appeals proceedings, subject to any restrictions in statutes, national and local rules, and such guidelines as the Judicial Conference may adopt.

[As amended March 3, 2008.]

1 Court unit executives include the Circuit Executive, Clerks of the Courts, and Chief Probation Officer.

2 Written notification may be done by e-mail, memo, letter, or court order.

CELL PHONES, LAPTOPS, AND OTHER ELECTRONIC DEVICES

I. Visitors may keep an electronic device (e.g., cell phone, laptop, iPhone, iPod, MP3 player, etc.) in the courthouse and annex if the device does not have a camera (still or video) or is not capable of recording audio.

II. The following individuals are allowed to bring electronic devices with camera and recording capabilities into the courthouse and annex:

- Members of the Bar - Attorneys who display a bar identification card or other proof of membership of the bar of the Court of Appeals, District Court, or D.C. Bar.
- Jurors - Jurors who display a juror summons or juror pass issued by the Jury Office.
- Members of the Media - Members of the media who are credentialed by either Court or who are credentialed by another federal or D.C. government entity, including the Supreme Court, Congress, a federal agency, or the D.C. government.
- Parole Commission Hearing Examiners - Individuals who display their credentials as Parole Commission hearing examiners are allowed to bring into the courthouse electronic devices with camera and recording capabilities and recording equipment used to record hearings.

III. All other visitors must check their electronic devices with cameras or recording capabilities at the entrances unless authorized in advance and in writing by a judge or court unit executive.

IV. All electronic devices must be turned off before entering a courtroom.

V. See also Policy Guidelines for the Use of Cameras and Recording and Videotaping Devices in the E. Barrett Prettyman United States Courthouse and the William B. Bryant Annex (as amended March 3, 2008).

INDEX TO THE UNITED STATES COURT OF APPEALS FOR THE DISTRICT OF COLUMBIA CIRCUIT

*

HANDBOOK OF PRACTICE AND INTERNAL PROCEDURES

As Amended Through December 1, 2011

PREFACE

The Handbook of Practice and Internal Procedures of the United States Court of Appeals for the District of Columbia Circuit was first published in 1978. That publication anticipated Section 208(a) of the Federal Courts Improvement Act of 1982, 96 Stat. 54, 28 U.S.C. § 2077, which provides, in pertinent part, "[t]he rules for the conduct of the business of each court of appeals, including the operating procedures of such court, shall be published."

The Handbook was revised in 1987 to reflect major changes in the operations of the D.C. Circuit. These changes included the implementation of the Civil Appeals Management Plan and, in August 1986, a comprehensive new program for managing the Court's entire caseload (Case Management Plan). The Court also began an appellate mediation program. In 1987 the Court issued a full revision of its General Rules—the first complete revision of those rules in nearly a decade.

The 1994 edition of the Handbook accompanied the Court's 1993 revision of its Circuit Rules. The rules were revised and renumbered to parallel more closely the Federal Rules of Appellate Procedure. Additionally, while the basic structure of the Case Management Plan remained, significant modifications were adopted, and the Court completely restructured its Appellate Mediation Program. The Handbook has been revised numerous times since then to reflect federal and local rules amendments as well as changes in court practice.

Cases in the Case Management/Electronic Case Files (CM/ECF) system are governed by the Court's Administrative Order, effective June 8, 2009. ECF filers must consult and comply with the Administrative Order and CM/ECF procedures posted on the Court's web site.

This Handbook is a practitioner's guide to the Court's rules and internal case management procedures. Counsel and litigants should bear in mind, however, that the Handbook is for guidance only. *The Federal Rules of Appellate Procedure and the Court's Circuit Rules, as well as any orders issued in a particular case, dictate the specific requirements for litigating a case in the D.C. Circuit, and counsel's first obligation is to consult and comply with those rules.*

The Court will continue to revise the Handbook periodically as necessary to reflect changes in its rules and case processing. The Court also encourages practitioners to forward their suggested revisions to the Clerk or the Court's Advisory Committee on Procedures. In publishing the Handbook, the Court seeks to facilitate the efficient disposition of its cases, while maintaining the high standards of appellate litigation and adjudication that are the tradition of the D.C. Circuit.

I. INTRODUCTION TO THE COURT

A. Physical Facilities. The United States Court of Appeals for the District of Columbia Circuit is located in the E. Barrett Prettyman United States Courthouse on Constitution Avenue between Third Street and John Marshall Park, Northwest, Washington, D.C. The mailing address is: E. Barrett Prettyman United States Courthouse, 333 Constitution Avenue, N.W., Washington, D.C. 20001–2866. The principal facilities of the Court are the judges' chambers, the courtroom, the Office of the Circuit Executive, the Office of the Clerk (which includes the Legal Division), and the Circuit Library. The judges' chambers are located on the third and fifth floors of the Courthouse. The Circuit Library is located on the third floor. The Office of the Circuit Executive is located on the fourth floor. The Office of the Clerk and the Legal Division are located on the fifth and third floors, respectively.

The United States District Court for the District of Columbia, the United States Bankruptcy Court, the United States Marshal's Office, and the United States Probation Office also are located in the Courthouse.

The Courthouse became a "smoke-free" building in 1996. Smoking is not permitted in the public areas or in any of the Courthouse offices.

1. *Chambers.* Access to the area of the judges' chambers, the Office of the Circuit Executive, and the Legal Division is limited to court personnel and others with legitimate reasons for visiting. All persons visiting these areas must be admitted through the security system on the third, fourth, and fifth floors. Visitors should make advance arrangements with the judges' chambers, the Circuit Executive's Office, or the Legal Division.

2. *Office of the Circuit Executive.* The Office of the Circuit Executive is located in Room 4726. Automation staff is in Room 5836. Mediation sessions set up by the Circuit Executive are held in Rooms A, B, and C of Room 5720, or in lawyer conference rooms, if needed.

3. *Office of the Clerk.* The public Office of the Clerk is located in Room 5523. This is where the dockets—the official records of cases before the Court—are kept, all filings with the Court are made, and orders of the Court are issued. The file room where the public may inspect filings also is located in Room 5523. Both the file room and the public office are open between 9 a.m. and 4 p.m., Monday through Friday, except federal holidays and any other day designated by the Chief Judge. A filing depository, available 24 hours a day, 7 days a week, is located inside the Third Street entrance to the Courthouse. *See* infra Part II.C.2.

4. *Legal Division.* The Legal Division is located in Room 3529. Conferences convened by the Director of the Legal Division are held in Room 3535.

5. *Library.* The Circuit Library, located on the third floor of the Courthouse, may be used by court personnel, members of the bar of the Court of Appeals or the District Court, and any person who is counsel or a party in a case pending in this Circuit, or by the permission of a judge of this Circuit. Any person wishing to use the government document collection will be admitted for that purpose, subject to generally applicable security and other restrictions. Library hours are 8:30 a.m. to 4:30 p.m., Monday through Friday, except federal holidays and any other day designated by the Chief Judge.

B. Personnel.

1. *Judges.* The Court has eleven authorized Circuit Judgeships. By statute, the administrative head of the Court is the Chief Judge, a position filled by the most senior judge under the age of 65 at the time the vacancy occurs. The Chief Judge serves until the age

of 70, or for a period of 7 years, whichever occurs first.

In addition to carrying a regular caseload, the Chief Judge is responsible for the administrative business of the Court and the Circuit. The Chief Judge presides in the courtroom, at the Judicial Council meetings, at the Court's Executive Sessions, and at the Circuit Judicial Conference. The Chief Judge is also a member of the Judicial Conference of the United States.

Supplementing the judges in full-time "active" service on the Court are Senior Circuit Judges, who handle as full a caseload as they are willing and able to undertake.

2. *Judges' Staffs.* All of the Circuit Judges employ one secretary or judicial assistant and up to four law clerks. In addition, the Chief Judge usually hires a Special Assistant for the duration of his or her term. No contact relating to court business is permitted between the judges' law clerks, judicial assistants, or secretaries and attorneys or other persons outside the Court. All communications must be made through the Clerk's Office.

3. *Legal Division.* The Legal Division is part of the Office of the Clerk. The Court's central legal staff consists of the Director, an Assistant to the Director, staff attorneys, and support staff. The office also occasionally employs law student interns. Staff attorneys are hired either on a permanent basis or for two-year terms on a staggered basis. Their primary duties fall into three broad categories: (1) screening and classifying cases and pleadings filed in the Court; (2) making recommendations to panels and preparing proposed dispositions in all contested motions and emergency matters; and (3) making recommendations and preparing proposed dispositions in cases decided without oral argument, pursuant to Circuit Rule 34(j).

In addition to supervising the work of the staff attorneys, the Director and Assistant assist merits panels in managing motions practice, briefing, and oral argument in major cases designated "Complex" under the Court's 1986 Case Management Plan, and in smaller cases deemed appropriate for management. The Legal Division also screens cases for inclusion in the Court's Appellate Mediation Program.

The Director is responsible for the hiring, training, and supervision of the central legal staff. He or she also works with the Court on major projects related to the Court's overall functioning, including the development and implementation of case processing procedures, and the revision of the Court's Circuit Rules and Handbook of Practice and Internal Procedures.

4. *Circuit Executive.* The Circuit Executive is appointed by the Circuit Judicial Council and serves the United States Court of Appeals, the United States District Court, and the United States Bankruptcy Court. While the clerks' offices within the Circuit handle case processing and other "line" responsibilities, the Circuit Executive facilitates these traditional functions by providing a bridge between each of these offices. The Circuit Executive works on projects with other court units and with judges and chambers staff, and works closely with the Administrative Office, the Federal Judicial Center, and Executive Branch agencies.

The Circuit Executive handles other responsibilities as well. He or she creates and implements alternative dispute resolution programs throughout the Circuit; oversees space and facilities projects and food service and mailroom operations in the Courthouse; and is responsible for developing and implementing security and emergency preparedness plans. In addition, the Circuit Executive carries out a wide variety of responsibilities for the Chief Judge of the Court of Appeals, such as preparing the annual budget for the Court; assisting with investitures, portrait unveilings, and other official ceremonies; administering the Court's non-appropriated fund; assisting in the resolution of personnel problems; and planning programs for visiting judges and other dignitaries.

As Secretary to the Historical Society of the District of Columbia Circuit, the Circuit Executive maintains the records and supports the operations of the Society.

As Secretary to the D.C. Circuit Judicial Conference, the Circuit Executive plans, administers, and records the conference.

As Secretary to the Circuit Judicial Council, the Circuit Executive serves as the executive officer of the Council. These duties include assisting with the development of new Court-related operations and handling problems that arise in such areas as space and facilities, and court and personnel management.

The Circuit Executive's staff includes a Deputy Circuit Executive, Assistant Circuit Executives, an Emergency Preparedness Coordinator, administrative analysts, and support staff. In addition, the staff includes a Chief Circuit Mediator and Circuit Mediator assisted by volunteer mediators.

5. *Clerk's Office.* The Clerk's Office is composed of an administrative division, a case administration division, and a legal division. *See* supra Part I.B.3. The Clerk's Office maintains the docket of the Court, the official record of all proceedings before the Court, and receives and maintains all filings in the Court, keeping them available for public inspection. It prepares and distributes the judges' sitting schedules and the Court's oral argument calendar; handles attorney admissions to the Court's bar; and prints, records, and distributes all opinions and orders of the Court. The Clerk's Office serves as the Court's liaison with attorneys, litigants, the media, and the general public.

The Clerk's Office also provides the Court with statistical, fiscal, personnel, training, and property and procurement services, as well as other administrative support services. The Clerk is also responsible for processing complaints of judicial misconduct or disability.

6. *Librarian.* The Circuit Library is administered by the Circuit Librarian and the Deputy Circuit Librarian.

C. Court Organization.

1. *Judicial Council.* The Judicial Council of the Circuit, as established by 28 U.S.C. § 332, is composed of the Chief Judge of the Court of Appeals and an equal number of the judges of this Court and of the District Court. The Chief Judge of this Court presides. The Circuit Executive serves as the secretary and administrative officer to the Council. Most business of the Council is conducted through e-mail discussions and votes. Meetings are closed.

The Council is empowered under 28 U.S.C. § 332(d)(1) to "make all necessary and appropriate orders for the effective and expeditious administration of justice within its circuit." Any member of the Council may place an item on the agenda by forwarding it to the Circuit Executive for inclusion.

2. *Meetings of the Court of Appeals in Executive Session.* Periodically, the judges of the Court of Appeals meet in executive session to discuss the business of the Court. The Chief Judge may also call special meetings to address specific issues. Both active and senior judges attend these meetings and vote on matters of concern to the entire Court. The Chief Judge presides; also generally present are the Circuit Executive and the Clerk. At each meeting the Circuit Executive and the Clerk report to the Court about the Court's caseload and other matters affecting Court operations. Any judge may place an item on the agenda by instructions to the Clerk, who serves as secretary at these meetings. The meetings of the Court in executive session are closed, although on occasion the Chief Judge may request an individual from outside the Court to attend to discuss a matter of concern to the Court.

Six items regularly included on the agenda of the executive sessions reflect the Court's concern with the status of its work: a report by the Circuit Executive on matters affecting Circuit and Court operations; a report by the Clerk on the Legal Division's caseload of motions, Rule 34(j) cases, and emergency matters; reports providing monthly caseload statistics such as the number of filings and dispositions; reports by each judge on the status of cases assigned to that judge for opinions; reports on cases that have been argued but not yet assigned for the writing of an opinion; and reports on motions or petitions pending before the judges.

3. *Committees.* The Court uses permanent, as well as ad hoc, committees in conducting its internal business. Of particular interest to the bar are the following:

(a) Advisory Committee on Procedures. Circuit Rule 47.4, in accordance with 28 U.S.C. § 2077(b), formally establishes this Committee. The Advisory Committee is composed of no less than 15 local attorneys representing all sectors of the profession—government, private, public interest, and academic. The Committee initiates recommended rule changes and evaluates internal operating procedures in effect or under consideration. The Committee also serves as a channel of communication between the Court, and the bar and the public.

(b) Committee on Admissions and Grievances. Rule II of the Court's Rules of Disciplinary Enforcement establishes this Committee, composed of 6 members of the Court's bar. The Court may refer to the Committee, for investigation, hearing, and report, any allegation of professional misconduct by any member of the Court's bar. The Committee also advises the Court on its admission policies and practices.

(c) Criminal Justice Act Panel Committee. Rule I.(b) of the Court's Plan to Implement the Criminal Justice Act of 1964 establishes a committee to review the operation and administration on the CJA list. The Committee consists of two active Circuit Judges, the Federal Public Defender, and one experienced criminal practitioner who is on the list and one who is not on the list.

4. *Judicial Conference.* As provided in 28 U.S.C. § 333, the Chief Judge may convene biennially or annually the judges of this Court, the District Court, and the Bankruptcy Court to discuss improvements in the administration of justice within the Circuit. Public officials especially concerned with the work of these courts, deans of law schools in the District of Columbia, and a representative group of local attorneys from the public and private sectors are also invited to participate in the Conference. The Circuit also will occasionally convene a Conference including only judges and court staff. Further information on the Conference is contained in Circuit Rule 47.3.

D. The Circuit Rules. Federal Rule of Appellate Procedure 47 permits each court of appeals to make local rules not inconsistent with the Federal Rules of Appellate Procedure. To become effective, local rules must be approved by a majority of the judges in active service. In this Circuit the local rules are called the Circuit Rules (cited as "D.C. Cir. Rule ___").

Circuit Rule 47 provides for notice and an opportunity to comment on proposed changes to the Court's local rules. Proposed rule changes are posted in the Court's public office and on the Court's Internet web site. Notice of proposed amendments is also published in *The Daily Washington Law Reporter* and sent to the presidents of the District of Columbia Bar, the Bar Association of the District of Columbia, the Washington Bar Association, the Women's Bar Association, and the presidents of any other organization described in Circuit Rule 47(c)(4)(E), who notify the Clerk of the Court that they wish to receive notice of proposed rule changes.

Comments on proposed changes may be submitted in writing to the Advisory Committee on Procedures. The Committee will consider them in formulating its recommendation to the Court and will transmit these comments to the Court, together with its recommendation. The comment period will ordinarily be no less than 45 days.

Circuit Rule 47(b) also provides that any person may propose a change in the rules by submitting a written request directly to the Court or to the Advisory Committee on Procedures.

II. PRELIMINARY MATTERS

A. Admission to Practice. (*See* Fed. R. App. P. 46; D.C. Cir. Rule 46.)

1. *When Required.* An attorney practicing before the Court must be a member of the bar of the Court, except as otherwise provided by law. Membership in the bar of another court does not confer membership in the bar of this Court. The Clerk's Office will not file briefs, motions, or other papers not signed by a member of this Court's bar. The pleading will, however, be lodged with the Court and filed once the attorney becomes a member of the bar of this Court.

There are three qualifications to this rule. First, in order to file a notice of appeal in the district court or a petition for review, an attorney need not be a member of the bar of this Court. The docketing statement and any further filing in the case, however, must be signed by a member of the bar of this Court. Second, the requirement is temporarily suspended whenever a problem of timeliness might arise. Where this is the case, the Clerk will file the pleading and immediately notify counsel of the admission requirement. Third, law students may participate in a case under the direction of a supervising attorney, as provided in Circuit Rule 46(g).

An attorney who is not a member of the Court's bar may be granted leave by the Court to present oral argument in a case. Counsel of record should advise the Clerk's Office at least 7 days in advance, at the time counsel submits Form 72, *Notification To The Court From Attorney Intending To Present Argument*, that a motion for leave to argue pro hac vice will be made. Permission is usually granted by the Court on the morning of oral argument. Were the Court, however, to deny the motion, counsel would be informed in advance of the argument date. The attorney who wishes to argue pro hac vice must arrive at the courtroom, accompanied by a sponsoring attorney who is a member of the bar of this Court, at least 20 minutes prior to the start of argument for the day and immediately notify the courtroom deputy clerk, who will furnish appropriate forms and advise counsel of the procedures for admission pro hac vice. Counsel who litigate regularly before the Court *may not* make repeated appearances pro hac vice, but must apply for admission to the bar of the Court. Similarly, counsel may not seek to appear pro hac vice in order to file pleadings; rather counsel must apply for admission to the bar of the Court. Counsel who are not members of the bar of the Court or who have not been granted leave to appear pro hac vice will not appear on the opinion heading.

2. *Obtaining Admission.* The Court admits to practice before it attorneys who have previously been admitted to the bar of the highest court of a state or to the bar of other federal courts. Applicants must fill out the forms supplied by the Clerk's Office and submit them with certification of their membership and good standing in the bar that qualifies them for admission. They must also remit the fee specified by order of the Court. Attorneys may be admitted on the written application without a personal appearance. The Clerk's Office will send the attorney a certificate of membership in the bar of the Court.

3. *Exclusion from Practice.* No person employed by the Court, including law clerks, after leaving the employ of the Court, may practice as an attorney in any case that was pending in the Court during the person's term of service. A case is pending in the Court from the moment the appeal or petition for review is docketed until final disposition of the appeal. This prohibition includes signing briefs and giving advice in connection with the case. As a general rule, employees of the Court may not engage in the practice of law. *See* D.C. Cir. Rule 1(c).

Suspension or disbarment by any other court of record may result in the suspension or disbarment of a member of this Court's bar. Before any reciprocal discipline is imposed, the attorney will be afforded an opportunity to show cause why he or she should not be suspended from practice in the Court or disbarred. The Court may refer to its Committee on Admissions and Grievances this or any other suggestion of professional misconduct on the part of a member of the bar.

B. Requests for Information.

1. *Procedural Questions.* Personnel in the Clerk's Office and the Legal Division are available to answer procedural questions about matters not covered in the Federal Rules of Appellate Procedure, the Circuit Rules, or this Handbook.

2. *Court Records.* The Clerk's Office will make available, and will assist in locating, all public records in the possession of the Court. Public records consist primarily of information entered in the docket of the

Court and any briefs, motions, or other filings not under seal.

3. *Electronic Public Access to Information.* The Court's Internet web site provides additional court information to the public. The site is located at: www.cadc.uscourts.gov. The site allows on-line viewing and printing of court forms; the Circuit Rules, Handbook, and Frequently Asked Questions (FAQs); the oral argument calendar; court opinions that are not sealed; and other information concerning the Court. Case information is also available on the PACER web site to individuals having a PACER account. There is a fee for access to PACER. To set up an account, interested parties must call the PACER Service Center at 1–800–676–6856. The PACER web site is accessible via a link from the Court's web site.

Persons and organizations funded by federal judiciary appropriations, *e. g.*, attorneys appointed under the Criminal Justice Act, are exempt from the PACER access fee. Anyone exempt under this provision must notify the account representative when establishing an account. In addition, the Court may, for good cause, exempt persons from the PACER access fee to avoid unreasonable burdens and promote public access. Anyone seeking an exemption under this provision should complete an exemption request form and return it to the Clerk's Office.

Under the Court's CM/ECF system, attorneys and pro se litigants who have registered as ECF filers will receive electronic notification of docket activity. Only pro se parties and attorneys who have entered an appearance and are listed on the Court's docket will receive electronic notices in a particular case. To register as an ECF filer, consult the PACER Service Center's web site at http://pacer.ps c.uscourts.gov/announcements/general/ea_filer.html. Additional information on the CM/ECF system is available on the Court's web site.

4. *Court Operations During Inclement Weather or Emergency Situations.* Counsel with filing deadlines or who are scheduled to appear for oral argument must check with the Clerk's Office when there is a possibility that the Court may be closed because of inclement weather or an emergency situation. Special announcements on closings can be obtained by calling the Clerk's Office general information number (202–216–7000) or by checking the Court's web site located at www.cadc.uscourts.gov.

5. *The Appeals Management Plan; Complex Cases.* Questions concerning multi-party, multi-issue cases handled pursuant to the Appeals Management Plan, or designated "Complex" under the Case Management Plan, should be directed to the Legal Division. Questions that must be answered by reference to the dockets should be resolved by consulting the PACER web site. *See* supra Part II.B.3. For further assistance, questions can be directed to the Clerk's Office. The Legal Division will, however, advise practitioners whether a case is being managed by the Legal Division, or whether such management would be appropriate.

6. *General Information.* Requests for information of a general nature about cases, such as whether a brief or specific pleading has been filed, or whether the Court has acted on a motion, should be directed to the Clerk's Office or obtained by accessing docket information through the PACER web site. *See* supra Part II.B.3.

7. *Pending Cases.* It is the strict policy of the Court that telephone calls to judges' chambers, or to judges' law clerks or secretaries, concerning the status of any pending case or motion will not be accepted. All such calls will be immediately referred to the Clerk or to the Legal Division.

If the inquiry as to a pending case involves procedural questions or matters of public record, it should be made in accordance with the instructions above. If counsel is experiencing a more specialized problem with a case, he or she should call the Clerk, the Chief Deputy Clerk, the Operations Manager of the Clerk's Office, or the Director of the Legal Division. If the problem does not require immediate attention, the Clerk will usually direct that counsel's inquiry be submitted in writing. The Clerk's Office will forward the letter or motion to the Court or Legal Division, as appropriate.

8. *Disclosure of Panels and Dates.*

(a) Merits Panels. Ordinarily, the Court discloses merits panels to counsel in the order setting the case for oral argument. In criminal appeals, unlike most civil appeals, the panel usually will not be disclosed until after the parties have filed briefs. This is because the Court does not make the tentative decision to schedule oral argument in most criminal cases until after both the appellant's and appellee's briefs have been filed.

In addition, the Clerk's Office posts in the Court's public office and on the Court's web site, the calendar for a sitting period approximately 2 months in advance. The panel is subject to unannounced change when regularly scheduled judges recuse themselves or otherwise become unavailable to sit.

The timing of disclosure of the merits panel when a case is decided without oral argument pursuant to Circuit Rule 34(j) depends on whether the case had been calendared for argument. If originally scheduled for argument, the panel (subject to substitutions) will be the one announced in the order setting the case for argument. If the case has not been calendared for argument, counsel will learn the identity of the panel from the order stating that the case will be decided without argument.

(b) Panels Deciding Motions. It is generally the policy of the Court not to reveal the identity of panels before whom motions are pending until the order disposing of the motion is issued.

(c) Disposition of Matters Under Submission. It is also the policy of the Court ordinarily not to reveal in advance the prospective date of disposition of any matter under submission. This policy applies to the Clerk's Office and to the Legal Division, as well as to chambers personnel. Requests for information of this nature are inappropriate. On the day an opinion designated for publication is issued, the Clerk's Office notifies counsel by telephone. In addition, the Clerk's Office provides a telephone recording on 202–216–7296 that lists the most recently issued opinions. Opinions are also available on the Court's web site and through PACER. *See* infra Part XII.E.

9. *Press Relations.* The Circuit Executive is the designated press officer of the Court. One copy of all unsealed opinions issued by the Court is made available to the media in the press box outside the Clerk's Office.

Requests by artists to sketch court proceedings should be directed to the Clerk's Office well in advance of the scheduled argument. The Court will accommodate all requests unless the panel for reasons of security decides otherwise. Additionally, if the Court receives multiple requests, space considerations may limit the number of sketch artists that can be accommodated.

C. Filings.

1. *Compliance with Rules.* The Clerk's Office examines all items submitted for filing to ensure that they comply with the Federal Rules of Appellate Procedure and the Circuit Rules. All filings must include the name of the attorney or party making the filing, the firm name, if any, the attorney's or party's postal address and telephone number, and e-mail address for ECF filers. The Clerk's Office has the authority to direct the correction of any filing that is not in compliance with the Federal Rules of Appellate Procedure or the Circuit Rules, or direct the filing of an appropriate motion. If a party fails to comply with the Clerk's direction, the matter will be submitted to a panel for disposition.

Pursuant to Federal Rule of Appellate Procedure 25(a)(2)(D) and 25(c), the Court has authorized the filing and service of documents by electronic means. *See* D.C. Cir. Rule 25(a), (c). Cases in the CM/ECF system are governed by the Court's Administrative Order, effective June 8, 2009. ECF filers must consult and comply with the Administrative Order and CM/ECF procedures posted on the Court's web site. Upon motion and a showing of good cause, the Court may exempt a party from the electronic filing requirements and authorize filing by means other than use of the CM/ECF system. *See* D.C. Cir. Rule 25(b).

2. *Timeliness.* (*See* Fed. R. App. P. 25(a), 26; D.C. Cir. Rules 25, 26, 27(h), 28(e).)

In computing times prescribed for filings, the day of the event from which the prescribed period begins to run is not included. All intermediate days are included. Furthermore, if the last day of the period falls on a Saturday, Sunday, legal holiday, or a day on which the Clerk's Office is otherwise closed or inaccessible, the period is extended to the next business day. Fed. R. App. P. 26(a)(1), (3); D.C. Cir. Rule 45(b). For forward-counted periods—that is, periods that are measured after an event—"legal holiday" is defined to include a day declared a holiday by the state in which the circuit clerk's principal office is located. Fed. R. App. P. 26(a)(6)(C). Because "state" includes the District of Columbia for purposes of these rules (Fed. R. App. P. 1(b)), any day that has been declared a holiday by the District of Columbia counts as a legal holiday that extends a deadline, but only when computing a forward-counted period. By contrast, if a filing is due 7 days before an event (for example, before a brief is due), that is considered a "backward-counted period," and if the 7th day falls on a District of Columbia holiday, the filing is due that day because state holidays are not legal holidays when computing a backward-counted deadline.

A document filed electronically is deemed filed on the date and at the time stated on the Notice of Docket Activity from the Court. To be considered timely filed that day, filing must be completed before midnight Eastern Time unless a specific time is set by Court order. Unless the Court has ordered filing by hand or other means, ECF filers may file paper copies of non-emergency documents by first-class mail, or other class of mail that is at least as expeditious, within 2 business days of the electronic filing.

For non-ECF filers, filing of a motion may be by mail addressed to the Clerk, but the papers must reach the Clerk's Office within the time prescribed. Only briefs, not motions or other pleadings, are timely if mailed on the date due. The Court, however, prefers to receive briefs on the date due. Briefs must be filed according to the schedule set by the Court.

Service by any method other than personal service extends by 3 calendar days the time for responding to the paper served (other than briefs, whose due dates are set by schedule). Papers are presumed to be served by mail unless the certificate of service indicates otherwise. In addition, upon motion for compelling reasons, the Court may extend the time prescribed for filing any papers or allow filings out of time. However, the Court lacks the authority to extend the time for filing papers that commence an appeal, such as a notice of appeal, a petition for review, or a petition filed pursuant to 28 U.S.C. § 1292(b) or Federal Rule of Civil Procedure 23(f).

Any filing or brief (with the exception of emergency, confidential, or sealed documents) may be left, on the date due, in the Court of Appeals filing depository, located inside the Third Street entrance to the Courthouse, unless the Court has ordered that the filing be made at a time certain. The filing depository is available 24 hours a day, 7 days a week. All filings must be enclosed in an envelope or otherwise securely wrapped. The maximum dimensions for documents deposited are 14 ½ inches by 11 ½ inches by 10 inches. Materials exceeding these dimensions must be split into separate packages and clearly marked. A form provided near the depository must be completed, date/time stamped, and affixed to each package.

Under the Court's Case Management Plan, briefing schedules are usually set after the case has been screened and classified by the Legal Division, and after all outstanding procedural and dispositive motions have been resolved. In cases classified as "Regular Merits" cases, the oral argument date might be included in the order establishing the briefing schedule, or might not be set until briefing is underway. In cases classified as potential "Rule 34(j)" cases, the briefing schedule is set in the order notifying counsel that the case might be disposed of without oral argument under Circuit Rule 34(j). Finally, in cases classified as "Complex," or otherwise identified for management under the Case Management Plan, the briefing format and schedule are formulated by the special panel in conjunction with the Legal Division, in most cases based on the parties' responses to an order to show cause concerning a proposed briefing schedule and format. The amount of time for briefing a case may vary, depending on whether it is a district court or agency case, whether there are intervenors or amici curiae, whether there are cross-appeals, and whether there is a deferred appendix.

Deadlines are monitored by the Clerk's Office; when the deadlines are not met, the matter is called to the party's attention by phone call, letter, or an order from the Court directing the party to show cause why certain action should not be taken. Depending on the nature of the deadline, such action could include dismissal for failure to prosecute the appeal.

The Clerk's Office has been directed to bring to the attention of the Court the names of counsel who repeatedly abuse the time limits in the rules. In extreme instances, this has led to a referral to the Court's Committee on Admissions and Grievances.

Counsel are advised that whenever there are serious settlement negotiations in progress, including post-argument settlement discussions, the parties should advise the Clerk of that fact.

3. *Service.* (*See* Fed. R. App. P. 25; D.C. Cir. Rule 25.)

Parties or counsel filing papers must serve copies on all other parties to the case, at or before the time of filing, unless the rules provide for service by the Clerk. Service must be on counsel if a party is represented by counsel. The Notice of Docket Activity that is generated by the CM/ECF system constitutes service on all parties who are registered ECF filers but does not replace the certificate of service. Parties who are not ECF filers must be served by an alternative method of service authorized by Federal Rule of Appellate Procedure 25(c). Service by mail or by commercial carrier is complete on mailing or delivery to the carrier. Service by electronic means is complete on transmission, unless the party making service is notified that the paper was not received by the party served. All filings must contain a certificate of service. In emergency situations, upon authorization by the Clerk, papers may be filed with the Court by facsimile transmission.

4. *Dockets.* When an appeal is filed in the Court, the Clerk's Office establishes a docket using an annual sequential numbering series. Docket numbers in agency cases begin with "1000" and are prefixed by the year, *e.g.*, 09–1000, 09–1001, *etc.* Docket numbers in criminal cases begin with "3000"; docket numbers in district court civil cases in which the federal government is a party begin with "5000"; docket numbers in district court civil cases involving private parties begin with "7000"; and docket numbers in cases which have not yet been accepted for filing begin with "8000."

5. *Privacy Protection.* Litigants must be aware of the federal rules and take all necessary precautions to protect the privacy of parties, witnesses, and others whose personal information appears in court filings. Sensitive personal data must be removed from documents filed with the Court and made available to the public—whether electronically or on paper. All filers must comply with Federal Rule of Appellate Procedure 25(a)(5) and must follow the guidance on redacting personal data identifiers, which is posted on the Court's web site. In addition, ECF filers must comply with the requirements for privacy protection set out in the Administrative Order—ECF–9, effective June 8, 2009.

D. Clerk's Fees. (*See* D.C. Cir. Rule 45.)

The Judicial Conference of the United States prescribes certain fees to be paid for services performed by the Clerk's Office, including docketing a case on appeal, searching records and certifying the results, providing copies of records or papers, certifying copies of records or papers, and providing copies of the Court's opinions. These fees, which change periodically, are set forth in a schedule appended to the Circuit Rules and posted on the Court's web site.

E. Complaints Against Judges. The procedure for filing complaints against judges is set forth in the

Rules for Judicial–Conduct and Judicial–Disability Proceedings. A copy of these rules may be obtained from the Clerk of the Court or the Court's web site.

III. COMMENCING THE APPEAL

A. Preliminary Matters—Jurisdiction. Before filing a notice of appeal or petition for review, parties should consider the following questions:

- Is there subject matter jurisdiction in this case?
- Has the district court or agency fully and finally resolved all issues in the case?
- Is the notice of appeal or petition for review timely?
- Is there a pending motion listed in Federal Rule of Appellate Procedure 4(a)(4) or 4(b)(3) that would make the filing of a notice of appeal ineffective?
- Have the points of error been properly preserved?
- Does the proposed appeal have genuine merit or is it frivolous?

It is critically important for parties to be certain that the Court has jurisdiction to entertain the appeal. In district court cases, parties should consult the relevant jurisdictional provisions of Titles 18 and 28 of the United States Code; in agency cases, parties should consult the particular statutory provisions and agency regulations bearing on jurisdiction. This Handbook does not purport to provide a complete and comprehensive guide to federal appellate jurisdiction. The following summary is intended only to identify generally the bases for the Court's review of district court and agency cases.

1. *Jurisdiction—District Court Cases.* The Court has jurisdiction over all criminal appeals and most civil appeals from the United States District Court for the District of Columbia. Ordinarily, only final judgments of the district court are reviewable. *See* 28 U.S.C. § 1291. The question whether an order is "final" may be very complex and requires careful examination of the rules and case law. *See Cohen v. Beneficial Industrial Loan Corp.*, 337 U.S. 541 (1949). In suits involving multiple claims or parties, parties should consult Federal Rule of Civil Procedure 54(b), which governs appeals from district court orders that do not dispose of the entire case.

There are certain interlocutory or non-final orders that also can be reviewed, some as a matter of right, and others as a matter of judicial discretion. Interlocutory civil orders reviewable as of right consist of orders granting, continuing, modifying, dissolving, or denying injunctions, and certain orders in receivership, bankruptcy, and admiralty. *See* 28 U. S.C. § 1292(a). With respect to many other interlocutory orders in civil actions, appellate review is possible only if the trial court certifies, pursuant to 28 U.S.C. § 1292(b), that the order "involves a controlling question of law as to which there is substantial ground for difference of opinion and that an immediate appeal from the order may materially advance the ultimate termination of the litigation." In that case, this Court, in its discretion, may permit an appeal from the order. Similarly, the Court may permit an appeal from an order of a district court granting or denying class action certification under Federal Rule of Civil Procedure 23(f). *See* Fed. R. App. P. 5.

With respect to appeals from district court cases, parties also should bear in mind the Federal Courts Improvement Act of 1982, which transferred to the United States Court of Appeals for the Federal Circuit the jurisdiction to hear certain types of cases formerly reviewable in this Court, including appeals where the district court's jurisdiction was based "in whole or in part" on the Tucker Act. *See* 28 U.S.C. § 1295(a)(2).

2. *Jurisdiction—Administrative Agency Cases.* The Court reviews final orders of many federal administrative agencies, as well as the Tax Court of the United States. In these cases, the Court's jurisdiction often depends on whether the petitioner resides, maintains its principal place of business, or does business within the Circuit. Moreover, the statutes providing for judicial review of certain agency decisions also may specify this Circuit as an alternative or a special forum, even where the petitioner has no contacts with the District of Columbia. Because the criteria vary from agency to agency, counsel must examine the statutes governing reviewability of the particular administrative action in each instance.

3. *Original Jurisdiction.* To aid its appellate jurisdiction, the Court may entertain original proceedings pursuant to the All Writs Act, 28 U.S.C. § 1651. These proceedings are usually petitions for writs of mandamus or prohibition. *See* Fed. R. App. P. 21.

4. *Collateral Review of Local Court Decisions.* The Court has no authority to entertain direct appeals from orders of the Superior Court of the District of Columbia or the District of Columbia Court of Appeals. Only where a party first makes a collateral challenge to a local court ruling by bringing suit in the United States District Court for the District of Columbia, and the district court enters an appealable order, may the matter be reviewed by this Court on appeal from that order.

B. Appeals From the District Court as of Right.

1. *How Taken.* (*See* Fed. R. App. P. 3, 7.)

Appeals from district court judgments are taken by filing a notice of appeal with the *Clerk of the district court*, at which time the fees for filing and docketing the appeal must be paid to the district court Clerk. The notice must state the court to which the appeal is taken, the ruling being appealed, and the party who is appealing. The Clerk of the district court notifies the other parties when the notice of appeal has been filed. As a matter of courtesy, however, the party taking an appeal also should serve all other parties a copy of the notice of appeal. In civil cases, the district court may require a bond or other security to cover the costs of appeal.

2. *Timing.* (*See* Fed. R. App. P. 4.)

(a) General Rules. The time for noting an appeal in civil and criminal cases is set forth in FRAP 4. Upon a showing of excusable neglect or good cause, however, the district court may enlarge the time for filing a notice of appeal in civil and criminal cases, but only for limited periods. *See* Fed. R. App. P. 4(a)(5), (b)(4).

In addition, the district court may reopen the time to appeal in a civil case if (1) the district court finds that the moving party did not receive notice under Federal Rule of Civil Procedure 77(d) of the entry of the judgment or order sought to be appealed within 21 days after entry; (2) the motion to reopen is filed within 180 days after the judgment or order is entered or within 14 days after the moving party receives notice under Federal Rule of Civil Procedure 77(d) of the entry, whichever is earlier; and (3) the district court finds that no party would be prejudiced by reopening the appeal period. *See* Fed. R. App. P. 4(a)(6).

(b) Civil Cases. Regardless of which party is appealing, if a party to a case in district court is the United States, one of its agencies, a federal officer or employee sued in an official capacity, or, under certain circumstances, a federal officer or employee sued in an individual capacity, the notice of appeal must be filed within 60 days after entry of the judgment or order, unless a statute provides otherwise. If no party fits into one of these categories, the notice of appeal must be filed within 30 days.

A notice of appeal filed after the announcement of a decision or order but before the entry of the judgment or order will ordinarily be treated as filed on the date of and after the entry. If any party has filed a timely motion in the district court for relief under Federal Rules of Civil Procedure 50(b), 52(b), 59, or 60(b) (if filed no later than 28 days after entry of judgment), however, the time for appeal begins to run from the entry of the order granting or denying that motion. A notice of appeal filed *before* the disposition of any of these motions has a limited effect, and a notice or an amended notice of appeal must be filed within the prescribed time measured from entry of the order disposing of the motion if the party wishes to appeal from an aspect of the judgment affected by the resolution of such a motion. *See* Fed. R. App. P. 4(a)(4).

If Federal Rule of Civil Procedure 58(a)(1) does not require the district court to set forth its judgment on a separate document, the district court's judgment or order is deemed entered for purposes of Federal Rule of Appellate Procedure 4(a) when it is entered on the civil docket under Federal Rule of Civil Procedure 79(a). If Federal Rule of Civil Procedure 58(a)(1) does require the district court to set forth its judgment on a separate document, the district court's judgment or order is deemed entered for purposes of Federal Rule of Appellate Procedure 4(a) when the judgment or order is entered in the civil docket under Federal Rule of Civil Procedure 79(a) and when either: (1) the judgment or order is set forth on a separate document or (2) 150 days have passed since the entry of the judgment or order in the civil docket, whichever occurs first.

The Clerk of the district court is required to provide notice of the entry of judgment to all parties not in default for failure to appear. A party also may serve an adversary with notice of entry. Lack of notice does not suspend the running of the time prescribed.

If one party files a timely notice of appeal, any other party may file a notice within 14 days thereafter if the usual time to appeal has expired. Thus, if one party files a notice of appeal on the 29th day in a case in which the federal government is not a party, another party may file a notice of appeal on the 43rd day. If one party files a notice of appeal on the 5th day, however, the other party may still wait until the 30th day to file a notice of appeal. If more than one timely appeal is filed, the 14–day period begins to run from the time the first appeal is filed.

(c) Criminal Cases. The defendant must appeal within 14 days after entry of the judgment or order being appealed or within 14 days of the government's notice of appeal. The government has 30 days to appeal in those limited situations when it is allowed to do so by statute. *See* 18 U.S.C. §§ 3731, 3742.

A timely motion for judgment of acquittal, arrest of judgment, or for a new trial on any ground other than newly discovered evidence, terminates the running of the time prescribed for appealing from a criminal conviction. A motion for a new trial on the ground of newly discovered evidence also terminates the running of time to file a notice of appeal, if the motion is made within 14 days of the entry of judgment. A new 14–day period within which to appeal from the judgment, as well as from the denial of any of the enumerated motions, begins to run after entry of the order disposing of the last such remaining motion or after entry of the judgment, whichever is later. *See* Fed. R. App. P. 4(b); Fed. R. Crim. P. 33, 34.

Absent extraordinary circumstances, direct criminal appeals will not be held in abeyance pending the filing and disposition of a postconviction motion in the district court. *See* D.C. Cir. Rule 47.5.

(d) Collateral Challenges in Criminal Proceedings. Petitions for writs of habeas corpus and motions attacking sentence under 28 U.S.C. § 2255 are civil cases for purposes of computing the time for appeal. Parties should consult appropriate authorities to determine whether other proceedings are deemed civil or criminal in nature to determine the appropriate filing period.

C. Appeals From the District Court by Permission. (*See* Fed. R. App. P. 5; D.C. Cir. Rule 5.)

1. *How Taken.* Currently, discretionary appeals from interlocutory decisions of the district court are authorized in two instances, under 28 U.S.C. § 1292(b) and Federal Rule of Civil Procedure 23(f). *See* 28 U.S.C. § 1292(e). Under either provision, interlocutory appeals from the district court are taken by filing with the Clerk of this Court an original and 4 copies of a petition for permission to appeal, with proof of service on all parties to the action in the district court, and must be accompanied by a certificate of parties and amici curiae as described in Circuit Rule 28(a)(1)(A), and any disclosure statement required by Circuit Rule 26.1. *See* D.C. Cir. Rule 5(a), (c). The petition is limited to 20 pages and must state the facts necessary to understand the question presented, the question itself, the relief sought, and the reasons why the appeal should be allowed and is authorized by a statute or rule. The petition must include a copy of the order complained of and any related opinion or memorandum, as well as any required order stating the district court's permission to appeal or finding that the necessary conditions to appeal are met.

Because the petition is not itself an appeal, but rather a request to the Court asking that docketing of the appeal be allowed, a docketing fee is not required unless the Court grants the petition.

The adverse party may respond to the petition within 10 days. A response may not exceed 20 pages. Any reply, limited to 10 pages, is due within 7 days thereafter. *See* D.C. Cir. Rule 5(b). There is no oral argument on the application unless the Court so orders. The Court refers these petitions to a special panel for disposition as soon as the matter has been fully briefed.

If the Court grants permission to appeal, a notice of appeal is unnecessary. This Court enters an order granting permission to appeal, and transmits a certified copy of it to the Clerk of the district court. This certified copy serves as a notice of appeal. The appellant must pay the docketing fee to the Clerk of the district court within 14 days after entry of the order granting permission to appeal. Once the Clerk is notified by the district court that the fee has been paid, the appeal will be docketed and the case transmitted to the Legal Division for screening.

2. *Timing.* The petition for permission to appeal under 28 U.S.C. § 1292(b) must be filed within 10 days after the entry of the interlocutory order containing the statement prescribed in the statute, or within 10 days after the entry of an order amending the prior interlocutory order to include the district judge's statement required by that section. The petition for permission to appeal under Federal Rule of Civil Procedure 23(f) must be filed within 14 days after entry of the order granting or denying class action certification.

D. Appeals From the Tax Court. (*See* Fed. R. App. P. 13, 14.)

1. *How Taken.* These appeals are taken by filing a notice of appeal with the Clerk of the Tax Court in the District of Columbia. Filing by mail is permitted. The notice must identify the court to which the appeal is taken, the ruling being appealed, and the party who is appealing. The Clerk of the Tax Court notifies the other parties that a notice of appeal has been filed, but it is good practice for the party taking an appeal also to serve all other parties with a copy of the notice of appeal.

2. *Timing.* The notice of appeal must be filed within 90 days after entry of the decision of the Tax Court. If a timely notice is filed, any other party may take an appeal by filing a notice of appeal within 120 days after entry of the decision. A notice of appeal mailed and postmarked *before* the prescribed time expires, but received *after* it expires, is treated as timely under 26 U.S.C. § 7502.

A motion to vacate or revise a decision, timely filed under the Rules of Practice of the Tax Court, terminates the running of time for filing a notice of appeal from that decision. The new time begins to run for all parties from entry of an order disposing of the motion, or from entry of a new decision, whichever is later.

E. Review of Administrative Agency Orders. (*See* Fed. R. App. P. 15; D.C. Cir. Rule 15.)

1. *How Obtained.* To obtain review of an administrative agency order, a party must file a petition for review (or other document prescribed by the applicable statute) with the Clerk of this Court. The petition for review must designate the party seeking relief, the respondent(s), and the order to be reviewed. The respondent is the appropriate agency or officer of that agency. Some statutes also require the United States to be named as a respondent, and some statutes require the petitioner to attach a copy of the agency order or rule for which review is sought. The petitioner must file an original and 4 copies of the petition for review. In addition, the petitioner must serve a copy of the petition on all other parties who were participants in the agency proceeding, except in informal rulemaking proceedings, such as, for example, those covered by the Administrative Procedure Act, 5 U.S.C. § 553, or other statutory authority. In these informal rulemaking cases, petitioner need serve copies only on the respondent agency, and on the United

States if required by statute. Petitioner also must file a list of those served. When the number of parties filing comments in informal rulemaking proceedings is not too great to impose an undue burden, it is courteous to serve those parties with a copy of the petition for review, although a copy of the agency order need not be attached.

2. *Timing.* The time for filing the petition for review is prescribed by the statute that sets forth the procedures for obtaining judicial review of the particular agency's orders.

3. *Intervention.* Unless the applicable statute provides otherwise, a party who wishes to intervene must file a motion for leave to intervene with service on all parties to the proceeding before this Court. The motion must contain a concise statement of the party's interest in the case, and the grounds for intervention. The motion must be filed within 30 days of the filing of the petition for review and must be accompanied by any disclosure statement required by Circuit Rule 26.1. A motion to intervene in a proceeding before this Court concerning direct review of an agency action will be deemed a motion to intervene in all cases before the Court involving the same agency action or order, including later filed cases, unless the moving party specifically advises otherwise. An order granting such a motion has the effect of granting intervention in all such cases.

F. Enforcement of Administrative Agency Orders.

1. *How Obtained.* (*See* Fed. R. App. P. 15(b).)

When authorized by statute, a party may seek enforcement of an administrative agency order by filing an application with the Clerk of this Court. A cross-application for enforcement also may be filed by a respondent to a petition for review, if the Court has jurisdiction to enforce the order. Any application for enforcement must contain a concise statement of the proceedings in which the order sought to be enforced was entered, the party against whom the order is to be enforced, the facts upon which jurisdiction and venue are based, and the relief sought. The applicant must file the original of the application for enforcement, 4 copies, and a copy for each respondent. The Clerk's Office serves the respondents; the petitioner serves all other parties who participated before the agency.

The respondent to the enforcement petition must serve and file an answer within 21 days. Where no answer is filed, the Court will enter a judgment in favor of the moving party.

2. *Timing.* The time for filing an enforcement application is prescribed by the applicable statute.

G. Original Proceedings. (*See* Fed. R. App. P. 21; D.C. Cir. Rule 21.)

1. *How Taken.* A party seeking a writ of mandamus or prohibition directed to a judge, or seeking any other extraordinary writ, must file an original and 4 copies of a petition with the Clerk of this Court, with proof of service on the respondent judge or agency, and on all parties to the action in the trial court or to proceedings before the agency. The petition is limited to 30 pages and must comply with the typeface requirements of Federal Rule of Appellate Procedure 32(a)(5) and the type-style requirements of Federal Rule of Appellate Procedure 32(a)(6). The petition must contain a statement of the issues, the necessary facts, the relief sought, and the reasons the writ should issue. It must include copies of any relevant order or opinion, necessary parts of the record, a certificate of parties and amici curiae as described in Circuit Rule 28(a)(1)(A), and any disclosure statement required by Circuit Rule 26.1. Circuit Rule 21 prescribes the manner of captioning the action.

The Court handles petitions for extraordinary writs in the same way as dispositive motions, referring them to a special panel for disposition. *See* infra Part VII.D. If the panel finds the petition to be without merit, it may deny the petition without calling for an answer. Otherwise, the panel issues an order fixing a time within which an answer must be filed. Unless otherwise provided, there is no oral argument.

2. *Timing.* No time limits are applicable.

3. *Petitions for Writs of Mandamus Challenging District Court Transfers.* Any order by the district court transferring a case to another district is not an appealable order. Therefore, litigants seeking to challenge such a transfer frequently file petitions for writ of mandamus with this Court. *See In re Scott*, 709 F.2d 717 (D.C. Cir. 1983) (per curiam); *see also* supra Part III.G.1. Unless the case was transferred to an improper forum or there is a substantial issue whether the district court had power to order the transfer, once physical transfer of the original record takes place, jurisdiction is exclusive in the transferee court, and this Court has no power to review the transfer decision. *See In re Briscoe*, 976 F.2d 1425 (D.C. Cir. 1992); *Starnes v. McGuire*, 512 F.2d 918, 924 (D.C. Cir. 1974) (en banc).

4. *Petitions for Writs of Mandamus Alleging Unreasonable Agency Delay.* The Court has identified a category of petitions for writ of mandamus to compel administrative agency action unreasonably delayed. *See In re GTE Serv. Corp.*, 762 F.2d 1024, 1026 n.5 (D.C. Cir. 1985); *Telecommunications Research & Action Ctr. v. FCC*, 750 F.2d 70 (D.C. Cir. 1984). These petitions are treated in the same manner as other petitions for writ of mandamus, *i.e.*, petitions are limited to 30 pages and must comply with the typeface requirements of Federal Rule of Appellate Procedure 32(a)(5) and the type-style requirements of Federal Rule of Appellate Procedure 32(a)(6), the petition is

initially considered by the special panel, and no petition will be granted unless the Court orders an answer.

H. Joint Appeals. (*See* Fed. R. App. P. 3(b), 15(a).)

Persons entitled to appeal whose interests make joinder practicable may file a joint notice of appeal or petition for review, or they may join in an appeal after filing separate timely notices or petitions. Parties taking joint appeals must list individually each appellant or petitioner. The Court also may consolidate appeals on its own or upon motion. *See* infra Part V.A.

I. Cross–Appeals. (*See* Fed. R. App. P. 28.1; D.C. Cir. Rule 28.1.)

Appellees, in cases appealed from the district court, may generally, without filing a cross-appeal, defend a judgment on any ground raised in the district court, even if that ground was rejected, not considered, or raised sua sponte by the district court. They may not, however, attack the judgment, either to enlarge their own rights or to lessen the rights of their adversary, except by filing a cross-appeal. A cross-appeal also is necessary where appellees seek to correct an error in, or to supplement, the district court's judgment. Unless the parties otherwise agree and notify the Clerk's Office, or the designation is modified by court order, the party that files the first notice of appeal files the first brief. *See* Fed. R. App. P. 28.1(b); D.C. Cir. Rule 28.1(a). The time for taking cross-appeals is set out supra at Part III.B.2.(b).

J. Appeals Expedited by Statute. (*See* Fed. R. App. P. 9(a); D.C. Cir. Rule 47.2.)

For several categories of appeals, the Federal Rules of Appellate Procedure and the Circuit Rules expressly prescribe special procedures. For example, the following matters are to be expedited, but this list is not exhaustive: appeals by the government from dismissal of an indictment or information or from suppression of evidence in a criminal proceeding, pursuant to 18 U.S.C. § 3731; appeals by recalcitrant witnesses from summary confinement, pursuant to 28 U.S.C. § 1826; appeals from denial or grant of pretrial release in criminal cases, pursuant to 18 U.S.C. § 3145; appeals from habeas corpus proceedings, pursuant to 28 U.S.C. chapter 153; appeals of certain orders entered in any case brought by the Federal Deposit Insurance Corporation, pursuant to 12 U.S.C. § 1821(q)(1); and appeals from any action for temporary or preliminary injunctive relief, pursuant to 28 U.S.C. § 1657(a). Counsel should consult these statutes and the relevant rules with care. Prompt notification to the Clerk's Office by counsel intending to file such an appeal is essential to enable the Court to begin immediate preparation for prompt disposition. It is particularly important that counsel notify the Court in writing of arrangements for preparation of all necessary transcripts and for transmittal of relevant portions of the record.

Other sections of this Handbook bear on emergency motions, motions for release pending appeal, and the calendaring of emergency and expedited appeals. *See* infra Parts VIII.A, B, C.

K. Cases with Records Under Seal. (*See* D.C. Cir. Rule 47.1.)

Any portion of the record that was placed under seal in the district court or before an agency remains under seal in this Court unless otherwise ordered. Parties and their counsel are responsible for assuring that materials under seal remain under seal and are not publicly disclosed. Matters under seal may not be filed in the Court of Appeals drop box. For privacy protections that govern all cases filed in this Court, see supra Part II.C.5.

In any case in which the record in the district court or before an agency is under seal in whole or in part, each party must review the record to determine whether any portions of the record under seal should remain under seal on appeal. If a party determines that some portion should be unsealed, that party must seek an agreement on the unsealing. Such agreement must be promptly presented to the district court or agency for its consideration and issuance of an appropriate order. *See* D.C. Cir. Rule 47.1(b); *see also* infra Parts VIII.H (discussing motions to unseal), IX.A.10 (discussing briefs containing material under seal), IX.B.7 (discussing appendices containing matters under seal). For procedures governing disposal of sealed records, see infra Part XIII.A.5.

A motion to file documents under seal, including any exhibits and attachments, and all documents containing material under seal may not be filed or served electronically unless the Court orders otherwise.

IV. DOCKETING THE APPEAL

A. Cases From the District Court and the Tax Court.

1. *Preliminary Record on Appeal and Preparation of Transcripts.* (*See* Fed. R. App. P. 10.)

The preliminary record on appeal, prepared in the district court Clerk's Office or the Tax Court Clerk's Office, consists of the notice of appeal and the district court docket entries. Upon receipt of the preliminary record, a case administrator in this Court's Clerk's Office dockets the appeal, assigns it a number, and gives notice of the filing to all parties by issuing an order scheduling certain submissions. In addition, a case administrator checks to see that the docketing fee has been paid and sends appropriate notice if it has not.

The documents and exhibits filed in the district court; the transcript of proceedings, if any; and the docket entries prepared by the Clerk of the district court, constitute the record on appeal. The parties may correct errors or omissions in the record by stipulation. In the event of a dispute, this Court has the power to require that the record be corrected or amplified, but disputes about the accuracy of the record must first be submitted to the district court.

Within 14 days of filing the notice of appeal in a civil case, or entry of an order disposing of the last timely remaining motion as specified in Federal Rule of Appellate Procedure 4(a)(4)(A), appellants must order from the court reporter a transcript of such parts of the proceedings not already on file as they consider necessary to dispose of the appeal.

It is the policy of this Court to expedite criminal appeals. Counsel has the responsibility for assuring expeditious preparation of the transcript in a criminal appeal. If any unusual problems arise with the court reporter, they should be brought to this Court's attention immediately. Where the defendant proceeded in forma pauperis in the district court, that court, by local practice, requires appointed counsel to order the transcript at the same time as filing the notice of appeal.

Unless the entire transcript is ordered, the appellant must file and serve on the appellee a designation of the parts of the transcript ordered, and a statement of the issues to be presented on appeal. The appellee has 14 days to file and serve a cross-designation of additional parts of the transcript. If the appellant refuses to order the additional portions, appellee should do so, or ask the district court to compel the appellant to comply.

When, as is often the case, a complete transcript has been made during the trial, and it is filed with the Clerk, no designation need be made. The parties, however, must include in the appendix to the briefs only those portions of the transcript that are pertinent to the appeal. Awards of costs and sanctions may be imposed where a party has included unnecessary material in the appendix. *See* infra Part IX.B.

If no transcript is available, the appellant may prepare and file with the district court a statement of the evidence or proceedings from the best available means, including recollection, and serve it on the appellee. The appellee has 14 days to serve objections or proposed amendments in response. The district court then approves the statement as submitted or amended, and certifies it to this Court as the record on appeal.

As with transcript designations, the parties are encouraged to agree on what exhibits are necessary to resolve the appeal, but in the absence of an agreement they may cross-designate exhibits.

In civil cases, the district court returns the exhibits to the parties who filed them. In criminal cases, the exhibits are given to the United States Attorney. If a party wants an exhibit in the courtroom during oral argument to this Court, counsel must notify the Court in writing at least 7 days before the argument date of his or her intention, and deliver the exhibit to the Clerk's Office. If the Court requests an exhibit, the parties will be notified and directed to deliver the exhibit to the Clerk's Office.

2. *Transmission of the Record.* (*See* Fed. R. App. P. 11; D.C. Cir. Rule 11.)

The district court transmits the preliminary record in all cases a few days after the notice of appeal is filed. Counsel should keep in mind that, unlike other federal circuits, briefing schedules in this Court, where the case has been scheduled for argument, are *not* computed from the date on which the record is filed in this Court. Rather, briefing schedules are established by order. *See* infra Part IX.A.1.

3. *Docketing the Appeal.* (*See* Fed. R. App. P. 12; D.C. Cir. Rule 12.)

After an appeal has been docketed, the Clerk's Office enters an initial scheduling order that specifies the dates on which the docketing statement and initial submissions, procedural motions, and dispositive motions are due. In civil cases, the order directs the appellant to file within 30 days a docketing statement on a form provided by the Clerk's Office and to serve a copy on all other parties and amici curiae. The docketing statement includes information about the type of case; the district court or agency case number; relevant dates; the order sought to be reviewed; related cases; relevant statutes; and counsel's name, e-mail address, postal address, and telephone number. A copy of the district court judgment under review must be submitted with the docketing statement, as well as a preliminary statement of the issues for appeal and a transcript status report. This material assists the Clerk's Office and the Legal Division in screening and classifying all new appeals, identifying related cases in this Court, and detecting possible jurisdictional problems. The information about preparation of the transcript is especially important to ensure against delays as the case is processed. The parties also may include a stipulation to be placed in the stand-by pool for argument or a request to be included in the Court's mediation program. *See* infra Part IV.D (discussing the Court's mediation program), and Part X.E.4 (discussing the requirements to enter the stand-by pool).

Appellants must provide with the docketing statement a provisional certificate setting forth the information specified in Circuit Rule 28(a)(1), identifying parties, intervenors, and amici in the district court proceedings and in this Court, including a disclosure statement required by Circuit Rule 26.1. Circuit Rule 26.1 requires corporations, associations, joint ventures, partnerships, syndicates, or other similar entities appearing before the Court to file a disclosure statement that identifies all parent companies and any publicly-held company that has a 10% or greater ownership interest (such as stock or partnership shares) in the entity. The statement also must identify the represented entity's general nature and purpose, as relevant to the litigation, and if the entity is unincorporated and its members have no ownership interests, the statement must include the names of any members of the entity that have issued shares or debt securities to the public. No listing need be made, however, of the names of members of a trade association or professional association.

In civil cases, the provisional certificate filed with the docketing statement is necessary to enable the Clerk's Office to avoid assigning matters to a judge who would be recused because of his or her association with a party or counsel in the case.

Appellees must file, within 7 days of service of the docketing statement, or upon filing a motion, response, or answer, whichever occurs first, any disclosure statement required by Circuit Rule 26.1. *See* Fed. R. App. P. 26.1(b). Any disclosure statement required by Circuit Rule 26.1 must also accompany a motion to intervene, a written representation of consent to participate as amicus curiae, and a motion for leave to participate as amicus. *See* D.C. Cir. Rules 12(f), 15(c)(6). This disclosure statement and a Rule 28(a)(1)(A) certificate of parties and amici must likewise accompany a petition for panel rehearing or rehearing en banc. *See* D.C. Cir. Rule 35(c). A revised corporate disclosure statement must also be filed any time there is a change in corporate ownership interests that would affect the disclosures required under Circuit Rule 26.1.

B. Cases from Administrative Agencies. (*See* Fed. R. App. P. 15, 16, 17; D.C. Cir. Rules 15, 17.)

In cases from administrative agencies, docketing occurs at the time the petition for review or notice of appeal is filed and precedes transmission of the record. The appellant or petitioner must remit the docketing fee to this Court at that time. For information the parties are required to provide with the docketing statement, motions, and rehearing petitions, see supra Part IV.A.3. In addition, in cases involving direct review of administrative agency actions, the docketing statement must contain a brief statement of the basis for the appellant's or petitioner's claim of standing. *See* D.C. Cir. Rule 15(c)(2).

The record on review consists of the order sought to be reviewed or enforced; the findings or report on which it is based; and the pleadings, evidence, and proceedings before the agency. The record may later be corrected or supplemented by stipulation or by order of this Court, as in the case of an appeal from the district court.

Because of a lack of storage space, the record before the administrative agency is not transmitted to this Court at the time of docketing; only a certified index to the record is submitted by the agency. Any party to the proceeding may, by motion, subsequently request that part or all of the record be transmitted to the Court, or the Court on its own may require transmission of the record. It is the duty of the agency to maintain the record so that it can be transmitted to the Court with a minimum of delay. In most cases, however, transmission of the actual record will be unnecessary because the appendix must contain those documents necessary for the Court's review.

The administrative agency submits to this Court the certified index to the record within 45 days of the filing of the petition for review or application for enforcement, unless the statute authorizing review fixes a different time. The date of filing the certified index is deemed to be the date the record is filed.

C. Original Proceedings. No record is prepared or transmitted to the Court in original proceedings. Any documents from the district court or agency proceedings that are necessary to understand the issues being presented must, however, be attached to the petition. An appendix may be utilized. The petitioner seeking a writ of mandamus or other extraordinary relief must remit the docketing fee to the Clerk of this Court before the petition will be accepted for filing.

D. Mediation Program. Program procedures are described in the Court's order establishing the mediation program, included as Appendix III to the Court's rules. Cases docketed in the Court are screened by the Legal Division, and those deemed appropriate for mediation are referred to the Director of the Appellate Mediation Program for further assessment and placement into the program. Procedures are explained to counsel when a case is selected for mediation. Counsel are advised that whenever there are serious settlement negotiations in progress, including post-argument settlement discussions, the parties should advise the Clerk of that fact.

V. MULTI–PARTY CASES

A. Consolidation. In order to achieve the most efficient use of the Court's resources, as well as to maintain consistency in its decisions, the Court generally will consolidate, on its own motion or on motion of the parties, all appeals and cross-appeals from the same district court judgment or order, and all petitions for review of agency orders entered in the same administrative proceeding. In addition, other cases involving essentially the same parties or the same, similar, or related issues, may be consolidated. When cases are consolidated, the Clerk's Office designates one case (usually the one with the lowest docket number) as the "lead" case but usually enters items filed in any of the consolidated cases on the dockets of all the cases.

As noted in Part III.H, supra, parties with common interests also may file a joint notice of appeal or petition for review.

Once cases are consolidated, they are treated as one appeal for most purposes. They generally follow a single briefing schedule, they are assigned for hearing on the same day before the same panel, argument time is allotted to the cases as a group, and they are decided at the same time. Each case retains some of its individual identity, however. For example, motions may be filed in one case and not in others, and extensions of time in one case do not necessarily extend the time in any others. Joint briefs are encouraged pursuant to Federal Rule of Appellate Procedure 28(i). Briefing by intervenors is governed by Circuit Rule 28(d). *See* infra Part IX.A.4.

B. Appeals Management Plan. The Director of the Legal Division administers the Court's plan for the management of its caseload. The objectives of this plan are: (1) to achieve an efficient and organized presentation of appeals in complex, multi-party litigation; (2) to identify early in the appellate process cases that either are not ripe for review or are appropriate for summary disposition; and (3) to enhance the Court's control of the pace of the appellate process. An important characteristic of the plan is its flexibility and informality. Although the Director of the Legal Division ordinarily determines which cases will require special attention or management under the plan, counsel for the parties are encouraged to notify the Director or the Clerk of cases that may be appropriate for such treatment.

In carrying out the plan, the Director of the Legal Division is authorized to obtain from counsel information that will assist the Court in making decisions about the appointment of lead or liaison counsel, joint briefing, briefing schedules, motions dispositions, and oral argument dates and formats. The Director may obtain this information informally by letter or telephone, by meeting with counsel, or by requesting the Clerk's Office to issue directives to counsel.

In any case pending before the Court, counsel may independently develop proposals to facilitate briefing and other matters and submit such proposals to the Legal Division. On the recommendation of the Director of the Legal Division, the Clerk's Office may issue procedural orders that reflect the agreement of counsel. Where agreement is not achieved, or where the Director believes the circumstances warrant it, the Court will issue procedural orders in cases managed under the plan.

VI. APPEALS IN FORMA PAUPERIS AND PURSUANT TO THE CRIMINAL JUSTICE ACT; APPOINTMENT OF COUNSEL

A. When Permitted. (*See* Fed. R. App. P. 24; D.C. Cir. Rule 24.)

The district court and this Court are authorized by 28 U.S.C. § 1915 and Federal Rule of Appellate Procedure 24 to allow an appeal, civil or criminal, to be taken without payment of the docketing fee or costs by a non-incarcerated person who makes an affidavit of indigence. While an incarcerated litigant may also proceed in forma pauperis, in civil cases the prisoner will be required to pay the full amount of the filing fee—albeit in monthly installments. *See* 28 U.S.C. § 1915(b). Any non-incarcerated person who has been permitted to proceed in forma pauperis in the district court may proceed in forma pauperis in this Court, unless the district court finds and states in writing that the appeal is not taken in good faith, or that the party is otherwise not entitled to that status. If a party wishes to claim in forma pauperis status for the first time in this Court, or if a prisoner seeks to appeal in forma pauperis, he or she must first apply to the district court and, if permission is granted, no further authorization from this Court is necessary. If that party is a prisoner, however, a fee will nonetheless be assessed by this Court.

If the district court denies permission to proceed on appeal in forma pauperis, or revokes in forma pauperis status previously granted in the district court, the party may, within 30 days of service of notice of the district court's action, move this Court for leave to proceed on appeal in forma pauperis. The filing of a new notice of appeal is not required. If the Court grants the motion, the docketing fee is waived for non-incarcerated parties but will be assessed for incarcerated parties in civil cases; if the Court denies the motion, the appellant must pay the docketing fee or the appeal will be dismissed.

A party to an administrative agency proceeding who wishes to take an appeal or file a petition for review in forma pauperis must file a motion with this Court for leave to so proceed.

B. District Court Dismissal of Suits Brought In Forma Pauperis. Under 28 U.S.C. § 1915(e), the district court must dismiss a civil suit in which the plaintiff seeks to proceed in forma pauperis if the court concludes that the action is "frivolous or malicious." *See Denton v. Hernandez*, 504 U.S. 25 (1992) (discussing the "frivolous or malicious" standard).

In *Sills v. Bureau of Prisons*, 761 F.2d 792 (D.C. Cir. 1985), this Court established procedures to be followed by the district court in dismissing a complaint under § 1915 in order to facilitate appellate review. The district court must provide a clear statement of reasons for its conclusion that the suit is frivolous or malicious, and the court also should revoke the plaintiff's in forma pauperis status when it dismisses the complaint. This latter procedure permits this Court to evaluate the correctness of the § 1915(e) dismissal in the context of ruling on appellant's motion to proceed in forma pauperis on appeal.

C. Procedural Consequences of In Forma Pauperis Status. (*See* D.C. Cir. Rules 24, 31.)

Parties proceeding in forma pauperis who are authorized to file electronically need not provide paper copies of any motions papers; those not authorized to file electronically need file only the original of any motions papers. The Clerk's Office will make the necessary copies for the Court. Litigants proceeding in forma pauperis who are *not* represented by counsel are also exempt from filing the usual number of briefs; such unrepresented parties need submit only the electronic version if authorized to file electronically, or the original of the brief if not authorized to file electronically. All other parties must file the standard number of briefs required by the Circuit Rules, but appointed counsel in criminal appeals may be reimbursed for the expense of reproducing the brief by photocopy process in accordance with the Criminal Justice Act (CJA).

Represented parties proceeding in forma pauperis and amicus curiae appointed by the Court must comply with the standard requirements for an appendix. *See* Fed. R. App. P. 30; D.C. Cir. Rule 30. If an appellant or petitioner proceeding in forma pauperis is unrepresented, the Court may decide the appeal on the original record without an appendix. Under Circuit Rule 24, however, the pro se appellant or petitioner must file with his or her brief 1 copy of those pages of the trial transcript the appellant or petitioner wishes to call to the Court's attention, 1 copy of a list designating those pages of the transcript, and 1 copy of any other portions of the record to which the appellant or petitioner wishes to direct the Court's attention. Although the Clerk's Office will reproduce enough copies of these items to provide them to the panel, parties are encouraged to provide the Court 4 copies of these items so as not to delay processing of the case. The appellee or respondent must furnish with the brief 4 copies of an appendix containing any additional pages of transcript or portions of the record to which the Court's attention is directed.

D. Appointment of Counsel.

1. *Time and Manner of Appointment.* The CJA, 18 U.S.C. § 3006A, does not provide for the appointment of counsel in non-criminal cases. Thus, even though a party in a civil appeal may be granted leave to proceed in forma pauperis, counsel will not ordinarily be provided by the Court. The appellant may file a motion for the appointment of counsel. If the Court grants the motion or elects to appoint amicus curiae in lieu of counsel, it may select a member of a legal aid organization or a law school clinical program, or it may appoint an attorney who has indicated a willingness to serve without compensation in non-criminal cases. The decision whether to appoint counsel or an amicus in a civil case is usually made by the special panel, and the Court will appoint a private attorney or amicus only when a panel determines it is in the interest of the Court.

Counsel who wish to be considered for appointment in civil cases should write to the Clerk, providing information about their background and experience, and listing any cases they have previously handled in this Court. Counsel and amici appointed in civil appeals serve without compensation. Counsel are encouraged to volunteer their services for civil matters.

2. *Withdrawal.* Appointed counsel who are unable to continue to represent an appellant in a civil or criminal appeal must promptly move this Court to withdraw, stating specific reasons.

In a criminal appeal, if counsel wishes to withdraw because of a belief there is no merit to the appeal, counsel should refer to *Anders v. California*, 386 U.S. 738 (1967), and *Suggs v. United States*, 391 F.2d 971 (D.C. Cir. 1968), for guidance. Counsel in a criminal appeal also should confer with the Office of the Federal Public Defender to help assure uniformity of practice in this regard.

Counsel must serve the appellant with the motion to withdraw. When filing a motion to withdraw because of lack of merit to the appeal in a criminal case, counsel also must submit to the Court and serve on the appellant, *but not on government counsel*, a confidential memorandum under seal setting forth the points the appellant wishes to assert, any other points counsel has considered, and the most effective arguments counsel can make on the appellant's behalf. The Court gives the appellant 30 days to respond to this memorandum; if the Court thereafter concludes there are no meritorious issues on appeal, it will grant counsel's motion to withdraw and ordinarily dismiss the appeal.

3. *Duties in Criminal Appeals.* Upon notice of appointment in a criminal appeal, counsel must so advise the defendant, and if the defendant is incarcerated, counsel must explore the possibility of obtaining release pending appeal. *See* infra Part VIII.C. Counsel also should check the district court record to ensure that the transcript has been or is being prepared. It is trial counsel's duty to order the transcript when the notice of appeal is filed, but counsel appointed on appeal must make sure that all necessary portions of the transcript have been designated. The failure of trial counsel to order the necessary transcript does not justify an extension of time for filing defendant's brief.

Appointed counsel ordinarily should interview the defendant in person at least once if the defendant is within the jurisdiction. If the defendant is incarcerated outside the jurisdiction, the Court may authorize counsel to visit the defendant at his or her place of incarceration. Such visits must be approved in advance and must be fully justified in order for counsel to be reimbursed. Requests for such advance authorization are first to be submitted to the Federal Public Defender.

If the defendant is dissatisfied with court-appointed counsel's handling of the appeal and wishes counsel to withdraw, counsel must file a motion for leave to withdraw, and the Clerk will refer the matter to the Legal Division for presentation to a panel. *See* infra Part VII.D. The Court does not respond favorably to general complaints about counsel, only to specific grievances.

Counsel's responsibility when appointed in a criminal case extends through the filing of a nonfrivolous petition for a writ of certiorari. Appointed counsel must advise the defendant of the right to file a certiorari petition and counsel's opinion as to the merit and likelihood of success in obtaining such a writ. If the defendant asks counsel to file a petition for writ of certiorari and there are nonfrivolous grounds for doing so, counsel must prepare and file one. If counsel determines that there are no nonfrivolous grounds for filing a petition, counsel must, within 20 days of the entry of judgment, notify the defendant in writing that counsel will not file a petition, briefly explaining why. Counsel must also inform the defendant about the procedures both for filing a petition for certiorari pro se and for asking this Court to appoint new counsel to prepare a petition for certiorari. Counsel should caution the defendant that it is unlikely the Court will appoint new counsel and that the client should be prepared to file a petition for certiorari pro se within the prescribed time. Once counsel has provided this notice to the client, counsel must notify the Court that counsel's representation has ceased. (A model letter withdrawing from representation at the certiorari stage can be found on the Court's web site under "Attorney & Pro Se Information>Criminal Justice Act Information.") The Clerk will notify the defendant in writing of the effective date of the termination of counsel's appointment. The cost of this work is recoverable in this Court pursuant to the original appointment, and counsel may not submit his or her voucher until all work is completed. Failure to comply with the foregoing procedures may result in the Court's refusal to approve counsel's voucher.

4. *Compensation.* The CJA prescribes the rate at which appointed counsel is compensated for time spent in court, and for time spent on the case out of court. While total compensation is limited to a specific dollar amount in direct criminal appeals and collateral proceedings, the Chief Judge, or another judge designated by the Chief Judge, may authorize payments in excess of these limitations. Awards of excess compensation are not made lightly in view of budgetary constraints, and require strong justification and documentation.

Counsel also may be reimbursed for certain out-of-pocket expenses, including the cost of reproducing the briefs. General office costs are not reimbursable.

Counsel must submit claims for reimbursement within 45 days of the date after which no further action before this Court or the Supreme Court is possible. Counsel's claims must be itemized on the voucher form sent to counsel by this Court at the time of the appointment. Records of time spent on the appeal must be indicated on the standard work-sheets available from the Clerk's Office. The Clerk reviews the claim form for mathematical and technical accuracy and for conformity with applicable regulations. The completed form is then sent for approval to the judge who wrote the opinion in the case, or, if no opinion was issued, to the presiding judge of the panel.

VII. MOTIONS PRACTICE

A. Formal Requirements. (*See* Fed. R. App. P. 27; D.C. Cir. Rules 27, 32(b).)

Motions practice in this Court has become a means of achieving early resolution of cases that would otherwise unnecessarily go the full route of briefing and oral argument. Parties are particularly encouraged to file dispositive motions where a sound basis exists for summary disposition. The result can be a major savings of time, effort, and resources for the parties, counsel, and the Court. In order to achieve this economy, however, it is essential for counsel to comply fully with the procedural requirements for motions practice. The following section discusses general motions practice; specific motions are discussed infra at Part VIII.

At the outset, there are two important time limits to observe: 30 days from docketing for filing procedural motions, and 45 days from docketing for filing dispositive motions. The actual dates when both types of motions are due are specified in the initial order sent out by the Clerk's Office at the time of docketing.

Procedural motions are those that may affect the progress of the case through the Court, *e.g.*, motions to intervene, motions to consolidate, motions to defer the appendix, motions to hold the case in abeyance, motions for stay, and motions to expedite.

Dispositive motions are defined in Circuit Rule 27(g) as those which, if granted, would dispose of the appeal or the petition for review in its entirety, or would transfer the case to another court. They include motions for summary affirmance or reversal, motions to dismiss (on any ground, including jurisdiction), and motions to transfer. Absent leave of the Court, dispositive motions may not be filed more than

45 days after docketing. This requirement does not apply to a motion by an appellant or a petitioner for voluntary dismissal, which may be filed at any time.

Normally, cases will not be given oral argument dates or briefing schedules until all pending motions have been resolved. Counsel can assist the Clerk's Office in processing the case by stipulating within the first 45 days that no dispositive motions will be filed. Any motions filed after the oral argument date is set are referred to the panel assigned to hear the case on the merits.

There are certain formal requirements common to most motions. Unless a party is proceeding in forma pauperis, or the Court directs otherwise, non-ECF filers must submit an original and 4 paper copies of any motion, except in en banc cases, in which event an original and 19 copies are required. ECF filers must, in addition to the electronic original, file 4 paper copies of any motion specified in the Court's Administrative Order Regarding Electronic Case Filing, ECF–6(B), or 19 paper copies in en banc cases. These motions include dispositive motions, contested procedural motions, and motions for emergency relief.

Motions, responses thereto, and replies must be prepared in conformity with Federal Rule of Appellate Procedure 27(d)(1) and (2). Thus, all papers relating to motions must be submitted in standard typographical printing or by any duplicating or copying process that produces a clear black image on light paper, in a plain, roman style, with a proportionally spaced typeface of 14–point or larger or a monospaced typeface containing no more than 10 and one-half characters per inch. Except by permission or direction of the Court, a motion may not, under any printing method utilized, exceed 20 pages. All legal arguments must be presented in the body of the motion; a separate brief or memorandum supporting or responding to a motion may not be filed. A copy of the trial court's opinion or agency's decision must accompany a motion seeking any substantive relief.

The front page of the motion must give the name of this Court, the title and file number of the case, and a brief descriptive title (*e.g.*, Motion for Summary Affirmance). If a case has been scheduled for oral argument, has already been argued, or is being submitted without oral argument, a motion, response, or reply must so state in capital letters at the top of the first page. Where applicable, the date of the argument also must be included.

The motion must specify the grounds and the relief sought. Parties may seek more than one form of relief in a single motion if the matters are related. For example, a single motion may be filed where, in addition to seeking dismissal, a party requests in the alternative summary affirmance. If a party seeks more than one form of relief in a single motion, the descriptive title on the front page of the motion must clearly set forth the matters presented in the pleading. If the matters are unrelated, parties should file separate motions. Requests for permission to file an untimely or overlong motion should not be included in the substantive motion but should be filed as a separate motion.

All motions must be signed by a party or by a member of the bar of the Court, with proof of service on all other parties to the proceeding before the Court. Except as prescribed by Federal Rule of Appellate Procedure 28(j), parties, other than pro se litigants proceeding in forma pauperis, may not plead by letter. *See* D.C. Cir. Rule 32(b). Generally, for motions, responses, and replies, filing is complete on *receipt* of the pleading in the Clerk's Office, *not* on mailing. A document filed electronically is deemed filed on the date and at the time stated on the Notice of Docket Activity from the Court. For incarcerated litigants, filing is complete upon deposit in the institution's internal mailing system in accordance with the federal rules. *See* Fed. R. App. P. 25(a)(2)(C).

Any response must be filed within 10 days after service of the motion. It may not exceed 20 pages. Any reply to the response must be filed within 7 days after service of the response and may not exceed 10 pages. The response may contain a motion for other relief. If so, the caption must clearly denote that the response includes the separate motion, and the document may not exceed 30 pages. When the response includes a motion for affirmative relief, the reply may be joined in the same pleading with a response to the motion for affirmative relief, and counsel has 10 days to file it. Such reply may not exceed 20 pages. The final reply on a combined filing is limited to 10 pages. Replies must not reargue positions presented in an opening paper and may not present any matters that are not strictly in reply to the response. After the filing of a reply, no further pleadings on a motion or petition are permitted, except by leave of the Court. The above filing times are extended by 3 days if service was effected on the responding party by any method of service authorized by Federal Rule of Appellate Procedure 25 other than personal service. *See* Fed. R. App. P. 26(c).

When a substantive motion is filed along with a motion for leave to file out of time or to exceed the length limitations, no response is required on the substantive motion until a decision is rendered on the motion to file out of time or to exceed the length limitations.

Circuit Rule 27(h) establishes the requirements for seeking extensions of time to file motions, responses, and replies, and for seeking leave to exceed the page limits. Such motions must be filed 5 days before the pleading is due. A motion to extend time for filing a motion, response, or reply must indicate in the first paragraph when the motion, response, or reply is currently due. On a showing of good cause, the Clerk may grant a late-filed motion for extension of time if it is unopposed. Otherwise, motions for extension of time to file a pleading or to exceed the page limits, which are filed less than 5 days before the pleading is due, will be denied as untimely, absent extraordinary circumstances.

Counsel should bear in mind that the federal rules set page limits on motions, responses, and replies. *See* Fed. R. App. P. 27(d)(2). The Circuit Rules explicitly state that requests to exceed those limits are disfavored and will be granted "only for extraordinarily compelling reasons." D.C. Cir. Rule 27(h)(3).

Circuit Rule 27(h)(2) establishes requirements for consulting the opposing side to obtain consent to motions for extension of time and motions to exceed the page limit, and to inquire whether an opposition or other form of response will be filed. The opening paragraph of any such motion must recite the position taken by the opposing party, or the efforts made to obtain a response. Where the other side has indicated an intention to file an opposition or other form of response, or has not been reached after reasonable effort, the moving party must serve the motion by personal service if the opposing party is not an ECF filer or if the motion is not filed electronically. If personal service is not feasible, the moving party must give telephone notice of the filing and serve the motion by another form of expedited service authorized by Federal Rule of Appellate Procedure 25. Where the moving party is unable to effect personal service or telephone notice at the time of the filing, the opening paragraph of the motion must recite the efforts made to do so.

Finally, Circuit Rule 27(h)(4) provides for an automatic extension of the original deadline for filing motions or petitions, or to exceed length limits for such pleadings, if the motion is filed in accordance with the requirements of subparagraphs (1) and (2) of Circuit Rule 27(h) and the Court does not act on the motion by the end of the second business day before the filing deadline. If the Court thereafter denies the motion, the filing deadline will be extended automatically for 7 days. If the Court denies the motion to extend the length, it ordinarily will allow time to file a conforming document. *This automatic extension provision applies **only** to motions deadlines; there are no comparable provisions in the Circuit Rules for automatic extension of the deadline for filing briefs.* Motions to extend time or length limits for filing briefs are separately addressed in Circuit Rule 28(e).

B. Processing. When counsel files a motion, it is handled in one of three ways, depending on the nature of the relief sought: by the Clerk, by a panel designated to decide motions, or by the merits panel in the case.

Motions are generally considered ripe for decision once a reply has been filed or the time allowed for a reply has expired. An exception is made for emergency motions, discussed below, and for procedural motions that reflect the consent of all parties. Motions filed in cases assigned to merits panels are delivered immediately to the judges. It is in the merits panel's discretion whether to await a response.

C. Disposition by the Clerk. (*See* Fed. R. App. P. 27(b); D.C. Cir. Rule 27(e).)

The Circuit Rules authorize the Clerk to dispose of procedural motions of a routine character, in accordance with the Court's instructions.

Any party adversely affected by the action of the Clerk on a motion may move for reconsideration within 10 days of entry of the Clerk's order. The motion for reconsideration will be submitted to a special panel or to the merits panel, if a merits panel has been assigned.

Motions disposed of by the Clerk can be identified by the form of the order. Orders are signed by the Clerk "For the Court." Clerk's orders never carry the phrase "Per Curiam" above the signature block.

D. Disposition by a Panel. The Clerk's Office refers dispositive and procedural motions to the Legal Division. Each motion (or all motions in a single case) is assigned to one of the staff attorneys, who reviews the motion, response, and reply, and any other papers filed; examines the record; and then prepares a confidential memorandum setting forth the issues, the facts, an analysis of the law, and a recommended disposition. The staff attorney also drafts a proposed order and, where appropriate, an accompanying memorandum disposing of the motion. Except for emergency matters and other matters requiring expedition or motions to hold a case in abeyance, matters are generally assigned chronologically by filing date, and staff attorneys work on them in that order.

Once the staff attorney has completed work on the motion, his or her recommendation, proposed disposition, and the underlying pleadings are routed either to the special panel or to the merits panel for resolution.

The special panel consists of judges who are assigned on a rotational basis throughout the year to consider and decide motions, cases recommended for disposition without oral argument under Circuit Rule 34(j), and emergency matters, presented by the Legal Division. *See* infra Part VIII and Part XI.C.2. The special panel members also are engaged in their regular merits sittings while they serve on the special panel.

The Legal Division circulates to the panel an agenda, the necessary papers, and recommendations of the staff attorneys regarding the motions that will be presented. The panel may adopt or reject the staff attorney's recommendation, request more research, take the matter under advisement, or refer the motion for disposition to the panel ultimately assigned to hear the case on the merits.

The Court does not publish or disclose in advance the names of the judges on the special panel, nor does it notify counsel or the public of the date on which a particular motion will be considered. The panel does not hear oral argument on motions, except, very rarely, in emergency matters or for extraordinary cause.

Orders of the special panel disposing of motions are usually not published, although in some cases the panel may decide that a published per curiam opinion will be useful to establish the law of the Circuit on a particular issue. The unpublished orders reflect the names of the panel members beneath the case caption. The order, or a separate memorandum accompanying the order, will explain the basis for the Court's disposition of the motion.

If a party disagrees with the special panel's disposition of a motion, it may move for reconsideration by the same panel or by the full Court. The Court rarely grants these motions.

E. Disposition by a Merits Panel. Once a case is assigned to a merits panel, everything relating to the case comes under the exclusive control of the panel. All motions filed in the case are submitted to the panel.

When a motion is filed, it is transmitted to the panel via an electronic vote sheet, which contains links to the motions papers, any supporting material, and any memorandum prepared by the Legal Division recommending a disposition. The panel members record electronically the disposition they wish to make of the motion. Once all votes are entered, an order is prepared disposing of the motion. The order usually shows the names of the panel members.

F. Distribution of Orders. The Clerk's Office files and distributes all orders. When an order or judgment is entered in a case assigned to the CM/ECF system, the Clerk's Office electronically transmits a Notice of Docket Activity to all parties who have consented to electronic service, and mails notice and a copy of any opinion or judgment to parties who are not ECF filers. *See* D.C. Cir. Rules 36(b), 45(d). The Clerk's Office maintains a record of all persons to whom copies of an order are sent.

VIII. SPECIFIC MOTIONS

A. Motions for Stay or Emergency Relief. (*See* Fed. R. App. P. 8, 18; D.C. Cir. Rules 8, 18, 27(f).)

Filing a notice of appeal, or obtaining permission to appeal, generally does not automatically stay the operation of the judgment or order under review. Except in cases involving money judgments against the United States or the District of Columbia, or where the appellant posts a supersedeas bond in accordance with Federal Rule of Civil Procedure 62(d), the losing party must move to obtain a stay or injunction pending appeal to prevent immediate execution of the judgment or order being appealed, or immediate enforcement of an agency order under review. Such motions are procedural motions; they can be filed as soon as possible, but usually no later than 30 days after docketing.

Application for a stay or any other appropriate emergency relief must first be made to the district court or agency whose order is being appealed, or the motion filed in this Court must explain why such relief was not sought. If the district court or agency denies the relief requested, an application may then be made to this Court. A motion for a stay must describe any prior applications for relief and their outcome.

If the facts are in dispute, evidentiary material supporting the request for a stay should be furnished. Relevant portions of the record must be included with the motion. At a minimum, these include a copy of the judgment or order involved, and any explanation, written or oral, that accompanied the ruling. The motion also should contain, in a prominent place, a specific statement of the time exigencies involved.

Because many motions for stay are filed on an emergency basis, Circuit Rules 8, 18, and 27(f), which prescribe the procedures for seeking emergency relief, should be reviewed carefully. In particular, counsel or a party must identify the motion as an "Emergency Motion," and file it at least 7 days before the date on which court action is necessary, or explain why the motion could not have been filed sooner. Where counsel or a party gives only a vague or general explanation as to why it was not filed at least 7 days before the date of the requested court action, the Court may conclude that expedited consideration of the motion is unwarranted.

Counsel or a party seeking expedition of a stay application or any other matter must communicate the request for emergency consideration in person or by telephone to the Clerk's Office and to the opposing side. If the motion is not filed electronically or if the opposing party has not consented to electronic service, the motion must be served by hand or, in the case of out-of-town parties, by another form of expedited service authorized by Federal Rule of Appellate Procedure 25. The motion must describe the efforts made to notify the opposing side.

When an emergency motion is filed in a case not yet assigned for hearing on the merits, it is referred to the Director of the Legal Division for assignment to a staff attorney and immediate referral to the special panel for disposition. The special panel does not normally grant the relief requested before receiving a response. However, it may enter an administrative stay of very short duration before receiving a response to give the Court more time to consider the matter. The administrative stay order will usually direct that responses to the motion be expedited. Alternatively, the special panel may order expedited responses without issuing a temporary stay. The judges might conclude that the matter does not require unusual expedition and take no action prior to the filing of a response, or they may deny the motion without awaiting a response.

The motion for stay or for emergency relief must specifically discuss four factors: (1) the likelihood that the moving party will prevail on the merits; (2) the prospect of irreparable injury to the moving party if relief is withheld; (3) the possibility of substantial harm to other parties if relief is granted; and (4) the public interest. *See Washington Metropolitan Area Transit Comm'n v. Holiday Tours, Inc.*, 559 F.2d 841 (D.C. Cir. 1977); *Virginia Petroleum Jobbers Ass'n v. Federal Power Comm'n*, 259 F.2d 921 (D.C. Cir. 1958). In seeking a stay or injunction pending appeal, counsel also should address the question whether the appeal should be expedited if a stay or injunction is granted.

A party filing or opposing a motion for stay or other emergency relief may, in addition or in the alternative, file a motion to dispose of the appeal or petition for review in its entirety. If the Court grants a motion for stay or for injunction pending appeal, it may, pursuant to Federal Rules of Appellate Procedure 8(a)(2)(E) and 18(b), condition the stay or injunction on the posting of a bond or other security in the appropriate court. No such bond is required where the federal government or the District of Columbia is the appellant. *See* Fed. R. Civ. P. 62(e); D.C. Superior Court Rule 62.

B. Motions to Expedite Consideration of the Appeal. (*See* 28 U.S.C. § 1657; D.C. Cir. Rules 27(f), 47.2.)

The Court accords expedited consideration to a case when required to do so by statute, or when the Court grants a motion for expedition.

Circuit Rule 47.2(a) lists many of those statutory provisions that mandate expedited appellate review: 18 U.S.C. §§ 3145, 3731; 28 U.S.C. chapter 153; and 28 U.S.C. § 1826. *See* supra Part III.J. Whenever a party takes an appeal pursuant to one of these provisions, counsel must advise the Clerk's Office of this Court immediately both orally and by letter. The district court Clerk will transmit the notice of appeal and certified docket entries forthwith to this Court, so that the appeal can be docketed and an expedited briefing and argument schedule set. Counsel must advise the Clerk of this Court in writing of counsel's arrangements to order any necessary portions of the transcript on an expedited basis, and make arrangements with the district court Clerk to send the record promptly to this Court.

When expedition is not required by statute, counsel seeking expedited review must file a motion. Like other procedural motions, motions to expedite must be filed within 30 days of the date the case is docketed. The Court grants expedited consideration very rarely. The movant must demonstrate that the delay will cause irreparable injury and that the decision under review is subject to substantial challenge. The Court also may expedite cases in which the public generally, or in which persons not before the Court, have an unusual interest in prompt disposition. The reasons must be strongly compelling.

When the Court disposes of a motion for stay or injunction pending appeal, it may at the same time expedite the case to minimize possible harm to the parties or the public. In moving for a stay or injunction pending appeal, counsel should address the appropriateness of expediting the appeal if a stay is entered.

An order granting expedition does not automatically shorten the briefing schedule. When time is a critical consideration, counsel may wish to propose a specific date for the hearing and to move for an abbreviated briefing schedule.

When counsel files a motion to expedite consideration of an appeal, the Clerk's Office refers it to the Legal Division. Staff attorneys give priority to such motions.

Parties might be able to have their appeal calendared earlier than normal by agreeing to place their case in the Court's stand-by pool of cases for oral argument. The requirements to enter the stand-by pool are discussed infra in Part X.E.4.

C. Motions for Release Pending Appeal. (*See* 18 U.S.C. § 3143; Fed. R. App. P. 9(b); D.C. Cir. Rule 9(b).)

A defendant who has filed a notice of appeal from a criminal conviction may apply for release while the appeal is pending. The defendant must apply first to the district court for release. If the district court denies the application, or imposes conditions of release, the defendant may then move this Court for release or for modification of the conditions. A new notice of appeal is not necessary. Circuit Rule 9 sets forth the required contents of this motion. The motion may not exceed 20 pages without leave of the Court, it must be prepared in conformity with Federal Rule of Appellate Procedure 27(d)(1) and (2), and it must be served on opposing counsel. Staff attorneys give priority to motions for release pending appeal and send them to the special panel for disposition as soon as a recommendation is prepared.

The criteria for release are specified by statute and rule. *See* Fed. R. App. P. 9. The burden is on the defendant to show that he or she will not flee or pose a danger to others if released, *and* that the appeal is not for purposes of delay and raises a substantial question of law or fact likely to result in reversal or an order for a new trial.

If this Court denies the motion for release, the defendant may seek Supreme Court review by submitting an application for release on conditions to the Circuit Justice for the District of Columbia Circuit, who is the Chief Justice of the United States. Counsel must file the application with the Clerk of the Supreme Court and serve the opposing party pursuant to Rule 29 of the Rules of the Supreme Court. Such motions are rarely granted.

D. Motions for Voluntary Dismissal. (*See* Fed. R. App. P. 42.)

An appeal from the district court not yet docketed in this Court may be dismissed by the district court. Once an appeal has been docketed, however, it can be dismissed only by this Court.

In a civil appeal or agency proceeding, the parties may stipulate that the case should be dismissed, or the appellant or the petitioner may file a motion, with service on the opposing party, requesting dismissal and indicating whether the other parties agree. Before joining in a request for dismissal, the parties also should attempt to reach an agreement as to who will pay costs, if any. A motion for dismissal or stipulation of dismissal predicated on mootness may not be acted on by the Clerk. *See Northern California Power Agency v. Nuclear Regulatory Comm'n*, 393 F.3d 223 (D.C. Cir. 2004). And conditional motions for dismissal or stipulations of dismissal, such as those requesting that the dismissal be without prejudice, will usually be denied by the Clerk.

In a criminal case, counsel *must* submit a motion to the Court requesting dismissal, with service on opposing counsel. The motion must be accompanied by an affidavit from the appellant, stating that the appellant has been fully informed of the circumstances of the case and of the consequences of a dismissal, and wishes to dismiss the appeal. The affidavit also must recite the appellant's satisfaction with the services of counsel.

E. Motions for Remand. (*See* Fed. R. App. P. 12.1; D.C. Cir. Rule 41(b).)

Parties may file a motion to remand either the case or the record for a number of reasons, including to have the district court or agency reconsider a matter, to adduce additional evidence, to clarify a ruling, or to obtain a statement of reasons. The Court also may remand a case or the record on its own motion.

If the *case* is remanded, this Court does not retain jurisdiction, and a new notice of appeal or petition for review will be necessary if a party seeks review of the proceedings conducted upon remand. *See* D.C. Cir. Rule 41(b). In general, a remand of the case occurs where district court or agency reconsideration is necessary. *See, e.g., Raton Gas Transmission Co. v. FERC*, 852 F.2d 612 (D.C. Cir. 1988); *Siegel v. Mazda Motor Co.*, 835 F.2d 1475 (D.C. Cir. 1987). By contrast, if only the *record* is remanded, such as where additional fact-finding is necessary, this Court retains jurisdiction over the case. *See* D.C. Cir. Rule 41(b).

It is important to note that where an appellant, either in a criminal or a civil case, seeks a new trial on the ground of newly discovered evidence while his or her appeal is pending, or where other relief is sought in the district court, the appellant must file the motion seeking the requested relief in the district court. *See Smith v. Pollin*, 194 F.2d 349, 350 (D.C. Cir. 1952); Fed. R. Crim. P. 33; Fed. R. Civ. P. 60. If that court indicates that it will grant the motion, the appellant should move this Court to remand the case to enable the district court to act. *See* Fed. R. App. P. 12.1; *Smith v. Pollin*, 194 F.2d at 350.

F. Motions to Transfer. Motions to transfer are dispositive motions that, pursuant to the initial scheduling order, must be filed within 45 days of the date the case is docketed.

In the context of administrative agency cases, a motion to transfer may be predicated on the Court's power under 28 U.S.C. § 2112(a) to transfer a case to any other court "[f]or the convenience of the parties in the interest of justice." In addition, where this Court concludes that it lacks jurisdiction over an appeal or a petition for review, the Court may, instead of dismissing the case outright, order it transferred to a court where jurisdiction exists. *See* 28 U.S.C. § 1631.

G. Motions for Summary Disposition. Motions for summary affirmance or summary reversal must be filed within 45 days of the date the case is docketed. Parties are encouraged to file such motions where a sound basis exists for summary disposition.

Motions for summary disposition may be granted in whole or in part. Summary affirmance is appropriate where the merits are so clear as to justify summary action. *See Cascade Broadcasting Group, Ltd. v. FCC*, 822 F.2d 1172, 1174 (D.C. Cir. 1987) (per curiam); *Taxpayers Watchdog, Inc. v. Stanley*, 819 F.2d 294, 297 (D.C. Cir. 1987) (per curiam). Summary reversal is rarely granted and is appropriate only where the merits are "so clear, plenary briefing, oral argument, and the traditional collegiality of the decisional process would not affect [the Court's] decision." *Sills v. Federal Bureau of Prisons*, 761 F.2d 792, 793–94 (D.C. Cir. 1985). Parties should avoid requesting summary disposition of issues of first impression for the Court.

H. Motions to Unseal. (*See* D.C. Cir. Rule 47.1.)

Parties or other interested persons may move at any time to unseal any portion of the record in this Court, including confidential briefs or appendices filed under Circuit Rule 47.1. *See* D.C. Cir. Rule 47.1(c).

If the case arises from the district court, the motion will ordinarily be referred to that court, and, if necessary, the record will be remanded for that purpose. This Court may, when the interests of justice require, decide such a motion itself. If unsealing is ordered by this Court, the record may be remanded to the district court for unsealing. Unless otherwise ordered, the filing of a motion to unseal any portion of the record does not delay the filing of any brief under any scheduling order.

IX. BRIEFS AND APPENDIX

A. Briefs. (*See* Fed. R. App. P. 28–32.1; D.C. Cir. Rules 25, 28–32.1)

A well-written brief is of prime importance to success on appeal. Three precepts should guide counsel in drafting briefs:

- Be clear.
- Cite the record and legal authorities fully, fairly, and accurately and, in particular, cite to controlling D.C. Circuit law.
- Be concise.

1. *Timing.* Normally, the Clerk's Office establishes a briefing schedule after the case has been screened and classified by the Legal Division, and after any pending motions in the case have been resolved. In cases designated as "Regular Merits" cases, counsel might receive a single order fixing the date for oral argument and setting the briefing dates back from the oral argument date, with the final brief usually due at least 50 days before the case is to be heard, or the argument date might not be set until after briefing has commenced.

In general, the appellee's or respondent's brief is due 30 days after that of the appellant or petitioner. A reply brief is due 14 days later. To avoid repetition of factual statements or legal arguments made in the principal briefs, the Clerk's Office will stagger the briefing so that intervenors and amici curiae file their briefs 15 days after the brief of the party they support. A briefing schedule also will contain additional time where the Court has granted the parties leave to file a deferred appendix, as provided in Federal Rule of Appellate Procedure 30(c). *See* infra Part IX.B.3.

Once a case has been calendared, the Court strongly disfavors motions to extend the briefing schedule. Such motions will be granted only for extraordinarily compelling reasons. In those extraordinary situations where counsel must seek such an extension, Circuit Rule 28(e)(2) requires the motion to be filed at least calendar 7 days before the brief is due. Circuit Rule 28(e)(3) requires that, before filing the motion, counsel attempt to obtain the consent of other counsel, and recite in the motion the result of such an attempt. Circuit Rule 28(e)(3) also specifies the requirements for service of motions to extend time or to exceed length limits. On a showing of good cause, the Clerk may grant a late-filed motion to extend time if it is unopposed and will not affect the oral argument schedule. Otherwise, motions for extension of time to file a brief that are filed less than 7 days before the brief is due will be denied as untimely, absent extraordinary circumstances. Counsel should be aware that, while the Court will attempt to rule on the motion prior to the date on which the brief is due, submission of a motion to extend time or exceed length limits does not toll the time for compliance with the filing requirements for briefs. Under Circuit Rule 28(e)(4), movants are required to meet all filing requirements absent an express order from the Court granting a waiver.

With respect to cases that have been calendared for oral argument, the Court has instructed the Clerk to deny motions for extensions of time to file briefs (except for very modest extensions of 1 or 2 days) where no explanation for the request is provided or where the need for the extension is attributed to: (1) production difficulties such as malfunctioning equipment, delivery problems, or the lack of secretarial help; or (2) the press of other business. The Clerk may, upon an appropriate showing, grant extensions of up to 7 days.

Untimely or unwarranted motions for extensions of time may result in the imposition of sanctions. If sanctions are appropriate, the Court will consider issuing an order to show cause that requires further explanation from counsel; imposing a fine payable to the Court; assessing attorneys' fees; or referring counsel to the Court's disciplinary committee. The failure by appellant or petitioner to file a timely brief may result in dismissal of the case.

If the appellant or petitioner fails to file the opening brief within the time allowed by the Court, the appellee or respondent may move to dismiss the case, or the Court may dismiss it on the Court's own motion. If the appellee or respondent fails to file a timely answering brief, the Court may order the case submitted on the appellant's or petitioner's brief alone. Circuit Rule 34(f) forecloses oral argument by any party who fails to file a brief, except by permission of the Court.

2. *Consolidated and Joint Appeals.* (*See* Fed. R. App. P. 3(b), 28, 32; D.C. Cir. Rules 28, 32.)

Parties with common interests in consolidated or joint appeals must join in a single brief where feasible. The Court has admonished counsel that it looks with extreme disfavor on the filing of duplicative briefs in consolidated cases. To avoid repetitious arguments, a party may adopt or incorporate by reference all or any part of the brief of another.

It is important in consolidated cases that the parties caption their briefs correctly and uniformly. Each brief cover must bear the lead docket number and corresponding case name and reflect the particular docket number and case name pertaining to that party.

3. *Cross–Appeals.* (*See* Fed. R. App. P. 28.1; D.C. Cir. Rule 28.1.)

In cross-appeals, the first party to appeal is deemed the appellant; if cross-notices are filed on the same day, the plaintiff is deemed the appellant. These designations may be modified by the Court, or by agreement of the parties if the parties notify the Clerk's Office at the time the docketing statements are filed in civil cases, or at the time the final transcript status report is filed in criminal cases. The brief of the appellee serves both as the response brief to appellant's appeal and as the main brief on appellee's appeal. For length limitation purposes, both appellant's opening and response/reply briefs are treated as principal briefs. They are limited to 30 pages each unless the briefs comply with the type-volume limitation of 14,000 words or use a monospaced face and contain no more than 1,300 lines of text. *See* Fed. R. App. P. 28.1(e). The appellee's opening brief is limited to 35 pages unless it complies with the type-volume limitation of 16,500 words or uses a monospaced face and contains no more than 1,500 lines of text. *See id.* The appellee may file a second brief, but only in reply to the appellant's answer on the appellee's cross-appeal. That brief is limited to half the type-volume of appellant's principal brief or 15 pages. *See* Fed. R. App. P. 28.1(e)(2)(C); *see also* Part IX.A. 6, 7. Further briefing requires permission of the Court. *See* Fed. R. App. P. 28.1(c)(5). The cover of appellant's opening brief must be blue; appellee's opening brief, red; appellant's second brief, yellow; and appellee's reply brief, gray. *See* Fed. R. App. P. 28.1(d).

4. *Amici Curiae and Intervenors.* (*See* Fed. R. App. P. 29; D.C. Cir. Rules 28(d), 29, 32.)

A brief of an amicus curiae may be filed only by consent of all the parties or by leave of the Court, unless the amicus is the United States or an officer or agency thereof, a state, a territory, a commonwealth, or the District of Columbia, or has been appointed by the Court. A motion for leave to file an amicus brief must set forth the movant's interest, the reason why briefing is desirable, and why the matters asserted are relevant. Motions for leave to participate as amicus curiae, or written representation of the consent of all parties to such participation, must be accompanied by any disclosure statement required by Circuit Rule 26.1. Parties seeking leave to participate as amicus curiae after the merits panel has been assigned or at the rehearing stage should be aware that the Court will not accept an amicus brief where it would result in the recusal of a member of the panel or recusal of a member of the en banc Court.

The Court encourages those who wish to participate as amici, including governmental entities, to notify the Court as soon as practicable after a case is docketed in this Court, by filing a notice of intent to participate, a representation of consent, or a motion for leave of court when necessary. Prompt notification will enable the Court to accommodate amici briefs in setting the briefing format and schedule in each case, and assist the Court in the early identification of potential recusals caused by the participation of amici. An amicus brief will be due as set by the briefing order in each case; in the absence of provision for such a brief in the order, the brief must be filed in accordance with the time limitations of FRAP 29(e).

An amendment to FRAP 29(c), which took effect December 1, 2010, requires an amicus (other than the United States or its officer or agency, or a state) to disclose whether a party's counsel authored the amicus brief in whole or in part and whether a party or a party's counsel contributed money with the intention of funding the preparation or submission of the brief, and to identify every person (other than the amicus, its members, and its counsel) who contributed money that was intended to fund the brief's preparation or submission.

The brief of an amicus curiae not appointed by the Court may not exceed one-half the maximum length authorized by the Federal Rules of Appellate Procedure for a party's main brief. *See* Fed. R. App. P. 29(d). The brief of an amicus appointed by the Court is usually subject to the length limitations set forth in Federal Rule of Appellate Procedure 32(a)(7).

This Court's rules define an "intervenor" as an interested person who has sought and obtained this Court's leave to participate in an already instituted proceeding. *See* D.C. Cir. Rule 28(d). The principal brief of an intervenor is limited to 19 pages unless the brief complies with the type-volume limitation of 8,750 words or uses a monospaced face and contains no more than 813 lines of text. *See* D.C. Cir. Rule 32(a)(2).

The briefs are due approximately 15 days after the brief of the party that the intervenor or amicus supports, and the briefs may not repeat facts or legal arguments made and adequately elaborated upon in the parties' briefs. Circuit Rule 28(d)(4) requires consolidated briefing by intervenors on the same side, to the extent practicable. Similarly, Circuit Rule 29(d) requires amici curiae on the same side to join in a single brief, to the extent practicable. Where an intervenor or amicus files a separate brief, counsel must certify in the brief why a separate brief is necessary. Grounds that are *not* acceptable as reasons for filing a separate brief include representations that the issues presented require greater length than allowed under the rules, that counsel cannot coordinate filing a single brief because of geographical dispersion, or that separate presentations were permitted in the proceedings below. When a governmental entity is an amicus curiae or an intervenor, it is not required to file a joint brief with other amici or intervenors. For this purpose, a governmental entity includes the United States or an officer or agency thereof, a state, a territory, a commonwealth, and the District of Columbia.

An intervenor supporting an appellant or petitioner may file a reply brief when the appellant's or petitioner's reply brief is due, but an amicus, other than one appointed by the Court, may not file a reply brief unless otherwise directed by the Court. An intervenor's reply brief is limited to half the type-volume of the intervenor's opening brief or 9 pages.

5. *Number of Copies.* (*See* Fed. R. App. P. 31(b); D.C. Cir. Rule 31.)

Except when the appeal is in forma pauperis, the original and 8 copies of each brief must be filed and 2 copies served on each party separately represented. Unrepresented parties proceeding in forma pauperis need file only the original brief, and the Clerk's Office will duplicate the necessary copies. If a deferred appendix is used (*see* infra Part IX.B.3), the parties are required to file only 6 copies of their briefs initially. ECF filers must submit the initial brief in electronic format, along with 5 paper copies.

6. *Format.* (*See* Fed. R. App. P. 32(a); D.C. Cir. Rules 28(a), 32.)

Briefs may use either a proportionally spaced or a monospaced face and must be set in a plain, roman style, although italics and boldface may be used for emphasis. Case names must be italicized or underlined. If a brief uses a proportionally spaced face, the typeface must be at least 14–point and must include serifs, but sans-serif type may be used in headings and captions. If a brief uses a monospaced face, it may have no more than 10 ½ characters per inch. *See* Fed. R. App. P. 32(a)(5), (6). Briefs must be double-spaced and printed on one side of the page only. Evasion of the length limitations may result in the Court's rejection of the brief.

Briefs other than those submitted by unrepresented parties proceeding in forma pauperis must have colored covers as follows: appellant—blue; appellee—red; intervenor or amicus curiae—green; appellant's reply—gray; supplemental brief—tan. In cases designated "Complex," the cover of the briefs and the first page of motions and other pleadings should indicate the designation "Complex." In cases being considered for disposition without oral argument under Circuit Rule 34(j), the cover of the briefs and the first page of motions and other pleadings should indicate "Case being considered for treatment pursuant to Rule 34(j)."

The front cover of the brief must set forth the following: (1) the name of this Court; (2) the docket number of the appeal and the caption of the case, including the docket number and caption of the lead case in a consolidated appeal; (3) the nature of the proceeding and the name of the court or agency below (*e.g.*, Appeal from the United States District Court for the District of Columbia; Petition for Review of an Order of the Federal Communications Commission); (4) the title of the document (*e.g.*, Brief for Appellant); (5) the names, postal addresses, and telephone numbers of an unrepresented party or counsel representing the party filing the brief, and e-mail addresses for ECF filers; and (6) the date on which the case has been scheduled for oral argument. One of the attorneys designated on the cover must be a member of the bar of the Court, except as otherwise provided by law.

The Court prefers spiral binding of briefs, because this method ensures briefs will lie flat when open. *See* Fed. R. App. P. 32(a)(3). Therefore parties are strongly encouraged to use spiral binding for their briefs.

If a brief does not conform to the Federal Rules of Appellate Procedure or to the Circuit Rules, the party will be called and directed either to file a conforming brief (if the problems are numerous) or an errata to the brief (if the problems are minor). If the brief exceeds the page, line, or word limitations, the party will be directed to submit either a corrected brief or a motion for leave to exceed the limits on length.

7. *Length.* (*See* Fed. R. App. P. 32(a); D.C. Cir. Rules 28(c), 28(e), 32.)

Briefs may not exceed the word, line, or page limitations set forth in the Federal and Circuit Rules absent the Court's permission. A principal brief is limited to 30 pages unless the brief complies with the type-volume limitation of 14,000 words or uses a monospaced face and contains no more than 1,300 lines of text. *See* Fed. R. App. P. 32(a)(7). A reply brief is limited to half the type-volume of the principal brief or 15 pages. The length limitations for briefs in cross-appeals are set out in Federal Rule of Appellate Procedure 28.1. *See* Part IX.A.3. These limits do not include the table of contents; table of citations; statement with respect to oral argument; certificate of parties, rulings, and related cases; the glossary; any addendum containing statutory material, regulations, or evidence supporting the claim of standing; and certificates of service and compliance with type-volume limitations. *The summary of argument, footnotes, and citations are included for purposes of computing the word or page limits.*

Parties submitting briefs under the type-volume limitations of Federal Rule of Appellate Procedure 32(a)(7)(B) must include in the brief a certificate, signed by counsel of record or, in the case of parties filing briefs pro se, by the party, stating the number of words in the brief or the number of lines of monospaced text. The person preparing this certificate may rely on word or line counts reported by word processing systems provided the word processing system counts words in footnotes and citations. Parties using word processing systems that do not count words may use the page limitations of 30 pages for principal briefs and 15 pages for reply briefs.

Parties wishing to submit a brief that exceeds the length limitations must, not less than 7 days before the brief is due, file a motion requesting permission to exceed the length limitations. Such motions are granted only for extraordinarily compelling reasons, and motions filed less than 7 days before the brief is due will be denied as untimely, absent exceptional circumstances. *See* D.C. Cir. Rule 28(e).

8. *Contents*. (*See* Fed. R. App. P. 28, 32.1; D.C. Cir. Rules 28, 32.1.)

Briefs must contain the following in the order indicated. Note, however, that intervenors and amici might not be required to include each of the specified items in their briefs.

(a) A "Certificate as to Parties, Rulings, and Related Cases" immediately inside the cover of the brief and preceding the table of contents. Three items must be included in this certificate:

i. The certificate must identify by name all parties, intervenors, and amici who appeared before the district court and all parties, intervenors, or amici in this Court. The appellee or the respondent may omit from the certificate those listed by the appellant or the petitioner but must identify the briefs in which the lists are set forth. The certificate also must include the name of any parent company and any publicly-held company that has a 10% or greater ownership interest in the certifying party. Circuit Rule 26.1 specifies precisely what must be included as to corporate entities, and counsel should consult that provision for greater detail.

ii. The certificate must identify the rulings under review, including the date, the name of the district court judge, the place in the appendix where the ruling is reproduced, and any official citation to the ruling, the Federal Register or other citation when the ruling is an agency decision, or a statement that no such citation exists. In briefs filed after the opening brief, the certificate may incorporate by reference the opening brief's certificate of rulings under review, but must so indicate.

iii. The certificate must indicate whether the case was previously before this or any other court, and, if so, identify it by court number and caption. The certificate also must identify "related cases," as defined in Circuit Rule 28(a)(1)(C), or state that there are none.

(b) A table of contents, with page references.

(c) A table of cases, statutes, and other authorities cited, arranged alphabetically and referring to the pages of the brief where they are cited. The table must either include asterisks in the left margin to denote those authorities upon which the brief chiefly relies or state that there are none. All sources listed in the table of authorities must refer to the specific pages of the brief on which a source is cited; passim or the use of similar terms is prohibited.

(d) A glossary defining abbreviations and acronyms, other than those that are part of common usage. *See* D.C. Cir. Rule 28(a)(3). In briefs the use of acronyms other than those that are widely known should be avoided.

(e) A statement indicating the basis for this Court's jurisdiction and the basis for the district court's or agency's subject matter jurisdiction, with statutory citations and, if necessary, relevant case citations. *See* Fed. R. App. P. 28(a)(4); D.C. Cir. Rule 28(a)(4). Only appellant's or petitioner's brief must contain this statement; any party, intervenor, or amicus may include a counter statement regarding jurisdiction. If the basis of the district court's or agency's subject matter jurisdiction or this Court's jurisdiction is in dispute, the parties should so state and should reference the pages in the brief that address this issue. In cases involving direct review of administrative actions, the petitioner or appellant must also recite in a separate section the basis on which it claims standing. *See* D.C. Cir. Rule 28(a)(7); *Sierra Club v. EPA*, 292 F.3d 895, 900–01 (D.C. Cir. 2002).

(f) A section containing pertinent statutes and regulations. *See* D.C. Cir. Rule 28(a)(5). If these are extensive, they may either be included as an addendum bound with the brief or be bound separately. If they are contained in another party's brief, they may be incorporated by reference.

(g) A statement of the issues presented for review, which appellee or respondent may omit if satisfied with appellant's or petitioner's statement.

(h) A statement of the facts relevant to the issues presented for review, with appropriate references to the record. *See* Fed. R. App. P. 28(a)(7). Appellee or respondent may omit or shorten the statement of the facts if satisfied with that of the appellant or petitioner.

(i) A summary of argument that contains a succinct, clear statement of the arguments made in the body of the brief. The summary must not merely repeat the argument headings.

(j) The argument, which contains the contentions of the parties on the issues presented, with citations to authorities, statutes, and portions of the record upon which the parties rely, and the standard of review for each issue. The appellee or respondent may omit this statement if satisfied with that of the appellant or petitioner.

(k) A succinct conclusion setting forth the precise relief sought.

(*l*) A certificate of compliance if required by Federal Rule of Appellate Procedure 32(a)(7).

Citation requirements for briefs are set out in Federal Rule of Appellate Procedure 32.1 and Circuit Rule 32.1. Counsel must cite D.C. Circuit decisions to the Federal Reporter and state court decisions to the National Reporter System. Parallel citations to the U.S. App. D.C. for D.C. Circuit decisions are not required. All federal statutes, including those applicable to the District of Columbia, must be cited by the current official code or its supplement, or, if there is no current official code, to the current unofficial code or its supplement. Citation to the official session laws is not required unless there is no code citation. When citing to the record, authorities, or any other material, citations must refer to specific pages of the source; passim or similar terms may not be used.

Unpublished orders, judgments, sealed dispositions, or explanatory memoranda entered by this Court before January 1, 2002, may not be cited as precedent. An unpublished disposition may, however, be cited for its res judicata, law of the case, or preclusive effect.

Unpublished dispositions of the D.C. Circuit entered on or after January 1, 2002, may be cited as precedent. Unpublished dispositions include any order, judgment, explanatory memorandum, or other disposition, including interlocutory rulings and summary orders (but not sealed dispositions). (As before, an unpublished disposition of this Court may always be cited for its res judicata, law of the case, or preclusive effect.)

Unpublished dispositions of other federal courts entered before January 1, 2007, may be cited where they are relevant for purposes of res judicata, law of the case, or their preclusive effect. Otherwise, unpublished dispositions of other courts of appeals entered before January 1, 2007, may be cited only in the circumstances and for the purposes allowed by the court issuing the disposition, and unpublished dispositions of district courts entered before that date may not be cited. Unpublished dispositions of other federal courts entered on or after January 1, 2007, may be cited in accordance with Federal Rule of Appellate Procedure 32.1.

If unpublished dispositions cited in a brief are not available in a publicly accessible electronic database, a copy of each must be included in an appropriately labeled addendum to the brief. The addendum may be bound together with the brief, but it should be separated from the body of the brief and any other addendum by a distinctly colored separation page. If the addendum is bound separately, it must be filed and served concurrently with, and in the same number of copies as, the brief itself.

It is important to understand an important caveat in connection with reliance upon unpublished dispositions of this Court. For example, counsel are permitted to argue that an unpublished disposition is binding precedent on a particular issue; they may also argue that an unpublished disposition establishes an intra-circuit conflict in decisions warranting a rehearing en banc. On the other hand, counsel are reminded that the Court's decision to issue an unpublished disposition means that the Court sees no precedential value in that disposition. *See* D.C. Cir. Rule 36(e)(2). Indeed, unpublished dispositions contain language to that very effect. Thus, counsel should recognize that the Court believes its published precedents already establish and adequately explain the legal principles applied in the unpublished disposition, and that there is accordingly no need for counsel to base their arguments on unpublished dispositions. (See generally Circuit Rule 36, which sets out the criteria for published and unpublished opinions.)

Counsel should avoid use of designations such as "appellant" and "appellee." In the interest of clarity, it is preferable to use the designations in the court or agency below, the actual names of the parties, or terms descriptive of them, such as "the employee." In addition, parties are strongly urged to limit the use of acronyms. While acronyms may be used for entities and statutes with widely recognized initials, such as FERC and FOIA, parties should avoid using acronyms that are not widely known.

The excessive use of footnotes also should be avoided. The Court prefers that substantive arguments not be made in footnotes. Footnotes should be used primarily for citations.

Finally, counsel may not refer this Court to sections of pleadings filed in the district court to support those contentions upon which it relies on appeal in lieu of addressing such arguments in the brief.

9. *Citation of Supplemental Authorities.* (*See* Fed. R. App. P. 28(j); D.C. Cir. Rule 28(f).)

When pertinent and significant authorities come to a party's attention after briefing or oral argument but before decision, a party may promptly advise the Clerk by letter, limited to 350 words, with copies to all other parties as provided in Federal Rule of Appellate

Procedure 28(j). Other parties may file a response to the letter, but any response must be similarly limited.

10. *Briefs Containing Material Under Seal.* (*See* D.C. Cir. Rule 47.1(d).)

If it is necessary to refer in a brief to material under seal, two sets of briefs must be filed. The briefs are to be identical except for references to sealed materials. One set of briefs must bear the legend "Under Seal" on the cover, and each page containing sealed material must bear the legend "Under Seal" at the top of the page. The second set of briefs must bear the legend "Public Copy—Sealed Material Deleted" on the cover, and each page from which material under seal has been deleted must bear a legend stating "Material Under Seal Deleted" at the top of the page. Seven copies of the sealed brief and 15 copies of the public brief must be filed, and 2 copies of the public brief and 2 copies of the brief under seal served on each party, if such party is entitled to receive the material under seal. *See, e.g.*, Fed. R. Crim. P. 6(e). Both sets of briefs must comply with the remainder of the rules, including Federal Rule of Appellate Procedure 32(a)(7) and Circuit Rule 32(a), on the length of briefs. Litigants proceeding in forma pauperis must file 1 copy of the sealed brief and 1 copy of the public brief. Briefs filed with the Court under seal are available only to authorized court personnel and are not made available to the public.

B. Appendix. (*See* Fed. R. App. P. 30; D.C. Cir. Rule 30.)

1. *Contents.* While the original record is available to the judges, it may contain far more than is necessary to a proper disposition of the case. To reduce the record to a manageable size, counsel must prepare an appendix, reproducing those parts of the record that are relevant to the issues on appeal. The Court does not require unrepresented parties proceeding in forma pauperis to file an appendix. *See* D.C. Cir. Rule 24.

The appendix must include the relevant docket entries in the proceeding below; the relevant portions of the pleadings, charge, findings, or opinion; the judgment or order in question; and any other parts of the record to which the parties intend to direct the Court's attention. The relevant portions of all pleadings, transcripts, and exhibits that are cited in the brief must also be included. Exhibits may be reproduced in a separate volume of the appendix. *See* Fed. R. App. P. 30(e). Memoranda of law must not be included in the appendix unless there is an issue as to which arguments were raised in the district court or some point that was admitted below. Failure to include relevant parts of the record in the appendix does not preclude the Court or the parties from relying on that material.

The appendix must contain a table of contents describing each item included, with the page of the appendix on which it can be found. This is followed by the relevant docket entries, and then by the other items from the record, set out in chronological order. All the material in the appendix must be consecutively paginated to facilitate citation to the appendix in the briefs.

2. *Preparation.* The appellant or the petitioner bears the burden of preparing the appendix, but the parties are encouraged to agree informally on the contents. If the parties do not agree, the appellant or the petitioner must, not later than 14 days after the date on which the record is filed, serve on the appellee or the respondent a designation of the parts of the record the appellant or petitioner intends to include in the appendix. If the appellee or the respondent wishes to direct the Court's attention to parts of the record not designated by the appellant or the petitioner, the appellee or the respondent must, within 14 days after receipt of the designation, serve upon the appellant or the petitioner a designation of those parts. The appellant or the petitioner must include in the appendix the parts thus designated with respect to the appeal and any cross-appeal. In designating parts of the record for inclusion in the appendix, the parties should have regard for the fact that the entire record is always available to the Court for reference and examination, and the parties should not engage in unnecessary designation.

The appellant or the petitioner pays for the appendix but may be reimbursed when costs are taxed at the conclusion of the case. Appointed counsel in criminal appeals may be reimbursed for the expense of reproducing the appendix by photocopy process in accordance with the Criminal Justice Act. If the appellant or the petitioner believes that opposing counsel is designating material that is unnecessary, the appellant or the petitioner may request the appellee or the respondent to advance the cost of reproducing the materials. If either party causes the inclusion of unnecessary material in the appendix, the Court may require that party to bear the cost of reproducing it, and the Court also may impose sanctions.

Parties to a joint appeal file a joint appendix. In consolidated cases where there are several appellants, the parties must designate someone to assume the primary responsibility for preparing the joint appendix. Intervenors may ask the appellant or the petitioner to include certain material in the appendix, or intervenors may include that material as an addendum to their brief or submit it as a separate volume of the appendix.

If anything material to the appeal is omitted from the appendix, the Clerk, on the written request of any party, may allow the appendix to be supplemented.

3. *Timing; Deferred Appendix.* (*See* Fed. R. App. P. 30; D.C. Cir. Rule 30.)

Federal Rule of Appellate Procedure 30 authorizes either of two timetables for preparing the appendix, and the appellant or petitioner must notify the Court as to which method will be utilized. Under one method, the appendix is complete and available to the parties as they prepare their briefs. In the absence of informal cooperation, the appellant or the petitioner serves the appellee or the respondent with a designation of the proposed contents of the appendix, plus a statement of the issues that the party intends to present for review. The appellee or the respondent then has 14 days to respond with a cross-designation. The appellant or petitioner thereafter files and serves the appendix at the time of filing the brief.

The alternate method allows preparation of the appendix *after* the briefs are filed. Absent informal cooperation, each party serves its designation of the proposed contents of the appendix at the time of filing that party's main brief. *See* Fed. R. App. P. 30(c)(1); D.C. Cir. Rule 30(c). The deferred appendix then must be filed in accordance with the briefing schedule issued by the Court. If a party objects to the use of a "deferred appendix," the matter will be submitted to the Court for resolution.

When parties file their briefs before the appendix has been prepared, they must nonetheless clearly cite to the record, and may do so in one of two ways. *See* Fed. R. App. P. 30(c)(2). They may cite in their briefs to the original pagination of the record (*e.g.*, "Tr. 1154"), in which case the original page numbers also must be indicated on the material reproduced in the appendix. The second and preferred procedure is to file 6 copies of the briefs containing references to the original record. Thereafter, the parties must, in accordance with the briefing schedule, serve and file their briefs in final form, inserting references to the appendix. *See* Fed. R. App. P. 30(c); D.C. Cir. Rule 31. No changes other than citations to the deferred appendix and correction of typographical errors may be made in the final briefs filed under this method.

4. *Format.* (*See* Fed. R. App. P. 32(b); D.C. Cir. Rule 30(a).)

Unlike the brief, the appendix may be duplicated on both sides of each page. If the appendix is separately produced, it must have a white cover.

5. *Number of Copies.* (*See* Fed. R. App. P. 30(e); D.C. Cir. Rule 30(a).)

The appellant or the petitioner must file 8 copies of the appendix, and serve 1 copy on counsel for each party separately represented. When an appendix is filed electronically, 7 paper copies must be filed in addition to the electronic version. If exhibits are reproduced in a separate volume, only 4 copies of that volume need be filed.

6. *In Forma Pauperis Appeals.* (*See* D.C. Cir. Rule 24.)

An unrepresented appellant or petitioner proceeding in forma pauperis is not required to file an appendix. The appellant or petitioner may instead furnish, with the brief, 1 copy of the transcript pages he or she wishes to call to the Court's attention; 1 copy of a list setting forth the page numbers of the transcript so furnished; and 1 copy of other portions of the record to which the appellant or petitioner directs the Court's attention. Pro se parties, however, are encouraged to submit 4 copies of these materials if they can. An appellee or respondent must furnish, with the brief, 4 copies of an appendix containing any pages of transcript or other portions of the record not furnished by appellant or petitioner to which the appellee or respondent directs the Court's attention.

7. *Appendix Containing Matters Under Seal.* (*See* D.C. Cir. Rule 47.1(e).)

If it is necessary to include material under seal in an appendix, the appendix must be filed in two segments. One segment must contain all sealed material and must bear the legend "Supplement—Under Seal" on the cover, and each page of that segment containing sealed material must bear the legend "Under Seal" at the top of the page. The second appendix segment must bear the legend "Public Appendix—Material Under Seal in Separate Supplement" on the cover; each page from which material under seal has been deleted must bear the legend "Material Under Seal Deleted" at the top of the page. Seven copies of the sealed segment and 7 copies of the public segment of the appendix must be filed, and 1 copy of the public segment of the appendix and 1 copy of the sealed segment served on each party, if such party is entitled to receive the material under seal. *See, e.g.*, Fed. R. Crim. P. 6(e). Segments of appendices filed with the Court under seal are available only to authorized court personnel and are not made available to the public.

X. THE COURT'S CALENDAR

The Court usually hears cases in 8 sitting periods consisting of 4 weeks each. Except when it is sitting en banc, the Court hears cases in panels of three judges. The Court usually does not hear cases on Wednesdays. Judges are usually assigned to no more than one regular merits panel during a sitting period.

A. Scheduling Sitting Periods. The sitting periods ordinarily begin in September and end in May. While there are usually no formal sitting periods in June, July, and August, panels of the Court are available throughout the summer to hear appeals in which there is an urgent need for immediate consideration. These summer panels also continue to decide motions and cases submitted without argument pursuant to Circuit Rule 34(j).

The sitting periods for each term are scheduled the preceding winter. The Clerk prepares a proposed schedule and submits it to the Court in executive session. The Court accepts the schedule as prepared by the Clerk or modifies it, if necessary.

B. Merits Panels. The Clerk assigns the judges in panels of three to the sitting weeks for which they are available for an entire term. The Clerk attempts to pair each active judge with each other active judge an equal number of weeks during the year, insofar as availability permits. If a judge becomes unavailable, he or she may arrange to switch sitting dates with another judge. Depending on their availability, senior judges of this Court also serve on panels.

C. Caseload and Case Mix. The Clerk's Office usually schedules at least three cases for each day of a panel's sitting period. The "mix" of cases (criminal appeals, private civil appeals, civil appeals where the federal government is a party, and administrative agency cases) in a given sitting period reflects roughly the proportions of the Court's overall caseload.

D. Scheduling Cases for Argument. Most appeals screened by the Legal Division are classified as "Regular Merits" cases. Normally, the Clerk's Office sets an oral argument date and a briefing schedule in these cases after all pending motions have been resolved. Scheduling is done by a computer program, which automatically checks for known recusals and makes certain that the case mix both for a specific date and for that week's sitting is acceptable. As a general rule, once they become ready, cases are calendared in order of age, with the oldest cases set first. Counsel are advised that whenever there are serious settlement negotiations in progress, the parties should advise the Clerk of that fact.

From time to time a judge must recuse himself or herself from consideration of a particular case. *See* 28 U.S.C. § 455; Canon 3C, Code of Conduct for United States Judges, Judicial Conference of the United States. The judge is not required to state the reasons for recusal. The provisional certificate of parties filed with the docketing statement, pursuant to Circuit Rules 12(c) and 15(c), or with a petition for permission to appeal or a petition for an extraordinary writ, pursuant to Circuit Rules 5 and 21, affords the Clerk's Office the opportunity to determine in advance of briefing those judges who would be recused. In most cases, this ensures that the case will not be set for hearing on a day when the recused judge is sitting. In some cases, however, a judge discovers the basis for recusal only after the case has been scheduled before a particular panel. In those cases, a replacement judge is assigned to hear the case on that date.

E. Scheduling in Particular Cases.

1. *Special Panel.* From time to time in deciding motions, the special panel may have considered in great detail a matter that is closely related to the merits of a case; this consideration may have included oral argument. If that panel determines that judicial efficiency would be served by the panel retaining the case, it will so advise the Clerk. The special panel then controls the case from that point on to disposition.

2. *Related Cases.* Most related cases are consolidated before they are calendared, as described supra in Parts III.H and V.A. Occasionally, however, a case is identified after a related case has been scheduled for argument or even argued. In these and other instances in which the cases would normally have been consolidated, or at least joined for hearing before the same panel, the Clerk's Office advises the panel to which the earlier case has been assigned. If the panel determines, in the interest of judicial economy and consistency of decisions, to take the new case, it will so advise the Clerk.

3. *Cases on Remand to this Court.* When the Supreme Court remands a case to this Court for further proceedings, the case is assigned to the same panel that previously considered it.

4. *Stipulated Stand-by Pool.* Parties may agree to enter the Court's stipulated stand-by pool, which would allow the case to be used as a replacement for cases that are removed from the calendar too close to the argument date to be replaced in the normal course. Utilization of the stand-by pool may result in significant expedition.

In order to enter the stand-by pool, parties must: (1) stipulate that they do not object to inclusion in the stand-by pool; (2) stipulate that they will not file any dispositive motions; and (3) agree to an expedited briefing schedule. Usually, counsel will be given at least 50 days' notice of the argument date and that date will be no earlier than 50 days after the last brief is due. If counsel is unavailable for the selected date, every effort will be made to calendar the case so that consideration is not delayed. Parties should note that the Court will not ordinarily include in the stand-by pool cases that are inappropriate for oral argument, *see* Circuit Rule 34(j), or cases that require special internal management pursuant to this Court's Appeals Management Plan.

XI. ORAL ARGUMENT

A. Notification. (*See* Fed. R. App. P. 34(b); D.C. Cir. Rule 34(c).)

In civil cases, parties may receive notice of the date for oral argument at the time the briefing schedule is set or after briefing has started. In criminal cases, the Clerk's Office ordinarily gives counsel notice of the date for oral argument after the briefs have been filed. Generally, the members of the panel of judges are named in the notice setting the date for oral argument; occasionally the panel is revealed in a later notice. The notice includes a form that counsel must complete and submit to the Clerk's Office, no less than 7 days before oral argument, giving the name of the attorney or attorneys who will present the argument to the Court. Counsel are advised that whenever there are serious settlement negotiations in progress, the parties should advise the Clerk of that fact.

Requests by artists to sketch court proceedings should be directed to the Clerk's Office well in advance of the scheduled argument. The Court will accommodate all requests unless the panel for reasons of security decides otherwise. Additionally, if the Court receives multiple requests, space considerations may limit the number of sketch artists that can be accommodated.

B. Postponements. (*See* Fed. R. App. P. 34(b); D.C. Cir. Rule 34(g).)

The Court disfavors motions to postpone oral argument and will grant them only upon a showing of "extraordinary cause." Unless the panel that grants a motion to postpone argument is prepared to retain the case and hear it outside its normal sitting period, the case will have to be rescheduled for the first available date on the calendar—possibly months later than the original date. Accordingly, it is in counsel's interest to avoid seeking to postpone argument.

C. Argument Time. (*See* D.C. Cir. Rule 34(b).)

1. *Screening by the Panel.* When cases are assigned to panels, the Clerk designates one judge of the Court on the panel for each day to have primary responsibility for screening cases for that day. The screening function is concerned with alignment of parties and issues, and allotment of times for the arguments. Senior judges of this Court do not serve as screening judges. The name of the screening judge is not made public.

The Clerk's Office distributes the briefs, appendices, and other relevant materials to the judges. In addition, the panel has before it any motions for allotment of argument time. The screening judge reviews the assigned cases and then sends a memorandum to the other judges on the panel containing his or her screening decisions.

There is no standard length of oral argument time, although the allotment of 15 minutes per side is perhaps the most common. The screening judge determines the amount of argument time and may set a particular format for oral argument. The argument may be limited to certain issues, counsel may be advised that the panel wishes additional questions to be addressed at oral argument, and the usual order of presentation contemplated by Federal Rule of Appellate Procedure 34(c) may be altered. The screening judge also advises the Clerk of the order in which cases set for a particular day will be heard.

When the screening judge allots time for argument, that decision is automatically effective, and no concurrences are necessary from the other members of the panel. If the screening judge recommends instead that the case be submitted without oral argument, pursuant to Circuit Rule 34(j), it is necessary that the other two members of the panel concur in this recommendation. After receiving the judge's screening memoranda, the Clerk's Office issues orders that reflect the screening decisions.

Parties allotted less time than they believe is warranted may move promptly for additional time. The Court rarely grants such motions. If the Court orders a case to be submitted without argument pursuant to Circuit Rule 34(j), counsel has 10 days from the date of the screening order within which to move to restore the case to the argument calendar. The Court rarely grants these motions. On the other hand, a party in a case that has been set for argument may wish to move to submit the case on the briefs alone. Counsel should file such a motion as soon as possible after receiving the argument date and briefing schedule.

If a case is screened and then postponed before oral argument, the screening decision will be subject to redetermination when the argument is rescheduled.

2. *Rule 34(j) Dispositions.* Pursuant to Federal Rule of Appellate Procedure 34(a)(2), the Court may, under certain circumstances, decide a case without oral argument. Among the factors the Court considers are: (1) whether the appeal is frivolous; (2) whether the dispositive issue has previously been authoritatively decided; and (3) whether the facts and legal arguments are adequately presented in the briefs and record so that oral argument would not significantly aid the decisional process. The decision to dispense with oral argument must be unanimously made by a three-judge panel.

The Court's Case Management Plan is designed to identify early in the appellate process cases suitable for disposition without oral argument under Circuit Rule 34(j). When a staff attorney screens a new appeal and concludes that Rule 34(j) treatment might be appropriate, that screening recommendation goes to the Clerk's Office, and a briefing schedule (but no oral argument date) is set. The staff attorney then reviews the briefs, and if he or she concludes that the case should be disposed of without oral argument, the staff attorney recommends to the special panel that it decide the case on the merits, pursuant to the Rule. The staff attorney also proposes a disposition, embodied in a draft judgment and, where appropriate, an accompanying memorandum. If the special panel accepts the recommendation for Rule 34(j) disposition, the panel issues an order advising the parties that the case will be decided without oral argument. Counsel may move within 10 days for reconsideration of that order. In the absence of a successful motion to reconsider, the special panel will decide the case on the merits, usually by an unpublished per curiam judgment.

The second way in which a case may be submitted for decision without oral argument is if the screening judge, with the concurrence of the other two members of the merits panel, determines that a case, originally set for argument as a "Regular Merits" case, should be removed from the calendar and handled pursuant to Rule 34(j). The Clerk's Office issues an order notifying counsel of that decision, and counsel has 10 days to move for reconsideration. The Court rarely grants such motions.

The merits panel discusses cases submitted without oral argument at a conference following oral argument on the day on which the case was originally scheduled to be heard. The disposition is usually in the form of an unpublished per curiam judgment.

D. Number of Counsel. (*See* D.C. Cir. Rules 34(c), (d).)

There is generally a limit of two counsel per side who may argue in cases allotted more than 15 minutes per side. In cases allotted 15 minutes or less per side, only one counsel may argue. This rule applies to consolidated cases, and it may be waived only by leave of the Court.

An intervenor may argue only to the extent that counsel whose side the intervenor supports is willing to share argument time. If counsel wishes to share time with an intervenor in a case in which at least 15 minutes per side has been allotted for argument, no leave of the Court is necessary. Counsel should inform the Clerk's Office of such arrangements no less than 7 days before the date of argument. The counsel for the intervenor will be counted as one of the two counsel per side permitted under the rules.

Counsel on the same side should make their own apportionment of time among themselves; otherwise the Court will do so. The courtroom deputy should be advised of the arrangement before the case is called; the attorney making the opening presentation should announce the arrangement to the Court. Each attorney is thereafter limited to the time specifically allotted, unless the Court permits otherwise.

E. Arguments by Amici Curiae. (*See* D.C. Cir. Rule 34(e).)

An amicus curiae, other than one appointed by the Court, may not present oral argument without permission of the Court, and such permission is sparingly granted. If counsel for the party supported by the amicus consents to share oral argument time with the amicus, no motion is necessary, subject to the limitation in Circuit Rule 34(c) that no more than two attorneys may argue. Otherwise, an amicus seeking leave to argue must file a motion no later than 14 days prior to the date oral argument is scheduled.

F. Form and Content of Argument. (*See* Fed. R. App. P. 34; D.C. Cir. Rule 34.)

The appellant is entitled to open and conclude the argument. If the case involves a cross-appeal, the first party to file a notice of appeal is deemed the appellant, unless the parties agree or the Court orders otherwise. *See* Fed. R. App. P. 28.1(b). In cases in which separate time is allotted to a number of parties, the screening order will indicate the order of presentation of argument to be followed by those parties.

The opening argument should include a brief introductory statement of the case and the issues presented. Counsel may not read from a prepared text, nor should counsel read at length from briefs, records, or authorities. *See* Fed. R. App. P. 34(c); D.C. Cir. Rule 34(a). Counsel should be prepared to answer questions from the bench, and attorneys on the same side should take care not to duplicate their arguments.

If counsel wishes to use any exhibits in the courtroom, counsel must make arrangements with the Clerk's Office and advise the Court and all other counsel by letter at least 7 days prior to the argument. The letter must set forth the justification for the use of the exhibits. After the argument, counsel should remove the exhibits, unless directed otherwise by the panel. *See* D.C. Cir. Rule 34(i).

In this Circuit, the judges will always have read the briefs prior to the hearing. Counsel should keep this in mind when preparing and presenting argument.

Argument for the day usually begins at 9:30 a.m. As a general rule, the panel will hear all cases scheduled for that day, even if it is necessary to recess for lunch and reconvene.

G. Court Closings. As noted in Part II.B.4, if there is any possibility that the Court will not be in session because of inclement weather or an emergency situation, counsel should call the Clerk's Office at 202–216–7000 (Option 2, Special Announcements), or check the Court's web site located at www.cadc.uscourts.gov, to determine whether the Court is open. In the absence of official notice *from the Court* to the contrary, counsel should assume that the Court *will* be in session. A general announcement by the media that the "government" is closed does not necessarily include this Court.

H. Procedures for Oral Argument. Counsel must arrive at the courtroom at least 20 minutes before the start of argument for the day. The identity of the panel and the order in which the cases will be heard will be posted outside the courtroom. Counsel also may call the Clerk's Office in the afternoon of the day before argument to find out the order in which the cases will be heard or consult the Court's web site. If more than one panel is sitting that morning, the notice also will disclose the other hearing location. The presiding judge may alter the order in which the cases are to be heard from the schedule posted. Counsel must sign in with the courtroom deputy upon arrival. Except as stated below, counsel must remain in the courtroom, or arrange with the courtroom deputy to be on call in the attorney waiting room next to the courtroom. Counsel scheduled to appear in the third and subsequent cases on the calendar, however, may be excused by the courtroom deputy after signing in, unless the panel directs otherwise. Prior to leaving the courtroom, excused counsel must inform the courtroom deputy of the places and, if available, telephone numbers, where they can be reached in the interim.

All counsel who have not remained in the courtroom must return to the courtroom 15 minutes before their cases are due to be heard, based on the time set for each preceding case.

The deputy will explain the warning light system used to signal the time remaining during the oral argument. Counsel for the appellant or petitioner also must inform the courtroom deputy whether he or she wishes to reserve time for rebuttal.

The presiding judge of the panel is the member of the panel in active service who is first in seniority. The presiding judge sits in the center of the bench, and the next ranking judge is seated to his or her right. The names and seating arrangement of the panel for the day are marked on the lectern.

Facing the bench, counsel for the appellant or the petitioner sits at the table to the right of the lectern, and counsel for the appellee or respondent to the left. Additional counsel may sit at the tables or elsewhere in the well of the courtroom.

Three lights—green, amber, and red—are on the lectern in front of counsel. The lectern lights also are visible to the Court. If counsel does not wish to reserve rebuttal time, the courtroom deputy will flash the amber light when there are 2 minutes remaining in the allotted time. The red light will be turned on when all the allotted time is used. Counsel wishing to reserve time for rebuttal must observe the timer and preserve the time he or she has reserved for rebuttal. During rebuttal, counsel will receive no amber light warning when time is about to expire; when the time has expired, the red light will be turned on.

When the questioning has been extensive, the presiding judge in his or her discretion may grant counsel additional time for argument. The Court also may terminate the hearing before the allotted time is up, if further argument appears unnecessary.

I. Transcription of Arguments. All arguments are recorded for future reference of the Court. Recordings are retained at the Court for a period of two years following issuance of the mandate. If counsel wishes to listen to the recording of an oral argument or to have the recording transcribed, counsel must make the request in a letter to the Clerk. Counsel must provide in the letter the name of the case, the case number, and the date of the argument. Counsel also must make appropriate arrangements with the company that is the Court's official reporter. The Clerk will release the recording to the company for preparation of the transcript. In addition, copies of oral argument recordings may be purchased upon written request *after the case has been completely closed.* This means all appeals, remands, or additional proceedings must be concluded before the recording will be reproduced.

XII. MAKING THE DECISION

A. Forms of Decision. (*See* Fed. R. App. P. 32.1, 36; D.C. Cir. Rules 32.1, 36.)

Four possible forms for disposing of cases that have been considered by a merits panel are currently used: a published signed opinion, a published per curiam opinion, an unpublished judgment or order with memorandum, and a judgment or order without memorandum. The first two forms are familiar to all attorneys. An unpublished judgment or order with memorandum is addressed primarily to those immediately concerned with the case. The memorandum usually is fairly brief, stating only the facts and law necessary for an understanding of the Court's decision. A judgment or order without memorandum indicates affirmance or reversal, or grant or denial of a petition for review, with a brief explanation, such as citation of a governing precedent. With the exception of orders filed under seal and some scheduling orders generated by the Court's docketing system, all orders and judgments, including Clerk's orders, issued on or after June 1, 2001, are available over the Internet via PACER, the Judiciary's electronic public access service. A small document icon appears next to the docket entry for any order or judgment that can be viewed online. A PACER account is required (available from the PACER Service Center), and a per page fee applies. The PACER Service Center can be accessed through a link at the Court's web site, www.cadc.uscourts.gov.

Circuit Rule 36(c)(2) sets out the criteria the Court employs in determining whether to publish an opinion. The Court's policy is to publish an opinion or memorandum if it meets one or more of the following criteria: (1) the opinion resolves a substantial issue of first impression generally or an issue presented for the first time in this Court; (2) the opinion alters, modifies, or significantly clarifies a rule of law previously announced by the Court; (3) the opinion calls attention to an existing rule of law that appears to have been generally overlooked; (4) the opinion criticizes or questions existing law; (5) the opinion resolves a conflict in decisions within the Circuit or creates a conflict with another circuit; (6) the opinion reverses a published district court or agency decision, or affirms it on grounds different from those in a published opinion of the district court; or (7) the opinion warrants publication in light of other factors that give it general public interest.

An unpublished disposition will be used where the Court's decision does not satisfy the criteria for publication under Circuit Rule 36(c). Citation of unpublished dispositions is governed by Federal Rule of Appellate Procedure 32.1 and Circuit Rule 32.1(b). Although Circuit Rule 32.1(b)(1) permits citation, as precedent, of unpublished dispositions of this Court issued on or after January 1, 2002, Circuit Rule 36(e)(2) makes clear that the Court's decision to issue an unpublished disposition means that the Court sees no precedential value in that disposition, *i.e.*, the order or judgment does not add anything to the body of law already established and explained in the Court's published precedents.

B. Case Conferences. In this Circuit, cases decided on the merits are generally discussed at a case conference. If the case was argued, the conference generally takes place later the same day; if the case was submitted without argument, it is usually discussed at the same conference as the cases with which it was originally scheduled. This Court does not ordinarily decide argued cases from the bench.

At the conference, the members of the panel reach agreement on the form as well as the substance of the decision. If the panel decides to issue an opinion or memorandum, the presiding judge assigns the responsibility for writing it, unless he or she is in the minority, in which event the senior member of the panel in the majority designates the author. When a case has been submitted without oral argument, the screening judge usually prepares the opinion or memorandum.

C. Preparation of Opinions. If the case is to be decided with an opinion or memorandum, the author circulates a draft to the other members of the panel. The other judges are free to suggest changes in the proposed text, or they may draft and circulate concurring or dissenting opinions. These may lead to further changes in the majority opinion.

Final drafts of all opinions to be published also are circulated to all active judges on the Court. Following circulation of the drafts to the panel and the Court, the opinion is printed in house.

D. Timing of Decisions. Each month there is a report on the status of every case that has been argued but not yet assigned, and each judge reports on the status of every opinion assigned to him or her that either has not been circulated or is awaiting clearance by other members of the panel.

Occasionally, a panel defers decision of a case pending disposition of another case in this Court or before another tribunal. The Clerk's Office usually notifies the parties by an order holding the case in abeyance pending a decision or some other event.

Counsel are advised that whenever there are serious post-argument settlement negotiations in progress, the parties should advise the Clerk of that fact.

E. Notice of Decisions. When an order or judgment is entered in a case assigned to the CM/ECF system, the Clerk's Office electronically transmits a Notice of Docket Activity to all parties who have consented to electronic service, and mails notice and a copy of any opinion or judgment to parties who are not ECF filers. For printed copies of opinions, each party (including ECF filers) will receive 2 paper copies of the decision without charge. *See* D.C. Cir. Rules 36(b), 45(d) and (f).

Opinions will be posted on the Court's web site, which can be accessed from a computer terminal in the public office of the Clerk's Office. Members of the bar should call the Clerk's attention to typographical or other errors in slip opinions.

Dockets and other Court records are available on the PACER web site. *See* supra Part II.B.3. Opinions issued since September 1997 are available on the Court's web site and PACER in PDF format.

Opinions are added to the Court's web site soon after they are publicly released. Docket sheets and opinions posted on the PACER web site provide case information in real time.

Although certain decisions are not published, all unsealed judgments and memoranda are available to the public upon proper application to the Clerk's Office, and those issued since June 2000 are posted on the Court's web site.

XIII. POST–DECISION PROCEDURES

A. Terminating the Case.

1. *Enforcement Judgments.* (*See* Fed. R. App. P. 19.)

After the Court files an opinion directing entry of judgment enforcing in part an agency order, the agency within 14 days must submit a proposed judgment to the Court. If a party disagrees with the agency's proposal, that party has 10 days thereafter to file an alternative judgment. The panel will then either settle the judgment and direct its entry, return the matter to the agency for redrafting, or craft its own judgment.

2. *Mandates.* (*See* Fed. R. App. P. 41; D.C. Cir. Rule 41.)

The Court will enter its judgment in a case on the same date its decision is issued. Ordinarily, the Clerk's Office will issue a certified copy of that judgment in lieu of a formal mandate 7 days after the period for seeking rehearing has expired or a petition for rehearing has been decided. The Court, however, retains discretion to direct immediate issuance of its mandate in an appropriate case, and any party may move at any time for expedited issuance of the mandate on a showing of good cause. Counsel should not confuse the mandate with the judgment itself because the time for filing a petition for a writ of certiorari with the United States Supreme Court runs from the date of this Court's judgment or disposition of a timely petition for rehearing or for rehearing en banc.

A motion for stay of the mandate must set forth facts showing good cause. Unless the motion recites that the other parties do not object to a stay, the motion will not be acted upon until the response time has expired. Subject to these limitations, the Clerk has been given authority to grant unopposed motions for stays for a period of up to 90 days. In his or her discretion, the Clerk may instead submit the motion to the panel that decided the case. Motions to reconsider a decision by the Clerk are referred to the panel that decided the case. If a motion to stay issuance of the mandate is denied, the mandate ordinarily will be issued 7 days thereafter. Stays ordinarily will not extend beyond 90 days from the date the mandate otherwise would have issued.

If the party who obtained a stay of the mandate files a petition for a writ of certiorari during the term of the stay issued by this Court, and so notifies the circuit Clerk in writing, the stay will continue until the Supreme Court's final disposition. A petition for a writ of certiorari filed under any other circumstances has no effect on the mandate.

3. *Remands.* (*See* Fed. R. App. P. 12.1; D.C. Cir. Rule 41(b).)

When the Court remands the *record* in any case to the district court or to an agency, the Court retains jurisdiction over the case. When the Court remands the *case*, the Court does not retain jurisdiction, and a new notice of appeal or petition for review is required if a party seeks review of the proceedings conducted on remand.

4. *Costs.* (*See* Fed. R. App. P. 39; D.C. Cir. Rule 39.)

Costs, when requested, are usually charged to the losing party or to an appellant who withdraws the appeal. When the government is a party to a suit, costs are governed by statute. Costs are not taxed for briefs of amici curiae or intervenors or separate replies thereto except on motion granted by the Court.

The items allowed as costs are set forth in Circuit Rule 39(a). Reimbursable printing costs are limited to the cost of the most economical means of reproduction. In addition to the docketing fee, costs are allowed for reproducing the number of copies of briefs and appendices that must be filed with the Court and served on parties, intervenors, and amici curiae, plus 3 for the submitting party.

Counsel has 14 days after entry of judgment to submit the bill of costs with service on opposing counsel. Printing and reproduction costs must be itemized and verified to show the charge per page. Opposing counsel may file objections. The Clerk's Office provides forms for itemizing bills of costs, and parties that submit bills not presented on these forms (or reasonable facsimiles thereof) will be directed to provide a conforming request.

The Clerk reviews the bill for compliance with the rules and then prepares a statement for inclusion in the mandate. Ordinarily, the directions as to costs are issued at the same time as the mandate. If the matter of costs has not been settled by that time, the Clerk's Office will at a later date send a supplemental statement to the district court or agency for insertion in the mandate.

Once a party is ordered to pay costs, there is usually no further action on the matter in this Court. Any action to enforce an award of costs is brought in the district court. In addition, various expenses incidental to the appeal must be settled in the district court. Among these are the costs of the reporter's transcript, the filing fee for the notice of appeal, the Clerk's fee for preparing and transmitting the record, and the premiums paid for any required appeal bond. The successful party on appeal must apply for recovery of these expenses in the district court after issuance of the mandate of this Court.

5. *Disposal of Sealed Records.* (*See* D.C. Cir. Rule 47.1(f).)

In any case in which all or part of the record has been maintained under seal, the Clerk will order the parties to show cause why the record should not be unsealed, unless the nature of the materials themselves (*e.g.*, grand jury material) makes it clear that unsealing would be impermissible. This order will be entered in conjunction with the issuance of the mandate. If the parties agree to unsealing, the record will be unsealed by Clerk's order. Otherwise, the matter will be referred to the Court for disposition. Counsel to an appeal involving sealed records must promptly notify the Court when it is no longer necessary to maintain the record or portions of the record under seal.

B. Reconsideration.

1. *Rehearing by the Panel.* (*See* Fed. R. App. P. 32, 35, 40; D.C. Cir. Rule 35.)

Very few petitions for rehearing are granted. Sanctions may be imposed as a penalty for filing a petition for rehearing found to be wholly without merit.

A party seeking rehearing must file a petition within 45 days after entry of the judgment in any case in which a party is either the United States, one of its agencies, a federal officer or employee sued in an official capacity, or, under certain circumstances, a federal officer or employee sued in an individual capacity. If no party fits into one of these categories, the petition must be filed within 30 days. These time limits will not be extended except for good cause shown. The petition must state with particularity the errors that the panel is claimed to have made. An original and 4 copies must be filed. A copy of the panel's opinion, a Rule 28(a)(1)(A) certificate of parties and amici, and any disclosure statement required by Circuit Rule 26.1 must be attached as an addendum to the petition. *See* D.C. Cir. Rule 35(c). The form of a petition for rehearing is governed by Federal Rule of Appellate Procedure 32, and the petition may not exceed 15 pages. *See* Fed. R. App. P. 35(b)(2), 40(b); D.C. Cir. Rule 35(b). Motions to exceed this page limitation are viewed with disfavor and will be granted only for extraordinarily compelling reasons.

A response to the petition is not permitted unless the panel requests one. A petition for rehearing, however, will not ordinarily be granted, nor will an opinion or judgment be modified in any significant respect, in the absence of a request by the Court for a response.

The Clerk does not send the mandate to the district court or agency until a timely petition for rehearing has been decided, unless the Court expressly so orders. The Clerk also will delay issuing the mandate when a party moves for an extension of the time within which to petition for rehearing or rehearing en banc. A timely petition for rehearing or rehearing en banc extends the time for petitioning the United States Supreme Court for a writ of certiorari.

The Clerk's Office transmits the petition to the panel members via an electronic vote sheet. When voting is complete, the Clerk enters an appropriate order for the Court. If a petition for rehearing en banc also has been filed, the Clerk will withhold entry of an order denying rehearing by the panel until the en banc question has been resolved. If rehearing en banc is granted, the panel's judgment, but ordinarily not its opinion, is vacated, but the panel may act on the petition for rehearing without waiting for final termination of the en banc proceeding. On termination of the en banc proceeding (including when the en banc Court divides evenly), a new judgment will be issued.

2. *Rehearing En Banc.* (*See* Fed. R. App. P. 35; D.C. Cir. Rule 35.)

Like petitions for rehearing by a panel, petitions for rehearing en banc are frequently filed but rarely granted. Federal Rule of Appellate Procedure 35(a) expressly states that en banc hearings are not favored and ordinarily will not be ordered except to secure or maintain uniformity of decisions among the panels of the Court, or to decide questions of exceptional importance.

The timing requirements for a petition for rehearing en banc are the same as those for panel rehearing. The formal requirements partly duplicate, and partly differ from, those for a petition for rehearing by the panel. The petition must begin with a section that sets forth why the case is of exceptional importance or cites the decisions with which the panel judgment is claimed to be in conflict. An original and 19 copies must be filed. As with panel rehearing petitions, a copy of the panel opinion, a Rule 28(a)(1)(A) certificate of parties and amici, and any disclosure statement required by Circuit Rule 26.1 must be attached as an addendum to the petition. *See* D.C. Cir. Rule 35(c). The petition may not exceed 15 pages in length. Motions to exceed this limitation are viewed with disfavor and will be granted only for extraordinarily compelling reasons.

If a party is submitting both a petition for rehearing by the panel and a petition for rehearing en banc, the two should be combined in the same document, in which event an original and 19 copies must be filed, and the page limit for the combined pleading is 15. If the two pleadings are filed separately, they may not, combined, exceed this page limit.

As in the case of petitions for panel rehearing, the rules do not provide for a response to a petition for rehearing en banc, except by request of the Court. If any member of the Court wishes a response, the Clerk will enter an order to that effect. There is no oral argument on the question whether rehearing en banc should be granted.

The Clerk's Office transmits a vote sheet and the petition for rehearing en banc electronically to all members of the original panel, including a senior judge of this Court, and to all other active judges of this Court. A vote may be requested by an active judge of the Court, or by any member of the panel. If no judge asks for a vote within a specified time, and none requests more time to consider the matter, the Clerk will enter an order denying the petition.

If a judge calls for a vote on the petition for rehearing en banc, the Clerk's Office transmits electronically to the full Court a new vote sheet, along with any response to the petition ordered by the Court. The question now is whether there should be a rehearing en banc. On this question only active judges of the Court may vote, and a majority of all active judges who are not recused must approve rehearing en banc in order for it to be granted.

When rehearing en banc is granted, the Clerk enters an order granting the rehearing en banc and vacating the judgment by the original panel, either in whole or in part, as circumstances warrant. This order is posted on the Court's web site and is published in the federal reporter system. An order granting rehearing en banc does not indicate the names of the judges who voted against rehearing, but an order denying rehearing en banc does indicate the names of the judges who voted to grant rehearing en banc, if they wish.

The Court has followed a variety of procedures in conducting rehearing en banc. On occasion, only the original briefs have been considered; in other cases, the Court has requested supplemental briefs. The Court almost always hears oral argument in considering a case en banc.

The Court sitting en banc consists of all active judges, plus any senior judges of the Court who were members of the original panel and wish to participate. When the Court sits en banc with an even number of judges, and the result is an evenly divided vote, the Court will enter a judgment affirming the order or judgment under review, and it may publish the en banc Court's divided views.

In the absence of a request from a party, any active judge of the Court, or member of the panel, may suggest that a case be reheard en banc. If a majority of the active judges who are not recused agree, the Court orders rehearing en banc.

In addition, a party may move for en banc consideration prior to a panel decision. Such a petition must include a concise statement of the issue and its importance and conform to the other requirements of Federal Rule of Appellate Procedure 35(c). If a party wishes a case to be heard initially en banc, counsel ideally should file the petition within the first 30 days after docketing, but in no event later than the date on which the appellee's or the respondent's brief is due. A judge also may suggest en banc consideration prior to the panel decision; on occasion this has been done by the panel itself.

C. Review by the Supreme Court of the United States. In general, a party has 90 days from the entry of judgment or the denial of a timely petition for rehearing, whichever is later, in which to petition for a writ of certiorari. A circuit court cannot enlarge this period; application for an extension must be made to the Supreme Court. Counsel should be mindful that the judgment is entered on the day of the Court's decision and not when the mandate—*i.e.*, a certified copy of the judgment—is issued.

Because of a problem of space, the Clerk of the Supreme Court has asked this Court not to transmit any record, or portion of a record, unless specifically requested by the Clerk or Deputy Clerk.

Federal Rule of Appellate Procedure 41(d) provides that a stay pending application for certiorari "must not exceed 90 days, unless the period is extended for good cause." When, however, a party files a petition for a writ of certiorari before the mandate of this Court is issued, the mandate is stayed until the Supreme Court disposes of the case *if* the party first obtained a stay of the mandate, filed the petition within the period the stay was in effect, and so notified the Clerk of this Court. Upon notification of the denial of the petition by the Supreme Court, this Court's mandate will be issued promptly.

[Amended April 1997; January 3, 2000; December 19, 2001, effective January 1, 2002; December 1, 2002; December 1, 2005; June 19, 2006, effective July 1, 2006; effective December 1, 2006; January 16, 2007; April 4, 2007; March 2, 2009; June 8, 2009; December 1, 2009; May 10, 2010; December 1, 2010; April 14, 2011; December 1, 2011.]

*

UNITED STATES COURT OF APPEALS
FOR THE
FEDERAL CIRCUIT

Including Amendments Received Through
January 1, 2012

Research Note

These rules may be searched electronically on Westlaw in the US-RULES database; updates to these rules may be found on Westlaw in US-RULESUPDATES. For search tips, and a detailed summary of database content, consult the Westlaw Scope Screen of each database.

TITLE I. APPLICABILITY OF RULES

TITLE II. APPEAL FROM A JUDGMENT OR ORDER OF A DISTRICT COURT

~~TITLE III. REVIEW OF A DECISION OF THE UNITED STATES TAX COURT~~

TITLE IV. REVIEW OR ENFORCEMENT OF AN ORDER OF AN ADMINISTRATIVE AGENCY, BOARD, COMMISSION, OR OFFICER

TITLE V. EXTRAORDINARY WRITS

TITLE VI. ~~HABEAS CORPUS~~; PROCEEDINGS IN FORMA PAUPERIS

PREFACE

This book contains information needed to conduct a proceeding in the United States Court of Appeals for the Federal Circuit. Counsel are assumed to be familiar with this information. The Federal Rules of Appellate Procedure are current as of the date of issuance of this volume. Litigants should check the Federal Rules of Appellate Procedure for amendments adopted after the publication date of this book. For the most current listing of Mediators please refer to the court's website at www.cafc.uscourts.gov.

Federal Rules of Appellate Procedure

The Federal Rules of Appellate Procedure not applicable in this court are indicated by strike-

throughs. Cite these rules as Federal Rules of Appellate Procedure.

Federal Circuit Rules

The court's own Federal Circuit Rules are in gray shaded areas and printed in this font.* A court rule implementing a specific Federal Rule follows and bears the same number as the rule implemented. Other court rules concerning procedural matters appear after Federal Rules of Appellate Procedure 47. Court rules concerning administrative matters appear after Federal Rules of Appellate Procedure 48. Cite the court's rules as Federal Circuit Rules.

Practice Notes

Practice Notes are in ruled boxes and are printed in this font.* Practice Notes follow the rule annotated. Counsel may rely on the notes but may not use them to avoid controlling statutes or rules, which govern in the event of conflict. As a general practice, do not cite the notes.

Appellate Mediation Program Guidelines

The Guidelines set forth the rules and procedures governing the court's mediation program are located at the end of the rules. Forms related to mediation at the court may be found in the Federal Circuit Forms.

Federal Circuit Forms

Forms prescribed by the Federal Rules of Appellate Procedure and selected Federal Circuit forms are an appendix to this volume. Forms also are available from the clerk or on the court's website.

Guide for Pro Se Petitioners and Appellants

The Guide provides an alternative method for conducting a proceeding in this court for those not represented by counsel. As a general practice, the Guide should not be cited by pro se petitioners or appellants.

Federal Circuit Attorney Discipline Rules

The court's rules provide the grounds for disciplining members of the bar, the types of discipline, and the procedures to be followed.

Courtroom Decorum

Provides proper conduct for participants and spectators during court sessions.

Inquiries and Comments

Telephone inquiries about the rules of practice may be made to the Clerk's Office at 202–275–8000. Public and telephone hours are 9:00 a.m. to 5:00 p.m. Monday thru Friday. Have these rules at hand when you call. Counsel receiving advice by telephone are expected to confirm it in writing to the clerk and to opposing counsel when that advice appears to authorize exceptions to these rules.

Comments on the rules are welcome. Send comments to Clerk of Court, United States Court of Appeals for the Federal Circuit, 717 Madison Place, NW, Washington, DC 20439.

United States Court of Appeals
for the Federal Circuit
717 Madison Place, NW
Washington, DC 20439

National Courts Building

Public access to the building is from 7:30 a.m. to 6:00 p.m. (EST).

Clerk's Office

Room 401—Hours are from 9:00 a.m. to 5:00 p.m.

Information—202–275–8000
Oral Argument Questions—202–275–8036
Facsimile—202–275–9678
Daily Disposition Sheet—202–275–8030

Questions concerning cases with docket numbers:	xxxx-1xxx, e.g., 2006–1467
Call	202–275–8026 202–275–8027 202–275–8028 202–275–8029
Questions concerning cases with docket numbers:	xxxx–3xxx, e.g., 2006–3740 xxxx–5xxx, e.g., 2006–5721 xxxx–7xxx, e.g., 2006–7800
Call	202–275–8031 202–275–8032 202–275–8033 202–275–8034
Questions concerning rehearings call:	202–275–8023
Questions concerning the Court's Mediation Program call:	202–275–8120

LIBRARY - Room 218

Hours are from 9:00 a.m. to 5:00 p.m.

Reference Desk	202–275–8411

PACER - pacer.cafc.uscourts.gov

Parties and attorneys

Compilation of case related information

Chronology of dates of case events entered in the case record.

WEBSITE - www.cafc.uscourts.gov

Current Announcements

Court Rules and Forms

Opinions, Calendars & Dispositions

Court Information

ORAL ARGUMENT TAPES OR OPINIONS - Room 410

Hours are from 8:00 a.m. to 5:00 p.m.

Phone 202–275–8154

Tapes are $26.00 each; Opinions are $2.00 each. The Court accepts Visa, MasterCard, Discover, American Express, checks and cash (exact amount required). Also available on website free of charge.

* **Publisher's Note:** Font style, shading, and ruled boxes are applied in the court copy that are not reproduced in this publication.

TITLE I. APPLICABILITY OF RULES

FRAP RULE 1. SCOPE OF RULES; DEFINITION; TITLE

(a) *Scope of Rules.*

(1) These rules govern procedure in the United States courts of appeals.

(2) When these rules provide for filing a motion or other document in the district court, the procedure must comply with the practice of the district court.

(b) *Definition.* In these rules, "state" includes the District of Columbia and any United States commonwealth or territory.

(c) *Title.* These rules are to be known as the Federal Rules of Appellate Procedure.

LOCAL RULE 1. SCOPE OF RULES; TITLE

(a) Reference to District and Trial Courts and Agencies.

(1) The terms "district court" and "trial court" include:

(A) the United States district courts;

(B) the United States Court of International Trade;

(C) the United States Court of Federal Claims; and

(D) if applicable, the United States Court of Appeals for Veterans Claims.

(2) The term "agency" includes an administrative agency, board, commission, bureau, or officer of the United States, including each of the following:

(A) the Board of Patent Appeals and Interferences of the Patent and Trademark Office;

(B) the Director of Patents and Trademarks;

(C) the Trademark Trial and Appeal Board;

(D) the United States International Trade Commission;

(E) the Secretary of Commerce acting under U.S. note 6 to subchapter X of chapter 98 of the Harmonized Tariff Schedule of the United States (relating to importation of instruments or apparatus);

(F) the Secretary of Agriculture acting under 7 U.S.C. § 2461;

(G) the Merit Systems Protection Board;

(H) certain arbitrators;

(I) the Boards of Contract Appeals in federal agencies;

(J) the Secretary of Veterans Affairs acting under 38 U.S.C. § 502;

(K) the Equal Employment Opportunity Commission acting under 3 U.S.C. § 454;

(L) the Federal Labor Relations Authority acting under part D of subchapter II of chapter 5 of title 3;

(M) the Secretary of Labor or the Occupational Safety and Health Review Commission, under part C of subchapter II of chapter 5 of title 3;

(N) the Office of Compliance acting under 2 U.S.C. § 1407(a)(1);

(O) the Government Accountability Office Personnel Appeals Board; or

(P) the Bureau of Justice Assistance.

(b) Rules of the Court of International Trade, Court of Federal Claims, and Court of Appeals for Veterans Claims.

(1) Reference in these rules to the Federal Rules of Civil Procedure includes analogous rules of the Court of International Trade and the Court of Federal Claims.

(2) Reference in these rules to the Federal Rules of Civil Procedure includes rules of the Court of Appeals for Veterans Claims only where applicable, because that court's rules are derived from the Federal Rules of Appellate Procedure.

(c) *Title.* ***These rules are to be known as the Federal Circuit Rules.***

[Effective July 1, 1997. Amended effective March 4, 1999; May 1, 2003; May 1, 2006; December 1, 2009; June 1, 2011.]

FRAP RULE 2. SUSPENSION OF RULES

On its own or a party's motion, a court of appeals may—to expedite its decision or for other good cause—suspend any provision of these rules in a particular case and order proceedings as it directs, except as otherwise provided in Rule 26(b).

TITLE II. APPEAL FROM A JUDGMENT OR ORDER OF A DISTRICT COURT

FRAP RULE 3. APPEAL AS OF RIGHT—HOW TAKEN

(a) *Filing the Notice of Appeal.*

(1) An appeal permitted by law as of right from a district court to a court of appeals may be taken only by filing a notice of appeal with the district clerk within the time allowed by Rule 4. At the time of filing, the appellant must furnish the clerk with enough copies of the notice to enable the clerk to comply with Rule 3(d).

(2) An appellant's failure to take any step other than the timely filing of a notice of appeal does not affect the validity of the appeal, but is ground only for the court of appeals to act as it considers appropriate, including dismissing the appeal.

(3) An appeal from a judgment by a magistrate judge in a civil case is taken in the same way as an appeal from any other district court judgment.

(4) An appeal by permission under 28 U.S.C. § 1292(b) ~~or an appeal in a bankruptcy case~~ may be taken only in the manner prescribed by Rule~~s~~ 5 ~~and 6, respectively~~.

(b) *Joint or Consolidated Appeals.*

(1) When two or more parties are entitled to appeal from a district-court judgment or order, and their interests make joinder practicable, they may file a joint notice of appeal. They may then proceed on appeal as a single appellant.

(2) When the parties have filed separate timely notices of appeal, the appeals may be joined or consolidated by the court of appeals.

(c) *Contents of the Notice of Appeal.*

(1) The notice of appeal must:

(A) specify the party or parties taking the appeal by naming each one in the caption or body of the notice, but an attorney representing more than one party may describe those parties with such terms as "all plaintiffs," "the defendants," "the plaintiffs A, B, et al.," or "all defendants except X";

(B) designate the judgment, order, or part thereof being appealed; and

(C) name the court to which the appeal is taken.

(2) A pro se notice of appeal is considered filed on behalf of the signer and the signer's spouse and minor children (if they are parties), unless the notice clearly indicates otherwise.

(3) In a class action, whether or not the class has been certified, the notice of appeal is sufficient if it names one person qualified to bring the appeal as representative of the class.

(4) An appeal must not be dismissed for informality of form or title of the notice of appeal, or for failure to name a party whose intent to appeal is otherwise clear from the notice.

(5) Form 1 in the Appendix of Forms is a suggested form of a notice of appeal.

(d) *Serving the Notice of Appeal.*

(1) The district clerk must serve notice of the filing of a notice of appeal by mailing a copy to each party's counsel of record—excluding the appellant's—or, if a party is proceeding pro se, to the party's last known address. ~~When a defendant in a criminal case appeals, the clerk must also serve a copy of the notice of appeal on the defendant, either by personal service or by mail addressed to the defendant.~~ The clerk must promptly send a copy of the notice of appeal and of the docket entries—and any later docket entries—to the clerk of the court of appeals named in the notice. The district clerk must note, on each copy, the date when the notice of appeal was filed.

(2) If an inmate confined in an institution files a notice of appeal in the manner provided by Rule 4(c), the district clerk must also note the date when the clerk docketed the notice.

(3) The district clerk's failure to serve notice does not affect the validity of the appeal. The clerk must note on the docket the names of the parties to whom the clerk mails copies, with the date of mailing. Service is sufficient despite the death of a party or the party's counsel.

(e) *Payment of Fees.* Upon filing a notice of appeal, the appellant must pay the district clerk all required fees. The district clerk receives the appellate docket fee on behalf of the court of appeals.

LOCAL RULE 3. APPEAL AS OF RIGHT—HOW TAKEN

(a) **Appeal Information Sheet; Opinion; Certified Copy of Docket Entries.** When a notice of appeal is filed, the trial court clerk must promptly send to this court's clerk the appeal information sheet prescribed by this court. The trial court clerk must attach a copy of the opinion, if any, that accompanied the judgment or order being appealed. The trial court clerk must certify the copy of the docket entries and send it with the notice of appeal and the appeal information sheet.

(b) Petition for Certification of Judgment of the High Court of the Trust Territory of the Pacific Islands. A petition for certification of a judgment of the High Court of the Trust Territory of the Pacific Islands under the Compact of Free Association: Federated States of Micronesia, Republic of Marshall Islands, Title II, Title One, Article VII, § 174(c), and the Compact of Free Association: Palau, Title II, Title One, Article VII, § 174(c), in 48 U.S.C. § 1901 note and § 1931 note, must be filed with this court's clerk, but otherwise is deemed to be an appeal from the judgment of a district court for purposes of these rules.

[Effective July 1, 1997. Amended effective March 4, 1999; May 1, 2006.]

Practice Notes

Failure to File a Notice of Appeal. Only a party that has filed a notice of appeal may attack all or any part of the trial court judgment. Any other party in the trial court not filing a notice of appeal may participate in the appeal as an appellee but may not seek to overturn or modify the judgment.

Fees. The fee schedule is set forth in Federal Circuit Rule 52. *See also* 28 U.S.C. § 1913, note 1 [Judicial Conference Schedule of Fees].

Filing and Docketing an Appeal. An appeal is filed when the notice of appeal is received by the trial court. An appeal sent to this court by the trial court clerk is docketed when it is assigned a docket number, a docket card for the appeal is made available to the public, and the names of the parties to the appeal are recorded in the party index that is available to the public.

Filing and Docketing Appeals Under 15 U.S.C. § 3416(c) and Petitions Under 42 U.S.C. § 300aa–12(f). Appeals under 15 U.S.C. § 3416(c) from the district courts and petitions under 42 U.S.C. § 300aa–12(f) from the Court of Federal Claims are filed in this court, unlike other appeals from those courts in which the notice of appeal is filed with the clerks of those courts. However, once these appeals or petitions are filed in this court, they are forwarded to the clerks of those courts with instructions to comply with Federal Rule of Appellate Procedure 3(d).

Appeal Information Sheet. The format to use for the appeal information sheet is found in Form 7.

FRAP RULE 3.1. APPEAL FROM A JUDGMENT OF A MAGISTRATE JUDGE IN A CIVIL CASE [ABROGATED]

FRAP RULE 4. APPEAL AS OF RIGHT—WHEN TAKEN

(a) *Appeal in a Civil Case.*

(1) Time for Filing a Notice of Appeal.

(A) In a civil case, except as provided in Rules 4(a)(1)(B), 4(a)(4), and 4(c), the notice of appeal required by Rule 3 must be filed with the district clerk within 30 days after the judgment or order appealed from is entered.

(B) When the United States or its officer or agency is a party, the notice of appeal may be filed by any party within 60 days after the judgment or order appealed from is entered.

(C) An appeal from an order granting or denying an application for a writ of error *coram nobis* is an appeal in a civil case for purposes of Rule 4(a).

(2) Filing Before Entry of Judgment. A notice of appeal filed after the court announces a decision or order—but before the entry of the judgment or order—is treated as filed on the date of and after the entry.

(3) Multiple Appeals. If one party timely files a notice of appeal, any other party may file a notice of appeal within 14 days after the date when the first notice was filed, or within the time otherwise prescribed by this Rule 4(a), whichever period ends later.

(4) Effect of a Motion on a Notice of Appeal.

(A) If a party timely files in the district court any of the following motions under the Federal Rules of Civil Procedure, the time to file an appeal runs for all parties from the entry of the order disposing of the last such remaining motion:

(i) for judgment under Rule 50(b);

(ii) to amend or make additional factual findings under Rule 52(b), whether or not granting the motion would alter the judgment;

(iii) for attorney's fees under Rule 54 if the district court extends the time to appeal under Rule 58;

(iv) to alter or amend the judgment under Rule 59;

(v) for a new trial under Rule 59; or

(vi) for relief under Rule 60 if the motion is filed no later than 28 days after the judgment is entered.

(B)(i) If a party files a notice of appeal after the court announces or enters a judgment—but before it disposes of any motion listed in Rule 4(a)(4)(A)—the notice becomes effective to appeal a judgment or order, in whole or in part, when the order disposing of the last such remaining motion is entered.

(ii) A party intending to challenge an order disposing of any motion listed in Rule 4(a)(4)(A), or a judgment's alteration or amendment upon such a motion, must file a notice of appeal, or an amended notice of appeal—in compliance with Rule 3(c)—within the time prescribed by this Rule measured from the entry of the order disposing of the last such remaining motion.

(iii) No additional fee is required to file an amended notice.

(5) Motion for Extension of Time.

(A) The district court may extend the time to file a notice of appeal if:

(i) a party so moves no later than 30 days after the time prescribed by this Rule 4(a) expires; and

(ii) regardless of whether its motion is filed before or during the 30 days after the time prescribed by this Rule 4(a) expires, that party shows excusable neglect or good cause.

(B) A motion filed before the expiration of the time prescribed in Rule 4(a)(1) or (3) may be ex parte unless the court requires otherwise. If the motion is filed after the expiration of the prescribed time, notice must be given to the other parties in accordance with local rules.

(C) No extension under this Rule 4(a)(5) may exceed 30 days after the prescribed time or 14 days after the date when the order granting the motion is entered, whichever is later.

(6) *Reopening the Time to File an Appeal.* The district court may reopen the time to file an appeal for a period of 14 days after the date when its order to reopen is entered, but only if all the following conditions are satisfied:

(A) the court finds that the moving party did not receive notice under Federal Rule of Civil Procedure 77(d) of the entry of the judgment or order sought to be appealed within 21 days after entry;

(B) the motion is filed within 180 days after the judgment or order is entered or within 14 days after the moving party receives notice under Federal Rule of Civil Procedure 77(d) of the entry, whichever is earlier; and

(C) the court finds that no party would be prejudiced.

(7) *Entry Defined.*

(A) A judgment or order is entered for purposes of this Rule 4(a):

(i) if Federal Rule of Civil Procedure 58(a) does not require a separate document, when the judgment or order is entered in the civil docket under Federal Rule of Civil Procedure 79(a); or

(ii) if Federal Rule of Civil Procedure 58(a) requires a separate document, when the judgment or order is entered in the civil docket under Federal Rule of Civil Procedure 79(a) and when the earlier of these events occurs:

- **the judgment or order is set forth on a separate document, or**
- **150 days have run from entry of the judgment or order in the civil docket under Federal Rule of Civil Procedure 79(a).**

(B) A failure to set forth a judgment or order on a separate document when required by Federal Rule of Civil Procedure 58(a) does not affect the validity of an appeal from that judgment or order.

~~**(b) *Appeal in a Criminal Case.***~~

(c) *Appeal by an Inmate Confined in an Institution.*

(1) If an inmate confined in an institution files a notice of appeal in ~~either~~ a civil ~~or a criminal~~ case, the notice is timely if it is deposited in the institution's internal mail system on or before the last day for filing. If an institution has a system designed for legal mail, the inmate must use that system to receive the benefit of this rule. Timely filing may be shown by a declaration in compliance with 28 U.S.C. § 1746 or by a notarized statement, either of which must set forth the date of deposit and state that first-class postage has been prepaid.

(2) If an inmate files the first notice of appeal in a civil case under this Rule 4(c), the 14-day period provided in Rule 4(a)(3) for another party to file a notice of appeal runs from the date when the district court dockets the first notice.

~~**(3) When a defendant in a criminal case files a notice of appeal under this Rule 4(c), the 30-day period for the government to file its notice of appeal runs from the entry of the judgment or order appealed from or from the district court's docketing of the defendant's notice of appeal, whichever is later.**~~

(d) *Mistaken Filing in the Court of Appeals.* If a notice of appeal in ~~either~~ a civil ~~or a criminal~~ case is mistakenly filed in the court of appeals, the clerk of that court must note on the notice the date when it was received and send it to the district clerk. The notice is then considered filed in the district court on the date so noted.

LOCAL RULE 4. APPEAL AS OF RIGHT—UNTIMELY NOTICE

The clerk may return a notice of appeal that is untimely on its face.

[Effective July 1, 1997. Amended effective March 4, 1999; May 1, 2006; June 1, 2011.]

Practice Notes

Time to Appeal. The table below is provided only as a convenience for counsel, who should refer to the statutes and case law before determining the period available for taking an appeal. Counsel should also be aware of the district court's authority under Federal Rule of Appellate Procedure 4 to extend or reopen the time for appeal.

Court	Statute	Time
District Courts	28 U.S.C. § 2107	30 days (60 days if U.S. is a party)
	15 U.S.C. § 3416(c)	30 days
Court of International Trade	28 U.S.C. § 2645(c)	60 days
Court of Federal Claims		
Appeals	28 U.S.C. § 2522	60 days
Petitions	42 U.S.C. § 300aa–12(f)	60 days
Court of Appeals for Veterans Claims	38 U.S.C. § 7292	60 days
High Court of the Trust Territory of the Pacific Islands	48 U.S.C. § 1901 note (1994) (Compact of Free Association: Federated States of Micronesia, Republic of Marshall Islands, Title II, Title One, Article VII, § 174(c)); 48 U.S.C. § 1931 note (1994) (Compact of Free Association: Palau, Title II, Title One, Article VII § 174(c))	60 days

Untimely Notice of Appeal. The United States Court of Appeals for the Federal Circuit cannot waive the untimely filing of a notice of appeal.

Duty to Notify the Clerk of Postjudgment Motions Pending in the Trial Court. Even though the district court clerk must forward copies of later docket entries under Federal Rule of Appellate Procedure 3(d), the appellant should promptly notify this court's clerk if any party in the case files a motion listed in Federal Rule of Appellate Procedure 4(a)(4). Any other party may also notify the clerk in such case. On receiving the appropriate docket entries from the district court, the clerk will deactivate the appeal. Deactivation of the appeal suspends all further action in the court of appeals. Upon reactivation of the appeal, the clerk will reschedule the next required filing and notify counsel.

FRAP RULE 5. APPEAL BY PERMISSION

(a) *Petition for Permission to Appeal.*

(1) To request permission to appeal when an appeal is within the court of appeals' discretion, a party must file a petition for permission to appeal. The petition must be filed with the circuit clerk with proof of service on all other parties to the district-court action.

(2) The petition must be filed within the time specified by the statute or rule authorizing the appeal or, if no such time is specified, within the time provided by Rule 4(a) for filing a notice of appeal.

(3) If a party cannot petition for appeal unless the district court first enters an order granting permission to do so or stating that the necessary conditions are met, the district court may amend its order, either on its own or in response to a party's motion, to include the required permission or statement. In that event, the time to petition runs from entry of the amended order.

(b) *Contents of the Petition; Answer or Cross-Petition; Oral Argument.*

(1) The petition must include the following:

(A) the facts necessary to understand the question presented;

(B) the question itself;

(C) the relief sought;

(D) the reasons why the appeal should be allowed and is authorized by a statute or rule; and

(E) an attached copy of:

(i) the order, decree, or judgment complained of and any related opinion or memorandum, and

(ii) any order stating the district court's permission to appeal or finding that the necessary conditions are met.

(2) A party may file an answer in opposition or a cross-petition within 10 days after the petition is served.

(3) The petition and answer will be submitted without oral argument unless the court of appeals orders otherwise.

(c) *Form of Papers; Number of Copies.* All papers must conform to Rule 32(c)(2). Except by the court's permission, a paper must not exceed 20 pages, exclusive of the disclosure statement, the proof of service, and the accompanying documents required by Rule 5(b)(1)(E). An original and 3 copies must be filed unless the court requires a different number by local rule or by order in a particular case.

(d) *Grant of Permission; Fees; Cost Bond; ~~Filing the Record~~.*

(1) Within 14 days after the entry of the order granting permission to appeal, the appellant must:

(A) pay the district clerk all required fees; and

(B) file a cost bond if required under Rule 7.

(2) A notice of appeal need not be filed. The date when the order granting permission to appeal is entered serves as the date of the notice of appeal for calculating time under these rules.

(3) The district clerk must notify the circuit clerk once the petitioner has paid the fees. Upon receiving this notice, the circuit clerk must enter the appeal on the docket. ~~The record must be forwarded and filed in accordance with Rules 11 and 12(c).~~

LOCAL RULE 5. APPEAL BY PERMISSION

(a) Appeal Information Sheet.

(1) A petition for permission to appeal must be accompanied by either:

(A) the appeal information sheet prescribed by this court prepared by the petitioner; or

(B) a copy of the docket entries in the trial court.

(2) If permission to appeal is granted, the trial court clerk must promptly prepare and send the appeal information sheet to this court's clerk.

(b) Record; Certified Copy of Docket Entries. In an allowed appeal, the trial court must retain the record as provided in Federal Rule of Appellate Procedure 11(e) and in Federal Circuit Rule 11(a). The trial court clerk must send a certified copy of the docket entries instead of the record.

[Effective July 1, 1997. Amended effective March 4, 1999; May 1, 2003; May 1, 2004.]

Practice Note

Appeal Information Sheet. The format for the appeal information sheet is found in Form 7.

FRAP RULE 5.1. APPEAL BY LEAVE UNDER 28 U.S.C. § 636(c)(5) [ABROGATED]

~~FRAP RULE 6. APPEAL IN A BANKRUPTCY CASE FROM A FINAL JUDGMENT, ORDER, OR DECREE OF A DISTRICT COURT OR BANKRUPTCY APPELLATE PANEL~~

FRAP RULE 7. BOND FOR COSTS ON APPEAL IN A CIVIL CASE

In a civil case, the district court may require an appellant to file a bond or provide other security in any form and amount necessary to ensure payment of costs on appeal. Rule 8(b) applies to a surety on a bond given under this rule.

FRAP RULE 8. STAY OR INJUNCTION PENDING APPEAL

(a) *Motion for Stay.*

(1) Initial Motion in the District Court. A party must ordinarily move first in the district court for the following relief:

(A) a stay of the judgment or order of a district court pending appeal;

(B) approval of a supersedeas bond; or

(C) an order suspending, modifying, restoring, or granting an injunction while an appeal is pending.

(2) Motion in the Court of Appeals; Conditions on Relief. A motion for the relief mentioned in Rule 8(a)(1) may be made to the court of appeals or to one of its judges.

(A) The motion must:

(i) show that moving first in the district court would be impracticable; or

(ii) state that, a motion having been made, the district court denied the motion or failed to afford the relief requested and state any reasons given by the district court for its action.

(B) The motion must also include:

(i) the reasons for granting the relief requested and the facts relied on;

(ii) originals or copies of affidavits or other sworn statements supporting facts subject to dispute; and

(iii) relevant parts of the record.

(C) The moving party must give reasonable notice of the motion to all parties.

(D) A motion under this Rule 8(a)(2) must be filed with the circuit clerk and normally will be considered by a panel of the court. But in an exceptional case in which time requirements make that procedure impracticable, the motion may be made to and considered by a single judge.

(E) The court may condition relief on a party's filing a bond or other appropriate security in the district court.

(b) *Proceeding Against a Surety.* If a party gives security in the form of a bond or stipulation or other undertaking with one or more sureties, each surety submits to the jurisdiction of the district court and irrevocably appoints the district clerk as the surety's agent on whom any papers affecting the surety's liability on the bond or undertaking may be served. On motion, a surety's liability may be enforced in the district court without the necessity of an independent action. The motion and any notice that the district court prescribes may be served on the district clerk, who must promptly mail a copy to each surety whose address is known.

~~(c) *Stay in a Criminal Case.* Rule 38 of the Federal Rules of Criminal Procedure governs a stay in a criminal case.~~

LOCAL RULE 8. STAY OR INJUNCTION PENDING APPEAL

(a) Notice of Appeal; Trial Court's Judgment or Order. A motion for a stay or injunction pending appeal must be accompanied by:

(1) a copy of the notice of appeal that has been filed with the trial court clerk;

(2) a copy of the trial court's judgment or order on the merits; and

(3) a copy of any order on the motion for a stay or injunction pending appeal.

(b) Length of Motion, Response, and Reply; Copies; Brief.

(1) A motion or a response to a motion for a stay or injunction pending appeal may not exceed 20 pages. A reply may not exceed 10 pages.

(2) An original and 4 copies of a motion, response, or reply must be filed.

(3) A separate brief supporting a motion, response, or reply is not permitted.

(c) Notice and Service When Requesting Immediate Action; Facsimile.

(1) A party moving for a stay or injunction pending appeal who requests immediate action by the court must—before filing—notify all parties that a motion will be filed and must utilize an expedited method of service.

(2) If a motion for a stay or injunction pending appeal is sent to the court by facsimile transmission, a certificate of interest must be included and opposing counsel must be served in the same manner. The filing must state the name, address, and, if applicable, the facsimile numbers of the persons served.

(d) Statement. If an initial motion for a stay or injunction pending appeal was not made in the district court under Federal Rule of Appellate Procedure 8(a)(1), movant must include in its motion in this court a statement explaining why it was not practicable to do so. If an initial motion for a stay or injunction pending appeal was made in the district court under Federal Rule of Appellate Procedure 8(a)(1) and remains pending, the movant must include in its motion in this court a statement specifically identifying when it filed the motion in the district court and why it is not practicable to await a ruling by the district court on that motion.

[Effective July 1, 1997. Amended effective March 4, 1999; May 1, 2003; May 1, 2004; May 1, 2006; December 1, 2009.]

Practice Notes

Form Requirements. See Federal Rule of Appellate Procedure 27(d) for form requirements concerning motions.

Certificate of Interest. The format for the certificate of interest is found in Form 9.

~~FRAP RULE 9. RELEASE IN A CRIMINAL CASE~~

FRAP RULE 10. THE RECORD ON APPEAL

(a) *Composition of the Record on Appeal.* The following items constitute the record on appeal:

(1) the original papers and exhibits filed in the district court;

(2) the transcript of proceedings, if any; and

(3) a certified copy of the docket entries prepared by the district clerk.

(b) *The Transcript of Proceedings.*

(1) Appellant's Duty to Order. Within 14 days after filing the notice of appeal or entry of an order disposing of the last timely remaining motion of a type specified in Rule 4(a)(4)(A), whichever is later, the appellant must do either of the following:

(A) order from the reporter a transcript of such parts of the proceedings not already on file as the appellant considers necessary, subject to a local rule of the court of appeals and with the following qualifications:

(i) the order must be in writing;

~~**(ii) if the cost of the transcript is to be paid by the United States under the Criminal Justice Act, the order must so state; and**~~

(iii) the appellant must, within the same period, file a copy of the order with the district clerk; or

(B) file a certificate stating that no transcript will be ordered.

(2) Unsupported Finding or Conclusion. If the appellant intends to urge on appeal that a finding or conclusion is unsupported by the evidence or is contrary to the evidence, the appellant must include in the record a transcript of all evidence relevant to that finding or conclusion.

(3) Partial Transcript. Unless the entire transcript is ordered:

(A) the appellant must—within the 14 days provided in Rule 10(b)(1)—file a statement of the issues that the appellant intends to present on the appeal and must serve on the appellee a copy of both the order or certificate and the statement;

(B) if the appellee considers it necessary to have a transcript of other parts of the proceedings, the appellee must, within 14 days after the service of the order or certificate and the statement of the issues, file and serve on the appellant a designation of additional parts to be ordered; and

(C) unless within 14 days after service of that designation the appellant has ordered all such parts, and has so notified the appellee, the appellee may within the following 14 days either order the parts or move in the district court for an order requiring the appellant to do so.

(4) Payment. At the time of ordering, a party must make satisfactory arrangements with the reporter for paying the cost of the transcript.

(c) *Statement of the Evidence When the Proceedings Were Not Recorded or When a Transcript Is Unavailable.* If the transcript of a hearing or trial is unavailable, the appellant may prepare a statement of the evidence or proceedings from the best available means, including the appellant's recollection. The statement must be served on the appellee, who may serve objections or proposed amendments within 14 days after being served. The statement and any objections or proposed amendments must then be submitted to the district court for settlement and approval. As settled and approved, the statement must be included by the district clerk in the record on appeal.

(d) *Agreed Statement as the Record on Appeal.* In place of the record on appeal as defined in Rule 10(a), the parties may prepare, sign, and submit to the district court a statement of the case showing how the issues presented by the appeal arose and were decided in the district court. The statement must set forth only those facts averred and proved or sought to be proved that are essential to the court's resolution of the issues. If the statement is truthful, it—together with any additions that the district court may consider necessary to a full presentation of the issues on appeal—must be approved by the district court and must then be certified to the court of appeals as the record on appeal. The district clerk must then send it to the circuit clerk within the time provided by Rule 11. A copy of the agreed statement may be filed in place of the appendix required by Rule 30.

(e) *Correction or Modification of the Record.*

(1) If any difference arises about whether the record truly discloses what occurred in the district court, the difference must be submitted to and settled by that court and the record conformed accordingly.

(2) If anything material to either party is omitted from or misstated in the record by error or accident, the omission or misstatement may be corrected and a supplemental record may be certified and forwarded:

(A) on stipulation of the parties;

(B) by the district court before or after the record has been forwarded; or

(C) by the court of appeals.

(3) All other questions as to the form and content of the record must be presented to the court of appeals.

LOCAL RULE 10. THE RECORD ON APPEAL

Delay in preparing the transcript. When a trial transcript is not filed in the trial court within 60 days after it was ordered, the clerk may direct the parties to proceed under Rule 10(c) or (d) of the Federal Rules of Appellate Procedure.

[Effective July 1, 1997. Amended effective March 4, 1999.]

Practice Notes

Daily Copy. Using daily transcript copy in lengthy trial proceedings can reduce or eliminate appellate delay in awaiting transcription after trial.

Procedures to Expedite Delivery of Transcripts. District courts and regional circuit councils have procedures to expedite transcripts that may be available to counsel experiencing difficulty with late delivery of transcripts by court reporters.

FRAP RULE 11. FORWARDING THE RECORD

(a) *Appellant's Duty.* An appellant filing a notice of appeal must comply with Rule 10(b) and must do whatever else is necessary to enable the clerk to assemble and forward the record. ~~If there are multiple appeals from a judgment or order, the clerk must forward a single record.~~

(b) *Duties of Reporter and District Clerk.*

(1) Reporter's Duty to Prepare and File a Transcript. The reporter must prepare and file a transcript as follows:

(A) Upon receiving an order for a transcript, the reporter must enter at the foot of the order the date of its receipt and the expected completion date and send a copy, so endorsed, to the circuit clerk.

(B) If the transcript cannot be completed within 30 days of the reporter's receipt of the order, the reporter may request the circuit clerk to grant additional time to complete it. The clerk must note on the docket the action taken and notify the parties.

(C) When a transcript is complete, the reporter must file it with the district clerk and notify the circuit clerk of the filing.

(D) If the reporter fails to file the transcript on time, the circuit clerk must notify the district judge and do whatever else the court of appeals directs.

~~(2) District Clerk's Duty to Forward.~~

~~(c) *Retaining the Record Temporarily in the District Court for Use in Preparing the Appeal.*~~

(d) [Abrogated.]

(e) *Retaining the Record by Court Order.*

(1) The court of appeals may, by order or local rule, provide that a certified copy of the docket entries be forwarded instead of the entire record. But a party may at any time during the appeal request that designated parts of the record be forwarded.

~~(2) The district court may order the record or some part of it retained if the court needs it while~~

~~**the appeal is pending, subject, however, to call by the court of appeals.**~~

~~**(3) If part or all of the record is ordered retained, the district clerk must send to the court of appeals a copy of the order and the docket entries together with the parts of the original record allowed by the district court and copies of any parts of the record designated by the parties.**~~

~~**(f)** ***Retaining Parts of the Record in the District Court by Stipulation of the Parties.***~~

~~**(g)** ***Record for a Preliminary Motion in the Court of Appeals.***~~

LOCAL RULE 11. FORWARDING THE RECORD

(a) Retaining the Record; Certified Copy of the Docket Entries; Physical Exhibits; Archival Storage.

(1) *The District Court Clerk Must:*

(A) retain the assembled record unless this court, on motion or sua sponte, orders otherwise; and

(B) send to this court a certified copy of the docket entries instead of the record.

(2) *Archival Storage.* The district court clerk must not send the record to archival storage until this court issues its mandate.

(b) Access of Parties and Counsel to the Original Record.

(1) *Material Not Subject to a Protective Order; Inspection and Copying.* When a notice of appeal is filed, the trial court clerk must permit a party or counsel for a party to inspect and copy the nonconfidential original papers, transcripts, and exhibits to prepare the appendix. This inspection and copying is subject to reasonable regulation by the trial court.

(2) *Material Subject to a Protective Order; Inspection and Copying.* A party or counsel for a party must be permitted to inspect and copy material in the record governed by a protective order of the trial court in accordance with that order. If this court modifies or annuls the protective order, the access of a party or counsel is governed by the order of this court.

(c) Preserving a Protective Order on Appeal. Any portion of the record that was subject to a protective order in the trial court remains subject to that order unless otherwise ordered.

(d) Agreement by Parties to Modify a Protective Order; Certificate of Compliance. If any portion of the record in the trial court is subject to a protective order and a notice of appeal has been filed, each party must promptly review the record to determine whether protected portions need to remain protected on appeal. If a party determines that some portions no longer need to be protected, that party must seek an agreement with the other party. Any agreement that is reached must be promptly presented to the trial court, which may issue an appropriate order. Whether or not an agreement is reached, each party must file a certificate of compliance within 45 days of docketing stating it complied with this rule. This Federal Circuit Rule 11(d) does not apply in a case arising under 19 U.S.C. § 1516a.

(e) Motion to Modify the Protective Order. A party may move at any time in this court to modify a protective order to remove protection from some material or to include another person within its terms. This court may decide the motion or may remand the case to the trial court. This court, sua sponte, may direct the parties to show cause why a protective order should not be modified.

[Effective July 1, 1997. Amended effective March 4, 1999.]

FRAP RULE 12. DOCKETING THE APPEAL; FILING A REPRESENTATION STATEMENT; FILING THE RECORD

(a) ***Docketing the Appeal.*** **Upon receiving the copy of the notice of appeal and the docket entries from the district clerk under Rule 3(d), the circuit clerk must docket the appeal under the title of the district-court action and must identify the appellant, adding the appellant's name if necessary.**

(b) ***Filing a Representation Statement.*** **Unless the court of appeals designates another time, the attorney who filed the notice of appeal must, ~~within 14 days after filing the notice,~~ file a statement with the circuit clerk naming the parties that the attorney represents on appeal.**

(c) ***Filing the Record, Partial Record, or Certificate.*** **Upon receiving the record, partial record, or district clerk's certificate as provided in Rule 11, the circuit clerk must file it and immediately notify all parties of the filing date.**

LOCAL RULE 12. DOCKETING THE APPEAL

The clerk must notify all parties of the date the appeal is docketed.

[Effective March 4, 1999. Amended effective December 1, 2009.]

Practice Notes

Date of Docketing. The date of docketing starts the time running for filing briefs. See Federal Circuit Rule 31(a).

Representation Statement. The requirements of Federal Rule of Appellate Procedure 12(b) are met by filing the entry of appearance and certificate of interest required under Federal Circuit Rules 47.3 and 47.4.

Official Caption; Participation in the Appeal by Appellees; Consolidation of Previously Consolidated Cases and Cross-Appeals. The clerk will provide the parties with the official caption in the case at the time of docketing. Any objection to the official caption should be made within 14 days of receipt. It is the court's usual practice to include in the caption all parties that participated in the court below, even if they are no longer participating in the case on appeal. Parties included in the trial court title who have an adverse interest to the appellant but who are not cross-appealing will be deemed appellees. Parties permitted to intervene in the trial court as plaintiffs or defendants will be identified only as plaintiff or defendant to avoid confusion with any third party permitted to intervene in the appeal. An appellee desiring not to file a brief or join in another party's brief must notify the clerk who will strike the party's designation as an appellee from the official caption. An appeal in a case that was consolidated in the trial court will be docketed under the title used for the consolidated case. When more than one party appeals from the same trial court case, the appeals or cross-appeals will be consolidated by the clerk. Other appeals may be consolidated on motion or by the court sua sponte.

Transferred Appeal. An appeal transferred from another court will be given a new docket number and will be consolidated by the clerk with any previously docketed appeal from the same judgment or order.

Filing and Docketing an Appeal. An appeal is filed when the notice of appeal is received by the trial court. An appeal sent to this court by the trial court clerk is docketed when it is assigned a docket number, a docket card for the appeal is made available to the public, and the names of the parties to the appeal are recorded in the party index that is available to the public.

FRAP RULE 12.1 REMAND AFTER AN INDICATIVE RULING BY THE DISTRICT COURT ON A MOTION FOR RELIEF THAT IS BARRED BY A PENDING APPEAL

(a) Notice to the Court of Appeals. If a timely motion is made in the district court for relief that it lacks authority to grant because of an appeal that has been docketed and is pending, the movant must promptly notify the circuit clerk if the district court states either that it would grant the motion or that the motion raises a substantial issue.

(b) Remand After an Indicative Ruling. If the district court states that it would grant the motion or that the motion raises a substantial issue, the court of appeals may remand for further proceedings but retains jurisdiction unless it expressly dismisses the appeal. If the court of appeals remands but retains jurisdiction, the parties must promptly notify the circuit clerk when the district court has decided the motion on remand.

~~TITLE III. REVIEW OF A DECISION OF THE UNITED STATES TAX COURT~~

~~FRAP RULE 13. REVIEW OF A DECISION OF THE TAX COURT~~

~~FRAP RULE 14. APPLICABILITY OF OTHER RULES TO THE REVIEW OF A TAX COURT DECISION~~

TITLE IV. REVIEW OR ENFORCEMENT OF AN ORDER OF AN ADMINISTRATIVE AGENCY, BOARD, COMMISSION, OR OFFICER

FRAP RULE 15. REVIEW OR ENFORCEMENT OF AN AGENCY ORDER—HOW OBTAINED; INTERVENTION

(a) *Petition for Review; Joint Petition.*

(1) Review of an agency order is commenced by filing, within the time prescribed by law, a petition for review with the clerk of a court of appeals authorized to review the agency order. If their interests make joinder practicable, two or more persons may join in a petition to the same court to review the same order.

(2) The petition must:

(A) name each party seeking review either in the caption or the body of the petition—using such terms as "et al.," "petitioners," or "respondents" does not effectively name the parties;

(B) name the agency as a respondent (even though not named in the petition, the United States is a respondent if required by statute); and

(C) specify the order or part thereof to be reviewed.

(3) Form 3 (Federal Circuit Form 5 herein) in the Appendix of Forms is a suggested form of a petition for review.

(4) In this rule "agency" includes an agency, board, commission, or officer; "petition for review" includes a petition to enjoin, suspend, modify, or otherwise review, or a notice of appeal, whichever form is indicated by the applicable statute.

(b) *Application or Cross-Application to Enforce an Order; Answer; Default.*

(1) An application to enforce an agency order must be filed with the clerk of a court of appeals

authorized to enforce the order. If a petition is filed to review an agency order that the court may enforce, a party opposing the petition may file a cross-application for enforcement.

(2) Within 21 days after the application for enforcement is filed, the respondent must serve on the applicant an answer to the application and file it with the clerk. If the respondent fails to answer in time, the court will enter judgment for the relief requested.

(3) The application must contain a concise statement of the proceedings in which the order was entered, the facts upon which venue is based, and the relief requested.

(c) *Service of the Petition or Application.* The circuit clerk must serve a copy of the petition for review, or an application or cross-application to enforce an agency order, on each respondent as prescribed by Rule 3(d), unless a different manner of service is prescribed by statute. At the time of filing, the petitioner must:

(1) serve, or have served, a copy on each party admitted to participate in the agency proceedings, except for the respondents;

(2) file with the clerk a list of those so served; and

(3) give the clerk enough copies of the petition or application to serve each respondent.

(d) *Intervention.* Unless a statute provides another method, a person who wants to intervene in a proceeding under this rule must file a motion for leave to intervene with the circuit clerk and serve a copy on all parties. The motion—or other notice of intervention authorized by statute—must be filed within 30 days after the petition for review is filed and must contain a concise statement of the interest of the moving party and the grounds for intervention.

(e) *Payment of Fees.* When filing any separate or joint petition for review in a court of appeals, the petitioner must pay the circuit clerk all required fees.

LOCAL RULE 15. REVIEW OF AN AGENCY ORDER—HOW OBTAINED

(a) Petition for Review or Notice of Appeal; Payment of Fees; Address and Telephone Number of Counsel or Pro Se Petitioner or Appellant; Number of Copies.

(1) *From the Patent and Trademark Office.* To appeal a decision of the Board of Patent Appeals and Interferences, the Trademark Trial and Appeal Board, or the Director under 15 U.S.C. § 1071(a), the appellant must file in the Patent and Trademark Office a notice of appeal within the time prescribed by law. The appellant must simultaneously send to the clerk three copies of the notice with the fee set forth in Federal Circuit Rule 52. The Director must promptly advise the clerk that the notice is or is not timely.

(2) *From Another Agency.*

(A) Except as provided in Federal Circuit Rule 15(a)(1), to petition or appeal from a decision or order of an agency, the petitioner must file a petition for review or notice of appeal with this court's clerk within the time prescribed by law. Upon filing, the petitioner must pay the clerk the fee set forth in Federal Circuit Rule 52.

(B) A petition filed by the Director of the Office of Personnel Management must be filed as prescribed in Federal Circuit Rule 47.9.

(3) *Address and Telephone Number of Counsel or Pro Se Petitioner or Appellant.* Each petition for review or notice of appeal must contain the counsel's—or the pro se petitioner's or appellant's—name, current address, and telephone number.

(4) *Copies.* A petition for review or notice of appeal must be filed in an original (except when the original is filed in the Patent and Trademark Office under 15 U.S.C. § 1071(a)) and three copies.

(b) Docketing Petition or Appeal; Notice of Docketing.

(1) *From the Patent and Trademark Office.*

(A) In an appeal from the Board of Patent Appeals and Interferences, the Trademark Trial and Appeal Board, or the Director under 15 U.S.C. § 1071(a)(2), the clerk will docket the appeal when the Director of Patents and Trademarks sends a copy of the notice of appeal and the certified list as required by Federal Circuit Rule 17(b)(1).

(B) If the Director advises the clerk concerning the untimeliness of an appeal, the clerk may order the appellant to show cause why the appeal should not be dismissed and refer appellant's response to the court.

(C) The clerk will notify all parties of the date the appeal is docketed.

(2) *From Another Agency.* In a petition for review or appeal from an administrative agency other than the Patent and Trademark Office, the clerk will docket a timely appeal or petition upon receipt.

(3) *Notice of Docketing.* The clerk must notify all parties of the date the appeal or petition for review is docketed.

(c) Statement Concerning Discrimination.

(1) *Petitioner's Statement.* Within 14 days after a petition for review of a decision of the Merit Systems Protection Board or a decision of an arbitrator under 5 U.S.C. § 7121 is docketed, the petitioner must serve

on the respondent and file with the clerk, see Form 10:

(A) one of the following statements:

(i) no claim of discrimination by reason of race, sex, age, national origin, or handicapped condition has been or will be made in the case;

(ii) any claim of discrimination by reason of race, sex, age, national origin, or handicapped condition raised before the Board has been abandoned and will not be raised or continued in this or any other court;

(iii) the petition seeks review only of the Board's or arbitrator's dismissal of the case for lack of jurisdiction or for untimeliness;

(iv) the case involves an application to the Office of Personnel Management for benefits; or

(v) the case was transferred to the Court of Appeals for the Federal Circuit from a district court and petitioner continues to contest the transfer; and

(B) a statement whether petitioner has filed a discrimination case:

(i) in a United States district court; or

(ii) in the Equal Employment Opportunity Commission.

(2) *Response When a Claim of Discrimination is Raised in a Motion or Brief.* ***If the petitioner in a case described in Federal Circuit Rule 15(c)(1) files a motion or brief making a claim of discrimination as to the case before the court, the respondent must:***

(A) state, in a responsive motion or brief, one of the following:

(i) the respondent concurs in the petitioner's statement concerning discrimination;

(ii) any claim of discrimination the petitioner made to the Merit Systems Protection Board was frivolous, with supporting reasons; or

(iii) the petitioner presented no evidence of discrimination to the Merit Systems Protection Board;

(B) state, if known, whether a discrimination claim has been filed in a United States district court or in the Equal Employment Opportunity Commission; and

(C) include in the response or brief any other information relevant to the statement concerning discrimination.

(d) Untimely Petition for Review or Notice of Appeal. The clerk may return a petition for review or notice of appeal that is untimely on its face.

(e) Notice of Election Under 35 U.S.C. § 141 or 15 U.S.C. § 1071(a)(1). A party filing a notice of election under 35 U.S.C. § 141 or 15 U.S.C. § 1071(a)(1) with the Director of Patents and Trademarks must file a copy of the notice with the clerk, and the clerk must dismiss the appeal.

(f) Judicial Review of Department of Veterans Affairs Rules and Regulations. See Federal Circuit Rule 47.12.

[Effective July 1, 1997. Amended effective March 4, 1999; May 1, 2003; May 1, 2004; May 1, 2006; December 1, 2009; June 1, 2011.]

Practice Notes

Time to Appeal or Petition. The table below is provided only as a convenience to counsel, who should refer to the statutes, rules, and case law before determining the period available for taking an appeal or filing a petition for review. Counsel should also note that the event that causes the period to run varies in each case.

Agency	Statute	Time
Arbitrator	5 U.S.C. §§ 7121, 7703	60 days
Merit Systems Protection Board	5 U.S.C. § 7703	60 days
Government Accountability Office Personnel Appeals Board	31 U.S.C. § 755	30 days
Board of Patent Appeals and Interferences; Trademark	35 U.S.C. § 142	2 months; 14 days for cross appeal
Trial and Appeal Board;	15 U.S.C. § 1071	
Director of Patents and Trademarks	37 C.F.R. §§ 1.304, 2.145	
International Trade Commission	19 U.S.C. § 1337	60 days
Board of Contract Appeals	41 U.S.C. § 607(g)	120 days
Secretary of Commerce	19 U.S.C. § 1202	20 days
Secretary of Agriculture	*See* 7 U.S.C. § 2461	60 days
Secretary of Veterans Affairs	38 U.S.C. § 502	60 days
Secretary of Labor; Occupational Safety and Health Review Commission; Federal Labor Relations Authority	28 U.S.C. § 1296	30 days
Office of Compliance, Congressional Accountability Act	2 U.S.C. § 1407(c)(3)	90 days
Equal Employment Opportunity Commission	3 U.S.C. § 454; 28 U.S.C. § 1296(b)	30 days
Bureau of Justice Assistance	42 U.S.C. § 3796c–2; 28 C.F.R. § 32.55	

Filing in the Patent and Trademark Office. A notice of appeal mailed to the Patent and Trademark Office should be addressed:

Office of the Solicitor
United States Patent
and Trademark Office
Mail Stop 8
Post Office Box 1450
Alexandria, Virginia 22313–1450

The general counsel requests that hand delivery, if any, be made to the Office of the General Counsel, Patent and Trademark Office, Madison East 10B20, 600 Dulaney Street, Alexandria, Virginia 22314, between the hours of 8:30 a.m. and 5:00 p.m.

Copy of Decision or Order. A party filing a petition for review or notice of appeal is urged to attach a copy of the decision or order of the agency for which review is sought.

Intervention. A party with the right to appeal or to petition for review may not, instead of exercising that right, intervene in another appeal or petition to seek relief in its own cause. Because the United States or an agency of the United States is the only appellee or respondent in cases under this rule, any other party seeking to intervene on the side of the appellee or respondent must move for leave to intervene within 30 days of the date when the petition for review or notice of appeal is filed. A motion for leave to intervene out of time will be granted only in extraordinary circumstances.

Discrimination Statement. A discrimination statement form with a preaddressed, postage-paid return envelope will be provided to any petitioner seeking review of a decision of the Merit Systems Protection Board or arbitrator. Failure to complete the discrimination statement will result in dismissal of the petition for review. *See* Form 10.

Timeliness. Except in inter partes appeals from decisions of the Board of Patent Appeals and Interferences or the Trademark Trial and Appeal Board, parties in agency proceedings do not have the 14-day "cross-appeal" period that Federal Rule of Appellate Procedure 4(a)(3) grants to parties appealing from trial courts. The court cannot waive the statutory time requirements for filing a petition for review or notice of appeal.

Consolidation. When more than one party files a petition for review or notice of appeal from the same decision or order, the parties should inform the clerk and the petitions or appeals may be consolidated and an adjusted briefing schedule may be issued.

Arbitration Awards in the United States Postal Service. These arbitration awards may not be appealed to this court.

Proper Governmental Party in Appeals from Boards of Contract Appeals. In appeals from the boards of contract appeals, the head of the federal agency is named in the caption along with the name of the agency he or she heads.

Filing and Docketing a Petition for Review or Appeal. A petition for review or appeal is filed when the petition for review or notice of appeal is received in the court or, in the case of an appeal from the Patent and Trademark Office, when the notice of appeal is received by the Director of Patents and Trademarks. A petition for review or appeal is docketed when it is assigned a docket number, a docket card for the petition for review or appeal is made available to the public, and the names of the parties to the petition for review or appeal are recorded in the party index that is available to the public.

Judicial Review of Department of Veterans Affairs Rules and Regulations. Federal Circuit Rule 47.12 governs actions for judicial review of Department of Veterans Affairs rules and regulations under 38 U.S.C. § 502. The procedures to be followed in such actions are the same as provided in this rule, except as provided in Federal Circuit Rule 47.12.

Change of Head of Agency. In appeals in which the proper governmental party is the head of the agency, counsel for the government should promptly notify the clerk of any change that would affect the accuracy of the caption.

Agency. The term agency in these rules includes a board, commission, bureau, or arbitrator.

~~FRAP RULE 15.1. BRIEFS AND ORAL ARGUMENT IN A NATIONAL LABOR RELATIONS BOARD PROCEEDING~~

FRAP RULE 16. THE RECORD ON REVIEW OR ENFORCEMENT

(a) *Composition of the Record.* The record on review or enforcement of an agency order consists of:

(1) the order involved;

(2) any findings or report on which it is based; and

(3) the pleadings, evidence, and other parts of the proceedings before the agency.

(b) *Omissions From or Misstatements in the Record.* The parties may at any time, by stipulation, supply any omission from the record or correct a misstatement, or the court may so direct. If necessary, the court may direct that a supplemental record be prepared and filed.

[Amended May 1, 2003.]

FRAP RULE 17. FILING THE RECORD

~~(a) *Agency to File; Time for Filing; Notice of Filing.*~~

(b) *Filing—What Constitutes.*

(1) The agency must file:

~~(A) the original or a certified copy of the entire record or parts designated by the parties; or~~

(B) a certified list adequately describing all documents, transcripts of testimony, exhibits, and other material constituting the record, or describing those parts designated by the parties.

~~(2) The parties may stipulate in writing that no record or certified list be filed. The date when the stipulation is filed with the circuit clerk is treated as the date when the record is filed.~~

(3) The agency must retain any portion of the record not filed with the clerk. All parts of the record retained by the agency are a part of the record on review for all purposes ~~and, if the court or a party so requests, must be sent to the court regardless of any prior stipulation~~.

LOCAL RULE 17. FILING THE RECORD

(a) Retaining the Record; Sending the Certified List. The agency must retain the record and send to this court a certified list or index unless this court, on motion or sua sponte, orders otherwise.

(b) Certified List or Index.

(1) *From the Patent and Trademark Office.* No later than 40 days after receiving the notice of appeal, the Director must send to the clerk the certified list and a copy of the decision or order appealed. This constitutes compliance with the requirement of 35 U.S.C. § 143 and 15 U.S.C. § 1071(a)(3) for sending a certified record to the court.

(2) *From Another Agency.* No later than 40 days after the court serves a petition for review or notice of appeal on an agency, the agency must send to the clerk the certified list or index and a copy of the decision or order being appealed.

(3) *Index of VA Rulemaking Record.* In petitions for review under 38 U.S.C. § 502, if a petitioner has not adequately identified the rulemaking proceeding complained of, so that the Secretary of Veterans Affairs cannot send the certified list or index within the time provided in Federal Circuit Rule 17(b)(2), the Secretary must promptly move to waive or extend the time for filing the certified list or index.

(c) Service of Certified List or Index by Agency. When an agency sends a certified list or index to the clerk, it must simultaneously serve a copy on the parties and provide a certificate of service to the clerk. Service must be made on counsel for the appellant or petitioner who has served the agency with a copy of an entry of appearance in this court; otherwise, service must be made on counsel who appeared before the agency or, if none, on the party. This service constitutes notice to the parties of the date the record was filed.

(d) Access of Parties and Counsel to Original Record.

(1) *Material Not Subject to a Protective Order; Inspection and Copying.* When a petition for review or notice of appeal is filed, the agency must permit a party or counsel for a party to inspect and copy the nonconfidential original papers, transcripts, and exhibits to prepare the appendix. This inspection and copying is subject to reasonable regulation by the agency.

(2) *Material Subject to a Protective Order; Inspection and Copying.* A party or counsel for a party must be permitted to inspect and copy material contained in the record governed by a protective order of an agency in accordance with that order. If this court modifies or annuls the protective order, the access of a party or counsel is governed by the order of this court.

(e) Preserving a Protective Order on Appeal. Any portion of the record that was subject to a protective order in an agency remains subject to that order unless otherwise ordered.

(f) Agreement by Parties to Modify Protective Order; Certificate of Compliance. If any portion of the record in an agency is subject to a protective order and a petition for review or notice of appeal has been filed, each party must promptly review the record to determine whether protected portions need to remain protected on appeal. If a party determines that some portions no longer need to be protected, that party must seek an agreement with the other party. Any agreement that is reached must be promptly presented to the agency, which may issue an appropriate order. Whether or not an agreement is reached, each party must file a certificate of compliance within 45 days of docketing stating it complied with this rule.

(g) Motion to Modify the Protective Order. A party may move at any time in this court to modify a protective order to remove protection from some material or to include another person within its terms. This court may decide the motion or may remand the case to the agency. This court, sua sponte, may direct the parties to show cause why a protective order should not be modified.

[Effective July 1, 1997. Amended effective March 4, 1999; May 1, 2003; May 1, 2006.]

Practice Notes

Transcript of Agency Proceeding at Government Expense. These rules do not require an agency to provide a party with a written transcript at the agency's expense. Any party seeking a written transcript of a hearing should direct the request to the agency, not the court.

Agency. The term agency in these rules includes a board, commission, bureau, or arbitrator.

FRAP RULE 18. STAY PENDING REVIEW

(a) *Motion for a Stay.*

(1) Initial Motion Before the Agency. A petitioner must ordinarily move first before the agency for a stay pending review of its decision or order.

(2) Motion in the Court of Appeals. A motion for a stay may be made to the court of appeals or one of its judges.

(A) The motion must:

(i) show that moving first before the agency would be impracticable; or

(ii) state that, a motion having been made, the agency denied the motion or failed to afford the relief requested and state any reasons given by the agency for its action.

(B) The motion must also include:

(i) the reasons for granting the relief requested and the facts relied on;

(ii) originals or copies of affidavits or other sworn statements supporting facts subject to dispute; and

(iii) relevant parts of the record.

(C) The moving party must give reasonable notice of the motion to all parties.

(D) The motion must be filed with the circuit clerk and normally will be considered by a panel of the court. But in an exceptional case in which time requirements make that procedure impracticable, the motion may be made to and considered by a single judge.

(b) *Bond.* The court may condition relief on the filing of a bond or other appropriate security.

LOCAL RULE 18. STAY PENDING REVIEW

(a) Petition for Review or Notice of Appeal; Agency Order. A petition for review or notice of appeal must be filed with this court before it will entertain a motion for a stay pending review. A motion for stay pending review must be accompanied by a copy of the agency decision on the merits and a copy of any agency order on the motion for a stay pending review.

(b) Length of Motion, Response, and Reply; Copies; Brief.

(1) A motion or a response to a motion for a stay pending review may not exceed 20 pages. A reply may not exceed 10 pages.

(2) An original and four copies of a motion, response, or reply must be filed.

(3) A separate brief supporting a motion, response, or reply is not permitted.

(c) Notice and Service When Requesting Immediate Action; Facsimile.

(1) A party moving for a stay pending review who requests immediate action by the court must—before filing—notify all parties that a motion will be filed and must utilize an expedited method of service.

(2) If a motion for stay pending review is sent to the court by facsimile transmission, a certificate of interest must be included and opposing counsel must be served in the same manner. The filing must state the name, address, and, if applicable, the facsimile numbers of the persons served.

(d) Statement. If an initial motion for a stay pending review was not made in the agency under Federal Rule of Appellate Procedure 18(a), movant must include in its motion in this court a statement explaining why it was not practicable to do so. If an initial motion for a stay pending review was made in the agency under Federal Rule of Appellate Procedure 18(a) and remains pending, the movant must include in its motion in this court a statement specifically identifying when it filed the motion in the agency and why it is not practicable to await a ruling by the agency.

[Effective July 1, 1997. Amended effective March 4, 1999; May 1, 2004; May 1, 2006; December 1, 2009.]

Practice Notes

Form Requirements. See Federal Rule of Appellate Procedure 27(d) for form requirements concerning motions.

Certificate of Interest. The form for the certificate of interest is found in Form 9.

Agency. The term agency in these rules includes a board, commission, bureau, or arbitrator.

FRAP RULE 19. SETTLEMENT OF A JUDGMENT ENFORCING AN AGENCY ORDER IN PART

When the court files an opinion directing entry of judgment enforcing the agency's order in part, the agency must within 14 days file with the clerk and serve on each other party a proposed judgment conforming to the opinion. A party who disagrees with the agency's proposed judgment must within 10 days file with the clerk and serve the agency with a proposed judgment that the party believes conforms to the opinion. The court will settle the judgment and direct entry without further hearing or argument.

[Amended May 1, 2003.]

FRAP RULE 20. APPLICABILITY OF RULES TO THE REVIEW OR ENFORCEMENT OF AN AGENCY ORDER

All provisions of these rules, except Rules 3–14 and 22–23, apply to the review or enforcement of an agency order. In these rules, "appellant" includes a petitioner or applicant, and "appellee" includes a respondent.

LOCAL RULE 20. APPLICABILITY OF RULES TO THE REVIEW OF AN AGENCY ORDER

All provisions of these Federal Circuit Rules, except Federal Circuit Rules 3–12, apply to the review of an agency order. In these Federal Circuit Rules, "appellant" includes a petitioner or applicant, and "appellee" includes a respondent.

[Effective March 4, 1999. Amended March 4, 1999; May 1, 2003.]

TITLE V. EXTRAORDINARY WRITS

FRAP RULE 21. WRITS OF MANDAMUS AND PROHIBITION, AND OTHER EXTRAORDINARY WRITS

(a) *Mandamus or Prohibition to a Court: Petition, Filing, Service, and Docketing.*

(1) A party petitioning for a writ of mandamus or prohibition directed to a court must file a petition with the circuit clerk with proof of service on all parties to the proceeding in the trial court. The party must also provide a copy to the trial-court judge. All parties to the proceeding in the trial court other than the petitioner are respondents for all purposes.

(2)(A) The petition must be titled "In re [name of petitioner]."

(B) The petition must state:

(i) the relief sought;

(ii) the issues presented;

(iii) the facts necessary to understand the issue presented by the petition; and

(iv) the reasons why the writ should issue.

(C) The petition must include a copy of any order or opinion or parts of the record that may be essential to understand the matters set forth in the petition.

(3) Upon receiving the prescribed docket fee, the clerk must docket the petition and submit it to the court.

(b) *Denial; Order Directing Answer; Briefs; Precedence.*

(1) The court may deny the petition without an answer. Otherwise, it must order the respondent, if any, to answer within a fixed time.

(2) The clerk must serve the order to respond on all persons directed to respond.

(3) Two or more respondents may answer jointly.

(4) The court of appeals may invite or order the trial-court judge to address the petition or may invite an amicus curiae to do so. The trial-court judge may request permission to address the petition but may not do so unless invited or ordered to do so by the court of appeals.

(5) If briefing or oral argument is required, the clerk must advise the parties, and when appropriate, the trial-court judge or amicus curiae.

(6) The proceeding must be given preference over ordinary civil cases.

(7) The circuit clerk must send a copy of the final disposition to the trial-court judge.

(c) ***Other Extraordinary Writs.*** An application for an extraordinary writ other than one provided for in Rule 21(a) must be made by filing a petition with the circuit clerk with proof of service on the respondents. Proceedings on the application must conform, so far as is practicable, to the procedures prescribed in Rule 21(a) and (b).

(d) ***Form of Papers; Number of Copies.*** All papers must conform to Rule 32(c)(2). Except by the court's permission, a paper must not exceed 30 pages, exclusive of the disclosure statement, the proof of service, and the accompanying documents required by Rule 21(a)(2)(C). An original and 3 copies must be filed unless the court requires the filing of a different number by local rule or by order in a particular case.

LOCAL RULE 21. WRITS OF MANDAMUS AND PROHIBITION, AND OTHER EXTRAORDINARY WRITS

(a) Title; Fee; Answer.

(1) A petition for writ of mandamus or prohibition directed to a court or an agency must be entitled: "In Re [name of petitioner], Petitioner."

(2) The petition must include a certificate of interest. An entry of appearance must accompany the petition, unless the petitioner is pro se.

(3) The petition must state the name, address, telephone number and, if applicable, facsimile number of each person served.

(4) The fee set forth in Federal Circuit Rule 52 must accompany the petition.

(5) No answer may be filed by any respondent unless ordered by the court.

(b) Copies; Brief.

(1) An original and four copies of the petition or answer must be filed.

(2) A separate brief supporting or answering a petition is not permitted.

(c) Reply. If the court directs the filing of a response to a petition, then the petitioner may file a reply within 7 days of the date of the filing of the response. The court may act on the petition before the receipt of any reply, and thus the filing of a reply should be expedited if appropriate. The reply may not exceed 15 pages.

(d) Service of Order Denying Petition. If the petition is denied, the petitioner must serve a copy of the order denying the petition on all persons served with the petition unless such a person has entered an appearance in the proceeding or has been sent a copy of the order by the clerk.

[Effective July 1, 1997. Amended effective March 4, 1999; May 1, 2003; December 1, 2009.]

TITLE VI. ~~HABEAS CORPUS;~~ PROCEEDINGS IN FORMA PAUPERIS

~~FRAP RULE 22. HABEAS CORPUS AND SECTION 2255 PROCEEDINGS~~

~~FRAP RULE 23. CUSTODY OR RELEASE OF A PRISONER IN A HABEAS CORPUS PROCEEDING~~

FRAP RULE 24. PROCEEDING IN FORMA PAUPERIS

(a) *Leave to Proceed In Forma Pauperis.*

(1) Motion in the District Court. Except as stated in Rule 24(a)(3), a party to a district-court action who desires to appeal in forma pauperis must file a motion in the district court. The party must attach an affidavit that:

(A) shows in the detail prescribed by Form 4 (Federal Circuit Form 6 herein) of the Appendix of Forms the party's inability to pay or to give security for fees and costs;

(B) claims an entitlement to redress; and

(C) states the issues that the party intends to present on appeal.

(2) Action on the Motion. If the district court grants the motion, the party may proceed on appeal without prepaying or giving security for fees and costs, unless a statute provides otherwise. If the district court denies the motion, it must state its reasons in writing.

(3) Prior Approval. A party who was permitted to proceed in forma pauperis in the district-court action, or who was determined to be financially unable to obtain an adequate defense in a criminal case, may proceed on appeal in forma pauperis without further authorization, unless:

(A) the district court—before or after the notice of appeal is filed—certifies that the appeal is not taken in good faith or finds that the party is not otherwise entitled to proceed in forma pauperis and states in writing its reasons for the certification or finding; or

(B) a statute provides otherwise.

(4) ***Notice of District Court's Denial.* The district clerk must immediately notify the parties and the court of appeals when the district court does any of the following:**

(A) denies a motion to proceed on appeal in forma pauperis;

(B) certifies that the appeal is not taken in good faith; or

(C) finds that the party is not otherwise entitled to proceed in forma pauperis.

(5) Motion in the Court of Appeals. A party may file a motion to proceed on appeal in forma pauperis in the court of appeals within 30 days after service of the notice prescribed in Rule 24(a)(4). The motion must include a copy of the affidavit filed in the district court and the district court's statement of reasons for its action. If no affidavit was filed in the district court, the party must include the affidavit prescribed by Rule 24(a)(1).

(b) ***Leave to Proceed In Forma Pauperis on Appeal or Review of an Administrative–Agency Proceeding.* When an appeal or review of a proceeding before an administrative agency, board, commission, or officer ~~(including for the purpose of this rule the United States Tax Court)~~ proceeds directly in a court of appeals, a party may file in the court of appeals a motion for leave to proceed on appeal in forma pauperis with an affidavit prescribed by Rule 24(a)(1).**

(c) ***Leave to Use Original Record.* A party allowed to proceed on appeal in forma pauperis may request that the appeal be heard on the original record without reproducing any part.**

LOCAL RULE 24. PROCEEDING IN FORMA PAUPERIS

(a) Form. If an appeal or petition for review is docketed without payment of the docketing fee, the clerk in providing notice of docketing will forward to the appellant or petitioner the form prescribed by this court for the motion to proceed on appeal in forma pauperis. (See Form 6.) Except as provided in Federal Rule of Appellate Procedure 24(a), if the clerk does not receive a completed motion, the docketing fee, or a completed Form 6B within 14 days of the date of docketing of the appeal or petition, the clerk is authorized to dismiss the appeal or petition. See also Federal Circuit Rule 52(d). The motion and affidavit may be made on the form provided in the Federal Rules of Appellate Procedure, but the court may request additional information from the movant.

(b) Supplemental Form. If movant is incarcerated, in addition to Form 6 movant must file a supplemental form for prisoners, Form 6A.

[Effective July 1, 1997. Amended effective March 4, 1999; May 1, 2003; May 1, 2004; May 1, 2006; December 1, 2009.]

Practice Notes

Docketing Fee; Transcript Request. A party permitted to proceed in forma pauperis on appeal is not required to pay the docketing fee. Any request for a transcript of an agency proceeding at government expense is governed by agency regulations and must be directed to the agency.

Proceeding on Original Record. A request under Federal Rule of Appellate Procedure 24(c) that an appeal be heard on the original record is rarely granted because the available informal brief procedure permits an appendix consisting only of a copy of the decision or order sought to be reviewed. *See* Federal Circuit Rules 28(g); 30(i); 31(e); and 32(c). *See* Forms 11–16.

Effect of Prison Litigation Reform Act. Under the Prison Litigation Reform Act of 1995, a prisoner granted pauper status before the district court is not automatically entitled to pauper status on appeal. See 28 U.S.C. § 1915. A prisoner seeking to proceed in forma pauperis is directed to the Guide for Pro Se Petitioners and Appellants for further information.

USERRA CASES. In a petition for review of a Merit Systems Protection Board decision, a petitioner is not required to pay the docketing fee or costs if the case involved a claim under the Uniformed Services Employment and Reemployment Rights Act of 1994 (USERRA). 38 U.S.C. § 4323. A petitioner claiming exemption from the fee pursuant to USERRA should submit Form 6B within 14 days of the date of docketing of the petition and may be required to submit documentation that his or her case before the Board involved a USERRA claim.

TITLE VII. GENERAL PROVISIONS

FRAP RULE 25. FILING AND SERVICE

(a) *Filing.*

(1) Filing With the Clerk. A paper required or permitted to be filed in a court of appeals must be filed with the clerk.

(2) Filing: Method and Timeliness.

(A) In General. Filing may be accomplished by mail addressed to the clerk, but filing is not timely unless the clerk receives the papers within the time fixed for filing.

(B) A Brief or Appendix. A brief or appendix is timely filed, however, if on or before the last day for filing, it is:

(i) mailed to the clerk by First–Class Mail, or other class of mail that is at least as expeditious, postage prepaid; or

(ii) dispatched to a third-party commercial carrier for delivery to the clerk within 3 days.

(C) Inmate Filing. A paper filed by an inmate confined in an institution is timely if deposited in the institution's internal mailing system on or before the last day for filing. If an institution has a system designed for legal mail, the inmate must use that system to receive the benefit of this rule. Timely filing may be shown by a declaration in compliance with 28 U.S.C. § 1746 or by a notarized statement, either of which must set forth the date of deposit and state that first-class postage has been prepaid.

(D) Electronic Filing. A court of appeals may by local rule permit papers to be filed, signed, or verified by electronic means that are consistent with technical standards, if any, that the Judicial Conference of the United States establishes. A paper filed by electronic means in compliance with a local rule constitutes a written paper for the purpose of applying these rules.

(3) Filing a Motion With a Judge. If a motion requests relief that may be granted by a single judge, the judge may permit the motion to be filed with the judge; the judge must note the filing date on the motion and give it to the clerk.

(4) Clerk's Refusal of Documents. The clerk must not refuse to accept for filing any paper presented for that purpose solely because it is not presented in proper form as required by these rules or by any local rule or practice.

(5) Privacy Protection. An appeal in a case whose privacy protection was governed by Federal Rule of Bankruptcy Procedure 9037, Federal Rule of Civil Procedure 5.2 or Federal Rule of Criminal Procedure 49.1 is governed by the same rule on appeal. In all other proceedings, privacy protection is governed by Federal Rule of Civil Procedure 5.2, except that Federal Rule of Criminal Procedure 49.1 governs when an extra ordinary writ is sought in a criminal case.

(b) *Service of All Papers Required.* Unless a rule requires service by the clerk, a party must, at or before the time of filing a paper, serve a copy on the other parties to the appeal or review. Service on a party represented by counsel must be made on the party's counsel.

(c) *Manner of Service.*

(1) Service may be any of the following:

(A) personal, including delivery to a responsible person at the office of counsel;

(B) by mail;

(C) by third-party commercial carrier for delivery within 3 days; or

(D) by electronic means, if the party being served consents in writing.

(2) If authorized by local rule, a party may use the court's transmission equipment to make electronic service under Rule 25(c)(1)(D).

(3) When reasonable considering such factors as the immediacy of the relief sought, distance, and cost, service on a party must be by a manner at least as expeditious as the manner used to file the paper with the court.

(4) Service by mail or by commercial carrier is complete on mailing or delivery to the carrier. Service by electronic means is complete on transmission, unless the party making service is notified that the paper was not received by the party served.

(d) *Proof of Service.*

(1) A paper presented for filing must contain either of the following:

(A) an acknowledgment of service by the person served; or

(B) proof of service consisting of a statement by the person who made service certifying:

(i) the date and manner of service;

(ii) the names of the persons served; and

(iii) their mail or electronic addresses, facsimile numbers, or the addresses of the places of delivery, as appropriate for the manner of service.

(2) When a brief or appendix is filed by mailing or dispatch in accordance with Rule 25(a)(2)(B), the proof of service must also state the date and manner by which the document was mailed or dispatched to the clerk.

(3) Proof of service may appear on or be affixed to the papers filed.

(e) *Number of Copies.* When these rules require the filing or furnishing of a number of copies, a court may require a different number by local rule or by order in a particular case.

LOCAL RULE 25. FILING AND SERVICE

(a) Facsimile Filing. A motion, response to a motion, reply to a response or letter may be filed by facsimile transmission if the certificate of service by facsimile transmission states that a copy has been served on all parties by facsimile transmission and that the appropriate number of copies of the motion, response, reply, or letter have been mailed or shipped for delivery to the clerk and the parties on the next business day.

(b) Facsimile Filing Limitation. No document other than a motion, response to a motion, reply to a response, or letter may be filed or served by facsimile transmission.

[Effective July 1, 1997. Amended effective March 4, 1999; May 1, 2003; May 1, 2004; May 1, 2008; December 1, 2009.]

Practice Notes

Location of Clerk's Office; Hours of Operation; Night Box. The clerk's office is in Room 401 of the National Courts Building, 717 Madison Place, NW, Washington, DC 20439, and is open from 9:00 a.m. to 5:00 p.m. on workdays. After the office closes on workdays, papers may be deposited until midnight in a night box at the garage entrance on H Street NW, between 15th Street and Madison Place.

Clerk's Mailing Address. Address mail as follows:

Clerk of Court
United States Court of Appeals for the Federal Circuit
717 Madison Place, NW
Washington, DC 20439

The clerk will not pay postage due.

Clerk's Facsimile Number. Documents which Federal Circuit Rule 25 permits to be sent by facsimile to the Clerk of Court should be sent to: 202–275–9678.

Proof of Service. Each brief, petition, motion, response, or reply must contain proof of service. Only the original filed with the court must be signed. A copy of the unsigned proof of service must be attached to any copies.

Return Copy Marked Received. When a brief or other paper presented for filing includes an extra copy, the clerk will mark it received and return it on request. If the filing is by mail or if the night box is used, a self-addressed, postage-paid (first class) return envelope must accompany the request.

Filing Rejected by the Clerk. The clerk may reject material submitted for filing that does not substantially conform with the Federal Rules of Appellate Procedure and the Federal Circuit Rules. The clerk will issue a rejection letter advising of the nature of the nonconformity and guidelines for resubmission. Opposing counsel will be notified of the rejection. The timeliness of a response is computed from date of service of the original material. Because of occasional delays with some mail transmitted by the United States Postal Service, due to screening or other issues, if a document such as a notice of appeal, petition for review, motion, or other document must be received by the court on a particular date, then the filer might consider using an alternative method of delivering the document to the court, such as a commercial carrier or hand-delivery. The court cannot waive the deadlines for filing a notice of appeal or petition for review, even if the document was deposited in the mail in a timely fashion. Federal Rule of Appellate Procedure 26(b).

FRAP RULE 26. COMPUTING AND EXTENDING TIME

(a) *Computing Time.* The following rules apply in computing any time period specified in these rules, in any local rule or court order, or in any statute that does not specify a method of computing time.

(1) Period Stated in Days or a Longer Unit. When the period is stated in days or a longer unit of time:

(A) exclude the day of the event that triggers the period;

(B) count every day, including intermediate Saturdays, Sundays, and legal holidays; and

(C) include the last day of the period, but if the last day is a Saturday, Sunday, or legal holiday, the period continues to run until the end of the next day that is not a Saturday, Sunday, or legal holiday.

(2) Period Stated in Hours. When the period is stated in hours:

(A) begin counting immediately on the occurrence of the event that triggers the period;

(B) count every hour, including hours during intermediate Saturdays, Sundays, and legal holidays; and

(C) if the period would end on a Saturday, Sunday, or legal holiday, the period continues to run until the same time on the next day that is not a Saturday, Sunday, or legal holiday.

(3) Inaccessibility of the Clerk's Office. Unless the court orders otherwise, if the clerk's office is inaccessible:

(A) on the last day for filing under Rule 26(a)(1), then the time for filing is extended to the first accessible day that is not a Saturday, Sunday, or legal holiday; or

(B) during the last hour for filing under Rule 26(a)(2), then the time for filing is extended to the same time on the first accessible day that is not a Saturday, Sunday, or legal holiday.

(4) "Last Day" Defined. Unless a different time is set by a statute, local rule, or court order, the last day ends:

(A) for electronic filing in the district court, at midnight in the court's time zone;

(B) for electronic filing in the court of appeals, at midnight in the time zone of the circuit clerk's principal office;

(C) for filing under Rules 4(c)(1), 25(a)(2)(B), and 25(a)(2)(C)—and filing by mail under Rule 13(b)—at the latest time for the method chosen for delivery to the post office, third-party commercial carrier, or prison mailing system; and

(D) for filing by other means, when the clerk's office is scheduled to close.

(5) "Next Day" Defined. The "next day" is determined by continuing to count forward when the period is measured after an event and backward when measured before an event.

(6) "Legal Holiday" Defined. "Legal holiday" means:

(A) the day set aside by statute for observing New Year's Day, Martin Luther King Jr.'s Birthday, Washington's Birthday, Memorial Day, Independence Day, Labor Day, Columbus Day, Veterans' Day, Thanksgiving Day, or Christmas Day;

(B) any day declared a holiday by the President or Congress; and

(C) for periods that are measured after an event, any other day declared a holiday by the state where either of the following is located: the district court that rendered the challenged judgment or order, or the circuit clerk's principal office.

(b) *Extending Time.* For good cause, the court may extend the time prescribed by these rules or by its order to perform any act, or may permit an act to be done after that time expires. But the court may not extend the time to file:

(1) a notice of appeal (except as authorized in Rule 4) or a petition for permission to appeal; or

(2) a notice of appeal from or a petition to enjoin, set aside, suspend, modify, enforce, or otherwise review an order of an administrative agency, board, commission, or officer of the United States, unless specifically authorized by law.

(c) *Additional Time after Service.* When a party may or must act within a specified time after service, 3 days are added after the period would otherwise expire under Rule 26(a), unless the paper is delivered on the date of service stated in the proof of service. For purposes of this Rule 26(c), a paper that is served electronically is not treated as delivered on the date of service stated in the proof of service.

LOCAL RULE 26. COMPUTING AND EXTENDING TIME

(a) Computation of Time; Closing the Clerk's Office. "Legal holiday" also means a day on which the clerk's office is closed by order of the court or the chief judge. Such an order will be posted publicly and its contents placed on a recording for telephone callers.

(b) Motion to Extend Time.

(1) A motion to extend the time prescribed by the Federal Rules of Appellate Procedure, the Federal Circuit Rules, or an order of this court must be made at least 7 days before the date sought to be extended, except that in extraordinary circumstances a motion may be made later than that deadline if accompanied by an affidavit or unsworn declaration under penalty of perjury under 28 U.S.C. § 1746 that describes the extraordinary circumstances.

(2) Before filing the motion, the movant must inform all other parties that it will seek an extension.

(3) The movant must state in the motion whether any other parties object and, if so, whether a response in opposition will be filed.

(4) In addition to showing good cause, the motion must state:

(A) the date to be extended;

(B) the revised date sought;

(C) the number of days of extension sought; and

(D) the total number of days of extension previously granted to the movant.

(5) A request for an extension of more than 14 days must be accompanied by an affidavit or unsworn declaration of counsel or a pro se party under penalty of perjury under 28 U.S.C. § 1746 showing good cause for the extension.

[Effective July 1, 1997. Amended effective March 4, 1999; February 4, 2000; May 1, 2004; May 1, 2006; December 1, 2009.]

Practice Notes

Opposition to Extension. If a party opposes a motion for extension of time, that party should file its response promptly. The court will not necessarily wait for an opposition before ruling on a motion.

Benefit of Timely Extension Request. Unless the court has previously ordered that there will be no further extensions, an appeal will not be dismissed for failure to file appellant's brief if appellant's motion to extend the time for filing was filed and served at least 7 days before the due date for the brief, but the motion has not been acted on by the due date.

Extension During Settlement Negotiations. Parties jointly stipulating that they are actively pursuing settlement of the case will be granted a reasonable extension of time to accomplish settlement.

Court Order. Federal Rule of Appellate Procedure 26(c) does not apply when a court order requires action within a specified time; the due date is as specified in the order.

FRAP RULE 26.1. CORPORATE DISCLOSURE STATEMENT

(a) *Who Must File.* Any nongovernmental corporate party to a proceeding in a court of appeals must file a statement that identifies any parent corporation and any publicly held corporation that owns 10% or more of its stock or states that there is no such corporation.

(b) *Time for Filing; Supplemental Filing.* A party must file the Rule 26.1(a) statement with the principal brief or upon filing a motion, response, petition, or answer in the court of appeals, whichever occurs first, unless a local rule requires earlier filing. Even if the statement has already been filed, the party's principal brief must include the statement ~~before the table of contents~~. A party must supplement its statement whenever the information that must be disclosed under Rule 26.1(a) changes.

(c) *Number of Copies.* If the Rule 26.1(a) statement is filed before the principal brief, or if a supplemental statement is filed, the party must file an original and 3 copies unless the court requires a different number by local rule or by order in a particular case.

LOCAL RULE 26.1. CORPORATE DISCLOSURE STATEMENT

The corporate disclosure statement must be included in the certificate of interest prescribed in Federal Circuit Rule 47.4. A certificate of interest must be filed by any party represented by counsel within 14 days of the date of docketing of the appeal or petition. *See* Federal Circuit Rule 47.4 for additional requirements.

[Effective July 1, 1997. Amended effective March 4, 1999; May 1, 2004; December 1, 2009.]

Practice Note

The requirements of Federal Rule of Appellate Procedure 26.1 are satisfied by filing a certificate of interest under Federal Circuit Rule 47.4. *See* Form 9.

FRAP RULE 27. MOTIONS

(a) *In General.*

(1) Application for Relief. An application for an order or other relief is made by motion unless these rules prescribe another form. A motion must be in writing unless the court permits otherwise.

(2) Contents of a Motion.

(A) Grounds and Relief Sought. A motion must state with particularity the grounds for the motion, the relief sought, and the legal argument necessary to support it.

(B) Accompanying Documents.

(i) Any affidavit or other paper necessary to support a motion must be served and filed with the motion.

(ii) An affidavit must contain only factual information, not legal argument.

(iii) A motion seeking substantive relief must include a copy of the trial court's opinion or agency's decision as a separate exhibit.

(C) Documents Barred or Not Required.

(i) A separate brief supporting or responding to a motion must not be filed.

(ii) A notice of motion is not required.

(iii) A proposed order is not required.

(3) Response.

(A) Time to File. Any party may file a response to a motion; Rule 27(a)(2) governs its contents. The response must be filed within 10 days after service of the motion unless the court shortens or extends the time. A motion authorized by Rules 8, 9, 18, or 41 may be granted before the 10-day period runs only if the court gives reasonable notice to the parties that it intends to act sooner.

(B) Request for Affirmative Relief. A response may include a motion for affirmative relief. The time to respond to the new motion, and to reply to that response, are governed by Rule 27(a)(3)(A) and (a)(4). The title of the response must alert the court to the request for relief.

(4) Reply to Response. Any reply to a response must be filed within 7 days after service of the response. A reply must not present matters that do not relate to the response.

(b) *Disposition of a Motion for a Procedural Order.* The court may act on a motion for a procedural order—including a motion under Rule 26(b)—at any time without awaiting a response, and may, by rule or by order in a particular case, authorize its clerk to act on specified types of procedural motions. A party adversely affected by the court's, or the clerk's, action may file a motion to reconsider, vacate, or modify that action. Timely opposition filed after the motion is granted in whole or in part does not constitute a request to reconsider, vacate, or modify the disposition; a motion requesting that relief must be filed.

(c) *Power of a Single Judge to Entertain a Motion.* A circuit judge may act alone on any motion, but may not dismiss or otherwise determine an appeal or other proceeding. A court of appeals may provide by rule or by order in a particular case that only the court may act on any motion or class of motions. The court may review the action of a single judge.

(d) *Form of Papers; Page Limits; and Number of Copies.*

(1) Format.

(A) Reproduction. A motion, response, or reply may be reproduced by any process that yields a clear black image on light paper. The paper must be opaque and unglazed. Only one side of the paper may be used.

(B) Cover. A cover is not required but there must be a caption that includes the case number, the name of the court, the title of the case, and a brief descriptive title indicating the purpose of the motion and identifying the party or parties for whom it is filed. If a cover is used, it must be white.

(C) Binding. The document must be bound in any manner that is secure, does not obscure the text, and permits the document to lie reasonably flat when open.

(D) Paper Size, Line Spacing, and Margins. The document must be on 8½ by 11 inch paper. The text must be double-spaced, but quotations more than two lines long may be indented and single-spaced. Headings and footnotes may be single-spaced. Margins must be at least one inch on all four sides. Page numbers may be placed in the margins, but no text may appear there.

(E) Typeface and Type Styles. The document must comply with the typeface requirements of Rule 32(a)(5) and the type-style requirements of Rule 32(a)(6).

(2) Page Limits. A motion or a response to a motion must not exceed 20 pages, exclusive of the corporate disclosure statement and accompanying documents authorized by Rule 27(a)(2)(B), unless the court permits or directs otherwise. A reply to a response must not exceed 10 pages.

(3) Number of Copies. An original and 3 copies must be filed unless the court requires a different number by local rule or by order in a particular case.

(e) *Oral Argument.* A motion will be decided without oral argument unless the court orders otherwise.

LOCAL RULE 27. MOTIONS

(a) Content of Motion. The preferred content and organization of a motion are:

(1) the name of this court;

(2) the caption. If the motion is for a procedural order on consent, the authorized abbreviated caption may be used. For any other motion, the official caption must be used;

(3) the title of the motion;

(4) the grounds for the motion, the relief sought, and the legal argument to support the motion;

(5) the movant's statement of consent or opposition to the motion. The movant must state in the motion that the movant has discussed the motion with the other parties, whether any party will object, and whether any party will file a response;

(6) counsel's or pro se party's signature;

(7) the certificate of interest. The certificate of interest (see Federal Circuit Rule 47.4) must be included in each motion;

(8) supporting affidavit. If the facts relied on in the motion are subject to dispute, an affidavit or unsworn declaration under penalty of perjury under 28 U.S.C. § 1746 must be attached to the motion;

(9) the proof of service (see Federal Rule of Appellate Procedure 25(d)).

(b) Response; When Filed; Content. If a motion states that it is consented to or unopposed, a response is not required. If a motion does not state whether—or incorrectly states that—it is consented to or unopposed, a response should be filed as soon as the omission or error becomes known. The preferred organization of a response is comparable to the organization of a motion provided in (a) of this rule and the preferred content of a response is:

(1) as provided in (a)(1), (2), (6), (7), (8), and (9) of this rule; and

(2) the grounds for denying the motion, limiting the relief granted, or modifying the order sought, and the legal argument to support the response; or the responding party's statement of consent or lack of opposition.

(c) Content of Reply. The preferred organization of a reply is comparable to the organization of a motion as provided in (a) of this rule and the preferred content of the reply is:

(1) as provided in (a)(1), (2), (6), (7), (8), and (9) of this rule; and

(2) the reply to the response and the legal argument to support it.

(d) Length of Motion, Response, or Reply; Cover and Backing; Attachments. Items listed in Federal Circuit Rule 27(a)(7)–(9) do not count toward the page limitation in Federal Rule of Appellate Procedure 27(d)(2). Cover and backing for a motion, response, or reply are not required. If a motion includes several attachments or exhibits, the court prefers that the attachments or exhibits be separately tabbed for ease of reference.

(e) Motion to Strike; Response. A motion to strike all or part of a brief, except to strike scandalous matter, is prohibited as long as the party seeking to strike has the right to file a responsive brief in which the objection could be made. A response, if any, in opposition to a motion to strike must be included in the responsive brief if one is authorized, or may be filed if leave is sought and obtained, or may be made at oral argument.

(f) Motion to Dismiss or to Remand; Response. A motion to dismiss for lack of jurisdiction or to remand should be made as soon after docketing as the grounds for the motion are known. After the appellant or petitioner has filed the principal brief, the argument supporting dismissal for lack of jurisdiction or remand should be made in the brief of the appellee or respondent. A response in opposition, if any, should be included in the responsive brief. Joint or unopposed motions or stipulations to dismiss or to remand may be made at any time.

(g) Motion Incorporated in a Brief. Except as provided in Federal Circuit Rule 27(e) and (f), a motion must not be incorporated in a brief.

(h) Delegation of Authority to the Clerk. The clerk is authorized to act on any procedural motion or unopposed nonprocedural motion, but may not act on an opposed nonprocedural motion or any motion that requires action by a judge or panel of judges. The clerk may also direct an expedited response to a motion or petition and may direct the parties to show cause why an appeal or petition should not be dismissed. Even if the clerk is authorized to act on a particular motion, the clerk may nonetheless refer the matter to a judge or panel, or may defer the matter to the merits panel, when appropriate.

(i) Ex Parte Application. Neither the court nor any judge of the court will conduct an ex parte hearing on an application for relief.

(j) Copies in an En Banc Case. When an appeal is pending before the court en banc, motions and responses must be filed in an original and 18 copies.

(k) Application for Consideration, Vacation, or Modification of Procedural Order. A party adversely affected by a procedural order entered on a motion without awaiting the response time or by an order of the clerk may move for relief within 14 days of the order or action. The application must be made by motion.

***(l)* Review or Reconsideration of the Order of a Single Judge or Panel of Judges.** Except for a dispositive order issued by a panel, which time will be governed by Federal Rule of Appellate Procedure 40(a)(1), a party seeking review by the court of the action of a single judge or reconsideration of the action of a panel of judges must file a motion for reconsideration within 14 days of the entry of the order.

(m) Motion Papers Containing Material Subject to a Protective Order.

(1) *Two Sets of Motion Papers.* If a party refers in motion papers to material subject to confidentiality mandated by statute or to a judicial or administrative protective order, two sets of motion papers must be filed.

(A) Confidential set; labeling; number of copies. One set of motion papers, consisting of the original and three copies, must be labeled "confidential" and filed with the court. If confidentiality will end on a date certain or upon the happening of an event, this must be stated on the cover, e.g., "CONFIDENTIAL UNTIL [DATE]," or "CONFIDENTIAL DURING JUDICIAL REVIEW." Each page containing confidential material must enclose this material in brackets or indicate this material by highlighting.

(B) Nonconfidential set; labeling; number of copies. The second set of motion papers, consisting of the original and three copies from which confidential matter has been deleted, must be labeled "nonconfidential" and filed with the court. Each page from which material subject to a protective order has been deleted must bear a legend so stating. The introductory paragraph of the nonconfidential motion or response must describe the general nature of the confidential material that has been deleted.

(2) *Service.* Each party to the appeal must be served two copies of the nonconfidential motion papers and, when permitted by the applicable protective order, two copies of the confidential motion papers.

(3) *Availability to the Public.* The confidential motion papers will be made available only to authorized court personnel and must not be made available to the public. After 5 years following the end of all proceedings in the court, the parties may be directed to show cause why confidential motion papers (except those protected by statute) should not be made available to the public.

[Effective July 1, 1997. Amended effective March 4, 1999; May 1, 2003; May 1, 2004; December 17, 2004; May 1, 2006; May 1, 2008; December 1, 2009.]

Practice Notes

Content of a Motion, Response, or Reply. Using Federal Circuit Rule 27's preferred content and organization for a motion, response, or reply will help avoid delays caused by the need for additional information. Although motions, responses, and replies need not have the formality of briefs, a motion, response, or reply may be rejected if it is not substantially complete.

Moot Response. A response to a motion for a procedural order that is received after the motion has been acted on is considered moot.

Authority to Act on Motions; Motions Referred to Panel. Neither the clerk nor the court is required to grant relief just because the parties agree it should be granted. The clerk's authority to act on procedural or unopposed nonprocedural motions includes the authority to grant or deny the requested relief in whole or in part or to refer the motion to a judge or a panel. Examples of procedural motions include motions for extensions of time, motions to reform the caption, motions for leave to file various documents, motions for leave to proceed in forma pauperis, etc. Examples of nonprocedural motions include motions to dismiss, motions to remand, motions to transfer, motions to summarily affirm judgments, motions for stays of injunctions, motions to strike portions of briefs or appendices, motions for leave to intervene, motions for leave to file briefs as amici curiae, etc. Motions to exceed the permitted word or page limitation for a brief will be decided by a judge. If the clerk grants a motion to extend the time to file a principal brief by 60 days, no further extensions should be anticipated. Once a case is assigned to a merits panel, the clerk refers all motions to the merits panel.

Telephone Inquiry About Pending Motions; Access to Orders on Website. Telephone inquiries about pending motions are discouraged because they divert the clerk's office staff from more pressing duties. When an order on a motion directs counsel to take prompt action, the clerk's office will telephone counsel. All other orders are considered routine, and counsel may await notification by mail. Alternatively, counsel or the parties may often determine the status of a pending motion and obtain copies of court orders on this court's website, http://www.cafc.uscourts.gov/index.html. First, one may view on PACER the court's current docket sheet in any pending appeal or petition to determine the current status of a motion. Second, if a motion has been processed by the court's senior staff attorney, the order will normally be available on the website the same day it is filed. Third, many other pertinent orders, including en banc orders, are promptly posted on the court's opinions and orders page. Under no circumstances should anyone telephone a judge or the office of the senior staff attorney about a motion. In an emergency, you may call the clerk's office.

FRAP RULE 28. BRIEFS

(a) *Appellant's Brief.* The appellant's brief must contain, under appropriate headings ~~and in the order indicated~~:

(1) a corporate disclosure statement if required by Rule 26.1;

(2) a table of contents, with page references;

(3) a table of authorities—cases (alphabetically arranged), statutes, and other authorities—with references to the pages of the brief where they are cited;

(4) a jurisdictional statement, including:

(A) the basis for the district court's or agency's subject-matter jurisdiction, with citations to applicable statutory provisions and stating relevant facts establishing jurisdiction;

(B) the basis for the court of appeals' jurisdiction, with citations to applicable statutory provisions and stating relevant facts establishing jurisdiction;

(C) the filing dates establishing the timeliness of the appeal or petition for review; and

(D) an assertion that the appeal is from a final order or judgment that disposes of all parties' claims, or information establishing the court of appeals' jurisdiction on some other basis;

(5) a statement of the issues presented for review;

(6) a statement of the case briefly indicating the nature of the case, the course of proceedings, and the disposition below;

(7) a statement of facts relevant to the issues submitted for review with appropriate references to the record (see Rule 28(e));

(8) a summary of the argument, which must contain a succinct, clear, and accurate statement of the arguments made in the body of the brief, and

which must not merely repeat the argument headings;

(9) the argument, which must contain:

(A) appellant's contentions and the reasons for them, with citations to the authorities and parts of the record on which the appellant relies; and

(B) for each issue, a concise statement of the applicable standard of review (which may appear in the discussion of the issue or under a separate heading placed before the discussion of the issues);

(10) a short conclusion stating the precise relief sought; and

(11) the certificate of compliance, if required by Rule 32(a)(7).

(b) *Appellee's Brief.* The appellee's brief must conform to the requirements of Rule 28(a)(1)–(9) and (11), except that none of the following need appear unless the appellee is dissatisfied with the appellant's statement:

(1) the jurisdictional statement;

(2) the statement of the issues;

(3) the statement of the case;

(4) the statement of the facts; and

(5) the statement of the standard of review.

(c) *Reply Brief.* The appellant may file a brief in reply to the appellee's brief. ~~An appellee who has cross-appealed may file a brief in reply to the appellant's response to the issues presented by the cross-appeal.~~ Unless the court permits, no further briefs may be filed. A reply brief must contain a table of contents, with page references, and a table of authorities—cases (alphabetically arranged), statutes, and other authorities—with references to the pages of the reply brief where they are cited.

(d) *References to Parties.* In briefs and at oral argument, counsel should minimize use of the terms "appellant" and "appellee." To make briefs clear, counsel should use the parties' actual names or the designations used in the lower court or agency proceeding, or such descriptive terms as "the employee," "the injured person," "the taxpayer," "the ship," "the stevedore."

(e) *References to the Record.* References to the parts of the record contained in the appendix filed with the appellant's brief must be to the pages of the appendix. ~~If the appendix is prepared after the briefs are filed, a party referring to the record must follow one of the methods detailed in Rule 30(c). If the original record is used under Rule 30(f) and is not consecutively paginated, or~~ if the brief refers to an unreproduced part of the record, any reference must be to the page of the original document. For example:

- Answer p. 7;
- Motion for Judgment p. 2;
- Transcript p. 231.

Only clear abbreviations may be used. A party referring to evidence whose admissibility is in controversy must cite the pages of the appendix or of the transcript at which the evidence was identified, offered, and received or rejected.

(f) *Reproduction of Statutes, Rules, Regulations, etc.* If the court's determination of the issues presented requires the study of statutes, rules, regulations, etc., the relevant parts must be set out in the brief or in an addendum at the end, or may be supplied to the court in pamphlet form.

(g) [Reserved]

(h) [Reserved]

(i) *Briefs in a Case Involving Multiple Appellants or Appellees.* In a case involving more than one appellant or appellee, including consolidated cases, any number of appellants or appellees may join in a brief, and any party may adopt by reference a part of another's brief. Parties may also join in reply briefs.

(j) *Citation of Supplemental Authorities.* If pertinent and significant authorities come to a party's attention after the party's brief has been filed—or after oral argument but before decision—a party may promptly advise the circuit clerk by letter, with a copy to all other parties, setting forth the citations. The letter must state the reasons for the supplemental citations, referring either to the page of the brief or to a point argued orally. The body of the letter must not exceed 350 words. Any response must be made promptly and must be similarly limited.

LOCAL RULE 28. BRIEFS

(a) Contents of Brief; Organization of Contents; Addendum; Binding. Briefs must be bound as prescribed in Rule 32 of the Federal Rules of Appellate Procedure and must contain the following in the order listed:

(1) the certificate of interest (see Federal Circuit Rule 47.4);

(2) the table of contents;

(3) the table of authorities;

(4) the statement of related cases (see Federal Circuit Rule 47.5);

(5) the jurisdictional statement including a representation that the judgment or order appealed from is final or, if not final, the basis for appealability (e.g.,

preliminary injunction, Fed. R. Civ. P. 54(b) certification of final judgment as to fewer than all of the claims or parties, etc.);

(6) the statement of the issues;

(7) the statement of the case, including the citation of any published decision of the trial tribunal in the proceedings;

(8) the statement of the facts;

(9) the summary of the argument;

(10) the argument, including statement of the standard of review;

(11) the conclusion and statement of relief sought;

(12) the judgment, order, or decision in question, and any opinion, memorandum, or findings and conclusions supporting it, as an addendum placed last within the initial brief of the appellant or petitioner. This requirement is met when the appendix is bound with the brief. (See Federal Circuit Rule 30(c)(1) and (d) for a duplicative requirement of the appendix.) Additionally, in an appeal involving a patent, the patent in suit may be included within the addendum of the initial brief and, if included, must be reproduced in its entirety. (See also Federal Circuit Rule 30(a)(2)(A)(iii) and Federal Circuit Rule 30(a)(3) for a requirement that the patent in suit be included in its entirety in the appendix);

(13) the proof of service (see Federal Rule of Appellate Procedure 25(d)); and

(14) the certificate of compliance, if required by Federal Rule of Appellate Procedure 32(a)(7).

(b) Appellee's Jurisdictional Statement and Statements of the Issues, the Case, the Facts, and the Standard of Review. The appellee's jurisdictional statement and statements of the issues, the case, the facts, and the standard of review must be limited to specific areas of disagreement with those of the appellant. Absent disagreement, the appellee must not include any of those statements. The statement of the case must include the citation of any published decision of the trial tribunal in the proceedings that is not included in the appellant's statement of the case.

(c) Motion to File Extended Brief. The court looks with disfavor on a motion to file an extended brief and grants it only for extraordinary reasons. Unless the order granting a motion to file an extended brief provides otherwise, when additional pages or words are allowed in the principal brief of an appellant or cross-appellant, a responsive brief permitted by the rules may contain the same number of additional pages or words.

(d) Brief Containing Material Subject to a Protective Order.

(1) *Two Sets of Briefs.* If a party refers in a brief to material subject to confidentiality mandated by statute or to a judicial or administrative protective order, two sets of briefs must be filed.

(A) Confidential set; labeling; number of copies. One set of briefs, consisting of the original and eleven copies, must be labeled "confidential" and filed with the court. If confidentiality will end on a date certain or upon the happening of an event, this must be stated on the cover, e.g., "CONFIDENTIAL UNTIL [DATE]," or "CONFIDENTIAL DURING JUDICIAL REVIEW." Each page containing confidential material must enclose this material in brackets or indicate this material by highlighting.

(B) Nonconfidential set; labeling; number of copies. The second set of briefs, consisting of the original and four copies from which confidential matter has been deleted, must be labeled "nonconfidential" and filed with the court. Each page from which material subject to a protective order has been deleted must bear a legend so stating. The table of contents of a nonconfidential brief must describe the general nature of the confidential material that has been deleted.

(2) *Service.* Each party to the appeal must be served two copies of the nonconfidential brief and, when permitted by the applicable protective order, two copies of the confidential brief.

(3) *Availability to the Public.* The confidential briefs will be made available only to authorized court personnel and must not be made available to the public. After 5 years following the end of all proceedings in the court, the parties may be directed to show cause why confidential briefs (except those protected by statute) should not be made available to the public.

(e) Citations. Opinions of this court and its predecessors should be cited as found in the Federal Reporter. Parallel citations to any other reporters are discouraged. Examples of acceptable citations are:

Guotos v. United States, 552 F.2d 992 (Ct. Cl. 1976).

In re Sponnable, 405 F.2d 578 (CCPA 1969).

South Corporation v. United States, 690 F.2d 1368 (Fed. Cir. 1982) (en banc).

Doe v. Roe, No. 12–345, slip op. (Fed. Cir. Oct. 1, 1982).

(f) Reference to Appendix. Reference in the brief to pages of the joint appendix and, if permitted, of a supplemental appendix must be as short as possible consistent with clarity, e.g., A206 or SA17.

(g) Informal Brief; Appellee's Brief. A pro se party may file an informal brief on the form prescribed by the court. When the appellant or petitioner files an informal brief, the appellee or respondent may elect to file an informal brief. An informal brief filed by an appellee or respondent must contain a statement of the case but otherwise follow the format prescribed for the pro se party.

(h) Briefs in a Transferred Case. When an appeal is transferred to this court by another court of appeals after briefs have been filed, the parties may stipulate to proceed on those briefs instead of filing briefs prescribed by these rules. The stipulation must be filed within 14 days of docketing, and the number of copies of briefs required by Federal Circuit Rule 31(b) must accompany the stipulation. The court may order supplemental briefs.

(i) Citation of Supplemental Authorities. An original and 6 copies of a citation of supplemental authorities must be filed.

[Effective July 1, 1997. Amended effective March 4, 1999; May 1, 2003; June 13, 2003; May 1, 2004; February 4, 2005; May 1, 2006; December 1, 2009.]

Practice Notes

Informal Brief. The informal brief procedure is explained in the Guide for Pro Se Petitioners and Appellants.

Multiple Parties. When there are multiple parties represented by the same counsel or counsel from the same firm, a combined brief must be filed on behalf of all the parties represented by that counsel or firm.

Describing the General Nature of Confidential Material Deleted from the Nonconfidential Brief. The following example is acceptable:

CONFIDENTIAL MATERIAL OMITTED

The material omitted on page 42 describes the circumstances of an alleged lost sale; the material omitted in the first line of page 43 indicates the dollar amount of an alleged revenue loss; the material omitted on page 44 indicates the quantity of the party's inventory and its market share; the material omitted in the text on page 45 describes the distributor's experiences concerning the inventories and order lead times; and the material omitted in the footnote on page 45 describes non-price factors affecting customers' preferences between competing methods.

Justification for Claim of Confidentiality. Unnecessarily designating material in the briefs and appendix as confidential may hinder the court's preparation and issuance of opinions. Counsel must be prepared to justify at oral argument any claim of confidentiality.

FRAP RULE 28.1. CROSS–APPEALS

(a) *Applicability.* This rule applies to a case in which a cross-appeal is filed. Rules 28(a)–(c), 31(a)(1), 32(a)(2), and 32(a)(7)(A)–(B) do not apply to such a case, except as otherwise provided in this rule.

(b) *Designation of Appellant.* The party who files a notice of appeal first is the appellant for the purposes of this rule and Rules 30 and 34. If notices are filed on the same day, the plaintiff in the proceeding below is the appellant. These designations may be modified by the parties' agreement or by court order.

(c) *Briefs.* In a case involving a cross-appeal:

(1) Appellant's Principal Brief. The appellant must file a principal brief in the appeal. That brief must comply with Rule 28(a).

(2) Appellee's Principal and Response Brief. The appellee must file a principal brief in the cross-appeal and must, in the same brief, respond to the principal brief in the appeal. That appellee's brief must comply with Rule 28(a), except that the brief need not include a statement of the case or a statement of the facts unless the appellee is dissatisfied with the appellant's statement.

(3) Appellant's Response and Reply Brief. The appellant must file a brief that responds to the principal brief in the cross-appeal and may, in the same brief, reply to the response in the appeal. That brief must comply with Rule 28(a)(2)–(9) and (11), except that none of the following need appear unless the appellant is dissatisfied with the appellee's statement in the cross-appeal:

(A) the jurisdictional statement;

(B) the statement of the issues;

(C) the statement of the case;

(D) the statement of the facts; and

(E) the statement of the standard of review.

(4) Appellee's Reply Brief. The appellee may file a brief in reply to the response in the cross-appeal. That brief must comply with Rule 28(a)(2)–(3) and (11) and must be limited to the issues presented by the cross-appeal.

(5) No further Briefs. Unless the court permits, no further briefs may be filed in a case involving a cross-appeal.

(d) *Cover.* Except for filings by unrepresented parties, the cover of the appellant's principal brief must be blue; the appellee's principal and response brief, red; the appellant's response and reply brief, yellow; the appellee's reply brief, gray; an intervenor's or amicus curiae's brief, green; and any supplemental brief, tan. The front cover of a brief must contain the information required by Rule 32(a)(2).

(e) *Length.*

(1) Page Limitation. Unless it complies with Rule 28.1(e)(2) and (3), the appellant's principal brief must not exceed 30 pages; the appellee's principal and response brief, 35 pages; the appellant's response and reply brief, 30 pages; and the appellee's reply brief, 15 pages.

(2) Type-Volume Limitation.

(A) The appellant's principal brief or the appellant's response and reply brief is acceptable if:

(i) it contains no more than 14,000 words; or

(ii) it uses a monospaced face and contains no more than 1,300 lines of text.

(B) The appellee's principal and response brief is acceptable if:

(i) it contains no more than 16,500 words; or

(ii) it uses a monospaced face and contains no more than 1,500 lines of text.

(C) The appellee's reply brief is acceptable if it contains no more than half of the type volume specified in Rule 28.1(e)(2)(A).

(3) Certificate of Compliance. A brief submitted under Rule 28.1(e)(2) must comply with Rule 32(a)(7)(C).

(f) *Time to Serve and File a Brief.* Briefs must be served and filed as follows:*

(1) the appellant's principal brief, within ~~40~~ days after the record is filed;

(2) the appellee's principal and response brief, within ~~30~~ days after the appellant's principal brief is served;

(3) the appellant's response and reply brief, within ~~30~~ days after the appellee's principal and response brief is served; and

(4) the appellee's reply brief, within ~~14~~ days after the appellant's response and reply brief is served, but at least ~~7~~ days before argument unless the court, for good cause, allows a later filing.

[Effective May 1, 2006.]

* [**Publisher's Note:** See Circuit Rule 31.]

Practice Notes

Cross-Appeals. A party may file a cross-appeal only when it seeks to modify or overturn the judgment of a trial tribunal. Although a party may present additional arguments in support of the judgment as an appellee, counsel are cautioned against improperly designating an appeal as a cross-appeal when they merely present arguments in support of the judgment. *See* Bailey v. Dart Container Corp., 292 F.3d 1360 (Fed. Cir. 2002). Further, counsel are cautioned, in cases involving a proper cross-appeal, to limit the fourth brief to the issues presented by the cross-appeal. In all cases, counsel should be prepared to defend the filing of a cross-appeal and the propriety of arguments presented in the fourth brief at oral argument.

Time to Serve and File a Brief. Please refer to Federal Circuit Rule 31(a) for brief due dates when there is a cross-appeal.

Clarification to Federal Rule of Appellate Procedure 28.1(4). Where the term "appellee" is used, it refers to the "cross-appellant".

FRAP RULE 29. BRIEF OF AN AMICUS CURIAE

(a) *When Permitted.* The United States or its officer or agency or a state may file an amicus-curiae brief without the consent of the parties or leave of court. Any other amicus curiae may file a brief only by leave of court or if the brief states that all parties have consented to its filing.

(b) *Motion for Leave to File.* The motion must be accompanied by the proposed brief and state:

(1) the movant's interest; and

(2) the reason why an amicus brief is desirable and why the matters asserted are relevant to the disposition of the case.

(c) *Contents and Form.* An amicus brief must comply with Rule 32. In addition to the requirements of Rule 32, the cover must identify the party or parties supported and indicate whether the brief supports affirmance or reversal. An amicus brief need not comply with Rule 28, but must include the following:

(1) if the amicus curiae is a corporation, a disclosure statement like that required of parties by Rule 26.1;

(2) a table of contents, with page references;

(3) a table of authorities—cases (alphabetically arranged), statutes and other authorities—with references to the pages of the brief where they are cited;

(4) a concise statement of the identity of the amicus curiae, its interest in the case, and the source of its authority to file;

(5) unless the amicus curiae is one listed in the first sentence of Rule 29(a), a statement that indicates whether:

(A) a party's counsel authored the brief in whole or in part;

(B) a party or a party's counsel contributed money that was intended to fund preparing or submitting the brief; and

(C) a person—other than the amicus curiae, its members, or its counsel—contributed money that was intended to fund preparing or submitting the brief and, if so, identifies each such person;

(6) an argument, which may be preceded by a summary and which need not include a statement of the applicable standard of review; and

(7) a certificate of compliance, if required by Rule 32(a)(7).

(d) *Length.* Except by the court's permission, an amicus brief may be no more than one-half the maximum length authorized by these rules for a party's principal brief. If the court grants a party permission to file a longer brief, that extension does not affect the length of an amicus brief.

(e) *Time for Filing.* An amicus curiae must file its brief, accompanied by a motion for filing when necessary, no later than 7 days after the principal brief of the party being supported is filed. An amicus curiae that does not support either party must file its brief no later than 7 days after the appellant's or petitioner's principal brief is filed. A court may grant leave for later filing, specifying the time within which an opposing party may answer.

(f) *Reply Brief.* Except by the court's permission, an amicus curiae may not file a reply brief.

(g) *Oral Argument.* An amicus curiae may participate in oral argument only with the court's permission.

LOCAL RULE 29. BRIEF OF AN AMICUS CURIAE

(a) Content; Form. In addition to the contents required by Federal Rule of Appellate Procedure 29, the brief of an amicus curiae must include a certificate of interest (see Federal Circuit Rule 47.4) in front of the table of contents.

(b) List of Amicus Curiae. The clerk will maintain a list of bar associations and other organizations to be invited to file amicus curiae briefs when the court directs. Bar associations and other organizations will be placed on the list if they request. The request must be renewed annually not later than October 1.

(c) Consent. If an amicus brief is filed on consent of all parties, then no motion for leave is required and the brief should state, pursuant to Federal Rule of Appellate Procedure 29(a), that all parties have consented to its filing.

[Effective July 1, 1997. Amended effective March 4, 1999; May 1, 2004; December 1, 2009; December 1, 2011.]

Practice Note

An amicus curiae must file an entry of appearance and a certificate of interest, if applicable. *See* Federal Circuit Rules 47.3, 47.4, and Forms 8 and 9.

FRAP RULE 30. APPENDIX TO THE BRIEFS

(a) *Appellant's Responsibility.*

(1) Contents of the Appendix. The appellant must prepare and file an appendix to the briefs containing:

(A) the relevant docket entries in the proceeding below;

(B) the relevant portions of the pleadings, charge, findings, or opinion;

(C) the judgment, order, or decision in question; and

~~(D) other parts of the record to which the parties wish to direct the court's attention.~~

(2) Excluded Material. ~~Memoranda of law in the district court should not be included in the appendix unless they have independent relevance.~~ Parts of the record may be relied on by the court or the parties even though not included in the appendix.

(3) Time to File; Number of Copies. Unless filing is deferred under Rule 30(c), the appellant must file ~~10~~ copies of the appendix with the brief and must serve one copy on counsel for each party separately represented. An unrepresented party proceeding in forma pauperis must file 4 legible copies with the clerk, and one copy must be served on counsel for each separately represented party. The court may by local rule or by order in a particular case require the filing or service of a different number.

(b) *All Parties' Responsibilities.*

~~(1) Determining the Contents of the Appendix.~~

(2) Costs of Appendix. Unless the parties agree otherwise, the appellant must pay the cost of the appendix. ~~If the appellant considers parts of the record designated by the appellee to be unnecessary, the appellant may advise the appellee, who must then advance the cost of including those parts.~~ The cost of the appendix is a taxable cost. But if any party causes unnecessary parts of the record to be included in the appendix, the court may impose the cost of those parts on that party. Each circuit must, by local rule, provide for sanctions against attorneys who unreasonably and vexatiously increase litigation costs by including unnecessary material in the appendix.

(c) *Deferred Appendix.*

(1) Deferral Until After Briefs Are Filed. The court may provide by rule for classes of cases or by order in a particular case that preparation of the appendix may be deferred until after the briefs have been filed ~~and that the appendix may be filed 21 days after the appellee's brief is served. Even though the filing of the appendix may be deferred, Rule 30(b) applies; except that a party must designate the parts of the record it wants included in the appendix when it serves its brief, and need not include a statement of the issues presented.~~

~~(2) References to the Record.~~

(d) *Format of the Appendix.* The appendix must begin with a table of contents identifying the page at which each part begins. The relevant docket entries must follow the table of contents. Other parts of the record must follow chronologically. ~~When pages from the transcript of proceedings are placed in the appendix, the transcript page numbers must be shown in brackets immediately before the included pages. Omissions in the text of papers or of the transcript must be indicated by asterisks. Immaterial formal matters (captions, subscriptions, acknowledgments, etc.) should be omitted.~~

(e) *Reproduction of Exhibits.* Exhibits designated for inclusion in the appendix may be reproduced in a separate volume, or volumes, suitably indexed. Four copies must be filed with the appendix, and one copy must be served on counsel for each separately represented party. If a transcript of a proceeding before an administrative agency, board, commission, or officer was used in a district-court action and has been designated for inclusion in the appendix, the transcript must be placed in the appendix as an exhibit.

(f) *Appeal on the Original Record Without an Appendix.* The court may, either by rule for all cases or classes of cases or by order in a particular case, dispense with the appendix and permit an appeal to proceed on the original record with any copies of the record, or relevant parts, that the court may order the parties to file.

LOCAL RULE 30. APPENDIX TO THE BRIEFS

(a) Purpose; Content of Appendix; Time for Filing; Number of Copies; Cover; Service.

(1) *Purpose.* The purpose of this rule is to limit the size of the appendix of documentary materials that is printed and filed with the court. The rule also authorizes a supplementary video recording media appendix under some circumstances.

(2) *Contents; Indiscriminate Referencing to Blocks of the Record Prohibited.*

(A) In addition to the matters required by Federal Rule of Appellate Procedure 30(a)(1)(A), (B), and (C), the appendix must include:

(i) the entire docket sheet from the proceedings below;

(ii) in an appeal from a jury case, the judge's charge, the jury's verdict, and the jury's responses to interrogatories;

(iii) in an appeal involving a patent, the patent in suit in its entirety. The patent in suit may also be included as an addendum to appellant's initial brief. Any other patents included in an appendix must be included in their entirety; and

(iv) any nonprecedential opinion or order cited in accordance with Federal Circuit Rule 32.1(c).

(B) Parts of the record authorized by Federal Rule of Appellate Procedure 30(a)(1)(D) must not be included in the appendix unless they are actually referenced in the briefs, but the parties are encouraged to include in the appendix sufficient surrounding transcript pages to provide context for a referenced transcript excerpt.

(C) Indiscriminate referencing in briefs to blocks of record pages or inclusion of unnecessary pages in the appendix is prohibited.

(D) If the appellant considers that parts of the record have been referenced in violation of this rule, the appellant may so advise the appellee and the appellee must advance the costs of including those parts in the appendix.

(E) The following must not be included in the appendix except by leave of the court, and any motion for leave must state the number of pages requested to be included:

(i) briefs and memoranda in their entirety (except as otherwise provided in Federal Circuit Rule 30);

(ii) notices;

(iii) subpoenas—except where the enforcement or validity of a subpoena is at issue;

(iv) summonses—except in appeals from the Court of International Trade;

(v) motions to extend time; or

(vi) jury lists.

(F) Nothing in this Federal Circuit Rule 30 prohibits from designation and inclusion in an appendix:

(i) an examiner's answer in an ex parte patent case;

(ii) a trademark examining attorney's appeal brief in an ex parte trademark case; or

(iii) the briefs and memoranda in their entirety in a case where the only issue is the propriety of summary judgment.

(3) *Additional Mandatory Appendix Items in Patent and Trademark Office Appeals.* In an appeal from the Patent and Trademark Office, unless the parties mutually agree otherwise, the appendix must include:

(A) a copy of all rejected claims in an ex parte patent appeal;

(B) a copy of all counts in a patent interference appeal; or

(C) a copy of the trademark sought to be registered or cancelled and a copy of any registration relied on to refuse or oppose registration or to seek cancellation of a registered mark in an ex parte or an inter partes trademark appeal.

(4) *Time for Filing.* The appellant must serve and file an appendix within 7 days after the last reply brief is served and filed. When there is no cross appeal, if the appellant does not file a reply brief, the appendix must be served and filed within the time for filing the reply brief. In a cross appeal, if the cross appellant does not file a reply brief, the appendix must be served and filed within 7 days after the time for filing the cross appellant's reply brief has expired.

(5) *Number of Copies.* Twelve copies of the appendix must be filed with the court.

(6) *Multi-Volume Appendix: Covers and Page Numbers.* A multi-volume appendix must have a volume number in roman numerals and the pages included in the volume listed at the top of the cover of each volume (e.g., Volume II, Pages 542 to 813).

(7) *Service.* Two copies of the appendix must be served on counsel for each party separately represented. One copy must be served on each pro se party.

(8) *Consequence of Failing to File an Appendix.* If the appellant fails to file an appendix, the clerk is authorized to dismiss the case.

(b) Determination of Contents of Appendix; Designation of Materials; Extension of Time.

(1) The parties are encouraged to agree on the contents of an appendix that will comply with this Federal Circuit Rule 30.

(2) In the absence of an agreement, the appellant must, within 14 days after docketing in an appeal from a court or after service of the certified list or index in a petition for review or appeal from an agency, serve on the appellee or cross appellant a designation of materials from which the appendix will be prepared and a statement of the issues to be presented for review. The appellee or cross appellant may, within 14 days after receiving the designation, serve on the appellant a counterdesignation of additional parts to be included in the appendix.

(3) A designation or counterdesignation must not be filed with the court.

(4) *Table of Page Numbers; Physical Compilation.*

(A) Within 14 days after the parties have designated the material for the appendix, the appellant must assign consecutive page numbers to the designated material and serve on all parties a table reflecting the page numbers of each item designated.

(B) If not prohibited in an outstanding protective order, instead of the table the appellant may—at the appellant's option—serve on the parties one copy of a physical compilation of the designated material with the assigned page numbers shown. This copy may be in micrographic format.

(C) The first page numbers in the designated material must be assigned to the judgment or order appealed from and any opinion, memorandum, or findings and conclusions supporting it.

(D) The table of page numbers or the physical compilation of the designated material, whichever is used, must not be filed with the court. If all designated material comprises no more than 100 pages, Federal Circuit Rule 30(d) applies.

(5) *Extension of Time Limits.* The time limits for designating, counterdesignating, and compiling the table may be extended by agreement of the parties without seeking leave of the court, as long as an extension of the time is not required for filing appellant's brief. But if a transcript of the proceedings is required before the material can be designated and if the transcript has been ordered but not completed within the time prescribed by this rule, the appellant must move for an extension of time within which to designate the material. An affidavit explaining in detail what has been done to expedite transcription of the trial proceedings must be attached to the motion.

(6) *Preparation of Appendix.* The appellant must prepare the appendix to be filed with the court from the designated material by selecting from that material only items required by these rules and pages specifically referred to in the briefs of the parties. Pages of the designated material not referenced in the briefs—other than items required by these rules—must be omitted from the appendix filed with the court.

(c) Format of Appendix; Pagination.

(1) *Arrangement of Appendix.* Federal Rule of Appellate Procedure 30(d) governs the arrangement of the appendix, except the judgment or order appealed from and any opinion, memorandum, or findings and conclusions supporting it must be placed first in the appendix. (See Federal Circuit Rule 28(a)(12) for a duplicative requirement of the appellant's or petitioner's initial brief.)

(2) *Pagination.* The page numbers used in the appendix must be the page numbers assigned by the appellant or petitioner to the designated material in accordance with Federal Circuit Rule 30(b). The page number must appear centered in the bottom margin of each page in the appendix. Other pagination marks must be redacted if necessary to avoid confusion. The materials in the appendix must be in numerical order according to the page numbers the appellant assigned to the designated materials. Omission of pages need not be noted, e.g., page 102 may be followed by page 230 without stating that pages 103–229 are not reproduced in the appendix. References in the briefs must be only to the page numbers of the appendix.

(3) *Printing.* Pages in an appendix—even when filing a combined brief and appendix—may be printed on both sides. To the extent possible, the court encourages this.

(d) Combined Brief and Appendix.

(1) When a brief and appendix are combined, the cover must so indicate.

(2) If all designated material comprises no more than 100 pages, all of it may be included in the appendix, in which case it may be bound together with the appellant's or petitioner's initial brief and the brief must be filed as provided in Federal Circuit Rule 31(a).

(e) Appendix in a Pro Se Case. If an appellant appearing pro se files an inadequate appendix, the appellee may file with its brief an appendix containing material permitted by Federal Circuit Rule 30(a)(2).

(f) Separate or Supplemental Appendix. If the appellant has failed to participate in determining the contents of an appendix or has filed an inadequate appendix, the United States or an officer or agency of the United States, as the appellee, may file a separate or supplemental appendix containing material permitted by Federal Circuit Rule 30(a)(2). The cover must be red. If the separate or supplemental appendix contains no more than 100 pages, it may be bound together with the appellee's initial brief. Except as provided in Federal Circuit Rule 30(e) and (f), no party may file a separate or supplemental appendix without leave of the court.

(g) Costs. The costs of the table of page numbers or the copy of the physical compilation of the designated material authorized in Federal Circuit Rule 30(b)(4) and of the appendix, including the separate segments authorized in Federal Circuit Rule 30(h), may be assessed as provided in Federal Rule of Appellate Procedure 30(b)(2).

(h) Appendices Containing Material Subject to a Protective Order.

(1) *Two Sets of Appendices.* If a party refers in appendices to material subject to confidentiality mandated by statute or to a judicial or administrative protective order, two sets of appendices must be filed.

(A) Confidential set; labeling; number of copies. One set of appendices, consisting of 12 copies of the complete appendix, must be labeled "confidential" and filed with the court. If confidentiality will end on a date certain or upon the happening of an event, this must be stated on the cover, e.g., "CONFIDENTIAL UNTIL [DATE]," or "CONFIDENTIAL DURING JUDICIAL REVIEW." The confidential appendix must include at the beginning (i.e., in front of the judgment or order appealed from) pertinent excerpts of any statutes imposing confidentiality or the entirety of any judicial or administrative protective order. Each page containing confidential material must enclose this material in brackets or indicate this material by highlighting.

(B) Nonconfidential set; labeling; number of copies. The second set of appendices, consisting of the original and four copies from which confidential matter has been deleted, must be labeled "nonconfidential" and filed with the court. Each page from which material subject to a protective order has been deleted must bear a legend so stating. The table of contents of a nonconfidential appendix must describe the general nature of the confidential material that has been deleted.

(2) *Service.* Each party to the appeal must be served two copies of the nonconfidential appendices and, when permitted by the applicable protective order, two copies of the confidential appendices.

(3) *Availability to the Public.* The confidential appendices will be made available only to authorized court personnel and must not be made available to the public. After 5 years following the end of all proceedings in the court, the parties may be directed to show cause why confidential appendices (except those protected by statute) should not be made available to the public.

(i) Appendix to Informal Brief. The appendix to an informal brief must contain the judgment and opinion of the trial court or the final order of an administrative agency. The initial decision of the administrative judge must also be included in the appendix in a Merit Systems Protection Board case.

(j) Supplementary Video Recording Media Appendix. When the record on appeal or review has been perpetuated in whole or in part on video recording media in accordance with the rules of the court or agency, those video recording media portions of the record that would properly be included in the appendix if they were in documentary form may be included in a supplementary video recording media appendix. Four copies must be filed.

[Effective July 1, 1997. Amended effective March 4, 1999; May 1, 2003; May 1, 2004; May 1, 2006; December 1, 2009.]

Practice Notes

Filing Page Proof Copies Prohibited; Notice of New References in Cross-Appellant's Reply Brief. Preparing the appendix requires extensive cooperation between the parties. Federal Circuit Rule 30, unlike Federal Rule of Appellate Procedure 30, does not permit filing page proof copies of briefs. An appendix prepared without careful attention to Federal Circuit Rule 30 may be rejected when submitted and may result in dismissal. To expedite preparing the joint appendix, a cross-appellant will notify the appellant promptly on being served appellant's reply brief whether the cross-appellant will file a reply brief and, if so, whether it will refer to pages not referenced in the briefs already filed, listing any such pages.

Dispensing with the Appendix. A motion to dispense with the appendix will be granted only in extraordinary circumstances.

Briefs and Memoranda. Briefs and memoranda presented to the trial court or agency may not ordinarily be included in their entirety in the appendix, but individual pages may be included when it is necessary to refer to them in the appellate briefs.

Table of Contents or Index. Parties are encouraged to include a table of contents or index in each volume of the appendix.

FRAP RULE 31. SERVING AND FILING BRIEFS

(a) *Time to Serve and File a Brief.*

(1) The appellant must serve and file a brief ~~within 40 days after the record is filed~~. The appel-

lee must serve and file a brief ~~within 30 days~~ after the appellant's brief is served. The appellant may serve and file a reply brief within 14 days after service of the appellee's brief but a reply brief must be filed at least 7 days before argument, unless the court, for good cause, allows a later filing.

(2) A court of appeals that routinely considers cases on the merits promptly after the briefs are filed may shorten the time to serve and file briefs, either by local rule or by order in a particular case.

(b) *Number of Copies.* ~~Twenty-five~~ copies of each brief must be filed with the clerk and 2 copies must be served on each unrepresented party and on counsel for each separately represented party. An unrepresented party proceeding in forma pauperis must file 4 legible copies with the clerk, and one copy must be served on each unrepresented party and on counsel for each separately represented party. The court may by local rule or by order in a particular case require the filing or service of a different number.

(c) *Consequence of Failure to File.* If an appellant fails to file a brief within the time provided by this rule, or within an extended time, an appellee may move to dismiss the appeal. An appellee who fails to file a brief will not be heard at oral argument unless the court grants permission.

LOCAL RULE 31. SERVING AND FILING BRIEFS

(a) Time for Service and Filing.

(1) *Brief of Appellant or Petitioner.*

(A) In an appeal from a court, the appellant must serve and file its initial brief within 60 days after docketing. Docketing a cross-appeal does not affect the time for serving and filing the appellant's initial brief.

(B) In an appeal from an agency, the petitioner or appellant must serve and file its initial brief within 60 days after the certified list or index is served pursuant to Federal Circuit Rule 17(c). In an appeal from the Patent and Trademark Office, the appellant's brief is due within 60 days after the date of docketing.

(C) When two or more appellants or petitioners choose to proceed by filing a single brief, the initial brief must be served and filed no later than the latest date on which the initial brief of any of these appellants or petitioners is due.

(2) *Brief of Appellee or Cross-Appellant.* The appellee or cross-appellant must serve and file its initial brief within 40 days after appellant's brief is served.

(3) *Cross-Appeal.* In a cross-appeal:

(A) the appellant must serve and file its reply brief within 40 days after cross-appellant's brief is served; and

(B) the cross-appellant must serve and file its reply brief within 14 days after appellant's reply brief is served.

(4) *Single Brief Responding to Multiple Parties.* A single brief that responds to the briefs of multiple parties must be served and filed within the time prescribed after service of the last of these briefs or, if no such brief is filed, after the time expires for filing the last of these briefs.

(5) *Reply Brief; Oral Argument.* A reply brief that is filed within 7 days of oral argument must be served so that it reaches all parties before the argument.

(b) Number of Copies. Except for briefs containing material subject to a protective order (see Federal Circuit Rule 28(d)), 12 copies of each brief, including the original or a copy designated as the original, must be filed with the court and 2 copies must be served on the principal counsel for each party, intervenor, and amicus curiae separately represented.

(c) Certain Motions Suspend the Due Date of the Next Brief. When a motion is filed that, if granted, would terminate the appeal, the time to serve and file the next brief due is suspended. If the motion is denied, the next brief becomes due, unless the court orders otherwise, within the balance of the time remaining under this rule when the motion was filed, but not fewer than 14 days from the date of the order.

(d) Consequence of Failure to File a Brief by Appellant or Petitioner. If the appellant fails to file an initial brief, the clerk is authorized to dismiss the case.

(e) Informal Brief; Time for Filing; Number of Copies.

(1) *Brief of Appellant or Petitioner.*

(A) In an appeal from a court, a pro se appellant filing an informal brief must serve and file the brief within 21 days after the appeal is docketed.

(B) In a petition for review or an appeal from an agency, a pro se petitioner or appellant filing an informal brief must serve and file the brief within 21 days after the certified list or index is served pursuant to Federal Circuit Rule 17(c) or within 21 days after docketing, whichever is later.

(2) *Brief of Appellee or Respondent.* An appellee or respondent filing an informal brief must serve and file the brief within 21 days after petitioner's or appellant's brief is served or within 21 days after the certified list or index is served pursuant to Federal Circuit Rule 17(c), whichever is later.

(3) *Reply Brief.* When an informal brief is used, any reply brief must be served within 14 days after respondent's or appellee's brief is served.

(4) *Number of Copies.* An original and 3 copies of each informal brief must be filed with the court and one copy must be served on each party.

[Effective July 1, 1997. Amended effective March 4, 1999; May 1, 2003; May 1, 2004; December 1, 2009.]

Practice Notes

Reply Briefs Due at Least 7 Days Before Oral Argument; Expedited Service. The reply brief of the appellant (or cross-appellant in a cross-appeal) is due to be served and filed within 14 days of the preceding brief. The 7–day provision of Federal Rule of Appellate Procedure 31(a)(1) means that the reply period is automatically shortened if the end of the 14–day period is within 7 days of oral argument. The briefing schedule will not ordinarily run so close to oral argument, but if it does—because of extensions or otherwise—the reply brief must be filed early. Federal Circuit Rule 31(a)(5) provides that when that happens, a reply brief filed within 7 days of oral argument must be filed and served in an expedited manner. Regular mail would be inappropriate.

Consolidated Appeals. In consolidated appeals in which more than one appellant filed a notice of appeal, the opening brief of all appellants will be governed by the docketing date of the last filed appeal.

Consolidated Cross-Appeals. In consolidated cross-appeals, the briefing schedule is computed according to the docketing date of the first appeal.

FRAP RULE 32. FORM OF BRIEFS, APPENDICES, AND OTHER PAPERS

(a) *Form of a Brief.*

(1) Reproduction.

(A) A brief may be reproduced by any process that yields a clear black image on light paper. The paper must be opaque and unglazed. Only one side of the paper may be used.

(B) Text must be reproduced with a clarity that equals or exceeds the output of a laser printer.

(C) Photographs, illustrations, and tables may be reproduced by any method that results in a good copy of the original; a glossy finish is acceptable if the original is glossy.

(2) Cover. Except for filings by unrepresented parties, the cover of the appellant's brief must be blue; the appellee's, red; an intervenor's or amicus curiae's, green; any reply brief, gray; and any supplemental brief, tan. The front cover of a brief must contain:

(A) the number of the case centered at the top;

(B) the name of the court;

(C) the title of the case (see Rule 12(a));

(D) the nature of the proceeding (e.g., Appeal, Petition for Review) and the name of the court, agency, or board below;

(E) the title of the brief, identifying the party or parties for whom the brief is filed; and

(F) the name, office address, and telephone number of counsel representing the party for whom the brief is filed.

(3) Binding. The brief must be bound in any manner that is secure, does not obscure the text, and permits the brief to lie reasonably flat when open.

(4) Paper Size, Line Spacing, and Margins. The brief must be on 8½ by 11 inch paper. The text must be double-spaced, but quotations more than two lines long may be indented and single-spaced. Headings and footnotes may be single-spaced. Margins must be at least one inch on all four sides. Page numbers may be placed in the margins, but no text may appear there.

(5) Typeface. Either a proportionally spaced or a monospaced face may be used.

(A) A proportionally spaced face must include serifs, but sans-serif type may be used in headings and captions. A proportionally spaced face must be 14–point or larger.

(B) A monospaced face may not contain more than 10½ characters per inch.

(6) Type Styles. A brief must be set in a plain, roman style, although italics or boldface may be used for emphasis. Case names must be italicized or underlined.

(7) Length.

(A) Page Limitation. A principal brief may not exceed 30 pages, or a reply brief 15 pages, unless it complies with Rule 32(a)(7)(B) and (C).

(B) Type-Volume Limitation.

(i) A principal brief is acceptable if:

• it contains no more than 14,000 words;

• or it uses a monospaced face and contains no more than 1,300 lines of text.

(ii) A reply brief is acceptable if it contains no more than half of the type volume specified in Rule 32(a)(7)(B)(i).

(iii) Headings, footnotes, and quotations count toward the word and line limitations. The corporate disclosure statement, table of contents, table of citations, statement with respect to oral argument, any addendum containing statutes, rules or regulations, and any certificates of counsel do not count toward the limitation.

(C) Certificate of Compliance.

(i) A brief submitted under Rules 28.1(e)(2) or 32(a)(7)(B) must include a certificate by the attorney, or an unrepresented party, that the brief complies with the type-volume limitation.

The person preparing the certificate may rely on the word or line count of the word-processing system used to prepare the brief. The certificate must state either:

- **the number of words in the brief; or**
- **the number of lines of monospaced type in the brief.**

(ii) Form 6 (Federal Circuit Form 19 herein) in the Appendix of Forms is a suggested form of a certificate of compliance. Use of Form 6 must be regarded as sufficient to meet the requirements of Rules 28.1(e)(3) and 32(a)(7)(C)(i).

(b) *Form of an Appendix.* An appendix must comply with Rule 32(a)(1), (2), (3), and (4), with the following exceptions:

(1) The cover of a separately bound appendix must be white.

(2) An appendix may include a legible photocopy of any document found in the record or of a printed judicial or agency decision.

(3) When necessary to facilitate inclusion of odd-sized documents such as technical drawings, an appendix may be a size other than 8½ by 11 inches, and need not lie reasonably flat when opened.

(c) *Form of Other Papers.*

(1) Motion. The form of a motion is governed by Rule 27(d).

(2) Other Papers. Any other paper, including a petition for panel rehearing and a petition for hearing or rehearing en banc, and any response to such a petition, must be reproduced in the manner prescribed by Rule 32(a), with the following exceptions:

(A) A cover is not necessary if the caption and signature page of the paper together contain the information required by Rule 32(a)(2). If a cover is used, it must be white.

(B) Rule 32(a)(7) does not apply.

(d) *Signature.* Every brief, motion, or other paper filed with the court must be signed by the party filing the paper or, if the party is represented, by one of the party's attorneys.

(e) *Local Variation.* Every court of appeals must accept documents that comply with the form requirements of this rule. By local rule or order in a particular case a court of appeals may accept documents that do not meet all of the form requirements of this rule.

LOCAL RULE 32. FORM OF BRIEFS, APPENDICES, AND OTHER PAPERS

(a) Nonconforming Brief. The clerk may refuse to file any brief that has not been printed or bound in conformity with Federal Rule of Appellate Procedure 32.

(b) Exclusion From Type–Volume Limitation. In addition to the items listed in Federal Rule of Appellate Procedure 32(a)(7)(B)(iii) that are not counted in the type-volume limitation of Federal Rule of Appellate Procedure 32(a)(7)(B), the following items do not count toward that limitation:

(1) the certificate of interest;

(2) the statement of related cases; and

(3) the addendum in an initial brief of an appellant or petitioner.

(c) Informal Brief. An informal brief must be prepared on a form provided by the clerk. The form contains instructions for preparing and filing an informal brief. An informal brief should be typewritten, but block printing or, as a last resort, legible handwriting is permitted. An informal brief including continuation pages must not exceed 30 pages of typewritten double-spaced text or its equivalent.

(d) Form of Appendix. Pages in an appendix—even when filing a combined brief and appendix—may be printed on both sides. To the extent possible, the court encourages this.

(e) Filing Corresponding Brief on Compact Disc. In addition to the filing of a paper brief, a party may file a corresponding brief contained on a compact disc—read only memory (CD–ROM), subject to the following requirements.

(1) *Consent; Motion.* Within 14 days of docketing an appeal, a party intending to file a corresponding brief must ascertain whether any other party consents or objects. If the other parties consent, the filing party must promptly file with the court a notice of intent to file a corresponding brief. If any other party does not consent, the party seeking to file a corresponding brief must promptly file a motion for leave with the court. If no response is filed within 7 days, the clerk will grant the motion for leave to file a corresponding brief. The court will deny a motion for leave to file a corresponding brief only if an opposing party demonstrates substantial prejudice.

(2) *Content.* A corresponding brief must be identical in content to the paper brief. A corresponding brief may provide hypertext links to the complete versions of material that was part of the record below. Hypertext links to other material must be confined to materials such as cases, statutes, treatises, law review

articles, and similar authorities. A corresponding brief must be self-contained and static.

(3) *Statement Concerning Instructions and Viruses.* A corresponding brief must be accompanied by a statement, preferably within or attached to the packaging, that:

(A) sets forth the instructions for viewing the brief and the minimum equipment required for viewing; and

(B) verifies the absence of computer viruses and lists the software used to ensure that the brief is virus-free.

(4) *Time for Filing.* A corresponding brief, if any, must be filed no later than the time for filing the joint appendix.

(5) *Filing and Service.* Except for the time of filing, a corresponding brief must be filed and served in the same manner and the same number of copies as the paper brief.

(6) *Single CD-ROM.* All parties to an appeal who intend to file a corresponding CD-ROM brief are encouraged to cooperate in placing all such briefs on a single CD-ROM.

(7) *Table of Contents.* Parties filing a corresponding brief are encouraged to include a table of contents with links to all of the items required in a joint appendix under Federal Rule of Appellate Procedure 30 and Federal Circuit Rule 30 and to all other parts of the record contained on the corresponding brief.

(8) *Labeling.* A label with the caption of the case, the number of the case, and the types of briefs included on the CD-ROM must be included on both the packaging and the CD-ROM.

[Effective July 1, 1997. Amended effective March 4, 1999; February 4, 2000; May 1, 2004; May 1, 2006.]

Practice Notes

Preferred Cover. In addition to the requirements of Federal Rule of Appellate Procedure 32(a)(2)(D), the court encourages inclusion on the cover of the name of the judge, when applicable, from whose judgment appeal is taken.

Preferred Binding. The court prefers that a brief be securely bound along the left margin to ensure that the bound copy will not loosen or fall apart; that a brief lie flat when open; that a ring-type binding, plastic or metal, or a binding that protrudes from the front and back covers (e.g., VeloBind) not be used; and that any externally positioned staple be covered with tape.

Print Size of Briefs. Counsel should avoid photoreproduction that reduces the print size of the original smaller than the size required by Federal Rule of Appellate Procedure 32.

Footnotes. The typeface requirements of Federal Rule of Appellate Procedure 32(a)(5) apply to all text in the brief, including footnotes.

Brief Covers in Cross-Appeals. The color of the cover of the cross-appellant's principal brief is red. The color of the covers of appellant's reply brief is yellow and cross-appellant's reply brief is gray.

Copies of Patent Documents. Oversize patent documents reproduced in a brief or appendix should be photoreduced to 8½ by 11 inches if readability can be maintained; otherwise, they should be folded and bound so they do not protrude from the covers of the brief or appendix.

Errata; Corrections to be made by Counsel or a Party. A brief may not be corrected merely by appending an errata sheet. Corrections, which must be limited to nonsubstantive matters, must be made by counsel or a party using suitable means directly in the briefs in the clerk's office. As a last resort, briefs may be replaced. Corrected or replacement briefs must be re-served, but the time to file a brief in response to a corrected or replaced brief runs from service of the original brief. A corrected or replacement brief should so indicate on the cover. Counsel or a party must file a "Notice of Correction" with the court and serve opposing counsel or unrepresented party, specifically delineating each correction. Any individual making corrections on briefs in the clerk's office must provide written authorization and present proper photo identification.

Testimony in the Appendix. To reduce bulk in the appendix, the use of condensed, columnar transcripts of testimony is encouraged.

Certificate of Compliance. Federal Rule of Appellate Procedure 32(a)(7)(C)(ii) states that the use of Federal Rules of Appellate Procedure Form 6 is sufficient to satisfy the requirements of Rule 32(a)(7)(C)(i). That form is reproduced as Federal Circuit Form 19. Parties are reminded that some software programs do not automatically include footnotes. When certain text is marked for word count or line count purposes, a party may need to separately mark text in footnotes and include those words or lines in the certified count. It is the responsibility of the filing party to ensure that its certificate of compliance is accurate.

FRAP RULE 32.1. CITING JUDICIAL DISPOSITIONS

(a) *Citation Permitted.* A court may not prohibit or restrict the citation of federal judicial opinions, orders, judgments, or other written dispositions that have been:

(i) designated as "unpublished," "not for publication," "non-precedential," "not precedent," or the like; and

(ii) issued on or after January 1, 2007.

(b) *Copies Required.* If a party cites a federal judicial opinion, order, judgment, or other written disposition that is not available in a publicly accessible electronic database, the party must file and serve a copy of that opinion, order, judgment, or disposition with the brief or other paper in which it is cited.

LOCAL RULE 32.1. CITING JUDICIAL DISPOSITIONS

(a) Disposition of Appeal, Motion, or Petition. Disposition of an appeal may be announced in an opinion; disposition of a motion or petition may be announced in an order. An appeal may also be disposed of in a judgment of affirmance without opinion pursuant to Federal Circuit Rule 36. A nonprecedential disposition shall bear a legend designating it as nonprecedential. A precedential disposition shall bear no legend.

(b) Nonprecedential Opinion or Order. An opinion or order which is designated as nonprecedential is one determined by the panel issuing it as not adding significantly to the body of law.

(c) Parties' Citation of Nonprecedential Dispositions. Parties are not prohibited or restricted from citing nonprecedential dispositions issued after January 1, 2007. This rule does not preclude assertion of claim preclusion, issue preclusion, judicial estoppel, law of the case, and the like based on a nonprecedential disposition issued before that date.

(d) Court's Consideration of Nonprecedential Dispositions. The court may refer to a nonprecedential disposition in an opinion or order and may look to a nonprecedential disposition for guidance or persuasive reasoning, but will not give one of its own nonprecedential dispositions the effect of binding precedent. The court will not consider nonprecedential dispositions of another court as binding precedent of that court unless the rules of that court so provide.

(e) Request to Make an Opinion or Order Precedential; Time for Filing. Within 60 days after any nonprecedential opinion or order is issued, any person may request, with accompanying reasons, that the opinion or order be reissued as precedential. An original and 6 copies of the request must be filed with the court. The request will be considered by the panel that rendered the disposition. The requester must notify the court and the parties of any case that person knows to be pending that would be determined or affected by reissuance as precedential. Parties to pending cases who have a stake in the outcome of a decision to make precedential must be given an opportunity to respond. If the request is granted, the opinion or order may be revised as appropriate.

(f) Public Records. All dispositions by the court in any form will be in writing and are public records.

[Effective December 1, 2006. Amended effective June 1, 2011.]

Practice Notes

Filing an Opinion. An opinion is issued when ready. No particular day of the week is considered a "down day." An opinion is not issued on a holiday, as defined in Federal Rule of Appellate Procedure 26 and Federal Circuit Rule 26. The judgment is entered on the day the opinion is filed with the clerk and mailed to the parties.

Availability of an Opinion. The court's precedential and nonprecedential opinions are available in a variety of commercially available print and electronic media.

Subscriptions. Subscriptions to opinions are not available from the court, but are available from several commercial sources.

Information About an Opinion. A disposition sheet containing information about decisions rendered, opinions issued, and actions taken on petitions for rehearing is posted daily in the Clerk's Office. The information about opinions is also available after 11:00 a.m. daily on a telephone recording; call (202) 275–8030. On Fridays, the opinions for the entire week are included on the recording.

The court's opinions, rules, and other information are also available on the Federal Circuit web site: www.cafc.uscourts.gov.

Copies of the court's opinions also may be purchased from the administrative services office of the court for $2.

Request to Make an Opinion or Order Precedential. It is improper to refer in a brief to a request to make an opinion or order precedential before the request has been acted on. The opinion or order that is subject to the request remains nonprecedential unless and until the court grants the request.

FRAP RULE 33. APPEAL CONFERENCES

The court may direct the attorneys—and, when appropriate, the parties—to participate in one or more conferences to address any matter that may aid in disposing of the proceedings, including simplifying the issues and discussing settlement. A judge or other person designated by the court may preside over the conference, which may be conducted in person or by telephone. Before a settlement conference, the attorneys must consult with their clients and obtain as much authority as feasible to settle the case. The court may, as a result of the conference, enter an order controlling the course of the proceedings or implementing any settlement agreement.

LOCAL RULE 33. APPEAL CONFERENCES

(a) Settlement Discussion; Joint Statement of Compliance or Agreement to Dismiss.

(1) When all the parties are represented by counsel, within 7 days after the first two briefs in an appeal or the first three briefs in a cross appeal are served and filed, the parties through counsel must discuss settlement in appeals under 28 U.S.C. §§ 1292(c)(1)–(2); 1295(a)(1); 1295(a)(4)(A) [with respect to patent interferences only]; 1295(a)(4)(B) [with respect to inter partes proceedings only]; 1295(a)(4)(C) [with respect to civil actions under 35 U.S.C. § 146 only]; and 1295(a)(6).

(2) No later than the time for filing a separate appendix under Federal Circuit Rule 30(a)(4), the parties must file one copy of either of the following (select only one):

(A) a joint statement of compliance with this rule indicating that settlement discussions have been conducted; or

(B) an agreement that the proceeding be dismissed under Federal Rule of Appellate Procedure 42(b).

(b) Other Settlement Discussions. This rule does not preclude the parties from discussing settlement or agreeing to dismiss the proceedings at other times, including after oral argument but before decision.

[Effective July 1, 1997. Amended effective March 4, 1999; May 1, 2003.]

FRAP RULE 34. ORAL ARGUMENT

(a) *In General.*

(1) Party's Statement. Any party may file, or a court may require by local rule, a statement explaining why oral argument should, or need not, be permitted.

(2) Standards. Oral argument must be allowed in every case unless a panel of three judges who have examined the briefs and record unanimously agrees that oral argument is unnecessary for any of the following reasons:

(A) the appeal is frivolous;

(B) the dispositive issue or issues have been authoritatively decided; or

(C) the facts and legal arguments are adequately presented in the briefs and record, and the decisional process would not be significantly aided by oral argument.

(b) *Notice of Argument; Postponement.* The clerk must advise all parties whether oral argument will be scheduled, and, if so, the date, time, and place for it, and the time allowed for each side. A motion to postpone the argument or to allow longer argument must be filed reasonably in advance of the hearing date.

(c) *Order and Contents of Argument.* The appellant opens and concludes the argument. Counsel must not read at length from briefs, records, or authorities.

(d) *Cross-Appeals and Separate Appeals.* If there is a cross-appeal, Rule 28.1(b) determines which party is the appellant and which is the appellee for purposes of oral argument. Unless the court directs otherwise, a cross-appeal or separate appeal must be argued when the initial appeal is argued. Separate parties should avoid duplicative argument.

(e) *Nonappearance of a Party.* If the appellee fails to appear for argument, the court must hear appellant's argument. If the appellant fails to appear for argument, the court may hear the appellee's argument. If neither party appears, the case will be decided on the briefs, unless the court orders otherwise.

(f) *Submission on Briefs.* The parties may agree to submit a case for decision on the briefs, but the court may direct that the case be argued.

(g) *Use of Physical Exhibits at Argument; Removal.* Counsel intending to use physical exhibits other than documents at the argument must arrange to place them in the courtroom on the day of the argument before the court convenes. After the argument, counsel must remove the exhibits from the courtroom, unless the court directs otherwise. The clerk may destroy or dispose of the exhibits if counsel does not reclaim them within a reasonable time after the clerk gives notice to remove them.

LOCAL RULE 34. ORAL ARGUMENT

(a) Reply Brief Instead of Oral Argument. If an appeal is not called for oral argument and the appellant declined to file a reply brief in anticipation of replying during oral argument, the appellant may file a reply brief within 14 days after the notice that the appeal will be submitted on the briefs.

(b) Time Allowed. The time allowed each side for oral argument will be determined by the court. The clerk will advise counsel of the time allotted. A party is not obliged to use all the time allowed. The court may terminate the argument if it deems further argument unnecessary.

(c) Visual Aids.

(1) *Visual Aids Used at a Trial or Administrative Hearing; Notice.* If counsel intends to use at oral argument a visual aid used at a trial or administrative hearing, counsel must advise the clerk by letter in an original and 3 copies and served no later than 14 days before argument of the proposed visual aid.

(2) *Visual Aids Not Used at a Trial or Administrative Hearing; Notice.* If counsel intends to use at oral argument a visual aid that was not used at a trial or administrative hearing, counsel must give written notice to opposing counsel no later than 21 days before the oral argument.

(3) *Objection to the Use of Visual Aids.* An objection to the proposed use of a visual aid at oral argument must be in writing, served on all parties, and filed no later than 7 days before the oral argument. If a party objects, the parties' written submissions will be treated as a motion and response and will be referred to the panel.

(4) *Scope.* This rule does not preclude use of a chalkboard or equivalent during oral argument.

(5) *Disposition.* The clerk may dispose of visual aids not removed by the parties.

[Effective July 1, 1997. Amended effective March 4, 1999; May 1, 2003; May 1, 2004; May 1, 2006; December 1, 2009; June 1, 2011.]

Practice Notes

Court Sessions; Hearing Date. Sessions of the court will be held as announced by the court. Sessions are held regularly in Washington, DC, but the court may sit elsewhere. Appeals are usually calendared for oral argument or submission without argument within 2 months after the briefs and joint appendix are filed. Counsel are advised of the firm date of hearing approximately 30 days before the session. Once scheduled, a case will not be postponed except on motion showing **compelling reasons**. Counsel should advise the clerk in writing within 30 days once briefing is completed of potential scheduling conflicts or as soon as they are known and should not wait until an actual conflict arises. Counsel requiring a courtroom accessible to the disabled, if oral argument is scheduled, should notify the clerk of this requirement when counsel files the entry of appearance. Counsel may elect to submit on the briefs to avoid delay in disposition or for any other reason.

Oral Argument. Counsel must report to the clerk's office at least 30 minutes before the scheduled session and before proceeding to the courtroom. The members of the panel will have read the briefs before oral argument. Counsel should, therefore, emphasize the dispositive issue or issues. Time allotted for oral argument is ordinarily 15 minutes, although the court may vary this depending on the nature of the case. The court may extend the allotted time during the argument, or it may terminate the argument, if it deems it appropriate.

Justification for Claim of Confidentiality. Unnecessarily designating material in the briefs and appendix as confidential may hinder the court's preparation and issuance of opinions. Counsel must be prepared to justify at oral argument any claim of confidentiality.

Pamphlet. When counsel are advised of the firm date of oral argument, they will be sent a pamphlet, Notice to Counsel on Oral Argument, which contains detailed instructions about the conduct of oral argument.

Copies of Recordings Available. Oral arguments are recorded for the convenience of the court. Copies of a recording may be purchased from the administrative services office of the court. Recordings are also available on the court's website www.cafc.uscourts.gov free of charge.

Open to Public. Unless held in camera, oral arguments are open to the public. Those in attendance whose attire or behavior reflects adversely on the dignity of the proceedings will be asked to leave.

Oral Argument on Motions. Oral argument is ordinarily not granted on motions. See Federal Rule of Appellate Procedure 27(e).

FRAP RULE 35. EN BANC DETERMINATION

(a) *When Hearing or Rehearing En Banc May Be Ordered.* A majority of the circuit judges who are in regular active service and who are not disqualified may order that an appeal or other proceeding be heard or reheard by the court of appeals en banc. An en banc hearing or rehearing is not favored and ordinarily will not be ordered unless:

(1) en banc consideration is necessary to secure or maintain uniformity of the court's decisions; or

(2) the proceeding involves a question of exceptional importance.

(b) *Petition for Hearing or Rehearing En Banc.* A party may petition for a hearing or rehearing en banc.

(1) The petition must begin with a statement that either:

(A) the panel decision conflicts with a decision of the United States Supreme Court or of the court to which the petition is addressed (with citation to the conflicting case or cases) and consideration by the full court is therefore necessary to secure and maintain uniformity of the court's decisions; or

(B) the proceeding involves one or more questions of exceptional importance, each of which must be concisely stated; for example, a petition may assert that a proceeding presents a question of exceptional importance if it involves an issue on which the panel decision conflicts with the authoritative decisions of other United States Courts of Appeals that have addressed the issue.

(2) Except by the court's permission, a petition for an en banc hearing or rehearing must not exceed 15 pages, excluding material not counted under Rule 32.

(3) For purposes of the page limit in Rule 35(b)(2), if a party files both a petition for panel rehearing and a petition for rehearing en banc, they are considered a single document even if they are filed separately, unless separate filing is required by local rule.

(c) *Time for Petition for Hearing or Rehearing En Banc.* A petition that an appeal be heard initially en banc must be filed by the date when the appellee's brief is due. A petition for a rehearing en banc must be filed within the time prescribed by Rule 40 for filing a petition for rehearing.

(d) *Number of Copies.* The number of copies to be filed must be prescribed by local rule and may be altered by order in a particular case.

(e) *Response.* No response may be filed to a petition for an en banc consideration unless the court orders a response.

(f) *Call for a Vote.* A vote need not be taken to determine whether the case will be heard or reheard en banc unless a judge calls for a vote.

RULE 35. EN BANC DETERMINATION

(a) General.

(1) *Arguing to a Panel to Overrule a Precedent.* Although only the court en banc may overrule a binding precedent, a party may argue, in its brief and oral argument, to overrule a binding precedent without petitioning for hearing en banc. The panel will decide whether to ask the regular active judges to consider hearing the case en banc.

(2) *Frivolous Petition.* A petition for hearing or rehearing en banc that does not meet the standards of Federal Rule of Appellate Procedure 35(a) may be deemed frivolous and subject to sanctions.

(b) Statement of Counsel.

(1) *Petition for Hearing En Banc.* A petition that an appeal be initially heard en banc must contain the following statement of counsel at the beginning:

> Based on my professional judgment, I believe this appeal requires an answer to one or more precedent-setting questions of exceptional importance:
>
> (set forth each question in a separate sentence).
>
> /s/ ____________________
>
> ATTORNEY OF RECORD FOR __________

(2) *Petition for Rehearing En Banc.* A petition that an appeal be reheard en banc must contain one or both of the following statements of counsel at the beginning:

> Based on my professional judgment, I believe the panel decision is contrary to the following decision(s) of the Supreme Court of the United States or the precedent(s) of this court: (cite specific decisions).
>
> Based on my professional judgment, I believe this appeal requires an answer to one or more precedent-setting questions of exceptional importance:
>
> (set forth each question in a separate sentence).
>
> /s/ ____________________
>
> ATTORNEY OF RECORD FOR __________

(c) Petition for Hearing or Rehearing En Banc; Response.

(1) *Certificate of Interest.* A certificate of interest (*see* Federal Circuit Rule 47.4) must be included in a petition for a hearing or rehearing en banc or a response to such a petition. The certificate must appear immediately following the cover.

(2) *Items Excluded from Page Limitation.* The following items do not count against the page limitation in Federal Rule of Appellate Procedure 35(b)(2):

(A) the certificate of interest;

(B) the table of contents;

(C) the table of citations; and

(D) any addendum containing statutes, rules, regulations, and similar matters.

(3) *Rehearing En Banc: Copy of Opinion or Judgment.* A petition for a rehearing must include a copy of the opinion or the judgment of affirmance without opinion. The copy must be bound with the petition as an addendum.

(4) *Number of Copies.* If only nonconfidential copies are filed, an original and eighteen copies of a petition for hearing or rehearing en banc must be filed with the court. Two copies must be served on each party separately represented. If confidential and nonconfidential copies are filed, an original and eighteen copies of the confidential petition and original and three copies of the nonconfidential petition must be filed with the court. Two copies of the confidential petition and one copy of the nonconfidential petition must be served on each party separately represented.

(d) Combined Petition for Panel Rehearing and Rehearing En Banc. If a party chooses to file both a petition for panel rehearing, see Federal Circuit Rule 40, and a petition for a rehearing en banc, then the two must not be filed separately, they must be combined. A combined petition for panel rehearing and rehearing en banc must comply with Federal Circuit Rule 35(c). The cover of a combined petition must indicate that it is a combined petition.

(e) Contents of Petition for Hearing En Banc, Rehearing En Banc, and Combined Petition; Response.

(1) *Petition for Hearing En Banc.* The preferred contents and organization for a petition for a hearing en banc are:

(A) white cover or first sheet with the information prescribed in Federal Rule of Appellate Procedure 32(a)(2);

(B) the certificate of interest (*see* Federal Circuit Rule 47.4);

(C) the table of contents;

(D) the table of authorities;

(E) the statement of counsel required in Federal Circuit Rule 35(b);

(F) the argument; and

(G) the proof of service (*see* Federal Rule of Appellate Procedure 25(d)).

(2) *Petition for Rehearing En Banc.* The preferred contents and organization for a petition for a rehearing en banc are:

(A) white cover or first sheet with the information prescribed in Federal Rule of Appellate Procedure 32(a)(2);

(B) the certificate of interest (*see* Federal Circuit Rule 47.4);

(C) the table of contents;

(D) the table of authorities;

(E) the statement of counsel required in Federal Circuit Rule 35(b);

(F) the argument;

(G) the addendum containing a copy of the court's opinion or judgment of affirmance without opinion sought to be reheard; and

(H) the proof of service (*see* Federal Rule of Appellate Procedure 25(d)).

(3) *Combined Petition for Panel Rehearing and Rehearing En Banc.* The preferred contents and organization for a combined petition for panel rehearing and a rehearing en banc are:

(A) white cover or first sheet with the information prescribed in Federal Rule of Appellate Procedure 32(a)(2);

(B) the certificate of interest (*see* Federal Circuit Rule 47.4);

(C) the table of contents;

(D) the table of authorities;

(E) the statement of counsel required in Federal Circuit Rule 35(b);

(F) the points of law or fact overlooked or misapprehended by the panel of the court;

(G) the argument in support of a rehearing;

(H) the argument in support of rehearing en banc;

(I) the addendum containing a copy of the court's opinion or judgment of affirmance without opinion sought to be reheard; and

(J) the proof of service (*see* Federal Rule of Appellate Procedure 25(d)).

(4) *Response.* If the court requests a response, which must not exceed 15 pages unless otherwise ordered, the preferred contents and organization are:

(A) white cover or first sheet with the information prescribed in Federal Rule of Appellate Procedure 32(a)(2);

(B) the certificate of interest (*see* Federal Circuit Rule 47.4);

(C) the table of contents;

(D) the table of authorities;

(E) argument against a rehearing, rehearing en banc, or both; and

(F) the proof of service (*see* Federal Rule of Appellate Procedure 25(d)).

(f) Additional Copies of Briefs in Cases to be Heard En Banc. Within 7 days after the order granting a rehearing en banc, counsel must file 30 sets of the briefs that were before the panel that initially heard the appeal, unless the court directs otherwise.

(g) Amicus Curiae Brief. Except by the court's permission or direction, an amicus curiae brief submitted in connection with a petition for hearing en banc, a petition for rehearing en banc, or a combined petition for panel rehearing and rehearing en banc, must be accompanied by a motion for leave and must not exceed 10 pages. Except by the court's permission or direction, any brief amicus curiae or any motion for leave to file a brief amicus curiae must be filed within 14 days of the date of filing of the petition or response that the amicus curiae supports. If the amicus curiae does not support either party, then the brief or motion for leave to file the brief must be filed within 14 days of the date of filing of the petition.

[Effective July 1, 1997. Amended effective March 4, 1999; May 1, 2003; May 1, 2006; February 6, 2009.]

Practice Notes

Hearing or Rehearing En Banc. The court may sua sponte order that an appeal be initially heard or be reheard en banc. The panel or a judge on the panel that is considering a case may at any time request the active judges of the court to hear or rehear the case en banc with or without further briefs or argument by counsel.

Rehearing En Banc; Senior Judges. If a senior judge participated in the original hearing and disposition of a case for which rehearing en banc is granted, that senior judge may participate fully in the rehearing.

Combined Petition for Panel Rehearing and Rehearing En Banc. When a combined petition for panel rehearing and petition for rehearing en banc is filed, the petition for panel rehearing is decided first in the same manner as a petition for panel rehearing without an accompanying petition for rehearing en banc. If the panel grants the requested relief, the petition for rehearing en banc is deemed moot.

Petition for Rehearing En Banc Referred to Panel. A petition for rehearing en banc is presumed to request relief that can be granted by the panel that heard the appeal, and action on the petition for rehearing en banc will be deferred until the panel has an opportunity to grant the relief requested.

Timeliness. A petition for hearing or rehearing en banc is filed when the court receives it, not on mailing. The clerk will return an untimely petition for hearing or rehearing en banc.

Nonprecedential Opinions. A petition for rehearing en banc is rarely appropriate if the appeal was the subject of a nonprecedential opinion by the panel of judges that heard it.

Writ of Certiorari. Filing a petition for a panel rehearing or for rehearing en banc is not a prerequisite to filing a petition for a writ of certiorari in the Supreme Court.

FRAP RULE 36. ENTRY OF JUDGMENT; NOTICE

(a) *Entry.* A judgment is entered when it is noted on the docket. The clerk must prepare, sign, and enter the judgment:

(1) after receiving the court's opinion—but if settlement of the judgment's form is required, after final settlement; or

(2) if a judgment is rendered without an opinion, as the court instructs.

(b) *Notice.* On the date when judgment is entered, the clerk must serve on all parties a copy of

the opinion—or the judgment, if no opinion was written—and a notice of the date when the judgment was entered.

LOCAL RULE 36. ENTRY OF JUDGMENT—JUDGMENT OF AFFIRMANCE WITHOUT OPINION

The court may enter a judgment of affirmance without opinion, citing this rule, when it determines that any of the following conditions exist and an opinion would have no precedential value:

(a) the judgment, decision, or order of the trial court appealed from is based on findings that are not clearly erroneous;

(b) the evidence supporting the jury's verdict is sufficient;

(c) the record supports summary judgment, directed verdict, or judgment on the pleadings;

(d) the decision of an administrative agency warrants affirmance under the standard of review in the statute authorizing the petition for review; or

(e) a judgment or decision has been entered without an error of law.

[Effective July 1, 1997. Amended effective March 4, 1999; May 1, 2003.]

Practice Note

Separate Judgment Not Prepared in Certain Instances. A separate judgment is not prepared when a case is dismissed on consent or on motion or for failure to prosecute. The order of dismissal serves as the judgment when entered.

FRAP RULE 37. INTEREST ON JUDGMENT

(a) *When the Court Affirms.* Unless the law provides otherwise, if a money judgment in a civil case is affirmed, whatever interest is allowed by law is payable from the date when the district court's judgment was entered.

(b) *When the Court Reverses.* If the court modifies or reverses a judgment with a direction that a money judgment be entered in the district court, the mandate must contain instructions about the allowance of interest.

FRAP RULE 38. FRIVOLOUS APPEAL—DAMAGES AND COSTS

If a court of appeals determines that an appeal is frivolous, it may, after a separately filed motion or notice from the court and reasonable opportunity to respond, award just damages and single or double costs to the appellee.

Practice Notes

Warning Against Filing or Proceeding with a Frivolous Appeal or Petition. The court's early decision in Asberry v. United States, 692 F.2d 1378 (Fed. Cir. 1982), established the policy of enforcing this rule vigorously. Since then, many precedential opinions have included sanctions under the rule. Damages, double costs, and attorney fees, singly or in varying combinations, have been imposed on counsel, parties, and pro se petitioners for pursuing frivolous appeals.

Challenging a Frivolous Appeal. If an appellee or respondent considers an appeal or petition frivolous, the appellee or respondent must file a separate motion with that allegation. The assertion that an appeal is frivolous must be accompanied by citation to the opposing brief or the record below with clear argument as to why those citations establish that the appeal is frivolous. A party whose case has been challenged as frivolous is expected to respond or to request dismissal of the case.

FRAP RULE 39. COSTS

(a) *Against Whom Assessed.* The following rules apply unless the law provides or the court orders otherwise:

(1) if an appeal is dismissed, costs are taxed against the appellant, unless the parties agree otherwise;

(2) if a judgment is affirmed, costs are taxed against the appellant;

(3) if a judgment is reversed, costs are taxed against the appellee;

(4) if a judgment is affirmed in part, reversed in part, modified, or vacated, costs are taxed only as the court orders.

(b) *Costs for and Against the United States.* Costs for or against the United States, its agency, or officer will be assessed under Rule 39(a) only if authorized by law.

(c) *Costs of Copies.* Each court of appeals must, by local rule, fix the maximum rate for taxing the cost of producing necessary copies of a brief or appendix, or copies of records authorized by Rule 30(f). The rate must not exceed that generally charged for such work in the area where the clerk's office is located and should encourage economical methods of copying.

(d) *Bill of Costs: Objections; Insertion in Mandate.*

(1) A party who wants costs taxed must—within 14 days after entry of judgment—file with the circuit clerk, with proof of service, an itemized and verified bill of costs.

(2) Objections must be filed within 14 days after service of the bill of costs, unless the court extends the time.

(3) The clerk must prepare and certify an itemized statement of costs for insertion in the mandate, but issuance of the mandate must not be delayed for taxing costs. If the mandate issues before costs are finally determined, the district clerk must—upon the circuit clerk's request—add

the statement of costs, or any amendment of it, to the mandate.

(e) *Costs on Appeal Taxable in the District Court.* The following costs on appeal are taxable in the district court for the benefit of the party entitled to costs under this rule:

(1) the preparation and transmission of the record;

(2) the reporter's transcript, if needed to determine the appeal;

(3) premiums paid for a supersedeas bond or other bond to preserve rights pending appeal; and

(4) the fee for filing the notice of appeal.

LOCAL RULE 39. COSTS

(a) Notice of Entitlement to Costs. When the clerk provides notice of judgment or order disposing of an appeal, the clerk must advise which party or parties are entitled to costs.

(b) Bill of Costs; Copies; Objection. A party must serve the bill of costs on the form prescribed by the court and must file an original and three copies with the court. An objection to a bill of costs must not exceed 5 pages and must be filed in an original and three copies and served on the other parties.

[Effective July 1, 1997. Amended effective March 4, 1999.]

Practice Notes

Costs When the United States is a Party; Costs in Ex Parte Appeals from the Patent and Trademark Office. 28 U.S.C. § 2412(a) authorizes costs to be taxed against the United States; thus, costs (as defined in 28 U.S.C. § 1920) may be awarded both for and against the United States in this court. An ex parte patent appeal under 35 U.S.C. § 141 and an ex parte trademark appeal under 15 U.S.C. § 1071 are not within the scope of 28 U.S.C. § 2412, however, and costs in these appeals are not awarded for or against the Patent and Trademark Office.

Limit on Printing Costs. The costs taxable under Federal Rule of Appellate Procedure 39 are limited to the costs of preparing typewritten briefs (even if a party elects to have a brief printed) and of copying briefs and appendices.

Current Rates. The following rates are the current maximum allowable costs:

$6.00 per page for the table of page numbers of designated materials, the originals of briefs, and the table of contents for the appendix (whether printed, typewritten, or word processed);

$0.08 per page for copying and collating; and

$2.00 per copy for covers and binding.

Allowable Costs. Costs may be billed for 16 copies of briefs and appendices, plus 2 copies for each additional party, plus any copies required or allowed, e.g., confidential briefs or appendices. The cost of service copies of the table or physical compilation of the designated materials may also be billed. Any other cost billed must be separately justified. The total billed for any item must be limited to the lesser of actual or allowable costs. Actual cost of briefs and appendices prepared in-house includes word processing, copying, and binding, at the amount normally billed to a client for these services. The United States may assume its actual costs are the allowable costs. The costs of correcting a nonconforming brief are not taxable. Counsel are urged to stipulate to costs.

Payment of Costs Taxed. Pay the party or parties in whose favor costs are taxed by check sent to counsel for the party or to the party if the party appeared pro se. Do not involve the court in collection matters.

Docketing Fee and Costs in a Case Involving a Claim Under the Uniformed Services Employment and Reemployment Rights Act of 1994. No costs are taxed, and the docketing fee does not have to be paid, in a petition for review of a decision of the Merits Systems Protection Board if the underlying appeal involved a claim under the Uniformed Services Employment and Reemployment Rights Act of 1994 (USERRA)). 38 U.S.C. § 4323. The petitioner must complete form 6B to inform the court that the case involves a claim under USERRA.

FRAP RULE 40. PETITION FOR PANEL REHEARING

(a) *Time to File; Contents; Answer; Action by the Court if Granted.*

(1) Time. Unless the time is shortened or extended by order or local rule, a petition for panel rehearing may be filed within 14 days after entry of judgment. But in a civil case, if the United States or its officer or agency is a party, the time within which any party may seek rehearing is 45 days after entry of judgment, unless an order shortens or extends the time.

(2) Contents. The petition must state with particularity each point of law or fact that the petitioner believes the court has overlooked or misapprehended and must argue in support of the petition. Oral argument is not permitted.

(3) Answer. Unless the court requests, no answer to a petition for panel rehearing is permitted. But ordinarily rehearing will not be granted in the absence of such a request.

(4) Action by the Court. If a petition for panel rehearing is granted, the court may do any of the following:

(A) make a final disposition of the case without reargument;

(B) restore the case to the calendar for reargument or resubmission; or

(C) issue any other appropriate order.

(b) *Form of Petition; Length.* The petition must comply in form with Rule 32. Copies must be served and filed as Rule 31 prescribes. Unless the court permits or a local rule provides otherwise, a petition for panel rehearing must not exceed 15 pages.

LOCAL RULE 40. PETITION FOR PANEL REHEARING

(a) Contents of Petition for Panel Rehearing. The preferred contents and organization for a petition for panel rehearing are:

(1) white cover or first page with the information prescribed in Federal Rule of Appellate Procedure 32(a)(2);

(2) the certificate of interest (*see* Federal Circuit Rule 47.4);

(3) the table of contents;

(4) the points of law or fact overlooked or misapprehended by the court;

(5) the argument;

(6) the addendum containing a copy of the court's opinion or judgment of affirmance without opinion sought to be reheard; and

(7) the proof of service (*see* Federal Rule of Appellate Procedure 25(d)).

(b) Addendum. A copy of the opinion or judgment of affirmance without opinion sought to be reheard must be bound with the petition for panel rehearing as an addendum.

(c) Items Excluded From Page Limitation; Other Material.

(1) *Items Excluded.* The following items do not count against the page limitation in Federal Rule of Appellate Procedure 40(b):

(A) the certificate of interest;

(B) the table of contents;

(C) the table of citations;

(D) the addendum containing a copy of the opinion or judgment of affirmance without opinion; and

(E) any addendum containing statutes, rules, regulations, and similar matters.

(2) *Other Material.* Material not listed in this Federal Circuit Rule 40 may not be included in the addendum or in an appendix without leave of the court.

(d) Answer. If the court requests an answer, which must not exceed 15 pages unless otherwise ordered, the preferred contents and organization for the answer are:

(1) white cover or first sheet with the information prescribed in Federal Rule of Appellate Procedure 32(a)(2);

(2) the certificate of interest (*see* Federal Circuit Rule 47.4);

(3) the table of contents;

(4) the argument; and

(5) the proof of service (*see* Federal Rule of Appellate Procedure 25(d)).

(e) Time. Except for a civil case in which the United States or its officer or agency is a party, a petition for panel rehearing may be filed within 30 days after entry of judgment. If the United States or its officer or agency is a party, a petition for panel rehearing may be filed within 45 days after entry of judgment. The time limits set forth in this rule also apply to a motion for panel reconsideration of a dispositive panel order.

(f) Informal Petition for Panel Rehearing; Answer.

(1) *Informal Petition.* A pro se party may file an original and 3 copies of an informal petition for panel rehearing in letter form not to exceed 15 typewritten double-spaced pages, attaching to each a copy of the opinion or judgment sought to be reheard.

(2) *Informal Answer.* If the court requests an answer to an informal petition for panel rehearing, or if the court requests a pro se party to answer a formal petition for panel rehearing, the answer may be informal, following the standards prescribed for informal briefs. The informal answer may not exceed 15 typewritten double-spaced pages, and must be filed in an original and 3 copies.

(g) Amicus Curiae Brief. Except by the court's permission or direction, an amicus curiae brief submitted in connection with a petition for panel rehearing must be accompanied by a motion for leave to file and must not exceed 10 pages. Except by the court's permission or direction, any brief amicus curiae or any motion for leave to file a brief amicus curiae must be filed within 14 days of the date of filing of the petition or response that the amicus curiae supports. If the amicus curiae does not support either party, then the brief or motion for leave to file the brief must be filed within 14 days of the date of filing of the petition.

[Effective July 1, 1997. Amended effective March 4, 1999; June 9, 2000; May 1, 2004; May 1, 2006; February 6, 2009.]

Practice Notes

Petition for Panel Rehearing Not Filed When Mailed. A petition for panel rehearing, unlike a brief, is not deemed filed when mailed; it must be received by the clerk within the time fixed for filing. The time provided in Federal Circuit Rule 40(e) runs from the date the judgment is entered (see Federal Rule of Appellate Procedure 36), not from the date counsel receives the opinion or order. Therefore, Federal Rule of Appellate Procedure 26(c) does not apply. The clerk may return an untimely petition for panel rehearing.

Action by the Court. When a petition for panel rehearing is filed, the clerk will transmit copies to the panel that decided the case. The clerk will enter an order denying the petition unless a majority of the panel agrees to rehear the case. Rehearing before the panel may take place with or without further briefing or oral argument by the parties as the court directs.

FRAP RULE 41. MANDATE: CONTENTS; ISSUANCE AND EFFECTIVE DATE; STAY

(a) *Contents.* Unless the court directs that a formal mandate issue, the mandate consists of a certified copy of the judgment, a copy of the court's opinion, if any, and any direction about costs.

(b) *When Issued.* The court's mandate must issue 7 days after the time to file a petition for rehearing expires, or 7 days after entry of an order denying a timely petition for panel rehearing, petition for rehearing en banc, or motion for stay of mandate, whichever is later. The court may shorten or extend the time.

(c) *Effective Date.* The mandate is effective when issued.

(d) *Staying the Mandate.*

(1) On Petition for Rehearing or Motion. The timely filing of a petition for panel rehearing, petition for rehearing en banc, or motion for stay of mandate, stays the mandate until disposition of the petition or motion, unless the court orders otherwise.

(2) Pending Petition for Certiorari.

(A) A party may move to stay the mandate pending the filing of a petition for a writ of certiorari in the Supreme Court. The motion must be served on all parties and must show that the certiorari petition would present a substantial question and that there is good cause for a stay.

(B) The stay must not exceed 90 days, unless the period is extended for good cause or unless the party who obtained the stay files a petition for the writ and so notifies the circuit clerk in writing within the period of the stay. In that case, the stay continues until the Supreme Court's final disposition.

(C) The court may require a bond or other security as a condition to granting or continuing a stay of the mandate.

(D) The court of appeals must issue the mandate immediately when a copy of a Supreme Court order denying the petition for writ of certiorari is filed.

LOCAL RULE 41. ISSUANCE OF MANDATE

An order dismissing a case on consent or for failure to prosecute, or dismissing, remanding, or transferring a case on motion, will constitute the mandate. The date of the certified order is the date of the mandate. In an appeal dismissed or transferred by the court sua sponte in an opinion, the mandate will issue in regular course.

[Effective July 1, 1997. Amended effective March 4, 1999; May 1, 2003.]

Practice Note

Relation of Mandate to Application for Certiorari; Stay. That a mandate has issued does not affect the right to apply to the Supreme Court for a writ of certiorari. Consequently, a motion to stay the mandate should advance reasons for the stay beyond the mere intention to apply for certiorari, e.g., to forestall action in the trial court or agency that would necessitate a remedial order of the Supreme Court if the writ of certiorari were granted.

FRAP RULE 42. VOLUNTARY DISMISSAL

(a) *Dismissal in the District Court.* Before an appeal has been docketed by the circuit clerk, the district court may dismiss the appeal on the filing of a stipulation signed by all parties or on the appellant's motion with notice to all parties.

(b) *Dismissal in the Court of Appeals.* The circuit clerk may dismiss a docketed appeal if the parties file a signed dismissal agreement specifying how costs are to be paid and pay any fees that are due. But no mandate or other process may issue without a court order. An appeal may be dismissed on the appellant's motion on terms agreed to by the parties or fixed by the court.

Practice Note

Request to Withdraw Appeal or Petition. An appellant or petitioner may request to withdraw an appeal or petition at any time before decision, and the request will be granted in all but the most unusual circumstances. An opposing party is ordinarily expected to consent to the withdrawal on terms requiring each party to bear its own costs on appeal. A stipulation of the parties that a case is withdrawn may refer to a settlement agreement, but the stipulation should not include the terms of the settlement.

FRAP RULE 43. SUBSTITUTION OF PARTIES

(a) *Death of a Party.*

(1) After Notice of Appeal Is Filed. If a party dies after a notice of appeal has been filed or while a proceeding is pending in the court of appeals, the decedent's personal representative may be substituted as a party on motion filed with the circuit clerk by the representative or by any party. A party's motion must be served on the representative in accordance with Rule 25. If the decedent has no representative, any party may suggest the death on the record, and the court of appeals may then direct appropriate proceedings.

(2) Before Notice of Appeal Is Filed—Potential Appellant. If a party entitled to appeal dies before filing a notice of appeal, the decedent's personal representative—or, if there is no personal representative, the decedent's attorney of record—may file

a notice of appeal within the time prescribed by these rules. After the notice of appeal is filed, substitution must be in accordance with Rule 43(a)(1).

(3) Before Notice of Appeal Is Filed—Potential Appellee. If a party against whom an appeal may be taken dies after entry of a judgment or order in the district court, but before a notice of appeal is filed, an appellant may proceed as if the death had not occurred. After the notice of appeal is filed, substitution must be in accordance with Rule 43(a)(1).

(b) *Substitution for a Reason Other Than Death.* If a party needs to be substituted for any reason other than death, the procedure prescribed in Rule 43(a) applies.

(c) *Public Officer: Identification; Substitution.*

(1) Identification of Party. A public officer who is a party to an appeal or other proceeding in an official capacity may be described as a party by the public officer's official title rather than by name. But the court may require the public officer's name to be added.

(2) Automatic Substitution of Officeholder. When a public officer who is a party to an appeal or other proceeding in an official capacity dies, resigns, or otherwise ceases to hold office, the action does not abate. The public officer's successor is automatically substituted as a party. Proceedings following the substitution are to be in the name of the substituted party, but any misnomer that does not affect the substantial rights of the parties may be disregarded. An order of substitution may be entered at any time, but failure to enter an order does not affect the substitution.

FRAP RULE 44. CASE INVOLVING A CONSTITUTIONAL QUESTION WHEN THE UNITED STATES OR THE RELEVANT STATE IS NOT A PARTY

(a) *Constitutional Challenge to Federal Statute.* If a party questions the constitutionality of an Act of Congress in a proceeding in which the United States or its agency, officer, or employee is not a party in an official capacity, the questioning party must give written notice to the circuit clerk immediately upon the filing of the record or as soon as the question is raised in the court of appeals. The clerk must then certify that fact to the Attorney General.

(b) *Constitutional Challenge to State Statute.* If a party questions the constitutionality of a statute of a State in a proceeding in which that State or its agency, officer, or employee is not a party in an official capacity, the questioning party must give written notice to the circuit clerk immediately upon the filing of the record or as soon as the question is raised in the court of appeals. The clerk must then certify that fact to the attorney general of the State.

FRAP RULE 45. CLERK'S DUTIES

(a) *General Provisions.*

(1) Qualifications. The circuit clerk must take the oath and post any bond required by law. Neither the clerk nor any deputy clerk may practice as an attorney or counselor in any court while in office.

(2) When Court Is Open. The court of appeals is always open for filing any paper, issuing and returning process, making a motion, and entering an order. The clerk's office with the clerk or a deputy in attendance must be open during business hours on all days except Saturdays, Sundays, and legal holidays. A court may provide by local rule or by order that the clerk's office be open for specified hours on Saturdays or on legal holidays other than New Year's Day, Martin Luther King, Jr.'s Birthday, Washington's Birthday, Memorial Day, Independence Day, Labor Day, Columbus Day, Veterans' Day, Thanksgiving Day, and Christmas Day.

(b) *Records.*

(1) The Docket. The circuit clerk must maintain a docket and an index of all docketed cases in the manner prescribed by the Director of the Administrative Office of the United States Courts. The clerk must record all papers filed with the clerk and all process, orders, and judgments.

(2) Calendar. Under the court's direction, the clerk must prepare a calendar of cases awaiting argument. In placing cases on the calendar for argument, the clerk must give preference to ~~appeals in criminal cases and to~~ other proceedings and appeals entitled to preference by law.

(3) Other Records. The clerk must keep other books and records required by the Director of the Administrative Office of the United States Courts, with the approval of the Judicial Conference of the United States, or by the court.

(c) *Notice of an Order or Judgment.* Upon the entry of an order or judgment, the circuit clerk must immediately serve a notice of entry on each party, with a copy of any opinion, and must note the date of service on the docket. Service on a party represented by counsel must be made on counsel.

(d) *Custody of Records and Papers.* The circuit clerk has custody of the court's records and papers. Unless the court orders or instructs otherwise, the clerk must not permit an original record or paper to be taken from the clerk's office. Upon disposition of the case, original papers constituting the

record on appeal or review must be returned to the court or agency from which they were received. The clerk must preserve a copy of any brief, appendix, or other paper that has been filed.

LOCAL RULE 45. CLERK'S DUTIES

(a) Dismissal by Clerk; Reconsideration. The clerk may dismiss an appeal for a failure to follow the Federal Rules of Appellate Procedure or these Federal Circuit Rules. A party may move that the court reconsider such dismissal. A motion for reconsideration must:

(1) be filed within 14 days after issuance of the order of dismissal;

(2) be in the form prescribed by Federal Rule of Appellate Procedure 27 and Federal Circuit Rule 27; and

(3) not exceed 5 pages.

(b) Informal Motion for Reconsideration. A pro se party may file an original and 3 copies of an informal motion, which may be in the form of a letter, for reconsideration of the dismissal. The informal motion must not exceed 5 typewritten double-spaced pages. A copy of the dismissal order must be attached to the original and each copy of the informal motion.

(c) Authority to Enter Orders. The clerk may enter an order "For the Court" only when authorized by these rules or at the direction of a judge or the court.

(d) Communication with the Court. All correspondence and telephone calls about cases and motions and all press inquiries must be directed to the clerk.

[Effective July 1, 1997. Amended effective March 4, 1999; May 1, 2003; May 1, 2006.]

FRAP RULE 46. ATTORNEYS

(a) *Admission to the Bar.*

(1) Eligibility. An attorney is eligible for admission to the bar of a court of appeals if that attorney is of good moral and professional character and is admitted to practice before the Supreme Court of the United States, the highest court of a state, another United States court of appeals, or a United States district court (including the district courts for Guam, the Northern Mariana Islands, and the Virgin Islands).

(2) Application. An applicant must file an application for admission, on a form approved by the court that contains the applicant's personal statement showing eligibility for membership. The applicant must subscribe to the following oath or affirmation:

"I, ______, do solemnly swear [or affirm] that I will conduct myself as an attorney and counselor of this court, uprightly and according to law; and that I will support the Constitution of the United States."

(3) *Admission Procedures.* On written or oral motion of a member of the court's bar, the court will act on the application. An applicant may be admitted by oral motion in open court. But, unless the court orders otherwise, an applicant need not appear before the court to be admitted. Upon admission, an applicant must pay the clerk the fee prescribed by local rule or court order.

(b) *Suspension or Disbarment.*

(1) Standard. A member of the court's bar is subject to suspension or disbarment by the court if the member:

(A) has been suspended or disbarred from practice in any other court; or

(B) is guilty of conduct unbecoming a member of the court's bar.

(2) Procedure. The member must be given an opportunity to show good cause, within the time prescribed by the court, why the member should not be suspended or disbarred.

(3) Order. The court must enter an appropriate order after the member responds and a hearing is held, if requested, or after the time prescribed for a response expires, if no response is made.

(c) *Discipline.* A court of appeals may discipline an attorney who practices before it for conduct unbecoming a member of the bar or for failure to comply with any court rule. First, however, the court must afford the attorney reasonable notice, an opportunity to show cause to the contrary, and, if requested, a hearing.

LOCAL RULE 46. ATTORNEYS

(a) Eligibility. An attorney is eligible for admission to the bar of this court if that attorney is of good moral and professional character and is admitted to practice before and of good standing in:

(1) any of the courts listed in Federal Rule of Appellate Procedure 46(a);

(2) the United States Court of International Trade;

(3) the United States Court of Federal Claims;

(4) the United States Court of Appeals for Veterans Claims; or

(5) the District of Columbia Court of Appeals.

(b) Procedure for Admission.

(1) *Motion in Open Court.* An attorney may be admitted to the bar in open court by appearing personally with a sponsor who is a member of the bar of

this court and who states the applicant's qualifications and moves the admission. Motions for admission to the bar will be entertained at the opening of each session of court.

(2) *Written Motion by Member of the Court's Bar.* An attorney may be admitted on written motion of a member of the bar of the court who states the applicant's qualifications.

(3) *Written Motion by Attorney.* An attorney may be admitted on that attorney's own motion, accompanied by a certificate of good standing from a court listed in Federal Rule of Appellate Procedure 46(a) or Federal Circuit Rule 46(a). The certificate must be dated within 30 days of the motion for admission and must bear the seal of the issuing court. A written motion for admission must be submitted on a form approved by this court. The clerk will furnish the form.

(4) *Oath.* Each attorney admitted to the bar of this court must take an oath prescribed by the court.

(c) Admission Fee. The fee for admission to the bar of the court is $50, in addition to the Judicial Conference fee of $150, payable to the clerk, for which the applicant will receive a certificate of admission. For a duplicate certificate, the fee is $10, in addition to the Judicial Conference fee of $15.

(d) Government Attorney. An attorney for any federal, state, or local government office or agency may appear before this court in connection with that attorney's official duties without formal admission to the bar of the court.

(e) Change of Name, Address, or Telephone Number. An attorney admitted to the bar of this court must promptly notify the clerk of a change of name, address, or telephone number.

(f) Disciplinary Action. Disciplinary action against an attorney will be conducted in accordance with the Federal Circuit Attorney Discipline Rules.

[Effective July 1, 1997. Amended effective March 4, 1999; January 1, 2005; May 1, 2006; April 7, 2009.]

FRAP RULE 47. LOCAL RULES BY COURTS OF APPEALS

(a) ***Local Rules.***

(1) Each court of appeals acting by a majority of its judges in regular active service may, after giving appropriate public notice and opportunity for comment, make and amend rules governing its practice. A generally applicable direction to parties or lawyers regarding practice before a court must be in a local rule rather than an internal operating procedure or standing order. A local rule must be consistent with—but not duplicative of—Acts of Congress and rules adopted under 28 U.S.C. § 2072 and must conform to any uniform numbering system prescribed by the Judicial Conference of the United States. Each circuit clerk must send the Administrative Office of the United States Courts a copy of each local rule and internal operating procedure when it is promulgated or amended.

(2) A local rule imposing a requirement of form must not be enforced in a manner that causes a party to lose rights because of a nonwillful failure to comply with the requirement.

(b) *Procedure When There Is No Controlling Law.* A court of appeals may regulate practice in a particular case in any manner consistent with federal law, these rules, and local rules of the circuit. No sanction or other disadvantage may be imposed for noncompliance with any requirement not in federal law, federal rules, or the local circuit rules unless the alleged violator has been furnished in the particular case with actual notice of the requirement.

LOCAL RULE 47.1 SESSIONS AND PLACES OF HOLDING COURT

(a) Sessions. Sessions of the court will be held as the court announces.

(b) Places of Holding Court. The court may hold sessions in any place named and permitted in 28 U.S.C. § 48.

[Effective July 1, 1997. Amended effective March 4, 1999; June 9, 2000.]

LOCAL RULE 47.2 PANELS

(a) Panels. Cases and controversies will be heard and determined by a panel consisting of an odd number of at least three judges, two of whom may be senior judges of the court.

(b) Assignment of Cases. Assignment of cases to panels will be made so as to provide each judge with a representative cross-section of the fields of law within the jurisdiction of the court.

[Effective July 1, 1997. Amended effective March 4, 1999; June 9, 2000.]

LOCAL RULE 47.3 APPEARANCE

(a) Party and Amicus Curiae Must Be Represented; Pro Se Party; Attorney of Record; Of Counsel. An individual (not a corporation, partnership, organization, or other legal entity) may choose to be represented by counsel or to represent himself or herself pro se, but may not be represented by a nonattorney. An individual represented by counsel, each other party in an action, each party seeking to intervene, and each amicus curiae must appear through an attorney authorized to practice before this court and must designate one attorney as the principal attorney of record. Any other attorney assisting the attorney of record must be designated as "of counsel." Every attorney named on a brief must enter an appearance, except that the filing of an entry of appearance does not apply to government officials who, by reason of their status as supervisors or heads of offices, are listed on briefs in their ex officio capacity. Documents that are sent by the court will be sent only to the principal attorney of record.

(b) Petition for Writ of Mandamus or Prohibition. The attorney whose name, address, and telephone number appears first on a petition for a writ of mandamus or a writ of prohibition will be deemed attorney of record.

(c) Appearance; Contents; Service of Papers Before Appearance; Withdrawal of Counsel.

(1) *Appearance.* Each attorney who intends to participate in an appeal must file, within 14 days of docketing, an entry of appearance on the form provided by the clerk. A pro se party must also file an entry of appearance unless all the necessary information appears on the petition for review or notice of appeal. Any attorney retained for the case later must file an entry of appearance within 14 days after being retained. An attorney representing a party seeking or permitted to intervene, and for each amicus curiae, must file an entry of appearance with the motion for leave to intervene (if required) or with the brief amicus curiae. If an attorney's entry of appearance is first submitted within 30 days of the scheduled argument, then the attorney must file a motion for leave to file the entry of appearance. The motion for leave will be transmitted to the merits panel assigned to the case.

(2) *Contents.* The appearance must include the name of the party or parties represented and the name, address, and telephone number of the attorney or the pro se party. An attorney's appearance must show the name of the law firm or public or quasi-public legal office with which the attorney is associated. A new entry of appearance must be filed and served any time the information on record changes.

(3) *Certificate of Interest.* A certificate of interest must be filed with the first-filed entry of appearance. See Federal Circuit Rule 47.4. Both documents are due within 14 days of the date of docketing of the appeal or petition.

(4) *Service of Papers Before Appearance.* Until an attorney files a written entry of appearance, service of all papers must be made on the attorney of record in the proceeding below at the last known address. In a pro se case, unless an attorney files an entry of appearance, service of all papers must be made on the pro se party at the last known address.

(5) *Withdrawal of Counsel.* An attorney other than a government attorney who has been properly replaced, may not withdraw from representing a party without notice to the party, filing a motion with the court, and obtaining the court's consent.

(d) Signature. At least one copy of each brief, petition, motion, application, notice, or other paper presented for filing must contain the signature of the pro se party or the attorney who has entered an appearance. When no attorney appearing for a party is available to sign, any person having actual authority may sign on behalf of the attorney of record, attaching an affidavit of authority or an unsworn declaration of authority under penalty of perjury pursuant to 28 U.S.C. § 1746.

[Effective July 1, 1997. Amended effective March 4, 1999; May 1, 2003; May 1, 2004; May 1, 2006; September 1, 2006; December 1, 2009; June 1, 2011.]

Practice Notes

Form for Entry of Appearance. See Form 8, for a form for entry of appearance.

Filings Requiring Signature and Appearance. After docketing, the clerk will accept no filing required to be signed unless it is signed by a pro se party or an attorney—who is a member of the bar, if required under Federal Circuit Rule 46—and unless the pro se party or attorney has entered an appearance in the case.

New Counsel on Appeal. New counsel on appeal should provide a copy of the entry of appearance form filed in this court to the lower court or agency to expedite service of the certified list and other communications.

LOCAL RULE 47.4 CERTIFICATE OF INTEREST

(a) Purpose; Contents. To determine whether recusal by a judge is necessary or appropriate, an attorney—except an attorney for the United States—for each party, including a party seeking or permitted to intervene, and for each amicus curiae, must file a certificate of interest. The certificate of interest must be filed within 14 days of the date of docketing of the appeal or petition, except that for an intervenor or amicus curiae, the certificate of interest must be filed with the motion and with the brief. A certificate of interest must be in the form set forth in the appendix to these rules, and must contain the information below in the order listed. Negative responses, if applicable, are required as to each item on the form.

(1) The full name of every party or amicus represented in the case by the attorney.

(2) The name of the real party in interest if the party named in the caption is not the real party in interest.

(3) The corporate disclosure statement prescribed in Federal Rule of Appellate Procedure 26.1.

(4) The names of all law firms and the partners and associates that have appeared for the party in the lower tribunal or are expected to appear for the party in this court.

(b) Filing. The certificate must be filed with the entry of appearance. The certificate—first filed—must also be filed with each motion, petition, or response thereto, and in each principal brief and brief amicus curiae.

(c) Changes. If any of the information required in Federal Circuit Rule 47.4(a) changes after the certificate is filed and before the mandate has issued, the party must file an amended certificate within 7 days of the change.

[Effective July 1, 1997. Amended effective March 4, 1999; May 1, 2003; December 1, 2009; June 1, 2011.]

LOCAL RULE 47.5 STATEMENT OF RELATED CASES

Each principal brief must contain a statement of related cases indicating:

(a) whether any other appeal in or from the same civil action or proceeding in the lower court or body was previously before this or any other appellate court, stating:

(1) the title and number of that earlier appeal;

(2) the date of decision;

(3) the composition of the panel; and

(4) the citation of the opinion in the Federal Reporter; and

(b) the title and number of any case known to counsel to be pending in this or any other court that will directly affect or be directly affected by this court's decision in the pending appeal. If there are many related cases, they may be described generally, but the title and case number must be given for any case known to be pending in the Supreme Court, this court, or any other circuit court of appeals.

[Effective July 1, 1997. Amended effective March 4, 1999; May 1, 2004.]

LOCAL RULE 47.6 OPINION AND ORDER OF THE COURT [RESERVED]

LOCAL RULE 47.7 ATTORNEY FEES AND EXPENSES INCURRED IN THIS COURT

(a) Time for Filing; Response.

(1) *Generally.* The court may award attorney fees and expenses when authorized by law. An award may be made by the court on its own motion or on application of a party.

(2) *Time for Filing.* An application for an award of attorney fees and expenses must be served and filed within the time prescribed by the statute authorizing the award. If the statute does not prescribe a time, the application must be made within 30 days after entry of the judgment or order denying rehearing, whichever is later. However, if a petition for writ of certiorari is filed, the application will not be due until 30 days after all proceedings in the Supreme Court are concluded.

(3) *Response.* No response may be filed to an application for attorney fees and expenses unless directed by the court, but no application will be granted without the court giving the party an opportunity to submit a response.

(4) *Award on the Court's Motion.* A party awarded attorney fees and expenses by the court on its own motion must file and serve a bill of attorney fees and expenses containing the information required in Federal Circuit Rule 47.7(b)(2)(A)–(C) with the bill of costs authorized by Federal Rule of Appellate Procedure 39. Any objection must be filed within the time prescribed in Federal Rule of Appellate Procedure 39.

(b) Content of Application.

(1) *Application Under the Equal Access to Justice Act.* An application for attorney fees and expenses under the Equal Access to Justice Act must be made on Form 20.

(2) *Other Applications.* Each other application for attorney fees and expenses must cite the authority for an award and must indicate how the prerequisites for an award, including timeliness, are met. In addition, each application must contain a statement, under oath, specifying:

(A) the nature of each service rendered;

(B) the amount of time expended rendering each type of service; and

(C) the customary charge for each type of service rendered.

[Effective July 1, 1997. Amended effective March 4, 1999; May 1, 2004.]

LOCAL RULE 47.8 IN CAMERA PROCEEDINGS

On motion showing that the interest of justice requires it, the court may sit in camera, seal its record, or both.

[Effective July 1, 1997. Amended effective March 4, 1999; June 9, 2000; May 1, 2003.]

LOCAL RULE 47.9 PETITION FOR JUDICIAL REVIEW UNDER 5 U.S.C. § 7703(D)

(a) Time for Filing. A petition for review of a final order or decision of the Merit Systems Protection

Board or of an arbitrator pursuant to 5 U.S.C. § 7703(d) must be filed by the Director of the Office of Personnel Management within 60 days after the date the Director received notice of the final order or decision of the Board or arbitrator.

(b) Contents. The Director's petition must contain:

(1) a statement of jurisdiction (see Federal Rule of Appellate Procedure 28(a)(4));

(2) the Director's determination that the Board or arbitrator erred in interpreting a civil service law, rule, or regulation affecting personnel management and the reasons supporting the determination;

(3) the Director's determination that the decision or order of the Board or arbitrator will have a substantial impact on a civil service law, rule, regulation, or policy directive, and the reasons supporting the determination; and

(4) an appendix including a copy of the order or decision for which review is sought and any relevant portion of the record on review; the appendix may also include documents not part of the record on review that are relevant to the determination that the decision will have substantial impact.

(c) Length of Petition, Answer and Reply; Separate Brief. A petition or answer must not exceed 20 pages. A reply must not exceed 10 pages. A separate brief supporting a petition, answer, or reply is not permitted.

(d) Service and Filing; Number of Copies. The Director must file with the clerk an original and 3 copies of the petition with proof of service and must serve a copy of the petition on the named respondents, all other parties before the Board or arbitrator, and the Board or arbitrator.

(e) Notice of Docketing. On receipt, the clerk will enter the petition on the miscellaneous docket and notify the Director, the named respondents, all other parties before the Board or arbitrator, and the Board or arbitrator of the docketing date.

(f) Appearance by Other Than the Named Respondent. The Board or arbitrator and any other party to the proceeding desiring to participate in the proceeding in this court must enter an appearance. Anyone entering an appearance will be deemed a respondent.

(g) Answer; Appendix; Reply. Within 21 days after service of a petition, any respondent may file an answer. The answer may include an appendix containing any relevant portion of the record on review not included in the appendix to the petition; the appendix may also include documents or affidavits not part of the record on review that are relevant to the determination that the decision will have substantial impact. Within 14 days after service of an answer, the Director may file a reply.

(h) Action by the Court. Granting a petition for review is at the discretion of the court. On receipt of an order granting review, the clerk must enter the petition for review on the general docket. The petition for review will then proceed as if filed under Federal Rule of Appellate Procedure 15.

[Effective July 1, 1997. Amended effective March 4, 1999; June 9, 2000; May 1, 2003.]

LOCAL RULE 47.10 DISMISSAL OF A BANKRUPTCY STAY CASE

An appeal stayed in accordance with the bankruptcy stay provisions of 11 U.S.C. § 362 may be dismissed by the clerk without prejudice to the appellant reinstating the appeal within 30 days after the stay is lifted or the bankruptcy proceeding ends.

[Effective July 1, 1997. Amended effective March 4, 1999; June 9, 2000.]

LOCAL RULE 47.11 QUORUM

A quorum is a simple majority of a panel of the court or of the court en banc. In determining whether a quorum exists for en banc purposes, more than half of all circuit judges in regular active service, including recused or disqualified judges, must be eligible to participate in the en banc process. If a judge of a panel that has heard oral argument or taken under submission any appeal, petition, or motion is unable to continue with consideration of the matter because of death, illness, resignation, incapacity, or recusal, the remaining judges will determine the matter if they are in agreement and no remaining judge requests the designation of another judge. If the remaining judges are not in agreement or if any remaining judge requests the designation of another judge, the remaining judges will promptly advise the chief judge who will secure another judge to sit with the panel. The clerk will advise the parties of the designation, but no further argument will be had or briefs received unless ordered by the court.

[Effective July 1, 1997. Amended effective March 4, 1999; May 1, 2006.]

LOCAL RULE 47.12 ACTION FOR JUDICIAL REVIEW UNDER 38 U.S.C. § 502

(a) Time for Filing. An action for judicial review under 38 U.S.C. § 502 of a rule and regulation of the Department of Veterans Affairs must be filed with the clerk within 60 days after issuance of the rule or regulation or denial of a request for amendment or waiver of the rule or regulation.

(b) Parties. Only a person or persons adversely affected by the rule or regulation or the rulemaking process may bring an action for judicial review. The

Secretary of Veterans Affairs must be named the respondent.

(c) Contents. The action for judicial review must describe how the person or persons bringing the action are adversely affected and must specifically identify either:

(1) the rule, regulation, opinion, or order of the Department of Veterans Affairs separately stated and published in the Federal Register pursuant to 5 U.S.C. § 552(a)(1) on which judicial review is sought; or

(2) the notice-and-comment rulemaking process by the Department of Veterans Affairs pursuant to 5 U.S.C. § 553 on which judicial review is sought.

(d) Procedure. Except as provided in this rule, the procedures applicable to an action for judicial review under 38 U.S.C. § 502 are the same as those for a petition for review under Federal Rule of Appellate Procedure 15.

[Effective July 1, 1997. Amended effective March 4, 1999; June 9, 2000.]

FRAP RULE 48. MASTERS

(a) *Appointment; Powers.* A court of appeals may appoint a special master to hold hearings, if necessary, and to recommend factual findings and disposition in matters ancillary to proceedings in the court. Unless the order referring a matter to a master specifies or limits the master's powers, those powers include, but are not limited to, the following:

(1) regulating all aspects of a hearing;

(2) taking all appropriate action for the efficient performance of the master's duties under the order;

(3) requiring the production of evidence on all matters embraced in the reference; and

(4) administering oaths and examining witnesses and parties.

(b) *Compensation.* If the master is not a judge or court employee, the court must determine the master's compensation and whether the cost is to be charged to any party.

LOCAL RULE 49. SEAL OF THE COURT

The clerk is the keeper of the seal, which is the means of authentication of all records and certificates issued from this court.

[Effective July 1, 1997. Amended effective March 4, 1999.]

LOCAL RULE 50. EMPLOYEE AND FORMER EMPLOYEE

No employee of the court may engage in the practice of law. No former employee of the court may participate or assist, by representation, consultation, or otherwise, in any case that was pending in the court during the period of employment. For purposes of this rule, a person serving at the court as an intern, whether in a judge's chambers or otherwise, is considered an employee of the court, whether such service is for pay, for law school credit, or voluntary.

[Effective July 1, 1997. Amended effective March 4, 1999; April 7, 2009.]

Practice Note

All future participation and assistance prohibited. A former employee of the court is prohibited from participating or assisting in any case after employment with the court if the case was before this court at any point during the person's employment. Thus, for example, a former employee is prohibited from participating or assisting in a case in a trial forum, agency, or other forum if the case was before this court during the person's employment and was remanded by this court or otherwise continued in the trial forum, agency, or other forum for any other reason. A former employee is also prohibited, for example, from participating or assisting in the case if it is subsequently before this court again or if it is before the Supreme Court of the United States.

LOCAL RULE 51. COMPLAINT OF JUDICIAL MISCONDUCT OR DISABILITY

The procedures for processing a complaint of judicial misconduct or disability are pursuant to 28 U.S.C. § 351, et seq. The clerk will provide copies of these procedures on request.

[Effective July 1, 1997. Amended effective March 4, 1999; May 1, 2006.]

LOCAL RULE 52. FEES

(a) Judicial Conference Schedule of Fees.

(1) *General.* The fees charged by the clerk must be the fees prescribed by the Judicial Conference of the United States pursuant to 28 U.S.C. § 1913 or by this rule. No fees are to be charged for services rendered on behalf of the United States, with the exception of those specifically prescribed in subsections (3)(B), (D) and (E) of this rule. No fees under this schedule shall be charged to federal agencies or programs which are funded from judiciary appropriations, including, but not limited to, agencies, organizations, and individuals providing services authorized by the Criminal Justice Act, 18 U.S.C. § 3006A, and Bankruptcy Administrator programs.

(2) *Docketing Fee.* The docketing fee will be paid to the trial court clerk on filing a notice of appeal in that court. The docketing fee will be paid to this court's

clerk on filing any other proceeding, including an appeal or petition for review from the Patent and Trademark Office or the Merit Systems Protection Board, or any other agency, and including an extraordinary writ.

(3) *Judicial Conference Schedule of Fees.*

(A) For docketing a case on appeal or review, or docketing any other proceeding, $450. A separate fee shall be paid by each party filing a notice of appeal in the district court, but parties filing a joint notice of appeal in the district court are required to pay only one fee. A docketing fee shall not be charged for the docketing of an application for the allowance of an interlocutory appeal under 28 U.S.C. § 1292(b), unless the appeal is allowed.

(B) For every search of the records of the court and certifying the results thereof, $26. This fee shall apply to services rendered on behalf of the United States if the information requested is available through electronic access.

(C) For certifying any document or paper, whether the certification is made directly on the document, or by separate instrument, $9.

(D) For reproducing any record or paper, 50 cents per page. This fee shall apply to paper copies made from either: (1) original documents; or (2) microfiche or microfilm reproductions of the original records. This fee shall apply to services rendered on behalf of the United States if the record or paper requested is available through electronic access.

(E) For reproduction of recordings of proceedings, regardless of the medium, $26, including the cost of materials. This fee shall apply to services rendered on behalf of the United States if the reproduction of the recording is available electronically.

(F) For reproduction of the record in any appeal in which the requirement of an appendix is dispensed with by any court of appeals pursuant to Rule 30(f), FRAP, a flat fee of $71.

(G) For each microfiche or microfilm copy of any court record, where available, $5.

(H) For retrieval of a record from a Federal Records Center, National Archives, or other storage location removed from the place of business of the court, $45.

(I) For a check paid into the court which is returned for lack of funds, $45.

(J) The court may charge and collect a fee of $200 per remote location for counsel's requested use of videoconferencing equipment in connection with each oral argument.

(K) For original admission of attorneys to practice, $150 each, including a certificate of admission. For a duplicate certificate of admission or certificate of good standing, $15. Federal Circuit Rule 46 requires an additional local fee of $50 for admission and $10 for a duplicate certificate.

(4) *Electronic Public Access Fee Schedule.* The fees for electronic public access are set forth in the note following 28 U.S.C. § 1913.

(b) Copies of Opinions. For each copy of an opinion (including any separate or dissenting opinions), the fee is $2. No charge may be assessed for the following:

(1) a copy of the opinion furnished to each party of record in the case; and

(2) copies of opinions furnished persons and organizations whose names are on a public interest list established by order of the court.

(c) Fees to Be Paid in Advance. The clerk is not required to docket any proceeding or perform any other service until all fees due the clerk are paid unless a party has been granted leave to proceed in forma pauperis.

(d) Dismissal of Appeal or Petition for Failing to Pay Docketing Fee. If a proceeding is docketed without prepayment of the docketing fee, the appellant or petitioner must pay the fee within 14 days after docketing. If the clerk does not receive the docketing fee, a completed motion for leave to proceed in forma pauperis, or a completed Form 6B within 14 days of the date of docketing of the appeal or petition, the clerk is authorized to dismiss the appeal or petition.

(e) Checks. Checks in payment of all fees must be made payable to the Clerk of Court, United States Court of Appeals for the Federal Circuit.

[Effective July 1, 1997. Amended effective March 4, 1999; May 1, 2003; May 1, 2004; January 1, 2005; May 1, 2006; May 1, 2008; December 1, 2009; June 1, 2011.]

Practice Notes

No Refund of Fees. Fees are deposited with the Treasury Department on receipt. The clerk cannot refund any fee once it is deposited.

Checks and Drafts. Checks and drafts are accepted subject to collection, and full credit will be given only when the check or draft is accepted by the financial institution on which it is drawn.

Docketing Fee and Costs in a Case Involving a Claim Under the Uniformed Services Employment and Reemployment Rights Act of 1994. The docketing fee does not have to be paid, and no costs are taxed, in a petition for review of a decision of the Merits Systems Protection Board if the underlying appeal involved a claim under the Uniformed Services Employment and Reemployment Rights Act of 1994 (USERRA)). 38 U.S.C. § 4323. The petitioner must complete Form 6B to inform the court that the case involves a claim under USERRA.

LOCAL RULE 53. JUDICIAL CONFERENCE

There will be held, at a time and place designated by the chief judge, a conference to consider the business of the court and to advise means of improving the administration of justice. The chief judge presides at the conference. All members of the bar of the court may be members of the conference and may participate in its discussions and deliberations. Registrants must pay a fee to be applied to the payment of expenses of the conference.

[Effective July 1, 1997. Amended effective March 4, 1999.]

LOCAL RULE 54. LIBRARY

(a) General. The library in the Howard T. Markey National Courts Building serves this court and the United States Court of Federal Claims.

(b) Authorized Users. The library's authorized users are limited to:

(1) the judges of the courts;

(2) their court staff;

(3) members of the bars of either court;

(4) pro se litigants with pending cases in either court;

(5) attorneys employed by the United States; and

(6) employees of the Administrative Office of the United States Courts and the Federal Judicial Center.

(c) Suspension; Closing. The librarian may suspend an authorized user for cause and may, when warranted, close the library to all except judges and the court staff.

(d) Books: Check Out and Removal. Only judges and the court staff may check out books from the library. Library books must not be removed from the premises of the Howard T. Markey National Courts Building without express permission from the librari an.

[Effective July 1, 1997. Amended effective March 4, 1999.]

APPENDICES

APPENDIX I. APPENDIX OF FEDERAL CIRCUIT FORMS

FORM 1. NOTICE OF APPEAL TO THE UNITED STATES COURT OF APPEALS FOR THE FEDERAL CIRCUIT FROM A JUDGMENT OR ORDER OF A UNITED STATES DISTRICT COURT

Name of United States District Court for the ________

Case Number ______________

_______________________, Plaintiff,

v. **NOTICE OF APPEAL**

_______________________, Defendant.

Notice is hereby given that ______ (name all parties* taking the appeal) in the above named case hereby appeal to the United States Court of Appeals for the Federal Circuit from the ______ (from the final judgment) ((from an order) (describe the order)) entered in this action on ______, ______ (date).

____

(Signature of appellant or attorney)

____

____

(Address of appellant or attorney)

**See* Fed. R. App. P. 3(c) for permissible ways of identifying appellants.

[Amended effective March 4, 1999; May 1, 2004.]

FORM 2. NOTICE OF APPEAL TO THE UNITED STATES COURT OF APPEALS FOR THE FEDERAL CIRCUIT FROM A JUDGMENT OR ORDER OF THE COURT OF FEDERAL CLAIMS

United States Court of Federal Claims

Case Number ______________

_________________________, Plaintiff,

v. **NOTICE OF APPEAL**

United States, Defendant.

Notice is hereby given that ______ (name all parties* taking the appeal) in the above named case hereby appeal to the United States Court of Appeals for the Federal Circuit from the ______ (from the final judgment) ((from an order) (describe the order)) entered in this action on ______, ______ (date).

____
(Signature of appellant or attorney)

____
(Address of appellant or attorney)

**See* Fed. R. App. P. 3(c) for permissible ways of identifying appellants.

[Effective May 1, 2004.]

FORM 3. NOTICE OF APPEAL TO THE UNITED STATES COURT OF APPEALS FOR THE FEDERAL CIRCUIT FROM A JUDGMENT OR ORDER OF THE COURT OF INTERNATIONAL TRADE

United States Court of International Trade

Case Number ______________

__________________________, Plaintiff,

v. **NOTICE OF APPEAL**

__________________________, Defendant.

Notice is hereby given that ______ (name all parties* taking the appeal) in the above named case hereby appeal to the United States Court of Appeals for the Federal Circuit from the ______ (from the final judgment) ((from an order) (describe the order)) entered in this action on ______, ______ (date).

____
(Signature of appellant or attorney)

____
(Address of appellant or attorney)

**See* Fed. R. App. P. 3(c) for permissible ways of identifying appellants.

[Effective May 1, 2004.]

FORM 4. NOTICE OF APPEAL TO THE UNITED STATES COURT OF APPEALS FOR THE FEDERAL CIRCUIT FROM A JUDGMENT OR ORDER OF THE UNITED STATES COURT OF APPEALS FOR VETERANS CLAIMS

The United States Court of Appeals for Veterans Claims

Case Number ______________

__________________________, Appellant,

v. **NOTICE OF APPEAL**

__________________________, Appellee.
Secretary of Veterans Affairs

Notice is hereby given that ______ (name all parties* taking the appeal) in the above named case hereby appeal to the United States Court of Appeals for the Federal Circuit from the ______ (from the final judgment) ((from an order) (describe the order)) entered in this action on ______, ______ (date).

____
(Signature of appellant or attorney)

____
(Address of appellant or attorney)

**See* Fed. R. App. P. 3(c) for permissible ways of identifying appellants.

[Effective May 1, 2004.]

FORM 5. PETITION FOR REVIEW OR NOTICE OF APPEAL OF AN ORDER OR DECISION OF AN AGENCY, BOARD, COMMISSION, OFFICE OR BUREAU

United States Court of Appeals for the Federal Circuit

________________________, Petitioner or Appellant,

v. **PETITION FOR REVIEW**

________________________, Respondent or Appellee.

_____ (name all parties* bringing the petition or appeal) hereby petition/appeal the court for review of the ______ (describe the order or decision and include decision number) of the ______ (name the agency, board, office or bureau) entered on ______, ______ (date). The order or decision was received on ______, ____ (date).

____
(Signature of petitioner, appellant or attorney)

____
(Address and phone number of petitioner, appellant or attorney)

**See* Fed. R. App. P. 15 for permissible ways of identifying petitioners.

[Former Form 3 redesignated Form 2 and amended effective March 4, 1999; redesignated Form 5 and amended effective May 1, 2004.]

FORM 6. MOTION AND DECLARATION FOR LEAVE TO PROCEED IN FORMA PAUPERIS

UNITED STATES COURT OF APPEALS FOR THE FEDERAL CIRCUIT

____________________ v. ____________________

No. __________

Motion and Declaration for Leave to Proceed In Forma Pauperis

INSTRUCTIONS: If you do not pay the fee, file this completed form with your petition for review or notice of appeal within 14 days of the date of docketing. Complete all questions in this application and then sign it. Do not leave any blanks; if the answer to a question is "0", "none", or "not applicable" (N/A), write in that response. If you need more space to answer a question or to explain your answer, attach a separate sheet of paper identified with your name, your case docket number, and the question number. Failure to fully answer the questions may result in a denial of the motion.

Petitioner/Appellant hereby moves for leave to proceed in forma pauperis, pursuant to 28 U.S.C. § 1915, in this case and submits the following declaration in support thereof:

I, ____________________, am the Petitioner/Appellant in the above-entitled case. In support of my motion to proceed on appeal without being required to pay the docketing fee, I state that I am unable to pay the fee because of my poverty; that I believe that I am entitled to redress; and that the issues which I desire to present on appeal are the following:

____

I further declare that the responses which I have made to the questions and instructions below relating to my ability to pay the docketing fee are true.

1. For both you and your spouse, estimate the average amount of money received from each of the following sources during the past 12 months. Adjust any amount that was received weekly, biweekly, quarterly, semiannually, or annually to show the monthly rate. Use gross amounts, that is, amounts before any deductions for taxes or otherwise.

Income source	**Average monthly amount during the past 12 months**		**Amount expected next month**	
	You	**Spouse**	**You**	**Spouse**
Employment	$______	$______	$______	$______
Self-employment	$______	$______	$______	$______
Income from real property (such as rental income)	$______	$______	$______	$______
Interest and dividends	$______	$______	$______	$______
Gifts	$______	$______	$______	$______
Alimony	$______	$______	$______	$______
Child support	$______	$______	$______	$______
Retirement (such as social security, pensions, annuities, insurance)	$______	$______	$______	$______
Disability (such as social security, insurance payments)	$______	$______	$______	$______

Income source	**Average monthly amount during the past 12 months**		**Amount expected next month**	
	You	**Spouse**	**You**	**Spouse**
Unemployment payments	$______	$______	$______	$______
Public assistance (such as welfare)	$______	$______	$______	$______
Other (specify) ______________	$______	$______	$______	$______
Total monthly income:	$______	$______	$______	$______

2. List your employment history for the past two years, most recent employer first. (Gross monthly pay is pay before taxes or other deductions.)

Employer	**Address**	**Dates of employment**	**Gross monthly pay**
______	______	______	______
______	______	______	______
______	______	______	______

3. List your spouse's employment history for the past two years, most recent employer first. (Gross monthly pay is pay before taxes or other deductions.)

Employer	**Address**	**Dates of employment**	**Gross monthly pay**
______	______	______	______
______	______	______	______
______	______	______	______

4. Are you presently incarcerated? ______Yes ______No If so, you must attach a statement certified by the appropriate institutional officer showing all receipts, expenditures, and balances during the last six months in your institutional accounts. If you have multiple accounts, perhaps because you have been in multiple institutions, attach one certified statement of each account.

5. How much cash do you and your spouse have? $______

Below, state any money you or your spouse have in bank accounts or in any other financial institution. State the average monthly balance.

Financial institution	**Type of account**	**Amount you have**	**Amount your spouse has**
______	______	$______	$______
______	______	$______	$______

6. List the assets, and their values, which you own or your spouse owns. Do not list clothing and ordinary household furnishings.

Home (Value)	**Other real estate** (Value)	**Other assets** (Value)
______	______	______
______	______	______
______	______	______

Other assets (Value)	**Motor vehicle #1**	**Motor vehicle #2**
	Make, model & year:	Make, model & year:
______	______	______
	Value:	Value:
______	______	______
	Registration #:	Registration #:
______	______	______

7. State every person, business, or organization owing you or your spouse money, and the amount owed:

Person, business or organization owing you or your spouse money	Amount owed to you	Amount owed to your spouse
______	______	______
______	______	______
______	______	______

8. State the persons who rely on you or your spouse for support:

Initials of Person	Relationship	Age
______	______	______
______	______	______
______	______	______

9. Estimate the average monthly expenses of you and your family. Show separately the amounts paid by your spouse. Adjust any payments that are made weekly, biweekly, quarterly, semiannually, or annually to show the monthly rate.

	You	Your spouse
Rent or home mortgage payment (include lot rented for mobile home)	$______	$______
Are real estate taxes included? __Yes __No		
Is property insurance included? __Yes __No		
Utilities (electricity, heating fuel, water, sewer, and telephone)	$______	$______
Home maintenance (repairs and upkeep)	$______	$______
Food	$______	$______
Clothing	$______	$______
Laundry and dry cleaning	$______	$______
Medical and dental expenses	$______	$______
Transportation (not including motor vehicle payments)	$______	$______
Recreation, entertainment, newspapers, magazines, etc.	$______	$______
Insurance (not deducted from wages or included in mortgage payments)		
Homeowner's or renter's	$______	$______
Life	$______	$______
Health	$______	$______
Motor vehicle	$______	$______
Other: ______	$______	$______
Taxes (not deducted from wages or included in mortgage payments) (specify): ______	$______	$______
Installment payments		
Motor vehicle	$______	$______
Credit card (name): ______	$______	$______
Department store (name): ______	$______	$______
Other: ______	$______	$______
Alimony, maintenance, and support paid to others	$______	$______
Regular expenses for operation of business, profession or farm (attach detailed statement)	$______	$______
Other (specify): ______	$______	$______
Total monthly expenses:	$______	$______

10. Do you expect any major changes to your monthly income or expenses or in your assets or liabilities during the next 12 months?

__Yes __No If yes, describe on an attached sheet.

11. Have you paid, or will you be paying, an attorney any money for services in connection with this case, including the completion of this form?

__Yes __No If yes, how much? $______

If yes, state the attorney's name, address, and telephone number:

____

____

12. Have you paid, or will you be paying, anyone other than an attorney (such as a paralegal or a typist) any money for services in connection with this case, including the completion of this form?

__Yes __No If yes, how much? $______

If yes, state the person's name, address, and telephone number:

____

____

13. Provide any other information that will help explain why you cannot pay the docketing fees for your appeal or petition for review.

____

____

14. Have you ever filed a motion for leave to proceed in forma pauperis in any other case in this court? __Yes __No If yes, state the name and docket number of that case.

____

15. State the address of your legal residence:

____

Your daytime phone number: (   ) ____________

Your age:__________ Your years of schooling:__________

____

You must sign and date the declaration under penalty of perjury.

DECLARATION UNDER PENALTY OF PERJURY

I declare under penalty of perjury, under the laws of the United States, that my answers on this form are true and correct.

________________ ____________________

Date Petitioner's/Appellant's signature

cc: ________________

ORDER OF THE COURT

The motion to proceed in forma pauperis is DENIED. The docketing fee must be paid within 14 days.		The motion to proceed in forma pauperis is GRANTED. Let the applicant proceed without prepayment of the docketing fee.	
__________	______	__________	______
Circuit Judge or Clerk	Date	Circuit Judge or Clerk	Date

[Former Form 4 redesignated Form 3 and amended effective March 4, 1999; redesignated Form 6 and amended effective May 1, 2004.]

FORM 6A. SUPPLEMENTAL IN FORMA PAUPERIS FORM FOR PRISONERS

SUPPLEMENTAL IN FORMA PAUPERIS FORM FOR PRISONERS

AUTHORIZATION FORM

I, ______________, request and authorize the agency holding me in custody, to send to the Clerk of the United States Court of Appeals for the Federal Circuit a certified copy of the statement for the past six months of my trust fund account (or institutional equivalent) at the institution where I am incarcerated. I further request and authorize the agency holding me in custody to calculate and disburse funds from my trust fund account (or institutional equivalent) in the amounts specified by 28 U.S.C. § 1915(b). This authorization is furnished in connection with an appeal, and I understand that the total appellate filing fees for which I am obligated are $450 or $455. I also understand that these fees will be debited from my account regardless of the outcome of my appeal. This authorization shall apply to any other agency into whose custody I may be transferred.

______________ ______________________________

Date Petitioner's/Appellant's Signature

You must sign and date above. You must also complete the following Disclosure and sign and date the Declaration Under Penalty of Perjury below.

DISCLOSURE OF PRIOR FEDERAL ACTIONS

If you are presently incarcerated, have you ever before brought an action or appeal in a federal court while you were incarcerated or detained? ____ Yes ____ No

If so, how many times? ____

Were any of the actions or appeals dismissed because they were frivolous, malicious, or failed to state a claim upon which relief may be granted? ____ Yes ____ No

If so, how many of them? ____

DECLARATION UNDER PENALTY OF PERJURY

I declare under penalty of perjury, under the laws of the United States, that the foregoing is true and correct.

______________ ______________________________

Date Petitioner's/Appellant's Signature

cc: ______________

[Former Form 3A effective May 1, 2003; redesignated Form 6A and amended effective May 1, 2004; May 1, 2008.]

FORM 6B. USERRA NOTIFICATION FORM

UNITED STATES COURT OF APPEALS FOR THE FEDERAL CIRCUIT

_______________ v. _______________

Case No. _____

USERRA Notification Form

INSTRUCTIONS: In a petition for review of a Merit Systems Protection Board decision, a petitioner is not required to pay the docketing fee or costs if the case involved a claim under the Uniformed Services Employment and Reemployments Rights Act of 1994 (USERRA). 38 U.S.C. § 4323. Check the statement below indicating that the Board appeal involved a USERRA claim and sign this form only if the underlying appeal at the Board involved a USERRA claim. The signed original should be sent within 14 days of the date of docketing to: Clerk, United States Court of Appeals for the Federal Circuit, 717 Madison Place, NW, Washington, DC 20439. One copy should be sent to counsel for the respondent.

☐ Because the underlying appeal at the Merit Systems Protection Board involved a USERRA claim, the petitioner is not required to pay the docketing fee or costs.

I certify that a copy of this form was sent to _______________, the attorney for the respondent, at the following address:

_______________	_______________
Date	Signature of pro se or counsel

Clerk of Court
United States Court of Appeals for the Federal Circuit
717 Madison Place, NW
Washington, DC 20439

[May 1, 2008.]

FORM 7. APPEAL INFORMATION SHEET

FEDERAL CIRCUIT APPEAL INFORMATION SHEET

____ United States District Court for the ______________________

____ United States Court of International Trade

____ United States Court of Federal Claims

____ United States Court of Appeals for Veterans Claims

Type of case: ______________________________

______________ v. ______________

(List all parties. Use an asterisk to indicate dismissed or withdrawn parties. Use a separate sheet if needed. Explain any discrepancy with the caption used on the judgment, order, or opinion.)

Docket No. ______________ Date of Judgment or Order ______

Cross or related appeal? ______ Date of Notice of Appeal ______

Appellant is: ______ Plaintiff ______ Defendant ______ Other (explain) ____

FEES: Court of Appeals docket fee paid? ____ Yes ____ No

U.S. Appeal? ____ Yes ____ No

In forma pauperis? ____ Yes ____ No

Is this matter under seal? ____ Yes ____ No

COUNSEL: (List name, firm, address, and telephone of lead counsel for each party. Indicate party represented. Use separate sheet if needed.)

______________ ______________________________

COURT REPORTER: (Name and telephone): ______________________

IMPORTANT: Attach a copy of the judgment or order appealed from and any supporting opinion or memorandum. Forward together with a copy of the notice of appeal and certified docket entries.

Clerk of Court
United States Court of Appeals for the Federal Circuit
717 Madison Place, NW
Washington, DC 20439

[Former Form 5 redesignated Form 4 and amended effective March 4, 1999; redesignated Form 7 effective May 1, 2004.]

FORM 8. ENTRY OF APPEARANCE

UNITED STATES COURT OF APPEALS FOR THE FEDERAL CIRCUIT

________________ v. ________________

No. ______

ENTRY OF APPEARANCE

(INSTRUCTIONS: Counsel should refer to Federal Circuit Rule 47.3. Pro se petitioners and appellants should read paragraphs 1 and 18 of the Guide for Pro Se Petitioners and Appellants. File this form with the clerk within 14 days of the date of docketing and serve a copy of it on the principal attorney for each party.)

Please enter my appearance (select one):

____ Pro Se ____ As counsel for: ____________________
Name of party

I am, or the party I represent is (select one):

____Petitioner ____Respondent ____Amicus curiae ____Cross-Appellant
____Appellant ____Appellee ____Intervenor

As amicus curiae or intervenor, this party supports (select one):

____Petitioner or appellant ____Respondent or appellee

My address and telephone are:

Name: ____________________
Law firm: ____________________
Address: ____________________
City, State and ZIP: ____________________
Telephone: ____________________
Fax #: ____________________
E-mail address: ____________________

Statement to be completed by counsel only (select one):

____ I am the principal attorney for this party in this case and will accept all service for the party. I agree to inform all other counsel in this case of the matters served upon me.

____ I am replacing __________ as the principal attorney who will/will not remain on the case. [Government attorneys only.]

____ I am not the principal attorney for this party in this case.

Date admitted to Federal Circuit bar (counsel only): __________

This is my first appearance before the United States Court of Appeals for the Federal Circuit (counsel only):

____Yes ____No

____A courtroom accessible to the handicapped is required if oral argument is scheduled.

________________ ____________________
Date Signature of pro se or counsel

cc: __________

[Former Form 6 redesignated Form 5 and amended effective March 4, 1999; redesignated Form 8 and amended effective May 1, 2004.]

FORM 9. CERTIFICATE OF INTEREST

UNITED STATES COURT OF APPEALS FOR THE FEDERAL CIRCUIT

______________ v. ______________

No. ______

CERTIFICATE OF INTEREST

Counsel for the (petitioner) (appellant) (respondent) (appellee) (amicus) (name of party) ______ certifies the following (use "None" if applicable; use extra sheets if necessary):

1. The full name of every party or amicus represented by me is:

____

____

____

2. The name of the real party in interest (if the party named in the caption is not the real party in interest) represented by me is:

____

____

____

3. All parent corporations and any publicly held companies that own 10 percent or more of the stock of the party or amicus curiae represented by me are:

____

____

____

4. ☐ The names of all law firms and the partners or associates that appeared for the party or amicus now represented by me in the trial court or agency or are expected to appear in this court are:

____

______________ ______________

Date Signature of counsel

____

Printed name of counsel

Please Note: All questions must be answered

cc: ______________

[Former Form 7 redesignated Form 6 and amended effective March 4, 1999; redesignated Form 9 effective May 1, 2004; May 1, 2008.]

FORM 10. STATEMENT CONCERNING DISCRIMINATION

UNITED STATES COURT OF APPEALS FOR THE FEDERAL CIRCUIT

__________________ v. __________________

No. ______

PETITIONER'S FED. CIR. R. 15(c) STATEMENT CONCERNING DISCRIMINATION

Please complete sections A, B, and C.

SECTION A:

Check the statements in section A that apply to your case. Usually, it is one statement, but it may be more. Do not alter or add to any of the statements.

___ (1) No claim of discrimination by reason of race, sex, age, national origin, or handicapped condition has been or will be made in this case.

___ (2) Any claim of discrimination by reason of race, sex, age, national origin, or handicapped condition raised before and decided by the Merit Systems Protection Board or arbitrator has been abandoned or will not be raised or continued in this or any other court.

___ (3) The petition seeks review only of the Board's or arbitrator's dismissal of the case for lack of jurisdiction or for untimeliness.

___ (4) The case involves an application to the Office of Personnel Management for benefits.

___ (5) The case was transferred to this court from a district court and I continue to contest the transfer.

SECTION B:

Answer the following: Have you filed a discrimination case in a United States district court from the Board's or arbitrator's decision? ___Yes ___No

If so, identify any case. ____

SECTION C:

Answer the following: Have you filed a discrimination case in the Equal Employment Opportunity Commission from the Board's or arbitrator's decision? ___Yes ___No

If so, identify any case ____

______________ ______________________________

Date Petitioner's signature

Mail this form with the petition for review or within 14 days of the date of docketing of the petition for review to:

Clerk of Court
United States Court of Appeals for the Federal Circuit
717 Madison Place, NW
Washington, DC 20439

cc: ______________

[Former Form 8 redesignated Form 7 and amended effective March 4, 1999; redesignated Form 10 effective May 1, 2004; revised May 1, 2006.]

FORM 11. INFORMAL BRIEF (MSPB OR ARBITRATOR CASES)

UNITED STATES COURT OF APPEALS FOR THE FEDERAL CIRCUIT

____________________ v. ____________________

No. ________

INFORMAL BRIEF OF PETITIONER

Read the Guide for Pro Se Petitioners and Appellants before completing this form. Attach a copy of the initial and final decision or order of the Merit Systems Protection Board or arbitrator. Answer the following questions as best you can. Your answers should refer to the decision or order you are appealing where possible. Use extra sheets if needed.

1. Have you ever had another case in this court? _______Yes _______No In a United States district court? _______Yes _______No In the Equal Employment Opportunity Commission? _______Yes _______No If so, identify each case.

2. Did the MSPB or arbitrator incorrectly decide or fail to take into account any facts? _______Yes _______No If so, what facts? (Refer to paragraph 7 of the Guide.)

3. Did the MSPB or arbitrator apply the wrong law? _______Yes _______No If so, what law should be applied?

4. Did the MSPB or arbitrator fail to consider important grounds for relief? _______Yes _______No If so, what grounds?

5. Are there other reasons why the MSPB's or arbitrator's decision was wrong? _______Yes _______No If so, what reasons?

6. What action do you want the court to take in this case?

7. Do you want to argue before the court in person? _______Yes _______No If yes, what are the reasons why argument will aid the court? (Refer to paragraph 15 of the Guide.)

____

____

____

____

____

____

8. Do you intend to represent yourself? _______Yes _______No If you have not filed an Entry of Appearance, indicate your full name, address, and telephone number.

____

____

____

____

____

____

9. I certify that a copy of this brief and any attachments was sent to. __________, the attorney for respondent, at the following address: __________. (Address is found on the Entry of Appearance served on you by the attorney for the respondent. If you do not send a copy of this brief to the respondent, the court will not file the brief.)

____________________ ______________________________

Date Petitioner's signature

In addition to mailing a copy to the attorney for the respondent, mail an original and three copies of this informal brief and attachments to:

Clerk of Court
United States Court of Appeals for the Federal Circuit
717 Madison Place, NW
Washington, DC 20439

[Former Form 9 redesignated Form 8 and amended effective March 4, 1999; redesignated Form 11 effective May 1, 2004.]

FORM 11A. INFORMAL BRIEF OF PRO SE APPELLEE/RESPONDENT

UNITED STATES COURT OF APPEALS FOR THE FEDERAL CIRCUIT

____________________ v. ____________________

No. ___

INFORMAL BRIEF OF PRO SE APPELLEE/RESPONDENT

Read the Guide for Pro Se Petitioners and Appellants before completing this form. Answer the following questions as best you can. Your answers should refer to the decision or order that was appealed, where possible. Use extra sheets if needed.

1. Have you ever had another case in this court? ☐ Yes ☐ No If so, state the name and number of each case.

   ____

2. What arguments do you make in response to the arguments made by the appellant or petitioner?

   ____

3. Are there other arguments you wish to make? ☐ Yes ☐ No If so, what are the arguments?

   ____

4. What action do you want the court to take in this case?

   ____

5. Do you want to argue before the court in person? ☐ Yes ☐ No What are the reasons why argument will aid the court? (Refer to paragraph 15 of the Guide.)

   ____

6. Do you intend to represent yourself? ☐ Yes ☐ No If you have not filed an Entry of Appearance, indicate your full name, address, and telephone number.

   ____

7. I certify that a copy of this brief and any attachments was sent to: ____________, the attorney for appellant or petitioner, at the following address: ____________. (Address is found on the Entry of Appearance served on you by the attorney for the appellant or petitioner. If you do not send a copy of this brief to the attorney for the appellant or petitioner, the court will not file the brief.)

____________________	____________________
Date	Signature

In addition to mailing a copy to the attorney for the appellant or petitioner, mail an original and three copies of this informal brief and attachments to:

Clerk of Court
United States Court of Appeals for the Federal Circuit
717 Madison Place, NW
Washington, DC 20439

[May 1, 2008.]

FORM 12. INFORMAL BRIEF (DISTRICT COURT, COURT OF INTERNATIONAL TRADE, AND COURT OF FEDERAL CLAIMS CASES)

UNITED STATES COURT OF APPEALS FOR THE FEDERAL CIRCUIT

____________________ v. ____________________

No. ______

INFORMAL BRIEF OF APPELLANT

Read the Guide for Pro Se Petitioners and Appellants before completing this form. Attach a copy of the final decision or order of the trial court. Answer the following questions as best you can. Your answers should refer to the decision or order you are appealing where possible. Use extra sheets if needed.

1. Have you ever had another case in this court? ______Yes ______No If so, state the name and number of each case.

____
____
____
____

2. Did the trial court incorrectly decide or fail to take into account any facts? ______Yes ______No If so, what facts? (Refer to paragraph 7 of the Guide.)

____
____
____
____

3. Did the trial court apply the wrong law? ______Yes ______No If so, what law should be applied?

____
____
____
____

4. Did the trial court fail to consider important grounds for relief? ______Yes ______No If so, what grounds?

____
____
____
____

5. Are there other reasons why the trial court's decision was wrong? ______Yes ______No If so, what reasons?

____
____
____
____

6. What action do you want the court to take in this case?
____
____
____
____
____

7. Do you want to argue before the court in person? ______Yes ______No If yes, what are the reasons why argument will aid the court? (Refer to paragraph 15 of the Guide.)
____
____
____
____
____

8. Do you intend to represent yourself? ______Yes ______No If you have not filed an Entry of Appearance, indicate your full name, address, and telephone number.
____
____
____
____
____

9. I certify that a copy of this brief and any attachments was sent to: __________, the attorney for appellee, at the following address: ______________. (Address is found on the Entry of Appearance served on you by the attorney for the appellee. If you do not send a copy of this brief to the appellee, the court will not file the brief.)

______________________ ______________________
Date Appellant's signature

In addition to mailing a copy to the attorney for the appellee, mail an original and three copies of this informal brief and attachments to:

Clerk of Court
United States Court of Appeals for the Federal Circuit
717 Madison Place, NW
Washington, DC 20439

[Former Form 10 redesignated Form 9 and amended effective March 4, 1999; redesignated Form 12 effective May 1, 2004.]

FORM 13. INFORMAL BRIEF (COURT OF APPEALS FOR VETERANS CLAIMS CASES)

UNITED STATES COURT OF APPEALS FOR THE FEDERAL CIRCUIT

____________________ v. ____________________

No. ______

INFORMAL BRIEF OF APPELLANT

Read the Guide for Pro Se Petitioners and Appellants before completing this form. Attach a copy of the final decision or order of the Court of Appeals for Veterans Claims. Answer the following questions as best you can. Your answers should refer to the decision or order you are appealing where possible. Use extra sheets if needed.

1. Have you ever had another case in this court? ______Yes ______No If so, state the name and number of each case.

2. Did the Court of Appeals for Veterans Claims decision involve the validity or interpretation of a statute or regulation? ____ Yes ____ No If so, what are your arguments concerning those issues? (Refer to paragraph 7 of the Guide.)

3. Did the Court of Appeals for Veterans Claims decide constitutional issues? ______Yes ______No If so, what are your arguments concerning those issues?

4. Did the Court of Appeals for Veterans Claims fail to decide any other issue correctly? ______Yes ______No If so, how?

5. Are there other arguments you wish to make? ______Yes ______No If so, what are the arguments?

6. What action do you want the court to take in this case?

____
____
____
____
____

7. Do you want to argue before the court in person? _____Yes _____No If yes, what are the reasons why argument will aid the court? (Refer to paragraph 15 of the Guide.)

____
____
____
____
____

8. Do you intend to represent yourself? _____Yes _____No If you have not filed an Entry of Appearance, indicate your full name, address, and telephone number.

____
____
____
____
____

9. I certify that a copy of this brief and any attachments was sent to: _________, the attorney for the Secretary of Veterans Affairs, at the following address: _____________. (Address is found on the Entry of Appearance served on you by the attorney for the Secretary of Veterans Affairs. If you do not send a copy of this brief to the attorney for the Secretary, the court will not file the brief.)

______________________ ______________________
Date Appellant's signature

In addition to mailing a copy to the attorney for the Secretary, mail an original and three copies of this informal brief and attachments to:

Clerk of Court
United States Court of Appeals for the Federal Circuit
717 Madison Place, NW
Washington, DC 20439

[Former Form 10 effective March 4, 1999; redesignated Form 13 effective May 1, 2004.]

FORM 14. INFORMAL BRIEF (BOARD OF CONTRACT APPEALS, BOARD OF PATENT APPEALS AND INTERFERENCES, TRADEMARK TRIAL AND APPEAL BOARD, AND INTERNATIONAL TRADE COMMISSION CASES)

UNITED STATES COURT OF APPEALS FOR THE FEDERAL CIRCUIT

________________ v. ________________

No. ______

INFORMAL BRIEF OF APPELLANT

Read the Guide for Pro Se Petitioners and Appellants before completing this form. Attach a copy of the final decision or order of the Board, Office, or Commission. Answer the following questions as best you can. Your answers should refer to the decision or order you are appealing where possible. Use extra sheets if needed.

1. Have you ever had another case in this court? ______Yes ______No If so, state the name and number of each case.

____

____

____

____

2. Did the Board or Commission incorrectly decide or fail to take into account any facts? ______Yes ______No If so, what facts? (Refer to paragraph 7 of the Guide.)

____

____

____

____

____

3. Did the Board or Commission apply the wrong law? ______Yes ______No If so, what law should be applied?

____

____

____

____

____

4. Did the Board or Commission fail to consider important grounds for relief? ______Yes ______No If so, what grounds?

____

____

____

____

____

5. Are there other reasons why the decision was wrong? ______Yes ______No If so, what reasons?

____

____

____

____

____

6. What action do you want the court to take in this case?

____
____
____
____
____

7. Do you want to argue before the court in person? _______Yes _______No If yes, what are the reasons why argument will aid the court? (Refer to paragraph 15 of the Guide.)

____
____
____
____
____

8. Do you intend to represent yourself? _______Yes _______No If you have not filed an Entry of Appearance, indicate your full name, address, and telephone number.

____
____
____
____
____

9. I certify that a copy of this brief and any attachments was sent to: __________, the attorney for appellee, at the following address: ________________. (Address is found on the Entry of Appearance served on you by the attorney for the appellee. If you do not send a copy of this brief to the attorney for the appellee, the court will not file the brief.)

______________________ ______________________
Date Appellant's signature

In addition to mailing a copy to the attorney for the appellee, mail an original and three copies of this informal brief and attachments to:

Clerk of Court
United States Court of Appeals for the Federal Circuit
717 Madison Place, NW
Washington, DC 20439

[Former Form 11 amended effective March 4, 1999; redesignated Form 14 effective May 1, 2004.]

FORM 15. INFORMAL BRIEF (SECRETARY OF VETERANS AFFAIRS CASES UNDER 38 U.S.C. § 502)

UNITED STATES COURT OF APPEALS FOR THE FEDERAL CIRCUIT

____________________ v. ____________________

No. ______

INFORMAL BRIEF OF PETITIONER

Read the Guide for Pro Se Petitioners and Appellants before completing this form. Attach a copy of the action or regulation of the Secretary of Veterans Affairs that is subject to judicial review. Answer the following questions as best you can. Your answers should refer to the Secretary's action or regulations where possible. Use extra sheets if needed.

1. Have you ever had another case in this court? ______Yes ______No If so, state the name and number of each case.

2. What action of the Secretary of Veterans Affairs do you want reviewed by this court?

3. What regulations, if any, of the Secretary of Veterans Affairs do you want reviewed by this court?

4. What errors of fact or law are found in the Secretary's action or regulations? Explain in detail.

5. Have you exhausted the administrative remedies available? ______Yes ______No Explain in detail all the steps you have taken within the Department of Veterans Affairs to obtain the relief you are seeking.

6. What action do you want the court to take in this case?
____
____
____
____
____

7. Do you want to argue before the court in person? ______Yes ______No If yes, what are the reasons why argument will aid the court? (Refer to paragraph 15 of the Guide.)
____
____
____
____
____

8. Do you intend to represent yourself? ______Yes ______No If you have not filed an Entry of Appearance, indicate your full name, address, and telephone number.
____
____
____
____
____

9. I certify that a copy of this brief and any attachments was sent to ________, the attorney for respondent, at the following address: ____________. (Address is found on the Entry of Appearance served on you by the attorney for the respondent. If you do not send a copy of this brief to the attorney for the respondent, the court will not file the brief.)

____________________ ____________________

Date Petitioner's signature

In addition to mailing a copy to the attorney for the respondent, mail an original and three copies of this informal brief and attachments to:

Clerk of Court
United States Court of Appeals for the Federal Circuit
717 Madison Place, NW
Washington, DC 20439

[Former Form 12 amended effective March 4, 1999; redesignated Form 15 effective May 1, 2004.]

FORM 16. INFORMAL BRIEF (GOVERNMENT ACCOUNTABILITY OFFICE PERSONNEL APPEALS BOARD, OFFICE OF COMPLIANCE, EQUAL EMPLOYMENT OPPORTUNITY COMMISSION, AND BUREAU OF JUSTICE ASSISTANCE CASES)

UNITED STATES COURT OF APPEALS FOR THE FEDERAL CIRCUIT

________________ v. ________________

No. ______

INFORMAL BRIEF OF PETITIONER

Read the Guide for Pro Se Petitioners and Appellants before completing this form. Attach a copy of the final decision or order of the Board, Office, or Commission. Answer the following questions as best you can. Your answers should refer to the decision or order you are appealing where possible. Use extra sheets if needed.

1. Have you ever had another case in this court? ______Yes ______No If so, state the name and number of each case.

____
____
____
____
____

2. Did the Board or Commission incorrectly decide or fail to take into account any facts? ______Yes ______No If so, what facts? (Refer to paragraph 7 of the Guide.)

____
____
____
____

3. Did the Board or Commission apply the wrong law? ______Yes ______No If so, what law should be applied?

____
____
____
____
____

4. Did the Board or Commission fail to consider important grounds for relief? ______Yes ______No If so, what grounds?

____
____
____
____
____

5. Are there other reasons why the decision was wrong? ______Yes ______No If so, what reasons?

____
____
____
____
____

6. What action do you want the court to take in this case?
____
____
____
____
____

7. Do you want to argue before the court in person? _______Yes _______No If yes, what are the reasons why argument will aid the court? (Refer to paragraph 15 of the Guide.)
____
____
____
____
____

8. Do you intend to represent yourself? _______Yes _______No If you have not filed an Entry of Appearance, indicate your full name, address, and telephone number.
____
____
____
____
____

9. I certify that a copy of this brief and any attachments was sent to: ________, the attorney for respondent, at the following address: ________________. (Address is found on the Entry of Appearance served on you by the attorney for respondent. If you do not send a copy of this brief to the attorney for the respondent, the court will not file the brief.)

______________________ ______________________
Date Petitioner's signature

In addition to mailing a copy to the attorney for the respondent, mail an original and three copies of this informal brief and attachments to:

Clerk of Court
United States Court of Appeals for the Federal Circuit
717 Madison Place, NW
Washington, DC 20439

[Former Form 13 amended effective March 4, 1999; redesignated Form 16 and amended effective May 1, 2004.]

FORM 17. SAMPLE BRIEF COVER (MSPB CASES)

2008–3333

UNITED STATES COURT OF APPEALS FOR THE FEDERAL CIRCUIT

JOANNE S. DOE,

Petitioner,

v.

DEPARTMENT OF THE NAVY,

Respondent.

PETITION FOR REVIEW FROM THE MERIT SYSTEMS PROTECTION BOARD IN CH0752991234–I–5.

BRIEF OF PETITIONER JOANNE S. DOE

MARY S. SMITH
SMITH & JONES
123 Main Street
Anytown, ST 12345
(555) 555–5555

Attorney for Petitioner

December 1, 2007

[Former Form 14 amended effective March 4, 1999; redesignated Form 17 and amended effective May 1, 2004; May 1, 2008.]

FORM 18. SAMPLE BRIEF COVER (DISTRICT COURT CASES)

2008–1111, –1112

UNITED STATES COURT OF APPEALS FOR THE FEDERAL CIRCUIT

ABC CORPORATION and DEF COMPANY, INC.,

Plaintiffs–Appellants,

v.

UVW, LTD. and XYZ, CO.,

Defendants–Cross Appellants.

APPEAL FROM THE UNITED STATES DISTRICT COURT FOR THE NORTHERN DISTRICT OF IOWA IN CV–99–1234, JUDGE ROBERT WASHINGTON.

BRIEF OF DEFENDANTS–CROSS APPELLANTS UVW, LTD. and XYZ, CO.

JOHN JONES, JR.
SMITH & JONES
123 Main Street
Anytown, ST 12345
(555) 555–5555

Attorney for Defendants–Cross Appellants

December 1, 2007

[Former Form 15 amended effective March 4, 1999; redesignated Form 18 and amended effective May 1, 2004; May 1, 2008.]

FORM 19. CERTIFICATE OF COMPLIANCE WITH RULE 32(A)

CERTIFICATE OF COMPLIANCE WITH TYPE–VOLUME LIMITATION, TYPEFACE REQUIREMENTS, AND TYPE STYLE REQUIREMENTS

1. This brief complies with the type-volume limitation of Federal Rule of Appellate Procedure 32(a)(7)(B) or Federal Rule of Appellate Procedure 28.1(e).

☐ The brief contains [*state the number of*] words, excluding the parts of the brief exempted by Federal Rule of Appellate Procedure 32(a)(7)(B)(iii), or

☐ The brief uses a monospaced typeface and contains [*state the number*] lines of text, excluding the parts of the brief exempted by Federal Rule of Appellate Procedure 32(a)(7)(B)(iii).

2. This brief complies with the typeface requirements of Federal Rule of Appellate Procedure 32(a)(5) or Federal Rule of Appellate Procedure 28.1(e) and the type style requirements of Federal Rule of Appellate Procedure 32(a)(6).

☐ The brief has been prepared in a proportionally spaced typeface using [*state name and version of word processing program*] in [*state font size and name of type style*], or

☐ The brief has been prepared in a monospaced typeface using [*state name and version of word processing program*] with [*state number of characters per inch and name of type style*].

____
(Signature of Attorney)

____
(Name of Attorney)

____
(State whether representing appellant, appellee, etc.)

____
(Date)

[Former Form 15 effective May 1, 2003; redesignated Form 19 and amended effective May 1, 2004; amended May 1, 2008.]

FORM 20. APPLICATION FOR FEES AND OTHER EXPENSES UNDER THE EQUAL ACCESS TO JUSTICE ACT

APPLICATION
FOR FEES AND OTHER EXPENSES UNDER THE EQUAL ACCESS TO JUSTICE ACT
Title 28 U.S.C. § 2412(d), Title II of Public Law 96–481, 94 STAT 2325

1. COURT
UNITED STATES COURT OF APPEALS FOR THE FEDERAL CIRCUIT

2. DATE FILED

3. DOCKET NO.

4. NAME OF APPLICANT (one per form)

5. GOVERNMENT AGENCY INVOLVED IN CLAIM

6. NATURE OF APPLICATION
- A. ☐ Original application under 28 U.S.C. § 2412(d)(1)(A) after judgment in civil action against U.S.
- B. ☐ Appeal of fees and expenses awarded by Lower Court. (If item 6B is checked go to item 7.)
- C. ☐ Original application under 28 U.S.C. § 2412(d)(3) after review of agency decision.
- D. ☐ Petition for leave to appeal an administrative agency fee determination under 5 U.S.C. § 504(c)(2).

7. APPEAL FROM:
☐ DISTRICT COURT ☐ BANKRUPTCY COURT
☐ OTHER: ______

7A. DATE FILED IN LOWER COURT

7B. DOCKET NO.

8. ADMINISTRATIVE AGENCY DOCKET NO.

9. DATED FILED IN ADMINISTRATIVE AGENCY

10. SHOWING OF "PREVAILING PARTY" STATUS (28 U.S.C. § 2412(d)(1)(B)):

IS AGENCY ORDER, COURT ORDER, OR OTHER RELEVANT DOCUMENT ATTACHED?
☐ YES ☐ NO

11. SHOWING OF ELIGIBILITY (28 U.S.C. § 2412(d)(2)(B)):

IS NET WORTH INFORMATION ATTACHED? ☐ YES ☐ NO

12. ENTER ALLEGATION THAT GOVERNMENT POSITION WAS NOT SUBSTANTIALLY JUSTIFIED (28 U.S.C. § 2412(d)(1)(B)):

13. FOR EACH AMOUNT CLAIMED, PLEASE ATTACH ITEMIZATION INFORMATION INDICATING SERVICE PROVIDED, DATE, HOURS, AND RATE (28 U.S.C. § 2412(d)(2)(B)):

	AMOUNT CLAIMED
A. ATTORNEY FEES	$ ______
B. STUDY	______
C. ANALYSIS	______
D. ENGINEERING REPORT	______
E. TEST	______
F. PROJECT	______
G. EXPERT WITNESS FEES	______
H. OTHER FEES AND EXPENSES—SPECIFY	
(1) ______	______
(2) ______	______
(3) ______	______
I. TOTAL FEES AND EXPENSES	$ ______

14. SIGNATURE

15. DATE

NOTE: THIS FORM SHOULD ACCOMPANY YOUR CLAIM WHEN FILED WITH THE CLERK OF COURT.

[Former Form 16 redesignated Form 17 effective May 1, 2003; redesignated Form 20 effective May 1, 2004.]

FORM 21. APPLICATION FOR ADMISSION TO THE BAR

United States Court of Appeals for the Federal Circuit
APPLICATION FOR ADMISSION TO THE BAR

I (print name), ______________________________ whose mailing address is:

Street/P.O. Box ____

City/State/Zip/Phone ____

do hereby apply for admission to the bar of the United States Court of Appeals for the Federal Circuit.

My personal statement showing my eligibility for membership is as follows:

I am admitted to practice before the highest court of these states (attach extra page if necessary):

State Court/Date of Admission (month and year) ________________________

State Bar Number (if any) ___________

I am admitted to practice before these federal courts (attach extra page if necessary):

Federal Court/Date of Admission (month and year) ______________________

Federal Bar Number (if any) ___________

I certify that I am not presently subject to discipline by another court. I will inform this court within 30 days of any disciplinary action taken against me by any court and will furnish the court with copies of relevant court orders and I will inform the court if any bar application is denied.

____________________________ ____________________________

Date of Birth Signature of Applicant

MOTION OF SPONSOR

(The motion of a sponsoring member of the bar is not required if the applicant attaches a certificate of good standing as described in Federal Circuit Rule 46(b).

I (print name), ________________, a member of the bar of this court, do hereby move the admission of the above attorney.

Date: ___________ Signature of sponsor:_______________________

OATH OF ADMISSION

(Execute the oath unless arrangements have been made to have the oath administered in open court)

I, ________________, do solemnly swear (or affirm) that I will comport myself as an attorney and counselor of this court, uprightly and in accordance with the law, and that I will support the Constitution of the United States.

__________ ____________________________

Date of Birth Signature of Applicant

Subscribed and sworn to before me on this date: _________. My commission expires on this date: _________. Signature of Notary: ______________________

[Seal]

INSTRUCTIONS FOR APPLYING FOR ADMISSION TO THE BAR OF THE UNITED STATES COURT OF APPEALS FOR THE FEDERAL CIRCUIT

Fill out the application on the reverse side. Print your name clearly on the first line. Your name as printed will be the name that appears on the court's attorney roster and on the certificate of admission.

You may submit a completed admission form accompanied by a certificate of good standing from one of the courts enumerated in Federal Rule of Appellate Procedure 46(a) or Federal Circuit Rule 46(a) (the certificate must be dated within 30 days of the motion for admission and must bear the seal of the issuing court) or you may submit a completed admission form and have a member of the bar move for your admission in the space provided on the form. Federal Circuit Rule 46(b) sets forth the admissions procedures fully.

The prescribed fee for admission is $226. The application must include a check in that amount payable to the Clerk of Court.

The application and check should be sent to:

Clerk of Court
United States Court of Appeals for the Federal Circuit
717 Madison Place, NW
Washington, DC 20439

FOR CLERK'S USE ONLY

Fee Paid:

___ Yes
___ No

Date Paid: ____________________

Admitted on: ____________________

____
Signature of Clerk or Deputy Clerk

[Former Form 17 effective March 4, 1999; redesignated Form 18 effective May 1, 2003; redesignated Form 21 effective May 1, 2004; April 24, 2009.]

FORM 22. TRANSCRIPT PURCHASE ORDER

United States Court of Appeals for the Federal Circuit

) Appeal from ☐ U.S. District Court for ________
☐ Court of International Trade
☐ Court of Federal Claims

—VERSUS—) TRIAL COURT NO. ________
) CIRCUIT COURT NO. ________

TRANSCRIPT PURCHASE ORDER

(See Rules 10(b) and 11(b) of the Federal Rules of Appellate Procedure)

PART I—TO BE COMPLETED BY THE APPELLANT WITHIN 14 DAYS OF FILING OF NOTICE OF APPEAL.

When filing this form, distribute copies as follows: 3 copies to the court reporter; 1 copy to the Trial Court; 1 copy to the appellee; 1 copy retained by appellant.

A. Complete one of the following:

( ) A transcript is not needed for the appeal

( ) A transcript is already on file

( ) Request is hereby made to the reporter for a transcript of the following proceedings (give particulars):

Note: voir dire and closing arguments are not prepared unless specifically requested.

Note: Unless the entire transcript is ordered, appellant must attach a statement of the issues to Copies 4 and 5.

B. I certify that financial arrangements have been made with the reporter. Payment is by:

( ) Private Funds

( ) Government expense (civil case). A motion for transcript has been submitted to the trial judge.

SIGNED ______ DATE _____ COUNSEL FOR ________

ADDRESS ________

TELEPHONE ________

PART II—TO BE COMPLETED BY THE COURT REPORTER

2 copies retained by the reporter; 1 copy to be transmitted to the Court of Appeals on same date transcript order is received.

Date Purchase Order received: ____________________

Estimated completion date: ____________________

Estimated number of pages: ____________________

I certify that satisfactory financial arrangements have/have not (strike one) been completed with appellant for payment of the cost of the transcript.

____
Signature and Date

Telephone ____________________

PART III—NOTIFICATION THAT TRANSCRIPT HAS BEEN FILED IN THE TRIAL COURT.

(To be completed by court reportor on date of filing transcript in Trial Court and this notification must be forwarded to Court of Appeals on the same date.)

This is to certify that the transcript has been completed. ____ volumes of transcript have been filed with the Trial Court today.

________________ ____________________________
Date Signature

[May 1, 2006.]

FORM 23. BILL OF COSTS INSTRUCTION SHEET

INSTRUCTIONS

Bill of Costs

Use this form to bill reimbursable costs for the table or compilation of designated materials (Fed. Cir. R. 30 (b)), briefs (Rule 28), appendices (Rule 30), and other items allowed or permitted.

Counsel should read Rule 39 before filing a bill of costs. Counsel are urged to agree upon the costs to be taxed. Costs must be claimed using this form. The total billed for each item must be limited to the lesser of actual or allowable costs. The additional costs of confidential briefs and appendices should be incorporated in the quantity billed, e.g., a 50–page brief that has 15 confidential pages will allow 65 original pages to be billed. Counsel must calculate and enter the total billed for each item and the grand total billed. Items on the form which do not apply should be marked N.A. The clerk will determine the total taxed for each item and the grand total taxed. Absent objection, costs will be taxed as billed.

The following items pertain to the letters appearing on the Bill of Costs form reprinted on the reverse side of these instructions:

(A) Insert docket number or numbers.

(B) Insert authorized abbreviated caption.

(C) Insert party to be taxed, e.g., ABC Inc., Plaintiff–Appellant.

(D) Docketing fees paid in a District Court, Court of International Trade or Court of Federal Claims must be claimed in those courts.

(E) Insert number of pages of original material in the master version. Do not bill as an original any page that is itself a photocopy of another document not created for this appeal.

(F) Attach copy of invoice or state in-house costs.

(G) Insert number of copies billable. See Rule 39.

(H) Insert number of photocopied pages in each copy.

(I) Any item not enumerated on the form but which has been filed at the request or with the leave of the court may be billed.

(J) If costs have been agreed upon by the parties, insert "Stipulated Costs" and enter the total and grand total billed, and disregard all other items on the form.

(K) Insert name of attorney verifying costs.

(L) Insert name of party claiming costs, e.g., XYZ Co., Defendant–Appellant.

[May 1, 2008.]

FORM 24. BILL OF COSTS

BILL OF COSTS (File original and three copies with the Clerk within 14 days of judgment.)

Docket No(s): A: ____________ Caption:B: ____________

The Clerk is requested to tax the following costs against: C:

ITEM	Number of copies	Number of pages	Actual cost	Allowable cost	Total billed	Total taxed
Docketing Fee (if paid in this court)	xxxxx	xxxxx	D:			
Table of Designated Materials (original)	xxxxx	E:	F:	6.00		
Table of Compilation of Designated Materials (copying and collating)	G:	H:		0.08		
Brief (original)	xxxxx	E:		6.00		
Brief (cover and binding)	G:	xxxxx		2.00		
Brief (copying and collating)	G:	H:		0.08		
Appendix (original—table of contents)	xxxxx	E:		6.00		
Appendix (covers and binding)	G:	xxxxx		2.00		
Appendix (copying and collating)	G:	H:		0.08		
Reply Brief (original)	xxxxx	E:		6.00		
Reply Brief (covers and binding)	G:	xxxxx		2.00		
Reply Brief (copying and collating)	G:	H:		0.08		
Other (describe):	I:	J:				
GRAND TOTALS						

City/County of ____________) District/State of ____________) SS
I, K: ____________, swear under penalty of perjury that the services for which costs are taxed were necessarily performed. Itemized statements of the costs incurred or invoices are attached. Copies of this bill were served on all parties. The certificate of service is attached.

Signature: ____________ Date: ____________ Attorney for: L: ____________

[May 1, 2008.]

FORM 25. MEDIATOR APPLICATION

UNITED STATES COURT OF APPEALS FOR THE FEDERAL CIRCUIT

Appellate Mediation Program

MEDIATOR APPLICATION

Mediators and applicants must not be in active practice as defined by the Federal Circuit Appellate Mediation Program Guidelines. Mediators are not paid for their services, but are reimbursed by the court for minor out-of-pocket expenses such as photocopying costs, telephone charges, facsimile charges, and transportation to the courthouse. Mediation proceedings may be held in the courthouse if desired. Reimbursement for reasonable travel and lodging expenses of the mediator is assumed by the litigants if the mediator must travel to conduct the mediation.

Information from Candidates:

Name ______________________________

Mailing Address ______________________________

____

Telephone Number ______________________________

FAX Number ______________________________

E-mail Address ______________________________

1. I am, and have been, a member in good standing of the bar of the following states or the District of Columbia (add extra pages if necessary):

State ____________________ Date of Admission _______________

State ____________________ Date of Admission _______________

2. I am admitted to practice before the bar of the United States Court of Appeals for the Federal Circuit.

☐ Yes ☐ No

Date of Admission __________. If retired, I retired from the practice of law on __________.

3. I have a working knowledge of the Federal Circuit's practice and procedures based on the following: ______________________________

____

4. ☐ No, I have not been disciplined by a court bar, a state bar or the District of Columbia, or the bar of an administrative agency, had a professional license revoked, or been convicted of a felony.

☐ Yes, I have (explain on an attached sheet).

5. ☐ Yes, I am experienced with the mediation process, having at a minimum (1) represented clients in at least 2 mediations or served as a mediator in at least 2 mediations; and (2) obtained at least 24 hours of CLE-accredited or court-approved mediation training. Please indicate any other experience that you believe is relevant: ______________________

☐ No, I do not have the requisite experience, but believe I am qualified. Please explain: ______________________

6. I am willing to attend mediation training on my own before being assigned as a mediator.

☐ Yes ☐ No

I am willing to attend court-sponsored mediation, if available.

☐ Yes ☐ No

7. Please outline any previous judicial experience. ______________________

8. List additional relevant experience including: (1) professional organizations and any leadership positions held; (2) relevant additional degrees or licenses; and (3) speaking or teaching about mediation (attach additional pages if necessary): ______________________

9. I confirm that I am not in active practice as defined by the Appellate Mediation Program Guidelines at the present time.

☐ Yes ☐ No

The following describes why I believe I am not in active practice: ______________________

10. I understand that mediators in the Federal Circuit Appellate Mediation Program will not be compensated for their services. I am willing to serve as a mediator on this pro bono basis.

☐ Yes ☐ No

11. If selected to be a pro bono Federal Circuit mediator, I expect my level of participation to be ______________________

12. I have practice experience in the following areas (check the appropriate boxes):

☐ Customs or International Trade
☐ Patent Litigation
☐ Government Contracts
☐ Personnel Law
☐ Patent and Trademark Office
☐ Veterans Law

☐ Other ______________________

13. Add any additional information that you wish to bring to the attention of the Federal Circuit ____

____

____________________ ____________________
Date Signature

Submit form to:

Federal Circuit Bar Association
1620 I Street, NW, Suite 900
Washington, DC 20006

AND

Wendy L. Dean
Circuit Mediation Officer
United States Court of Appeals
for the Federal Circuit
717 Madison Place, NW
Washington, DC 20439

[May 1, 2008.]

FORM 26. DOCKETING STATEMENT

UNITED STATES COURT OF APPEALS
FOR THE FEDERAL CIRCUIT

No. ________

____

v.

____

DOCKETING STATEMENT

This Docketing Statement must be completed by all counsel and filed with the court within 14 days of the date of docketing. When the United States or its officer or agency is a party, this Docketing Statement must be completed by all counsel and filed with the court within 30 days of docketing. All questions must be answered or the statement will be rejected.

Name of the party you represent ______________________________

Party is (select one) ☐ Appellant/Petitioner ☐ Cross–Appellant
☐ Appellee/Respondent ☐ Intervenor

Tribunal appealed from and Case No. ______________________________

Date of Judgment/Order ________ Type of Case ______________________________

Relief sought on appeal

____

Relief awarded below (if damages, specify) ______________________________

Briefly describe the judgment/order appealed from ______________________________

____

____

____

Nature of judgment (select one)

☐ Final Judgment, 28 USC 1295
☐ Rule 54(b)
☐ Interlocutory Order (specify type) ______________________________
☐ Other (explain; *see* Fed. Cir. R. 28(a)(5)) ______________________________

____

Name and docket number of any related cases pending before this court plus the name of the writing judge if an opinion was issued ______________________________

____

____

____

Brief statement of the issues to be raised on appeal ______________________________

____

____

____

Have there been discussions with other parties relating to settlement of this case?
☐ Yes ☐ No

If "yes," when were the last such discussions?

☐ Before the case was filed below?
☐ During the pendency of the case below?
☐ Following the judgment/order appealed from?

If "yes," were the settlement discussions mediated? ☐ Yes ☐ No

If they were mediated, by whom? ______________________________

Do you believe that this case may be amenable to mediation? ☐ Yes ☐ No

If you answered no, explain why not ______________________________

Provide any other information relevant to the inclusion of this case in the court's mediation program. ______________________________

I certify that I filed an original and one copy of this Docketing Statement with the Clerk of the United States Court of Appeals for the Federal Circuit and served a copy on counsel of record, this ___ day of ________, ________ by: ______________________________

(manner of service)

______________________________	______________________________
Name of Counsel	Signature of Counsel

Law Firm ______________________________
Address ______________________________
City, State, ZIP ______________________________
Telephone Number ______________________________
FAX Number ______________________________
E-mail Address ______________________________

[May 1, 2008. Amended effective June 29, 2011.]

FORM 27. CONFIDENTIAL JOINT REQUEST TO ENTER APPELLATE MEDIATION PROGRAM

UNITED STATES COURT OF APPEALS FOR THE FEDERAL CIRCUIT

CONFIDENTIAL JOINT REQUEST TO ENTER APPELLATE MEDIATION PROGRAM

______________ v. ______________

No. ____

We would like the above case considered for entry into the Appellate Mediation Program (counsel for all parties must sign).

______________________	______________________
Signature of Counsel for:	Signature of Counsel for:
☐ Appellant/Petitioner ☐ Cross–Appellant	☐ Appellant/Petitioner ☐ Cross–Appellant
☐ Appellee/Respondent ☐ Intervenor	☐ Appellee/Respondent ☐ Intervenor
Name of Party represented: ________	Name of Party represented ________
______________________	______________________
Law Firm ________________	Law Firm ________________
Address ________________	Address ________________
City/State/ZIP ________________	City/State/ZIP ________________
Telephone Number ________________	Telephone Number ________________
FAX Number ________________	FAX Number ________________
E-mail Address ________________	E-mail Address ________________

This Joint Mediation Request must be submitted to the Circuit Mediation Officer.

Please send completed form to:

Wendy Dean, Circuit Mediation Officer
United States Court of Appeals for the Federal Circuit
717 Madison Place, NW
Washington, DC 20439

[May 1, 2008.]

FORM 28. CONFIDENTIAL MEDIATION SURVEY FOR PARTIES

UNITED STATES COURT OF APPEALS
FOR THE FEDERAL CIRCUIT

CONFIDENTIAL MEDIATION SURVEY
FOR PARTIES

Short Caption ______________________________

Case Number ______________________________

Attorney for ______________________________

Was a settlement agreement reached through mediation? ☐ Yes ☐ No

When did you decide to participate in mediation?

- ☐ When completing the Docketing Statement.
- ☐ After filing a brief.
- ☐ After all briefing had been completed but before oral argument.
- ☐ After oral argument.

Did your client attend any of the mediation sessions? ☐ Yes ☐ No

Did the mediator have expertise in the legal issues in the case? ☐ Yes ☐ No

What impact did this have on the mediation? ______________________________

Do you consider the mediation to have been successful;? ☐ Yes ☐ No

Why? ______________________________

____

Please provide a candid evaluation of the mediator assigned to this case. ____________

Was the Circuit Mediation Office responsive? ☐ Yes ☐ No

Will you recommend the mediation program to others? ☐ Yes ☐ No

Will you participate in the mediation program again? ☐ Yes ☐ No

Comments/suggestions please: ______________________________

Thank you for your participation in the program. Please return this completed form to:

Annette Young
Circuit Mediation Administrator
United States Court of Appeals for the Federal Circuit
717 Madison Place, NW
Washington, DC 20439

[May 1, 2008; revised April 19, 2009.]

FORM 29. CONFIDENTIAL MEDIATOR REPORT

UNITED STATES COURT OF APPEALS
FOR THE FEDERAL CIRCUIT

Appellate Mediation Program

CONFIDENTIAL MEDIATOR REPORT

Short Caption ______________________________

Case Number ______________________________

Mediator's Name and Control Information:

____

Was a settlement agreement reached? ☐ Yes ☐ No

☐ Full ☐ Partial

Date of First Contact with the Parties ______________________________

Date Settlement Agreement Signed/Mediation Terminated ______________________________

Total Mediator Time ______________________________

Who Participated:

☐ Lawyers Only ☐ Lawyers and Clients ☐ Nonparties

How did you conduct the mediation?

☐ Number of Face-to-Face Meetings

☐ Number of Telephone Conferences

☐ Number of Written Submissions

☐ Number of Other Contacts/Conferences

If the case was settled, please describe any elements in the settlement (*e.g.*, an apology) that could not have been obtained through judicial disposition:

____

On a separate sheet of paper, please evaluate the mediation. For example, were the techniques you used effective? Did the mediation present any unusual problems? If the case settled, what did you do to achieve that result? In hindsight, would you do anything differently? How can the mediation program be improved?

Did you have expertise in the legal issues involved in the case?

☐ Yes ☐ No

What impact, if any, did this have on the mediation? ____________________

____

Was the Circuit Mediation Office responsive/supportive?
☐ Yes ☐ No

Will you recommend others join the program as volunteer mediators?
☐ Yes ☐ No

Will you participate in the mediation program again? ☐ Yes ☐ No

Comments/suggestions, please: ____________________

____

Thank you for your participation in the program. Please return this completed form to:

Annette Young
Circuit Mediation Administrator
United States Court of Appeals for the Federal Circuit
717 Madison Place, NW
Washington, DC 20439

[May 1, 2008; revised April 19, 2009.]

APPENDIX II. GUIDE FOR PRO SE PETITIONERS AND APPELLANTS

1. **Appearing pro se or by counsel; unions; veterans organizations; nonlawyer representatives; deceased appellants or petitioners; corporations; associations.** You as an individual may conduct your own case pro se in the United States Court of Appeals for the Federal Circuit. ("Pro se" means "in his own behalf.") If you are pro se, you must file a written entry of appearance, after your case is docketed, on the form provided by the clerk. Alternatively, you may be represented by a lawyer admitted to practice before this court. If legal counsel enters an appearance, only counsel may communicate with or will receive communications from the court. The court has no procedure to appoint counsel for you. A union, veterans organization, or other non-lawyer representative may not represent you in this court even if such represented you before the Merit Systems Protection Board, an arbitrator, the Court of Appeals for Veterans Claims, or other tribunal. Nor may other lay spokespersons like relatives or friends represent you in this court. An executor or administrator of the estate of an appellant or petitioner also must be represented by counsel. Corporations and associations cannot proceed pro se and must be represented by counsel.

2. **Available materials.** Your pro se case is subject to the United States Code, Federal Rules of Appellate Procedure, and Federal Circuit Rules. You may obtain the Rules of Practice from the clerk and you will be sent a copy when your case is docketed. You will find the statutes governing this court's jurisdiction and related matters in the United States Code, the United States Code Annotated, or the United States Code Service, and the decisions of the court in the Federal Reporter, Second and Third Series (F.2d, F. 3d), all available in many public libraries.

3. **Filing petitions for review or notices of appeal; postmark does not establish timeliness; forms.** You must file your petition for review or notice of appeal within the time allowed by the statute that authorizes it. Your petition or notice is not considered filed at the time it is postmarked by the U.S. Postal Service; it must actually be received in the place for filing within the time allowed by statute. You may not file a petition for review or notice of appeal by facsimile transmission. The statutes allow these times for filing:

Merit Systems Protection Board. You may seek review of a Merit Systems Protection Board decision in one of two ways. First, you may petition this court for review of an initial decision of an administrative judge within 60 days of the date that decision becomes final. The initial decision will clearly state the date that the decision becomes final. If you choose to petition this court for review at that time, you may not petition the three-member Board for review of the administrative judge's decision and you may not file a petition for review in both this court and before the Board. If you file in both places, your petition here will be dismissed as premature. Second, you may, after an administrative judge issues an initial decision, petition the three-member Board for review of that decision. When the Board issues a decision, you may file a petition for review in this court within 60 days of receipt of the Board's decision.

Either your employing agency or the Office of Personnel Management as named in the order of the Merit Systems Protection Board, or the board itself, will be the respondent in your petition for review. In your petition for review, you should name as respondent the agency captioned in the board's order on your appeal. If the board should be the respondent rather than the agency, you will be notified by the clerk.

Arbitrator. You have 60 days after you receive notice of the Arbitrator's decision to file a petition for review with the clerk of this court. Arbitration awards in the U.S. Postal Service, however, are not appealable.

Government Accountability Office Personnel Appeals Board. You have 30 days after you receive notice of the Board's decision to file a petition for review with the clerk of this court.

Patent and Trademark Office Boards. You have 2 months from the date of a final decision of the Board of Patent Appeals and Interferences or the Trademark Trial and Appeal Board in which to file a notice of appeal with the Patent and Trademark Office. If you asked the board to reconsider your case, you have 2 months from the date of the decision on reconsideration in which to file a notice of appeal with the Patent and Trademark Office. A notice of appeal must actually reach the Patent and Trademark Office within the 2–month period. If mailed, the notice should be addressed:

General Counsel
United States Patent and Trademark Office
Post Office Box 15667
Arlington, Virginia 22215

A copy of the notice of appeal must also be sent to the clerk of this court.

Certified Lists should be received from the Patent and Trademark Office within 40 days. The Federal

Circuit docket number is assigned once the appeal is docketed in the Federal Circuit

Boards of Contract Appeals. You have 120 days after receiving the decision of a Board of Contract Appeals in which to file a notice of appeal with the clerk of this court.

International Trade Commission. You have 60 days after a determination of the International Trade Commission becomes final to file a notice of appeal with the clerk of this court.

District Courts; Court of International Trade; Court of Federal Claims; and Court of Appeals for Veterans Claims. You have 30 days from the date of entry of the judgment or order to file a notice of appeal with the clerk of the district court, the Court of International Trade, the Court of Federal Claims, or the Court of Appeals for Veterans Claims. You have 60 days when the government was the other party in one of these courts. If your Court of Federal Claims case involved vaccine compensation, file your petition for review with the clerk of this court.

Judicial review under the Administrative Procedure Act of rule making by the Department of Veterans Affairs (VA). You may seek judicial review in this court of VA rule making only if you are challenging the publication or promulgation of a VA rule or regulation. If you have a VA claim and you seek to challenge the VA's application of the veterans' benefits statutes to the facts of your particular claim as it has been adjudicated in the VA, you may not do so under the guise of seeking judicial review of VA rule making concerning the rules used to adjudicate your claim. If you want your claim reviewed in this court, it must first be reviewed in the Court of Appeals for Veterans Claims. When reviewing your claim, both this court and the Court of Appeals for Veterans Claims will review the legality of the VA rules used to adjudicate your claim to the extent permitted by statute.

Office of Compliance. You have 90 days after the entry of a final decision in the records of the Office of Compliance to file a petition for review with the clerk of this court.

Equal Employment Opportunity Commission (or other entity designated by the President). You have 30 days after the receipt of a final order to file a petition for review with the clerk of this court. EEOC orders reviewable in this court pertain only to certain Presidential appointees. EEOC orders pertaining to discrimination claims in MSPB appeals are not reviewable in this court.

Timeliness. If a notice of appeal or petition for review filed with the clerk shows on its face that it is not timely filed within the time allowed by statute to appeal or petition, the clerk will reject the notice of appeal or petition. When it cannot be determined from the facts set forth whether a notice of appeal or petition for review is timely, but the clerk has reason to believe it may be untimely, the clerk will ascertain from the board or agency whose decision is the subject of the appeal or petition when notice of its decision was received by the appellant or petitioner and will thereupon make a determination of timeliness. If the clerk determines that the appeal or petition for review is untimely, the clerk will reject it. Thereafter, if the appellant or petitioner submits proof of timeliness, the clerk will enter the appeal or petition for review upon the docket of the court.

Extensions of time to appeal or to petition for review requested in the court of appeals; in the district court. This court lacks authority to extend the time to appeal or to petition for review because the applicable statutes do not confer on the court the power to waive or extend the time to appeal or petition. When an application or request to extend the time to appeal or petition is received, if the time to appeal or petition has not yet passed, the application or request will be deemed to be the appeal or petition for review, and it will be placed on the docket by the clerk. However, if the time to appeal or petition has passed, the application or request will be returned by the clerk without judicial action as the court lacks authority to extend the time to appeal or to petition for review. An application or request to extend the time to file a notice of appeal from the judgment of a district court, the Court of International Trade, or the Court of Federal Claims should be filed in those courts.

Forms. You do not need a special form for a petition for review or a notice of appeal, but you may use the forms provided in the Forms section of the court's Rules of Practice. You will also find these forms wherever the Federal Rules of Appellate Procedure are reprinted. You should put your current mailing address and telephone number on the petition or notice. You should include on the petition or notice the file number of the case when it was in the board, commission, or court and the date you received notice of the decision or judgment. You should attach a copy of the board's, commission's, or court's judgment, decision or opinion to the petition or notice. All papers must be 8½ by 11 inches.

4. Fees. You are required to pay a docketing fee of $450 to the clerk of this court when you petition for review of, or appeal, a decision of a board or commission. If you appeal a judgment of a court, you must pay a docketing fee of $450 and also pay a filing fee of $5, both to the clerk of that court when you file a notice of appeal in that court. If the fees have not been paid or if you have not filed a motion for leave to proceed in forma pauperis within 14 days after the case is docketed in this court, the case will be dismissed.

If your petition for review seeks review of a Merit Systems Protection Board decision that involves a claim under the Uniformed Services Employment and Reemployment Rights Act of 1994 (USERRA), then you are not required to pay the docketing fee or costs. 38 U.S.C. § 4323. To advise the court that your case is covered by 38 U.S.C. § 4323, you must complete form 6B (USERRA Notification Form), return it to the clerk's office within 14 days after your case is docketed, and mail a copy to the attorney for the respondent.

5. Permission to proceed in forma pauperis; waiving fees. You may qualify to proceed in forma pauperis if the court determines that you are unable to pay the fees. Permission to proceed in forma pauperis means that the filing and docketing fees are waived; it does not mean that a free transcript of the hearing or trial will be provided, or that a free lawyer will be appointed, or that the assessment of costs will be waived. Unless you are a prisoner, you are automatically qualified to proceed in forma pauperis if the district court, Court of International Trade, Court of Federal Claims, or Court of Appeals for Veterans Claims has granted you that right and not revoked it. Otherwise, you may request to proceed in forma pauperis on a form available from the clerk of this court. You are required to disclose all your financial resources on the form. You should file the form with your petition for review, but if you do not file it at that time, it must be filed within 14 days of the date of docketing.

If you are a prisoner and file a notice of appeal in this court, the Clerk's Office will forward to you a blank motion and affidavit for leave to proceed in forma pauperis and a supplemental authorization and affidavit form. You must complete and file the supplemental form, and the Clerk's Office will send a copy to the institution in which you are incarcerated. The form authorizes the institution to (1) furnish to this court a certified copy of your prison account statement and (2) calculate and disburse funds from the prison account, including the initial partial filing fee payment and subsequent monthly payments. Your institution will forward the certified statement, the initial payment, and the subsequent payments to this court. If you file the proper form, the failure of the institution to send the statement or to remit the payments shall not adversely affect your appeal. If, however, you do not submit the motion and affidavit for leave to proceed IFP and the supplemental in forma pauperis form within 14 days of the date of docketing, the prisoner's appeal shall be dismissed. See also Form 6B, which may be used to seek waiver of the fee if the underlying decision involved a claim under the Uniformed Services Employment and Reemployment Rights Act of 1994.

6. Discrimination claims in Merit Systems Protection Board cases. This court does not have jurisdiction to review cases involving bona fide claims of discrimination based on race, sex, age, national origin, or handicap that were raised before and considered by the Merit Systems Protection Board. If your case involves such claims and you are unwilling to abandon them forever, you must proceed in a district court (which will hear all your claims, both discrimination and nondiscrimination) or before the Equal Employment Opportunity Commission (which will hear your discrimination claims only). You may waive your discrimination claims on the Federal Circuit Rule 15(c) form sent to you by the clerk. If you fail to complete and return the form within 14 days after the date of docketing, the clerk will dismiss your petition for review. A discrimination issue raised for the first time in this court does not affect the jurisdiction of the court to decide the issues raised before the Board, and such a discrimination claim will be disregarded.

7. This court does not conduct new trials or hearings; additional limitations in appeals from the Court of Appeals for Veterans Claims. This court reviews only what a board, commission, or court did in your case. You cannot retry the facts before this court. Review is limited to the written record of proceedings that were held in the board, commission, or court. You cannot raise in this court matters that you did not present first before the board, commission, or court. You must show that the version of the facts accepted by the board or commission is not supported by substantial evidence or that the version of the facts accepted by the court is clearly erroneous. If you show that the board, commission, or court erred, you must also show that the error materially affected the outcome of your case. Minor procedural errors rarely affect the outcome of a case. Procedural errors are usually deemed waived if not raised first before the board, commission, or court. If you are successful before this court, the court may issue a decision in your favor or it may send the case back (remand) for further proceedings before the board, commission, or court.

If you are appealing from the Court of Appeals for Veterans Claims, the statute contains additional limitations. If you make challenges not contemplated by the statute, your appeal will be dismissed. See 38 U.S.C. § 7292.

8. Cases dismissed for lack of jurisdiction or for untimeliness. If the board, commission, or court dismissed your case for lack of jurisdiction or because you did not file on time, you must limit your petition for review or appeal to these issues. In that situation, this court will not consider the merits of your case (whether you deserve to win or lose your case on the facts and the law) and, if this court were to reverse the board, commission, or court on its jurisdictional or timeliness ruling, your case would be remanded to the board, commission, or court to consider the merits. If jurisdiction or timeliness was the basis of the decision you are appealing, you will waste your time and effort, and will unduly burden this court, if you discuss the merits.

9. Frivolous petitions for review and appeals will be penalized. If you file and proceed with a frivolous petition for review or appeal, you are subject to the imposition of damages, double costs, and attorney fees payable to the other party. "Frivolous" means clearly hopeless and unquestionably without any basis whatever in fact or law. You may require the advice of an attorney in making your decision that your case is not frivolous.

10. Withdrawing a pro se petition for review or appeal. You may ordinarily withdraw your pro se petition for review or appeal at any time before this court decides your case. To withdraw your case simply advise the clerk by letter, "I withdraw my case." Serve a copy of your letter on the other party. The Department of Justice will ordinarily consent to the withdrawal of a pro se case on the condition that each party bear its own costs. This court will ordinarily not assess damages, double costs, or attorney fees for filing a frivolous petition for review or appeal if it is voluntarily withdrawn within 14 days after you receive the other party's brief. Serious consideration should be given to voluntarily withdrawing your case if the other party's brief makes a strong argument that you are pursuing a frivolous case.

11. Record. If you need access to the original record of the board, commission, or court proceedings, you must contact the board, commission, or court because the original record is not forwarded to this court.

12. Service of notice of appearance, briefs, appendices, motions, letters, and other documents. You must serve on counsel for the other party (by mail or by personal hand delivery) a copy of all notices of appearance, briefs, appendices, motions, letters, and other documents you send to the court. Make sure this court's docket number appears on every document. You must serve opposing counsel using the name and address contained on the entry of appearance form filed by that counsel and served on you. If an entry of appearance has not been filed, please serve the person listed on the notice of docketing. The clerk will not file and may return any material that is not accompanied by a certificate from you stating that you have served the other party with a copy of all the material sent to the court. A sample certificate follows:

CERTIFICATE OF SERVICE

I certify that I mailed my informal brief to

John Doe, Esq.
111 Main Street, Suite 911
Washington, DC 74891–2000

The certificate of service may be included at the end of the material you are filing or it may be on a separate paper attached to that material. You may also make the certification of service on a photocopy of the opposing counsel's copy of the entry of appearance that was served on you and attach it to whatever you file with the clerk.

13. Informal briefs; appendix; petitions for rehearing; motions; length; new evidence; correspondence generally. You may file an **informal brief** (original and three copies) using a form (Forms 11, 11A, 12, 13, 14, 15, or 16) provided by the clerk of this court. The informal brief is the only permissible substitute for the brief required by the Federal Rules of Appellate Procedure and Federal Circuit Rules. The informal brief, together with any continuation pages needed for answers that will not fit on the form, may not exceed 30 typewritten, double-spaced pages with 1–inch margins, or their equivalent in content.

You must include an **appendix** with your opening brief containing, as appropriate, the initial and final decision of the Merit Systems Protection Board, the final decision of another board or commission, the judgment and opinion of the trial court, or the rule or rules that are the subject of your petition for judicial review of the VA rule making. Do not attempt to supplement the record on appeal with new evidence that was not considered at your hearing or trial. The clerk can return such new evidence. Copies of correspondence with others about your appeal are not part of the record on appeal and can also be returned by the clerk.

You may, but are not required to, file a **reply brief** to respond to issues raised in appellee's or respondent's brief. It may not exceed 15 typewritten, double-spaced pages with 1–inch margins, or their equivalent in content.

Motions and **responses to motions** may not exceed 20 pages. A **petition for rehearing** of an opinion or a **motion for reconsideration** of an order may not exceed 15 pages.

All filings with the court must be on 8½ by 11–inch paper, be double spaced, have 1–inch margins, and the type size must be at least 14 point. An original and three copies must be filed. The title of the filing and the courts' case number should appear at the top of the first page.

If attachments to the informal brief are included, an original and three copies are required otherwise the attachment will be rejected.

If your informal brief is handwritten, please write as clearly as possible. Make sure your brief is dated and signed.

Please note: Briefs cannot be filed if the fee has not been paid. If there is a pending In Forma Pauperis motion or the certified list has not been filed, briefs submitted prior to such action will be held in abeyance.

14. Timetable for filing briefs; dismissal for default.

Informal briefs. In a petition for review or appeal from a board or commission or for judicial review of VA rule making, you must file an informal brief within 21 days after the certified list or index is served. In an appeal from a court or the Patent and Trademark Office, you must file an informal brief within 21 days after the appeal is docketed. The other party may file either an informal brief within 21 days or a formal brief within 40 days after service of your informal brief. If you file a brief before the certified list or index is served and filed, the other party's time runs from service and filing of the certified list or index. If you attempt to serve government counsel using a name and address other than that contained on the entry of appearance served on you, the time for filing the government's informal brief will not begin to run until the government attorney appearing in the case has actually received your brief. You may choose to file a reply brief within 14 days after service of the other party's brief.

Formal briefs. If you elect to file a formal brief, the brief and appendix must comply with the strict requirements of the Federal Rules of Appellate Procedure and the Federal Circuit Rules or the brief and appendix will not be accepted. A formal brief is due 60 days after the certified list is served in board or commission cases or 60 days after the case is docketed in court or Patent and Trademark Office cases. The other party must file a formal brief within 40 days of service of your formal brief or the certified list, whichever is later. Any reply must be a formal reply brief filed within 14 days of service of the other party's brief.

Dismissal for default. If you fail to file a brief or comply with other rules, the clerk will dismiss your appeal or petition. However, if the appellee or respondent fails to comply with the rules, you are not entitled to the relief you seek solely by reason of that noncompliance, because the appellant or petitioner always has the burden to establish entitlement to relief in the court of appeals and cannot meet that burden by the failure of another to comply with the rules.

15. Oral argument. Oral argument (usually 15 minutes or less) is rarely needed in pro se cases. However, you may request to argue your case before the court, giving reasons why that would aid the court. If you are granted oral argument you must bear your own travel expenses to the court.

16. Recovery of costs. If you lose before this court, you will normally be responsible for paying the costs of the other party. If you prevail, you will normally have your own costs paid by the other party. "Costs" means the expenses of printing or copying briefs and appendices, and may amount to several hundred dollars. Attorney fees are not costs. If you are responsible for costs, the matter is between you and the other party, and the court will not resolve any dispute between the parties once the costs have been taxed. In ex parte appeals from the Patent and Trademark Office, each party bears its own costs on appeal. Please refer to Practice Note 39.

17. Attorney fees. You are not entitled to payment for your own services in pursuing your case pro se, because only an attorney may be awarded attorney fees. Before filing a petition for review or an appeal you may wish to seek a lawyer who might be willing to undertake the case on the contingency that the attorney fees may be payable under the Equal Access to Justice Act.

18. Change of address. You must file and serve a new notice of appearance if you change your address while your case is pending.

19. Notice of the court's decision. You will be sent a copy of the court's opinion in your case by mail on the day it is filed with the clerk. If the court decides your appeal without preparing an opinion, you will be sent a copy of the judgment of affirmance without opinion. If you file a petition for rehearing, it must be received within 30 days of the date of the court's opinion. If the United States is a party, then you have 45 days to file a petition for rehearing. Untimely petitions for rehearing will be returned. Rehearings are rarely granted. Do not file a motion to alter or amend a judgment or a motion for relief from judgment as those motions are appropriate only in proceedings governed by Federal Rules of Civil Procedure 59 and 60, which do not apply in this court.

20. Additional information. For information, you may call the Clerk's Office at 202–275–8000 or write to the Clerk of Court, United States Court of Appeals for the Federal Circuit, 717 Madison Place, NW, Washington, DC 20439. Collect calls are not accepted. The staff of the Clerk's Office will answer questions about procedures, but they are not permitted to give you legal advice or to recommend how you should pursue your appeal. For additional information please refer to the court's website at www.cafc.uscourts.gov.

[Amended effective June 1, 2011.]

APPENDIX III. FEDERAL CIRCUIT ATTORNEY DISCIPLINE RULES

INTRODUCTION

The United States Court of Appeals for the Federal Circuit, in furtherance of its power and responsibility under Federal Rule of Appellate Procedure 46 and its inherent power and responsibility to supervise the conduct of attorneys who are members of its bar, promulgates the following Attorney Discipline Rules.

The rules contemplate that a disciplinary proceeding stemming from most misconduct that occurs before a merits or motions panel will be conducted by that panel. A proceeding stemming from more serious misconduct, based on conviction of a serious crime, or imposing reciprocal discipline will be conducted by a Standing Panel on Attorney Discipline composed of three judges. In conformance with Federal Rule of Appellate Procedure 46, a hearing, if requested, will be available in any proceeding. The record in an ongoing proceeding will be confidential unless otherwise ordered. At the conclusion of a proceeding in which discipline is imposed, the final order and the record will be made a public record. A final order issued by a panel will be reviewable in a manner analogous to review under Federal Rules of Appellate Procedure 35 and 40.

RULE 1. DEFINITIONS

(a) Another Court. Another court means any Court of the United States or any court of a state, the District of Columbia, a territory, or a commonwealth of the United States. For purposes of these rules, another court also includes the United States Court of Appeals for Veterans Claims and the United States Court of Federal Claims.

(b) Agency. Agency means any agency of the United States as defined in 5 U.S.C. § 551.

(c) Serious Crime. Serious crime means (1) any felony or (2) any lesser crime a necessary element of which, as determined by statutory or common law definition of such crime in the jurisdiction where the conviction occurred, is (i) interference with the administration of justice, (ii) false swearing, (iii) misrepresentation, (iv) fraud, (v) willful failure to file an income tax return, (vi) deceit, (vii) bribery, (viii) extortion, (ix) misappropriation, (x) theft, or (xi) an attempt or conspiracy or solicitation of another to commit a serious crime.

RULE 2. GROUNDS FOR DISCIPLINE

(a) Conviction. Conviction in another court of a serious crime may be the basis for discipline.

(b) Disbarment or Suspension. Reciprocal discipline may be imposed based on disbarment or suspension by another court or by an agency.

(c) Resignation. Disbarment may be imposed based on an attorney's disbarment on consent or resignation from the bar of another court or an agency while an investigation into an allegation of misconduct is pending.

(d) Act or Omission. An act or omission by an attorney that violates the Federal Rules of Appellate Procedure, the Federal Circuit Rules, these rules, or orders or instructions of the court, other than an act or omission contemplated by Rule 3(d) of these rules, may be the basis for discipline. A failure to notify the court in compliance with Rule 6(a) may itself be the basis for discipline.

(e) Conduct Unbecoming. Any conduct before the court unbecoming a member of the bar may be the basis for discipline.

RULE 3. TYPES OF DISCIPLINE

(a) Discipline for Misconduct. Discipline for attorney misconduct may consist of disbarment, suspension for a definite period, monetary sanction, public reprimand, private reprimand, or any other disciplinary action that the court deems appropriate.

(b) Disbarment. Disbarment is the presumed discipline for conviction of a serious crime.

(c) Reciprocal Discipline. The imposition of reciprocal disbarment or suspension is the presumed discipline based on the disbarment or suspension of an attorney by another court or an agency. Disbarment based on an attorney's disbarment on consent or resignation from a bar of another court or an agency while an investigation into an allegation of misconduct is pending constitutes reciprocal discipline.

(d) Sanctions Under Other Provisions. Assessment of damages, costs, expenses, or attorney fees under Federal Rule of Appellate Procedure 38, 28 U.S.C. § 1927, or similar statutory provision are not disciplinary sanctions within the meaning of these rules and are not governed by these rules.

RULE 4. DISCIPLINARY MATTERS REFERRED TO THE COURT

(a) Docketing. The Clerk shall maintain a miscellaneous attorney disciplinary matter docket and shall assign a number to each matter.

(b) Merits or Motions Panel. When attorney misconduct under these rules occurs within the context of a case before a merits panel or a motions panel, that panel may impose any discipline except disbarment, suspension, or a monetary sanction over $1,000. The proceeding is conducted in accordance with Rule 5. In lieu of conducting its own proceeding, a majority of the panel may refer the matter to the Standing Panel on Attorney Discipline.

(c) Standing Panel on Attorney Discipline.

(1) The Standing Panel shall conduct proceedings in any matter in which disbarment, suspension, or a monetary sanction over $1000 may be considered, or in any matter referred by a merits or motions panel.

(2) The Standing Panel shall consist of three judges, at least two of whom shall be active judges, appointed by the Chief Judge. The Chief Judge may serve as a member of the Standing Panel. The initial appointments shall be for one, two, and three year terms, so that the members' terms are staggered. Thereafter, a member shall be appointed for a three-year term. A member who has served on the Standing Panel for three years shall not be eligible for appointment to another term until three years after termination of his or her last appointment.

(3) The chairperson of the Standing Panel shall be the senior active judge.

(4) If a member of the Standing Panel is unable or unavailable to hear a particular matter, the Chief Judge shall appoint another judge to be a member of the Standing Panel for that matter. If a member of the Standing Panel is unable to complete the remainder of his or her term for any reason, e.g., retirement, incapacity, death, the Chief Judge shall appoint another judge to serve the remainder of the term.

RULE 5. MERITS/MOTIONS PANEL OR STANDING PANEL PROCEDURE

(a) Representation. An attorney may be represented by counsel in any disciplinary proceeding. Counsel must enter an appearance promptly, and in any event prior to submitting any documents or at least 14 days before appearing at a hearing, whichever is earlier. Except as provided by Federal Circuit Rule 46(d), counsel must be a member of the bar of this court.

(b) Show Cause Order. Any panel may issue an order describing an attorney's misconduct and ordering the attorney to show cause (1) why a specific discipline should not be imposed or (2) why a discipline to be determined later should not be imposed. Unless otherwise ordered, a response shall be due within 30 days. Any request for a hearing shall be included in a response.

(c) Uncontested Matter. If an attorney does not respond to a show cause order or does not object to the imposition of a specified discipline, the Clerk may then issue a final order imposing such discipline.

(d) Contested Matter. If an attorney contests the imposition of discipline or requests a hearing, further proceedings shall be conducted in accordance with Rule 8.

(e) Referral to State Bar Association or Other Disciplinary Entity. The Standing Panel or any merits or motions panel may in its discretion refer a pending disciplinary matter or a matter that has been concluded to an appropriate state bar association or other disciplinary entity.

(f) Final Order. At the conclusion of a proceeding, a panel shall issue a final order in the matter. The order may direct the attorney or the Clerk to send a copy of the order to all other courts and agencies before which an attorney is admitted. The Clerk may also be directed to notify the American Bar Association's National Lawyer Regulatory Data Bank of the discipline.

(g) Review by the Panel or the Active Judges of the Court. An attorney may file a petition for rehearing by the panel or a combined petition for rehearing by the panel and suggestion for rehearing by the active judges of the court, or a majority of the active judges may order that a disciplinary matter be heard or reheard by them. Such a hearing or rehearing is not favored and ordinarily will not be ordered except when necessary to secure or maintain uniformity of the court's decisions or when the proceeding involves a question of exceptional importance. Any such petition shall be filed within 30 days of the date of the panel's final order. The procedures governing a petition for rehearing or a combined petition/suggestion will otherwise be in accordance with the provisions of Federal Rules of Appellate Procedure 35 and 40 and Federal Circuit Rules 35 and 40.

[Amended effective June 1, 2011.]

RULE 6. CONVICTION OR DISCIPLINE IMPOSED BY ANOTHER COURT OR AN AGENCY

(a) Duty of Attorney to Notify. An attorney who is a member of the bar of this court shall notify the Clerk in writing within 14 days of the member's (1) conviction of a serious crime, (2) disbarment or suspension by another court or by an agency, or (3) disbarment on consent or resignation from the bar of another court or an agency while an investigation into an allegation of misconduct is pending. Upon receipt of such information, the Clerk shall follow the procedures set forth in Rule 7.

(b) Notification From Another Court or Agency; Sua Sponte. Upon receipt of a copy of a judgment, order, or other document demonstrating that a member of the bar of this court has been disbarred or suspended from the practice of law by another court or an agency, or has resigned while an investigation into an allegation of misconduct is pending, the Clerk shall follow the procedures set forth in Rule 7.

[Amended effective June 1, 2011.]

RULE 7. PROCEEDINGS FOR RECIPROCAL DISCIPLINE OR CONVICTION OF SERIOUS CRIME

(a) Show Cause Order. On notification of an attorney's disbarment or suspension by another court or agency, the Clerk shall issue a show cause order why the court should not impose the identical discipline. On notification of an attorney's conviction of a serious crime or resignation from the bar of another court or agency while a misconduct investigation is pending, the Clerk shall issue a show cause order why disbarment should not be imposed.

(b) Response. Unless otherwise ordered, a response to a show cause order shall be due within 30 days. The response should be in an envelope marked "Direct to Chief Deputy Clerk" and should indicate the docket number of the matter.

Any request for a hearing shall be included in a response. In any response, the attorney must (1) list all bars to which the attorney is admitted, including all bar numbers and other bar identification information and (2) list all cases pending before this court in which the attorney is involved.

(c) Uncontested Matter. If an attorney does not object to the imposition of reciprocal discipline or does not respond to the show cause order, the Clerk may then issue a final order imposing such reciprocal discipline.

(d) Contested Matter. If an attorney contests the imposition of reciprocal discipline, further proceedings shall be conducted in accordance with Rule 8.

(e) Final Order and Further Review. At the conclusion of a proceeding, the Standing Panel shall issue a final order in the matter. Any further review will be in accordance with Rule 5(g).

RULE 8. CONTESTED PROCEEDINGS

(a) No Request for a Hearing. If an attorney does not request a hearing in response to a show cause order, then the panel shall prepare the record consisting of the show cause order, the response, and any other documents obtained by the panel. If the record includes documents in addition to the show cause order and the response, then an attorney shall be given notice that he or she may inspect and copy the record at his or her expense and may file a supplemental response. Information will be withheld from an attorney only in extraordinary circumstances, e.g., for national security or criminal investigation reasons. Any supplemental response shall be due within 14 days of the date of the notice concerning inspection and copying.

(b) Request for Hearing. On request by an attorney, the panel shall schedule a hearing. A hearing scheduled by a merits or motions panel will be an oral hearing. If a merits or motions panel determines that an evidentiary hearing is necessary, that panel shall refer the matter to the Standing Panel. In matters that have not been referred by a merits or motions panel, the Standing Panel shall determine whether a hearing is oral or evidentiary. An attorney shall be given at least 30 days' notice of the time, date, and place of a hearing.

(1) The record consists of the show cause order, the response, and any other documents obtained by the panel. If the record includes documents in addition to the show cause order and the response, then an attorney shall be given notice that he or she may inspect and copy the record at his or her expense. Information will be withheld from an attorney only in extraordinary circumstances, e.g., for national security or criminal investigation reasons.

(2) The Standing Panel may compel by subpoena the attendance of witnesses, including the attorney subject to the proceeding, and the production of documents.

(3) During an evidentiary hearing, an attorney shall be afforded an opportunity to cross-examine any witnesses called by the Standing Panel and to introduce evidence in defense or mitigation.

(4) A hearing shall be recorded on tape unless an attorney arranges to have a reporting service present at his or her own expense.

(c) Reciprocal Disciplinary Matter. Notification that an attorney has been disbarred or suspended by another court or agency shall establish that the conduct in fact occurred and that the discipline was appropriate unless an attorney shows that:

(1) the procedure was so lacking in notice or opportunity to be heard that it constituted a deprivation of due process; or

(2) there was such an infirmity of proof establishing the misconduct that it gave rise to the clear conviction that this court could not, consistent with its duty, accept as final the conclusion on the matter; or

(3) the imposition of the same discipline by this court would result in grave injustice; or

(4) the misconduct established is deemed by this court to warrant substantially different discipline.

(d) Conviction of a Serious Crime. Notification of a conviction of a serious crime shall be conclusive evidence of the commission of that crime for purposes of these disciplinary proceedings. If an attorney notifies the court that a conviction has been vacated or reversed, the Standing Panel shall promptly review the matter.

RULE 9. REINSTATEMENT

(a) After Reciprocal Disbarment or Suspension. If disbarment by this court was based on a disbarment by another court or agency or a suspension was directed to run concurrently with a suspension ordered by another court or agency, then an attorney shall be eligible for reinstatement when the original discipline is lifted or expires. An attorney must submit an affidavit notifying this court of the action of the court that imposed the original discipline. The Clerk shall refer an attorney's notification affidavit to the Standing Panel. Unless otherwise ordered, the Clerk shall issue an order reinstating the attorney within 14 days after reference to the Standing Panel.

(b) After Disbarment. An attorney who has been disbarred as a result of misconduct before this court may not apply for reinstatement until the expiration of five years from the effective date of the disbarment.

(c) After Suspension.

(1) An attorney who has been suspended with automatic reinstatement as a result of misconduct before this court may file an affidavit of compliance with the suspension order after the suspension period has expired. The Clerk shall issue an order reinstating the attorney within 14 days.

(2) An attorney who has been suspended conditioned on applying for reinstatement as a result of misconduct before this court may file an application after the suspension period expires.

(d) Application for Reinstatement. The Clerk shall refer an application for reinstatement to the Standing Panel. Any request for a hearing shall be included in an application.

(1) The Standing Panel may issue an order granting an application or, if no hearing is requested, may issue an order denying an application.

(2) If the Standing Panel is not satisfied initially that reinstatement is appropriate and a hearing is requested, the Standing Panel shall schedule a hearing. The Standing Panel shall decide whether a hearing shall be oral or evidentiary. At a hearing the applicant has the burden of showing that he or she has the moral qualifications, competency, and learning in the law required for readmission and that the resumption of practice will not be detrimental to the integrity and standing of the bar or to the administration of justice.

(3) At the conclusion of a proceeding, the Standing Panel shall issue a final order. Further review shall be in accordance with Rule 5(g).

(e) Successive Application. A successive application for reinstatement may not be filed until one year has elapsed after an adverse decision on an earlier application.

RULE 10. ACCESS TO INFORMATION

(a) Confidentiality During Proceedings. An ongoing disciplinary proceeding shall be confidential (1) unless the attorney subject to the proceeding requests that it be made a public record or (2) except to the extent that a panel may disclose the subject matter and status of a proceeding if the proceeding is based on a conviction of a serious crime, or an allegation that has become generally known to the public, or there is a need to notify another person or entity to protect the public, the legal profession, or the administration of justice.

(b) Confidentiality Upon Issuance of a Final Order. A final order issuing a private reprimand or imposing no discipline and the record of those proceedings shall be confidential unless the attorney subject to the proceeding requests that it be made a public record. If other discipline is imposed, a final order and the record shall be made a public record at the time of issuance of a final order. However, a panel may issue a permanent protective order prohibiting the disclosure of any part of the record to protect the interest of a complainant, a witness, a third party or nonparty, or the attorney.

RULE 11. EFFECTIVE DATE

These rules shall become effective June 1, 2010.

APPENDIX IV. COURTROOM DECORUM

App. IV. Courtroom Decorum

- The dignity of the Court is to be respected and maintained at all times.
- Attire for counsel and spectators should be restrained and appropriate to the dignity of a Court of Appeals of the United States.
- Court security officers and Court staff are authorized to open and inspect any item carried into a courtroom.
- Everyone in the courtroom, unless physically challenged, must rise when the judges enter and remain standing until the presiding judge invites everyone to be seated. Similarly, when court adjourns, everyone stands in place until the judges are no longer visible.
- Standing in the courtroom may be permitted only at the discretion of the Clerk. Areas marked as reserved are for Court Staff and Federal Circuit Law Clerks.
- Counsel may address the Court when invited to do so. Only counsel associated with the appeal being argued may address the court, unless a judge directs otherwise.
- Coat racks in the hallways outside the courtrooms are to be utilized.
- Only material related to the Court's business can be read in the courtroom while court is in session.
- When Court is in session, no one should be heard except for counsel making argument or a judge.
- The following items are prohibited in the courtroom and adjacent lobby area:
  - Recording or broadcasting devices
  - Cameras, including those contained in computers and other electronic devices
  - Food and drink except for the water provided at the counsel table
  - Computers (except for those to be used by counsel in argued cases)
  - Phones must be turned off
- Inappropriate facial gestures or exaggerated gesticulating is forbidden.
- Repeated entrances and departures are to be avoided.
- Doorways and passageways should be kept clear at all times.

[Effective June 4, 1998. Amended effective May 1, 2008; October 1, 2009.]

APPENDIX V. RULES FOR JUDICIAL CONDUCT AND JUDICIAL DISABILITY PROCEEDINGS

INTRODUCTION

On March 11, 2008, the Judicial Conference of the United States approved binding Rules for Judicial Conduct and Judicial Disability Proceedings ("Rules"). The Rules take effect on April 10, 2008. These Rules replace the United States Court of Appeals for the Federal Circuit's previous Rules Governing Complaints of Judicial Misconduct and Disability.

Pursuant to Title 28 of the United States Code, sections 351 et al., and the Rules, any person may file a written complaint with the circuit executive concerning the actions or behavior of a judge of this court. The form that may be used for a complaint is provided at the end of the rules.

Complaints should be sent to:

Circuit Executive
United States Court of Appeals
for the Federal Circuit
717 Madison Place, NW
Washington, DC 20439

The United States Court of Appeals for the Federal Circuit is now posting public orders pertaining to judicial conduct and disability complaints on its website. The orders generally do not disclose the name of the complainant or of the judge about whom the complaint is made. Pursuant to the Rules, an order is posted when final action on a complaint has been taken and the order is no longer subject to review. Paper copies of the orders are also available to the public from the circuit executive's office.

PREFACE

These Rules were promulgated by the Judicial Conference of the United States, after public comment, pursuant to 28 U.S.C. §§ 331 and 358, to establish standards and procedures for addressing complaints filed by complainants or identified by chief judges, under the Judicial Conduct and Disability Act, 28 U.S.C. §§ 351–364.

ARTICLE I. GENERAL PROVISIONS

RULE 1. SCOPE

These Rules govern proceedings under the Judicial Conduct and Disability Act, 28 U.S.C. §§ 351–364 (the Act), to determine whether a covered judge has engaged in conduct prejudicial to the effective and expeditious administration of the business of the courts or is unable to discharge the duties of office because of mental or physical disability.

[Adopted March 11, 2008, effective April 10, 2008.]

Commentary on Rule 1

In September 2006, the Judicial Conduct and Disability Act Study Committee, appointed in 2004 by Chief Justice

Rehnquist and known as the "Breyer Committee," presented a report, known as the "Breyer Committee Report," 239 F.R.D. 116 (Sept. 2006), to Chief Justice Roberts that evaluated implementation of the Judicial Conduct and Disability Act of 1980, 28 U.S.C. §§ 351–364. The Breyer Committee had been formed in response to criticism from the public and the Congress regarding the effectiveness of the Act's implementation. The Executive Committee of the Judicial Conference directed the Judicial Conference Committee on Judicial Conduct and Disability to consider the recommendations made by the Breyer Committee and to report on their implementation to the Conference.

The Breyer Committee found that it could not evaluate implementation of the Act without establishing interpretive standards, Breyer Committee Report, 239 F.R.D. at 132, and that a major problem faced by chief judges in implementing the Act was the lack of authoritative interpretive standards. *Id.* at 212–15. The Breyer Committee then established standards to guide its evaluation, some of which were new formulations and some of which were taken from the "Illustrative Rules Governing Complaints of Judicial Misconduct and Disability," discussed below. The principal standards used by the Breyer Committee are in Appendix E of its report. *Id.* at 238.

Based on the findings of the Breyer Committee, the Judicial Conference Committee on Judicial Conduct and Disability concluded that there was a need for the Judicial Conference to exercise its power under Section 358 of the Act to fashion standards guiding the various officers and bodies who must exercise responsibility under the Act. To that end, the Judicial Conference Committee proposed rules that were based largely on Appendix E of the Breyer Committee Report and the Illustrative Rules.

The Illustrative Rules were originally prepared in 1986 by the Special Committee of the Conference of Chief Judges of the United States Courts of Appeals, and were subsequently revised and amended, most recently in 2000, by the predecessor to the Committee on Judicial Conduct and Disability. The Illustrative Rules were adopted, with minor variations, by circuit judicial councils, to govern complaints under the Judicial Conduct and Disability Act.

RULE 2. EFFECT AND CONSTRUCTION

(a) Generally. These Rules are mandatory; they supersede any conflicting judicial council rules. Judicial councils may promulgate additional rules to implement the Act as long as those rules do not conflict with these Rules.

(b) Exception. A Rule will not apply if, when performing duties authorized by the Act, a chief judge, a special committee, a judicial council, the Judicial Conference Committee on Judicial Conduct and Disability, or the Judicial Conference of the United States expressly finds that exceptional circumstances render application of that Rule in a particular proceeding manifestly unjust or contrary to the purposes of the Act or these Rules.

[Adopted March 11, 2008, effective April 10, 2008.]

Commentary on Rule 2

Unlike the Illustrative Rules, these Rules provide mandatory and nationally uniform provisions governing the substantive and procedural aspects of misconduct and disability proceedings under the Act. The mandatory nature of these Rules is authorized by 28 U.S.C. § 358(a) and (c). Judicial councils retain the power to promulgate rules consistent with these Rules. For example, a local rule may authorize the electronic distribution of materials pursuant to Rule 8(b).

Rule 2(b) recognizes that unforeseen and exceptional circumstances may call for a different approach in particular cases.

RULE 3. DEFINITIONS

(a) Chief Judge. "Chief judge" means the chief judge of a United States Court of Appeals, of the United States Court of International Trade, or of the United States Court of Federal Claims.

(b) Circuit Clerk. "Circuit clerk" means a clerk of a United States court of appeals, the clerk of the United States Court of International Trade, the clerk of the United States Court of Federal Claims, or the circuit executive of the United States Court of Appeals for the Federal Circuit.

(c) Complaint. A complaint is:

(1) a document that, in accordance with Rule 6, is filed by any person in his or her individual capacity or on behalf of a professional organization; or

(2) information from any source, other than a document described in (c)(1), that gives a chief judge probable cause to believe that a covered judge, as defined in Rule 4, has engaged in misconduct or may have a disability, whether or not the information is framed as or is intended to be an allegation of misconduct or disability.

(d) Court of Appeals, District Court, and District Judge. "Courts of appeals," "district court," and "district judge," where appropriate, include the United States Court of Federal Claims, the United States Court of International Trade, and the judges thereof.

(e) Disability. "Disability" is a temporary or permanent condition rendering a judge unable to discharge the duties of the particular judicial office. Examples of disability include substance abuse, the inability to stay awake during court proceedings, or a severe impairment of cognitive abilities.

(f) Judicial Council and Circuit. "Judicial council" and "circuit," where appropriate, include any courts designated in 28 U.S.C. § 363.

(g) Magistrate Judge. "Magistrate judge," where appropriate, includes a special master appointed by the Court of Federal Claims under 42 U.S.C. § 300aa–12(c).

(h) Misconduct. Cognizable misconduct:

(1) is conduct prejudicial to the effective and expeditious administration of the business of the courts. Misconduct includes, but is not limited to:

(A) using the judge's office to obtain special treatment for friends or relatives;

(B) accepting bribes, gifts, or other personal favors related to the judicial office;

(C) having improper discussions with parties or counsel for one side in a case;

(D) treating litigants or attorneys in a demonstrably egregious and hostile manner;

(E) engaging in partisan political activity or making inappropriately partisan statements;

(F) soliciting funds for organizations; or

(G) violating other specific, mandatory standards of judicial conduct, such as those pertaining to restrictions on outside income and requirements for financial disclosure.

(2) is conduct occurring outside the performance of official duties if the conduct might have a prejudicial effect on the administration of the business of the courts, including a substantial and widespread lowering of public confidence in the courts among reasonable people.

(3) does not include:

(A) an allegation that is directly related to the merits of a decision or procedural ruling. An allegation that calls into question the correctness of a judge's ruling, including a failure to recuse, without more, is merits-related. If the decision or ruling is alleged to be the result of an improper motive, e.g., a bribe, ex parte contact, racial or ethnic bias, or improper conduct in rendering a decision or ruling, such as personally derogatory remarks irrelevant to the issues, the complaint is not cognizable to the extent that it attacks the merits.

(B) an allegation about delay in rendering a decision or ruling, unless the allegation concerns an improper motive in delaying a particular decision or habitual delay in a significant number of unrelated cases.

(i) Subject Judge. "Subject judge" means any judge described in Rule 4 who is the subject of a complaint.

[Adopted March 11, 2008, effective April 10, 2008.]

Commentary on Rule 3

Rule 3 is derived and adapted from the Breyer Committee Report and the Illustrative Rules.

Unless otherwise specified or the context otherwise indicates, the term "complaint" is used in these Rules to refer both to the complaints identified by a chief judge under Rule 5 and to complaints filed by complainants under Rule 6.

Under the Act, a "complaint" may be filed by "any person" or "identified" by a chief judge. *See* 28 U.S.C. § 351(a) and (b). Under Rule 3(c)(1), complaints may be submitted by a person, in his or her individual capacity, or by a professional organization. Generally, the word "complaint" brings to mind the commencement of an adversary proceeding in which the contending parties are left to present the evidence and legal arguments, and judges play the role of an essentially passive arbiter. The Act, however, establishes an administrative, inquisitorial process. For example, even absent a complaint under Rule 6, chief judges are expected in some circumstances to trigger the process—"identify a complaint," *see* 28 U.S.C. § 351(b) and Rule 5—and conduct an investigation without becoming a party. *See* 28 U.S.C. § 352(a); Breyer Committee Report, 239 F.R.D. at 214; Illustrative Rule 2(j). Even when a complaint is filed by someone other than the chief judge, the complainant lacks many rights that a litigant would have, and the chief judge, instead of being limited to the "four corners of the complaint," must, under Rule 11, proceed as though misconduct or disability has been alleged where the complainant reveals information of misconduct or disability but does not claim it as such. *See* Breyer Committee Report, 239 F.R.D. at 183–184.

An allegation of misconduct or disability filed under Rule 6 is a "complaint," and the Rule so provides in subsection (c)(1). However, both the nature of the process and the use of the term "identify" suggest that the word "complaint" covers more than a document formally triggering the process. The process relies on chief judges considering known information and triggering the process when appropriate. "Identifying" a "complaint," therefore, is best understood as the chief judge's concluding that information known to the judge constitutes probable cause to believe that misconduct occurred or a disability exists, whether or not the information is framed as, or intended to be, an accusation. This definition is codified in (c)(2).

Rule 3(e) relates to disability and provides only the most general definition, recognizing that a fact-specific approach is the only one available.

The phrase "prejudicial to the effective and expeditious administration of the business of the courts" is not subject to precise definition, and subsection (h)(1) therefore provides some specific examples. Although the Code of Conduct for United States Judges may be informative, its main precepts are highly general; the Code is in many potential applications aspirational rather than a set of disciplinary rules. Ultimately, the responsibility for determining what constitutes misconduct under the statute is the province of the judicial council of the circuit subject to such review and limitations as are ordained by the statute and by these Rules.

Even where specific, mandatory rules exist—for example, governing the receipt of gifts by judges, outside earned income, and financial disclosure obligations—the distinction between the misconduct statute and the specific, mandatory rules must be borne in mind. For example, an inadvertent, minor violation of any one of these Rules, promptly remedied when called to the attention of the judge, might still be a violation but might not rise to the level of misconduct under the statute. By contrast, a pattern of such violations of the Code might well rise to the level of misconduct.

An allegation can meet the statutory standard even though the judge's alleged conduct did not occur in the course of the performance of official duties. The Code of Conduct for United States Judges expressly covers a wide range of extra-official activities, and some of these activities may constitute misconduct. For example, allegations that a judge solicited funds for a charity or participated in a partisan political event are cognizable under the Act.

On the other hand, judges are entitled to some leeway in extra-official activities. For example, misconduct may not include a judge being repeatedly and publicly discourteous to a spouse (not including physical abuse) even though this might cause some reasonable people to have diminished confidence in the courts.

Rule 3(h)(2) states that conduct of this sort is covered, for example, when it might lead to a "substantial and widespread" lowering of such confidence.

Rule 3(h)(3)(A) tracks the Act, 28 U.S.C. § 352(b)(1)(A)(ii), in excluding from the definition of misconduct allegations "[d]irectly related to the merits of a decision or procedural ruling." This exclusion preserves the independence of judges in the exercise of judicial power by ensuring that the complaint procedure is not used to collaterally attack the substance of a judge's ruling. Any allegation that calls into question the correctness of an official action of a judge—without more—is merits-related. The phrase "decision or procedural ruling" is not limited to rulings issued in deciding Article III cases or controversies. Thus, a complaint challenging the correctness of a chief judge's determination to dismiss a prior misconduct complaint would be properly dismissed as merits-related—in other words, as challenging the substance of the judge's administrative determination to dismiss the complaint—even though it does not concern the judge's rulings in Article III litigation. Similarly, an allegation that a judge had incorrectly declined to approve a Criminal Justice Act voucher is merits-related under this standard.

Conversely, an allegation—however unsupported—that a judge conspired with a prosecutor to make a particular ruling is not merits-related, even though it "relates" to a ruling in a colloquial sense. Such an allegation attacks the propriety of conspiring with the prosecutor and goes beyond a challenge to the correctness—"the merits"—of the ruling itself. An allegation that a judge ruled against the complainant because the complainant is a member of a particular racial or ethnic group, or because the judge dislikes the complainant personally, is also not merits-related. Such an allegation attacks the propriety of arriving at rulings with an illicit or improper motive. Similarly, an allegation that a judge used an inappropriate term to refer to a class of people is not merits-related even if the judge used it on the bench or in an opinion; the correctness of the judge's rulings is not at stake. An allegation that a judge treated litigants or attorneys in a demonstrably egregious and hostile manner while on the bench is also not merits-related.

The existence of an appellate remedy is usually irrelevant to whether an allegation is merits-related. The merits-related ground for dismissal exists to protect judges' independence in making rulings, not to protect or promote the appellate process. A complaint alleging an incorrect ruling is merits-related even though the complainant has no recourse from that ruling. By the same token, an allegation that is otherwise cognizable under the Act should not be dismissed merely because an appellate remedy appears to exist (for example, vacating a ruling that resulted from an improper ex parte communication). However, there may be occasions when appellate and misconduct proceedings overlap, and consideration and disposition of a complaint under these Rules may be properly deferred by a chief judge until the appellate proceedings are concluded in order to avoid, inter alia, inconsistent decisions.

Because of the special need to protect judges' independence in deciding what to say in an opinion or ruling, a somewhat different standard applies to determine the merits-relatedness of a non-frivolous allegation that a judge's language in a ruling reflected an improper motive. If the judge's language was relevant to the case at hand—for example a statement that a claim is legally or factually "frivolous"—then the judge's choice of language is presumptively merits-related and excluded, absent evidence apart from the ruling itself suggesting an improper motive. If, on the other hand, the challenged language does not seem relevant on its face, then an additional inquiry under Rule 11 is necessary.

With regard to Rule 3(h)(3)(B), a complaint of delay in a single case is excluded as merits-related. Such an allegation may be said to challenge the correctness of an official action of the judge—in other words, assigning a low priority to deciding the particular case. But, by the same token, an allegation of a habitual pattern of delay in a significant number of unrelated cases, or an allegation of deliberate delay in a single case arising out of an illicit motive, is not merits-related.

The remaining subsections of Rule 3 provide technical definitions clarifying the application of the Rules to the various kinds of courts covered.

RULE 4. COVERED JUDGES

A complaint under these Rules may concern the actions or capacity only of judges of the United States courts of appeals, judges of the United States district courts, judges of United States bankruptcy courts, United States magistrate judges, and judges of the courts specified in 28 U.S.C. § 363.

[Adopted March 11, 2008, effective April 10, 2008.]

Commentary on Rule 4

This Rule tracks the Act. Rule 8(c) and (d) contain provisions as to the handling of complaints against persons not covered by the Act, such as other court personnel, or against both covered judges and noncovered persons.

ARTICLE II. INITIATION OF A COMPLAINT

RULE 5. IDENTIFICATION OF A COMPLAINT

(a) Identification. When a chief judge has information constituting reasonable grounds for inquiry into whether a covered judge has engaged in misconduct or has a disability, the chief judge may conduct an inquiry, as he or she deems appropriate, into the accuracy of the information even if no related complaint has been filed. A chief judge who finds probable cause to believe that misconduct has occurred or that a disability exists may seek an informal resolution that he or she finds satisfactory. If no informal resolution is achieved or is feasible, the chief judge may identify a complaint and, by written order stating the reasons, begin the review provided in Rule 11. If the evidence of misconduct is clear and convincing and no informal resolution is achieved or is feasible, the chief judge must identify a complaint. A chief judge must not decline to identify a complaint merely because the person making the allegation has not filed a complaint under Rule 6. This Rule is subject to Rule 7.

(b) Noncompliance with Rule 6(d). Rule 6 complaints that do not comply with the requirements of Rule 6(d) must be considered under this Rule.

[Adopted March 11, 2008, effective April 10, 2008.]

Commentary on Rule 5

This Rule is adapted from the Breyer Committee Report, 239 F.R.D. at 245–46.

The Act authorizes the chief judge, by written order stating reasons, to identify a complaint and thereby dispense with the filing of a written complaint. *See* 28 U.S.C. § 351(b). Under Rule 5, when a chief judge becomes aware of information constituting reasonable grounds to inquire into possible misconduct or disability on the part of a covered judge, and no formal complaint has been filed, the chief judge has the power in his or her discretion to begin an appropriate inquiry. A chief judge's decision whether to informally seek a resolution and/or to identify a complaint is guided by the results of that inquiry. If the chief judge concludes that there is probable cause to believe that misconduct has occurred or a disability exists, the chief judge may seek an informal resolution, if feasible, and if failing in that, may identify a complaint. Discretion is accorded largely for the reasons police officers and prosecutors have discretion in making arrests or bringing charges. The matter may be trivial and isolated, based on marginal evidence, or otherwise highly unlikely to lead to a misconduct or disability finding. On the other hand, if the inquiry leads the chief judge to conclude that there is clear and convincing evidence of misconduct or a disability, and no satisfactory informal resolution has been achieved or is feasible, the chief judge is required to identify a complaint.

An informal resolution is one agreed to by the subject judge and found satisfactory by the chief judge. Because an informal resolution under Rule 5 reached before a complaint is filed under Rule 6 will generally cause a subsequent Rule 6 complaint alleging the identical matter to be concluded, *see* Rule 11(d), the chief judge must be sure that the resolution is fully appropriate before endorsing it. In doing so, the chief judge must balance the seriousness of the matter against the particular judge's alacrity in addressing the issue. The availability of this procedure should encourage attempts at swift remedial action before a formal complaint is filed.

When a complaint is identified, a written order stating the reasons for the identification must be provided; this begins the process articulated in Rule 11. Rule 11 provides that once the chief judge has identified a complaint, the chief judge, subject to the disqualification provisions of Rule 25, will perform, with respect to that complaint, all functions assigned to the chief judge for the determination of complaint filed by a complainant.

In high-visibility situations, it may be desirable for the chief judge to identify a complaint without first seeking an informal resolution (and then, if the circumstances warrant, dismiss or conclude the identified complaint without appointment of a special committee) in order to assure the public that the allegations have not been ignored.

A chief judge's decision not to identify a complaint under Rule 5 is not appealable and is subject to Rule 3(h)(3)(A), which excludes merits-related complaints from the definition of misconduct.

A chief judge may not decline to identify a complaint solely on the basis that the unfiled allegations could be raised by one or more persons in a filed complaint, but none of these persons has opted to do so.

Subsection (a) concludes by stating that this Rule is "subject to Rule 7." This is intended to establish that only: (i) the chief judge of the home circuit of a potential subject judge, or (ii) the chief judge of a circuit in which misconduct is alleged to have occurred in the course of official business while the potential subject judge was sitting by designation, shall have the power or a duty under this Rule to identify a complaint.

Subsection (b) provides that complaints filed under Rule 6 that do not comply with the requirements of Rule 6(d), must be considered under this Rule. For instance, if a complaint has been filed but the form submitted is unsigned, or the truth of the statements therein are not verified in writing under penalty of perjury, then a chief judge must nevertheless consider the allegations as known information, and proceed to follow the process described in Rule 5(a).

RULE 6. FILING A COMPLAINT

(a) Form. A complainant may use the form reproduced in the appendix to these Rules or a form designated by rules of the judicial council in the circuit in which the complaint is filed. A complaint form is also available on each court of appeals' website or may be obtained from the circuit clerk or any district court or bankruptcy court within the circuit. A form is not necessary to file a complaint, but the complaint must be written and must include the information described in (b).

(b) Brief Statement of Facts. A complaint must contain a concise statement that details the specific facts on which the claim of misconduct or disability is based. The statement of facts should include a description of:

(1) what happened;

(2) when and where the relevant events happened;

(3) any information that would help an investigator check the facts; and

(4) for an allegation of disability, any additional facts that form the basis of that allegation.

(c) Legibility. A complaint should be typewritten if possible. If not typewritten, it must be legible. An illegible complaint will be returned to the complainant with a request to resubmit it in legible form. If a resubmitted complaint is still illegible, it will not be accepted for filing.

(d) Complainant's Address and Signature; Verification. The complainant must provide a contact address and sign the complaint. The truth of the statements made in the complaint must be verified in writing under penalty of perjury. If any of these requirements are not met, the complaint will be accepted for filing, but it will be reviewed under only Rule 5(b).

(e) Number of Copies; Envelope Marking. The complainant shall provide the number of copies of the complaint required by local rule. Each copy should be in an envelope marked "Complaint of Misconduct" or "Complaint of Disability." The envelope must not show the name of any subject judge.

[Adopted March 11, 2008, effective April 10, 2008.]

Commentary on Rule 6

The Rule is adapted from the Illustrative Rules and is self-explanatory.

RULE 7. WHERE TO INITIATE COMPLAINTS

(a) Where to File. Except as provided in (b),

(1) a complaint against a judge of a United States court of appeals, a United States district court, a United States bankruptcy court, or a United States magistrate judge must be filed with the circuit clerk in the jurisdiction in which the subject judge holds office.

(2) a complaint against a judge of the United States Court of International Trade or the United States Court of Federal Claims must be filed with the respective clerk of that court.

(3) a complaint against a judge of the United States Court of Appeals for the Federal Circuit must be filed with the circuit executive of that court.

(b) Misconduct in Another Circuit; Transfer. If a complaint alleges misconduct in the course of official business while the subject judge was sitting on a court by designation under 28 U.S.C. §§ 291–293 and 294(d), the complaint may be filed or identified with the circuit clerk of that circuit or of the subject judge's home circuit. The proceeding will continue in the circuit of the first-filed or first-identified complaint. The judicial council of the circuit where the complaint was first filed or first identified may transfer the complaint to the subject judge's home circuit or to the circuit where the alleged misconduct occurred, as the case may be.

[Adopted March 11, 2008, effective April 10, 2008.]

Commentary on Rule 7

Title 28 U.S.C. § 351 states that complaints are to be filed with "the clerk of the court of appeals for the circuit." However, in many circuits, this role is filled by circuit executives. Accordingly, the term "circuit clerk," as defined in Rule 3(b) and used throughout these Rules, applies to circuit executives.

Section 351 uses the term "the circuit" in a way that suggests that either the home circuit of the subject judge or the circuit in which misconduct is alleged to have occurred is the proper venue for complaints. With an exception for judges sitting by designation, the Rule requires the identifying or filing of a misconduct or disability complaint in the circuit in which the judge holds office, largely based on the administrative perspective of the Act. Given the Act's emphasis on the future conduct of the business of the courts, the circuit in which the judge holds office is the appropriate forum because that circuit is likely best able to influence a judge's future behavior in constructive ways.

However, when judges sit by designation, the non-home circuit has a strong interest in redressing misconduct in the course of official business, and where allegations also involve a member of the bar—ex parte contact between an attorney and a judge, for example—it may often be desirable to have the judicial and bar misconduct proceedings take place in the same venue. Rule 7(b), therefore, allows transfer to, or filing or identification of a complaint in, the non-home circuit. The proceeding may be transferred by the judicial council of the filing or identified circuit to the other circuit.

RULE 8. ACTION BY CLERK

(a) Receipt of Complaint. Upon receiving a complaint against a judge filed under Rule 5 or 6, the circuit clerk must open a file, assign a docket number according to a uniform numbering scheme promulgated by the Judicial Conference Committee on Judicial Conduct and Disability, and acknowledge the complaint's receipt.

(b) Distribution of Copies. The clerk must promptly send copies of a complaint filed under Rule 6 to the chief judge or the judge authorized to act as chief judge under Rule 25(f), and copies of complaints filed under Rule 5 or 6 to each subject judge. The clerk must retain the original complaint. Any further distribution should be as provided by local rule.

(c) Complaints Against Noncovered Persons. If the clerk receives a complaint about a person not holding an office described in Rule 4, the clerk must not accept the complaint for filing under these Rules.

(d) Receipt of Complaint about a Judge and Another Noncovered Person. If a complaint is received about a judge described in Rule 4 and a person not holding an office described in Rule 4, the clerk must accept the complaint for filing under these Rules only with regard to the judge and must inform the complainant of the limitation.

[Adopted March 11, 2008, effective April 10, 2008.]

Commentary on Rule 8

This Rule is adapted from the Illustrative Rules and is largely self-explanatory.

The uniform docketing scheme described in subsection (a) should take into account potential problems associated with a complaint that names multiple judges. One solution may be to provide separate docket numbers for each subject judge. Separate docket numbers would help avoid difficulties in tracking cases, particularly if a complaint is dismissed with respect to some, but not all of the named judges.

Complaints against noncovered persons are not to be accepted for processing under these Rules but may, of course, be accepted under other circuit rules or procedures for grievances.

RULE 9. TIME FOR FILING OR IDENTIFYING A COMPLAINT

A complaint may be filed or identified at any time. If the passage of time has made an accurate and fair investigation of a complaint impractical, the complaint must be dismissed under Rule 11(c)(1)(E).

[Adopted March 11, 2008, effective April 10, 2008.]

Commentary on Rule 9

This Rule is adapted from the Act, 28 U.S.C. §§ 351, 352(b)(1)(A)(iii), and the Illustrative Rules.

RULE 10. ABUSE OF THE COMPLAINT PROCEDURE

(a) Abusive Complaints. A complainant who has filed repetitive, harassing, or frivolous complaints, or has otherwise abused the complaint procedure, may be restricted from filing further complaints. After giving the complainant an opportunity to show cause in writing why his or her right to file further complaints should not be limited, a judicial council may prohibit, restrict, or impose conditions on the complainant's use of the complaint procedure. Upon written request of the complainant, the judicial council may revise or withdraw any prohibition, restriction, or condition previously imposed.

(b) Orchestrated Complaints. When many essentially identical complaints from different complainants are received and appear to be part of an orchestrated campaign, the chief judge may recommend that the judicial council issue a written order instructing the circuit clerk to accept only a certain number of such complaints for filing and to refuse to accept further ones. The clerk must send a copy of any such order to anyone whose complaint was not accepted.

[Adopted March 11, 2008, effective April 10, 2008.]

Commentary on Rule 10

This Rule is adapted from the Illustrative Rules.

Rule 10(a) provides a mechanism for a judicial council to restrict the filing of further complaints by a single complainant who has abused the complaint procedure. In some instances, however, the complaint procedure may be abused in a manner for which the remedy provided in Rule 10(a) may not be appropriate. For example, some circuits have been inundated with submissions of dozens or hundreds of essentially identical complaints against the same judge or judges, all submitted by different complainants. In many of these instances, persons with grievances against a particular judge or judges used the Internet or other technology to orchestrate mass complaint-filing campaigns against them. If each complaint submitted as part of such a campaign were accepted for filing and processed according to these Rules, there would be a serious drain on court resources without any benefit to the adjudication of the underlying merits.

A judicial council may, therefore, respond to such mass filings under Rule 10(b) by declining to accept repetitive complaints for filing, regardless of the fact that the complaints are nominally submitted by different complainants. When the first complaint or complaints have been dismissed on the merits, and when further, essentially identical submissions follow, the judicial council may issue a second order noting that these are identical or repetitive complaints, directing the circuit clerk not to accept these complaints or any further such complaints for filing, and directing the clerk to send each putative complainant copies of both orders.

ARTICLE III. REVIEW OF A COMPLAINT BY THE CHIEF JUDGE

RULE 11. REVIEW BY THE CHIEF JUDGE

(a) Purpose of Chief Judge's Review. When a complaint is identified by the chief judge or is filed, the chief judge must review it unless the chief judge is disqualified under Rule 25. If the complaint contains information constituting evidence of misconduct or disability, but the complainant does not claim it as such, the chief judge must treat the complaint as if it did allege misconduct or disability and give notice to the subject judge. After reviewing the complaint, the chief judge must determine whether it should be:

(1) dismissed;

(2) concluded on the ground that voluntary corrective action has been taken;

(3) concluded because intervening events have made action on the complaint no longer necessary; or

(4) referred to a special committee.

(b) Inquiry by Chief Judge. In determining what action to take under Rule 11(a), the chief judge may conduct a limited inquiry. The chief judge, or a designee, may communicate orally or in writing with the complainant, the subject judge, and any others who may have knowledge of the matter, and may review transcripts or other relevant documents. In conducting the inquiry, the chief judge must not determine any reasonably disputed issue.

(c) Dismissal.

(1) Allowable grounds. A complaint must be dismissed in whole or in part to the extent that the chief judge concludes that the complaint:

(A) alleges conduct that, even if true, is not prejudicial to the effective and expeditious administration of the business of the courts and does not indicate a mental or physical disability resulting in inability to discharge the duties of judicial office;

(B) is directly related to the merits of a decision or procedural ruling;

(C) is frivolous;

(D) is based on allegations lacking sufficient evidence to raise an inference that misconduct has occurred or that a disability exists;

(E) is based on allegations which are incapable of being established through investigation;

(F) has been filed in the wrong circuit under Rule 7; or

(G) is otherwise not appropriate for consideration under the Act.

(2) Disallowed grounds. A complaint must not be dismissed solely because it repeats allegations of a previously dismissed complaint if it also contains material information not previously considered and does not constitute harassment of the subject judge.

(d) Corrective Action. The chief judge may conclude the complaint proceeding in whole or in part if:

(1) an informal resolution under Rule 5 satisfactory to the chief judge was reached before the complaint was filed under Rule 6; or

(2) the chief judge determines that the subject judge has taken appropriate voluntary corrective action that acknowledges and remedies the problems raised by the complaint.

(e) Intervening Events. The chief judge may conclude the complaint proceeding in whole or in part upon determining that intervening events render some or all of the allegations moot or make remedial action impossible.

(f) Appointment of Special Committee. If some or all of the complaint is not dismissed or concluded, the chief judge must promptly appoint a special committee to investigate the complaint or any relevant portion of it and to make recommendations to the judicial council. Before appointing a special committee, the chief judge must invite the subject judge to respond to the complaint either orally or in writing if the judge was not given an opportunity during the limited inquiry. In the chief judge's discretion, separate complaints may be joined and assigned to a single special committee. Similarly, a single complaint about more than one judge may be severed and more than one special committee appointed.

(g) Notice of Chief Judge's Action; Petitions for Review.

(1) When special committee is appointed. If a special committee is appointed, the chief judge must notify the complainant and the subject judge that the matter has been referred to a special committee and identify the members of the committee. A copy of the order appointing the special committee must be sent to the Judicial Conference Committee on Judicial Conduct and Disability.

(2) When chief judge disposes of complaint without appointing special committee. If the chief judge disposes of the complaint under Rule 11(c), (d), or (e), the chief judge must prepare a supporting memorandum that sets forth the reasons for the disposition. Except as authorized by 28 U.S.C. § 360, the memorandum must not include the name of the complainant or of the subject judge. The order and the supporting memorandum, which may be one document, must be provided to the complainant, the subject judge, and the Judicial Conference Committee on Judicial Conduct and Disability.

(3) Right of petition for review. If the chief judge disposes of a complaint under Rule 11(c), (d), or (e), the complainant and subject judge must be notified of the right to petition the judicial council for review of the disposition, as provided in Rule 18. If a petition for review is filed, the chief judge must promptly transmit all materials obtained in connection with the inquiry under Rule 11(b) to the circuit clerk for transmittal to the judicial council.

(h) Public Availability of Chief Judge's Decision. The chief judge's decision must be made public to the extent, at the time, and in the manner provided in Rule 24.

[Adopted March 11, 2008, effective April 10, 2008.]

Commentary on Rule 11

Subsection (a) lists the actions available to a chief judge in reviewing a complaint. This subsection provides that where a complaint has been filed under Rule 6, the ordinary doctrines of waiver do not apply. A chief judge must identify as a complaint any misconduct or disability issues raised by the factual allegations of the complaint even if the complainant makes no such claim with regard to those issues. For example, an allegation limited to misconduct in fact-finding that mentions periods during a trial when the judge was asleep must be treated as a complaint regarding disability. Some formal order giving notice of the expanded scope of the proceeding must be given to the subject judge.

Subsection (b) describes the nature of the chief judge's inquiry. It is based largely on the Breyer Committee Report, 239 F.R.D. at 243–45. The Act states that dismissal is appropriate "when a limited inquiry . . . demonstrates that the allegations in the complaint lack any factual foundation or are conclusively refuted by objective evidence." 28 U.S.C. § 352(b)(1)(B). At the same time, however, Section 352(a) states that "[t]he chief judge shall not undertake to make findings of fact about any matter that is reasonably in dispute." These two statutory standards should be read together, so that a matter is not "reasonably" in dispute if a limited inquiry shows that the allegations do not constitute misconduct or disability, that they lack any reliable factual foundation, or that they are conclusively refuted by objective evidence.

In conducting a limited inquiry under subsection (b), the chief judge must avoid determinations of reasonably disputed issues, including reasonably disputed issues as to whether the facts alleged constitute misconduct or disability, which are ordinarily left to a special committee and the judicial council. An allegation of fact is ordinarily not "refuted" simply because the subject judge denies it. The limited inquiry must reveal something more in the way of refutation before it is appropriate to dismiss a complaint that is otherwise cognizable. If it is the complainant's word against the subject judge's—in other words, there is simply no other significant evidence of what happened or of the complainant's unreliability—then there must be a special committee investigation. Such a credibility issue is a matter "reasonably in dispute" within the meaning of the Act.

However, dismissal following a limited inquiry may occur when the complaint refers to transcripts or to witnesses and the chief judge determines that the transcripts and witnesses all support the subject judge. Breyer Committee Report, 239 F.R.D. at 243. For example, consider a complaint alleging that the subject judge said X, and the complaint mentions, or it is independently clear, that five people may have heard what the judge said. *Id.* The chief judge is told by the subject judge and one witness that the judge did not say X, and the chief judge dismisses the complaint without questioning the other four possible witnesses. *Id.* In this example, the matter remains reasonably in dispute. If all five witnesses say the judge did not say X, dismissal is appropriate, but if potential witnesses who are reasonably accessible have not been questioned, then the matter remains reasonably in dispute. *Id.*

Similarly, under (c)(1)(A), if it is clear that the conduct or disability alleged, even if true, is not cognizable under these Rules, the complaint should be dismissed. If that issue is reasonably in dispute, however, dismissal under (c)(1)(A) is inappropriate.

Essentially, the standard articulated in subsection (b) is that used to decide motions for summary judgment pursuant to Fed. R. Civ. P. 56. Genuine issues of material fact are not resolved at the summary judgment stage. A material fact is one that "might affect the outcome of the suit under the governing law," and a dispute is "genuine" if "the evidence is such that a reasonable jury could return a verdict for the nonmoving party." *Anderson v. Liberty Lobby*, 477 U.S. 242, 248 (1986). Similarly, the chief judge may not resolve a genuine issue concerning a material fact or the existence of misconduct or a disability when conducting a limited inquiry pursuant to subsection (b).

Subsection (c) describes the grounds on which a complaint may be dismissed. These are adapted from the Act, 28 U.S.C. § 352(b), and the Breyer Committee Report, 239 F.R.D. at 239–45. Subsection (c)(1)(A) permits dismissal of an allegation that, even if true, does not constitute misconduct or disability under the statutory standard. The proper standards are set out in Rule 3 and discussed in the Commentary on that Rule. Subsection (c)(1)(B) permits dismissal of complaints related to the merits of a decision by a subject judge; this standard is also governed by Rule 3 and its accompanying Commentary.

Subsections (c)(1)(C)–(E) implement the statute by allowing dismissal of complaints that are "frivolous, lacking sufficient evidence to raise an inference that misconduct has occurred, or containing allegations which are incapable of being established through investigation." 28 U.S.C. § 352(b)(1)(A)(iii).

Dismissal of a complaint as "frivolous," under Rule 11(c)(1)(C), will generally occur without any inquiry beyond the face of the complaint. For instance, when the allegations are facially incredible or so lacking in indicia of reliability that no further inquiry is warranted, dismissal under this subsection is appropriate.

A complaint warranting dismissal under Rule 11(c)(1)(D) is illustrated by the following example. Consider a complainant who alleges an impropriety and asserts that he knows of it because it was observed and reported to him by a person who is identified. The judge denies that the event occurred. When contacted, the source also denies it. In such a case, the chief judge's proper course of action may turn on whether the source had any role in the allegedly improper conduct. If the complaint was based on a lawyer's statement that he or she had an improper ex parte contact with a judge, the lawyer's denial of the impropriety might not be taken as wholly persuasive, and it would be appropriate to conclude that a real factual issue is raised. On the other hand, if the complaint quoted a disinterested third party and that disinterested party denied that the statement had been made, there would be no value in opening a formal investigation. In such a case, it would be appropriate to dismiss the complaint under Rule 11(c)(1)(D).

Rule 11 (c)(1)(E) is intended, among other things, to cover situations when no evidence is offered or identified, or when the only identified source is unavailable. Breyer Committee Report, 239 F.R.D. at 243. For example, a complaint alleges that an unnamed attorney told the complainant that the judge did X. *Id.* The subject judge denies it. The chief judge requests that the complainant (who does not purport to have observed the judge do X) identify the unnamed witness, or that the unnamed witness come forward so that the chief judge can learn the unnamed witness's account. *Id.* The complainant responds that he has spoken with the unnamed witness, that the unnamed witness is an attorney who practices in federal court, and that the unnamed witness is unwilling to be identified or to come forward. *Id.* at 243–44. The allegation is then properly dismissed as containing allegations that are incapable of being established through investigation. *Id.*

If, however, the situation involves a reasonable dispute over credibility, the matter should proceed. For example, the complainant alleges an impropriety and alleges that he or she observed it and that there were no other witnesses; the subject judge denies that the event occurred. Unless the complainant's allegations are facially incredible or so lacking indicia of reliability warranting dismissal under Rule 11(c)(1)(C), a special committee must be appointed because there is a material factual question that is reasonably in dispute.

Dismissal is also appropriate when a complaint is filed so long after an alleged event that memory loss, death, or changes to unknown residences prevent a proper investigation.

Subsection (c)(2) indicates that the investigative nature of the process prevents the application of claim preclusion principles where new and material evidence becomes available. However, it also recognizes that at some point a renewed investigation may constitute harassment of the subject judge and should be foregone, depending of course on the seriousness of the issues and the weight of the new evidence.

Rule 11(d) implements the Act's provision for dismissal if voluntary appropriate corrective action has been taken. It is largely adapted from the Breyer Committee Report, 239 F.R.D. 244–45. The Act authorizes the chief judge to conclude the proceedings if "appropriate corrective action has been taken." 28 U.S.C. § 352(b)(2). Under the Rule, action taken after the complaint is filed is "appropriate" when it acknowledges and remedies the problem raised by the complaint. Breyer Committee Report, 239 F.R.D. at 244. Because the Act deals with the conduct of judges, the emphasis is on correction of the judicial conduct that was the subject of the complaint. *Id.* Terminating a complaint based on corrective action is premised on the implicit understanding that voluntary self-correction or redress of misconduct or a disability is preferable to sanctions. *Id.* The chief judge may facilitate this process by giving the subject judge an objective view of the appearance of the judicial conduct in question and by suggesting appropriate corrective measures. *Id.* Moreover, when corrective action is taken under Rule 5 satisfactory to the chief judge before a complaint is filed, that informal resolution will be sufficient to conclude a subsequent complaint based on the identical conduct.

"Corrective action" must be voluntary action taken by the subject judge. Breyer Committee Report, 239 F.R.D. at 244. A remedial action directed by the chief judge or by an appellate court without the participation of the subject judge in formulating the directive or without the subject judge's subsequent agreement to such action does not constitute the requisite voluntary corrective action. *Id.* Neither the chief judge nor an appellate court has authority under the Act to impose a formal remedy or sanction; only the judicial council can impose a formal remedy or sanction under 28 U.S.C. § 354(a)(2). *Id.* Compliance with a previous council order may serve as corrective action allowing conclusion of a later complaint about the same behavior. *Id.*

Where a judge's conduct has resulted in identifiable, particularized harm to the complainant or another individual, appropriate corrective action should include steps taken by that judge to acknowledge and redress the harm, if possible, such as by an apology, recusal from a case, or a pledge to refrain from similar conduct in the future. *Id.* While the Act is generally forward-looking, any corrective action should, to the extent possible, serve to correct a specific harm to an individual, if such harm can reasonably be remedied. *Id.* In some cases, corrective action may not be "appropriate" to justify conclusion of a complaint unless the complainant or other individual harmed is meaningfully apprised of the nature of the corrective action in the chief judge's order, in a direct communication from the subject judge, or otherwise. *Id.*

Voluntary corrective action should be proportionate to any plausible allegations of misconduct in the complaint. The form of corrective action should also be proportionate to any sanctions that a judicial council might impose under Rule 20(b), such as a private or public reprimand or a change in case assignments. Breyer Committee Report, 239 F.R.D. at 244–45. In other words, minor corrective action will not suffice to dispose of a serious matter. *Id.*

Rule 11(e) implements Section 352(b)(2) of the Act, which permits the chief judge to "conclude the proceeding," if "action on the complaint is no longer necessary because of intervening events," such as a resignation from judicial office. Ordinarily, however, stepping down from an administrative post such as chief judge, judicial council member, or court committee chair does not constitute an event rendering unnecessary any further action on a complaint alleging judicial misconduct. Breyer Committee Report, 239 F.R.D. at 245. As long as the subject of the complaint performs judicial duties, a complaint alleging judicial misconduct must be addressed. *Id.*

If a complaint is not disposed of pursuant to Rule 11(c), (d), or (e), a special committee must be appointed. Rule 11(f) states that a subject judge must be invited to respond to the complaint before a special committee is appointed, if no earlier response was invited.

Subject judges, of course, receive copies of complaints at the same time that they are referred to the chief judge, and they are free to volunteer responses to them. Under Rule 11(b), the chief judge may request a response if it is thought necessary. However, many complaints are clear candidates for dismissal even if their allegations are accepted as true, and there is no need for the subject judge to devote time to a defense.

The Act requires that the order dismissing a complaint or concluding the proceeding contain a statement of reasons and that a copy of the order be sent to the complainant. 28 U.S.C. § 352(b). Rule 24, dealing with availability of information to the public, contemplates that the order will be made public, usually without disclosing the names of the complainant or the subject judge. If desired for administrative purposes, more identifying information can be included in a non-public version of the order.

When complaints are disposed of by chief judges, the statutory purposes are best served by providing the complainant with a full, particularized, but concise explanation, giving reasons for the conclusions reached. *See also* Commentary on Rule 24, dealing with public availability.

Rule 11(g) provides that the complainant and subject judge must be notified, in the case of a disposition by the chief judge, of the right to petition the judicial council for review. A copy of the chief judge's order and memorandum, which may be one document, disposing of a complaint must be sent by the circuit clerk to the Judicial Conference Committee on Judicial Conduct and Disability.

ARTICLE IV. INVESTIGATION AND REPORT BY SPECIAL COMMITTEE

RULE 12. COMPOSITION OF SPECIAL COMMITTEE

(a) Membership. Except as provided in (e), a special committee appointed under Rule 11(f) must consist of the chief judge and equal numbers of circuit and district judges. If the complaint is about a district judge, bankruptcy judge, or magistrate judge, then, when possible, the district judge members of the committee must be from districts other than the district of the subject judge. For the courts named in 28 U.S.C. § 363, the committee must be selected from the judges serving on the subject judge's court.

(b) Presiding Officer. When appointing the committee, the chief judge may serve as the presiding officer or else must designate a committee member as the presiding officer.

(c) Bankruptcy Judge or Magistrate Judge as Adviser. If the subject judge is a bankruptcy judge or magistrate judge, he or she may, within 14 days after being notified of the committee's appointment, ask the chief judge to designate as a committee adviser another bankruptcy judge or magistrate judge, as the case may be. The chief judge must grant such a request but may otherwise use discretion in naming the adviser. Unless the adviser is a Court of Federal Claims special master appointed under 42 U.S.C. § 300aa–12(c), the adviser must be from a district other than the district of the subject bankruptcy judge or subject magistrate judge. The adviser cannot vote but has the other privileges of a committee member.

(d) Provision of Documents. The chief judge must certify to each other member of the Committee and to any adviser copies of the complaint and statement of facts in whole or relevant part, and any other relevant documents on file.

(e) Continuing Qualification of Committee Members. A member of a special committee who was qualified to serve when appointed may continue to serve on the committee even though the member relinquishes the position of chief judge, active circuit judge, or active district judge, as the case may be, but only if the member continues to hold office under Article III, Section 1, of the Constitution of the United States, or under 28 U.S.C. § 171.

(f) Inability of Committee Member to Complete Service. If a member of a special committee can no longer serve because of death, disability, disqualification, resignation, retirement from office, or other reason, the chief judge must decide whether to appoint a replacement member, either a circuit or district judge as needed under (a). No special committee appointed under these Rules may function with only a single member, and the votes of a two-member committee must be unanimous.

(g) Voting. All actions by a committee must be by vote of a majority of all members of the committee.

[Adopted March 11, 2008, effective April 10, 2008.]

Commentary on Rule 12

This Rule is adapted from the Act and the Illustrative Rules.

Rule 12 leaves the size of a special committee flexible, to be determined on a case-by-case basis. The question of committee size is one that should be weighed with care in view of the potential for consuming the members' time; a large committee should be appointed only if there is a special reason to do so.

Although the Act requires that the chief judge be a member of each special committee, 28 U.S.C. § 353(a)(1), it does not require that the chief judge preside. Accordingly, Rule 12(b) provides that if the chief judge does not preside, he or she must designate another committee member as the presiding officer.

Rule 12(c) provides that the chief judge must appoint a bankruptcy judge or magistrate judge as an adviser to a special committee at the request of a bankruptcy or magistrate subject judge.

Subsection (c) also provides that the adviser will have all the privileges of a committee member except a vote. The adviser, therefore, may participate in all deliberations of the committee, question witnesses at hearings, and write a separate statement to accompany the special committee's report to the judicial council.

Rule 12(e) provides that a member of a special committee who remains an Article III judge may continue to serve on the committee even though the member's status otherwise changes. Thus, a committee that originally consisted of the chief judge and an equal number of circuit and district judges, as required by the law, may continue to function even though changes of status alter that composition. This provision reflects the belief that stability of membership will contribute to the quality of the work of such committees.

Stability of membership is also the principal concern animating Rule 12(f), which deals with the case in which a special committee loses a member before its work is complete. The Rule permits the chief judge to determine whether a replacement member should be appointed. Generally, appointment of a replacement member is desirable in these situations unless the committee has conducted evidentiary hearings before the vacancy occurs. However, cases may arise in which a committee is in the late stages of its work, and in which it would be difficult for a new member to play a meaningful role. The Rule also preserves the collegial character of the committee process by prohibiting a single surviving member from serving as a committee and by providing that a committee of two surviving members will, in essence, operate under a unanimity rule.

Rule 12(g) provides that actions of a special committee must be by vote of a majority of all the members. All the members of a committee should participate in committee decisions. In that circumstance, it seems reasonable to require that committee decisions be made by a majority of the membership, rather than a majority of some smaller quorum.

RULE 13. CONDUCT OF AN INVESTIGATION

(a) Extent and Methods of Special Committee Investigations. Each special committee must determine the appropriate extent and methods of the investigation in light of the allegations of the complaint. If, in the course of the investigation, the committee has cause to believe that the subject judge may have engaged in misconduct or has a disability that is beyond the scope of the complaint, the committee must refer the new matter to the chief judge for action under Rule 5 or Rule 11.

(b) Criminal Conduct. If the committee's investigation concerns conduct that may be a crime, the committee must consult with the appropriate prosecutorial authorities to the extent permitted by the Act to avoid compromising any criminal investigation. The committee has final authority over the timing and extent of its investigation and the formulation of its recommendations.

(c) Staff. The committee may arrange for staff assistance to conduct the investigation. It may use existing staff of the judicial branch or may hire special staff through the Director of the Administrative Office of the United States Courts.

(d) Delegation of Subpoena Power; Contempt. The chief judge may delegate the authority to exercise the committee's subpoena powers. The judicial council or special committee may institute a contempt proceeding under 28 U.S.C. § 332(d) against anyone who fails to comply with a subpoena.

[Adopted March 11, 2008, effective April 10, 2008.]

Commentary on Rule 13

This Rule is adapted from the Illustrative Rules.

Rule 13, as well as Rules 14, 15, and 16, are concerned with the way in which a special committee carries out its mission. They reflect the view that a special committee has two roles that are separated in ordinary litigation. First, the committee has an investigative role of the kind that is characteristically left to executive branch agencies or discovery by civil litigants. 28 U.S.C. § 353(c). Second, it has a formalized fact-finding and recommendation-of-disposition role that is characteristically left to juries, judges, or arbitrators. *Id.* Rule 13 generally governs the investigative stage. Even though the same body has responsibility for both roles under the Act, it is important to distinguish between them in order to ensure that appropriate rights are afforded at appropriate times to the subject judge.

One of the difficult questions that can arise is the relationship between proceedings under the Act and criminal investigations. Rule 13(b) assigns responsibility for coordination to the special committee in cases in which criminal conduct is suspected, but gives the committee the authority to determine the appropriate pace of its activity in light of any criminal investigation.

Title 28 U.S.C. § 356(a) provides that a special committee will have full subpoena powers as provided in 28 U.S.C. § 332(d). Section 332(d)(1) provides that subpoenas will be issued on behalf of judicial councils by the circuit clerk "at the direction of the chief judge of the circuit or his designee." Rule 13(d) contemplates that, where the chief judge designates someone else as presiding officer of a special committee, the presiding officer also be delegated the authority to direct the circuit clerk to issue subpoenas related to committee proceedings. That is not intended to imply, however, that the decision to use the subpoena power is exercisable by the presiding officer alone. *See* Rule 12(g).

RULE 14. CONDUCT OF HEARINGS BY SPECIAL COMMITTEE

(a) Purpose of Hearings. The committee may hold hearings to take testimony and receive other evidence, to hear argument, or both. If the committee is investigating allegations against more than one judge, it may hold joint or separate hearings.

(b) Committee Evidence. Subject to Rule 15, the committee must obtain material, nonredundant evidence in the form it considers appropriate. In the committee's discretion, evidence may be obtained by committee members, staff, or both. Witnesses offering testimonial evidence may include the complainant and the subject judge.

(c) Counsel for Witnesses. The subject judge has the right to counsel. The special committee has discretion to decide whether other witnesses may have counsel present when they testify.

(d) Witness Fees. Witness fees must be paid as provided in 28 U.S.C. § 1821.

(e) Oath. All testimony taken at a hearing must be given under oath or affirmation.

(f) Rules of Evidence. The Federal Rules of Evidence do not apply to special committee hearings.

(g) Record and Transcript. A record and transcript must be made of all hearings.

[Adopted March 11, 2008, effective April 10, 2008.]

Commentary on Rule 14

This Rule is adapted from Section 353 of the Act and the Illustrative Rules.

Rule 14 is concerned with the conduct of fact-finding hearings. Special committee hearings will normally be held only after the investigative work has been completed and the committee has concluded that there is sufficient evidence to warrant a formal fact-finding proceeding. Special committee proceedings are primarily inquisitorial rather than adversarial. Accordingly, the Federal Rules of Evidence do not apply to such hearings. Inevitably, a hearing will have something of an adversary character. Nevertheless, that tendency should be moderated to the extent possible. Even though a proceeding will commonly have investigative and hearing stages, committee members should not regard themselves as prosecutors one day and judges the next. Their duty—and that of their staff—is at all times to be impartial seekers of the truth.

Rule 14(b) contemplates that material evidence will be obtained by the committee and presented in the form of affidavits, live testimony, etc. Staff or others who are organizing the hearings should regard it as their role to present evidence representing the entire picture. With respect to testimonial evidence, the subject judge should normally be called as a committee witness. Cases may arise in which the judge will not testify voluntarily. In such cases, subpoena powers are available, subject to the normal testimonial privileges. Although Rule 15(c) recognizes the subject judge's statutory right to call witnesses on his or her own behalf, exercise of this right should not usually be necessary.

RULE 15. RIGHTS OF SUBJECT JUDGE

(a) Notice.

(1) Generally. The subject judge must receive written notice of:

(A) the appointment of a special committee under Rule 11(f);

(B) the expansion of the scope of an investigation under Rule 13(a);

(C) any hearing under Rule 14, including its purposes, the names of any witnesses the committee intends to call, and the text of any statements that have been taken from those witnesses.

(2) Suggestion of additional witnesses. The subject judge may suggest additional witnesses to the committee.

(b) Report of the Special Committee. The subject judge must be sent a copy of the special committee's report when it is filed with judicial council.

(c) Presentation of Evidence. At any hearing held under Rule 14, the subject judge has the right to present evidence, to compel the attendance of witnesses, and to compel the production of documents. At the request of the subject judge, the chief judge or the judge's designee must direct the circuit clerk to issue a subpoena to a witness under 28 U.S.C. § 332(d)(1). The subject judge must be given the opportunity to cross-examine committee witnesses, in person or by counsel.

(d) Presentation of Argument. The subject judge may submit written argument to the special committee and must be given a reasonable opportunity to present oral argument at an appropriate stage of the investigation.

(e) Attendance at Hearings. The subject judge has the right to attend any hearing held under Rule 14 and to receive copies of the transcript, of any documents introduced, and of any written arguments submitted by the complainant to the committee.

(f) Representation by Counsel. The subject judge may choose to be represented by counsel in the exercise of any right enumerated in this Rule. As provided in Rule 20(e), the United States may bear the costs of representation.

[Adopted March 11, 2008, effective April 10, 2008.]

Commentary on Rule 15

This Rule is adapted from the Act and the Illustrative Rules.

The Act states that these Rules must contain provisions requiring that "the judge whose conduct is the subject of a complaint ... be afforded an opportunity to appear (in person or by counsel) at proceedings conducted by the investigating panel, to present oral and documentary evidence, to compel the attendance of witnesses or the production of documents, to cross-examine witnesses, and to present argument orally or in writing." 28 U.S.C. § 358(b)(2). To implement this provision, Rule 15(e) gives the judge the right to attend any hearing held for the purpose of receiving evidence of record or hearing argument under Rule 14.

The Act does not require that the subject judge be permitted to attend all proceedings of the special committee. Accordingly, the Rules do not give a right to attend other proceedings—for example, meetings at which the committee is engaged in investigative activity, such as interviewing persons to learn whether they ought to be called as witnesses or examining for relevance purposes documents delivered pursuant to a subpoena duces tecum, or meetings in which the committee is deliberating on the evidence or its recommendations.

RULE 16. RIGHTS OF COMPLAINANT IN INVESTIGATION

(a) Notice. The complainant must receive written notice of the investigation as provided in Rule 11(g)(1). When the special committee's report to the judicial council is filed, the complainant must be notified of the filing. The judicial council may, in its discretion, provide a copy of the report of a special committee to the complainant.

(b) Opportunity to Provide Evidence. If the committee determines that the complainant may have evidence that does not already exist in writing, a representative of the committee must interview the complainant.

(c) Presentation of Argument. The complainant may submit written argument to the special committee. In its discretion, the special committee may permit the complainant to offer oral argument.

(d) Representation by Counsel. A complainant may submit written argument through counsel and, if permitted to offer oral argument, may do so through counsel.

(e) Cooperation. In exercising its discretion under this Rule, a special committee may take into account the degree of the complainant's cooperation in preserving the confidentiality of the proceedings, including the identity of the subject judge.

[Adopted March 11, 2008, effective April 10, 2008.]

Commentary on Rule 16

This Rule is adapted from the Act and the Illustrative Rules.

In accordance with the view of the process as fundamentally administrative and inquisitorial, these Rules do not give the complainant the rights of a party to litigation, and leave the complainant's role largely to the discretion of the special committee. However, Rule 16(b) provides that, where a special committee has been appointed and it determines that the complainant may have additional evidence, the complainant must be interviewed by a representative of the committee. Such an interview may be in person or by telephone, and the representative of the committee may be either a member or staff.

Rule 16 does not contemplate that the complainant will ordinarily be permitted to attend proceedings of the special committee except when testifying or presenting oral argument. A special committee may exercise its discretion to permit the complainant to be present at its proceedings, or to permit the complainant, individually or through counsel, to participate in the examination or cross-examination of witnesses.

The Act authorizes an exception to the normal confidentiality provisions where the judicial council in its discretion provides a copy of the report of the special committee to the complainant and to the subject judge. 28 U.S.C. § 360(a)(1). However, the Rules do not entitle the complainant to a copy of the special committee's report.

In exercising their discretion regarding the role of the complainant, the special committee and the judicial council should protect the confidentiality of the complaint process. As a consequence, subsection (e) provides that a special committee may consider the degree to which a complainant has cooperated in preserving the confidentiality of the proceedings in determining what role beyond the minimum required by these Rules should be given to that complainant.

RULE 17. SPECIAL COMMITTEE REPORT

The committee must file with the judicial council a comprehensive report of its investigation, including findings and recommendations for council action. The report must be accompanied by a statement of the vote by which it was adopted, any separate or dissenting statements of committee members, and the record of any hearings held under Rule 14. A copy of the report and accompanying statement must be sent to the Judicial Conference Committee on Judicial Conduct and Disability.

[Adopted March 11, 2008, effective April 10, 2008.]

Commentary on Rule 17

This Rule is adapted from the Illustrative Rules and is self-explanatory. The provision for sending a copy of the special committee report and accompanying statement to the Judicial Conference Committee is new.

ARTICLE V. JUDICIAL COUNCIL REVIEW

RULE 18. PETITIONS FOR REVIEW OF CHIEF JUDGE DISPOSITIONS UNDER RULE 11(C), (D) OR (E)

(a) Petitions for Review. After the chief judge issues an order under Rule 11(c), (d) or (e), a complainant or subject judge may petition the judicial council of the circuit to review the order. By rules promulgated under 28 U.S.C. § 358, the judicial council may refer a petition for review filed under this Rule to a panel of no fewer than five members of the council, at least two of whom must be district judges.

(b) When to File; Form; Where to File. A petition for review must be filed in the office of the circuit clerk within 35 days of the date on the clerk's letter informing the parties of the chief judge's order. The petition should be in letter form, addressed to the circuit clerk, and in an envelope marked "Misconduct Petition" or "Disability Petition." The name of the subject judge must not be shown on the envelope. The letter should be typewritten or otherwise legible. It should begin with "I hereby petition the judicial council for review of ..." and state the reasons why the petition should be granted. It must be signed.

(c) Receipt and Distribution of Petition. A circuit clerk who receives a petition for review filed within the time allowed and in proper form must:

(1) acknowledge its receipt and send a copy to the complainant or subject judge, as the case may be;

(2) promptly distribute to each member of the judicial council, or its relevant panel, except for any member disqualified under Rule 25, or make available in the manner provided by local rule, the following materials:

(A) copies of the complaint;

(B) all materials obtained by the chief judge in connection with the inquiry;

(C) the chief judge's order disposing of the complaint;

(D) any memorandum in support of the chief judge's order;

(E) the petition for review; and

(F) an appropriate ballot;

(3) send the petition for review to the Judicial Conference Committee on Judicial Conduct and Disability. Unless the Judicial Conference Committee requests them, the clerk will not send copies of the materials obtained by the chief judge.

(d) Untimely Petition. The clerk must refuse to accept a petition that is received after the deadline in (b).

(e) Timely Petition Not in Proper Form. When the clerk receives a petition filed within the time allowed but in a form that is improper to a degree that would substantially impair its consideration by the judicial council—such as a document that is ambiguous about whether it is intended to be a petition for review—the clerk must acknowledge its receipt, call the filer's attention to the deficiencies, and give the filer the opportunity to correct the deficiencies within 21 days of the date of the clerk's letter about the deficiencies or within the original deadline for filing the petition, whichever is later. If the deficiencies are corrected within the time allowed, the clerk will proceed according to paragraphs (a) and (c) of this Rule. If the deficiencies are not corrected, the clerk must reject the petition.

[Adopted March 11, 2008, effective April 10, 2008.]

Commentary on Rule 18

Rule 18 is adapted largely from the Illustrative Rules.

Subsection (a) permits a subject judge, as well as the complainant, to petition for review of a chief judge's order dismissing a complaint under Rule 11(c), or concluding that appropriate corrective action or intervening events have remedied or mooted the problems raised by the complaint pursuant to Rule 11(d) or (e). Although the subject judge may ostensibly be vindicated by the dismissal or conclusion of a complaint, a chief judge's order may include language disagreeable to the subject judge. For example, an order may dismiss a complaint, but state that the subject judge did in fact engage in misconduct. Accordingly, a subject judge may wish to object to the content of the order and is given the opportunity to petition the judicial council of the circuit for review.

Subsection (b) contains a time limit of thirty-five days to file a petition for review. It is important to establish a time limit on petitions for review of chief judges' dispositions in order to provide finality to the process. If the complaint requires an investigation, the investigation should proceed; if it does not, the subject judge should know that the matter is closed.

The standards for timely filing under the Federal Rules of Appellate Procedure should be applied to petitions for review. *See* Fed. R. App. P. 25(a)(2)(A) and (C).

Rule 18(e) provides for an automatic extension of the time limit imposed under subsection (b) if a person files a petition that is rejected for failure to comply with formal requirements.

RULE 19. JUDICIAL COUNCIL DISPOSITION OF PETITIONS FOR REVIEW

(a) Rights of Subject Judge. At any time after a complainant files a petition for review, the subject judge may file a written response with the circuit clerk. The clerk must promptly distribute copies of the response to each member of the judicial council or of the relevant panel, unless that member is disqualified under Rule 25. Copies must also be distributed to the chief judge, to the complainant, and to the Judicial Conference Committee on Judicial Conduct and Disability. The subject judge must not otherwise communicate with individual council members about the matter. The subject judge must be given copies of any communications to the judicial council from the complainant.

(b) Judicial Council Action. After considering a petition for review and the materials before it, a judicial council may:

(1) affirm the chief judge's disposition by denying the petition;

(2) return the matter to the chief judge with directions to conduct a further inquiry under Rule 11(b) or to identify a complaint under Rule 5;

(3) return the matter to the chief judge with directions to appoint a special committee under Rule 11(f); or

(4) in exceptional circumstances, take other appropriate action.

(c) Notice of Council Decision. Copies of the judicial council's order, together with any accompanying memorandum in support of the order or separate concurring or dissenting statements, must be given to the complainant, the subject judge, and the Judicial Conference Committee on Judicial Conduct and Disability.

(d) Memorandum of Council Decision. If the council's order affirms the chief judge's disposition, a supporting memorandum must be prepared only if the judicial council concludes that there is a need to supplement the chief judge's explanation. A memorandum supporting a council order must not include the name of the complainant or the subject judge.

(e) Review of Judicial Council Decision. If the judicial council's decision is adverse to the petitioner, and if no member of the council dissented on the ground that a special committee should be appointed under Rule 11(f), the complainant must be notified that he or she has no right to seek review of the decision. If there was a dissent, the petitioner must be informed that he or she can file a petition for review under Rule 21(b) solely on the issue of whether a special committee should be appointed.

(f) Public Availability of Judicial Council Decision. Materials related to the council's decision must be made public to the extent, at the time, and in the manner set forth in Rule 24.

[Adopted March 11, 2008, effective April 10, 2008.]

Commentary on Rule 19

This Rule is largely adapted from the Act and is self-explanatory.

The council should ordinarily review the decision of the chief judge on the merits, treating the petition for review for all practical purposes as an appeal. The judicial council may respond to a petition by affirming the chief judge's order, remanding the matter, or, in exceptional cases, taking other appropriate action.

RULE 20. JUDICIAL COUNCIL CONSIDERATION OF REPORTS AND RECOMMENDATIONS OF SPECIAL COMMITTEES

(a) Rights of Subject Judge. Within 21 days after the filing of the report of a special committee, the subject judge may send a written response to the members of the judicial council. The judge must also be given an opportunity to present argument through counsel, written or oral, as determined by the council. The judge must not otherwise communicate with council members about the matter.

(b) Judicial Council Action.

(1) Discretionary actions. Subject to the judge's rights set forth in subsection (a), the judicial council may:

(A) dismiss the complaint because:

(i) even if the claim is true, the claimed conduct is not conduct prejudicial to the effective and expeditious administration of the business of the courts and does not indicate a mental or physical disability resulting in inability to discharge the duties of office;

(ii) the complaint is directly related to the merits of a decision or procedural ruling;

(iii) the facts on which the complaint is based have not been established; or

(iv) the complaint is otherwise not appropriate for consideration under 28 U.S.C. §§ 351–364.

(B) conclude the proceeding because appropriate corrective action has been taken or intervening events have made the proceeding unnecessary.

(C) refer the complaint to the Judicial Conference of the United States with the council's recommendations for action.

(D) take remedial action to ensure the effective and expeditious administration of the business of the courts, including:

(i) censuring or reprimanding the subject judge, either by private communication or by public announcement;

(ii) ordering that no new cases be assigned to the subject judge for a limited, fixed period;

(iii) in the case of a magistrate judge, ordering the chief judge of the district court to take action specified by the council, including the initiation of removal proceedings under 28 U.S.C. § 631(i) or 42 U.S.C. § 300aa–12(c)(2);

(iv) in the case of a bankruptcy judge, removing the judge from office under 28 U.S.C. § 152(e);

(v) in the case of a circuit or district judge, requesting the judge to retire voluntarily with the provision (if necessary) that ordinary length-of-service requirements will be waived; and

(vi) in the case of a circuit or district judge who is eligible to retire but does not do so, certifying the disability of the judge under 28 U.S.C. § 372(b) so that an additional judge may be appointed.

(E) take any combination of actions described in (b)(1)(A)–(D) of this Rule that is within its power.

(2) Mandatory actions. A judicial council must refer a complaint to the Judicial Conference if the council determines that a circuit judge or district judge may have engaged in conduct that:

(A) might constitute ground for impeachment; or

(B) in the interest of justice, is not amenable to resolution by the judicial council.

(c) Inadequate Basis for Decision. If the judicial council finds that a special committee's report, recommendations, and record provide an inadequate basis for decision, it may return the matter to the committee for further investigation and a new report, or it may conduct further investigation. If the judicial council decides to conduct further investigation, the subject judge must be given adequate prior notice in writing of that decision and of the general scope and purpose of the additional investigation. The judicial council's conduct of the additional investigation must generally accord with the procedures and powers set forth in Rules 13 through 16 for the conduct of an investigation by a special committee.

(d) Council Vote. Council action must be taken by a majority of those members of the council who are not disqualified. A decision to remove a bankruptcy judge from office requires a majority vote of all the members of the council.

(e) Recommendation for Fee Reimbursement. If the complaint has been finally dismissed or concluded under (b)(1)(A) or (B) of this Rule, and if the subject judge so requests, the judicial council may recommend that the Director of the Administrative Office of the United States Courts use funds appropriated to the Judiciary to reimburse the judge for reasonable expenses incurred during the investigation, when those expenses would not have been incurred but for the requirements of the Act and these Rules. Reasonable expenses include attorneys' fees and expenses related to a successful defense or prosecution of a proceeding under Rule 21(a) or (b).

(f) Council Action. Council action must be by written order. Unless the council finds that extraordinary reasons would make it contrary to the interests of justice, the order must be accompanied by a memorandum setting forth the factual determinations on which it is based and the reasons for the council action. The order and the supporting memorandum must be provided to the complainant, the subject judge, and the Judicial Conference Committee on Judicial Conduct and Disability. The complainant and the subject judge must be notified of any right to review of the judicial council's decision as provided in Rule 21(b).

[Adopted March 11, 2008, effective April 10, 2008.]

Commentary on Rule 20

This Rule is largely adapted from the Illustrative Rules.

Rule 20(a) provides that within twenty-one days after the filing of the report of a special committee, the subject judge may address a written response to all of the members of the judicial council. The subject judge must also be given an opportunity to present oral argument to the council, personally or through counsel. The subject judge may not otherwise communicate with council members about the matter.

Rule 20(c) provides that if the judicial council decides to conduct an additional investigation, the subject judge must be given adequate prior notice in writing of that decision and of the general scope and purpose of the additional investigation. The conduct of the investigation will be generally in accordance with the procedures set forth in Rules 13 through 16 for the conduct of an investigation by a special committee. However, if hearings are held, the council may limit testimony or the presentation of evidence to avoid unnecessary repetition of testimony and evidence before the special committee.

Rule 20(d) provides that council action must be taken by a majority of those members of the council who are not disqualified, except that a decision to remove a bankruptcy judge from office requires a majority of all the members of the council as required by 28 U.S.C. § 152(e). However, it is inappropriate to apply a similar rule to the less severe actions that a judicial council may take under the Act. If some members of the council are disqualified in the matter, their disqualification should not be given the effect of a vote against council action.

With regard to Rule 20(e), the judicial council, on the request of the subject judge, may recommend to the Director of the Administrative Office of the United States Courts that the subject judge be reimbursed for reasonable expenses, including attorneys' fees, incurred. The judicial council has the authority to recommend such reimbursement where, after investigation by a special committee, the complaint has been finally dismissed or concluded under subsection (b)(1)(A) or (B) of this Rule. It is contemplated that such reimbursement may be provided for the successful prosecution or defense of a proceeding under Rule 21(a) or (b), in other words, one that results in a Rule 20(b)(1)(A) or (B) dismissal or conclusion.

Rule 20(f) requires that council action normally be supported with a memorandum of factual determinations and reasons and that notice of the action be given to the complainant and the subject judge. Rule 20(f) also requires that the notification to the complainant and the subject judge include notice of any right to petition for review of the council's decision under Rule 21(b).

ARTICLE VI. REVIEW BY JUDICIAL CONFERENCE COMMITTEE ON CONDUCT AND DISABILITY

RULE 21. COMMITTEE ON JUDICIAL CONDUCT AND DISABILITY

(a) Review by Committee. The Committee on Judicial Conduct and Disability, consisting of seven members, considers and disposes of all petitions for review under (b) of this Rule, in conformity with the Committee's jurisdictional statement. Its disposition of petitions for review is ordinarily final. The Judicial Conference of the United States may, in its sole discretion, review any such Committee decision, but a complainant or subject judge does not have a right to this review.

(b) Reviewable Matters.

(1) Upon petition. A complainant or subject judge may petition the Committee for review of a judicial council order entered in accordance with:

(A) Rule 20(b)(1)(A), (B), (D), or (E); or

(B) Rule 19(b)(1) or (4) if one or more members of the judicial council dissented from the order on the ground that a special committee should be appointed under Rule 11(f); in that event, the Committee's review will be limited to the issue of whether a special committee should be appointed.

(2) Upon Committee's initiative. At its initiative and in its sole discretion, the Committee may review any judicial council order entered under Rule 19(b)(1) or (4), but only to determine whether a special committee should be appointed. Before undertaking the review, the Committee must invite that judicial council to explain why it believes the appointment of a special committee is unnecessary, unless the reasons are clearly stated in the judicial council's order denying the petition for review. If the Committee believes that it would benefit from a submission by the subject judge, it may issue an appropriate request. If the Committee determines that a special committee should be appointed, the Committee must issue a written decision giving its reasons.

(c) Committee Vote. Any member of the Committee from the same circuit as the subject judge is disqualified from considering or voting on a petition for review. Committee decisions under (b) of this Rule must be by majority vote of the qualified Committee members. If only six members are qualified to vote on a petition for review, the decision must be made by a majority of a panel of five members drawn from a randomly selected list that rotates after each decision by a panel drawn from the list. The members who will determine the petition must be selected based on committee membership as of the date on which the petition is received. Those members selected to hear the petition should serve in that capacity until final disposition of the petition, whether or not their term of committee membership has ended. If only four members are qualified to vote, the Chief Justice must appoint, if available, an ex-member of the Committee or, if not, another United States judge to consider the petition.

(d) Additional Investigation. Except in extraordinary circumstances, the Committee will not conduct an additional investigation. The Committee may return the matter to the judicial council with directions to undertake an additional investigation. If the Committee conducts an additional investigation, it will exercise the powers of the Judicial Conference under 28 U.S.C. § 331.

(e) Oral Argument; Personal Appearance. There is ordinarily no oral argument or personal appearance before the Committee. In its discretion, the Committee may permit written submissions from the complainant or subject judge.

(f) Committee Decisions. Committee decisions under this Rule must be transmitted promptly to the Judicial Conference of the United States. Other distribution will be by the Administrative Office at the direction of the Committee chair.

(g) Finality. All orders of the Judicial Conference or of the Committee (when the Conference does not exercise its power of review) are final.

[Adopted March 11, 2008, effective April 10, 2008.]

Commentary on Rule 21

This Rule is largely self-explanatory.

Rule 21(a) is intended to clarify that the delegation of power to the Judicial Conference Committee on Judicial Conduct and Disability to dispose of petitions does not preclude review of such dispositions by the Conference. However, there is no right to such review in any party.

Rules 21(b)(1)(B) and (b)(2) are intended to fill a jurisdictional gap as to review of dismissals or conclusions of complaints under Rule 19(b)(1) or (4). Where one or more members of a judicial council reviewing a petition have dissented on the ground that a special committee should have been appointed, the complainant or subject judge has the right to petition for review by the Committee but only as to that issue. Under Rule 21(b)(2), the Judicial Conference Committee on Judicial Conduct and Disability may review such a dismissal or conclusion in its sole discretion, whether or not such a dissent occurred, and only as to the appointment of a special committee. No party has a right to such review, and such review will be rare.

Rule 21(c) provides for review only by Committee members from circuits other than that of the subject judge. To avoid tie votes, the Committee will decide petitions for review by rotating panels of five when only six members are qualified. If only four members are qualified, the Chief Justice must appoint an additional judge to consider that petition for review.

Under this Rule, all Committee decisions are final in that they are unreviewable unless the Judicial Conference, in its discretion, decides to review a decision. Committee decisions, however, do not necessarily constitute final action on a complaint for purposes of Rule 24.

RULE 22. PROCEDURES FOR REVIEW

(a) Filing a Petition for Review. A petition for review of a judicial council decision may be filed by sending a brief written statement to the Judicial Conference Committee on Judicial Conduct and Disability, addressed to:

Judicial Conference Committee on Judicial Conduct and Disability
Attention: Office of General Counsel
Administrative Office of the United States Courts
One Columbus Circle, N.E.
Washington, D.C. 20544

The Administrative Office will send a copy of the petition to the complainant or subject judge, as the case may be.

(b) Form and Contents of Petition for Review. No particular form is required. The petition must contain a short statement of the basic facts underlying the complaint, the history of its consideration before the appropriate judicial council, a copy of the judicial council's decision, and the grounds on which the petitioner seeks review. The petition for review must specify the date and docket number of the judicial council order for which review is sought. The petitioner may attach any documents or correspondence arising in the course of the proceedings before the judicial council or its special committee. A petition should not normally exceed 20 pages plus necessary attachments.

(c) Time. A petition must be submitted within 63 days of the date of the order for which review is sought.

(d) Copies. Seven copies of the petition for review must be submitted, at least one of which must be signed by the petitioner or his or her attorney. If the petitioner submits a signed declaration of inability to pay the expense of duplicating the petition, the Administrative Office must accept the original petition and must reproduce copies at its expense.

(e) Action on Receipt of Petition for Review. The Administrative Office must acknowledge receipt of a petition for review submitted under this Rule, notify the chair of the Judicial Conference Committee on Judicial Conduct and Disability, and distribute the petition to the members of the Committee for their deliberation.

[Adopted March 11, 2008, effective April 10, 2008.]

Commentary on Rule 22

Rule 22 is self-explanatory.

ARTICLE VII. MISCELLANEOUS RULES

RULE 23. CONFIDENTIALITY

(a) General Rule. The consideration of a complaint by the chief judge, a special committee, the judicial council, or the Judicial Conference Committee on Judicial Conduct and Disability is confidential. Information about this consideration must not be disclosed by any judge or employee of the judicial branch or by any person who records or transcribes testimony except as allowed by these Rules. In extraordinary circumstances, a chief judge may disclose the existence of a proceeding under these Rules when necessary to maintain public confidence in the federal judiciary's ability to redress misconduct or disability.

(b) Files. All files related to complaints must be separately maintained with appropriate security precautions to ensure confidentiality.

(c) Disclosure in Decisions. Except as otherwise provided in Rule 24, written decisions of the chief judge, the judicial council, or the Judicial Conference Committee on Judicial Conduct and Disability, and dissenting opinions or separate statements of members of the council or Committee, may contain information and exhibits that the authors consider appropriate for inclusion, and the information and exhibits may be made public.

(d) Availability to Judicial Conference. On request of the Judicial Conference or its Committee on Judicial Conduct and Disability, the circuit clerk must furnish any requested records related to a complaint. For auditing purposes, the circuit clerk must provide access to the Committee to records of proceedings under the Act at the site where the records are kept.

(e) Availability to District Court. If the judicial council directs the initiation of proceedings for removal of a magistrate judge under Rule 20(b)(1)(D)(iii), the circuit clerk must provide to the chief judge of the district court copies of the report of the special committee and any other documents and records that were before the judicial council at the time of its decision. On request of the chief judge of the district court, the judicial council may authorize release to that chief judge of any other records relating to the investigation.

(f) Impeachment Proceedings. If the Judicial Conference determines that consideration of impeachment may be warranted, it must transmit the record of all relevant proceedings to the Speaker of the House of Representatives.

(g) Subject Judge's Consent. If both the subject judge and the chief judge consent in writing, any materials from the files may be disclosed to any person. In any such disclosure, the chief judge may require that the identity of the complainant, or of witnesses in an investigation conducted by a chief judge, a special committee, or the judicial council, not be revealed.

(h) Disclosure in Special Circumstances. The Judicial Conference, its Committee on Judicial Conduct and Disability, or a judicial council may authorize disclosure of information about the consideration of a complaint, including the papers, documents, and transcripts relating to the investigation, to the extent that disclosure is justified by special circumstances and is not prohibited by the Act. Disclosure may be made to judicial researchers engaged in the study or evaluation of experience under the Act and related modes of judicial discipline, but only where the study or evaluation has been specifically approved by the Judicial Conference or by the Judicial Conference Committee on Judicial Conduct and Disability. Appropriate steps must be taken to protect the identities of the subject judge, the complainant, and witnesses from public disclosure. Other appropriate safeguards to protect against the dissemination of confidential information may be imposed.

(i) Disclosure of Identity by Subject Judge. Nothing in this Rule precludes the subject judge from acknowledging that he or she is the judge referred to in documents made public under Rule 24.

(j) Assistance and Consultation. Nothing in this Rule precludes the chief judge or judicial council acting on a complaint filed under the Act from seeking the help of qualified staff or from consulting other judges who may be helpful in the disposition of the complaint.

[Adopted March 11, 2008, effective April 10, 2008.]

Commentary on Rule 23

Rule 23 was adapted from the Illustrative Rules.

The Act applies a rule of confidentiality to "papers, documents, and records of proceedings related to investigations conducted under this chapter" and states that they may not be disclosed "by any person in any proceeding," with enumerated exceptions. 28 U.S.C. § 360(a). Three questions arise: Who is bound by the confidentiality rule, what proceedings are subject to the rule, and who is within the circle of people who may have access to information without breaching the rule?

With regard to the first question, Rule 23(a) provides that judges, employees of the judicial branch, and those persons involved in recording proceedings and preparing transcripts are obliged to respect the confidentiality requirement. This of course includes subject judges who do not consent to identification under Rule 23(i).

With regard to the second question, Rule 23(a) applies the rule of confidentiality broadly to consideration of a complaint at any stage.

With regard to the third question, there is no barrier of confidentiality among a chief judge, judicial council, the Judicial Conference, and the Judicial Conference Committee on Judicial Conduct and Disability. Each may have access to any of the confidential records for use in their consideration of a referred matter, a petition for review, or monitoring the administration of the Act. A district court may have similar access if the judicial council orders the district court to initiate proceedings to remove a magistrate judge from office, and Rule 23(e) so provides.

In extraordinary circumstances, a chief judge may disclose the existence of a proceeding under these Rules. The disclosure of such information in high-visibility or controversial cases is to reassure the public that the federal judiciary is capable of redressing judicial misconduct or disability. Moreover, the confidentiality requirement does not prevent the chief judge from "communicat[ing] orally or in writing with ... [persons] who may have knowledge of the matter," as part of a limited inquiry conducted by the chief judge under Rule 11(b).

Rule 23 recognizes that there must be some exceptions to the Act's confidentiality requirement. For example, the Act requires that certain orders and the reasons for them must be made public. 28 U.S.C. § 360(b). Rule 23(c) makes it explicit that memoranda supporting chief judge and council orders, as well as dissenting opinions and separate statements, may contain references to information that would otherwise be confidential and that such information may be made public. However, subsection (c) is subject to Rule 24(a) which provides the general rule regarding the public availability of decisions. For example, the name of a subject judge cannot be made public in a decision if disclosure of the name is prohibited by that Rule.

The Act makes clear that there is a barrier of confidentiality between the judicial branch and the legislative. It provides that material may be disclosed to Congress only if it is believed necessary to an impeachment investigation or trial of a judge. 28 U.S.C. § 360(a)(2). Accordingly, Section 355(b) of the Act requires the Judicial Conference to transmit the record of the proceedings to the House of Representatives if the Conference believes that impeachment of a subject judge may be appropriate. Rule 23(f) implements this requirement.

The Act provides that confidential materials may be disclosed if authorized in writing by the subject judge and by the chief judge. 28 U.S.C. § 360(a)(3). Rule 23(g) implements this requirement. Once the subject judge has consented to the disclosure of confidential materials related to a complaint, the chief judge ordinarily will refuse consent only to the extent necessary to protect the confidentiality interests of the complainant or of witnesses who have testified in investigatory proceedings or who have provided information in response to a limited inquiry undertaken pursuant to Rule 11. It will generally be necessary, therefore, for the chief judge to require that the identities of the complainant or of such witnesses, as well as any identifying information, be shielded in any materials disclosed, except insofar as the chief judge has secured the consent of the complainant or of a particular witness to disclosure, or there is a demonstrated need for disclosure of the information that, in the judgment of the chief judge, outweighs the confidentiality interest of the complainant or of a particular witness (as may be the case where the complainant is delusional or where the complainant or a particular witness has already demonstrated a lack of concern about maintaining the confidentiality of the proceedings).

Rule 23(h) permits disclosure of additional information in circumstances not enumerated. For example, disclosure may be appropriate to permit a prosecution for perjury based on testimony given before a special committee. Another example might involve evidence of criminal conduct by a judge discovered by a special committee.

Subsection (h) also permits the authorization of disclosure of information about the consideration of a complaint, including the papers, documents, and transcripts relating to the investigation, to judicial researchers engaged in the study or evaluation of experience under the Act and related modes of judicial discipline. The Rule envisions disclosure of information from the official record of complaint proceedings to a limited category of persons for appropriately authorized research purposes only, and with appropriate safeguards to protect individual identities in any published research results that ensue. In authorizing disclosure, the judicial council may refuse to release particular materials when such release would be contrary to the interests of justice, or that constitute purely internal communications. The Rule does not envision disclosure of purely internal communications between judges and their colleagues and staff.

Under Rule 23(j), chief judges and judicial councils may seek staff assistance or consult with other judges who may be helpful in the process of complaint disposition; the confidentiality requirement does not preclude this. The chief judge, for example, may properly seek the advice and assistance of another judge who the chief judge deems to be in the best position to communicate with the subject judge in an attempt to bring about corrective action. As another example, a new chief judge may wish to confer with a predecessor to learn how similar complaints have been handled. In consulting with other judges, of course, the chief judge should disclose information regarding the complaint only to the extent the chief judge deems necessary under the circumstances.

RULE 24. PUBLIC AVAILABILITY OF DECISIONS

(a) General Rule; Specific Cases. When final action has been taken on a complaint and it is no longer subject to review, all orders entered by the chief judge and judicial council, including any supporting memoranda and any dissenting opinions or separate statements by members of the judicial council, must be made public, with the following exceptions:

(1) if the complaint is finally dismissed under Rule 11(c) without the appointment of a special committee, or if it is concluded under Rule 11(d) because of voluntary corrective action, the publicly available materials must not disclose the name of the subject judge without his or her consent.

(2) if the complaint is concluded because of intervening events, or dismissed at any time after a special committee is appointed, the judicial council must determine whether the name of the subject judge should be disclosed.

(3) if the complaint is finally disposed of by a privately communicated censure or reprimand, the publicly available materials must not disclose either the name of the subject judge or the text of the reprimand.

(4) if the complaint is finally disposed of under Rule 20(b)(1)(D) by any action other than private censure or reprimand, the text of the dispositive order must be included in the materials made public, and the name of the subject judge must be disclosed.

(5) the name of the complainant must not be disclosed in materials made public under this Rule unless the chief judge orders disclosure.

(b) Manner of Making Public. The orders described in (a) must be made public by placing them in a publicly accessible file in the office of the circuit clerk or by placing the orders on the court's public website. If the orders appear to have precedential value, the chief judge may cause them to be published. In addition, the Judicial Conference Committee on Judicial Conduct and Disability will make available on the Federal Judiciary's website, www.uscourts.gov, selected illustrative orders described in paragraph (a), appropriately redacted, to provide additional information to the public on how complaints are addressed under the Act.

(c) Orders of Judicial Conference Committee. Orders of this Committee constituting final action in a complaint proceeding arising from a particular circuit will be made available to the public in the office of the clerk of the relevant court of appeals. The Committee will also make such orders available on the Federal Judiciary's website, www.uscourts.gov. When authorized by the Committee, other orders related to complaint proceedings will similarly be made available.

(d) Complaints Referred to the Judicial Conference of the United States. If a complaint is referred to the Judicial Conference under Rule 20(b)(1)(C) or 20(b)(2), materials relating to the complaint will be made public only if ordered by the Judicial Conference.

[Adopted March 11, 2008, effective April 10, 2008.]

Commentary on Rule 24

Rule 24 is adapted from the Illustrative Rules and the recommendations of the Breyer Committee.

The Act requires the circuits to make available only written orders of a judicial council or the Judicial Conference imposing some form of sanction. 28 U.S.C. § 360(b). The Judicial Conference, however, has long recognized the desirability of public availability of a broader range of orders and other materials. In 1994, the Judicial Conference "urge[d] all circuits and courts covered by the Act to submit to the West Publishing Company, for publication in Federal Reporter 3d, and to Lexis all orders issued pursuant to [the Act] that are deemed by the issuing circuit or court to have significant precedential value to other circuits and courts covered by the Act." Report of the Proceedings of the Judicial Conference of the United States, Mar. 1994, at 28. Following this recommendation, the 2000 revision of the Illustrative Rules contained a public availability provision very similar to Rule 24. In 2002, the Judicial Conference again voted to encourage the circuits "to submit non-routine public orders disposing of complaints of judicial misconduct or disability for publication by on-line and print services." Report of the Proceedings of the Judicial Conference of the United States, Sept. 2002, at 58. The Breyer Committee Report further emphasized that "[p]osting such orders on the judicial branch's public website would not only benefit judges directly, it would also encourage scholarly commentary and analysis of the orders." Breyer Committee Report, 239 F.R.D. at 216. With these considerations in mind, Rule 24 provides for public availability of a wide range of materials.

Rule 24 provides for public availability of orders of the chief judge, the judicial council, and the Judicial Conference Committee on Judicial Conduct and Disability and the texts of any memoranda supporting their orders, together with any dissenting opinions or separate statements by members of the judicial council. However, these orders and memoranda are to be made public only when final action on the complaint has been taken and any right of review has been exhausted. The provision that decisions will be made public only after final action has been taken is designed in part to avoid public disclosure of the existence of pending proceedings. Whether the name of the subject judge is disclosed will then depend on the nature of the final action. If the final action is an order predicated on a finding of misconduct or disability (other than a privately communicated censure or reprimand) the name of the judge must be made public. If the final action is dismissal of the complaint, the name of the subject judge must not be disclosed. Rule 24(a)(1) provides that where a proceeding is concluded under Rule 11(d) by the chief judge on the basis of voluntary corrective action, the name of the subject judge must not be disclosed. Shielding the name of the subject judge in this circumstance should encourage informal disposition.

If a complaint is dismissed as moot, or because intervening events have made action on the complaint unnecessary, after appointment of a special committee, Rule 24(a)(2) allows the judicial council to determine whether the subject judge will be identified. In such a case, no final decision has been rendered on the merits, but it may be in the public interest—particularly if a judicial officer resigns in the course of the investigation—to make the identity of the judge known.

Once a special committee has been appointed, and a proceeding is concluded by the full council on the basis of a remedial order of the council, Rule 24(a)(4) provides for disclosure of the name of the subject judge.

Finally, Rule 24(a)(5) provides that the identity of the complainant will be disclosed only if the chief judge so orders. Identifying the complainant when the subject judge is not identified would increase the likelihood that the identity of the subject judge would become publicly known, thus circumventing the policy of nondisclosure. It may not always be practicable to shield the complainant's identity while making public disclosure of the judicial council's order and supporting memoranda; in some circumstances, moreover, the complainant may consent to public identification.

RULE 25. DISQUALIFICATION

(a) General Rule. Any judge is disqualified from participating in any proceeding under these Rules if the judge, in his or her discretion, concludes that circumstances warrant disqualification. If the complaint is filed by a judge, that judge is disqualified from participating in any consideration of the complaint except to the extent that these Rules provide for a complainant's participation. A chief judge who has identified a complaint under Rule 5 is not automatically disqualified from considering the complaint.

(b) Subject Judge. A subject judge is disqualified from considering the complaint except to the extent that these Rules provide for participation by a subject judge.

(c) Chief Judge Not Disqualified from Considering a Petition for Review of a Chief Judge's Order. If a petition for review of the chief judge's order entered under Rule 11(c), (d), or (e) is filed with the judicial council in accordance with Rule 18, the chief judge is not disqualified from participating in the council's consideration of the petition.

(d) Member of Special Committee Not Disqualified. A member of the judicial council who serves on a special committee, including the chief judge, is not disqualified from participating in council consideration of the committee's report.

(e) Subject Judge's Disqualification After Appointment of a Special Committee. Upon appointment of a special committee, the subject judge is automatically disqualified from participating in any proceeding arising under the Act or these Rules as a member of any special committee, the judicial council of the circuit, the Judicial Conference of the United States, and the Judicial Conference Committee on Judicial Conduct and Disability. The disqualification continues until all proceedings on the complaint against the subject judge are finally terminated with no further right of review.

(f) Substitute for Disqualified Chief Judge. If the chief judge is disqualified from participating in consideration of the complaint, the duties and responsibilities of the chief judge under these Rules must be assigned to the most-senior active circuit judge not disqualified. If all circuit judges in regular active service are disqualified, the judicial council may determine whether to request a transfer under Rule 26, or, in the interest of sound judicial administration, to permit the chief judge to dispose of the complaint on the merits. Members of the judicial council who are named in the complaint may participate in this determination if necessary to obtain a quorum of the judicial council.

(g) Judicial Council Action When Multiple Judges Are Disqualified. Notwithstanding any other provision in these Rules to the contrary,

(1) a member of the judicial council who is a subject judge may participate in its disposition if:

(A) participation by one or more subject judges is necessary to obtain a quorum of the judicial council;

(B) the judicial council finds that the lack of a quorum is due to the naming of one or more judges in the complaint for the purpose of disqualifying that judge or judges, or to the naming of one or more judges based on their participation in a decision excluded from the definition of misconduct under Rule 3(h)(3); and

(C) the judicial council votes that it is necessary, appropriate, and in the interest of sound judicial administration that one or more subject judges be eligible to act.

(2) otherwise disqualified members may participate in votes taken under (g)(1)(B) and (g)(1)(C).

(h) Disqualification of Members of the Judicial Conference Committee. No member of the Judicial Conference Committee on Judicial Conduct and Disability is disqualified from participating in any proceeding under the Act or these Rules because of consultations with a chief judge, a member of a special committee, or a member of a judicial council about the interpretation or application of the Act or these Rules, unless the member believes that the consultation would prevent fair-minded participation.

[Adopted March 11, 2008, effective April 10, 2008.]

Commentary on Rule 25

Rule 25 is adapted from the Illustrative Rules.

Subsection (a) provides the general rule for disqualification. Of course, a judge is not disqualified simply because the subject judge is on the same court. However, this subsection recognizes that there may be cases in which an appearance of bias or prejudice is created by circumstances other than an association with the subject judge as a colleague. For example, a judge may have a familial relationship with a complainant or subject judge. When such circumstances exist, a judge may, in his or her discretion, conclude that disqualification is warranted.

Subsection (e) makes it clear that the disqualification of the subject judge relates only to the subject judge's participation in any proceeding arising under the Act or these Rules as a member of a special committee, judicial council, Judicial Conference, or the Judicial Conference Committee. The Illustrative Rule, based on Section 359(a) of the Act, is ambiguous and could be read to disqualify a subject judge from service of any kind on each of the bodies mentioned. This is undoubtedly not the intent of the Act; such a disqualification would be anomalous in light of the Act's allowing a subject judge to continue to decide cases and to continue to exercise the powers of chief circuit or district judge. It would also create a substantial deterrence to the appointment of special committees, particularly where a special committee is needed solely because the chief judge may not decide matters of credibility in his or her review under Rule 11.

While a subject judge is barred by Rule 25(b) from participating in the disposition of the complaint in which he or she is named, Rule 25(e) recognizes that participation in proceedings arising under the Act or these Rules by a judge who is the subject of a special committee investigation may lead to an appearance of self-interest in creating substantive and procedural precedents governing such proceedings; Rule 25(e) bars such participation.

Under the Act, a complaint against the chief judge is to be handled by "that circuit judge in regular active service next senior in date of commission." 28 U.S.C. § 351(c). Rule 25(f) provides that seniority among judges other than the chief judge is to be determined by date of commission, with the result that complaints against the chief judge may be routed to a former chief judge or other judge who was appointed earlier than the chief judge. The Rules do not purport to prescribe who is to preside over meetings of the judicial council. Consequently, where the presiding member of the judicial council is disqualified from participating under these Rules, the order of precedence prescribed by Rule 25(f) for performing "the duties and responsibilities of the chief circuit judge under these Rules" does not apply to determine the acting presiding member of the judicial council. That is a matter left to the internal rules or operating practices of each judicial council. In most cases the most senior active circuit judge who is a member of the judicial council and who is not disqualified will preside.

Sometimes a single complaint is filed against a large group of judges. If the normal disqualification rules are observed in such a case, no court of appeals judge can serve as acting chief judge of the circuit, and the judicial council will be without appellate members. Where the complaint is against all circuit and district judges, under normal rules no member of the judicial council can perform the duties assigned to the council under the statute.

A similar problem is created by successive complaints arising out of the same underlying grievance. For example, a complainant files a complaint against a district judge based on alleged misconduct, and the complaint is dismissed by the chief judge under the statute. The complainant may then file a complaint against the chief judge for dismissing the first complaint, and when that complaint is dismissed by the next senior judge, still a third complaint may be filed. The threat is that the complainant will bump down the seniority ladder until, once again, there is no member of the court of appeals who can serve as acting chief judge for the purpose of the next complaint. Similarly, complaints involving the merits of litigation may involve a series of decisions in which many judges participated or in which a rehearing en banc was denied by the court of appeals, and the complaint may name a majority of the judicial council as subject judges.

In recognition that these multiple-judge complaints are virtually always meritless, the judicial council is given discretion to determine: (1) whether it is necessary, appropriate, and in the interest of sound judicial administration to permit the chief judge to dispose of a complaint where it would otherwise be impossible for any active circuit judge in the circuit to act, and (2) whether it is necessary, appropriate, and in the interest of sound judicial administration, after appropriate findings as to need and justification are made, to permit subject judges of the judicial council to participate in the disposition of a petition for review where it would otherwise be impossible to obtain a quorum.

Applying a rule of necessity in these situations is consistent with the appearance of justice. *See, e.g., In re Complaint of Doe*, 2 F.3d 308 (8th Cir. Jud. Council 1993) (invoking the rule of necessity); *In re Complaint of Judicial Misconduct*, No. 91–80464 (9th Cir. Jud. Council 1992) (same). There is no unfairness in permitting the chief judge to dispose of a patently insubstantial complaint that names all active circuit judges in the circuit.

Similarly, there is no unfairness in permitting subject judges, in these circumstances, to participate in the review of a chief judge's dismissal of an insubstantial complaint. The remaining option is to assign the matter to another body. Among other alternatives, the council may request a transfer of the petition under Rule 26. Given the administrative inconvenience and delay involved in these alternatives, it is desirable to request a transfer only if the judicial council determines that the petition is substantial enough to warrant such action.

In the unlikely event that a quorum of the judicial council cannot be obtained to consider the report of a special committee, it would normally be necessary to request a transfer under Rule 26.

Rule 25(h) recognizes that the jurisdictional statement of the Judicial Conference Committee contemplates consultation between members of the Committee and judicial participants in proceedings under the Act and these Rules. Such consultation should not automatically preclude participation by a member in that proceeding.

RULE 26. TRANSFER TO ANOTHER JUDICIAL COUNCIL

In exceptional circumstances, a chief judge or a judicial council may ask the Chief Justice to transfer a proceeding based on a complaint identified under Rule 5 or filed under Rule 6 to the judicial council of another circuit. The request for a transfer may be made at any stage of the proceeding before a reference to the Judicial Conference under Rule 20(b)(1)(C) or 20(b)(2) or a petition for review is filed under Rule 22. Upon receiving such a request, the Chief Justice may refuse the request or select the transferee judicial council, which may then exercise the powers of a judicial council under these Rules.

[Adopted March 11, 2008, effective April 10, 2008.]

Commentary on Rule 26

Rule 26 is new; it implements the Breyer Committee's recommended use of transfers. Breyer Committee Report, 239 F.R.D. at 214–15.

Rule 26 authorizes the transfer of a complaint proceeding to another judicial council selected by the Chief Justice. Such transfers may be appropriate, for example, in the case of a serious complaint where there are multiple disqualifications among the original council, where the issues are highly visible and a local disposition may weaken public confidence in the process, where internal tensions arising in the council as a result of the complaint render disposition by a less involved council appropriate, or where a complaint calls into question policies or governance of the home court of appeals. The power to effect a transfer is lodged in the Chief Justice to avoid disputes in a council over where to transfer a sensitive matter and to ensure that the transferee council accepts the matter.

Upon receipt of a transferred proceeding, the transferee council shall determine the proper stage at which to begin consideration of the complaint—for example, reference to the transferee chief judge, appointment of a special committee, etc.

RULE 27. WITHDRAWAL OF COMPLAINTS AND PETITIONS FOR REVIEW

(a) Complaint Pending Before Chief Judge. With the chief judge's consent, a complainant may withdraw a complaint that is before the chief judge for a decision under Rule 11. The withdrawal of a complaint will not prevent a chief judge from identifying or having to identify a complaint under Rule 5 based on the withdrawn complaint.

(b) Complaint Pending before Special Committee or Judicial Council. After a complaint has been referred to a special committee for investigation and before the committee files its report, the complainant may withdraw the complaint only with the consent of both the subject judge and either the special committee or the judicial council.

(c) Petition for Review. A petition for review addressed to a judicial council under Rule 18, or the Judicial Conference Committee on Judicial Conduct and Disability under Rule 22 may be withdrawn if no action on the petition has been taken.

[Adopted March 11, 2008, effective April 10, 2008.]

Commentary on Rule 27

Rule 27 is adapted from the Illustrative Rules and treats the complaint proceeding, once begun, as a matter of public business rather than as the property of the complainant. Accordingly, the chief judge or the judicial council remains responsible for addressing any complaint under the Act, even a complaint that has been formally withdrawn by the complainant.

Under subsection 27(a), a complaint pending before the chief judge may be withdrawn if the chief judge consents. Where the complaint clearly lacked merit, the chief judge may accordingly be saved the burden of preparing a formal order and supporting memorandum. However, the chief judge may, or be obligated under Rule 5, to identify a complaint based on allegations in a withdrawn complaint.

If the chief judge appoints a special committee, Rule 27(b) provides that the complaint may be withdrawn only with the consent of both the body before which is it pending (the special committee or the judicial council) and the subject judge. Once a complaint has reached the stage of appointment of a special committee, a resolution of the issues may be necessary to preserve public confidence. Moreover, the subject judge is given the right to insist that the matter be resolved on the merits, thereby eliminating any ambiguity that might remain if the proceeding were terminated by withdrawal of the complaint.

With regard to all petitions for review, Rule 27(c) grants the petitioner unrestricted authority to withdraw the petition. It is thought that the public's interest in the proceeding is adequately protected, because there will necessarily have been a decision by the chief judge and often by the judicial council as well in such a case.

RULE 28. AVAILABILITY OF RULES AND FORMS

These Rules and copies of the complaint form as provided in Rule 6(a) must be available without charge in the office of the clerk of each court of appeals, district court, bankruptcy court, or other federal court whose judges are subject to the Act. Each court must also make these Rules and the complaint form available on the court's website, or provide an Internet link to the Rules and complaint form that are available on the appropriate court of appeals' website.

[Adopted March 11, 2008, effective April 10, 2008.]

RULE 29. EFFECTIVE DATE

These Rules will become effective 30 days after promulgation by the Judicial Conference of the United States.

[Adopted March 11, 2008, effective April 10, 2008.]

APPENDIX—COMPLAINT FORM

COMPLAINT FORM

COMPLAINT FORM
COMPLAINT OF JUDICIAL MISCONDUCT OR DISABILITY

Mail this form to: Circuit Executive, United States Court of Appeals for the Federal Circuit, 717 Madison Place, NW, Washington, DC 20439. Mark the envelope "Judicial Misconduct Complaint" or "Judicial Disability Complaint." DO NOT PUT THE NAME OF THE JUDGE ON THE ENVELOPE. This form may be used, but it is not required. *See* Rule 6.

If the complaint is about a single judge, three copies of the form and any attachments should be filed. If the complaint is about more than one judge, enough copies must be filed to provide one for the circuit executive, one for the chief judge, and one for each judge complained about.

1. Complainant's Name: ______________________

Address: ______________________

____

Daytime Telephone: (___) ______________________

2. Federal judge complained about: ______________________

3. Does this complaint concern the behavior of a judge in a particular appeal?

[ ] Yes [ ] No

If yes, give the following information about each appeal (use an additional sheet of paper if there is more than one appeal):

Docket number: ______________________

Are you or were you a party or lawyer in the appeal?

[ ] Party [ ] Lawyer [ ] Neither

If a party, give the name, address, and telephone number of your lawyer, if you had one:

____

____

4. Have you filed any lawsuits against this judge?

[ ] Yes [ ] No

If yes, give the following information about each lawsuit (use an additional sheet of paper if more than one lawsuit).

Court: ______________________

Docket number: ______________________

Present status of suit: ______________________

Name, address, and telephone of your lawyer, if you have one:

____

____

Court to which any appeal has been taken: ______________________

Docket number of the appeal: ______________________

Present status of appeal: ______________________

5. On separate sheets of paper, not larger than the paper this form is printed on, describe the conduct or the evidence of disability that is the subject of this complaint.
6. You should check the box below and sign the form.

[ ] I declare under penalty of perjury that—

(a) I have read Rules 3, 6, and 10 of the Judicial Conduct and Judicial Disability Proceedings; and

(b) The statements made in this complaint are true and correct to the best of my knowledge.

____

(Signature)

____

(Date)

Judicial Misconduct or Disability Complaint Form Rule 6(a)

[Adopted March 11, 2008, effective April 10, 2008.]

[APPENDIX A]. APPELLATE MEDIATION PROGRAM[1]

(Effective May 1, 2008)

1. Introduction.

The United States Court of Appeals for the Federal Circuit established an appellate mediation program pursuant to Federal Rule of Appellate Procedure 33, which commenced on October 3, 2005.

The program is administered by the Chief Circuit Mediator, James M. Amend, and the Circuit Mediation Officer, Wendy L. Dean ("mediation officers"). A three-judge committee monitors the program and makes recommendations to the Chief Judge. The program is periodically assessed by the court.

The purpose of the program is to help the parties achieve settlement. The mediation program provides a confidential, risk-free opportunity for parties to resolve their dispute with the help of the circuit mediation officers or an experienced volunteer neutral, third-party mediator. Mediation, unlike arbitration where a decision that may be binding is issued, will result in a settlement only if all parties agree on that resolution.

2. Eligible Cases.

All cases where the parties are represented by counsel are eligible for the program.

3. Case Selection Process.

Participation in the court's mediation program is mandatory for all cases selected for participation in the program that were docketed after September 18, 2006. The circuit mediation officers contact principal counsel in cases selected for mediation to determine whether the case is a good candidate for mediation and seek the opinion of counsel regarding participation in the program. At that time, the circuit mediation officers ask counsel to determine whether the appeal and, if pertinent, the cross-appeal, present any jurisdictional defects. If at the outset it appears to the circuit mediation officers that mediation will not be fruitful, then court mediation efforts cease. Counsel may jointly request that a case be included in the mediation program. A Confidential Joint Request to Enter Mediation Program form is available from the Clerk's Office and on the court's website. Such a request should be submitted to:

Circuit Mediation Office
United States Court of Appeals
for the Federal Circuit
717 Madison Place, NW
Washington, DC 20439

The circuit mediation officers may review the notice of appeal, the trial tribunal's docket sheet, the decision of the trial tribunal, the court's docketing statement, and briefs to aid in selecting cases for mediation. The docketing statement is a three-page form to be completed by counsel. The form is included in the docketing packet sent to counsel by the Clerk of Court. All counsel must complete the form in duplicate and return it to the Clerk of Court within 14 days of docketing. When the United States or its officer or agency is a party, all counsel must complete the form in duplicate and return it to the clerk within 30 days of docketing. The docketing statement is not part of the formal mediation process, but assists the circuit mediation officers with the selection process. One copy is retained in the Clerk's Office case file and the other copy is transmitted to the Circuit Mediation Office.

4. Mediators.

In appropriate cases, the Chief Circuit Mediator or the Circuit Mediation Officer or both may serve as mediator. In other cases, the mediator is an outside volunteer mediator. The court has selected a roster of outside mediators. The court's mediators include distinguished, experienced attorneys, and academicians with expertise in the substantive areas of the court's jurisdiction, as well as attorneys with experience mediating. The court invites more applicants. The application is available on the Federal Circuit Bar Association and the court's websites. The candidates are encouraged to be members of the bar of the court, but are not required to be members.

Mediators and applicants to be mediators must not be in active practice. For purposes of these guidelines "not be in active practice" means that the applicant or mediator is not appearing, and will not appear while a member of the court's mediation panel (i) as counsel for a party or amicus in any matter that would or could be appealed to this court, or (ii) as counsel for a party or amicus in any appeal to this court.

Mediators are not paid for their services, but are reimbursed by the court for minor out-of-pocket expenses such as photocopying costs, telephone charges, facsimile charges, and transportation to the courthouse. Mediation proceedings may be held in the courthouse if desired. Reimbursement for reasonable travel and lodging expenses of the mediator is assumed by the litigants if the mediator must travel to conduct the mediation.

If the circuit mediation officers do not conduct the mediation, the circuit mediation officers select a mediator from the court's list with the following exception. If counsel, under the program, jointly propose a mediator not on the list, then the circuit mediation officers have the option of appointing that mediator, provided the parties agree to pay any travel, lodging, and out-of-pocket expenses of the mediator and the mediator agrees to serve pro bono. Parties are free, of course, to participate in mediation outside the court's program under terms to which they agree, whether or not the case is selected for mediation under the court program.

If the mediator is affiliated with a law firm and that law firm represents or has represented a party to an appeal within the last 5 years, the mediator will recuse him or herself if appointed to mediate any case involving that party. Before final selection of a mediator, the circuit mediation officers inquire about conflicts of interest. The mediator must not presently represent either party or any amicus for any purpose, must disclose any past relationships that he or she had with counsel, counsels' firms, and the parties, and must disclose any potential "issues" conflicts. Mediators are required to decline from participating in any cases in which there is a conflict of interest, in which they perceive a conflict, or in which a reasonable person would perceive a conflict.

5. Confidentiality.

Confidentiality is ensured throughout the mediation process except as noted in these guidelines. The circuit mediation officers do not communicate with the judges about the substance of mediation proceedings. During the program, however, the mediation committee from time to time has discussions with the circuit mediation officers with a view to revising the program while it is ongoing, as appropriate and necessary. Communications concerning statistical information and information needed to assess the program are not prohibited. All mediators must protect the confidentiality of the substance of all proceedings and are prohibited from complying with subpoenas or other requests for information about mediated cases except in response to a final court order requiring such disclosure. All communication with the court about mediation matters is between the mediator and the circuit mediation officers.

The substance of mediation is confidential and may not be disclosed by any participants, except in the course of litigation concerning enforceability of any agreements reached through mediation. The fact that a case is in mediation is not confidential. Any motions for extensions of time that are filed because the parties are engaged in mediation are part of the public file in the Clerk's Office. Section 7 sets forth the procedures for seeking extensions of time.

6. Mandatory Mediation Process.

Mediation is a flexible process. The mediator is not bound by a defined formula or approach to mediating a case and the mediator conducts the mediation as he or she deems appropriate. Mediation ceases at any time the mediator concludes that further efforts will not be fruitful.

The purpose of mediation is a settlement of the case. This may include a global settlement. Under the program, the mediator is not asked to narrow the issues on appeal. To the extent that the parties agree to narrow the issues, that may be reflected in their briefs.

If the circuit mediation officers determine that mediation may be fruitful, then principal counsel must participate in any initial telephone conference that is ordered. The initial telephone conference may be arranged and conducted in any manner by the circuit mediation officers, by an outside mediator, or both. If an initial telephone conference is ordered, then participation is mandatory. If the participants agree that a telephone conference is not necessary and that they wish to meet for a mediation session, then no telephone conference will be ordered. If, in the judgment of the mediator, a mediation session might be fruitful, then participation in at least one session is mandatory.

The court requires that the principal attorney attend all sessions and that at the initial session a party representative with actual settlement authority also attend. "Actual settlement authority" does not simply mean sending a person allowed to accept or offer a minimum or maximum dollar amount. Rather, the party representative should be a person who can make independent decisions and has the knowledge necessary to generate and consider creative solutions. These requirements may be modified or waived by the mediator, if the circuit mediation officers concur and if circumstances dictate. When the United States government is one of the parties, the requirement that a party representative with actual settlement authority attend any mediation session is waived because government settlement decisions must be made collectively and approved by the authorized representative of the Attorney General, as set forth in 28 C.F.R. Part 0, Subpart Y. A government attorney with authority to negotiate on behalf of the government and to make recommendations concerning settlement must participate in the mediation session.

7. Briefing and Oral Argument Schedule Extensions.

It is contemplated that after a case is referred to a mediator, mediation should be completed in 90 days. At the outside, mediation should be completed within 150 days of the date of reference. Cases generally are selected before the first brief is filed. However, cases in which briefs have been filed may also be selected. While cases in mediation remain subject to the normal scheduling for briefs and oral argument by the Clerk of Court, counsel are of course free to file a consent motion for an extension of time pursuant to Fed. Cir. R. 27(h)(4) in the ordinary course. If the mediator believes that multiple mediation sessions are required, that the filing of a brief or the scheduling of oral argument will interfere with good faith settlement efforts, and that additional extensions of time are needed, then motions for additional extensions may be filed. A motion for an extension, beyond the time granted under Rule 27(h)(4), is referred to the circuit mediation officers. The court has given the circuit mediation officers the authority to grant motions for extensions, upon the showing of good cause, up to a date that is generally no more than 150 days after a case is referred to a mediator. Any consent motion for an extension of time under this paragraph need not disclose that the extension is sought in order to facilitate mediation. Opposed motions will be decided by the court.

Any motions for extensions of time are entered on the docket in the ordinary course. In addition to an original and three copies, movant must file one additional copy prominently stamped "Direct to the Circuit Mediation Officer."

8. The Conclusion of Mediation.

The purpose of the mediation program is to help the parties achieve settlement. If settlement is reached, then the agreement must be in writing and binding on all parties. The appellant or the parties jointly must file a motion or stipulation of voluntary dismissal or other appropriate motion. If the case is not settled, then it remains on the docket and proceeds as if mediation had not been initiated.

9. Noncompliance Sanctions.

Any party, counsel or outside mediator who fails to materially comply with any of the provisions of this document, including failing to cooperate with the circuit mediation officers may be subject to appropriate sanction by the court. Notwithstanding the confidentiality provisions of Paragraph 5, the court may be apprised by the circuit mediation officers of the substance of a mediation only to the extent necessary to explain any recommendation for sanctions. Any judge ruling on such a recommendation shall be recused from hearing the case on the merits.

10. Evaluation.

At the conclusion of the mediation process in an individual case, the mediator notifies the circuit mediation officers of the resolution of the mediation. The circuit mediation officers send a questionnaire to counsel and the mediator inviting their candid confidential responses, which are not provided to the judges or others, about the effectiveness of the program. The questionnaire responses are summarized by the circuit mediation office—without identification of any specific case – for purposes of evaluating the program, compiling statistics, etc. The summary is provided to the court for purposes of assessing the program, but it does not reveal any details about or names of specific cases. In a case in which the Chief Circuit Mediator or the Circuit Mediation Officer or both serve as the mediator, the circuit mediation officers shall prepare the response to the mediation questionnaire.

1 Appendix designation added by publisher.

INDEX TO THE UNITED STATES COURT OF APPEALS FOR THE FEDERAL CIRCUIT

RULES OF THE UNITED STATES DISTRICT COURT FOR THE DISTRICT OF COLUMBIA

Effective August 1, 1999

Including Amendments Received Through January 1, 2012

Research Note

These rules may be searched electronically on Westlaw in the DC-RULES database; updates to these rules may be found on Westlaw in DC-RULESUPDATES. For search tips, and a detailed summary of database content, consult the Westlaw Scope Screen of each database.

TELEPHONE NUMBERS AND OTHER U.S. COURTHOUSE NUMBERS

UNITED STATES DISTRICT COURT
FOR THE DISTRICT OF COLUMBIA
333 CONSTITUTION AVENUE, NW
WASHINGTON, DC 20001

Clerk's Office Information	(202) 354–3000
Clerk, Committee on Grievances	(202) 354–3320
Court Reporter	(202) 354–3044
Probation Office Information	(202) 565–1300

OTHER U.S. COURTHOUSE NUMBERS

Alternative Dispute Resolution Programs	(202) 216–7350
Bankruptcy Court Clerk's Office	(202) 354–3150
Court of Appeals for the D.C. Circuit/Information	(202) 216–7000
Circuit Executive	(202) 216–7340
US Marshals Service Information	(202) 353–0600
Cafeteria	(202) 289–4015
Health Unit	(202) 219–4739

RELATED PHONE NUMBERS

U.S. Attorney's Office Information	(202) 514–7566
D.C. Superior Court Information	(202) 879–1010
Federal Public Defender	(202) 208–7500

COURT PERSONNEL

Chief Judge

Royce C. Lamberth, Rm. 2010A	(202) 354–3380

Active Judges

Emmet G. Sullivan, Rm. 4935A	(202) 354–3260
Colleen Kollar–Kotelly, Rm. 6939A	(202) 354–3340
Henry H. Kennedy, Jr., Rm. 6903A	(202) 354–3350
Richard W. Roberts, Rm. 4435	(202) 354–3400
Ellen Segal Huvelle, Rm. 4423A	(202) 354–3230
Reggie B. Walton, Rm. 6403A	(202) 354–3290
John D. Bates, Rm. 4114	(202) 354–3430
Richard J. Leon, Rm. 6315	(202) 354–3580
Rosemary M. Collyer, Rm. 2528	(202) 354–3560
Beryl A. Howell, Rm. 6600	(202) 354–3450
Robert L. Wilkins, Rm. 6305	(202) 354-3480
James E. Boasberg, Rm. 6321 e	(202) 354-330
Amy B. Jackson, Rm. 2528	(202) 354-3460

Senior Judges

Thomas F. Hogan, Rm. 4012A	(202) 354–3420
Gladys Kessler, Rm. 4006A	(202) 354–3440
Paul L. Friedman, Rm. 6012A	(202) 354–3490
Ricardo M. Urbina, Rm. 6006A	(202) 354–3390

Magistrate Judges

Deborah A. Robinson, Rm. 2315	(202) 354–3070
Alan Kay, Rm. 2333	(202) 354–3030
John M. Facciola, Rm. 2321	(202) 354–3130

Bankruptcy Judge

S. Martin Teel, Jr., Rm. 2114	(202) 565–2534

Clerk of the Court

Angela D. Caesar, Rm. 1130	(202) 354–3050

[Effective March 2008.]

CIVIL RULES

LCvR 1.1 SCOPE, CONSTRUCTION AND AMENDMENTS

(a) Scope and Construction. These Rules govern all proceedings in the United States District Court for the District of Columbia. These Rules supplement the Federal Rules of Civil and Criminal Procedure and shall be construed in harmony therewith.

(b) Publication of Amendments. Any amendment to these Rules shall be published in The Daily Washington Law Reporter before its adoption. The notice shall state that the proposed amendment will be adopted unless modified or withdrawn after receiving comments from organized bar associations, members of the bar, and the public. Such comments shall be submitted in writing within 45 days of publication to the Chairman of the Advisory Committee on District Court Rules. If the court determines there is an immediate need for a particular local rule or amendment to an existing local rule, it may proceed without public notice and opportunity for comment, but the court shall promptly thereafter afford such notice and opportunity for comment.

[Effective August 1, 1999.]

LCvR 5.1 FORM AND FILING OF PLEADINGS AND OTHER PAPERS

(a) Place and Manner of Filing. All papers relating to a pending action shall be filed with the Clerk unless otherwise directed by the court.

(b) Correspondence With Court. Except when requested by a judge, correspondence shall not be directed by the parties or their attorneys to a judge, nor shall papers be left with or mailed to a judge for filing.

(c) Number of Copies. The original and one copy of every pleading, motion or other paper shall be filed with the Clerk.

(d) Electronic Transmission. No pleading, motion or other document shall be transmitted to the Clerk for filing by means of electronic facsimile transmission except with express leave of Court.

(e) Name and Address of Parties and Attorneys.

(1) The first filing by or on behalf of a party shall have in the caption the name and full residence address of the party. Where a person is sued in an official capacity, the person's official address shall be used. If the party is appearing pro se, the caption shall also include the party's telephone number. Those filing pro se in forma pauperis must provide in the caption the name and full residence address or official address of each party. Failure to provide the address information within 30 days upon filing may result in the dismissal of the case against the defendant. All papers signed by an attorney shall contain the name, address, telephone number, and D.C. Bar identification number of the attorney if the attorney is a member of the D.C. Bar. All attorneys listed on any pleading or paper who are members of the D.C. Bar must include their D.C. Bar identification numbers regardless of whether they sign the pleading. Notice of a change in address or telephone number of an attorney or a party not represented by an attorney must be filed within 14 days of the change. Unless changed by notice filed with the Clerk, the address and telephone number of a party or an attorney noted on the first filing shall be conclusively taken as the last known address and telephone number of the party or attorney.

(2) By signing a pleading or paper that is presented to the Court, an attorney is certifying that the attorney, and all other attorneys appearing with the attorney on the pleading or paper, are members of, or have a pending application for admission to, the Bar of this Court, or has complied with LCvR 83.2(c) or (d), or is covered by LCvR 83.2(e) as an attorney employed by the United States or one of its agencies.

(f) Form of Papers. All papers shall be typed (double spaced) or reproduced by any duplicating or copying process that produces a clear black image on opaque white paper 11 inches long and 8–1/2 inches wide, unfolded, without back or cover, fastened at the top. Every paper shall contain a heading under the caption describing the nature of the pleading, motion or other paper. Papers should also be punched at the top with two holes, 2 3/4 inches apart and 3/8 inch from the top, to facilitate insertion in the file jacket. The case number on every paper shall be followed by the initials of the judge to whom the case has been assigned. If the case has been referred to a magistrate judge, the magistrate judge's initials shall also be shown. All exhibits or attachments to papers should reflect the number of the case in which they are filed.

(g) Attachments to Pleadings. No complaint, amended complaint, counterclaim, cross claim or third party complaint shall have appended thereto any document that is not essential to determination of the action. Whenever any such pleading is sought to be filed with an attached document, the Clerk shall bring this Rule to the attention of the person filing the pleading.

(h) Verification. Whenever any matter is required or permitted by law or by rule to be supported by the sworn written statement of a person (other than a deposition, oath of office, or oath required to be taken before a specified official other than a notary public), the matter may, with the same force and effect, be supported by the unsworn declaration, certificate, verification, or statement, in writing of such person which is subscribed as true under penalty of perjury, and dated, in substantially the following form:

(1) If executed without the United States "I declare (or certify, verify, or state) under penalty of perjury under the laws of the United States of America that the foregoing is true and correct. Executed on (date).

(Signature)".

(2) If executed within the United States, its territories, possessions, or commonwealths: "I declare (or certify, verify, or state) under penalty of perjury that the foregoing is true and correct. Executed on (date).

(Signature)".

(i) Nonconforming Papers. A paper that does not conform to the requirements of this Rule and Rule 10(a) of the Federal Rules of Civil Procedure shall not be accepted for filing.

(j) Sealed or Confidential Documents.

(1) Absent statutory authority, no cases or documents may be sealed without an order from the Court. Any pleading filed with the intention of being sealed shall be accompanied by a motion to seal. The document will be treated as sealed, pending the outcome of the ruling on the motion. Failure to file a motion to seal will result in the pleading being placed in the public record.

(2) Unless otherwise ordered or otherwise specifically provided in these Local Rules, all documents submitted for a confidential in camera inspection by the Court, which are the subject of a Protective Order, which are subject to an existing order that they be sealed, or which are the subject of a motion for such orders, shall be submitted to the Clerk securely sealed in an envelope/box needed to accommodate the documents. The envelope/box containing such documents shall contain a conspicuous notation that carries

"DOCUMENT UNDER SEAL" or "DOCUMENTS SUBJECT TO PROTECTIVE ORDER," or the equivalent.

(3) The face of the envelope/box shall also contain the case number, the title of the Court, a descriptive title of the document and the case caption unless such information is to be, or has been, included among the information ordered sealed. The face of the envelope/box shall also contain the date of any order, or the reference to any statute permitting the item sealed.

(4) Filings of sealed materials must be made in the Clerk's Office during the business hours of 9:00 a.m. and 4:00 p.m. daily except Saturdays, Sundays and legal holidays. Filings at the security desk are prohibited because the Security Officers are not authorized to accept this material.

[Effective August 1, 1999. Amended effective December 13, 2000; December 1, 2009.]

Comment

COMMENT TO LCvR 5.1(e)(1) and (2): Section (e)(1) was amended to make clear that the reference to the requirement that all papers include "the bar identification number of the attorney" requires a D.C. Bar identification number. Because members of the bar of this Court are not assigned bar identification numbers, Section (e)(2) was added to assist the Clerk's Office in verifying the bar membership status of attorneys who appear in this Court.

LCvR 5.2 FILING OF DISCOVERY REQUESTS AND RESPONSES

(a) Nonfiling of Discovery Materials. Except as otherwise provided by this Rule, interrogatories, depositions, requests for documents, requests for admissions, and answers and responses thereto shall be served upon other counsel and parties but shall not be filed with the Clerk until they are used in the proceeding or upon order of the Court as required below. The party responsible for service of the discovery material shall retain the original and become its custodian and, with respect to depositions, the deposing party shall retain the original deposition and become its custodian and shall make it available for inspection by any party to the action upon request. The Court may in its discretion order that all or any portion of discovery materials in a particular case be filed with the Clerk.

(b) Filing of Discovery Materials With Motions and at Trial. Any motion concerning discovery matters shall be accompanied by a copy of, or shall set forth verbatim, the relevant portion of any nonfiled discovery materials to which the motion is addressed. Discovery materials may be used and filed as exhibits or evidence in support of any motion or at a trial or evidentiary hearing in accordance with the Federal Rules of Evidence.

(c) Filing for Purpose of Appeal. When discovery materials not previously in the record are needed for the purpose of an appeal, they may be filed with the Clerk by stipulation of counsel or upon application to and order of the Court.

[Effective August 1, 1999. Amended effective December 1, 2000 subject to further review. Amended effective May 17, 2001.]

LCvR 5.3 PROOF OF SERVICE

Proof of service of papers required or permitted to be served, other than those for which a different method of proof is prescribed by the Federal Rules of Civil Procedure or by statute, shall be filed with such papers. The proof shall show the date and manner of service, and may be by certificate of an attorney of record or other proof satisfactory to the Court. Failure to make proof of service does not affect the validity of service. The Court may at any time allow the proof to be amended or supplied, unless to do so would unfairly prejudice a party.

[Effective August 1, 1999.]

LCvR 5.4 CASES ASSIGNED TO CASE MANAGEMENT/ELECTRONIC CASE FILING (CM/ECF) SYSTEM

(a) Documents to Be Filed by Electronic Means. Except as otherwise provided in this Rule 5.4, all documents to be filed with the Court must be filed by electronic means in a manner authorized by the Clerk.

(b) Obtaining and Using Electronic Filing Password; Signature; Consent to Service by Electronic Means.

(1) An attorney must obtain a CM/ECF password from the Clerk in order to file documents with the Court or to receive copies of opinions and orders of the Court.

(2) A pro se party may obtain a CM/ECF password from the Clerk with leave of Court. Whether leave of Court should be granted is within the discretion of the judge to whom the case is assigned. To obtain leave of Court, the pro se party must file a written motion entitled "Motion for CM/ECF Password," describing the party's access to the internet and confirming the capacity to file documents and receive the filings of other parties electronically on a regular basis. If leave of Court is granted, the pro se party must complete the CM/ECF training provided by the Clerk to all electronic filers before the Clerk issues a CM/ECF password.

(3) A CM/ECF password may be used only by the person to whom it is assigned, or, in the case of an attorney, by that attorney or an authorized employee or agent of that attorney's law office or organization.

(4) The use of a CM/ECF password to login and submit documents creates an electronic record that operates and serves as the signature of the person to

whom the password is assigned for all purposes under the Federal Rules of Civil Procedure and the Local Rules of this Court.

(5) The electronic filing of a document that contains a sworn declaration, verification, certificate, statement, oath or affidavit certifies that the original signed document is in the possession of the attorney or pro se party responsible for the filing and that it is available for review upon request by a party or by the Court.

(6) An attorney or pro se party who obtains a CM/ECF password consents to electronic service of all documents, subsequent to the original complaint, that are filed by electronic means pursuant to F.R.Civ.P. 5(b)(2)(E). Such counsel and pro se parties are responsible for monitoring their e-mail accounts, and, upon receipt of notice of an electronic filing, for retrieving the noticed filing.

(c) Filing by Electronic Means.

(1) The filing of any document electronically following procedures set forth in this Rule constitutes filing for all purposes under the Federal Rules of Civil Procedure and the Local Rules of this Court.

(2) A person filing a document by electronic means is responsible for insuring the accuracy of the official docket entry generated by the CM/ECF software.

(3) Any document, order, or notice filed or docketed electronically by the Court or by the Clerk shall have the same binding authority as one filed on paper.

(d) Service.

(1) Electronic filing of any document operates to effect service of the document on counsel or pro se parties who have obtained CM/ECF passwords. Counsel or parties who have not yet obtained CM/ECF passwords must serve and be served as otherwise provided in F.R.Civ.P. 5(b).

(2) The requirement of a certificate or other proof of service is satisfied by the automatic notice of filing sent by the CM/ECF software to counsel or pro se parties who have obtained CM/ECF passwords. A separate certificate or other proof of service showing that a paper copy was served on a party or counsel is required when that party or counsel does not receive electronic notification of filings.

(e) Exceptions to Requirement of Electronic Filing.

(1) Exhibits or attachments that (A) exceed 500 pages (including administrative records and records of state court proceedings); or (B) are not in a format that readily permits electronic filing, such as large maps, charts, video tapes, and similar materials; or (C) are illegible when scanned into electronic format; or (D) are filed under seal, may be filed in paper form. Documents or things filed pursuant to this subsection (e)(1), and in compliance with LCvR 5.1, must be served by mail or by hand delivery, unless counsel have otherwise agreed, and must be identified in an electronically filed notice of filing.

(2) A motion pursuant to LCvR 5.1(j) for leave to file a document under seal shall be filed by electronic means, but sealed documents accompanying such a motion shall be filed in paper form together with the notice of filing required by subsection (e)(1).

(3) A party appearing pro se shall file documents in paper form with the Clerk and must be served with documents in paper form, unless the pro se party has obtained a CM/ECF password.

(f) Privacy Requirements. The following personal identifiers shall be excluded, or redacted where inclusion is necessary, from all electronically filed documents unless otherwise ordered by the Court.

(1) *Social Security Numbers.* If an individual's Social Security number must be included in a pleading, only the last four digits of that number should be used.

(2) *Names of Minor Children.* If the involvement of a minor child must be mentioned, only the initials of that child should be used.

(3) *Dates of Birth.* If an individual's date of birth must be included in a pleading, only the year should be used.

(4) *Financial Account Numbers.* If a financial account number is relevant, only the last four digits should be used.

A party wishing to file a document containing unredacted personal identifiers listed in LCvR 5.4(f)(1)–(4) may file an unredacted document under seal. This document shall be retained by the Court as part of the record.

(g) Incorrect Filings and Technical Difficulties.

(1) The Clerk may direct an attorney or pro se party to re-file a document that has been incorrectly filed, or to correct an erroneous or inaccurate docket entry.

(2) If an attorney or pro se party who has been given leave to file electronically presents a document for filing in paper form, the Clerk may direct the attorney or pro se party to file the document electronically or present it in a format compatible with CM/ECF filing. The document will be deemed filed on the date it was first presented for filing if electronically filed or presented in proper electronic format no later than the next business day.

(3) The inability to complete an electronic filing because of technical problems may constitute "cause" for an order enlarging time or "excusable neglect" for the failure to act within the specified time, within the meaning of F.R.Civ.P. 6(b). Counsel or parties encountering technical problems with CM/ECF filing shall

immediately notify a Clerk's Office employee of the problem by telephone and immediately send written confirmation of that notification to the Office of the Clerk. This Rule does not provide authority to extend statutory and jurisdictional time limits.

[Effective April 11, 2003.]

Comments

COMMENT to LCvR 5.4(a): This Rule does not apply to cases that are filed in paper form and are not assigned to the CM/ECF system. Eventually, however, all new civil cases will be assigned to the CM/ECF system.

COMMENT to LCvR 5.4(c)(3): An opinion, memorandum, order, judgment, default, or other notice issued electronically by the Court or by the Clerk bears an electronic "signature" and does not require a handwritten signature to be official and binding. Also, an order or notice (such as a minute entry or scheduling notice) entered on the docket without an attached document is official and binding.

COMMENT to LCvR 5.4(g): Notice to the Clerk that technical problems interfered with electronic filing can provide a contemporaneous record in support of a party's motion under F.R.Civ.P. 6(b) for an order enlarging time. Only the Court, not the Clerk, may enlarge time. However, if the filing deadline is statutory and jurisdictional, electronic filers should take care not to wait until the last minute to file since not even technical difficulties will provide a means for the Court to extend the deadline.

LCvR 7. MOTIONS

(a) Statement of Points and Authorities. Each motion shall include or be accompanied by a statement of the specific points of law and authority that support the motion, including where appropriate a concise statement of facts. If a table of cases is provided, counsel shall place asterisks in the margin to the left of those cases or authorities on which counsel chiefly relies.

(b) Opposing Points and Authorities. Within 14 days of the date of service or at such other time as the Court may direct, an opposing party shall serve and file a memorandum of points and authorities in opposition to the motion. If such a memorandum is not filed within the prescribed time, the Court may treat the motion as conceded.

(c) Proposed Order. Each motion and opposition shall be accompanied by a proposed order.

(d) Reply Memorandum. Within seven days after service of the memorandum in opposition the moving party may serve and file a reply memorandum.

(e) Page Limitations. A memorandum of points and authorities in support of or in opposition to a motion shall not exceed 45 pages and a reply memorandum shall not exceed 25 pages, without prior approval of the court. Documents that fail to comply with this provision shall not be filed by the Clerk.

(f) Oral Hearings. A party may in a motion or opposition request an oral hearing, but its allowance shall be within the discretion of the court. If at the time of the hearing the moving party fails to appear, the court may treat the motion as withdrawn; if the opposing party fails to appear, the court may treat the motion as conceded.

(g) Motions to Vacate Default; Verified Answer. A motion to vacate an entry of default, or a judgment by default, or both, shall be accompanied by a verified answer presenting a defense sufficient to bar the claim in whole or in part.

(h) Motions for Summary Judgment.

(1) Each motion for summary judgment shall be accompanied by a statement of material facts as to which the moving party contends there is no genuine issue, which shall include references to the parts of the record relied on to support the statement. An opposition to such a motion shall be accompanied by a separate concise statement of genuine issues setting forth all material facts as to which it is contended there exists a genuine issue necessary to be litigated, which shall include references to the parts of the record relied on to support the statement. Each such motion and opposition must also contain or be accompanied by a memorandum of points and authorities and proposed order as required by LCvR 7(a), (b) and (c). In determining a motion for summary judgment, the court may assume that facts identified by the moving party in its statement of material facts are admitted, unless such a fact is controverted in the statement of genuine issues filed in opposition to the motion.

(2) Paragraph (1) shall not apply to cases in which judicial review is based solely on the administrative record. In such cases, motions for summary judgment and oppositions thereto shall include a statement of facts with references to the administrative record.

(i) Motions to Amend Pleadings. A motion for leave to file an amended pleading shall be accompanied by an original of the proposed pleading as amended. The amended pleading shall be deemed to have been filed and served by mail on the date on which the order granting the motion is entered.

(j) Motion to Intervene. A motion to intervene as a party pursuant to Rule 24(c), Federal Rules of Civil Procedure, shall be accompanied by an original of the pleading setting forth the claim or defense for which intervention is sought. The pleading shall be deemed to have been filed and served by mail on the date on which the order granting the motion is entered.

(k) Names of Persons to Be Served With Proposed Orders, Judgments and Stipulations. Each proposed order, judgment and stipulation shall have appended to it or endorsed upon it a list of the names and addresses of all attorneys entitled to be notified of its entry. If a party is not represented by an attorney, the name and address of the party shall be included.

(*l*) Time for Filing Dispositive Motions. A dispositive motion in a civil action shall be filed sufficiently in advance of the pretrial conference that it may be fully briefed and ruled on before the conference.

(m) Duty to Confer on Nondispositive Motions. Before filing any nondispositive motion in a civil action, counsel shall discuss the anticipated motion with opposing counsel, either in person or by telephone, in a good faith effort to determine whether there is any opposition to the relief sought and, if there is opposition, to narrow the areas of disagreement. The duty to confer also applies to non-incarcerated parties appearing pro se. A party shall include in its motion a statement that the required discussion occurred, and a statement as to whether the motion is opposed.

(n) Motions Involving Judicial Review of Administrative Agency Actions.

(1) In cases involving the judicial review of administrative agency actions, counsel shall provide the Court with an appendix containing copies of those portions of the administrative record that are cited or otherwise relied upon in any memorandum in support of or in opposition to any dispositive motion. Counsel shall not burden the appendix with excess material from the administrative record that does not relate to the issues raised in the motion or opposition.

(2) The appendix shall be prepared jointly by the parties and filed within 14 days following the final memorandum on the subject motion. The parties are encouraged to agree on the contents of the appendix which shall be filed by plaintiff. In the absence of an agreement, the plaintiff must serve on all other parties an initial designation and provide all other parties the opportunity to designate additional portions of the administrative record. Plaintiff shall include all parts of the record designated by all parties in the appendix.

(3) In appropriate cases, the parties may request the option to submit separate appendices to be filed with any memorandum in support of, or in opposition to, the dispositive motion.

[Former LCvR 7.1 effective August 1, 1999; redesignated LCvR 7 effective September 1, 2003. Amended effective October 12, 2006; April 10, 2007; September 2, 2008; December 1, 2009.]

Comments

Comment to LCvR 7(h): This provision recognizes that in cases where review is based on an administrative record the court is not called upon to determine whether there is a genuine issue of material fact, but rather to test the agency action against the administrative record. As a result the normal summary judgment procedures requiring the filing of a statement of undisputed material facts is not applicable.

COMMENT TO LCvR 7(m): The changes to this rule are designed to bring non-incarcerated pro se litigants within the scope of the duty to confer on nondispositive motions, so as to extend the benefits of the rule to cases in which such litigants are parties.

Comment to LCvR7(n): This rule is intended to assist the Court in cases involving a voluminous record (e.g., environmental impact statements) by providing the Court with copies of relevant portions of the record relied upon in any dispositive motion. This rule is patterned after Local Rule 30 of the D.C. Circuit and Rule 30 of the Federal Rules of Appellate Procedure. The rule does not relieve any party from any obligation to file the complete record with the Clerk of Court. Pages should retain the original pagination from the administrative record.

LCvR 7.1 DISCLOSURE OF CORPORATE AFFILIATIONS AND FINANCIAL INTERESTS*

In all civil or agency cases where a corporation is a party or intervenor, counsel of record for that party or intervenor shall file a certificate listing any parent, subsidiary or affiliate of that party or intervenor which, to the knowledge of counsel, has any outstanding securities in the hands of the public. Such certificate shall be filed at the time the party's first pleading is filed. The purpose of this certificate is to enable the judges of this court to determine the need for recusal. Counsel shall have the continuing obligation to advise the court of any change. The form of the certificate is:

"Number and Title of Case"

Certificate required by LCvR 7.1 of the Local Rules of the United States District Court for the District of Columbia:

I, the undersigned, counsel of record for ______, certify that to the best of my knowledge and belief, the following are parent companies, subsidiaries or affiliates of ______ which have any outstanding securities in the hands of the public.

(Here list all such parent companies, subsidiaries and affiliates of the corporation.)

These representations are made in order that judges of this court may determine the need for recusal.

Attorney of Record for ______________

[Effective September 1, 2003.]

* **Publisher's Note:** As of the press time for this publication, the Court's official copy, effective as of March 2010 (updated July 2010), also included LCvR 26.1 ("Disclosure of Corporate Affiliations and Financial Interests"). *See post.*

LCvR 9.1 APPLICATIONS FOR A STATUTORY THREE–JUDGE COURT

In every case in which by statute a Three–Judge Court is required, there shall be filed with the complaint a separate document entitled "Application for Three–Judge Court," together with a memorandum of points and authorities in support of the application. Upon the convening of a Three–Judge Court, each party shall submit to the Clerk two additional copies of all pleadings and papers previously filed by the party, and all subsequent filings shall be in quadruplicate.

[Effective August 1, 1999.]

LCvR 9.2 HABEAS CORPUS PETITIONS, SECTION 1983 COMPLAINTS, AND SECTION 2255 MOTIONS

Petitions for a writ of habeas corpus and complaints pursuant to 42 U.S.C. § 1983 filed by a petitioner incarcerated in the District of Columbia, and motions filed pursuant to 28 U.S.C. § 2255 (attacking a sentence imposed by the court), must be filed on standard forms to be supplied upon request to the petitioner or plaintiff by the Clerk without cost. Counsel filing a petition for a writ of habeas corpus, a complaint under 42 U.S.C. § 1983, or a motion under 28 U.S.C. § 2255 need not use a standard form, but any such petition, complaint or motion shall contain essentially the same information set forth on the standard form.

[Effective August 1, 1999.]

LCvR 11.1 NAMES AND ADDRESSES OF PARTIES AND ATTORNEYS

The first filing by or on behalf of a party shall have in the caption the name and full residence address of the party. Where a person is sued in an official capacity, the person's official address shall be used. If the party is appearing pro se, the caption shall also include the party's telephone number. Those filing pro se in forma pauperis must provide in the caption the name and full residence address or official address of each party. Failure to provide the address information within 30 days upon filing may result in the dismissal of the case against the defendant. All papers signed by an attorney shall contain the name, address, telephone number, and bar identification number of the attorney. Notice of change in address or telephone number of an attorney or a party not represented by an attorney must be filed within 14 days of the change. Unless changed by notice filed with the Clerk, the address and telephone number of a party or an attorney noted on the first filing shall be conclusively taken as the last known address and telephone number of the party or attorney.

[Effective August 1, 1999. Amended effective December 1, 2009.]

LCvR 11.2 VERIFICATION

Whenever any matter is required or permitted by law or by rule to be supported by the sworn written statement of a person (other than a deposition, oath of office, or oath required to be taken before a specified official other than a notary public), the matter may, with the same force and effect, be supported by the unsworn declaration, certificate, verification, or statement, in writing of such person which is subscribed as true under penalty of perjury, and dated, in substantially the following form:

(1) If executed without the United States: "I declare (or certify, verify, or state) under penalty of perjury under the laws of the United States of America that the foregoing is true and correct. Executed on (date).

(Signature)".

(2) If executed within the United States, its territories, possessions, or commonwealths: "I declare (or certify, verify, or state) under penalty of perjury that the foregoing is true and correct. Executed on (date).

(Signature)".

[Effective August 1, 1999.]

LCvR 15.1 MOTIONS TO AMEND PLEADINGS

A motion for leave to file an amended pleading shall be accompanied by an original of the proposed pleading as amended. The amended pleading shall be deemed to have been filed and served by mail on the date on which the order granting the motion is entered.

[Effective August 1, 1999.]

LCvR 16.1 SCHEDULING AND CONTINUANCES

(a) Scheduling. All hearings, conferences and trials shall be scheduled by the judge to whom the case is assigned, except that matters referred to a magistrate judge shall be scheduled by the magistrate judge. Each party is responsible for arranging a conference among the parties to plan discovery in accordance with Rule 26(f), F.R.Civ.P.

(b) Continuances. No application for a continuance of a hearing, conference or trial shall be made unless notice of the application has been given to all other parties. An application for a continuance shall be ruled upon by the judge or magistrate judge before whom the hearing, conference or trial is to be held.

(c) Notice. The Clerk shall give notice to counsel of every matter set by the court, unless the matter is scheduled orally in open court in the presence of counsel for all parties, in which case further notice is not required. All scheduling orders pursuant to Rule 16(b), Federal Rules of Civil Procedure must be in writing.

[Effective August 1, 1999. Amended effective December 1, 2000 subject to further review. Amended effective May 17, 2001.]

Comment

COMMENT TO LCvR 16.1: This Rule implements Rule 26(f), F.R.Civ.P., as amended in December 2000. Rule 26(f) is amended to require only a conference of the parties rather than a meeting. The Federal Rule 26(f) amendments removed the word "meeting" and replaced it with "conference."

LCvR 16.2 AVOIDANCE AND RESOLUTION OF CONFLICTS IN ENGAGEMENTS OF COUNSEL AMONG THE COURTS IN THE DISTRICT OF COLUMBIA

The following provisions, which implement the "Procedure for Avoiding and Resolving Conflicts in Engagements of Counsel to Appear Before the Courts in the District of Columbia" dated April 18, 1973, adopted by and applicable to the United States Court of Appeals for the District of Columbia Circuit, the District Court for the District of Columbia, the District of Columbia Court of Appeals, and the Superior Court of the District of Columbia, shall apply to matters scheduled in this Court:

(a) Priority to Be Accorded Appellate Courts. Trial proceedings in this court will yield, and, if under way, will be held in abeyance, during argument by trial counsel in an appellate court.

(b) Priorities in Trial Courts. Actual trials of civil or criminal cases in this court or in the Superior Court will be accorded priority over any nontrial matters in either court. For the purpose of this Rule, a hearing on a preliminary injunction shall be regarded as a trial. A judge shall set a date for trial only after ascertaining that trial counsel have no conflicting trial or appellate engagement in any court within the District of Columbia. If, despite the foregoing and the obligations imposed on counsel by section (c) of this Rule, counsel should have more than one trial set on one day, the following priorities will be recognized:

(1) That case which is first set to commence trial on a specific day will receive priority over cases which are later set to commence trial on that day. A continued case shall be treated as set as of the last setting date.

(2) Any trial in progress, including a trial in progress from day to day, shall take precedence over trial or nontrial engagements of counsel which are set for times during which the trial is still in progress.

(3) If a scheduled trial conflicts with a previously set nontrial matter and, because of the urgency or complexity of the nontrial matter or the number of persons involved, it would be difficult to reschedule the nontrial matter, counsel shall immediately advise the court in which or the judge before whom the conflicting trial is scheduled. The court or the judge will be receptive to counsel's application for a change of the trial date or an adjustment of the hours of trial, but shall retain discretion to grant or deny such an application.

(4) The judges of this court insofar as practical will attempt to adjust their schedules to enable an attorney to attend to brief nontrial matters such as pleas, sentences, or status and pretrial conferences pending in another court. It is recognized that emergency situations will arise and that certain types of cases may require special consideration. The judges of this court will attempt to accommodate these situations by recognizing the need to depart, on occasion, from rigid scheduling rules when such situations are brought to their attention by counsel.

(c) Responsibilities of Counsel. It is the professional responsibility of attorneys to avoid the setting of conflicting engagements in the courts, to inform the courts of expected difficulties or conflicts which may arise, and to achieve the resolution of such conflicts or problems at the earliest possible time. The following particular obligations are imposed upon counsel:

(1) Attorneys are expected to carry with them at all times they are in court a calendar of their future court appearances.

(2) Attorneys shall appear personally before the judge when a case is being set, reset, or continued except as otherwise specified below. They shall in every case inform the court fully as to any matters which may conflict with a setting, resetting, or continued date being considered by the court. Counsel shall not schedule engagements which they cannot reasonably expect to attend at the time scheduled. They shall observe such limitations on the number of matters they schedule as are imposed herein, or are imposed by the individual courts of this jurisdiction, or which arise by reason of their professional obligations to their clients. The sole exception to the requirement that counsel appear personally before the judge when a case is being reset or continued arises when counsel is physically unable to be present. In such event counsel should leave three open dates with the judge in question, and the trial may be reset in counsel's absence. It shall, however, be the attorney's duty to appear personally as soon as possible before the judge who reset the case to confirm the reset date.

(3) Attorneys are obliged to take action immediately upon becoming aware of any conflict and specifically to call the conflicting engagements to the attention of the judge being asked to yield, and to pursue the matter until the conflict is resolved. Such matters may be presented to the judge in open court as a preliminary matter, with advance notice to other counsel.

(4) If counsel cannot avoid being unexpectedly late for, or absent from any scheduled appearance before any judge, they shall in advance of the scheduled appearance notify by telephone the judge's courtroom deputy of that fact, the reason therefore and the nature and duration of the conflicting engagements.

(5) If an attorney has a criminal felony case set for trial in any court on a given day, the attorney shall not schedule any other case for trial on that day or for any date thereafter during which that felony trial may reasonably be expected to continue. If an attorney has a misdemeanor case set for jury trial on a given date, the attorney shall not schedule more than one other misdemeanor case for trial on that day. These restrictions do not apply to cases as to which an attorney is certain there will be a nontrial disposition.

(6) This court will take appropriate disciplinary action when an attorney fails to conduct himself or herself in accordance with the requirements and obligations imposed by this Rule.

[Effective August 1, 1999.]

LCvR 16.3 DUTY TO CONFER

(a) Time for Conference. Counsel (including any non-prisoner pro se party) must confer in accordance with this Rule and Rule 26(f), Federal Rules of Civil Procedure, within 21 days before a scheduling conference is held or a scheduling order is due under Rule 16(b), F.R.Civ.P., to:

(1) Discuss the matters set forth in Rule 16.3(c).

(2) Make or arrange for disclosures required by Rule 26(a)(1), F.R.Civ.P.; and

(3) Develop a discovery plan that indicates the parties' views and proposals.

In a case involving multiple defendants, the 21–day period shall run from the date of appearance or first filing in the form of an answer or motion, pursuant to Rule 12, F.R.Civ.P., by the defendant who is given the longest time to answer under the Federal Rules of Civil Procedure. Any party may move to extend the deadline to a time fixed by the court on the ground that another defendant has not been served or has not yet appeared in the case, or for other sufficient reasons.

If necessary to comply with its expedited schedule for Rule 16(b) conferences, a court may require the conference between the parties to occur fewer than 21 days before the scheduling conference is held or a scheduling order is due under Rule 16(b), F.R.Civ.P.

(b) Exempted Cases. The requirement of this Rule, of LCvR 16.3 of these Rules, and Rules 16(b) and 26(f), Federal Rules of Civil Procedure, shall not apply in the following categories of proceedings exempted from initial disclosure under Rule 26(a)(1)(E), F.R.Civ. P., or when otherwise ordered. The following categories of proceedings are exempted from both initial disclosure under Rule 26(a)(1)(E), F.R.Civ.P., and the Rule 26(f) conference, F.R.Civ.P.:

(1) an action for review on an administrative record;

(2) a petition for habeas corpus or other proceeding to challenge a criminal conviction or sentence;

(3) an action brought without counsel by a person in custody of the United States, a state, or a state subdivision;

(4) an action to enforce or quash an administrative summons or subpoena;

(5) an action by the United States to recover benefit payments;

(6) an action by the United States to collect on a student loan guaranteed by the United States;

(7) a proceeding ancillary to proceedings in other courts;

(8) an action to enforce an arbitration award; and

(9) FOIA actions.

(c) Matters to Be Discussed by the Parties. At the conference required by this Rule, the parties must confer to discuss the following matters:

(1) Whether the case is likely to be disposed of by dispositive motion; and whether, if a dispositive motion has already been filed, the parties should recommend to the court that discovery or other matters should await a decision on the motion.

(2) The date by which any other parties shall be joined or the pleadings amended, and whether some or all the factual and legal issues can be agreed upon or narrowed.

(3) Whether the case should be assigned to a magistrate judge for all purposes, including trial.

(4) Whether there is a realistic possibility of settling the case.

(5) Whether the case could benefit from the Court's alternative dispute resolution (ADR) procedures (or some other form of ADR); what related steps should be taken to facilitate such ADR; and whether counsel have discussed ADR and their response to this provision with their clients. In assessing the above, counsel shall consider:

(i) the client's goals in bringing or defending the litigation;

(ii) whether settlement talks have already occurred and, if so, why they did not produce an agreement;

(iii) the point during the litigation when ADR would be most appropriate, with special consideration given to:

(aa) whether ADR should take place after the informal exchange or production through discovery of specific items of information; and

(bb) whether ADR should take place before or after the judicial resolution of key legal issues;

(iv) whether the parties would benefit from a neutral evaluation of their case, which could include suggestions regarding the focus of discovery, the legal merits of the claim, an assessment of damages and/or the potential settlement value of the case; and

(v) whether cost savings or any other practical advantages would flow from a stay of discovery or of other pre-trial proceedings while an ADR process is pending.

(6) Whether the case can be resolved by summary judgment or motion to dismiss; dates for filing dispositive motions and/or cross-motions, oppositions, and replies; and proposed dates for a decision on the motions.

(7) Whether the parties should stipulate to dispense with the initial disclosures required by Rule 26(a)(1), F.R.Civ.P., and if not, what if any changes should be made in the scope, form or timing of those disclosures.

(8) The anticipated extent of discovery, how long discovery should take, what limits should be placed on discovery; whether a protective order is appropriate; and a date for the completion of all discovery, including answers to interrogatories, document production, requests for admissions, and depositions.

(9) Whether the requirement of exchange of expert witness reports and information pursuant to Rule 26(a)(2), F.R.Civ.P., should be modified, and whether and when depositions of experts should occur.

(10) In class actions, appropriate procedures for dealing with Rule 23, F.R.Civ.P., proceedings, including the need for discovery and the timing thereof, dates for filing a Rule 23 motion, and opposition and reply, and for oral argument and/or an evidentiary hearing on the motion and a proposed date for decision.

(11) Whether the trial and/or discovery should be bifurcated or managed in phases, and a specific proposal for such bifurcation.

(12) The date for the pretrial conference (understanding that a trial will take place 30 to 60 days thereafter).

(13) Whether the Court should set a firm trial date at the first scheduling conference or should provide that a trial date will be set at the pretrial conference from 30 to 60 days after that conference.

(14) Such other matters that the parties believe may be appropriate for inclusion in a scheduling order.

(d) Report to the Court and Proposed Order. Not later than 14 days following the conference required by this Rule, the attorneys of record and all unrepresented parties that have appeared in the case shall submit to the court a written report outlining the discovery plan and including a succinct statement of all agreements reached with respect to any of the 14 matters set forth in paragraph (c), a description of the positions of each party on any matters as to which they disagree, and a proposed scheduling order. The report shall be submitted jointly, but the parties may submit alternative proposed orders that reflect any disagreements. The plaintiff shall have the duty to ensure timely filing of the report. If, by the time the report is due, any defendant has not responded to the plaintiff's proposed report or declines to join in the report, the plaintiff shall certify in the report that efforts were made to secure that defendant's participation.

If necessary to comply with its expedited schedule for Rule 16(b) conferences, a court may require the written report outlining the discovery plan be filed fewer than 14 days after the conference between the parties, or excuse the parties from submitting a written report and permit them to report orally on their discovery plan at the Rule 16(b) conference as per Rule 26(f), F.R.Civ.P.

[Effective August 1, 1999. Amended effective December 1, 2000 subject to further review. Amended effective May 17, 2001.]

Comments

COMMENT TO LCvR 16.3(a): LCvR 16.3(a) has been modified to conform to the amendments to the Federal Rules of Civil Procedure as amended in December 2000. The amendment (1) modified the date by which the Rule 26(f), F.R.Civ.P., conference is to be held and (2) removed the requirement that the Rule 16(b), F.R.Civ.P., conference be a face-to-face meeting. The court, however, encourages face-to-face meetings and retains its authority to require that the conference be conducted face-to-face in a particular case.

COMMENT TO LCvR 16.3(b): The amendment to Rule 26(f), F.R.Civ.P., removed the authority to exempt cases by local rule from the discovery conference requirement. The amendment exempts the same categories of proceedings from the conference requirement that are exempted from the initial disclosure requirement. Accordingly, LCvR 16.3(b) lists the proceedings exempted under LCvR 26.2(a) and Rule 26 (a)(1)(E), F.R.Civ.P., and removes the cases previously exempted by local rule (viz., proceedings involving a non-prisoner pro se plaintiff in which a dispositive motion is filed before the deadline for the meeting expires). Although the first eight enumerated exempt categories of cases were intended to be exclusive and are considered actions that are brought in most, if not all of the Federal District Courts, we have included Freedom of Information Act actions to this list, as item number (9) because they are actions that typically do not require discovery or actions in which an initial disclosure requirement would not make sense. A significant portion of the nation's FOIA actions are pending in this court.

COMMENT TO LCvR 16.3(c): LCvR 16.3(c) has been amended slightly to conform to the amendments to the Federal Rules of Civil Procedure as amended in December 2000.

COMMENT TO LCvR 16.3(d): The submission date for the report, following the Rule 26(f) conference, F.R.Civ.P., has been extended from 10 to 14 days.

LCvR 16.4 SCHEDULING ORDERS

Scheduling Conference and Order. After receiving the report of the parties pursuant to LCvR 16.3(d) of these Rules, the court will hold a scheduling conference unless it determines, on the basis of the report, that a conference is unnecessary. At or after the scheduling conference, or after receiving the report of the parties where no scheduling conference is held, the court will issue a scheduling order governing future proceedings in accordance with Rule 16(b), Federal Rules of Civil Procedure. The Scheduling Order will include the limits if any on the number of interrogatories, the number and duration of depositions, and the use of other forms of discovery. The court may modify the scheduling order at any time upon a showing of good cause. Objections made to the discovery plan during the Rule 26(f) conference are to be ruled on by the court in the scheduling conference or order. In its ruling on the objection, the court must determine what disclosures if any are to be made and set the time for disclosure.

[Effective August 1, 1999. Amended effective December 1, 2000 subject to further review. Amended effective May 17, 2001.]

Comment [2001]

COMMENT TO LCvR 16.4(a): The amendment to Rule 26(f), F.R.Civ.P., requires that the conference between parties be held 21 days before the Rule 16(a) scheduling conference or scheduling order is due, as per the Federal Rules of Civil Procedure. The reference to the track assignment has been deleted from the rule above.

LCvR 16.5 PRETRIAL STATEMENTS

(a) General.

(1) In any case scheduled for trial or evidentiary hearing the court may order a final Pretrial Conference before the court or a magistrate judge. Trial counsel for each party must be present at the final Pretrial Conference unless the court authorizes otherwise.

(2) Not less than 14 days prior to the final Pretrial Conference, each party shall file and serve on every other party a Pretrial Statement, in the form prescribed by subparagraph (b) of this Rule. Amendments to a party's Pretrial Statement shall be permitted for excusable neglect until entry by the court or magistrate judge of a final Pretrial Order.

(3) As soon as practicable following the final Pretrial Conference the court or magistrate judge shall enter a final Pretrial Order which shall govern the trial of the case. The final Pretrial Order may incorporate, in whole or part, the parties' Pretrial Statements. Objections to the final Pretrial Order shall be promptly made, and shall be determined by the court before trial. Thereafter no departures from the final Pretrial Order shall be permitted except to prevent manifest injustice.

(b) Pretrial Statements.

(1) A party's Pretrial Statement shall contain the following:

(i) a statement of the case;

(ii) a statement of claims made by the party;

(iii) a statement of defenses raised by the parties;

(iv) a schedule of witnesses to be called by the party;

(v) a list of exhibits to be offered in evidence by the party;

(vi) a designation of depositions, or portions thereof, to be offered in evidence by the party;

(vii) an itemization of damages the party seeks to recover; and

(viii) a request for other relief sought by the party.

(2) The statement of the case shall set forth a brief description of the nature of the case, the identities of the parties, and the basis of the court's jurisdiction.

(3) The statement of claims shall set forth each claim a party has against any other party (including counter-, cross-, and third-party claims), and the party or parties against whom the claim is made.

(4) The statement of defenses shall set forth each defense a party interposes to a claim asserted against it by any other party, including defenses raised by way of general denial, without regard to which party has the burden of persuasion.

(5) The schedule of witnesses shall set forth the full names and addresses of all witnesses the party may call if not earlier called by another party, separately identifying those whom the party expects to present and those whom the party may call if the need arises including rebuttal witnesses. The schedule shall also set forth a brief description of the testimony to be elicited from the witness; and an estimate of the time the party will take in eliciting such testimony. Expert

witnesses shall be designated by an asterisk. A party need not list any witness who will be called solely for impeachment purposes.

No objection shall be entertained to a witness or to testimony on the ground that the witness or testimony was disclosed for the first time in a party's Pretrial Statement, unless the party objecting has unsuccessfully sought to learn the identity of the witness or the substance of the testimony by discovery, and the court or magistrate judge finds the information to have been wrongfully withheld.

(6) The list of exhibits shall set forth a description of each exhibit the party may offer in evidence (other than those created at trial), separately identifying those which the party expects to offer and those which the party may offer if the need arises. Exhibits shall be listed by title and date.

Exhibits will be presumed to be authentic unless objection to their authenticity is made at or before the final Pretrial Conference and the objection is sustained.

(7) The designation of depositions shall identify each deposition or portion thereof (by page and line numbers) the party intends to offer in evidence. Any cross-designation sought by any other party pursuant to Rule 106, Federal Rules of Evidence, must be made at or before the final Pretrial Conference.

(8) The itemization of damages shall set forth separately each element of damages, and the monetary amount thereof, the party claims to be entitled to recover of any other party, including prejudgment interest, punitive damages and attorneys' fees. No monetary amount need be set forth for elements of intangible damage (e.g., pain and suffering, mental anguish, or loss of consortium).

(9) The request for other relief shall set forth all relief, other than judgment for a sum of money, the party claims to be entitled to receive against any other party.

(c) Exempted Cases. The following categories of actions are exempt from this Rule:

(1) Actions brought pursuant to the Freedom of Information Act;

(2) Petitions for writ of habeas corpus brought by a petitioner incarcerated in the District of Columbia;

(3) Motions filed pursuant to 28 U.S.C. section 2255;

(4) All other petitions brought by prisoners incarcerated in federal facilities, in the District of Columbia;

(5) Appeals from bankruptcy decisions;

(6) All actions brought by the United States to collect student loans or other debts owed to the United States Government.

(7) Actions involving the review of Social Security benefit denials;

(8) All applications for attorneys' fees and costs;

(9) Multi-district litigation;

(10) Condemnation proceedings;

(11) Forfeiture actions by the United States;

(12) Appeals from a decision by a United States Magistrate Judge; and

(13) Motions to quash or enforce administrative subpoenas.

(d) Orders Affecting Content of Pretrial Statements. Nothing in this Rule shall preclude the court in a particular case from entering an order requiring the parties to submit, in addition to the foregoing contents of pretrial statements, the following:

(1) Stipulations of fact agreed upon or proposed by the parties;

(2) A trial brief incorporating a concise statement of law supporting the party's claims or defenses, and addressing any unusual issues of fact or evidence not already submitted to the court;

(3) In jury cases, proposed voir dire questions, jury instructions and verdict forms;

(4) In nonjury cases, proposed findings of fact and conclusions of law; and

(5) A joint pretrial statement.

(e) Objections to Depositions and Exhibits. The statement of objections to the use of depositions and to the admissibility of exhibits required by Rule 26(a)(3), Federal Rules of Civil Procedure, shall be filed at or before the pretrial conference.

(f) Compliance With Federal Rules of Civil Procedure. Compliance with the requirements of this Rule shall constitute full compliance with Rules 26(a)(3) and (4), Federal Rules of Civil Procedure. Those rules shall apply, however, in cases exempted from this Rule.

[Effective August 1, 1999. Amended effective December 1, 2009.]

Comment

COMMENT TO LCvR 16.5: The changes in this Rule are made to conform to the recent amendments to Rule 26(a)(3), Federal Rules of Civil Procedure. Categories of cases exempted from this Rule are not exempted from the scheduling order provisions of Rule 16(b), F.R.Civ.P., and LCvR 16.3 of these Rules.

LCvR 16.6 STIPULATIONS

A stipulation need not be considered by the court unless it is in writing and signed by the parties thereto or their attorneys, or stenographically recorded in court or during a deposition.

[Effective August 1, 1999.]

LCvR 23.1 CLASS ACTIONS

(a) Class Action Allegations. In any case sought to be maintained as a class action, the complaint shall contain under a separate heading styled "Class Action Allegations":

(1) A reference to the portion or portions of Rule 23, Federal Rules of Civil Procedure, under which the suit is claimed properly to be maintainable as a class action.

(2) Appropriate allegations justifying such claim, including, but not necessarily limited to:

(i) the size (or approximate size) and definition of the alleged class;

(ii) the basis upon which the plaintiff claims to be an adequate representative of the class, or if the class is comprised of defendants, that those named as parties are adequate representatives of the class;

(iii) the alleged questions of law and fact claimed to be common to the class; and

(iv) in actions claimed to be maintainable as class actions under Rule 23(b)(3) of the Federal Rules of Civil Procedure, allegations supporting the findings required by that subdivision.

(b) Motion for Certification. Within 90 days after the filing of a complaint in a case sought to be maintained as a class action, unless the court in the exercise of its discretion has extended this period, the plaintiff shall move for a certification under Rule 23(c)(1), Federal Rules of Civil Procedure, that the case may be so maintained. In ruling upon the motion, the court may allow the action to be so maintained, may deny the motion, or may order that a ruling be postponed pending discovery or other appropriate preliminary proceedings. A defendant may move at any time to strike the class action allegations or to dismiss the complaint.

(c) Provisions as to Notice. In an action maintained under Rule 23(b)(3) of the Federal Rules of Civil Procedure, the plaintiff shall include in the motion for certification a statement proposing (1) how, when, by whom, and to whom the notice required by Rule 23(c)(2) shall be given, (2) how and by whom payment therefore is to be made, and (3) by whom the response to the notice is to be received. In lieu of such a statement the movant may state reasons why a determination of these matters cannot then be made, and offer a proposal as to when the determination should be made. In certifying a class action as maintainable under Rule 23(b)(3), the court may include in its order the provisions for notice pursuant to Rule 23(c)(2) or may postpone a determination of the matter.

(d) Applicability to Counterclaims and Cross–claims. The foregoing provisions shall apply, with appropriate adaptations, to any counterclaim or cross claim alleged to be brought for or against a class.

[Effective August 1, 1999.]

Comment

COMMENT TO LCvR 23.1(b) AS AMENDED 10/10/90: This amendment makes clear that the court may enlarge the 90–day period within which the motion for certification is to be filed.

LCvR 26.1 DISCLOSURE OF CORPORATE AFFILIATIONS AND FINANCIAL INTERESTS*

In all civil, agency, or criminal cases where a corporation is a party or intervenor, counsel of record for that party or intervenor shall file a certificate listing any parent, subsidiary, affiliate, or any company which owns 10% or more of the stock of that party or intervenor which, to the knowledge of counsel, has any outstanding securities in the hands of the public. Such certificate shall be filed at the time the party's first pleading is filed. The purpose of this certificate is to enable the judges of this court to determine the need for recusal.

Counsel shall have the continuing obligation to advise the court of any change. The form of the certificate is:

"Number and Title of Case"

Certificate required by LCvR 26.1 of the Local Rules of the United States District Court for the District of Columbia:

I, the undersigned, counsel of record for ______, certify that to the best of my knowledge and belief, the following are parent companies, subsidiaries, affiliates, or companies which own at least 10% of the stock of ______ which have any outstanding securities in the hands of the public.

(Here list all such parent companies, subsidiaries, affiliates, and companies which own at least 10% of the stock of the corporation.)

These representations are made in order that judges of this court may determine the need for recusal.

Attorney of Record for ______________

* **Publisher's Note:** As of the press time for this publication, the Court's official copy, effective as of March 2010 (updated July 2010), also included LCvR 7.1 ("Disclosure of Corporate Affiliations and Financial Interests"). *See post.*

Comment

COMMENT TO RULE LCvR 26.1: Language has been added in order to identify any publicly held companies which own 10% or more of the stock of the party or interve-

nor. This language mirrors a recommendation by the Judicial Conference's Committee on Codes of Conduct.

LCvR 26.2 DISCOVERY

(a) Initial Disclosure Requirements. Unless otherwise provided by the court in its scheduling order, the requirement of Rule 26(a)(1), F.R.Civ. P., for initial disclosure of information are applicable in all cases except for cases exempted by order of the court and in the following categories of proceedings:

(1) an action for review on an administrative record;

(2) a petition for habeas corpus or other proceeding to challenge a criminal conviction or sentence;

(3) an action brought without counsel by a person in custody of the United States, a state, or a state subdivision;

(4) an action to enforce or quash an administrative summons or subpoena;

(5) an action by the United States to recover benefit payments;

(6) an action by the United States to collect on a student loan guaranteed by the United States;

(7) a proceeding ancillary to proceedings in other courts;

(8) an action to enforce an arbitration award; and

(9) FOIA actions.

Initial disclosures must be made at or within 14 days after the Rule 26(f) conference, F.R. Civ.P., unless the parties agree or the court orders a different date or unless a party objects during the conference that initial disclosures are not appropriate in the circumstances of the action and states the objection in the Rule 26(f) discovery plan, F.R. Civ.P.

Any party first served or otherwise joined after the Rule 26(f) conference, F.R.Civ. P., must make these disclosures within 30 days after being served or joined unless a different time is set by stipulation or court order. A party must make its initial disclosures based on the information then reasonably available to it and is not excused from making its disclosures because it has not fully completed its investigation of the case or because it challenges the sufficiency of another party's disclosures or because another party has not made its disclosures.

A party that without substantial justification fails to disclose information required by this Rule or by Rule 26(a) or 26(e)(1), F.R.Civ. P., or to amend a prior response to discovery as required by Rule 26(e)(2), F.R.Civ. P., is not, unless such failure is harmless, permitted to use as evidence at a trial, at a hearing, or on a motion any witness or information not so disclosed. In addition to or in lieu of this sanction, the court, on motion and after affording an opportunity to be heard, may impose other appropriate sanctions. These sanctions may include any of the actions authorized under Rule 37(b)(2)(A),(B), and (C), F.R.Civ. P., in addition to requiring payment of reasonable expenses, including attorney's fees, caused by the failure, and may also include informing the jury of the failure to make the disclosure.

Except in categories of proceedings exempted from initial disclosure under Rule 26(a)(1)(E), F.R.Civ. P., or when authorized under these rules or by order or agreement of the parties, a party may not seek discovery from any sources before the parties have conferred as required by Rule 26(f), F.R. Civ.P.

(b) Presumptive Limits on Interrogatories and Depositions. Whether and to what extent limitations shall be placed on the permitted number of interrogatories and depositions will be determined by the court in the scheduling order and may thereafter be changed on motion of the parties or the court's own motion. When the scheduling order sets limits different from those contained in Rules 30(1)(2)(1)* and 33(a), Federal Rules of Civil Procedure, the scheduling order shall govern.

By order in a particular case, the court may alter the limits on the number of depositions and interrogatories or the length of depositions under Rule 30, F.R.Civ.P. The court may also limit by order in a particular case the number of requests under Rule 36, F.R.Civ.P.

(c) Duration of Depositions. A deposition is limited to one day of seven hours, however, the court may authorize or the parties may agree to different limits on the length of a deposition. The court must allow additional time consistent with Rule 26(b)(2), F.R.Civ. P., if needed for a fair examination of the deponent or if the deponent or another person, or other circumstance impedes or delays the examination. If the court finds that the fair examination of the deponent has been frustrated by any impediment or delay, it may impose an appropriate sanction upon the persons responsible, including the reasonable costs and attorney's fees incurred by any parties as a result thereof.

(d) Form of Responses to Interrogatories and Requests for Admission or Production of Documents. Answers, responses and objections to interrogatories and requests for admissions or for production of documents and motions to compel answers or responses, shall identify and quote each interrogatory or request in full immediately preceding the answer, response or objection thereto.

[Effective August 1, 1999. Amended effective December 1, 2000 subject to further review. Amended effective May 17, 2001; December 1, 2009.]

* So in original. See Fed. R. Civ. P. Rule 30(a).

Comments

COMMENT TO LCvR 26.2(a): LCvR 26.2(a) has been amended to conform with the Rules of this Court to the amendments to the Federal Rules of Civil Procedure as amended in December 2000. Also, FOIA actions have been added as item (9). See comment to Local Rule 16.3(b). The 1993 amendment permitted local rules to "opt out" of disclosure requirements or to alter its operation. According to the committee notes for the amendment, the 1994 "opt out" provision was a response to opposition to initial disclosure in some districts and permitted districts to tailor their rules to their preference. The purpose of the present amendment is to "restore" national uniformity.

COMMENT TO LCvR 26.2(b): LCvR 26.2(b) has been modified to conform to the amendments to the Federal Rules of Civil Procedure as amended in December 2000. The amendment established a presumptive national limit on the number of depositions and interrogatories. The amendment, however, purposefully removed previous permission for local rules that established different presumptive limits on these discovery activities. Limits can, however, be made by court order or agreement in individual actions, but "standing" orders imposing different presumptive limits are not authorized.

COMMENT TO LCvR 26.2(c): LCvR 26.2(c) has been modified to conform to the amendments to Federal Rules of Civil Procedure as amended in December 2000. Partial reasoning for this amendment included removing the "deponent veto," the requirement that the deponent consent to extension of a deposition beyond the presumptive time limitation. Additionally, the committee was guided by concern that overlong depositions resulted in undue costs and delays. The limitation contemplates that there will be reasonable breaks during the day for lunch and other reasons, and that the only time to be counted is the time occupied by the actual deposition.

COMMENT TO LCrR 26.2(d): No change appears to be intended by amendment to the F.R.Civ.P., however, discovery requests and responses (including depositions, interrogatories, requests for documents or to permit entry upon land, and requests for admission) must not be filed until they are used in the proceeding or the court orders filing.

LCvR 30.1 SERVICE OF NOTICE OF DEPOSITION

Service of a notice of deposition seven days in advance of the date set for taking the deposition shall constitute "reasonable notice" to a party as required by Rule 30(b), Federal Rules of Civil Procedure, unless the deposition is to be taken at a place more than 50 miles from the District of Columbia, in which case 14 days shall constitute reasonable notice. The computation of time under this Rule shall be governed by Rule 6, Federal Rules of Civil Procedure. The court may enlarge or shorten the time on application of a party for good cause shown. Nothing in this Rule modifies the provision in Rule 32(a), Federal Rules of Civil Procedure, prohibiting the use of depositions against certain parties who with due diligence are unable to obtain counsel to represent them, or against parties with less than 14 days' notice who file a motion for protective order.

[Effective August 1, 1999. Amended effective December 1, 2009.]

LCvR 30.4 FORM OF RESPONSES TO INTERROGATORIES AND REQUESTS FOR ADMISSION OR PRODUCTION OF DOCUMENTS

Answers, responses and objections to interrogatories and requests for admissions or for production of documents and motions to compel answers or responses, shall identify and quote each interrogatory or request in full immediately preceding the answer, response or objection thereto.

[Effective August 1, 1999.]

LCvR 40.1 ASSIGNMENT SYSTEM

(a) Cases to Be Assigned to a Single Judge. Unless otherwise provided in these Rules, each civil and criminal case shall be assigned to a single judge in the manner provided herein.

(b) Calendar and Case Management Committee. The assignment of cases to judges of this Court shall be performed by the Clerk under the direction of the Calendar and Case Management Committee. The Committee shall be composed of no less than three and no more than five active judges appointed by the Chief Judge for two year terms. All matters dealing with the assignment of cases, including but not limited to any efforts to restrain or avoid the enforcement or application of rules under this Part shall be referred to the Chairman of the Calendar and Case Management Committee for resolution by the Committee.

(c) Emergency Judge. A judge of this Court will be available, in accordance with a schedule of assignments announced from time to time by the Chief Judge, to hear emergency civil or criminal matters on all legal holidays and weekends. The emergency judge's assignment starts at 4:30 p.m. on the day preceding the weekend and ends at 9:00 a.m. the next business day. The judge designated for emergency assignments will not be present in the Courthouse but will be reasonably available, on call, in the area.

(d) Notice of Transfers and Reassignments. All case transfers and reassignments shall be accompanied by formal notice to the Chairman of the Calendar and Case Management Committee and to the Clerk's Office Liaison. The Clerk will notify each of the judges involved and all counsel in the case of the reassignment.

[Effective August 1, 1999. Amended effective March 8, 2004; March 2008.]

Comment

COMMENT TO LCvR 40.1: The rule has been changed to reflect a change in scope and to provide the court with greater flexibility with respect to this Committee.

LCvR 40.2 CLASSES OF CASES

(a) Classification. In order to assure a more even distribution of each type of case among the judges of this Court, each civil and criminal case will be classified for assignment purposes in accordance with a set of categories established by the court on the recommendation of the Calendar and Case Management Committee.

(b) Designation at Time of Filing. Upon filing the complaint in a civil action, the attorney for the plaintiff shall note the proper classification of the case on a form provided by the Clerk. In criminal cases the United States Attorney shall, at the time of the return of an indictment, note the proper classification of the case on a form provided by the Clerk.

[Effective August 1, 1999. Amended March 2008.]

LCvR 40.3 MANNER OF ASSIGNMENT

(a) Random Assignment. Except as otherwise provided by these Rules, civil, criminal and miscellaneous cases shall be assigned to judges of this court selected at random in the following manner:

(1) The Clerk shall create a separate assignment deck in the automated system for each subclassification of civil and criminal cases established by the Court pursuant to LCvR 40.2 of these Rules and a separate deck for miscellaneous cases[1]. The decks will be created by the Liaison to the Calendar and Case Management Committee or the Liaison's backup and access to this function shall be restricted to these individuals to protect the integrity and confidentiality of the random assignment of cases. The Calendar and Case Management Committee will, from time to time determine and indicate by order the frequency with which each judge's name shall appear in each designated deck, to effectuate an even distribution of cases among the active judges.

(2) At the time a civil complaint is filed or an indictment or information is returned in a criminal case, the case shall be assigned to the judge whose name appears on the screen when the appropriate deck is selected. The Clerk shall also stamp on the indictment, information, complaint or other initial pleading of each case, and on the file jacket, the number of the case and the name of the judge to whom it is assigned. The numbering and assignment of each case shall be completed before processing of the next case is begun. Notwithstanding the foregoing, a civil case, requiring an emergency hearing, which is filed after normal business hours, shall not be assigned to a judge until the next business day.

(b) Three–Judge Court Cases. Civil, including miscellaneous, cases requested or required to be heard by a Three–Judge Court shall be randomly assigned to a District Court judge, excluding the Chief Judge.

(c) Bankruptcy Matters. Bankruptcy matters requiring the attention of a District Judge shall be submitted to the Motions Judge, except as otherwise provided in D.C. LBR 5011–1(f) and except that appeals from a Bankruptcy Judge's decisions and cases requiring a jury trial shall be randomly assigned.

(d) Prisoner Petitions. Petitions for a writ of habeas corpus and complaints filed pursuant to 42 U.S.C. § 1983 filed by a petitioner incarcerated in the District of Columbia shall be randomly assigned, except that related petitions from the same petitioner may be assigned to the judge who received the initial petition after consultation with that judge. Motions filed under 28 U.S.C. § 2255 shall, if possible, be assigned to the sentencing judge.

(e) Assignment to Visiting and Senior Judges. Cases may be assigned to visiting and senior judges in accordance with procedures adopted from time to time by the Calendar and Case Management Committee.

(f) Proceedings After Assignment. All proceedings in a case after its assignment shall be conducted by the judge to whom the case is assigned, except as otherwise provided in these Rules. A judge who declares a mistrial shall retain the case for subsequent proceedings including, where appropriate, retrial.

[Effective August 1, 1999. Amended March 2008.]

1 For the purpose of this Rule, miscellaneous cases that will be randomly assigned will include, but not be limited to, these proceedings: (a) actions to perpetuate testimony as in Rule 27, Federal Rules of Civil Procedure; (b) actions to enforce administrative subpoenas and summonses; (c) proceedings ancillary to an action pending in another district; (d) supplementary proceedings brought in aid of execution; (e) motions for return of property in criminal proceedings; and (f) requests for judicial assistance. Grand Jury Miscellaneous cases will continue to be assigned to the Chief Judge and Pen Register Applications will continue to be assigned to magistrate judges.

Comment

COMMENT TO LCvR 40.3: To ensure an even distribution of cases filed on the miscellaneous docket these cases will now be randomly assigned to a judge of this Court at the time of filing. The assigned judge will maintain jurisdiction of the miscellaneous case for all purposes. The assignment of miscellaneous cases does not affect the duties of the Motions Judge as specified in LCvR 40.8.

LCvR 40.4 SUSPENSION OF NEW ASSIGNMENTS

A judge shall be relieved by the Calendar and Case Management Committee from any new assignment of indictments and civil cases accompanied by motions for temporary restraining orders and preliminary injunctions or civil cases in which an intention to file a motion for a preliminary injunction is expressed, upon notification by the judge or the Chief Judge to the Committee that the judge:

(1) has continued in a protracted trial or hearing for 10 consecutive trial days;[2] (2) is confined to a

hospital; (3) is confined at home due to illness for seven days; (4) has had a death in the judge's immediate family; or (5) is performing judicial duties out of this jurisdiction pursuant to assignment. New cases shall be assigned to the judge in accordance with normal procedures upon the conclusion of any such condition.

Whenever a judge begins what is expected to be an unusually protracted criminal trial (one lasting four weeks or more) he or she may refer to the Calendar and Case Management Committee for routine reassignment such other criminal cases assigned to such judge as the judge was unable to dispose of prior thereto and which are expected to require disposition pursuant to the Speedy Trial Act within the time period of the unusually protracted trial.

[Effective August 1, 1999. Amended March 2008.]

2 If a judge, after suspension based upon 10 consecutive days in a trial or hearing, thereafter devotes an occasional day to other court business, that judge shall not by virtue thereof be reinstated in the complete draw.

LCvR 40.5 RELATED CASES

(a) Definition. A related case for the purpose of this Rule means as follows:

(1) Criminal cases are deemed related when (i) a superseding indictment has been filed, or (ii) more than one indictment is filed or pending against the same defendant or defendants, or (iii) prosecution against different defendants arises from a common wiretap, search warrant, or activities which are a part of the same alleged criminal event or transaction. A case is considered pending until a defendant has been sentenced.

(2) If a civil forfeiture proceeding is filed concerning a criminal defendant, or a defendant is charged in a criminal case while a civil forfeiture proceeding is pending concerning that defendant, the civil and criminal cases are to be deemed related.

(3) Civil, including miscellaneous, cases are deemed related when the earliest is still pending on the merits in the District Court and they (i) relate to common property, or (ii) involve common issues of fact, or (iii) grow out of the same event or transaction, or (iv) involve the validity or infringement of the same patent. Notwithstanding the foregoing, a case filed by a pro se litigant with a prior case pending shall be deemed related and assigned to the judge having the earliest case. However, if a judge in the interest of judicial economy, consolidates a significant number of similar pro se prisoner complaints, or has a single case with a significant number of pro se prisoner plaintiffs, and any of those prisoners later files a new complaint which is unrelated to the subject matter of the consolidated cases or the multiple plaintiffs' case, the judge who receives the new case as related may, if he or she chooses, refer the new case to the Calendar and Case Management Committee for random assignment.

(4) Additionally, cases whether criminal or civil, including miscellaneous, shall be deemed related where a case is dismissed, with prejudice or without, and a second case is filed involving the same parties and relating to the same subject matter.

(b) Notification of Related Cases. The parties shall notify the Clerk of the existence of related cases as follows:

(1) At the time of returning an indictment the United States Attorney shall indicate, on a form to be provided by the Clerk, the name, docket number and relationship of any related case pending in this court or in any other United States District Court. The form shall be mailed to all defense counsel along with the notification of the arraignment. Any objection by the defendant to the related case designation shall be served on the U.S. Attorney and filed with the Clerk within 14 days after arraignment.

(2) At the time of filing any civil, including miscellaneous, action, the plaintiff or his attorney shall indicate, on a form to be provided by the Clerk, the name, docket number and relationship of any related case pending in this court or in any other United States Court. The plaintiff shall serve this form on the defendant with the complaint. Any objection by the defendant to the related case designation shall be filed and served with the defendant's first responsive pleading or motion.

(3) Whenever an attorney for a party in a civil, including miscellaneous, or criminal action becomes aware of the existence of a related case or cases, the attorney shall immediately notify, in writing, the judges on whose calendars the cases appear and shall serve such notice on counsel for all other parties. Upon receiving information from any source concerning a relationship between pending cases, the Clerk shall transmit that information in writing to the judges on whose calendars the cases appear and to all parties to the proceeding.

(c) Assignment of Related Cases. Related cases noted at or after the time of filing shall be assigned in the following manner:

(1) Where the existence of a related case in this court is noted at the time the indictment is returned or the complaint is filed, the Clerk shall assign the new case to the judge to whom the oldest related case is assigned. If a judge who is assigned a case under this procedure determines that the cases in question are not related, the judge may transfer the new case to the Calendar and Case Management Committee. If the Calendar and Case Management Committee finds that good cause exists for the transfer, it shall cause the case to be reassigned at random. If the Calendar and Case Management Committee finds that good

cause for the transfer does not exist, it may return the case to the transferring judge.

(2) Where the existence of related cases in this court is revealed after the cases are assigned, the judge having the later-numbered case may transfer that case to the Calendar and Case Management Committee for reassignment to the judge having the earlier case. If the Calendar and Case Management Committee finds that good cause exists for the transfer, it shall assign the case to the judge having the earlier case. If the Calendar and Case Management Committee finds that good cause for the transfer does not exist, it may return the case to the transferring judge.

(3) Where a party objects to a designation that cases are related pursuant to subparagraphs (b)(1) or (b)(2) of this Rule, the matter shall be determined by the judge to whom the case is assigned.

(d) Motions to Consolidate. Motions to consolidate cases assigned to different judges of this court shall be heard and determined by the judge to whom the earlier-numbered case is assigned. If the motion is granted, the later-numbered case shall be reassigned in accordance with section (c) of this Rule.

(e) Referrals to a Single Judge by the Calendar and Case Management Committee. Upon a finding by the Calendar and Case Management Committee that two or more cases assigned to different judges should be referred for a specific purpose to one judge in order to avoid a duplication of judicial effort, the Calendar and Case Management Committee may enter such an order of referral. The order shall be with the consent of the judge to whom the cases will be referred and shall set forth the scope of authority of said judge. Unless otherwise provided, such an order shall not transfer any cases nor affect the assignment of future cases.

[Effective August 1, 1999. Amended effective May 31, 2002; March 2008; December 1, 2009.]

Comment

COMMENT TO LCvR 40.5(c)(3): The Court has eliminated the provision in this Rule that permitted a party to appeal to the Calendar and Case Management Committee an individual judge's decision with respect to whether cases are related because the Court does not believe it is appropriate for a party to be able to seek review of a decision of one judge of this Court by three of that judge's co-equal colleagues. As amended, the Rule would make the individual judge's decision final.

LCvR 40.6 OTHER TRANSFERS AND REASSIGNMENTS

(a) Transfers by Consent. A judge, upon written advice to the Calendar and Case Management Committee, may transfer directly all or part of any case on the judge's docket to any consenting judge.

(b) Death, Retirement, Appointment of New Judges, etc. When reassignments are necessitated by the death, retirement, resignation or incapacity of any judge or by the appointment of a new judge, or by any other circumstances, the Calendar and Case Management Committee shall determine and indicate by order the method by which such reassignments shall be made.

(c) Reassignment of Criminal Cases. If the Calendar and Case Management Committee, giving due consideration to LCrR 45.1 of these Rules, determines in its discretion that the interests of justice require the transfer of any criminal case from one judge to another, it may reassign the case.

(d) Calendar and Case Management Committee Calendar. Any criminal case in which the only defendant is a fugitive or is mentally incompetent to stand trial shall be assigned to the Calendar and Case Management Committee by the judge upon whose calendar it appears after the case has been pending for 90 days or more. In cases involving two or more defendants, in the event that one or more are fugitives or are mentally incompetent to stand trial, the case may go to trial as to those defendants who are not fugitives and are not mentally incompetent to stand trial. Upon the entry of a final judgment as to such defendants, the case shall be assigned to the Calendar and Case Management Committee for further action as to those defendants who are fugitives or mentally incompetent to stand trial. Additionally, the case of any criminal defendant who becomes a fugitive subsequent to a guilty plea but prior to sentencing shall be assigned to the Calendar and Case Management Committee by the judge upon whose calendar the case appeared after such a fugitive has been an absconder for 90 days or more. The Calendar and Case Management Committee may assign one or more judges for the purpose of making a periodic call of such cases. The judge or judges so assigned shall from time to time consult with the United States Attorney to ascertain whether dismissals of particular criminal actions or civil commitment of defendants incompetent to stand trial shall be deemed advisable. If the reasons which made a case untriable cease to exist, the case shall be reassigned for trial to the transferring judge.

(e) Transfers Not Provided for by Other Rules. Calendar. If a case is transferred to the Calendar and Case Management Committee for any reason not otherwise provided for in this title, and the Calendar and Case Management Committee approves the transfer, it shall cause the case to be reassigned by random lot or otherwise as these Rules provide.

[Effective August 1, 1999. Amended March 2008.]

LCvR 40.7 DUTIES OF THE CHIEF JUDGE

In addition to the trial of such cases as he/she may undertake and other duties provided by these Rules, the Chief Judge shall:

(a) preside at the assignment of criminal cases;

(b) hear and determine requests for excuse from service on grand and petit juries;

(c) empanel the grand jury and hear and determine all matters relating to proceedings before the grand jury;

(d) receive indictments from the grand jury;

(e) consider application for allowance under the Criminal Justice Act in a case not already assigned;

(f) dispose of matters requiring immediate action in criminal cases already assigned to any judge of the Court if that judge is unavailable or otherwise unable to hear the matters;

(g) hear and determine requests for review of rulings by magistrate judges in criminal cases not already assigned to a judge of the Court; and

(h) take such other administrative actions, after consultation with appropriate committees of the Court, as in his/her judgment are necessary to assure the just, speedy and inexpensive determination of cases, and are not inconsistent with these Rules.

The Chief Judge may, from time to time, reassign any of the foregoing duties to an active judge for a reasonable period.

[Effective August 1, 1999.]

LCvR 40.8 MOTIONS JUDGE

(a) Assignment by Rotation. The active judges of this court except the Chief Judge shall be assigned in rotation according to seniority to serve one month as Motions Judge. Part or all of the Motions Judge assignment may be discharged by a volunteer senior judge designated by the Chief Judge.

(b) Matters Heard by Motions Judge. The Motions Judge shall hear and determine the following matters:

(1) Any petition, application or other proceeding of a civil nature which is not assigned to a judge of this court;

(2) Matters requiring action by a District Court Judge in bankruptcy cases, except that appeals from decisions of the Bankruptcy Judge shall be randomly assigned;

(3) Matters requiring immediate action in civil cases already assigned to a judge of the court, if that judge is absent or indicates that he or she is unavailable or otherwise unable to hear the matter;

(4) Naturalization proceedings; and

(5) Proceedings for admissions to the Bar of this court.

(c) Extended Proceedings in Matters Assigned to the Motions Judge. A judge who first takes a matter described in paragraph (b)(1) of this Rule may decide to retain all further proceedings in the same matter, and in this event the judge shall promptly so advise the Calendar and Case Management Committee. If the judge determines at the outset that the matter appears to require a substantial investment of judicial time and the judge decides not to retain it for all further proceedings, the judge shall promptly so advise the Calendar and Case Management Committee for reassignment by lot.

[Effective August 1, 1999. Amended March 2008.]

LCvR 40.9 SANCTIONS IMPOSED

(a) Court Officers and Employees. The Clerk or his/her designee may respond to or describe, in general terms, the process of creating case assignment decks for the automated case assignment system. In addition, the Clerk or his/her designee is also authorized to reveal the name of a judge assigned a case and the procedure by which the assignment was made. No employee of the court may reveal to any other person, other than members of the Calendar and Case Management Committee and the Chief Judge, any list that may show the composition of any deck. No court employee may number or assign any case other than in the manner provided in these rules or in the manner ordered by the Calendar and Case Management Committee. An employee who violates this provision shall be subject to discharge from service.

(b) Third Parties. No person shall directly or indirectly cause, or procure, or attempt to cause or procure, a court officer or employee to reveal to any person, other than the members of the Calendar and Case Management Committee, the sequence of the judges' names within each block of assignment cards, or to number or assign any case otherwise than herein provided or as ordered by the Calendar and Case Management Committee. A violation of this Rule may be punished as a contempt of court.

[Effective August 1, 1999. Amended January 15, 2002; March 2008.]

Comment

COMMENT TO LCvR 40.9(a): This amendment provides the Clerk's Office with sufficient latitude to generally discuss the creation of the case assignment decks. Further, it permits the Chief Judge to be apprised of the composition of any deck.

LCvR 40.10 COMPLAINTS AGAINST JUDGES

The Judicial Conduct and Disability Act of 1980, 28 U.S.C. § 372(c), authorizes that complaints against United States circuit, district, bankruptcy, and magistrate judges who have "engaged in conduct prejudicial to the effective, and expeditious administration of the business of the courts" or who are "unable to discharge all the duties of office by reason of mental or physical disability" may be submitted to a judicial committee for review.

Written complaints may be filed with the Clerk of the United States Court of Appeals for the District of Columbia Circuit, 333 Constitution Avenue, N.W., Room 5409, Washington, D.C. 20001.

[Effective August 1, 1999.]

LCvR 47.1 JURY

(a) Selection and Assignment. Grand and petit jurors shall be selected at random in accordance with a plan adopted by the court and available from the Jury Office. Petit jurors shall be assigned to a single jury pool and reassigned for service upon the requisition of each trial judge.

(b) Notification of Settlement in Civil Jury Cases. Whenever any civil action scheduled for jury trial is settled or otherwise resolved by the parties after the final pretrial conference, counsel shall notify the Clerk of the resolution of the action promptly and no later than one business day prior to the day on which the trial is scheduled to commence. In the event that the action is resolved by the parties less than one business day prior to the scheduled trial date, counsel shall notify the Clerk as soon as practicable after resolution of the action. The court may assess against the settling parties any juror costs incurred if the parties fail to provide notification as set forth in this Rule, unless good cause for such failure is shown. Any such costs shall be assessed equally among the settling parties unless otherwise ordered by the Court.

[Effective August 1, 1999.]

Comment

COMMENT TO LCvR 47.1: This Rule is intended to address situations where the parties resolve a civil action shortly before a scheduled jury trial. While the court encourages the settlement of cases, budgetary constraints require that increased attention be paid to jury utilization practices. This Rule requires the parties to notify the Clerk of any resolution as soon as possible in order to avoid the unnecessary cost to the court as well as the inconvenience to jurors that result when jurors are required to appear for a case that will not go forward as scheduled. To the extent available, the Clerk in this situation should be the Deputy Clerk assigned to the presiding judge. The Rule authorizes the court to assess juror costs against the parties for a violation of the Rule.

LCvR 47.2 COMMUNICATION WITH A JUROR

(a) During Trial. No party, attorney for a party, or person acting on behalf of a party or attorney, shall communicate directly or indirectly with a juror or an excused juror or a member of a juror's, or an excused juror's family during the trial.

(b) After Trial. After a verdict is rendered or a mistrial is declared but before the jury is discharged, an attorney or party may request leave of court to speak with members of the jury after their discharge. Upon receiving such a request, the court shall inform the jury that no juror is required to speak to anyone but that a juror may do so if the juror wishes. If no request to speak with jurors is made before discharge of the jury, no party or attorney shall speak with a juror concerning the case except when permitted by the court for good cause shown in writing. The court may grant permission to speak with a juror upon such conditions as it deems appropriate, including but not limited to a requirement that the juror be examined only in the presence of the court.

[Effective August 1, 1999.]

Comment

COMMENT TO LCvR 47.2: This Rule gives the court greater flexibility by stating that where the request to converse with jurors is made after their discharge, the court may impose such conditions as it deems appropriate.

LCvR 53.1 EXPENSES OF A MASTER

In each order referring a matter to a special master pursuant to Rule 53 of the Federal Rules of Civil Procedure, the court shall direct the allocation of costs among the parties.

[Effective August 1, 1999.]

LCvR 54.1 TAXATION OF COSTS

(a) Bill of Costs. Costs shall be taxed as provided in Rule 54(d), Federal Rules of Civil Procedure. A prevailing party may serve and file a bill of costs which shall include all costs the party seeks to have taxed. This bill of costs shall specifically designate which costs fall within paragraph (d) of this Rule. A bill of costs must be filed within 21 days after entry of judgment terminating the case as to the party seeking costs, unless the time is extended by the court. Any cost omitted from the bill of costs shall not be allowed, except for post-judgment costs.

(b) Opposition to the Bill of Costs. A party from whom costs are sought may file an opposition to the bill of costs within 14 days after service of the bill. The opposition shall identify each item objected to, and the grounds for the objection. If no objection is filed, the Clerk shall tax those costs specified in the bill which are permitted by paragraph (d) of this Rule.

(c) Taxation of Costs by the Clerk. The Clerk shall tax costs after the judgment has become final or at such earlier time as the parties may agree or the court may order. A judgment is final when the time for appeal has expired and no appeal has been taken, or when the court of appeals issues its mandate.

(d) Costs Taxable by the Clerk. When requested to do so in the bill of costs, the Clerk shall tax the following costs:

(1) Clerk's fees;

(2) costs of service of summons and complaint;

(3) Marshal's fees and expenses specified in 28 U.S.C. § 1921;

(4) docket fees and costs specified in 28 U.S.C. § 1923;

(5) the cost of a bond or other security furnished by reason of a statute, court order or rule;

(6) the costs, at the reporter's standard rate, of the original and one copy of any deposition noticed by the prevailing party, and of one copy of any deposition noticed by any other party, if the deposition was used on the record, at a hearing or trial;

(7) the cost, at the reporter's standard rate, of the original and one copy of the reporter's transcript of a hearing or trial if the transcript: (i) is alleged by the prevailing party to have been necessary for the determination of an appeal within the meaning of Rule 39(e), Federal Rules of Appellate Procedure, or (ii) was required by the court to be transcribed;

(8) costs of copying those exhibits which are introduced into evidence, are used for impeachment, or are filed with the Clerk;

(9) other costs of copying up to $300.00;

(10) witness fees pursuant to 28 U.S.C. § 1821(b), and travel and subsistence costs pursuant to 28 U.S.C. § 1821(c), paid to each witness who testified at a hearing or trial;

(11) costs of service of a subpoena on a witness who testified at a deposition, hearing or trial;

(12) fees of court-appointed experts, fees of interpreters used at a trial or hearing, and fees and expenses of special interpretation services under 28 U.S.C. § 1828; and

(13) any costs of the kind enumerated in this Rule which were incurred in the District of Columbia courts prior to removal which are recoverable under the rules of the District of Columbia Court of Appeals and the Superior Court of the District of Columbia;

(14) costs as shown on the mandate of the court of appeals.

(e) Motion to Retax. A review of the decision of the Clerk in the taxation of costs may be taken to the court on motion to retax by any party in accordance with Rule 54(d), Federal Rules of Civil Procedure. The court, on a motion to retax, for good cause shown may tax additional costs or may deny costs allowed by the Clerk pursuant to Section (d). A motion to retax shall specify the ruling of the Clerk excepted to and no other costs will be considered, except that the opposing party may, within 14 days of service of the motion to retax, file an opposition and/or a cross-motion to retax.

(f) Costs and Attorneys Fees. In a case in which the court has, at the time of the entry of final judgment, entered an order pursuant to LCvR 54.2(a), and in which a party wishes to present its claim for costs at the same time as its claim for attorneys' fees under LCvR 54.2, the requirements of this Rule shall not apply.

[Effective August 1, 1999. Amended effective December 1, 2009.]

LCvR 54.2 DETERMINATION OF ATTORNEYS FEES

(a) Post-Judgment Conference. In any case in which a party may be entitled to an attorney's fee from another party, the court may, at the time of entry of final judgment, enter an order directing the parties to confer and to attempt to reach agreement on fee issues. The order shall provide an extension of time for filing a motion under Rule 54(d)(2)(B). Such an order shall also set a status conference, ordinarily not more than 60 days thereafter, at which the court will (1) determine whether settlement of any and or all aspects of the fee matter has been reached, (2) enter judgment for any fee on which agreement has been reached, (3) make the determination required by paragraph (b) of this Rule, and (4) set an appropriate schedule for completion of the fee litigation. If the court does not enter an order and schedule a status conference pursuant to this Rule, the parties are to proceed with motions for attorneys fees pursuant to Rule 54(d)(2), Federal Rules of Civil Procedure.

(b) Determination of Attorneys Fees Pending Appeal. If a status conference described in paragraph (a) is held, the court shall ascertain whether an appeal is being taken by either party, and if so, whether the appeal is on all or fewer than all issues. If a party has not finally decided whether to appeal, the court may allow the party reasonable additional time to reach such a decision. After a decision has been made that there will be an appeal, the court shall make a specific determination as to whether, in the interest of justice, the fee issues, in whole or in part, should be considered or be held in abeyance pending the outcome of the appeal.

(c) Interim Awards. Nothing in this Rule precludes interim applications for attorneys fees prior to final judgment, nor does this Rule apply to attorneys fees sought as sanctions under Rules 11, 16, 26, or 27, Federal Rules of Civil Procedure.

[Effective August 1, 1999.]

LCvR 56.1 MOTIONS FOR SUMMARY JUDGMENT

[Effective August 1, 1999. Amended effective October 12, 2006; deleted effective September 8, 2008.]

Comment

COMMENT TO LCvR 56.1: This rule is deleted as it repeats verbatim current LCvR 7(h).

LCvR 65.1 TEMPORARY RESTRAINING ORDERS AND PRELIMINARY INJUNCTIONS

(a) Applications for Temporary Restraining Orders. An application for a temporary restraining order shall be made in a motion separate from the complaint. The application shall be accompanied by a certificate of counsel, or other proof satisfactory to the court, stating (1) that actual notice of the time of making the application, and copies of all pleadings and papers filed in the action to date or to be presented to the court at the hearing, have been furnished to the adverse party; or (2) the efforts made by the applicant to give such notice and furnish such copies. Except in an emergency, the court will not consider an ex parte application for a temporary restraining order.

(b) Emergency Applications Outside Business Hours. If an application for a temporary restraining order is to be made to a judge outside regular business hours, the party seeking relief shall, if possible, notify the Clerk of such a forthcoming application during business hours so that proper arrangements can be made to handle the matter. If notice is not given to the Clerk as provided herein, the party shall file with its application an affidavit stating why such notice was not given. The court may decline to hear an application on an emergency basis if the affidavit fails to state sufficient reason for failure to give notice as provided herein.

(c) Applications for Preliminary Injunctions. An application for a preliminary injunction shall be made in a document separate from the complaint. The application shall be supported by all affidavits on which the plaintiff intends to rely. The opposition shall be served and filed within seven days after service of the application for preliminary injunction, and shall be accompanied by all affidavits on which the defendant intends to rely. Supplemental affidavits either to the application or the opposition may be filed only with permission of the court.

(d) Hearings on Applications for Preliminary Injunction. On request of the moving party together with a statement of the facts which make expedition essential, a hearing on an application for preliminary injunction shall be set by the court no later than 21 days after its filing, unless the court earlier decides the motion on the papers or makes a finding that a later hearing date will not prejudice the parties. The practice in this jurisdiction is to decide preliminary injunction motions without live testimony where possible. Accordingly, any party who wishes to offer live testimony or cross-examine an affiant at the hearing shall so request in writing 72 hours before the hearing and shall provide the court and all other parties a list of the witnesses to be examined and an estimate of the time required. The court may decline to hear witnesses at the hearing where the need for live testimony is outweighed by considerations of undue delay, waste of time, or needless presentation of cumulative evidence. If practicable, the court shall notify all parties of its ruling on the request to adduce live testimony one business day before the hearing.

[Effective August 1, 1999. Amended effective December 1, 2009.]

Comment

COMMENT TO LCvR 65.1: Paragraph (a), is applicable to temporary restraining orders. Paragraph (b) is designed to prevent "judge-shopping" by making application to the Emergency Judge rather than to a judge chosen at random through the Clerk's normal procedures. The Committee believes that a rule is needed to regulate the use of affidavits and live testimony on applications for preliminary injunctions and to entitle the applicant to a prompt hearing where necessary. The grounds for exclusion of live testimony are taken from Rule 403, Federal Rules of Evidence.

LCvR 65.1.1 BONDS AND SURETIES

Any bond or undertaking required in a proceeding must be set by an order or by consent. The bond or undertaking may be in the form of a surety, cash or check. A surety holding authority from the Secretary of the Treasury to do business in the District of Columbia and having an agent for service of process therein may be approved by the Clerk and filed. In all other cases, the person seeking approval of the bond shall serve on all parties to be secured two days written notice of the application, stating the name and address of the surety. Court approval is required. No officer of the court or member of the bar in active practice will be accepted as a surety.

[Effective August 1, 1999.]

LCvR 67.1 COURT REGISTRY INVESTMENT SYSTEM

The following procedure shall govern deposits into the registry of the Court in all civil actions.

(a) Receipt of Funds.

(1) Unless the statute requires the deposit of funds without leave of Court, no money shall be sent to the court or its officers for deposit into the Court's registry without a court order signed by the presiding Judge in the case or proceeding.

(2) Unless provided for elsewhere in this Rule, all money ordered to be paid into the Court or received by its officers in any case pending or adjudicated shall be deposited with the Treasurer of the United States in the name and to the credit of this Court pursuant to 28 U.S.C. 2041 through depositaries designated by the Treasury to accept such deposit on its behalf.

(3) The party making the deposit or transferring funds to the court's registry shall serve the order permitting the deposit or transfer on the Clerk.

(b) Investment of Registry Funds.

(1) All funds deposited into the registry of the court will be placed in some form of interest bearing account. Unless otherwise ordered, the Court Registry Investment System (CRIS), administered through the United States District Court for the Southern District of Texas, shall be the investment mechanism authorized.

(2) Under CRIS, monies deposited in each case under (a)(1) will be "pooled" together with those on deposit with the Treasury to the credit of other courts in the Court Registry Investment System and used to purchase Treasury Securities which will be held at the Federal Reserve Bank of the Dallas/Houston Branch, in a Safekeeping account in the name and to the credit of the Clerk, United States Court for the Southern District of Texas, hereby designated custodian for the Court Registry Investment System.

(3) An account for each case will be established in the CRIS titled in the name of the case giving rise to the investment in the system. Income received from fund investments will be distributed to each case based on the ratio each account's principal and income has to the aggregate principal and income total in the fund each week. Weekly reports showing the income earned and the principal amounts contributed in each case will be prepared and distributed to each court participating in CRIS and made available to litigants and/or their counsel.

(c) Registry Investment Fee.

(1) The custodian is authorized and directed by this Rule to deduct, for maintaining accounts in the Fund, a fee equal to 10% of the income earned.

(2) No additional fee shall be assessed with respect to investments for which a fee has already been deducted prior to the establishment of CRIS in this district.

[Effective August 1, 1999.]

LCvR 72.1 DUTIES AND POWERS OF MAGISTRATE JUDGES

(a) General Duties. The United States Magistrate Judges appointed by this Court pursuant to 28 U.S.C. § 631 shall have the duty and the power to:

(1) Administer oaths and affirmations and take acknowledgments, affidavits and depositions.

(2) Order the return or the forfeiture of collateral or surety bonds.

(3) Issue subpoenas, writs of *habeas corpus ad testificandum*, or *habeas corpus ad prosequendum*, or other orders necessary to obtain the presence of parties or witnesses or evidence needed for court proceedings.

(4) Supervise proceedings conducted pursuant to letters rogatory in accordance with 28 U.S.C. § 1782.

(5) Conduct proceedings and enter orders as described in LCvR 73.1.

(6) Conduct hearings and enter orders regarding persons believed to be mentally ill found in certain federal reservations, in accordance with 21 D.C. Code §§ 901 909.

(7) Consider petitions by adopted persons to open adoption records of the Court.

(b) Powers Exercised at the Request of a District Judge. At the request of the district judge to whom the case is assigned, a magistrate judge shall have the duty and power to:

(1) Conduct proceedings and enter orders or recommendations as described in LCvR 72.2 and LCvR 72.3 of these Rules.

(2) Enter scheduling orders and exercise other powers provided in Rules 16 and 26(f), Federal Rules of Civil Procedure, and LCvR 16.4 and LCvR 16.5 of these Rules.

(3) Serve as a special master in civil actions pursuant to Rule 53, Federal Rules of Civil Procedure.

(4) Conduct voir dire and select petit juries in civil cases with the consent of the parties.

(5) Accept petit jury verdicts in civil cases in the absence of a district judge.

(6) Conduct examinations of judgment debtors and other persons in accordance with Rule 69, Federal Rules of Civil Procedure.

(7) Perform any additional duty not inconsistent with the Constitution and laws of the United States.

[Effective August 1, 1999. Amended effective April 10, 2007.]

Comment

COMMENT TO LCvR 72.1: The Rule has been revised to remove any references to criminal procedure. Section (a)(7) has been added to preserve the responsibility that was originally located in Section 8(B) of the Civil Justice Expense and Delay Reduction Plan, which has been eliminated. Section (b)(7) has been moved from section (a) to make clear that the stated duties may be performed only at the request of a district judge.

LCvR 72.2 REFERRAL OF MOTIONS AND PRETRIAL MATTERS TO MAGISTRATE JUDGES

(a) Matters Determinable by a Magistrate Judge. At the request of the district judge to whom the case is assigned, a magistrate judge may hear and determine any pretrial motion or matter other than those specified in LCvR 72.3 of these Rules, and may conduct proceedings and enter orders pursuant to LCvR 16.4 of these Rules.

(b) Objections to Magistrate Judge's Ruling. Any party may file written objections to a magistrate judge's ruling under paragraph (a) within 14 days after being served with the order of the magistrate judge, unless a different time is prescribed by the magistrate judge or the district judge. The objections shall specifically designate the order or part thereof to which objection is made, and the basis for the objection. The filing of oppositions and replies shall be governed by LCvR 7(b) and (d).

(c) Determination of Objections. Upon consideration of objections filed in accordance with this Rule, a district judge may modify or set aside any portion of a magistrate judge's order under this Rule found to be clearly erroneous or contrary to law. A district judge may modify or set aside any portion of a magistrate judge's order pursuant to LCvR 16.5 of these Rules whenever the district judge deems such a modification necessary or appropriate.

[Effective August 1, 1999. Amended effective April 10, 2007; December 1, 2009.]

Comment

COMMENT TO LCvR 72.2: The Rule is intended to make clear that objections to the magistrate judge's proposed findings and recommendations should not be called motions for reconsideration and are to be directed to the district judge.

LCvR 72.3. REFERRAL OF MATTERS FOR REPORT AND RECOMMENDATION BY MAGISTRATE JUDGES

(a) Matters Referable to a Magistrate Judge for Report and Recommendation. At the request of the district judge to whom the case is assigned, a magistrate judge may conduct hearings, including evidentiary hearings, and submit to the district judge proposed findings of fact and recommendations for the disposition of:

(1) prisoner petitions challenging conditions of confinement;

(2) motions for injunctive relief (including temporary restraining orders and preliminary injunctions);

(3) motions for judgment on the pleadings, for summary judgment, to dismiss or to permit maintenance of a class action, to dismiss for failure to state a claim upon which relief can be granted, or otherwise to dismiss an action involuntarily;

(4) motions to set aside default judgments;

(5) petitions for judicial review of administrative determinations; and

(6) petitions for civil commitment arising under Title III of the Narcotic Addict Rehabilitation Act of 1966, 18 U.S.C. § 4251, et. seq.

(b) Objections to Recommendations of the Magistrate Judge. Any party may file for consideration by the district judge written objections to the magistrate judge's proposed findings and recommendations issued under paragraph (a) within 14 days after being served with a copy thereof. The objections shall be denominated "Objections to the Magistrate Judge's Proposed Findings and Recommendations." The objections shall specifically identify the portions of the proposed findings and recommendations to which objection is made and the basis for the objection. The filing of oppositions and replies shall be governed by LCvR 7(b) and (d).

Failure to file timely objections may waive appellate review of a District Court order adopting the magistrate judge's report. All magistrate judge's reports shall contain a notice substantially as follows:

> Failure to file timely objections to the findings and recommendations set forth in this report may waive your right of appeal from an order of the District Court adopting such findings and recommendations. See *Thomas v. Arn*, 474 U.S. 140 (1985).

(c) Determination by the Court. A district judge shall make a *de novo* determination of those portions of a magistrate judge's findings and recommendations to which objection is made as provided in paragraph (b). A district judge may make a determination based solely on the record developed before the magistrate judge, or may conduct a new hearing, receive further evidence, and recall witnesses. A district judge may accept, reject, or modify, in whole or in part, the findings and recommendations of the magistrate judge, or may recommit the matter to the magistrate judge with instructions.

[Effective August 1, 1999. Amended effective April 10, 2007; December 1, 2009.]

Comment

COMMENT TO LCvR 72.3: The Rule has been revised to remove any references to criminal procedure. Moreover, the Rule is intended to make clear that objections to the magistrate judge's proposed findings and recommendations should not be called motions for reconsideration and are to be directed to the district judge.

LCvR 73.1 REFERRAL OF CIVIL CASES TO MAGISTRATE JUDGES FOR ALL PURPOSES

(a) Consent to Assignment. By consent of all parties, a magistrate judge may conduct any and all proceedings in a civil case, including trials (with or without a jury), and may thereafter order entry of judgment, in accordance with 28 U.S.C. § 636(c).

(b) Procedure for Consent. The Clerk shall notify the parties of their voluntary right to consent to assignment of a civil case to a magistrate judge as soon as practicable after the action is filed. If the parties consent to such an assignment, a notice of consent signed by the parties or their attorneys shall be filed with the Clerk. The notice of consent should be filed prior to entry of a pretrial order under LCvR 16.5 of these Rules. Thereafter, either the district judge or the magistrate judge may again advise the parties of the availability of the magistrate judge, but in so doing, shall also advise the parties that they are free to withhold consent without adverse substantive consequences.

(c) Appeal to the United States Court of Appeals. An appeal from a judgment of a magistrate judge, entered in proceedings under this Rule, shall be taken to the United States Court of Appeals for the District of Columbia Circuit, in the same manner as an appeal from any other judgment of the district court in a civil case.

[Effective August 1, 1999. Amended effective April 10, 2007.]

Comment

COMMENT TO LCvR 73.1: The Rule has been amended to make clear that if all parties consent to the assignment to a magistrate judge, then the district judge need not formally approve that decision.

LCvR 77.1 CLERK'S OFFICE

The Clerk's Office shall remain open for the transaction of business from 9:00 A.M. until 4:30 P.M. daily except Saturdays, Sundays and legal holidays. Papers, except for sealed material, that must be filed on a given date may be delivered after 4:30 P.M. to the security desk at the Third Street entrance to the courthouse. Papers found to be in compliance with these Rules will be filed as of the date they were delivered to the security desk. Documents that are being filed under seal pursuant to a protective order must be filed in the Clerk's Office during business hours because the Security Officers are not authorized to accept this material.

[Effective August 1, 1999.]

LCvR 78.1 ORAL HEARINGS

A party may in a motion or opposition request an oral hearing, but its allowance shall be within the discretion of the court. If at the time of the hearing the moving party fails to appear, the court may treat the motion as withdrawn; if the opposing party fails to appear, the court may treat the motion as conceded.

[Effective August 1, 1999.]

LCvR 79.1 CUSTODY AND REMOVAL OF RECORDS

Removal of Records. No original paper, document or record in any case shall be removed from its place of filing or custody, except under the following conditions:

(a) The Clerk or one of the Clerk's deputies, any attorney or party to the case, or any person designated by a judge, may remove any paper, document or record, when required or ordered for use before a judge or a person to whom the case has been referred for consideration, for the use required or ordered.

(b) No paper, document or record shall be taken from the courthouse by any person other than the Clerk or one of the Clerk's deputies except by permission of the court.

(c) Where a paper, document or record is removed by a person other than the Clerk or one of the Clerk's deputies, a receipt shall be given to the Clerk.

(d) Any person removing a record shall return it immediately upon completion of the purpose for which it was removed.

[Effective August 1, 1999.]

LCvR 79.2 CUSTODY OF EXHIBITS IN CIVIL CASES

All exhibits offered by a party in a civil proceeding whether or not received as evidence, shall be retained after trial by the party or the attorney offering the exhibit, unless otherwise ordered by the court. In the event an appeal is prosecuted, each party to the action in this court, upon notification from the Clerk that the record is to be transmitted and upon request of a party to the appeal, shall file with the Clerk any exhibits to be transmitted as part of the record on appeal. Those exhibits not transmitted as part of the record on appeal shall be retained by the parties, who shall make them available for use by the appellate court upon request. Within thirty days after final disposition of the case by the appellate court, the exhibits shall be removed by the parties who offered them. If any party, having received notice from the Clerk to remove exhibit as provided herein, fails to do so within thirty days of the date of such notice, the

Clerk may destroy or otherwise dispose of those exhibits.

[Effective August 1, 1999. Amended effective December 1, 2009.]

LCvR 83.1 PHOTOGRAPH, TAPE RECORDING, BROADCASTING IN THE COURTHOUSE

The taking of photographs and operation of tape recorders inside the United States Courthouse and radio or television broadcasting from inside the courthouse during the progress of or in connection with judicial proceedings, including proceedings before a United States Magistrate Judge, whether or not court is actually in session, are prohibited. A judge may, however, permit (1) the use of electronic or photographic means for the presentation of evidence or the perpetuation of a record, (2) the broadcasting, televising, recording, or photographing of investitive, ceremonial, or naturalization proceedings, and (3) the videotaping or audio taping of educational programs with prior approval of the Chief Judge and under such conditions as he or she may prescribe. The use of the above equipment is permissible within a judge's chambers at the discretion of the judge. Contents of official tapes that are made as part of the record in a case will be treated in the same manner as official stenographic notes.

[Effective August 1, 1999.]

LCvR 83.2 PRACTICE BY ATTORNEYS

(a) Practice by Members of the Bar of This Court. An attorney who is a member in good standing of the Bar of this Court may appear, file papers and practice in this Court, provided that the attorney complies with section (b) of this Rule.

(b) Appearance as Sole or Lead Counsel in a Contested Evidentiary Hearing or Trial on the Merits. Each attorney who acts as sole or lead counsel in any contested evidentiary hearing or trial on the merits, civil or criminal, must have on file with the Clerk's Office a certificate, in a form prescribed by the Clerk, that the attorney

(1) has previously acted as sole or lead counsel in a federal district court or the Superior Court of the District of Columbia or a state trial court of general jurisdiction in a contested jury or bench trial or other contested evidentiary hearing in which testimony was taken in open court and an order or other appealable judgment was entered; or

(2) has participated in a junior capacity in an entire contested jury or bench trial in a federal district court or the Superior Court of the District of Columbia or a state trial court of general jurisdiction; or

(3) has satisfactorily completed a continuing legal education trial advocacy course of at least 30 hours sponsored by the District of Columbia Bar or accredited by a state bar.

(c) Practice by Non-Members of the Bar of This Court.

(1) An attorney who is a member in good standing of the bar of any United States Court or of the highest court of any State, but who is not a member of the Bar of this Court, may file papers in this Court only if such attorney joins of record a member in good standing of the Bar of this Court. All papers submitted by non-members of the Bar of this Court must be signed by such counsel and by a member of the Bar of this Court joined in compliance with this Rule.

(2) Paragraph (1) above is not applicable to an attorney who engages in the practice of law from an office located in the District of Columbia. An attorney who engages in the practice of law from an office located in the District of Columbia must be a member of the District of Columbia Bar and the Bar of this Court to file papers in this Court.

(d) Participation by Non-Members of This Court's Bar in Court Proceedings. An attorney who is not a member of the Bar of this Court may be heard in open court only by permission of the judge to whom the case is assigned. Any attorney seeking to appear pro hac vice must file a motion signed by a sponsoring member of the Bar of this Court, accompanied by a declaration by the non-member that sets forth: (1) the full name of the attorney; (2) the attorney's office address and telephone number; (3) a list of all bars to which the attorney has been admitted; (4) a certification that the attorney either has or has not been disciplined by any bar, and if the attorney has been disciplined by any bar, the circumstances and details of the discipline; (5) the number of times the attorney has been admitted pro hac vice in this Court within the last two years; and (6) whether the attorney, if the attorney engages in the practice of law from an office located in the District of Columbia, is a member of the District of Columbia Bar or has an application for membership pending.

(e) Attorneys Employed by the United States. An attorney who is employed or retained by the United States or one of its agencies may appear, file papers and practice in this court in cases in which the United States or the agency is a party, irrespective of (c) and (d) above.

(f) Attorneys Employed by a State. A State Attorney General or that official's designee, who is a member in good standing of the bar of the highest court in any State or of any United States Court, may appear and represent the State or any agency thereof, irrespective of (c) and (d) above.

(g) Attorneys Representing Indigents. Notwithstanding (c) and (d) above, an attorney who is a member in good standing of the District of Columbia Bar or who is a member in good standing of the bar of any United States Court or of the highest court of any State may appear, file papers and practice in any case handled without a fee on behalf of indigents upon filing a certificate that the attorney is providing representation without compensation.

(h) Entry and Withdrawal of Appearance. Attorneys may enter and withdraw appearances in civil actions as provided in LCvR 83.6 of these Rules, and in criminal actions as provided in LCrR 44.5 of these Rules.

(i) Striking Appearance for Non-Attendance at Court Proceedings. The court may, upon notice and after affording an opportunity to be heard, strike the appearance of any attorney in a particular case for failure, without adequate cause, to attend any hearing, conference or other proceeding. The fact that an attorney's residence or office is located at a place distant from the District of Columbia does not constitute grounds for rescheduling or failing to attend court proceedings.

(j) Certification by Non-Members of the Bar of This Court. An attorney who appears, files papers and practices in this Court pursuant to (e), (f) or (g) above, shall file certification of personal familiarity with the Local Rules of this Court and, as appropriate, the other materials set forth in Rules LCvR 83.8(b) and LCvR 83.9(a) simultaneously with each initial appearance by the attorney before a judge of this Court.

[Effective August 1, 1999. Amended effective December 13, 2000; April 11, 2003.]

Comments

COMMENT TO LCvR 83.2(c)(2): LCvR 83.2(c)(2) has been added to conform the Rules of this Court to the current practice of the District of Columbia Committee on Unauthorized Practice, and to recognize that, as a general matter, attorneys who engage in the practice of law from an office located in the District of Columbia and who file papers in this Court should be a member of the Bar of this Court and the District of Columbia Bar.

COMMENT TO LCvR 83.2(d): The original intent of this rule was that the "submission" by nonmembers of the Bar seeking pro hac vice admission be provided in the form of a declaration or affidavit as is customary in such circumstances. This section has now been amended to clarify the responsibility of non-members of this Court's Bar.

COMMENT TO LCvR 83.2(g): The provision under LCvR 83.10 has been deleted to avoid any confusion between this rule and the deleted rule, and to make clear that attorneys can represent parties pro bono without being approved by the Court.

LCvR 83.3 NUMBER OF COUNSEL

Except by permission of the court only one attorney on each side shall examine a witness, address the court on a question arising in a trial, or address the court or jury in final argument.

[Effective August 1, 1999.]

LCvR 83.4 PRACTICE BY LAW STUDENTS

(a) Activities. A law student certified pursuant to this Rule may:

(1) Enter an appearance in this court in any criminal or civil case if the client on whose behalf the law student is appearing has consented in writing to that appearance, and a "supervising lawyer", as hereinafter defined, has also indicated written approval of that appearance.

(2) Engage in activities on behalf of the client in all ways that a licensed attorney may, under the general supervision of the supervising lawyer; however, a student may make no binding commitments on behalf of a client absent prior client and supervisory approval; and in any matters, including depositions, in which testimony is taken the student must be accompanied by the supervising lawyer. Documents or papers filed with the court must be read, approved, and co-signed by the supervising lawyer.

(3) The court retains the authority to establish exceptions to such activities, and also to limit a student's participation in any individual case.

(b) Student, Program and Supervisor Requirements.

(1) *Student Requirements.* In order to be certified pursuant to this Rule a law student shall:

(i) Be a law student in good standing, enrolled in and attending a law school approved by the American Bar Association;

(ii) Have completed at least four semesters of legal studies, or the equivalent;

(iii) Have knowledge of the Federal Rules of Civil and Criminal Procedure, Evidence, and the Code of Professional Responsibility;

(iv) Be enrolled for credit in a law school clinical program which has been certified by this court;

(v) Be certified by the dean of the law school, or the dean's designee, as being of good character and sufficient legal ability, and as being adequately trained, in accordance with paragraphs (i)-(iv) above, to fulfill the responsibilities as a legal intern to both the client and the court;

(vi) Be certified by this court to practice pursuant to this Rule;

(vii) Neither ask for nor receive any fee or compensation of any kind from the client on whose behalf service is rendered, nor under the Criminal Justice Act, under this Rule; but this shall not prevent a lawyer, legal aid bureau, law school, public defender agency or the government from paying compensation to the eligible law student nor shall it prevent any agency from making such charges for its services as it may otherwise properly require.

(2) *Program Requirements.* The program:

(i) Must be a law school clinical practice program for credit, in which a law student obtains academic and practice advocacy training, utilizing attorneys certified by the dean of the law school for practice supervision;

(ii) Must be certified by this court;

(iii) Must be conducted in such a manner as not to conflict with normal court schedules;

(iv) May accept compensation other than from a client such as Criminal Justice Act (CJA) payments;

(v) Must maintain malpractice insurance for its activities.

(3) *Supervisor Requirements.* The person under whose supervision an eligible law student does any of the things permitted by this Rule shall:

(i) Be a member in good standing of the Bar of this court;

(ii)(a) Have faculty or adjunct faculty status at the responsible law school and be certified by the dean of the law school as being of good character and sufficient legal ability and as being adequately trained to fulfill the responsibilities of a supervisor; or

(b) Be a member of the Bar of this court for at least two years, who after the certification by the dean of the law school as being of good character and adequately trained to fulfill the responsibilities of a supervisor, is determined by the court to be competent to carry out the role of supervising attorney;

(iii) Be certified by this court as a student supervisor;

(iv) Be present with the student at all times in court, and at other proceedings in which testimony is taken;

(v) Co-sign all pleadings or other documents filed with the court;

(vi) Supervise concurrently no more than 10 students carrying clinical practice as their entire academic program, with a proportionate increase in the number of students as their percentage of time devoted to clinical practice may be less;

(vii) Assume full personal professional responsibility for student's guidance in any work undertaken and for the quality of a student's work, and be available for consultation with represented clients;

(viii) Assist and counsel the student in activities mentioned in this Rule, and review such activities with the student, all to the extent required for the proper practical training of the student and the protection of the client;

(ix) Be responsible to supplement oral or written work of the student as necessary to ensure proper representation of the client.

(c) Certification of Student, Program and Supervisor.

(1) *Student.* Certification by the law school dean and approval by the Court shall be filed with the Clerk, and unless it is sooner withdrawn, shall remain in effect until expiration of 18 months;

(i) Certification to appear in a particular case may be withdrawn by the court at any time, in the discretion of the court, and without any showing of cause.

(2) *Program.*

(i) Certification of a program by the court shall be filed with the Clerk and shall remain in effect indefinitely unless withdrawn by the court;

(ii) Certification of a program may be withdrawn by the court at the end of any academic year without cause, or at any time, provided notice stating the cause for such withdrawal is furnished to the law school dean and supervisor.

(3) *Supervisor.*

(i) Certification of a supervisor must be filed with the Clerk, and shall remain in effect indefinitely unless withdrawn by the court;

(ii) Certification of a supervisor may be withdrawn by the court at the end of any academic year without cause, or at any time upon notice and a showing of cause;

(iii) Certification of a supervisor may be withdrawn by the dean by mailing a notice to that effect to the Clerk.

[Effective August 1, 1999.]

LCvR 83.5 PRACTICE BY LAW CLERKS AND COURT EMPLOYEES

Law clerks and secretaries to judges of this court, and all other persons employed in any capacity by this court, shall not engage in the practice of law while so employed. A law clerk or secretary to a particular judge of this court shall not, at any time after separating from that position, engage in any activity as an attorney or advisor, nor permit his or her name to appear as an attorney on any paper filed in this court, in connection with any case that was pending on that judge's docket during his or her term of service. Any other person employed in any capacity by this court shall not, for a period of two years after separating from that position, engage in any activity as an attorney or advisor in connection with any case that was pending in this court during his or her term of service. Each former law clerk, secretary or other employee of this court, as well as persons employing or associating with them in the practice of law before this court, shall have the responsibility of enforcing the provisions of this Rule. Evidence of a failure to comply with this Rule shall be referred to this court's Committee on Grievances.

[Effective August 1, 1999.]

LCvR 83.6 ENTRY AND WITHDRAWAL OF APPEARANCES BY ATTORNEYS IN CIVIL ACTIONS

(a) Entry of Appearance. An attorney eligible to appear may enter an appearance in a civil action by signing any pleading described in Rule 7(a), Federal Rules of Civil Procedure, or by filing a written notice of entry of an appearance listing the attorney's correct address, telephone number and bar identification number.

(b) Withdrawal of Appearance by Notice. If no trial date has been set, an attorney may withdraw an appearance in a civil action by filing a notice of withdrawal signed by the attorney and the party represented, if another attorney has previously entered an appearance on behalf of the party.

(c) Withdrawal of Appearance by Motion. If a trial date has been set, or if a party's written consent is not obtained, or if the party is not represented by another attorney, an attorney may withdraw an appearance for a party only by order of the court upon motion by the attorney served upon all parties to the case. Unless the party is represented by another attorney or the motion is made in open court in the party's presence, a motion to withdraw an appearance shall be accompanied by a certificate of service listing the party's last known address and stating that the attorney has served upon the party a copy of the motion and a notice advising the party to obtain other counsel, or, if the party intends to conduct the case pro se or to object to the withdrawal, to so notify the Clerk in writing within seven days of service of the motion.

(d) Ruling on Motion to Withdraw Appearance. The court may deny an attorney's motion for leave to withdraw if the withdrawal would unduly delay trial of the case, or be unfairly prejudicial to any party, or otherwise not be in the interest of justice. The Clerk shall mail to the affected party a copy of the order granting or denying the motion for leave to withdraw.

[Effective August 1, 1999. Amended effective December 1, 2009.]

Comment

COMMENT TO LCvR 83.6: This Rule requires, as in LCvR 5.1, that an attorney's appearance notice contain the attorney's District of Columbia Bar identification number.

LCvR 83.7 REVIEW OF ORDERS AS TO ADMISSION OR EXCLUSION OF PRACTITIONERS BEFORE THE PATENT OFFICE

A person refused recognition to practice or suspended or excluded from practice before the Patent Office may file a petition in this court against the Commissioner of Patents for review of such action within 30 days after the date of the order recording the Commissioner's action. The Commissioner shall answer the petition within 21 days after receiving service of the summons. Within 14 days after filing of the answer, the petitioner shall file a certified copy of the record and proceedings before the Patent Office, which shall constitute the sole basis for the court's review.

[Effective August 1, 1999. Amended effective December 1, 2009.]

LCvR 83.8 ADMISSION TO THE BAR

(a) Who May Be Admitted. Admission to and continuing membership in the Bar of this Court are limited to attorneys who are (1) active members in good standing in the District of Columbia Bar; or (2) active members in good standing of the highest court of any state in which the attorney maintains his/her principal law office and is a member in good standing of a United States District Court that provides for reciprocal admission to members of the Bar of this Court.

(b) Petition for Admission. Each applicant for admission shall file with the Clerk at least 14 days prior to hearing thereon (unless for good cause shown the judge shall shorten the time) a written petition for admission on a form supplied by the Clerk stating:

(1) applicant's residence and office addresses and office telephone number;

(2) the court where and date when admitted;

(3) applicant's legal training and experience;

(4) whether the applicant has ever been held in contempt of court and, if so, the nature of the contempt and the final disposition thereof;

(5) whether the applicant has ever been convicted of any crime (other than minor traffic offenses) or

publicly reprimanded, publicly censured, suspended, disciplined or disbarred by any court, and, if so, the facts and circumstances connected therewith; and

(6) that the applicant is familiar with:

(i) the provisions of the Judicial Code (Title 28 U.S.C.) which pertain to the jurisdiction of and practice in the United States District Courts;

(ii) the Federal Rules of Civil or Criminal Procedure;

(iii) the Rules of the United States District Court for the District of Columbia;

(iv) the Rules of Professional Conduct as adopted by the District of Columbia Court of Appeals except as otherwise provided by specific rule of this Court, and that he/she will faithfully adhere thereto; and

(v) D.C. Bar Voluntary Standards for Civility in Professional Conduct, adopted by the Bar on June 18, 1996 (attached as Appendix B).

(c) Affidavit of a Member of the Bar. The petition shall be accompanied by an affidavit or declaration of an attorney who is a member in good standing of the Bar of this Court who has known the applicant for at least one year stating when the affiant was admitted to practice in this Court and how long and under what circumstances the attorney has known the applicant and a statement of the applicant's character and experience at the bar. The affidavit shall be on a form supplied by the Clerk.

(d) Hearing on the Petition. The petition for admission shall be placed on the calendar of the Motions Judge and shall be heard on the first Monday of each month. If the first Monday is a holiday, the petition shall be heard on the following Monday. If the petition is granted, the applicant shall take the oath of office.

(e) Oath. The oath which each applicant for admission to the Bar of this Court shall take shall be as follows:

> I do solemnly swear (or affirm) that I will support the Constitution of the United States; that I will respect courts of justice and judicial officers; that I will well and faithfully discharge my duties as an attorney and as an officer of the court; and in the performance of those duties I will conduct myself with dignity and according to both the law and the recognized standards of ethics of our profession.

(f) Admission Fee. Each petition shall be accompanied by payment in such amount and form as determined by the Court, which the Clerk shall deposit to the credit of a fund to be used for such purposes as inure to the benefit of the members of the bench and the Bar in the administration of justice which are determined to be appropriate by the Court from time to time. This fee shall be in addition to the statutory fee for administering the oath of office and issuing the certificate of admission.

(g) Clerk as Agent for Service. By being admitted to the Bar of this Court or by being permitted to practice in this Court under Local Rule 83.2 and 83.12 or in fact practicing in this Court, the attorney shall be deemed to have designated the Clerk of the Court as agent for service of process in any disciplinary proceeding before this Court.

[Effective August 1, 1999. Amended effective December 13, 2000; December 1, 2009.]

Comments

COMMENT TO LCvR 83.8: This Rule clarifies the intention that continuing membership in the Bar is premised on a continuing duty to meet the requirements of this Rule. Section (a) parallels revised LCvR 83.2 regarding practice by attorneys.

COMMENT TO LCvR 83.8(b)(6)(ii): Section (v) was added to LCvR 83.8(b)(6) to stress the importance that the Court places on the need for civility among lawyers who practice in the Court.

LCvR 83.9 RENEWAL OF MEMBERSHIP

(a) Renewal of Membership Every Three Years. Each member of the Bar of this Court shall renew his or her membership every three years by filing with the Clerk of the Court, on or before July 1st of every third year, a certificate in a form prescribed by the Clerk that the member is familiar with the then-current version of the Federal Rules of Civil Procedure, Federal Rules of Evidence, the Local Rules of this Court, Rules of Professional Conduct and the D.C. Bar Voluntary Standards for Civility in Professional Conduct. If the attorney appears in criminal cases, he or she must also certify familiarity with the then-current version of the Federal Rules of Criminal Procedure and the Sentencing Guidelines. (See LCrR 44.5(b)). Members of the Bar of this Court on the effective date of this Rule shall file certificates by March 1, 1990, and by July 1 of every third calendar year thereafter. Subsequently admitted members shall file certificates by July 1st of every third calendar year after the year in which they were admitted. The Clerk shall notify members of this certification requirement at least 60 days before the date for filing such certificates and renewals.

(b) Renewal Fee. Each certificate required by (a) above shall be accompanied by a payment of $25 in a form determined by the Clerk. The fee shall be $10 for the initial certificate filed by any person admitted to the Bar of this Court after July 1, 1986. The Clerk shall deposit the fees received to the credit of the fund described in LCvR 83.8(f) to be used for the purposes specified in that Rule, including the defraying of expenses of maintaining a current register of members in good standing and to administer the counseling program outlined in LCvR 83.21.

(c) Failure to Renew. An attorney who fails to file the required certifications and pay the renewal fee shall be provisionally removed from the list of members in good standing and pursuant to LCrR 44.1(a) shall not be permitted to practice before this Court until restored as a member in good standing. The name of the attorney shall be restored to the list of members in good standing upon filing of the required certificates and payment of the delinquent fee within five years after the due date. At the end of five years from the due date, the name will be permanently removed from the roll, without prejudice to an application for admission as a new member.

[Effective August 1, 1999. Amended effective December 13, 2000; April 11, 2003.]

Comments

COMMENT TO LCvR 83.9(a): This amendment brings the rule in compliance with LcvR 83.8(b)(6)(v).

LCvR 83.10 COURT APPOINTED REPRESENTATION

(a) Attorneys who are members in good standing of the Bar of this Court shall be required to assist or represent the needy in civil matters before this Court whenever requested by the Court and, if necessary, without compensation and to accept appointments under the Criminal Justice Act unless exempted by rule or statute.

(b) [Deleted].

[Effective August 1, 1999. Amended effective April 11, 2003.]

Comment

COMMENT TO LCvR 83.10(b): LCvR 83.10(b) has been deleted to avoid confusion with LCvR 83.2(g), and to make clear that attorneys can represent parties pro bono without being appointed by the courts.

LCvR 83.11 CIVIL PRO BONO PANEL

(a) Attorneys who are members in good standing of the Bar of this Court are required under Rule 83.10(a) to assist or represent the needy in civil matters before this Court whenever requested by the Court, and, if necessary, without compensation. As one way to assist attorneys in meeting this requirement, and in light of the need for attorneys to represent indigent pro se litigants in civil matters before this Court, the Court hereby establishes a Civil Pro Bono Panel ("Panel") of attorneys who are members in good standing of the Bar of this Court and who have agreed to accept pro bono appointments to represent indigent pro se litigants in civil cases before this Court. Members of the Bar of this Court are urged to volunteer to serve on this Panel.

(b) The following procedures shall govern the appointment of attorneys from the Civil Pro Bono Panel to represent pro se parties who are proceeding in forma pauperis in civil actions and cannot obtain counsel by any other means.

(1) *Committee on Pro Se Litigation.* The Chief Judge shall appoint a Committee on Pro Se Litigation, which shall include private practitioners and of government attorneys who are members of the District of Columbia Bar and who practice in this Court, to oversee the Civil Pro Bono Panel established herein and annually report to the Court on the operation of the Panel.

(2) *Civil Pro Bono Panel.*

(i) Attorneys, law firms, and clinical legal education programs ("Clinics") at law schools accredited by the American Bar Association that are willing to accept appointment to represent indigent pro se parties in civil actions may apply to join the Panel. Appropriate forms shall be available from the Clerk of Court ("Clerk"). Each application shall set forth, among other things:

(aa) in the case of a law firm, the name of a member of the firm designated as the Panel Liaison, to whom orders of appointment may be directed; and

(bb) that the individual attorney, Panel Liaison, or supervisor of the Clinic is a member in good standing of the Bar of this Court or is in compliance with Rule 83.10(b) of the Rules of this Court;

(cc) the attorney's prior civil trial experience or trial advocacy training;

(dd) whether the attorney, law firm or Clinic has the ability to consult and advise in languages other than English;

(ee) the number of cases per calendar year the applicant is willing to accept;

(ff) any particular experience or interest in specific types of civil cases to which attorneys from the Panel are most often appointed (e.g. FOIA cases, habeas corpus petitions, social security claims, section 1983 actions, and employment discrimination cases) and any types of civil cases to which the applicant desires not to be assigned.

(ii) Information on an application may be amended at any time by letter to the Clerk. An attorney, law firm or Clinic may by letter withdraw from the Panel at any time.

(3) *Appointment of Counsel.* When leave has been granted pursuant to 28 U.S.C. § 1915 for a pro se litigant to proceed in forma pauperis, the judge to whom the case is assigned may, on application by the pro se party or otherwise, appoint an attorney from the Panel to represent such party. The appointment should be made taking into account:

(i) the nature and complexity of the action;

(ii) the potential merit of the pro se party's claims;

(iii) the demonstrated inability of the pro se party to retain counsel by other means; and

(iv) the degree to which the interests of justice will be served by appointment of counsel, including the benefit the Court may derive from the assistance of the appointed counsel.

(4) *Appointment Procedure.*

(i) The judge shall not direct the appointment of a specific attorney from the Panel but may advise the Clerk to attempt to select an attorney with particular expertise. If service of the summons and complaint has not yet been made, the judge may direct that service be made by the Marshal or by other appropriate method.

(ii) Upon receiving the Appointment Order, the Clerk shall select a member of the Panel. In making the selection, the Clerk shall take into consideration the experience and preferences of Panel members regarding specific types of cases and the equitable distribution of cases among Panel members.

(iii) Before selecting any attorney, the Clerk shall determine whether the litigant has any other case pending before the Court and whether an attorney has been retained or appointed in such case. If so, such retained or appointed counsel shall be contacted by the Clerk and encouraged, but not required, to accept appointment to represent the litigant in the new action. If such counsel declines, the Clerk shall select another attorney in accordance with this Rule.

(iv) The Clerk shall send a copy of the Appointment Order, this Rule, any pleadings, and any relevant correspondence or other documents to the appointed attorney.

(5) *Responsibilities of the Appointed Attorney.*

(i) Upon receiving the Appointment Order, and unless a conflict of interest is apparent from the materials sent by the Clerk under subparagraph (b)(4) above, the appointed attorney shall promptly communicate with the pro se party regarding the action. Such communication shall include exploration of any actual or potential conflicts of interest and whether the dispute could be resolved more appropriately in other forums or by other means.

(ii) After any such consultation with the pro se party, the appointed attorney shall, within 30 days of receiving notice of the appointment or within such additional time permitted by the assigned judge for good cause shown, file either:

(aa) a notice of appearance pursuant to Local Civil Rule 83.6(a); or

(bb) a notice of withdrawal or a motion for withdrawal from the appointment pursuant to paragraph (b)(6) of this Rule.

(iii) If a notice of appearance is filed by the appointed attorney, the appointed attorney shall represent the party in the action from the date he or she files an appearance until (1) he or she has been relieved of the appointment by the Court according to the provisions of this Rule, (2) the case has been dismissed, (3) the case has been transferred to another Court, or (4) a final judgment has been entered in the action by this Court.

(iv) The appointed attorney accepting the appointment shall not be required to represent the client in any other matter.

(v) If an order of appointment has been directed to a participating law firm or Clinic, the action shall remain the responsibility of the firm or of the Clinic, notwithstanding the firm's or the program's assignment of the case to one of its attorneys.

(vi) An attorney appointed under this Rule may, but is not required to, represent the pro se party:

(aa) in any appeal taken either by the pro se party or an opposing party from a final judgment entered by this Court, provided, however, that if the appointed attorney elects not to represent the pro se party on such appeal, he or she shall advise the party of the requirements for filing a notice of appeal or cross-appeal within sufficient time for the party to file such a notice pro se.

(bb) in any proceeding, in any forum, that is related or collateral to the action in this Court or that may ensue upon an order of dismissal or remand of the action in this Court.

(6) *Relief From Appointment.*

(i) An appointed attorney may be relieved of an order of appointment only on the following grounds:

(aa) a conflict of interest precludes the attorney from representing the party in the action; or

(bb) a substantial disagreement exists between the attorney and the party on litigation strategy; or

(cc) in the attorney's opinion, formed after reasonable inquiry, the claim or defense is not well grounded in fact; or is not warranted under existing law and cannot be supported by good faith argument for extension, modification, or reversal of existing law; or the party is proceeding for purposes of harassment or other improper purpose; or

(dd) because of the temporary burden of other professional commitments, the attorney lacks the time necessary to represent the party; or (ee) the client has refused to enter into a reasonable fee agreement pursuant to subparagraphs (b)(9)(i)(aa) or (bb); or

(ff) on such other grounds acceptable to the Court for good cause shown.

(ii) An attorney seeking to be relieved from appointment for the reasons set forth in subparagraph (b)(6)(i)(aa), (bb), or (cc) above shall file a Notice of Withdrawal with the Court, with proof of service on the pro se litigant, stating without identification of reasons, that "grounds for relief from appointment under subparagraph (b)(6)(i)(aa), (bb), or (cc) exist." Such notice will effect withdrawal without any Court action.

(iii) An attorney wishing to be relieved for the reasons set forth in subparagraph (b)(6)(i)(dd) or (ff) shall file a motion for withdrawal setting forth the circumstances constituting cause for withdrawal, with proof of service on the pro se litigant. A motion citing (b)(6)(i)(ee) shall include the fee agreement that the pro se litigant would not accept. This motion shall be filed under seal and shall not be served upon or otherwise made available to the opposing party. A withdrawal on motion will require Court approval, distribution of which shall be given to all parties if the withdrawing attorney had filed a notice of appearance.

(iv) An attorney wishing to be relieved for the reasons set forth in subparagraph (b)(6)(i)(ee) shall file a motion for withdrawal prior to entering an appearance, and shall submit with the motion a copy of the proposed fee agreement which the client has refused to sign.

(v) If an appointed attorney is relieved from an order of appointment, the judge may issue an order directing appointment of another attorney to represent the party, or may issue such other orders as may be deemed appropriate.

(7) *Discharge.*

(i) A party for whom an attorney has been appointed shall be permitted to request the judge to discharge the attorney from the representation and either to appoint another attorney or let the party proceed pro se.

(ii) When such a request is made, the judge shall forthwith issue an order discharging the appointed attorney from further representation of the party in the action and may, in his or her discretion, order appointment of another attorney to undertake the representation pursuant to paragraph (b)(4). Where a party requests discharge of a second appointed attorney, no additional appointments shall ordinarily be made.

(8) *Expenses.*

(i) The Indigent Civil Litigation Fund, Inc. ("Fund") is a private, non-profit organization established to defray some reasonable expenses incurred in the course of representations pursuant to appointments under this Rule. A description of this Fund, its requirements, and application forms for reimbursement are available from the Clerk's Office. Because the Fund's assets are limited, and because no public funds are available to defray expenses, the appointed attorney or the law firm or Clinic with which he or she is affiliated should be prepared to advance the reasonable expenses of the litigation but may seek reimbursement from the Fund.

(ii) The appointed attorney shall not condition the representation upon the client's advancing the cost of the litigation expenses. The appointed attorney may enter into an agreement with the client wherein the client agrees:

(aa) to reimburse the attorney for reasonable litigation expenses from any monetary recovery that may be obtained through the representation, and/or

(bb) to assign to the attorney any amounts awarded to the client as reasonable litigation expenses pursuant to law, including case law, authorizing the award of such expenses.

(iii) For purpose of this Rule, reasonable litigation expenses shall include, but not be limited to, filing fees, witness fees (including consultant and expert witness fees), travel expenses, reproduction and printing costs, computerized legal research, long distance telephone charges and the cost of deposition and trial transcripts. Reasonable litigation expenses shall not include the attorney's normal office and overhead expenses, such as secretarial services and local telephone charges.

(iv) The appointed attorney may waive, at any time, his or her entitlement to reimbursement for expenses under this Rule; such waiver must be in writing.

(9) *Attorney Fees.*

(i) The appointed attorney shall represent the client without receiving a fee, except that in cases where the client may be entitled to recover attorney fees or a monetary award or monetary settlement, the appointed attorney shall advise the client of the possibility of such recovery and may:

(aa) condition the representation on the client's entering into a written agreement assigning to the attorney any amounts recovered by the client as attorney fees pursuant to laws, including case law, authorizing the award of attorney fees; and/or

(bb) propose to the client a contingent fee arrangement providing for the payment of a reasonable fee out of any funds recovered by the client as a result of the representation. A contingent fee arrangement shall provide that the amount of any payment received by the attorney pursuant to an assignment agreement under subparagraph (i) above shall be credited against the client's fee obligations under such a contingent fee arrangement. Any such contingent fee arrangement shall be in writing, executed by both the attorney and the client, and submitted to the Court ex parte for its approval; or

(cc) seek to assist the client in retaining other counsel on a compensated basis, subject to the client's consent to such a change in representation and to the Court's approval of a request for relief from appointment under subparagraph (6)(i)(ff) on the ground that the party no longer requires appointed counsel for the purpose of pursuing claim, but, if the appointed attorney is unable to obtain such other counsel for the client, he or she shall then continue the representation to its conclusion unless relieved by the Court, either without receiving a fee, or pursuant to an assignment or contingent fee arrangement as provided in subparagraphs (i) and (ii) above.

(ii) Any attorney fee agreement permitted under subparagraphs (i)(aa) and (ii) shall be entered into prior to the entry of the attorney's notice of appearance pursuant to paragraph 5(ii).

(iii) In cases in which the applicable statute authorizes the award of attorneys' fees to be paid out of the amounts awarded to the plaintiff, the appointed attorney shall advise the client of the possibility of such an award.

(10) *Training Sessions.* The Committee on Pro Se Litigation shall, in cooperation with the District of Columbia Bar, organize and conduct educational programs to train and advise attorneys on the Panel in the preparation and trial of the most common types of civil actions involving pro se parties brought before this Court.

(11) *Appointment of Non-Panel Attorneys or Legal Organizations.* Nothing in this Rule shall be interpreted as preventing a judge from requesting an attorney, law firm or legal organization that is not on the Panel to represent a litigant who is otherwise proceeding pro se in this Court. In addition, nothing in this Rule shall be interpreted as preventing an attorney who is not a member of the Bar of this Court, but who qualifies under Local Civil Rule 83.2(g) to practice before this Court, from representing an indigent litigant under Local Civil Rule 83.10 subject to the conditions of Local Civil Rule 83.2(g).

[Effective August 1, 1999. Amended effective November 19, 2001; December 1, 2009.]

Comments

COMMENT TO LCvR 83.11: This Rule, promulgated in 1991, created the Court's Civil Pro Bono Panel and an Advisory Committee on Pro Se Litigation to oversee the operation of the Panel. The Rule was amended in 2001 to reflect the Court's experience with appointments from the Panel. Because the Rule applies to cases filed by both prisoners and non-prisoners, no amendments expressly address changes made by the Prison Litigation Reform Act. The Court notes, however, that the calculation of any contingent fee agreement with a prisoner-plaintiff under subparagraph (b)(9)(i)(bb) should be reduced by the amount of any judgment that has been used to pay a portion of attorney fees under 42 U.S.C. § 1997e(d)(2).

The 2001 amendments to LCvR 83.11 were published with the following comments:

COMMENT TO LCvR 83.11(a): This amendment moves material previously in Paragraph (2) reminding lawyers of their obligation to provide representation to the needy in civil matters are requested by the Court and recites the establishment and purposes of the Civil Pro Bono Panel.

COMMENT TO LCvR 83.11(b)(1): This amendment alters the criteria for membership on the Committee on Pro Se Litigation from D.C. Bar members "who practice primarily in federal courts" to members "practicing in this Court."

COMMENT TO LCvR 83.11(b)(2): This amendment consolidates the requirements for membership on the Panel, but the requirements are not substantively changed. Applicants for participation in the Panel will be invited to identify types of cases they do not want, in addition to types of cases they do want.

COMMENT TO LCvR 83.11(b)(3): The amendment consolidates three subsections into one to improve readability. The section retains the requirement that the party be granted leave to proceed in forma pauperis before being appointed counsel from the Panel. In (ii), the provision limiting the Court to only the pleadings in deciding the "merit" of a pro se litigant's case was removed and in (iii) added "demonstrated" to the "inability to pay" criterion.

COMMENT TO LCvR 83.11(b)(4): This amendment changes paragraph (i) to allow a judge to ask the Clerk for the appointment of an attorney with particular expertise, but still does not allow a judge to request a Panel member by name. In addition, the requirement that Panel members be selected randomly was removed from Paragraph (ii) in favor of a more considered approach by the Clerk to allow for a Panel member's preferences and the equitable distribution of cases among Panel members.

COMMENT TO LCvR 83.11(b)(5): This paragraph was rewritten to include in one place all of the responsibilities of appointed counsel, including material that was listed in former paragraphs (5)(v), (5)(vi) and (11). In addition, the amendment clarifies that the responsibility of an attorney to represent the litigant commences when a notice of appearance is filed and continues until the matter is concluded at the District Court or until the attorney is otherwise relieved. The amendment also clarifies that the appointed attorney has no obligation to represent the client in any other case or in an appeal or in any collateral action following a dismissal or remand.

COMMENT TO LCvR 83.11(b)(6): This amendment clarifies the procedures for filing a notice of withdrawal and a motion for withdrawal and adds a provision (i)(ee) permitting withdrawal on motion in the event the appointed attorney and the litigant are unable to come to terms on a contingent fee agreement, pursuant to paragraph (b)(9).

COMMENT TO LCvR 83.11(b)(7): This amendment makes no substantive changes.

COMMENT TO LCvR 83.11(b)(8): This amendment reminds Panel members of the potential for recovery of some expenses under the Indigent Civil Litigation Fund. It also limits reimbursement to reasonable litigation expenses and clarifies what constitutes reasonable litigation expenses.

COMMENT TO LCvR 83.11(b)(9): This amendment allows a Panel member to condition their entry of an appearance upon the client entering into a contingent fee agreement approved by the Court. Because the Rule applies to cases filed by both prisoners and non-prisoners, no amendment expressly addresses changes made by the Prison Litigation Reform Act. However, the calculation of any contingent fee agreement with a prisoner-plaintiff under subparagraph (b)(9)(i)(aa) should be reduced by the amount of any judgment that has been used to pay a portion of attorney fees under 42 U.S.C. § 1997e(d)(2).

COMMENT TO LCvR 83.11(b)(11): This amendment makes no substantive changes, but clarifies that attorneys who are not members of the Bar of this Court may be members of the Panel if they comply with the conditions of Local Civil Rule 83.2(g), involving attorneys representing indigents.

LCvR 83.12 RULES OF DISCIPLINARY ENFORCEMENT

(a) Promulgation of Rules. This Court, in furtherance of its inherent power and responsibility to supervise the conduct of attorneys who are admitted to practice before it under LCvR 83.2 or 83.8 of these Rules, or who are admitted for the purpose of a particular proceeding (pro hac vice), or who otherwise appear before the Court, promulgates the following Rules of Disciplinary Enforcement superseding all of its other Rules pertaining to disciplinary enforcement heretofore promulgated. These Rules shall become effective on May 1, 1987, provided, however, that any formal disciplinary proceeding then pending before this Court shall be concluded under the procedure existing prior to the effective date of these Rules.

(b) Attorneys Subject to Rules. These Rules shall apply to all attorneys admitted to membership in the Bar of this Court, to all attorneys permitted to practice before this Court under LCvR 83.2, and to all attorneys who appear before this Court or who participate in proceedings, whether admitted or not. All attorneys to whom these Rules apply shall be subject to the disciplinary jurisdiction of this Court for any alleged misconduct arising in connection with such proceeding. All such attorneys shall also be deemed thereby to have designated the Clerk of the Court as agent for service of process under these Rules governing discipline and disciplinary proceedings.

[Effective August 1, 1999.]

Comment

COMMENT TO LCvR 83.12: Section (a) incorporates the former Preamble to the Rules of Disciplinary Enforcement. Section (b) was added to make clear that the Court has authority to discipline all attorneys who appear before it, whether admitted or not. Because this Rule is broader in its application than either LCvR 83.2 or 83.8, it restates the provision that all attorneys subject to these Rules shall be deemed to have designated the Clerk of the Court as agent for service of process for purpose of the disciplinary rules.

LCvR 83.13 DISCIPLINARY PANEL

(a) Appointment. The Chief Judge shall appoint three judges of the Court to be known as the Disciplinary Panel and shall appoint two additional judges to serve as alternate members. The Disciplinary Panel shall have jurisdiction over all judicial proceedings involving the disbarment, suspension, censure or other discipline of attorneys subject to these Rules.

(b) Powers of Individual Judges. Nothing contained in these Rules shall be construed to deny to this Court or to any individual judge or United States Magistrate Judge thereof or to the United States Bankruptcy Judge such powers as are necessary for the Court to maintain control over proceedings conducted before it, such as proceedings for contempt under Title 18 of the United States Code or under Rule 42 of the Federal Rules of Criminal Procedure, or to deprive any judge or magistrate judge of his/her inherent power of discipline for conduct committed in the presence of the Court.

[Effective August 1, 1999.]

Comment

COMMENT TO LCvR 83.13: Section (b) makes clear the power of an individual judge, Bankruptcy Judge or Magistrate Judge, to maintain control over proceedings through the contempt power or otherwise to discipline for conduct in the presence of the Court.

LCvR 83.14 COMMITTEE ON GRIEVANCES

(a) Appointment. There shall be established a standing committee appointed by the Court to be known as the Committee on Grievances (the "Committee") consisting of six or more members of the Bar of this Court appointed for terms of three years and until their successors have been appointed. The terms of the members shall be staggered so as to provide continuity. No member of the Committee on Grievances shall serve more than two consecutive terms. The Court shall designate a Chairman of the Committee and a Vice Chairman who shall act in the absence or disability of the Chairman. Members of the Committee shall serve without compensation except that the Court may authorize payments in lieu of expenses from fees collected by the Clerk pursuant to Rule LCvR 83.8(f).

(b) Duties. The Committee shall be charged with receiving, investigating, considering and acting upon complaints against all attorneys subject to these Rules, LCvR 83.12(b) relating to disbarment, suspension, censure, reprimand or other disciplinary action, and petitions for reinstatement of attorneys.

(c) Clerk. The Clerk shall with approval of the Court, appoint a Clerk to the Committee who shall have all powers vested in a Deputy Clerk of the Court. The Clerk to the Committee shall assist the Committee, maintain records of its proceedings, investigations and prosecutions, and proceed as otherwise set forth in these Rules.

(d) Confidentiality and Immunity. All proceedings before the Committee involving allegations of misconduct of an attorney and all documents and charges presented to the Committee shall remain confidential and privileged. All formal charges prepared by the Committee and directed to be filed by the Court, attorney or grievance cases filed with the Clerk of the Court, court orders, and subsequent pleadings, answers or responses filed therein shall be matters of public record.

All meetings and hearings of the Committee shall be held in camera and the business conducted therein shall remain confidential and privileged. The Committee's Chairman or, in the Chairman's absence or disability, the Vice Chairman shall have discretion in determining the manner and extent of cooperating with disciplinary agencies from other jurisdictions. All records and minutes of the Committee shall be maintained under seal and shall not be disclosed except by order or direction of the Chief Judge (or the designee of the Chief Judge).

When exercising the power delegated by the Court, Committee members shall be absolutely immune from suit for any conduct in connection with their duties. Complaints submitted to the Committee on Grievances pursuant to LCvR 83.16 shall be absolutely privileged and no claim or action predicated thereon may be instituted or maintained.

[Effective August 1, 1999.]

Comment

COMMENT TO LCvR 83.14: Section (c) governs the responsibilities of the Clerk to the Committee. The most important change is section (d) which is added to describe the practice of the Committee on Grievances and the Court relating to confidentiality and disclosure of disciplinary proceedings. It clarifies existing practice by explicitly stating which proceedings are confidential and which are not. The Rule does not bar disclosure of information by order of the Chief Judge or his/her designee in connection with judicial appointments. In addition, consistent with rules of other courts and case law, the Rule provides that Committee members shall be immune from suit for conduct in the course of their duties in exercising the power delegated to the Committee members by the Court.

LCvR 83.15 OBLIGATIONS OF ATTORNEYS

(a) Rules of Professional Conduct. Violations of the Rules of Professional Conduct (as adopted by the District of Columbia Court of Appeals except as otherwise provided by specific Rule of this Court) by attorneys subject to these Rules shall be grounds for discipline, whether or not the act or omission occurred in the course of an attorney-client relationship.

(b) Duty to Notify the Court. It shall be the duty of each attorney subject to these Rules to notify promptly the Clerk of this Court of:

(1) conviction of any crime other than minor traffic offenses, giving the name of the court in which the attorney was convicted, the date of conviction, docket number, the offense for which the attorney was convicted and the sentence;

(2) any disbarment, suspension or other public discipline imposed by any federal, state or local court, giving the name of the court, the date of such disbarment, suspension or other public discipline, the docket number, and a description of the discipline imposed and the offense committed in connection therewith; or any disbarment by consent or resignation while an investigation into allegations of misconduct is pending;

(3) whether the attorney has ever been held in contempt of court and if so, the nature of the contempt and the final disposition thereof; and

(4) any change in the attorney's office address or telephone number as provided for in (c) below.

Failure to provide the notice required by this paragraph may constitute a separate ground for discipline.

(c) Changes in Address. Notice to the Clerk of any change in the attorney's address or telephone number (see (b)(4) above) shall be filed in writing within 14 days of the change. The attorney shall also within 14 days file a praecipe reflecting such change in each case which the attorney has pending before this Court, serving a copy upon each of the attorneys in these cases.

(d) Duties of the Clerk Upon Notification. Upon being informed that an attorney subject to these Rules has been convicted of any crime, disciplined by any court, held in contempt by any court, disbarred by consent, or resigned from any Bar pending an investigation into allegations of misconduct, the Clerk shall promptly obtain a certified or exemplified copy of such conviction, disciplinary judgment or other court order and present it to the Committee which shall proceed in accordance with these Rules.

[Effective August 1, 1999. Amended effective December 1, 2009.]

Comment

COMMENT TO LCvR 83.15: Section (b) combines several former Rules relating to an attorney's obligations under these Rules to notify the Court of certain facts: (1) conviction of crime; (2) disbarment, suspension or public discipline; (3) citation for contempt; (4) change in address or telephone number. The duty of notification in LCvR 83.15(b) regarding public discipline does not include sanctions imposed under civil rules other than contempt as specified in subsection (b)(3). Failure to provide notice may constitute grounds for disciplinary action.

Section (c) has been added to impose on the Clerk to the Grievance Committee the duty to obtain a certified or exemplified copy of such conviction, disciplinary judgment or court order.

LCvR 83.16 GROUNDS AND PROCEDURES FOR DISCIPLINE

(a) Service of Process. Service of process under these Rules shall be made by certified mail addressed to the attorney (hereinafter attorney or respondent) at the last known address or at the last recorded address filed with the Clerk of the Court as required pursuant to LCvR 83.8(g). If service cannot be so made, service shall be sufficient when served on the Clerk of this Court and all time periods specified in these Rules shall run from the time of such service. If service is made by serving the Clerk, a courtesy copy shall be mailed to the respondent by first class mail at his/her last known address.

(b) Attorneys Convicted of Crimes.

(1) *Felonies.* Upon presentation to the Disciplinary Panel of a certified copy of a court record demonstrating that an attorney subject to these Rules has been found guilty of a felony in any court, the attorney shall be immediately suspended from practicing before this court by order of the Disciplinary Panel, whether the finding resulted from a plea of guilty or nolo contendere or from a verdict after trial or otherwise, and regardless of the pendency of an appeal. The Disciplinary Panel may defer entry of the order or set aside an order of suspension when it appears to the Panel in the interest of justice to do so.

Upon presentation of proof that the conviction is final, and regardless of the pendency of an appeal or other review of the conviction or of a Petition for Writ of Certiorari, the respondent shall be disbarred and the attorney's name shall be struck from the roll of members of the Bar of this Court by order of the Disciplinary Panel, unless within a period of 30 days from the date of the order, the respondent shows cause why disbarment would not be in the interest of justice.

(2) *Misdemeanors.* An attorney subject to these Rules who shall be convicted in any court of a misdemeanor may be disciplined in such manner and to such extent as the Disciplinary Panel may determine and may upon petition of the Committee and for good cause shown, be temporarily suspended pending a final decision of the Disciplinary Panel.

Upon receipt of a certified copy of such judgment of conviction, the Committee shall obtain an order from the Disciplinary Panel requiring the respondent to show cause within thirty days after service in accordance with LCvR 83.16(a) why the attorney should not be disciplined. If the respondent files a timely Answer, the Committee shall have 30 days within which to file a response thereto if it so desires. The Committee shall serve a copy of its response, if any, upon the respondent or respondent's counsel of record by first class mail or, failing that, in accordance with LCvR 83.16(a).

Upon the filing of the respondent's Answer to the Order to Show Cause and any response thereto by the Committee, or if no answer has been filed, upon the filing of a recommendation by the Committee, the matter shall be promptly submitted to the Disciplinary Panel for its consideration. The Disciplinary Panel may, in its discretion, schedule a hearing. If a hearing is scheduled, the Chairman or designated member(s) of the Committee shall appear at the hearing and offer proof or arguments pertinent to the issues. After the hearing or, if no hearing is scheduled, upon a review of the papers submitted, the Disciplinary Panel shall take such action as these Rules and justice may require. In all proceedings hereunder the certified copy of the judgment of conviction shall constitute conclusive proof of the respondent's guilt of the conduct for which the respondent was convicted. The pendency of an appeal or other review of the conviction or of a petition for Writ of Certiorari will not constitute a ground for failing to proceed in accordance with this Rule absent extraordinary circumstances and for good cause shown.

(3) *Reinstatement Following Suspension.* An attorney suspended under LCvR 83.16(b)(1) or (2) will be reinstated immediately upon the filing of a certificate demonstrating that the conviction has been reversed, vacated, or set aside, but the reinstatement will not terminate any formal disciplinary proceeding then pending against the attorney, the disposition of which shall be determined by the Committee on the basis of the available evidence.

(c) Discipline Imposed by Other Courts.

(1) *Policy of Reciprocal Discipline.* An attorney subject to these Rules who has been suspended for more than 30 days or disbarred by another court shall be automatically suspended from practice in this Court. The suspension shall be effective upon service of a Temporary Suspension and Show Cause Order in accordance with these Rules. An attorney who has been suspended for 30 days or less by another court shall have the fact of that discipline noted by the

Clerk on the Lawyer's Register maintained by this Court, and no further proceedings shall be had thereon, unless the Committee on Grievances shall determine that the facts underlying the discipline warrant a proceeding for the imposition of discipline by this Court. Notations on the Lawyers' Register do not constitute discipline imposed by the Court and they shall be available only to the Court and to the Committee and shall not be matters of public record.

(2) *Issuance of Temporary Suspension and Show Cause Order.* Upon receipt of a certified or exemplified copy of a judgment or order from another court suspending or disbarring an attorney subject to these Rules, the Disciplinary Panel of this Court shall issue a Temporary Suspension and Show Cause Order, suspending the attorney from practice before this Court pending a final disposition under these Rules, except where it finds extraordinary circumstances. Respondent may answer and show cause within 30 days after service of the Order why the imposition of the identical discipline by the Court would be unwarranted and the reasons therefor.

(3) *Duties of the Clerk.* The Clerk to the Committee thereupon shall cause to be served on the attorney the following documents: a copy of the judgment or order of discipline imposed by the other court; a certified copy of this Court's Temporary Suspension and Show Cause Order; and a copy of LCvR 83.16.

(4) *Procedures When Respondent Fails to Answer.* If a respondent fails to answer to show cause within 30 days from service of the Temporary Suspension and Show Cause Order, this Court shall issue an Order vacating the Temporary Suspension and Show Cause Order and imposing the identical discipline or such other discipline it deems appropriate, unless it finds that upon the face of the record on which the discipline by the other court is predicated it clearly appears:

(i) that the procedure was so lacking in notice or opportunity to be heard as to constitute a deprivation of due process; or

(ii) that proof establishing the misconduct gives rise to a reasonable doubt that this Court could not, consistent with its duty, accept as final the conclusion of the disciplining court; or

(iii) that the imposition of the same discipline by this Court would result in grave injustice; or

(iv) that the misconduct established is deemed by this Court to warrant substantially different discipline; or

(v) that the misconduct on which the discipline was imposed by the other court does not constitute misconduct in the District of Columbia.

Where this Court determines that any of these elements exist, it shall enter such other order as it deems appropriate.

(5) *Procedures When Respondent Answers.* If the respondent files a timely Answer, the Committee shall have 30 days within which to file a response and make a recommendation to the Court. Upon consideration of the papers submitted by the respondent and by the Committee, the Court shall either (1) enter an Order vacating the Temporary Suspension and Show Cause Order and imposing the identical discipline or such other discipline it might find appropriate, or (2) if the Court finds that, upon the face of the record on which the discipline in another jurisdiction is predicated it clearly appears that one or more of the factors listed in subparagraphs (4)(i)-(v) exists, it shall enter such other order as it deems appropriate.

(6) *Censure or Reprimand.* Where discipline imposed by the other court is a public censure or reprimand, the Clerk shall note the fact of that discipline on the Lawyers' Register maintained by this Court, and no further proceedings shall be had thereon. Notations on the Lawyers' Register do not constitute discipline imposed by this Court and they shall be available only to the Court and to the Committee and shall not be matters of public record.

(7) *Stays.* If the discipline imposed by another court has been stayed, any reciprocal discipline proceeding in this Court may, upon motion of the respondent, be deferred by order of this Court until the stay expires and until further order of this Court. In the absence of a stay of discipline imposed by such other court, neither a motion for reconsideration or motion for rehearing or rehearing en banc filed in the other court or petition for a writ of certiorari will be the basis for a deferral of the proceedings in this Court absent good cause shown.

(d) Complaints of Misconduct Filed in This Court.

(1) *Complaints Generally.* Any person seeking to charge an attorney subject to the Rules with any act or omission which may justify disbarment, suspension, censure, reprimand or other discipline shall do so by a clear and concise written statement of facts in support of the allegations, subscribed and under oath or affirmed under the penalty of perjury pursuant to the United States Code, Title 28, Section 1746. The Complaint shall be presented to the Committee by lodging it with the Clerk to the Committee. The Committee shall have the inherent power without any formal Complaint to inquire into misconduct of attorneys subject to these Rules.

(2) *Complaints by a Court or a Judge.* Any court, judge or United States magistrate judge in the District of Columbia may refer to the Committee the name of any attorney subject to these Rules on a Complaint that such attorney has engaged in conduct which, if substantiated, would warrant the imposition of discipline.

(3) *Investigation.* Complaints received by the Committee shall be reviewed to determine if the Complaint is appropriate for action. If the Complaint is insufficient on its face to warrant investigation, the Committee may discharge the Complaint and advise the complainant that no action will be taken. If the Committee decides that the Complaint or information otherwise received by the Committee requires action, the Committee is authorized to (1) investigate the matter itself; (2) refer the matter to the Office of Bar Counsel, the Board on Professional Responsibility, District of Columbia Court of Appeals; (3) informally seek information from the respondent; or (4) require a formal Answer from the respondent in accordance with subsection (d)(4). To further any investigation, the Chairman, or in his absence, the Vice Chairman is authorized to issue subpoenas commanding the production of books, papers, documents, records or tangible items. If following any of these actions the Committee decides no further action is warranted, the Committee may, if its investigation was based on receipt of a complaint, discharge the Complaint and so inform the complainant and the respondent. If the Committee's investigation was based on information otherwise received and the respondent was made aware by the Committee of its investigation, the Committee shall notify the respondent that it has decided that no further action is warranted. The Committee may, as part of its notice to the respondent discharging the Complaint, provide an informal, non-reportable cautionary or educational statement, which shall not be considered discipline.

(4) *Service of Complaint; Answer.* If the Committee determines that a formal Answer is required from the respondent, a copy of the Complaint as received by the Committee or as prepared by it based on information otherwise received shall be served upon the respondent and he/she shall be required to answer within 30 days after the date of service. An Answer to a Complaint shall be in writing, subscribed and under oath or affirmed under the penalty of perjury in a form prescribed by the provisions of the United States Code, Title 28, Section 1746 and shall be accompanied by a list of all courts before which the respondent is admitted to practice. Upon receipt of the Answer, the Clerk to the Committee shall mail a copy thereof to the complainant, if there is one, who may reply to the Answer within 14 days of the date of the transmittal letter from the Clerk of the Committee. A copy of any reply to the Answer to the Complaint shall be served upon the respondent. If a respondent is served with a copy of a Complaint by the Committee and fails to answer within the time allowed by these Rules, the matters shall be certified to the Disciplinary Panel for its appropriate action.

(5) *Subcommittee of Inquiry.* The Chairman may designate three members of the Committee to sit as a Subcommittee of Inquiry and shall designate one as Chairman of the Subcommittee. The Chairman of the Subcommittee of Inquiry is hereby designated and appointed a Master with authority to cause subpoenas to be issued commanding the attendance of witnesses and/or parties at any hearings, as well as commanding the production of books, papers, documents, records or tangible things designated therein at such hearing. The Chairman of the Subcommittee as such Master is further authorized to administer oaths to the parties and witnesses. Should any witness and/or party fail or refuse to attend or to testify under oath, the witness' or party's name may be certified to the Disciplinary Panel of the Court, whereupon the Disciplinary Panel may refer the matter to the United States Attorney or the U.S. Department of Justice to bring formal criminal contempt charges against such witness and/or party for so refusing. If the witness or party is found guilty of contempt, the Court shall administer such punishment as may be appropriate.

(6) *Right to Counsel in Disciplinary Proceedings.* The respondent shall be entitled to be represented by counsel who may appear on the respondent's behalf at any time during the investigation or after a Complaint has been served upon respondent.

(7) *Submission of Charges.* If following investigation the Subcommittee of Inquiry recommends, and a majority of the Committee concurs, the Committee shall prepare charges and submit them to the Disciplinary Panel of the Court or, in its discretion with or without preparing charges refer the matter to the Office of Bar Counsel, the Board on Professional Responsibility, District of Columbia Court of Appeals with a request that that Office take whatever action it deems appropriate. If submitted to the Disciplinary Panel and the Panel orders the charges to be filed, the Clerk shall file them and issue a summons directed to the respondent, commanding respondent to answer. The summons and a copy of the charges shall be served in accordance with these Rules. The respondent shall answer the charges within 30 days after the effective date of service and shall file with the Answer a list of all courts before which the attorney is admitted to practice. If no Answer is received within 30 days or such additional time as the Disciplinary Panel may allow, the charges may be taken as admitted and the Disciplinary Panel may reprimand, censure, suspend, disbar or otherwise discipline the respondent by entering an appropriate order.

(8) *Hearings and Orders of the Disciplinary Panel of the Court.* When the respondent has filed an Answer, the case shall be set down for hearing before the Disciplinary Panel and a member of the Committee designated by the Chairman shall appear at the hearing to offer proof or arguments pertinent to the issues. If the charges are sustained by clear and convincing evidence, the Disciplinary Panel may reprimand, censure, suspend, disbar or otherwise discipline the respondent by entering an appropriate order. Any

knowing violation of the order of judgment shall be deemed a contempt of court.

(e) Disbarment on Consent.

(1) *By This Court.* Any attorney admitted to practice before this Court who is the subject of an investigation into, or a pending proceeding involving, allegations of misconduct may not resign from this bar, but may consent to disbarment. The attorney must deliver to this Court an affidavit stating that the attorney desires to consent to disbarment and that:

(i) the attorney's consent is freely and voluntarily given; the attorney is not being subjected to coercion or duress; the attorney is fully aware of the implications of so consenting; and

(ii) the attorney is aware that there is presently pending an investigation or proceeding involving allegations that there exist grounds for the attorney's discipline the nature of which the attorney shall specifically set forth.

Upon receipt of the required affidavit, the Disciplinary Panel shall enter an order disbarring the attorney. The order disbarring the attorney on consent shall be a matter of public record, but the affidavit shall be sealed and not be publicly disclosed or made available for use in any other proceeding except upon order of this Court.

(2) *By Other Courts.* An attorney admitted to practice before this Court who shall be disbarred on consent or who shall resign from the bar of any court of the United States or from the bar of any State, Territory, District, Commonwealth or Possession of the United States while an investigation into allegations of misconduct is pending, shall so advise this Court and submit a certified or exemplified copy of the judgment or order accepting such disbarment on consent or resignation. If no such order or judgment is submitted, the Clerk shall obtain it from the other court. The Disciplinary Panel thereupon shall enter an order disbarring the attorney and directing that the attorney's name be stricken from the roll of attorneys admitted to practice before this Court unless the attorney shows why it would not be in the interest of justice to do so. A certified or exemplified copy of the judgment or order accepting such disbarment on consent or resignation is conclusive proof of such disbarment on consent or resignation.

[Effective August 1, 1999. Amended effective April 10, 2007; December 1, 2009.]

Comments

COMMENT TO LCvR 83.16: LCvR 83.16 outlines the grounds and procedures for discipline of: attorneys convicted of crimes; attorneys disciplined by other courts; attorneys who are the subject of complaints of misconduct filed in this Court; and attorneys disbarred on consent.

Section (a) governs service of process in disciplinary proceedings. It makes clear that the primary method of service is by mail and the alternative method is by service on the Clerk of the Court.

Section (b) provides for immediate suspension upon proof of a felony conviction. The Disciplinary Panel may defer or set aside entry of the order in the interest of justice. This provision is to be invoked only in extraordinary circumstances. The Rule further provides for disbarment upon final conviction, regardless of the pendency of an appeal or other review, unless respondent shows cause within 30 days why disbarment would not be in the interest of justice.

With respect to misdemeanors, the Rule essentially maintains the show cause procedures in effect under former Rule 4–3(I)(b). With respect to both felonies and misdemeanors, the Rule makes clear that the pendency of an appeal or other review of conviction or of a petition for writ of certiorari does not affect the imposition of discipline. This provision was added to solve the recurring problem of a year or more delay attendant on petitions for certiorari, during which time the attorney might be permitted to practice before this Court.

Subsection (b)(3) has been added to provide for reinstatement after suspension upon proof that the underlying conviction has been reversed, vacated or set aside.

Section (c) governs discipline imposed by other courts and is a significant change from former Rule 4–3(II). The Rule provides that an attorney subject to these Rules who is suspended or disbarred by another court shall be suspended from practice in this court during the pendency of disciplinary proceedings. The procedures adopted are consistent with the practice in the United States Supreme Court, many United States Court of Appeals and a number of other district courts. By providing the attorney an opportunity to show cause why reciprocal discipline should not be imposed, the Rule satisfies the due process requirements of the relevant Supreme Court cases. See, e.g., In Re Ruffalo, 390 U.S. 544 (1968); Theard v. United States, 354 U.S. 278 (1957); Selling v. Radford, 243 U.S. 46 (1917). The Rule corrects the inadequacies of the former show cause procedures that permitted a respondent to continue to practice during the pendency of disciplinary proceedings. The revised procedure, requiring immediate temporary suspension followed by a show cause order, shifts the burden of going forward to the respondent to show cause why identical reciprocal discipline should not be imposed.

The provision for suspension eliminates the procedure of noting short-term suspensions imposed by other courts on this Court's records, rather than imposing reciprocal discipline. Those procedures were unworkable and caused inequities. Under the new procedures, censures and reprimands will be noted, but reciprocal discipline proceedings will be followed in the case of all suspensions or disbarments.

Subsection (c)(7) makes clear that if discipline imposed by another court has been stayed, reciprocal discipline in this Court may be deferred. However, in the absence of a stay, neither a motion for reconsideration nor a motion for rehearing or rehearing en banc nor a petition for writ of certiorari serves to defer disciplinary proceedings in this Court absent good cause shown.

Subsection (d) sets forth in one section all the procedures relating to Complaints filed in this Court. Subsection (d)(1): This rule was modified to require that written complaints of misconduct contain a clear and concise statement of facts supporting the allegations made against attorneys. Subsec-

tion (d)(3) was amended to clarify that the Committee on Grievances may include an informal, non-reportable cautionary or educational statement as a part of a notice discharging a Complaint without further action.

Subsection (d)(7) provides that if a respondent fails to respond after a formal complaint is filed, the Disciplinary Panel has the power to take the allegations as admitted and impose appropriate discipline. Subsection (d)(8) sets forth the clear and convincing standard of proof for the imposition of discipline.

Section (e) governs disbarment on consent. It makes clear that there can be disbarment on consent in this Court or reciprocal disbarment for disbarment on consent by another court. It changes the former Rule by providing that an attorney under investigation or subject to pending proceedings involving allegations of misconduct may not resign from the Bar of this Court, but may only consent to disbarment.

Revised subsection (e)(1) governing disbarment on consent by this Court makes two substantive changes. First it permits the attorney affidavit, which is the predicate for disbarment on consent, to be filed under seal. Second, it eliminates the former requirement that an affidavit filed by an attorney seeking disbarment on consent contain an acknowledgment that the material facts alleged are true. This revision was adopted because it was felt that it was in the public interest to encourage consent disbarments.

With respect to disbarment on consent or resignation in other courts, subsection (e)(2) is changed only to the extent of providing the attorney an opportunity to show cause why such disbarment would not be in the interest of justice.

COMMENT TO LCvR 83.16(c)(1): Typically, an order of suspension entered by the District of Columbia Court of Appeals by its terms is effective 30 days from the date of its entry. The Disciplinary Panel of this Court signs its Temporary Suspension and Show Cause Order after the effective date of suspension order in the other court.

Since a respondent has 30 days within which to answer an order to show cause in this Court, a short-term suspension by another court has often expired and a respondent automatically reinstated in the other court before the time an answer is due in this Court. Thus, no useful purpose is served by initiating reciprocal disciplinary proceedings in cases involving suspensions of 30 days or less.

LCvR 83.17 NOTIFICATION TO DISCIPLINARY AUTHORITIES

(a) Notification to Other Courts. When any person subject to these Rules has been convicted of any crime or disbarred, suspended, reprimanded, censured or disbarred on consent by this Court, the Clerk shall within ten days transmit to the disciplinary authorities in any other jurisdictions or courts in which the attorney is admitted to practice, a certified copy of the conviction or a certified copy of the judgment or order of disbarment, suspension, reprimand, censure or disbarment on consent. The Clerk shall also serve a certified copy of such judgment or order and a copy of such notice upon the respondent in accordance with LCvR 83.16(a).

(b) Notification to National Discipline Data Bank. The Clerk shall promptly notify the National Discipline Data Bank operated by the American Bar Association of any order imposing public discipline upon any attorney admitted to practice before this Court.

[Effective August 1, 1999.]

Comment

COMMENT TO LCvR 83.17: LCvR 83.17 has been adopted from the Model Rules of Disciplinary Enforcement. The purpose is to foster cooperation in reporting disciplinary actions.

LCvR 83.18 REINSTATEMENT

(a) After Disbarment or Suspension. An attorney suspended for a specific period shall be automatically reinstated at the end of the period upon the filing with the Court of an affidavit of compliance with the provisions of the order of suspension (including, in the case of reciprocal discipline, proof that the attorney has been reinstated by the court in which the attorney was disciplined). An attorney suspended for an indefinite period may not resume practice until the suspension is terminated by an order of the Disciplinary Panel. A disbarred attorney may not resume practice until reinstated by order of the Disciplinary Panel.

(b) Time of Application Following Disbarment or Suspension for Indefinite Period. A person who has been disbarred may not apply for reinstatement until the expiration of at least five years from the effective date of the order of disbarment. A person who has been suspended for an indefinite period may not apply for termination of the suspension until after the expiration of the minimum period fixed by the order of suspension or, if no minimum period is fixed, for a period of three years, or, in the case of reciprocal discipline, upon proof that the attorney has been reinstated by the court in which the attorney was disciplined.

(c) Hearing on Application. Petitions for reinstatement under this Rule shall be filed with the Clerk to the Committee. The Committee shall have 30 days within which to respond. The attorney shall have the burden of demonstrating by clear and convincing evidence that he/she has met the conditions of reinstatement or termination of suspension as provided for under these Rules. The Disciplinary Panel may hold a hearing on the application or, in its discretion, decide the matter on the basis of the papers filed.

(d) Conditions of Reinstatement or Termination of Suspension. If the Disciplinary Panel finds the attorney unfit to resume the practice of law, the petition for reinstatement shall be denied. If the Disciplinary Panel finds the attorney fit to resume the practice of law, it shall issue an order reinstating the attorney or terminating the suspension. The order may make reinstatement or termination of the suspension conditional upon the payment of all or part of the costs of the proceedings and upon the making of partial or complete restitution to parties harmed by the attorney's misconduct which led to the suspension or disbarment. In the discretion of the Disciplinary Panel, reinstatement or termination of suspension may also be conditioned upon the furnishing of proof of competency and learning in the law, which proof may include certification by the Bar Examiners of a State or other jurisdiction of the attorney's successful completion of an examination for admission to practice subsequent to the date of indefinite suspension or disbarment.

(e) Successive Petitions. No petition for reinstatement or for termination of suspension under this Rule shall be filed within one year following an order denying a petition for reinstatement or termination of suspension filed by or on behalf of the same person.

(f) Notification of Reinstatement. Upon entry of an Order of Reinstatement or an Order Terminating Suspension, the Clerk shall promptly notify the same persons who notified of the disciplinary order.

[Effective August 1, 1999.]

Comments

COMMENT TO LCvR 83.18: Section (a) provides that to apply for reinstatement in the case of reciprocal discipline, the attorney must submit proof of reinstatement by the court in which the attorney was disciplined. Section (c) provides that the Committee will have 30 days to respond to a petition for reinstatement. The provision outlining the respondent's burden in obtaining reinstatement requires proof that the respondent has met the conditions of reinstatement under these Rules.

Section (d) sets forth the conditions for reinstatement. It provides that the Disciplinary Panel has the discretion to condition reinstatement or termination of suspension upon proof of competency and learning in the law, eliminating the provision that such proof would only be required if the disbarment or suspension lasted for five years or more. Section (f) provides for notification of reinstatement to the attorney.

LCvR 83.19 PROCEEDINGS WHERE AN ATTORNEY IS DECLARED TO BE MENTALLY INCOMPETENT OR IS ALLEGED TO BE INCAPACITATED

(a) Attorneys Declared Incompetent or Physically Infirm. If an attorney who is subject to these Rules has been judicially declared incompetent or involuntarily committed to a mental hospital, or has resigned from the bar of any court or been suspended from such a bar on the basis of such mental incompetence or incapacity or on the basis of physical infirmity or illness, the Disciplinary Panel, upon proper proof of the fact, shall enter an order suspending such attorney from the practice of law effective immediately and for an indefinite period until further order of the Court. A copy of such order shall be served upon such attorney, his/her guardian and the administrator of any hospital or other institution if the Court is informed such attorney is a patient thereof in such manner as the Disciplinary Panel may direct.

(b) Attorneys Alleged to Be Incapacitated. Whenever the Committee shall petition the Disciplinary Panel to determine whether an attorney who is subject to these Rules is incapacitated from continuing the practice of law by reason of mental infirmity or illness or because of the use of drugs or intoxicants, the Disciplinary Panel may take or direct such action as it deems necessary or proper to determine whether the attorney is so incapacitated, including the examination of the attorney by such qualified medical experts as the Disciplinary Panel shall designate. Failure or refusal to submit to such examination shall be prima facie evidence of incapacity. If upon due consideration of the matter the Disciplinary Panel concludes that the attorney is incapacitated from continuing to practice law it shall enter an order suspending the attorney on the ground of such disability for an indefinite period and until further order of the Court.

The Disciplinary Panel may provide for such notice to the attorney of proceedings in the matter as it deems proper and advisable and may appoint an attorney to represent the attorney if the attorney is without representation.

(c) Claim of Disability During Disciplinary Proceedings. If during the course of a disciplinary proceeding the attorney contends that he/she is suffering from a disability by reason of mental or physical infirmity or illness or because of the use of drugs or intoxicants which makes it impossible for the attorney to defend adequately, the Disciplinary Panel shall enter an order immediately suspending the attorney from continuing to practice law until a determination is made of the attorney's capacity to continue to practice law in a proceeding instituted in accordance with the provisions of paragraph (b) above.

(d) Application for Reinstatement. Any attorney suspended under this Rule for incompetency, mental illness, physical infirmity or because of the use of drugs or intoxicants may apply to the Disciplinary Panel for reinstatement immediately and thereafter once a year or at such shorter intervals as the Disciplinary Panel may direct in the order of suspension. The application shall be granted by the Disciplinary Panel upon a showing by clear and convincing evidence that the attorney's disability has been removed and that the attorney is fit to resume the practice of law provided, however, that if the suspension was based on resignation from the bar of another court the attorney must provide proof that the attorney has been reinstated in the other court, or that, if the suspension from practice before this Court was based on a finding of incompetence or incapacity by another court, it clearly appears on the face of the record that any of the five elements set forth in LCvR 83.16(c)(4) exist. The Disciplinary Panel may take or direct such action as it deems necessary or proper to a determination of whether the attorney's disability has been removed including a direction for an examination of the attorney. The Disciplinary Panel may direct that the expenses of such an examination shall be paid for by the attorney.

If an attorney has been suspended because of a judicial declaration of incompetence or involuntary commitment to a mental hospital and has thereafter been judicially declared to be competent, the Disciplinary Panel may dispense with further evidence and direct the reinstatement of the attorney upon such terms as it deems proper and advisable.

(e) Evidentiary Hearing. If the Disciplinary Panel holds an evidentiary hearing to determine whether an attorney is incapacitated or on an attorney's application for reinstatement under this Rule, the Chairman of the Committee shall appoint one or more members of the Committee to appear for the purpose of examining and cross-examining witnesses and/or offering proof or argument pertinent to the issues.

(f) Waiver of Physician–Patient Privilege. The filing of an application for reinstatement by an attorney who has been suspended for disability shall constitute a waiver of any physical patient privilege with respect to any treatment of the attorney during the period of the attorney's disability. The attorney shall be required to disclose the name of every psychiatrist, psychologist, physician and hospital by whom or in which the attorney has been examined or treated since the attorney's suspension and the attorney shall furnish the Disciplinary Panel with written consents for such psychiatrists, psychologists, physicians or hospital to disclose such information or records as may be requested by the medical experts designated by the Disciplinary Panel.

[Effective August 1, 1999.]

LCvR 83.20 LAWYER COUNSELING PANEL

(a) Referral of Attorneys for Counseling. Judges or the Committee on Grievances may refer to the Lawyer Counseling Panel established by this Rule any member of the Bar of this Court who exhibits a deficiency in performance and who, in the judge's or the Committee's opinion, would likely benefit from counseling by other trial attorneys on matters of litigation practice, ethics, or apparent abuse of alcohol or drugs. The judge or the Committee will notify both the panel and the attorney of the referral and the basis therefor. The referral shall be confidential.

(b) The Counseling Panel. The counseling panel shall be composed of experienced litigation practitioners appointed by the Court, one of whose members shall be designated chairperson.

(c) Panel Proceedings. The chairperson of the Lawyer Counseling Panel shall receive references from judges or the Committee on Grievances and assign the referred member to a particular panel member for counseling. Participation in the counseling program by referred attorneys shall be voluntary. Any conversations between the referred attorney and members of the panel shall be confidential and shall not waive any attorney client privilege. The panel will make no findings or report of its action as to any referred attorney, other than a report to the referring judge, or the Committee on Grievances, as to whether the attorney did or did not participate in counseling.

(d) Confidentiality and Immunity. All documents and communications relating or referring to the Panel's referrals shall remain confidential and privileged.

All meetings and discussions of the Lawyer Counseling Panel shall be held in camera and the business conducted therein shall remain confidential and privileged. All records, reports, correspondence and minutes of the Panel shall be maintained by the Chairperson of the Lawyer Counseling Panel and shall not be disclosed except by order or direction of the Chief Judge (or the designee of the Chief Judge).

When exercising the power relegated by the Court, Panel members shall be absolutely immune from suit for any conduct in connection with their duties. Referrals and counseling with respect thereto shall be absolutely privileged and no claim or action predicated thereon may be instituted or maintained.

[Effective August 1, 1999. Amended effective April 10, 2007.]

Comment

COMMENT TO LCvR 83.20(a) and (c): This rule was modified to permit the Committee on Grievances to refer attorneys to the Lawyer Counseling Panel and receive reports from the Panel concerning whether the referred attorney participated in counseling.

LCvR 83.21 PUBLICATION OF AMENDMENTS

Any amendment to these Rules shall be published in The Daily Washington Law Reporter before its adoption. The notice shall state that the proposed amendment will be adopted unless modified or withdrawn after receiving comments from organized bar associations, members of the bar, and the public. Such comments shall be submitted in writing within 45 days of publication to the Chairman of the Advisory Committee on District Court Rules. If the Court determines there is an immediate need for a particular local rule or amendment to an existing local rule, it may proceed without public notice and opportunity for comment, but the Court shall promptly thereafter afford such notice and opportunity for comment.

[Effective August 1, 1999.]

LCvR 83.22 PUBLICATION AND PROOF THEREOF

A notice relating to a proceeding that requires publication shall be published in *The Daily Washington Law Reporter* for the time fixed by statute or directed by the Court, in addition to any newspaper or periodical specifically designated by the Court. Publication shall be proved by affidavit of an officer or agent of the publisher, stating the dates of publication with an attached copy of the notice as published.

[Effective August 1, 1999.]

LCvR 83.23 DISMISSAL FOR FAILURE TO PROSECUTE

A dismissal for failure to prosecute may be ordered by the Court upon motion by an adverse party, or upon the Court's own motion. An order dismissing a claim for failure to prosecute shall specify that the dismissal is without prejudice, unless the Court determines that the delay in prosecution of the claim has resulted in prejudice to an opposing party.

[Effective August 1, 1999.]

LCvR 84. MEDIATION—PURPOSE AND SCOPE OF RULES

(a) These Rules govern the administration of the United States District Court Mediation Program. The Mediation Program was designed to give litigants an opportunity to discuss settlement of their claims with the help of a trained, neutral third party. Mediation, while not appropriate in all cases, can benefit many litigants. It can, for example, lead to resolutions more quickly, with less expense and with results that are more satisfying to the litigants than those that result from judicial disposition of a claim. The Court makes mediation services available to litigants on a pro bono basis.

(b) These Rules apply only to mediation proceedings that are formally conducted through the United States District Court's Mediation Program. Nothing in these Rules shall preclude litigants from independently retaining a private mediator or other ADR professional to facilitate negotiations in their case.

[Effective May 17, 2001.]

LCvR 84.1 ADMINISTRATION OF MEDIATION PROGRAM

(a) The United States District Court Mediation Program is administered by the Office of the Circuit Executive for the United States Courts for the District of Columbia Circuit. The mediation staff consists of a Director and Deputy Director of Dispute Resolution, who are responsible for assigning cases to qualified volunteer mediators and providing parties with the proper notification and instructions. They also oversee volunteer training, monitor the progress of mediated cases, collect pertinent statistical information and serve as a resource for program mediators as they work on cases.

(b) The Director and Deputy Director of Dispute Resolution may be reached at the following address and phone numbers:

Office of the Circuit Executive
E. Barrett Prettyman United States Courthouse
333 Constitution Avenue, N.W.
Washington D.C., 20001
(202) 216–7350
fax: (202) 273–0331

The Court encourages litigants and counsel to contact these officials to secure general information about the Mediation Program, to discuss the suitability of mediation for a particular case, or to raise any concerns they may have about the operation of the Program.

[Effective May 17, 2001.]

LCvR 84.2 DESCRIPTION OF THE MEDIATION PROCESS

(a) Description. Mediation is a flexible, non-binding, confidential process in which a neutral lawyer-mediator facilitates settlement negotiations. The mediator improves communication across party lines, helps parties articulate their interests and understand those of their opponent, probes the strengths and weaknesses of each party's legal position, helps identify key legal and factual issues, identifies common interests and areas of agreement and helps generate options for a mutually agreeable resolution of the dispute. If appropriate, the mediator may provide an evaluation of the merits of the case. A hallmark of mediation is its capacity to expand traditional settlement discussion and broaden resolution options, often by exploring litigant needs and interests that may be independent of the legal issues in controversy.

(b) Limits on Role of Mediator. The mediator has no authority to render a decision or to dictate a settlement.

[Effective May 17, 2001.]

LCvR 84.3 MEDIATORS

(a) Panel. The Court shall maintain a panel of mediators serving in the Mediation Program. Mediators will be selected from time to time by the Court from applications submitted by lawyers willing to serve on a volunteer basis. The Director and Deputy Director of Dispute Resolution may also serve as mediators.

(b) Qualifications and Training. Each lawyer serving as a mediator in the Court's Mediation Program shall be a member of the Bar of this Court and shall successfully complete training as required by the Court. Additional minimum requirements for serving on the Court's panel of mediators, which the Court may modify in individual circumstances, are as follows:

(1) Mediators shall have been admitted to the practice of law for at least ten years and shall be knowledgeable about civil litigation in federal court.

(2) Mediators shall have strong mediation process skills and the temperament and training to listen well, facilitate communication across party lines and assist the parties with settlement negotiations.

(c) Mediator Immunity. All lawyers serving as mediators in the Court's Mediation Program are performing quasi-judicial functions and shall be entitled to absolute quasi-judicial immunity for acts performed within the scope of their official duties.

(d) Complaints Against Mediators. Complaints against a mediator or concerns about a mediator's performance shall be brought to the attention of the Director of Dispute Resolution. The parties shall not bring such complaints to the attention of the assigned judge.

[Effective May 17, 2001.]

LCvR 84.4 REFERRAL TO MEDIATION

(a) Method of Referral. District judges may refer civil cases to mediation, subject to the availability of qualified mediators:

(1) by encouraging litigants to submit to mediation voluntarily and entering a consent order referring the case to the Circuit Executive's Office, or

(2) by requiring litigants to participate after giving them an opportunity, in response to an order to show cause, to explain why mediation would not be appropriate in their case.

Cross Reference

Local Civil Rule 16.3 requires counsel to meet, within 14 days after defendant enters an appearance in a case, to discuss whether mediation might be appropriate and to submit their views to the Court within 14 days after the meeting. Counsel must also indicate whether they discussed mediation with their clients before filing their report.

(b) Timing of Referral. Cases may be referred to mediation, with the consent of the assigned judge, at any point during the course of the litigation.

Cross Reference

Local Civil Rule 16.3 requires counsel to discuss the question of timing. Litigants may refer to the Court's brochure, "Mediation in the United States District Court for the District of Columbia," for a discussion of timing considerations.

(c) Pro Se Cases. Cases in which one of the parties is proceeding pro se are generally considered ineligible for mediation, unless the pro se party is represented by counsel for the purpose of mediation.

(d) Magistrate Judges Consent Cases. In cases in which the parties have consented to jurisdiction by a magistrate judge under 28 U.S.C. § 636(c), the magistrate judge shall have the same authority to refer cases to the Mediation Program as do district judges under Local Rule 84.1(b) above.

(e) Bankruptcy Proceedings. Mediation is also available to litigants in bankruptcy proceedings.

[Effective May 17, 2001. Amended effective December 1, 2009.]

LCvR 84.5 APPOINTMENT OF MEDIATOR

(a) Appointment by Circuit Executive. After entry of an order referring a case to mediation, the mediation staff will appoint from the Court's panel a mediator who is available during the appropriate period and who has confirmed, following such inquiry as may be appropriate, that no personal or professional conflict precludes his/her participation as mediator. The Circuit Executive's Office will notify the parties of the appointment.

(b) Objections to Appointment. Litigants who object to the appointment of a particular mediator for any reason shall make their concerns known to the Director of Dispute Resolution, who will make every reasonable effort to substitute a new mediator who is acceptable to all parties. Such concerns may be brought to the Director's attention at any point during the course of the mediation.

[Effective May 17, 2001.]

LCvR 84.6 MEDIATION STATEMENTS

(a) Content and Timing. No later than seven days prior to the first mediation session, each party shall submit directly to the mediator a confidential mediation statement. The mediation statement shall not exceed ten pages and shall outline the underlying facts of the dispute, the key legal issues in the case, possible areas of agreement and options for settlement, and the settlement history of the dispute, if any.

The mediation statement shall also identify, by name and title or status:

(1) the person(s) with decision-making authority, who, in addition to counsel, will attend the mediation as representative(s) of the party; and

(2) persons connected with either party (including insurer representatives) whose presence might substantially improve the utility of the mediation or the prospects for settlement.

(b) Confidential Nature of Statement. Mediation statements shall not be filed with the Court or served upon other parties to the lawsuit.

[Effective May 17, 2001.]

LCvR 84.7 THE MEDIATION PROCESS

(a) Scheduling. Promptly after being appointed to a case, the mediator shall fix the date and time of the first mediation session, which shall be held within three weeks of the date of the mediator's appointment.

(b) Discretion of Mediator. The mediation shall be informal. Mediators shall have discretion to structure the mediation so as to maximize prospects for settling all or part of the case.

(c) Joint and Separate Meetings. The mediator typically begins with a joint mediation session, to be attended by all counsel and parties. S/he may hold separate, private caucuses with each side or each lawyer or, if the parties agree, with the clients only. The mediator may choose to conduct any joint session or private caucus by telephone or e-mail.

(d) Completion of Process.

(1) The mediation ends when one of the following events occurs:

(i) the parties settle the dispute;

(ii) the mediator and the parties conclude that further discussion would be fruitless; or

(iii) the *mediation deadline*—a date established in the assigned judge's order of referral—is reached.

(2) If a settlement is reached, counsel shall notify the Court by filing a stipulation of dismissal or other appropriate document.

(3) Mediators shall notify the Court of the outcome of a mediation by promptly completing a Mediator Evaluation Form and returning it to the Circuit Executive's Office.

(e) Extension of Mediation Deadline. The assigned judge may alter or extend the mediation deadline sua sponte or at the parties' request.

(f) Agreements to Be Reduced to Writing. Agreements reached during mediation shall not bind the parties unless they are reduced to writing and signed by counsel and the parties. In cases involving government or corporate parties, an authorized representative of the governmental or corporate entity may sign.

[Effective May 17, 2001.]

LCvR 84.8 ATTENDANCE REQUIREMENTS

(a) In General. The Court requires counsel and parties with settlement authority to attend mediation sessions.

(b) Corporation or Other Entity. A party other than a natural person (e.g., a corporation or an association) satisfies this attendance requirement if it sends a representative (other than outside counsel) who possesses authority to settle, or if it makes such a person immediately available to the mediator by telephone.

(c) Government Entities. A party that is a government or governmental agency, in addition to counsel, shall send a representative with settlement authority or, alternatively, a representative who is knowledgeable about the facts of the case and will play a major role in submitting a recommendation to the person or body with decision-making authority.

(d) Exception. Notwithstanding (b) or (c) above, mediators may require the presence of or participation by telephone of the ultimate governmental or corporate decision-maker, or other appropriate senior manager, if they conclude, with the concurrence of the Director of Dispute Resolution, that such participation is advisable.

[Effective May 17, 2001.]

LCvR 84.9 CONFIDENTIALITY

(a) Confidential Treatment.

(1) The Court hereby prohibits the mediator, all counsel and parties and any other persons attending the mediation from disclosing any written or oral communications made in connection with or during any mediation session.

(2) There shall be no communication between the mediator and the assigned judge regarding a case that has been referred to mediation. Disputes and complaints of any kind, the resolution of which may require the disclosure of information acquired through a mediation, shall not be heard by the assigned judge but shall be brought to the attention of the Compliance Judge as outlined in Local Rule 84.10 below.

(3) Information acquired through mediation shall not be used for any purpose, including impeachment, in any pending or future proceeding in this or any other court or forum. Mediators shall not respond to subpoenas or requests for such information or disclose such information voluntarily. Mediators who are served with a subpoena or otherwise asked for infor-

mation about any mediation in which they have participated shall immediately inform the Director of Dispute Resolution of the request.

(b) Confidentiality Agreement. The mediator may ask the parties and all persons attending the mediation to sign a confidentiality agreement on a form provided by the Court, but the confidentiality requirements of this section apply regardless of whether a confidentiality agreement is signed.

(c) Exceptions.

(1) Nothing in this Rule shall be construed to prohibit disclosures to persons not directly participating in a mediation (such as corporate or government officials) whose possession of mediation-related information counsel believe to be necessary to further the progress of the talks in the case; or to help the institution respond to the mediation program generally. Persons not attending a mediation who are given information on this "need to know" basis shall also be bound by this Rule regarding confidentiality.

(2) This Rule shall not be construed to prohibit parties from entering written agreements resolving some or all of the case or from entering and filing procedural or factual stipulations based on suggestions or agreements made in connection with a mediation.

(3) Information which is obtained through discovery or other means outside the mediation process shall not be rendered inadmissable or non-discoverable because it is used or presented in mediation.

(4) This Rule does not preclude a report to or an inquiry by the Compliance Judge pursuant to Local Rule 84.10 below regarding a possible violation of these Rules.

(5) Nothing in this Rule shall be construed to prohibit the mediator, counsel or litigants from discussing, with the Court's ADR staff, the progress of a mediation or the specific facts and ideas discussed in the course of mediated negotiations. Such communications are encouraged to permit the staff to monitor the quality of the mediation services being provided.

(6) This Rule does not preclude dissemination of information about the types of cases going through the Mediation Program or about overall program results. Generic information about the program and cases entering mediation is available, and reports are generated for analysis and evaluation. Individual cases that have been resolved through mediation may be publicly identified, discussed or brought to the Court's attention if the parties consent to such a disclosure.

[Effective May 17, 2001.]

LCvR 84.10 DISPUTE RESOLUTION COMPLIANCE JUDGE

The Court has designated a district judge to serve as the Dispute Resolution Compliance Judge. Complaints alleging a material violation of these mediation local rules or of a judicial order referring a case to mediation must be made to the Director of Dispute Resolutions, who may then refer them to the Compliance Judge for appropriate action. If the Compliance Judge believes judicial intervention is necessary, s/he will so inform the parties and will ask them to address the matter. The Compliance Judge will have the authority to impose sanctions as s/he deems appropriate. *Litigants and mediators may not bring compliance issues directly to the attention of the Compliance Judge or to the attention of the judge who is assigned to the lawsuit.*

[Effective May 17, 2001.]

LCvR 85. FILINGS UNDER THE DODD–FRANK WALL STREET REFORM & CONSUMER PROTECTION ACT

This rule governs petitions by the Secretary of the Treasury ("Secretary") under the Dodd–Frank Wall Street Reform and Consumer Protection Act ("Act"), Pub.L. No. 111–203, 124 Stat. 1376, 1444 (Jul. 21, 2010), 12 U.S.C. § 5382(a)(1), for orders authorizing the Secretary to appoint the Federal Deposit Insurance Corporation as receiver for financial companies.

(a) Filing of the Petition. A petition under this Act must contain all relevant findings and recommendations under the Act, and must be filed under seal. The original and one copy of the petition and a PDF version on a CD–ROM shall be tendered to the Clerk. The original and copy of the petition and all related documents shall be submitted securely in an envelope/box appropriate to accommodate the documents. The envelope/box containing such documents shall have a conspicuous notation as follows: "DOCUMENT UNDER SEAL."

(b) Notice to the Court. The Secretary shall provide written notice under seal to the Clerk of the Court that a petition will likely be filed with the Court, and to the extent feasible, the notice will be provided at least 48 hours prior to filing the petition.

(c) Notice to the Financial Company. A petition shall be accompanied by a certificate of counsel or other proof satisfactory to the Court, stating (1) that actual notice of the time of filing the petition, and copies of all papers filed to date or to be presented to the Court at any hearing, have been or are being furnished to the financial company; or (2) the efforts made by the Secretary to give such notice and furnish such copies. The certificate shall also contain the name and contact information of the individual at the financial company to whom notice was given and upon whom service was effected.

(d) Opposition to the Petition. The financial company named in the petition may file an opposition to the petition under seal and may appear at a hearing to oppose the petition. The opposition shall be served on the Secretary by the most expeditious means available.

(e) Proposed Order. Each petition and opposition shall be accompanied by a proposed order.

(f) Assignment of the Petition. The petition shall be assigned to the Chief Judge or Acting Chief Judge.

(g) Consideration of Petition: Notification of Decision. In considering a petition, the Court shall, on a confidential basis and without public disclosure, determine whether the Secretary's decision that the covered financial company (1) is in default or in danger of default and (2) satisfies the definition of a financial company under the Act is arbitrary and capricious.*

(1) Upon a finding that the Secretary's determination is not arbitrary and capricious, the Court shall issue an order immediately authorizing the Secretary to appoint the Corporation as receiver of the covered financial company.

(2) Upon a finding that the Secretary's determination is arbitrary and capricious, the Court shall provide immediately for the record a written statement of each reason supporting the determination of the Court, and shall provide copies thereof to the Secretary and the covered financial company, and must afford the Secretary an immediate opportunity to amend and refile the petition.

(h) Timing of Decision. The Court shall attempt to rule on a properly filed petition within twenty-four (24) hours of receipt of the petition. In the event that the Court does not do so, the petition is deemed granted by operation of law under the Act.

(i) Maintaining Petitions and Subsequent Filings Under Seal. The petition and subsequent filings must be maintained under seal pending further order of the Court. Upon the granting of a petition, the Secretary shall promptly notify the Court of the appointment of the receiver. The Court shall then issue an Order to Show Cause to the Secretary as to why the proceedings, or any part thereof, shall not be unsealed.

(j) Stay Pending Appeal. The decision of the Court on a petition shall not be subject to a stay or injunction pending appeal.

(k) Effect of FRCP 6. The time periods found in subsections (b) and (h) of this Rule are not subject to Rule 6 of the Federal Rules of Civil Procedure.

[Effective January 19, 2011. Amended effective July 6, 2011.]

* So in original.

APPENDIX A. DISPUTE RESOLUTION PROGRAMS

"THE DISTRICT COURT IS COMMITTED TO MAKING DISPUTE RESOLUTION AN EFFECTIVE AND INTEGRAL PART OF THE ADMINISTRATION OF JUSTICE IN THIS JURISDICTION..."

Thomas F. Hogan
Chief Judge

INTRODUCTION

This introduction is provided to litigants and attorneys as an overview of the Mediation Program of the United States District Court for the District of Columbia. The Mediation Program was created in 1989 to give litigants an opportunity to discuss—with a trained, neutral third person—the possibility of settling their dispute consensually, without trying the case in court. Mediation, while not appropriate in all cases can offer numerous advantages over both formal litigation and direct negotiations in many situations. Mediation may, for example, lead to resolutions that are:

- faster
- less expensive
- more creative
- better able to address the underlying interests of all parties

This introduction has a two-fold purpose: (1) to explain mediation to litigants and their counsel; and (2) to help counsel meet their obligations under Local Rule 16.3 to "meet and confer" early in the litigation process about whether mediation would be appropriate in particular cases.

WHAT IS MEDIATION?

Mediation is an informal process in which a specially-trained neutral third person helps the parties in a lawsuit attempt to reach a mutually agreeable settlement. The mediation process involves one or more sessions in which counsel, litigants and the mediator participate and may continue over a period of time. The mediator has no power to render a decision or dictate a settlement. She or he can, however, help the parties improve communication, clarify interests and prove the strengths and weaknesses of their own and their opponents' positions. The mediator can also identify areas of agreement and help generate options that lead to a settlement.

HOW DOES A CASE GET INTO THE MEDIATION PROGRAM?

Voluntary participation. Participation in the District Court's Mediation Program is voluntary. Parties may request mediation or the presiding judge may suggest it at a status conference. If all parties consent, the judge issues an order referring the case to the Office of the Circuit Executive, where the program is administered. The referral may take place at any time while the case is pending.

Local Rule LCvR 16.3(a). Local Rule 16.3(a) requires counsel to meet, within 21 days after the defendant enters an appearance in a case to discuss—among other things—whether mediation might be appropriate. In assessing the possibility of mediation, counsel must consider:

- their clients' goals and objectives;
- the status of any prior settlement talks;
- the potential timing of any referral to mediation;
- whether their clients might benefit from a neutral evaluation of the merits of the case; and
- whether mediation might result in cost savings or any other practical benefits.

Within 14 days following this meeting, the parties must submit a joint report to the Court describing their views on the application of mediation to their case and outlining the steps that might be taken to facilitate that process. The report must also tell the Court whether counsel discussed mediation with their clients before filing the report.

Thus, even if the presiding judge does not suggest that counsel consider mediation, LCvR 16.3(a) requires them to do so.

WHICH CASES ARE ELIGIBLE FOR MEDIATION?

All civil cases in which parties are represented by counsel are eligible for mediation. Each case should be assessed on an individual basis to determine whether a referral would be appropriate.

WHAT MAKES A PARTICULAR CASE APPROPRIATE FOR MEDIATION?

Deciding whether a particular case has "mediation potential" is an art, not a science. Thinking about the factors listed below should help you make that determination.

Relationship between parties. Do the parties in your case have a business or other ongoing relationship? If so, is this an incentive to try to resolve the problems that generate the lawsuit? Are emotions so high that the intervention of a third person might help the parties communicate?

Receptivity of the lawyers. Are the lawyers in the case receptive to the mediation process?

Reluctance to exchange information in direct negotiation. Can a mediator help the parties identify and exchange information that will enable them to begin serious settlement discussions?

Adequacy of a judicial remedy. Will a judicial ruling give the parties what they really want and need? In certain kinds of lawsuits, for example, the plaintiff may want an apology in addition to money damages. Courts generally do not order litigants to apologize. But some form of apology might be available through a mediation.

Divergent views about the value of the case. Do the parties have widely divergent views about the value of a case; that is, about what will happen if the case goes to trial? Would they benefit from a neutral evaluation of their case by a Court mediator who is an expert in this type of litigation?

Need for a precedent. Do one or more of the parties seek to establish a legal precedent and therefore require a judicial ruling? Government or institutional litigants may frequently be in this position. In such a case, mediation might not be appropriate.

Need for privacy. Do the parties want to avoid a public airing of their dispute? A case involving the break-up of a law firm or claims of sexual harassment might be examples.

Difficulty in fashioning a remedy. Has liability been established, leaving the Court with the sometimes more difficult problem of fashioning a remedy? Could a mediator help the parties in this task? Class-action employment discrimination cases often present this problem. In such cases the Court may have decided that the institution's past practices are unlawful but left it to the parties to craft injunctive relief for the future.

Need for mediation to resolve continuing disputes. Can a mediator help the parties agree upon a dispute resolution mechanism they can use after the lawsuit is settled to resolve disputes that flow from the lawsuit? For example, can a mediator help litigants in a class-action discrimination case devise a mechanism to be used to decide the monetary value of each class member's claims, once class-wide liability is established?

WHEN SHOULD MEDIATION OCCUR?

Cases can be referred to mediation at any point during the litigation process. There are no hard-and-fast rules about when intervention might be most useful. As with case selection, the best way to think about the timing of a referral is to consider a series of questions:

- Do the parties have enough information to engage in serious conversations about settlement?
- Are there outstanding legal issues that the Court must resolve before settlement talks can take place?

- Have the parties' circumstances changed in a way that would make settlement talks more productive than in the past?
- Has the imminence of trial, with its attendant costs, anxieties and potential for publicity, heightened the parties' interest in settlement?
- Has liability been decided? Could a mediator assist the parties in devising a proposal for injunctive relief?

Your answers to these questions should help you confirm whether mediation is appropriate and, if so, when it should take place.

WHO ARE THE MEDIATORS?

The mediators are members of the United States District Court Bar who are selected by the Court and trained by professional trainers to provide mediation services to litigants on a pro bono basis. The Court typically maintains a roster of approximately 150 mediators.

HOW IS A MEDIATOR ASSIGNED TO A CASE?

When a case enters the program, a member of the dispute resolution staff in the Circuit Executive's Office appoints a qualified mediator from the Court's roster. The staff welcome any suggestions or ideas counsel may have about the type of mediator who is likely to be most helpful.

Mediators with particular expertise in the subject-matter of the lawsuit are available if the judge and the parties believe a neutral evaluation of the case is needed. In such a case the mediator would not only assist the parties in identifying their interests and the options for settlement, she or he would also give them an informal, non-binding assessment of the merits of the action. That assessment may be given to each side privately or to all parties in a joint mediation session.

WHAT TAKES PLACE IN A MEDIATION?

A mediation typically begins with a joint meeting of all parties and their counsel and the mediator, held within three weeks of the mediator's appointment. During that session, each participant has the opportunity to voice his or her perception of the dispute and to ask questions. The mediator then meets with each party separately to explore the issues further and to suggest settlement options. Mediation may continue over a period of time; with additional joint or individual sessions. The mediator may also confer with the parties by telephone. The process ends when one of the following events occur:

- the parties settle their dispute
- the mediator and the parties conclude that further discussions would be fruitless; or
- the mediation deadline—a date that is established by the judge's order of referral—is reached.

KEY POINTS ABOUT THE MEDIATION PROCESS

Mediation in the U.S. District Court is based on the following principles:

- All mediation proceedings are confidential. Documents generated for the mediation are also confidential and may not be introduced during a subsequent trial should the case not settle. The judge who is assigned to the case is not told the identity of the mediator or given any information about the transpires during the mediation process.
- Counsel and parties with settlement authority must attend mediation sessions. Certain exceptions may be granted for institutional parties or if a party is a unit of government.
- At least seven days prior to the first mediation session, each party must give the mediator a mediation statement that outlines the key facts and legal issues in the case. Mediation statements are not briefs and are not filed with the Court.
- Unless the presiding judge indicates otherwise, referral of a case to mediation does not stay other proceedings in the case or alter applicable litigation deadlines.
- The parties may seek an extension of the Court-imposed mediation deadline by filing an appropriate motion. The motion may represent the mediator's views about whether an extension is advisable, but may not disclose the mediator's identity.
- The Office of the Circuit Executive monitors the progress of mediated cases on a confidential basis. Questions or problems arising during the course of a mediation may be brought to the attention of the dispute resolution staff by any party.

COMPLIANCE JUDGE

Information about the mediation is confidential and may not be disclosed to the presiding judge in any referred action. To protect confidentiality while at the same time preserving the Court's ability to ensure compliance with its dispute resolution policies and orders, the Court has designated one judge to serve as the Dispute Resolution Compliance Judge. Complaints that litigants have not complied in good faith with the Court's mediation guidelines or with a judicial order referring a case to the program must be brought to the attention of the Director of Dispute Resolution, who may then refer them to the Compliance Judge for appropriate action. Litigants may not bring such matters to the attention of the Compliance Judge directly or to the attention of the judge who is presiding in the lawsuit.

PROGRAM ADMINISTRATION

The District Court's Mediation Program as well as the Appellate Mediation Program in the United States Court of Appeals for the District of Columbia Circuit are administered by the Office of the Circuit Executive. The Office is responsible for assigning cases to qualified neutrals and providing parties with the proper notification and instructions. Attorneys in the Circuit Executive's Office also monitor the progress of cases, collect pertinent statistical information and serve as a resource for program mediators as they handle cases.

WHERE CAN I GET MORE INFORMATION: CLERK'S OFFICE

The District Court Clerk's Office supplies copies of:

- The Rules of the United States District Court for the District of Columbia, including Local Rule 16.3 and the Court's mediation procedure.
- Mediation in the United States District Court for the District of Columbia

OFFICE OF THE CIRCUIT EXECUTIVE

For information about using the Court's Mediation Program or about the procedures that apply once a case is referred, or for other information about dispute resolution, contact:

Director of Dispute Resolution
Office of the Circuit Executive
United States Courts for the
District of Columbia Circuit
333 Constitution Avenue, N.W.
Washington, D.C. 20001
(202) 216–7350

[Effective August 1, 1999. Amended effective December 1, 2009.]

APPENDIX B. D.C. BAR VOLUNTARY STANDARDS FOR CIVILITY IN PROFESSIONAL CONDUCT

Civility in professional conduct is the responsibility of every lawyer. While lawyers have an obligation to represent clients zealously, we must also be mindful of our obligations to the administration of justice. Incivility to opposing counsel, adverse parties, judges, court personnel, and other participants in the legal process demeans the legal profession, undermines the administration of justice, and diminishes respect for both the legal process and the results of our system of justice.

Our judicial system is a truth-seeking process designed to resolve human and societal problems in a rational, peaceful, and efficient manner and designed to be perceived as producing fair and just results. We must be careful to avoid actions or statements which undermine the system or the public's confidence in it.

The organized bar and the judiciary, in partnership with each other, have a responsibility to promote civility in the practice of law and the administration of justice. Uncivil conduct of lawyers or judges impedes the fundamental goal of resolving disputes rationally, peacefully and efficiently. Such conduct may delay or deny justice and diminish the respect of law, which is a cornerstone of our society and our profession.

Civility and professionalism are hallmarks of a learned profession dedicated to public service. These standards are designed to encourage us, as lawyers and judges, to meet our obligations of civility and professionalism, to each other, to litigants, and to the system of justice. The goal is to ensure that lawyers and judges will conduct themselves at all times, in both litigated and nonlitigated matters, with personal courtesy and professionalism in the fullest sense of those terms.

While these standards are voluntary and are not intended by the D.C. Bar Board of Governors to be used as a basis of litigation or sanctions, we expect that lawyers and judges in the District of Columbia will make a commitment to adhere to these standards in all aspects of their dealings with one another and with other participants in the legal process.

Finally, we believe these standards should be incorporated as an integral component of the teaching of professionalism to law students and practicing lawyers alike. We therefore believe that it is important for law schools in our community to incorporate these standards in their curricula and for the District of Columbia Bar, the voluntary bar associations, law firms, government agencies, and other legal institutions in our community to teach and promote these standards as part of their continuing legal education programs.

PRINCIPLES OF GENERAL APPLICABILITY: LAWYERS DUTIES TO OTHER COUNSEL, PARTIES AND THE JUDICIARY

GENERAL PRINCIPLES:

1. In carrying out our professional responsibilities, we will treat all participants in the legal process, including counsel and their staff, parties, witnesses, judges, and court personnel, in a civil, professional, and courteous manner, at all times and in all communications, whether oral or written. We will refrain from acting upon or manifesting racial, gender, or other bias or prejudice toward any participant in the legal process. We will treat all participants in the legal process with respect.

2. Except within the bounds of fair argument in pleadings or in formal proceedings, we will not reflect in our conduct, attitude, or demeanor our clients' ill feelings, if any, toward other participants in the legal process.

3. We will not, even if called upon by a client to do so, engage in offensive conduct directed toward other participants in the legal process nor will we abuse other such participants in the legal process. Except within the bounds of fair argument in pleadings or in formal proceedings, we will abstain from disparaging personal remarks or acrimony toward such participants and treat adverse witnesses and parties with fair consideration. We will encourage our clients to act civilly and respectfully to all participants in the legal process.

4. We will not encourage or authorize any person under our control to engage in conduct that would be inappropriate under these standards if we were to engage in such conduct.

5. We will not bring the profession into disrepute by making unfounded accusations of impropriety or making ad hominem attacks on counsel, and, absent good cause, we will not attribute bad motives or improper conduct to other counsel.

6. While we owe our highest loyalty to our clients, we will discharge that obligation in the framework of the judicial system in which we apply our learning, skill, and industry in accordance with professional norms. In this context, we will strive for orderly, efficient, ethical, fair, and just disposition of litigation as well as disputed matters that are not, or not yet, the subject of litigation, and for the efficient, ethical and fair negotiation and consummation of business transactions.

7. The foregoing General Principles apply to all aspects of legal proceedings, both in the presence and outside the presence of a court or tribunal.

SCHEDULING MATTERS:

8. We will endeavor to schedule dates for trials, hearings, depositions, meetings, negotiations, conferences, vacations, seminars, and other functions to avoid creating calendar conflicts for other participants in the legal process, provided our clients' interests will not be adversely affected.

9. We will notify other counsel and, if appropriate, the court or other persons, at the earliest possible time when hearings, depositions, meetings, or conferences need to be canceled or postponed. Early notice avoids unnecessary travel and expense and may enable the court and the other participants in the legal process to use the previously reserved time for other matters.

10. We will agree to reasonable requests for extensions of time and for waiver of procedural formalities provided our clients' interests will not be adversely affected.

11. We will not request an extension of time for the purpose of unjustified delay.

PRINCIPLES PARTICULARLY APPLICABLE TO LITIGATION PROCEDURAL AGREEMENTS:

12. We will confer with opposing counsel about procedural issues that arise during the course of litigation, such as requests for extensions of time, discovery matters, pre-trial matters, and the scheduling of meetings, depositions, hearings, and trial. We will seek to resolve by agreement such procedural issues that do not require court order. For those that do, we will seek to reach agreement with opposing counsel before presenting the matter to court.

13. We accept primary responsibility, after consultation with the client, for making decisions about procedural agreements. We will explain to our clients that cooperation between counsel in such matters is the professional norm and may be in the client's interest. We will explain the nature of the matter at issue in any such proposed agreements and explain how such agreements do not compromise the client's interests.

DISCOVERY:

14. We will not use any form of discovery or discovery scheduling for harassment, unjustified delay, to increase litigation expenses, or any other improper purpose.

15. We will make good faith efforts to resolve by agreement any disputes with respect to matters contained in pleadings and discovery requests and objections.

16. We will not engage in any conduct during a deposition that would not be appropriate if a judge were present. Accordingly, we will not obstruct questioning during a deposition or object to deposition questions, unless permitted by the applicable rules to preserve an objection or privilege and we will ask only those questions we reasonably believe are appropriate in discovery under the applicable rules.

17. We will carefully craft document production requests so they are limited to those documents we reasonably believe are appropriate under the applicable rules. We will not design production requests for the purpose of placing an undue burden or expense on a party.

18. We will respond to document requests reasonably. We will not interpret the request in an artificially restrictive manner to avoid disclosure of relevant and non-privileged documents. We will not produce documents in a manner designed to hide or obscure the existence of particular documents.

19. We will carefully craft interrogatories so they are limited to those matters we reasonably believe are appropriate under the applicable rules, and we will not design them for the purpose of placing an undue burden or expense on a party.

20. We will respond to interrogatories reasonably. We will not interpret interrogatories in an artificially restrictive manner to avoid disclosure of relevant and non-privileged information.

21. We will base our discovery objections on a good faith belief in their merit. We will not object solely for the purpose of withholding or delaying the disclosure of properly discoverable information.

22. During discovery, we will not engage in acrimonious conversations or exchanges with opposing counsel, parties, or witnesses. We will advise our clients to conduct themselves in accordance with these provisions. We will not engage in undignified or discourteous conduct which degrades the legal proceeding.

SANCTIONS:

23. We will not seek court sanctions or disqualification of counsel unless reasonably justified by the circumstances after conducting a reasonable investigation, which includes attempting to confer with opposing counsel.

LAWYERS' DUTIES TO THE COURT:

24. We recognize that the public's perception of our system of justice is influenced by the relationship between lawyers and judges, and that judges perform a symbolic role. At the same time, lawyers have the right and, at times, the duty to be critical of judges and their rulings. Thus, in all communications with the court, we will speak and write civilly. In expressing criticism of the court, we shall seek to use language that minimizes disrespect for courts and the system of justice.

25. We will not engage in conduct that offends the dignity and decorum of judicial proceedings, brings disorder or disruption to the courtroom, or undermines the image of the legal profession.

26. We will advise clients and witnesses to act civilly and respectfully toward the court, educate them about proper courtroom decorum, and, to the best of our ability, prevent them from creating disorder or disruption in the courtroom.

27. We will not knowingly misrepresent, mischaracterize, misquote, or miscite facts or authorities.

28. We will not degrade the intelligence, ethics, morals, integrity or personal behavior of others, unless such matters are legitimately at issue in the proceeding.

29. We will act and speak civilly and respectfully to the judge's staff, the courtroom staff, and other court personnel with an awareness that they, too, are an integral part of the judicial system. We will also advise clients and witnesses to act civilly and respectfully toward these participants in the legal process.

30. We recognize that judicial resources are scarce, that court dockets are crowded, and that justice is undermined when cases are delayed and/or disputes remain unresolved. Therefore, we will be considerate of the time constraints and pressures on the court and court staff inherent in their efforts to administer justice.

31. We recognize that tardiness and neglect show disrespect to the court and the judicial system. Therefore, we will be punctual and prepared for all court appearances so that all hearings, conferences, and trials may commence on time and proceed efficiently. We will also educate clients and witnesses concerning the need to be punctual and prepared. If delayed, we will promptly notify the court and counsel, if at all possible.

32. Before dates for hearing or trials are set, or, if that is not feasible, immediately after such a date has been set, we will attempt to verify the availability of necessary participants and witnesses so we can promptly notify the court of any likely problems.

33. We will avoid *ex parte* communications with the court, including the judge's staff, on pending matters in person (whether in social, professional, or other contexts), by telephone, and in letters and other forms of written communication, unless such communications relate solely to scheduling or other non-substantive administrative matters, or are made with the consent of all parties, or are otherwise expressly authorized by law or court rule.

JUDGES' DUTIES TO LAWYERS:

34. We will be courteous, respectful, and civil to lawyers, parties, and witnesses. We will maintain control of the proceedings, recognizing that judges have both the obligation and the authority to ensure that judicial proceedings are conducted with dignity, decorum, and courtesy.

35. We will not employ hostile, demeaning, or humiliating words in opinions or in written or oral communications with lawyers, parties, or witnesses.

36. We will be punctual in convening hearings, meetings, and conferences; if delayed, we will notify counsel as promptly as possible.

37. In scheduling hearings, meetings, and conferences, we will be considerate of time schedules of lawyers, parties, and witnesses and of other courts and tribunals. We will inform counsel promptly of any rescheduling, postponement, or cancellation of hearings, meetings, or conferences.

38. While endeavoring to resolve disputes efficiently, we will be considerate of the time constraints and pressures imposed on lawyers by the exigencies of litigation practice. We will make all reasonable efforts promptly to decide matters presented to us for decision.

39. We recognize that a lawyer has a right and duty to present a cause fully and properly, and that a litigant has a right to a fair and impartial hearing. Within the practical limits of time, we will allow lawyers to present proper arguments, to make a complete and accurate record, and to present a case free from unreasonable or unnecessary judicial interruption.

40. We will not impugn the integrity or professionalism of any lawyer on the basis of the clients whom or the causes which a lawyer represents.

41. We will do our best to ensure that court personnel act civilly toward lawyers, parties and witnesses.

42. At an appropriate time and in an appropriate manner, we will bring to a lawyer's attention conduct which we observe that is inconsistent with these standards.

JUDGES' DUTIES TO EACH OTHER:

43. We will treat other judges with courtesy and respect.

44. In written opinions and oral remarks, we will refrain from personally attacking, disparaging, or demeaning other judges.

45. We will endeavor to work cooperatively with other judges with respect to the availability of lawyers, witnesses, parties, and court resources.

PRINCIPLES PARTICULARLY APPLICABLE TO REPRESENTATION INVOLVING BUSINESS TRANSACTIONS AND OTHER NEGOTIATIONS

46. We will not knowingly misrepresent or mischaracterize facts or authorities or affirmatively mislead another party or its counsel in negotiations.

47. We will not engage in personal vilification or other abusive or discourteous conduct in negotiations. We will not engage in acrimonious exchanges with opposing counsel or parties at the negotiating table. We will encourage our clients to conduct themselves in accordance with these principles.

48. We will honor all understandings with, and commitments we have made to, other attorneys. We will stand by proposals we have made in negotiations unless newly received information or unforeseen circumstances provide a good faith basis for rescinding them, and we will encourage our clients to conduct themselves in accordance with this principle.

49. We will not make changes to written documents under negotiation in a manner calculated to cause the opposing party or counsel to overlook or fail to appreciate the changes. We will clearly and accurately identify for other counsel and parties all changes that we have made in documents submitted to us for review.

50. In memorializing oral agreements the parties have reached, we will do so without making changes in substance and will strive in good faith to state the oral understandings accurately and completely. In drafting proposed agreements based on letters of intent, we will strive to draft documents that fairly reflect the agreements of the parties.

[Adopted by the D.C. Bar Board of Governors June 18, 1996. Amended March 11, 1997; August 1, 1999.]

CRIMINAL

LCrR 1.1 SCOPE AND CONSTRUCTION

These Rules govern all proceedings in the United States District Court for the District of Columbia. These Rules supplement the Federal Rules of Civil and Criminal Procedure and shall be construed in harmony thereafter.

[Effective August 1, 1999.]

LCrR 6.1 GRAND JURY MATTERS

A motion or application filed in connection with a grand jury subpoena or other matter occurring before a grand jury, all other papers filed in support of or in opposition to such a motion or application, and all orders entered by the Court in connection therewith, shall be filed under seal. Such a motion or application shall be assigned a Miscellaneous case number. All hearings on matters affecting a grand jury proceeding shall be closed, except for contempt proceedings in which the alleged contemnor requests a public hearing. Papers, orders and transcripts of hearings subject to this Rule, or portions thereof, may be made public by the Court on its own motion or on motion of any person upon a finding that continued secrecy is not necessary to prevent disclosure of matters occurring before the grand jury.

[Effective August 1, 1999.]

LCrR 16.1 DISCOVERY

Defense counsel shall consult with the attorney for the United States prior to the first status conference in a criminal case and shall attempt to obtain voluntary discovery of all materials and information to which the defense may be entitled. No discovery motion shall be heard unless it states that defense counsel has previously requested that the information sought from the attorney for the United States and that such attorney has not complied with the request.

[Effective August 1, 1999.]

LCrR 17.1 ISSUANCE OF SUBPOENAS FOR APPOINTED COUNSEL

Defense counsel appointed under the Criminal Justice Act and staff attorneys of the Public Defender Service may apply to the Clerk for witness subpoenas where the witness will be served within a 25 mile radius of the boundaries of this district. The Clerk shall issue such subpoenas signed and sealed and designated in forma pauperis, but otherwise in blank. By filling in such a subpoena, defense counsel certifies that in counsel's opinion, the presence of the witness is necessary to an adequate defense. No subpoena so issued in blank may be served at a place more than 25 miles from the district. Where a witness to be subpoenaed will be served at a place more than 25 miles from the district, an application for the issuance of a subpoena in forma pauperis shall be made to the Court. The application may be made ex parte.

[Effective August 1, 1999.]

LCrR 17.2 CLOSURE OF PRETRIAL PROCEEDINGS

(a) General Rule. Unless otherwise provided by law or by this Rule, all criminal proceedings, including preliminary examinations and hearings on pretrial motions, shall be held in open court and shall be available for attendance and observation by the public. This Rule does not apply to bench conferences, conferences in chambers, and other matters normally handled in camera.

(b) Motion for Closure. Upon motion made or agreed to by the defendant, the Court may in the exercise of its discretion order a pretrial proceeding to be closed to the public in whole or in part, on the grounds:

(1) that there is a substantial probability that the dissemination of information disclosed at the proceeding would impair the defendant's right to a fair trial or another overriding public interest; and

(2) that no reasonable alternative to closure will adequately protect the defendant's right to a fair trial or another overriding public interest.

If the Court enters such an order, it shall state the specific findings which require closure.

(c) Opposition by Non-Parties. Any news organization or other interested person may be heard orally or in writing in opposition to a closure motion by a party. When any papers are filed by a non-party opposing closure, the matter shall be assigned a Miscellaneous docket number and shall be governed by LCrR 57.6. A non-party seeking to appeal from an order of closure shall be responsible for filing in the Miscellaneous proceeding the order from which the appeal is taken, and such other parts of the record of the criminal case as may be necessary to determination of the appeal.

[Effective August 1, 1999. Amended effective October 12, 2006.]

Comment

COMMENT TO LCrR 17.2(c): The changes to this rule correct a referencing error.

LCrR 24.1 JURY SELECTION AND ASSIGNMENT

Grand and petit jurors shall be selected at random in accordance with a plan adopted by the Court and available from the Jury Office. Petit jurors shall be assigned to a single jury pool and reassigned for service upon the requisition of each trial judge.

[Effective August 1, 1999.]

LCrR 24.2 COMMUNICATION WITH A JUROR

(a) During Trial. No party, attorney for a party, or person acting on behalf of a party or attorney, shall communicate directly or indirectly with a juror or an excused juror or a member of a juror's, or an excused juror's, family during the trial.

(b) After Trial. After a verdict is rendered or a mistrial is declared but before the jury is discharged, an attorney or party may request leave of court to speak with members of the jury after their discharge. Upon receiving such a request, the Court shall inform the jury that no juror is required to speak to anyone but that a juror may do so if the juror wishes. If no request to speak with jurors is made before discharge of the jury, no party or attorney shall speak with a juror concerning the case except when permitted by the Court for good cause shown in writing. The Court may grant permission to speak with a juror upon such conditions as it deems appropriate, including but not limited to a requirement that the juror be examined only in the presence of the Court.

[Effective August 1, 1999.]

Comment

COMMENT TO LCrR 24.2: This Rule gives the Court greater flexibility by stating that where the request to converse with jurors is made after their discharge, the Court may impose such conditions as it deems appropriate.

LCrR 32.1 PROBATION AND REVOCATION OF PROBATION

(a) Assignment to a Probation Officer. Immediately following a sentence of probation or a split sentence, the defendant shall be assigned to a probation officer.

(b) Conditions of Probation. The Court shall impose such conditions of probation as are necessary to provide a benefit to the probationer and protection to the public and may modify or enlarge such conditions at any time prior to the expiration or termination of the sentence as deemed advisable. The probationer shall be provided by the probation office with a written statement and an explanation of the conditions imposed. If the matter cannot be resolved by the probation office, the probationer may request clarification of any condition from the sentencing judge and may petition the sentencing judge for a modification of the conditions imposed.

(c) Hearing on Alleged Violations of Probation.

(1) Unless waived by the probationer after due notification of rights, a hearing shall be held on all alleged violations of probation where revocation is a possibility to determine whether a violation has occurred and, if so, the appropriate disposition. Prior to the hearing, the probationer shall be provided by the probation office with written notice of all alleged violations, and notice of the rights guaranteed by subsection (2), including the right to counsel and the right to appointed counsel if indigent.

(2) At the probation revocation hearing, which shall be held on the record in open court, the probationer shall be afforded:

(i) access to records regarding the probation violation;

(ii) the right to be represented by counsel, including the right to appointed counsel if indigent;

(iii) the right to subpoena and present witnesses and documentary evidence; and

(iv) the right to confront and cross-examine witnesses against the probationer.

(3) The government shall be represented by counsel at the probation revocation hearing.

(4) Before probation is revoked the Court, in cases where the facts of violation are contested, shall make findings of fact and shall find that the government has established by a preponderance of evidence that the probationer has violated a condition of probation.

(d) Violation of a Probation Condition; Resentencing. Upon finding a violation of a condition of probation the Court may: continue the existence* with or without modification; enlarge the conditions of probation; revoke the probation and require the probationer to serve the sentence imposed, or any lesser sentence, and, if imposition of sentence was suspended, may impose any sentence which might originally have been imposed. In resentencing a probation violator the procedures governing initial sentencing decisions shall apply.

(e) Hearings Delegated to the Magistrate Judge. A hearing on an alleged violation of probation as provided in sub-section (c)(2) may be delegated by the Court to the magistrate judge. Following a hearing before the magistrate judge, the magistrate judge shall file written findings and recommendations. The Court shall make a de novo determination of those portions of the magistrate judge's report to which objections are made and may accept, reject, or modify in whole or in part, the findings and recommendations made by the magistrate judge. The Court, however, need not conduct a new hearing and may make a determination based on the record, evidence, recall witnesses, or recommit the matter to the magistrate judge. The Court may also receive further evidence, recall witnesses, or recommit the matter to the magistrate judge with instructions. While the matter is pending before the magistrate judge, the magistrate judge shall have the authority to issue a bench warrant for the apprehension of the probationer for failure to appear before the magistrate judge as directed, or for failure to comply with any release conditions imposed by the magistrate judge.

[Effective August 1, 1999.]

* So in original. Probably should be "existing sentence".

LCrR 32.2 SENTENCING GUIDELINES

(a) Not less than 28 days prior to the date set for the sentencing, the probation officer shall disclose the initial presentence report to the defendant and the prosecution. Within 14 days thereafter, counsel shall communicate to the probation officer any objections they may have as to any material information, sentencing classifications, sentencing guideline ranges, and policy statements contained in or omitted from the report. Such communication may be oral or written, but the probation officer may require that any oral objection be promptly confirmed in writing.

(b) After receiving counsels' objections, the probation officer shall conduct any further investigation and make any revisions to the presentence report that may be necessary. The officer may require counsel for both parties to meet with the officer to discuss unresolved factual and legal issues.

(c) Not less than 7 days prior to the date of the sentencing, the probation officer shall submit the final presentence report to the sentencing judge. The report shall be accompanied by an addendum setting forth any objections counsel may have made that have not been resolved in the report, together with the officer's comments thereon. The probation officer shall certify that the contents of the final presentence report have been disclosed to the defendant and to counsel for the defendant and prosecution, that the addendum has been communicated to counsel, and the addendum fairly states any remaining objections.

(d) A hearing shall be held not more than 7 days prior to the date of sentencing to resolve any disputed issues of fact, and to gather any other information the

Court finds to be relevant to the sentencing guideline calculation. The Court may consider any reliable information presented by the probation officer, the defendant, or the prosecution.

(e) When necessary to make consistent findings as to the role of each defendant in a multiple defendant case, the Court may, in lieu of or in addition to the evidentiary hearing authorized for by subsection (d), convene a joint evidentiary hearing on the same or other appropriate date.

(f) To the extent that the final presentence investigation report is undisputed by the parties, it may be accepted by the Court as accurate. The Court, however, for good cause shown, may allow a new objection to be raised any time before the imposition of sentence. The Court shall ensure that the probation officer and the other party has ample notice of the objection and an opportunity fairly to robut or support the assertion.

(g) Any of the time periods set forth in this Rule may be modified by the Court on its own motion, or at the request of a party or the probation officer for good cause shown, and the Court may direct that the evidentiary hearing provided for in subsection (d) shall be held on the sentencing date. However, the 14–day period set forth in subsection (a) may be diminished only with the consent of the defendant.

(h) Nothing in this Rule requires the disclosure of any portions of the presentence report that are not disclosable under Rule 32 of the Federal Rules of Criminal Procedure.

(i) The presentence report shall be deemed to have been disclosed (1) when a copy of the report is physically delivered, (2) one day after the report's availability for inspection is orally communicated, or (3) three days after a copy of the report or notice of its availability is mailed.

[Effective August 1, 1999. Amended effective December 1, 2009.]

LCrR 44.1 PRACTICE BY ATTORNEYS

(a) Practice by Members of the Bar of This Court. An attorney who is a member in good standing of the Bar of this Court may appear, file papers and practice in this Court, provided that the attorney complies with section (b) of this Rule.

(b) Appearance as Sole or Lead Counsel in a Contested Evidentiary Hearing or Trial on the Merits. Each attorney who acts as sole or lead counsel in any contested evidentiary hearing or trial on the merits, civil or criminal, must have on file with the Clerk's office a certificate, in a form prescribed by the Clerk, that the attorney

(1) has previously acted as sole or lead counsel in a federal district court or the Superior Court of the District of Columbia or a state trial court of general jurisdiction in a contested jury or bench trial or other contested evidentiary hearing in which testimony was taken in open court and an order or other appealable judgment was entered; or

(2) has participated in a junior capacity in an entire contested jury or bench trial in a federal district court or the Superior Court of the District of Columbia or a state trial court of general jurisdiction; or

(3) has satisfactorily completed a continuing legal education trial advocacy course of at least 30 hours sponsored by the District of Columbia Bar or accredited by a State Bar.

(c) Practice by Non-Members of the Bar of This Court.

(1) An attorney who is a member in good standing of the bar of any United States Court or of the highest court of any State, but who is not a member of the Bar of this Court, may file papers in this Court only if such attorney joins of record a member in good standing of the Bar of this Court. All papers submitted by non-members of the Bar of this Court must be signed by such counsel and by a member of the Bar of this Court joined in compliance with this Rule.

(2) Paragraph (1) above is not applicable to an attorney who engages in the practice of law from an office located in the District of Columbia. An attorney who engages in the practice of law from an office located in the District of Columbia must be a member of the District of Columbia Bar and the Bar of this Court to file papers in this Court.

(d) Participation by Non-Members of This Court's Bar in Court Proceedings. An attorney who is not a member of the Bar of this Court may be heard in open court only by permission of the judge to whom the case is assigned. Any attorney seeking to appear pro hac vice must file a motion signed by a sponsoring member of the Bar of this Court, accompanied by a declaration by the non-member that sets forth: (1) the full name of the attorney; (2) the attorney's office address and telephone number; (3) a list of all bars to which the attorney has been admitted; (4) a certification that the attorney either has or has not been disciplined by any bar, and if the attorney has been disciplined by any bar, the circumstances and details of the discipline; (5) the number of times the attorney has been admitted pro hac vice in this Court within the last two years; and (6) whether the attorney, if the attorney engages in the practice of law from an office located in the District of Columbia, is a member of the District of Columbia Bar or has an application for membership pending.

(e) Attorneys Employed by the United States. An attorney who is employed or retained by the United States or one of its agencies may appear, file papers and practice in this Court in cases in which the

United States or the agency is a party, irrespective of (c) and (d) above.

(f) Entry and Withdrawal of Appearance. Attorneys may enter and withdraw appearances in civil actions as provided in LCvR 83.6 of these Rules, and in criminal actions as provided in LCrR 44.5 of these Rules.

(g) Striking Appearance for Nonattendance at Court Proceedings. The Court may, upon notice and after affording an opportunity to be heard, strike the appearance of any attorney in a particular case for failure, without adequate cause, to attend any hearing, conference or other proceeding. The fact that an attorney's residence or office is located at a place distant from the District of Columbia does not constitute grounds for rescheduling or failing to attend court proceedings.

(h) Certification by Non-Members of the Bar of This Court. An attorney who appears, files papers and practices in this Court pursuant to (e), (f) or (g) above, shall file certification of personal familiarity with the Local Rules of this Court and, as appropriate, the other materials set forth in LCrR 57.21(b) and LCrR 57.21.1(a) simultaneously with each initial appearance by the attorney before a judge of this Court.

[Effective August 1, 1999. Amended effective December 13, 2000; April 11, 2003.]

Comment

COMMENT TO LCrR 44.1(c)(2): LCrR 44.1(c)(2) has been added to conform the Rule of this Court to the current practice of the District of Columbia Committee on Unauthorized Practice, and to recognize that, as a general matter, attorneys who engage in the practice of law from an office located in the District of Columbia and who file papers in Court should be a member of the Bar of this Court and the District of Columbia Bar.

COMMENT TO LCrR 44.1(d): The original intent of this rule was that the "submission" by nonmembers of the Bar seeking pro hac vice admission be provided in the form of a declaration or affidavit as is customary in such circumstances. This section has now been amended to clarify the responsibility of non-members of this Court's Bar.

LCrR 44.2 NUMBER OF COUNSEL

Except by permission of the Court only one attorney on each side shall examine a witness, address the Court on a question arising in a trial, or address the Court or jury in final argument.

[Effective August 1, 1999.]

LCrR 44.3 PRACTICE BY LAW STUDENTS

[Effective August 1, 1999; deleted April 11, 2003.]

Comment

COMMENT TO LCrR 44.3: This rule is being deleted because law students have not been certified to practice criminal law in recent years and we do not anticipate beginning such a program.

LCrR 44.4 PRACTICE BY LAW CLERKS AND COURT EMPLOYEES

Law clerks and secretaries to judges of this Court, and all other persons employed in any capacity by this Court, shall not engage in the practice of law while so employed. A law clerk or secretary to a particular judge of this Court shall not, at any time after separating from that position, engage in any activity as an attorney or advisor, nor permit his or her name to appear as an attorney on any paper filed in this Court, in connection with any case that was pending on that judge's docket during his or her term of service. Any other person employed in any capacity by this Court shall not, for a period of two years after separating from that position, engage in any activity as an attorney or advisor in connection with any case that was pending in this Court during his or her term of service. Each former law clerk, secretary or other employee of this Court, as well as persons employing or associating with them in the practice of law before this Court, shall have the responsibility of enforcing the provisions of this Rule. Evidence of a failure to comply with this Rule shall be referred to this Court's Committee on Grievances.

[Effective August 1, 1999.]

LCrR 44.5 ENTRY AND WITHDRAWAL OF APPEARANCES BY ATTORNEYS IN CRIMINAL ACTION

(a) Entry of Appearance. An attorney appearing for a defendant in a criminal case, whether appointed or retained, shall file with the Clerk a notice of appearance on a court-approved form. If a defendant appears without counsel at arraignment, the Court shall set a date and time by which counsel shall enter an appearance or the defendant, after being fully advised of his right to counsel, shall waive such right and elect to proceed pro se.

(b) Certificate of Familiarity With Sentencing Guidelines. Every attorney who appears as sole or lead counsel in a criminal case must have on file with the Clerk's Office a certificate, in a form prescribed by the Clerk, in which the attorney states that he or she is familiar with the Federal Sentencing Guidelines. If the attorney has filed such a certificate during the previous three years (see Rule 701.1), a new certificate is not necessary.

(c) Continuing Duty of Representation. An attorney who enters an appearance shall continue to represent the defendant until the case is dismissed, the defendant is acquitted, or the time for filing post-trial motions and a notice of appeal has expired, unless the attorney is granted leave to withdraw by the Court.

(d) Withdrawal of Counsel. An attorney who has appeared in a criminal case may thereafter withdraw only by written motion served upon the defendant personally or at the defendant's last-known address, and upon all other parties. The Court may deny a motion to withdraw if the attorney's withdrawal would unduly delay trial of the case or be unfairly prejudicial to any party, or otherwise not be in the interests of justice.

(e) Counsel for the Government. Upon the return of an indictment or bill of information, the United States shall designate an Assistant United States Attorney or other attorney of the Department of Justice as its representative. The United States Attorney shall advise the Clerk and the judge to whom the case is assigned regarding any change in the attorney for the United States responsible for the prosecution.

[Effective August 1, 1999.]

LCrR 44.6 DISCLOSURE OF CORPORATE AFFILIATIONS AND FINANCIAL INTERESTS

In all criminal cases where a corporation is a party, counsel of record for that party shall file a certificate listing any parent, subsidiary, affiliate, or any company which, to the knowledge of counsel, has any outstanding securities in the hands of the public. Such certificate shall be filed at the time counsel first enters his or her appearance in the case. The purpose of this certificate is to enable the judges of this Court to determine the need for recusal. Counsel shall have the continuing obligation to advise the Court of any change. The form of the certificate is:

"Number and Title of Case"

Certificate required by LCrR 44.6 of the Local Rules of the United States District Court for the District of Columbia:

I, the undersigned, counsel of record for ______, certify that to the best of my knowledge and belief, the following are parent companies, subsidiaries or affiliates of ______ which have any outstanding securities in the hands of the public.

(Here list all such parent companies, subsidiaries and affiliates of the corporation.)

These representations are made in order that judges of this Court may determine the need for recusal.

Attorney of Record for ______

[Effective December 13, 2000.]

Comment

COMMENT TO LCrR 44.6: LCrR 44.6 has been added to make clear that attorneys in criminal cases are under a duty to disclose any corporate parent, subsidiary or affiliate when a corporation is a defendant so that judges will be able to determine whether there is a need for recusal. Although LCvR 7.1 purports to cover criminal cases, placing this provision in the criminal rules will insure it is not overlooked by criminal law practitioners.

LCrR 45.1 SPEEDY TRIAL

Pursuant to the requirements of Rule 50(b) of the Federal Rules of Criminal Procedure, the Speedy Trial Act of 1974 (18 U.S.C. Chapter 208), the Speedy Trial Amendments Act of 1979 (Pub. L. No. 96–43, 93 Stat. 327), and the Federal Juvenile Delinquency Act, as amended (18 U.S.C. §§ 5036, 5037), the judges of the United States District Court for the District of Columbia have adopted a Speedy Trial Plan to minimize undue delay and to further the prompt disposition of criminal cases and certain juvenile proceedings. A copy of the Speedy Trial Plan is available from the Clerk's Office.

[Effective August 1, 1999.]

Comment

COMMENT TO LCrR 45.1: This Rule incorporates the Speedy Trial Plan but removes the full text from the Rule. Copies of the Plan are available upon request from the Clerk's office. Many federal courts utilize this procedure and do not restate the full Plan in the rules.

LCrR 46.1 CONDITIONS OF RELEASE

(a) Report of the Pretrial Services Agency. The District of Columbia Pretrial Services Agency shall make personnel available in the courthouse to interview arrested defendants at all times during which magistrate judges are available for presentments. The Pretrial Services Agency shall interview each arrested defendant, verify the information obtained and prepare a report. A copy of the report shall be provided to the court file, to the United States Attorney, and to the defendant's counsel. The Clerk shall notify the Pretrial Services Agency of the action taken by the magistrate judge or Court with regard to conditions of release.

(b) Setting Conditions of Release. Conditions of release shall be set by a magistrate judge or by the judge to whom the case is assigned. An application to the Court for review of conditions of release fixed by a magistrate judge shall be heard upon the record certified by the magistrate judge, together with additional information that may be presented.

(c) Advice to the Defendant. When a defendant is initially released on conditions, the defendant shall be specifically informed of the consequences of a failure to appear at subsequent court dates pursuant to 18 U.S.C. 3146.

[Effective August 1, 1999.]

LCrR 47 MOTIONS

(a) Statement of Points and Authorities. Each motion shall include or be accompanied by a statement of the specific points of law and authority that support the motion, including where appropriate a concise statement of facts. If a table of cases is provided, counsel shall place asterisks in the margin to the left of those cases or authorities on which counsel chiefly relies.

(b) Opposing Points and Authorities. Within 14 days of the date of service or at such other time as the Court may direct, an opposing party shall serve and file a memorandum of points and authorities in opposition to the motion. If such a memorandum is not filed within the prescribed time, the Court may treat the motion as conceded.

(c) Proposed Order. Each motion shall be accompanied by a proposed order.

(d) Reply Memorandum. Within seven days after service of the memorandum in opposition the moving party may serve and file a reply memorandum.

(e) Page Limitations. A memorandum of points and authorities in support of or in opposition to a motion shall not exceed 45 pages and a reply memorandum shall not exceed 25 pages, without prior approval of the Court. Documents that fail to comply with this provision shall not be filed by the Clerk.

(f) Oral Hearings. A party may in a motion or opposition request an oral hearing, but its allowance shall be within the discretion of the Court. If at the time of the hearing the moving party fails to appear, the Court may treat the motion as withdrawn; if the opposing party fails to appear, the Court may treat the motion as conceded.

(g) Motions to Amend Pleadings. A motion for leave to file an amended pleading shall be accompanied by an original of the proposed pleading as amended. The amended pleading shall be deemed to have been filed and served by mail on the date on which the order granting the motion is entered.

(h) Names of Persons to Be Served With Proposed Orders, Judgments and Stipulations. Each proposed order, judgment and stipulation shall have appended to it or endorsed upon it a list of the names and addresses of all attorneys entitled to be notified of its entry. If a party is not represented by an attorney, the name and address of the party shall be included.

[Effective August 1, 1999. Amended effective December 1, 2009.]

LCrR 49.1 FORM AND FILING OF PLEADINGS AND OTHER PAPERS

(a) Place and Manner of Filing. All papers relating to pending action shall be filed with the Clerk unless otherwise directed by the Court.

(b) Correspondence With Court. Except when requested by a judge, correspondence shall not be directed by the parties or their attorneys to a judge, nor shall papers be left with or mailed to a judge for filing.

(c) Number of Copies. The original and one copy of every pleading, motion or other paper shall be filed with the Clerk.

(d) Electronic Transmission. No pleading, motion or other document shall be transmitted to the Clerk for filing by means of electronic facsimile transmission except with express leave of Court.

(e) Name and Address of Parties and Attorneys.

(1) All papers signed by an attorney shall contain the name, address, telephone number, and D.C. Bar identification number of the attorney if the attorney is a member of the D.C. Bar. All attorneys listed on any pleading or paper who are members of the D.C. Bar must include their D.C. Bar identification numbers regardless of whether they sign the pleading. Notice of a change in address or telephone number of an attorney or a party not represented by an attorney must be filed within 14 days of the change. Unless changed by notice filed with the Clerk, the address and telephone number of a party or an attorney noted on the first filing shall be conclusively taken as the last known address and telephone number of the party or attorney.

(2) By signing a pleading or paper that is presented to the Court, an attorney is certifying that the attorney, and all other attorneys appearing with the attorney on the pleading or paper, are members of, or have a pending application for admission to the Bar of this Court, or has complied with LCrR 44.1(c) or (d), or is covered by LCrR 44.1(e) as counsel for the United States.

(f) Form of Papers. All papers shall be typed (double spaced) or reproduced by any duplicating or copying process that produces a clear black image on opaque white paper 11 inches long and 8½ inches wide, unfolded, without back or cover, fastened at the top. Every paper shall contain a heading under the caption describing the nature of the pleading, motion or other paper. Papers should also be punched at the top with two holes, 2¾ inches apart and ⅜ inch from the top, to facilitate insertion in the file jacket. The case number on every paper shall be followed by the initials of the judge to whom the case has been assigned. If the case has been referred to a magistrate judge, the magistrate judge's initials shall also be shown. All exhibits or attachments to papers should reflect the number of the case in which they are filed.

(g) Verification. Whenever any matter is required or permitted by law or by rule to be supported by the sworn written statement of a person (other than a deposition, oath of office, or oath required to be taken before a specified official other than a notary public), the matter may, with the same force and effect, be supported by the unsworn declaration, certificate, verification, or statement, in writing of such person which is subscribed as true under penalty of perjury, and dated, in substantially the following form:

(1) If executed without the United States: "I declare (or certify, verify, or state) under penalty of perjury under the laws of the United States of America that the foregoing is true and correct. Executed on (date).

(Signature)".

(2) If executed within the United States, its territories, possessions, or commonwealths: "I declare (or certify, verify, or state) under penalty of perjury that the foregoing is true and correct. Executed on (date).

(Signature)"

(h) Sealed or Confidential Documents.

(1) Absent statutory authority, no cases or documents may be sealed without an order from the Court. Any pleading filed with the intention of being sealed shall be accompanied by a motion to seal. The document will be treated as sealed, pending the outcome of the ruling on the motion. Failure to file a motion to seal will result in the pleading being placed on the public record.

(2) Unless otherwise ordered or otherwise specifically provided in these Local Rules, all documents submitted for a confidential in camera inspection by the Court, which are the subject of a Protective Order, which are subject to an existing order that they be sealed, or which are the subject of a motion for such orders, shall be submitted to the Clerk securely sealed in an envelope/box needed to accommodate the documents. The envelope/box containing such documents shall contain a conspicuous notation that carries "DOCUMENTS UNDER SEAL" or "DOCUMENTS SUBJECT TO PROTECTIVE ORDER," or the equivalent.

(3) The face of the envelope/box shall also contain the case number, the title of the Court, a descriptive title of the document and the case caption unless such information is to be, or has been, included among the information ordered sealed. The face of the envelope/box shall also contain the date of any order, or the reference to any statute permitting the item sealed.

(4) Filings of sealed materials must be made in the Clerk's Office during the business hours of 9:00 a.m. and 4:00 p.m., daily except Saturdays, Sundays and legal holidays. Filings at the security desk are prohibited because the Security Officers are not authorized to accept this material.

[Effective August 1, 1999. Amended effective December 13, 2000; December 1, 2009.]

Comment

COMMENT TO LCrR 49.1(e)(1) and (2): Section (e)(1) was amended to make clear that the reference to the requirement that all papers include "the Bar identification number of the attorney" requires a D.C. Bar identification number. Because members of the Bar of this Court are not assigned bar identification numbers, Section (e)(2) was added to assist the Clerk's Office in verifying the bar membership status of attorneys who appear in this Court.

LCrR 49.2 PROOF OF SERVICE

Proof of service of papers required or permitted to be served, other than those for which a different method of proof is prescribed by the Federal Rules of Civil Procedure or by statute, shall be filed with such papers. The proof shall show the date and manner of service, and may be by certificate of an attorney of record or other proof satisfactory to the Court. Failure to make proof of service does not affect the validity of service. The Court may at any time allow the proof to be amended or supplied, unless to do so would unfairly prejudice a party.

[Effective August 1, 1999.]

LCrR 53.1.1 PHOTOGRAPH, TAPE RECORDING, AND BROADCASTING IN THE COURTHOUSE

The taking of photographs and operation of tape recorders inside the United States Courthouse and radio or television broadcasting from inside the courthouse during the progress of or in connection with judicial proceedings, including proceedings before a United States Magistrate Judge, whether or not court is actually in session, are prohibited. A judge may, however, permit (1) the use of electronic or photographic means for the presentation of evidence or the perpetuation of a record, and (2) the broadcasting, televising, recording, or photographing of investitive, ceremonial, or naturalization proceedings. Contents of official tapes that are made as part of the record in a case will be treated in the same manner as official stenographic notes.

[Effective August 1, 1999.]

LCrR 56.1 CLERK'S OFFICE

The Clerk's Office shall remain open for the transaction of business from 9:00 A.M. until 4:30 P.M. daily except Saturdays, Sundays and legal holidays. Papers, except for sealed material, that must be filed on a given date may be delivered after 4:30 P.M. to the security desk at the Third Street entrance to the courthouse. Papers found to be in compliance with these Rules will be filed as of the date they were delivered to the security desk. Documents that are being filed under seal pursuant to a protective order must be filed in the Clerk's Office during business hours because the Security Officers are not authorized to accept this material.

[Effective August 1, 1999.]

LCrR 56.2 CUSTODY OF EXHIBITS IN CRIMINAL CASES

(a) Prior to Verdict. A party in a criminal proceeding shall retain its exhibits until they are marked for identification and received in evidence. All exhibits shall thereafter be retained by the Clerk until verdict except that exhibits consisting of narcotics, weapons, money or articles of high monetary value shall be retained by the United States Attorney during adjournment.

(b) After Verdict. In cases where a verdict of not guilty or a judgment of acquittal is entered or a mistrial declared, each party shall immediately retake its exhibits from the Clerk unless otherwise ordered by the Court. In cases where a verdict of guilty is entered the Clerk shall retain all exhibits, except those exhibits described in section (c) of this Rule. If no appeal is perfected, each party shall retake its exhibits from the Clerk within 30 days after the date of final disposition of the case in this Court. If an appeal is perfected, each party shall retake its exhibits from the Clerk within 30 days after final disposition of the case by the appellate courts.

(c) Special Exhibits. Exhibits consisting of narcotics, weapons, money or articles of high monetary value shall be transmitted by the Clerk to the United States Attorney or a designee who shall receipt for them. Exhibits offered by any party which are large and unwieldy, such as diagrams, models, physical displays, etc., shall also be so transmitted unless otherwise ordered by the Court. The United States Attorney shall preserve and maintain in custody all exhibits so transmitted for the periods of time specified in section (b) of this Rule.

(d) Destruction of Exhibits. If any party, having received notice from the Clerk to retake exhibits as provided in section (b) of this Rule, fails to do so within 30 days of the date of such notice, the Clerk may destroy or otherwise dispose of those exhibits.

[Effective August 1, 1999.]

LCrR 57.1 PUBLICATION OF AMENDMENTS

Any amendment to these Rules shall be published in The Daily Washington Law Reporter before its adoption. The notice shall state that the proposed amendment will be adopted unless modified or withdrawn after receiving comments from organized bar associations, members of the bar, and the public. Such comments shall be submitted in writing within 45 days of publication to the Chairman of the Advisory Committee on District Court Rules. If the Court determines there is an immediate need for a particular local rule or amendment to an existing local rule, it may proceed without public notice and opportunity for comment, but the Court shall promptly thereafter afford such notice and opportunity for comment.

[Effective August 1, 1999.]

LCrR 57.2 SCHEDULING AND CONTINUANCES

(a) Scheduling. All hearings, conferences and trials shall be scheduled by the judge to whom the case is assigned, except that matters referred to a magistrate judge shall be scheduled by the magistrate judge.

(b) Continuances. No application for a continuance of a hearing, conference or trial shall be made unless notice of the application has been given to all other parties. An application for a continuance shall be ruled upon by the judge or magistrate judge before whom the hearing, conference or trial is to be held.

(c) Notice. The Clerk shall give notice to counsel of every matter set by the Court, unless the matter is scheduled orally in open court in the presence of counsel for all parties, in which case further notice is not required.

[Effective August 1, 1999.]

LCrR 57.3 STIPULATIONS

A stipulation need not be considered by the Court unless it is in writing and signed by the parties thereto or their attorneys, or stenographically recorded in court or during a deposition.

[Effective August 1, 1999.]

LCrR 57.4 BONDS AND SURETIES

Any bond or undertaking required in a proceeding must be set by an order or by consent. The bond or undertaking may be in the form of a surety, cash or check. A surety holding authority from the Secretary of the Treasury to do business in the District of Columbia and having an agent for service of process therein may be approved by the Clerk and filed. No officer of the Court or member of the bar in active practice will be accepted as a surety.

[Effective August 1, 1999.]

LCrR 57.5 AVOIDANCE AND RESOLUTION OF CONFLICTS IN ENGAGEMENTS OF COUNSEL AMONG THE COURTS IN THE DISTRICT OF COLUMBIA

The following provisions, which implement the "Procedures for Avoiding and Resolving Conflicts in Engagements of Counsel to Appear Before the Courts in the District of Columbia" dated April 18, 1973, adopted by and applicable to the United States Court of Appeals for the District of Columbia Circuit, the United States District Court for the District of Columbia, the District of Columbia Court of Appeals and the Superior Court of the District of Columbia, shall apply to matters scheduled in this Court:

(a) Priority to Be Accorded Appellate Courts. Trial proceedings in this Court will yield, and if under way will be held in abeyance, during argument by trial counsel in an appellate court.

(b) Priorities in Trial Courts. Actual trials of civil or criminal cases in this Court or in the Superior Court will be accorded priority over any nontrial matters in either court. For the purpose of this Rule, a hearing on a preliminary injunction shall be regarded as a trial. A judge shall set a date for trial only after ascertaining that trial counsel have no conflicting trial or appellate engagement in any court within the District of Columbia. If, despite the foregoing and the obligations imposed on counsel by section (c) of this Rule, counsel should have more than one trial set on one day, the following priorities will be recognized:

(1) That case which is first set to commence trial on a specific day will receive priority over cases which are later set to commence trial on that day. A continued case shall be treated as set as of the last setting date.

(2) Any trial in progress, including a trial in progress from day to day, shall take precedence over trial or nontrial engagements of counsel which are set for times during which the trial is still in progress.

(3) If a scheduled trial conflicts with a previously set nontrial matter and, because of the urgency or complexity of the nontrial matter or the number of persons involved, it would be difficult to reschedule the nontrial matter, counsel shall immediately advise the court in which or the judge before whom the conflicting trial is scheduled. The court or the judges will be receptive to counsel's application for change of the trial date or an adjustment of the hours of trial, but shall retain discretion to grant or deny such an application.

(4) The judges of this Court insofar as practical, will attempt to adjust their schedules to enable an attorney to attend to brief nontrial matters such as pleas, sentences, or status and pretrial conferences pending in another court. It is recognized that emergency situations will arise and that certain types of cases may require special consideration. The judges of this Court will attempt to accommodate these situations by recognizing the need to depart, on occasion, from rigid scheduling rules when such situations are brought to their attention by counsel.

(c) Responsibilities of Counsel. It is the professional responsibility of attorneys to avoid the setting of conflicting engagements in the courts, to inform the courts of expected difficulties or conflicts which may arise, and to achieve the resolution of such conflicts or problems at the earliest possible time. The following particular obligations are imposed upon counsel:

(1) Attorneys are expected to carry with them at all times they are in court a calendar of their future court appearances.

(2) Attorneys shall appear personally before the judge when a case is being set, reset, or continued except as otherwise specified below. They shall in every case inform the Court fully as to any matters which may conflict with a setting, resetting, or continued date being considered by the Court. Counsel shall not schedule engagements which they cannot reasonably expect to attend at the time scheduled.

They shall observe such limitations on the number of matters they schedule as are imposed herein, or are imposed by the individual courts of this jurisdiction, or which arise by reason of their professional obligations to their clients. The sole exception to the requirement that counsel appear personally before the judge when a case is being reset or continued arises when counsel is physically unable to be present. In such event counsel should leave three open dates with the judge in question, and the trial may be reset in counsel's absence. It shall, however, be the attorney's duty to appear personally as soon as possible before the judge who reset the case to confirm the reset date.

(3) Attorneys are obliged to take action immediately upon becoming aware of any conflict and specifically to call the conflicting engagements to the attention of the judge being asked to yield, and to pursue the matter until the conflict is resolved. Such matters may be presented to the judge in open court as a preliminary matter, with advance notice to other counsel.

(4) If counsel cannot avoid being unexpectedly late for, or absent from any scheduled appearance before any judge, they shall in advance of the scheduled

appearance notify by telephone the judge's courtroom deputy of that fact, the reason therefore and the nature and duration of the conflicting engagements.

(5) If an attorney has a criminal felony case set for trial in any court on a given day, the attorney shall not schedule any other case for trial on that day or for any date thereafter during which that felony trial may reasonably be expected to continue. If an attorney has a misdemeanor case set for jury trial on a given date, the attorney shall not schedule more than one other misdemeanor case for trial on that day. These restrictions do not apply to cases as to which an attorney is certain there will be a nontrial disposition.

(6) This Court will take appropriate disciplinary action when an attorney fails to conduct himself or herself in accordance with the requirements and obligations imposed by the Rule.

[Effective August 1, 1999.]

LCrR 57.6 APPLICATIONS FOR RELIEF IN A CRIMINAL CASE BY PERSONS NOT PARTIES TO THE CASE

Any news organization or other interested person, other than a party or a subpoenaed witness, who seeks relief relating to any aspect of the proceedings in a criminal case shall file an application for such relief in the Miscellaneous Docket of the Court. The application shall include a statement of the applicant's interest in the matter as to which relief is sought, a statement of facts and a specific prayer for relief. The application shall be served on the parties to the criminal case and shall be referred by the Clerk to the trial judge assigned to the criminal case for determination.

[Effective August 1, 1999.]

LCrR 57.7 RELEASE OF INFORMATION BY ATTORNEYS AND COURT PERSONNEL

(a) Conduct of Court Personnel. Courthouse supporting personnel, including, among others, marshals, court clerks, law clerks, messengers, court reporters and employees or subcontractors retained by the court-appointed official reporters, shall not disclose to any person without specific authorization by the Court, information relating to any pending criminal proceeding, including a grand jury proceeding, that is not part of the public records of the Court, nor shall any such personnel discuss the merits involved in any such proceeding with any members of the public.

(b) Conduct of Attorneys in Criminal Cases.

(1) It is the duty of the lawyer or law firm not to release or authorize the release of information or opinion which a reasonable person would expect to be disseminated by means of public communication, in connection with pending or imminent criminal litigation with which the lawyer or the law firm is associated, if there is a reasonable likelihood that such dissemination will interfere with a fair trial or otherwise prejudice the due administration of justice.

(2) With respect to a grand jury or other pending investigation of any criminal matter, a lawyer participating in or associated with the investigation shall refrain from making any extrajudicial statement which a reasonable person would expect to be disseminated by means of public communication, that goes beyond the public record or that is not necessary to inform the public that the investigation is underway, to describe the general scope of the investigation, to obtain assistance in the apprehension of a suspect, to warn the public of any dangers, or otherwise to aid in the investigation.

(3) From the time of arrest, issuance of an arrest warrant, or the filing of a complaint, information or indictment in any criminal matter until the commencement of trial or disposition without trial, a lawyer or law firm associated with the prosecution or defense shall not release or authorize the release of any extrajudicial statement which a reasonable person would expect to be disseminated by means of public communication, relating to that matter and concerning:

(i) The prior criminal record (including arrests, indictments, or other charges of crime), or the character or reputation of the accused, except that the lawyer or law firm may make a factual statement of the accused's name, age, residence, occupation, and family status, and if the accused has not been apprehended, a lawyer associated with the prosecution may release any information necessary to aid in apprehension of the accused or to warn the public of any dangers he or she may present;

(ii) The existence or contents of any confession, admission, or statement given by the accused, or the refusal or failure of the accused to make any statement;

(iii) The performance of any examinations or tests or the accused's refusal or failure to submit to an examination or test;

(iv) The identity, testimony, or credibility of prospective witnesses, except that the lawyer or law firm may announce the identity of the victim if the announcement is not otherwise prohibited by the law;

(v) The possibility of a plea of guilty to the offense charged or a lesser offense;

(vi) Any opinion as to the accused's guilt or innocence or as to the merits of the case or the evidence in the case.

The foregoing shall not be construed to preclude the lawyer or law firm during this period, in the proper discharge of official or professional obligations, from announcing the fact and circumstances of arrest (including time and place of arrest, resistance, pursuit, and use of weapons), the identity of the investigating and arresting officer or agency, and the length of the investigation; from making an announcement, at the time of seizure of any physical evidence other than a confession, admission or statement, which is limited to a description of the evidence seized; from disclosing the nature, substance, or text of the charge, including a brief description of the offense charged; from quoting or referring without comment to public records of the court in the case; from announcing the scheduling or result of any stage in the judicial process; from requesting assistance in obtaining evidence; or from announcing without further comment that the accused denies the charges.

(4) During a jury trial of any criminal matter, including the period of selection of the jury, no lawyer or law firm associated with the prosecution or defense shall give or authorize any extrajudicial statement or interview, relating to the trial or the parties or issues in the trial which a reasonable person would expect to be disseminated by means of public communication if there is a reasonable likelihood that such dissemination will interfere with a fair trial, except that the lawyer or law firm may quote from or refer without comment to public records of the court in the case.

(5) Nothing in this Rule is intended to preclude the formulation or application of more restrictive rules relating to the release of information about juvenile or other offenders, to preclude the holding of hearings or the lawful issuance of reports by legislative, administrative, or investigative bodies, or to preclude any lawyer from replying to charges of misconduct that are publicly made against him or her.

(c) Orders in Widely Publicized or Sensational Cases. In a widely publicized or sensational criminal case, the Court, on motion of either party or on its own motion, may issue a special order governing such matters as extrajudicial statements by parties, witnesses and attorneys likely to interfere with the rights of the accused to a fair trial by an impartial jury, the seating and conduct in the courtroom of spectators and news media representatives, the management and sequestration of jurors and witnesses, and any other matters which the Court may deem appropriate for inclusion in such an order.

[Effective August 1, 1999.]

LCrR 57.8 ASSIGNMENT SYSTEM

(a) Cases to Be Assigned to a Single Judge. Unless otherwise provided in these Rules, each civil and criminal case shall be assigned to a single judge in the manner provided herein.

(b) Calendar and Case Management Committee. The assignment of cases to judges of this Court shall be performed by the Clerk under the direction of the Calendar and Case Management Committee. The Committee shall be composed of no less than three and no more than five active judges appointed by the Chief Judge for two year terms. All matters dealing with the assignment of cases, including but not limited to any efforts to restrain or avoid the enforcement or application of rules under this Part shall be referred to the Chairman of the Calendar and Case Management Committee for resolution by the Committee.

(c) Emergency Judge. A judge of this Court will be available, in accordance with a schedule of assignments announced from time to time by the Chief Judge, to hear emergency civil or criminal matters on all legal holidays and weekends. The emergency judge's assignment starts at 4:30 p.m. on the day preceding the weekend and ends at 9:00 a.m. the next business day. The judge designated for emergency assignments will not be present in the Courthouse but will be reasonably available, on call, in the area.

(d) Notice of Transfers and Reassignments. All case transfers and reassignments shall be accompanied by formal notice to the Chairman of the Calendar and Case Management Committee and to the Clerk's Office Liaison. The Clerk will notify each of the judges involved and all counsel in the case of the reassignment.

[Effective August 1, 1999. Amended effective March 8, 2004; March 2008.]

Comment

COMMENT: The rule has been changed to reflect a change in scope and to provide the court with greater flexibility with respect to this Committee.

LCrR 57.9 CLASSES OF CASES

(a) Classification. In order to assure a more even distribution of each type of case among the judges of this Court, each civil and criminal case will be classified for assignment purposes in accordance with a set of categories established by the Court on the recommendation of the Calendar and Case Management Committee.

(b) Designation at Time of Filing. Upon filing the complaint in a civil action, the attorney for the plaintiff shall note the proper classification of the case on a form provided by the Clerk. In criminal cases the United States Attorney shall, at the time of the return of an indictment, note the proper classification of the case on a form provided by the Clerk.

[Effective August 1, 1999. Amended March 2008.]

LCrR 57.10 MANNER OF ASSIGNMENT

(a) Random Assignment. Except as otherwise provided by these Rules, civil, criminal and miscellaneous cases shall be assigned to judges of this Court selected at random in the following manner:

(1) The Clerk shall create a separate assignment deck in the automated system for each subclassification of civil and criminal cases established by the Court pursuant to LCrR 57.9 of these Rules and a separate deck for miscellaneous cases[3]. The decks will be created by the Liaison to the Calendar and Case Management Committee or the Liaison's backup and access to this function shall be restricted to these individuals to protect the integrity and confidentiality of the random assignment of cases. The Calendar and Case Management Committee will, from time to time determine and indicate by order the frequency with which each judge's name shall appear in each designated deck, to effectuate an even distribution of cases among the active judges.

(2) At the time a civil complaint is filed or an indictment or information is returned in a criminal case, the case shall be assigned to the judge whose name appears on the screen when the appropriate deck is selected. The Clerk shall also stamp on the indictment, information, complaint or other initial pleading of each case, and on the file jacket, the number of the case and the name of the judge to whom it is assigned. The numbering and assignment of each case shall be completed before processing of the next case is begun. Notwithstanding the foregoing, a civil case, requiring an emergency hearing, which is filed after normal business hours, shall not be assigned to a judge until the next business day.

(b) Assignment to Visiting and Senior Judges. Cases may be assigned to visiting and senior judges in accordance with procedures adopted from time to time by the Calendar and Case Management Committee.

(c) Proceedings After Assignment. All proceedings in a case after its assignment shall be conducted by the judge to whom the case is assigned, except as otherwise provided in these Rules. A judge who declares a mistrial shall retain the case for subsequent proceedings including, where appropriate, retrial.

(d) Wiretap Order Applications. Applications by the United States Attorney for orders authorizing interception of wire or oral communications shall be assigned in rotation by seniority among the active judges, excluding the Chief Judge.

[Effective August 1, 1999; paragraph (c) rescinded effective February 1, 2000. Amended March 2008.]

[3] For the purpose of this Rule, miscellaneous cases that will be randomly assigned will include, but not be limited to, these proceedings: (a) actions to perpetuate testimony as in Rule 27, Federal Rules of Civil Procedure; (b) actions to enforce administrative subpoenas and summonses; (c) proceeding ancillary to an action pending in another district; (d) supplementary proceedings brought in aid of execution; (e) motions for return of property in criminal proceedings; and (f) requests for judicial assistance. Grand Jury Miscellaneous cases will continue to be assigned to the Chief Judge and Pen Register Applications will continue to be assigned to magistrate judges.

Comment

COMMENT TO LCrR 57.10: To ensure an even distribution of cases filed on the miscellaneous docket these cases will now be randomly assigned to a judge of this Court at the time of filing. The assigned judge will maintain jurisdiction of the miscellaneous case for all purposes. The assignment of miscellaneous cases does not affect the duties of the Motions Judge as specified in LCvR 40.8(a), (b), (c).

LCrR 57.11 SUSPENSION OF NEW ASSIGNMENTS

A judge shall be relieved by the Calendar and Case Management Committee from any new assignment of indictments and civil cases accompanied by motions for temporary restraining orders and preliminary injunctions or civil cases in which an intention to file a motion for a preliminary injunction is expressed, upon notification by the judge or the Chief Judge to the Committee that the judge: (1) has continued in a protracted trial or hearing for 10 consecutive trial days;[4] (2) is confined to a hospital; (3) is confined at home due to illness for seven days; (4) has had a death in the judge's immediate family; or (5) is performing judicial duties out of this jurisdiction pursuant to assignment. New cases shall be assigned to the judge in accordance with normal procedures upon the conclusion of any such condition.

Whenever a judge begins what is expected to be an unusually protracted criminal trial (one lasting four weeks or more) he or she may refer to the Calendar and Case Management Committee for routine reassignment such other criminal cases assigned to such judge as the judge was unable to dispose of prior thereto and which are expected to require disposition pursuant to the Speedy Trial Act within the time period of the unusually protracted trial.

[Effective August 1, 1999. Amended March 2008.]

[4] If a judge, after suspension based upon 10 consecutive days in a trial or hearing, thereafter devotes an occasional day to other court business, that judge shall not by virtue thereof be reinstated in the complete draw.

LCrR 57.12 RELATED CASES

(a) Definition. A related case for the purpose of this Rule means as follows:

(1) Criminal cases are deemed related when (i) a superseding indictment has been filed, or (ii) more than one indictment is filed or pending against the same defendant or defendants, or (iii) prosecution against different defendants arises from a common wiretap, search warrant, or activities which are a part of the same alleged criminal event or transaction. A

case is considered pending until a defendant has been sentenced.

(2) If a civil forfeiture proceeding is filed concerning a criminal defendant, or a defendant is charged in a criminal case while a civil forfeiture proceeding is pending concerning that defendant, the civil and criminal cases are to be deemed related.

(3) Civil cases are deemed related when the earliest is still pending on the merits in the District Court and they (i) relate to common property, or (ii) involve common issues of fact, or (iii) grow out of the same event or transaction or (iv) involve the validity or infringement of the same patent. Notwithstanding the foregoing, a case filed by a pro se litigant with a prior case pending shall be deemed related and assigned to the judge having the earliest case. However, if a judge in the interest of judicial economy, consolidates a significant number of similar pro se prisoner complaints, or has a single case with a significant number of pro se prisoner plaintiffs, and any of those prisoners later files a new complaint which is unrelated to the subject matter of the consolidated cases or the multiple plaintiffs' case, the judge who receives the new case as related may, if he or she chooses, refer the new case to the Calendar and Case Management Committee for random assignment.

(4) Additionally, cases whether criminal or civil shall be deemed related where a case is dismissed, with prejudice or without, and a second case is filed involving the same parties and relating to the same subject matter.

(b) Notification of Related Cases. The parties shall notify the Clerk of the existence of related cases as follows:

(1) At the time of returning an indictment the United States Attorney shall indicate, on a form to be provided by the Clerk, the name, docket number and relationship of any related case pending in this Court or in any other United States District Court. The form shall be mailed to all defense counsel along with the notification of the arraignment. Any objection by the defendant to the related case designation shall be served on the U.S. Attorney and filed with the Clerk within 21 days after arraignment.

(2) At the time of filing any civil action, the plaintiff or his attorney shall indicate, on a form to be provided by the Clerk, the name, docket number and relationship of any related case pending in this Court or in any other United States Court. The plaintiff shall serve this form on the defendant with the complaint. Any objection by the defendant to the related case designation shall be filed and served with the defendant's first responsive pleading or motion.

(3) Whenever an attorney for a party in a civil or criminal action becomes aware of the existence of a related case or cases, the attorney shall immediately notify, in writing, the judges on whose calendars the cases appear and shall serve such notice on counsel for all other parties. Upon receiving information from any source concerning a relationship between pending cases, the Clerk shall transmit that information in writing to the judges on whose calendars the cases appear and to all parties to the proceeding.

(c) Assignment of Related Cases. Related cases noted at or after the time of filing shall be assigned in the following manner:

(1) Where the existence of a related case in this Court is noted at the time the indictment is returned or the complaint is filed, the Clerk shall assign the new case to the judge to whom the oldest related case is assigned. If a judge who is assigned a case under this procedure determines that the cases in question are not related, the judge may transfer the new case to the Calendar and Case Management Committee. If the Calendar and Case Management Committee finds that good cause exists for the transfer, it shall cause the case to be reassigned at random. If the Calendar and Case Management Committee finds that good cause for the transfer does not exist, it may return the case to the transferring judge.

(2) Where the existence of related cases in this Court is revealed after the cases are assigned, the judge having the later-numbered case may transfer that case to the Calendar and Case Management Committee for reassignment to the judge having the earlier case. If the Calendar and Case Management Committee finds that good cause exists for the transfer, it shall assign the case to the judge having the earlier case. If the Calendar and Case Management Committee finds that good cause for the transfer does not exist, it may return the case to the transferring judge.

(3) Where a party objects to a designation that cases are related pursuant to subparagraphs (b)(1) or (b)(2) of this Rule, the matter shall be determined by the judge to whom the case is assigned.

(d) Referrals to a Single Judge by the Calendar and Case Management Committee. Upon a finding by the Calendar and Case Management Committee that two or more cases assigned to different judges should be referred for a specific purpose to one judge in order to avoid a duplication of judicial effort, the Calendar and Case Management Committee may enter such an order of referral. The order shall be with the consent of the judge to whom the cases will be referred and shall set forth the scope of authority of said judge. Unless otherwise provided, such an order shall not transfer any cases nor affect the assignment of future cases.

[Effective August 1, 1999. Amended effective May 31, 2002; March 2008; December 1, 2009.]

Comment

COMMENT TO LCvR 57.12(c)(3): The Court has eliminated the provision in this Rule that permitted a party to appeal to the Calendar and Case Management Committee an individual judge's decision with respect to whether cases are related because the Court does not believe it is appropriate for a party to be able to seek review of a decision of one judge of this Court by three of that judge's co-equal colleagues. As amended, the Rule would make the individual judge's decision final.

LCrR 57.13 OTHER TRANSFERS AND REASSIGNMENTS

(a) Transfers by Consent. A judge, upon written advice to the Calendar and Case Management Committee, may transfer directly all or part of any case on the judge's docket to any consenting judge.

(b) Death, Retirement, Appointment of New Judges, etc. When reassignments are necessitated by the death, retirement, resignation or incapacity of any judge or by the appointment of a new judge, or by any other circumstances, the Calendar and Case Management Committee shall determine and indicate by order the method by which such reassignments shall be made.

(c) Reassignment of Criminal Cases. If the Calendar and Case Management Committee, giving due consideration to LCrR 45.1 of these Rules, determines in its discretion that the interest of justice require the transfer of any criminal case from one judge to another, it may reassign the case.

(d) Calendar and Case Management Committee Calendar. Any criminal case in which the only defendant is a fugitive or is mentally incompetent to stand trial shall be assigned to the Calendar and Case Management Committee by the judge upon whose calendar it appears after the case has been pending for 90 days or more. In cases involving two or more defendants, in the event that one or more are fugitives or are mentally incompetent to stand trial, the case may go to trial as to those defendants who are not fugitives and are not mentally incompetent to stand trial. Upon the entry of a final judgment as to such defendants, the case shall be assigned to the Calendar and Case Management Committee for further action as to those defendants who are fugitives or mentally incompetent to stand trial. Additionally, the case of any criminal defendant who becomes a fugitive subsequent to a guilty plea but prior to sentencing shall be assigned to the Calendar and Case Management Committee by the judge upon whose calendar the case had appeared after such a fugitive has been an absconder for 90 days or more. The Calendar and Case Management Committee may assign one or more judges for the purpose of making a periodic call of such cases. The judge or judges so assigned shall from time to time consult with the United States Attorney to ascertain whether dismissals of particular criminal actions or civil commitment of defendants incompetent to stand trial shall be deemed advisable. If the reasons which made a case untriable cease to exist, the case shall be reassigned for trial to the transferring judge.

(e) Transfers Not Provided for by Other Rules. If a case is transferred to the Calendar and Case Management Committee for any reason not otherwise provided for in this title, and the Calendar and Case Management Committee approves the transfer, it shall cause the case to be reassigned by random lot or otherwise as these Rules provide.

[Effective August 1, 1999. Amended March 2008.]

LCrR 57.14 DUTIES OF THE CHIEF JUDGE

In addition to the trial of such cases as he may undertake and other duties provided by these Rules, the Chief Judge shall:

(1) preside at the assignment of criminal cases;

(2) hear and determine requests for excuse from service on grand and petit juries;

(3) empanel the grand jury and hear and determine all matters relating to proceedings before the grand jury;

(4) receive indictments from the grand jury;

(5) consider applications for allowance under the Criminal Justice Act in a case not already assigned;

(6) dispose of matters requiring immediate action in criminal cases already assigned to any judge of the Court if that judge is unavailable or otherwise unable to hear the matters;

(7) hear and determine requests for review of rulings by magistrate judges in criminal cases not already assigned to a judge of the Court; and

(8) take such other administrative actions, after consultation with appropriate committees of the Court, as in his judgment are necessary to assure the just, speedy and inexpensive determination of cases, and are not inconsistent with these Rules.

The Chief Judge may, from time to time, reassign any of the foregoing duties to an active judge for a reasonable period.

[Effective August 1, 1999.]

Comment

COMMENT TO LCrR 57.14: Paragraph (8) has been added to affirm the power of the Chief Judge to take other appropriate administrative actions not inconsistent with the Rules.

LCrR 57.15 SANCTIONS IMPOSED

(a) Court Officers and Employees. The Clerk or his/her designee may respond to or describe, in general terms, the process of creating case assignment decks for the automated case assignment system. In addition, the Clerk or his/her designee is also authorized to reveal the name of a judge assigned a case and the procedure by which the assignment was made. No employee of the Court may reveal to any other person, other than members of the Calendar and Case Management Committee and the Chief Judge, any list that may show the composition of any deck. No court employee may number or assign any case other than in the manner provided in these Rules or in the manner ordered by the Calendar and Case Management Committee. An employee who violates this provision may be subject to discharge from service.

(b) Third Parties. No person shall directly or indirectly cause, or procure, or attempt to cause or procure, a court officer or employee to reveal to any person, other than the members of the Calendar and Case Management Committee, the sequence of the judges' names within each block of assignment cards, or to number or assign any case otherwise than herein provided or as ordered by the Calendar and Case Management Committee. A violation of this Rule may be punished as a contempt of court.

[Effective August 1, 1999. Amended January 15, 2002; March 2008.]

Comment

COMMENT TO LCrR 57.15(a): This amendment provides the Clerk's Office with sufficient latitude to generally discuss the creation of the case assignment decks. Further, it permits the Chief Judge to be apprised of the composition of any deck.

LCrR 57.16 COMPLAINTS AGAINST JUDGES

The Judicial Conduct and Disability Act of 1980, 28 U.S.C. § 372(c), authorizes that complaints against United States circuit, district, bankruptcy, and magistrate judges who have "engaged in conduct prejudicial to the effective, and expeditious administration of the business of the courts" or who are "unable to discharge all the duties of office by reason of mental or physical disability" may be submitted to a judicial committee for review.

Written complaints may be filed with the Clerk of the United States Court of Appeals for the District of Columbia Circuit, 333 Constitution Avenue, N.W., Room 5409, Washington, D.C. 20001.

[Effective August 1, 1999.]

LCrR 57.17 DUTIES AND POWERS OF MAGISTRATE JUDGES

(a) General Duties. The United States Magistrate Judges appointed by this Court pursuant to 28 U.S.C. § 631 shall have the duty and the power to:

(1) Act as committing magistrate judge in holding preliminary hearings for violations of the United States Code.

(2) Issue arrest warrants or summonses for violations of the United States Code.

(3) Issue search warrants.

(4) Conduct transfer proceedings and conduct proceedings incident to the transfer of criminal cases, as provided in Rules 5, 5.1 and 40, Federal Rules of Criminal Procedure.

(5) Receive indictments returned by the grand jury and issue bench warrants, when necessary, for defendants named in indictments.

(6) Conduct international extradition proceedings pursuant to 18 U.S.C. § 3181 et seq.

(7) Administer oaths and affirmations and take acknowledgments, affidavits and depositions.

(8) Impose or review conditions of release under applicable federal law.

(9) Order the return or the forfeiture of collateral or surety bonds.

(10) Issue subpoenas, writs of habeas corpus ad testificandum, or habeas corpus ad prosequendum, or other orders necessary to obtain the presence of parties or witnesses or evidence needed for court proceedings.

(11) Order lineups, photographs, fingerprinting, palm-printing, voice identification, medical or physical examinations, and the taking of blood, urine, fingernail, hair and bodily secretion sampling (with any appropriate medical safeguards required by due process considerations) and handwriting exemplars.

(12) Ascertain whether defendants or any other persons entitled to counsel in criminal matters are represented by counsel and, in instances where any such person is financially unable to obtain counsel, appoint counsel to represent the person.

(13) Conduct proceedings and enter orders as described in LCrR 58.

(14) Refer a defendant to an available facility for a preliminary opinion; hear motions and enter orders for examinations to determine mental competency; and conduct competency hearings to determine a defendant's ability to understand and to participate in any proceeding which a magistrate judge is authorized to conduct.

(b) Powers Exercised Upon Referral From a District Judge. At the request of the district judge to whom the case is assigned, a magistrate judge shall:

(1) Conduct proceedings and enter orders or recommendations as described in LCrR 59.1 and LCrR 59.2 of these Rules.

(2) Dismiss indictments on motion of the United States and with the consent of the defendants.

(3) Conduct arraignments in felony cases pursuant to Rule 10, Federal Rules of Criminal Procedure.

(4) Conduct voir dire and select petit juries in felony cases, upon consent of the defendant.

(5) Conduct guilty plea proceedings in felony cases upon consent of the parties, and forward recommendations to the district judge to whom the case is assigned.

(6) Perform any additional duty not inconsistent with the Constitution and laws of the United States.

[Effective August 1, 1999. Amended effective April 10, 2007; March 2008.]

COMMENT

COMMENT TO LCrR 57.17: The Rule has been revised to remove references to civil procedure. Section (a)(5) has been moved from the previous section (c) to clarify that indictments may be returned to magistrate judges in accordance with Rule 6(f), Federal Rules of Criminal Procedure. Other changes have also been made to conform to the Federal Rules of Criminal Procedure. Section (b)(4) has been amended to make explicit that, in order for voir dire to be conducted before a magistrate judge in a felony case, the parties must consent, in accordance with Peretz v. United States, 501 U.S. 923 (1991). Section (b)(5) has been added to give magistrate judges the authority to conduct guilty plea proceedings in felony cases upon the consent of the parties. Section (b)(6) has been moved from section (a) to make clear that it is one of the duties that may be performed only at the request of a judge.

LCrR 57.18 REFERRAL OF MOTIONS AND PRETRIAL MATTERS TO MAGISTRATE JUDGES [REDESIGNATED LCrR 59.1]

[Effective August 1, 1999. Redesignated LCrR 59.1 effective April 10, 2007.]

LCrR 57.19 REFERRAL OF MATTERS FOR HEARING AND RECOMMENDATION BY MAGISTRATE JUDGES [REDESIGNATED LCrR 59.2]

[Effective August 1, 1999. Redesignated LCrR 59.2 effective April 10, 2007.]

LCrR 57.20 REFERRAL OF MISDEMEANOR CASES TO MAGISTRATE JUDGES FOR ALL PURPOSES [REDESIGNATED LCrR 58]

[Effective August 1, 1999. Redesignated LCrR 58 effective April 10, 2007.]

LCrR 57.21 ADMISSION TO THE BAR

(a) Who May Be Admitted. Admission to and continuing membership in the Bar of this Court are limited to attorneys who are (1) active members in good standing in the District of Columbia Bar; or (2) active members in good standing of the highest court of any state in which the attorney maintains his/her principal law office and is a member in good standing of a United States District Court that provides for reciprocal admission to members of the Bar of this Court.

(b) Petition for Admission. Each applicant for admission shall file with the Clerk at least 14 days prior to hearing thereon (unless for good cause shown the judge shall shorten the time) a written petition for admission on a form supplied by the Clerk stating:

(1) applicant's residence and office addresses and office telephone number;

(2) the court where and date when admitted;

(3) applicant's legal training and experience;

(4) whether the applicant has ever been held in contempt of court and, if so, the nature of the contempt and the final disposition thereof;

(5) whether the applicant has ever been convicted of any crime (other than minor traffic offenses) or publicly reprimanded, publicly censured, suspended, disciplined or disbarred by any court, and, if so, the facts and circumstances connected therewith; and

(6) that the applicant is familiar with:

(i) the provisions of the Judicial Code (Title 28 U.S.C.) which pertain to the jurisdiction of and practice in the United States District Courts;

(ii) the Federal Rules of Civil or Criminal Procedure;

(iii) the Rules of the United States District Court for the District of Columbia; and

(iv) the *Rules of Professional Conduct* as adopted by the District of Columbia Court of Appeals except as otherwise provided by specific rule of this Court, and that he/she will faithfully adhere thereto; and

(v) D.C. Bar Voluntary Standards for Civility in Professional Conduct, adopted by the Bar on June 18, 1996 (attached as Appendix B to the Local Civil Rules).

(c) Affidavit of a Member of the Bar. The petition shall be accompanied by an affidavit of an attorney who is a member in good standing of the Bar of this Court who has known the applicant for at least one year stating when the affiant was admitted to practice in this Court and how long and under what circumstances the attorney has known the applicant and a statement of the applicant's character and experience at the bar. The affidavit shall be on a form supplied by the Clerk.

(d) Hearing on the Petition. The petition for admission shall be placed on the calendar of the Motions Judge and shall be heard on the first Monday of each month. If the first Monday is a holiday, the petition shall be heard on the following Monday. If the petition is granted, the applicant shall take the oath of office.

(e) Oath. The oath which each applicant for admission to the Bar of this Court shall take shall be as follows:

> I do solemnly swear (or affirm) that I will support the Constitution of the United States; that I will respect courts of justice and judicial officers; that I will well and faithfully discharge my duties as an attorney and as an officer of the court; and in the performance of those duties I will conduct myself with dignity and according to both the law and the recognized standards of ethics of our profession.

(f) Admission Fee. Each petition shall be accompanied by payment in such amount and form as determined by the Court, which the Clerk shall deposit to the credit of a fund to be used for such purposes as inure to the benefit of the members of the bench and the Bar in the administration of justice which are determined to be appropriate by the Court from time to time. This fee shall be in addition to the statutory fee for administering the oath of office and issuing the certificate of admission.

(g) Clerk as Agent for Service. By being admitted to the Bar of this Court or by being permitted to practice in this Court under LCrR 44.1 and LCrR 57.23 or in fact practicing in this Court, the attorney shall be deemed to have designated the Clerk of the Court as agent for service of process in any disciplinary proceeding before this Court.

[Effective August 1, 1999. Amended effective December 13, 2000; December 1, 2009.]

Comments

COMMENT TO LCrR 57.21: This Rule clarifies the intention that continuing membership in the Bar is premised on a continuing duty to meet the requirements of this Rule. Section (a) parallels revised LCrR 44.1 regarding practice by attorneys.

COMMENT TO LCrR 57.21(b)(6)(v): Section (v) was added to LCrR 57.21(b)(6) to stress the importance that the Court places on the need for civility among lawyers who practice in the Court.

LCrR 57.21.1 RENEWAL OF MEMBERSHIP

(a) Renewal of Membership Every Three Years. Each member of the Bar of this Court shall renew his or her membership every three years by filing with the Clerk of the Court, on or before July 1st of every third year, a certificate in a form prescribed by the Clerk that the member is familiar with the then-current version of the Federal Rules of Civil Procedure, Federal Rules of Evidence, the Local Rules of this Court, Rules of Professional Conduct and the D.C. Bar Voluntary Standards for Civility in Professional Conduct. If the attorney appears in criminal cases, he or she must also certify familiarity with the then-current version of the Federal Rules of Criminal Procedure and the Sentencing Guidelines. (See LCrR 44.5(b).) Members of the Bar of this Court on the effective date of this Rule shall file certificates by March 1, 1990, and by July 1 of every third calendar year thereafter. Subsequently admitted members shall file certificates by July 1st of every third calendar year after the year in which they were admitted. The Clerk shall notify members of this certification requirement at least 60 days before the date for filing such certificates and renewals.

(b) Renewal Fee. Each certificate required by (a) above shall be accompanied by a payment of $25 in a form determined by the Clerk. The fee shall be $10 for the initial certificate filed by any person admitted to the Bar of this Court after July 1, 1986. The Clerk shall deposit the fees received to the credit of the fund described in LCvR 83.8(f) to be used for the purposes specified in that Rule, including the defraying of expenses of maintaining a current register of members in good standing and to administer the counseling program outlined in LCrR 57.31.

(c) Failure to Renew. An attorney who fails to file the required certifications and pay the renewal fee shall be provisionally removed from the list of members in good standing and pursuant to LCrR 44.1(a) shall not be permitted to practice before this Court until restored as a member in good standing. The name of the attorney shall be restored to the list of members in good standing upon filing of the required certificates and payment of the delinquent fee within five years after the due date. At the end of five years from the due date, the name will be permanently removed from the roll, without prejudice to an application for admission as a new member.

[Effective August 1, 1999. Amended effective December 13, 2000; April 11, 2003.]

Comments

COMMENT TO LCrR 57.21.1(a): This amendment brings the rule in compliance with LCrR57.21(b)(6)(v).

LCrR 57.22 COURT APPOINTED REPRESENTATION

(a) Attorneys who are members in good standing of the Bar of this Court shall be required to assist or represent the needy in civil matters before this Court whenever requested by the Court and, if necessary, without compensation and to accept appointments under the Criminal Justice Act unless exempted by rule or statute.

(b) Attorneys who are members in good standing of the Bar of the District of Columbia or of any United States Court or of the highest court of any state may assist or represent the needy in civil matters before this Court without compensation, provided that such attorneys file a certificate under LCrR 44.1(g) and comply with the provisions of LCrR 57.26.

[Effective August 1, 1999.]

LCrR 57.23 RULES OF DISCIPLINARY ENFORCEMENT

(a) Promulgation of Rules. This Court, in furtherance of its inherent power and responsibility to supervise the conduct of attorneys who are admitted to practice before it under LCrR 44.1 or LCrR 57.21 of these Rules, or who are admitted for the purpose of a particular proceeding (pro hac vice), or who otherwise appear before the Court, promulgates the following Rules of Disciplinary Enforcement superseding all of its other Rules pertaining to disciplinary enforcement heretofore promulgated. These Rules shall become effective on May 1, 1987, provided, however, that any formal disciplinary proceeding then pending before this Court shall be concluded under the procedure existing prior to the effective date of these Rules.

(b) Attorneys Subject to Rules. These Rules shall apply to all attorneys admitted to membership in the Bar of this Court, to all attorneys permitted to practice before this Court under LCrR 44.1, and to all attorneys who appear before this Court or who participate in proceedings, whether admitted or not. All attorneys to whom these Rules apply shall be subject to the disciplinary jurisdiction of this Court for any alleged misconduct arising in connection with such proceeding. All such attorneys shall also be deemed thereby to have designated the Clerk of the Court as agent for service of process under these Rules governing discipline and disciplinary proceedings.

[Effective August 1, 1999.]

Comment

COMMENT TO LCrR 57.23: Section (a) incorporates the former Preamble to the Rules of Disciplinary Enforcement. Section (b) was added to make clear that the Court has authority to discipline all attorneys who appear before it, whether admitted or not. Because this Rule is broader in its application than either LCvR 83.2 or 83.8, it restates the provision that all attorneys subject to these Rules shall be deemed to have designated the Clerk of the Court as agent for service of process for purposes of the disciplinary rules.

LCrR 57.24 DISCIPLINARY PANEL

(a) Appointment. The Chief Judge shall appoint three judges of the Court to be known as the Disciplinary Panel and shall appoint two additional judges to serve as alternate members. The Disciplinary Panel shall have jurisdiction over all judicial proceedings involving the disbarment, suspension, censure or other discipline of attorneys subject to these Rules.

(b) Powers of Individual Judges. Nothing contained in these Rules shall be construed to deny to this Court or to any individual judge or United States Magistrate Judge thereof or to the United States Bankruptcy Judge such powers as are necessary for the Court to maintain control over proceedings conducted before it, such as proceedings for contempt under Title 18 of the United States Code or under Rule 42 of the Federal Rules of Criminal Procedure, or to deprive any judge or magistrate judge of his/her inherent power of discipline for conduct committed in the presence of the Court.

[Effective August 1, 1999.]

Comment

COMMENT TO LCrR 57.24: Section (b) makes clear the power of an individual judge, Bankruptcy Judge or Magistrate Judge to maintain control over proceedings through the contempt power or otherwise to discipline for conduct in the presence of the Court.

LCrR 57.25 COMMITTEE ON GRIEVANCES

(a) Appointment. There shall be established a standing committee appointed by the Court to be known as the Committee on Grievances (the "Committee") consisting of six or more members of the Bar of this Court appointed for terms of three years and until their successors have been appointed. The terms of the members shall be staggered so as to provide continuity. No members of the Committee on Grievances shall serve more than two consecutive terms.

The Court shall designate a Chairman of the Committee and a Vice Chairman who shall act in the absence or disability of the Chairman. Members of the Committee shall serve without compensation except that the Court may authorize payments in lieu of expenses from fees collected by the Clerk pursuant to Rule LCrR 57.21(f).

(b) Duties. The Committee shall be charged with receiving, investigating, considering and acting upon complaints against all attorneys subject to these Rules. LCrR 57.23(b) relating to disbarment, suspension, censure, reprimand or other disciplinary action, and petitions for reinstatement of attorneys.

(c) Clerk. The Clerk shall with approval of the Court, appoint a Clerk to the Committee who shall have all powers vested in a Deputy Clerk of the Court. The Clerk to the Committee shall assist the Committee, maintain records of its proceedings, investigations and prosecutions, and proceed as otherwise set forth in these Rules.

(d) Confidentiality and Immunity. All proceedings before the Committee involving allegations of misconduct of an attorney and all documents and charges presented to the Committee shall remain confidential and privileged. All formal charges prepared by the Committee and directed to be filed by the Court, attorney or grievance cases filed with the Clerk of the Court, court orders, and subsequent pleadings, answers or responses filed therein shall be matters of public record.

All meetings and hearings of the Committee shall be held in camera and the business conducted therein shall remain confidential and privileged. The Committee's Chairman or, in the Chairman's absence or disability, the Vice Chairman shall have discretion in determining the manner and extent of cooperating with disciplinary agencies from other jurisdictions. All records and minutes of the Committee shall be maintained under seal and shall not be disclosed except by order or direction of the Chief Judge (or the designee of the Chief Judge).

When exercising the power delegated by the Court, Committee members shall be absolutely immune from suit for any conduct in connection with their duties. Complaints submitted to the Committee on Grievances pursuant to LCrR 57.27 shall be absolutely privileged and no claim or action predicated thereon may be instituted or maintained.

[Effective August 1, 1999.]

Comment

COMMENT TO LCrR 57.25: Section (c) governs the responsibilities of the Clerk to the Committee. The most important change is Section (d) which is added to describe the practice of the Committee on Grievances and the Court relating to confidentiality and disclosure of disciplinary proceedings. It clarifies existing practice by explicitly stating which proceedings are confidential and which are not. The Rule does not bar disclosure of information by order of the Chief Judge or his/her designee in connection with judicial appointments. In addition, consistent with rules of other courts and case law, the Rule provides that Committee members shall be immune from suit for conduct in the course of their duties in exercising the power delegated to the Committee members by the Court.

LCrR 57.26 OBLIGATIONS OF ATTORNEYS

(a) Rules of Professional Conduct. Violations of the Rules of Professional Conduct (as adopted by the District of Columbia Court of Appeals except as otherwise provided by specific Rule of this Court) by attorneys subject to these Rules shall be grounds for discipline, whether or not the act or omission occurred in the course of an attorney-client relationship.

(b) Duty to Notify the Court. It shall be the duty of each attorney subject to these Rules to notify promptly the Clerk of this Court of:

(1) conviction for any crime other than minor traffic offenses, giving the name of the court in which the attorney was convicted, the date of conviction, docket number, the offense for which the attorney was convicted and the sentence;

(2) any disbarment, suspension or other public discipline imposed by any federal, state or local court, giving the name of the court, the date of such disbarment, suspension or other public discipline, the docket number, and a description of the discipline imposed and the offense committed in connection therewith; or any disbarment by consent or resignation while an investigation into allegations of misconduct is pending;

(3) whether the attorney has ever been held in contempt of court and if so, the nature of the contempt and the final disposition thereof; and

(4) any change in the attorney's office address or telephone number as provided for in (c) below.

Failure to provide the notice required by this paragraph may constitute a separate ground for discipline.

(c) Changes in Address. Notice to the Clerk of any change in the attorney's address or telephone number (see (b)(4) above) shall be filed in writing within 14 days of the change. The attorney shall also within 14 days file a praecipe reflecting such change in each case which the attorney has pending before this Court, serving a copy upon each of the attorneys in these cases.

(d) Duties of the Clerk Upon Notification. Upon being informed that an attorney subject to these Rules has been convicted of any crime, disciplined by any court, held in contempt by any court, disbarred by consent, or resigned from any Bar pending an investigation into allegations of misconduct, the Clerk shall promptly obtain a certified or exemplified copy of such conviction, disciplinary judgment or other court order and present it to the Committee which shall proceed in accordance with these Rules.

[Effective August 1, 1999. Amended effective December 1, 2009.]

Comment

COMMENT TO LCrR 57.26: Section (b) combines several former Rules relating to an attorney's obligations under these Rules to notify the Court of certain facts: (1) conviction of crime; (2) disbarment, suspension or public discipline; (3) citation for contempt; and (4) change in address or telephone number. The duty of notification in LCrR 57.26(b) regarding public discipline does not include sanctions imposed under civil rules other than contempt as specified in subsection (b)(3). Failure to provide notice may constitute grounds for disciplinary action.

Section (c) has been added to impose on the Clerk to the Grievance Committee the duty to obtain a certified or exemplified copy of such conviction, disciplinary judgment or court order.

LCrR 57.27 GROUNDS AND PROCEDURES FOR DISCIPLINE

(a) Service of Process. Service of process under these Rules shall be made by certified mail addressed to the attorney (hereinafter attorney or respondent) at the last known address or at the last recorded address filed with the Clerk of the Court as required pursuant to LCrR 57.21(g). If service cannot be so made, service shall be sufficient when served on the Clerk of this Court and all time periods specified in these Rules shall run from the time of such service. If service is made by serving the Clerk, a courtesy copy shall be mailed to the respondent by first class mail at his/her last known address.

(b) Attorneys Convicted of Crimes.

(1) *Felonies.* Upon presentation to the Disciplinary Panel of a certified copy of a court record demonstrating that an attorney subject to these Rules has been found guilty of a felony in any court, the attorney shall be immediately suspended from practicing before this Court by order of the Disciplinary Panel, whether the finding resulted from a plea of guilty or nolo contendere or from a verdict after trial or otherwise, and regardless of the pendency of an appeal. The Disciplinary Panel may defer entry of the order or set aside an order of suspension when it appears to the Panel in the interest of justice to do so.

Upon presentation of proof that the conviction is final, and regardless of the pendency of an appeal or other review of the conviction or of a Petition for Writ of Certiorari, the respondent shall be disbarred and the attorney's name shall be struck from the roll of members of the Bar of this Court by order of the Disciplinary Panel, unless within a period of 30 days from the date of the order, the respondent shows cause why disbarment would not be in the interest of justice.

(2) *Misdemeanors.* An attorney subject to these Rules who shall be convicted in any court of a misdemeanor may be disciplined in such manner and to such extent as the Disciplinary Panel may determine and may upon petition of the Committee and for good cause shown, be temporarily suspended pending a final decision of the Disciplinary Panel.

Upon receipt of a certified copy of such judgment of conviction, the Committee shall obtain an order from the Disciplinary Panel requiring the respondent to show cause within thirty days after service in accordance with LCrR 57.27(a) why the attorney should not be disciplined. If the respondent files a timely Answer, the Committee shall have 30 days within which to file a response thereto if it so desires. The Committee shall serve a copy of its response, if any, upon the respondent or respondent's counsel of record by first class mail, or, failing that, in accordance with LCrR 57.27(a).

Upon the filing of the respondent's Answer to the Order to Show Cause and any response thereto by the Committee, or if no answer has been filed, upon the filing of a recommendation by the Committee, the matter shall be promptly submitted to the Disciplinary Panel for its consideration. The Disciplinary Panel may, in its discretion, schedule a hearing. If a hearing is scheduled, the Chairman or designated member(s) of the Committee shall appear at the hearing and offer proof or arguments pertinent to the issues. After the hearing or, if no hearing is scheduled, upon a review of the papers submitted, the Disciplinary Panel shall take such action as these Rules and justice may require. In all proceedings hereunder the certified copy of judgment of conviction shall constitute conclusive proof of the respondent's guilt of the conduct for which the respondent was convicted. The pendency of an appeal or other review of the conviction or of a petition for writ of certiorari will not constitute a ground for failing to proceed in accordance with this Rule absent extraordinary circumstances and for good cause shown.

(3) *Reinstatement Following Suspension.* An attorney suspended under LCrR 57.27(b)(1) or (2) will be reinstated immediately upon the filing of a certificate demonstrating that the conviction has been reversed, vacated, or set aside, but the reinstatement will not terminate any formal disciplinary proceeding then pending against the attorney, the disposition of which shall be determined by the Committee on the basis of the available evidence.

(c) Discipline Imposed by Other Courts.

(1) *Policy of Reciprocal Discipline.* An attorney subject to these Rules who has been suspended for more than 30 days or disbarred by another court shall be automatically suspended from practice in this Court. The suspension shall be effective upon service of Temporary Suspension and Show Cause Order in accordance with these Rules. An attorney who has been suspended for 30 days or less by another court shall have the fact of that discipline noted by the

Clerk on the Lawyers' Register maintained by this Court, and no further proceedings shall be had thereon, unless the Committee on Grievances shall determine that the facts underlying the discipline warrant a proceeding for the imposition of discipline by this Court. Notations on the Lawyers' Register do not constitute discipline imposed by the Court and they shall be available only to the Court and to the Committee and shall not be matters of public record.

(2) *Issuance of Temporary Suspension and Show Cause Order.* Upon receipt of a certified or exemplified copy of a judgment or order from another court suspending or disbarring an attorney subject to these Rules, the Disciplinary Panel of this Court shall issue a Temporary Suspension and Show Cause Order suspending the attorney from practice before this Court pending a final disposition under these Rules, except where it finds extraordinary circumstances. Respondent may answer and show cause within 30 days after service of the Order why the imposition of the identical discipline by the Court would be unwarranted and the reasons thereof.

(3) *Duties of the Clerk.* The Clerk to the Committee thereupon shall cause to be served on the attorney the following documents: a copy of the judgment or order of discipline imposed by the other court; a certified copy of this Court's Temporary Suspension and Show Cause Order; and a copy of LCrR 57.27.

(4) *Procedures When Respondent Fails to Answer.* If respondent fails to answer to show cause within 30 days from service of the Temporary Suspension and Show Cause Order, this Court shall issue an Order vacating the Temporary Suspension and Show Cause Order and imposing the identical discipline or such other discipline it deems appropriate, unless it finds that upon the face of the record on which the discipline by the other court is predicated it clearly appears:

(i) that the procedure was so lacking in notice or opportunity to be heard as to constitute a deprivation of due process; or

(ii) that proof establishing the misconduct gives rise to a reasonable doubt that this Court could not, consistent with its duty, accept as final the conclusion of the disciplining court; or

(iii) that the imposition of the same discipline by this Court would result in grave injustice; or

(iv) that the misconduct established is deemed by this Court to warrant substantially different discipline; or

(v) that the misconduct on which the discipline was imposed by the other court does not constitute misconduct in the District of Columbia.

Where this Court determines that any of these elements exist, it shall enter such other order as it deems appropriate.

(5) *Procedures When Respondent Answers.* If the respondent files a timely Answer, the Committee shall have 30 days within which to file a response and make a recommendation to the Court. Upon consideration of the papers submitted by the respondent and by the Committee, the Court shall either (1) enter an Order vacating the Temporary Suspension and Show Cause Order and imposing the identical discipline or such other discipline it might find appropriate, or (2) if the Court finds that, upon the face of the record on which the discipline in another jurisdiction is predicated it clearly appears that one or more of the factors listed in subparagraphs (4)(i)-(v) exists, it shall enter such other order as it deems appropriate.

(6) *Censure or Reprimand.* Where discipline imposed by the other court is a public censure or reprimand, the Clerk shall note the fact of that discipline on the Lawyers' Register maintained by this Court, and no further proceedings shall be had thereon. Notations on the Lawyers' Register do not constitute discipline imposed by this Court and they shall be available only to the Court and to the Committee and shall not be matters of public record.

(7) *Stays.* If the discipline imposed by another court has been stayed, any reciprocal discipline proceeding in this Court may, upon motion of the respondent, be deferred by order of this Court until the stay expires and until further order of this Court. In the absence of a stay of discipline imposed by such other court, neither a motion for reconsideration or motion for rehearing or rehearing en banc filed in the other court or petition for a writ of certiorari will be the basis for a deferral of the proceedings in this Court absent good cause shown.

(d) Complaints of Misconduct Filed in This Court.

(1) *Complaints Generally.* Any person seeking to charge an attorney subject to the Rules with any act or omission which may justify disbarment, suspension, censure, reprimand or other discipline shall do so by a clear and concise written statement of facts in support of the allegations, subscribed and under oath or affirmed under the penalty of perjury pursuant to the United States Code, Title 28, Section 1746. The Complaint shall be presented to the Committee by lodging it with the Clerk to the Committee. The Committee shall have the inherent power without any formal Complaint to inquire into misconduct of attorneys subject to these Rules.

(2) *Complaints by a Court or a Judge.* Any court, judge or United States magistrate judge in the District of Columbia may refer to the Committee the name of any attorney subject to these Rules on a Complaint that such attorney has engaged in conduct, which, if substantiated, would warrant the imposition of discipline.

(3) *Investigation.* Complaints received by the Committee shall be reviewed to determine if the Complaint is appropriate for action. If the Complaint is insufficient on its face to warrant investigation, the Committee may discharge the complaint and advise the complainant that no action will be taken. If the Committee decides that the Complaint or information otherwise received by the Committee requires action, the Committee is authorized to (1) investigate the matter itself; (2) refer the matter to the Office of Bar Counsel, the Board on Professional Responsibility, District of Columbia Court of Appeals; (3) informally seek information from the respondent; or (4) require a formal Answer from the respondent in accordance with subsection (d)(4). To further any investigation, the Chairman, or in his absence, the Vice Chairman is authorized to issue subpoenas commanding the production of books, papers, documents, records or tangible items. If following any of these actions the Committee decides no further action is warranted, the Committee may, if its investigation was based on receipt of a complaint, discharge the Complaint and so inform the complainant and the respondent. If the Committee's investigation was based on information otherwise received and the respondent was made aware by the Committee of its investigation, the Committee shall notify the respondent that it has decided that no further action is warranted. The Committee may, as part of its notice to the respondent discharging the Complaint, provide an informal, non-reportable cautionary or educational statement, which shall not be considered discipline.

(4) *Service of Complaint; Answer.* If the Committee determines that a formal Answer is required from the respondent, a copy of the Complaint as received by the Committee or as prepared by it based on information otherwise received shall be served upon the respondent and he/she shall be required to answer within 30 days after the date of service. An Answer to a Complaint shall be in writing, subscribed and under oath or affirmed under the penalty of perjury in a form prescribed by the provisions of the United States Code, Title 28, Section 1746 and shall be accompanied by a list of all courts before which the respondent is admitted to practice. Upon receipt of the Answer, the Clerk to the Committee shall mail a copy thereof to the complainant, if there is one, who may reply to the Answer within 14 days of the date of the transmittal letter from the Clerk of the Committee. A copy of any reply to the Answer to the Complaint shall be served upon the respondent. If a respondent is served with a copy of a Complaint by the Committee and fails to answer within the time allowed by these Rules, the matter shall be certified to the Disciplinary Panel for its appropriate action.

(5) *Subcommittee of Inquiry.* The Chairman may designate three members of the Committee to sit as a Subcommittee of Inquiry and shall designate one as Chairman of the Subcommittee. The Chairman of the Subcommittee of Inquiry is hereby designated and appointed a Master with authority to cause subpoenas to be issued commanding the attendance of witnesses and/or parties at any hearings, as well as commanding the production of books, papers, documents, records or tangible things designated therein at such hearing. The Chairman of the Subcommittee as such Master is further authorized to administer oaths to the parties and witnesses. Should any witness and/or party fail or refuse to attend or to testify under oath, the witness' or party's name may be certified to the Disciplinary Panel of the Court, whereupon the Disciplinary Panel may refer the matter to the United States Attorney or to the U.S. Department of Justice to bring formal criminal contempt charges against such witness and/or party for so refusing. If the witness or party is found guilty of contempt, the Court shall administer such punishment as may be appropriate.

(6) *Right to Counsel in Disciplinary Proceedings.* The respondent shall be entitled to be represented by counsel who may appear in the respondent's behalf at any time during the investigation or after a Complaint has been served upon respondent.

(7) *Submission of Charges.* If following investigation the Subcommittee of Inquiry recommends, and a majority of the Committee concurs, the Committee shall prepare charges and submit them to the Disciplinary Panel of the Court or, in its discretion with or without preparing charges refer the matter to the Office of Bar Counsel, the Board on Professional Responsibility, District of Columbia Court of Appeals with a request that that Office take whatever action it deems appropriate. If submitted to the Disciplinary Panel and the Panel orders the charges to be filed, the Clerk shall file them and issue a summons directed to the respondent, commanding respondent to answer. The summons and a copy of the charges shall be served in accordance with these Rules. The respondent shall answer the charges within 30 days after the effective date of service and shall file with the Answer a list of all courts before which the attorney is admitted to practice. If no Answer is received within 30 days or such additional time as the Disciplinary Panel may allow, the charges may be taken as admitted and the Disciplinary Panel may reprimand, censure, suspend, disbar or otherwise discipline the respondent by entering an appropriate order.

(8) *Hearings and Orders of the Disciplinary Panel of the Court.* When the respondent has filed an Answer, the case shall be set down for hearing before the Disciplinary Panel and a member of the Committee designated by the Chairman shall appear at the hearing to offer proof or arguments pertinent to the issues. If the charges are sustained by clear and convincing evidence, the Disciplinary Panel may reprimand, censure, suspend, disbar or otherwise discipline the respondent by entering an appropriate order. Any

knowing violation of the order of judgment shall be deemed a contempt of court.

(e) Disbarment on Consent.

(1) *By This Court.* Any attorney admitted to practice before this Court who is the subject of an investigation into, or a pending proceeding involving, allegations of misconduct may not resign from this Bar, but may consent to disbarment. The attorney must deliver to this Court an affidavit stating that the attorney desires to consent to disbarment and that:

(i) the attorney's consent is freely and voluntarily given; the attorney is not being subjected to coercion or duress; the attorney is fully aware of the implications of so consenting; and

(ii) the attorney is aware that there is presently pending an investigation or proceeding involving allegations that there exist grounds for the attorney's discipline the nature of which the attorney shall specifically set forth.

Upon receipt of the required affidavit, the Disciplinary Panel shall enter an order disbarring the attorney. The order disbarring the attorney on consent shall be a matter of public record, but the affidavit shall be sealed and not be publicly disclosed or made available for use in any other proceeding except upon order of this Court.

(2) *By Other Courts.* Any attorney admitted to practice before this Court who shall be disbarred on consent or who shall resign from the Bar of any court of the United States or from the bar of any State, Territory, District, Commonwealth or Possession of the United States while an investigation into allegations of misconduct is pending, shall so advise this Court and submit a certified or exemplified copy of the judgment or order accepting such disbarment on consent or resignation. If no such order or judgment is submitted, the Clerk shall obtain it from the other court. The Disciplinary Panel thereupon shall enter an order disbarring the attorney and directing that the attorney's name be stricken from the roll of attorneys admitted to practice before this Court unless the attorney shows why it would not be in the interest of justice to do so. A certified or exemplified copy of the judgment or order accepting such disbarment on consent or resignation is conclusive proof of such disbarment on consent or resignation.

[Effective August 1, 1999. Amended effective April 10, 2007.]

Comments

COMMENT TO LCrR 57.27: LCrR 57.27 outlines the grounds and procedures for discipline of: attorneys convicted of crimes; attorneys disciplined by other courts; attorneys who are the subject of complaint of misconduct filed in this Court; and attorneys disbarred on consent.

Section (a) governs service of process in disciplinary proceedings. It makes clear that the primary method of service is by mail and the alternative method is by service on the Clerk of the Court.

Section (b) provides for immediate suspension upon proof of a felony conviction. The Disciplinary Panel may defer or set aside entry of the order in the interest of justice. This provision is to be invoked only in extraordinary circumstances. The Rule further provides for disbarment upon final conviction, regardless of the pendency of an appeal or other review, unless respondent shows cause within 30 days why disbarment would not be in the interest of justice.

With respect to misdemeanors, the Rule essentially maintains the show cause procedures in effect under former Rule 4-3(i)(b). With respect to both felonies and misdemeanors, the Rule makes clear that the pendency of an appeal or other review of conviction or of a petition for writ of certiorari does not affect the imposition of discipline. This provision was added to solve the recurring problem of a year or more delay attendant on petitions for certiorari, during which time the attorney might be permitted to practice before this Court.

Subsection (b)(3) has been added to provide for reinstatement after suspension upon proof that the underlying conviction has been reversed, vacated or set aside.

Section (c) governs discipline imposed by other courts and is a significant change from former Rule 4-3(II). The Rule provides that an attorney subject to these Rules who is suspended or disbarred by another court shall be suspended from practice in this court during the pendency of disciplinary proceedings. The procedures adopted are consistent with the practice in the United States Supreme Court, many United States Court of Appeals and a number of other district courts. By providing the attorney an opportunity to show cause why reciprocal discipline should not be imposed, the Rule satisfies the due process requirements of the relevant Supreme Court cases. See, e.g., In Re Ruffalo, 390 U.S. 544 (1968); Theard v. United States, 354 U.S. 278 (1957); Selling v. Radford, 243 U.S. 46 (1917). The Rule corrects the inadequacies of the former show cause procedures that permitted a respondent to continue to practice during the pendency of disciplinary proceedings. The revised procedure, requiring immediate temporary suspension followed by a show cause order, shifts the burden of going forward to the respondent to show cause why identical reciprocal discipline should not be imposed.

The provision for suspension eliminates the procedure of noting short-term suspensions imposed by other courts on this Court's records, rather than imposing reciprocal discipline (former Rule 4-3(i)(e)). Those procedures were unworkable and caused inequities. Under the procedures, censures and reprimands will be noted, but reciprocal discipline proceeding will be followed in the case of all suspensions or disbarments.

Subsection (c)(7) makes clear that if discipline imposed by another court has been stayed, reciprocal discipline in this Court may be deferred. However, in the absence of a stay, neither a motion for reconsideration nor a motion for rehearing or rehearing en banc nor a petition for writ of certiorari serves to defer disciplinary proceedings in this Court absent good cause shown.

Section (d) sets forth in one section all the procedures relating to Complaints filed in this Court. Subsection (d)(1) specifies that the Committee has the inherent power to inquire into misconduct of attorneys subject to these Rules, without formal Complaint. Subsection (d)(3) was amended to clarify that the Committee on Grievances may include an informal, non-reportable cautionary or educational statement as part of a notice discharging a Complaint without further actions.

Subsection (d)(7) provides that if a respondent fails to respond after a formal complaint is filed, the Disciplinary Panel has the power to take the allegations as admitted and impose appropriate discipline. Subsection (d)(8) sets forth the clear and convincing standard of proof for the imposition of discipline.

Section (e) governs disbarment on consent. It makes clear that there can be disbarment on consent in this Court or reciprocal disbarment for disbarment on consent by another court. It changes the former Rule by providing that an attorney under investigation or subject to pending proceedings involving allegations of misconduct may not resign from the Bar of this Court, but may only consent to disbarment.

Revised subsection (e)(1) governing disbarment on consent by this Court makes two substantive changes. First it permits the attorney affidavit, which is the predicate for disbarment on consent, to be filed under seal. Second, it eliminates the former requirement that an affidavit filed by an attorney seeking disbarment on consent contain an acknowledgment that the material facts alleged are true. This revision was adopted because it was felt that it was in the public interest to encourage consent disbarments.

With respect to disbarment on consent or resignation in other courts, subsection (e)(2) is changed only to the extent of providing the attorney an opportunity to show cause why such disbarment would not be in the interest of justice.

COMMENT TO LCrR 57.27(c)(1): Typically, an order of suspension entered by the District of Columbia Court of Appeals by its terms is effective 30 days from the date of its entry. The Disciplinary Panel of this Court signs its Temporary Suspension and Show Cause Order after the effective date of suspension order in the other court.

Since a respondent has 30 days within which to answer an order to show cause in this Court, a short-term suspension by another court has often expired and a respondent automatically reinstated in the other court before the time an answer is due in this Court. Thus, no useful purpose is served by initiating reciprocal disciplinary proceedings in cases involving suspensions of 30 days or less.

COMMENT TO LCrR 57.27(d)(1): This rule was modified to require that written complaints of misconduct contain a clear and concise statement of facts supporting the allegations made against attorneys.

LCrR 57.28 NOTIFICATION TO DISCIPLINARY AUTHORITIES

(a) Notification to Other Courts. When any person subject to these Rules has been convicted of any crime or disbarred, suspended, reprimanded, censured or disbarred on consent by this Court, the Clerk shall within ten days transmit to the disciplinary authorities in any other jurisdictions or courts in which the attorney is admitted to practice, a certified copy of the conviction or a certified copy of the judgment or order of disbarment, suspension, reprimand, censure or disbarment on consent. The Clerk shall also serve a certified copy of such judgment or order and a copy of such notice upon the respondent in accordance with LCrR 57.27(a).

(b) Notification to National Discipline Data Bank. The Clerk shall promptly notify the National Discipline Data Bank operated by the American Bar Association of any order imposing public discipline upon any attorney admitted to practice before this Court.

[Effective August 1, 1999.]

Comment

COMMENT TO LCrR 57.28: LCrR 57.28 has been adopted from the Model Rules of Disciplinary Enforcement. The purpose is to foster cooperation in reporting disciplinary actions.

LCrR 57.29 REINSTATEMENT

(a) After Disbarment or Suspension. An attorney suspended for a specific period shall be automatically reinstated at the end of the period upon the filing with the Court of an affidavit of compliance with the provisions of the order of suspension (including, in the case of reciprocal discipline, proof that the attorney has been reinstated by the court in which the attorney was disciplined). An attorney suspended for an indefinite period may not resume practice until the suspension is terminated by an order of the Disciplinary Panel. A disbarred attorney may not resume practice until reinstated by order of the Disciplinary Panel.

(b) Time of Application Following Disbarment or Suspension for Indefinite Period. A person who has been disbarred may not apply for reinstatement until the expiration of at least five years from the effective date of the order of disbarment. A person who has been suspended for an indefinite period may not apply for termination of the suspension until after the expiration of the minimum period fixed by the order of suspension or, if no minimum period is fixed, for a period of three years, or, in the case of reciprocal discipline, upon proof that the attorney has been reinstated by the court in which the attorney was disciplined.

(c) Hearing on Application. Petitions for reinstatement under this Rule shall be filed with the Clerk to the Committee. The Committee shall have 30 days within which to respond. The attorney shall have the burden of demonstrating by clear and convincing evidence that he/she has met the conditions of reinstatement or termination of suspension as provided for under these Rules. The Disciplinary Panel may hold a hearing on the application or, in its discretion, decide the matter on the basis of the papers filed.

(d) Conditions of Reinstatement or Termination of Suspension. If the Disciplinary Panel finds the attorney unfit to resume the practice of law, the petition for reinstatement shall be denied. If the Disciplinary Panel finds the attorney fit to resume the practice of law, it shall issue an order reinstating the attorney or terminating the suspension. The order may make reinstatement or termination of the suspension conditional upon the payment of all or part of the costs of the proceedings and upon the making of partial or complete restitution to parties harmed by the attorney's misconduct which led to the suspension or disbarment. In the discretion of the Disciplinary Panel, reinstatement or termination of suspension may also be conditioned upon the furnishing of proof of competency and learning in the law, which proof may include certification by the Bar Examiners of a State or other jurisdiction of the attorney's successful completion of an examination for admission to practice subsequent to the date of indefinite suspension or disbarment.

(e) Successive Petitions. No petition for reinstatement or for termination of suspension under this Rule shall be filed within one year following an order denying a petition for reinstatement or termination of suspension filed by or on behalf of the same person.

(f) Notification of Reinstatement. Upon entry of an Order of Reinstatement or an Order Terminating Suspension, the Clerk shall promptly notify the same persons who notified of the disciplinary orders.

[Effective August 1, 1999.]

Comment

COMMENT TO LCrR 57.29: Section (a) provides that to apply for reinstatement in the case of reciprocal discipline, the attorney must submit proof of reinstatement by the court in which the attorney was disciplined. Section (c) provides that the Committee will have 30 days to respond to a petition for reinstatement. The provision outlining the respondent's burden in obtaining reinstatement requires proof that the respondent has met the conditions of reinstatement under these Rules.

Section (d) sets forth the conditions for reinstatement. It provides that the Disciplinary Panel has the discretion to condition reinstatement or termination of suspension upon proof of competency and learning in the law, eliminating the provision that such proof would only be required if the disbarment or suspension lasted for five years or more. Section (f) provides for notification of reinstatement to the attorney.

LCrR 57.30 PROCEEDINGS WHERE AN ATTORNEY IS DECLARED TO BE MENTALLY INCOMPETENT OR IS ALLEGED TO BE INCAPACITATED

(a) Attorneys Declared Incompetent or Physically Infirm. If an attorney who is subject to these Rules has been judicially declared incompetent or involuntarily committed to a mental hospital, or has resigned from the bar of any court or been suspended from such a bar on the basis of such mental incompetence or incapacity or on the basis of physical infirmity or illness, the Disciplinary Panel, upon proper proof of the fact, shall enter an order suspending such attorney from the practice of law effective immediately and for an indefinite period until further order of the Court. A copy of such order shall be served upon such attorney, his/her guardian and the administrator of any hospital or other institution if the Court is informed such attorney is a patient thereof in such manner as the Disciplinary Panel may direct.

(b) Attorneys Alleged to Be Incapacitated. Whenever the Committee shall petition the Disciplinary Panel to determine whether an attorney who is subject to these Rules is incapacitated from continuing the practice of law by reason of mental infirmity or illness or because of the use of drugs or intoxicants, the Disciplinary Panel may take or direct such action as it deems necessary or proper to determine whether the attorney is so incapacitated, including the examination of the attorney by such qualified medical experts as the Disciplinary Panel shall designate. Failure or refusal to submit to such examination shall be prima facie evidence of incapacity. If upon due consideration of the matter the Disciplinary Panel concludes that the attorney is incapacitated from continuing to practice law it shall enter an order suspending the attorney on the ground of such disability for an indefinite period and until further order of the Court.

The Disciplinary Panel may provide for such notice to the attorney of proceedings in the matter as it deems proper and advisable and may appoint an attorney to represent the attorney if the attorney is without representation.

(c) Claim of Disability During Disciplinary Proceedings. If during the course of a disciplinary proceeding the attorney contends that he/she is suffering from a disability by reason of mental or physical infirmity or illness or because of the use of drugs or intoxicants which makes it impossible for the attorney to defend adequately, the Disciplinary Panel shall enter an order immediately suspending the attorney from continuing to practice law until a determination is made of the attorney's capacity to continue to practice law in a proceeding instituted in accordance with the provisions of paragraph (b) above.

(d) Application for Reinstatement. Any attorney suspended under this Rule for incompetency, mental illness, physical infirmity or because of the use of drugs or intoxicants may apply to the Disciplinary Panel for reinstatement immediately and thereafter once a year or at such shorter intervals as the Disciplinary Panel may direct in the order of suspension. The application shall be granted by the Disciplinary Panel upon a showing by clear and convincing evidence that the attorney's disability has been removed and that the attorney is fit to resume the practice of law provided, however, that if the suspension was based on resignation from the bar of another court the attorney must provide proof that the attorney has been reinstated in the other court, or that, if the suspension from practice before this Court was based on a finding of incompetence or incapacity by another court, it clearly appears on the face of the record that any of the five elements set forth in LCrR 57.27(c)(4) exist. The Disciplinary Panel may take or direct such action as it deems necessary or proper to a determination of whether the attorney's disability has been removed including a direction for an examination of the attorney. The Disciplinary Panel may direct that the expenses of such an examination shall be paid for by the attorney.

If an attorney has been suspended because of a judicial declaration of incompetence or involuntary commitment to a mental hospital and has thereafter been judicially declared to be competent, the Disciplinary Panel may dispense with further evidence and direct the reinstatement of the attorney upon such terms as it deems proper and advisable.

(e) Evidentiary Hearing. If the Disciplinary Panel holds an evidentiary hearing to determine whether an attorney is incapacitated or on an attorney's application for reinstatement under this Rule, the Chairman of the Committee shall appoint one or more members of the Committee to appear for the purpose of examining and cross-examining witnesses and/or offering proof or argument pertinent to the issues.

(f) Waiver of Physician–Patient Privilege. The filing of an application for reinstatement by an attorney who has been suspended for disability shall constitute a waiver of any physical patient privilege with respect to any treatment of the attorney during the period of the attorney's disability. The attorney shall be required to disclose the name of every psychiatrist, psychologist, physician and hospital by whom or in which the attorney has been examined or treated since the attorney's suspension and the attorney shall furnish the Disciplinary Panel with written consents for such psychiatrists, psychologists, physicians or hospital to disclose such information or records as may be requested by the medical experts designated by the Disciplinary Panel.

[Effective August 1, 1999.]

LCrR 57.31 LAWYER COUNSELING PANEL

(a) Referral of Attorneys for Counseling. Judges or the Committee on Grievances may refer to the lawyer counseling panel established by this Rule any member of the Bar of this Court who exhibits a deficiency in performance and who, in the judge's or the Committee's opinion, would likely benefit from counseling by other trial attorneys on matters of litigation practice, ethics, or apparent abuse of alcohol or drugs. The judge or the Committee will notify both the panel and the attorney of the referral and the basis therefor. The referral shall be confidential.

(b) The Counseling Panel. The counseling panel shall be composed of experienced litigation practitioners appointed by the Court, one of whose members shall be designated chairperson.

(c) Panel Proceedings. The chairperson of the lawyer counseling panel shall receive references from judges or the Committee on Grievances and assign the referred member to a particular panel member for counseling. Participation in the counseling program by referred attorneys shall be voluntary. Any conversations between the referred attorney and members of the panel shall be confidential and shall not waive any attorney client privilege. The panel will make no findings or report of its action as to any referred attorney, other than a report to the referring judge, or the Committee on Grievances, as to whether the attorney did or did not participate in counseling.

(d) Confidentiality and Immunity. All documents and communications relating or referring to the panel's referrals shall remain confidential and privileged.

All meetings and discussions of the counseling panel shall be held in camera and the business conducted therein shall remain confidential and privileged. All records, reports, correspondence and minutes of the panel shall be maintained by the Chairperson of the Counseling Panel and shall not be disclosed except by order or direction of the Chief Judge (or the designee of the Chief Judge).

When exercising the power relegated by the court, panel members shall be absolutely immune from suit for any conduct in connection with their duties. Referrals and counseling with respect thereto shall be absolutely privileged and no claim or action predicated thereon may be instituted or maintained.

[Effective August 1, 1999. Amended effective April 10, 2007.]

Comment

COMMENT TO LCrR 57.31(a) and (c): This rule was modified to permit the Committee on Grievances to refer attorneys to the Lawyer Counseling Panel and receive reports from the Panel concerning whether the referred attorney participated in counseling.

LCrR 58. MISDEMEANOR CASES BEFORE MAGISTRATE JUDGES

(a) Jurisdiction to Conduct Trials of Misdemeanor Cases. A magistrate judge may conduct trials (with or without a jury), accept pleas, impose sentence, and otherwise exercise jurisdiction in cases of misdemeanor offenses in accordance with 18 U.S.C. § 3401 and Rule 58, Federal Rules of Criminal Procedure.

(b) Recording the Proceedings. The court must record any proceedings under this rule by using a court reporter or a suitable recording device.

(c) Presentence Investigation at the Request of a Magistrate Judge. When requested by a magistrate judge, the Probation Office shall conduct a presentence investigation and render a report on any person convicted or who pleads guilty or nolo contendere before the magistrate judge.

(d) Payment of Fixed Sum in Lieu of Appearance.

(1) In accordance with Rule 58(d), Federal Rules of Criminal Procedure, the magistrate judge may in suitable misdemeanor cases accept payment of a fixed sum in lieu of appearance. In such cases, payment of the fixed sum shall terminate the proceeding. A schedule of fixed sums for misdemeanor cases subject to this Rule shall be approved by the Court on recommendation of the magistrate judges. The schedule may provide that the fixed sums will be increased depending on the stage of the proceedings at which the sum is paid, but the sum may not exceed the maximum fine allowed by law.

(2) If the defendant fails to pay a fixed sum, request a hearing, or appear in response to a citation or violation notice, the Clerk or a magistrate judge may issue a notice for the defendant to appear before the court on a date certain. The notice may give the defendant an additional opportunity to pay a fixed sum in lieu of appearance. The Clerk must serve the notice on the defendant by mailing a copy to the defendant's last known address.

(3) Upon an indictment, or upon a showing by one of the other charging documents specified in Federal Rules of Criminal Procedure 58(b)(1) of probable cause to believe that an offense has been committed and that the defendant has committed it, the court may issue an arrest warrant or, if no warrant is requested by an attorney for the government, a summons. The showing of probable cause must be made under oath or under penalty of perjury, but the affiant need not appear before the court. If the defendant fails to appear before the court in response to a summons, the court may summarily issue a warrant for the defendant's arrest.

(e) Appeal. Appeal from a magistrate judge's order or judgment under this Rule is governed by Federal Rule of Criminal Procedure 58(g).

[Former LCrR 57.20 effective August 1, 1999. Redesignated LCrR 58 and amended effective April 10, 2007.]

Comment

COMMENT TO LCrR 58: The Rule has been renumbered as LCrR 58 to conform with the numbering of Federal Rule of Criminal Procedure 58. Changes and additions have been made to conform with Federal Rule of Criminal Procedure 58.

LCrR 59.1. REFERRAL OF MOTIONS AND PRETRIAL MATTERS TO MAGISTRATE JUDGES

(a) Matters Determinable by a Magistrate Judge. At the request of the district judge to whom a felony case is assigned, a magistrate judge may hear and determine any nondispositive pretrial motion or matter other than those motions specified in LCrR 59.2 of these Rules, and may conduct pretrial proceedings and enter orders pursuant to LCrR 57.2 of these Rules.

(b) Objections to Magistrate Judge's Ruling. Any party may file written objections to a magistrate judge's ruling under paragraph (a) within 14 days after being served with the order of the magistrate judge or after the oral order is stated on the record, unless a different time is prescribed by the magistrate judge or the district judge. The objections shall specifically designate the order or part thereof to which objection is made, and the basis for the objection. The filing of oppositions and replies shall be governed by LCrR 47(b) and (d).

(c) Determination of Objections. Upon consideration of objections filed in accordance with this Rule, a district judge may modify or set aside any portion of a magistrate judge's order under this Rule found to be clearly erroneous or contrary to law.

[Former LCrR 57.18 effective August 1, 1999. Redesignated LCrR 59.1 and amended effective April 10, 2007. Amended effective December 1, 2009.]

Comment

COMMENT TO LCrR 59.1:.The Rule has been revised to remove references to civil procedure. Section (a) has been amended to make clear that magistrate judges may determine only nondispositive motions or matters in a felony case. See Federal Rule of Criminal Procedure 59(a). Additionally, the Rule has been renumbered as LCrR 59.1 to conform with the numbering of Federal Rule of Criminal Procedure 59. Finally, the Rule is intended to make clear that objections to the magistrate judge's proposed findings and recommendations should not be called motions for reconsideration and are to be directed to the district judge.

LCrR 59.2. REFERRAL OF MATTERS FOR HEARING AND RECOMMENDATION BY MAGISTRATE JUDGES

(a) Matters Referable to a Magistrate Judge for Hearing and Recommendation. At the request of the district judge to whom the case is assigned, a magistrate judge may conduct hearings, including evidentiary hearings, and submit to the district judge proposed findings of fact and recommendations for the disposition of:

(1) application for post-trial relief made by individuals convicted of criminal offenses;

(2) applications for revocation or modification of probation or supervised release, in accordance with LCrR 32.1(e) and Federal Rules of Criminal Procedure 32.1(b) and (c); and

(3) motions to dismiss or quash an indictment or information, motions to suppress evidence, or any matter that may dispose of a charge or defense.

(b) Objections to Recommendations of the Magistrate Judge. Any party may file for consideration by the district judge written objections to the magistrate judge's proposed findings and recommendations issued under paragraph (a) within 14 days after being served with a copy thereof. The objections shall be denominated "Objections to the Magistrate Judge's Proposed Findings and Recommendations." The objections shall specifically identify the portions of the proposed findings and recommendations to which objection is made and the basis for the objection. The filing of oppositions and replies shall be governed by LCrR 47(b) and (d).

Failure to file timely objections may waive appellate review of a District Court order adopting the magistrate judge's report. All magistrate judge's reports shall contain a notice substantially as follows:

> Failure to file timely objections to the findings and recommendations set forth in this report may waive your right of appeal from an order of the District Court adopting such findings and recommendations. See *Thomas v. Arn*, 474 U.S. 140 (1985).

(c) Determination by the Court. A district judge shall make a *de novo* determination of those portions of a magistrate judge's findings and recommendations to which objection is made as provided in paragraph (b). A district judge may make a determination based solely on the record developed before the magistrate judge, or may conduct a new hearing, receive further evidence, and recall witnesses. A district judge may accept, reject, or modify, in whole or in part, the findings and recommendations of the magistrate judge, or may recommit the matter to the magistrate judge with instructions.

[Former LCrR 57.19 effective August 1, 1999. Redesignated LCrR 59.2 and amended effective April 10, 2007. Amended effective December 1, 2009.]

Comment

COMMENT TO LCrR 59.2: The Rule has been revised to remove references to civil procedure. Additionally, the Rule has been renumbered as LCrR 59.2 to conform with the numbering of new Federal Rule of Criminal Procedure 59. Finally, the Rule is intended to make clear that objections to the magistrate judge's proposed findings and recommendations should not be called motions for reconsideration and are to be directed to the trial district judge.

ADMINISTRATION OF THE BANKRUPTCY SYSTEM[1]

[1] Rules 5011-1 - 9033-1 deal with the interrelationship of matters (references, de novo review, appeals, etc.) between the United States District Court and the United States Bankruptcy Court. The United States Bankruptcy Court has its own local rules governing procedures within that court. Those local rules, which were last revised on January 1, 1997, remain in effect.

DCt.LBR 5011-1. REFERENCE TO BANKRUPTCY JUDGE

Pursuant to 28 U.S.C. § 157(a), all cases under Title 11 and all proceedings arising under Title 11 or arising in or related to a case under Title 11 are referred to the Bankruptcy Judge of this District. All papers filed in any such case or proceeding, including the original petition, shall be filed with the Clerk of the Bankruptcy Court and shall be captioned "United States Bankruptcy Court for the District of Columbia."

[Effective August 1, 1999.]

DCt.LBR 5011-2. WITHDRAWAL OF REFERENCE

(a) Form of Request; Place for Filing. A request for withdrawal in whole or in part of the reference of a case or proceeding referred to the Bankruptcy Judge, other than a sua sponte request by the Bankruptcy Judge, shall be by motion filed timely with the Clerk of the Bankruptcy Court. All such motions shall conform to Local Rule LCvR 7 of the Local Rules of this Court. In addition, all such motions shall clearly and conspicuously state that "RELIEF IS SOUGHT FROM A UNITED STATES DISTRICT JUDGE."

(b) Time for Filing. Except as provided below as to adversary proceedings and contested matters, motion to withdraw the reference of a whole bankruptcy case or any part of a bankruptcy case shall be served and filed at or before the time first scheduled for the meeting of creditors held pursuant to 11 U.S.C. § 341(a). Except as provided below as to contested matters, a motion to withdraw the reference of a whole adversary proceeding or any part of an adversary proceeding shall be served and filed on or before the date on which an answer, reply or motion under Bankruptcy Rule 7012 or 7015 is first due. A motion to withdraw the reference of a contested matter within a case shall be served and filed not later than 14 days after service of the motion, application or objection which initiates the contested matter. Notwithstanding the foregoing, a motion to withdraw the reference may be served and filed not later than 14 days after service of any timely filed pleading or paper in which the basis for the motion first arises.

(c) Stay. The filing of a motion to withdraw the reference does not stay proceedings in the Bankruptcy Court. The procedures relating to stay shall be the same as set forth in Bankruptcy Rule 8005.

(d) Designation of Record. The moving party shall serve and file, together with the motion to withdraw the reference, a designation of those portions of the record of the proceedings in the Bankruptcy Court that the moving party believes will reasonably be necessary or pertinent to the District Court's consideration of the motion. Within 14 days after service of such designation of record, any other party may serve and file a designation of additional portions of the record. If the record designated by any party includes a transcript of any proceeding or a part thereof, that party shall immediately after filing the designation deliver to the reporter and file with the Clerk of the Bankruptcy Court a written request for the transcript and make satisfactory arrangements for payment of its cost. All parties shall take any other action necessary to enable the Clerk to assemble and transmit the record. The parties shall submit only that part or parts of a transcript of proceedings relevant to the issues raised on the motion for withdrawal of reference. If the issues involve only questions of law, the parties may submit an agreed statement of facts or such part or parts of the record as are relevant to such questions of law, unless the District Judge considering the motion directs otherwise.

(e) Responses to Motions to Withdraw the Reference; Reply. Opposing parties shall file with the Clerk of the Bankruptcy Court, and serve on all parties to the matter as to which withdrawal of the reference has been requested, their written responses to the motion to withdraw the reference, within 14 days after being served a copy of the motion. The moving party may serve and file a reply within 14 days after service of a response.

(f) Transmittal to and Proceedings in District Court. When the record is complete for the purpose of transmittal, but without awaiting the filing of any transcripts, the Clerk of the Bankruptcy Court shall promptly transmit to the Clerk of the District Court the motion papers and the portions of the record designated. After the opening of a docket in the District Court, documents pertaining to the matter under review by the District Court shall be filed with the Clerk of the District Court, but all documents relating to other matters in the bankruptcy case or adversary proceeding or contested matter shall continue to be filed with the Clerk of the Bankruptcy Court. Any motion and any sua sponte request by the Bankruptcy Judge to withdraw the reference shall be referred to the Chief Judge or the Chief Judge's designee for decision, but if the matter is withdrawn it shall be assigned to a District Judge in accordance with this court's usual system for assigning civil cases, unless the Chief Judge determines that exceptional circumstances warrant special assignment to a District Judge. Upon request of this Court, the Bankruptcy Judge shall determine, pursuant to 28 U.S.C. § 157(b)(3), whether or not any proceeding, as to which withdrawal of the reference is sought in whole or in part, is a core proceeding. This Court may, in its discretion, grant or deny the motion to withdraw the reference, in whole or in part. After such withdrawal, this Court may retain the entire matter withdrawn or may refer part or all of it back to the Bankruptcy Judge with or without instructions for further proceedings.

[Effective August 1, 1999. Amended effective December 1, 2009.]

DCt.LBR 8003–1. INTERLOCUTORY APPEALS

Whenever the Bankruptcy Judge has entered an interlocutory order, decree or judgment as to which a motion for leave to appeal has been filed pursuant to 28 U.S.C. § 158 and Rule 8003 of the Bankruptcy Rules, the Bankruptcy Judge shall, upon request of this Court, submit to this Court a written certification stating whether, in the Bankruptcy Judge's opinion, such order, decree or judgment involves a controlling question of law as to which there is substantial ground for difference of opinion and whether an immediate appeal from the order may materially advance the ultimate termination of the case. This Court may thereupon, in its discretion, grant or deny the motion for leave to appeal.

[Effective August 1, 1999.]

DCt.LBR 8006–1. FAILURE TO DESIGNATE RECORD OR ISSUES

If, after an appeal to the District Court has been noted, the appellant fails to designate the contents of the record on appeal or to file a statement of the issues to be presented on appeal within the time required by Bankruptcy Rule 8006, the Clerk of the Bankruptcy Court shall forward forthwith to the Clerk of the District Court a partial record consisting of a copy of the order or judgment appealed from, the notice of appeal, a copy of the docket entries and any other part of the record that the Clerk of the Bankruptcy Court deems appropriate. On request of the District Court, the Clerk of the Bankruptcy Court shall in addition transmit any other part of the record to the Clerk of the District Court. The District Court may, upon motion of the appellee filed in the office of the Clerk of the District Court, or upon its own order, dismiss the appeal for failure to comply with Bankruptcy Rule 8006.

[Effective August 1, 1999.]

DCt.LBR 8007–1. RETENTION OF RECORD IN BANKRUPTCY COURT

Unless the District Court or the Bankruptcy Court otherwise orders in any particular case, the record on appeal as designated pursuant to Bankruptcy Rule 8006 shall be retained by the Clerk of the Bankruptcy Court until such time as it is requested by the District Judge to whom the appeal is assigned.

[Effective August 1, 1999.]

DCt.LBR 8009–1. FAILURE TO FILE BRIEF

If, after an appeal has been noted and the appellant has complied with Bankruptcy Rule 8006, the appellant fails to serve and file a brief within the time required by Bankruptcy Rule 8009, the District Court may, upon motion of the appellee filed in the office of the Clerk of the District Court, or upon its own order, dismiss the appeal for failure to comply with Bankruptcy Rule 8009.

[Effective August 1, 1999.]

DCt.LBR 9033–1. DE NOVO REVIEW

(a) Form of Request; Time and Place for Filing. Pursuant to 28 U.S.C. § 157(c)(1), any party may request de novo review of proposed findings of fact and conclusions of law and a proposed final order or judgment by the Bankruptcy Judge by filing with the Clerk of the Bankruptcy Court, and serving on all parties to the matter under review within 14 days after service of a copy of such proposed findings, conclusions and order or judgment, written objections which shall specifically identify the portions of the proposed findings, conclusions, and order or judgment to which objection is made and the basis for such objection. All such objections shall conform to Local Rule 7.1 of the Local Rules of this Court and in addition shall clearly and conspicuously state that "RELIEF IS SOUGHT FROM A UNITED STATES DISTRICT JUDGE."

(b) Designation of Record; Response to Objections; Reply; Transmittal to and Proceedings in District Court. The procedures for designation of record, responses to objections, reply, and transmittal to and proceedings in the District Court shall be the same as set forth in Rule 5011–2 but the matter under review shall be assigned to a District Judge in accordance with this Court's usual system for assigning civil cases.

(c) De Novo Consideration by District Judge. A District Judge shall make a de novo determination of those portions of the Bankruptcy Judge's proposed findings, conclusions, and order or judgment to which objection is made and may accept, reject, or modify, in whole or in part, the proposed findings, conclusions, and order or judgment by the Bankruptcy Judge. The District Judge, however, need not normally conduct a new hearing and may consider the record developed before the Bankruptcy Judge and may make a determination on the basis of that record. The District Judge may also receive further evidence, recall witnesses or re-refer the matter to the Bankruptcy Judge with instructions.

(d) Effect of Failure to Object. Failure to file a timely objection to the Bankruptcy Judge's proposed findings, conclusions and order or judgment shall constitute consent to determination of the proceeding by the Bankruptcy Judge, pursuant to 28 U.S.C. § 157(c)(2); in such event the proposed findings, conclusion and order or judgment shall become the findings, conclusions and order or judgment of the Bankruptcy Court as of the date of their original entry.

[Effective August 1, 1999. Amended effective December 1, 2009.]

ORDERS AND NOTICES

NOTICE REGARDING PRIVACY AND PUBLIC ACCESS TO ELECTRONIC CIVIL CASE FILES

The United States District Court for the District of Columbia is an electronic case management court (CM/ECF) which has been accepting electronically filed pleadings and making the content of these pleadings available on the court's Internet website. Any subscriber to PACER will be able to read, download, store and print the full content of electronically filed documents from the Court's CM/ECF internet web site.

In compliance with the Judicial Conference of the United States, and the E–Government Act of 2002, as amended, and in order to promote electronic access to case files while also protecting personal privacy and other legitimate interests, parties shall refrain from including, or shall partially redact where inclusion is necessary, the following personal identifiers from all pleadings filed with the court, including exhibits thereto, whether filed electronically or in paper, unless otherwise ordered by the Court.

1) **Social Security Numbers.** If an individual's social security number must be included in a pleading, only the last four digits of that number should be used.

2) **Names of Minor Children.** If the involvement of a minor child must be mentioned, only the initials of that child should be used.

3) **Dates of Birth.** If an individual's date of birth must be included in a pleading, only the year should be used.

4) **Financial Account Information.** If financial account numbers are relevant, only the last four digits of these numbers should be used.

In compliance with the E–Government Act of 2002, as amended in August 2004, a party wishing to file a document containing the personal data identifiers listed above may:

(a) file an unredacted version of the document under seal. This document shall be retained by the court as part of the record, or

(b) file a reference list under seal. The reference list shall contain the complete personal data identifier(s) and the redacted identifier(s) used in its (their) place in the filing. All references in the case to the redacted identifiers included in the reference list will be construed to refer to the corresponding complete identifier. The reference list must be filed under seal, and may be amended as a matter of right. It shall be retained by the court as part of the record.

The unredacted version of the document or the reference list shall be retained by the court as part of the record. The court may, however, still require the party to file a redacted copy for the public file.

Exercise caution when filing documents that contain the following information and consider accompanying such filings with a motion to seal.

1) any personal identifying number, such as a driver's license number;

2) medical records, treatment and diagnosis;

3) employment history;

4) individual financial information;

5) proprietary or trade secret information;. If the Court seals a document after it has already been included in the public file, the Clerk shall restrict viewing of the document from both the electronic and paper files as soon as the order sealing the document is entered.

The responsibility for redacting personal identifiers rests solely with counsel and the parties. The Clerk will not review each pleading for compliance with this rule.

* Although not addressed in this civil privacy notice, it is important to redact such information relating to national security information.

[September 2004.]

NOTICE REGARDING PRIVACY AND PUBLIC ACCESS TO ELECTRONIC CRIMINAL CASE FILES

The United States District Court for the District of Columbia is an electronic case management court (CM/ECF) and will be accepting electronically filed criminal pleadings and making the content of these pleadings available on the court's Internet website in the near future. Any subscriber to PACER will be able to read, download, store and print the full content of electronically filed documents from the Court's CM/ECF Internet Web Site.

In compliance with the Judicial Conference of the United States, and the E–Government Act of 2002, as amended, and in order to promote electronic access to case files while also protecting personal privacy and other legitimate interests, parties shall refrain from including, or shall partially redact where inclusion is necessary, the following personal identifiers from all pleadings filed with the court, including exhibits thereto, whether filed electronically or in paper, unless otherwise ordered by the Court.

1) **Social Security Numbers.** If an individual's social security number must be included in a pleading,

only the last four digits of that number should be used.

2) **Names of Minor Children.** If the involvement of a minor child must be mentioned, only the initials of that child should be used.

3) **Dates of Birth.** If an individual's date of birth must be included in a pleading, only the year should be used.

4) **Financial Account Information.** If financial account numbers are relevant, only the last four digits of these numbers should be used.

5) **Home Address of an Individual.** If home address is in the pleading, only use city and state.

In compliance with the E–Government Act of 2002, as amended in August 2004, a party wishing to file a document containing the personal data identifiers listed above may:

(a) file an unredacted version of the document under seal. This document shall be retained by the court as part of the record. or

(b) file a reference list under seal. The reference list shall contain the complete personal data identifier(s) and the redacted identifier(s) used in its (their) place in the filing. All references in the case to the redacted identifiers included in the reference list will be construed to refer to the corresponding complete identifier. The reference list must be filed under seal, and may be amended as a matter of right. It shall be retained by the court as part of the record.

The unredacted version of the document or the reference list shall be retained by the court as part of the record. The court may, however, still require the party to file a redacted copy for the public file.

Exercise caution when filing documents that contain the following information and consider accompanying such filings with a motion to seal:

1. any personal identifying number, such as a driver's license number;

2. medical records, treatment and diagnosis;

3. employment history;

4. individual financial information;

5. proprietary or trade secret information;.

6. information regarding an individual's cooperation with the government;

7. information regarding the victim of any criminal activity;

8. national security information; and

9. sensitive security information as described in 49 U.S.C. Section 114(s).

The following documents shall not be included in the public case file and should not be made available to the public at the courthouse or via remote electronic access:

- Unexecuted summons or warrants of any kind (e.g. search warrants, arrest
- warrants;
- pretrial bail or presentence investigation reports;
- statement of reasons in the judgment of conviction;
- juvenile records;
- documents containing identifying information about jurors or potential jurors;
- financial affidavits filed in seeking representation pursuant to the Criminal Justice Act;
- ex parte request for authorization of investigative, expert or other services pursuant to the Criminal Justice Act;
- sealed documents (e.g. motions for downward departure for substantial assistance, plea agreements indicating cooperation)

If the Court seals a document after it has already been included in the public file, the Clerk shall restrict viewing of of the document from both the electronic and paper files as soon as the order sealing the document is entered.

The responsibility for redacting personal identifiers rests solely with counsel and the parties. The Clerk will not review each pleading for compliance with this rule.

[September 2004.]

TRANSCRIPT FILING INSTRUCTIONS FOR ATTORNEYS AND PRO SE LITIGANTS

In compliance with the Judicial Conference Policy to Make Transcript of Court Proceedings Available Electronically via CM/ECF and PACER, the following procedure will become effective on **May 19, 2008** for the U.S. District Court for the District of Columbia.

Official Court Transcript Filing Procedure:

- The official court transcript will be filed into CM/ECF by the court reporter and all filing users in the case will receive a Notice of Electronic Filing. For a period of 90 calendar days the transcript will be restricted in CM/ECF to court users, public terminal users, attorneys who have purchased a copy from the court reporter and others as directed by the court. However, copies may be purchased from the court reporter during this period. Attorneys for parties in the case purchasing a copy of the transcript will be given remote electronic access through CM/ECF and PACER by the court reporter upon payment of the transcript fee. Since Pro Se litigants are not registered users in ECF, electronic access cannot be granted until the transcript is available through PACER for public access.

- All filed transcripts are subject to redaction of personal identifiers as identified by counsel of record or parties to the case. If applicable, the redacted transcript must be filed within 31 days after the filing of the original transcript. It will not be available through PACER until the 90–day period has ended. See requirements below.
- Charges for access through PACER will accrue during and after the 90–day restriction period. Charges will accrue for the entire transcript and will not be capped at 30 pages. There will not be a free copy of the transcript. When purchasing the transcript from the court reporter, the attorney can receive the original and/or redacted transcript in both paper and/or electronic format.
- After the 90 day period has ended the filed transcript (or redacted transcript) will be available for inspection and copying in the Clerk's Office as well as through CM/ECF and PACER.

Redaction Requirements:

- Attorneys and parties in the case must review the transcript for redaction of these personal identifiers:

  Individuals' Social Security numbers

  Names of minor children

  Financial account numbers

  Dates of birth

  Home addresses in criminal cases

- Attorneys and parties must review the following portions of the transcript:

  Opening and closing statements made on the party's behalf

  Statements of the party

  Testimony of any witnesses called by the party

  Any other portion of the transcript as ordered by the court

- If only part of the transcript is ordered, attorneys and parties are not responsible for ordering and reviewing other parts of the proceeding.
- Parties have the responsibility of requesting redaction even if the requestor of the transcript is a judge or a member of the public/media.
- An attorney serving as court appointed standby counsel for a pro se defendant in defense of a criminal case must review the same portions of the transcript as if the pro se defendant were their client.
- Neither court reporters nor the Clerk's Office are responsible for the identification of the need for redaction of transcripts. Instead, it rests on the attorneys to tell the court reporter where to redact, and on the court reporter to perform the redaction.

Redaction Procedure:

- Attorneys and parties must file a Redaction Request in CM/ECF and by emailing the court reporter within **21 calendar days** of the filing of the transcript, listing the information to be redacted by page and line number. If the party wishes to redact other information, a motion must be filed. The transcript will remain restricted until this motion is ruled on, even though the 90 day period may have expired.
- The court reporter will then file a redacted transcript within 10 calendar days which also remain restricted from remote access for the 90 day period.
- After the 90 day period has expired, the redacted transcript will be available through PACER and the un-redacted transcript will remain restricted, except at the public terminal unless otherwise directed by the court.
- Access privileges for non-court users automatically propagate forward but not backward. If an attorney purchases the un-redacted transcript, and subsequently a redacted transcript is filed, the attorney will be granted access to it. However, if an attorney purchases only a redacted transcript, he does not acquire access rights to the un-redacted version.

Note to CJA Attorneys:

An attorney appointed under CJA is entitled to reimbursement for the costs of obtaining a transcript for purposes of review as well as for functions performed to fulfill his or her obligations including the following:

(1) traveling to gain access to the transcript, if needed;

(2) reviewing a transcript to determine whether to file a notice of intent to redact;

(3) filing a notice of intent to redact or a motion for extension of time;

(4) reviewing a transcript to determine the location of information to be redacted or whether to file a motion for additional redaction;

(5) preparing and filing a redaction request or motion; and

(6) other actions (including creating pleadings, attend hearings, or other follow-up).

If a case is closed, the CJA attorney may submit a supplemental voucher for compensation, if a final voucher has already been filed. If the original attorney is no longer available, a new attorney may be appointed under CJA and compensated as set out above.

Note to Appellate Attorneys:

If an attorney of record for the appellate case only, wants remote access to a transcript within the 90 day restriction period, the attorney is required to purchase the transcript from the court reporter, who will inform the court that this transaction has occurred. After the appellate attorney has requested access and provided the required information, the district court will create an ECF account for the appellate attorney and enable remote access to the transcript. The appellate attorney will not be added to the ECF case record.

[Effective May 19, 2008.]

INDEX TO

RULES OF THE UNITED STATES DISTRICT COURT FOR THE DISTRICT OF COLUMBIA

LOCAL RULES FOR THE UNITED STATES BANKRUPTCY COURT FOR THE DISTRICT OF COLUMBIA

Effective January 1, 1997

Including Amendments Received Through January 1, 2012

Research Note

These rules may be searched electronically on Westlaw in the DC-RULES database; updates to these rules may be found on Westlaw in DC-RULESUPDATES. For search tips, and a detailed summary of database content, consult the Westlaw Scope Screen of each database.

RULE 1001–1. SCOPE OF RULES; TITLE

(a) Scope of Rules and Title. These Rules govern practice and procedure in the United States Bankruptcy Court for the District of Columbia, referred to in these Rules as the "Court". These Rules supplement the Federal Rules of Bankruptcy Procedure. They may be cited as the "Local Bankruptcy Rules" or "LBRs" and an individual rule may be cited as

"LBR" (or, to distinguish the Rule from other districts' rules, "D.C. LBR").

(b) Cross-References. LBR 5005–4 (Electronic Filing); LBR 9029–1 (Suspension of Local Rules); LBR 9029–2 (Standing Orders); LBR 9029–3 (Local Rules—District Court).

Note: These Rules follow the Uniform Numbering System for Local Bankruptcy Court Rules (Revised May 2003), found at http://www.uscourts.gov/rules/newrules10.html (under Rules Committee Publications). Accordingly, what may be perceived as gaps in the numbering of these Rules merely reflects that these Rules do not cover every topic for which a uniform national number exists and that the uniform national numbers themselves intentionally have gaps. These Rules have been drafted with reliance placed on Bryan A. Garner, Guidelines for Drafting and Editing Court Rules (1996), found at http://www.uscourts.gov/rules/newrules10.html *(under Administrative Office Publications). The rules governing bankruptcy proceedings in the District Court are set forth in the D. Ct. LBRs. found in Appendix B.*

[Effective January 1, 1997. Amended effective July 1, 2011.]

PART I. COMMENCEMENT OF CASE; PROCEEDINGS RELATING TO PETITION AND ORDER FOR RELIEF

RULE 1002–1. PETITION—GENERAL*

(a) Verification of Authority to File.

(1) *Corporations.* In the case of a corporate debtor (including, but not limited to, a limited liability company or professional corporation) there must be filed with any voluntary petition, or any consent to an involuntary petition, a copy of the corporate resolution authorizing such filing.

(2) *Partnerships.* LBR 1004–1 governs the certificate required to accompany the petition of a partnership.

(b) Requirement of Filing Fee. A petition is not deemed filed as to a debtor and must be returned by the Clerk to the filer if the petition is not accompanied by payment of the required fee, tendered in an acceptable form, as set forth in LBR 1006–1, unless:

(1) the case is one in which:

(A) the petition is a voluntary petition filed by a debtor who is an individual (or filed by spouses in a joint case); and

(B) the petition is accompanied by an application, conforming to the form prescribed by the Clerk and posted on the Court's website (or conforming to the Official Form), signed by the debtor, and stating that the debtor is unable to pay the filing fee except in installments; or

(2) the case is one in which:

(A) the petition is a voluntary chapter 7 petition filed by a debtor who is an individual (or filed by spouses in a joint case); and

(B) the petition is accompanied by an application, signed by the debtor, on the appropriate Official Form for waiver of the filing fee.

(c) Mailing Matrix. For the requirements regarding the mailing matrix which must accompany the petition, see LBR 1007–1.

(d) Requirement to Utilize Current Official Form B1 (Petition). A petition must be submitted on the current Official Form B1 (Petition).

Note: This Rule 1002–1 sets forth certain documents that must be filed with the petition. There are additional documents, however, that a debtor must file under Rule 1007, and some of those must be filed with the petition. Lists of all the documents a debtor is required to file are available on the Court's website http://www.dcb.uscourts.gov/dcb/ under Bankruptcy Information/Statutes, Rules, Guides, etc./Guides/ Filing Instructions.

[Effective January 1, 1997. Amended effective July 1, 2011.]

* **Publisher's Note:** See also Standing Order In re Clerk's Office Operations, effective November 1, 2011, *post.*

RULE 1004–1. PETITION—PARTNERSHIP

In the case of a debtor that is a partnership, there must be filed with any voluntary petition or any consent to an involuntary petition:

(1) a statement signed by a general partner stating that all general partners have consented to such filing; and

(2) a notice to all general partners who have not signed the petition (or the consent to the involuntary petition):

(A) giving notice of the date on which the voluntary petition or the consent is being filed;

(B) attaching a copy of the voluntary petition (or of the consent to the involuntary petition); and

(C) bearing a certificate certifying that a copy of the notice has been mailed to all general partners who have not signed the petition (or the consent to the involuntary petition).

[Effective January 1, 1997. Amended effective July 1, 2011.]

RULE 1006–1. FILING FEE AND OTHER FEES AND AMOUNTS REQUIRED TO BE PAID TO CLERK

(a) Acceptable Forms of Tendering Payment. A fee required to be paid to the Clerk, pursuant to 28

U.S.C. § 1930(a) and the Appendix to § 1930 (Bankruptcy Court Miscellaneous Fee Schedule) (28 U.S.C. § 1930), and any other amount required to be paid to the Clerk, may be paid only:

(1) in cash;

(2) by cashier's check, certified check, or negotiable money order:

(A) issued by an FDIC–insured entity, or a credit union (as defined in section 19(b)(1)(A)(iv) of the Federal Reserve Act), or other entity recognized by the Clerk's Office to be a financially sound issuer; and

(B) made payable to "Clerk, United States Bankruptcy Court";

(3) by a member of the bar of the Court using a credit card in the electronic case filing system; or

(4) by a check made payable to "Clerk, United States Bankruptcy Court" drawn on the account of an attorney who is a member of the bar of the Court (or of the law firm of which such an attorney is a member, partner, associate, or of counsel), but the fee may not be paid by such a check if the Clerk refuses the check because a prior check or prior checks of that attorney or law firm have been dishonored.

[Effective July 1, 2011.]

RULE 1007–1. INITIAL LIST OF CREDITORS AND MAILING MATRIX; OBLIGATION TO AMEND*

(a) Requirement to File List of Creditors and Mailing Matrix. The debtor must file a List of Creditors and Mailing Matrix (which will serve as both the list required by Fed. R. Bankr. P. 1007(a)(1) or 1007(a)(2), and a mailing matrix):

(1) with the petition in a voluntary case; or

(2) within 14 days after entry of the order for relief in an involuntary case.

(b) Coversheet. An initial List of Creditors and Mailing Matrix must include a signed coversheet conforming to the form coversheet prescribed by the Clerk and posted on the Court's website. The coversheet must be dated and must contain a signed verification or declaration under 28 U.S.C. § 1746 establishing that the appended list is an accurate and complete listing of all entities required to be listed under Rule 1007(a)(1) or 1007(a)(2).

(c) Contents of List. The list appended to the coversheet must:

(1) list all entities required to be included on the list required by Fed. R. Bankr. P. 1007(a)(1) (or 1007(a)(2)) (the entities required to be listed on Schedules D, E, F, G, and H);

(2) list the entities in alphabetical order of the names of the entities; and

(3) include, after the name of each entity, the address of the entity, including postal ZIP Code.

(d) Format of List. The list appended to the coversheet must be submitted in the format (regarding font and so forth) set by the Clerk and posted on the Court's website.

(e) Obligation to File an Amendment to List of Creditors and Mailing Matrix. If the debtor discovers that an entity required to be listed under Rule 1007(a)(1) (or 1007(a)(2)) was omitted from the List of Creditors and Mailing Matrix (as amended by any amendment), or an entity was incorrectly listed thereon, the debtor must promptly file the appropriate type of amendment specified by LBR 1009–2.

(f) Cross–Reference. For the mailing list to be used for notices required to be sent to all creditors, and the right of a creditor to request to be added to that list, see LBR 2002–2 (Mailing List).

Note: The Court posts the Clerk's mailing matrix format instructions and matrix coversheet forms on its website (www.dcb.uscourts.gov) under "Court's Local Forms" (www.dcb.uscourts.gov/dcb/local–forms) (found under "Statutes, Rules, Forms, Guides, etc."). The List of Creditors and Mailing Matrix is used to prepare the LBR 2002–2 mailing list for notices to creditors, but that mailing list can differ because, for example, it uses creditors' preferred addresses.

[Effective January 1, 1997. Amended effective December 1, 2009; July 1, 2011.]

* **Publisher's Note:** See also Standing Order In re Clerk's Office Operations, effective November 1, 2011, *post.*

RULE1007–2. SCHEDULE OR AMENDED SCHEDULE FILED AFTER FILING OF INITIAL LIST OF CREDITORS AND MAILING MATRIX*

When a Schedule D, E, F, G, or H (or an amended Schedule D, E, F, G, or H) is filed after the date of filing of the initial List of Creditors and Mailing Matrix, the debtor must simultaneously file either:

(a) an Amendment to the List of Creditors and Mailing Matrix complying with LBR 1009–2, or

(b) a statement conforming with Local Official Form No. 12 that the schedule:

(1) does not add any entity not included on the existing List of Creditors and Mailing Matrix (as amended by any amendments that have been made thereto); and

(2) does not change the name or address of any entity as listed on the existing List of Creditors and Mailing Matrix (as amended by any amendments that have been made thereto).

[Effective January 1, 1997. Amended effective July 1, 2011.]

* **Publisher's Note:** See also Standing Order In re Clerk's Office Operations, effective June 1, 2011, *post.*

RULE 1007–3. NOTICE REQUIRED IN A CHAPTER 11 CASE WHEN A CREDITOR'S CLAIM IS SCHEDULED AS DISPUTED, CONTINGENT, OR UNLIQUIDATED

If a creditor's claim is listed on a schedule or amended schedule as disputed, contingent, or unliquidated, and the case is pending in chapter 11, then:

(a) within 14 days after the filing of the first schedule or amended schedule that so lists the creditor's claim (or within 14 days after the case was converted to chapter 11, if later), the debtor must file and serve on the creditor a notice of the listing and a certificate of service complying with LBR 5005–1(h); and

(b) the notice must state that the creditor has a right to file a proof of claim by the later of the bar date that would otherwise apply or 28 days after the date of mailing of the notice, and that the creditor's failure timely to do so may prevent the creditor from voting upon the plan or participating in any distribution thereunder.

[Effective July 1, 2011.]

RULE 1007–4. MAILING MATRIX FOR EQUITY SECURITY HOLDERS IN CHAPTER 11 CASE

(a) General Requirement. Except as provided in paragraph (b), the debtor in a chapter 11 case must file with the list required by Fed. R. Bankr. P. 1007(a)(3) a separate mailing matrix listing the names and addresses of the equity security holders, identified as a mailing matrix of equity security holders, utilizing the format specified by the Clerk for the mailing matrix required by LBR 1007–1, and accompanied by a coversheet attesting to the accuracy of the mailing matrix.

(b) Exception. If there are no more than 10 equity security holders in the case, the debtor may include those entities on the mailing matrix required by LBR 1007–1(a) with an appropriate modification to the LBR 1007–1(b) coversheet indicating that the mailing matrix also includes on it the names and addresses of the equity security holders required by Fed. R. Bankr. P. 1007(a)(3) to be included on the separate list of equity security holders.

Note: The exception in paragraph (b) does not relieve the debtor of filing a "list of equity security holders of each class showing the number and kind of interests registered in the name of each holder," etc., as required by Rule 1007(a)(3). This LBR recognizes that in cases in which there are many equity security holders, it could impose significantly increased noticing costs if equity security holders were added to the LBR 2002–2 mailing list (which includes creditors derived from the LBR 1007–1(a) mailing matrix and which is utilized for sending notices to all creditors under Fed. R. Bankr. P. 2002). Not all notices required to be sent to creditors under Rule 2002 are required to be sent to equity security holders under Fed. R. Bankr. P. 2002(d).

[Effective July 1, 2011.]

RULE 1007–5. FILING OF PAYMENT ADVICES (OR OTHER EVIDENCE OF PAYMENT), OR STATEMENT THAT NO SUCH DOCUMENTS EXIST

(a) At least 7 days before the date of the meeting of creditors under 11 U.S.C. § 341, the debtor must:

(1) separately file, with a cover sheet conforming with Local Official Form No. 9, copies of all payment advices or other evidence of payment received by the debtor from any employer within 60 days before the filing of the petition; and

(2) mail copies of the filed documents to any creditor who, at least 14 days before the date of the meeting of creditors under 11 U.S.C. § 341, has filed a request to receive such copies.

(b) The debtor must redact from the copies filed under paragraph (a)(1) any information entitled to privacy protection under Fed. R. Bankr. P. 9037.

(c) To protect against disclosure to the general public of information entitled to privacy protection under Fed. R. Bankr. P. 9037, the Court's electronic case filing system, upon the filing being docketed using the correct docketing event, will permit the documents filed under paragraph (a)(1) to be viewed by only:

(1) the trustee (if any);

(2) the Office of the United States Trustee;

(3) the debtor;

(4) the debtor's attorney; and

(5) the Court and Court staff,

but the docket entry will be a matter of public record and reflect the filing of the documents.

(d) If the debtor has received no payment advices or other evidence of payment from any employer within 60 days before the filing of the petition, the debtor must, by the deadline set forth in paragraph (a)(1), file a statement (utilizing Local Official Form No. 9) that the debtor received no such statements.

[Effective July 1, 2011.]

RULE 1007–6. STATEMENT REGARDING INTEREST IN ACCOUNT OR PROGRAM OF THE TYPE DESCRIBED BY § 521(C) OF THE BANKRUPTCY CODE

Within 14 days after the filing of a voluntary petition, or within 14 days after an involuntary petition is granted, an individual debtor must file a statement complying with Local Official Form No. 10, either appending thereto a record of any interest the debtor has in an account or program of the type described in 11 U.S.C. § 521(c) or certifying that the debtor has no such interest.

[Effective July 1, 2011.]

RULE 1009-1. AMENDED SCHEDULES

(a) Requirement to Amend Schedules. A debtor must promptly file an amended schedule whenever the existing schedule is materially inaccurate or whenever the debtor adds or changes the name or address of an entity required to be on the LBR 1007-1 mailing matrix.

(b) Requirement of Amended Summary of Schedules and Signed Declaration Page When Schedules Are Amended. When a debtor amends schedules, the debtor must include:

(1) an Amended Summary of Schedules that:

(A) indicates as to each required schedule whether an amendment is attached and indicates as to each amended schedule the number of sheets attached; and

(B) sets forth the dollar amounts on the debtor's schedules as amended by the attached amendments to the schedules; and

(2) a signed declaration under penalty of perjury, attesting to the number of sheets of amended schedules, and attesting that the Summary and the schedules, as amended, are true and correct to the best of the debtor's knowledge, information, and belief.

(c) Amendments to Schedule D, E, F, G, or H. When a debtor amends Schedule D, E, F, G, or H, the debtor must comply with LBR 1007-2 (requiring the filing of a LBR 1009-2 amendment to the mailing matrix or a statement explaining why no amendment is needed).

(d) Amended Schedules in a Chapter 11 Case That Treat Creditor's Claim as Disputed, Contingent, or Unliquidated. LBR 1007-3 governs an amended schedule in a chapter 11 case that lists a creditor's claim as disputed, contingent, or unliquidated.

[Effective January 1, 1997. Amended effective July 1, 2011.]

RULE 1009-2. AMENDMENT TO LIST OF CREDITORS AND MAILING MATRIX

(a) Requirement to File Separate and Distinct Amendments for the Four Different Types of Amendments to List of Creditors and Mailing Matrix. When a debtor amends the LBR 1007(a)(1) List of Creditors and Mailing Matrix, the four different types of amendment (which must be filed separately and distinctly from one another) are:

(1) to add entities;

(2) to delete entities;

(3) to change the address of an entity; and

(4) to change the name of an entity.

(b) Coversheet. An Amendment must include the form of coversheet (prescribed by the Clerk and posted on the court's website) that applies to the particular type of Amendment to the List of Creditors and Mailing Matrix being filed. The coversheet must be dated and must contain a signed verification or declaration under 28 U.S.C. § 1746 establishing that the mailing matrix, as amended by the attached list, is an accurate and complete listing of all entities required to be listed under Rule 1007(a)(1) or Rule 1007(a)(2) (and, additionally, under Rule 1019 in a case converted to chapter 7).

(c) Contents of List Appended to an Amendment's Coversheet. The list appended to the coversheet to the Amendment must:

(1) list the entities who, as the case may be, are being added, deleted, having an address changed, or having a name changed;

(2) list the entities in alphabetical order of the names of the entities; and

(3) include after the name of each entity, the address of the entity, including postal ZIP Code.

An Amendment that deletes an entity must list the entity-to-be-deleted as it was previously listed.

(d) Format of List. The list appended to the Amendment's coversheet must be submitted in the same format (regarding font and so forth) set by the Clerk for the list to be appended to an initial List of Creditors and Mailing Matrix under LBR 1007-1(a).

(e) Notice to Entities Affected by an Amendment (Other Than Entities Being Deleted from the List of Creditors and Mailing Matrix). The party filing the Amendment must file, separate from the Amendment, a certificate of service complying with Local Official Form No. 13 reciting that the party has mailed by first class mail, to each entity affected by the Amendment (other than an entity being deleted from the List of Creditors and Mailing Matrix):

(1) the notice of the commencement of the bankruptcy case;

(2) any notice from the clerk regarding conversion of the case;

(3) any notice of the meeting of creditors;

(4) any notice sent to all creditors regarding a deadline for opposing any motion not yet decided or any hearing not yet held;

(5) any notice to creditors of the deadline for filing any of the following:

(A) a proof of claim; and

(B) an objection to a disclosure statement not yet approved or to a plan not yet confirmed; and

(6) any currently proposed or already confirmed plan affecting the entities and any order confirming the plan, but the party need not mail a copy of the certificate of service to the affected entities.

(f) Requirement Either to Pay Fee Triggered by Filing of an Amendment or to File Certification That the Amendment Did Not Trigger a Fee. When an Amendment of the List of Creditors and Mailing Matrix, other than an Amendment changing only the addresses of previously listed entities, is filed, the filer must either:

(1) pay the fee (standing at $26 as of the adoption of these LBRs) imposed by the Bankruptcy Court Miscellaneous Fee Schedule (an appendix to 28 U.S.C. § 1930), but need pay only one such fee for multiple documents filed on the same date to make amendments to the List of Creditors and Mailing Matrix or to the debtor's Schedules; or

(2) file a certification that no fee is owed because the Amendment:

(A) only changed the address of a creditor or an attorney for a creditor listed on the debtor's schedules;

(B) only adds the name or address of an attorney for a creditor listed on the schedules; or

(B)* only relates to the debtor's initial schedule filed to comply with Fed. R. Bankr. P. 1019(5)(A)(i), (B)(i), (C)(ii), or (C)(iii) upon the conversion of a case to chapter 7.

[Effective July 1, 2011.]

* So in original.

RULE 1009-3. AMENDED CHAPTER 11 LIST OF EQUITY SECURITY HOLDERS

When an amended list of equity security holders adds, deletes, or changes the name or address of an equity security holder:

(1) the debtor must file with the amendment an amendment to the LBR 1007-4 mailing matrix for equity security holders (or the LBR 1007-1 mailing matrix if equity security holders were included on that mailing matrix), accompanied by a coversheet (as in the case of an amendment under LBR 1009-2) that addresses the particular type of change; and

(2) the debtor must additionally mail to the equity security holder a copy of the amendment and copies of any notices that were mailed to equity security holders in the case.

[Effective July 1, 2011.]

RULE 1013-1. DISPOSITION OF INVOLUNTARY PETITION

Dismissal of an involuntary petition is governed by LBR 1017-2(a). Consents to an involuntary petition are governed in the case of corporations and partnerships, respectively, by LBR 1002-1(a)(1) and LBR 1004-1.

[Effective January 1, 1997.]

RULE 1017-1. CONVERSION UNDER § 706(A) OF THE BANKRUPTCY CODE

(a) Unless otherwise ordered by the Court, a motion to convert a case under chapter 7 to a case under chapter 11, 12, or 13 pursuant to § 706(a) of the Bankruptcy Code requires no notice and opportunity for a hearing under Federal Rule of Bankruptcy Procedure 9014 and no corresponding notice of opportunity to object under LBR 9013-1(b)(3).

(b) A motion to convert under § 706(a) must be served by first class mail on the Chapter 7 Trustee and the Office of the United States Trustee.

(c) The Court may enter an order converting a case on the motion of the debtor filed pursuant to § 706(a) without the necessity of a hearing if the following conditions are met:

(1) no opposition to the motion is filed within 7 days of its entry on the docket; and

(2) the Court determines based on the information available to it on the docket that there is no reason to believe the conversion is being undertaken in bad faith or, for a motion to convert to chapter 13, that the debtor would be ineligible to be a debtor in chapter 13 under § 109(e).

Note: This LBR implements the holding of In re Pricer, 2001 WL 2855801 (Bankr. D.D.C. June 29, 2009).

[Effective July 1, 2011.]

RULE 1017-2. DISMISSAL OF CASE

(a) Dismissal of Involuntary Petition. Prior to dismissal of an involuntary petition on motion of a petitioner or on consent of all petitioners and the debtor, or for want of prosecution, the debtor must prepare and file a list of all creditors. Notice under LBR 2002-1 on a petitioner's motion to dismiss, or on a motion to dismiss on consent of all petitioners and the debtor, or on a motion to dismiss for want of prosecution, must contain the following additional information:

(1) A disclosure by the moving party of the reasons dismissal is sought;

(2) The terms of any settlement reached with the debtor, including any consideration received; and

(3) A notice that any creditor may file objections or may join in the petition under 11 U.S.C. § 303(c).

(b) Automatic Dismissal Under 11 U.S.C. § 521(i). To dismiss a case under the automatic dismissal provisions of 11 U.S.C. § 521(i), a motion is required, and the notice of the motion may set a deadline for opposing the motion of 3 days after the filing of the notice. Unless the court orders otherwise, the motion must be filed within 21 days after the date on which the case became subject to automatic dismissal under § 521(i).

(c) Cross–Reference. For the rejection of a petition for failure to pay the filing fee, see LBR 1002–1(b). For the effect of a motion to dismiss for failure to attend the meeting of creditors on certain bar dates, including the Rule 1017(e)(1) bar date for motions to dismiss for substantial abuse, see LBR 2003–1(b).

Note: LBR 1017–2(a) supplements 11 U.S.C. § 303(j) and imposes requirements suggested by Collier. LBR 9013–1 governs motions generally, and LBR 2002–1 governs notice to creditors of the opportunity to oppose a motion to dismiss.

[Effective January 1, 1997. Amended effective July 1, 2011.]

RULE 1019–1. CONVERSION OF CASE TO CHAPTER 7

(a) Form of Schedule Filed Under Fed. R. Bankr. P. 1019(5) Listing Unpaid Debt. A schedule filed under Fed. R. Bankr. P. 1019(5) that lists an unpaid debt must:

(1) list the name and address of the entity to whom the unpaid debt is owed; and

(2) state the nature and amount of the debt.

(b) Form of Schedule Filed Under Fed. R. Bankr. P. 1019(5)(C)(iii) of Executory Contracts or Unexpired Leases. A schedule filed under Fed. R. Bankr. P. 1019(5)(C)(iii) must:

(1) list the name and address (including ZIP Code) of each of the other parties to the executory contract or unexpired lease; and

(2) describe the contract or lease.

(c) Adding to Mailing Matrix Entities Scheduled Under Fed. R. Bankr. P. 1019(5). Upon filing a schedule (or amended schedule) of post-petition debts or post-petition executory contracts or post-petition unexpired leases under Fed. R. Bankr. P. 1019(5):

(1) the filer must file on the same date an amendment to the mailing matrix complying with LBR 1009–2(a)(1) (consisting of a coversheet under LBR 1009–2(b) and an attached list complying with LBR 1009–2(c) and (d)) in order to add to the mailing matrix the entities listed on the schedule; and

(2) if after conversion of the case and prior to docketing of the amendment to the mailing matrix required by the preceding paragraph (1), the Clerk has issued any notice under Fed. R. Bankr. P. 2002(f), then by the date of the filing of the supplemental mailing matrix, the debtor shall mail, by first class mail, to each entity listed on the schedule a copy of each such notice, and file a certificate of mailing.

(d) Statement That There Are No Unpaid Debts, Executory Contracts, Unexpired Leases, or Property To Schedule Under Rule 1019(5). If there are no unpaid debts, executory contracts, unexpired leases, or property to schedule under Fed. R. Bankr. P. 1019(5), then by the deadline for filing a schedule of such matters under Fed. R. Bankr. P. 1019(5), the debtor must file a verified statement or declaration under 28 U.S.C. § 1746 attesting to that fact.

[Effective July 1, 2011.]

PART II. OFFICERS AND ADMINISTRATION; NOTICES; MEETINGS; EXAMINATIONS; ATTORNEYS AND ACCOUNTANTS

RULE 2002–1. NOTICE TO CREDITORS AND OTHER INTERESTED PARTIES

(a) Scope of Rule. This Rule governs notices required under Fed. R. Bankr. P. 2002(a) regarding certain motions, applications, or proposed acts.

(b) Rule 2002(a) Notice of Period for Objections. Unless otherwise ordered by the court:

(1) *General Requirement of 21–Day Deadline.* Except as provided in paragraphs (2) and (3), a notice under Rule 2002(a) must conspicuously give the recipient notice that by the date (calculated by the movant) that is 21 days after the later of the date of filing or the date of service of the notice, the recipient must file an objection to the relief sought or the relief may be authorized without an actual hearing. The add-three-days rule of Fed. R. Bankr. P. 9006(f) does not apply to computation of the 21–day period because the notice is of a specific deadline date.

(2) *Optional Exception for Notice Under Fed. R. Bankr. P. 6004(b).* When Fed. R. Bankr. P. 6004(b)

(regarding a proposed use, sale, or lease of property, other than cash collateral) applies, a party may instead give notice that any objection, as provided by that Rule, "shall be filed and served not less than seven days before the date set for the proposed action," with notice of a hearing date (if one proves necessary) that is a date that is at least 21 days after the later of the date of filing or the date of service of the notice.

(3) *Optional Exception for Notice Under Fed. R. Bankr. P. 6004(d).* When Fed. R. Bankr. P. 6004(d) (regarding sales of property under $2,500) applies, a party may instead give notice that any objection to the sale must be filed and served within 14 days of the mailing of the notice.

(4) *Inapplicability of Three–Days–Added Provision of Fed. R. Bankr. P. 9006(f) to paragraphs (1) and (2).* The add-three-days provision of Fed. R. Bankr. P. 9006(f) shall not apply to the computation of the deadline under paragraph (1) above or the 21–day notice of the hearing date under paragraph (2) above, but shall apply to computation of the 14–day deadline under paragraph (3) above.

(c) Content of Notice. The notice must substantially conform to Official Form No. 20A, and, in addition to the information required by specific notices, a notice:

(1) may state that if the Court determines that as a matter of law the explanation for an objection does not establish a valid basis for objection, the Court may proceed to dispose of the objection without a hearing;

(2) must contain sufficient information to enable a party in interest to make a reasonably well-informed decision whether to object to the action proposed in the notice;

(3) must state the address, telephone number, and email address of the party to be contacted if parties in interest have questions regarding the subject of the notice; and

(4) may not state that an objecting party must attend a Court hearing in support of any objection made.

Notice is sufficient under this paragraph if it is substantially in the form of Local Official Form No. 4.

(d) Service of Notices—General. A party serving a notice under this Rule must serve it based on the current mailing list maintained by the Clerk under LBR 2002–2.

(e) Limitation of Notice—Chapter 7. Unless otherwise directed by the Court, in a chapter 7 case service of a notice to creditors under Fed. R. Bankr. P. 2002(a) is limited, as set forth in Fed. R. Bankr. P. 2002(h), to (1) creditors that hold claims for which proofs of claim have been filed, and (2) such other creditors who may file timely claims.

(f) Limitation of Notice—Chapter 11. In a chapter 11 case, if an official committee of unsecured creditors has been appointed and the number of creditors exceeds 30, service of a notice under Fed. R. Bankr. P. 2002(a)(2), (3), or (7) may, at the option of the party giving notice, be limited to the debtor, any trustee, the U.S. Trustee, the members of all official committees (or committee counsel, if appointed), and to those creditors and equity security holders who have served on the debtor in possession (or the trustee when a trustee has been appointed) and filed a request under LBR 2002–1(k) that all notices be mailed to them.

(g) Limitation of Notice—Chapter 13. In a chapter 13 case, notice of a professional's application for approval of compensation and reimbursement of expenses need only be sent to the Chapter 13 Trustee, the debtor, the debtor's attorney (if different from the applicant), and creditors who have filed and served on the trustee a request under LBR 2002–1(k) to receive all notices in the case.

(h) Proponent to Give Notice. Except as stated elsewhere in the Bankruptcy Code, the Federal Rules of Bankruptcy Procedure, these Local Rules, or by order of the Court, the proponent of any action requiring notice governed by this Rule must transmit the notice, unless the Clerk determines to give the notice.

(i) Certificate of Service. Within 2 days after completion of service of a Rule 2002(a) notice, the entity that made service must file a certificate of service complying with LBR 5005–3.

(j) Entities Requesting to Receive All Notices. Any entity entitled generally to receive notices in the case who wishes to receive all notices under Fed. R. Bankr. P. 2002 must file a document styled "Request to Receive All Notices Under Rule 2002 in Case" which the Clerk must docket. The request must be served on the trustee or debtor in possession. The Clerk shall add the entity to the mailing list under LBR 2002–2 if it is not already on that mailing list.

(k) Hearing. In a proceeding to which this Rule applies, the Court may set a hearing if timely objection is filed to the proposed action or the Court otherwise deems a hearing appropriate. Other procedures governing the setting of a hearing are set forth in LBR 5070–1. The conduct of a hearing is governed by LBR 9073–1.

(*l*) Cross–References. LBR 9013–1(c) governs the entities to be served with a motion itself as distinct from the entities to be given notice of the motion.

Note: Pursuant to 11 U.S.C. § 102, an act may be authorized without an actual hearing if no hearing is timely requested after notice of an opportunity to oppose the act. Except where a Fed. R. Bankr. P. such as Fed. R. Bankr. P. 6007 specifies a deadline "after mailing of the notice," paragraph (b) authorizes notice to object by a set date, instead of, for example, a deadline of 21 days after the service of the notice, thereby avoiding the requirement of Fed. R. Bankr. P. 9006(f) of adding 3 days to the response time when the time to act is measured from the date of mailing.

[Effective January 1, 1997. Amended effective December 1, 2009; July 1, 2011.]

RULE 2002-2. MAILING LIST

(a) Mailing List for Notice to Creditors. The Clerk maintains in the Court's Case Management/Electronic Case Filing system (or such other entity as the Court shall direct shall maintain) a mailing list to be utilized whenever notice is required to be sent to all creditors. That mailing list consists of the names and addresses of entities listed on the LBR 1007-1 mailing matrix, as modified by any supplemental mailing matrix, and as further adjusted by the Clerk to take into account, for example, preferred addresses (as under 11 U.S.C. § 342(f) or Fed. R. Bankr. P. 2002(g)(1)) that have been submitted, and addresses that result in mail being undeliverable.

(b) Mailing List for Notices to Equity Security Holders. In a chapter 11 case, the Clerk maintains in the Court's Case Management/Electronic Case Filing system a separate mailing list for equity security holders unless the equity security holders were listed on the mailing matrix required by LBR 1007-1.

(c) Request to Be Added to the Mailing List. An entity having an interest in the case may file a request to the Clerk to be added to the mailing list under paragraph (a) or (b) above, as the case may be. If the entity is a creditor, an equity security holder, or an attorney for any of the foregoing, the Clerk must add that entity to the mailing list, but otherwise the Clerk may exercise discretion whether to add the entity to the mailing list. A request under this LBR 2002-1(c) shall not suffice to comply with LBR 2002-1(k) regarding a creditor's request to receive all notices.

(d) Request to Change Address on the Mailing List. An entity may file a request directing how notices under Rule 2002 must be addressed to it and requesting that the list under LBR 2002-2(a) or LBR 2002-2(b), as the case may be, be changed accordingly.

[Effective January 1, 1997. Amended effective July 1, 2011.]

RULE 2002-3. FILING OF DESIGNATION UNDER § 342(f) OF THE BANKRUPTCY CODE OF A CREDITOR'S PREFERRED ADDRESS

Under 11 U.S.C. § 342(f), an entity may file with any bankruptcy court a notice of address, to be used by all bankruptcy courts or by particular bankruptcy courts, to provide notice to such entity in chapter 7 and 13 cases in which the entity is a creditor. Any § 342(f) notice of a preferred address must be filed with the National Creditor Registration Service (NCRS). Forms for registration of a preferred address are available at https://ncrs.uscourts.gov/.

[Effective July 1, 2011.]

RULE 2003-1. MEETING OF CREDITORS AND EQUITY SECURITY HOLDERS

(a) A request by the debtor or the debtor's attorney to continue a meeting of creditors must, except in extraordinary circumstances, be made in advance or at the meeting of creditors, and made as follows: in chapter 13 cases to the standing Chapter 13 Trustee; in chapter 7 cases to the interim Chapter 7 Trustee; and in chapter 11 cases to the Office of the U.S. Trustee:

(1) Upon denial of or a failure to act upon the request, a motion may be filed with the Court.

(2) If the request is granted, then within 3 days of receiving the new date and time for the meeting of creditors, the attorney for the debtor (or the debtor if the debtor is not represented by counsel) must serve written notice of the rescheduled meeting of creditors on all creditors and other parties in interest and file a certificate of such service complying with LBR 5005-3. Notice must be given in the form, if any, approved by the Clerk and posted on the Court's website.

(b) In cases under chapter 7 or 11, if the debtor fails to appear at a meeting of creditors:

(1) any motion to dismiss on that basis is deemed to include a motion to enlarge the time, if not already expired, for objecting to discharge or moving to dismiss the case on other grounds, until the later of 60 days after resolution of the motion to dismiss or 60 days after resolution of any motion to vacate an order granting the motion to dismiss; and

(2) an order acting on the motion, unless it indicates otherwise, is deemed to grant such enlargement of time.

(c) If the debtor does not appear as required at the meeting of creditors under 11 U.S.C. § 341 or at a continuation of that meeting of creditors, the meeting is deemed not to have been concluded for purposes of Fed. R. Bankr. P. 4003(b).

[Effective January 1, 1997. Amended effective July 1, 2011.]

RULE 2004-1. EXAMINATIONS

A motion under Fed. R. Bankr. P. 2004 for an examination of or the production of documents by an entity other than the debtor (or for permission to issue a subpoena to the debtor for such an examination or production) need not include the notice required by LBR 9013-1(b)(3) to accompany motions commencing contested matters and the movant may submit a praecipe requesting the Clerk to bring the motion to the Court for a ruling without awaiting a response.

Note: This Rule is designed to expedite the granting of orders allowing examinations under Fed. R. Bankr. P. 2004 of entities other than the debtor. Such an order must be enforced by service of a subpoena, such that any defenses to the examination can be raised in response to the subpoena under Fed. R. Civ. P. 45 (made applicable by Fed. R. Bankr. P. 9016). When a motion seeks to compel the debtor to appear for an examination and to produce records, any defenses to the examination of the debtor or to the production of the debtor's records should be raised in response to the motion because the order will adjudicate the parties' rights and will be subject to enforcement by the Court's contempt powers, with the propriety of the order no longer at issue except on appeal. This would not be the case when the motion only seeks permission to issue a subpoena to the debtor for an examination or production of records (as opposed to an order requiring the debtor, whether subpoenaed or not, to appear for examination or to produce records).

[Effective January 1, 1997. Amended effective July 1, 2011.]

RULE 2014–1. APPLICATIONS TO EMPLOY PROFESSIONALS

Unless otherwise ordered by the Court, when a debtor in possession in a chapter 11 case or a trustee in any case files an application to employ a professional, the application must include:

(1) a notice of opportunity to object to the application by the later of 21 days after the filing of the petition and 14 days after the date of filing of the application; and

(2) a certificate of service reflecting that the application was mailed to:

(A) the Office of the United States Trustee;

(B) any committee appointed in the case (or its counsel); and

(C) if no committee of unsecured creditors has been appointed in a chapter 11 case, the creditors listed under Fed. R. Bankr. P. 1007(d).

Note: The limitation that oppositions to the application are due no earlier than 21 days after the filing of the petition is derived from Fed. R. Bankr. P. 6003(a).

[Effective July 1, 2011.]

RULE 2015–1. MONTHLY OPERATING REPORTS

In a chapter 11 case, the debtor in possession or the trustee must file with the Court all monthly operating reports that are transmitted to the United States Trustee.

[Effective July 1, 2011.]

RULE 2016–1. COMPENSATION OF PROFESSIONALS

(a) Applications of Professionals for Compensation and Reimbursement—Contents. Any professional seeking interim or final compensation for services and reimbursement of expenses under 11 U.S.C. §§ 330, 331, or 503(b)(2) or (4) must file an application for compensation and reimbursement. In addition to the information specifically required by Fed. R. Bankr. P. 2016(a), the application must also include:

(1) the time period during which the services were performed;

(2) the date of any order authorizing the employment;

(3) the date and amount of any pending fee application, of any prior fee allowance, and of any retainer or payment;

(4) a brief narrative statement concerning the services performed, the total time spent performing the services, and the results achieved, including, in the case of an attorney, how the attorney's efforts have contributed to the estate (in light of its present status and the anticipated additional time and fees that will be necessary to conclude the case);

(5) if the applicant intends to seek compensation as both attorney and trustee, a recitation that fees are not being sought by the individual as attorney for work which is the responsibility of the trustee (it being advisable separately to list time spent as trustee);

(6) when the fees sought exceed $50,000, a summary or cover sheet that provides a synopsis of the following information:

(A) total compensation and expenses requested and any amount(s) previously requested;

(B) total compensation and expenses previously awarded by the Court;

(C) name and applicable billing rate for each person who billed time during the period, and date of bar admission for each attorney;

(D) total hours billed and total amount of billing for each person who billed time during the billing period; and

(E) computation of blended hourly rate for persons who billed time during period, excluding paralegal or other paraprofessional time;

(7) a chronological itemization of services performed which includes the date each service was performed, the amount of time spent in performing each service, and a narrative description of each service performed. If the itemization of services is extensive or complex, as in the case of multiple adversary proceedings or substantial contested matters, the chronological itemization must be done by project,

dispute, or subject matter and include a summary setting forth the information required by paragraphs (6)(D) and (6)(E) above with respect to the time spent on such project, dispute or subject matter. Such "project billing" is presumptively required when the application seeks in excess of $50,000;

(8) a separate document styled "List of Each Day on Which an Employee Spent More Than 12 Hours" listing each employee who is being billed for more than 12 hours in a given day, the amount of time the employee is billing and the tasks performed for that day;

(9) an itemization of actual, necessary expenses incurred:

(A) stating that, except for expenses listed in the amount charged by the vendor of the service or item to the applicant, each charge is in an amount reflecting the applicant's ordinary rate of charge and indicating what the ordinary unit rate of charge is for each separate category of service (*e.g.*, photocopying and facsimile transmission or receipt charges); and

(B) when charges are made for travel and related expenses, itemizing each travel expense (including the class of travel), with each hotel and meal expense separately stated and limited to an amount that is charged for a class other than luxury, deluxe, or first class; and

(10) when an attorney seeking interim compensation was employed by the Chapter 7 Trustee, the application must additionally include the following:

(A) a summary of the status of the case, including, to the best of the applicant's knowledge, the projected date for the trustee's final report;

(B) an estimate of the funds that will be available to unsecured creditors; and

(C) the amount of funds then on hand in the chapter 7 case.

(b) Notice. Notice of an application for compensation and reimbursement of expenses is governed by LBR 2002-1. When Fed. R. Bankr. P. 2002(a) does not require service on creditors (because of the small amount applied for), a notice as described in LBR 2002-1 must be served on the debtor, the debtor's attorney (if different from the applicant), the trustee, and, in cases under chapter 7 or 11, the Office of the U.S. Trustee.

[Effective January 1, 1997. Amended effective July 1, 2011.]

RULE 2016-2. RULE 2016(B) DISCLOSURES AND TREATMENT OF PAYMENTS FROM PROPERTY OF THE ESTATE

(a) Sanctions for Failure to Make Timely Fed. R. Bankr. P. 2016(b) Disclosure. Failure to make timely disclosure under Fed. R. Bankr. P. 2016(b) may lead to disallowance of compensation and disgorgement of fees.

(b) Disclosing Payment Received From a Source Already Disclosed or a Deposit for Payment of Fees. The requirement under Fed. R. Bankr. P. 2016(b) that an attorney disclose any payment of fees or arrangement for payment of fees extends to:

(1) any payment received even if the initial Fed. R. Bankr. P. 2016(b) statement disclosed the source of future payment of fees; and

(2) any deposit made with the attorney for possible payment of fees, but a statement need not be filed disclosing a receipt of a payment authorized by order of the Court.

(c) Collection of Fees Out of Payment From Property of the Estate Requires a Court Order. An attorney may not collect a fee from property of the estate without an order of the Court authorizing the payment.

(d) Postpetition Deposit of Property of the Estate for Eventual Payment of Fees. After the commencement of a case, an attorney may accept a deposit of estate funds to be held in the attorney's trust account to be used for possible payment of attorney's fees, but only if the debtor and the attorney have agreed in writing that, until otherwise ordered by the Court, the funds remain subject to the debtor's direction and control.

Note: This Rule implements In re Taylor, 2004 WL 1746112 (Bankr. D.D. C. Aug. 4, 2004) (available on Court's website), and In re Williams, 2008 WL 2890933 (Bankr. D.D.C. July 21, 2008) (available on Court's website). Paragraph (d) has particular relevance in chapter 13 cases. In this District, the order confirming a chapter 13 plan usually provides that property of the estate remains property of the estate and thus such property does not revest in the debtor notwithstanding 11 U.S.C. § 1327(b). Payment of fees from estate funds requires a court order. An attorney may not accept a deposit of estate funds for possible payment of attorney's fees unless the debtor and the attorney have agreed in writing that, until the Court orders otherwise, the funds are to remain subject to the debtor's direction and control, and the attorney discloses the deposit.

[Effective July 1, 2011.]

RULE 2016-3. COMPENSATION OF DEBTOR OR DEBTOR'S OFFICERS, PARTNERS, AND DIRECTORS IN CHAPTER 11

(a) Unless otherwise ordered by the Court, the rate of compensation paid in a chapter 11 case to members of a debtor partnership, or to an officer or director of a debtor corporation, or to an individual debtor after the filing of the petition must not exceed the rate of compensation paid to those persons 90 days prior to the filing of the petition.

(b) Within 21 days after the date of filing of the petition, the debtor must file and serve on the U.S. Trustee and any committee of unsecured creditors (or, if no such committee has been appointed, the creditors listed under Fed. R. Bankr. P. 1007(d)) a statement:

(1) listing the names of the individual(s) who, depending on the type of debtor involved, are:

(A) the debtor, if the debtor is an individual;

(B) members of the debtor partnership;

(C) the officers and directors of the debtor corporation; and

(D) other insiders drawing compensation from the debtor; and

(2) listing as to each individual listed in paragraph (1);

(A) the position and duties of the individual; and

(B) the rates of compensation of the individual:

(i) at the point of 90 days prior to the filing of the petition;

(ii) at the time of the filing of the petition; and

(iii) as of the time the statement is filed.

[Effective January 1, 1997. Amended effective December 1, 2009; July 1, 2011.]

RULE 2016–4. ADMINISTRATIVE CLAIMS OF ENTITIES OTHER THAN PROFESSIONALS

Except for fees and expenses subject to 11 U.S.C. § 330, a Chapter 7 Trustee has authority, prior to approval of the final report, without further order of the Court, to pay:

(1) reasonable and necessary administrative expenses (other than administrative taxes) in an aggregate amount not exceeding the amount that is double the permissible exemption amount, as of the date of the last payment, under 11 U.S.C. § 522(d)(6); and

(2) administrative taxes.

Note: As of March 2011, the § 522(d)(6) exemption amount is $2,175, and under this Rule permissible aggregate expenses as of March 2011 would be $4,350. But the § 522(d)(6) exemption amount is adjusted under 11 U.S.C. § 104(b)(1) every three years commencing April 1, 1998.

[Effective January 1, 1997. Amended effective July 1, 2011.]

RULE 2090–1. ATTORNEYS—ADMISSION TO PRACTICE

(a) Attorneys Authorized to Practice Pursuant to DCt.LCvR 83.2. Attorneys may practice before this Court, as a unit of the District Court, in accordance with DCt.LCvR 83.2 (Practice By Attorneys), but:

(1) DCt.LCvR 83.2(h) (Entry and Withdrawal of Appearance) is supplanted by LBR 9010–1, 9010–2 and 9010–3; and

(2) DCt.LCvR 83.2(j) (Certification by Non–Members of Bar of this Court) does not apply (but all counsel are nevertheless required to be familiar with the Local Rules of this Court).

(b) Other District Court Local Rules Applicable to Practice of Attorneys in Bankruptcy Court. The following District Court Local Civil Rules apply to attorneys practicing in this Court as a unit of the District Court, and attorneys practicing before this Court will be subject to the disciplinary procedures of those rules:

(1) DCt.LCvR 16.2 (Avoidance and Resolution of Conflicts in Engagements);

(2) DCt.LCvR 83.2(b) (Appearance as Sole or Lead Counsel in a Contested Evidentiary Hearing or Trial on the Merits) (with any certificate required by DCt. LCvR 83.2(b) to be filed with the Clerk of the District Court in a form prescribed by that Clerk);

(3) DCt.LCvR 83.3 (Number of Counsel);

(4) DCtLCvR 83.5 (Practice by Law Clerks and Court Employees);

(5) DCtLCvRs 83.8 (Admission to the Bar) and 83.9 (Renewal of Membership);

(6) DCtLCvR 83.15 (Obligations of Attorneys) (with any notification under Rule 83.15(b) to be filed with the Clerk of the District Court); and

(7) DCtLCvRs 83.12 through 83.14 and 83.16 through 83.20 (relating principally to discipline of attorneys).

(c) Entry of Appearance; Scope of Duties Imposed by Entry of Appearance. The entry of appearance of counsel and the duties arising from such entry are governed by LBRs 9010–1 through 9010–4.

(d) Law Students. Law students may practice before this Court in accordance with DCt.LCvR 83.4, with the following modifications:

(1) Subsection (b)(1)(ii) is modified to read: "Have completed at least 2 semesters of legal studies, or the equivalent, and have completed or are in the midst of completing three semester hours, or the equivalent, in bankruptcy law or a clinic specializing or concentrating in the handling of bankruptcy cases";

(2) Subsection (b)(1)(iii) is modified to strike the words "and Criminal" and have added after the words "Professional Responsibility" the following: "and have knowledge of the Bankruptcy Code, the Federal Rules of Bankruptcy Procedure, the Local Bankruptcy Rules, and such other statutes or rules that may be or

become applicable to bankruptcy cases and proceedings";

(3) Subsection (b)(3)(vi) is modified to read: "Supervise concurrently no more than twenty-five (25) students carrying clinical practice in bankruptcy as part of their academic program, with a total of not more than five (5) students per semester, or equivalent, being certified and practicing under this Rule".

Note: LBR 2090–1(d) is changed to permit second-year law students engaged in a bankruptcy course or bankruptcy clinic to practice in this Court under the guidance of a supervising attorney.

[Effective January 1, 1997. Amended effective July 1, 2011.]

RULE 2090–2. COURT APPOINTED REPRESENTATION

Attorneys who are members in good standing of the Bar of the United States District Court for the District of Columbia are urged whenever requested by the Court to assist or represent parties who cannot afford to retain counsel to represent them in bankruptcy matters before this Court and, if necessary, without compensation unless exempted by rule or statute.

[Effective September 22, 2006.]

RULE 2090–3. ATTORNEYS REPRESENTING INDIGENT PARTIES

An attorney who is a member in good standing of the District of Columbia Bar or who is a member in good standing of the bar of any United States Court or of the highest court of any State may appear, file papers, and practice in any case handled without a fee on behalf of indigent parties upon filing a certificate that the attorney is providing representation without compensation.

[Effective September 22, 2006.]

RULE 2090–4. BANKRUPTCY PRO BONO PANEL

(a) Attorneys who are members in good standing of the Bar of the United States District Court for the District of Columbia are urged whenever requested by the Court under LBR 2090–2 to assist or represent litigants who cannot afford to retain counsel to represent them in bankruptcy matters before this Court and, if necessary, without compensation unless exempted by rule or statute. As one way to assist attorneys in meeting this request, and in light of the need for attorneys to represent indigent pro se litigants in bankruptcy matters before this Court, the Court hereby establishes a Bankruptcy Pro Bono Panel (the "Panel") of attorneys who are members in good standing of the Bar of the United States District Court for the District of Columbia or who are otherwise eligible to practice before this Court pursuant to LBR 2090–3, and who have agreed to accept pro bono appointments to represent indigent parties in bankruptcy matters before this Court. Members of the Bar of the United States District Court for the District of Columbia are urged to volunteer to serve on this Panel.

(b) The following procedures shall govern the assignment of attorneys from the Bankruptcy Pro Bono Panel to represent pro se parties who cannot obtain counsel by any other means:

(1) *Bankruptcy Task Force.* The Bankruptcy Court shall appoint a Bankruptcy Task Force, which shall include private practitioners and government attorneys who are members of the District of Columbia Bar and who practice in this Court, to oversee the Bankruptcy Pro Bono Panel established herein and annually report to the Court and to the D.C. Circuit Judicial Conference Standing Committee on Pro Bono Legal Services on the operation of the Panel.

(2) *Bankruptcy Pro Bono Panel.*

(A) Attorneys, law firms, and clinical legal education programs ("Clinics") at law schools accredited by the American Bar Association that are willing to accept appointment to represent indigent pro se parties in bankruptcy matters may apply to join the Panel. Application forms shall be available from the Clerk. Each application must set forth, among other things:

(i) in the case of a law firm, the name of an attorney in the firm designated as the Panel Liaison, to whom orders of appointment may be directed;

(ii) that the individual attorney, Panel Liaison, or supervisor of the Clinic is a member in good standing of the Bar of the United States District Court for the District of Columbia or eligible to practice pursuant to LBR 2090–3;

(iii) the attorney's prior bankruptcy representation and/or trial experience;

(iv) whether the attorney, law firm, or Clinic has the ability to consult and advise in languages other than English;

(v) the number of cases per calendar year that the applicant is willing to accept; and

(vi) any particular experience or interest of the applicant that should be considered when assigning bankruptcy matters, as well as any types of bankruptcy matters to which the applicant desires not to be assigned.

(B) Information on an application may be amended at any time by letter to the Clerk. An attorney, law firm, or Clinic may by letter withdraw from the Panel at any time.

(3) *Appointment of Counsel.* When documentation or other evidence is submitted certifying that a pro se party cannot afford to retain counsel by other means, the judge to whom the case is assigned may, whether by application of the pro se party, or otherwise, refer such party to an attorney from the Panel for representation. The referral should be made taking into account:

(A) whether the party is a party (or prospective party) in an adversary proceeding or a contested matter;

(B) the nature and complexity of the action;

(C) the potential merit of the pro se party's claims or defenses;

(D) the degree to which the interests of justice will be served by appointment of counsel, including the benefit that the Court may derive from the assistance of the appointed counsel; and

(E) any other relevant factors.

(4) *Appointment Procedure.*

(A) Whenever the presiding judge concludes that the services of pro bono counsel are warranted, the judge shall issue a referral ("Referral Form") to the Clerk requesting an assignment from the Panel to represent the pro se party. The judge may suggest a specific attorney from the Panel to receive the referral or may advise the Clerk to attempt to select an attorney with particular expertise or experience.

(B) Upon receiving the Referral Form, the Clerk shall select a member of the Panel. In making the selection, the Clerk shall take into consideration the experience and preferences of Panel members regarding specific types of cases and the equitable distribution of cases among Panel members.

(C) The Clerk shall contact the Panel attorney and, if that attorney is interested and available, so advise the Court. The Court will then enter an order (the "Appointment Order") directing the appointment of the attorney, subject to the attorney's right under paragraph (5)(B)(ii), below, and directing the Clerk to send a copy to the Panel attorney of the Appointment Order, this Rule and any pleadings, relevant correspondence or other documents not readily accessible from the Court's electronic docket.

(5) *Acceptance of Appointment by Appointed Attorney.*

(A) Upon receiving the Appointment Order, and unless a conflict of interest is apparent from the materials obtained through the Court's electronic docket or sent by the Clerk under paragraph (b)(4) above, the appointed attorney shall promptly communicate with the pro se party regarding the proceeding. Such communication shall include exploration of any actual or potential conflicts of interest and, if the absence of any conflicts can be established, whether the party has meritorious claims and/or defenses to raise, and whether the dispute can be resolved more appropriately in other forums or by other means.

(B) After any such consultation with the pro se party, the appointed attorney shall, within 14 days of entry of the order of appointment or within such other time ordered by the Court for good cause shown, file either:

(i) a notice of appearance by the appointed attorney (and by any other attorney in the appointed attorney's law firm or Clinic who will also represent the party) pursuant to LBR 9010–1(d); or

(ii) a notice declining representation and, to the extent possible, the justification.

(C) If a notice of appearance is filed pursuant to paragraph (5)(B)(i) above, each attorney entering an appearance shall represent the party in the proceeding from the date that the attorney files an appearance until (i) the attorney has been relieved of the assignment by the Court according to the provisions of this Rule and LBRs 9010–2, (ii) the proceeding has been dismissed, (iii) the proceeding has been transferred (other than by way of withdrawal of the reference under 28 U.S.C. § 157(d)) to another Court, or (iv) a final appealable judgment or order has been entered in the proceeding by the Court. The notice of appearance shall state with respect to each attorney making an appearance whether that attorney agrees to file a notice of appeal on behalf of the party (but not necessarily to further pursue the appeal on the party's behalf) should an adverse final appealable judgment or order be entered by the Court.

(D) Limits of Representation.

(i) Notwithstanding LBR 9010–3, an attorney accepting an appointment pursuant to this Rule shall not be required to represent the party in any other matter or proceeding.

(ii) However, the appointed attorney may upon agreement with the party submit a proposed order amending the earlier appointment order to reflect an expansion of the proceedings for which representation is being provided.

(iii) The appointed attorney is not required to pursue an appeal on behalf of the party from any adverse order or judgment of the Court, but, pursuant to paragraph (ii) above, the Court may expand the attorney's representation to include representation of the party with respect to part or all of the pursuit of an appeal. By way of illustration and not limitation, the Court may, upon the submission of a proposed order by the party's attorney, expand the appointment to include (1) the filing of a notice of appeal only, (2) the filing of a notice of appeal and the designation of the record and statement of issues presented on appeal required by Federal Rule of Bankruptcy Procedure 8006, but not the appeal itself, or (3) the entire appeal, including representation of the party before the District Court.

(6) *Relief from Appointment.*

(A) An appointed attorney may be relieved of an order of appointment, after acceptance of that appointment, only as provided in LBR 9010–2 or, where the appointment is with regards to a proceeding that is transferred to the District Court for the District of Columbia pursuant to an order withdrawing the reference to this Court, as provided in DCt.LCvR 83.11(b)(6).

(B) If an appointed attorney is relieved from an order of appointment, the Court may issue an order directing appointment of another attorney to represent the party, or may issue such other orders as may be deemed appropriate.

(7) *Discharge of Appointment.*

(A) A party for whom an attorney has been appointed shall be permitted to request the Court to discharge the attorney from the representation and either to attempt to appoint another attorney or allow the party to proceed pro se.

(B) When such a request is made, the Court may, in its discretion, forthwith issue an order discharging the attorney from further representation of the party in the action and may, in its discretion, refer the party to another attorney to undertake the representation pursuant to paragraph (b)(4). If a party requests discharge of a second attorney, no additional referrals shall ordinarily be made.

(8) *Attorney Fees.*

(A) The attorney shall represent the party without receiving a fee, except upon order of the Court (i) where a party makes material misrepresentations regarding assets or the ability to afford counsel or where there is a material change in the financial circumstances of the party or it is otherwise determined by the Court that the circumstances of the party are such that the payment of a fee is reasonable, or (ii) where a fee or expenses may be recoverable by a litigant under an applicable rule, statute or other law. The appointed attorney shall advise the party of the possibility of such a fee.

(B) Any recovery of attorney fees pursuant to subpart (8)(A) of this Rule shall be permitted only if the retainer agreement provides for the recovery of such fees.

(9) *Training Sessions.* The Bankruptcy Task Force may, in cooperation with the District of Columbia Bar, organize and conduct educational programs to train and advise attorneys on the Panel in the preparation for and representation of the most common types of bankruptcy matters involving pro se parties brought before this Court.

(10) *Appointment of Non–Panel Attorneys or Legal Organizations.* Nothing in this Rule shall be interpreted to preclude a judge from requesting an attorney, law firm, Clinic, or legal organization that is not on the Panel to represent a party who is otherwise proceeding pro se in this Court. In addition, nothing in this Rule shall be interpreted to preclude an attorney who is not a member of the Bar of the United States District Court for the District of Columbia, but who qualifies under LBR 2090–3 to practice before this Court, from representing an indigent party subject to the conditions of LBR 2090–3.

[Effective September 22, 2006. Amended effective July 1, 2011.]

RULE 2091–1. WITHDRAWALS

Rules governing withdrawals of an attorney's appearance are contained in LBR 9010–2.

[Effective January 1, 1997. Amended effective December 1, 2009; July 1, 2011.]

PART III. CLAIMS AND DISTRIBUTION TO CREDITORS AND EQUITY INTEREST HOLDERS; PLANS

RULE 3003–1. NOTICE REQUIRED IN A CHAPTER 11 CASE WHEN A CREDITOR'S CLAIM IS SCHEDULED AS DISPUTED, CONTINGENT, OR UNLIQUIDATED

Cross Reference. LBR 1007–3 governs the required notice when a creditor's claim is scheduled as disputed, contingent, or unliquidated in a chapter 11 case.

[Effective July 1, 2011.]

RULE 3007–1. CLAIMS—OBJECTIONS TO

(a) Inapplicability of Rule When the Objection to Claim is Asserted in an Adversary Proceeding. This Rule does not apply when an objection to a claim is joined with a request for relief of a kind specified in Fed. R. Bankr. P. 7001 and is thereby filed as part of a complaint in an adversary proceeding, or the objection to claim is asserted in a counterclaim or other pleading in an adversary proceeding.

(b) General Requirements. An objection to claim must:

(1) state with particularity the grounds of the objection;

(2) set forth the relief requested;

(3) attach any affidavit (or 28 U.S.C. § 1746 declaration under penalty of perjury) or memorandum filed in support of the objection;

(4) attach a notice complying with paragraph (d);

(5) include the proposed order required by LBR 9072–1; and

(6) include a certificate of service complying with LBR 5005–3 and reflecting service as required by paragraph (f).

(c) Hearing When Objection Is Unopposed. When the creditor fails to respond to an objection to its claim and the claim constitutes prima facie evidence of the validity and amount of the claim under Fed. R. Bankr. P. 3001(f), the Court may set a hearing to take evidence to rebut the prima facie validity and amount of the claim unless the party filing the objection to claim has attached an affidavit or affidavits to the objection that suffice to rebut the prima facie validity of the claim or its amount.

(d) Notice. An objection to claim must include a notice, substantially conforming to Official Form 20B with the following modifications:

(1) the notice shall not include the paragraph in Official Form 20B directing the creditor to "Attend the hearing . . . ";

(2) the notice must advise that the creditor may attach any affidavits, documents, and other evidence the creditor wishes to attach in support of its claim; and

(3) the notice must advise the creditor that if as a matter of law, the response fails to set forth an adequate defense to the objection to the claim, the Court may rule on the objection without a hearing.

(e) Local Form of Notice. A notice complies with this Rule if it is in substantially the form of Local Official Form No. 6.

(f) Service. The objecting party must serve copies of the objection to claim and the papers that must accompany it under paragraph (b) by mailing the copies to the creditor at the address for notices that appears on the proof of claim, and additionally:

(1) in the case of a creditor which is an insured depository institution to whom Fed. R. Bankr. P. 7004(h) applies, by complying with Fed. R. Bankr. P. 7004(h);

(2) in the case of a creditor which is the United States or an agency of the United States, by mailing copies to the Attorney General and the United States Attorney; and

(3) in the case of a creditor which is the District of Columbia or an agency of the District of Columbia, by mailing copies to the Attorney General of the District of Columbia.

(g) Cross–References. LBRs 5070–1, 5071–1, and 9073–1 govern hearings. LBR 9014–1 makes certain Part VII (Adversary Proceedings) rules applicable.

[Effective January 1, 1997. Amended effective July 1, 2011.]

RULE 3015–1. CHAPTER 13—PLAN

(a) Service. In a chapter 13 case, the debtor or the attorney for the debtor must mail a copy of the debtor's plan to all creditors and the additional entities specified on the form chapter 13 plans available at the Clerk's Office and on the Court's website.

(b) Notice of Deadline for Objections. The plan must include a conspicuous notice of the date that is the deadline for filing an objection to confirmation of the plan and serving the objection on the debtor, the debtor's attorney, and the Chapter 13 Trustee.

(c) Certificate of Mailing. A certificate of the mailing of the plan and notice must be filed with the plan.

(d) Deadline for Objecting to an Initial Plan. Unless the Court approves notice of a different deadline, the deadline for a creditor to file and serve an objection to an initial plan is the date that is 28 days after the filing date of the initial plan. The deadline for objecting to an amended plan is governed by LBR 3015–2.

Note: The Chapter 13 Trustee and the Clerk's Office have available a form Chapter 13 Plan and Notice of Deadline to Object to Confirmation which includes the notice required by this Rule. These forms may also be found on the Court's website (www.dcb.uscourts.gov).

[Effective January 1, 1997. Amended effective December 1, 2009; July 1, 2011.]

RULE 3015–2. CHAPTER 13—AMENDMENTS TO PLAN

(a) Service. The service requirements of LBR 3015–1 apply to amended chapter 13 plans except that:

(1) a plan that only increases payments to the trustee need be served only on the trustee; and

(2) the Court when appropriate may allow the debtor to amend the plan by a praecipe not served on creditors or by oral amendment at the confirmation hearing, in which event the order of confirmation must reflect any such amendments.

(b) Notice of Date by Which Objections to an Amended Plan Must be Filed. An amended chapter 13 plan must include a conspicuous notice of the date set by paragraph (c) below as the deadline for filing an objection to confirmation of the plan and serving the objection on the debtor, the debtor's attorney, and the Chapter 13 Trustee.

(c) Deadline for Objecting to an Amended Plan. Unless the Court approves notice of a different deadline, the deadline for a creditor to object to an amended chapter 13 plan is the later of:

(1) the date that is the deadline for objecting to the initial plan; or

(2) the date that is 21 days after the filing date of the amended plan.

(d) Confirmation of Amended Plan When It Does Not Materially Adversely Affect Any Creditor. The Court may confirm an amended chapter 13 plan (without awaiting the expiration of the time for objections thereto) if:

(1) there was a prior plan as to which the time to object expired before any amended plan was filed;

(2) any entity who objected to that prior plan consents to confirmation of the amended plan or the amended plan moots that entity's objection;

(3) no one else timely objected to that prior plan and the changes proposed by the amended plan do not adversely affect such entities; and

(4) the Court determines that the plan otherwise meets the requirements for confirmation.

Note: LBR 3015-2(a)(2) allows amendments to be made at the confirmation hearing when appropriate (for example, when the amendments are not adverse to any creditor or when all adversely affected creditors consent).

[Effective January 1, 1997. Amended effective December 1, 2009; July 1, 2011.]

RULE 3015-3. CHAPTER 13—CONFIRMATION HEARING AND NOTICE OF CONFIRMATION OF PLAN

(a) Attendance of Debtor and Counsel at Confirmation Hearing. A debtor and the debtor's counsel need not attend the confirmation hearing if:

(1) the Chapter 13 Trustee has recommended confirmation of the chapter 13 plan and no objections to confirmation of that plan have been timely filed or, if filed, have been withdrawn; or

(2) the Chapter 13 Trustee has objected to confirmation of the plan, and the trustee and any other entity who timely objected to confirmation of the plan have agreed to a continuance.

(b) Notice of Confirmation of Plan. Whenever a chapter 13 plan is confirmed, the Clerk will transmit to all entities on the mailing list under LBR 2002-2:

(1) a copy of the confirmation order; or

(2) a notice of entry of the order confirming the plan and specifying which plan was confirmed and, if there were any amendments thereto, that there were amendments thereto reflected in the order of confirmation.

Note: LBR 3015-2(a) allows certain amendments to be made orally or by praecipe not served on creditors. In addition, when multiple plans are filed in a case a creditor may not have received the latest version. Accordingly, LBR 3015-3(b) assures that when creditors begin receiving payments they will know what plan is controlling in the event that something different from the original plan was confirmed.

[Effective January 1, 1997. Amended effective July 1, 2011.]

RULE 3018-1. CHAPTER 11 PLANS: BALLOTS AND TALLY OF BALLOTS

(a) Filing Tally of Ballots. The tally of ballots voting on a plan in a chapter 11 case must be filed with the Clerk no later than 3 business days prior to the confirmation hearing. It must substantially conform to any format prescribed by the Court. A copy must be brought to the confirmation hearing.

(b) Retention of Ballots. The ballots must be retained by the proponent of the plan, including after being received into evidence at the confirmation hearing as an exhibit (with the disposition of the exhibit being controlled by LBR 9070-1).

[Effective January 1, 1997. Amended effective July 1, 2011.]

RULE 3022-1. FINAL REPORT/DECREE IN CHAPTER 11 CASE

Within 6 months of confirmation or such other time as the Court orders, the entity responsible for making distributions under a confirmed chapter 11 plan must file a Final Report and Motion for Final Decree in accordance with the form available in the Clerk's Office.

[Effective January 1, 1997. Amended effective July 1, 2011.]

PART IV. THE DEBTOR: DUTIES AND BENEFITS

RULE 4001-1. AUTOMATIC STAY—RELIEF FROM

(a) Title; Requirement of Separate Motion. In addition to complying with Fed. R. Bankr. P. 4001(a), each motion under 11 U.S.C. § 362(d) for relief from the automatic stay:

(1) must be filed separately from any other motion (other than a motion for relief from the co-debtor stay);

(2) must bear a title clearly identifying it as a motion for relief from the automatic stay;

(3) must bear a title that identifies any property involved, with (A) the street address of real property or (B) the make and model of motor vehicle or other tangible personal property;

(4) must be submitted with a proposed order that identifies any property involved as in the case of the motion itself; and

(5) in a chapter 7 case, must include a conspicuous statement regarding whether the movant has provided to the Chapter 7 Trustee (or included as part of the motion) the information specified by LBR 4001-1(e)(1) unless the Chapter 7 Trustee has consented to the motion or has filed a report of no distribution.

(b) Discovery in Automatic Stay Litigation. The time to respond to a motion to shorten the time for responses to discovery requests shall be 7 days after filing of the motion to shorten time, but conspicuous notice of that response time must be included with the motion.

(c) Obtaining Hearing Date for § 362(d) Motion.

(1) *General.* Prior to filing a motion for relief from the stay, the moving party must contact the Courtroom Deputy Clerk or consult the Court's website to obtain a date and time for the hearing from the dates that are available.

(2) *Preserving Right to Insist That Hearing Date be Within 30 Days of Filing of Motion.* If the moving party believes that a hearing date within 30 days of the intended date of filing of the motion is not being made available, and the moving party will not consent to the hearing date being held on an available date that is beyond that 30 days, then:

(A) the moving party must file and serve with its motion for relief from the automatic stay a notice certifying (subject to the requirements of Fed. R. Bankr. P. 9011(a)) that the Clerk failed to make available a hearing date within the 30-day period specified by 11 U.S.C. § 362(e) and demanding that the Court make available a hearing date, of the Court's choosing, that is within 30 days of the date on which such motion for relief from stay is filed;

(B) the Clerk must, on such written notice being filed, make available at least one hearing date and time of the Clerk's choosing that is within the indicated 30-day period; and

(C) upon the Clerk's issuing notice of the hearing date and time chosen by the Clerk, the moving party must within 1 day thereafter file and serve on the other parties to the motion a notice that the hearing on its motion will be held on the date and at the time specified by the Clerk.

(d) Filing of Notice of § 362(d) Hearing with Motion. Except as provided in paragraph (c)(2) above, the moving party must file and serve, with the motion, a notice of the hearing (in addition to the notice required by LBR 9013-1). The moving party will be deemed to have waived the 30-day automatic termination rule of 11 U.S.C. § 362(e) if the hearing date chosen by the moving party is more than 30 days after the motion is filed with the Court or if the moving party fails to file the required notice of hearing.

(e) Conditions to Granting Motion as Unopposed in a Chapter 7 Case. In a chapter 7 case, when the movant seeks to enforce a security interest in collateral, and the Chapter 7 Trustee has not consented to the motion or filed a report of no distribution, the motion will not be granted against the Chapter 7 Trustee as not timely opposed by the Chapter 7 Trustee unless the movant has at least 7 days beforehand:

(1) served on the Chapter 7 Trustee evidence of perfection of the security interest and an explanation of the value of the collateral; and

(2) filed a certificate of such service, which may be included in the certificate of service of the motion.

(f) Obligation to Disclose Payment History. If a motion seeking relief from the automatic stay includes as a ground for relief failure to make post-petition payments, then at least 7 days prior to the hearing, the movant shall file and serve upon the debtor's counsel (or the debtor, if pro se) a statement showing a history of payments received post-petition.

(g) Inapplicability of Rule 55 and the Soldiers' and Sailors' Relief Act. Unless the Court otherwise directs, neither Rule 55 nor the Soldiers' and Sailors' Relief Act of 1940 applies with respect to the granting of an unopposed motion for relief from the automatic stay.

(h) Cross-References. LBR 9013-1 sets forth the general requirements for motions which are applicable as well to motions under Fed. R. Bankr. P. 4001(a) (and other motions under Fed. R. Bankr. P. 4001). LBRs 5070-1, 5071-1, 9070-1, and 9073-1 govern hearings. LBR 9014-1 makes certain Part VII (Adversary Proceedings) rules applicable.

Note: Paragraph (e) governs unopposed lift stay motions. It contemplates that the movant will provide the Chapter 7 Trustee with (1) a title report or some other evidence of a perfected security interest and (2) an explanation of the property's value. With respect to explaining value, the movant might rely on a tax assessment, a debtor's own valuation of the property, a real estate agent's market analysis, or an actual appraisal. Paragraph (g) recognizes that the automatic stay is akin to a preliminary injunction having been granted against certain entities. Accordingly, the party seeking relief from the automatic stay is akin to an entity against whom a judgment has been imposed, and ordinarily is not viewed as akin to a plaintiff to whom Rule 55 and other provisions regarding default judgments apply when seeking to have the motion for relief from the automatic stay granted as unopposed.

[Effective January 1, 1997. Amended effective December 1, 2009; July 1, 2011.]

RULE 4003-1. OBJECTIONS TO EXEMPTIONS

(a) Any party objecting to exemptions must file a certificate of service reflecting service of a copy of the objection to exemptions and memorandum in support, if any, and the proposed order required by LBR 9072-1 upon the debtor, the debtor's counsel, the trustee, and, in a case under chapter 7 or 11, the Office of the U.S. Trustee. The objection must include a notice substantially conforming to Official Form 20A, advising the debtor conspicuously that:

(1) within 21 days of filing of the objection, the debtor must file and serve an opposition to the objection, which may include supporting documents and other evidence, together with the proposed order required by LBR 9072-1;

(2) an interested party may request a hearing, which may be held in the Court's discretion; and

(3) if no opposition is filed, the Court may sustain the objection.

(b) Notice is sufficient if substantially in the form of Local Official Form No. 7.

(c) Cross-References. For the effect of the debtor's failure to attend a meeting of creditors on computing the bar date for objecting to exemptions, see LBR 2003-1(c). LBRs 5070-1, 5071-1, 9070-1, and 9073-1 govern hearings. LBR 9014-1 makes certain Part VII (Adversary Proceedings) rules applicable.

[Effective January 1, 1997. Amended effective December 1, 2009; July 1, 2011.]

RULE 4004-2. OBJECTIONS TO DISCHARGE

(a) Dismissals. Dismissals of adversary proceedings in which there has been an objection to discharge are governed by LBR 7041-1.

(b) Cross-Reference. For the effect of a debtor's failure to appear at the meeting of creditors on the bar date for filing a complaint objecting to discharge, see LBR 2003-1(b).

[Effective January 1, 1997.]

RULE 4008-1. CHAPTER 13 MOTION FOR ENTRY OF DISCHARGE UNDER BANKRUPTCY CODE § 1328(a)

Within 49 days of the filing by the Chapter 13 Trustee of a Final Report and Account indicating the debtor's completion of Chapter 13 plan payments, the debtor must file a Motion for Entry of § 1328(a) Chapter 13 Discharge and Notice of Deadline and Opportunity to Object utilizing Local Official Form No. 11. Failure to timely file the Motion may result in the case being closed without entry of discharge.

[Effective July 1, 2011.]

PART V. COURT AND CLERK

RULE 5005-1. FILING PAPERS—MECHANICS OF FILING; PAYING FEES

(a) Requirement of Filing Fee. This paragraph governs papers that require a filing fee:

(1) LBR 1006-1 governs the permissible forms of payment of any required filing fee;

(2) LBR 1002-1(b) governs the Clerk's rejection of a petition for filing when it is unaccompanied by the filing fee; and

(3) the Court may strike any other filing if, after notice of failure to pay the filing fee, the required filing fee is not paid in the proper form.

(b) Filing in Clerk's Office. Unless otherwise directed by the Court, if an entity is not required under LBR 5005-4 to file a paper electronically and is filing the paper in paper form, the paper must be filed with the Clerk in the Clerk's Office (or in the speedy filing box as set forth in paragraph (d)), and no paper may be (1) submitted to the Courtroom Deputy Clerk in open court for filing or (2) delivered or mailed to the judge for filing.

(c) Filing Documents Under Seal.

(1) Absent statutory authority, no paper may be filed under seal without an order of the Court. Any paper filed with the intention of being sealed must be accompanied by a motion to seal. The document will

be treated as sealed, pending the outcome of the ruling on the motion. If a motion to seal is denied, and unless the filer consented to the paper being filed in the event that the Court denied the motion to seal, the Clerk will return the paper by mail to the entity that filed the motion to seal. Failure to file a motion to seal will result in the paper being placed in the public record.

(2) Unless otherwise ordered or otherwise specifically provided in these Rules, all documents which are submitted for a confidential in camera inspection by the Court, which are the subject of a Protective Order, which are subject to an existing order that they be sealed, or which are the subject of a motion for such orders, must be submitted to the Clerk securely sealed in an envelope or box needed to accommodate the documents. The envelope or box containing such documents must contain a conspicuous notation that carries "DOCUMENT UNDER SEAL" or "DOCUMENTS SUBJECT TO PROTECTIVE ORDER" or the equivalent.

(3) The face of the envelope or box must also contain the number of the case or adversary proceeding or miscellaneous matter in which the paper is being filed; the title of the Court; a descriptive title of the document; and the caption for the case or adversary proceeding or miscellaneous matter caption, unless such information is to be or has been included among the information ordered sealed. The face of the envelope/box must also contain the date of any order, or the reference to any statute permitting the item to be sealed.

(4) Filings of sealed materials must be made in the Clerk's Office during the business hours of 9:00 a.m. to 4:00 p.m. daily except Saturdays, Sundays, and legal holidays. No one may file sealed materials using the speedy filing box at the Third Street entrance to the Courthouse.

(d) Filing a Paper Using Speedy Filing Box. Subject to paragraph (a) regarding a petition that may be rejected for filing, and unless the paper is being filed under seal (or is sought to be filed under seal), a paper that is authorized to be filed in paper form may be filed using the Bankruptcy Court's special filing box at the Third Street entrance to the Courthouse (when that entrance is open to the public) subject to the following provisions:

(1) the back of the last page of the document must be time-stamped using the Bankruptcy Court's time-stamp machine that is next to the speedy filing box;

(2) the document must be deposited in the speedy filing box in accordance with instructions of the Clerk of the Bankruptcy Court that are posted on the front of the speedy filing box;

(3) the document will be presumed filed as of the date and time stamped on the back of the last page of the document (and the Clerk shall include a copy of that page showing a date and time stamp as part of the document as filed electronically in the Electronic Case Filing system); and

(4) in the absence of a date and time stamped on the back of the last page of the document pursuant to paragraph (1) above, the document will be treated as filed when the Clerk retrieves the document from the speedy filing box and marks the document as filed.

(e) Correspondence With the Court. Except when requested by a judge, correspondence must not be directed by the parties or their attorneys to a judge, nor shall papers be left with or mailed to a judge for filing.

(f) Filings Made Shortly Before a Hearing. When a filing is made less than one full business day prior to a hearing, counsel must have two extra copies of the filing available for the Court's use at the hearing or deliver the two copies to chambers before the hearing.

(g) Cross–References. For the non-filing of discovery materials, see LBR 7026–1(b). For the requirement of filing a proposed order with papers, see LBR 9072–1. For special filing requirements relating to the petition and to the lists, schedules and statements, see LBRs 1002–1, 1007–1, and 1009–1. For special requirements regarding the captioning of motions for relief from the automatic stay, see LBR 4001–1(a). For the prohibition against combining multiple motions in the same document, see LBR 9013–1(a).

Note: Providing a copy of a filing for the judge should be in rare instances and attorneys should use their common sense as to when a chambers copy would be helpful for the judge-in routine cases, an unnecessary chambers copy can be a nuisance.

[Effective January 1, 1997. Amended effective December 1, 2009; July 1, 2011.]

RULE 5005–2. FORMATTING AND STYLE OF PAPERS

(a) Size of Papers; Print; Margins. Any paper filed:

(i) must be in black typographical print (doubled spaced except for notice or quotations);

(ii) must be on opaque white paper, 8–1/2 inches wide by 11 inches long,

(iii) must have a top margin of not less than 1 1/2 inches, except in the case of the first page of a proposed order (which requires a 4 inch top margin); and

(iv) if filed in paper form:

(A) must be unfolded, without back or cover, and fastened at the top left corner only; and

(B) must include on any exhibit or attachment to the paper the number of the case or, if applicable, adversary proceeding in which the paper is filed.

(b) Style. All papers filed must bear the caption required by the Official Bankruptcy Forms. Under the caption, the paper must contain a heading describing the nature of the pleading, motion, or other paper. LBR 9072–1 governs the format of proposed orders.

(c) Notation of Date of Hearing. When a paper relates to a matter for which a hearing has been scheduled, the date of the hearing, if known, must be noted in the caption underneath the adversary proceeding number or (if not an adversary proceeding) underneath the case number. See, e.g., Local Official Forms No. 1 and 2.

(d) Names, Addresses, and Telephone Numbers of Entities and Attorneys. Papers filed by an entity not represented by counsel must contain the name, full residence or business address, and telephone number of the entity filing the paper. If an entity is represented by an attorney, all papers signed by the attorney must include the name, office address, email address, telephone number, and D.C. Bar identification number of the attorney.

Note: Paragraph (c) assists the court when a paper is filed shortly before a hearing. The Rule enhances the chances that the Clerk may be able to alert the judge to the filing (and docket any paper filed in paper form) before the hearing.

[Effective July 1, 2011.]

RULE 5005–3. CERTIFICATE OF SERVICE

(a) Requirement of Filing of Certificate of Service. Proof of service of papers required or permitted to be served, other than those for which a different method of proof is prescribed by these Rules, the Federal Rules of Bankruptcy Procedure, or by statute, must be filed in the form of a certificate of service either attached to the paper served or docketed separately.

(b) Recitation of Manner of Service. The proof must show the date and manner of service on each entity served. Care must be taken that when the paper commences a contested matter that service of the papers complies with the Federal Rules of Bankruptcy Procedure: electronic service is not good service when a paper commences a contested matter.

(c) Recitation of List of Entities Served. The proof must list the names and addresses of persons served, including, where applicable, whom they represent, except that:

(1) when the paper has been served on all entities on the mailing list maintained by the Court, it suffices as to those entities to recite that those served included "all entities on the mailing list maintained by the Court on the Case Management, Electronic Case Filing system as that list appeared at __: __ __.m. on [insert date]";

(2) in an adversary proceeding, it suffices with respect to parties who have already entered an appearance on the record to recite that service was made on all counsel (including pro se parties) who have entered an appearance of record as of the date of service; and

(3) in a contested matter, after the contested matter has already been commenced, the proof may recite with respect to attorneys who have registered to receive electronic notification that the paper was served on the attorney by electronic transmission (for example, by reciting that the paper was served "on the following via electronic notification through the Court's Case Management/Electronic Case Filing system: John Jones, Esq. (counsel for Debtor); . . .").

(d) Execution of Certificate of Service. The certification of service must be made by:

(1) a certificate of an identified attorney of record (including an attorney filing papers under DCt.LCvR 83.2(c));

(2) a certificate of a named member in good standing of the bar of this Court (with an indication of the attorney's bar identification number); or

(3) an affidavit or a certificate under penalty of perjury pursuant to 28 U.S.C. § 1746 which identifies the signer.

(e) Effect of Failure to File a Certificate of Service. Failure to file a certificate of service does not affect the validity of service. The Court may at any time allow the proof to be amended or supplied, unless to do so would unfairly prejudice a party.

Note: Paragraph (d)(3) specifies how someone other than an attorney of record (or an attorney who is a member in good standing of the bar of the District Court) may certify service of a paper. With respect to documents executed within the United States, 28 U.S.C. § 1746 provides that in lieu of an affidavit, it suffices to submit a writing subscribed by the person as true under penalty of perjury, and dated, in substantially the following form:

I declare (or certify, verify, or state) under penalty of perjury that the foregoing is true and correct. Executed on (date).

(Signature)

(In the case of documents executed outside the United States, the form is: "I declare (or certify, verify, or state) under penalty of perjury under the laws of the United States of America that the foregoing is true and correct. Executed on (date)" followed by the signature.)

[Effective July 1, 2011.]

RULE 5005-4. ELECTRONIC FILING

Unless the Court orders otherwise, an attorney filing a paper on behalf of a client must file the paper electronically in compliance with the Court's Administrative Order Relating to Electronic Case Filing (available on the Court's website). Documents that are being filed under seal must be filed in the Clerk's Office during business hours.

[Effective July 1, 2011.]

RULE 5070-1. CALENDARS AND SCHEDULING

(a) Optional Scheduling of Motion, Application, or Objection for Hearing. Instead of awaiting the setting of a hearing by the Court a party may obtain and set a hearing date on a motion, application, or objection, subject to the power of the Court to decide the matter on the papers in advance if:

(1) the movant (A) submits to the Clerk a request for a hearing on Local Official Form No. 1 and obtains a hearing date from the Clerk's Office, or (B) the movant obtains a hearing date provided by the Clerk either on the Court's website or through contacting the Courtroom Deputy Clerk; and

(2) within 3 days of notification of the hearing date, and by any deadline set by the Federal Rules of Bankruptcy Procedure or these Rules, the movant files a separate notice of said scheduled hearing and a certificate of service, complying with LBR 5005-3, regarding service of the notice; and

(3) any required notice of an opportunity to file an opposition to the matter is filed and served sufficiently in advance of the hearing that the deadline for filing an opposition expires prior to the date of the hearing.

(b) Emergency Matters. When any motion or application or objection requires the Court's immediate attention or an immediate hearing, the movant must file a separate one-sentence Praecipe Re Emergency Matter stating "The attached motion [or application or objection] requires a ruling by the Court no later than [insert date] for reasons set forth in [insert name of document explaining reasons]" or "The attached motion [or application or objection] requires a hearing before [insert date] for reasons set forth in [insert name of document explaining reasons]." The movant must explain the reasons an emergency exists in the motion or application or objection itself or in a motion for an emergency hearing or ruling. Frivolous assertions of an emergency may result in sanctions under Fed. R. Bankr. P. 9011.

(c) Section 362(d) Motions. LBR 4004-1(c) governs scheduling a hearing on a motion for relief from the automatic stay, and sets deadlines for giving notice of the hearing.

[Effective January 1, 1997. Amended effective July 1, 2011.]

RULE 5071-1. CONTINUANCES

(a) Motions for Continuances. Motions for continuances, except when made in open Court, must be in writing, and:

(1) must include a recital that the party has attempted to contact all other interested parties for their consent;

(2) must state whether any previous requests for continuance have been made or granted and for what date the hearing was first scheduled;

(3) must state, if known, the dates on which the parties will be unavailable for a continued hearing; and

(4) must contain a certificate of service indicating service on the interested parties on or before the date of filing.

LBR 5070-1(b) governs obtaining an emergency ruling on the motion prior to the scheduled hearing.

(b) Matters That Will Be Automatically Continued by Stipulation. Unless the Court has previously directed that further continuances will not be automatic, the following matters will be continued, but not for more than 120 days, to a date suitable to the Court, when all parties who have appeared in the matter stipulate to the continuance:

(1) a motion for relief from the automatic stay;

(2) a hearing on confirmation of a chapter 13 plan (and only the debtor and all parties who have timely objected to the plan need to have agreed to the continuance);

(3) a chapter 13 motion to dismiss; and

(4) a scheduling conference or pretrial conference in an adversary proceeding or contested matter.

(c) Manner of Communicating Stipulation for Continuance. A stipulation for a continuance under paragraph (b) may be communicated to the Court:

(1) by filing a written stipulation continuing the matter and fixing a continued hearing date and time that has been obtained from the Courtroom Deputy Clerk;

(2) by filing a written stipulation that requests the Clerk to issue notice of a continued hearing date;

(3) by one of the attorneys contacting the Courtroom Deputy Clerk to advise the parties have agreed to a continuance, in which event, at the time of the scheduled hearing, the failure of any parties to appear in the courtroom will be taken as verifying that there was a stipulation, and the Courtroom Deputy Clerk will either issue a notice continuing the matter or will prepare a case hearing summary continuing the matter (with the filing of that case hearing summary

constituting notice of the continued hearing date and time);

(4) by an oral statement by one of the attorneys at the hearing on the matter; or

(5) by the Chapter 13 Trustee's filing a notice of a continued hearing on confirmation of a plan or on a motion to dismiss.

(d) Appearance at Hearing Required Unless Continuance Granted. Except as provided in paragraphs (b) and (c), and in LBR 3015-3(a) (regarding Chapter 13 confirmation hearings), the pendency of a motion to continue does not excuse the obligations of counsel under LBRs 9010-4 regarding appearing at hearings.

(e) Continuances Based on Settlements. A matter may in the Court's discretion be taken off the Court's calendar because a settlement has been reached, but only:

(1) on written motion under paragraph (a) reciting that a written settlement signed by all parties and resolving all issues has been reached; or

(2) by representations of all counsel and any pro se parties in open Court at the time of the scheduled hearing.

If the continuance is granted, a stipulation of settlement or proposed consent order must be submitted within 14 days after the previously scheduled hearing date, or such other time as the Court allows.

(f) Counsel's Availability on Possible Continued Hearing Dates. Whenever an attorney appears at a hearing in the Court, the attorney must have a calendar of future engagements in order to assist the Court in fixing any continued hearing date.

(g) Meeting of Creditors. Continuance of a meeting of creditors is governed by LBR 2003-1.

[Effective January 1, 1997. Amended effective December 1, 2009; July 1, 2011.]

PART VI. COLLECTION AND LIQUIDATION OF THE ESTATE

RULE 6004-1. USE, SALE, OR LEASE OF ESTATE PROPERTY

(a) Notice of Sale. In addition to the information required by Fed. R. Bankr. P. 2002(c) and LBR 2002-1 (concerning notices in general) a notice of a private sale out of the ordinary course of business must include:

(1) if an appraisal has been performed, the appraised value of the asset proposed to be sold, the date of the appraisal, and the name and address of the appraiser;

(2) if no appraisal has been performed, the scheduled value of the asset proposed to be sold;

(3) the purchaser's identity;

(4) the relationship, if any, between the purchaser and the debtor, the trustee, or any other party in interest; and

(5) all consideration paid and to be paid by the purchaser and the terms of payment.

(b) Notice of Use or Lease. Notice of a proposed agreement out of the ordinary course of business for the lease or use of estate property must include information similar to that required by paragraph (a).

(c) Uses, Sales, or Leases Authorized Without Court Order. Uses, sales, or leases out of the ordinary course of business that do not require a motion shall be deemed automatically authorized upon expiration of the notice period if no written objections have been filed with the Clerk. Notice of such a use, sale, or lease is sufficient if substantially as set out in Local Official Form No. 5. Any party in interest may request a certification by the Clerk that no objections to the notice have been filed, for which a certification fee shall be charged.

(d) Buyer's Premium. Any buyer's premium, break-up fee, topping fee, or similar arrangement is prohibited, unless Court approval is obtained.

(e) Report of Sale. Upon completion of a private sale out of the ordinary course of business, the trustee, debtor in possession, or chapter 13 debtor, as the case may be, must file with the court an itemized statement complying with the requirements of Fed. R. Bankr. P. 6004(f).

[Effective January 1, 1997. Amended effective July 1, 2011.]

RULE 6005-1. AUCTIONEERS

LBR 2016-1 governs compensation of auctioneers.

[Effective January 1, 1997. Amended effective July 1, 2011.]

RULE 6007-1. ABANDONMENT

(a) Abandonment—Generally. A notice of a proposed abandonment or disposition given pursuant to Fed. R. Bankr. P. 6007(a), or a motion requiring the trustee or debtor-in-possession to abandon property of the estate, must describe the property with specificity and state the justification for the abandonment.

(b) Abandonment by Notice.

(1) *Notice.* LBR 2002-1 governs the form of a notice of a proposed abandonment or disposition given

pursuant to Fed. R. Bankr. P. 6007(a) except that the notice may give notice of the shorter deadline set by Rule 6007(a) for filing objections to the proposed abandonment.

(2) *Effect of Lack of Objection.* If no objection is timely filed under Fed. R. Bankr. P. 6007(a) to a notice of a proposed abandonment (or disposition) of property of the estate, the property shall be deemed abandoned (or the disposition authorized) without the necessity of court order. On motion of a party in interest, accompanied by a proposed order and without the necessity of notice under LBR 9013-1, the court shall enter an order confirming that property has been abandoned when property has been abandoned by notice.

(c) Motion to Compel Abandonment. A motion to require abandonment filed pursuant to Fed. R. Bankr. P. 6007(b) must be served by the movant upon all parties entitled to notice under Fed. R. Bankr. P. 6007(a).

(d) Cross-References. LBRs 5070-1, 5071-1, and 9073-1 govern hearings. LBR 9013-1 sets forth requirements applicable to all motions. LBR 9014-1 makes certain Part VII (Adversary Proceedings) rules applicable.

[Effective January 1, 1997. Amended effective July 1, 2011.]

RULE 6070-1. TAX REFUNDS

Unless otherwise directed by the trustee or ordered by the Court, Federal and state and local tax authorities are authorized to make income tax refunds, in the ordinary course of business, directly to debtors in chapter 7, 12, and 13 cases, except that in chapter 7 cases no refunds may be made to a debtor within the first 60 days after a petition has been filed.

Note: The purpose of LBR 6070-1 is to avoid the burden on both the bankruptcy system and the tax system of constant filings concerning tax refunds.

[Effective January 1, 1997. Amended effective December 1, 2009; July 1, 2011.]

PART VII. ADVERSARY PROCEEDINGS

RULE 7003-1. ADVERSARY PROCEEDING COVER SHEET

Any complaint or other document initiating an adversary proceeding that is not electronically filed shall be accompanied by a completed adversary cover sheet conforming to Procedural Bankruptcy Form B104.

[Effective July 1, 2011.]

RULE 7015-1. AMENDED PLEADINGS

DCt.LCvR 15.1 applies in the Bankruptcy Court.

Note: DCt.LCvR 15.1 (Motions to Amend Pleadings) provides:

A motion for leave to file an amended pleading shall be accompanied by an original of the proposed pleading as amended. The amended pleading shall be deemed to have been filed and served by mail on the date on which the order granting the motion is entered.

[Effective January 1, 1997. Amended effective July 1, 2011.]

RULE 7024-1. INTERVENTION

DCt.LCvR 7(j) applies in the Bankruptcy Court.

Note: DCt.LCvR 7(j) (Motion to Intervene) provides:

A motion to intervene as a party pursuant to Rule 24(c), Federal Rules of Civil Procedure, must be accompanied by an original of the pleading setting forth the claim or defense for which intervention is sought. The pleading will be deemed to have been filed and served by mail on the date on which the order granting the motion is entered.

[Effective January 1, 1997. Amended effective July 1, 2011.]

RULE 7026-1. DISCOVERY—GENERAL

(a) Form of Responses to Written Discovery. DCt.LCvR 26.2(d) applies to discovery.

(b) Non-Filing of Certain Discovery Materials. DCt.LCvR 5.2(a) applies to all contested matters and adversary proceedings.

(c) Motions to Compel Discovery and Other Discovery Disputes: Conference of Counsel Required. Counsel (including any pro se party) must confer with one another concerning a discovery dispute (other than a failure to respond at all to written discovery or a failure to appear for deposition) and make sincere attempts to resolve the differences between them. The Court will not consider any discovery motion unless the moving party has filed a certificate reciting (1) the date and time of the discovery conference, the names of all persons participating therein, and any issues remaining to be resolved, or (2) the moving party's attempts to hold such a conference without success.

(d) Application of Provisions of Fed. R. Civ. P. 26(a). Unless otherwise ordered by the Court, all bankruptcy contested matters and adversary proceedings are exempted from the provisions set out in Fed. R. Civ. P. 26(a)(1) and 26(d), and contested matters are exempted from the provisions set out in Fed. R. Civ. P. 26(a)(2) and 26(a)(3).

(e) Application of Provisions of Fed. R. Civ. P. 26(f). The requirement for a meeting of the parties set out in Fed. R. Civ. P. 26(f) applies, but the parties may confer by telephone.

(f) Cross–Reference. For the shortening of discovery response times with respect to motions for relief from the automatic stay, see LBR 4001–1(b).

Note: DCt.LCvR 26.2(d) (Form of Responses to Interrogatories and Requests or Production of Documents) provides:

Answers, responses and objections to interrogatories and requests for admissions or for production of documents and motions to compel answers or responses, shall identify and quote each interrogatory or request in full immediately preceding the answer, response or objection thereto.

DCt.LCvR 5.2(a) (Filing of Discovery Requests and Responses) provides:

(a) NONFILING OF DISCOVERY MATERIALS. *Except as otherwise provided by this Rule, interrogatories, depositions, requests for documents, requests for admissions, and answers and responses thereto shall be served upon other counsel and parties but shall not be filed with the Clerk until they are used in the proceeding or upon order of the Court as required below. The party responsible for service of the discovery material shall retain the original and become its custodian and, with respect to depositions, the deposing party shall retain the original deposition and become its custodian and shall make it available for inspection by any party to the action upon request. The Court may in its discretion order that all or any portion of discovery materials in a particular case be filed with the Clerk.*

(b) FILING OF DISCOVERY MATERIALS WITH MOTIONS AND AT TRIAL. *Any motion concerning discovery matters shall be accompanied by a copy of, or shall set forth verbatim, the relevant portion of any non-filed discovery materials to which the motion is addressed. Discovery materials may be used and filed as exhibits or evidence in support of any motion or at a trial or evidentiary hearing in accordance with the Federal Rules of Evidence.*

(c) FILING FOR PURPOSE OF APPEAL. *When discovery materials not previously in the record are needed for the purpose of an appeal, they may be filed with the Clerk by stipulation of counsel or upon application to and order of the Court.*

[Effective January 1, 1997. Amended effective July 1, 2011.]

RULE 7030–1. DEPOSITIONS

DCt.LCvR 30.1 (Service of Notice of Deposition) applies to the Bankruptcy Court.

Note: DCt.LCvR 30.1 (Service of Notice of Deposition) provides:

Service of a notice of deposition seven days in advance of the date set for taking the deposition shall constitute "reasonable notice" to a party as required by Rule 30(b), Federal Rules of Civil Procedure, unless the deposition is to be taken at a place more than 50 miles from the District of Columbia, in which case 14 days shall constitute reasonable notice. The computation of time under this Rule shall be governed by Rule 6, Federal Rule of Civil Procedure. The court may enlarge or shorten the time on application of a party for good cause shown. Nothing in this Rule modifies the provision in Rule 32(a), Federal Rules of Civil Procedure, prohibiting the use of depositions against certain parties who with due diligence are unable to obtain counsel to represent them, or against parties with less than 14 days' notice who file a motion for protective order.

Ordinarily, however, the Court expects counsel to have first attempted to schedule an agreeable date.

[Effective January 1, 1997. Amended effective July 1, 2011.]

RULE 7041–1. DISMISSAL OF ADVERSARY PROCEEDING

(a) Dismissal of Complaint Objecting to Debtor's Discharge. An adversary proceeding initiated by a complaint objecting to the discharge of the debtor shall be dismissed at the plaintiff's instance only by motion and not by stipulation or notice and only if (1) the debtor and the debtor's attorney, or the plaintiff and the plaintiff's attorney, file affidavits stating any consideration promised in any way to the plaintiff in exchange for the withdrawal of the objection to discharge and (2) the plaintiff has mailed a notice to all creditors and other parties in interest in the bankruptcy case giving them an opportunity to object within 21 days of the mailing of such notice.

(b) Dismissal for Failure to Prosecute. DCt. LCvR 83.23 applies to adversary proceedings in the Bankruptcy Court.

Note: This Rule contemplates notice similar to the notice required in In re Short, 60 B.R. 951 (Bankr. M.D. La. 1986), except that no notice is to be given suggesting that a creditor has an automatic right to be substituted as the plaintiff. For example, the trustee may have settled the objection to discharge and if the Court determines that the settlement is in the best interest of creditors, a creditor's request to be substituted as the plaintiff would not be granted. The Rule also preserves for adjudication in the adversary proceeding itself, instead of by local rule, any argument by the debtor that the bar date for objecting to discharge precludes a creditor from being substituted as the plaintiff.

DCt.LCvR 83.23 (Dismissal for Failure to Prosecute) provides:

A dismissal for failure to prosecute may be ordered by the Court upon motion by an adverse party or upon the Court's own motion. An order dismissing a claim for failure to prosecute shall specify that the dismissal is without prejudice, unless the Court determines that the delay in prosecution of the claim has resulted in prejudice to an opposing party.

[Effective January 1, 1997. Amended effective December 1, 2009; July 1, 2011.]

RULE 7054–1. ALLOWANCE OF COSTS

No costs will be allowed in adversary proceedings unless the entitled party files a bill of costs within 21 days after the entry of a judgment or final order in favor of the entitled party. Any opposition to a bill of costs must be filed within 14 days after the filing of the bill of costs.

[Effective January 1, 1997. Amended effective July 1, 2011.]

RULE 7054-2. ATTORNEY'S FEES

Unless a longer period is fixed by statute or by the Court, any motion by a prevailing party for an award of attorney's fees must be filed within 21 days after the entry of a judgment or final order in favor of the prevailing party. Any opposition to a motion for an award of attorney's fees must be filed within 14 days after the filing of the motion.

[Effective July 1, 2011.]

RULE 7055-1. DEFAULT—FAILURE TO PROSECUTE

(a) Motions to Vacate Default. DCt.LCvR 7(g) applies to a motion to vacate a default.

(b) Requirements for Default Motion. All motions for default judgment must recite whether the opponent has appeared, either informally or formally, and be accompanied by any notice required by paragraph (c), and must in the case of an individual be accompanied by a non-conclusory affidavit complying with the Soldiers' and Sailors' Civil Relief Act of 1940 § 200, 50 U.S.C. Appendix, § 520.

(c) Time for Response to Default Motion. When a party seeks default judgment against an entity who has made an appearance, conspicuous notice must be given that an opposition may be filed within 7 days of service of the motion. When an opponent has not appeared, no notice need be provided and the movant may request the Clerk to bring the motion to the Court's immediate attention.

(d) Cross-References. LBRs 4001-1 and 9014-1 contain exceptions making this Rule 7055-1 inapplicable in certain instances.

Note: DCt.LCvR 7(g) (Motions to Vacate Default; Verified Answer) provides:

A motion to vacate an entry of default, or a judgment by default, or both, shall be accompanied by a verified answer presenting a defense sufficient to bar the claim in whole or in part.

Under Fed. R. Civ. P. 55(b)(1) a party has "appeared" if the party has engaged in settlement negotiations or has mailed an acknowledgment of service. H.F. Livermore Corp. v. Aktiengesellschaft Gebruder Loepfe, 432 F.2d 689 (D.C. Cir. 1987); Practical Concepts, Inc. v. Republic of Bolivia, 811 F.2d 1543, 1546 n.6 (D.C. Cir. 1987) (dictum). Affidavits under § 200 of the Soldiers' and Sailors' Relief Act should be non-conclusory, reciting facts showing that the opponent is not in the military service, as defined in 50 U.S.C. Appendix § 511(1). Government offices will apprise the public whether an individual identified by Social Security Number is in the military service.

[Effective January 1, 1997. Amended effective December 1, 2009; July 1, 2011.]

RULE 7056-1. SUMMARY JUDGMENT

DCt.LCvR 7(h) applies in the Bankruptcy Court except that the third sentence thereof ("Each such motion . . .") shall be read as requiring compliance with the requirements of LBR 9013-1.

Note: DCt.LCvR 7(h) (Motions for Summary Judgment) provides:

Each motion for summary judgment shall be accompanied by a statement of material facts as to which the moving party contends there is no genuine issue, which shall include references to the parts of the record relied on to support the statement. An opposition to such a motion shall be accompanied by a separate concise statement of genuine issues setting forth all material facts as to which it is contended there exists a genuine issue necessary to be litigated, which shall include references to the parts of the record relied on to support the statement. Each such motion and opposition must also contain or be accompanied by a memorandum of points and authorities and proposed order as required by LCvR 7(a), (b) and (c). In determining a motion for summary judgment, the court may assume that facts identified by the moving party in its statement of material facts are admitted, unless such a fact is controverted in the statement of genuine issues filed in opposition to the motion.

[Effective January 1, 1997. Amended effective July 1, 2011.]

RULE 7062-1. STAYS OF APPEALS: EXEMPTION FROM APPEAL BOND

The District of Columbia Government, or any political subdivision or any officer or agent thereof sued or suing in an official capacity, shall not be required, unless otherwise ordered by the Court, to post a supersedeas bond or other undertaking which includes security for the payment of costs on appeal.

[Effective January 1, 1997. Amended effective July 1, 2011.]

RULE 7065-1. INJUNCTIONS

The following rules of the District Court apply in this Court: DCt.LCvR 65.1(a) (Applications for Temporary Restraining Orders); DCt.LCvR 65.1(c) (Applications for Preliminary Injunctions); DCt.LCvR 65.1(d) (Hearings on Applications for Preliminary Injunctions).

Note: DCt.LCvRs 65.1(a), (c) and (d) provide:

(a) APPLICATIONS FOR TEMPORARY RESTRAINING ORDERS. *An application for a temporary restraining order shall be made in a motion separate from the complaint. The application shall be accompanied by a certifi-*

cate of counsel, or other proof satisfactory to the Court, stating (1) that actual notice of the time of making the application, and copies of all pleadings and papers filed in the action to date or to be presented to the Court at the hearing, have been furnished to the adverse party; or (2) the efforts made by the applicant to give such notice and furnish such copies. Except in an emergency, the Court will not consider an ex parte application for a temporary restraining order.

* * *

(c) APPLICATIONS FOR PRELIMINARY INJUNCTIONS. *An application for a preliminary injunction shall be made in a document separate from the complaint. The application shall be supported by affidavits on which the plaintiff intends to rely. The opposition shall be served and filed within seven days after service of the application for preliminary injunction, and shall be accompanied by all affidavits on which the defendant intends to rely. Supplemental affidavits either to the application or the opposition may be filed only with permission of the Court.*

(d) HEARINGS ON APPLICATIONS FOR PRELIMINARY INJUNCTIONS. *On request of the moving party together with a statement of the facts which make expedition essential, a hearing on an application for preliminary injunction shall be set by the Court no later than 21 days after its filing, unless the Court earlier decides the motion on the papers or makes a finding that a later hearing date will not prejudice the parties. The practice in this jurisdiction is to decide preliminary injunction motions without live testimony where possible. Accordingly, any party who wishes to offer live testimony or cross-examine an affiant at the hearing shall so request in writing 72 hours before the hearing and shall provide the Court and all other parties a list of the witnesses to be examined and an estimate of the time required. The Court may decline to hear witnesses at the hearing where the need for live testimony is outweighed by considerations of undue delay, waste of time, or needless presentation of cumulative evidence. If practicable, the Court shall notify all parties of its ruling on the request to adduce live testimony one business day before the hearing.*

[Effective January 1, 1997. Amended effective July 1, 2011.]

RULE 7067–1. REGISTRY FUND

(a) All monies paid into the Court or received by the Clerk in any case or proceeding must be deposited by the Clerk in the registry of the Court. Except when the Clerk determines in the case of an unclaimed distribution that the small amount of the distribution does not warrant it, all deposits in the registry of the Court are subject to the provisions of DCt.LCvR 67.1 (Court Registry Investment System) as though the reference in that Rule 67.1 to "Court" and "Clerk" are to the Bankruptcy Court and its Clerk.

(b) Any claimant entitled to withdraw such monies from the registry of the Court may, on motion filod and served on the United States Attorney and the U.S. Trustee and full proof of the right thereto, including in the case of unclaimed distributions deposited under 11 U.S.C. § 347(a) notarized proof of identity, obtain an order directing payment to the claim.

Note: DCt.LCvR 67.1 opts into the Court Registry Investment System, a vehicle for earning interest on registry deposits, subject to a fee equal to 10% of the interest earned. It additionally imposes an obligation of an order for the receipt of funds "unless the statute requires deposit of funds without leave of court." Because 11 U.S.C. § 347(a) requires deposits of unclaimed distributions by Chapter 7 and 13 Trustees without leave of Court, the requirement of an order does not apply to such deposits.

[Effective January 1, 1997. Amended effective July 1, 2011.]

PART VIII. APPEALS TO DISTRICT COURT

RULE 8001–1. APPEALS IN GENERAL; DESIGNATION OF RECORD

Rules governing appeals to the District Court are contained in the DCt.LBRs.

[Effective July 1, 2011.]

RULE 8014–1. COSTS OF AN APPEAL

If the Court is to rule on a bill of costs incurred in the appeal, the procedures regarding a bill of costs set forth in LBR 7054–1 apply.

[Effective July 1, 2011.]

PART IX. GENERAL PROVISIONS

RULE 9006–1. COMPUTING AND EXTENDING TIME

(a) Computing Time When Deadline is a Specific Date. Unless the Court directs that this LBR 9006–1(a) does not apply, if an order or notice sets a specific date for performing an act, and

(1) if the date set (by the notice, order, or by reason of paragraph (2) below) is a Saturday, Sunday, or legal holiday, the date set for performing the act becomes the next day on which the Clerk's Office is accessible and that is not a Saturday, Sunday, or legal holiday; and

(2) if the date set is a date on which the Clerk's Office is inaccessible, the date set for performing the act becomes the first accessible day that is not a Saturday, Sunday, or legal holiday.

(b) "Last Day" Defined. The "last day" set for filing a paper ends at midnight in the Court's time zone, whether the filing is an electronic filing or a filing in paper form.

Note: LBR 9006–1(b) alters the default rule of Fed. R. Bankr. P. 9006(a)(4) because the Court has a "speedy filing box" under LBR 5005–1(d) that can be utilized for filing a paper document when the Clerk's office is closed.

[Effective July 1, 2011.]

RULE 9008–1. PUBLICATION

DCt.LCvR 83.22 applies in the Court.

Note: DCt.LCvR 83.22 (Publication and Proof Thereof) provides:

A notice relating to a proceeding that requires publication shall be published in The Daily Washington Law Reporter for the time fixed by statute or directed by the Court, in addition to any newspaper or periodical specifically designated by the Court. Publication shall be proved by affidavit of an officer or agent of the publisher, stating the dates of publication with an attached copy of the notice as published.

[Effective January 1, 1997. Amended effective July 1, 2011.]

RULE 9010–1. ATTORNEYS—ENTRY OF APPEARANCE

(a) Appearance. Except as provided in paragraphs (c) and (d), an attorney eligible under LBR 2090–1 to practice in this Court enters an appearance in a case or proceeding by filing a paper or a notice of appearance signed by the attorney. Such paper or notice of appearance must list the attorney's:

(1) mailing address;

(2) telephone number;

(3) bar identification number; and

(4) e–mail address.

An attorney whose authorization to appear requires an order of the Court is deemed to have entered an appearance upon the Court's entry of an order granting a motion to authorize the attorney to appear in the case or proceeding.

(b) Appearance on Behalf of Debtor in Meeting of Creditors, Rule 2004 Examination, or Deposition. If an attorney represents the debtor at a meeting of creditors, Rule 2004 examination, or deposition, and no other attorney has entered an appearance on behalf of the debtor, that representation shall constitute an entry of appearance and the attorney must file a notice of appearance prior to the meeting, examination, or deposition.

(c) Acts Not Constituting an Appearance. The following acts do not constitute an appearance by an attorney:

(1) filing a proof of claim;

(2) filing a Fed. R. Bankr. P. 2002(g) request;

(3) casting a ballot accepting or rejecting a plan;

(4) casting a ballot in an election of a trustee under §§ 702 or 1104(b)(1);

(5) except as provided in paragraph (b), participating in a meeting of creditors on behalf of a party other than the debtor or in a meeting of a committee of creditors or a committee of equity security holders; or

(6) filing a § 1111(b) election.

(d) Notice of Appearance of Counsel. For an attorney to enter an appearance in a proceeding for a party who previously has been represented by another attorney (or by the party pro se), that new attorney must file a notice of appearance.

(e) Appearance at a Hearing. An attorney who has not entered an appearance may not participate in a hearing on behalf of a client until the attorney files with the Courtroom Deputy Clerk at the hearing a notice of appearance.

(f) Effect of Appearance on Requirements Regarding Service on Client in Other Contested Matters or Adversary Proceedings. Except as provided by LBR 9010–3 (representation of a debtor), an appearance by an attorney does not alter, or impose additional requirements with respect to, service of papers under Fed. R. Bankr. P. 7004 and 9014. The attorney may, however, apply for an order imposing additional requirements regarding such service.

Note: Requirement of Separate Notice of Appearance. Paragraphs (d) and (e) of this Rule are intended to insure that the Clerk will note an attorney's appearance for purposes of receiving notices of electronic filings in a proceeding when another attorney previously represented or also represents the client or when the attorney first appears at a hearing in the proceeding.

Note: Effect of Entry of Appearance on Service Requirements Regarding Future Adversary Proceedings or Contested Matters. Paragraph (f) of this Rule is adopted to clarify that a socalled general appearance in a case does not modify the requirements regarding making service on the attorney's client when a new adversary proceeding or contested matter is commenced.

[Effective January 1, 1997. Amended effective July 1, 2011.]

RULE 9010–2. WITHDRAWAL OF AN ATTORNEY'S APPEARANCE

(a) Withdrawal of Appearance by Notice of Substitution of Attorney. An attorney may withdraw an appearance in the specified matter(s) by filing a notice of withdrawal signed by the attorney and the party represented if:

(1) no trial date has been set with respect to the specific matter(s) for which withdrawal is to be effected; and

(2) another attorney has previously or contemporaneously entered an appearance on behalf of the client.

(b) Withdrawal of Appearance by Motion. DCt. LCvR 83.6(c) governs withdrawal of an appearance by motion except that:

(1) the motion must identify the specific matter(s) as to which withdrawal is sought; and

(2) the requirement of service "upon all parties to the case" means:

(A) all parties to the contested matter or adversary proceeding or other specific matter involved; and

(B) in the case of an attorney representing the debtor or debtor-in-possession or trustee, means additionally the debtor, the U.S. Trustee and any trustee in the case.

(c) Requirement of Separate Withdrawal in Each Adversary Proceeding. When an attorney seeks to withdraw as counsel in an adversary proceeding, the withdrawal papers must be filed in the adversary proceeding itself. An order in the main case authorizing the attorney's withdrawal does not constitute a withdrawal in the adversary proceeding.

(d) Ruling on Motion to Withdraw Appearance. DCt.LCvR Rule 83.6(d) (Ruling on Motion to Withdraw Appearance) applies to motions for leave to withdraw.

Note: DCt.LCvR 83.6(d) (Ruling on Motion to Withdraw Appearance) provides:

The court may deny an attorney's motion for leave to withdraw if the withdrawal would unduly delay trial of the case, or be unfairly prejudicial to any party, or otherwise not be in the interest of justice. The Clerk shall mail to the affected party a copy of the order granting or denying the motion for leave to withdraw.

[Effective July 1, 2011.]

RULE 9010–3. REPRESENTATION OF A DEBTOR

(a) Effect of Entry of Appearance as Counsel for Debtor on Requirements Regarding Service Upon the Debtor. When an attorney is deemed under paragraph (b)(1) of this Rule to be representing the debtor generally in the case, and without regard to any limits on representation under paragraph (b)(2)(A), the attorney is deemed to be the debtor's attorney for purposes of Fed. R. Bankr. P. 7004(b)(9).

(b) Extent of Representation of Debtor Required by Entry of Appearance. This Rule governs how long an attorney must continue to represent a debtor or debtor-in-possession.

(1) *General Rule.* Except as provided in subparagraph (2) below, the filing of a petition in bankruptcy by an attorney on behalf of a debtor, or the subsequent entry of an appearance on behalf of the debtor by an attorney constitutes an entry of an appearance on behalf of the debtor in all matters arising during the administration of the case until the case is closed, including adversary proceedings, contested matters, the meeting of creditors, Fed. R. Bankr. P. 2004 examinations, and disclosure statement and confirmation hearings.

(2) *Exceptions.* The following exceptions apply to paragraph (1).

(A) Allowable Limitation of Representation by Agreement. An attorney may reduce the scope of representation of the debtor (thereby limiting the extent of counsel's appearance) by filing a statement under Fed. R. Bankr. P. 2016(b) disclosing a written agreement with the debtor to such limitation as long as the agreement meets the minimum scope of representation set forth below:

(i) In a case under chapter 7, representation of an individual debtor must continue until the date of discharge (or denial of discharge) and continue as to any matter pending at the time of the discharge, except that representation may exclude adversary proceedings if counsel's Fed. R. Bankr. P 2016(b) Statement discloses an agreement with the debtor to exclude adversary proceedings and the debtor has consented in writing to that limitation.

(ii) In a case under chapter 7, representation of a non-individual debtor continues until closing of the case.

(iii) In a case under chapter 11, representation of a debtor continues until entry of a Final Decree.

(iv) In a case under chapter 12 or 13, representation of a debtor continues until the earlier of: 120 days after entry of an order confirming the debtor's plan, or dismissal of the case and expiration of the time for seeking an enlargement of the time for taking an appeal.

(v) If a case is converted to a case under another chapter, the Rule under the latter chapter governs.

(B) Withdrawal by Notice When Substitute Counsel Has Entered Appearance. An attorney for a debtor may file a notice of withdrawal under LBR 9010–2(a).

(C) Withdrawal by Motion for Cause. An attorney for a debtor may file a motion to withdraw for cause under LBR 9010–2(b).

(D) Limited Appearance When Another Attorney Is Already Representing Debtor Generally. When one attorney has already entered an appearance for the debtor and is representing the debtor as to all matters, another attorney may limit representation to specific matters.

Note: Debtor's Counsel's Limitations on the Scope of Representation. Paragraph (b)(2)(A) governs all retainer agreements for representation of a debtor and makes ineffective any inconsistent provision therein unless otherwise ordered by the Court for cause.

[Effective July 1, 2011.]

RULE 9010-4. OBLIGATION OF ATTORNEY TO ATTEND HEARINGS

(a) General Requirement. Except as provided in paragraph (b):

(1) an attorney who has entered an appearance in a case or an adversary proceeding on behalf of a client must attend all hearings relating to the matter for which an appearance has been entered (and not withdrawn under LBR 9010-2); and

(2) an attorney for a debtor (whose appearance has not been withdrawn under LBR 9010-2) must attend all hearings relating to matters affecting the debtor.

(b) Exceptions. An attorney need not attend a hearing if:

(1) the client has expressly instructed the attorney not to appear and the attorney so notifies the Court and other counsel in writing before the hearing;

(2) the attorney has filed a paper stating that the client has no objection to, or does not oppose, the relief requested, or the attorney has endorsed without objection a proposed order (or a stipulation such as a stipulation of dismissal) that has been docketed and that would resolve the matter without the necessity of a motion or notice regarding approval of the proposed order;

(3) the attorney has been excused by the Court;

(4) the hearing is only a scheduling conference and the attorney has provided another counsel appearing at the scheduling conference with the attorney's views regarding the topics set forth in Fed. R. Civ. P. 16(b), together with available dates for any further conferences before trial and for trial;

(5) the attorney has arranged with the Courtroom Deputy Clerk's consent to be available by telephone and appears by telephone;

(6) the hearing is being automatically continued by stipulation under LBR 5071-1(b) via a stipulation communicated to the Court, under LBR 5071-1(c), before or at the hearing;

(7) a motion for approval of a proposed settlement of the matter has been filed; or

(8) another attorney represents the party at the hearing.

Note: Cause for Not Appearing. An attorney may be excused from appearing for cause. Such cause might include a showing that the client has not authorized counsel to take a position at the hearing despite a good faith effort by counsel to contact the client concerning the hearing. A motion to be excused may be filed on an emergency basis, and by alerting the Clerk to the emergency nature of the motion. See LBR 5070-1(b).

[Effective July 1, 2011.]

RULE 9013-1. MOTION PRACTICE

(a) Multiple Requests for Relief in Same Motion Paper. Multiple requests for unrelated relief must not be sought in the same written motion. When a motion requests multiple forms of related relief: (1) the title of the motion must clearly identify the requested relief, (2) a separate proposed order must be submitted for each form of relief, and (3) each form of relief must be docketed separately.

(b) General Procedure for Motions.

(1) *Grounds and Proposed Order.* All motions must state with particularity the grounds therefor, must set forth the relief or order sought, and must be accompanied by a proposed order conforming with LBR 9072-1 and a certificate of service complying with LBR 5005-3.

(2) *Optional Supporting Materials.* A memorandum of facts and law may be filed with or combined with a motion. Supporting affidavits or documents entitling the movant to the relief requested may be filed with a motion.

(3) *Required Notice When Motion Commences A Contested Matter.* Unless LBR 2002-1(b) applies to the motion, a motion commencing a contested matter must include or be accompanied by a conspicuous notice of the opportunity to oppose the motion:

(A) Content of Notice. The notice must conform substantially to Official Form 20A and state:

(i) that a party may append to its objection an opposing memorandum and supporting affidavits or documents; and

(ii) that if the objection states inadequate grounds for denial, the Court may grant the motion without a hearing.

(B) When the notice is included in the motion, either the title of the motion must include a reference to the notice as in Local Official Form No. 3 or the notice must appear immediately following the title of the motion.

(C) Impermissible Content of Notice. Unless otherwise ordered by the Court, a notice may not compel an objecting party to attend a Court hearing in support of the objection.

(D) Suggested Form of Notice. Notice is sufficient if in substantially the form of Local Official Form No. 3.

(4) *Deadline For Objection.* Within 14 days of service of the motion (or such other time as provided by the Fed. R. Bankr. P.), the party upon whom the motion is served must file and serve an objection containing a complete specification of the factual and legal grounds upon which the motion is opposed, together with a proposed order setting forth the requested disposition.

(5) *Default.* If no objection is timely filed, the Court may grant the motion without a hearing. If the motion is one commencing a contested matter, default is governed by Fed. R. Bankr. P. 7055 and LBR 7055-1 (and in the case of "lift stay motions," LBR 4001-1(e)).

(6) *Reply Memorandum.* A reply momorandum may be filed within 7 days after the date of filing of the objection to the motion.

(7) *Action On Motion If Grounds Inadequate.* Except as otherwise provided by the Bankruptcy Code and the Fed. R. Bankr. P., the Court may grant or deny a motion on the papers without a hearing if the motion sets forth inadequate grounds for relief or if the objection sets forth inadequate grounds for denying the motion.

(c) Entities to be Served.

(1) In an adversary proceeding and in a contested matter already commenced, every motion must be served as provided by Fed. R. Bankr. P. 7005.

(2) Every motion commencing a contested matter must be served upon the parties against whom relief is sought as provided by Fed. R. Bankr. P. 9014 and 7004, the parties specified by Fed. R. Bankr. P. 9013, the U.S. Trustee when required by Fed. R. Bankr. P. 9034, and any other parties specified in the Fed. R. Bankr. P. (such as in Fed. R. Bankr. P. 4001). In addition, unless the Court orders otherwise, copies of the motion must be transmitted to (A) the debtor, (B) the debtor's attorney (if any), (C) the U.S. Trustee in chapters 7 and 11, (D) all parties that to the movant's actual knowledge have asserted any concern as to or would be directly adversely affected by the outcome of the particular motion or have or claim any interest in (as opposed to an unsecured claim against) any property that is the subject of the motion; (E) counsel who has to the movant's actual knowledge been representing any party described in part (D); (F) chair and counsel for any appointed committees; and (G) the creditors or equity security holders who have served on the trustee or debtor-in-possession and filed with the Clerk a request that all notices be mailed to them.

(3) Motions under 11 U.S.C. § 1121(d) to reduce or extend the periods of 11 U.S.C. § 1121(b) and (c) (the exclusivity periods for filing a plan and gaining acceptances) must be served on the persons specified in paragraph (2) above and if no committee of unsecured creditors has been appointed, the creditors listed on the list filed under Fed. R. Bankr. P. 1007(d).

(d) Cross-References. Special rules for motions for relief from the automatic stay are set forth in LBR 4001-1. LBRs 5070-1, 5071-1, and 9073-1 govern hearings. Emergency motions requiring the Court's immediate attention or an emergency hearing are governed by LBR 5070-1(b). Proposed orders must be submitted with motions and objections as provided by LBR 9072-1. Exceptions to certain parts of this Rule apply under LBR 2004-1 to motions for Fed. R. Bankr. P. 2004 examinations. LBR 9014-1 makes certain Part VII (Adversary Proceedings) Rules applicable.

Note: LBR 9013-1(a) contemplates that motions seeking relief in the alternative, as in the case of a motion to dismiss or convert, may be filed in a single document. But motions for different forms of relief that are not in the alternative ought not be combined in a single document. This will better facilitate the Court's docketing and disposing of such motions.

[Effective January 1, 1997. Amended effective December 1, 2009; July 1, 2011.]

RULE 9014-1. CONTESTED MATTERS

(a) Local Bankruptcy Rules 7004-1, 7026-1, 7030-1, 7041-1, 7054-1, 7056-1, 7062-1, and 7067-1 apply in contested matters. Fed. R. Bankr. P. 7007.1 applies to any contested matter.

(b) When the motion or objection commencing the contested matter is not timely opposed and seeks relief against a debtor who has already subjected the debtor to the jurisdiction of the Court by filing a petition commencing a case, the provisions of LBR 7055-1 and the Soldiers' and Sailors' Relief Act of 1940 will be deemed inapplicable unless the Court orders otherwise.

(c) The other Rules of Part VII of these Rules apply to contested matters when directed by the Court.

[Effective January 1, 1997. Amended effective July 1, 2011.]

RULE 9015-1. JURY TRIAL

(a) Voir Dire Examination. Counsel desiring questions propounded to the jury on voir dire examination must submit the same in writing to the Court, with copies to opposing counsel, prior to the commencement of the trial or at such earlier date as may be directed by the Court.

(b) Jury Selection; Communication With a Juror. DCt.LCvRs 47.1 (Jury) and 47.2 (Communication With a Juror) apply in the Court, with the Court drawing upon the District Court's jury selection plan and Jury Office.

[Effective January 1, 1997. Amended effective July 1, 2011.]

RULE 9029–1. SUSPENSION OF LOCAL RULES

For good cause shown, the Court may suspend the requirements or provisions of any of these Rules in a particular case or proceeding, on the motion of a party or upon its own motion, and may enter such other orders as are appropriate.

[Effective January 1, 1997. Amended effective July 1, 2011.]

RULE 9029–2. STANDING ORDERS

The Court may issue standing orders to the Clerk's Office affecting procedures which that office must follow generally unless ordered otherwise. Such standing orders will be available for public inspection.

Note: LBR 9029–2 reflects a long-standing practice of issuance of standing orders to the Clerk to act in a set fashion on certain procedural matters arising in cases. Such standing orders are in the nature of internal directives and do not impose obligations on parties. But pursuant to such standing orders, the Clerk may, on behalf of the Court, issue notices or orders which do fix rights or obligations. For example, one standing order instructs the Clerk to give creditors in chapter 11 cases notice that the bar date for filing proofs of claim is the date that is 100 days after the first date set for the meeting of creditors under 11 U.S.C. § 341.

[Effective January 1, 1997. Amended effective July 1, 2011.]

RULE 9029–3. LOCAL RULES—DISTRICT COURT

(a) Non-Applicability of Local Bankruptcy Rules to District Court. These Local Bankruptcy Rules do not govern proceedings pending in the District Court except as may be expressly provided by the District Court by rule or directive.

(b) Effect of Amendment of Local District Court Rules. The Local District Court Rules made applicable by these Rules are the Local District Court Rules in effect on the effective date of these Rules and as thereafter amended, unless otherwise provided by such amendment or by these Rules.

(c) Local District Court Rules Applicable to Bankruptcy Court. In addition to Local District Court Rules made applicable to the Court by other provisions of these Rules, the following Local District Court Civil Rules apply to bankruptcy cases and proceedings in the Court:

(1) Rule 83.1 (Photography, tape recording and broadcasting in the courthouse);

(2) Rule 83.5 (Practice by law clerks and court employees); and

(3) Rule 40.10 (Complaints Against Judges).

(d) Meanings of Words in the Local District Court Rules When Applicable to these Rules. Unless the context otherwise indicates, references in the Local District Court Rules, other than Title VI, to "action" or "civil action" mean case or proceeding (including contested matters and adversary proceedings), to "Clerk" mean Clerk of the Bankruptcy Court, to "Judge" mean Bankruptcy Judge, and to "Court" mean Bankruptcy Court.

Note: LBR 9029–3(a) reflects that these Rules do not attempt to decide which of these Rules the District Court ought to make applicable after the District Court withdraws from the Bankruptcy Court the reference of a bankruptcy case or proceeding or when the District Court reviews a matter de novo. Such matters remain subject to the Federal Rules of Bankruptcy Procedure. See Fed. R. Civ. P. 81(a) and Fed. R. Bankr. P. 1001. The Local District Court Rules provide any further rules applicable to the withdrawn matter and the District Court can invoke Fed. R. Bankr. P. 9029(b) to regulate practice in the matter in a manner not inconsistent with any federal rules or local rules that do apply. The same applies to the handling of appeals in the District Court. See Fed. R. Bankr. P. 8018. LBR 9029–3(c) reflects a philosophy followed in promulgating these Rules. As a unit of the District Court, the Bankruptcy Court has the same bar as the District Court, subject generally to the same rules of practice and discipline of attorneys. These Rules accordingly attempt to minimize the differences in practice between the District Court and the Bankruptcy Court.

These Rules reprint many of the incorporated Local District Court Rules as they read on the effective date of these Local Bankruptcy Rules, and the District Court's website's Local Rules page should be consulted regarding any changes to those rules. Bankruptcy cases and proceedings are subject to Title VI of the Local District Court Rules (relating to administration of the bankruptcy system), and to Title VII of those rules (relating to admission and discipline of attorneys). Title VI is reprinted in Appendix B hereto.

Local District Court Rules incorporated into these Rules with no or only minor changes include:

Local District Court Rule	*LBR Analog*
Rule LCvR83.2 (Practice by attorneys)	*2090–1(a)*
Rule LCvR83.3 (Number of Counsel)	*9073–1(a)*
Rule LCvR5.2(a) (Filing of Discovery Requests and Responses)	*7026–1(b)*
Rule LCvR7(g) (Motions to Vacate Default; Verified Answer)	*7055–1(a)*
Rule LCvR7(h) (Motions for Summary Judgment)	*7056–1*
Rule LCvR7(i) (Motions to Amend Pleadings)	*7015–1*
Rule LCvR7(j) (Motion to Intervene)	*7024–1*
Rule LCvR7.1 (Disclosure of Corporate Affiliations, etc.)	*5004–1*
Rule LCvR16.6(Stipulations)	*9071–1*

Local District Court Rule	*LBR Analog*
Rule LCvR83.22(Publication and Proof Thereof)	*9008–1*
Rule LCvR47.1 (Jury)	*9015–1(c)*
Rule LCvR47.2 (Communication with Juror)	*9015–1(c)*
Rule LCvR16.2 (Avoidance of conflicts in engagements of counsel)	*9073–1(d)*
Rule LCvR83.6(c) (Withdrawal of Appearances by Motion)	*9010–2(b)*
Rule LCvR65.1(a) (Applications for Temporary Restraining Orders)	*7065–1*
Rule LCvR65.1(c) (Applications for Preliminary Injunctions)	*7065–1*
Rule LCvR65.1(d) (Hearings on Applications re Prelim. Injns.)	*7065–1*
Rule LCvR26.2(d) (Form of Interrogatories and Requests for Admissions or Production of Documents)	*7026–1(a)*
Rule LCvR30.1 (Service of Notice of Deposition)	*7030–1(b)*
Rule LCvR83.23 (Dismissal for Failure to Prosecute)	*7041–1(b)*
Rule LCvR79.2 (Custody of Exhibits)	*9070–1(f) & (g)*
Rule LCvR54.1 (Taxation of Costs)	*7054–1*
Rule LCvR54.2 (Determination of Attorneys Fees)	*7054–1*
Rule LCvR67.1 (Court Registry Investment System)	*7067–1(a)*

Local District Court Rules not incorporated which nevertheless have analogs in these Rules, sometimes with significant differences, include:

Local District Court Rule	*LBR Analog*
Rule LCvR79.1 (Clerk's Office; Custody and Removal of Records)	*5001–2; 5003–2*
Rule LCvR5.1 (Form and Filing of Pleadings and Other Papers)	
(a) Place and Manner of Filing	*5005–1(a)*
(b) Correspondence With Court	*5005–1(b)*
(d) Electronic Transmission	*5005–1(d)*
(e) Name and Address of Parties and Attorneys	*5005–1(g)*
(f) Form of Papers	*5005–1(e)&(f)*
(g) Attachments to Pleadings	*5005–1(e)*
(h) Verification	*5005–3(b))*
Rule LCvR7(a), (b), (d), (e) and (f) (Motions rules)	*9013–1*
Rule LCvR7(c) & (k) (Proposed Order and Names of Persons to be Served With Proposed Orders, Judgments and Stipulations)	*9072–1*
Rule LCvR5.3 (Proof of Service)	*5005–3*
Rule LCvR16.1(Scheduling and Continuances)	*5070–1 & 5071–1*
Rule LCvR83.6(a) (Entry of Appearance)	*9010–1*
Rule LCvR83.6(b) (Withdrawal of Appearance by Notice)	*9010–2*

Some of the Local District Court Rules made applicable to bankruptcy cases by these Rules are not reprinted for the reason that they will seldom be encountered (as in the rare event of a jury trial) or for other obvious reasons.

LBR 9029–3(d) is modeled after Fed. R. Bankr. P. 9002 ("Meanings of Words in the Federal Rules of Civil Procedure When Applicable to Cases Under the Code").

[Effective January 1, 1997. Amended effective July 1, 2011.]

RULE 9070–1. EXHIBITS AND WITNESSES

(a) Pre–Numbering, Pre–Marking, and Pre–Listing Exhibits.

(1) Prior to any trial (including any hearing at which evidence is to be taken) exhibits to be offered at the trial (other than those created at trial) must be numbered sequentially, with movant or plaintiff to use numbers and the respondent or defendant to use letters (A, B, C, etc., followed by AA, AB, AC, etc., then BA, BB, BC, etc.).

(2) All exhibits must be marked prior to the trial with an exhibit sticker bearing the exhibit number and the case or adversary proceeding number.

(3) Prior to the trial the exhibits must be listed sequentially by exhibit number on a Witness and Exhibit Record in substantially the form of Local Official Form No. 8. The list must describe each exhibit by title and date.

(4) Prior to the commencement of a trial or hearing, each party shall furnish to its opponents a copy of the Witness and Exhibit Record and copies of its premarked exhibits.

(b) Listing Witnesses. Prior to any trial (including any hearing at which evidence is to be taken), each party must set forth on the party's Witness and Exhibit List the full names of all witnesses the party intends to call if not earlier called by another party; a brief description of the testimony to be elicited from the witness; and an estimate of the time the party will take in eliciting such testimony. Any expert witness must be designated as such by including the designation "expert witness" after the witness's name.

(c) Presentation of Witness and Exhibit Record and of Copies of Exhibits. At the commencement of the trial or evidentiary hearing, each party must present to the Courtroom Deputy Clerk (1) the original of the party's Witness and Exhibit Record and (2) two copies of the party's exhibits.

(d) Binding of Numerous Exhibits. Whenever the exhibits in any trial or evidentiary hearing, to be presented by any party, exceed 15, the party intending to offer such exhibits must place them in a binder or notebook, numbered and indexed, unless otherwise ordered by the Court.

(e) Retention of Witness and Exhibit Record. At the conclusion of the trial or evidentiary hearing, the Clerk must maintain the Witness and Exhibit Record with the sleeve for logs and tapes of electronic recordings for the last day the trial or hearing was conducted.

(f) Retention by Parties of Exhibits.

(1) *Requirement of Retention.* All exhibits offered by a party in a proceeding, whether or not received as evidence, must be retained after trial by the party or the attorney offering the exhibit, unless otherwise ordered by the Court. The Clerk shall note the return of exhibits on the Witness and Exhibit Record.

(2) *Appeals.* In the event an appeal is prosecuted, each party or attorney retaining exhibits must, upon request of a party to the appeal, make a copy of any exhibit available to that requesting party at the usual and customary photocopying charge of the custodian party or attorney, or allow the requesting party temporarily to take custody of the exhibit to photocopy it. The originals of exhibits must be retained by the parties, who must make them available for use by the appellate court upon request.

(3) *Period of Retention.* After a judgment disposing of the proceeding becomes final, each party or the party's attorney must maintain custody of any exhibits for a period of at least 30 days after the time for appeal has expired, or, in the event an appeal is pursued, for a period of at least 30 days after any judgment not resulting in a remand has become final and the time for seeking further appellate or Supreme Court review has expired.

(g) Disposition of Exhibits Retained by Clerk.

(1) *Thirty Day Period to Retrieve.* When the Clerk has kept custody of exhibits, the exhibits must be removed by the parties who offered them within 30 days after the time for appeal has expired, or in the event an appeal is pursued, within 30 days after any judgment not resulting in a remand has become final and the time for seeking further appellate or Supreme Court review has expired.

(2) *Disposition in Case of Apparent Failure Timely to Retrieve.* If the Clerk believes that a party has failed timely to retrieve exhibits from the Clerk, the Clerk may forward the exhibits to the counsel or party who offered them. Alternatively, the Clerk may give the party or attorney notice of a 30–day opportunity to remove the exhibits; if the party or attorney fails to do so within 30 days of the date of such notice, the Clerk may destroy or otherwise dispose of the exhibits.

(3) *Notation of Disposition.* The Clerk shall make an appropriate notation on the Witness and Exhibit Record reflecting any disposition of exhibits.

[Effective January 1, 1997. Amended effective July 1, 2011.]

RULE 9071–1. STIPULATIONS

DCt.LCvR 16.6 applies in the Bankruptcy Court (with the clarification that a stipulation is additionally effective if electronically recorded in a Bankruptcy Court hearing).

Note: DCt.LCvR 16.6 (Stipulations) provides:

A stipulation need not be considered by the Court unless it is in writing and signed by the parties thereto or their attorneys, or stenographically recorded in Court or during a deposition.

[Effective January 1, 1997. Amended effective July 1, 2011.]

RULE 9072–1. ORDERS—PROPOSED

(a) Submission of Proposed Orders.

(1) Each motion, application, objection to claim, objection to exemptions, or other written request for a Court order (other than a complaint in an adversary proceeding), and each opposition thereto (except a responsive pleading under Fed. R. Bankr. P. 7007 in an adversary proceeding) must be accompanied by a proposed order.

(2) Unless the Court directs otherwise, or a sufficient proposed order has already been submitted, an entity that prevails at a hearing must, within 14 days after the Court's oral ruling, submit to the Clerk and serve upon all other parties who appeared or against whom the relief is directed a proposed order in accordance with the ruling.

(b) Form of Proposed Orders. A proposed order must:

(1) contain a specific title describing the nature and effect of the order, preferably referring to the verbatim name of the motion giving rise to the order;

(2) include a 4″ margin at the top of the first page; and

(3) include at the foot of the last page (or carried over to a separate additional page) a "Copies to" section listing the full names and complete addresses of all entities that are to receive copies of the Court's order when entered, except that:

(A) attorneys who are registered e-filers and have entered an appearance in the case or proceeding may be listed by only name or listed as "All attorneys who have entered an appearance and who are registered e-filers";

(B) in an adversary proceeding it suffices as to attorneys representing a party in the proceeding to list "Copies to: All of attorneys of record," but for an entity who is not a party (*e.g.*, a witness who is the subject of a motion to compel) the entity's attorney must be listed separately; and

(C) if the debtor, the debtor's attorney, the trustee, and all creditors are required to receive notice of the Court order, those entities may be listed as "All entities on court's mailing list."

[Effective January 1, 1997. Amended effective December 1, 2009; July 1, 2011.]

RULE 9073–1. HEARINGS

(a) Number of Counsel. DCt.LCvR 83.3 applies to hearings in the Bankruptcy Court.

(b) Judicial Notice. Unless otherwise ordered by the Court, the Court will not take judicial notice of a paper unless the party both requests the Court to do so before the close of evidence and either (1) submits as an exhibit a copy of the paper of which judicial notice is sought, or (2) alternatively, in the case of a paper in a case or an adversary proceeding, can identify the document by docket entry number or date. Any copy of such paper to be submitted must be listed on any Witness and Exhibit Record required to be filed.

(c) Courtroom Decorum. Counsel must direct statements and objections made on the record to the Court and not to other counsel. Unless otherwise directed by the Court, counsel need not ask permission to approach a witness.

(d) Conflicts in Engagements of Counsel. DCt. LCvR 16.2 (Avoidance and Resolution of Conflicts in Engagement of Counsel Among the Courts in the District of Columbia) applies to the Bankruptcy Court as a unit of the District Court.

(e) Cross–References. LBR 9070–1 governs exhibits and witnesses. LBR 5071–1 governs continuances (and the duty of counsel to have at any hearing a calendar of future engagements). LBR 5070–1(b) governs emergency hearings. LBR 9010–1(e) governs the obligation of an attorney whose first appearance is at a hearing to file a notice of entry of appearance at the hearing.

Note: DCt.LCvR 83.3 (Number of Counsel) provides.

Except by permission of the Court only one attorney on each side shall examine a witness, address the Court on a question arising in a trial, or address the Court or jury in final argument.

[Effective January 1, 1997. Amended effective July 1, 2011.]

APPENDICES

APPENDIX A. LOCAL OFFICIAL FORMS

LOCAL OFFICIAL FORM NO. 1 REQUEST UNDER LBR 5070–1 FOR HEARING

IN THE UNITED STATES BANKRUPTCY COURT
FOR THE DISTRICT OF COLUMBIA

In re)
) Case No. __________
)
______________________________,) (Chapter ___)
)
Debtor(s).) [Hearing Date: Not yet set]

[If this is an Adversary Proceeding, the Adversary Proceeding caption, Official Form No. 16C, Fed. R. Bankr. Proc., should be used with the note regarding the hearing date underneath the Adversary Proceeding Number instead of the Case Number.]

REQUEST FOR HEARING PURSUANT TO LBR 5070–1

1. Pursuant to LBR 5070–1, the undersigned requests that the Clerk assign a hearing date for the following matter: [describe motion or other matter that requires a hearing].

2. It is estimated that the hearing will take [state the estimated time the hearing will take].

3. I will need to mail the notice of the hearing at least ___ days ahead of the hearing.

4. The following dates should not be used as the hearing date (because of unavailability of counsel or witnesses or other reasons): __________.

5. [State any other information which will be useful to the Clerk in deciding what date to assign for the hearing of the matter, including any urgency in the need for a ruling.]

Dated: ____________ ____
[Requestor's Name, Address, and Phone No.]

[CERTIFICATE OF SERVICE UNDER LBR 5005–1(h)]

NOTE: In compliance with LBR 5070–1, the party requesting a hearing must file a notice of the hearing, see Official Form No. 2, within three (3) days after being given notification of the hearing date. A party need not request a hearing: if the party's motion or other matter is not ruled upon on the papers, the Court will set a hearing in due course. This form is intended for use when the party knows in advance that a matter will require a hearing or to assure that a hearing is already set if someone files an objection to the action the party proposes. It may also be used when a party desires a hearing on a matter already ripe for a hearing and the Court has not set a hearing.

[Effective January 1, 1997. Amended effective July 1, 2011.]

LOCAL OFFICIAL FORM NO. 2 NOTICE UNDER LBR 5070–1 OF HEARING

IN THE UNITED STATES BANKRUPTCY COURT
FOR THE DISTRICT OF COLUMBIA

In re)
) Case No. ________
)
____________________,) (Chapter ___)
)
Debtor(s).) [Hearing Date: ___ / ___ / ___ at ___: ___ ___.m.]

[If this is an Adversary Proceeding, the Adversary Proceeding caption, Official Form No. 16C, Fed. R. Bankr. P., should be used with the note regarding the hearing date underneath the Adversary Proceeding Number instead of the Case Number.]

NOTICE OF HEARING ON
[INSERT TITLES OF MOTIONS
OR OTHER MATTERS BEING HEARD]

Please take notice that a hearing will be held on ________ at ___: ___ ___.m. on the following matters:

[insert matters to be heard]

in the Bankruptcy Court's courtroom in the E. Barrett Prettyman United States Courthouse, 3rd and Constitution Avenue, N.W., Washington, D.C. 20001. Parties in interest with questions may contact the undersigned.

Date: ____________ ______________________________________

[Signer's Name, Address, E–Mail Address, and Phone No.]

[CERTIFICATE OF SERVICE UNDER LBR 5005–1(h)]

[Effective January 1, 1997.]

LOCAL OFFICIAL FORM NO. 3. NOTICE OF DEADLINE TO OBJECT TO MOTION COMMENCING CONTESTED MATTER

[CAPTION]

NOTICE OF DEADLINE TO FILE AND SERVE
OBJECTION TO [NAME OF MOTION]

__________________ has filed a [insert name of motion] seeking [describe the relief sought in the motion].

Your rights may be affected. You should read these papers carefully and discuss them with your attorney, if you have one in this bankruptcy case. (If you do not have an attorney, you may wish to consult one.)

If you do not want the Court to [relief sought in motion], or if you want the Court to consider your views on the [motion] then:

on or before [date of deadline], you or your attorney must file with the Court a written objection to the [motion], together with the proposed order required by Local Bankruptcy Rule 9072–1. The objection and proposed order must be filed with the Clerk of the Bankruptcy Court, U.S. Courthouse, 3rd and Constitution Avenue, N.W., Washington, D.C. 20001. You may append affidavits and documents in support of your objection.

If you mail your objection to the Court for filing, you must mail it early enough so the Court will receive it on or before the date stated above.

You must also mail a copy of your objection to:

[movant's attorney's name and address]

[names and addresses of others to be served]

If you or your attorney do not take these steps, the Court may decide that you do not oppose the relief sought in the [motion] and may enter an order granting relief. The Court may grant the [motion] without a hearing if the objection filed states inadequate grounds for denial of the [relief sought in motion or other filing].

Dated: __________ ______________________________

[Movant's Attorney's Name, Addr., E-Mail Addr., and Phone No.]

[CERTIFICATE OF SERVICE UNDER LBR 5005–1(h)]

NOTES:

1. The Notice of Deadline optionally may appear conspicuously in the Motion, with the title of the Motion to read "MOTION . . . AND NOTICE OF DEADLINE TO FILE AND SERVE OBJECTION TO MOTION."

2. When a Rule requires that the deadline be measured from the date of service, instead of from the date of filing, and service is made by mail, Fed. R. Bankr. P. 9006(f) requires that the date of the deadline is changed to three (3) days after the deadline date that would otherwise apply.

3. Once the paper commencing a contested matter has been served, generally there is no need, when a later motion is filed in the contested matter, to include a notice of the deadline to object to that motion. An exception would be a motion for contempt against a witness (for example, for failing to comply with a subpoena).

4. Official Local Form No. 4 is substantially similar, but is tailored to be used for such miscellaneous filings as a notice of a proposed abandonment, and it includes Notes pertinent to service on the entire creditor body.

[Effective January 1, 1997; amended effective December 1, 2009. Amended effective July 1, 2011.]

LOCAL OFFICIAL FORM NO. 4. NOTICE TO CREDITOR BODY AND OTHERS OF OPPORTUNITY TO OBJECT TO MOTION OR OTHER FILING

[CAPTION]

NOTICE OF OPPORTUNITY TO OBJECT TO [NAME OF MOTION OR PROPOSED ACTION (E. G., AN ABANDONMENT) TO BE TAKEN]

____________________ has filed a [insert name of motion or other filing] seeking [describe the relief sought].

<u>Your rights may be affected.</u> You should read these papers carefully and discuss them with your attorney, if you have one in this bankruptcy case. (If you do not have an attorney, you may wish to consult one.)

If you do not want the Court to [relief sought in motion or proposed action to be taken], or if you want the Court to consider your views on the matter, then:

> on or before [date of deadline], you or your attorney must file with the Court a written objection to the [motion] [proposed action], together with the proposed order required by Local Bankruptcy Rule 9072–1. The objection and proposed order must be filed with the Clerk of the Bankruptcy Court, E. Barrett Prettyman U.S. Courthouse, 3rd and Constitution Avenue, N.W., Washington, D.C. 20001. You may append affidavits and documents in support of your objection.
>
> If you mail your objection to the Court for filing, you must mail it early enough so the Court will receive it on or before the date stated above.
>
> You must also mail a copy of your objection to:
>
> [movant's attorney's name and address]
>
> [names and addresses of others to be served]

If you or your attorney do not take these steps, the Court may decide that you do not oppose the relief sought in the motion and may enter an order granting relief. The Court may grant the [motion or proposed action] without a hearing if the objection filed states inadequate grounds for denial of the [motion] [proposed action to be taken]. Parties in interest with questions may contact the undersigned.

Dated: __________ ____

[Movant's Attorney's Name, Addr., E–Mail Addr., and Phone No.]

[CERTIFICATE OF SERVICE UNDER LBR 5005–1(h)]

NOTES:

1. Matters governed by Fed. R. Bankr. P. 2002(a) provide for 21–day notice, measured under LBR 2002–1 from the date of filing.

2. Some rules, such as Fed. R. Bankr. P. 6007, provide for a different period than twenty-one (21) days for objections.

3. In addition, some rules, such as Fed. R. Bankr. P. 6007, measure the objection period from the date of the mailing of the notice, with the result that Fed. R. Bankr. P. 9006(f) applies to require that the date of the deadline is changed to three (3) days after the deadline date that would otherwise apply.

4. LBR 2002–1 sets forth instances in which notice may be limited.

5. Local Official Form 5 applies to a notice of a proposed use, sale, or lease of property.

6. Local Official Form 6 applies to an objection to a claim.

7. Local Official Form 7 applies to an objection to exemptions.

8. The Notice of Deadline optionally may appear conspicuously in the Motion or other paper), with the title of the paper to read (for example) "MOTION . . . AND NOTICE OF DEADLINE TO FILE AND SERVE OBJECTION TO MOTION."

[Effective January 1, 1997; amended effective December 1, 2009. Amended effective July 1, 2011.]

LOCAL OFFICIAL FORM NO. 5. NOTICE UNDER LBR 6004–1 OF PROPOSED USE, SALE, OR LEASE OF PROPERTY

[CAPTION]

NOTICE OF PROPOSED [SALE, USE, OR LEASE] OF [DESCRIBE PROPERTY]

PLEASE TAKE NOTICE that [sale, use, or lease] of the following-described property of the estate, not in the ordinary course of business, is proposed in accordance with Fed. R. Bankr. P. 6004(a):

[Detailed Property Description]

It is proposed that the property be [describe sale, use, or lease]. [Insert information required by LBR 6004–1(a) and Fed. R. Bankr. P. 2002(c).]

Your rights may be affected. You should read these papers carefully and discuss them with your attorney, if you have one in this bankruptcy case. (If you do not have an attorney, you may wish to consult one.)

If you do not want the [sale, use, or lease] to become effective, or if you want the Court to consider your views on the proposed [sale, use, or lease], then:

on or before [deadline] [the 5th day before the date set for the proposed [sale, use, or lease], you or your attorney must file with the Court a written objection to the proposed [sale, use, or lease], together with the proposed order required by Local Bankruptcy Rule 9072–1. The objection and proposed order must be filed with the Clerk of the Bankruptcy Court, E. Barrett Prettyman U.S. Courthouse, 3rd and Constitution Avenue, N.W., Washington, D.C. 20001. You may append affidavits and documents in support of your objection.

If you or your attorney mail your objection to the Court for filing, you must mail it early enough so the Court will receive it on or before the date stated above.

You or your attorney must also mail a copy of your objection to:

[movant's attorney's name and address]

[names and addresses of others to be served]

IN THE ABSENCE OF A TIMELY OBJECTION, THE [SALE, USE, OR LEASE] WILL BE AUTHORIZED BY THE BANKRUPTCY CODE AND BY THE RULES OF THE COURT WITHOUT THE NECESSITY OF A COURT ORDER. The Court may authorize the [sale, use, or lease] without a hearing if the objection filed states inadequate grounds for denial. Parties in interest with questions may contact the undersigned.

Dated: __________ ______________________________

[Movant's Attorney's Name, Addr., E–Mail Addr., and Phone No.]

[CERTIFICATE OF SERVICE UNDER LBR 5005–1(h)]

NOTE: This form is to be used when a sale, use, or lease out of the ordinary course of business can be authorized on notice without the necessity of Court order, if there is no objection. A sale free and clear of liens requires a motion and a proposed order.

[Effective January 1, 1997; amended effective December 1, 2009. Amended effective July 1, 2011.]

LOCAL OFFICIAL FORM NO. 6. NOTICE UNDER LBR 3007–1 OF TIME TO RESPOND TO OBJECTION TO CLAIM

[CAPTION]

NOTICE OF TIME TO RESPOND TO OBJECTION TO CLAIM

_________ has filed an objection to your claim in this bankruptcy case.

Your claim may be reduced, modified, or eliminated. You should read these papers carefully and discuss them with your attorney, if you have one in this bankruptcy case. (If you do not have an attorney, you may wish to consult one.)

If you do not want the Court to [reduce, modify, or eliminate] your claim, or if you want the Court to consider your views on the objection, then:

on or before [date of deadline] [30 days of the date of the objection—see LBR 3007–1], you or your attorney must file with the Court a written opposition to the objection to your claim and a proposed order under Local Bankruptcy Rule 9072–1. The opposition and proposed order must be filed with the Clerk of the Bankruptcy Court, E. Barrett Prettyman U.S. Courthouse, 3rd and Constitution Avenue, N.W., Washington, D.C. 20001. You may append affidavits, documents, and other evidence you wish to attach in support of your claim.

If you mail your opposition to the Court for filing, you must mail it early enough so the Court will receive it on or before the date stated above.

You must also mail a copy of your opposition to:

[movant's attorney's name and address]

[names and addresses of others to be served]

If you or your attorney do not take these steps, the Court may decide that you do not oppose the relief sought in the objection and may enter an order sustaining the objection. The Court may sustain the objection without a hearing if the opposition filed states inadequate grounds for overruling the objection.

Dated: _________ ______________________________

[Movant's Attorney's Name, Addr., E–Mail Addr., and Phone No.]

[CERTIFICATE OF SERVICE UNDER LBR 5005–1(h)]

NOTE: See LBR 3007–1 for the rules regarding service of the objection. The Notice of Deadline optionally may appear conspicuously in the Objection to Claim, with the title of the Motion to read "OBJECTION TO CLAIM OF . . . AND NOTICE OF DEADLINE TO FILE AND SERVE OPPOSITION TO OBJECTION."

[Effective January 1, 1997. Amended effective July 1, 2011.]

LOCAL OFFICIAL FORM NO. 7. NOTICE UNDER LBR 4003–1 OF TIME TO RESPOND TO OBJECTION TO EXEMPTIONS

[CAPTION]

NOTICE OF TIME TO RESPOND TO OBJECTION TO EXEMPTIONS

________________ has filed an objection to your claim of exemptions.

Your rights may be affected. You should read these papers carefully and discuss them with your attorney, if you have one in this bankruptcy case. (If you do not have an attorney, you may wish to consult one.)

If you do not want the Court to sustain the objection to your claimed exemptions, or if you want the Court to consider your views on the objection, then:

on or before [deadline] [the date that is 15 days after the date of service of the objection, adding three (3) days if service is by mail], you or your attorney must file with the Court a written opposition to the objection to your claimed exemptions, together with the proposed order required by Local Bankruptcy Rule 9072–1. The opposition and proposed order must be filed with the Clerk of the Bankruptcy Court, E. Barrett Prettyman U. S. Courthouse, 3rd and Constitution Avenue, N.W., Washington, D.C. 20001. You may append affidavits and documents in support of your opposition.

If you mail your opposition to the Court for filing, you must mail it early enough so the Court will receive it on or before the date stated above.

You must also mail a copy of your opposition to:

[movant's attorney's name and address]

[names and addresses of others to be served]

If you or your attorney do not take these steps, the Court may decide that you do not oppose the relief sought in the objection and may enter an order sustaining the objection. The Court may sustain the objection without a hearing if the opposition filed states inadequate grounds for denial.

Dated: ________ ______________________________

[Movant's Attorney's Name, Addr., E–Mail Addr., and Phone No.]

[CERTIFICATE OF SERVICE UNDER LBR 5005–1(h)]

NOTE: See LBR 4003–1 for the rules regarding service of the objection. The Notice of Deadline optionally may appear conspicuously in the Objection to Claim, with the title of the Motion to read "OBJECTION TO CLAIM OF . . . AND NOTICE OF DEADLINE TO FILE AND SERVE OPPOSITION TO OBJECTION."

[Effective January 1, 1997; amended effective December 1, 2009. Amended effective July 1, 2011.]

LOCAL OFFICIAL FORM NO. 8. ________'S WITNESS AND EXHIBIT RECORD

Date	Case or Adv. Pro. No.	Operator*	Page Number

Name of Witness	Brief Description of Testimony to be Elicited	Estimated Time to Elicit Testimony	Date Called*

* For Court Use

Exhibit Number*	Description	ID	Date Admitted*

* For Court Use

* When there are two parties, the plaintiff or movant should number its exhibits by numbers, and the defendant or respondent should number its exhibits by letters (A, B, . . ., Z, AA, AB, . . ., AZ, BA, BB, . . ., BE, etc.).

Exhibit Number	Description	ID*	Date Admitted*

* For Court Use

[Effective January 1, 1997. Amended effective July 1, 2011.]

LOCAL OFFICIAL FORM NO. 9. LBR 1007–5 COVERSHEET

In re)
) Case No. ________
)
______________________________,) (Chapter ___)
)
Debtor(s).)

LBR 1007–5 DECLARATION OF DEBTOR REGARDING PAYMENT ADVICES

Select one of the following:

___ The attached (consisting of ___ pages) represent complete and accurate copies of all payment advices or other evidence of payment I have received from any employer within sixty (60) days before the commencement of this bankruptcy case. (Attach all payment advices received, redacting any information entitled to privacy protection under Fed. R. Bankr. P. 9037.)[1]

___ I have received no payment advices or other evidence of payment from any employer within sixty (60) days before the commencement of this bankruptcy case.

I declare under penalty of perjury under the laws of the United States of America that the foregoing is true and correct.

Executed on: ________ ______________________ (Signature)
______________________ (Printed Name)
______________________ (Address)
______________________ (Phone No.)

[1] Federal Rule of Bankruptcy Procedure 9037(a) provides that the following personal information must be redacted from any payment advices:

- All but the last four digits of a social-security number or taxpayer-identification number;
- The month and day of the individual's birth (but not the year);
- All but the initials of any minor's name; and
- All but the last four digits of any financial account number.

[Effective July 1, 2011.]

LOCAL OFFICIAL FORM NO. 10. LBR 1007–6 STATEMENT REGARDING INTEREST IN ACCOUNT OR PROGRAM OF THE TYPE DESCRIBED BY § 521(c) OF THE BANKRUPTCY CODE

UNITED STATES BANKRUPTCY COURT
FOR THE DISTRICT OF COLUMBIA

In re)
) Case No. ________
) (Chapter ___)
Debtor(s).)

STATEMENT OF RECORD OF THE DEBTOR'S INTEREST OR LACK OF AN INTEREST UNDER AN ACCOUNT OR PROGRAM OF THE TYPE SPECIFIED IN 11 U.S.C. § 521(c)

___ I do not have any interest in an education individual retirement account (as defined in § 530(b)(1) of the Internal Revenue Code of 1986) or under a State tuition program (as defined in § 529(b)(1) of the Internal Revenue Code of 1986)

___ I have the following interest(s) in an education individual retirement account (as defined in § 530(b)(1) of the Internal Revenue Code of 1986) or under a State tuition program (as defined in § 529(b)(1) of the Internal Revenue Code of 1986):

____

____

____

____

and as to each such interest attached hereto (with all but the last four digits of any account number redacted) is a record of that interest

I HEREBY CERTIFY under penalty of perjury that the information on this Certificate including any additional sheets provided, is true, correct, and complete as of the date on which I filed my petition commencing this case.

Debtor's Signature: ________________________

Printed name of Debtor: ________________________

Date: ___/___/___

[Effective July 1, 2011.]

LOCAL OFFICIAL FORM NO. 11. DEBTOR'S MOTION FOR ENTRY OF § CHAPTER 13 DISCHARGE AND NOTICE OF DEADLINE AND OPPORTUNITY TO OBJECT

UNITED STATES BANKRUPTCY COURT
FOR THE DISTRICT OF COLUMBIA

In re)
) Case No. ________
) (Chapter ___)
Debtor(s).)

DEBTOR'S MOTION FOR ENTRY OF § 1328(a) CHAPTER 13 DISCHARGE AND NOTICE OF DEADLINE AND OPPORTUNITY TO OBJECT

Comes now the debtor and respectfully moves this court to enter a Chapter 13 Discharge pursuant to 11 U.S.C. § 1328(a), and in support thereof, states as follows:

1. The debtor has completed in full all plan payments under the confirmed Chapter 13 plan including all modifications thereof and the Trustee has accordingly filed a Final Report and Account.
2. The debtor has completed, **after the filing of this case**, the required instructional course concerning Personal Financial Management described in § 111 and has filed, no later than the last payment made under the plan, the requisite certification (Official Form 23).
3. The debtor has not received a discharge in a case filed under Chapter 7, 11, or 12 during the 4–year period preceding the date of the order of relief under this Chapter.

4A. The debtor has not been required by a judicial or administrative order, or by statute to pay any domestic support obligation as defined in 11 U.S.C. § 101(14A) either before this bankruptcy was filed or at any time after the filing of this bankruptcy.

OR

4B. The debtor has made all pre-petition and post-petition domestic support obligations required by judicial or administrative order or by statute and the name of each holder of a domestic support obligation is as follows:

Name: Address:

________________ ________________________________

________________ ________________________________

5. The debtor's most recent/current address is:

____

____

6. The name and address of the debtor's most recent/current employer/income source is:

Name: Address:

____________________ ______________________________

____

7. The debtor hereby certifies that there is no action pending in which the debtor may be found guilty of a felony as described in § 522(q)(1)(A) or liable for a debt as described in § 522(q)(1)(B).

WHEREFORE, the debtor respectfully moves this court to enter a Chapter 13 Discharge pursuant to 11 U.S.C. § 1328(a).

___/___/______ ______________________________

DATE Debtor/Debtor's Attorney

____

____

NOTICE OF OPPORTUNITY AND DEADLINE TO OBJECT TO MOTION FOR ENTRY OF CHAPTER 13 DISCHARGE

***PLEASE TAKE NOTICE THAT WITHIN TWENTY–ONE (21) DAYS AFTER THE SERVICE OF THIS NOTICE** you must file and serve a written objection to the motion, together with the proposed order required by Local Bankruptcy Rule 9072–1. The objection and proposed order must be filed with the Clerk of the Bankruptcy Court, U.S. Courthouse, 3rd and Constitution Ave., N.W., Washington, D.C. 20001, and served by mailing a copy to the Debtor/Debtor's Attorney and to the Chapter 13 Trustee.

***IF YOU FAIL TO FILE A TIMELY OBJECTION, THE MOTION MAY BE GRANTED BY THE COURT WITHOUT A HEARING.** The court may grant the motion without a hearing if the objection filed states inadequate grounds for denial. Parties in interest with questions may contact the Debtor/Debtor's Attorney.

___/___/______ ______________________________

DATE Debtor/Debtor's Attorney

CERTIFICATE OF SERVICE UNDER LBR 5005–3

I hereby certify that a copy of the Motion for Entry of § 1328(a) Chapter 13 Discharge and Notice of Deadline and Opportunity to Object has been mailed, postage pre-paid, on the date that appears below to all **scheduled creditors and to:**

Cynthia A. Niklas, Esq.,
Chapter 13 Trustee DC
4545 42nd St. NW #211
Washington, DC 200016–4623

United States Attorney
Civ. Div., Fin. Litigation
555 4th St., NW
Washington, DC 20530

Internal Revenue Service
P.O. Box 7346
Philadelphia, PA 19101–7346

D.C. Tax and Revenue.
1101 4th St., SW 6th Fl.
Washington, DC 20024

IRS Chief Counsel
P.O. Box 77085
Washington, DC 20013

Attorney General for D.C.
441 4th St. NW
Washington, DC 20001

Child Support Serv. Div.
Office of Attorney General
441 4th St., NW 5th Fl.
Washington, DC 2001

___ / ___ / ________
DATE

____
Debtor/Debtor's Attorney

[Effective July 1, 2011.]

LOCAL OFFICIAL FORM NO. 12. LBR 1007–2(b) STATEMENT OF NO ALTERATIONS

UNITED STATES BANKRUPTCY COURT
FOR THE DISTRICT OF COLUMBIA

In re)
) Case No. __________
) (Chapter 13)
Debtor(s).)

LBR 1007–2(b) STATEMENT OF NO ALTERATIONS

The schedules filed herewith:

(1) do not add any entity not included on the existing List of Creditors and Mailing Matrix (as amended by any amendments that have been made thereto); and

(2) do not change the name or address of any entity as listed on the existing List of Creditors and Mailing Matrix (as amended by any amendments that have been made thereto).

I HEREBY CERTIFY under penalty of perjury that the information on this statement is true, correct, and complete.

Debtor's Signature: ____

Printed name of Debtor: ____

Date: ____ / ____ / __________

[Effective July 1, 2011.]

LOCAL OFFICIAL FORM NO. 13. LBR 1009–2(e) CERTIFICATE OF SERVICE OF PAPERS REQUIRED TO BE MAILED TO ENTITIES AFFECTED BY AMENDMENT OF LIST OF CREDITORS AND MAILING MATRIX

UNITED STATES BANKRUPTCY COURT
FOR THE DISTRICT OF COLUMBIA

In re)
) Case No. ________
) (Chapter ___)
Debtor(s).)

LBR 1009–2(e) CERTIFICATE OF SERVICE OF PAPERS REQUIRED TO BE MAILED TO ENTITIES AFFECTED BY AMENDMENT OF LIST OF CREDITORS AND MAILING MATRIX

In compliance with LBR 1009–2(e), I certify that I have mailed to each entity affected by the amendments, filed this date, to the debtor's list of creditors and mailing matrix (other than entities being deleted by the amendments) copies of the following documents:

(1) the notice of the commencement of the bankruptcy case;

(2) any notice from the clerk regarding conversion of the case;

(3) any notice of the meeting of creditors;

(4) any notice sent to all creditors regarding a deadline for opposing any motion not yet decided or any hearing not yet held;

(5) any notice to creditors of the deadline for filing any of the following:

(A) a proof of claim; and

(B) an objection to a disclosure statement not yet approved or to a plan not yet confirmed; and

(6) any currently proposed or already confirmed plan affecting the entities and any order confirming the plan, but the party need not mail a copy of the certificate of service to the affected entities.

I declare under penalty of perjury under the laws of the United States that the foregoing is true and correct.

Executed on: ___ / ___ / ___

Signature: ____________________

Type or Print Name: ____________________

[Effective July 1, 2011.]

APPENDIX B. TITLE VI. LOCAL RULES OF THE UNITED STATES DISTRICT COURT FOR THE DISTRICT OF COLUMBIA

[**Publisher's Note:** See the Rules of the U.S. District Court for the District of Columbia, *ante*, for the text of DCt. LBR 5011–1, DCt. LBR 5011–2, DCt. LBR 8003–1, DCt. LBR 8006–1, DCt. LBR 8007–1, DCt. LBR 8009–1, DCt. LBR 9033–1.]

OTHER FORMS AND GUIDELINES

APPLICATION TO PAY FILING FEE IN INSTALLMENTS

Form 3A
(12/07)

United States Bankruptcy Court
_______ District Of _______

In re _______________________________, Case No. _______
Debtor
Chapter _______

APPLICATION TO PAY FILING FEE IN INSTALLMENTS

1. In accordance with Fed. R. Bankr. P. 1006, I apply for permission to pay the filing fee amounting to $_______ in installments.
2. I am unable to pay the filing fee except in installments.
3. Until the filing fee is paid in full, I will not make any additional payment or transfer any additional property to an attorney or any other person for services in connection with this case.
4. I propose the following terms for the payment of the Filing Fee.*

____Check one ☐ With the filing of the petition, or
☐ On or before _______

$____ on or before _______

$____ on or before _______

$____ on or before _______

DEAR FILER, PLEASE BE ADVISED THAT PER STANDING ORDER § 5, THE INITIAL INSTALLMENT MUST BE AT LEAST $61.00 AND PER STANDING ORDER § 6, THE TIME SPAN BETWEEN EACH INDIVIDUAL PAYMENT CANNOT EXCEED 45 DAYS

* The number of installments proposed shall not exceed four (4), and the final installment shall be payable not later than 120 days after filing the petition. For cause shown, the court may extend the time of any installment, provided the last installment is paid not later than 180 days after filing the petition. Fed. R. Bankr. P. 1006(b)(2).

5. I understand that if I fail to pay any installment when due, my bankruptcy case may be dismissed and I may not receive a discharge of my debts.

____
Signature of Attorney Date

____
Signature of Debtor Date
(In a joint case, both spouses must sign.)

____
Name of Attorney

____
Signature of Joint Debtor (if any) Date

DECLARATION AND SIGNATURE OF NON–ATTORNEY BANKRUPTCY PETITION PREPARER (See 11 U.S.C. § 110)

I declare under penalty of perjury that: (1) I am a bankruptcy petition preparer as defined in 11 U.S.C. § 110; (2) I prepared this document for compensation and have provided the debtor with a copy of this document and the notices and information required under 11 U.S.C. §§ 110(b), 110(h), and 342(b); (3) if rules or guidelines have been promulgated pursuant to 11 U.S.C. § 110(h) setting a maximum fee for services chargeable by bankruptcy petition preparers, I have given the debtor notice of the maximum amount before preparing any document for filing for a debtor or accepting any fee from the debtor, as required under that section; and (4) I will not accept any additional money or other property from the debtor before the filing fee is paid in full.

______________________________ ______________________________

Printed or Typed Name and Title, if any, of Bankruptcy Petition Preparer

Social Security No. (Required by 11 U.S.C. § 110.)

If the bankruptcy petition preparer is not an individual, state the name, title (if any), address, and social security number of the officer, principal, responsible person, or partner who signs the document.

____

____

Address

______________________________ __________

Signature of Bankruptcy Petition Preparer Date

Names and Social Security numbers of all other individuals who prepared or assisted in preparing this document, unless the bankruptcy petition preparer is not an individual:

If more than one person prepared this document, attach additional signed sheets conforming to the appropriate Official Form for each person. A bankruptcy petition preparer's failure to comply with the provisions of title 11 and the Federal Rules of Bankruptcy Procedure may result in fines or imprisonment or both. 11 U.S.C. § 110; 18 U.S.C. § 156.

UNITED STATES BANKRUPTCY COURT
______ DISTRICT OF ______

In re ______________________________,
Debtor

Case No. ______

Chapter ______

ORDER APPROVING PAYMENT OF FILING FEE IN INSTALLMENTS

☐ IT IS ORDERED that the debtor(s) may pay the filing fee in installments on the terms proposed in the foregoing application.

☐ IT IS ORDERED that the debtor(s) shall pay the filing fee according to the following terms:

_____Check one ☐ With the filing of the petition, or
☐ On or before _____

$_____ on or before ______
$_____ on or before ______
$_____ on or before ______

☐ IT IS FURTHER ORDERED that until the filing fee is paid in full the debtor(s) shall not make any additional payment or transfer any additional property to an attorney or any other person for services in connection with this case.

BY THE COURT

Date: ______

____

United States Bankruptcy Judge

MAILING MATRIX

MAILING MATRIX GUIDELINES

A mailing matrix must conform to the following guidelines:

- A mailing matrix consists of eight or nine creditors per page with their complete addresses, clearly typed[1], left justified and centered in a single column down the middle of one side of an 8½″ × 11″ sheet of paper.
- The mailing matrix must be typed on blank, white, 20 lb. paper. Do not use textured, onion skin, or colored paper. This will cause our scanner to misread information. The paper should not have any stray lines, staples, or holes.
- The mailing matrix must be typed in one of the following standard typefaces or font styles: Courier 10 pitch or 12 pitch on a word processor; Prestige Elite 12 pitch; Letter Gothic 10 pitch on a typewriter. To ensure the scanner can read the matrix, it must be printed from a laser quality printer or typewriter.
- Each creditor's address must be single-spaced. Triple-spaced between each address. A margin of at least one inch should appear at the top and bottom of each page.
- Each creditor's address must consist of no more than five total lines, including the creditor's name, street address, city, state and zip code.
- No account numbers should be included on the matrix.
- The city, state and zip code must all appear together on the final line of each creditor's address. The zip code should never be dropped down to a separate line. No other lines of address information should appear after the city, state and zip code line.
- Commas must be placed between the city and state in the address.
- All state names must be abbreviated, in capital letters, as delineated by the United States Postal Service. Each state must have a two letter abbreviation code - No Period Following.
- Creditor addresses should never be printed in all capital letters. The standardized English format is preferred; i.e. first letters of proper names are capitalized, all others are in lower case.
- Do Not include the debtors' or debtors' attorney's addresses on the mailing matrix as this information is added to the BANCAP system when the case is opened.
- Do Not include any taxing authorities unless monies are owed. This information is mailed separately by the court.
- Do Not two-hole punch or staple the mailing matrix. This will cause the scanner to misread the address.
- The "Amended Matrix" should conform to all of the aforementioned guidelines, with one additional provision; in order to avoid needless duplication, the "Amended Matrix" must include only the creditors not appearing on the previously filed list or lists. Similarly, an amended matrix should include only the address or addresses actually being amended.
- Adherence to these guidelines will greatly enhance the speed and efficiency with which the Bankruptcy Court scans, edits, prints, and completes its noticing. On the reverse side of this page is an example of a Perfect Mailing Matrix.
- A "List of Creditors and Mailing Matrix" cover sheet should accompany the mailing matrix.[2] This cover sheet should not be stapled to the mailing matrix but should be attached by a paper clip or a clamp. These pages should not be hole punched.

1 A pdf-fillable form for preparing the mailing matrix is available on our website. You may use the computer in the intake area at the clerk's office to gain access to the website and to prepare and print out the mailing matrix.

2 The list required by Fed. R. Bankr. P. 1007(a) of creditors and certain other entities (the so-called List of Creditors) can be combined with the Mailing Matrix, and that simplifies the filing of the two documents. The requirement in the Guidelines of a List of Creditors and Mailing Matrix cover sheet assumes that the debtor is combining the two documents in a single document. The form cover sheet is available on our website in a pdf-fillable format. Debtors may use the computer in the intake area at the clerk's office to gain access to the website and to prepare and print out the cover sheet.

STANDING ORDER: IN RE CLERK'S OFFICE OPERATIONS

STANDING ORDER. IN RE CLERK'S OFFICE OPERATIONS

Effective November 1, 2011, this standing order replaces all prior standing and administrative orders, except for the court's administrative order(s) regarding electronic case filing and the court's administrative order relating to deadlines in local rules.

§ 1. Definition.

Clerk. As used in this order, the term "clerk" includes the clerk of the court and the deputy in charge, and further includes members of the clerk's office who have been delegated from the clerk of court or the deputy in charge authority to handle the matter involved.

Example: In the case of a reference to a form prescribed by the clerk, this means a form prescribed by the Clerk of Court or the Chief Deputy Clerk, or a form prescribed by a Deputy Clerk who has been delegated the authority to prescribe the form to be used: it does not include every Deputy Clerk who utilizes that form in the course of the Deputy Clerk's work.

§ 2. Verification and Recordation of Identity of Entity Presenting Petition for Filing.

(a) When someone presents for filing a bankruptcy petition for a debtor who is not represented by an attorney, the clerk is authorized to request such individual to produce for photocopying (with the individual's permission):

(1) a picture identification (preferably a driver's license) of the individual; and

(2) in the case of a messenger service, a copy of the messenger log showing for whom the messenger is acting.

(b) Based on examination of the materials produced and the clerk's other inquiries, the clerk is authorized to make a notation on the docket entry for the petition regarding who presented the petition for filing and on whose behalf the individual was acting. The clerk shall notify the court in the event that it appears that the petition was filed without the debtor's authorization or that the petition was prepared by a petition preparer (as defined in 11 U.S.C. § 110) who has failed to note such capacity on the petition.

(c) If the individual presenting the petition has no picture identification or refuses to produce an identification, the clerk is authorized to:

(1) request, on behalf of the court, that the individual sign a verified statement identifying the individual and acknowledging that the individual presented the petition for filing (and a suggested form is attached hereto);

(2) docket the verified statement, if one is signed; and

(3) note on the docket entry for the petition that the individual failed or refused to produce a picture identification, and note any refusal to sign a verified statement as requested pursuant to paragraph (1) of this subsection.

§ 3. Rejecting or Accepting Petition for Filing; Acceptance of Other Papers for Filing Despite Absence of Filing Fee.

(a) *Rejecting Petitions for Filing.* The clerk may not mark a petition as filed and must reject the petition for filing if the petition submitted for filing is unaccompanied by one of the following:

(1) the payment of the filing fee in full in an acceptable form, as defined in paragraph (b) of this section;

(2) an application to pay the filing fee in installments, which the clerk has not rejected for filing under paragraph (d) of this section; or

(3) an application to waive the filing fee which the clerk has not rejected for filing under paragraph (e) of this section.

(b) *Acceptable Forms of Payment of Filing Fee.* The filing fee may be paid only by:

(1) U.S. currency;

(2) a cashier's check (or certified check) or money order made payable to "Clerk, U.S. Bankruptcy Court"; or

(3) if an attorney has not been given notice under paragraph (c)(1) below, a check drawn on the account of the attorney for the debtor or on the account of a law firm of which the attorney for the debtor is a member, partner, or associate.

(c) *Notification of an Attorney Whose Checks Will no Longer Be Accepted; Maintenance of Records.*

(1) The clerk, in the exercise of the clerk's discretion, is authorized to notify an attorney (and is authorized to do so by letter, or by a notice or order prepared, signed, and entered by the clerk in a particular bankruptcy case) that the clerk will not accept for payment of filing fees (and other fees) in any bankruptcy case:

(A) a check drawn on the account of the attorney; and

(B) a check drawn on the account of the law firm of which the attorney is a member, partner or associate.

(2) At the clerk's office's intake counter, the clerk will maintain a log, available for public inspection, of all notifications issued under this paragraph.

(d) *Grounds for Rejecting for Filing Applications to Pay the Filing Fee in Installments.*

(1) The clerk shall reject for filing any application to pay the filing fee in installments if:

(A) the debtor is not an individual;

(B) the petition is not a voluntary petition;

(C) the application was not signed;

(D) the application was not prepared on the appropriate Official Form; or

(E) the application does not state that the debtor is unable to pay the filing fee except in installments.

(e) *Grounds for Rejecting for Filing Requests to Waive the Filing Fee.*

(1) The clerk shall reject for filing any request to waive the filing fee if:

(A) the debtor is not an individual;

(B) the petition is not a voluntary chapter 7 petition;

(C) the application was not signed; or

(D) the application was not prepared on the appropriate Official Form.

(2) If an application to waive the filing fee is not required to be rejected under the foregoing, the clerk shall transmit the application to chambers for a ruling on the application.

(f) *Marking and Retaining Rejected Petition.* When the clerk rejects a petition for filing, the clerk shall:

(1) mark on the rejected petition, any rejected application to pay the filing fee in installments, and any rejected application to waive the filing fee the date and time the petition was submitted for filing;

(2) mark the petition and any accompanying installment payment or waiver application as rejected;

(3) retain but not file or docket the petition and any accompanying installment payment or waiver application; and

(4) deliver by hand or by mail a photocopy of the pages of the petition and any accompanying installment payment application or fee waiver application bearing the foregoing marks regarding submission and rejection to the person who tendered the petition and applications.

(g) *Accepting Petition for Filing; Marking Time of Filing of Petition Accepted for Filing.*

(1) Unless the clerk is required to reject the petition for filing under paragraph (a), the clerk must accept the petition for filing even if it is defective due to:

(A) if the debtor is not an individual, lack of a signature by an attorney who is a member of the bar of the United States District Court for the District of Columbia;

(B) lack of a list of creditors signed under penalty of perjury (or notarized);

(C) lack of a mailing matrix or a mailing matrix in proper form;

(D) lack of a list under F.R. Bankr. P. 1007(d) in a chapter 11 case of the 20 largest unsecured creditors;

(E) an order of dismissal of a prior case with prejudice;

(F) lack of the debtor's signature;

(G) lack of any of the details required by the petition (for example, the debtor's tax identification number); or

(H) any other defect.

(2) The clerk shall mark the accepted petition as filed as of the time the clerk was required to accept it for filing. But the clerk shall promptly address any defect in the petition, in the application to pay the filing fee in installments, or in the application to waive the filing fee.

(h) *Accepting Other Papers for Filing.* Except for a paper authorized to be rejected for filing under paragraph (a), (d), or (e), the clerk shall not reject any other paper submitted for filing in the clerk's office (as opposed to the courtroom) for lack of an associated fee, including:

(1) a notice of conversion;

(2) an adversary proceeding complaint;

(3) a notice of appeal; and

(4) an amended schedule, mailing matrix, or list of creditors that adds creditors.

§ 4. Certificates of Credit Counseling.

(a) *Failure to File a Certificate of Credit Counseling.*

(1) Order to Show Cause. If a debtor who is an individual fails to either file a certificate of credit counseling or an Exhibit D selecting boxes 3 or 4 with the petition or within 14 days thereafter, the clerk is authorized to:

(A) prepare, sign, and enter, on behalf of the court, an order directing the debtor to file a credit counseling certificate or to show cause why the case ought not be dismissed;

(B) include in the order a 7–day notice to respond to the order; and

(C) transmit copies of the order to the debtor, the debtor's attorney, if any, any trustee in the case, and, in a case under chapter 7 or 11, to the U.S. Trustee.

(2) Order of Dismissal. If the debtor neither submits a written response to the order nor files a certificate of credit counseling (that is not invalid as too old or as issued postpetition) or an Exhibit D selecting boxes 3 or 4 within 7 days of entry of the order under paragraph (a)(1) of this section, the clerk shall:

(A) prepare a proposed order dismissing the case; and

(B) transmit the proposed order to chambers.

(b) *Out of Time and Post–Petition Credit Counseling Certificates.*

(1) Order to Show Cause. When a debtor who is an individual files either a credit counseling certificate that is dated more than 180 days before the filing of the petition or a credit counseling certificate that is dated after the petition, and the debtor has not checked box 3 or 4 of Exhibit D to the petition, the clerk is authorized to:

(A) prepare, sign, and enter, on behalf of the court, an order directing the debtor to either file a valid prepetition credit counseling certificate or show cause why the case ought not be dismissed;

(B) include in the order a 7–day notice to respond to the order; and

(C) transmit copies of the order to the debtor, the debtor's attorney, if any, any trustee in the case, and, in a case under chapter 7 or 11, to the U.S. Trustee.

(2) Order of Dismissal. If the debtor neither submits a written response to the order nor files a valid certificate of credit counseling within 7 days of entry of the order under paragraph (b)(1) of this section, the clerk shall:

(A) prepare a proposed order dismissing the case; and

(B) transmit the proposed order to chambers.

(C) If the clerk prepares and enters an order pursuant to paragraphs (a)(1) or (b)(1) of this section in error, the clerk is authorized to enter an order vacating the erroneous order.

§ 5. Clerk's Prescribing Acceptable Amounts that Clerk's Office May Authorize for Payment of the Filing Fee in Installments. In prescribing acceptable amounts and timing of installment fees under Rule 1006(b) that the clerk's office may authorize, the clerk shall:

(a) require payment at filing of an initial installment equal to the sum of:

(1) the miscellaneous administrative fee imposed by the Bankruptcy Court Miscellaneous Fee Schedule that is an Appendix to 28 U.S.C. § 1930 (**currently $46.00**, but subject to change);

(2) regardless of the chapter of the case, an amount equal to the fee (**currently $15.00**, but subject to change) imposed in a chapter 7 case by the Bankruptcy Court Miscellaneous Fee Schedule that is an Appendix to 28 U.S.C. § 1930 for payment to a trustee serving in a chapter 7 case as provided in 11 U.S.C. § 330(b)(2); and

(3) any additional amount prescribed by the clerk, provided that:

(A) in a chapter 7 or 13 case, the prescribed additional amount is the same amount in both a chapter 7 and a chapter 13 case, and

(B) in a chapter 11 case, the prescribed amount is at least as much as the additional amount required in a chapter 7 or 13 case;

(b) assure that the required installments, in the aggregate, equal the total amount of fees required by statute and by the Bankruptcy Miscellaneous Fee Schedule to be paid as a result of the filing of the case;

(c) require that the final installment be paid by a date that is no later than 120 days after the filing date of the petition;

(d) require that each installment after the initial installment be paid by a date that is no later than 45 days after the date of the previous installment. (Example 1: 2nd installment by Day 30 of the case; 3rd installment by Day 60 of the case; 4th installment by Day 90 of the case. Example 2: 2nd installment by Day 45 of the case; 3rd installment by Day 90 of the case; 4th installment by Day 120 of the case.).

§ 6. Granting and Denying Applications to Pay Filing Fee in Installments.

(a) The clerk is authorized to prepare, sign, and enter, on behalf of the court, an order granting an application filed by an individual debtor (or joint individual debtors) under F.R. Bankr. P. 1006(b) to pay the filing fee in installments, provided that:

(1) the application complies with Rule 1006(b) and with the Official Form;

(2) the application provides for making installment payments in the amounts and by the times prescribed by the clerk as acceptable, and as of February 28, 2009 (but subject to further change), the clerk has prescribed the following installments as being acceptable:

Installment	Ch.7	Ch.13	Ch.11
1st Installment pd. with petition	$61.00	$61.00	$337.00
2nd Installment pd. by Day 45 of the case (meaning the 45th day after the pet. date)	$81.70	$73.33	$236.33
3rd Installment pd. by Day 90 of the case	$81.70	$73.33	$236.33
4th Installment pd. by Day 120 of the case	$81.60	$73.34	$236.34;

(3) the application is accompanied by the fee that must be paid at filing under the preceding paragraph; and

(4) the clerk is unaware of any prior case in which the debtor failed fully to pay the filing fee, and is unaware of any bar against the debtor filing a new bankruptcy case.

(b) *Denying Application.* The clerk is authorized to deny any application that the clerk is not authorized to grant pursuant to paragraph (a).

(c) *Order to Show Cause Based on Denial of Application and Non–Payment of Fee.* When the clerk denies an application to pay the filing fee in installments the clerk is authorized to:

(1) prepare, sign, and enter, on behalf of the court, an order

(A) if the application is denied due to a defect in the application under paragraphs (a)(1), (a)(2), or (a)(3) of this section, directing the debtor to either pay the filing fee in full, submit an amended application to pay the filing fee in installments accompanied by the required first installment if not previously paid, or show cause why the case ought not be dismissed, and directing any trustee, and, in a chapter 7 or chapter 11 case, the Office of the U.S. Trustee to show cause why the case ought not be dismissed for failure to pay the filing fee;

(B) if the application is denied because the debtor was subject to a prior dismissal for failure to pay the filing fee under (a)(4) of this section, directing the debtor to either pay the filing fee in full, submit an application to waive the filing fee, or show cause why the case ought not be dismissed, and directing any trustee, and, in a chapter 7 or chapter 11 case, the Office of the U.S. Trustee to show cause why the case ought not be dismissed for failure to pay the filing fee

(2) advise that if the case is dismissed based on such non-payment:

(A) the debtor will not receive a discharge;

(B) the debtor will still remain liable for the unpaid portion of the filing fee;

(C) that if the debtor fails to pay, the debt could be referred to the Department of Treasury's Financial Management Service for collection;

(D) the debtor will not be allowed, absent extraordinary circumstances, in any future case to pay the filing fee in installments if the debtor fails to pay the filing fee in this case;

(E) if the debtor files a new case within one year after dismissal of this case, the provisions of 11 U.S.C. § 362(c)(3) or § 362(c)(4) will apply and may lessen or eliminate the protection of the automatic stay of 11 U.S.C. § 362(a) against collection efforts by creditors; and

(F) if prior to dismissal of the case a motion for relief from the automatic stay is filed, or if the court determines that the failure to pay was willful, the court may make the dismissal a dismissal with prejudice for 180 days.

(3) include in the order 14–day notice to respond to the order to show cause; and

(4) transmit copies of the order to the debtor, the debtor's attorney, if any, any trustee in the case, and, in a case under chapter 7 or 11, to the U.S. Trustee.

(d) *Order Dismissing Case After Issuance of Order Under Paragraph (c).* If within 14 days of entry of the order under paragraph (c) the debtor fails to either pay the filing fee in full, submit an amended application to pay the filing fee in installments (if order is issued pursuant to (c)(1)(A)) accompanied by the fee that must be paid at filing under paragraph (a)(2) if not previously paid, or submit an application to waive the filing fee (if order is issued pursuant to (c)(1)(B)), or the debtor, an appointed trustee, or the U.S. Trustee fails to file a document attempting to show cause, the clerk is authorized to:

(1) prepare, sign, and enter, on behalf of the court, an order dismissing the case and providing:

(A) that the debtor will not be allowed, absent extraordinary circumstances, in any future case to pay the filing fee in installments unless the filing fee in the dismissed case has been paid in full;

(B) that within 60 days of the entry of this order the debtor(s) shall either:

(i) pay the outstanding balance due, with interest at a rate of 3% per annum accruing 30 days from the date of this order; or

(ii) make arrangements with the clerk of the court to pay the amount due in installments over a period not to exceed 90 days;

(C) that the clerk shall refer such claim on the amount outstanding to the Bureau of Financial Management Services for collection if the debtor fails:

(i) to make payment of the outstanding balance in full, plus interest, within 60 days;

(ii) to make arrangements to pay the outstanding balance within 60 days; or

(iii) to make any payment pursuant to an arrangement made with the clerk of the court; and

(2) provide copies of the order to all entities on the BNC mailing list.

(e) *Referral of Outstanding Balance to Financial Management Service.* If within 60 days of the order for dismissal under paragraph (d) of this section the debtor has not paid in full any balance outstanding, made arrangements to pay the amount outstanding in installments, or failed to make an installment payment pursuant to an agreement to pay the amount outstanding over 90 days, the clerk shall:

(1) refer the amount due to the Department of Treasury's Financial Management Service for collection; and

(2) provide notice to the debtor of the referral.

(f) If the clerk prepares and enters an order pursuant to paragraph (d) of this section in error, the clerk is authorized within 14 days after entry of the erroneous order to enter an order vacating the erroneous order.

§ 7. Orders Striking Appearances.

(a) The clerk is authorized to prepare, sign, and enter, on behalf of the court, an order striking the attempted appearance (by filing of a paper bearing that attorney's name and signature) in any case or proceeding of an attorney who is not a member in good standing of the bar of the district court.

(b) Notwithstanding paragraph (a) of this section, the clerk may not strike the attorney if:

(1) the attorney is employed or retained by the United States or one of its agencies to represent the United States or the agency as a party;

(2) the attorney is a State Attorney General or that official's designee representing the State or any agency of the State;

(3) the attorney has filed a certificate that the attorney is providing representation without compensation;

(4) the attorney has joined of record a member in good standing of the bar of the district court who has signed the paper in question on behalf of the client (in which event, the clerk shall treat the attorney who is a member of the bar of the district court as the attorney entering an appearance);

(5) the appearance is on a notice of appeal, motion to withdraw the reference, or objection to the court's proposed findings of fact (in which event, the clerk shall notify the district court of any improper attempted appearance when the clerk transmits the paper to the district court); or

(6) the paper is one of the following types of paper (whose signing shall not be treated as an attempt to enter an appearance):

(A) a proof of claim;

(B) an assignment of a claim;

(C) a request under F.R. Bankr. P. 2002(g) to receive notices in the case; or

(D) a notice to perfect, or to maintain or continue the perfection of, any interest in property pursuant to 11 U.S.C. § 362(b)(4) and § 546(b)(1).

(c) If the clerk prepares and enters an order pursuant to paragraph (a) of this section in error, the clerk is authorized to enter an order vacating the erroneous order.

(d) When an attorney's appearance is stricken, the clerk may proceed to treat as unsigned by the attorney any paper signed by the attorney pursuant to that defective appearance.

§ 8. Unsigned Filings.

(a) *Notice.* If a party filing a paper, except:

a petition;[1]

a mailing matrix;[2] or

a schedule;[3]

fails to sign the paper or, if the party is represented by an attorney, the party's attorney (except when the filing is a petition,[4] list, schedule, or statement, or an amendment thereto) fails to sign the paper, the clerk is authorized to issue a notice advising the party or, if the party is represented by an attorney, the party's attorney that if the party fails to correct the deficiency within 3 days, the submission will be stricken.

(b) *Striking Filing.* If within 3 days after the clerk issues the notice in paragraph (a) of this section the party does not submit an amended filing that includes the signature of the party or, if the party is represented by an attorney, the party's attorney, the clerk is authorized to:

(1) prepare, sign, and enter, on behalf of the court, an order striking the unsigned filing;

(2) transmit copies of the order to the party, the party's attorney, if any, any trustee appointed in the case, and, in a case under chapter 7 or 11, the U.S. Trustee; and

(3) transmit copies to all counsel of record in an adversary proceeding or contested matter when the filing relates to a previously commenced adversary proceeding or contested matter.

(c) If the clerk prepares and enters an order pursuant to paragraph (b) of this section in error, the clerk is authorized to enter an order vacating the erroneous order.

§ 9. Failure to File Mailing Matrix, Chapter 13 Plan, and Rule 1007 Documents.

(a) *Failure to file a mailing matrix.*

(1) Chapters 7 and 11.

(A) Order to Show Cause. If the debtor in a case under chapter 7 or 11 of the Bankruptcy Code fails to file a mailing matrix with the petition, the clerk is authorized to:

(i) prepare, sign, and enter, on behalf of the court, an order attaching a copy of the court's recommended verification form and matrix preparation instructions, and directing the debtor and any other party in interest to show cause within 14 days of the entry of the order why the case ought not be dismissed if the debtor fails to file a mailing matrix within 7 days of entry of the order; and

(ii) transmit copies of the order to all entities on the BNC mailing list.

(B) Transmittal to Chambers. If within 14 days after the entry of the order to show cause issued pursuant to paragraph (a)(1)(A) of this section the debtor has failed to file a mailing matrix and neither the debtor nor any other party in interest has filed a paper to attempt to show cause why the case ought not be dismissed, the clerk shall prepare an order dismissing the case and transmit the order to chambers.

(2) Chapter 13.

(A) Order to Show Cause. If the debtor fails to file a mailing matrix with the bankruptcy petition in a case under chapter 13 of the Bankruptcy Code, the clerk is authorized to:

(i) prepare, sign, and enter, on behalf of the court, an order attaching a copy of the court's recommended verification form and matrix preparation instructions, and directing the debtor, within 7 days of entry of the order, to either file a mailing matrix or show cause why the case ought not be dismissed; and

(ii) transmit copies of the order to the debtor, the debtor's attorney, if any, and the Chapter 13 Trustee.

(B) Dismissal. If within 7 days after entry of the order to show cause issued pursuant to paragraph (a)(2)(A) of this section the debtor fails to either file a mailing matrix or file a paper to attempt to show cause, the clerk is authorized to:

(i) prepare, sign, and enter, on behalf of the court, an order dismissing the case; and

(ii) transmit copies of the order to all entities on the BNC mailing list.

(b) *Failure to file a chapter 13 plan.*

(1) Notice. In a chapter 13 case, if the debtor does not file a chapter 13 plan with the petition, the clerk is authorized to:

(A) issue, on behalf of the court, a notice advising the debtor that it must file a plan within 14 days after the debtor files the petition and that if the debtor fails to file the plan by that date, the case may be dismissed; and

(B) transmit copies of the notice to the debtor, the debtor's attorney, if any, and the chapter 13 trustee.

(2) Order. In a chapter 13 case, if the debtor fails to file a plan within 14 days after the filing of the petition, the clerk is authorized to:

(A) prepare, sign, and enter, on behalf of the court, an order to file the plan, warning the debtor that a continued failure to file may result in dismissal of the case; and

(B) transmit copies of the order to the debtor, the debtor's attorney, if any, and to the chapter 13 trustee.

(c) *Failure to file documents required by Fed. R. Bankr. Proc. 1007.*

(1) Notice. If the debtor has not filed the documents required by Fed. R. Bankr. Proc. 1007 with the petition, the clerk is authorized to:

(A) issue, on behalf of the court, a notice advising the debtor that it must file the documents within 14 days after the debtor files the petition and that if the debtor fails to file the documents by that date, the case may be dismissed; and

(B) transmit copies of the notice to the debtor, the debtor's attorney, if any, any trustee in the case, and, in a case under chapter 7 or 11, to the U.S. Trustee.

(2) Order. If the debtor fails to file the documents required by Rule 1007 within 14 days after the petition date, the clerk is authorized to:

(A) prepare, sign, and enter, on behalf of the court, an order to file the required documents, warning the debtor that a continued failure to file the missing documents may result in dismissal of the case and alerting the debtor to the automatic dismissal provision of 11 U.S.C. § 521(i); and

(B) transmit copies of the order to the debtor, the debtor's attorney, if any, any trustee in the case, and, in a case under chapter 7 or 11, to the U.S. Trustee.

(d) If the clerk prepares and enters an order pursuant to this section in error, the clerk is authorized to enter an order vacating the erroneous order, but not an order of dismissal of the case entered more than 14 days beforehand.

§ 10. Mailing Matrix Verification. This section does not apply to an amended mailing matrix filed after the debtor has filed a properly verified matrix; instead § 11 applies.

(a) *Failure to File Verification.*

(1) Order to show cause. If a debtor files a mailing matrix (including a combined mailing matrix and Rule 1007(a)(1) list), but fails to include with the matrix a signed verification, the clerk is authorized to:

(A) prepare, sign, and enter, on behalf of the court, an order directing the debtor to file an amended matrix with a signed verification;

(B) include in the order a 7–day notice to respond to the order;

(C) transmit copies of the order to the debtor, the debtor's attorney, if any, any trustee in the case, and, in a case under chapter 7 or 11, to the U.S. Trustee; and

(D) attach a copy of the court's recommended verification form to the order.

(2) Order Striking Matrix and to Show Cause. If within 7 days of entry of the order under paragraph (a)(1) of this section the debtor fails to file an amended matrix that includes a verification, the clerk is authorized to:

(A) prepare, sign, and enter, on behalf of the court, an order striking the matrix, and:

(i) in a case under chapter 7 or 11, directing the debtor and any other party in interest to show cause within 14 days of the entry of the order why the case ought not be dismissed if the debtor fails to file a mailing matrix within 7 days of entry of the order; or

(ii) in a case under chapter 13, directing the debtor, within 7 days of entry of the order, to either file a mailing matrix or show cause why the case ought not be dismissed; and

(B) transmit copies of the order to the debtor, the debtor's attorney, if any, any trustee in the case, and, in a case under chapter 7 or 11, to the U.S. Trustee.

(3) Dismissal Order.

(A) Chapter 7 or 11. If the clerk strikes the debtor's matrix pursuant to paragraph (a)(2) of this section in a case under chapter 7 or 11 and the debtor fails to file a new mailing matrix and no one files a writing attempting to show cause within the allowed time, the clerk is then authorized to prepare and transmit to chambers an order dismissing the case, providing for copies to be transmitted to the debtor, the debtor's attorney, if any, any trustee appointed in a case, and, in a case under chapter 7 or 11, to the United States Trustee; or

(B) Chapter 13. If the clerk strikes the debtor's matrix pursuant to paragraph (a)(2) of this section in a case under chapter 13 and the debtor fails to either file a new mailing matrix or file a writing attempting to show cause within the allowed time, the clerk is authorized to prepare, sign, and enter, on behalf of the court, an order dismissing the case and transmit copies of the order to the debtor, the debtor's attorney, if any, and the chapter 13 trustee.

(b) *Improper Form of Verification.*

(1) Order to Show Cause. If a debtor files a mailing matrix (including a combined mailing matrix and Rule 1007(a)(1) list) and includes a verification with the matrix, but the verification is not executed under penalty of perjury or does not substantially conform to the recommended verification provided by the court, the clerk is authorized to:

(A) prepare, sign, and enter, on behalf of the court, an order directing the debtor to file an amended matrix with a verification executed under penalty of perjury and that conforms in substance to the court's recommended form;

(B) include in the order a 7–day notice to respond to the order;

(C) transmit copies of the order to the debtor, the debtor's attorney, if any, any trustee in the case, and, in a case under chapter 7 or 11, to the U.S. Trustee; and

(D) attach a copy of the court's recommended verification form to the order.

(2) Order Striking Matrix. If within 7 days of entry of the order under paragraph (b)(1) of this section the debtor fails to file an amended matrix that includes a verification in proper form, the clerk is authorized to:

(A) prepare, sign, and enter, on behalf of the court, an order striking the matrix, and:

(i) in a case under chapter 7 or 11, directing the debtor and any other party in interest to show cause within 14 days of the entry of the order why the case ought not be dismissed if the debtor fails to file a mailing matrix within 7 days of entry of the order; or

(ii) in a case under chapter 13, directing the debtor, within 7 days of entry of the order, to either file a mailing matrix or show cause why the case ought not be dismissed; and

(B) transmit copies of the order to the debtor, the debtor's attorney, if any, any trustee in the case, and, in a case under chapter 7 or 11, to the U.S. Trustee.

(3) Dismissal Order.

(A) Chapter 7 or 11. If the clerk strikes the debtor's matrix pursuant to paragraph (b)(2) of this section in a case under chapter 7 or 11 and the debtor fails to file a new mailing matrix and no one files a writing attempting to show cause within the allowed time, the clerk is then authorized to prepare and transmit to chambers an order dismissing the case, providing for copies to be transmitted to the debtor, the debtor's attorney, if any, any trustee appointed in a case, and, in a case under chapter 7 or 11, to the United States Trustee; or

(B) Chapter 13. If the clerk strikes the debtor's matrix pursuant to paragraph (b)(2) of this section in a case under chapter 13 and the debtor fails to either file a new mailing matrix or file a writing attempting to show cause within the allowed time, the clerk is authorized to prepare, sign, and enter, on behalf of the court, an order dismissing the case and transmit copies of the order to the debtor, the debtor's attorney, if any, and the chapter 13 trustee.

§ 11. Amended Mailing Matrix Verification.

(a) *Failure to File Verification.*

(1) Order to show cause. If a debtor files an amended mailing matrix (including a combined mailing matrix and Rule 1007(a)(1) list) attempting to amend a previous mailing matrix that was in proper form, but fails to include with the amended matrix a verification, the clerk is authorized to:

(A) prepare, sign, and enter, on behalf of the court, an order directing the debtor to file an amended matrix with a verification;

(B) include in the order a 7–day notice to respond to the order;

(C) transmit copies of the order to the debtor, the debtor's attorney, if any, any trustee in the case, and, in a case under chapter 7 or 11, to the U.S. Trustee; and

(D) attach to the order a copy of the court's recommended verification form that applies (depending on whether the amended matrix adds, or deletes, or changes the name, or changes the address of entities).

(2) Order Striking Matrix and to Show Cause. If within 7 days of entry of the order under paragraph (a)(1) of this section the debtor fails to file an amended matrix that includes a verification, the clerk is authorized to:

(A) prepare, sign, and enter, on behalf of the court, an order striking the amended matrix; and

(B) transmit copies of the order to the debtor, the debtor's attorney, if any, any trustee in the case, and, in a case under chapter 7 or 11, to the U.S. Trustee.

(b) *Improper Form of Verification.*

(1) Order to Show Cause. If a debtor files an amended mailing matrix (including a combined mailing matrix and Rule 1007(a)(1) list) and includes a verification with the matrix, but the verification is not executed under penalty of perjury or does not substantially conform to the recommended verification provided by the court, the clerk is authorized to:

(A) prepare, sign, and enter, on behalf of the court, an order directing the debtor to file an amended matrix with a verification executed under penalty of perjury and that conforms in substance to the court's recommended form;

(B) include in the order a 7–day notice to respond to the order;

(C) transmit copies of the order to the debtor, the debtor's attorney, if any, any trustee in the case, and, in a case under chapter 7 or 11, to the U.S. Trustee; and

(D) attach to the order a copy of the court's recommended verification form that applies (depending on whether the amended matrix adds, or deletes, or changes the names, or changes the addresses of entities).

(2) Order Striking Matrix. If within 7 days of entry of the order under paragraph (b)(1) of this section the debtor fails to file an amended matrix that includes a verification in proper form, the clerk is authorized to:

(A) prepare, sign, and enter, on behalf of the court, an order striking the matrix; and

(B) transmit copies of the order to the debtor, the debtor's attorney, if any, any trustee in the case, and, in a case under chapter 7 or 11, to the U.S. Trustee.

§ 12. Schedules Not in Proper Form.

(a) *Summary of Schedules and Statistical Summary.*

(1) Order to Show Cause. If a debtor fails to file a summary of schedules or statistical summary, or in the case of amended schedules, an amended summary of schedules or amended statistical summary, the clerk is authorized to:

(A) prepare, sign, and enter, on behalf of the court, an order directing the debtor to either file a summary of schedules, amended summary of schedules, statistical summary, or amended statistical summary, as the case may be, with a declaration under penalty of perjury (Official Form 6—Declaration) or show cause why the debtor's schedules ought not be stricken;

(B) include in the order a 7–day notice to respond to the order; and

(C) transmit copies of the order to the debtor, the debtor's attorney, if any, any trustee in the case, and, in a case under chapter 7 or 11, to the U.S. Trustee.

(2) Striking Schedules. If within 7 days of entry of the order under paragraph (a)(1) of this section, the debtor fails to file a summary of schedules, an amended summary of schedules, a statistical summary, or an amended statistical summary, as the case may be, or fails to file a writing attempting to show cause, the clerk is authorized to:

(A) prepare, sign, and enter, on behalf of the court, an order striking the schedules or amended schedules, as the case may be, to which the debtor failed to include a summary of schedules, amended summary of schedules, statistical summary, or amended statistical summary, as the case may be; and

(B) transmit copies of the order to the debtor, the debtor's attorney, if any, any trustee in the case, and, in a case under chapter 7 or 11, to the U.S. Trustee.

(b) *Declaration.*

(1) Order to Show Cause. If a debtor fails to include a signed declaration in proper form when the debtor files schedules or amended schedules, the clerk is authorized to:

(A) prepare, sign, and enter, on behalf of the court, an order directing the debtor to either file amended schedules that include a signed declaration in proper form or show cause why the debtor's schedules ought not be stricken;

(B) include in the order a 7–day notice to respond to the order; and

(C) transmit copies of the order to the debtor, the debtor's attorney, if any, any trustee in the case, and, in a case under chapter 7 or 11, to the U.S. Trustee.

(2) Striking Schedules. If within 7 days of entry of the order under paragraph (b)(1) of this section, the debtor fails to file amended schedules that include a proper declaration or fails to file a writing attempting to show cause, the clerk is authorized to:

(A) prepare, sign, and enter, on behalf of the court, an order striking the schedules or amended schedules, as the case may be, which the debtor failed to include a declaration; and

(B) transmit copies of the order to the debtor, the debtor's attorney, if any, any trustee in the case, and, in a case under chapter 7 or 11, to the U.S. Trustee.

(c) *LBR 1007–1(a)(3) Statement or Supplemental Matrix.*

(1) Order to Show Cause. If a debtor files amended schedules but fails to include either a statement under LBR 1007–1(a)(3) or to file a supplemental matrix with a 1009–1(c) certificate, the clerk is authorized to:

(A) prepare, sign, and enter, on behalf of the court, an order directing the debtor to either submit an LBR 1007–1(a)(3) statement, submit a supplemental mailing matrix and LBR 1009–1(c) certificate, or show cause why the debtor's amended schedules ought not be stricken;

(B) include in the order a 7–day notice to respond to the order; and

(C) transmit copies of the order to the debtor, the debtor's attorney, if any, any trustee in the case, and, in a case under chapter 7 or 11, to the U.S. Trustee.

(2) Striking Schedules. If within 7 days of entry of the order under paragraph (c)(1) of this section, the debtor fails either to submit an LBR 1007–1(a)(3) statement, submit a supplemental mailing matrix and LBR 1009–1(c) certificate, or file a writing attempting to show cause, the clerk is authorized to

(A) prepare, sign, and enter, on behalf of the court, an order striking the amended schedules to which the debtor failed to include either the LBR 1007–1(a)(3) statement or file a supplemental mailing matrix and LBR 1009–1(c) certificate; and

(B) transmit copies of the order to the debtor, the debtor's attorney, if any, any trustee in the case, and, in a case under chapter 7 or 11, to the U.S. Trustee.

(d) If the clerk prepares and enters an order pursuant to this section in error, the clerk is authorized to enter an order vacating the erroneous order.

§ 13. Notices or Orders re Deficient Filings.

(a) *Issuing Deficiency Notices.* For any deficiency in a filing not covered by §§ 4, 6, 7, 8, 9, 10, 11, 12 or 17, the clerk is authorized to:

(1) prepare, sign, and enter a notice (including an electronic deficiency notice) directing a party filing a paper (or required to file a paper or pay a fee relating to a filing) to cure, by a specified date (or a period of time after issuance of the notice or order), any specified deficiency regarding that filing;

(2) include a warning, if appropriate, that failure to cure the deficiency by the specified deadline may result in the paper being stricken; and

(3) transmit copies of the notice to the party, the party's attorney, if any, any trustee appointed in the case, and, in a case under chapter 7 or 11, the U.S. Trustee.

(b) *Types of Notice.* The clerk is authorized to issue deficiency notices including, but not limited to, the following:

(1) failure of an individual debtor to sign the petition or, in the case of a debtor who is not an individual (e.g., a corporation or partnership), failure of the petition to be signed by a member of the bar of the district court;[5]

(2) payment of any filing fee not tendered as required;

(3) failure to file papers required for an amendment of the schedules not covered by §§ 10 & 11 of this standing order, such as a missing amended schedule (for example, when only the matrix has been amended) or a missing Notice to Creditors;

(4) failure to file a proposed order in proper form; and

(5) correction in the electronic case filing system of any deficiency in the electronic filing of a paper (including correcting mis-docketing of a paper).

(c) Upon failure of the entity timely to cure the deficiency, the clerk shall, as appropriate, either:

(1) submit to the court a proposed order, or request the court to issue a minute order, striking the paper;

(2) send the matter to chambers for further guidance if the clerk is uncertain whether any of the foregoing steps is appropriate; or

(3) decide in the clerk's discretion that the deficiency does not warrant further action.

§ 14. Discharging and Referring Orders To Show Cause.

(a) *Discharging Order to Show Cause.* If the clerk issues an order to show cause pursuant to the authority granted by this standing order and the party to whom the order is issued cures the deficiency that prompted the order by filing a corrective entry, the clerk is authorized to:

(1) prepare, sign, and enter, on behalf of the court, an order discharging the order to show cause;

(2) transmit copies of the order to the party, the party's attorney, if any, any trustee appointed in the case, and, in a case under chapter 7 or 11, the U.S. Trustee.

(b) *Referral To Chambers.* If the clerk issues an order to show cause pursuant to the authority granted by this standing order and the party to whom the order is issued files a writing purporting to show cause and the order to show cause is not discharged by the clerk under paragraph (a) above (i.e., the deficiency still remains uncured), the clerk shall refer the matter to chambers for disposition.

§ 15. Bar Date for Filing Proofs of Claims in Chapter 11 Cases. In chapter 11 cases, the clerk shall set the deadline for the filing of claims as (1) 100 days after the date first set for the meeting of creditors in the case of creditors who are not governmental units, and (2) 180 days after the date of the order for relief in the case of creditors who are governmental units. The clerk shall give notice of such bar dates with the notice of the first meeting of creditors.

§ 16. Order Setting Disclosure Statement Hearing. The clerk is authorized to prepare, sign, and enter an order setting the date and time for hearing on a disclosure statement, including the time for objections to the disclosure statement.

§ 17. Enforcing Payment of Filing Fee Installments.

(a) *Order to Show Cause.* If a debtor fails to make a timely installment payment of the filing fee pursuant to an order approving the debtor's application to pay the filing fee in installments, the clerk is authorized to:

(1) prepare, sign, and enter, on behalf of the court, an order directing the debtor and any other party in interest to show cause why the case ought not be dismissed for failure to pay the filing fee;

(2) advise that:

(A) the debtor will not receive a discharge;

(B) the debtor will still remain liable for the unpaid portion of the filing fee;

(C) that if the debtor fails to pay the debt could be referred to the Department of Treasury's Financial Management Service for collection;

(D) the debtor will not be allowed, absent exceptional circumstance, in any future case to pay the filing fee in installments if the debtor fails to pay the filing fee in this case;

(E) if the debtor files a new case within one year after dismissal of this case, the provisions of 11 U.S.C. § 362(c)(3) or § 362(c)(4) will apply and may lessen or eliminate the protection of the automatic stay of 11 U.S.C. § 362(a) against collection efforts by creditors; and

(F) if prior to dismissal of the case, a motion for relief from the automatic stay is filed, or if the court determines that the failure to pay was willful, the court may make the dismissal a dismissal with prejudice for 180 days.

(3) include in the order a 14–day notice to respond to the order; and

(4) transmit copies of the order to the debtor, the debtor's attorney, if any, any trustee in the case, and, in a case under chapter 7 or 11, to the U.S. Trustee.

(b) *Order Dismissing Case After Issuance of Order Under Paragraph (a).* If within 14 days of entry of the order under paragraph (a) of this section

(A) the debtor (or any other party in interest) fails to make even partial payment of the filing fee installment that was the subject of an order to show cause under paragraph (a);

(B) the debtor (or any other party in interest) fails timely to respond in writing to that order to show cause (including making a partial payment of the missing installment or requesting more time to make the payment);

(C) the clerk is unaware of sufficient payments held by the standing chapter 13 trustee under a chapter 13 plan to be a source for making payment within 180 days after the filing of the petition; and

(D) no motion for relief from the automatic stay has been filed in the case,

the clerk is authorized to:

(1) prepare, sign, and enter, on behalf of the court, an order dismissing the case and providing:

(A) that, absent exceptional circumstances, the debtor will not be allowed in any future case to pay the filing fee in installments unless the filing fee in the dismissed case has been paid in full;

(B) that within 60 days of the entry of this order the debtor(s) shall either:

(i) pay the outstanding balance due, with interest at a rate of 3% per annum accruing 30 days from the date of this order; or

(ii) make arrangements with the clerk of the court to pay the amount due in installments over a period not to exceed 90 days;

(C) that the clerk shall refer such claim on the amount outstanding to the Bureau of Financial Management Services for collection if the debtor fails:

(i) to make payment of the outstanding balance in full, plus interest, within 60 days;

(ii) to make arrangements to pay the outstanding balance within 60 days; or

(iii) to make any payment pursuant to an arrangement made with the clerk of the court; and

(2) transmit copies of the order to all entities on the BNC mailing list.

(c) *Referral to Chambers When Order of Dismissal Not Authorized.* When the clerk is *not* authorized by paragraph (b) of this section to issue a dismissal order and the filing fee installment still remains delinquent, the clerk should transmit the matter to chambers. Examples of these instances include:

(1) if the debtor makes only a partial payment of the delinquent installment of the filing fee, and the clerk views that payment as insufficient cause to justify not dismissing the case;

(2) if the debtor makes a response that the clerk views as stating insufficient cause to justify not dismissing the case; or

(3) if a motion to lift the automatic stay has been filed in the case.

(d) *Order in Chapter 13 Case for Trustee to Pay Fee.* At the outset of a chapter 13 case (or upon conversion of a case to chapter 13), the clerk is authorized to prepare, sign, and enter, on behalf of the court an order directing the standing chapter 13 trustee in due course to pay to the clerk, from funds paid to the trustee under the debtor's plan, the unpaid balance of the filing fee required by F.R. Bankr. P. 1006(a) (even if the debtor is not in default in making timely payment of an installment).

(e) *Order Vacating Order in Chapter 13 Case for Trustee to Pay Fee.* The clerk is authorized to prepare, sign, and enter, on behalf of the court an order partially or fully vacating an order under paragraph (d) above to the extent that the debtor makes payment of the filing fee.

(f) *Order To Pay Filing Fee if Case is Dismissed with Portion of Filing Fee Unpaid.* If a case is dismissed while the debtor(s) still owes a portion of the filing fee and the order dismissing the case does not contain the language provided by paragraphs (b)(1)(A), (B), and (C) of this section (e.g., case is dismissed on motion of the trustee and judge signs trustee's proposed order), the clerk is authorized to:

(1) prepare, sign, and enter, on behalf of the court, an order providing:

(A) that, absent exceptional circumstances, the debtor will not be allowed in any future case to pay the filing fee in installments unless the filing fee in the dismissed case has been paid in full;

(B) that within 60 days of the entry of this order the debtor(s) shall either:

(i) pay the outstanding balance due, with interest at a rate of 3% per annum accruing 30 days from the date of this order; or

(ii) make arrangements with the clerk of the court to pay the amount due in installments over a period not to exceed 90 days;

(C) that the clerk shall refer such claim on the amount outstanding to the Bureau of Financial Management Services for collection if the debtor fails:

(i) to make payment of the outstanding balance in full, plus interest, within 60 days;

(ii) to make arrangements to pay the outstanding balance within 60 days; or

(iii) to make any payment pursuant to an arrangement made with the clerk of the court; and

(2) transmit copies of the order to the debtor, the debtor's attorney, if any, any trustee appointed in the case, and, in cases under chapters 7 or 11, to the United States Trustee.

§ 18. Dismissal or Conversion.

(a) *Chapter 7.*

(1) Conversion to chapter 11. Upon the filing by the debtor of a motion to convert a chapter 7 case **that was not previously converted to chapter 7 from another chapter** to a case under chapter 11, the clerk is authorized to prepare and transmit to chambers a proposed order:

(A) granting the debtor's motion to convert the case to a case under chapter 11;

(B) directing the debtor(s) to file the list required by Fed. R. Bankr. Proc. 1007(d), Official Form B 22B (Chapter 11 Statement of Current Monthly Income) if the debtor is an individual, and, if not previously filed, the other schedules, lists, and statement of financial affairs required by Fed. R. Bankr. Proc. 1007;

(C) directing the chapter 7 trustee to file and serve on the debtor(s) and counsel for the debtor(s) and the United States Trustee, a final report and account, and to turn over to the debtor(s) in possession (or to the chapter 11 trustee, if appointed) all records and property of the estate in the chapter 7 trustee's custody, possession or control;

(D) directing the debtor to pay the additional fee required by 28 U.S.C. § 1930(a); and

(E) providing on the order for transmittal of copies of the order to all entities on the BNC mailing list.

(2) Conversion to chapter 13. Upon the filing by the debtor of a motion to convert a chapter 7 case **that was not previously converted to chapter 7 from another chapter** to a case under chapter 13, the clerk is authorized to prepare and transmit to chambers a proposed order:

(A) granting the debtor's motion to convert the case to a case under chapter 13;

(B) providing that within 14 days of the order, the debtor shall:

(i) file a form 22C;

(ii) if not previously filed, file, as required by Fed. R. Bankr. Proc. 1007(b)(1), schedules, statement of financial affairs, payment advices, and a record of any interest that the debtor has in an account or program of the type specified in 11 U.S.C. § 521(c);

(iii) file, if after the conversion of the case the debtor files schedules or any amended schedules, a supplemental mailing matrix and LBR 1009 statement; and

(iv) file and serve a chapter 13 plan in conformance with LBR 3015–1, with service to be evidenced by a certificate of service complying with LBRs 5005–1(h)(3) and 3015–1; and

(C) providing for transmittal of copies of the order to the debtor, the debtor's attorney, if any, the chapter 7 trustee, the chapter 13 trustee, and the office of the United States Trustee.

(b) *Chapter 11: Conversion to Chapter 7.* Upon the filing by the debtor of a motion to convert a chapter 11 case to a case under chapter 7, the clerk is authorized to prepare and submit to chambers a proposed order that shall:

(1) grant the debtor's motion to convert the case to a case under chapter 7;

(2) provide that pursuant to Fed. R. Bankr. Proc. 1019 and 11 U.S.C. § 521(a)(4) that after qualification of, or assumption of duties by the chapter 7 trustee, whichever occurs earlier, the debtor shall turn over to the chapter 7 trustee, upon request, all records and property of the estate in the debtor's possession or control;

(3) provide that within 14 days of the entry of the order, the debtor shall, in conformance with Fed. R. Bankr. Proc. 1019(5)(A) and LBR 1009–1:

(A) file a schedule of unpaid debts incurred after the filing of the original petition to the date of conversion (or a statement that no such debts were incurred or that they are reflected on original schedules filed after the conversion of the case);

(B) file with the schedule a dated supplemental mailing matrix, as required by LBR 1007–2(e), clearly titled as such, which includes the names and correct mailing addresses of all newly scheduled creditors;

(C) serve the schedule (or the statement that there are no additional creditors not already scheduled) on the chapter 7 trustee and the United States Trustee;

(D) serve on each creditor added by the schedule a copy of any Notice of Commencement of Case issued in the chapter 7 case, or, if the Notice has not yet been issued, a copy of the schedule; and

(D)* file a certificate of service complying with LBR 5005–1(h)(3) reflecting service of the paper(s) required to be served; and

(4) provide that the debtor shall file, if not previously filed, the schedules and the statement of financial affairs required by F.R. Bankr. P. 1007, and the copies and supplemental mailing matrix required by LBR 1007–1(a).

(5) provide that within 30 days of the entry of the order the debtor shall file and transmit to the United States Trustee a final report and account; and

(6) provide on the order for transmittal of copies of the order to the debtor, the debtor's attorney, if any, and the U.S. Trustee.

(c) *Chapter 13.*

(1) Dismissal. Immediately upon the filing by the debtor of a motion to dismiss a chapter 13 case that was not converted to chapter 13 from another chapter,

(A) the clerk is authorized to prepare, sign, and enter, on behalf of the court, an order granting the debtor's motion to dismiss, **except when the motion seeks to condition the dismissal (for example, by requesting that the dismissal be without prejudice).** The order may:

(i) direct that if the debtor fails to pay any unpaid filing fee in full, the debtor will not be allowed in any future case, absent exceptional circumstances, to pay the filing fee in installments; and

(ii) recite, when applicable, that "The clerk has ascertained that a motion for relief from the automatic stay was filed on a date prior to the filing date of the debtor's motion which will make the voluntary dismissal one with prejudice for 180 days pursuant to 11 U.S.C. § 109(g)(2)" and decree that it is "ORDERED that this case be and it hereby is DISMISSED and the dismissal is with prejudice for 180 days pursuant to 11 U.S.C. § 109(g)(2) to the extent that provision applies," and

(B) the order shall transmit copies of the order to all entities on the BNC mailing list.

(2) Conversion to chapter 7. Immediately upon the filing by the debtor of a motion to convert a chapter 13 case to a case under chapter 7, the clerk is authorized to:

(A) prepare, sign, and enter, on behalf of the court, an order granting the debtor's motion to convert, effective as of the date of the debtor's filing of the motion (which shall be treated as a notice of conversion);

(B) transmit copies of the order to the debtor, the debtor's attorney, if any, and the office of the U.S. Trustee.

(d) *Vacate.* The clerk is authorized to prepare and enter an order vacating any of the foregoing orders under this section if the clerk determines that the order was issued in administrative error and if the erroneous order was entered no more than 14 days beforehand.

§ 19. Locking Down Docket Entry When it Includes Matter That Should Have Been Redacted; Order to File Redacted Material.

(a) When an attorney or a party files a document that includes material that should have been redacted in accordance with the Judiciary's policy re preserving privacy under the E–Government Act, the clerk is authorized to:

(1) issue a notice advising the party or, if the party is represented by an attorney, the party's attorney, that if the party fails to file an amended document with the offending material redacted within 3 days, the submission will be stricken; and

(2) lock down the docket entry containing that document (making it inaccessible by the public).

(b) If the party filing the document that includes material that should have been redacted in accordance with the Judiciary's policy re preserving privacy under the E–Government Act does not file an amended document with the offended information within 3 days of the deficiency notice issued pursuant to paragraph (a)(1) of this section, the clerk is authorized to

(1) prepare, sign, and enter, on behalf of the court, an order striking the document, containing the unredacted information; provided, however, that the clerk shall not issue the order if the document containing the information is the petition; and

(2) transmit copies of the order to the party, the party's attorney, if any, any trustee in the case, and, in a case under chapter 7 or 11, to the U.S. Trustee.

§ 20. Miscellaneous Orders of Discharge or Closing Case. The clerk is authorized to prepare, sign, and enter:

(a) an order closing the case and discharging the trustee in the following circumstances, unless a contested matter (such as a motion to avoid lien), an adversary proceeding, or an appeal from an order in the main case is still pending:

(1) in a chapter 13 case, upon the trustee's filing a final report after the completion of plan payments or the dismissal of the case, and after expiration of the time for the debtor to file any papers required to obtain a discharge;

(2) in a no-asset chapter 7 case, upon the trustee filing a report that insufficient assets are available to make a distribution to creditors,

(3) in an asset chapter 7 case, upon the trustee filing a Report of Final Account and Application for Order Discharging Trustee and Closing the case that includes a statement of the U.S. Trustee's Office indicating "Trustee's Final Distribution reviewed by the United States Trustee's Office."

(b) an order granting the debtor a discharge upon the debtor becoming entitled to a discharge; and

(c) an order vacating any order entered under the paragraphs above if the clerk determines that the order was entered in administrative error (e.g., vacating a discharge that was entered before the time for objections had expired or before a ruling on a pending objection to discharge).

§ 21. Returned Mail.

(a) *Using Debtor's Attorney's Return Address on Mailing of Rule 2002 Notices.* The clerk is authorized to cause the debtor's attorney's or pro se debtor's return address to be placed on the envelopes containing notices mailed to creditors and other interested parties pursuant to the requirements of F.R. Bankr. P. 2002, including (but not limited to) the following which are mailed to all creditors:

(1) a notice (whether the first or a later notice) of a meeting of creditors;

(2) a notice of a bar date for filing a claim (including any order setting such a bar date);

(3) a notice of a bar date for filing a complaint objecting to discharge or a complaint to determine the dischargeability of a debt;

(4) a notice (or an order to show cause which includes such notice to all creditors) of an opportunity to object to the dismissal or conversion of a case;

(5) a notice of the granting or denial of a discharge;

(6) an order that dismisses a case and that is mailed to all creditors as notice of the dismissal; and

(7) a notice of the conversion of the case.

(b) *Destroying Returned Mail After Docketing the Returning of the Mail.* Any mailed copy of an item entered on the docket, and the envelope containing the same, which are returned to the clerk as the return addressee may be destroyed by the clerk after making a notation in the docket reflecting the return of the mailed item. The clerk may, but is not required, to note any notation that was placed on the envelope by the U.S. Postal Service.

(c) *Destroying Returned Mail Received Prior to April 1, 2005.* Any mailed copy of an item entered on the docket on or after October 6, 2003 (when this court converted to a paperless Case Management/Electronic Case Filing system without placing documents filed after that date in a paper file for the case or adversary proceeding or miscellaneous matter), and the envelope containing the same, which have been returned to the clerk as the return addressee and received prior to April 1, 2005 may be destroyed by the clerk without making any notation in the docket.

[Signed October 27, 2011, effective November 1, 2011.]

* So in original.

[1] See § 13(b)(1) addressing unsigned petitions.

[2] See § 10(a) addressing unsigned mailing matrices (including unsigned mailing matrix under Rule 1007(a)(1) list).

[3] See § 10(b) addressing unsigned schedules.

[4] When an attorney for a debtor that is not an individual fails to sign the petition *see* § 13(b)(1). When an attorney for a debtor who is an individual fails to sign the petitions *see* § 13(a)

[5] Such notices should give notice that if a properly signed petition is not filed within 7 days of entry of the notice (or the notice may specify a date that is 3 business days after issuance of the notice), the petition will be stricken and the case dismissed (but in a joint case, not dismissed as to any debtor who did sign the petition).

UNITED STATES BANKRUPTCY COURT
FOR THE DISTRICT OF COLUMBIA

STATEMENT OF INDIVIDUAL PRESENTING PETITION FOR FILING WITHOUT PRESENTING A PHOTOGRAPHIC IDENTIFICATION OF THE INDIVIDUAL

I, ____, state
[Print Full Name]
that I am the individual who this day, the _____ day of ___________________,
_____, has presented for filing a petition for the debtor or debtors named:
____.
[Print the name of the debtor(s) appearing on the petition].
I declare under penalty of perjury that the foregoing statement is true and correct.

____
[Signature of Individual]

Executed on __________________________.
[Insert date.]

ELECTRONIC CASE FILING

ADMINISTRATIVE ORDER RELATING TO ELECTRONIC CASE FILING

Federal Rule of Civil Procedure 5(d)(3) and Federal Rules of Bankruptcy Procedure 5005(a)(2), 9011, 9029, and 9036 authorize this Court to establish practices and procedures for the filing, signing, and verification of filings and documents by electronic means. This Order sets forth those practices and procedures.

IT IS ORDERED that:

1. The *Administrative Procedures for Filing, Signing, and Verifying Documents by Electronic Means* with amendments effective July 7, 2011, have been presented to this Court and are hereby approved. The Court will revise and update the *Administrative Procedures* as needed and notify the bar of such revisions. The *Administrative Procedures* and subsequent revisions will be posted on the Court's web site at http://www.dcb.uscourts.gov

2. Beginning June 1, 2005, Electronic Case Filing (ECF) will be mandatory for:

- all active members, in good standing, of the United States District Court for the District of Columbia bar and all attorneys of the U.S. Trustee's office filing and practicing in the United States Bankruptcy Court for the District of Columbia.
- creditors and claimants who annually file more than ten (10) proofs of claim or similar documents (such as assignments of claims, and Federal Rule of Bankruptcy Procedure ("FRBP") 2002(g) requests) must file electronically. Creditors and claimants who annually file fewer than ten (10) proofs of claim or similar documents may file electronically, but are not required to do so.

Pro se debtors and other parties (other than creditors and claimants) not represented by counsel **may not** file electronically; therefore, the *Administrative Procedures* do **not** apply to such filers.

3. The provisions of this Order shall apply to all cases previously filed, proceedings presently pending, and those subsequently filed in the United States Bankruptcy Court for the District of Columbia.

4. Any Order/Paperless Minute Order signed electronically and hence without the original signature of the judge shall have the same force and effect as if the judge had affixed his signature to a paper copy of the order and entered it in a conventional manner. Papers (such as discharges of debtors and notices) that are issued and entered by the Clerk's Office are similarly effective when signed electronically.

5. Electronically filed documents may be filed twenty-four (24) hours a day in the Court's Case Management/Electronic Case Filing ("CM/ECF") system. Electronically filed documents will constitute simultaneous filing of the document and entry of that document on the docket kept by the Clerk of Court in accordance with FRBP 5003.

6. The electronic filing of documents shall be suspended if, under extraordinary circumstances, CM/ECF is out of service. The Clerk's Office will maintain a log of these occurrences for reference purposes. If and when CM/ECF will be unavailable due to routine maintenance, the Clerk's Office will post advance notice on the Court's web site at http://www.dcb.uscourts.gov and on the CM/ECF login screen.

7. When the Clerk's Office scans paper documents filed by pro se filers and non-CM/ECF participants and dockets such filings in CM/ECF, the electronically scanned document shall constitute the official record of the Court. With the exception of the Voluntary Petition and the Statement of Social Security Number (Form B–21), the Clerk's Office may discard all filed paper documents that have been scanned electronically.

8. Amendments to this Order and the *Administrative Procedures for Filing, Signing, and Verifying Documents by Electronic Means* may be entered as necessary.

9. Nothing contained in this Order is intended, or shall be construed to alter or modify any party's duties under the provisions of the Bankruptcy Code or the Federal Rules of Bankruptcy Procedure.

[Effective July 7, 2011.]

ADMINISTRATIVE PROCEDURES FOR FILING, SIGNING, AND VERIFYING DOCUMENTS BY ELECTRONIC MEANS

(Note: Pro se debtors and other parties **(other than creditors and claimants)** ***not represented by counsel may not file electronically; therefore, these Administrative Procedures do not apply to such filers.)***

As amended Effective July 7, 2011

I. REGISTRATION FOR ELECTRONIC CASE FILING (ECF)

A. Terms.

1. "CM/ECF" refers to the Court's Case Management/Electronic Case Filing system that receives documents filed in electronic form.

2. "Electronic User" (or "User") refers to both of the following:

a. "Limited–Rights User" refers to users who can file with the limits as set forth in Part I.C.2.

b. "Full–Rights User" refers to users who can file without limitations.

3. "Filing Agent" refers to a person who a Full–Rights User has designated in CM/ECF to have authority to file documents on the User's behalf.

4. "Notice of Electronic Filing" ("NEF") refers to the notice automatically generated by CM/ECF each time a document is filed or a docket event is entered.

B. Designation of Cases. Cases filed **on and after October 6, 2003,** are completely electronic and are part of the Court's CM/ECF system. All cases opened **prior to October 6, 2003,** are in paper form prior to this date and in electronic form thereafter. Therefore, all petitions, motions, memoranda of law, or other documents filed after October 6, 2003, in cases opened prior to October 6, 2003, must be filed electronically, except as expressly provided or in circumstances where the User is prevented from filing electronically (i.e., CM/ECF system failure). Notwithstanding the foregoing, parties who are not Users in CM/ECF are not required to file documents electronically.

C. Registration. All Users must complete and submit a registration form even if the User uses CM/ECF in another federal court. Both the Attorney/Full–Rights User and Creditor/Claimant/Limited–Rights User Registration Forms are available on the Court's web site at http://www.dcb.uscourts.gov/dcb/

1. An Attorney/Full–Rights User Registration Form, in the form attached hereto as Exhibit A, must be submitted for each attorney User. A separate registration form must be submitted for each attorney within a particular law firm.

a. In order for an attorney User to register for CM/ECF, the attorney must be an active member, in good standing, of the bar of the United States District Court for the District of Columbia.

b. Failure to maintain good standing with the U.S. District Court for the District of Columbia will result in non-issuance of a login and password (See District Court LCvR 83.9).

c. Attorney Users must provide the Clerk's Office with a current e-mail account for use in CM/ECF. When an attorney changes his or her e-mail address, the attorney must update his or her CM/ECF account information to include the new e-mail address.

2. A Creditor/Claimant/Limited–Rights User Registration Form, in the form attached hereto as Exhibit B, may be submitted by any entity desiring to use CM/ECF for the following limited purposes that do not require the appearance of legal counsel:

a. Modification of Creditor Information

b. Notices of Appearance and Request to Add Party to Matrix

c. Notices of Appearance (for Attorneys representing Creditors)

d. Proofs of Claim

e. Reaffirmation Agreements

f. Reclassifications of Claims

g. Request to Withdraw Document

h. Transfers of Claims

i. Withdrawals of Claims

3. Registration forms may be hand-delivered, mailed, or faxed to the Clerk's Office at 202–354–3128.

4. Upon approval of the submitted registration form, each User will receive training information from the Clerk's Office via e-mail. After successful completion of the Court's training, each User will receive a CM/ECF login and password.

a. Experienced Attorney Users. Attorney Users who received classroom CM/ECF instruction in another federal court are required to complete on-line training exercises in this Court's CM/ECF training database. This on-line training is in lieu of additional classroom training. The exercises will be e-mailed to the attorney after the Clerk's Office receives the attorney's registration form.

b. New Attorney Users. Attorneys who are new to CM/ECF are required to attend one of the Clerk's Office's CM/ECF training sessions. Training dates and times are posted on the Court's web site at: http://www.dcb.uscourts.gov/dcb/ecf-training Attorneys may call the Clerk's Office CM/ECF Help Desk at 202–354–3281 in advance to schedule training, or sign up electronically via the "ECF Training (Sign Up) & Help Desk" link on the court's home page.

5. The Clerk's Office has prepared training materials and User resources, including an Attorney User's Guide and a Creditor/Claimant/Limited–Rights User tutorial. These resources will be updated as necessary and are available on the Court's web site at http://www.dcb.uscourts.gov/dcb/. The Clerk's Office will send an e-mail notice to all Users when materials are updated and posted to the Court's web site or post them in a quarterly newsletter.

6. Upon successful completion of the training, each User will receive a login and password to the Court's live CM/ECF system.

Users may wish to change their Court-issued password. User account information may be modified by using the Account Maintenance option in the CM/ECF Utilities menu. After a User changes his or her password, the Court no longer has knowledge of the User's password. Therefore, if a User changes his or her password and subsequently loses or forgets the new password, the User will need to contact the Clerk's Office for issuance of a new password.

7. If any of the information on the registration form changes (e.g., mailing address, e-mail address, etc.) it is the responsibility of the User to update this information in CM/ECF's "Maintain User Account" menu option. Likewise, when an attorney changes law firms, the attorney must submit an amended registration form and receive a new password from the Clerk's Office. It is the attorney's responsibility to notify the Clerk's Office as soon as such changes occur.

D. Passwords. The login and password required to submit documents to CM/ECF serves as the User's original signature on all electronic documents filed with the Court. The login and password also serves as a signature for purposes of FRBP 9011, other Federal Rules of Bankruptcy Procedure, the local rules of this Court, and any other purpose for which a signature is required in connection with proceedings before this Court.

Electronically filed documents that are required to include a signature of the filer must include a signature block that sets forth the name, address, telephone number, and (in the case of an attorney) the attorney's bar registration number. In addition, the name of the User who is submitting a document (or on whose behalf a Filing Agent is submitting the document) must be preceded by an "/s/" and typed in the space where the signature would otherwise appear. (e.g., "/s/ Jane Doe") Also acceptable is /s/ ________ with a signature block below listing the name of that User as the signatory.

A User may not delegate or share the User's password with associates, paralegals, secretaries, and other individuals. A Full–Rights User may, however, designate in CM/ECF a Filing Agent or Filing Agents authorized to file documents on the User's behalf. The User is solely responsible for <u>all</u> documents filed via the User's password. The User is solely responsible for <u>all</u> documents filed via the User's Filing Agent's password: a filing under a Filing Agent's password is deemed to be a filing by the User. Likewise, if a User has e-mail Notices of Electronic Filing sent to associates, paralegals, secretaries, and other individuals, the User is solely responsible for managing, maintaining, and, when necessary, responding to <u>all</u> Notices of Electronic Filing.

1. Participation in CM/ECF, by receipt of a login and password from the Court, shall constitute a request from the User for electronic service and notice pursuant to FRBP 9036, except as provided by FRBP 9014 (papers commencing a contested matter), which in the case of service upon an individual, requires service by first class mail. For example, a motion for relief from stay must be mailed or hand delivered. Users, by receiving a login and password from the Court, agree to receive notice and service by electronic means. Registration and receipt of a CM/ECF login and password constitutes:

a. waiver of the right to receive notice by first class or certified mail and consent to receive notice electronically; and

b. waiver of the right to service by personal service, first class or certified mail, and consent to electronic service, except with regard to service commencing an adversary proceeding or a contested matter. Waiver of service and notice by first class or certified mail also applies to notice of the entry of an order or judgment under FRBP 9022.

2. The Court may revoke a User's login and password, and, therefore, the User's authority and ability to electronically file documents, for:

a. failure to comply with any provision of the agreement contained in the User's registration form;

b. failure to adequately protect his or her login and password;

c. failure to comply with the provisions of this *Administrative Procedures for Filing, Signing, and Verifying Documents by Electronic Means*;

d. failure to pay fees required for documents filed electronically;

e. failure to maintain active membership in the Federal District and Bankruptcy Courts for the District of Columbia Bar;

f. as a sanction ordered by the Court after notice and opportunity for hearing; or

g. other misuse of CM/ECF.

II. ELECTRONIC FILING AND SERVICE

A. Filing.

1. All petitions, motions, memoranda of law, or other documents, except for creditor matrices, are to be converted into Portable Document Format (PDF) and filed directly into CM/ECF. Creditor matrices are to be filed in a similar manner, but in text (.txt) format.

2. In order for a User to submit filings or documents in paper format, the User must request a judicial waiver via a motion and proposed order to the Court. If paper filings or documents are submitted without a request for waiver, the Clerk's Office may proceed with steps to possibly strike the document.

a. All documents less than 1500 pages must be filed electronically. Exhibits or attachments, including sealed material, that (A) exceed 1500 pages of text; or (B) are illegible when scanned into electronic format, may be filed by hand with the Clerk in original format, and may be viewed in the Clerk's Office during business hours. Documents or items filed pursuant to this subsection shall be served, if it is necessary to serve them, by mail or hand delivery, unless counsel have otherwise agreed. All other exhibits or attachments filed under seal shall be filed in paper form in conformity with the requirements of LCvR 5.1(j). Items not in a format that readily permits electronic filing, such as maps, charts or video tapes, are to be maintained in the possession of the attorney or pro se party responsible for the filing. These items must be made available for a party or the Court, and must be identified as such in a filed Notice with the Clerk.

3. For entities that file more than ten (10) proofs of claims in a calendar year, a judicial waiver will be required to file such documents in paper format. If paper documents are submitted without a waiver, the Clerk's Office may proceed with steps to strike the document.

4. Parties not represented by counsel (other than creditors filing proofs of claims) shall file documents in paper format with the Clerk's Office. These documents will be scanned into PDF format by the Clerk's Office. The Clerk's Office will then docket or file the documents in CM/ECF.

With the exception of the Voluntary Petition, photo identification if applicable, and Statement of Social Security Number (Form B–21), the paper documents filed by pro se filers after being docketed will be discarded without further notice. (In March 2005, the Judicial Conference determined that the electronic record is the official record for all bankruptcy cases.)

5. Because CM/ECF is a "real-time" system, the receipt of filing will show the actual date and time a document was filed in CM/ECF. Documents submitted electronically in CM/ECF outside of normal business hours will be deemed filed on the date and time received. For example, if a document is received at 7:30 P.M. on April 13, 2005, the receipt of filing will show that date and time, and the document will be deemed filed as of that date and time. Deadlines will not change as a result of this policy. The deadline for filing, unless otherwise specifically set, is 11:59:59 P.M. of the due date (Eastern Time).

6. The User must designate a title for the filing by selecting the appropriate event title from the categories provided in CM/ECF. (See also paragraph II.D. of these *Administrative Procedures.*) Once a document is submitted and becomes part of the case docket, corrections to the docket are made only by the Clerk's Office.

7. Users seeking to file emergency motions or other expedited matters shall contact the Clerk's Office by telephone at 202–354–3106 immediately after filing such documents. Failure to notify the Clerk's Office of such filing within one hour of the time stated on the Notice of Electronic Filing may result in denial of the request for expedited or emergency relief, or a delay in action on the motion.

8. Filings relating to matters scheduled for hearing such as motions to continue, proposed consent orders, and similar filings that affect a matter that is scheduled for hearing, must be filed by 4:30 P.M. the day before the scheduled hearing or the matter will remain on the calendar and counsel will be required to attend the hearing. If a User files a document that affects a matter on the calendar after 4:30 P.M. the day before a scheduled hearing, the User shall also notify the Courtroom Deputy of such filing by telephone at 202–354–3148.

B. Signature.

1. The electronic filing of a petition, motion, claim, or other document by a User or by a User's Filing Agent purporting to bear the User's signature shall constitute a submission by that User under FRBP 9011 and other applicable rules.

2. Except as provided in paragraph 3, all documents electronically filed shall either contain a scanned image of any signature or indicate the signature by an "/s/" followed by the name of the signatory typed in the space where the signature would otherwise appear. Also acceptable is /s/ __________ with a signature block below.

3. Except in the case of an affidavit or a document signed under penalty of perjury, a filed document may indicate that a signature has been authorized in writing (with the form of authorization-e.g., "faxed signature" or "e-mail-authorized signature"-indicated on the electronically filed document).

4. When filing a document, the User must have the paper document containing the original signature of each person (other than the User) who signed the document or proof of authorization under paragraph 3 to affix such signature. The user must retain that paper document (and any document that is proof of authorization under paragraph 3 to affix any signature) **for a period of five (5) years from the filing of the document. The document may be retained in either paper or electronically (i.e., a scanned copy of the originally-signed document).** This requirement does not apply to a document filed with a scanned image of the original signature.

C. Service.

1. Whenever a document is filed electronically in accordance with these *Administrative Procedures*, CM/ECF will automatically generate a "Notice of Electronic Filing" ("NEF") at the time of docketing. The NEF will be sent automatically to all entities who are Full–Rights Users in CM/ECF who, in a bankruptcy case, have entered an appearance in the case or have requested to receive notice in the case or, in an adversary proceeding, have entered an appearance.

2. Participation in CM/ECF, by receipt of a login and password provided by the Court, shall constitute (1) a request for notice by electronic means pursuant to FRBP 9036, and (2) consent under FRCP 5(b)(2)(E) to service of papers by electronic means, with the transmission of the notice or paper being complete upon the transmission of the NEF relating to such notice or paper. Users in CM/ECF, by possessing a login and password from the Court, agree to receive such notice and service by electronic means, through NEFs, both from the Court and from other ECF Users. This does not apply to the commencement of an adversary proceeding (which requires service of a summons and complaint under FRBP 7004) or to service commencing a contested matter, or service prior to the filing of Rule 9011(c)(1)(A) motions, but does apply to other motions filed in an adversary proceeding or a contested matter that has already been commenced.

3. When an attorney files a document electronically, CM/ECF automatically e-mails an NEF with the document as a hyperlinked attachment ***if and only if*** the recipient is a Full-Rights User.

4. The attorney User must make service upon all entities not receiving electronic service in accordance with applicable rules.

5. Except when a paper commences an adversary proceeding or a contested matter, an acceptable form of certificate of service is to recite that: (a) "The following entities were served by Notice of Electronic Filing:"; and (b) "The following entities were served by first class mail at the indicated addresses:"

6. When a paper commences an adversary proceeding or a contested matter, electronic service is not adequate service.

7. The return of service on a summons in an adversary proceeding may be filed electronically by using the "summons service executed" event.

D. Title of Docket Entries. Users are responsible for designating appropriate docket entry titles for all filings by using one of the docket event categories prescribed by the Court. If a User is unable to locate an appropriate docket entry title for a filing, the User should call the Clerk's Office CM/ECF Help Desk at 202–354–3281 for clarification and further instruction.

E. Correcting Docket Entries. Once a document is filed in CM/ECF and the NEF is generated, the document becomes part of the case docket. If errors are found in documents filed by Users, the Clerk's Office may issue an Electronic Deficiency Notice ("EDN") in the case. The EDN advises the User of the problem and provides general instructions on how to correct it. Although the EDN is sent to all Users in the case, it is the responsibility of the User who submitted the deficient filing to correct the error within seventy-two (72) hours of the issuance of the EDN. If the User does not respond to the EDN or otherwise correct the filing within 72 hours, the Clerk's Office may strike the document, or set a hearing in which the User must show cause why he or she has failed to comply with the EDN.

Users who repeatedly receive EDNs or who do not respond to EDNs in a timely manner may be required to attend additional training provided by the Clerk's Office.

F. Consequence of Electronic Filing.

i.* Electronic transmission of a filing or document into CM/ECF or the docketing of an event in CM/ECF, consistent with these rules, together with the transmission of a Notice of Electronic Filing from the Court, constitute filing of the document for all purposes of the Federal Rules of Bankruptcy Procedure and the local rules of this Court, and constitute entry of the document on the docket kept by the Clerk of Court under FRBP 5003.

2. Whenever a document has been filed, whether, in paper and subsequently imaged or via an electronically docketed event, the official record is the electronic recording of the document as stored in CM/ECF. The filing party is bound by the document as filed or event docketed.

G. Fees Payable to the Clerk. The payment of fees generated by a filing is the responsibility of the User **at the time of filing, and the User is liable for such fees.** In the case of joint filings, the User who files the document is responsible for paying the fee at the time of filing. In CM/ECF, all filing fees must be paid electronically with a valid credit card by the User. All required fees must be paid via valid credit card within twenty-four (24) hours of the time of filing. Failure to make payment within this time period will result in the User being "locked out" of CM/ECF until the fee is paid. If fees are not received in a timely manner, steps may be taken to either reject the document or dismiss the case.

Users who are locked out of CM/ECF for failure to pay required fees at the time of filing may file subsequent documents in paper pursuant to paragraph II. A.2 of these *Administrative Procedures.*

If an attorney User encounters a problem with the CM/ECF payment screen or is not prompted to pay a filing fee that is due, the User must call the Clerk's Office CM/ECF Help Desk at 202–354–3128. If a filing fee error occurs with a credit card payment the User may petition the court for a refund.

H. System Failure. When a document must be filed or an event must be docketed immediately during normal business hours, but electronic filing cannot be accomplished because of a CM/ECF system failure, the filing party shall, after making at least two attempts to file electronically, contact the Clerk's Office at **202–354–3281** to confirm that CM/ECF is not accessible. If it is confirmed that CM/ECF is not accessible, or, if CM/ECF cannot be accessed due to a system failure during non-business hours, the filing or document shall be sent as an attachment in PDF format via e-mail to the following address: Michael_Wint@dcb.uscourts.gov with a carbon copy to Elizabeth_Nelson@dcb.uscourts.gov.

The User must file with the document an affidavit stating the reason(s) why the document is being filed via e-mail, demonstrating compliance with the prerequisites of these *Administrative Procedures.* Users who experience a CM/ECF system failure and file documents via e-mail must call the Clerk's Office prior to 10:00 a.m. the next business day to advise that a document has been filed via e-mail. The Clerk's Office will download and file the PDF document, which will be deemed filed on the date and time of the e mail transmission. Nothing contained in this paragraph is intended to alter rights contained elsewhere in these *Administrative Procedures* or in local or federal rules.

I. Exhibits.

1. *Exhibits to Motions/Pleadings:* Exhibits, including but not limited to leases, notes, and the like, shall be filed in electronic form.

2. *Trial Exhibits:* Three copies (the original plus two photocopies for the court, plus additional copies for opposing counsel and any witnesses) of trial exhibits must be provided in paper format to the courtroom deputy prior to any hearing. Pursuant to the judge's ruling, the paper copies may be marked as received into evidence and docketed to the file as an attachment to the case hearing summary. Trial exhibits over 50 pages will not be scanned by the Court. Exhibits over 50 pages shall be presented to the courtroom deputy in CD format in addition to paper copies. Exhibits may be filed electronically in PDF format as part of a pre-trial statement or they may be filed electronically and linked to the pre-trial statement. Paper exhibits will be marked as received into evidence.

3. *Exhibits to Proofs of Claim:* Exhibits in support of a proof of claim shall be filed electronically whenever possible and shall be docketed as one event with the proof of claim. The exhibits should be scanned and filed in PDF format together with the proof of claim.

J. Appeals. As with other electronically filed documents, Users are **no longer** required to file paper copies or courtesy copies of the Notice of Appeal with the Clerk's Office.

Pursuant to FRBP 8006, when filing the Designation of Record, Users must provide a list of documents, by docket entry number, to be included in the Designation of Records.

Pursuant to FRBP 8004, the Clerk's Office will mail a paper copy of the Notice of Appeal to any and all parties to the appeal as well as to the U. S. Trustee.

III. PAPER FILING OF SEALED DOCUMENTS

Notwithstanding Local Bankruptcy Rule 5005–1(c), a motion to file documents under seal shall be filed electronically without attaching the documents that are the subject of the motion. Contemporaneously with filing the motion to file documents under seal, the User shall conventionally file, in paper format, the documents sought to be placed under seal with the Court for its review. If the motion to file under seal is granted, the related documents will be maintained by the Clerk's Office under seal until further order.

The motion to file documents under seal should include a date or deadline for the unsealing of the documents.

IV. ORDERS

A. Proposed Orders.

1. *Requirement to Both Docket and Upload Proposed Orders.* In CM/ECF, Users must file and docket all proposed orders as attachments to the related filings, or, if the proposed order is filed later, must file and docket the proposed order with a link to the filing to which it relates. **Additionally,** Users must upload all proposed orders into CM/ECF for the Court's use in the Electronic Order Processing System ("E–Orders"). Proposed orders in bankruptcy cases must be uploaded via the CM/ECF Bankruptcy menu. Likewise, proposed orders in adversary cases must be uploaded via the CM/ECF Adversary menu.

ii.** *Format of Proposed Orders.*

a. All proposed orders must have a four (4) inch margin on the top of the first page.

b. The proposed order must be in PDF format.

B. Consent Orders/Reaffirmation Agreements/Court–Directed Orders. A User seeking to file a consent order or reaffirmation agreement shall conform to the standards set forth in Section II.B. regarding signatures.

Unless otherwise ordered by the Court, the submission of consent orders and court-directed orders (i.e., proposed orders directed by the Court to be submitted following a hearing or trial) shall be accomplished by electronic means by using one of the following two CM/ECF docketing events located in the "Bankruptcy or Adversary" and "Other or Miscellaneous" menus:

1. Proposed Consent Order;

2. Proposed Order (Corrections, Deficiencies, OTBS, etc.).

C. Notice of Orders and Judgments by the Court.

1. Immediately upon the entry of an order or judgment, CM/ECF will automatically generate to all Users in the case, an electronic NEF. Electronic transmission of the NEF constitutes the notice required by FRBP 9022. In accordance with the Federal Rules of Bankruptcy Procedure, the Clerk will provide paper notice to all parties who are not Users.

2. All orders signed electronically (i.e., utilizing the Judge's electronic signature and seal of the court) shall have the same force and effect as conventionally signed orders (i.e., paper orders with the Judge's signature signed by hand).

V. PUBLIC ACCESS TO CM/ECF DOCKETS

A. Internet Access. Documents filed in CM/ECF are not viewable via the Internet without a Public Access to Court Electronic Records (PACER) login and password. A PACER login and password can be secured by contacting the PACER Service Center to establish an account. Registration may be made online at http://pacer.psc.uscourts.gov or by calling the PACER Service Center at 800–676–6856.

PACER allows **only** for the **viewing** of docket sheets and documents. Upon receipt of the NEF, Users are allowed one free viewing of the document filed and thereafter must pay for all subsequent viewings. Documents **cannot** be filed electronically in or via PACER, they may be viewed only. Likewise documents **cannot** be viewed in CM/ECF, they may be filed only. Thus, PACER is for viewing docket sheets and documents, while CM/ECF is for filing documents.

Charges required by the Judicial Conference of the United States, as set out in 28 U.S.C. § 1930, for the usage of the electronic access to the Court's records, are assessed in accordance with the fees and procedures established by the Administrative Office of the United States Courts.

B. Public Access at the Court. The public will have electronic access at the Clerk's Office during regular business hours for viewing the docket sheet and documents filed in CM/ECF. Filings and documents may be printed in the Clerk's Office at a cost of ten cents ($.10) per page.

C. Privacy Provisions. In accordance with the E–Government Act of 2002 and its own policy regarding privacy and public access, the Judicial Conference of the United States (Judicial Conference), at its September 2003 session, promulgated Official Bankruptcy Form 21 (Form B 21), Statement of Social Security Number(s). This form has been created to satisfy the requirement set forth in FRBP 1007(f) that a debtor must submit a verified statement of his or her social security number along with the debtor's petition. All debtors, whether filing electronically (via counsel) or in paper, must file Form B 21.

For additional information regarding privacy provisions, please see the *Court's Rules and Policies Re Protecting Data Identifiers in Filed Documents and Transcripts* on the Court's website at: http://www.dcb.uscourts.gov/dcb/sit es/www.dcb.uscourts.gov.dcb/files/privacy2.pdf

Form B 21 is a "restricted" filing or event in the Court's CM/ECF system; therefore, only court personnel are able to view the PDF document. Neither the public nor any User is able to access or view Form B 21 in the Court's CM/ECF system.

1. *Debtors Represented by Attorney Users.* The attorney User must file electronically Form B 21 in CM/ECF. The filing attorney shall retain the signed original Form B 21 for five (5) years from the filing of the document.

2. *Pro Se Filers.* Pro se and pro bono filers shall submit a signed, original Form B 21, in paper format, to the Clerk's Office at the same time the voluntary petition is filed. The Clerk's Office will scan and file Form B 21, and retain the original document for five (5) years from the filing of the document.

D. Antiviral Software. All Users who retrieve and effect filings must have purchased, installed, utilized, and daily updated antiviral software on all computers used to access CM/ECF.

E. Conventional Paper Copies and Certified Copies. Conventional Paper and certified copies of electronically filed documents may be purchased at the Clerk's Office during regular business hours. The fee for copying and certification will be in accordance with the provisions of 28 U.S.C. § 1930.

EXHIBIT A

UNITED STATES BANKRUPTCY COURT FOR THE DISTRICT OF COLUMBIA

ELECTRONIC CASE FILING (ECF) SYSTEM

ATTORNEY/FULL–RIGHTS USER
REGISTRATION FORM

This form shall be used to register for an account on the U.S. Bankruptcy Court's Electronic Case Filing (ECF) System (hereafter "ECF"). Full–Rights Users will have privileges both to submit documents electronically, and to view and retrieve docket sheets and documents for all cases in the District of Columbia ECF system. (NOTE: a PACER account is necessary to view and retrieve docket sheets and documents. You may register for a PACER account either online at http://pacer.psc.uscourts.gov/ or by calling 1–800–676–6856.)

The following information is required for ECF registration:

First/Middle/Last Name: ____________________

Firm Name: ____________________

Mailing Address: ____________________

____

Attorney Phone Number: ________________

E–Mail Address: ________________

U.S. District Court for the District of Columbia Bar ID#:

____

Currently E–File in the Following Jurisdictions: ______

Name of Staff Member(s) Who Will be Authorized to E–File on Behalf of Attorney

____

Attorney Contact Person(s) and Phone Number(s) to be used when Clerk's Office Has Questions re: E–Filed Pleadings:

____

By submitting this registration form the applicant agrees to adhere to the Court's Administrative Order Relating to Electronic Case Filing, including any amendments thereto as may be made from time to time, and the following rules:

1. This access is for use only in ECF cases filed in the U.S. Bankruptcy Court for the District of Columbia. It may be used to file and view electronic documents, docket sheets, and reports. NOTE: a PACER account is necessary to view and retrieve docket sheets and documents. (see above for registration information).
2. Pursuant to Federal Rule of Bankruptcy Procedure 9011, every pleading, motion, and other paper (except lists, schedules, statements or amendments thereto) shall be signed by at least one attorney of record or, if the party is not represented by an attorney, all papers shall be signed by the party. An attorney's/full-rights user's password issued by the court combined with the User's identification, serves as and constitutes the attorney's/full-rights user's signature. Therefore, an attorney/full-rights user must protect and secure the password issued by the Court. If there is any reason to suspect the password has been compromised in any way, it is the duty and responsibility of the attorney/full-rights user to immediately notify the Court. This would include the resignation or reassignment of the person with authority to use the password. The Court will immediately delete that password from ECF and issue a new password.
3. An attorney's/full-rights user's registration will not waive paper service of a summons and complaint, subpoena, or other judicial process; submit the client to the jurisdiction of the Court; or operate as a consent to accept service of pleadings, documents, and orders in actions in which such attorney/full-rights user has not entered an appearance. An attorney's/full-rights user's registration will constitute a waiver in law only of paper service of other non-process pleadings, documents, and orders in the case. The attorney/full-rights user agrees to accept, on behalf of the client, service of notice of the electronic filing by hand, facsimile, or authorized e-mail.
4. To file documents electronically in the U. S. Bankruptcy Court for the District of Columbia, an attorney must:

a) be an active member of the bar of the U. S. District Court for the District of Columbia, or

b) be an attorney who is a member in good standing of the bar of any United States Court or of the highest court of any State who is representing the attorney's client without compensation.

But, if the attorney is an e-filer pursuant to paragraph (b), that attorney is restricted to e-filing only in cases in which the attorney files a certificate that he is providing representation without compensation.

5. Attorneys/full-rights users are required to pay ALL filing fees via an Internet credit card at the time of filing. If you have any questions regarding the payment of a fee, you MUST contact the Court's Finance Department at 202–354–3103 or the CM/ECF Help Desk at 202–354–3281 **BEFORE** filing the pleading.

6. By e-filing a document, the User certifies that the User has complied with the requirement that if the document purports via the use of "/s/" to have been signed by someone other than the User, then the User has a document (in paper or scanned electronic form) bearing the original signature. Attorneys/full-rights users are required to retain the original signed document of all e-filed pleadings for a period of five (5) years in either paper or electronically.

____

Applicant Signature Date

Please return this form to:

CM/ECF Help Desk; U.S. Bankruptcy Court for the District of Columbia;
Room 1225; 333 Constitution Avenue, NW; Washington, DC 20001
or FAX to: 202–354–3128
Our CM/ECF Help Desk staff are available at 202–354–3281 to answer questions.

EXHIBIT B
UNITED STATES BANKRUPTCY COURT FOR THE DISTRICT OF COLUMBIA
ELECTRONIC CASE FILING (ECF) SYSTEM
LIMITED–RIGHTS USER REGISTRATION FORM

This form shall be used to register for an account as a Limited–Rights User ("User") in the U.S. Bankruptcy Court's Electronic Case Filing ("ECF") System. Users will have privileges both to submit documents electronically, and to view and retrieve docket sheets and documents for all cases in the District of Columbia ECF system. (**Note**: a PACER account is necessary to view and retrieve docket sheets and documents. You may register for a PACER account either online at http://pacer.psc.uscourts.gov/ or by calling 1–800–676–6856.)

Registering User's Name: ____________________
[Name of individual registering as a User]

Business/Firm Name: ____________________
[Name of business/firm on whose behalf User is authorized to act]

Business/Firm Address: ____________________
City: ____________ **State:** ________ **Zip:** ____
Phone: ____________ **Fax:** ____________

E–Mail Address: ____________________
Currently E–File in the Following Jurisdictions:
____

Bar Identification Number (if applicable): ________ **State of:** ____________

1. I affirm that I am authorized to prepare and file Proofs of Claim, Requests for Notice, Reaffirmation Agreements, Assignments of Claims and other similar creditor papers on behalf of the above named business/firm.
2. The above-named business/firm, through its authorized officers, directors and agents, understands that the use of its Limited–Rights User password to file a document in a bankruptcy case or proceeding in the United States Bankruptcy Court for the District of Columbia will constitute an act on behalf of the above-named business/firm under the United States Code, the Federal Rules of Bankruptcy Procedure, and any applicable nonbankruptcy law. For example, the User's signature on the document by way of the password constituting a signing of the document on behalf of the business/firm under Federal Rule of Bankruptcy Procedure 9011.
3. The above-named business/firm, through its authorized officers, directors and agents, understands that it is its responsibility to protect and secure the confidentiality of its password. If the above-named business/firm believes that its password has been compromised, then it is the responsibility of the above-named business/firm, through its authorized officers, directors and agents, to notify the Court in writing, immediately.
4. The registering User understands that it is the User's responsibility to notify the Court, immediately, of any change in my address, telephone number, fax number, or e-mail address.
5. Registration as a User constitutes waiver of the above-named business/firm's right, that would otherwise arise from a filing made by the User using the User's password to receive notice by first class mail (including a right arising from such filing to notice of entry of an order or judgment), and constitutes consent to receive such notice electronically instead. This waiver does not apply to service of a summons and complaint in an adversary proceeding under F.R. Bankr. P. 7004 or to service of papers commencing a contested matter (e.g., an objection to a proof of claim).
6. By affixing a User's electronic signature to a document and e-filing that document with the Court, the User certifies that the User has on file in the User's office the original signature of each other party whose signature appears on the document via the use of "/s/" (or proof that the signature was authorized, in writing, to be affixed to the document). The User is required to retain the original signed document (or the proof of written authorization to sign) of all e-filed documents for a period of five (5) years in either paper or electronically.
7. By submitting this registration form the applicant agrees to adhere to the Court's Administrative Order Relating to Electronic Case Filing, including any amendments thereto as may be made from time to time.
8. I, ____________________, hereby state that I am the
Name of registering User

____________________ of ____________________
Title **Name of Business/Firm**

and am authorized to enter into this Limited–Rights User Registration on its behalf.

____________________ ____________
Signature of Individual Signing on Behalf of Business **Date**

Send Electronic Notices to these Additional E-mail Addresses:

____

I would like to receive electronic notification in the following cases (check as applicable):

____All cases and proceedings in which I am entitled to notice.

____The following additional cases or adversary proceedings (notification of all docket activity in each) (list case numbers):

Send Electronic Notice (check one): ___ of Each Filing or ___ as an End of Day Summary

Send Electronic Notices in the following format (check one):

____HTML or Netscape, ISP mail service (e.g. AOL, Hotmail, Yahoo, etc.)

____Text for cc:mail; Groupwise, Outlook, Outlook Express, Other (please list)

Please return this form to:

CM/ECF Help Desk
U.S. Bankruptcy Court for the District of Columbia
Room 1225
333 Constitution Avenue, NW
Washington, DC 20001

or FAX to: 202–354–3128

Our CM/ECF Help Desk staff are available at 202–354–3281 to answer questions.

[Amended effective July 7, 2011.]

* So in original.

** So in original.

RULES AND POLICIES RE PROTECTING PERSONAL DATA IDENTIFIERS IN FILED DOCUMENTS AND TRANSCRIPTS

I. YOUR OBLIGATION TO PROTECT PERSONAL DATA IDENTIFIERS WHEN YOU FILE A DOCUMENT

Under Rule 9037 of the Federal Rules of Bankruptcy Procedure, when you make a filing in a case, and that filing would otherwise show any of the following personal data identifiers:

- an individual's:
  - ▶ social-security number,
  - ▶ taxpayer-identification number, or
  - ▶ birth date;
- the name of an individual, other than the debtor, known to be and identified as a minor, or
- a financial-account number,

you are generally required to make the filing include only:

(1) the last four digits of the social-security number and taxpayer-identification number;

(2) the year of the individual's birth;

(3) the minor's initials; and

(4) the last four digits of the financial-account number.

Read Rule 9037 for exceptions to this requirement.

II. PROTECTING PERSONAL DATA IDENTIFIERS IN COURTROOM PROCEEDINGS

Trials and hearings in bankruptcy cases (unless sealed) are open to the public, and exhibits received into evidence may be examined by the public. A cumbersome procedure exists to redact personal data identifiers listed in Rule 9037(a) from any transcript of a hearing or trial before the transcript is accessible electronically on the internet, and a motion for a protective order can be filed with respect to an exhibit received into evidence that contained any personal data identifier. But the better course is to avoid unnecessarily placing personal data identifiers in the court record in the first place.

Unless necessary, don't:

- ask a witness for,
- place in evidence a document that reveals, or
- make statements that reveal

any personal data identifiers:

- any individual's birth date (versus year of birth);
- more than the last four numbers of an individual's social security (or taxpayer-identification) number;
- the name of any individual identified as a minor (instead of using initials); or
- more than the last four digits of a financial account number.

III. POLICY RE REDACTING PERSONAL IDENTIFIERS FROM TRANSCRIPTS

Responsibility to Review Transcript for Personal Data Identifiers. Prior to being made electronically available, transcripts must conform to Fed. R. Bankr. P. 9037(a). Once a prepared transcript is delivered to the clerk's office, the attorneys in the case are (or, where there is a self-represented party, the party is) responsible for reviewing it for the personal data identifiers required by Rule 9037(a) to be redacted, and providing the court reporter or transcriber with a statement of the redactions to be made to comply with the rules.

Seven-Day Deadline After Filing of the Transcript to Give Notice of Intent to Direct Redactions. Within seven calendar days of the delivery by the court reporter or transcriber of the official transcript to the clerk's office, each attorney must inform the court, by filing a Notice of Intent to Request Redaction with the clerk and serve a copy of the Notice on the transcriber. If no such Notice is filed within the allotted time, the court will assume redaction of personal data identifiers from the transcript is not necessary.

Twenty-one-Day Deadline to Submit List of Necessary Redactions. A party is to submit to the court reporter or transcriber, within 21 calendar days of the transcript's delivery to the clerk, or longer if a court so orders, a statement indicating where the personal data identifiers to be redacted appear in the transcript. The court reporter or transcriber must redact the identifiers as directed by the party. These procedures are limited to the redaction of the specific personal data identifiers listed in the rules. During the 21-day period, or longer if the court so orders, an attorney may move the court for additional redactions to the transcript.

Electronic Posting of Transcript. The transcript will not be made available on the internet until the time for directing redactions has expired and the court has acted on any motion for additional time to be allowed to direct redactions. The court reporter or transcriber must, within 31 calendar days of the delivery of the transcript to the clerk of court, or longer if the court so orders, perform the requested redactions, and file a redacted version of the transcript with the clerk of court. The original unredacted electronic transcript will be retained by the clerk of court.

Effect of Policy. Nothing in this policy creates a private right of action. Nothing in this policy changes any rules or policies with respect to sealing or redaction of court records for any other purpose.

[May 29, 2009.]

*

RULES OF PROCEDURE OF THE JUDICIAL PANEL ON MULTIDISTRICT LITIGATION

Renumbered and Amended Effective November 2, 1998

Including Amendments Effective July 6, 2011

I. RULES FOR MULTIDISTRICT LITIGATION UNDER 28 U.S.C. § 1407

RULE 1.1. DEFINITIONS

(a) "Panel" means the members of the United States Judicial Panel on Multidistrict Litigation appointed by the Chief Justice of the United States pursuant to 28 U.S.C. § 1407.

(b) "Chair" means the Chair of the Panel appointed by the Chief Justice of the United States pursuant to Section 1407, or the member of the Panel properly designated to act as Chair.

(c) "Clerk of the Panel" means the official that the Panel appoints to that position. The Clerk of the Panel shall perform such duties that the Panel or the Panel Executive delegates.

(d) "Electronic Case Filing (ECF)" refers to the Panel's automated system that receives and stores documents filed in electronic form. All attorneys filing pleadings with the Panel must do so using ECF. All pro se individuals are non-ECF users, unless the Panel orders otherwise.

(e) "MDL" means a multidistrict litigation docket which the Panel is either considering or has created by transferring cases to a transferee district for coordinated or consolidated pretrial proceedings pursuant to Section 1407.

(f) "Panel Executive" means the official appointed to act as the Panel's Chief Executive and Legal Officer. The Panel Executive may appoint, with the approval of the Panel, necessary deputies, clerical assistants and other employees to perform or assist in the performance of the duties of the Panel Executive. The Panel Executive, with the approval of the Panel, may make such delegations of authority as are necessary for the Panel's efficient operation.

(g) "Pleadings" means all papers, motions, responses, or replies of any kind filed with the Panel, including exhibits attached thereto, as well as all orders and notices that the Panel issues.

(h) "Tag-along action" refers to a civil action pending in a district court which involves common questions of fact with either (1) actions on a pending motion to transfer to create an MDL or (2) actions previously transferred to an existing MDL, and which the Panel would consider transferring under Section 1407.

(i) "Transferee district" is the federal district court to which the Panel transfers an action pursuant to Section 1407, for inclusion in an MDL.

(j) "Transferor district" is the federal district court where an action was pending prior to its transfer pursuant to Section 1407, for inclusion in an MDL, and where the Panel may remand that action at or before the conclusion of pretrial proceedings.

[Former Rule 1 adopted May 3, 1993, effective July 1, 1993. Renumbered Rule 1.1 September 1, 1998, effective November 2, 1998. Amended September 8, 2010, effective October 4, 2010.]

RULE 2.1. RULES AND PRACTICE

(a) Customary Practice. The Panel's customary practice shall govern, unless otherwise fixed by statute or these Rules.

(b) Failure to Comply With Rules. When a pleading does not comply with these Rules, the Clerk of the Panel may advise counsel of the deficiencies and set a date for full compliance. If counsel does not fully comply within the established time, the Clerk of the Panel shall file the non-complying pleading, but the Chair may thereafter order it stricken.

(c) Admission to Practice Before the Panel. Every member in good standing of the Bar of any district court of the United States is entitled to practice before the Panel, provided, however, that he or she has established and maintains a CM/ECF account with any United States federal court. Any attorney of record in any action transferred under Section 1407 may continue to represent his or her client in any district court of the United States to which such action is transferred. Parties are not required to obtain local counsel.

(d) Pendency of Motion or Conditional Order. The pendency of a motion, order to show cause, conditional transfer order or conditional remand order before the Panel pursuant to 28 U.S.C. § 1407 does not affect or suspend orders and pretrial proceedings in any pending federal district court action and does not limit the pretrial jurisdiction of that court. An order to transfer or remand pursuant to 28 U.S.C. § 1407 shall be effective only upon its filing with the clerk of the transferee district court.

(e) Reassignment. If for any reason the transferee judge is unable to continue those responsibilities, the Panel shall make the reassignment of a new transferee judge.

[Former Rule 5 adopted May 3, 1993, effective July 1, 1993. Renumbered Rule 1.2 September 1, 1998, effective November 2, 1998. Former Rule 4 adopted May 3, 1993, effective July 1, 1993. Renumbered Rule 1.3 and amended September 1, 1998, effective November 2, 1998. Former Rule 6 adopted May 3, 1993, effective July 1, 1993. Renumbered Rule 1.4 September 1, 1998, effective November 2, 1998. Former Rule 18 adopted May 3, 1993, effective July 1, 1993. Renumbered Rule 1.5 September 1, 1998, effective November 2, 1998. Former Rules 1.2, 1.3, 1.4, and 1.5 redesignated and amended September 8, 2010, effective October 4, 2010.]

RULE 3.1. ELECTRONIC RECORDS AND FILES; COPY FEES

(a) Electronic Record. Effective October 4, 2010, the official Panel record shall be the electronic file maintained on the Panel's servers. This record includes, but is not limited to, Panel pleadings, documents filed in paper and then scanned and made part of the electronic record, and Panel orders and notices filed. The official record also includes any documents or exhibits that may be impractical to scan. These documents and exhibits shall be kept in the Panel offices.

(b) Maintaining Records. Records and files generated prior to October 4, 2010, may be (i) maintained at the Panel offices, (ii) temporarily or permanently removed to such places at such times as the Clerk of the Panel or the Chair shall direct, or (iii) transferred whenever appropriate to the Federal Records Center.

(c) Fees. The Clerk of the Panel may charge fees for duplicating records and files, as prescribed by the Judicial Conference of the United States.

[Former Rule 2 adopted May 3, 1993, effective July 1, 1993. Renumbered Rule 5.1 and amended September 1, 1998, effective November 2, 1998. Former Rule 5.1 redesignated and amended September 8, 2010, effective October 4, 2010.]

RULE 3.2. ECF USERS: FILING REQUIREMENTS

(a) Form of Pleadings. This Rule applies to pleadings that ECF users file with the Panel.

(i) Each pleading shall bear the heading "Before the United States Judicial Panel on Multidistrict Litigation," the identification "MDL No. ___" and the descriptive title designated by the Panel. If the Panel has not yet designated a title, counsel shall use an appropriate description.

(ii) The final page of each pleading shall contain the name, address, telephone number, fax number and email address of the attorney or party designated to receive service of pleadings in the case, and the name of each party represented.

(iii) Each brief submitted with a motion and any response to it shall not exceed 20 pages, exclusive of exhibits. Each reply shall not exceed 10 pages and shall address arguments raised in the response(s). Absent exceptional circumstances and those set forth in Rule 6.1(d), the Panel will not grant motions to exceed page limits.

(iv) Each pleading shall be typed in size 12 point font (for both text and footnotes), double spaced (text only), in a letter size document (8 ½ × 11 inch) with sequentially numbered pages.

(v) Each exhibit shall be separately numbered and clearly identified.

(vi) Proposed Panel orders shall not be submitted.

(b) Place of Filing. Counsel shall sign and verify all pleadings electronically in accordance with these Rules and the Panel's Administrative Policies and Procedures for Electronic Case Filing found at www.jpml.uscourts.gov. A pleading filed electronically constitutes a written document for the purpose of these Rules and the Federal Rules of Civil Procedure and is deemed the electronically signed original thereof. All pleadings, except by pro se litigants, shall conform with this Rule beginning on October 4, 2010.

(i)* Pleadings shall not be transmitted directly to any Panel member.

(c) Attorney Registration. Only attorneys identified, or to be identified, pursuant to Rule 4.1, shall file pleadings. Each of these attorneys must register as a Panel CM/ECF user through www.jpml.uscourts.gov. Registration/possession of a CM/ECF account with any United States federal court shall be deemed consent to receive electronic service of all Panel orders and notices as well as electronic service of pleadings from other parties before the Panel.

(d) Courtesy Copy of Specified Pleadings. Counsel shall serve the Clerk of the Panel, for delivery within 1 business day of filing, with a courtesy paper copy of any of the following pleadings: (i) a motion to transfer and its supporting brief; (ii) a response to a show cause order; (iii) a motion to vacate a conditional transfer order or a conditional remand order; (iv) any response, reply, supplemental information or interested party response related to the pleadings listed in (i), (ii) and (iii); and (v) a corporate disclosure statement. No courtesy copies of any other pleadings are required. Courtesy copies of pleadings totaling 10 pages or less (including any attachments) may be faxed to the Panel. The courtesy copy shall include all exhibits, shall be clearly marked "Courtesy Copy—Do Not File," shall contain the CM/ECF pleading number (if known), and shall be mailed or delivered to:

Clerk of the Panel
United States Judicial Panel on Multidistrict Litigation
Thurgood Marshall Federal Judiciary Building
One Columbus Circle, NE,
Room G–255, North Lobby
Washington, DC 20002–8041

(e) Privacy Protections. The privacy protections contained in Rule 5.2 of the Federal Rules of Civil Procedure shall apply to all Panel filings.

[Former Rule 3 adopted May 3, 1993, effective July 1, 1993. Renumbered Rule 5.11 and amended September 1, 1998, effective November 2, 1998; renumbered Rule 5.1.1 and amended March 25, 2010, effective April 1, 2010. Former Rule 7 adopted May 3, 1993, effective July 1, 1993. Renumbered Rule 5.12 and amended September 1, 1998, effective November 2, 1998. Amended April 2, 2001, effective April 2, 2001; paragraph (a) suspended in part by Order filed April 19, 2005; renumbered Rule 5.1.2 and amended March 25, 2010, effective April 1, 2010. Former Rule 9 adopted May 3, 1993, effective July 1, 1993. Renumbered Rule 7.1 and amended September 1, 1998, effective November 2, 1998. Amended April 2, 2001, effective April 2, 2001. Former Rules 5.1.1, 5.1.2, and 7.1 redesignated in part and amended September 8, 2010, effective October 4, 2010. Amended effective July 6, 2011.]

* So in original. No subdivision (ii) promulgated.

RULE 3.3. NON–ECF USERS: FILING REQUIREMENTS

(a) Definition of Non–ECF Users. Non–ECF users are all pro se individuals, unless the Panel orders otherwise. This Rule shall apply to all motions, responses and replies that non-ECF users file with the Panel.

(b) Form of Pleadings. Unless otherwise set forth in this Rule, the provisions of Rule 3.2 shall apply to non-ECF users.

(i) Each pleading shall be flat and unfolded; plainly written or typed in size 12 point font (for both text and footnotes), double spaced (text only), and printed single-sided on letter size (8 ½ × 11 inch) white paper with sequentially numbered pages; and fastened at the top-left corner without side binding or front or back covers.

(ii) Each exhibit shall be separately numbered and clearly identified. Any exhibits exceeding a cumulative total of 50 pages shall be bound separately.

(c) Place of Filing. File an original and one copy of all pleadings with the Clerk of the Panel by mailing or delivering to:

Clerk of the Panel
United States Judicial Panel on Multidistrict Litigation
Thurgood Marshall Federal Judiciary Building
One Columbus Circle, NE,
Room G–255, North Lobby
Washington, DC 20002–8041

(i) Pleadings not exceeding a total of 10 pages, including exhibits, may be faxed to the Panel office.

(ii) The Clerk of the Panel shall endorse the date for filing on all pleadings submitted for filing.

[Former Rule 3 adopted May 3, 1993, effective July 1, 1993. Renumbered Rule 5.11 and amended September 1, 1998, effective November 2, 1998; renumbered Rule 5.1.1 and amended March 25, 2010, effective April 1, 2010. Former Rule 7 adopted May 3, 1993, effective July 1, 1993. Renumbered Rule 5.12 and amended September 1, 1998, effective November 2, 1998. Amended April 2, 2001, effective April 2, 2001; paragraph (a) suspended in part by Order filed April 19, 2005; renumbered Rule 5.1.2 and amended March 25, 2010, effective April 1, 2010. Former Rule 9 adopted May 3, 1993, effective July 1, 1993. Renumbered Rule 7.1 and amended September 1, 1998, effective November 2, 1998. Amended April 2, 2001, effective April 2, 2001. Former Rules 5.1.1, 5.1.2, and 7.1 redesignated in part and amended September 8, 2010, effective October 4, 2010.]

RULE 4.1. SERVICE OF PLEADINGS

(a) Proof of Service. The Panel's notice of electronic filing shall constitute service of pleadings. Registration/possession by counsel of a CM/ECF account with any United States federal court shall be deemed consent to receive electronic service of all pleadings. All pleadings shall contain a proof of service on all other parties in all involved actions. The proof of service shall indicate the name and manner of service. If a party is not represented by counsel, the proof of service shall indicate the name of the party and the party's last known address. The proof of service shall indicate why any person named as a party in a constituent complaint was not served with the Section 1407 pleading.

(b) Service Upon Transferor Court. The proof of service pertaining to motions for a transfer or remand pursuant to 28 U.S.C. § 1407 shall certify that counsel has transmitted a copy of the motion for filing to the clerk of each district court where an affected action is pending.

(c) Notice of Appearance. Within 14 days after the issuance of a (i) notice of filing of a motion to initiate transfer under Rule 6.2, (ii) notice of filed opposition to a CTO under Rule 7.1, (iii) a show cause order under Rules* 8.1, (iv) notice of filed opposition to a CRO under Rule 10.2, or (v) notice of filing of a motion to remand under Rule 10.3, each party or designated attorney as required hereinafter shall file a Notice of Appearance notifying the Clerk of the Panel of the name, address and email address of the attorney designated to file and receive service of all pleadings. Each party shall designate only one attorney. Any party not represented by counsel shall be served by mailing such pleadings to the party's last known address. Except in extraordinary circumstances, the Panel will not grant requests for an extension of time to file the Notice of Appearance.

(d) Liaison Counsel. If the transferee district court appoints liaison counsel, this Rule shall be satisfied by serving each party in each affected action and all liaison counsel. Liaison counsel shall receive copies of all Panel orders concerning their particular litigation and shall be responsible for distribution to the parties for whom he or she serves as liaison counsel.

[Former Rule 8 adopted May 3, 1993, effective July 1, 1993. Renumbered Rule 5.2 and amended September 1, 1998, effective November 2, 1998; March 26, 2009, effective December 1, 2009. Former Rule 5.2 redesignated and amended September 8, 2010, effective October 4, 2010. Technical revisions effective July 6, 2011.]

* So in original.

RULE 5.1. CORPORATE DISCLOSURE STATEMENT

(a) Requirements. A nongovernmental corporate party must file a disclosure statement that: (1) identifies any parent corporation and any publicly held corporation owning 10% or more of its stock; or (2) states that there is no such corporation.

(b) Deadline. A party shall file the corporate disclosure statement within 14 days after issuance of a notice of the filing of a motion to transfer or remand, an order to show cause, or a motion to vacate a conditional transfer order or a conditional remand order.

(c) Updating. Each party must update its corporate disclosure statement to reflect any change in the information therein (i) until the matter before the Panel is decided, and (ii) within 14 days after issuance of a notice of the filing of any subsequent motion to transfer or remand, order to show cause, or motion to vacate a conditional transfer order or a conditional remand order in that docket.

[Former Rule 2 adopted May 3, 1993, effective July 1, 1993. Renumbered Rule 5.1 and amended September 1, 1998, effective November 2, 1998. Former Rule 5.3 redesignated and amended September 8, 2010, effective October 4, 2010. Amended effective July 6, 2011.]

RULE 5.1.3. FILING OF PAPERS: COMPUTER GENERATED DISK REQUIRED [DELETED SEPT. 8, 2010, EFF. OCT. 4, 2010

[Added May 22, 2000, effective June 1, 2000. And amended July 30, 2007, effective July 30, 2007; renumbered Rule 5.1.3 and amended March 25, 2010, effective April 1, 2010. Deleted September 8, 2010, effective October 4, 2010.]

RULE 6.1. MOTION PRACTICE

(a) Application. This Rule governs all motions requesting Panel action generally. More specific provisions may apply to motions to transfer (Rule 6.2), miscellaneous motions (Rule 6.3), conditional transfer orders (Rule 7.1), show cause orders (Rule 8.1), conditional remand orders (Rule 10.2) and motions to remand (Rule 10.3).

(b) Form of Motions. All motions shall briefly describe the action or relief sought and shall include:

(i) a brief which concisely states the background of the litigation and movant's factual and legal contentions;

(ii) a numbered schedule providing

(A) the complete name of each action involved, listing the full name of each party included as such on the district court's docket sheet, not shortened by the use of references such as "et al." or "etc.";

(B) the district court and division where each action is pending;

(C) the civil action number of each action; and

(D) the name of the judge assigned each action, if known;

(iii) a proof of service providing

(A) a service list listing the full name of each party included on the district court's docket sheet and the complaint, including opt-in plaintiffs not listed on the docket sheet; and

(B) in actions where there are 25 or more plaintiffs listed on the docket sheet, list the first named plaintiff with the reference "et al." if all the plaintiffs are represented by the same attorney(s);

(iv) a copy of all complaints and docket sheets for all actions listed on the Schedule; and

(v) exhibits, if any, identified by number or letter and a descriptive title.

(c) Responses and Joinders. Any other party may file a response within 21 days after filing of a motion. Failure to respond to a motion shall be treated as that party's acquiescence to it. A joinder in a motion shall not add any action to that motion.

(d) Replies. The movant may file a reply within 7 days after the lapse of the time period for filing a response. Where a movant is replying to more than one response in opposition, the movant may file a consolidated reply with a limit of 20 pages.

(e) Alteration of Time Periods. The Clerk of the Panel has the discretion to shorten or enlarge the time periods set forth in this Rule as necessary.

(f) Notification of Developments. Counsel shall promptly notify the Clerk of the Panel of any development that would partially or completely moot any Panel matter.

[Former Rule 10 adopted May 3, 1993, effective July 1, 1993. Renumbered Rule 7.2 and amended September 1, 1998, effective November 2, 1998. Amended April 2, 2001, effective April 2, 2001; March 26, 2009, December 1, 2009. Former Rule 7.2 redesignated in part and amended September 8, 2010, effective October 4, 2010.]

RULE 6.2. MOTIONS TO TRANSFER FOR COORDINATED OR CONSOLIDATED PRETRIAL PROCEEDINGS

(a) Initiation of Transfer. A party to an action may initiate proceedings to transfer under Section 1407 by filing a motion in accordance with these Rules. A copy of the motion shall be filed in each district court where the motion affects a pending action.

(b) Notice of Filing of Motion to Transfer. Upon receipt of a motion, the Clerk of the Panel shall issue a "Notice of Filing of Motion to Transfer" to the service list recipients. The Notice shall contain the following: the filing date of the motion, caption, MDL docket number, briefing schedule and pertinent Panel policies. After a motion is filed, the Clerk of the Panel shall consider any other pleading to be a response unless the pleading adds an action. The Clerk of the Panel may designate such a pleading as a motion, and distribute a briefing schedule applicable to all or some of the parties, as appropriate.

(c) Notice of Appearance. Within 14 days of issuance of a "Notice of the Filing of a Motion to Transfer," each party or designated attorney shall file a Notice of Appearance in accordance with Rule 4.1(c).

(d) Notice of Potential Tag-along Actions. Any party or counsel in a new group of actions under consideration for transfer under Section 1407 shall promptly notify the Clerk of the Panel of any potential tag-along actions in which that party is also named or in which that counsel appears.

(e) Interested Party Responses. Any party or counsel in one or more potential tag-along actions as well as amicus curiae may file a response to a pending motion to transfer. Such a pleading shall be deemed an Interested Party Response.

(f) Amendment to a Motion. Before amending a motion to transfer, a party shall first contact the Clerk of the Panel to ascertain whether such amendment is feasible and permissible considering the Panel's hearing schedule. Any such amendment shall be entitled "Amendment to Motion for Transfer," and shall clearly and specifically identify and describe the nature of the amendment.

(i) Where the amended motion includes new civil actions, the amending party shall file a "Schedule of Additional Actions" and a revised Proof of Service.

(ii) The Proof of Service shall state (A) that all new counsel have been served with a copy of the amendment and all previously-filed motion papers, and (B) that all counsel previously served with the original motion have been served with a copy of the amendment.

(iii) The Clerk of the Panel may designate the amendment with a different denomination (*e.g.*, a notice of potential tag-along action(s)) and treatment.

(h) Oral Argument.* The Panel shall schedule oral arguments as needed and as set forth in Rule 11.1.

[Former Rule 10 adopted May 3, 1993, effective July 1, 1993. Renumbered Rule 7.2 and amended September 1, 1998, effective November 2, 1998. Amended April 2, 2001, effective April 2, 2001; March 26, 2009, December 1, 2009. Former Rule 15 adopted May 3, 1993, effective July 1, 1993. Renumbered Rule 6.2 and amended September 1, 1998, effective November 2, 1998. Former Rule 7.2 redesignated in part and amended September 8, 2010, effective October 4, 2010. Technical revisions effective July 6, 2011.]

* So in original.

RULE 6.3. MOTIONS FOR MISCELLANEOUS RELIEF

(a) Definition. Motions for miscellaneous relief include, but are not limited to, requests for extensions of time, exemption from ECF requirements, page limit extensions, or expedited consideration of any motion.

(b) Panel Action. The Panel, through the Clerk, may act upon any motion for miscellaneous relief, at any time, without waiting for a response. A motion for extension of time to file a pleading or perform an act under these Rules must state specifically the revised date sought and must be filed before the deadline for filing the pleading or performing the act. Any party aggrieved by the Clerk of the Panel's action may file objections for consideration. Absent exceptional circumstances, the Panel will not grant any extensions of time to file a notice of opposition to either a conditional transfer order or a conditional remand order.

[Former Rule 15 adopted May 3, 1993, effective July 1, 1993. Renumbered Rule 6.2 and amended September 1, 1998, effective November 2, 1998. Former Rule 6.2 redesignated and amended September 8, 2010, effective October 4, 2010.]

RULE 7.1. CONDITIONAL TRANSFER ORDERS (CTO) FOR TAG-ALONG ACTIONS

(a) Notice of Potential Tag-along Actions. Any party or counsel in actions previously transferred under Section 1407 shall promptly notify the Clerk of the Panel of any potential tag-along actions in which that party is also named or in which that counsel appears. The Panel has several options: (i) filing a CTO under Rule 7.1, (ii) filing a show cause order under Rule 8.1, or (iii) declining to act (Rule 7.1(b)(i)).

(b) Initiation of CTO. Upon learning of the pendency of a potential tag-along action, the Clerk of the Panel may enter a conditional order transferring that action to the previously designated transferee district court for the reasons expressed in the Panel's previous opinions and orders. The Clerk of the Panel shall serve this order on each party to the litigation but shall not send the order to the clerk of the transferee district court until 7 days after its entry.

(i)* If the Clerk of the Panel determines that a potential tag-along action is not appropriate for inclusion in an MDL proceeding and does not enter a CTO, an involved party may move for its transfer pursuant to Rule 6.1.

(c) Notice of Opposition to CTO. Any party opposing the transfer shall file a notice of opposition with the Clerk of the Panel within the 7-day period. In such event, the Clerk of the Panel shall not transmit the transfer order to the clerk of the transferee district court, but shall notify the parties of the briefing schedule.

(d) Failure to Respond. Failure to respond to a CTO shall be treated as that party's acquiescence to it.

(e) Notice of Appearance. Within 14 days after the issuance of a "Notice of Filed Opposition" to a CTO, each opposing party or designated attorney shall file a Notice of Appearance in accordance with Rule 4.1(c).

(f) Motion to Vacate CTO. Within 14 days of the filing of its notice of opposition, the party opposing transfer shall file a motion to vacate the CTO and brief in support thereof. The Clerk of the Panel shall set the motion for the next appropriate hearing session. Failure to file and serve a motion and brief shall be treated as withdrawal of the opposition and the Clerk of the Panel shall forthwith transmit the order to the clerk of the transferee district court.

(g) Notification of Developments. Parties to an action subject to a CTO shall notify the Clerk of the Panel if that action is no longer pending in its transferor district court.

(h) Effective Date of CTO. CTOs are effective when filed with the clerk of the transferee district court.

[Former Rule 12 adopted May 3, 1993, effective July 1, 1993. Renumbered Rule 7.4 and amended September 1, 1998, effective November 2, 1998. Amended April 2, 2001, effective April 2, 2001; March 26, 2009, December 1, 2009. Former Rule 7.4 redesignated and amended September 8, 2010, effective October 4, 2010. Technical revisions effective July 6, 2011.]

* So in original. No subdivision (ii) promulgated.

RULE 7.2. MISCELLANEOUS PROVISIONS CONCERNING TAG-ALONG ACTIONS

(a) Potential Tag-alongs in Transferee Court. Potential tag-along actions filed in the transferee district do not require Panel action. A party should request assignment of such actions to the Section 1407 transferee judge in accordance with applicable local rules.

(b) Failure to Serve. Failure to serve one or more of the defendants in a potential tag-along action with the complaint and summons as required by Rule 4 of the Federal Rules of Civil Procedure does not preclude transfer of such action under Section 1407. Such failure, however, may constitute grounds for denying the proposed transfer where prejudice can be shown. The failure of the Clerk of the Panel to serve a CTO on all plaintiffs or defendants or their counsel may constitute grounds for the Clerk to reinstate the CTO or for the aggrieved party to seek § 1407(c) remand.

[Former Rule 13 adopted May 3, 1993, effective July 1, 1993. Renumbered Rule 7.5 and amended September 1, 1998, effective November 2, 1998. Amended April 2, 2001, effective April 2, 2001. Former Rule 7.5 redesignated and amended September 8, 2010, effective October 4, 2010. Amended effective July 6, 2011.]

RULE 8.1. SHOW CAUSE ORDERS

(a) Entry of Show Cause Order. When transfer of multidistrict litigation is being considered on the initiative of the Panel pursuant to 28 U.S.C. § 1407(c)(i), the Clerk of the Panel may enter an order directing the parties to show cause why a certain civil action or actions should not be transferred for coordinated or consolidated pretrial proceedings. Any party shall also promptly notify the Clerk of the Panel whenever they learn of any other federal district court actions which are similar to those which the show cause order encompasses.

(b) Notice of Appearance. Within 14 days of the issuance of an order to show cause, each party or designated attorney shall file a Notice of Appearance in accordance with Rule 4.1(c).

(c) Responses. Unless otherwise provided by order, any party may file a response within 21 days of the filing of the show cause order. Failure to respond to a show cause order shall be treated as that party's acquiescence to the Panel action.

(d) Replies. Within 7 days after the lapse of the time period for filing a response, any party may file a reply.

(e) Notification of Developments. Counsel shall promptly notify the Clerk of the Panel of any development that would partially or completely moot any matter subject to a show cause order.

[Former Rule 7.3 adopted May 3, 1993, effective July 1, 1993. Renumbered Rule 7.3 and amended September 1, 1998, effective November 2, 1998; March 26, 2009, effective December 1, 2009. Former Rule 7.3 redesignated and amended September 8, 2010, effective October 4, 2010.]

RULE 9.1. TRANSFER OF FILES; NOTIFICATION REQUIREMENTS

(a) Notice to Transferee Court Clerk. The Clerk of the Panel, via a notice of electronic filing, will notify the clerk of the transferee district whenever a Panel transfer order should be filed in the transferee district court. Upon receipt of an electronically certified copy of a Panel transfer order from the clerk of the transferee district, the clerk of the transferor district shall transmit the record of each transferred action to the transferee district and then, unless Rule 9.1(b) applies, close the transferred action in the transferor district.

(b) Retention of Claims. If the transfer order provides for the separation and simultaneous remand of any claim, cross-claim, counterclaim, or third-party claim, the clerk of the transferor district shall retain jurisdiction over any such claim and shall not close the action.

(c) Notice to Clerk of Panel. The clerk of the transferee district shall promptly provide the Clerk of the Panel with the civil action numbers assigned to all transferred actions and the identity of liaison counsel, if or when designated. The clerk of the transferee district shall also promptly notify the Clerk of the Panel of any dispositive ruling that terminates a transferred action.

[Former Rule 19 adopted May 3, 1993, effective July 1, 1993. Renumbered Rule 1.6 and amended September 1, 1998, effective November 2, 1998. Former Rule 1.6 redesignated in part and amended September 8, 2010, effective October 4, 2010.]

RULE 10.1. TERMINATION AND REMAND

(a) Termination. Where the transferee district court terminates an action by valid order, including but not limited to summary judgment, judgment of dismissal and judgment upon stipulation, the transferee district court clerk shall transmit a copy of that order to the Clerk of the Panel. The terminated action shall not be remanded to the transferor court and the transferee court shall retain the original files and records unless the transferee judge or the Panel directs otherwise.

(b) Initiation of Remand. Typically, the transferee judge recommends remand of an action, or a part of it, to the transferor court at any time by filing a suggestion of remand with the Panel. However, the

Panel may remand an action or any separable claim, cross-claim, counterclaim or third-party claim within it, upon

(i) the transferee court's suggestion of remand,

(ii) the Panel's own initiative by entry of an order to show cause, a conditional remand order or other appropriate order, or

(iii) motion of any party.

[Former Rule 14 adopted May 3, 1993, effective July 1, 1993. Renumbered Rule 7.6 and amended September 1, 1998, effective November 2, 1998. Amended April 2, 2001, effective April 2, 2001; March 26, 2009, effective December 1, 2009. Former Rule 7.6 redesignated in part and amended September 8, 2010, effective October 4, 2010.]

RULE 10.2. CONDITIONAL REMAND ORDERS (CRO)

(a) Entering a CRO. Upon the suggestion of the transferee judge or the Panel's own initiative, the Clerk of the Panel shall enter a conditional order remanding the action or actions to the transferor district court. The Clerk of the Panel shall serve this order on each party to the litigation but shall not send the order to the clerk of the transferee district court for 7 days from the entry thereof.

(i)* The Panel may, on its own initiative, also enter an order that the parties show cause why a matter should not be remanded. Rule 8.1 applies to responses and replies with respect to such a show cause order.

(b) Notice of Opposition. Any party opposing the CRO shall file a notice of opposition with the Clerk of the Panel within the 7–day period. In such event, the Clerk of the Panel shall not transmit the remand order to the clerk of the transferee district court and shall notify the parties of the briefing schedule.

(c) Failure to Respond. Failure to respond to a CRO shall be treated as that party's acquiescence to it.

(d) Notice of Appearance. Within 14 days after the issuance of a "Notice of Filed Opposition" to a CRO, each opposing party or designated attorney shall file a Notice of Appearance in accordance with Rule 4.1(c).

(e) Motion to Vacate CRO. Within 14 days of the filing of its notice of opposition, the party opposing remand shall file a motion to vacate the CRO and brief in support thereof. The Clerk of the Panel shall set the motion for the next appropriate Panel hearing session. Failure to file and serve a motion and brief shall be treated as a withdrawal of the opposition and the Clerk of the Panel shall forthwith transmit the order to the clerk of the transferee district court.

(f) Effective Date of CRO. CROs are not effective until filed with the clerk of the transferee district court.

[Former Rule 14 adopted May 3, 1993, effective July 1, 1993. Renumbered Rule 7.6 and amended September 1, 1998, effective November 2, 1998. Amended April 2, 2001, effective April 2, 2001; March 26, 2009, effective December 1, 2009. Former Rule 7.6 redesignated in part and amended September 8, 2010, effective October 4, 2010. Technical revisions effective July 6, 2011.]

* So in original. No subdivision (ii) promulgated.

RULE 10.3. MOTION TO REMAND

(a) Requirements of the Motion. If the Clerk of the Panel does not enter a CRO, a party may file a motion to remand to the transferor court pursuant to these Rules. Because the Panel is reluctant to order a remand absent the suggestion of the transferee judge, the motion must include:

(i) An affidavit reciting whether the movant has requested a suggestion of remand and the judge's response, whether the parties have completed common discovery and other pretrial proceedings, and whether the parties have complied with all transferee court orders.

(ii) A copy of the transferee district court's final pretrial order, if entered.

(b) Filing Copy of Motion. Counsel shall file a copy of the motion to remand in the affected transferee district court.

(c) Notice of Appearance. Within 14 days of the issuance of a "Notice of Filing" of a motion to remand, each party or designated attorney shall file a Notice of Appearance in accordance with Rule 4.1(c).

[Former Rule 14 adopted May 3, 1993, effective July 1, 1993. Renumbered Rule 7.6 and amended September 1, 1998, effective November 2, 1998. Amended April 2, 2001, effective April 2, 2001; March 26, 2009, effective December 1, 2009. Former Rule 7.6 redesignated in part and amended September 8, 2010, effective October 4, 2010. Technical revisions effective July 6, 2011.]

RULE 10.4. TRANSFER OF FILES ON REMAND

(a) Designating the Record. Upon receipt of an order to remand from the Clerk of the Panel, the parties shall furnish forthwith to the transferee district clerk a stipulation or designation of the contents of the record or part thereof to be remanded.

(b) Transfer of Files. Upon receipt of an order to remand from the Clerk of the Panel, the transferee district shall transmit to the clerk of the transferor district the following concerning each remanded action:

(i) a copy of the individual docket sheet for each action remanded;

(ii) a copy of the master docket sheet, if applicable;

(iii) the entire file for each action remanded, as originally received from the transferor district and augmented as set out in this Rule;

(iv) a copy of the final pretrial order, if applicable; and

(v) a "record on remand" as designated by the parties in accordance with 10.4(a).

[Former Rule 19 adopted May 3, 1993, effective July 1, 1993. Renumbered Rule 1.6 and amended September 1, 1998, effective November 2, 1998. Former Rule 1.6 redesignated in part and amended September 8, 2010, effective October 4, 2010.]

RULE 11.1. HEARING SESSIONS AND ORAL ARGUMENT

(a) Schedule. The Panel shall schedule sessions for oral argument and consideration of other matters as desirable or necessary. The Chair shall determine the time, place and agenda for each hearing session. The Clerk of the Panel shall give appropriate notice to counsel for all parties. The Panel may continue its consideration of any scheduled matters.

(b) Oral Argument Statement. Any party affected by a motion may file a separate statement setting forth reasons why oral argument should, or need not, be heard. Such statements shall be captioned "Reasons Why Oral Argument Should [Need Not] Be Heard" and shall be limited to 2 pages.

(i)* The parties affected by a motion to transfer may agree to waive oral argument. The Panel will take this into consideration in determining the need for oral argument.

(c) Hearing Session. The Panel shall not consider transfer or remand of any action pending in a federal district court when any party timely opposes such transfer or remand without first holding a hearing session for the presentation of oral argument. The Panel may dispense with oral argument if it determines that:

(i) the dispositive issue(s) have been authoritatively decided; or

(ii) the facts and legal arguments are adequately presented and oral argument would not significantly aid the decisional process.

Unless otherwise ordered, the Panel shall consider all other matters, such as a motion for reconsideration, upon the basis of the pleadings.

(d) Notification of Oral Argument. The Panel shall promptly notify counsel of those matters in which oral argument is scheduled, as well as those matters that the Panel will consider on the pleadings. The Clerk of the Panel shall require counsel to file and serve notice of their intent to either make or waive oral argument. Failure to do so shall be deemed a waiver of oral argument. If counsel does not attend oral argument, the matter shall not be rescheduled and that party's position shall be treated as submitted for decision on the basis of the pleadings filed.

(i) Absent Panel approval and for good cause shown, only those parties to actions who have filed a motion or written response to a motion or order shall be permitted to present oral argument.

(ii) The Panel will not receive oral testimony except upon notice, motion and an order expressly providing for it.

(e) Duty to Confer. Counsel in an action set for oral argument shall confer separately prior to that argument for the purpose of organizing their arguments and selecting representatives to present all views without duplication. Oral argument is a means for counsel to emphasize the key points of their arguments, and to update the Panel on any events since the conclusion of briefing.

(f) Time Limit for Oral Argument. Barring exceptional circumstances, the Panel shall allot a maximum of 20 minutes for oral argument in each matter. The time shall be divided among those with varying viewpoints. Counsel for the moving party or parties shall generally be heard first.

[Former Rule 16 adopted May 3, 1998, effective July 1, 1993. Renumbered Rule 16.1 and amended September 1, 1998, effective November 2, 1998. Amended April 2, 2001, effective April 2, 2001. Former Rule 16.1 redesignated and amended September 8, 2010, effective October 4, 2010.]

* So in original. No subdivision (ii) promulgated.

RULE 12 TO 15. [RESERVED]

II. RULES FOR MULTICIRCUIT PETITIONS FOR REVIEW UNDER 28 U.S.C. § 2112(a)(3)

RULE 25.1. DEFINITIONS

The Panel promulgates these Rules pursuant to its authority under 28 U.S.C. § 2112(a)(3) to provide a means for the random selection of one circuit court of appeals to hear consolidated petitions for review of agency decisions.

An "Agency" means an agency, board, commission or officer of the United States government, that has received two or more petitions for review in a circuit court of appeals to enjoin, set aside, suspend, modify or otherwise review or enforce an action.

[Former Rule 20 adopted May 3, 1993, effective July 1, 1993. Renumbered Rule 25.1 and amended September 1, 1998, effective November 2, 1998. Amended September 8, 2010, effective October 4, 2010.]

RULE 25.2. FILING OF NOTICES

(a) Submitting Notice. An affected agency shall submit a notice of multicircuit petitions for review pursuant to 28 U.S.C. § 2112(a)(3) to the Clerk of the Panel by electronic means in the manner these Rules require and in accordance with the Panel's Administrative Policies and Procedures for Electronic Case Filing, except that the portion of Rule 3.2(d) requiring a courtesy copy is suspended in its entirety.

(b) Accompaniments to Notices. All notices of multicircuit petitions for review shall include:

(i) a copy of each involved petition for review as the petition for review is defined in 28 U.S.C. § 2112(a)(2);

(ii) a schedule giving

(A) the date of the relevant agency order;

(B) the case name of each petition for review involved;

(C) the circuit court of appeals in which each petition for review is pending;

(D) the appellate docket number of each petition for review;

(E) the date of filing by the court of appeals of each petition for review; and

(F) the date of receipt by the agency of each petition for review; and

(iii) proof of service (*see* Rule 25.3).

(c) Scope of Notice. All notices of multicircuit petitions for review shall embrace exclusively petitions for review filed in the courts of appeals within 10 days after issuance of an agency order and received by the affected agency from the petitioners within that 10–day period.

(d) Filing at the Panel. The Clerk of the Panel shall file the notice of multicircuit petitions for review and endorse thereon the date of filing.

(e) Filing With Each Circuit Clerk. The affected agency shall file copies of notices of multicircuit petitions for review with the clerk of each circuit court of appeals in which a petition for review is pending.

[Former Rule 21 adopted May 3, 1993, effective July 1, 1993. Renumbered Rule 25.2 and amended September 1, 1998, effective November 2, 1998. Amended September 8, 2010, effective October 4, 2010. Technical revisions effective July 6, 2011.]

RULE 25.3. SERVICE OF NOTICES

(a) Proof of Service. Notices of multicircuit petitions for review shall include proof of service on all other parties in the petitions for review included in the notice. Rule 25 of the Federal Rules of Appellate Procedure governs service and proof of service. The proof of service shall state the name, address and email address of each person served and shall indicate the party represented by each and the manner in which service was accomplished on each party. If a party is not represented by counsel, the proof of service shall indicate the name of the party and his or her last known address. The affected party shall submit proof of service for filing with the Clerk of the Panel and shall send copies thereof to each person included within the proof of service.

(b) Service on Clerk of Circuit. The proof of service pertaining to notices of multicircuit petitions for review shall certify the affected party has mailed or delivered copies of the notices to the clerk of each circuit court of appeals in which a petition for review is pending that is included in the notice. The Clerk shall file the notice with the circuit court.

[Former Rule 22 adopted May 3, 1993, effective July 1, 1993. Renumbered Rule 25.3 September 1, 1998, effective November 2, 1998. Amended September 8, 2010, effective October 4, 2010.]

RULE 25.4. FORM OF NOTICES; PLACE OF FILING

(a) Unless otherwise provided here, Rule 3.2 governs the form of a notice of multicircuit petitions for review. Each notice shall bear the heading Notice to the United States Judicial Panel on Multidistrict Litigation of Multicircuit Petitions for Review," followed by a brief caption identifying the involved agency, the relevant agency order, and the date of the order.

(b) Rule 3.2(b) and (c) govern the manner of filing a notice of multicircuit petitions for review.

[Former Rule 23 adopted May 3, 1993, effective July 1, 1993. Renumbered Rule 25.4 and amended September 1, 1998, effective November 2, 1998. Amended September 8, 2010, effective October 4, 2010.]

RULE 25.5. RANDOM SELECTION

(a) Selection Process. Upon filing a notice of multicircuit petitions for review, the Clerk of the Panel shall randomly select a circuit court of appeals from a drum containing an entry for each circuit wherein a constituent petition for review is pending. Multiple petitions for review pending in a single circuit shall be allotted only a single entry in the drum. A designated deputy other than the random selector shall witness the random selection. Thereafter, an order on behalf of the Panel shall be issued, signed by the random selector and the witness,

(i) consolidating the petitions for review in the court of appeals for the circuit that was randomly selected; and

(ii) designating that circuit as the one in which the record is to be filed pursuant to Rules 16 and 17 of the Federal Rules of Appellate Procedure.

(b) Effective Date. A consolidation of petitions for review shall be effective when the Clerk of the Panel enters the consolidation order.

[Former Rule 24 adopted May 3, 1993, effective July 1, 1993. Renumbered Rule 17.1 September 1, 1998, effective November 2, 1998. Former Rule 17.1 redesignated and amended September 8, 2010, effective October 4, 2010.]

RULE 25.6. SERVICE OF PANEL CONSOLIDATION ORDER

(a) The Clerk of the Panel shall serve the Panel's consolidation order on the affected agency through the individual or individuals, as identified in Rule 25.2(a), who submitted the notice of multicircuit petitions for review on behalf of the agency.

(b) That individual or individuals, or anyone else designated by the agency, shall promptly serve the Panel's consolidation order on all other parties in all petitions for review included in the Panel's consolidation order, and shall promptly submit a proof of that service to the Clerk of the Panel. Rule 25.3 governs service.

(c) The Clerk of the Panel shall serve the Panel's consolidation order on the clerks of all circuit courts of appeals that were among the candidates for the Panel's random selection.

[Former Rule 25 adopted May 3, 1993, effective July 1, 1993. Renumbered Rule 25.5 and amended September 1, 1998, effective November 2, 1998. Former Rule 25.5 redesignated and amended September 8, 2010, effective October 4, 2010.]

III. CONVERSION TABLE

New to Old:

New Rule	Previous Rule
1.1	1.1
2.1	1.2, 1.3, 1.4, 1.5
3.1	5.1
3.2	5.1.1, 5.1.2, 7.1
3.3	5.1.1, 5.1.2, 7.1
4.1	5.2
5.1	5.3
6.1	7.2
6.2	7.2
6.3	6.2
7.1	7.4
7.2	7.5
8.1	7.3
9.1	1.6
10.1	7.6
10.2	7.6
10.3	7.6
10.4	1.6
11.1	16.1
25.1	25.1
25.2	25.1, 25.2
25.3	25.3
25.4	25.1, 25.4
25.5	17.1
25.6	25.5

Old to New:

Previous Rule	New Rule
1.1	1.1
1.2	2.1
1.3	2.1
1.4	2.1
1.5	2.1
1.6	10.4
5.1	3.1
5.1.1	3.2, 3.3
5.1.2	3.2, 3.3
5.1.3	-
5.2	4.1
5.3	5.1
6.2	6.3
7.1	3.2, 3.3
7.2	6.1
7.3	8.1
7.4	7.1
7.5	7.2
7.6	10.1
16.1	11.1
17.1	25.5
25.1	25.1, 25.2, 25.4
25.2	25.2
25.3	25.3
25.4	25.4
25.5	25.6

[October 2010.]

*

FEDERAL COURTS MISCELLANEOUS FEE SCHEDULES

COURT OF APPEALS FEE SCHEDULE

(Issued in accordance with 28 U.S.C. § 1913)

(Effective November 1, 2011)

The fees included in the Court of Appeals Miscellaneous Fee Schedule are to be charged for services provided by the courts of appeals.

- The United States should not be charged fees under this schedule, except as prescribed in Items 2, 4, and 5 when the information requested is available through remote electronic access.
- Federal agencies or programs that are funded from judiciary appropriations (agencies, organizations, and individuals providing services authorized by the Criminal Justice Act, 18 U.S.C. § 3006A, and bankruptcy administrators) should not be charged any fees under this schedule.

(1) For docketing a case on appeal or review, or docketing any other proceeding, $450.

- Each party filing a notice of appeal pays a separate fee to the district court, but parties filing a joint notice of appeal pay only one fee.
- There is no docketing fee for an application for an interlocutory appeal under 28 U.S.C. § 1292(b) or other petition for permission to appeal under Fed. R. App. P. 5, unless the appeal is allowed.
- There is no docketing fee for a direct bankruptcy appeal or a direct bankruptcy cross appeal, when the fee has been collected by the bankruptcy court in accordance with item 14 of the Bankruptcy Court Miscellaneous Fee Schedule.

(2) For conducting a search of the court of appeals records, $30 per name or item searched. This fee applies to services rendered on behalf of the United States if the information requested is available through remote electronic access.

(3) For certification of any document, $11.

(4) For reproducing any document, $.50 per page. This fee applies to services rendered on behalf of the United States if the document requested is available through remote electronic access.

(5) For reproducing recordings of proceedings, regardless of the medium, $30, including the cost of materials. This fee applies to services rendered on behalf of the United States if the recording is available through remote electronic access.

(6) For reproducing the record in any appeal in which the court of appeals does not require an appendix pursuant to Fed. R. App. P.30(f), $83.

(7) For retrieving a record from a Federal Records Center, National Archives, or other storage location removed from the place of business of the court, $53.

(8) For a check paid into the court which is returned for lack of funds, $53.

(9) For copies of opinions, a fee commensurate with the cost of printing, as fixed by each court.

(10) For copies of the local rules of court, a fee commensurate with the cost of distributing the copies. The court may also distribute copies of the local rules without charge.

(11) For filing:

- Any separate or joint notice of appeal or application for appeal from the Bankruptcy Appellate Panel, $5.
- A notice of the allowance of an appeal from the Bankruptcy Appellate Panel, $5.

(12) For counsel's requested use of the court's videoconferencing equipment in connection with each oral argument, the court may charge and collect a fee of $200 per remote location.

(13) For original admission of an attorney to practice, including a certificate of admission, $176. For a duplicate certificate of admission or certificate of good standing, $18.

DISTRICT COURT MISCELLANEOUS FEE SCHEDULE[1]

(Effective November 1, 2011)

The fees included in the District Court Miscellaneous Fee Schedule are to be charged for services provided by the district courts.

- The United States should not be charged fees under this schedule, with the exception of those specifically prescribed in Items 2, 4 and 5, when the information requested is available through remote electronic access.
- Federal agencies or programs that are funded from judiciary appropriations (agencies, organizations, and individuals providing services authorized by the Criminal Justice Act, 18 U.S.C. § 3006 and bankruptcy administrators) should not be charged any fees under this schedule.

1. For filing any document that is not related to a pending case or proceeding, $46.
2. For conducting a search of the district court records, $30 per name or item searched. This fee applies to services rendered on behalf of the United States if the information requested is available through electronic access.
3. For certification of any document, $11. For exemplification of any document, $18.
4. For reproducing any record or paper, $.50 per page. This fee shall apply to paper copies made from either: (1) original documents; or (2) microfiche or microfilm reproductions of the original records. This fee shall apply to services rendered on behalf of the United States if the record or paper requested is available through electronic access.
5. For reproduction of an audio recording of a court proceeding, $30. This fee applies to services rendered on behalf of the United States, if the recording is available electronically.
6. For each microfiche sheet of film or microfilm jacket copy of any court record, where available, $6.
7. For retrieval of a record from a Federal Records Center, National Archives, or other storage location removed from the place of business of the court, $53.
8. For a check paid into the court which is returned for lack of funds, $53.
9. For an appeal to a district judge from a judgment of conviction by a magistrate judge in a misdemeanor case, $37.
10. For original admission of attorneys to practice, $176 each, including a certificate of admission. For a duplicate certificate of admission or certificate of good standing, $18.
11. The court may charge and collect fees commensurate with the cost of providing copies of the local rules of court. The court may also distribute copies of the local rules without charge.
12. The clerk shall assess a charge for the handling of registry funds deposited with the court, to be assessed from interest earnings and in accordance with the detailed fee schedule issued by the Director of the Administrative Office of the United States Courts.
    For management of registry funds invested through the Court Registry Investment System, a fee at a rate of 2.5 basis points shall be assessed from interest earnings.
13. For filing an action brought under Title III of the Cuban Liberty and Democratic Solidarity (LIBERTAD) Act of 1996, P.L. 104-114, 110 Stat. § 785 (1996), $6,355. (This fee is in addition to the filing fee prescribed in 28 U.S.C. § 1914(a) for instituting any civil action other than a writ of habeas corpus.)

[1] Issued in accordance with 28 U.S.C. § 1914.

BANKRUPTCY COURT MISCELLANEOUS FEE SCHEDULE (28 U.S.C. § 1930)

(Effective November 1, 2011)

The fees included in the Bankruptcy Court Miscellaneous Fee Schedule are to be charged for services provided by the bankruptcy courts.

- The United States should not be charged fees under this schedule, with the exception of those specifically prescribed in Items 1, 3 and 5 when the information requested is available through remote electronic access.
- Federal agencies or programs that are funded from judiciary appropriations (agencies, organizations, and individuals providing services authorized by the Criminal Justice Act, 18 U.S.C. § 3006A, and bankruptcy administrators) should not be charged any fees under this schedule.

(1) For reproducing any document, $.50 per page. This fee applies to services rendered on behalf of the United States if the document requested is available through electronic access.

(2) For certification of any document, $11.

For exemplification of any document, $21.

(3) For reproduction of an audio recording of a court proceeding, $30. This fee applies to services rendered on behalf of the United States if the recording is available electronically.

(4) For filing an amendment to the debtor's schedules of creditors, lists of creditors, or mailing list, $30, except:

- The bankruptcy judge may, for good cause, waive the charge in any case.
- This fee must not be charged if -
  - the amendment is to change the address of a creditor or an attorney for a creditor listed on the schedules; or
  - the amendment is to add the name and address of an attorney for a creditor listed on the schedules.

(5) For conducting a search of the bankruptcy court records, $30 per name or item searched. This fee applies to services rendered on behalf of the United States if the information requested is available through electronic access.

(6) For filing a complaint, $293, except:

- If the trustee or debtor-in-possession files the complaint, the fee must be paid only by the estate, to the extent there is an estate.
- This fee must not be charged if -
  - the debtor is the plaintiff; or
  - a child support creditor or representative files the complaint and submits the form required by § 304(g) of the Bankruptcy Reform Act of 1994.

(7) For filing any document that is not related to a pending case or proceeding, $46.

(8) Administrative fee for filing a case under Title 11 or when a motion to divide a joint case under Title 11 is filed, $46.

(9) For payment to trustees pursuant to 11 U.S.C. § 330(b)(2), a $15 fee applies in the following circumstances:

- For filing a petition under Chapter 7.
- For filing a motion to reopen a Chapter 7 case.
- For filing a motion to divide a joint Chapter 7 case.
- For filing a motion to convert a case to a Chapter 7 case.
- For filing a notice of conversion to a Chapter 7 case.

(10) In addition to any fees imposed under Item 9, above, the following fees must be collected:

- For filing a motion to convert a Chapter 12 case to a Chapter 7 case or a notice of conversion pursuant to 11 U.S.C. § 1208(a), $45.
- For filing a motion to convert a Chapter 13 case to a Chapter 7 case or a notice of conversion pursuant to 11 U.S.C. § 1307(a), $10.

The fee amounts in this item are derived from the fees prescribed in 28 U.S.C. § 1930(a).

If the trustee files the motion to convert, the fee is payable only from the estate that exists prior to conversion.

If the filing fee for the chapter to which the case is requested to be converted is less than the fee paid at the commencement of the case, no refund may be provided.

(11) For filing a motion to reopen, the following fees apply:

- For filing a motion to reopen a Chapter 7 case, $245.
- For filing a motion to reopen a Chapter 9 case, $1000.
- For filing a motion to reopen a Chapter 11 case, $1000.
- For filing a motion to reopen a Chapter 12 case, $200.

- For filing a motion to reopen a Chapter 13 case, $235.
- For filing a motion to reopen a Chapter 15 case, $1000.

The fee amounts in this item are derived from the fees prescribed in 28 U.S.C. § 1930(a).

The reopening fee must be charged when a case has been closed without a discharge being entered.

The court may waive this fee under appropriate circumstances or may defer payment of the fee from trustees pending discovery of additional assets. If payment is deferred, the fee should be waived if no additional assets are discovered.

The reopening fee must not be charged in the following situations:

- to permit a party to file a complaint to obtain a determination under Rule 4007(b); or
- when a debtor files a motion to reopen a case based upon an alleged violation of the terms of the discharge under 11 U.S.C. § 524; or
- when the reopening is to correct an administrative error.

(12) For retrieval of a record from a Federal Records Center, National Archives, or other storage location removed from the place of business of the court, $53.

(13) For a check paid into the court which is returned for lack of funds, $53.

(14) For filing an appeal or cross appeal from a judgment, order, or decree, $293.

This fee is collected in addition to the statutory fee of $5 that is collected under 28 U.S.C. § 1930(c) when a notice of appeal is filed.

Parties filing a joint notice of appeal should pay only one fee.

If a trustee or debtor-in-possession is the appellant, the fee must be paid only by the estate, to the extent there is an estate.

Upon notice from the court of appeals that a direct appeal or direct cross-appeal has been authorized, an additional fee of $157* must be collected.

(15) For filing a case under Chapter 15 of the Bankruptcy Code, $1000.

This fee is derived from and equal to the fee prescribed in 28 U.S.C. § 1930(a)(3) for filing a case commenced under Chapter 11 of Title 11.

(16) The court may charge and collect fees commensurate with the cost of providing copies of the local rules of court. The court may also distribute copies of the local rules without charge.

(17) The clerk shall assess a charge for the handling of registry funds deposited with the court, to be assessed from interest earnings and in accordance with the detailed fee schedule issued by the Director of the Administrative office of the United States Courts.

For management of registry funds invested through the Court Registry Investment System, a fee at a rate of 2.5 basis points shall be assessed from interest earnings.

(18) For a motion filed by the debtor to divide a joint case filed under 11 U.S.C. § 302, the following fees apply:

- For filing a motion to divide a joint Chapter 7 case, $245.
- For filing a motion to divide a joint Chapter 11 case, $1000.
- For filing a motion to divide a joint Chapter 12 case, $200.
- For filing a motion to divide a joint Chapter 13 case, $235.

These fees are derived from and equal to the filing fees prescribed in 28 U.S.C. § 1930(a).

(19) For filing the following motions, $176:

- To terminate, annul, modify or condition the automatic stay;
- To compel abandonment of property of the estate pursuant to Rule 6007(b) of the Federal Rules of Bankruptcy Procedure; or
- To withdraw the reference of a case or proceeding under 28 U.S.C. § 157(d).

This fee must not be collected in the following situations:

- For a motion for relief from the co-debtor stay;
- For a stipulation for court approval of an agreement for relief from a stay; or
- For a motion filed by a child support creditor or its representative, if the form required by § 304(g) of the Bankruptcy Reform Act of 1994 is filed.

* The approved increase in the notice of appeal fee necessitates that the supplemental direct appeal fee be reduced to ensure that the total fee for filing a direct appeal does not exceed the established appellate filing fee of $450.

JUDICIAL PANEL ON MULTIDISTRICT LITIGATION FEE SCHEDULE

(28 U.S.C. § 1932)

(Effective November 1, 2011)

Following are fees to be charged for services provided by the Judicial Panel on Multidistrict Litigation. No fees are to be charged for services rendered on behalf of the United States, with the exception of those specifically prescribed in items 1 and 3. No fees under this schedule shall be charged to federal agencies or programs which are funded from judiciary appropriations, including, but not limited to, agencies, organizations, and individuals providing services authorized by the Criminal Justice Act, 18 U.S.C. § 3006A.

(1) For every search of the records of the court conducted by the clerk of the court or a deputy clerk, $30 per name or item searched. This fee shall apply to services rendered on behalf of the United States if the information requested is available through electronic access.

(2) For certification of any document or paper, whether the certification is made directly on the document or by separate instrument, $11.

(3) For reproducing any record or paper, $.50 per page. This fee shall apply to paper copies made from either: (1) original documents; or (2) microfiche or microfilm reproductions of the original records. This fee shall apply to services rendered on behalf of the United States if the record or paper requested is available through electronic access.

(4) For retrieval of a record from a Federal Records Center, National Archives, or other storage location removed from the place of business of the court, $53.

(5) For a check paid into the Panel which is returned for lack of funds, $53.

ELECTRONIC PUBLIC ACCESS FEE SCHEDULE

(Effective September 7, 2011)

(Issued in Accordance with 28 U.S.C. §§ 1913, 1914, 1926, 1930, 1932)

As directed by Congress, the Judicial Conference has determined that the following fees are necessary to reimburse expenses incurred by the judiciary in providing electronic public access to court records. These fees shall apply to the United States unless otherwise stated. No fees under this schedule shall be charged to federal agencies or programs which are funded from judiciary appropriations, including, but not limited to, agencies, organizations, and individuals providing services authorized by the Criminal Justice Act, 18 U.S.C. § 3006A, and bankruptcy administrator programs.

I. For electronic access to court data via a federal judiciary Internet site: eight cents per page, with the total for any document, docket sheet, or case-specific report not to exceed the fee for thirty pages—provided however that transcripts of federal court proceedings shall not be subject to the thirty-page fee limit. For electronic access to an audio file of a court hearing via a federal judiciary Internet site: $2.40 per audio file. Attorneys of record and parties in a case (including *pro se* litigants) receive one free electronic copy of all documents filed electronically, if receipt is required by law or directed by the filer. No fee is owed under this provision until an account holder accrues charges of more than $10 in a quarterly billing cycle. Consistent with Judicial Conference policy, courts may, upon a showing of cause, exempt indigents, bankruptcy case trustees, individual researchers associated with educational institutions, courts, section 501(c)(3) not-for-profit organizations, court appointed pro bono attorneys, and pro bono ADR neutrals from payment of these fees. Courts must find that parties from the classes of persons or entities listed above seeking exemption have demonstrated that an exemption is necessary in order to avoid unreasonable burdens and to promote public access to information. For individual researchers, courts must also find that the defined research project is intended for academic research, and not for commercial purposes or internet redistribution. Any user granted an exemption agrees not to sell for profit the data obtained as a result. Any transfer of data obtained as the result of a fee exemption is prohibited unless expressly authorized by the court. Exemptions may be granted for a definite period of time and may be revoked at the discretion of the court granting the exemption.

II. For printing copies of any record or document accessed electronically at a public terminal in the courthouse: ten cents per page. This fee shall apply to services rendered on behalf of the United States if the record requested is remotely available through electronic access.

III. For every search of court records conducted by the PACER Service Center, $26 per name or item searched.

IV. For the PACER Service Center to reproduce on paper any record pertaining to a PACER account, if this information is remotely available through electronic access, 50 cents per page.

V. For a check paid to the PACER Service Center which is returned for lack of funds, $45.

JUDICIAL CONFERENCE POLICY NOTES

Courts should not exempt local, state or federal government agencies, members of the media, attorneys or others not members of one of the groups listed above. Exemptions should be granted as the exception, not the rule. A court may not use this exemption language to exempt all users. An exemption applies only to access related to the case or purpose for which it was given. The prohibition on transfer of information received without fee is not intended to bar a quote or reference to information received as a result of a fee exemption in a scholarly or other similar work.

The electronic public access fee applies to electronic court data viewed remotely from the public records of individual cases in the court, including filed documents and the docket sheet. Audio files of court hearings do not include naturalization ceremonies or appellate oral arguments. Electronic court data may be viewed free at public terminals at the courthouse and courts may provide other local court information at no cost. Examples of information that can be provided at no cost include: local rules, court forms, news items, court calendars, opinions, and other information—such as court hours, court location, telephone listings—determined locally to benefit the public and the court.

PUBLISHER'S APPENDIX—FEDERAL RULES OF EVIDENCE COMPARISON CHART

The following table sets forth a side-by-side comparison of the Federal Rules of Evidence in effect until December 1, 2011 and the revised Federal Rules of Evidence that became effective December 1, 2011. The side-by-side format offers a concise tool for counsel's reference in examining the revised text of a given rule.

Text Effective Until 12/1/11	Text Effective 12/1/11
ARTICLE I. GENERAL PROVISIONS **Rule 101. Scope**	**ARTICLE I. GENERAL PROVISIONS** **Rule 101. Scope; Definitions**
These rules govern proceedings in the courts of the United States and before the United States bankruptcy judges and United States magistrate judges, to the extent and with the exceptions stated in rule 1101.	**(a) Scope.** These rules apply to proceedings in United States courts. The specific courts and proceedings to which the rules apply, along with exceptions, are set out in Rule 1101. **(b) Definitions.** In these rules: **(1)** "civil case" means a civil action or proceeding; **(2)** "criminal case" includes a criminal proceeding; **(3)** "public office" includes a public agency; **(4)** "record" includes a memorandum, report, or data compilation; **(5)** a "rule prescribed by the Supreme Court" means a rule adopted by the Supreme Court under statutory authority; and **(6)** a reference to any kind of written material or any other medium includes electronically stored information.

Text Effective Until 12/1/11	Text Effective 12/1/11
Rule 102. Purpose and Construction	**Rule 102. Purpose**
These rules shall be construed to secure fairness in administration, elimination of unjustifiable expense and delay, and promotion of growth and development of the law of evidence to the end that the truth may be ascertained and proceedings justly determined.	These rules should be construed so as to administer every proceeding fairly, eliminate unjustifiable expense and delay, and promote the development of evidence law, to the end of ascertaining the truth and securing a just determination.
Rule 103. Rulings on Evidence	**Rule 103. Rulings on Evidence**
(a) **Effect of erroneous ruling.** Error may not be predicated upon a ruling which admits or excludes evidence unless a substantial right of the party is affected, and (1) **Objection.** In case the ruling is one admitting evidence, a timely objection or motion to strike appears of record, stating the specific ground of objection, if the specific ground was not apparent from the context; or (2) **Offer of proof.** In case the ruling is one excluding evidence, the substance of the evidence was made known to the court by offer or was apparent from the context within which questions were asked. Once the court makes a definitive ruling on the record admitting or excluding evidence, either at or before trial, a party need not renew an objection or offer of proof to preserve a claim of error for appeal.	(a) **Preserving a Claim of Error.** A party may claim error in a ruling to admit or exclude evidence only if the error affects a substantial right of the party and: (1) if the ruling admits evidence, a party, on the record: (A) timely objects or moves to strike; and (B) states the specific ground, unless it was apparent from the context; or (2) if the ruling excludes evidence, a party informs the court of its substance by an offer of proof, unless the substance was apparent from the context. (b) **Not Needing to Renew an Objection or Offer of Proof.** Once the court rules definitively on the record—either before or at trial—a party need not renew an objection or offer of proof to preserve a claim of error for appeal.
(b) **Record of offer and ruling.** The court may add any other or further statement which shows the	(c) **Court's Statement About the Ruling; Directing an Offer of Proof.** The court may make any

Text Effective Until 12/1/11	Text Effective 12/1/11
character of the evidence, the form in which it was offered, the objection made, and the ruling thereon. It may direct the making of an offer in question and answer form.	statement about the character or form of the evidence, the objection made, and the ruling. The court may direct that an offer of proof be made in question-and-answer form.
(c) **Hearing of jury.** In jury cases, proceedings shall be conducted, to the extent practicable, so as to prevent inadmissible evidence from being suggested to the jury by any means, such as making statements or offers of proof or asking questions in the hearing of the jury.	(d) **Preventing the Jury from Hearing Inadmissible Evidence.** To the extent practicable, the court must conduct a jury trial so that inadmissible evidence is not suggested to the jury by any means.
(d) **Plain error.** Nothing in this rule precludes taking notice of plain errors affecting substantial rights although they were not brought to the attention of the court.	(e) **Taking Notice of Plain Error.** A court may take notice of a plain error affecting a substantial right, even if the claim of error was not properly preserved.
Rule 104. Preliminary Questions	**Rule 104. Preliminary Questions**
(a) **Questions of admissibility generally.** Preliminary questions concerning the qualification of a person to be a witness, the existence of a privilege, or the admissibility of evidence shall be determined by the court, subject to the provisions of subdivision (b). In making its determination it is not bound by the rules of evidence except those with respect to privileges.	(a) **In General.** The court must decide any preliminary question about whether a witness is qualified, a privilege exists, or evidence is admissible. In so deciding, the court is not bound by evidence rules, except those on privilege.
(b) **Relevancy conditioned on fact.** When the relevancy of evidence depends upon the fulfillment of a condition of fact, the court shall admit it upon, or subject to, the introduction of evidence sufficient to support a finding of the fulfillment of the condition.	(b) **Relevance That Depends on a Fact.** When the relevance of evidence depends on whether a fact exists, proof must be introduced sufficient to support a finding that the fact does exist. The court may admit the proposed evidence on the condition that the proof be introduced later.

Text Effective Until 12/1/11	Text Effective 12/1/11
(c) **Hearing of jury.** Hearings on the admissibility of confessions shall in all cases be conducted out of the hearing of the jury. Hearings on other preliminary matters shall be so conducted when the interests of justice require, or when an accused is a witness and so requests.	(c) **Conducting a Hearing So That the Jury Cannot Hear It.** The court must conduct any hearing on a preliminary question so that the jury cannot hear it if: (1) the hearing involves the admissibility of a confession; (2) a defendant in a criminal case is a witness and so requests; or (3) justice so requires.
(d) **Testimony by accused.** The accused does not, by testifying upon a preliminary matter, become subject to cross-examination as to other issues in the case.	(d) **Cross–Examining a Defendant in a Criminal Case.** By testifying on a preliminary question, a defendant in a criminal case does not become subject to cross-examination on other issues in the case.
(e) **Weight and credibility.** This rule does not limit the right of a party to introduce before the jury evidence relevant to weight or credibility.	(e) **Evidence Relevant to Weight and Credibility.** This rule does not limit a party's right to introduce before the jury evidence that is relevant to the weight or credibility of other evidence.
Rule 105. Limited Admissibility	**Rule 105. Limiting Evidence That Is Not Admissible Against Other Parties or for Other Purposes**
When evidence which is admissible as to one party or for one purpose but not admissible as to another party or for another purpose is admitted, the court, upon request, shall restrict the evidence to its proper scope and instruct the jury accordingly.	If the court admits evidence that is admissible against a party or for a purpose—but not against another party or for another purpose—the court, on timely request, must restrict the evidence to its proper scope and instruct the jury accordingly.

Text Effective Until 12/1/11	Text Effective 12/1/11
Rule 106. Remainder of or Related Writings or Recorded Statements	**Rule 106. Remainder of or Related Writings or Recorded Statements**
When a writing or recorded statement or part thereof is introduced by a party, an adverse party may require the introduction at that time of any other part or any other writing or recorded statement which ought in fairness to be considered contemporaneously with it.	If a party introduces all or part of a writing or recorded statement, an adverse party may require the introduction, at that time, of any other part—or any other writing or recorded statement—that in fairness ought to be considered at the same time.

Text Effective Until 12/1/11	Text Effective 12/1/11
ARTICLE II. JUDICIAL NOTICE **Rule 201. Judicial Notice of Adjudicative Facts**	**ARTICLE II. JUDICIAL NOTICE** **Rule 201. Judicial Notice of Adjudicative Facts**
(a) **Scope of rule.** This rule governs only judicial notice of adjudicative facts.	(a) **Scope.** This rule governs judicial notice of an adjudicative fact only, not a legislative fact.
(b) **Kinds of facts.** A judicially noticed fact must be one not subject to reasonable dispute in that it is either (1) generally known within the territorial jurisdiction of the trial court or (2) capable of accurate and ready determination by resort to sources whose accuracy cannot reasonably be questioned.	(b) **Kinds of Facts That May Be Judicially Noticed.** The court may judicially notice a fact that is not subject to reasonable dispute because it: (1) is generally known within the trial court's territorial jurisdiction; or (2) can be accurately and readily determined from sources whose accuracy cannot reasonably be questioned.
(c) **When discretionary.** A court may take judicial notice, whether requested or not. (d) **When mandatory.** A court shall take judicial notice if requested by a party and supplied with the necessary information.	(c) **Taking Notice.** The court: (1) may take judicial notice on its own; or (2) must take judicial notice if a party requests it and the court is supplied with the necessary information.
(e) **Opportunity to be heard.** A party is entitled upon timely request to an opportunity to be heard as to the propriety of taking judicial notice and the tenor of the matter noticed. In the absence of prior notification, the request may be made after judicial notice has been taken.	(d) **Timing.** The court may take judicial notice at any stage of the proceeding.
(f) **Time of taking notice.** Judicial notice may be taken at any stage of the proceeding.	(e) **Opportunity to Be Heard.** On timely request, a party is entitled to be heard on the propriety of taking judicial notice and the na-

Text Effective Until 12/1/11	Text Effective 12/1/11
	ture of the fact to be noticed. If the court takes judicial notice before notifying a party, the party, on request, is still entitled to be heard.
(g) **Instructing jury.** In a civil action or proceeding, the court shall instruct the jury to accept as conclusive any fact judicially noticed. In a criminal case, the court shall instruct the jury that it may, but is not required to, accept as conclusive any fact judicially noticed.	(f) **Instructing the Jury.** In a civil case, the court must instruct the jury to accept the noticed fact as conclusive. In a criminal case, the court must instruct the jury that it may or may not accept the noticed fact as conclusive.

Text Effective Until 12/1/11	Text Effective 12/1/11
ARTICLE III. PRESUMPTIONS IN CIVIL ACTIONS AND PROCEEDINGS **Rule 301. Presumptions in General in Civil Actions and Proceedings**	**ARTICLE III. PRESUMPTIONS IN CIVIL CASES** **Rule 301. Presumptions in Civil Cases Generally**
In all civil actions and proceedings not otherwise provided for by Act of Congress or by these rules, a presumption imposes on the party against whom it is directed the burden of going forward with evidence to rebut or meet the presumption, but does not shift to such party the burden of proof in the sense of the risk of nonpersuasion, which remains throughout the trial upon the party on whom it was originally cast.	In a civil case, unless a federal statute or these rules provide otherwise, the party against whom a presumption is directed has the burden of producing evidence to rebut the presumption. But this rule does not shift the burden of persuasion, which remains on the party who had it originally.
Rule 302. Applicability of State Law in Civil Actions and Proceedings	**Rule 302. Applying State Law to Presumptions in Civil Cases**
In civil actions and proceedings, the effect of a presumption respecting a fact which is an element of a claim or defense as to which State law supplies the rule of decision is determined in accordance with State law.	In a civil case, state law governs the effect of a presumption regarding a claim or defense for which state law supplies the rule of decision.

Text Effective Until 12/1/11	Text Effective 12/1/11
ARTICLE IV. RELEVANCY AND ITS LIMITS	**ARTICLE IV. RELEVANCE AND ITS LIMITS**
Rule 401. Definition of "Relevant Evidence"	**Rule 401. Test for Relevant Evidence**
"Relevant evidence" means evidence having any tendency to make the existence of any fact that is of consequence to the determination of the action more probable or less probable than it would be without the evidence.	Evidence is relevant if: (a) it has any tendency to make a fact more or less probable than it would be without the evidence; and (b) the fact is of consequence in determining the action.
Rule 402. Relevant Evidence Generally Admissible; Irrelevant Evidence Inadmissible	**Rule 402. General Admissibility of Relevant Evidence**
All relevant evidence is admissible, except as otherwise provided by the Constitution of the United States, by Act of Congress, by these rules, or by other rules prescribed by the Supreme Court pursuant to statutory authority. Evidence which is not relevant is not admissible.	Relevant evidence is admissible unless any of the following provides otherwise: • the United States Constitution; • a federal statute; • these rules; or • other rules prescribed by the Supreme Court. Irrelevant evidence is not admissible.
Rule 403. Exclusion of Relevant Evidence on Grounds of Prejudice, Confusion, or Waste of Time	**Rule 403. Excluding Relevant Evidence for Prejudice, Confusion, Waste of Time, or Other Reasons**
Although relevant, evidence may be excluded if its probative value is substantially outweighed by the danger of unfair prejudice, confusion of the issues, or misleading the jury, or by considerations of undue delay, waste of time, or needless presentation of cumulative evidence.	The court may exclude relevant evidence if its probative value is substantially outweighed by a danger of one or more of the following: unfair prejudice, confusing the issues, misleading the jury, undue delay, wasting time, or needlessly presenting cumulative evidence.

Text Effective Until 12/1/11	Text Effective 12/1/11
Rule 404. Character Evidence Not Admissible to Prove Conduct; Exceptions; Other Crimes	**Rule 404. Character Evidence; Crimes or Other Acts**
(a) **Character evidence generally.** Evidence of a person's character or a trait of character is not admissible for the purpose of proving action in conformity therewith on a particular occasion, except:	(a) **Character Evidence.**
(1) **Character of accused.** In a criminal case, evidence of a pertinent trait of character offered by an accused, or by the prosecution to rebut the same, or if evidence of a trait of character of the alleged victim of the crime is offered by an accused and admitted under Rule 404(a)(2), evidence of the same trait of character of the accused offered by the prosecution;	(1) ***Prohibited Uses.*** Evidence of a person's character or character trait is not admissible to prove that on a particular occasion the person acted in accordance with the character or trait.
(2) **Character of alleged victim.** In a criminal case, and subject to the limitations imposed by Rule 412, evidence of a pertinent trait of character of the alleged victim of the crime offered by an accused, or by the prosecution to rebut the same, or evidence of a character trait of peacefulness of the alleged victim offered by the prosecution in a homicide case to rebut evidence that the alleged victim was the first aggressor;	(2) ***Exceptions for a Defendant or Victim in a Criminal Case.*** The following exceptions apply in a criminal case: (A) a defendant may offer evidence of the defendant's pertinent trait, and if the evidence is admitted, the prosecutor may offer evidence to rebut it; (B) subject to the limitations in Rule 412, a defendant may offer evidence of an alleged victim's pertinent trait, and if the evidence is admitted, the prosecutor may: (i) offer evidence to rebut it; and (ii) offer evidence of the defendant's same trait; and (C) in a homicide case, the prosecutor may offer evidence of the alleged victim's trait of peacefulness to rebut evidence that the victim was the first aggressor.
(3) **Character of witness.** Evidence of the character of a witness, as provided in Rules 607, 608, and 609.	(3) **Exceptions for a Witness.** Evidence of a witness's char-

Text Effective Until 12/1/11	Text Effective 12/1/11
	acter may be admitted under Rules 607, 608, and 609.
(b) **Other crimes, wrongs, or acts.** Evidence of other crimes, wrongs, or acts is not admissible to prove the character of a person in order to show action in conformity therewith. It may, however, be admissible for other purposes, such as proof of motive, opportunity, intent, preparation, plan, knowledge, identity, or absence of mistake or accident, provided that upon request by the accused, the prosecution in a criminal case shall provide reasonable notice in advance of trial, or during trial if the court excuses pretrial notice on good cause shown, of the general nature of any such evidence it intends to introduce at trial.	(b) **Crimes, Wrongs, or Other Acts.** (1) ***Prohibited Uses.*** Evidence of a crime, wrong, or other act is not admissible to prove a person's character in order to show that on a particular occasion the person acted in accordance with the character. (2) ***Permitted Uses; Notice in a Criminal Case.*** This evidence may be admissible for another purpose, such as proving motive, opportunity, intent, preparation, plan, knowledge, identity, absence of mistake, or lack of accident. On request by a defendant in a criminal case, the prosecutor must: (A) provide reasonable notice of the general nature of any such evidence that the prosecutor intends to offer at trial; and (B) do so before trial—or during trial if the court, for good cause, excuses lack of pretrial notice.
Rule 405. Methods of Proving Character	**Rule 405. Methods of Proving Character**
(a) **Reputation or opinion.** In all cases in which evidence of character or a trait of character of a person is admissible, proof may be made by testimony as to reputation or by testimony in the form of an opinion. On cross-examination, inquiry is allowable into relevant specific instances of conduct.	(a) **By Reputation or Opinion.** When evidence of a person's character or character trait is admissible, it may be proved by testimony about the person's reputation or by testimony in the form of an opinion. On cross-examination of the character witness, the court may allow an inquiry into relevant

Text Effective Until 12/1/11	Text Effective 12/1/11
	specific instances of the person's conduct.
(b) **Specific instances of conduct.** In cases in which character or a trait of character of a person is an essential element of a charge, claim, or defense, proof may also be made of specific instances of that person's conduct.	(b) **By Specific Instances of Conduct.** When a person's character or character trait is an essential element of a charge, claim, or defense, the character or trait may also be proved by relevant specific instances of the person's conduct.
Rule 406. Habit; Routine Practice	**Rule 406. Habit; Routine Practice**
Evidence of the habit of a person or of the routine practice of an organization, whether corroborated or not and regardless of the presence of eyewitnesses, is relevant to prove that the conduct of the person or organization on a particular occasion was in conformity with the habit or routine practice.	Evidence of a person's habit or an organization's routine practice may be admitted to prove that on a particular occasion the person or organization acted in accordance with the habit or routine practice. The court may admit this evidence regardless of whether it is corroborated or whether there was an eyewitness.
Rule 407. Subsequent Remedial Measures	**Rule 407. Subsequent Remedial Measures**
When, after an injury or harm allegedly caused by an event, measures are taken that, if taken previously, would have made the injury or harm less likely to occur, evidence of the subsequent measures is not admissible to prove negligence, culpable conduct, a defect in a product, a defect in a product's design, or a need for a warning or instruction. This rule does not require the exclusion of evidence of subsequent measures when offered for another purpose, such as proving ownership, control, or feasibility of precautionary measures, if controverted, or impeachment.	When measures are taken that would have made an earlier injury or harm less likely to occur, evidence of the subsequent measures is not admissible to prove: • negligence; • culpable conduct; • a defect in a product or its design; or • a need for a warning or instruction. But the court may admit this evidence for another purpose, such as impeachment or—if disputed—proving ownership, control, or the feasibility of precautionary measures.

Text Effective Until 12/1/11	Text Effective 12/1/11
Rule 408. Compromise and Offers to Compromise	**Rule 408. Compromise Offers and Negotiations**
(a) **Prohibited uses.** Evidence of the following is not admissible on behalf of any party, when offered to prove liability for, invalidity of, or amount of a claim that was disputed as to validity or amount, or to impeach through a prior inconsistent statement or contradiction: (1) furnishing or offering or promising to furnish—or accepting or offering or promising to accept—a valuable consideration in compromising or attempting to compromise the claim; and (2) conduct or statements made in compromise negotiations regarding the claim, except when offered in a criminal case and the negotiations related to a claim by a public office or agency in the exercise of regulatory, investigative, or enforcement authority.	(a) **Prohibited Uses.** Evidence of the following is not admissible—on behalf of any party—either to prove or disprove the validity or amount of a disputed claim or to impeach by a prior inconsistent statement or a contradiction: (1) furnishing, promising, or offering—or accepting, promising to accept, or offering to accept—a valuable consideration in compromising or attempting to compromise the claim; and (2) conduct or a statement made during compromise negotiations about the claim—except when offered in a criminal case and when the negotiations related to a claim by a public office in the exercise of its regulatory, investigative, or enforcement authority.
(b) **Permitted uses.** This rule does not require exclusion if the evidence is offered for purposes not prohibited by subdivision (a). Examples of permissible purposes include proving a witness's bias or prejudice; negating a contention of undue delay; and proving an effort to obstruct a criminal investigation or prosecution.	(b) **Exceptions.** The court may admit this evidence for another purpose, such as proving a witness's bias or prejudice, negating a contention of undue delay, or proving an effort to obstruct a criminal investigation or prosecution.

Text Effective Until 12/1/11	Text Effective 12/1/11
Rule 409. Payment of Medical and Similar Expenses	**Rule 409. Offers to Pay Medical and Similar Expenses**
Evidence of furnishing or offering or promising to pay medical, hospital, or similar expenses occasioned by an injury is not admissible to prove liability for the injury.	Evidence of furnishing, promising to pay, or offering to pay medical, hospital, or similar expenses resulting from an injury is not admissible to prove liability for the injury.
Rule 410. Inadmissibility of Pleas, Plea Discussions, and Related Statements	**Rule 410. Pleas, Plea Discussions, and Related Statements**
Except as otherwise provided in this rule, evidence of the following is not, in any civil or criminal proceeding, admissible against the defendant who made the plea or was a participant in the plea discussions: (1) a plea of guilty which was later withdrawn; (2) a plea of nolo contendere; (3) any statement made in the course of any proceedings under Rule 11 of the Federal Rules of Criminal Procedure or comparable state procedure regarding either of the foregoing pleas; or (4) any statement made in the course of plea discussions with an attorney for the prosecuting authority which do not result in a plea of guilty or which result in a plea of guilty later withdrawn. However, such a statement is admissible (i) in any proceeding wherein another statement made in the course of the same plea or plea discussions has been introduced and the statement ought in fairness be considered contemporaneously with it, or (ii) in a criminal proceeding for perjury or false statement	(a) **Prohibited Uses.** In a civil or criminal case, evidence of the following is not admissible against the defendant who made the plea or participated in the plea discussions: (1) a guilty plea that was later withdrawn; (2) a nolo contendere plea; (3) a statement made during a proceeding on either of those pleas under Federal Rule of Criminal Procedure 11 or a comparable state procedure; or (4) a statement made during plea discussions with an attorney for the prosecuting authority if the discussions did not result in a guilty plea or they resulted in a later-withdrawn guilty plea. (b) **Exceptions.** The court may admit a statement described in Rule 410(a)(3) or (4): (1) in any proceeding in which another statement made during the same plea or plea discussions has been introduced, if in fairness the statements ought to be con-

Text Effective Until 12/1/11	Text Effective 12/1/11
if the statement was made by the defendant under oath, on the record and in the presence of counsel.	sidered together; or (2) in a criminal proceeding for perjury or false statement, if the defendant made the statement under oath, on the record, and with counsel present.
Rule 411. Liability Insurance	**Rule 411. Liability Insurance**
Evidence that a person was or was not insured against liability is not admissible upon the issue whether the person acted negligently or otherwise wrongfully. This rule does not require the exclusion of evidence of insurance against liability when offered for another purpose, such as proof of agency, ownership, or control, or bias or prejudice of a witness.	Evidence that a person was or was not insured against liability is not admissible to prove whether the person acted negligently or otherwise wrongfully. But the court may admit this evidence for another purpose, such as proving a witness's bias or prejudice or proving agency, ownership, or control.
Rule 412. Sex Offense Cases; Relevance of Alleged Victim's Past Sexual Behavior or Alleged Sexual Predisposition	**Rule 412. Sex-Offense Cases: The Victim's Sexual Behavior or Predisposition**
(a) **Evidence Generally Inadmissible.** The following evidence is not admissible in any civil or criminal proceeding involving alleged sexual misconduct except as provided in subdivisions (b) and (c): (1) Evidence offered to prove that any alleged victim engaged in other sexual behavior. (2) Evidence offered to prove any alleged victim's sexual predisposition.	(a) **Prohibited Uses.** The following evidence is not admissible in a civil or criminal proceeding involving alleged sexual misconduct: (1) evidence offered to prove that a victim engaged in other sexual behavior; or (2) evidence offered to prove a victim's sexual predisposition.
(b) **Exceptions.** (1) In a criminal case, the following evidence is admissible, if otherwise admissible under these rules:	(b) **Exceptions.** (1) ***Criminal Cases.*** The court may admit the following evidence in a criminal case:

Text Effective Until 12/1/11	Text Effective 12/1/11
(A) evidence of specific instances of sexual behavior by the alleged victim offered to prove that a person other than the accused was the source of semen, injury or other physical evidence;	(A) evidence of specific instances of a victim's sexual behavior, if offered to prove that someone other than the defendant was the source of semen, injury, or other physical evidence;
(B) evidence of specific instances of sexual behavior by the alleged victim with respect to the person accused of the sexual misconduct offered by the accused to prove consent or by the prosecution; and	(B) evidence of specific instances of a victim's sexual behavior with respect to the person accused of the sexual misconduct, if offered by the defendant to prove consent or if offered by the prosecutor; and
(C) evidence the exclusion of which would violate the constitutional rights of the defendant.	(C) evidence whose exclusion would violate the defendant's constitutional rights.
(2) In a civil case, evidence offered to prove the sexual behavior or sexual predisposition of any alleged victim is admissible if it is otherwise admissible under these rules and its probative value substantially outweighs the danger of harm to any victim and of unfair prejudice to any party. Evidence of an alleged victim's reputation is admissible only if it has been placed in controversy by the alleged victim.	(2) ***Civil Cases.*** In a civil case, the court may admit evidence offered to prove a victim's sexual behavior or sexual predisposition if its probative value substantially outweighs the danger of harm to any victim and of unfair prejudice to any party. The court may admit evidence of a victim's reputation only if the victim has placed it in controversy.
(c) Procedure To Determine Admissibility.	**(c) Procedure to Determine Admissibility.**
(1) A party intending to offer evidence under subdivision (b) must—	(1) ***Motion.*** If a party intends to offer evidence under Rule 412(b), the party must:
(A) file a written motion at least 14 days before trial specifically describing the evidence	(A) file a motion that specifically describes the evidence and states the purpose for which it is

Text Effective Until 12/1/11	Text Effective 12/1/11
and stating the purpose for which it is offered unless the court, for good cause requires a different time for filing or permits filing during trial; and (B) serve the motion on all parties and notify the alleged victim or, when appropriate, the alleged victim's guardian or representative. (2) Before admitting evidence under this rule the court must conduct a hearing in camera and afford the victim and parties a right to attend and be heard. The motion, related papers, and the record of the hearing must be sealed and remain under seal unless the court orders otherwise.	to be offered; (B) do so at least 14 days before trial unless the court, for good cause, sets a different time; (C) serve the motion on all parties; and (D) notify the victim or, when appropriate, the victim's guardian or representative. (2) ***Hearing.*** Before admitting evidence under this rule, the court must conduct an in camera hearing and give the victim and parties a right to attend and be heard. Unless the court orders otherwise, the motion, related materials, and the record of the hearing must be and remain sealed.
	(d) **Definition of "Victim."** In this rule, "victim" includes an alleged victim.
Rule 413. Evidence of Similar Crimes in Sexual Assault Cases	**Rule 413. Similar Crimes in Sexual-Assault Cases**
(a) In a criminal case in which the defendant is accused of an offense of sexual assault, evidence of the defendant's commission of another offense or offenses of sexual assault is admissible, and may be considered for its bearing on any matter to which it is relevant.	(a) **Permitted Uses.** In a criminal case in which a defendant is accused of a sexual assault, the court may admit evidence that the defendant committed any other sexual assault. The evidence may be considered on any matter to which it is relevant.
(b) In a case in which the Government intends to offer evidence under this rule, the attorney for the Government shall disclose the evidence to the defendant, including statements of witnesses or a summary of the substance of any testi-	(b) **Disclosure to the Defendant.** If the prosecutor intends to offer this evidence, the prosecutor must disclose it to the defendant, including witnesses' statements or a summary of the expected testimony. The prosecutor must do so at

Text Effective Until 12/1/11	Text Effective 12/1/11
mony that is expected to be offered, at least fifteen days before the scheduled date of trial or at such later time as the court may allow for good cause.	least 15 days before trial or at a later time that the court allows for good cause.
(c) This rule shall not be construed to limit the admission or consideration of evidence under any other rule.	(c) **Effect on Other Rules.** This rule does not limit the admission or consideration of evidence under any other rule.
(d) For purposes of this rule and Rule 415, "offense of sexual assault" means a crime under Federal law or the law of a State (as defined in section 513 of title 18, United States Code) that involved— (1) any conduct proscribed by chapter 109A of title 18, United States Code; (2) contact, without consent, between any part of the defendant's body or an object and the genitals or anus of another person; (3) contact, without consent, between the genitals or anus of the defendant and any part of another person's body; (4) deriving sexual pleasure or gratification from the infliction of death, bodily injury, or physical pain on another person; or (5) an attempt or conspiracy to engage in conduct described in paragraphs (1)–(4).	(d) **Definition of "Sexual Assault."** In this rule and Rule 415, "sexual assault" means a crime under federal law or under state law (as "state" is defined in 18 U.S.C. § 513) involving: (1) any conduct prohibited by 18 U.S.C. chapter 109A; (2) contact, without consent, between any part of the defendant's body—or an object—and another person's genitals or anus; (3) contact, without consent, between the defendant's genitals or anus and any part of another person's body; (4) deriving sexual pleasure or gratification from inflicting death, bodily injury, or physical pain on another person; or (5) an attempt or conspiracy to engage in conduct described in subparagraphs (1)–(4).
Rule 414. Evidence of Similar Crimes in Child Molestation Cases	**Rule 414. Similar Crimes in Child–Molestation Cases**
(a) In a criminal case in which the defendant is accused of an offense of child molestation, evidence of the defendant's commission of another offense or offenses of child	(a) **Permitted Uses.** In a criminal case in which a defendant is accused of child molestation, the court may admit evidence that the defendant committed any other

Text Effective Until 12/1/11	Text Effective 12/1/11
molestation is admissible, and may be considered for its bearing on any matter to which it is relevant.	child molestation. The evidence may be considered on any matter to which it is relevant.
(b) In a case in which the Government intends to offer evidence under this rule, the attorney for the Government shall disclose the evidence to the defendant, including statements of witnesses or a summary of the substance of any testimony that is expected to be offered, at least fifteen days before the scheduled date of trial or at such later time as the court may allow for good cause.	(b) **Disclosure to the Defendant.** If the prosecutor intends to offer this evidence, the prosecutor must disclose it to the defendant, including witnesses' statements or a summary of the expected testimony. The prosecutor must do so at least 15 days before trial or at a later time that the court allows for good cause.
(c) This rule shall not be construed to limit the admission or consideration of evidence under any other rule.	(c) **Effect on Other Rules.** This rule does not limit the admission or consideration of evidence under any other rule.
(d) For purposes of this rule and Rule 415, "child" means a person below the age of fourteen, and "offense of child molestation" means a crime under Federal law or the law of a State (as defined in section 513 of title 18, United States Code) that involved—	(d) **Definition of "Child" and "Child Molestation."** In this rule and Rule 415: (1) "child" means a person below the age of 14; and
(1) any conduct proscribed by chapter 109A of title 18, United States Code, that was committed in relation to a child;	(2) "child molestation" means a crime under federal law or under state law (as "state" is defined in 18 U.S.C. § 513) involving:
(2) any conduct proscribed by chapter 110 of title 18, United States Code;	**(A)** any conduct prohibited by 18 U.S.C. chapter 109A and committed with a child;
(3) contact between any part of the defendant's body or an object and the genitals or anus of a child;	**(B)** any conduct prohibited by 18 U.S.C. chapter 110;
(4) contact between the genitals or anus of the defendant and any part of the body of a child;	**(C)** contact between any part of the defendant's body—or an object—and a child's genitals or anus;

Text Effective Until 12/1/11	Text Effective 12/1/11
(5) deriving sexual pleasure or gratification from the infliction of death, bodily injury, or physical pain on a child; or (6) an attempt or conspiracy to engage in conduct described in paragraphs (1)–(5).	(D) contact between the defendant's genitals or anus and any part of a child's body; (E) deriving sexual pleasure or gratification from inflicting death, bodily injury, or physical pain on a child; or (F) an attempt or conspiracy to engage in conduct described in subparagraphs (A)–(E).
Rule 415. Evidence of Similar Acts in Civil Cases Concerning Sexual Assault or Child Molestation	**Rule 415. Similar Acts in Civil Cases Involving Sexual Assault or Child Molestation**
(a) In a civil case in which a claim for damages or other relief is predicated on a party's alleged commission of conduct constituting an offense of sexual assault or child molestation, evidence of that party's commission of another offense or offenses of sexual assault or child molestation is admissible and may be considered as provided in Rule 413 and Rule 414 of these rules.	(a) **Permitted Uses.** In a civil case involving a claim for relief based on a party's alleged sexual assault or child molestation, the court may admit evidence that the party committed any other sexual assault or child molestation. The evidence may be considered as provided in Rules 413 and 414.
(b) A party who intends to offer evidence under this Rule shall disclose the evidence to the party against whom it will be offered, including statements of witnesses or a summary of the substance of any testimony that is expected to be offered, at least fifteen days before the scheduled date of trial or at such later time as the court may allow for good cause.	(b) **Disclosure to the Opponent.** If a party intends to offer this evidence, the party must disclose it to the party against whom it will be offered, including witnesses' statements or a summary of the expected testimony. The party must do so at least 15 days before trial or at a later time that the court allows for good cause.
(c) This rule shall not be construed to limit the admission or consideration of evidence under any other rule.	(c) **Effect on Other Rules.** This rule does not limit the admission or consideration of evidence under any other rule.

Text Effective Until 12/1/11	Text Effective 12/1/11
ARTICLE V. PRIVILEGES **Rule 501. General Rule**	**ARTICLE V. PRIVILEGES** **Rule 501. Privilege in General**
Except as otherwise required by the Constitution of the United States or provided by Act of Congress or in rules prescribed by the Supreme Court pursuant to statutory authority, the privilege of a witness, person, government, State, or political subdivision thereof shall be governed by the principles of the common law as they may be interpreted by the courts of the United States in the light of reason and experience. However, in civil actions and proceedings, with respect to an element of a claim or defense as to which State law supplies the rule of decision, the privilege of a witness, person, government, State, or political subdivision thereof shall be determined in accordance with State law.	The common law—as interpreted by United States courts in the light of reason and experience—governs a claim of privilege unless any of the following provides otherwise: • the United States Constitution; • a federal statute; or • rules prescribed by the Supreme Court. But in a civil case, state law governs privilege regarding a claim or defense for which state law supplies the rule of decision.
Rule 502. Attorney–Client Privilege and Work Product; Limitations on Waiver	**Rule 502. Attorney–Client Privilege and Work Product; Limitations on Waiver**
The following provisions apply, in the circumstances set out, to disclosure of a communication or information covered by the attorney-client privilege or work-product protection.	The following provisions apply, in the circumstances set out, to disclosure of a communication or information covered by the attorney-client privilege or work-product protection.
(a) **Disclosure made in a Federal proceeding or to a Federal office or agency; scope of a waiver.** When the disclosure is made in a Federal proceeding or to a Federal office or agency and waives the attorney-client privilege or work-product protection, the waiver extends to an undisclosed communication or information in a Federal or State proceeding only if: (1) the waiver is intentional; (2) the disclosed and undisclosed	(a) **Disclosure Made in a Federal Proceeding or to a Federal Office or Agency; Scope of a Waiver.** When the disclosure is made in a federal proceeding or to a federal office or agency and waives the attorney-client privilege or work-product protection, the waiver extends to an undisclosed communication or information in a federal or state proceeding only if: (1) the waiver is intentional;

Text Effective Until 12/1/11	Text Effective 12/1/11
communications or information concern the same subject matter; and (3) they ought in fairness to be considered together.	(2) the disclosed and undisclosed communications or information concern the same subject matter; and (3) they ought in fairness to be considered together.
(b) **Inadvertent disclosure.** When made in a Federal proceeding or to a Federal office or agency, the disclosure does not operate as a waiver in a Federal or State proceeding if: (1) the disclosure is inadvertent; (2) the holder of the privilege or protection took reasonable steps to prevent disclosure; and (3) the holder promptly took reasonable steps to rectify the error, including (if applicable) following Federal Rule of Civil Procedure 26(b)(5)(B).	(b) **Inadvertent Disclosure.** When made in a federal proceeding or to a federal office or agency, the disclosure does not operate as a waiver in a federal or state proceeding if: (1) the disclosure is inadvertent; (2) the holder of the privilege or protection took reasonable steps to prevent disclosure; and (3) the holder promptly took reasonable steps to rectify the error, including (if applicable) following Federal Rule of Civil Procedure 26(b)(5)(B).
(c) **Disclosure made in a State proceeding.** When the disclosure is made in a State proceeding and is not the subject of a State-court order concerning waiver, the disclosure does not operate as a waiver in a Federal proceeding if the disclosure: (1) would not be a waiver under this rule if it had been made in a Federal proceeding; or (2) is not a waiver under the law of the State where the disclosure occurred.	(c) **Disclosure Made in a State Proceeding.** When the disclosure is made in a state proceeding and is not the subject of a state-court order concerning waiver, the disclosure does not operate as a waiver in a federal proceeding if the disclosure: (1) would not be a waiver under this rule if it had been made in a federal proceeding; or (2) is not a waiver under the law of the state where the disclosure occurred.
(d) **Controlling effect of a court order.** A Federal court may order that the privilege or protection is not waived by disclosure connected with the litigation pending before the court—in which event the	(d) **Controlling Effect of a Court Order.** A federal court may order that the privilege or protection is not waived by disclosure connected with the litigation pending before the court—in which event the

Text Effective Until 12/1/11	Text Effective 12/1/11
disclosure is also not a waiver in any other Federal or State proceeding.	disclosure is also not a waiver in any other federal or state proceeding.
(e) **Controlling effect of a party agreement.** An agreement on the effect of disclosure in a Federal proceeding is binding only on the parties to the agreement, unless it is incorporated into a court order.	(e) **Controlling Effect of a Party Agreement.** An agreement on the effect of disclosure in a federal proceeding is binding only on the parties to the agreement, unless it is incorporated into a court order.
(f) **Controlling effect of this rule.** Notwithstanding Rules 101 and 1101, this rule applies to State proceedings and to Federal court-annexed and Federal court-mandated arbitration proceedings, in the circumstances set out in the rule. And notwithstanding Rule 501, this rule applies even if State law provides the rule of decision.	(f) **Controlling Effect of this Rule.** Notwithstanding Rules 101 and 1101, this rule applies to state proceedings and to federal court-annexed and federal court-mandated arbitration proceedings, in the circumstances set out in the rule. And notwithstanding Rule 501, this rule applies even if state law provides the rule of decision.
(g) **Definitions.** In this rule: (1) "attorney-client privilege" means the protection that applicable law provides for confidential attorney-client communications; and (2) "work-product protection" means the protection that applicable law provides for tangible material (or its intangible equivalent) prepared in anticipation of litigation or for trial.	(g) **Definitions.** In this rule: (1) "attorney-client privilege" means the protection that applicable law provides for confidential attorney-client communications; and (2) "work-product protection" means the protection that applicable law provides for tangible material (or its intangible equivalent) prepared in anticipation of litigation or for trial.

Text Effective Until 12/1/11	Text Effective 12/1/11
ARTICLE VI. WITNESSES	**ARTICLE VI. WITNESSES**
Rule 601. General Rule of Competency	**Rule 601. Competency to Testify in General**
Every person is competent to be a witness except as otherwise provided in these rules. However, in civil actions and proceedings, with respect to an element of a claim or defense as to which State law supplies the rule of decision, the competency of a witness shall be determined in accordance with State law.	Every person is competent to be a witness unless these rules provide otherwise. But in a civil case, state law governs the witness's competency regarding a claim or defense for which state law supplies the rule of decision.
Rule 602. Lack of Personal Knowledge	**Rule 602. Need for Personal Knowledge**
A witness may not testify to a matter unless evidence is introduced sufficient to support a finding that the witness has personal knowledge of the matter. Evidence to prove personal knowledge may, but need not, consist of the witness' own testimony. This rule is subject to the provisions of rule 703, relating to opinion testimony by expert witnesses.	A witness may testify to a matter only if evidence is introduced sufficient to support a finding that the witness has personal knowledge of the matter. Evidence to prove personal knowledge may consist of the witness's own testimony. This rule does not apply to a witness's expert testimony under Rule 703.
Rule 603. Oath or Affirmation	**Rule 603. Oath or Affirmation to Testify Truthfully**
Before testifying, every witness shall be required to declare that the witness will testify truthfully, by oath or affirmation administered in a form calculated to awaken the witness' conscience and impress the witness' mind with the duty to do so.	Before testifying, a witness must give an oath or affirmation to testify truthfully. It must be in a form designed to impress that duty on the witness's conscience.
Rule 604. Interpreters	**Rule 604. Interpreter**
An interpreter is subject to the provisions of these rules relating to qualification as an expert and the administra-	An interpreter must be qualified and must give an oath or affirmation to make a true translation.

Text Effective Until 12/1/11	Text Effective 12/1/11
tion of an oath or affirmation to make a true translation.	
Rule 605. Competency of Judge as Witness	**Rule 605. Judge's Competency as a Witness**
The judge presiding at the trial may not testify in that trial as a witness. No objection need be made in order to preserve the point.	The presiding judge may not testify as a witness at the trial. A party need not object to preserve the issue.
Rule 606. Competency of Juror as Witness	**Rule 606. Juror's Competency as a Witness**
(a) **At the trial.** A member of the jury may not testify as a witness before that jury in the trial of the case in which the juror is sitting. If the juror is called so to testify, the opposing party shall be afforded an opportunity to object out of the presence of the jury.	(a) **At the Trial.** A juror may not testify as a witness before the other jurors at the trial. If a juror is called to testify, the court must give a party an opportunity to object outside the jury's presence.
(b) **Inquiry into validity of verdict or indictment.** Upon an inquiry into the validity of a verdict or indictment, a juror may not testify as to any matter or statement occurring during the course of the jury's deliberations or to the effect of anything upon that or any other juror's mind or emotions as influencing the juror to assent to or dissent from the verdict or indictment or concerning the juror's mental processes in connection therewith. But a juror may testify about (1) whether extraneous prejudicial information was improperly brought to the jury's attention, (2) whether any outside influence was improperly brought to bear upon any juror, or (3) whether there was a mistake in entering the verdict onto the verdict form. A juror's affidavit or evidence of any statement by the juror may not be received on a	(b) **During an Inquiry Into the Validity of a Verdict or Indictment.** (1) ***Prohibited Testimony or Other Evidence.*** During an inquiry into the validity of a verdict or indictment, a juror may not testify about any statement made or incident that occurred during the jury's deliberations; the effect of anything on that juror's or another juror's vote; or any juror's mental processes concerning the verdict or indictment. The court may not receive a juror's affidavit or evidence of a juror's statement on these matters. (2) ***Exceptions.*** A juror may testify about whether:

Text Effective Until 12/1/11	Text Effective 12/1/11
matter about which the juror would be precluded from testifying.	**(A)** extraneous prejudicial information was improperly brought to the jury's attention; **(B)** an outside influence was improperly brought to bear on any juror; or **(C)** a mistake was made in entering the verdict on the verdict form.
Rule 607. Who May Impeach	**Rule 607. Who May Impeach a Witness**
The credibility of a witness may be attacked by any party, including the party calling the witness.	Any party, including the party that called the witness, may attack the witness's credibility.
Rule 608. Evidence of Character and Conduct of Witness	**Rule 608. A Witness's Character for Truthfulness or Untruthfulness**
(a) **Opinion and reputation evidence of character.** The credibility of a witness may be attacked or supported by evidence in the form of opinion or reputation, but subject to these limitations: (1) the evidence may refer only to character for truthfulness or untruthfulness, and (2) evidence of truthful character is admissible only after the character of the witness for truthfulness has been attacked by opinion or reputation evidence or otherwise.	(a) **Reputation or Opinion Evidence.** A witness's credibility may be attacked or supported by testimony about the witness's reputation for having a character for truthfulness or untruthfulness, or by testimony in the form of an opinion about that character. But evidence of truthful character is admissible only after the witness's character for truthfulness has been attacked.
(b) **Specific instances of conduct.** Specific instances of the conduct of a witness, for the purpose of attacking or supporting the witness' character for truthfulness, other than conviction of crime as provided in rule 609, may not be proved by extrinsic evidence. They may, however, in the discretion of the court, if probative of	(b) **Specific Instances of Conduct.** Except for a criminal conviction under Rule 609, extrinsic evidence is not admissible to prove specific instances of a witness's conduct in order to attack or support the witness's character for truthfulness. But the court may, on cross-examination, allow them to be inquired into if they are probative of the

Text Effective Until 12/1/11	Text Effective 12/1/11
truthfulness or untruthfulness, be inquired into on cross-examination of the witness (1) concerning the witness' character for truthfulness or untruthfulness, or (2) concerning the character for truthfulness or untruthfulness of another witness as to which character the witness being cross-examined has testified. The giving of testimony, whether by an accused or by any other witness, does not operate as a waiver of the accused's or the witness' privilege against self-incrimination when examined with respect to matters that relate only to character for truthfulness.	character for truthfulness or untruthfulness of: (1) the witness; or (2) another witness whose character the witness being cross-examined has testified about. By testifying on another matter, a witness does not waive any privilege against self-incrimination for testimony that relates only to the witness's character for truthfulness.
Rule 609. Impeachment by Evidence of Conviction of Crime	**Rule 609. Impeachment by Evidence of a Criminal Conviction**
(a) **General rule.** For the purpose of attacking the character for truthfulness of a witness, (1) evidence that a witness other than an accused has been convicted of a crime shall be admitted, subject to Rule 403, if the crime was punishable by death or imprisonment in excess of one year under the law under which the witness was convicted, and evidence that an accused has been convicted of such a crime shall be admitted if the court determines that the probative value of admitting this evidence outweighs its prejudicial effect to the accused; and (2) evidence that any witness has been convicted of a crime shall be admitted regardless of the punishment, if it readily can be determined that establishing the elements of the crime required proof or admission of an act of dishonesty or false statement by the witness.	(a) **In General.** The following rules apply to attacking a witness's character for truthfulness by evidence of a criminal conviction: (1) for a crime that, in the convicting jurisdiction, was punishable by death or by imprisonment for more than one year, the evidence: (A) must be admitted, subject to Rule 403, in a civil case or in a criminal case in which the witness is not a defendant; and (B) must be admitted in a criminal case in which the witness is a defendant, if the probative value of the evidence outweighs its prejudicial effect to that defendant; and (2) for any crime regardless of the punishment, the evidence must be admitted if the court can readily determine that establishing the elements of

Text Effective Until 12/1/11	Text Effective 12/1/11
	the crime required proving—or the witness's admitting—a dishonest act or false statement.
(b) Time limit. Evidence of a conviction under this rule is not admissible if a period of more than ten years has elapsed since the date of the conviction or of the release of the witness from the confinement imposed for that conviction, whichever is the later date, unless the court determines, in the interests of justice, that the probative value of the conviction supported by specific facts and circumstances substantially outweighs its prejudicial effect. However, evidence of a conviction more than 10 years old as calculated herein, is not admissible unless the proponent gives to the adverse party sufficient advance written notice of intent to use such evidence to provide the adverse party with a fair opportunity to contest the use of such evidence.	**(b) Limit on Using the Evidence After 10 Years.** This subdivision (b) applies if more than 10 years have passed since the witness's conviction or release from confinement for it, whichever is later. Evidence of the conviction is admissible only if: (1) its probative value, supported by specific facts and circumstances, substantially outweighs its prejudicial effect; and (2) the proponent gives an adverse party reasonable written notice of the intent to use it so that the party has a fair opportunity to contest its use.
(c) Effect of pardon, annulment, or certificate of rehabilitation. Evidence of a conviction is not admissible under this rule if (1) the conviction has been the subject of a pardon, annulment, certificate of rehabilitation, or other equivalent procedure based on a finding of the rehabilitation of the person convicted, and that person has not been convicted of a subsequent crime that was punishable by death or imprisonment in excess of one year, or (2) the conviction has been the subject of a pardon, annulment, or other equivalent procedure based on a finding of innocence.	**(c) Effect of a Pardon, Annulment, or Certificate of Rehabilitation.** Evidence of a conviction is not admissible if: (1) the conviction has been the subject of a pardon, annulment, certificate of rehabilitation, or other equivalent procedure based on a finding that the person has been rehabilitated, and the person has not been convicted of a later crime punishable by death or by imprisonment for more than one year; or (2) the conviction has been the subject of a pardon, annulment, or other equivalent procedure based on a finding of innocence.

Text Effective Until 12/1/11	Text Effective 12/1/11
(d) **Juvenile adjudications.** Evidence of juvenile adjudications is generally not admissible under this rule. The court may, however, in a criminal case allow evidence of a juvenile adjudication of a witness other than the accused if conviction of the offense would be admissible to attack the credibility of an adult and the court is satisfied that admission in evidence is necessary for a fair determination of the issue of guilt or innocence.	(d) **Juvenile Adjudications.** Evidence of a juvenile adjudication is admissible under this rule only if: (1) it is offered in a criminal case; (2) the adjudication was of a witness other than the defendant; (3) an adult's conviction for that offense would be admissible to attack the adult's credibility; and (4) admitting the evidence is necessary to fairly determine guilt or innocence.
(e) **Pendency of appeal.** The pendency of an appeal therefrom does not render evidence of a conviction inadmissible. Evidence of the pendency of an appeal is admissible.	(e) **Pendency of an Appeal.** A conviction that satisfies this rule is admissible even if an appeal is pending. Evidence of the pendency is also admissible.
Rule 610. Religious Beliefs or Opinions	**Rule 610. Religious Beliefs or Opinions**
Evidence of the beliefs or opinions of a witness on matters of religion is not admissible for the purpose of showing that by reason of their nature the witness' credibility is impaired or enhanced.	Evidence of a witness's religious beliefs or opinions is not admissible to attack or support the witness's credibility.
Rule 611. Mode and Order of Interrogation and Presentation	**Rule 611. Mode and Order of Examining Witnesses and Presenting Evidence**
(a) **Control by court.** The court shall exercise reasonable control over the mode and order of interrogating witnesses and presenting evidence so as to (1) make the interrogation and presentation effective for the ascertainment of the truth, (2) avoid needless con-	(a) **Control by the Court; Purposes.** The court should exercise reasonable control over the mode and order of examining witnesses and presenting evidence so as to: (1) make those procedures effective for determining the

Text Effective Until 12/1/11	Text Effective 12/1/11
sumption of time, and (3) protect witnesses from harassment or undue embarrassment.	truth; (2) avoid wasting time; and (3) protect witnesses from harassment or undue embarrassment.
(b) Scope of cross-examination. Cross-examination should be limited to the subject matter of the direct examination and matters affecting the credibility of the witness. The court may, in the exercise of discretion, permit inquiry into additional matters as if on direct examination.	**(b) Scope of Cross–Examination.** Cross-examination should not go beyond the subject matter of the direct examination and matters affecting the witness's credibility. The court may allow inquiry into additional matters as if on direct examination.
(c) Leading questions. Leading questions should not be used on the direct examination of a witness except as may be necessary to develop the witness' testimony. Ordinarily leading questions should be permitted on cross-examination. When a party calls a hostile witness, an adverse party, or a witness identified with an adverse party, interrogation may be by leading questions.	**(c) Leading Questions.** Leading questions should not be used on direct examination except as necessary to develop the witness's testimony. Ordinarily, the court should allow leading questions: (1) on cross-examination; and (2) when a party calls a hostile witness, an adverse party, or a witness identified with an adverse party.
Rule 612. Writing Used To Refresh Memory	**Rule 612. Writing Used to Refresh a Witness's Memory**
Except as otherwise provided in criminal proceedings by section 3500 of title 18, United States Code, if a witness uses a writing to refresh memory for the purpose of testifying, either— (1) while testifying, or (2) before testifying, if the court in its discretion determines it is necessary in the interests of justice, an adverse party is entitled to have the writing produced at the hearing, to inspect it, to cross-examine the witness	**(a) Scope.** This rule gives an adverse party certain options when a witness uses a writing to refresh memory: (1) while testifying; or (2) before testifying, if the court decides that justice requires the party to have those options. **(b) Adverse Party's Options; Deleting Unrelated Matter.** Unless 18 U.S.C. § 3500 provides otherwise in a criminal case, an adverse par-

Text Effective Until 12/1/11	Text Effective 12/1/11
thereon, and to introduce in evidence those portions which relate to the testimony of the witness. If it is claimed that the writing contains matters not related to the subject matter of the testimony the court shall examine the writing in camera, excise any portions not so related, and order delivery of the remainder to the party entitled thereto. Any portion withheld over objections shall be preserved and made available to the appellate court in the event of an appeal. If a writing is not produced or delivered pursuant to order under this rule, the court shall make any order justice requires, except that in criminal cases when the prosecution elects not to comply, the order shall be one striking the testimony or, if the court in its discretion determines that the interests of justice so require, declaring a mistrial.	ty is entitled to have the writing produced at the hearing, to inspect it, to cross-examine the witness about it, and to introduce in evidence any portion that relates to the witness's testimony. If the producing party claims that the writing includes unrelated matter, the court must examine the writing in camera, delete any unrelated portion, and order that the rest be delivered to the adverse party. Any portion deleted over objection must be preserved for the record. (c) **Failure to Produce or Deliver the Writing.** If a writing is not produced or is not delivered as ordered, the court may issue any appropriate order. But if the prosecution does not comply in a criminal case, the court must strike the witness's testimony or—if justice so requires—declare a mistrial.
Rule 613. Prior Statements of Witnesses	**Rule 613. Witness's Prior Statement**
(a) **Examining witness concerning prior statement.** In examining a witness concerning a prior statement made by the witness, whether written or not, the statement need not be shown nor its contents disclosed to the witness at that time, but on request the same shall be shown or disclosed to opposing counsel.	(a) **Showing or Disclosing the Statement During Examination.** When examining a witness about the witness's prior statement, a party need not show it or disclose its contents to the witness. But the party must, on request, show it or disclose its contents to an adverse party's attorney.
(b) **Extrinsic evidence of prior inconsistent statement of witness.** Extrinsic evidence of a prior inconsistent statement by a witness is not admissible unless the witness is afforded an opportunity to explain or deny the same and the opposite party is afforded an opportunity to interrogate the witness thereon, or the interests of justice otherwise require. This provision does not apply to admis-	(b) **Extrinsic Evidence of a Prior Inconsistent Statement.** Extrinsic evidence of a witness's prior inconsistent statement is admissible only if the witness is given an opportunity to explain or deny the statement and an adverse party is given an opportunity to examine the witness about it, or if justice so requires. This subdivision (b) does not apply to an opposing party's statement under Rule

Text Effective Until 12/1/11	Text Effective 12/1/11
sions of a party-opponent as defined in rule 801(d)(2).	801(d)(2).
Rule 614. Calling and Interrogation of Witnesses by Court	**Rule 614. Court's Calling or Examining a Witness**
(a) Calling by court. The court may, on its own motion or at the suggestion of a party, call witnesses, and all parties are entitled to cross-examine witnesses thus called.	**(a) Calling.** The court may call a witness on its own or at a party's request. Each party is entitled to cross-examine the witness.
(b) Interrogation by court. The court may interrogate witnesses, whether called by itself or by a party.	**(b) Examining.** The court may examine a witness regardless of who calls the witness.
(c) Objections. Objections to the calling of witnesses by the court or to interrogation by it may be made at the time or at the next available opportunity when the jury is not present.	**(c) Objections.** A party may object to the court's calling or examining a witness either at that time or at the next opportunity when the jury is not present.
Rule 615. Exclusion of Witnesses	**Rule 615. Excluding Witnesses**
At the request of a party the court shall order witnesses excluded so that they cannot hear the testimony of other witnesses, and it may make the order of its own motion. This rule does not authorize exclusion of (1) a party who is a natural person, or (2) an officer or employee of a party which is not a natural person designated as its representative by its attorney, or (3) a person whose presence is shown by a party to be essential to the presentation of the party's cause, or (4) a person authorized by statute to be present.	At a party's request, the court must order witnesses excluded so that they cannot hear other witnesses' testimony. Or the court may do so on its own. But this rule does not authorize excluding: **(a)** a party who is a natural person; **(b)** an officer or employee of a party that is not a natural person, after being designated as the party's representative by its attorney; **(c)** a person whose presence a party shows to be essential to presenting the party's claim or defense; or **(d)** a person authorized by statute to be present.

Text Effective Until 12/1/11	Text Effective 12/1/11
ARTICLE VII. OPINIONS AND EXPERT TESTIMONY	**ARTICLE VII. OPINIONS AND EXPERT TESTIMONY**
Rule 701. Opinion Testimony by Lay Witnesses	**Rule 701. Opinion Testimony by Lay Witnesses**
If the witness is not testifying as an expert, the witness' testimony in the form of opinions or inferences is limited to those opinions or inferences which are (a) rationally based on the perception of the witness, and (b) helpful to a clear understanding of the witness' testimony or the determination of a fact in issue, and (c) not based on scientific, technical, or other specialized knowledge within the scope of Rule 702.	If a witness is not testifying as an expert, testimony in the form of an opinion is limited to one that is: **(a)** rationally based on the witness's perception; **(b)** helpful to clearly understanding the witness's testimony or to determining a fact in issue; and **(c)** not based on scientific, technical, or other specialized knowledge within the scope of Rule 702.
Rule 702. Testimony by Experts	**Rule 702. Testimony by Expert Witnesses**
If scientific, technical, or other specialized knowledge will assist the trier of fact to understand the evidence or to determine a fact in issue, a witness qualified as an expert by knowledge, skill, experience, training, or education, may testify thereto in the form of an opinion or otherwise, if (1) the testimony is based upon sufficient facts or data, (2) the testimony is the product of reliable principles and methods, and (3) the witness has applied the principles and methods reliably to the facts of the case.	A witness who is qualified as an expert by knowledge, skill, experience, training, or education may testify in the form of an opinion or otherwise if: **(a)** the expert's scientific, technical, or other specialized knowledge will help the trier of fact to understand the evidence or to determine a fact in issue; **(b)** the testimony is based on sufficient facts or data; **(c)** the testimony is the product of reliable principles and methods; and **(d)** the expert has reliably applied the principles and methods to the facts of the case.

Text Effective Until 12/1/11	Text Effective 12/1/11
Rule 703. Bases of Opinion Testimony by Experts	**Rule 703. Bases of an Expert's Opinion Testimony**
The facts or data in the particular case upon which an expert bases an opinion or inference may be those perceived by or made known to the expert at or before the hearing. If of a type reasonably relied upon by experts in the particular field in forming opinions or inferences upon the subject, the facts or data need not be admissible in evidence in order for the opinion or inference to be admitted. Facts or data that are otherwise inadmissible shall not be disclosed to the jury by the proponent of the opinion or inference unless the court determines that their probative value in assisting the jury to evaluate the expert's opinion substantially outweighs their prejudicial effect.	An expert may base an opinion on facts or data in the case that the expert has been made aware of or personally observed. If experts in the particular field would reasonably rely on those kinds of facts or data in forming an opinion on the subject, they need not be admissible for the opinion to be admitted. But if the facts or data would otherwise be inadmissible, the proponent of the opinion may disclose them to the jury only if their probative value in helping the jury evaluate the opinion substantially outweighs their prejudicial effect.
Rule 704. Opinion on Ultimate Issue	**Rule 704. Opinion on an Ultimate Issue**
(a) Except as provided in subdivision (b), testimony in the form of an opinion or inference otherwise admissible is not objectionable because it embraces an ultimate issue to be decided by the trier of fact.	**(a) In General—Not Automatically Objectionable.** An opinion is not objectionable just because it embraces an ultimate issue.
(b) No expert witness testifying with respect to the mental state or condition of a defendant in a criminal case may state an opinion or inference as to whether the defendant did or did not have the mental state or condition constituting an element of the crime charged or of a defense thereto. Such ultimate issues are matters for the trier of fact alone.	**(b) Exception.** In a criminal case, an expert witness must not state an opinion about whether the defendant did or did not have a mental state or condition that constitutes an element of the crime charged or of a defense. Those matters are for the trier of fact alone.

Text Effective Until 12/1/11	Text Effective 12/1/11
Rule 705. Disclosure of Facts or Data Underlying Expert Opinion	**Rule 705. Disclosing the Facts or Data Underlying an Expert's Opinion**
The expert may testify in terms of opinion or inference and give reasons therefor without first testifying to the underlying facts or data, unless the court requires otherwise. The expert may in any event be required to disclose the underlying facts or data on cross-examination.	Unless the court orders otherwise, an expert may state an opinion—and give the reasons for it—without first testifying to the underlying facts or data. But the expert may be required to disclose those facts or data on cross-examination.
Rule 706. Court Appointed Experts	**Rule 706. Court–Appointed Expert Witnesses**
(a) **Appointment.** The court may on its own motion or on the motion of any party enter an order to show cause why expert witnesses should not be appointed, and may request the parties to submit nominations. The court may appoint any expert witnesses agreed upon by the parties, and may appoint expert witnesses of its own selection. An expert witness shall not be appointed by the court unless the witness consents to act. A witness so appointed shall be informed of the witness' duties by the court in writing, a copy of which shall be filed with the clerk, or at a conference in which the parties shall have opportunity to participate. A witness so appointed shall advise the parties of the witness' findings, if any; the witness' deposition may be taken by any party; and the witness may be called to testify by the court or any party. The witness shall be subject to cross-examination by each party, including a party calling the witness.	(a) **Appointment Process.** On a party's motion or on its own, the court may order the parties to show cause why expert witnesses should not be appointed and may ask the parties to submit nominations. The court may appoint any expert that the parties agree on and any of its own choosing. But the court may only appoint someone who consents to act. (b) **Expert's Role.** The court must inform the expert of the expert's duties. The court may do so in writing and have a copy filed with the clerk or may do so orally at a conference in which the parties have an opportunity to participate. The expert: (1) must advise the parties of any findings the expert makes; (2) may be deposed by any party; (3) may be called to testify by the court or any party; and (4) may be cross-examined by any party, including the party that called the expert.

Text Effective Until 12/1/11	Text Effective 12/1/11
(b) **Compensation.** Expert witnesses so appointed are entitled to reasonable compensation in whatever sum the court may allow. The compensation thus fixed is payable from funds which may be provided by law in criminal cases and civil actions and proceedings involving just compensation under the fifth amendment. In other civil actions and proceedings the compensation shall be paid by the parties in such proportion and at such time as the court directs, and thereafter charged in like manner as other costs.	(c) **Compensation.** The expert is entitled to a reasonable compensation, as set by the court. The compensation is payable as follows: (1) in a criminal case or in a civil case involving just compensation under the Fifth Amendment, from any funds that are provided by law; and (2) in any other civil case, by the parties in the proportion and at the time that the court directs—and the compensation is then charged like other costs.
(c) **Disclosure of appointment.** In the exercise of its discretion, the court may authorize disclosure to the jury of the fact that the court appointed the expert witness.	(d) **Disclosing the Appointment to the Jury.** The court may authorize disclosure to the jury that the court appointed the expert.
(d) **Parties' experts of own selection.** Nothing in this rule limits the parties in calling expert witnesses of their own selection.	(e) **Parties' Choice of Their Own Experts.** This rule does not limit a party in calling its own experts.

Text Effective Until 12/1/11	Text Effective 12/1/11
ARTICLE VIII. HEARSAY **Rule 801. Definitions**	**ARTICLE VIII. HEARSAY** **Rule 801. Definitions That Apply to This Article; Exclusions From Hearsay**
The following definitions apply under this article: (a) **Statement.** A "statement" is (1) an oral or written assertion or (2) nonverbal conduct of a person, if it is intended by the person as an assertion.	(a) **Statement.** "Statement" means a person's oral assertion, written assertion, or nonverbal conduct, if the person intended it as an assertion.
(b) **Declarant.** A "declarant" is a person who makes a statement.	(b) **Declarant.** "Declarant" means the person who made the statement.
(c) **Hearsay.** "Hearsay" is a statement, other than one made by the declarant while testifying at the trial or hearing, offered in evidence to prove the truth of the matter asserted.	(c) **Hearsay.** "Hearsay" means a statement that: (1) the declarant does not make while testifying at the current trial or hearing; and (2) a party offers in evidence to prove the truth of the matter asserted in the statement.
(d) **Statements which are not hearsay.** A statement is not hearsay if— (1) **Prior statement by witness.** The declarant testifies at the trial or hearing and is subject to cross-examination concerning the statement, and the statement is (A) inconsistent with the declarant's testimony, and was given under oath subject to the penalty of perjury at a trial, hearing, or other proceeding, or in a deposition, or (B) consistent with the declarant's testimony and is of-	(d) **Statements That Are Not Hearsay.** A statement that meets the following conditions is not hearsay: (1) ***A Declarant-Witness's Prior Statement.*** The declarant testifies and is subject to cross-examination about a prior statement, and the statement: (A) is inconsistent with the declarant's testimony and was given under penalty of perjury at a trial, hearing, or other proceeding or in a de-

Text Effective Until 12/1/11	Text Effective 12/1/11
fered to rebut an express or implied charge against the declarant of recent fabrication or improper influence or motive, or (C) one of identification of a person made after perceiving the person; or	position; **(B)** is consistent with the declarant's testimony and is offered to rebut an express or implied charge that the declarant recently fabricated it or acted from a recent improper influence or motive in so testifying; or **(C)** identifies a person as someone the declarant perceived earlier.
(2) **Admission by party-opponent.** The statement is offered against a party and is (A) the party's own statement, in either an individual or a representative capacity or (B) a statement of which the party has manifested an adoption or belief in its truth, or (C) a statement by a person authorized by the party to make a statement concerning the subject, or (D) a statement by the party's agent or servant concerning a matter within the scope of the agency or employment, made during the existence of the relationship, or (E) a statement by a coconspirator of a party during the course and in furtherance of the conspiracy. The contents of the statement shall be considered but are not alone sufficient to establish the declarant's authority under subdivision (C), the agency or employment relationship and scope thereof under subdivision (D), or the existence of the conspiracy and the participation therein of the declarant and the party against whom the statement is offered under subdivision (E).	(2) ***An Opposing Party's Statement.*** The statement is offered against an opposing party and: **(A)** was made by the party in an individual or representative capacity; **(B)** is one the party manifested that it adopted or believed to be true; **(C)** was made by a person whom the party authorized to make a statement on the subject; **(D)** was made by the party's agent or employee on a matter within the scope of that relationship and while it existed; or **(E)** was made by the party's coconspirator during and in furtherance of the conspiracy. The statement must be considered but does not by itself establish the declarant's authority under (C); the existence or scope of the relationship under (D); or the

Text Effective Until 12/1/11	Text Effective 12/1/11
	existence of the conspiracy or participation in it under (E).
Rule 802. Hearsay Rule	**Rule 802. The Rule Against Hearsay**
Hearsay is not admissible except as provided by these rules or by other rules prescribed by the Supreme Court pursuant to statutory authority or by Act of Congress.	Hearsay is not admissible unless any of the following provides otherwise: • a federal statute; • these rules; or • other rules prescribed by the Supreme Court.
Rule 803. Hearsay Exceptions; Availability of Declarant Immaterial	**Rule 803. Exceptions to the Rule Against Hearsay—Regardless of Whether the Declarant Is Available as a Witness**
The following are not excluded by the hearsay rule, even though the declarant is available as a witness: (1) **Present sense impression.** A statement describing or explaining an event or condition made while the declarant was perceiving the event or condition, or immediately thereafter.	The following are not excluded by the rule against hearsay, regardless of whether the declarant is available as a witness: (1) ***Present Sense Impression.*** A statement describing or explaining an event or condition, made while or immediately after the declarant perceived it.
(2) **Excited utterance.** A statement relating to a startling event or condition made while the declarant was under the stress of excitement caused by the event or condition.	(2) ***Excited Utterance.*** A statement relating to a startling event or condition, made while the declarant was under the stress of excitement that it caused.
(3) **Then existing mental, emotional, or physical condition.** A statement of the declarant's then existing state of mind, emotion, sensation, or physical condition (such as intent, plan, motive, design, mental feeling, pain, and bodily health), but	(3) ***Then-Existing Mental, Emotional, or Physical Condition.*** A statement of the declarant's then-existing state of mind (such as motive, intent, or plan) or emotional, sensory, or physical condition (such as mental feeling, pain, or bodily

Text Effective Until 12/1/11	Text Effective 12/1/11
not including a statement of memory or belief to prove the fact remembered or believed unless it relates to the execution, revocation, identification, or terms of declarant's will.	health), but not including a statement of memory or belief to prove the fact remembered or believed unless it relates to the validity or terms of the declarant's will.
(4) **Statements for purposes of medical diagnosis or treatment.** Statements made for purposes of medical diagnosis or treatment and describing medical history, or past or present symptoms, pain, or sensations, or the inception or general character of the cause or external source thereof insofar as reasonably pertinent to diagnosis or treatment.	(4) ***Statement Made for Medical Diagnosis or Treatment.*** A statement that: **(A)** is made for—and is reasonably pertinent to—medical diagnosis or treatment; and **(B)** describes medical history; past or present symptoms or sensations; their inception; or their general cause.
(5) **Recorded recollection.** A memorandum or record concerning a matter about which a witness once had knowledge but now has insufficient recollection to enable the witness to testify fully and accurately, shown to have been made or adopted by the witness when the matter was fresh in the witness' memory and to reflect that knowledge correctly. If admitted, the memorandum or record may be read into evidence but may not itself be received as an exhibit unless offered by an adverse party.	(5) ***Recorded Recollection.*** A record that: **(A)** is on a matter the witness once knew about but now cannot recall well enough to testify fully and accurately; **(B)** was made or adopted by the witness when the matter was fresh in the witness's memory; and **(C)** accurately reflects the witness's knowledge. If admitted, the record may be read into evidence but may be received as an exhibit only if offered by an adverse party.
(6) **Records of regularly conducted activity.** A memorandum, report, record, or data compilation, in any	(6) ***Records of a Regularly Conducted Activity.*** A record of an act, event, condition, opinion, or diagnosis

Text Effective Until 12/1/11	Text Effective 12/1/11
form, of acts, events, conditions, opinions, or diagnoses, made at or near the time by, or from information transmitted by, a person with knowledge, if kept in the course of a regularly conducted business activity, and if it was the regular practice of that business activity to make the memorandum, report, record or data compilation, all as shown by the testimony of the custodian or other qualified witness, or by certification that complies with Rule 902(11), Rule 902(12), or a statute permitting certification, unless the source of information or the method or circumstances of preparation indicate lack of trustworthiness. The term "business" as used in this paragraph includes business, institution, association, profession, occupation, and calling of every kind, whether or not conducted for profit.	if: **(A)** the record was made at or near the time by—or from information transmitted by—someone with knowledge; **(B)** the record was kept in the course of a regularly conducted activity of a business, organization, occupation, or calling, whether or not for profit; **(C)** making the record was a regular practice of that activity; **(D)** all these conditions are shown by the testimony of the custodian or another qualified witness, or by a certification that complies with Rule 902(11) or (12) or with a statute permitting certification; and **(E)** neither the source of information nor the method or circumstances of preparation indicate a lack of trustworthiness.
(7) **Absence of entry in records kept in accordance with the provisions of paragraph (6).** Evidence that a matter is not included in the memoranda reports, records, or data compilations, in any form, kept in accordance with the provisions of paragraph (6), to prove the nonoccurrence or nonexistence of the matter, if the matter was of a kind of which a memoran-	(7) ***Absence of a Record of a Regularly Conducted Activity.*** Evidence that a matter is not included in a record described in paragraph (6) if: **(A)** the evidence is admitted to prove that the matter did not occur or exist; **(B)** a record was regularly kept for a matter of

Text Effective Until 12/1/11	Text Effective 12/1/11
dum, report, record, or data compilation was regularly made and preserved, unless the sources of information or other circumstances indicate lack of trustworthiness.	that kind; and (C) neither the possible source of the information nor other circumstances indicate a lack of trustworthiness.
(8) **Public records and reports.** Records, reports, statements, or data compilations, in any form, of public offices or agencies, setting forth (A) the activities of the office or agency, or (B) matters observed pursuant to duty imposed by law as to which matters there was a duty to report, excluding, however, in criminal cases matters observed by police officers and other law enforcement personnel, or (C) in civil actions and proceedings and against the Government in criminal cases, factual findings resulting from an investigation made pursuant to authority granted by law, unless the sources of information or other circumstances indicate lack of trustworthiness.	(8) ***Public Records.*** A record or statement of a public office if: (A) it sets out: (i) the office's activities; (ii) a matter observed while under a legal duty to report, but not including, in a criminal case, a matter observed by law-enforcement personnel; or (iii) in a civil case or against the government in a criminal case, factual findings from a legally authorized investigation; and (B) neither the source of information nor other circumstances indicate a lack of trustworthiness.
(9) **Records of vital statistics.** Records or data compilations, in any form, of births, fetal deaths, deaths, or marriages, if the report thereof was made to a public office pursuant to requirements of law.	(9) ***Public Records of Vital Statistics.*** A record of a birth, death, or marriage, if reported to a public office in accordance with a legal duty.

Text Effective Until 12/1/11	Text Effective 12/1/11
(10) **Absence of public record or entry.** To prove the absence of a record, report, statement, or data compilation, in any form, or the nonoccurrence or nonexistence of a matter of which a record, report, statement, or data compilation, in any form, was regularly made and preserved by a public office or agency, evidence in the form of a certification in accordance with rule 902, or testimony, that diligent search failed to disclose the record, report, statement, or data compilation, or entry.	(10) ***Absence of a Public Record.*** Testimony—or a certification under Rule 902—that a diligent search failed to disclose a public record or statement if the testimony or certification is admitted to prove that: **(A)** the record or statement does not exist; or **(B)** a matter did not occur or exist, if a public office regularly kept a record or statement for a matter of that kind.
(11) **Records of religious organizations.** Statements of births, marriages, divorces, deaths, legitimacy, ancestry, relationship by blood or marriage, or other similar facts of personal or family history, contained in a regularly kept record of a religious organization.	(11) ***Records of Religious Organizations Concerning Personal or Family History.*** A statement of birth, legitimacy, ancestry, marriage, divorce, death, relationship by blood or marriage, or similar facts of personal or family history, contained in a regularly kept record of a religious organization.
(12) **Marriage, baptismal, and similar certificates.** Statements of fact contained in a certificate that the maker performed a marriage or other ceremony or administered a sacrament, made by a clergyman, public official, or other person authorized by the rules or practices of a religious organization or by law to perform the act certified, and purporting to have been issued at the time of the act or within a reasonable time thereafter.	(12) ***Certificates of Marriage, Baptism, and Similar Ceremonies.*** A statement of fact contained in a certificate: **(A)** made by a person who is authorized by a religious organization or by law to perform the act certified; **(B)** attesting that the person performed a marriage or similar ceremony or administered a sacrament; and

Text Effective Until 12/1/11	Text Effective 12/1/11
	(C) purporting to have been issued at the time of the act or within a reasonable time after it.
(13) **Family records.** Statements of fact concerning personal or family history contained in family Bibles, genealogies, charts, engravings on rings, inscriptions on family portraits, engravings on urns, crypts, or tombstones, or the like.	(13) ***Family Records.*** A statement of fact about personal or family history contained in a family record, such as a Bible, genealogy, chart, engraving on a ring, inscription on a portrait, or engraving on an urn or burial marker.
(14) **Records of documents affecting an interest in property.** The record of a document purporting to establish or affect an interest in property, as proof of the content of the original recorded document and its execution and delivery by each person by whom it purports to have been executed, if the record is a record of a public office and an applicable statute authorizes the recording of documents of that kind in that office.	(14) ***Records of Documents That Affect an Interest in Property.*** The record of a document that purports to establish or affect an interest in property if: (A) the record is admitted to prove the content of the original recorded document, along with its signing and its delivery by each person who purports to have signed it; (B) the record is kept in a public office; and (C) a statute authorizes recording documents of that kind in that office.
(15) **Statements in documents affecting an interest in property.** A statement contained in a document purporting to establish or affect an interest in property if the matter stated was relevant to the purpose of the document, unless dealings with the property since the document was made have been inconsistent with the	(15) ***Statements in Documents That Affect an Interest in Property.*** A statement contained in a document that purports to establish or affect an interest in property if the matter stated was relevant to the document's purpose—unless later dealings with the property are inconsistent with the truth of the statement or the pur-

Text Effective Until 12/1/11	Text Effective 12/1/11
truth of the statement or the purport of the document.	port of the document.
(16) **Statements in ancient documents.** Statements in a document in existence twenty years or more the authenticity of which is established.	(16) ***Statements in Ancient Documents.*** A statement in a document that is at least 20 years old and whose authenticity is established.
(17) **Market reports, commercial publications.** Market quotations, tabulations, lists, directories, or other published compilations, generally used and relied upon by the public or by persons in particular occupations.	(17) ***Market Reports and Similar Commercial Publications.*** Market quotations, lists, directories, or other compilations that are generally relied on by the public or by persons in particular occupations.
(18) **Learned treatises.** To the extent called to the attention of an expert witness upon cross-examination or relied upon by the expert witness in direct examination, statements contained in published treatises, periodicals, or pamphlets on a subject of history, medicine, or other science or art, established as a reliable authority by the testimony or admission of the witness or by other expert testimony or by judicial notice. If admitted, the statements may be read into evidence but may not be received as exhibits.	(18) ***Statements in Learned Treatises, Periodicals, or Pamphlets.*** A statement contained in a treatise, periodical, or pamphlet if: **(A)** the statement is called to the attention of an expert witness on cross-examination or relied on by the expert on direct examination; and **(B)** the publication is established as a reliable authority by the expert's admission or testimony, by another expert's testimony, or by judicial notice. If admitted, the statement may be read into evidence but not received as an exhibit.
(19) **Reputation concerning personal or family history.** Reputation among members of a person's family by	(19) ***Reputation Concerning Personal or Family History.*** A reputation among a person's family by blood,

Text Effective Until 12/1/11	Text Effective 12/1/11
blood, adoption, or marriage, or among a person's associates, or in the community, concerning a person's birth, adoption, marriage, divorce, death, legitimacy, relationship by blood, adoption, or marriage, ancestry, or other similar fact of personal or family history.	adoption, or marriage—or among a person's associates or in the community—concerning the person's birth, adoption, legitimacy, ancestry, marriage, divorce, death, relationship by blood, adoption, or marriage, or similar facts of personal or family history.
(20) **Reputation concerning boundaries or general history.** Reputation in a community, arising before the controversy, as to boundaries of or customs affecting lands in the community, and reputation as to events of general history important to the community or State or nation in which located.	(20) ***Reputation Concerning Boundaries or General History.*** A reputation in a community—arising before the controversy—concerning boundaries of land in the community or customs that affect the land, or concerning general historical events important to that community, state, or nation.
(21) **Reputation as to character.** Reputation of a person's character among associates or in the community.	(21) ***Reputation Concerning Character.*** A reputation among a person's associates or in the community concerning the person's character.
(22) **Judgment of previous conviction.** Evidence of a final judgment, entered after a trial or upon a plea of guilty (but not upon a plea of nolo contendere), adjudging a person guilty of a crime punishable by death or imprisonment in excess of one year, to prove any fact essential to sustain the judgment, but not including, when offered by the Government in a criminal prosecution for purposes other than impeachment, judgments against persons other than the accused. The pendency of an appeal may be shown but does not affect admissibility.	(22) ***Judgment of a Previous Conviction.*** Evidence of a final judgment of conviction if: (A) the judgment was entered after a trial or guilty plea, but not a nolo contendere plea; (B) the conviction was for a crime punishable by death or by imprisonment for more than a year; (C) the evidence is admitted to prove any fact essential to the judgment; and

Text Effective Until 12/1/11	Text Effective 12/1/11
	(D) when offered by the prosecutor in a criminal case for a purpose other than impeachment, the judgment was against the defendant. The pendency of an appeal may be shown but does not affect admissibility.
(23) Judgment as to personal, family, or general history, or boundaries. Judgments as proof of matters of personal, family or general history, or boundaries, essential to the judgment, if the same would be provable by evidence of reputation.	(23) ***Judgments Involving Personal, Family, or General History, or a Boundary.*** A judgment that is admitted to prove a matter of personal, family, or general history, or boundaries, if the matter: **(A)** was essential to the judgment; and **(B)** could be proved by evidence of reputation.
(24) [Other exceptions.] [Transferred to Rule 807.]	(24) [***Other Exceptions.***] [Transferred to Rule 807.]
Rule 804. Hearsay Exceptions; Declarant Unavailable	**Rule 804. Exceptions to the Rule Against Hearsay—When the Declarant Is Unavailable as a Witness**
(a) Definition of unavailability. "Unavailability as a witness" includes situations in which the declarant— **(1)** is exempted by ruling of the court on the ground of privilege from testifying concerning the subject matter of the declarant's statement; or **(2)** persists in refusing to testify concerning the subject matter of the declarant's statement despite an order of the	**(a) Criteria for Being Unavailable.** A declarant is considered to be unavailable as a witness if the declarant: **(1)** is exempted from testifying about the subject matter of the declarant's statement because the court rules that a privilege applies; **(2)** refuses to testify about the subject matter despite a court order to do so;

Text Effective Until 12/1/11	Text Effective 12/1/11
court to do so; or	
(3) testifies to a lack of memory of the subject matter of the declarant's statement; or	(3) testifies to not remembering the subject matter;
(4) is unable to be present or to testify at the hearing because of death or then existing physical or mental illness or infirmity; or	(4) cannot be present or testify at the trial or hearing because of death or a then-existing infirmity, physical illness, or mental illness; or
(5) is absent from the hearing and the proponent of a statement has been unable to procure the declarant's attendance (or in the case of a hearsay exception under subdivision (b)(2), (3), or (4), the declarant's attendance or testimony) by process or other reasonable means. A declarant is not unavailable as a witness if exemption, refusal, claim of lack of memory, inability, or absence is due to the procurement or wrongdoing of the proponent of a statement for the purpose of preventing the witness from attending or testifying.	(5) is absent from the trial or hearing and the statement's proponent has not been able, by process or other reasonable means, to procure: (A) the declarant's attendance, in the case of a hearsay exception under Rule 804(b)(1) or (6); or (B) the declarant's attendance or testimony, in the case of a hearsay exception under Rule 804(b)(2), (3), or (4). But this subdivision (a) does not apply if the statement's proponent procured or wrongfully caused the declarant's unavailability as a witness in order to prevent the declarant from attending or testifying.
(b) **Hearsay exceptions.** The following are not excluded by the hearsay rule if the declarant is unavailable as a witness: (1) **Former testimony.** Testimony given as a witness at another hearing of the same or a different proceeding, or in a deposition taken in compliance with law in the course of the same or another proceeding, if the party against whom the testimony is now offered, or, in a civil	(b) **The Exceptions.** The following are not excluded by the rule against hearsay if the declarant is unavailable as a witness: (1) ***Former Testimony.*** Testimony that: (A) was given as a witness at a trial, hearing, or lawful deposition, whether given during the current proceeding or a different one; and

Text Effective Until 12/1/11	Text Effective 12/1/11
action or proceeding, a predecessor in interest, had an opportunity and similar motive to develop the testimony by direct, cross, or redirect examination.	**(B)** is now offered against a party who had—or, in a civil case, whose predecessor in interest had—an opportunity and similar motive to develop it by direct, cross-, or redirect examination.
(2) **Statement under belief of impending death.** In a prosecution for homicide or in a civil action or proceeding, a statement made by a declarant while believing that the declarant's death was imminent, concerning the cause or circumstances of what the declarant believed to be impending death.	(2) ***Statement Under the Belief of Imminent Death.*** In a prosecution for homicide or in a civil case, a statement that the declarant, while believing the declarant's death to be imminent, made about its cause or circumstances.
(3) **Statement against interest.** A statement that: **(A)** a reasonable person in the declarant's position would have made only if the person believed it to be true because, when made, it was so contrary to the declarant's proprietary or pecuniary interest or had so great a tendency to invalidate the declarant's claim against someone else or to expose the declarant to civil or criminal liability; and **(B)** is supported by corroborating circumstances that clearly indicate its trustworthiness, if it is offered in a criminal case as one that tends to expose the declarant to criminal liability.	(3) ***Statement Against Interest.*** A statement that: **(A)** a reasonable person in the declarant's position would have made only if the person believed it to be true because, when made, it was so contrary to the declarant's proprietary or pecuniary interest or had so great a tendency to invalidate the declarant's claim against someone else or to expose the declarant to civil or criminal liability; and **(B)** is supported by corroborating circumstances that clearly indicate its trustworthiness, if it is offered in a criminal case as one that tends to expose the declarant to criminal liability.

Text Effective Until 12/1/11	Text Effective 12/1/11
(4) **Statement of personal or family history.** (A) A statement concerning the declarant's own birth, adoption, marriage, divorce, legitimacy, relationship by blood, adoption, or marriage, ancestry, or other similar fact of personal or family history, even though declarant had no means of acquiring personal knowledge of the matter stated; or (B) a statement concerning the foregoing matters, and death also, of another person, if the declarant was related to the other by blood, adoption, or marriage or was so intimately associated with the other's family as to be likely to have accurate information concerning the matter declared.	(4) ***Statement of Personal or Family History.*** A statement about: **(A)** the declarant's own birth, adoption, legitimacy, ancestry, marriage, divorce, relationship by blood, adoption, or marriage, or similar facts of personal or family history, even though the declarant had no way of acquiring personal knowledge about that fact; or **(B)** another person concerning any of these facts, as well as death, if the declarant was related to the person by blood, adoption, or marriage or was so intimately associated with the person's family that the declarant's information is likely to be accurate.
(5) **[Other exceptions.]** [Transferred to Rule 807.]	(5) [***Other Exceptions.***] [Transferred to Rule 807.]
(6) **Forfeiture by wrongdoing.** A statement offered against a party that has engaged or acquiesced in wrongdoing that was intended to, and did, procure the unavailability of the declarant as a witness.	(6) ***Statement Offered Against a Party That Wrongfully Caused the Declarant's Unavailability.*** A statement offered against a party that wrongfully caused—or acquiesced in wrongfully causing—the declarant's unavailability as a witness, and did so intending that result.

Text Effective Until 12/1/11	Text Effective 12/1/11
Rule 805. Hearsay Within Hearsay	**Rule 805. Hearsay Within Hearsay**
Hearsay included within hearsay is not excluded under the hearsay rule if each part of the combined statements conforms with an exception to the hearsay rule provided in these rules.	Hearsay within hearsay is not excluded by the rule against hearsay if each part of the combined statements conforms with an exception to the rule.
Rule 806. Attacking and Supporting Credibility of Declarant	**Rule 806. Attacking and Supporting the Declarant's Credibility**
When a hearsay statement, or a statement defined in Rule 801(d)(2)(C), (D), or (E), has been admitted in evidence, the credibility of the declarant may be attacked, and if attacked may be supported, by any evidence which would be admissible for those purposes if declarant had testified as a witness. Evidence of a statement or conduct by the declarant at any time, inconsistent with the declarant's hearsay statement, is not subject to any requirement that the declarant may have been afforded an opportunity to deny or explain. If the party against whom a hearsay statement has been admitted calls the declarant as a witness, the party is entitled to examine the declarant on the statement as if under cross-examination.	When a hearsay statement—or a statement described in Rule 801(d)(2)(C), (D), or (E)—has been admitted in evidence, the declarant's credibility may be attacked, and then supported, by any evidence that would be admissible for those purposes if the declarant had testified as a witness. The court may admit evidence of the declarant's inconsistent statement or conduct, regardless of when it occurred or whether the declarant had an opportunity to explain or deny it. If the party against whom the statement was admitted calls the declarant as a witness, the party may examine the declarant on the statement as if on cross-examination.
Rule 807. Residual Exception	**Rule 807. Residual Exception**
A statement not specifically covered by Rule 803 or 804 but having equivalent circumstantial guarantees of trustworthiness, is not excluded by the hearsay rule, if the court determines that (A) the statement is offered as evidence of a material fact; (B) the statement is more probative on the point for which it is offered than any other evidence which the proponent can procure through reasonable efforts; and (C) the general purposes of these rules and the	(a) **In General.** Under the following circumstances, a hearsay statement is not excluded by the rule against hearsay even if the statement is not specifically covered by a hearsay exception in Rule 803 or 804: (1) the statement has equivalent circumstantial guarantees of trustworthiness;

Text Effective Until 12/1/11	Text Effective 12/1/11
interests of justice will best be served by admission of the statement into evidence. However, a statement may not be admitted under this exception unless the proponent of it makes known to the adverse party sufficiently in advance of the trial or hearing to provide the adverse party with a fair opportunity to prepare to meet it, the proponent's intention to offer the statement and the particulars of it, including the name and address of the declarant.	(2) it is offered as evidence of a material fact; (3) it is more probative on the point for which it is offered than any other evidence that the proponent can obtain through reasonable efforts; and (4) admitting it will best serve the purposes of these rules and the interests of justice. (b) **Notice.** The statement is admissible only if, before the trial or hearing, the proponent gives an adverse party reasonable notice of the intent to offer the statement and its particulars, including the declarant's name and address, so that the party has a fair opportunity to meet it.

Text Effective Until 12/1/11	Text Effective 12/1/11
ARTICLE IX. AUTHENTICATION AND IDENTIFICATION **Rule 901. Requirement of Authentication or Identification**	**ARTICLE IX. AUTHENTICATION AND IDENTIFICATION** **Rule 901. Authenticating or Identifying Evidence**
(a) **General provision.** The requirement of authentication or identification as a condition precedent to admissibility is satisfied by evidence sufficient to support a finding that the matter in question is what its proponent claims.	(a) **In General.** To satisfy the requirement of authenticating or identifying an item of evidence, the proponent must produce evidence sufficient to support a finding that the item is what the proponent claims it is.
(b) **Illustrations.** By way of illustration only, and not by way of limitation, the following are examples of authentication or identification conforming with the requirements of this rule:	(b) **Examples.** The following are examples only—not a complete list—of evidence that satisfies the requirement:
(1) **Testimony of witness with knowledge.** Testimony that a matter is what it is claimed to be.	(1) ***Testimony of a Witness with Knowledge.*** Testimony that an item is what it is claimed to be.
(2) **Nonexpert opinion on handwriting.** Nonexpert opinion as to the genuineness of handwriting, based upon familiarity not acquired for purposes of the litigation.	(2) ***Nonexpert Opinion About Handwriting.*** A nonexpert's opinion that handwriting is genuine, based on a familiarity with it that was not acquired for the current litigation.
(3) **Comparison by trier or expert witness.** Comparison by the trier of fact or by expert witnesses with specimens which have been authenticated.	(3) ***Comparison by an Expert Witness or the Trier of Fact.*** A comparison with an authenticated specimen by an expert witness or the trier of fact.
(4) **Distinctive characteristics and the like.** Appearance, contents, substance, internal patterns, or other distinctive characteristics, taken in con-	(4) ***Distinctive Characteristics and the Like.*** The appearance, contents, substance, internal patterns, or other distinctive characteristics of the

Text Effective Until 12/1/11	Text Effective 12/1/11
junction with circumstances.	item, taken together with all the circumstances.
(5) **Voice identification.** Identification of a voice, whether heard firsthand or through mechanical or electronic transmission or recording, by opinion based upon hearing the voice at any time under circumstances connecting it with the alleged speaker.	(5) ***Opinion About a Voice.*** An opinion identifying a person's voice—whether heard firsthand or through mechanical or electronic transmission or recording—based on hearing the voice at any time under circumstances that connect it with the alleged speaker.
(6) **Telephone conversations.** Telephone conversations, by evidence that a call was made to the number assigned at the time by the telephone company to a particular person or business, if (A) in the case of a person, circumstances, including self-identification, show the person answering to be the one called, or (B) in the case of a business, the call was made to a place of business and the conversation related to business reasonably transacted over the telephone.	(6) ***Evidence About a Telephone Conversation.*** For a telephone conversation, evidence that a call was made to the number assigned at the time to: **(A)** a particular person, if circumstances, including self-identification, show that the person answering was the one called; or **(B)** a particular business, if the call was made to a business and the call related to business reasonably transacted over the telephone.
(7) **Public records or reports.** Evidence that a writing authorized by law to be recorded or filed and in fact recorded or filed in a public office, or a purported public record, report, statement, or data compilation, in any form, is from the public office where items of this nature are kept.	(7) ***Evidence About Public Records.*** Evidence that: **(A)** a document was recorded or filed in a public office as authorized by law; or **(B)** a purported public record or statement is from the office where items of this kind are kept.
(8) **Ancient documents or data compilation.** Evidence that	(8) ***Evidence About Ancient Documents or Data Compi-***

Text Effective Until 12/1/11	Text Effective 12/1/11
a document or data compilation, in any form, (A) is in such condition as to create no suspicion concerning its authenticity, (B) was in a place where it, if authentic, would likely be, and (C) has been in existence 20 years or more at the time it is offered.	***lations.*** For a document or data compilation, evidence that it: **(A)** is in a condition that creates no suspicion about its authenticity; **(B)** was in a place where, if authentic, it would likely be; and **(C)** is at least 20 years old when offered.
(9) **Process or system.** Evidence describing a process or system used to produce a result and showing that the process or system produces an accurate result.	(9) ***Evidence About a Process or System.*** Evidence describing a process or system and showing that it produces an accurate result.
(10) **Methods provided by statute or rule.** Any method of authentication or identification provided by Act of Congress or by other rules prescribed by the Supreme Court pursuant to statutory authority.	(10) ***Methods Provided by a Statute or Rule.*** Any method of authentication or identification allowed by a federal statute or a rule prescribed by the Supreme Court.
Rule 902. Self-authentication	**Rule 902. Evidence That Is Self-Authenticating**
Extrinsic evidence of authenticity as a condition precedent to admissibility is not required with respect to the following: (1) **Domestic public documents under seal.** A document bearing a seal purporting to be that of the United States, or of any State, district, Commonwealth, territory, or insular possession thereof, or the Panama Canal Zone, or the Trust Territory of the Pacific Islands, or of a political subdivision, department, officer, or agency thereof,	The following items of evidence are self-authenticating; they require no extrinsic evidence of authenticity in order to be admitted: (1) ***Domestic Public Documents That Are Sealed and Signed.*** A document that bears: **(A)** a seal purporting to be that of the United States; any state, district, commonwealth, territory, or insular possession of the United States; the former

Text Effective Until 12/1/11	Text Effective 12/1/11
and a signature purporting to be an attestation or execution.	Panama Canal Zone; the Trust Territory of the Pacific Islands; a political subdivision of any of these entities; or a department, agency, or officer of any entity named above; and **(B)** a signature purporting to be an execution or attestation.
(2) **Domestic public documents not under seal.** A document purporting to bear the signature in the official capacity of an officer or employee of any entity included in paragraph (1) hereof, having no seal, if a public officer having a seal and having official duties in the district or political subdivision of the officer or employee certifies under seal that the signer has the official capacity and that the signature is genuine.	(2) ***Domestic Public Documents That Are Not Sealed but Are Signed and Certified.*** A document that bears no seal if: **(A)** it bears the signature of an officer or employee of an entity named in Rule 902(1)(A); and **(B)** another public officer who has a seal and official duties within that same entity certifies under seal—or its equivalent—that the signer has the official capacity and that the signature is genuine.
(3) **Foreign public documents.** A document purporting to be executed or attested in an official capacity by a person authorized by the laws of a foreign country to make the execution or attestation, and accompanied by a final certification as to the genuineness of the signature and official position (A) of the executing or attesting person, or (B) of any foreign official whose certificate of genuineness of signature and official position relates to the execution or attestation or is in a chain of certificates of genuineness of signature and	(3) ***Foreign Public Documents.*** A document that purports to be signed or attested by a person who is authorized by a foreign country's law to do so. The document must be accompanied by a final certification that certifies the genuineness of the signature and official position of the signer or attester—or of any foreign official whose certificate of genuineness relates to the signature or attestation or is in a chain of certificates of genuineness relating to the signature or attestation. The certification may be made by a secretary of a

Text Effective Until 12/1/11	Text Effective 12/1/11
official position relating to the execution or attestation. A final certification may be made by a secretary of an embassy or legation, consul general, consul, vice consul, or consular agent of the United States, or a diplomatic or consular official of the foreign country assigned or accredited to the United States. If reasonable opportunity has been given to all parties to investigate the authenticity and accuracy of official documents, the court may, for good cause shown, order that they be treated as presumptively authentic without final certification or permit them to be evidenced by an attested summary with or without final certification.	United States embassy or legation; by a consul general, vice consul, or consular agent of the United States; or by a diplomatic or consular official of the foreign country assigned or accredited to the United States. If all parties have been given a reasonable opportunity to investigate the document's authenticity and accuracy, the court may, for good cause, either: **(A)** order that it be treated as presumptively authentic without final certification; or **(B)** allow it to be evidenced by an attested summary with or without final certification.
(4) **Certified copies of public records.** A copy of an official record or report or entry therein, or of a document authorized by law to be recorded or filed and actually recorded or filed in a public office, including data compilations in any form, certified as correct by the custodian or other person authorized to make the certification, by certificate complying with paragraph (1), (2), or (3) of this rule or complying with any Act of Congress or rule prescribed by the Supreme Court pursuant to statutory authority.	(4) ***Certified Copies of Public Records.*** A copy of an official record—or a copy of a document that was recorded or filed in a public office as authorized by law—if the copy is certified as correct by: **(A)** the custodian or another person authorized to make the certification; or **(B)** a certificate that complies with Rule 902(1), (2), or (3), a federal statute, or a rule prescribed by the Supreme Court.
(5) **Official publications.** Books, pamphlets, or other publications purporting to be issued by public authority.	(5) ***Official Publications.*** A book, pamphlet, or other publication purporting to be issued by a public authority.
(6) **Newspapers and periodicals.** Printed materials pur-	(6) ***Newspapers and Periodicals.*** Printed material pur-

Text Effective Until 12/1/11	Text Effective 12/1/11
porting to be newspapers or periodicals.	porting to be a newspaper or periodical.
(7) **Trade inscriptions and the like.** Inscriptions, signs, tags, or labels purporting to have been affixed in the course of business and indicating ownership, control, or origin.	(7) ***Trade Inscriptions and the Like.*** An inscription, sign, tag, or label purporting to have been affixed in the course of business and indicating origin, ownership, or control.
(8) **Acknowledged documents.** Documents accompanied by a certificate of acknowledgment executed in the manner provided by law by a notary public or other officer authorized by law to take acknowledgments.	(8) ***Acknowledged Documents.*** A document accompanied by a certificate of acknowledgment that is lawfully executed by a notary public or another officer who is authorized to take acknowledgments.
(9) **Commercial paper and related documents.** Commercial paper, signatures thereon, and documents relating thereto to the extent provided by general commercial law.	(9) ***Commercial Paper and Related Documents.*** Commercial paper, a signature on it, and related documents, to the extent allowed by general commercial law.
(10) **Presumptions under Acts of Congress.** Any signature, document, or other matter declared by Act of Congress to be presumptively or prima facie genuine or authentic.	(10) ***Presumptions Under a Federal Statute.*** A signature, document, or anything else that a federal statute declares to be presumptively or prima facie genuine or authentic.
(11) **Certified domestic records of regularly conducted activity.** The original or a duplicate of a domestic record of regularly conducted activity that would be admissible under Rule 803(6) if accompanied by a written declaration of its custodian or other qualified person, in a manner complying with any Act of Congress or rule prescribed by the Supreme Court pursuant to statutory authority,	(11) ***Certified Domestic Records of a Regularly Conducted Activity.*** The original or a copy of a domestic record that meets the requirements of Rule 803(6)(A)–(C), as shown by a certification of the custodian or another qualified person that complies with a federal statute or a rule prescribed by the Supreme Court. Before the trial or hearing, the proponent must give an adverse

Text Effective Until 12/1/11	Text Effective 12/1/11
certifying that the record— **(A)** was made at or near the time of the occurrence of the matters set forth by, or from information transmitted by, a person with knowledge of those matters; **(B)** was kept in the course of the regularly conducted activity; and **(C)** was made by the regularly conducted activity as a regular practice. A party intending to offer a record into evidence under this paragraph must provide written notice of that intention to all adverse parties, and must make the record and declaration available for inspection sufficiently in advance of their offer into evidence to provide an adverse party with a fair opportunity to challenge them.	party reasonable written notice of the intent to offer the record—and must make the record and certification available for inspection—so that the party has a fair opportunity to challenge them.
(12) **Certified foreign records of regularly conducted activity.** In a civil case, the original or a duplicate of a foreign record of regularly conducted activity that would be admissible under Rule 803(6) if accompanied by a written declaration by its custodian or other qualified person certifying that the record— **(A)** was made at or near the time of the occurrence of the matters set forth by, or from information transmitted by, a person with knowledge of those matters;	(12) ***Certified Foreign Records of a Regularly Conducted Activity.*** In a civil case, the original or a copy of a foreign record that meets the requirements of Rule 902(11), modified as follows: the certification, rather than complying with a federal statute or Supreme Court rule, must be signed in a manner that, if falsely made, would subject the maker to a criminal penalty in the country where the certification is signed. The proponent must also meet the notice requirements of Rule 902(11).

Text Effective Until 12/1/11	Text Effective 12/1/11
(B) was kept in the course of the regularly conducted activity; and **(C)** was made by the regularly conducted activity as a regular practice. The declaration must be signed in a manner that, if falsely made, would subject the maker to criminal penalty under the laws of the country where the declaration is signed. A party intending to offer a record into evidence under this paragraph must provide written notice of that intention to all adverse parties, and must make the record and declaration available for inspection sufficiently in advance of their offer into evidence to provide an adverse party with a fair opportunity to challenge them.	
Rule 903. Subscribing Witness' Testimony Unnecessary	**Rule 903. Subscribing Witness's Testimony**
The testimony of a subscribing witness is not necessary to authenticate a writing unless required by the laws of the jurisdiction whose laws govern the validity of the writing.	A subscribing witness's testimony is necessary to authenticate a writing only if required by the law of the jurisdiction that governs its validity.

Text Effective Until 12/1/11	Text Effective 12/1/11
ARTICLE X. CONTENTS OF WRITINGS, RECORDINGS, AND PHOTOGRAPHS	**ARTICLE X. CONTENTS OF WRITINGS, RECORDINGS, AND PHOTOGRAPHS**
Rule 1001. Definitions	**Rule 1001. Definitions That Apply to This Article**
For purposes of this article the following definitions are applicable:	In this article:
(1) **Writings and recordings.** "Writings" and "recordings" consist of letters, words, or numbers, or their equivalent, set down by handwriting, typewriting, printing, photostating, photographing, magnetic impulse, mechanical or electronic recording, or other form of data compilation.	(a) A "writing" consists of letters, words, numbers, or their equivalent set down in any form. (b) A "recording" consists of letters, words, numbers, or their equivalent recorded in any manner.
(2) **Photographs.** "Photographs" include still photographs, X-ray films, video tapes, and motion pictures.	(c) A "photograph" means a photographic image or its equivalent stored in any form.
(3) **Original.** An "original" of a writing or recording is the writing or recording itself or any counterpart intended to have the same effect by a person executing or issuing it. An "original" of a photograph includes the negative or any print therefrom. If data are stored in a computer or similar device, any printout or other output readable by sight, shown to reflect the data accurately, is an "original".	(d) An "original" of a writing or recording means the writing or recording itself or any counterpart intended to have the same effect by the person who executed or issued it. For electronically stored information, "original" means any printout—or other output readable by sight—if it accurately reflects the information. An "original" of a photograph includes the negative or a print from it.
(4) **Duplicate.** A "duplicate" is a counterpart produced by the same impression as the original, or from the same matrix, or by means of photography, including enlargements and miniatures, or by mechanical or electronic rerecording, or by chemical reproduction, or by other	(e) A "duplicate" means a counterpart produced by a mechanical, photographic, chemical, electronic, or other equivalent process or technique that accurately reproduces the original.

Text Effective Until 12/1/11	Text Effective 12/1/11
equivalent techniques which accurately reproduces the original.	
Rule 1002. Requirement of Original	**Rule 1002. Requirement of the Original**
To prove the content of a writing, recording, or photograph, the original writing, recording, or photograph is required, except as otherwise provided in these rules or by Act of Congress.	An original writing, recording, or photograph is required in order to prove its content unless these rules or a federal statute provides otherwise.
Rule 1003. Admissibility of Duplicates	**Rule 1003. Admissibility of Duplicates**
A duplicate is admissible to the same extent as an original unless (1) a genuine question is raised as to the authenticity of the original or (2) in the circumstances it would be unfair to admit the duplicate in lieu of the original.	A duplicate is admissible to the same extent as the original unless a genuine question is raised about the original's authenticity or the circumstances make it unfair to admit the duplicate.
Rule 1004. Admissibility of Other Evidence of Contents	**Rule 1004. Admissibility of Other Evidence of Content**
The original is not required, and other evidence of the contents of a writing, recording, or photograph is admissible if—	An original is not required and other evidence of the content of a writing, recording, or photograph is admissible if:
(1) **Originals lost or destroyed.** All originals are lost or have been destroyed, unless the proponent lost or destroyed them in bad faith; or	(a) all the originals are lost or destroyed, and not by the proponent acting in bad faith;
(2) **Original not obtainable.** No original can be obtained by any available judicial process or procedure; or	(b) an original cannot be obtained by any available judicial process;
(3) **Original in possession of opponent.** At a time when an original was under the control of the party against whom offered, that party was put on notice, by the	(c) the party against whom the original would be offered had control of the original; was at that time put on notice, by pleadings or otherwise, that the original would be a subject of proof at the trial or

Text Effective Until 12/1/11	Text Effective 12/1/11
pleadings or otherwise, that the contents would be a subject of proof at the hearing, and that party does not produce the original at the hearing; or	hearing; and fails to produce it at the trial or hearing; or
(4) **Collateral matters.** The writing, recording, or photograph is not closely related to a controlling issue.	(d) the writing, recording, or photograph is not closely related to a controlling issue.
Rule 1005. Public Records	**Rule 1005. Copies of Public Records to Prove Content**
The contents of an official record, or of a document authorized to be recorded or filed and actually recorded or filed, including data compilations in any form, if otherwise admissible, may be proved by copy, certified as correct in accordance with rule 902 or testified to be correct by a witness who has compared it with the original. If a copy which complies with the foregoing cannot be obtained by the exercise of reasonable diligence, then other evidence of the contents may be given.	The proponent may use a copy to prove the content of an official record—or of a document that was recorded or filed in a public office as authorized by law—if these conditions are met: the record or document is otherwise admissible; and the copy is certified as correct in accordance with Rule 902(4) or is testified to be correct by a witness who has compared it with the original. If no such copy can be obtained by reasonable diligence, then the proponent may use other evidence to prove the content.
Rule 1006. Summaries	**Rule 1006. Summaries to Prove Content**
The contents of voluminous writings, recordings, or photographs which cannot conveniently be examined in court may be presented in the form of a chart, summary, or calculation. The originals, or duplicates, shall be made available for examination or copying, or both, by other parties at reasonable time and place. The court may order that they be produced in court.	The proponent may use a summary, chart, or calculation to prove the content of voluminous writings, recordings, or photographs that cannot be conveniently examined in court. The proponent must make the originals or duplicates available for examination or copying, or both, by other parties at a reasonable time and place. And the court may order the proponent to produce them in court.

Text Effective Until 12/1/11	Text Effective 12/1/11
Rule 1007. Testimony or Written Admission of Party	**Rule 1007. Testimony or Statement of a Party to Prove Content**
Contents of writings, recordings, or photographs may be proved by the testimony or deposition of the party against whom offered or by that party's written admission, without accounting for the nonproduction of the original.	The proponent may prove the content of a writing, recording, or photograph by the testimony, deposition, or written statement of the party against whom the evidence is offered. The proponent need not account for the original.
Rule 1008. Functions of Court and Jury	**Rule 1008. Functions of the Court and Jury**
When the admissibility of other evidence of contents of writings, recordings, or photographs under these rules depends upon the fulfillment of a condition of fact, the question whether the condition has been fulfilled is ordinarily for the court to determine in accordance with the provisions of rule 104. However, when an issue is raised (a) whether the asserted writing ever existed, or (b) whether another writing, recording, or photograph produced at the trial is the original, or (c) whether other evidence of contents correctly reflects the contents, the issue is for the trier of fact to determine as in the case of other issues of fact.	Ordinarily, the court determines whether the proponent has fulfilled the factual conditions for admitting other evidence of the content of a writing, recording, or photograph under Rule 1004 or 1005. But in a jury trial, the jury determines—in accordance with Rule 104(b)—any issue about whether: **(a)** an asserted writing, recording, or photograph ever existed; **(b)** another one produced at the trial or hearing is the original; or **(c)** other evidence of content accurately reflects the content.

Text Effective Until 12/1/11	Text Effective 12/1/11
ARTICLE XI. MISCELLANEOUS RULES **Rule 1101. Applicability of Rules**	**ARTICLE XI. MISCELLANEOUS RULES** **Rule 1101. Applicability of the Rules**
(a) **Courts and judges.** These rules apply to the United States district courts, the District Court of Guam, the District Court of the Virgin Islands, the District Court for the Northern Mariana Islands, the United States courts of appeals, the United States Claims Court, and to United States bankruptcy judges and United States magistrate judges, in the actions, cases, and proceedings and to the extent hereinafter set forth. The terms "judge" and "court" in these rules include United States bankruptcy judges and United States magistrate judges.	(a) **To Courts and Judges.** These rules apply to proceedings before: • United States district courts; • United States bankruptcy and magistrate judges; • United States courts of appeals; • the United States Court of Federal Claims; and • the district courts of Guam, the Virgin Islands, and the Northern Mariana Islands.
(b) **Proceedings generally.** These rules apply generally to civil actions and proceedings, including admiralty and maritime cases, to criminal cases and proceedings, to contempt proceedings except those in which the court may act summarily, and to proceedings and cases under title 11, United States Code.	(b) **To Cases and Proceedings.** These rules apply in: • civil cases and proceedings, including bankruptcy, admiralty, and maritime cases; • criminal cases and proceedings; and • contempt proceedings, except those in which the court may act summarily.
(c) **Rule of privilege.** The rule with respect to privileges applies at all stages of all actions, cases, and proceedings.	(c) **Rules on Privilege.** The rules on privilege apply to all stages of a case or proceeding.
(d) **Rules inapplicable.** The rules (other than with respect to privileges) do not apply in the following situations: (1) **Preliminary questions of fact.** The determination of questions of fact preliminary	(d) **Exceptions.** These rules—except for those on privilege—do not apply to the following: (1) the court's determination, under Rule 104(a), on a preliminary question of fact gov-

Text Effective Until 12/1/11	Text Effective 12/1/11
to admissibility of evidence when the issue is to be determined by the court under rule 104.	erning admissibility;
(2) **Grand jury.** Proceedings before grand juries.	(2) grand-jury proceedings; and
(3) **Miscellaneous proceedings.** Proceedings for extradition or rendition; preliminary examinations in criminal cases; sentencing, or granting or revoking probation; issuance of warrants for arrest, criminal summonses, and search warrants; and proceedings with respect to release on bail or otherwise.	(3) miscellaneous proceedings such as: • extradition or rendition; • issuing an arrest warrant, criminal summons, or search warrant; • a preliminary examination in a criminal case; • sentencing; • granting or revoking probation or supervised release; and • considering whether to release on bail or otherwise.
(e) **Rules applicable in part.** In the following proceedings these rules apply to the extent that matters of evidence are not provided for in the statutes which govern procedure therein or in other rules prescribed by the Supreme Court pursuant to statutory authority: the trial of misdemeanors and other petty offenses before United States magistrate judges; review of agency actions when the facts are subject to trial de novo under section 706(2)(F) of title 5, United States Code; review of orders of the Secretary of Agriculture under section 2 of the Act entitled "An Act to authorize association of producers of agricultural products" approved February 18, 1922 (7 U.S.C. 292), and under sections 6 and 7(c) of the Perishable Agricultural Commodities Act, 1930 (7 U.S.C. 499f, 499g(c)); naturalization and revocation of naturalization under sections 310–318 of the Immigration and Nationality Act (8 U.S.C. 1421–1429); prize pro-	(e) **Other Statutes and Rules.** A federal statute or a rule prescribed by the Supreme Court may provide for admitting or excluding evidence independently from these rules.

Text Effective Until 12/1/11	Text Effective 12/1/11
ceedings in admiralty under sections 7651–7681 of title 10, United States Code; review of orders of the Secretary of the Interior under section 2 of the Act entitled "An Act authorizing associations of producers of aquatic products" approved June 25, 1934 (15 U.S.C. 522); review of orders of petroleum control boards under section 5 of the Act entitled "An Act to regulate interstate and foreign commerce in petroleum and its products by prohibiting the shipment in such commerce of petroleum and its products produced in violation of State law, and for other purposes", approved February 22, 1935 (15 U.S.C. 715d); actions for fines, penalties, or forfeitures under part V of title IV of the Tariff Act of 1930 (19 U.S.C. 1581–1624), or under the Anti–Smuggling Act (19 U.S.C. 1701–1711); criminal libel for condemnation, exclusion of imports, or other proceedings under the Federal Food, Drug, and Cosmetic Act (21 U.S.C. 301–392); disputes between seamen under sections 4079, 4080, and 4081 of the Revised Statutes (22 U.S.C. 256–258); habeas corpus under sections 2241–2254 of title 28, United States Code; motions to vacate, set aside or correct sentence under section 2255 of title 28, United States Code; actions for penalties for refusal to transport destitute seamen under section 4578 of the Revised Statutes (46 U.S.C. 679); actions against the United States under the Act entitled "An Act authorizing suits against the United States in admiralty for damage caused by and salvage service rendered to public vessels belonging to the United States, and for other purposes", approved March 3, 1925 (46 U.S.C. 781–790), as implemented by section 7730 of title 10, United States Code.	

Text Effective Until 12/1/11	Text Effective 12/1/11
Rule 1102. Amendments	**Rule 1102. Amendments**
Amendments to the Federal Rules of Evidence may be made as provided in section 2072 of title 28 of the United States Code.	These rules may be amended as provided in 28 U.S.C. § 2072.
Rule 1103. Title	**Rule 1103. Title**
These rules may be known and cited as the Federal Rules of Evidence.	These rules may be cited as the Federal Rules of Evidence.

†